The Encyclopædia of
OXFORD

Edited by Christopher Hibbert
Associate editor Edward Hibbert

PAPERMAC

Copyright © Christopher Hibbert and Edward Hibbert 1988

Designed by Robert Updegraff
Picture research by Juliet Brightmore

First published 1988 by
Macmillan London Limited

First published in paperback in 1992 by
PAPERMAC
a division of Pan Macmillan Publishers Limited
Cavaye Place London SW10 9PG
and Basingstoke

Associated companies in Auckland, Delhi, Dublin, Gaborone,
Hamburg, Harare, Hong Kong, Johannesburg, Kuala Lumpur,
Lagos, Manzini, Melbourne, Mexico City, Nairobi, New York,
Singapore and Tokyo

British Library Cataloguing in Publication Data

Hibbert, Christopher
The encyclopædia of Oxford.
1. Oxford (Oxfordshire)—Dictionaries
and encyclopedia
I. Title
942.5′74′00321   DA690.098

ISBN 0-333-39917-X (cased)
ISBN 0-333-48614-5 (Papermac)

Filmset by Pindar Graphics, Scarborough
Printed in Hong Kong

Contents

The Entries   1

Guide to the use of the Encyclopædia

The names of places, buildings and institutions which no longer exist are printed in funereal gothic, thus:

𝕺𝖘𝖊𝖓𝖊𝖞 𝕬𝖇𝖇𝖊𝖞

There are, of course, many entries under **Oxford**, but if a particular subject is not found there it will probably appear under the second word in its title. For example, Oxford Union Society is listed under **Union Society**.

A number of subjects are grouped together: for example, **Academic Halls**, **Fairs**, **Gardens**, **Portraits**, **Riots**, **Statues and Busts**.

There are also many special subject entries: for instance, **Printing**, **Real Tennis**, **Rowing**, **Transport**, **Water Supply**.

Place entries are not limited strictly to the city of Oxford. A selection has been made of certain places which lie beyond the boundaries of the city but which are closely connected with it: for instance, **Boar's Hill**, **Cumnor Hill**, **Godstow** and **Wytham**.

Cross-references are indicated by the use of SMALL CAPITALS in the body of the entry. The names of colleges are not printed thus, however, since all colleges, of course, have separate entries. Several other frequently occurring subjects are also not cross-referenced in this way: chair, degree, faculties, University.

INDEX OF PEOPLE (pages 537–550). The Encyclopædia includes entries for people. The selection is necessarily controversial, but information about persons who have not been given their own entries will be found in the body of other entries by reference to the Index of People. In this index the page numbers against the name of Thomas Combe, for example, refer the reader to **Edward Burne-Jones**, **Jericho**, **William Morris**, **Oxford University Press**, **Printing**, **Church of St Barnabas** and **Wolvercote Paper Mill**. Living persons have not been given separate entries.

The GENERAL INDEX (pages 551–562) gives page references for every place, building, institution, business, subject or event, irrespective of whether or not it has a separate entry. Page numbers in the index for Canterbury College, for instance, refer the reader to **Monastic Colleges**, among other entries.

Acknowledgements

A list of contributors to the *Encyclopædia* is given on pages vii–ix; but we would also like to express our thanks to all those whose help and encouragement have contributed so much to its completion. We are most grateful to the heads of houses for suggesting suitable contributors for the college entries, and to Mr Malcolm Graham and the staff of the Local History Collections of the Central Library for their invaluable help. We would also like to thank the following for checking entries for us, answering innumerable questions or making valuable suggestions: Mrs Nina Armstrong; the late T. H. Aston, Senior Research Fellow and Librarian, Corpus Christi College; Miss Norma Aubertin-Potter, Sub-Librarian, Codrington Library, All Souls College; Mr Giles Barber, Fellow of Linacre College and Librarian of the Taylor Institution; Mr B. Berryman; Mr John Billingham, Director of Planning, Estates and Architecture; Mr Arthur Bissell, Custodian of Records, the Religious Society of Friends; Mr David Butler, City Engineer, and the staff of the Department of the City Engineer; Mr H. M. Colvin, Fellow of St John's College; Mr Alan Cook; Mr Peter Crane, Assistant Registrar; Mr John Critchley; Mrs Ruth Deech, Fellow of St Anne's College and Senior Proctor; Mother Frances Dominica of Helen House; Dr A. J. Dorey, Fellow of Linacre College and Registrar; Mr John Eckersley; Mr Ralph Evans, of *The History of the University*; Dr Robin Fletcher, Warden of Rhodes House; Mr H. George, General Manager, Oxford Stadium; Mr A. J. Gray; Mr Harold Gray; Mr A. H. Greenwood; Mr David Hay, Director of the Alister Hardy Research Centre; Mrs Vera Hibbert; Mr R. M. Hoby, Secretary to the Committee for Scientific Collections, the University Museum; Professor Sir Michael Howard, Fellow of Oriel College and Regius Professor of Modern History; Dr S. Jameson, Registrar, Warnborough College; Sir Leslie Kirkley, former Director of Oxfam; Miss J. M. Knight, Registrar of Queen Elizabeth House; Mr Alan Knowles; Professor Nicholas Kurti, Emeritus Professor of Physics; Mr Colin Leach, Fellow of Pembroke College; Miss E. A. Livingstone; Mr Antonio Lopez; Dr Pat Lund; Mr F. R. Maddison, Curator of the Museum of the History of Science; Mr W. Meeuws;

The Encyclopædia of
OXFORD

Christopher Hibbert, who read History at Oriel College, is a Fellow of the Royal Society of Literature and winner of the Heinemann Award for Literature. He is the author and editor of many distinguished books, including biographies of Samuel Johnson, Dickens, George IV and Edward VII; *The Great Mutiny: India 1857*; *The Dragon Wakes: China and the West*; *The Rise and Fall of the House of Medici*; *The French Revolution*; *London: Biography of a City*; *The English*; and, with Ben Weinreb, this book's companion volume, *The London Encyclopædia*.

Edward Hibbert has lived and worked for over forty years in Oxford, where he practised as a solicitor. He is a Fellow of the Royal Philatelic Society, London, and is the author of *St Helena Postal History and Stamps*. He has also written a short history of Vanbrugh House, the building in St Michael's Street, Oxford, which was his office. He is married and has two sons.

also available

The London Encyclopædia
(edited by Ben Weinreb and Christopher Hibbert)

Dr Michael Metcalf, Keeper of the Heberden Coin Room; Mr W. H. Miller; Mr Edward Minty; Mr Peter Newell, Chairman of Wolsey Hall; Mr T. C. Newell, Assistant Regional Director, Home Office Prisons Department; Roger Northcote-Green; Mr Leslie Ody; Mr John Osmond-Smith; Mr C. R. Paine; Mrs L. Palm; Dr Jessie Parfit; Mr E. P. Payne; Mr A. Pearson; Mr Stephen Penney; Mr G. M. Phillips; the staff of the Pitt Rivers Museum; Mr Robert Potter; Mr Philip Powell, Assistant Curator, University Museum; Mr K. C. Revis; Mr Peter Reynolds; Mr Arthur Salter; Mr H. E. Smith; The Rev. Alberic Stacpoole, Senior Tutor, St Benet's Hall; Mr Anthony Thwaite; Mr David Tolson; Mr Steven Tomlinson, Deputy Keeper of the University Archives; Mr G. C. Tyack; Mr J. R. Venables; Miss Ruth Vyse, former Assistant Archivist, University Archives; Dr Charles Webster, Fellow of Corpus Christi College and Director of the Wellcome Unit for the History of Medicine;

Mr D. J. Wenden, Fellow and Bursar of All Souls College; Dr Christopher White, Director of the Ashmolean Museum; Mr Harold Williams, the Lord Mayor's Secretary.

We are most grateful to Brenda Thomson, the editor responsible for the *Encyclopædia* at Macmillan; to Robert Updegraff, who has designed the book; to Juliet Brightmore, who has collected and chosen the illustrations; to Barbara Britton and Susan Hibbert of the Society of Indexers who have compiled the indexes; and to Alison Riley, Margaret Lewendon, Mabel Armstrong and Lesley Caswell, who have typed and retyped so many of the entries. Finally, we would like to express our gratitude to Mr J. S. G. Simmons, Emeritus Fellow of All Souls College, for his generous help and for having read the proofs.

CHRISTOPHER HIBBERT
EDWARD HIBBERT
Spring 1988

Contributors

PAULINE ADAMS Fellow and Librarian of Somerville College
LUCY AITCHISON
BRIGID ALLEN sometime commoner of Somerville College
STEPHEN ASHLEY
PHYLLIS AUTY sometime commoner of St Hilda's College
GERALD AYLMER Master of St Peter's College
J. F. BAMBOROUGH Principal of Linacre College
T. C. BARNARD Fellow of Hertford College
CATHERINE BARRINGTON-WARD Principal of Beechlawn Tutorial College
MICHAEL BARSLEY sometime editor of *Cherwell*
E. A. BASKERVILLE Secretary, Oxford College Admissions Office
MAVIS BATEY author of *Oxford Gardens* (1982)
PETER BAYLEY sometime Fellow of University College
JOHN BLAIR Fellow of The Queen's College
LORD BRIGGS Provost of Worcester College
BEN BROWN Fellow of Oriel College
RICHARD BURNELL Oxford University Eight, 1939
PETER BURROWS Managing Director of Holywell Press Ltd
JOAN CAMPBELL sometime commoner of St Hugh's College
ESTHER CAPLIN
HUMPHREY CARPENTER sometime commoner of Keble College
JEREMY CATTO Dean and Fellow of Oriel College
The late SIR NORMAN CHESTER Warden of Nuffield College
NIGEL COLLINSON Minister of Wesley Memorial Methodist Church
JANET COOPER *Victoria History of the County of Oxford*

H. E. J. COWDREY Fellow of St Edmund Hall
TONY CROSS Principal of Manchester College
ALAN CROSSLEY Editor, *Victoria History of the County of Oxford*
CLIFFORD DAVIES Fellow of Wadham College
CHRISTOPHER DAY *Victoria History of the County of Oxford*
P. G. DICKENS Fellow of New College
BERNARD DOD Senior Editor, Phaidon Press Ltd
The late RUTH FASNACHT author of *A History of the City of Oxford* (1954)
JOHN M. FLETCHER sometime commoner of Merton College
W. G. G. FORREST Wykeham Professor of Ancient History
M. J. O. FRANCIS Fellow of Wolfson College
KENNETH GARLICK former Keeper of Western Art, Ashmolean Museum
V. H. H. GREEN Rector of Lincoln College
JAMES GRIFFIN Fellow of Keble College
W. D. HACKMAN Assistant Curator, Museum of the History of Science
G. L. HARRISS Fellow of Magdalen College
T. G. HASSALL Secretary of the Royal Commission on the Historical Monuments of England and
    former Director, Oxford Archaeological Unit
W. O. HASSALL former Deputy Keeper of Western Manuscripts, Bodleian Library
J. G. HEMSLEY Managing Director, Oxford and County Newspapers
CHRISTOPHER HIBBERT sometime commoner of Oriel College
EDWARD HIBBERT author of *Vanbrugh House* (1982)
GUY HIBBERT former Playwright in Residence at the Oxford Playhouse
SUSAN HIBBERT sometime commoner of St Anne's College
C. H. JAQUES late master at the Dragon School and author of *A Dragon Century 1877–1977* (1977)
JOHN JONES Dean and Archivist, Balliol College
PETER WARD JONES Music Librarian, Bodleian Library
MICHAEL KASER Fellow of St Antony's College
JOHN KAYE Fellow of The Queen's College
MAURICE KEEN Fellow of Balliol College
J. D. R. KEWLEY sometime exhibitioner of St John's College
J. H. C. LEACH Fellow of Pembroke College
JAMES LEASOR sometime commoner of Oriel College
DAPHNE LENNIE sometime commoner of St Hugh's College and Secretary of the Oxford Society
ANGUS MACINTYRE Fellow of Magdalen College
MICHAEL MACLAGAN Emeritus Fellow of Trinity College and Richmond Herald
JOHN MADDICOTT Fellow of Exeter College
PAUL J. MARRIOTT author of *Early Oxford Picture Palaces* (1978) and *Oxford Pubs Past and
    Present* (1978)
J. F. A. MASON Student of Christ Church
PAUL MORGAN author of *Oxford Libraries outside the Bodleian* (second edition, 1980)
HELEN O'MALLEY commoner of Balliol College
JESSIE PARFIT author of *The Health of a City: Oxford 1770–1974* (1987)
BRENDA PARRY-JONES Archivist of Magdalen College and of the Oxfordshire Health Authority
HELEN MARY PETTER author of *The Oxford Almanacks* (1974)
The late IAN PHILIP sometime Secretary and Keeper of Printed Books, Bodleian Library
THÉRÈSE POLLEN
HAROLD POLLINS author of *The History of Ruskin College* (1984)
S. R. PORTER Fellow of St Cross College
JEREMY POTTER sometime exhibitioner of The Queen's College
J. A. N. RAILTON Secretary of the Oxford University Sports Centre
D. A. REES Fellow of Jesus College
MARJORIE REEVES Honorary Fellow of St Anne's College
SUSAN REYNOLDS Fellow of Lady Margaret Hall
BERNARD RICHARDS Fellow of Brasenose College
R. T. RIVINGTON author of *Punts and Punting* (1982)

A. H. T. ROBB-SMITH author of *A Short History of the Radcliffe Infirmary* (1970)
GEOFFREY ROWELL Chaplain of Keble College
JOHN RYAN graduate, Oxford Polytechnic
J. S. G. SIMMONS Emeritus Fellow of All Souls College
DAVID STEEL author of *Shotover: The Natural History of a Royal Forest* (1984)
TESSA STREET
DAVID STURDY sometime commoner of Christ Church and Assistant Keeper, Ashmolean Museum
P. H. SUTCLIFFE Senior Editor, Oxford University Press
ANN SPOKES SYMONDS Oxford City Councillor, Lord Mayor (1976–7) and Chairman Oxfordshire
    County Council (1981–3)
RICHARD SYMONDS Senior Associate Member, St Antony's College
ALAN TAYLER Fellow of St Catherine's College
RACHEL TRICKETT Principal of St Hugh's College
SIR JOHN WALTON Warden of Green College
PETER WAY sometime commoner of St John's College
JOHN WEBB Senior Administrator of St Clare's
B. R. WHITE Principal of Regent's Park College
ROLAND WILCOCK sometime commoner of Wadham College and author of *The Examination
    Schools, 1876–1882* (1983)
PENRY WILLIAMS Fellow of New College
HUGH WILLIAMSON Editor, *The Printing Historical Society Bulletin*
JAN L. WOMER Acting Principal of Mansfield College

(The appointments shown are those held when the entries were written)

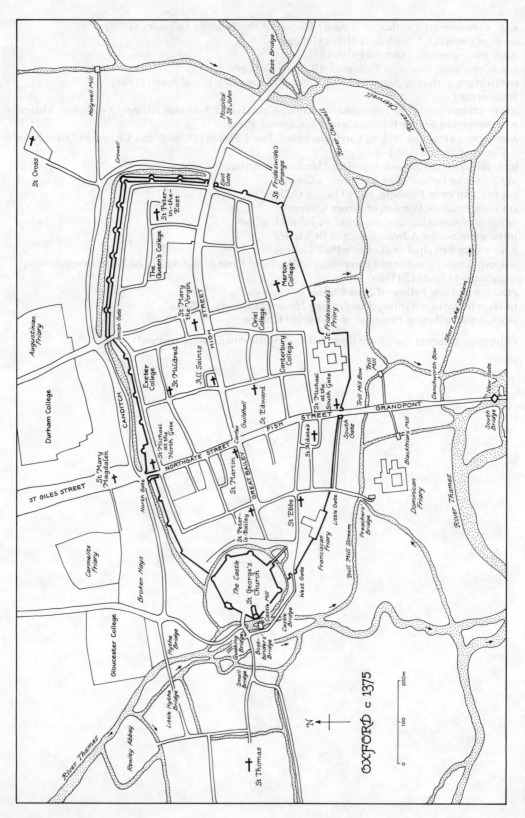

OXFORD c 1375

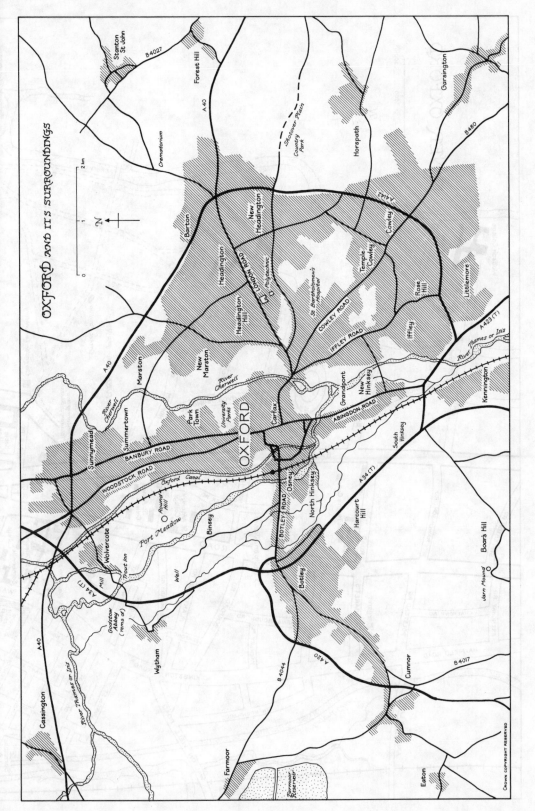

OXFORD AND ITS SURROUNDINGS

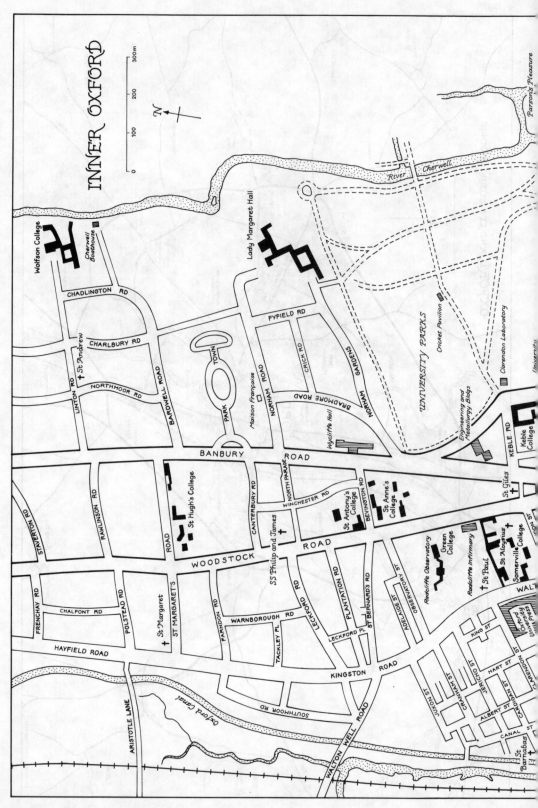

INNER OXFORD

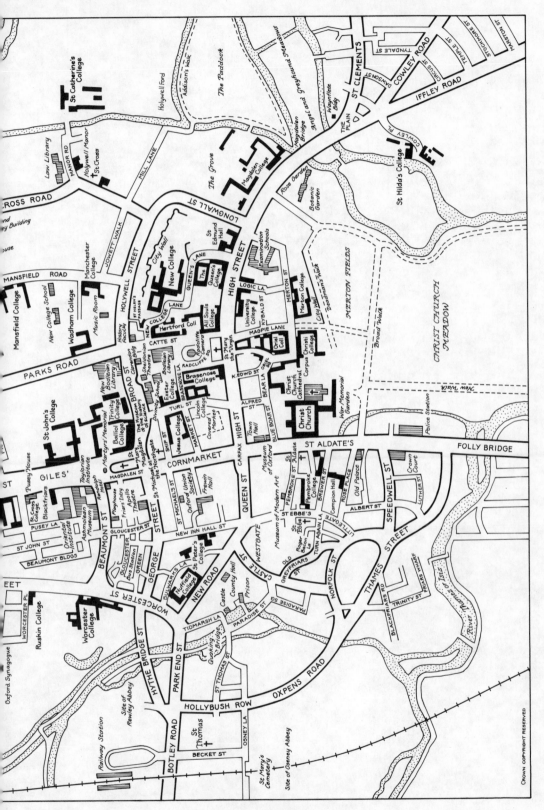

A

Abbots of Oseney Founded as an Augustinian priory in 1129, OSENEY ABBEY was the largest and richest monastery in the county. Its abbots exercised considerable influence in both town and University. During the abbacy of John Leech from 1235 to 1249 many of the abbey's extensive buildings were reconstructed and the fine abbey church begun. Thomas Kidlington, abbot from 1330 to 1372, added the Lady Chapel to the north of the presbytery. The last abbot, Robert King, who had spent some of his early years with the Cistercians at REWLEY ABBEY, was elected on 22 December 1537 through the influence of Thomas Cromwell, with whose family his own was connected. When the see of Oxford was created out of part of the huge see of Lincoln in 1542, King became the first BISHOP OF OXFORD. He died in 1557 and was buried in CHRIST CHURCH CATHEDRAL where a tomb was erected to his memory.

Abingdon Arms 7 *Market Street*. Began as a coaching inn during the 17th century and was at first called the Red Lion. From 1750 to 1800 it was known as the Earl or Lord Abingdon Arms, after the owner of the site, and thereafter as the Abingdon Arms. It was demolished in 1961 and replaced by the Oxford Trustee Savings Bank.

Abingdon Road Described by Herbert Hurst in 1899 as a 'very early and very necessary way from Abingdon', this road runs between FOLLY BRIDGE and the city boundary. It was known until the 17th century as the Causey (or Causy) as far as Lake Street, taking its name from the great Causeway (or GRANDPONT) of at least forty arches which once ran from ST ALDATE'S to the foot of Hinksey Hill. In the time of Faritius, Abbot of Abingdon between about 1100 and 1117, the Causeway was also known as the Bridge. The Folly from which its new name was derived was the ruin of what was once known as Friar Bacon's Study, or the New Gate, which was pulled down when the road was widened in 1779 (*see* FOLLY BRIDGE).

The Abingdon–Oxford–Banbury Turnpike is a small section of the ancient Saxon highway which ran between Southampton and Northampton via Winchester, Newbury and Oxford. A section of the original Saxon causeway was discovered in 1971. An inscribed milestone which marks this turnpike remains outside No. 309 Abingdon Road (near RIVERMEAD REHABILITATION CENTRE). One mile north of this was the toll-gate on Folly Bridge, which was built in 1844 and recently restored.

The name Abingdon is derived from the Old English name *Abba*. *Dun* means hill or down, and it

Abingdon Road in flood in 1894.

was thus known as Abba's Hill, or Abbandun(e), with its earliest recording in 977. Most of the Abingdon Road, except Grandpont House and Eastwyke Farm House (early 17th century) was not built until the 19th century. Before the building of Folly Bridge the river was crossed here by a ford, which, it has been suggested, may have given Oxford its name.

Places of note in Abingdon Road (from Folly Bridge southwards) include Grandpont House (*see* GRAND-PONT). No. 5 Folly Bridge was built in 1849 for Joseph Caudwell, an accountant, and was originally known as North Hinksey House. It is an eccentric, folly-like brick 'castle' with Gothic windows and statues. Isis House, just off the road on the other side of the backwater, was built in about 1850. HOLY ROOD CHURCH was completed in 1961 to designs by Gilbert Flavel. Grandpont Villas (Nos 65–83) were built in about 1859. Eastwyke Farmhouse is a Grade II listed building of the early 17th century. The Old White House public house (Grade II) was built in 1897 by H.T. Hare. Nearby is the White House Ground, home of Oxford City Football Club. The old Infectious Diseases Hospital (1886) is now the Rivermead Rehabilitation Centre and opposite is the City Council's Park and Ride site (*see* PARKING). To the east of the road, at the side of the river, is the OXFORD UNIVERSITY BOAT CLUB, a Grade II listed building erected in 1881 by J.O. Scott with a five-door boat-house at ground level.

Hogarth's The Lecture *of 1737 shows various styles of academic head-dress. Reading the lecture is Henry Fisher of Jesus College, University Registrar.*

Academic Dress In 1222 the Archbishop of Canterbury decreed that all clerks should wear the *cappa clausa*, a development of the pluvial – a loose, hooded cape with a hole for the head and a slit in front for the arms. Thereafter the *cappa clausa* became the first recognised form of academic dress at Oxford for Doctors of Theology and Masters of Arts, who, as priests, were obliged to wear it. The hood was at first

a purely utilitarian head covering, but it remained a distinctive feature of the dress of academical persons when it was abandoned in ordinary dress in the middle of the 15th century; and, as a feature of academic dress, it became greatly extended. The academical bonnet was derived from a French fashion of 1449 and the square cap, or mortar-board, from a head-dress which apparently originated in Italy and was introduced at the University of Paris in about 1520. The square cap was adorned with a 'tump' or knob. To this was added a tassel during the 1730s, an addition which was made official in 1770. The sons of noblemen were permitted to wear gold tassels or tufts – hence the phrase 'tuft-hunting'.

As FACULTIES, NATIONS and COLLEGES developed at the University, so did the use of colours in academical dress to differentiate one from another. By the 13th century Doctors of the University had, for example, adopted various shades of red for their *cappae*. The hood worn by Bachelors of Arts was already lined with lamb's wool or rabbit's fur in the 15th century. SUBFUSC was unknown before the 16th century.

Sometimes the founder of a college left directions about what colours the members of his foundation should wear. For the Fellows of The Queen's College, Robert Eglesfeld prescribed that they were to dine in hall in purple cloaks, the Doctors wearing theirs trimmed with fur, while the Masters were to wear theirs 'plain'. The colour was 'to suit the dignity of their position and to be like the blood of the Lord'.

From time to time enactments were passed to ensure that the rules governing the wearing of academical dress were observed. In 1358 tailors, who were evidently endeavouring to shorten the length of University gowns, were informed that it was 'honourable and in accordance with reason that clerks to whom God has given an advantage over the lay folk in their adornments within, should likewise differ from the lay folks outwardly in dress'. Masters of Arts were later reminded that they must wear 'boots either black or as near black as possible', and that they must never give 'ordinary lectures' when wearing 'shoes cut down or short in any way'. And in 1489 it was ordained that 'whereas the insolence of many scholars in our days is reaching such a pitch of audacity that they are not afraid to wear hoods like Masters', henceforth they were to wear only the '*liripipium consutum et non contextum*' (an adornment that survived in Oxford until the 19th century).

On his visit to Oxford in 1654, John Evelyn noted that the old ceremonial dress was still maintained, though in the republican and presbyterian atmosphere of the times it seemed then doubtful that it would long survive. However, an influential PROCTOR of the time, Walter Pope, came out strongly in opposition to any change. He persuaded his friends to resist it in CONVOCATION and he eventually succeeded in preserving academical dress and the 'distinctions of Degrees'.

Some years before this, title XIV of the LAUDIAN CODE of 1636 had required the heads of colleges and halls (*see* ACADEMIC HALLS) to make 'diligent enquiry' to determine what were the correct robes for each faculty of the University. A specimen of each robe was then to be deposited in a chest and any persons thereafter found wearing incorrect robes, or any tailor manufacturing them, were to be punished at the discretion of the VICE-CHANCELLOR. It is not known if the chest and its contents were ever provided, but certainly they cannot now be found. In 1956, however, a book of patterns of robes, gowns and hoods by D.R. Venables of SHEPHERD AND WOODWARD was submitted to a Committee on Academic Dress on behalf of the Oxford branch of the National Federation of Merchant Tailors. The committee recommended that the patterns should be approved. Soon afterwards, on 12 February 1957, HEBDOMADAL COUNCIL accordingly gave its approval to the patterns, which were made up in fur, silk and other materials and, with the University requirements inscribed over each, were deposited in a leather-bound register with the University ARCHIVES. A copy of the register was deposited with Shepherd and Woodward. That same year *Academic Dress of the University of Oxford* by D.R. Venables and R.E. Clifford (head clerk in the UNIVERSITY OFFICES) was published. A sixth edition of this work, revised and enlarged by Venables's son, J.R. Venables, and by R.E. Clifford's successor in the University Offices, Philip Moss, was issued in 1985 as the authoritative work on academic dress in Oxford.

The wearing of academic dress is compulsory at all formal ceremonies of the University, such as ENCAENIA, and is generally required at examinations and at most official meetings. Subfusc clothing is worn with full academic dress. Caps are also worn with full academic dress, at all times by women, by men when out of doors, and by the CHANCELLOR, the Vice-Chancellor and the Proctors at all times, except in church, a college or a private place. The square black cap, or mortar-board, is worn by both men and women, though women, if they prefer to do so, may wear a soft black cap. A black bonnet is worn by the holders of the degrees of Doctor of Civil Law, Doctor of Medicine and Doctor of Music by both sexes when in full dress robes. The Chancellor's cap is of black velvet with a gold tassel.

The Chancellor's long, trailing robe is of heavy black brocaded silk with gold lace trimmings on the collar, facings, back and sleeves. The Vice-Chancellor has no special robe but wears the robe or gown of the degree to which he is entitled.

The patterns and colours of the various robes and GOWNS are illustrated and fully described in *Academic Dress of the University of Oxford*. The colours and materials of the hoods are as follows:

Doctor of Divinity: scarlet cloth lined with black silk or art silk.
Doctor of Music: cream silk or art silk brocade with apple-blossom embroidery lined with cherry crimson silk or art silk.
Doctor of Civil Law and *Doctor of Medicine*: scarlet cloth lined with crimson silk or art silk.
Master of Surgery: black silk or art silk lined and edged with blue silk or art silk.
Doctor of Letters and *Doctor of Science*: scarlet cloth lined with grey silk or art silk.
Doctor of Philosophy: scarlet cloth lined with blue silk or art silk.
Master of Letters and *Master of Science*: blue ribbed silk or art silk, edged and lined with grey silk or art silk.
Master of Philosophy and *Bachelor of Philosophy*: blue ribbed silk or art silk lined with white silk or art silk.
Bachelor of Music: lilac ribbed silk or art silk trimmed with white fur.
Bachelor of Medicine, Bachelor of Surgery and

Bachelor of Civil Law: blue corded silk or poplin with white fur.
Bachelor of Letters and *Bachelor of Science*: steel-blue corded silk or poplin with white fur.
Master of Studies: deep-green ribbed silk or art silk lined with white silk or art silk.
Bachelor of Divinity: black corded silk or art silk lined with a fine black ribbed silk or art silk.
Master of Arts: black corded silk or art silk lined with crimson or shot-crimson silk or art silk.
Bachelor of Arts: black corded silk or art silk lined and trimmed with white fur (the use of a synthetic fur forbidden in 1956 was allowed by the Hebdomadal Council in July 1979 because of the rising cost of real fur and the reluctance of conservationists to wear it).
Bachelor of Fine Art: black silk or art silk lined with gold silk or art silk.
Bachelor of Education: black corded silk or art silk lined with green silk or art silk. (This degree is no longer conferred and has been replaced by the Bachelor's degree of the Council for National Academic Awards, whose hood is of gold panama lined with turquoise-blue art silk.)

As well as full dress robes and their undress gown, Doctors of Divinity, Civil Law, Medicine, Letters, Science and Philosophy also have what is known as a Convocation Habit, which is worn for meetings of the Ancient House of CONGREGATION when presenting students for degrees. Convocation Habits are also worn at UNIVERSITY SERMONS which are not marked as Scarlet Days (*see* Glossary), with the exception of Quinquagesima, in Lent and at ASSIZE SERMONS on weekdays. On Scarlet Days, or those indicated in the *University Gazette* or in other notices as occasions on which 'Doctors will wear their robes', full dress robes are worn with white ties and bands. Bands are also worn by the Vice-Chancellor and Proctors and by Pro-Proctors when representing Proctors and by Pro-Vice-Chancellors when representing the Vice-Chancellor. (*See also* GOWNS *and* SUBFUSC.)

(Venables, D.R., and Clifford, R.E., *Academic Dress of the University of Oxford*, 6th edition, Oxford, 1985; Hargreaves-Mawdsley, W.N., *A History of Academical Dress in Europe until the End of the Eighteenth Century*, Oxford, 1963; Dudley Buxton, L.H., and Gibson, Strickland, *Oxford University Ceremonies*, Oxford, 1935.)

Academic Halls The mediaeval forerunners of the Oxford colleges. At the close of the 12th century individual teachers – 'masters' – were beginning to collect groups of pupils – 'scholars' – for the teaching, by lecture, of Canon and Roman Law, Liberal Arts and Theology. These masters, mostly obscure figures, hired for their lectures rooms in dwelling houses in the town, many concentrated in the area north of the University Church, ST MARY THE VIRGIN. For living quarters both masters and scholars used houses scattered over various parts of the town, mostly within the CITY WALLS, but a few outside.

Very little is known about this period – the last two decades of the 12th century – of very rapid growth in the academic population in Oxford, a community with a well-defined interest but having only the rudiments of an informal organisation, with no corporate existence, endowments or property. An episode early in the 13th century sheds light on the conditions in

One of the largest of the University's academic halls, Magdalen Hall was once the grammar school of Magdalen College.

which the embryo scholastic community was developing and gives an early indication of the importance its members attached to accommodation. Included in the terms, drawn up by a papal legate, of the settlement of a serious quarrel between the masters and scholars on one side and the townsmen on the other was the provision that 'from Michaelmas AD 1214 for the ten years next following there shall be remitted to the scholars studying in Oxford one half of the rent of all *hospicia* let to clerks'. It is this final phrase that in due course gave rise to the category of buildings termed 'academic halls'.

For three hundred years an academic hall was the society in which the great majority of those studying at the University lived and worked. At their most numerous, in the early 14th century, halls numbered over 120; probably a greater number of buildings in all was used for academic halls between the beginnings of the 12th and 17th centuries, by which time colleges had taken their place. The typical academic hall owed its existence to the initiative of an individual graduate, normally a master, who took the lease of a house from a landlord for the purpose of providing a boarding house, for profit, for a group of scholars.

Because academic halls were enterprises in the hands of private proprietors, virtually no records of their operation have come down from the days in which they flourished. Such written evidence as does exist is derived from the rent-rolls of the monastic landlords – and later the colleges – who owned many of the houses used; and from the mid-13th century there are also University documents recording the steps taken by the authorities to regulate academic halls. Thus, almost everything which can now be said about them, particularly in their earlier decades, must be considered tentative.

By the second quarter of the 13th century the

University was able to act as a corporate body, and over the following fifty years was able to deal, to its own satisfaction, with the questions of control of rents and security of tenure for the proprietors of academic halls. By 1290 a series of royal decisions provided for rents to be determined by taxors representing both town and University, and for the permanent use of a building for scholastic purposes once it had been so used.

Control by the University over the inhabitants of the halls took a much longer time. It appears that from a very early date it had become the custom for all 'Principals' – heads of academic halls – to come yearly before the CHANCELLOR or his representative by six o'clock on the morning after the Feast of the Nativity of the Blessed Virgin (8 September) to establish their right to the tenancy concerned and to deposit a 'caution' – normally a pledge in money or kind (*see* CAUTION MONEY) – as security for paying the rent in the year ahead. Only those establishments whose Principals did this were recognised as academic halls. The first positive attempt at the direct control of scholars was the Royal Ordinance of 1231, which laid down that every scholar must place his name on the roll (*matricula*) of a master, who was required to monitor his attendance at lectures. A few years later a University statute provided for inquisitions to be made at halls, without notice, to identify unruly scholars. This proving ineffectual, in 1313 the Principals themselves were made responsible for the discipline of their scholars, being bound under oath to report wrongdoers. Finally, a statute of the early 15th century provided that thenceforth every scholar must reside in an academic hall. Thus disappeared 'chamberdeacons' – individual scholars living on their own in lodgings – who had been a source of disorder over the centuries (though it is said that some survived till 1612). Between 1483 and 1490 the Aularian

4

Statutes (*aula* meaning a hall) drew together the various ordinances and statutes of the previous two centuries.

By the beginning of the 14th century academic halls were well established and for the following two hundred years they were the normal home for the great majority of scholars. Although scattered about the town, the majority lay to the east of CARFAX. They were particularly thick on the ground north-west and south-east of St Mary the Virgin, in areas lying between what is now TURL STREET and CATTE STREET, and in a square bordered by MERTON STREET (either side), ORIEL STREET and HIGH STREET. There was a smaller concentration in the area now occupied by Christ Church. They had a great variety of names, indicative of ancient local families, saints, trades, inns, or were derived from the position of the site or a feature of the building: Cary's Hall, St Mary's Hall, Spicer's Hall, the Dolphin, Corner Hall, Chimney Hall. Many halls changed their names more than once over the centuries, and there were often duplications in names. In addition to the neighbouring monastic houses, their owners were prominent citizens; others were clergy with livings in the Oxford area. They were mostly typical mediaeval town houses of two storeys with a hall rising from ground floor to the rafters, a feature which caused almost any substantial dwelling to be called a 'hall'. Off the hall would be a few smaller rooms. Many halls had a narrow frontage on to the street, in some cases occupied by a row of shops. If the layout so required, the hall and rooms would be reached via a narrow covered passage or 'entry' – a term forming part of the name of several academic halls. Few were purpose-built. Some of those in use early on were amalgamated with adjoining halls to create more extensive accommodation; others were rebuilt for the same purpose. Nearly all halls had a buttery and a kitchen; but there is only one case of a chapel being permitted by the local clergy, and St Mary Hall alone possibly had a library.

It is almost impossible to tell, from surviving records, what were the physical conditions of learning in academic halls. The typical room for scholars was small – about 20 feet by 15 – shared for sleeping and study purposes by four or five scholars. Small 'studies' might be partitioned off from the communal area. In course of time the typical academic hall developed, from providing merely board and lodging, into a community exhibiting features that later characterised the colleges, with a daily and weekly routine of lectures, academic exercises, studies, sermons and Masses. Towards the end of the 15th century the germ of the tutorial system can be discerned (*see* TUTORIALS).

In the formative years of the University the present pattern of undergraduates and graduates hardly existed. The scholar population of an academic hall could range from Doctors to boys at one of Oxford's five grammar schools. By the mid-15th century, however, some halls had become occupied exclusively by graduates studying for higher degrees in Law – the 'legists' – and others by undergraduates in the Liberal Arts – the 'artists' – with about six scholars on average in a legists' hall and twenty on average in one for artists. By this time all Principals were required by the University to be Masters of Arts; many were men who later had distinguished careers in the Church or in the academic world. Their assistant staff always included a manciple (housekeeper) and sometimes a cook in addition. By the mid-15th century there might also be graduate tutors.

When at the height of their importance, around 1450, the academic halls, though fewer in number – seventy or so – than at the opening of the 14th century as a result of amalgamations and acquisition by the emerging colleges, contained about 1450 of the total University population of 1600. One hundred years later only eight were still in existence, with a total population of 260 out of a University reduced by the Reformation to about 1150, though some of the halls were larger than the smaller colleges. The eclipse of the academic halls was caused by the rise of the colleges. Their weakness was their lack of corporate identity, property or endowment; an academic hall's continued existence depended on the continued willingness of its Principal to maintain his enterprise and the annual renewal of his authority by the University. By contrast, the colleges had permanence in the form of statutes, endowments, property and buildings; and the means to provide better conditions for scholars. The foundation of the earliest colleges – University (1249), Balliol (1263), Merton (1264), Exeter (1314), Oriel (1326) and Queen's (1341) – had little immediate effect on the role of academic halls, since their founders intended them primarily for graduate scholars. However, the founder of New College (1379) provided in his foundation for seventy young boys from his school at Winchester to be scholars in his college; and, with the exception of Lincoln (1427) and All Souls (1438), all the colleges founded from then until the mid-16th century – Magdalen (1458), Brasenose (1509), Corpus Christi (1517), Christ Church (1546), Trinity (1555) and St John's (1555) – provided for undergraduates from their foundation. From the early 17th century commoners began to form a significant proportion of the population of a college. All of the above colleges physically absorbed adjoining academic halls; in some cases there was a smooth transition from a group of halls into a college, with the Principal of one of them as its first head.

Only eight academic halls survived from the reign of Elizabeth – BROADGATES, GLOUCESTER, HART, MAGDALEN, ST ALBAN, ST MARY, NEW INN and ST EDMUND – and from that time the Chancellor appointed Principals, with the exception of St Edmund Hall, whose Principal was appointed by The Queen's College. By 1800 the first three had been incorporated into colleges; the others survived into the 19th century, providing a less expensive Oxford University education for a small proportion of students. Magdalen Hall formed the core of the second – successful – foundation of Hertford College. The others were absorbed into colleges, not without protest, by the University Commission of 1877 (*see* ROYAL COMMISSIONS), but St Edmund Hall avoided absorption and in 1957 became a college by royal charter, and, as a college, retained its ancient title.

(*See also* COLLEGES, BEAM HALL, POSTMASTERS' HALL, TACKLEY'S INN and PRIVATE HALLS.)

(The History of the University of Oxford – Vol. I: *The Early Oxford Schools*, J.I. Catto (ed.), Oxford, 1984, and Vol. III: *The Collegiate University*, James McConica (ed.), Oxford, 1986; Emden, A.B., *An Oxford Hall in Medieval Times*, Oxford, reprinted 1968, and 'Oxford Academical Halls in the Later Middle Ages' in *Medieval Learning and Literature – Essays presented to R.W. Hunt*, Alexander, J.J.G, and

Rudolph Ackermann's History of the University of Oxford *(1814). This print shows the Clarendon Building with the Sheldonian Theatre and the Old Ashmolean to the right.*

Gibson, M.T. (eds), Oxford, 1976; Pantin, W.A., 'The Halls and Schools of Medieval Oxford' in *Oxford Studies presented to Daniel Callus*, OHS New Series Vol. XVI, Oxford, 1964; Salter, H.E., and Lobel, Mary D., *Victoria County History of the County of Oxford*, Vol. III, Oxford, 1954.)

Ackermann, Rudolph *(1764–1834)*. A fine-art publisher and bookseller. He settled in London as a coach designer, but in 1795 opened a print shop in the Strand. He established fine-art lithography in England and published numerous illustrated books. Among these was his *History of the University of Oxford: Its Colleges, Halls and Public Buildings*, published in 1814 in two volumes. The work was dedicated to Lord Grenville, CHANCELLOR of the University, and includes a portrait of him. It contains sixty-nine coloured aquatints of views of the colleges and University buildings drawn by Pugin, Mackenzie, Nash and Westall. There are sections on each of the colleges then in existence, as well as the ACADEMIC HALLS, the Chancellor, OFFICERS OF THE UNIVERSITY, degrees, and sections on 'founders' (thirty-two plates), and on ACADEMIC DRESS (called 'Costumes') with seventeen coloured plates after Unwins. Among the illustrations, many of which have been reproduced for the OXFORD ALMANACK, are 'Alban Hall' (Mackenzie), 'Magdalen Tower' (Nash), 'Wadham College from the Parks' (Pugin), 'The Statue Gallery' (showing the Arundel Marbles, by Westall) and 'The Clarendon Printing House, Theatre & Museum' (Mackenzie). The theatre referred to is the SHELDONIAN and the museum the OLD ASHMOLEAN, now the MUSEUM OF THE HISTORY OF SCIENCE. This drawing shows the EMPERORS' HEADS and a flock of sheep being driven down BROAD STREET.

Acland, Sir Henry Wentworth *(1815–1900)*. The son of Sir Thomas Dyke Acland, the politician and philanthropist who was one of the founders of Grillion's Club, Acland was educated at Harrow and in 1834 matriculated at Christ Church, where he began a life-long friendship with JOHN RUSKIN. Elected a Fellow of All Souls in 1840, he studied medicine in London and Edinburgh before being appointed Lee's Lecturer in Anatomy in 1845. In 1847 he became physician to the RADCLIFFE INFIRMARY and Aldrichian Professor of Clinical Medicine, and, in

1857, was appointed Regius Professor of Medicine. He held that appointment for thirty-seven years, during which he vastly improved the status of the University medical school. He was largely responsible for the establishment of the UNIVERSITY MUSEUM, and he founded and endowed the nursing home which developed into the ACLAND HOSPITAL. (*See also* MEDICINE.)

Acland Hospital Sir Henry Acland was Regius Professor of Medicine from 1857–94. His wife, Sarah, died in 1878 and to perpetuate her memory a home for district nurses and private nurses was established at No. 37 WELLINGTON SQUARE. In 1882, No. 38 Wellington Square was opened as a medical and surgical home to take six cases. When Sir Henry Acland retired he gave the £3000 raised to mark his retirement to assist the transfer of the nursing home to its present site at No. 25 BANBURY ROAD. The new building, designed by SIR THOMAS JACKSON, was opened in 1897 by King Edward VII, then Prince of Wales. The home was extended in 1906 and an operating theatre added. Until then, operations had been carried out in the patient's own room. A gift from LORD NUFFIELD enabled a new wing to be added and the present front, built in neo-Georgian style in 1937, was designed by R. Fielding Dodd. In 1962 Nuffield Nursing Homes Trust took over the Acland Home. After a successful appeal in 1977, work began on the building of a new wing, with two major operating theatres, which was opened in June 1979. In 1964 the Acland Home was renamed the Acland Hospital.

Act, The The old name for ENCAENIA, the ceremony at the close of the academic year.

Sir Henry Wentworth Acland with his pet monkey. Acland was Regius Professor of Medicine for thirty-seven years from 1857.

Addison's Walk This walk, within the grounds of Magdalen College, was formerly known as the Water Walks but was renamed after Joseph Addison in the 19th century. It runs northwards from the college buildings between Long Meadow and the Fellows' Garden until it reaches MESOPOTAMIA in the north. Joseph Addison, the essayist and poet (1672–1719), is probably best known for his contributions to the *Spectator* (1711–12). SAMUEL JOHNSON said of him that 'whoever wishes to attain an English style must give his days and nights to the volumes of Addison'. Addison's association with Magdalen began in 1689 when he gained a DEMYSHIP. He was a Fellow of the college until 1711. A champion of landscape gardening, Addison was a critic of formal gardens and in articles for the *Spectator* in 1712 attacked topiary (which had 'the marks of the scissors on every plant and bush') and moveable plants with which the 'shops are plentifully stocked'. His rooms in Magdalen overlooked the Water Walks, fields and the meadows, which are still a nature reserve (the famous snake's-head fritillaries flower there in the spring). Addison said that a poet 'must love to hide himself in woods and to haunt the springs and meadows. His head must be full of the humming of bees, the bleating of flocks and the melody of birds. The verdure of the grass, the embroidery of the flowers and the glist'ning of the

dew must be painted strong in his imagination'. His inspiration can still be appreciated in Addison's Walk.

Admissions All Oxford candidates are required to complete two documents, both of which have to be submitted between 1 September and 15 October of the year before they wish to commence their university career. The first is the UCCA form (*see* UCCA); the second is the Oxford application card, which must be completed and returned to the Oxford Colleges Admissions Office (see address at end of this entry). This provides Oxford with the following information on each candidate: mode of application; the papers they wish to take, if they are applying through the entrance examination; their choice of up to three colleges (if such a choice has been made); and the subject they wish to study at Oxford.

There are two modes of application: Mode E and Mode N. Candidates who, at the time of making application, will not have passed more than one subject at Advanced level are designated pre-A-level and may choose between the two modes (except that pre-A-level candidates for Medicine must enter through Mode E).

Mode E involves taking the Oxford entrance examination, which is set towards the end of November each year. In this examination candidates take two or three (or, exceptionally, four) papers in the subject(s) of their choice. This examination is available only to pre-A-level candidates and special care has been taken to set the papers at a level suitable for the selection of students who are at the end of their fourth term in the sixth form. Candidates who are offered a place after they have taken the examination are not required to obtain stipulated grades in their A-level examinations still to be taken, other than attainment of two A-level grade passes at grade E or better, which are necessary for the satisfaction of the University's MATRICULATION requirements.

Mode N is available to those pre-A-level candidates who choose not to apply through the entrance examination, and is the only mode available to post-A-level candidates (those who, at the time of applying, will have passed two or more subjects at A-level). Although this mode does not involve taking the entrance examination, candidates may be asked either to submit some samples of written work or to take a short written test while they are in Oxford for interview. The interview for Mode N candidates is likely to be more stringent than that for Mode E and may take the form of an oral test, and pre-A-level candidates who are offered places through Mode N may well be required to achieve high A-level results in their GCE examinations the following summer. Most commonly the grades sought are A, A, B, but some offers are made on higher or slightly lower conditions. For post-A-level candidates the A-level results already achieved are a major factor in the selection procedure, and any offers made are unconditional, providing the candidate has obtained the O-level qualifications required for matriculation.

Before making decisions on candidates for either mode, the tutors also take into account all the information given in the reference and in the GCE results already obtained.

Candidates attend Oxford for interview in the first half of December, after which selection meetings are held. Letters offering places to successful candidates

Addison's Walk takes its name from Joseph Addison, a Fellow of Magdalen College, the tower of which can be seen in the background.

are usually despatched in time for them to reach their destinations before Christmas.

The dossiers of candidates who narrowly fail to be offered a place are made available to all colleges during January, and no candidate is finally rejected until the end of January.

There are twenty-eight undergraduate colleges in Oxford: twenty-six are mixed, and two are for women only (St Hilda's and Somerville). In addition, for admission purposes only, Mansfield College is grouped with the colleges, although it is a private hall. Candidates are encouraged to name the three colleges by which they wish to be considered. For about half the subjects taught, candidates may choose any three colleges, but for the main arts subjects the colleges are divided into three groups as below, and for these subjects candidates are required to restrict their choice of colleges to any one group. The attention of applicants is drawn to a table printed in the Undergraduate Prospectus which shows any preference for either mode of application held by any subject within each college.

Any candidate who does not wish to name colleges may submit an 'open application'. Through this procedure candidates may leave the selection of one, two or all three colleges to the Admissions Office. Such candidates are allocated to colleges by computer, which takes into account the number of candidates applying to each college for each subject.

In recent years, about 7500 school leavers have applied to Oxford each year, of whom approximately 3000 have been admitted; about 1200 (40 per cent) of the intake have been women and there has been an almost equal number of students coming from state schools and from the independent sector. About two-thirds of the places have been given mainly on performance in the entrance examination; nevertheless, the standard of the Oxford intake as judged by A-level results is very high, with 40 per cent of the intake obtaining grade A in three subjects and 80 per cent gaining grades of A, B, B or better.

Grouping of Colleges

Group 1	Group 2	Group 3
Brasenose	Balliol	Corpus Christi
Christ Church	Exeter	Hertford
Jesus	Keble	Lady Margaret
Lincoln	Pembroke	Hall
Magdalen	St Anne's	New College
Merton	St Edmund Hall	The Queen's
Oriel	St John's	College
St Hilda's (W)	St Peter's	St Catherine's
Somerville (W)	Wadham	St Hugh's
Mansfield		Trinity
		University
		Worcester

Information about courses available at Oxford, descriptions of each of the twenty-eight colleges and details of the admissions procedure are included in the Undergraduate Prospectus which is published annually and is available from the Oxford Colleges Admissions Office, University Offices, Wellington Square, Oxford OX1 2JD.

Airport In November 1935 Oxford City Council purchased land for development as a municipal airport. The airfield is about 7 miles north-west of Oxford on the road to Woodstock. Flying started in June 1938 by No. 26 Elementary & Reserve Flying Training School, operated by Marshall's of Cambridge, training pilots for the RAFVR. In July 1939 the Oxford Flying Club began flying under the Civil Air Guard scheme. The aerodrome was requisitioned by the RAF on 5 September 1939 and, after sporadic use by various units, RAF Kidlington became the base for two Glider Operational Training Units, training pilots for the Glider Pilot Regiment. In 1946, with civil flying restrictions lifted, the Oxford Flying Club resumed private flying. Renamed the Oxford Aeroplane Club later, it changed ownership several times and almost ceased to exist in the 1950s; but in 1959, operated by Oxford Aviation, it began to expand, using modern aircraft.

In September 1962 the Pressed Steel Company acquired the lease of the airfield to develop air-taxi and charter flying, and took over Oxford Aviation two years later. Thus was created British Executive Air Services, whose air training division was renamed the Oxford Air Training School in spring 1963. In March 1964 Pressed Steel gave up their flying interests at Kidlington, except for helicopter sales and operations, and the fixed-wing activities were taken over by CSE Aviation. In May, under new government regulations, the Oxford Air Training School became one of only three schools to receive government approval to train commercial pilots. In the following years OATS expanded to become the biggest flying school in Europe.

In 1971 aircraft movements at Oxford Airport reached 175,000 – second only to Heathrow. CSE Aviation purchased the aerodrome freehold from the City Council in September 1981 and now operates a fleet of fixed-wing aircraft and helicopters, in addition to aircraft sales and maintenance, and an engineering training school.

Alden An old Oxford family connected with various Oxford businesses. In 1939 there were thirteen different businesses in the city with the name Alden, but by 1978 the number had dropped to three. The firm of butchers of that name was founded in 1793, but closed at the end of 1986. Robert Rhodes Alden gave his name to the firm of R.R. Alden & Sons, butchers of Eastwyke Farm, ABINGDON ROAD. One of his sons, Leonard Henry Alden, was MAYOR of Oxford in 1936 but was killed in a road accident during his term of office. Another son, Frederick George Alden, founded the firm of Fred. G. Alden (Heating) Ltd, the Oxford heating engineers. The third business with the Alden name is that of printing (see ALDEN PRESS).

Alden Press *Osney Mead.* This printing firm was founded by Henry Alden (see ALDEN), who opened his shop in 1832 and traded there and elsewhere near the centre of the city for forty years. He was joint publisher of the weekly *Oxford Chronicle* (see NEWSPAPERS), publisher of books by local authors, and proprietor, printer and publisher of two local monthly magazines and a local almanac. His son Edward went on for another forty years, introducing local maps and books about Oxford, including *Alden's Oxford Guide*, which has been in print since 1874. His son, H.J.C. Alden, set up a printing works in Binsey Lane in 1926 and closed the retail shop. The firm was closely linked at this time with the publisher Jonathan Cape. The Alden Press, now in a modern factory at OSNEY MEAD and managed by John F. Alden, prints academic and other books and journals for publishers and learned societies in several countries, from Scandinavia to the Middle East and the United States.

Aldrich, Henry   *(1647–1710)*. Installed as Dean of Christ Church in 1689 after the flight of his Roman Catholic predecessor (*see* ROMAN CATHOLICS), Aldrich held that office for the rest of his life, becoming VICE-CHANCELLOR of the University in 1692, the year after the publication of his *Artis Logicae Compendium*, which remained the standard textbook in the 19th century. A convivial host and talented musician – he was composer of the popular catch *Hark the bonny Christ Church bells* – as well as a 'polite though not profound scholar', as Macaulay described him, Aldrich was also a skilled amateur architect. He probably designed The Queen's College library (1692–6) and ALL SAINTS CHURCH, HIGH STREET (1706–8), and he certainly designed Peckwater Quad at Christ Church (1705–14). He was buried – as he requested, without any memorial – in CHRIST CHURCH CATHEDRAL. Some twenty years later, however, the memorial by Henry Cheere, with Aldrich's profile in a roundel, was erected in the nave. There is also a good bust of him by an unknown artist in the college library.

Details from a portrait of Henry Aldrich. 'A polite though not profound scholar', he was Dean of Christ Church from 1689 until his death in 1710.

Alfred Street   Running from the south side of HIGH STREET to the junction of BLUE BOAR STREET and (the present) BEAR LANE, this narrow street was in existence in 1220. It was then called Venella Sancti Edwardi after St Edward's Church on the west side of the lane, which was destroyed in about 1500. In the 16th century it was known as Vine Hall Street after Vine Hall, which was further to the south at the north-west

corner of the Peckwater Quadrangle of Christ Church. Before Christ Church was built, the lane ran southwards to ST FRIDESWIDE'S CHURCH. In the 17th and 18th centuries it was called Bear Lane after the BEAR inn. When and why it was renamed Alfred Street is not known. H.E. SALTER, in his booklet on Oxford street-names (1921), merely says 'Its last and very pointless name is Alfred Street'. Perhaps it was named after King Alfred, who has been credited with the foundation of University College.

At the corner of Alfred Street and High Street is the National Westminster Bank (1866 by F. & H. Francis). The new National Westminster House now takes up most of the east side of the street. Further down on the west side is ST COLUMBA'S UNITED REFORMED CHURCH. On the southern corner is the BEAR INN.

Alice   *Alice's Adventures in Wonderland* and *Through the Looking-glass*, which capture the essence of childhood, grew out of a unique relationship between Alice Liddell, the daughter of the Dean of Christ Church (*see* HENRY GEORGE LIDDELL), and the REV. CHARLES DODGSON (Lewis Carroll), a Mathematics lecturer at the college. This shy bachelor don was never happier than when in the company of children and entering wholeheartedly into their world. Alice, whose favourite phrase was 'Let's pretend', was the ideal child-friend to stimulate Lewis Carroll's genius for make-believe. She was born in 1852 at Westminster School, where her father was headmaster, and was four years old when the family moved into the Christ Church Deanery. An acquaintance was soon struck up with Lewis Carroll, who photographed her and her sisters in the Deanery garden. In the summer term Lewis Carroll took the Liddell children on the river and, in his words, stories lived and died 'like summer midges'. But after one memorable expedition up the river to GODSTOW on 4 July 1862, Alice persuaded him to write the stories down for her. When he wrote the little book 'for a dear child in memory of a summer's day' he had no thought of publishing it, but friends who saw it insisted that he must do so. The book was published by Macmillan in 1865 as *Alice's Adventures in Wonderland* and a second volume of the stories was published much later, in 1871, and called *Through the Looking-glass and What Alice Found There*.

Wonderland and Looking-glass world were fantasy indeed, but based on real experiences shared by Alice and Lewis Carroll and some of the observant remarks in the book are Alice's own. Figuring prominently in the stories are Alice's sisters, Lorina and Edith (the Lory and the Eaglet) and her governess Miss Prickett, called 'Pricks' by the children (the Red Queen, 'one of the thorny kind'), Alice's cat, Dinah, and Lewis Carroll's friend from Trinity College, the Rev. Robinson Duckworth (the Duck) and his brothers and sister, who accompanied the children on some of the river excursions. Things they saw together in Oxford include the Dodo in the UNIVERSITY MUSEUM, the BOTANIC GARDEN, the BINSEY treacle well, the deer in Magdalen Park, the Anglo-Saxons in the Caedmon Ms in the BODLEIAN LIBRARY, and Alice's shop in ST ALDATE'S, opposite Christ Church, where she bought her favourite barley-sugar. The visit of the Prince and Princess of Wales to Oxford in 1863, when they stayed at the Deanery, was a highlight in the life of the Liddell children and provided much of the background to the

Alice Liddell, the little girl to whom Lewis Carroll told his famous story, was the daughter of Henry George Liddell, Dean of Christ Church.

Looking-glass stories: the bonfire, the royal banquet, the fireworks, the Lion and the Unicorn illuminated on Oxford buildings, and the crown which figured so persistently in Alice's thoughts. Everything in the books relates to incidents Alice would have recognised. Even the date of the Mad Tea-party is subtly given as 4 May – her birthday.

When Lewis Carroll told children stories, he would make a little drawing to illustrate a particular character or situation and then toss it into the waste-paper basket; and when he was persuaded to publish he thought that if he received tuition his own drawings might be used, but JOHN RUSKIN discouraged him. The *Punch* artist, John Tenniel, was approached. He was given Carroll's illustrations to work on and studied the Oxford background, having been given minute instructions about what was required – as were Macmillan when they came to set Tenniel's illustrations in the text. It was agreed that the heroine's face should not be a real likeness, and although Tenniel did not like using models, he was introduced to Mary Badcock, the daughter of Canon Badcock of Ripon, whose face he immortalised as Alice.

Alice married Reginald Hargreaves, who had been up at Christ Church from 1872–8, and had very little contact with Lewis Carroll after she moved to Cuffnells in Lyndhurst, but in 1885 he wrote to ask her if she would return the original *Alice* and give permission for it to be published in facsimile form. In his letter he refers to 'my ideal child-friend', saying, 'I have had scores of child-friends since your time, but they have been quite a different thing.'

Alister Hardy Research Centre *Westminster College*. Formerly the Religious Experience Research Unit, the centre was renamed in honour of Sir Alister Hardy (*d*.1986), Linacre Professor of Zoology, who founded the unit in 1969 and was the inspiration behind its work. Appeals by the Centre for reports of personal religious and spiritual experiences resulted in some 5000 detailed replies, which are now being collated. Its research programme includes large-scale survey work and studies of the nature and function of religious experience. Hardy's working hypothesis is that religious awareness is biologically natural in the human species and has evolutionary survival value (*see* his *The Spiritual Nature of Man*, 1979). In 1986 the director was David Hay. He was succeeded in November 1989 by the Revd Dr Gordon Wakefield.

All Saints Church *High Street* (now Lincoln College library). Founded in 1122, the original church was granted to ST FRIDESWIDE'S PRIORY, which kept the advowson until it passed to the Bishop of Lincoln in 1326. In 1427 All Saints was used for the endowment of Lincoln College, which was granted the patronage in 1475, remaining the patron until the church was closed in 1971 and converted into a library for the college. After its demolition in 1896, ST MARTIN'S CHURCH, CARFAX, joined All Saints as a united benefice under the patronage of Lincoln College, and All Saints became the City Church. In 1943 the united benefice was held in plurality with ST MICHAEL AT THE NORTH GATE, and in 1971 the three benefices of St Michael, St Martin and All Saints were united, with Lincoln College as patron, St Michael's remaining in use for public worship. During his incumbency, W.W. Merry (vicar 1861–84), later Rector of Lincoln College, drew large congregations; and in 1908 the church was described as being 'in a most extra-ordinary way typical of the Church of England', its congregation following a middle-churchmanship that 'had never been over-excited by any religious movement either wise or unwise.' Between the two world wars, All Saints continued to draw considerable congregations from beyond its own declining parish.

The mediaeval church of All Saints, perhaps converted from a domestic building in the 11th or 12th century, and consisting of nave, chancel, and probably a west tower with a later spire, was enlarged in the 13th century. When in 1662 the spire rocked, local inhabitants left their houses in trepidation; in 1700 it collapsed, destroying much of the church. An appeal for £4800 to rebuild the church was made to 'the Nobility, Gentry and Clergy and to all other Pious and well disposed Persons', Queen Anne being among the contributors. HENRY ALDRICH, Dean of Christ Church, had, as one of the 'able judges in architecture', given advice on the building of the chapel (1691–4) of Trinity College, and the rebuilding of All Saints, containing 350 seats, was almost certainly to his designs. In his *Unbuilt Oxford* (1983) H.M. Colvin describes Aldrich's All Saints as 'a rectangle without any suggestion of a chancel' and as a building which can 'be regarded as an academic version of a Wren church of the simpler type'. Aldrich died in 1710 and the original steeple he designed was not built, nor was NICHOLAS HAWKSMOOR'S proposed dome-and-peristyle design adopted. The eventual version, completed by 1720, was a combination of Aldrich's design strengthened by Hawksmoor features. The result is one of Oxford's architectural landmarks. It has been suggested that Aldrich positioned the 153-foot steepled tower so it would be linked to Trinity College Chapel by the line of TURL STREET, each visible from the other – an attractive if unproven theory.

The poor quality of the local STONE used in Aldrich's church made repairs necessary in 1783, 1803 and 1804; and in 1872 the tower and steeple were rebuilt to the 1720 designs under the supervision of E.G. Bruton. Further repairs were carried out to the exterior (1887–90) under the direction of H.W. Moore; and T.G. JACKSON supervised interior alterations in 1896 when All Saints became the City Church.

In 1971, when the church was declared redundant, work began under the supervision of Robert Potter to convert it into a library for Lincoln College. Re-roofing was carried out and eroded stone replaced with new stone from Besace, near Cambrai, carved by the stonemasons of Chichester Cathedral. The floor was raised to provide a lower reading room and the

All Saints Church from Turl Street, as depicted by J.C. Buckler in 1824. The building is now the library for Lincoln College.

former Senior Library was moved complete into the lower east end of the building. At the upper level the effect of lofty classical columns, tall clear-glazed windows, fine woodwork and redecoration is both graceful and impressive. The conversion, completed in 1975 at a cost of £420,000, was begun when Sir Walter Oakeshott was Rector (1953–72) and owes much to his inspiration and expert knowledge.

All Saints Church *Lime Walk, Headington.* In 1870 a mission church was built in Lime Walk to assist ST ANDREW'S, OLD HEADINGTON, in catering for the growing population of new HEADINGTON. It was replaced in 1910 by the present red-brick church, designed in Early English style by Arthur Blomfield & Son, and described by Pevsner as having 'an exceptionally impressive interior'. The chancel was added in 1937 to the designs of N.W. Harrison. Five clear-glazed 'stepped' lancet windows at the north end and three at the west end, with clerestory windows above four-bay arches to north and south aisles, provide a light and airy interior. Five aisle windows by Christopher Webb are dedicated to St Francis (1959), St Nicholas (1961), St Michael (1962), St Andrew (1964, in memory of A.D. Gilbertson, sometime Chaplain of the Fleet) and St Clement (1965). The Lady Chapel, equipped in 1947, has a window (1955) by Joseph Nuttgens depicting 'Christian beholds the Celestial City'. In 1986 the previous organ was replaced by the organ from the church of ST PHILIP AND ST JAMES, which had been built for the chapel of Merton College in about 1860 by William Hill & Son, and moved to St Philip and St James in 1904. In 1967 All Saints Church House in New High Street, Headington, designed by Gray & Baynes and costing £21,000, was opened by HRH Princess Margaret.

The living is in the gift of the BISHOP OF OXFORD, and the parish includes the NUFFIELD ORTHOPAEDIC CENTRE, ST LUKE'S NURSING HOME, and HEADINGTON SCHOOL, whose boarders attend Sunday services at All Saints. The former Archbishop of York, the Most Rev. Stuart Blanch, was curate at All Saints (1949–52) and the Rt Rev. David Porter, Bishop of Aston, was vicar (1935–43).

All Saints Church *Wytham.* The earliest mention of a church at Wytham is an entry in the English Register of the nuns at nearby GODSTOW ABBEY in 1135. The church was extensively restored around 1490, but was rebuilt in 1811 by the 5th Earl of Abingdon using material from Cumnor Place, which he had pulled down, and from the earlier church. Parish registers going back to 1559 are preserved. Two windows in the nave of the church contain five 14th-century glass roundels, depicting a king (probably Richard II), a queen (Anne of Bohemia), the Good Shepherd, St Mary in an Annunciation scene, and the eagle, emblem of St John. The east window is an early 18th-century version of the Adoration of the Shepherds. The church contains a memorial brass of 1406 to Robert de Wytham and memorials to Robert Lydall, who was Rector from 1712 to 1742 and who assisted in the management of the Earl of Abingdon's estates as well as being his chaplain, and to Henry Octavius Coxe, who was librarian of the BODLEIAN LIBRARY and Rector from 1868 to 1881. There is also an unusual 14th-century corbel of a bagpipe player.

All Souls College The College of All Souls of the Faithful Departed was established by HENRY CHICHELE, Archbishop of Canterbury, with King Henry VI as its formal co-founder. The Archbishop was making preparations for this, his second Oxford foundation (*see* ST BERNARD'S COLLEGE), as early as 1436, but its foundation stone was not laid until St Scholastica's Day (10 February) 1437/8. Between then and 1443, when its original buildings were effectively complete and it received its final statutes, Chichele's college had cost him some £9500 (say £3 million at current prices). Of this, over £5000 went to endow it with estates, chiefly in Kent and Middlesex, together with other properties in Bedfordshire and Buckinghamshire, and substantial confiscated alien priory lands in Leicestershire, Northamptonshire, Shropshire and Wales.

The college statutes, though largely modelled on those of New College (of which Chichele had once been a Fellow), made clear the unique nature of this ninth Oxford college. Chichele demonstrated his personal interest by making himself and his successors in the see of Canterbury VISITORS of his foundation. Its numbers he restricted to a Warden and forty Fellows, all of whom were to have studied for three years in the University and to be between eighteen and twenty-five years of age on election. They were to be of legitimate birth, to receive (apart from quarters and commons) an annual livery of cloth, and were to be sufficiently instructed in grammar (these requirements were doubtless responsible for the *bene nati, bene vestiti et mediocriter docti* gibe first recorded in Thomas Fuller's *Church History* in 1655). Chichele's twofold aim was that his college should produce a learned clerical 'militia' to serve Church and State,

and that it should also be a chantry where the Fellows should pray for the souls of the faithful departed and of those killed in the French wars – in particular for members of the House of Lancaster, with which Chichele had close political connections. The Fellows were accordingly under a double obligation: to take Orders and to engage in higher studies. Twenty-four of them were to study for the doctorate of Theology and sixteen for doctorates in the two Laws, Canon and Civil. The statutes do not refer to Medicine, the third higher faculty, but a number of Fellows (including THOMAS LINACRE, Fellow in 1484) proceeded to medical doctorates.

As was not uncommon at the time, the' statutes accorded a preference in elections to students in certain categories: in the first place, to those who could claim to be of the kin of the founder (the FOUNDERS' KIN provision), and then to those born on college land. Birth in the Province of Canterbury was an absolute requirement.

Chichele was able to acquire an enviable site for his college on the corner of HIGH STREET and CATTE STREET, and immediately to the east of ST MARY THE VIRGIN, where much University business was then conducted. The college buildings, like its statutes, were modelled to a considerable degree on those of New College. However, the narrowness of the site-frontage on the High meant that the original hall, unlike that of New College (which was a prolongation of the axis of its chapel), had to be awkwardly placed with its kitchen and offices at the east end of the chapel and at right-angles to it. The east, south and west ranges of the front quadrangle accommodated the forty Fellows on two floors in chambers for two or three with small studies leading off them. The Warden's quarters

David Loggan's view of All Souls College from the High Street in 1675, before the construction of Hawksmoor's North Quadrangle.

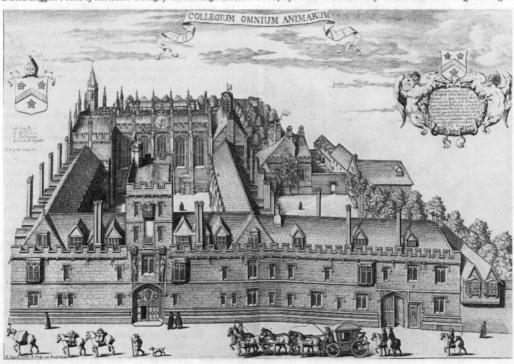

COLLEGIUM OMNIUM ANIMARUM

probably included the room on the first floor of the gate-tower and certainly the rooms to the east of it. The second and third floors of the tower were used as the college treasury and for storage of records. The T-plan chapel formed the north range of the quadrangle and was consecrated in June 1442; as at New College, the original college library took up the bulk of the upper floor of the east range. The windows of both chapel and library had contemporary painted glass by John Prudde and John Glasier, some of which still survives in the antechapel (*see* STAINED GLASS). Battlements were added to the front quadrangle in 1510, and its lofts were brought into occupation in the 16th and 17th centuries. Its once cusped window-heads have been squared off and some unobtrusive dormers have been added in recent years, but otherwise the quadrangle is unusual among Oxford colleges in retaining its original appearance.

Only two substantial additions were made to the college buildings before the beginning of the 18th century. Between 1460 and 1515 a cloister was constructed to the north of the chapel, with its west wall along the line of Catte Street, and in 1550 a range of buildings was erected on land acquired on the High immediately to the east of the original quadrangle. This range provided more ample accommodation for the Warden, who moved eastwards into it from his earlier more spartan quarters in the front quadrangle. This development may be connected with the post-Reformation possibility of a married Warden – though the first such (Robert Hovenden) was not elected until 1571.

The Reformation and the religious changes of the mid-16th century left their mark on the college. John Warner, the Regius Professor of Medicine (Warden from 1536 to 1556 and again from 1559 to 1565) showed notable flexibility in retaining office under Henry VIII, Edward VI, Mary (for two years) and Elizabeth I, but some Fellows were deprived of their fellowships in both Protestant and Catholic times (*see* ROMAN CATHOLICS). The chapel lost its altars, its reredos statuary, its organ, and some of its vestments and ornaments; changes in fashion as well as religion caused many manuscripts to be withdrawn from the college library, some of which (thanks to the enterprise of Christopher Plantin) are now in the Plantin-Moretus Museum in Antwerp. Such restoration as occurred under Philip and Mary was reversed under their successor, when the chantry functions of the college became much attenuated and a clean sweep was ultimately made of 'idolatrous monuments'. The religious changes of the 16th century also affected the college's academic bias. Greek and Latin lecturerships and a Civil Law lecture (seemingly shortlived) were established by the Royal Visitors in 1535, and the Commissioners of 1549 even proposed that the college should become devoted exclusively to legal studies. This did not come about (the twenty-four Theology Fellowships continued to be formally 'artist' places), but the college's reputation as a nursery of lawyers, and especially of civil lawyers practising in the ecclesiastical and admiralty courts, dates from this period.

The post-Reformation years were a time of indiscipline within the college. Archbishop Cranmer's VISITATION of 1541 had shown that non-residence, failure to take degrees and enter Holy Orders, sumptuary extravagance, brawling and drunkenness were not unknown among the Fellows,

and that – more seriously – the practice of corrupt resignation (the acceptance of payment for nomination of a successor to an arranged vacancy in the fellowship) was already rife. The college clearly needed a strong guiding hand; it found one in Warden Hovenden.

Robert Hovenden, a Canterbury man, was elected Warden in 1571 at the age of twenty-seven. He was the youngest Warden ever to be elected and was to serve longer than any other before or since, dying in office forty-three years later. During his long tenure he showed himself to be a notable disciplinarian and a man jealous of the college's property. He defended tooth and nail the college's interest, even against Queen Elizabeth when she claimed college land at nearby Stanton Harcourt and demanded a peppercorn lease of the college's woods at Edgware in Middlesex; he commissioned over 100 cadastral maps of the college's estates; and he set its archive in order. He was also (and less admirably) successful in furthering the interests of his own kin in the bestowal of fellowships and beneficial leases, and in introducing a large number of undergraduates as *servientes* into the college – an influx which did not survive the Commonwealth, though there were four Bible Clerks on the establishment until 1924. He acquired land to the east and north of the range added in 1550 and built on part of it the twin-gabled study (shown in DAVID LOGGAN's view of 1675) which was pulled down in 1703 when the new lodgings were built. But his most notable addition to the college fabric is the fine heraldic ceiling in the Old Library. This was inserted in 1598 when the original – and by then overflowing – lectern desks were replaced by standing presses on the Merton model.

Hovenden's two successors were unremarkable, but under one of them, Richard Astley (Warden 1618–36), we have, in 1633, the first reference to the college totem – the mallard – and to the ceremonies connected with it. These included a circumambulation of the college by the Fellows, which, according to the Visitor's letter, had led in the previous year to 'barbarously unbeseeming conduct' involving doors and gates. Rooftop mallard circumambulations are known to have taken place on All Souls Day or St Hilary's Day (14 January, the first day of Hilary Term) in 1701, 1801 and – in a more seemly fashion – in 1901, and the accompanying Mallard Song is still sung at college GAUDIES. (*For a fuller description, see* CEREMONIES.)

Astley's successor, GILBERT SHELDON, the future Archbishop of Canterbury, who was Warden from 1636 to 1648 and from 1660 to 1661, made his mark in office. Not surprisingly, with ARCHBISHOP LAUD as college Visitor and CHANCELLOR of the University, and with Sheldon as Warden, attention was given to the fabric and arrangement of the chapel. Later writers have, however, erred in suggesting that it was Sheldon rather than Astley who courageously but vainly opposed Laud's high-handed if well-judged 'nomination' of Jeremy Taylor to a fellowship in 1635.

Sheldon was the leader of a strongly royalist college whose Fellows were to be put to the test by the events of the CIVIL WAR and the Commonwealth. Almost all of them contributed generously to the royalist cause and sacrificed their fellowships rather than swear allegiance to Parliament. The college was second only to Magdalen in the amount of PLATE (over 250 lb) that it supplied to the royal MINT, and it lent the King a further £654 14s 3d – a bad debt not finally written off until 1857. In spite of failure of rents, it provided maintenance for royalist soldiers and contributed towards fortifications and stores. Small wonder that Sheldon was forcibly removed from the lodgings in April 1648 and that only seven of the forty Fellows avoided the loss of their fellowships. John Palmer was brought in to take the place of Warden Sheldon, and between 1648 and 1652 forty-three men (thirteen of them from Cambridge) were intruded into fellowships by the Commissioners (*see* VISITATIONS). Most of the intruders were academically undistinguished, but they included Thomas Sydenham – one of a number of medical and scientific Fellows of the college in the second half of the century, some of whom were early recruits to the ranks of the Royal Society. In 1653, when regular elections commenced, CHRISTOPHER WREN joined All Souls after three years at Wadham. He held college office and in 1659 (the year of his bursarship) designed the fine and accurate sun-dial which surmounted the south wall of the chapel until its removal to the Great Quadrangle in 1877.

The Restoration of King Charles II in 1660 brought welcome relief to the college. All the intruded fellows save one (Edward Greene) were sent packing, Sheldon was reinstated as Warden, and the few surviving pre-Civil War Fellows who wished to resume their fellowships rejoined the college. The chapel received attention in the early 1660s: a screen based on a design by Wren was installed, a *Last Judgement* fresco was painted over the east end and painted wooden panels were inserted between the roof-trusses in the chancel. These paintings were the work of Isaac Fuller, whose fresco was to justify John Evelyn's comment that it would not 'hold long', being 'too full of nakeds'. Parts only of some of the painted panels have defied the prophecy and are preserved in the antechapel.

In 1681 Warden Jeames, supported by the Visitor, Archbishop Sancroft, at last succeeded by the use of his veto in stamping out the abuse of corrupt resignations, and the quality of the fellowship notably improved when men of the stamp of GEORGE CLARKE (Fellow 1680), Nathaniel Lloyd (1689) and CHRISTOPHER CODRINGTON (1690) joined the college. Jeames's successor as Warden, however, represented a falling-off. This was the Hon. Leopold Finch, a Fellow of only five years' standing in the college when in January 1687 he was, at the age of twenty-four, unconstitutionally nominated to the wardenship by King James II (he was not formally admitted Warden until 1698). A man of some learning, with a passion for sash windows and with low moral standards, he died in the lodgings (which he was sharing with bailiffs) in November 1702.

Finch was succeeded by Bernard Gardiner, who for a quarter of a century fought an ultimately unsuccessful campaign to enforce the statutes relating to residence and the taking of Holy Orders. His failure in the former respect was to have regrettable consequences for the college's future. In another area, however, he presided over a brilliant success – the replanning of the college buildings. The initiative came from Dr George Clarke, politician, lawyer, virtuoso and capable amateur architect. In 1703 he offered to build a house on college land which on his death would become college property. The offer was accepted and the cloister to the north of the chapel (apart from its Catte Street wall) was demolished to provide a site for the house. Then came a change of mind and the present lodgings were built in 1704 on a site in the High immediately to the east of the 1550 range. Now that the cloister area was available for development, Dr Clarke was able to entertain large designs for the *aggiornamento* of the college. In about 1705 he planned a double-quadrangle college with a chapel and hall as a continuous east–west range dividing a southern quadrangle, with a central north–south library over a colonnade, from a northern quadrangle with a 'grand dormitory' as its northern range. Variations on this theme were offered by, among others, NICHOLAS HAWKSMOOR, DEAN ALDRICH, John Talman and William Townesend (*see* TOWNESENDS), but before a decision had been reached, the college received news in 1710 that Christopher Codrington had died in Barbados, leaving £10,000 to the college to build and endow a library – together with his own collection of some 12,000 volumes. By 1715 Hawksmoor had submitted a design which, not surprisingly, substituted a 'grand library' for the 'grand dormitory' and removed the Fellows' lavish accommodation from the north to the east range of the north quadrangle and also to the east range of a new south quadrangle. A loggia was retained as the western range of the northern quadrangle, while a north–south colonnade, shorn of its library over, remained (on paper) the central feature of the southern quadrangle.

Clarke and Lloyd were among a number of generous benefactors who helped to finance the building campaign and were appointed to oversee Hawksmoor's plans. A start was made with the chapel,

All Souls' twin towers were built between 1716 and 1720 to the design of Nicholas Hawksmoor.

where between 1713 and 1716 Sir James Thornhill rebuilt the Wren screen, painted the chancel walls with huge *trompe-l'œil* vases and figures of saints and Lancastrian nobles, inserted painted coffered canvas panels in the roof, and covered Fuller's *Last Judgement* with an *Apotheosis of Archbishop Chichele*, which crowned a marble reredos and wooden panelling given by Clarke to classicise the east end of the chapel. This work was done by 1716, and in that year the construction began of the CODRINGTON LIBRARY and the east range of the new Great Quadrangle. This range consisted of a common room flanked by twin towers and link-blocks to the north and south. The north tower was the gift of General William Steuart, and the college owed the two link-blocks to the Duke of Wharton (Edward Young, Fellow 1708, had been his secretary) and to Nathaniel Lloyd. The range was built by 1724 and the hall (1730) and the loggia (1728–34) completed Hawksmoor's remarkable northern quadrangle, in which all the buildings combined 'Gothic' exteriors (matching the chapel) with classical interiors. But by the time of his and Clarke's deaths in 1736 the college had tired of 'Hawksmooring' and the ambitious plans for the new front quadrangle were not proceeded with.

In other respects, too, 18th-century All Souls lacked ambition. Non-residence became commonplace (and remained so for two centuries), and now that the fellowships were financially more attractive, during the second half of the century graduates claiming kinship with the founder (and often with little else to recommend them) began to swamp the college. There were exceptions to the low intellectual standards, however: 18th-century All Souls can claim the poet Edward Young (Fellow 1708), a couple of Lord Chancellors, nine bishops and, above all, WILLIAM BLACKSTONE (Fellow from 1743 to 1762), the first man to lecture on the Common Law at Oxford (in 1753) and the author of the *Essay on Collateral Consanguinity* (1750), in which he vainly attempted to stem by argument the tide of founder's kin. But the flood continued: between 1750 and 1857 more than half of those elected to fellowships were of the kin of the founder, and almost as many came to the college from aristocratic Christ Church. A mere 12 per cent of those elected between 1802 and 1857 had been awarded first classes in the SCHOOLS; more than half of them were destined for the Church. The tone of the college was unambiguous.

The year 1857 marked the end of an age for the college. It was the year of the Ordinance which followed the activities of the 1850 ROYAL COMMISSION of enquiry into the University and the subsequent Executive Commission of 1854. This new dispensation swept away the founder's kin and other privileges and also the obligation to take Orders. Candidature for fellowships became restricted to those who had either taken a first class in the Schools or won a University PRIZE – a restriction which was to revolutionise the intellectual level of the college within a very few years. The new examination was to be in subjects in the School of Jurisprudence and Modern History – a specialisation reinforced by the suppression of ten fellowships to fund the Chichele Professorships of International Law and Diplomacy (1859) and of Modern History (1862). It became possible for the college to elect to fellowships, without examination, professors or other members of the University 'of eminence', and also Honorary Fellows (WILLIAM GLADSTONE and the University BURGESS Sir William Heathcote were the first to be so elected, in 1858). The marriage prohibition did not apply to the non-examination Fellows, and in 1858 Max Müller (Professor of Modern European Languages) became, within a few months of his election, the first married Fellow of All Souls.

The change of tone introduced by the workings of the 1857 Ordinance reinforced an already existing movement towards the 'academicisation' of the college. Its examinations, previously perfunctory, became a severe test, and in 1867 its library was opened to all members of the University, an extension to the north of the Great Library (now the Anson Reading Room) being built to accommodate readers who were not members of the college. The specialisation of the library in the fields of History and Law dates from this period. Other buildings of the college were also given attention. Between 1869 and 1879 the chapel was thoroughly restored in the Gothic style under the direction of Henry Clutton and (from 1873) SIR GEORGE GILBERT SCOTT. As part of the process, new stained-glass windows were installed in the chancel, the 15th-century glass in the antechapel (some of it originally in the Old Library) was restored, and the Old Library itself, which had been partitioned into rooms after its books had been transferred to the Codrington Library in 1750, became a lecture room.

In the 1870s there was much soul-searching over the best way in which the college could employ its resources, and the admission of undergraduates (to reinforce the surviving four Bible Clerks) or of Indian Civil Service candidates were two of the proposals which found support. But before these exotic measures could be adopted, the Act of Parliament of 1877, which followed the second University Commission (of 1872), altered the situation radically. The Act appointed executive Commissioners (two of whom were Fellows of All Souls), who were to draw up new statutes for the colleges in consultation with governing bodies. One of the All Souls Fellows who was especially active in this process was SIR WILLIAM ANSON (Fellow since 1867 and Baronet on the death of his father in 1873), who was to become the college's first lay Warden in 1881. He was an outstanding constitutional lawyer and an active Liberal politician, and under his aegis the college developed along two lines: in the direction of the advancement of learning by research and teaching, and towards the production of 'men-of-the-world' with high academic qualifications. He envisaged some of the latter as men who, after serving the State as lawyers, politicians and administrators, might ultimately be invited to strengthen the governing body of the college as non-stipendiary ('Distinguished') or near-non-stipendiary ('Fifty-pound') Fellows.

The statutes of 1881, as finally agreed with the Commissioners, reflected Anson's views. They preserved the rights of the existing Life Fellows, but ensured that future examination fellowships should terminate after seven years. The marriage restriction was done away with (save for the surviving Life Fellows), as was the limitation of examination candidates to those with first-class degrees or University prizes (few candidates without one or other of these distinctions now offered themselves). In future there were to be twenty-one seven-year

Thomas Rowlandson's 1790 incorrectly titled watercolour drawing of All Souls with the Radcliffe Camera to the left.

examination (or prize) fellowships (two-thirds of them specifically connected with historical and legal studies), up to seven research fellowships, and ten fifty-pound fellowships. There were to be three distinguished fellowships and the three existing professorial fellowships in International Law, History and Political Economy were increased by the addition of the holders of the Regius Chair of Civil Law and the Vinerian Chair of English Law. The college provided financial support for all five chairs and for new readerships in Indian Law and Roman Law (1878 and 1881 respectively).

The new statutes set the tone for the college's development for many years to come. On the academic side, the seven-year examination fellowships offered for competitive entry every October became Oxford's most sought-after prizes and attracted outstanding candidates: for example, the future LORD CURZON (1883) and Archbishop Lang (1888); and in 1897 L.S. Amery and the future Lord Simon were elected, with Ramsay Muir and William Holdsworth as two of the unsuccessful candidates. Two of the Fellows, G.E. Buckle (Fellow 1877) and Geoffrey Dawson (Fellow 1898) became successive editors of *The Times* from 1884 to 1941 (with a hiatus in 1919–23). Such careers chimed well with Warden Anson's conception of the dual role of the college, but the stress since the 1881 statutes has increasingly been on the academic side: the college elected the first of its many Research Fellows (the historian S.R. Gardiner) in 1884.

The year 1914 marked another turning-point in All Souls history. It saw the end of Warden Anson's life

and of his thirty-three years of active, generous and fruitful wardenship. Within a few weeks of his death the First World War broke out and took its toll (two of the college's most brilliant members, Raymond Asquith and Patrick Shaw Stewart, were among its victims). Elections were halted for four years after 1914.

In November 1919 four Fellows were elected, and within a few days of their election the third Universities Commission was appointed. Among the Commissioners were three actual or past Fellows of the college and they were among those who signed a report (published in 1922) which recommended that All Souls should increase the number of its Research Fellows and contribute especially to the advanced teaching of graduate students. The report also commended the college's declared intention to invite 'distinguished senior students' to become associated with it. These recommendations were prophetic of the path that the college was to follow – though hardly precipitately (it was not until 1936 that T.E. Lawrence, Fellow from 1919 to 1926, and Lionel Curtis, elected in 1921, had a Research Fellow successor). The Distinguished and Fifty-pound Fellows continued to play their part in college life in spite of the fact that they were almost all non-resident, and a few of them were active in academic matters. It was among their number that the All Souls 'appeasers' of the 1930s were to be found – Dawson (editing *The Times*), Simon and Halifax – but other views were well represented in the college, especially among the younger Examination Fellows, who combined high intellectual standards with youthful radicalism.

The Second World War, like the First, brought college elections to a halt. The fellowship examinations were not resumed until 1946, when the record number of six Fellows was elected. Between 1948 and 1965 eleven Research Fellows were appointed and in the latter year discussions about the college's role, which had been rumbling on since the mid-1920s, came to a head. Development had become increasingly feasible with the growth since the 1890s of the college's income (especially from its London estates), a substantial proportion of which it had been diverting to general University purposes. Moves in the 1920s to build on the existing chairs of Political Economy and Political Theory, thereby adding a third special field to the traditional disciplines of Law and History, had made little headway and were effectively halted by the establishment of Nuffield College in 1937. By 1963 there were fourteen Professorial Fellows of All Souls. Most of them were in the fields of Law, History, and Political Economy, but other disciplines represented ranged from Ecological Genetics to Eastern Religions. The ten Research Fellows were in the main concerned with legal, historical and philosophical studies, as were the eleven Examination Fellows. In addition to these academic Fellows, there were eighteen ex-Examination Fellows holding distinguished or fifty-pound fellowships (the so-called 'London Fellows').

This was the college which in 1963 eventually decided that its future lay in accepting graduate students – a decision which was to be rescinded twelve months later after detailed and sometimes bitter discussion. The ultimately accepted alternative was the development of a large-scale scheme for Visiting Fellows from Britain and overseas, who were to be invited to spend up to a year at All Souls pursuing their researches. This change of heart, which was to result over the next twenty years in some 300 distinguished scholars from twenty-five countries joining the college, was in effect a belated implementation of the most important recommendation of the 1919 Commission's report. But the college's alleged 'infirmity of purpose' did not commend itself to the University's FRANKS COMMISSION of 1964, though the Commissioners in their report (1966) approved of the visiting fellowships scheme in principle. At the same time they recommended that the 'London' fellowships should be phased out, as they considered that their holders did not contribute to 'the vigour of the academic community of the College' – an opinion which the college did not share.

Providing accommodation for the Visiting Fellows resulted in the first major building works at All Souls since the completion of the chapel restoration in 1879: studies for them were built in 1966, and at IFFLEY, in the garden of a house bought for the purpose, a block of flats was constructed in the same year. A systematic restoration programme for the college's older buildings was simultaneously initiated – a long-term project which it is expected will be completed by the end of the 1980s.

In the twenty or so years since the Franks Commission, the changes in the academic field have involved a strengthening and broadening of the college as a centre for the advancement of learning by research and teaching – the latter especially in the form of the supervision by Fellows of graduate students, and the eventual taking up by Examination Fellows of teaching posts in Oxford and other universities. All Souls maintains its regular chapel services, but its Fellows are no longer all Anglicans and the last Fellow to become a bishop, A.T.P. Williams, was consecrated in 1939. Emeritus fellowships were instituted in 1974; they were followed in 1978 by two-year fellowships open to ex-Fellows organising seminars and lecture courses; women became eligible for fellowships in 1979; and in 1980 five-year 'fellowships by thesis' in a wide range of subjects, including the Mathematical Sciences, were introduced. These new categories of Fellowship have enriched and rejuvenated the time-honoured ones – themselves broadened by the addition of special papers in English (1970) and Classical Studies (1976) to the existing ones in Law, History, Politics, Economics and Philosophy, from which would-be Examination Fellows can make a choice.

The last three Wardens of All Souls have been, respectively, an economist, a scholar-bibliophile and a lawyer: Sir Hubert Henderson (1952), J.H.A. Sparrow (1952–77) and Sir Patrick Neill (1977 to date). The present (1986) sixty-seven holders of All Souls fellowships can claim that they continue to fill Archbishop Chichele's aims, if for 'service to Church and State' we read 'service to learning and society'. They also fulfil Warden Anson's vision of the college's dual function, if we recall that they include among their number a Nobel prizewinner in Economics, an OM and past-President of the British Academy, a Lord Chancellor, a retired Senior Law Lord, and past and present cabinet ministers.

The corporate designation of the college is The Warden and College of the Souls of all Faithful People deceased in the University of Oxford.

(Royal Commission on Historic Monuments, *Oxford*, 1939, pp. 15–19; *Victoria History of the County of Oxford*, Vol. III, Oxford, 1954, pp. 173–93; Burrows, M., *Worthies of All Souls*, 1874 (includes an appendix on the All Souls mallard); Robertson, C. Grant, *All Souls College*, 1899; Rowse, A.L., *Appeasement: a study in political decline, 1933–9*, New York, 1961 (fuller than his *All Souls and Appeasement: a study in contemporary history*, London, 1961); Caute, J.D., 'Crisis in All Souls: a case-history in reform', in *Collisions*, London, 1974, pp. 12–45 (fuller than his article in *Encounter*, March 1966); Eason, R.E., and Snoxall, R.A., *The Last of Their Line: the Bible Clerks of All Souls College, Oxford*, Oxford, 1976; Colvin, H.M., *Unbuilt Oxford*, New Haven and London, 1983; Hutchinson, F.E., *Medieval Glass at All Souls College*, London, 1949. The college betting books, 1815–1919, were privately printed in two volumes by C.W.C. Oman, 1912–38.)

Almanacks *see* OXFORD ALMANACKS.

Anchor *2 Hayfield Road*. Otherwise known as 'Dolly's Hut', after William Dolley, the landlord from 1852 to 1877. Originally a house called Heathfield's Hut, it became an inn in 1796 to cater for the local trade from Midland coal bargees at the nearby CANAL wharf. The present Anchor was rebuilt by the Ind Coope brewery to the designs of J.C. Leed, architect of the UNIVERSITY AND CITY ARMS. It re-opened in June 1937.

Angel Inn *High Street*. This large, ancient inn stood partly on the site of the present EXAMINATION

SCHOOLS. From 1391 to 1510 it was a small inn called the Tabard (a herald's overtunic), leased from St John's Hospital. It was enlarged in 1510 when Magdalen College owned it and its name was changed to the Angel. It became Oxford's first COFFEE HOUSE in 1650 (*see also* COOPER'S 'OXFORD' MARMALADE). In 1663 it was rebuilt or extended and had a frontage of about 110 feet. The lane behind had been closed in 1442, enabling the extensive stabling to be built. It became Oxford's most important coaching inn and remained so throughout the coaching era (*see* TRANSPORT). In the 18th century ten coaches started from the Angel at 8 o'clock each morning. The section of MERTON STREET near the East Gate was appropriately called Coach and Horses Lane. ANGEL MEADOW was leased by the inn for grazing the horses.

The Angel had many distinguished customers. Christian VII, King of Denmark, stayed here in 1768. In 1835 Queen Adelaide, consort of William IV, visited Oxford and stayed with her suite at the Angel, where, so it is recorded, 'she could scarcely have been so conveniently and comfortably accommodated in any of our monastic edifices, as in this excellent house'. The morning after her arrival she went for a walk in CHRIST CHURCH MEADOW, entering the Meadow from the hotel's stables. She then paid a visit to The Queen's College opposite the hotel. The hotel closed in 1866 and was sold to the University for the building of the Examination Schools.

Angel Meadow   Borders the River Cherwell (*see* THAMES) by MAGDALEN BRIDGE. From 1585 this meadow and the adjoining Greyhound Meadow were leased from Magdalen College, to whom they belong, by the tenants of the ANGEL INN and the GREYHOUND INN respectively, to provide grazing for customers' horses (*see also* TRANSPORT). In 1925 the city leased both meadows from the college for use as a children's playground. The Queen's College's Florey Building overlooks Angel Meadow.

Anson, Sir William Reynell   (*1843–1914*). Warden of All Souls and BURGESS for the University, passed from Eton to Balliol College in 1862 and to a fellowship at All Souls in 1867. Thereafter he read for (and, for a short time, practised at) the Bar, succeeded as 3rd baronet in 1873, and a year later was elected to the Vinerian Readership in English Law, thus beginning an outstanding career as a teacher of the Law. A Liberal Unionist in national politics and a moderate reformer in University and college affairs, he was elected Warden of All Souls in 1881 (the first layman to hold the office). As Warden he set the future tone of the college – on the one hand personally subsidising its first Research Fellow (1884), and on the other encouraging its members to look forward to playing active roles in the legal, political and administrative life of the nation. He published his pioneering *Principles of the Law of Contract* in 1879, and the two volumes of his classic *Law and Custom of the Constitution* followed between 1886 and 1892. Remarkably, he continued as Warden to take pupils until he became VICE-CHANCELLOR in 1898. After only six months in office he resigned on his election as Parliamentary Burgess for the University in April 1899. Anson was from 1902 to 1905 a conscientious and well-informed secretary to the Board of Education in Balfour's administration. After the Liberal

A 'Spy' cartoon of the lawyer Sir William Anson, who was elected Warden of All Souls in 1881 and Burgess for the University in 1899.

débâcle he continued to be active in opposition and devoted himself single-mindedly (he was a bachelor) to the affairs of his University and to his college and parliamentary responsibilities. He died on 4 June 1914.

Apollo Theatre   There has been a theatre on the site of the Apollo in GEORGE STREET since 1836. The first was built in Victoria Court, off George Street, and was called the New Theatre, but also, more commonly, the Vic. From 1868 it was also known as the Theatre Royale, after the company which played there. However, this was not a permanent, resident company: it was forbidden to perform plays during the University terms and the lessee of the theatre resorted to presenting 'concerts' which were music-hall entertainments. By 1880 the theatre had become run down and members of both town and gown were demanding the erection of a new theatre on the site, to be used by University and town players as well as by professionals. In 1885 a company was formed to raise money for the theatre and it was only one year later that the OXFORD UNIVERSITY DRAMATIC SOCIETY opened the second New Theatre with a Shakespearean production. Designed by H.G.W. Drinkwater, the theatre had a 1000-seat capacity. Badly damaged by fire in 1892 and altered in 1908, when the seating capacity was increased to 1200, the theatre survived until 1933, when it was demolished.

The most significant event in the history of the New occurred in 1908 when Charles Dorrill became managing director, thus beginning a sixty-four-year reign in which his family managed the theatre. When Charles died in 1912, his son Stanley took over at the age of seventeen. Stanley was determined to build 'the most luxurious and comfortable house of entertainment in England'. In 1933 he commissioned a new building designed by Milburn Bros of Sunderland, with an art-deco interior by T.P. Bennet and Sons, who had designed the Saville in London. The Drury Lane hit *Wild Violets* opened the third New Theatre on 26 February 1934. The theatre was now capable of seating over 1700 people. Stanley Dorrill brought almost all the great dramatic actors and actresses of the age to Oxford, performing classic and modern roles in touring West End productions. He also brought in the best popular and operatic singers, music-hall entertainers, matinée idols, dancers and musicians. This was the golden age of the New. Dorrill built up a large clientèle who came every week, having permanently reserved seats. With the advent of television in the 1950s, running a large theatre became increasingly difficult. In 1965 Stanley Dorrill's son John took over as managing director, but he was unable to keep the family business going and in 1972 he was bought out by Howard and Wyndam's, a company owning a chain of provincial theatres. Howard and Wyndam's style of management was not popular with Dorrill's regular theatregoers or his staff and, though Stanley was made president of the company set up by Howard and Wyndam's to run the theatre, the Dorrill atmosphere had gone.

In 1977 Paul Gregg, the impresario and managing director of Apollo Leisure, took over the theatre and renamed it the Apollo. Though audiences can still see the leading opera and ballet companies, West End musicals and the annual pantomime (which became an Oxford family ritual in the Dorrill days), play productions have, for the most part, been superseded by pop and rock performances.

Archives, City Most of the city's archives are housed in the TOWN HALL. The earliest title deed of a city property is a grant dated 1229 from Henry III of the site of part of the present town hall (*see* COURTS). The town's common seal attached to a confirmation of a grant of Medley Island to OSENEY ABBEY in 1191 is the earliest known municipal seal in Great Britain. A charter of privileges granted by King John in 1199 is the town's earliest surviving charter. Other charters in the archives are that of 1555 confirming previous charters, the charter of incorporation granted by King James I in 1605, and one of 1974 whereby the borough was granted the status of a city. These and many other documents were shown in an exhibition of Oxford City Archives held in the town hall in March 1985. The city also has an extensive collection of local records in the local history section of the CENTRAL LIBRARY. Other documents concerning the history of the city and its inhabitants have been deposited by various bodies in the County Record Office in the basement under COUNTY HALL.

Archives, University *Bodleian Library*. Originally kept, so it seems, in the chapter house of ST FRIDESWIDE'S PRIORY, the University's archives were transferred to the CONGREGATION HOUSE at ST MARY THE VIRGIN in the 14th century and kept there with other valuables, including the UNIVERSITY CHEST. When the Congregation House was broken into and plundered in 1544, the archives were strewn about and never properly catalogued until the appointment of BRIAN TWYNE as first Keeper of the Archives in 1634. They were thereafter transferred to the tower of the BODLEIAN. In the middle of the 19th century they were moved up to the highest room in the tower, together with the records of the Chancellor's Court (*see* COURTS). The archives, which date back to 1214, have been constantly added to since.

Aristotle Lane An old unadopted road which runs westwards to PORT MEADOW from No. 1 HAYFIELD ROAD, and so called after Aristotle's Well in the vicinity. ANTHONY WOOD suggested that it was once called Brumman's Well because a certain Brumman the Rich (also known as Brumman of Walton) may have owned lands, including several wells, nearby. He gave these to Oxford CASTLE 'by the favour' of ROBERT D'OILLY, his lord and master. Wood says that after the time of Brumman the well was 'christened by the name of Aristotle ... because it was ... frequented in the Summer season by the Peripateticks'. These were followers of the philosopher, and perhaps so called either because he used to walk about while lecturing or after the covered walk where the lectures were held (the Lyceum). There was also a Plato's Well in what is now WORCESTER STREET. In the 19th century Aristotle's Well was found in a neglected state (shown in Cole's plan near Heathfield's Hutts – *see* HAYFIELD ROAD). In the late 19th century it was covered over by a house. In some unpublished notes Anthony Wood expresses doubt about whether Brumman's Well might have been Walton Well and Aristotle's Well really Wolward's (or Ulward's) Well, called after John Ulward who held lands in GODSTOW. This now seems more likely. The hump-back, single-arch bridge in the lane, which takes the road over the CANAL, was designed in the office of James Brindley in about 1790.

Arnold, Matthew (*1822–1888*). The eldest son of THOMAS ARNOLD, he won a classical scholarship from Rugby to Balliol College in 1841. In 1843 he won the NEWDIGATE PRIZE for a poem on Cromwell; in 1845 he was elected to a fellowship at Oriel; and in 1857 became Professor of Poetry, an appointment he held for ten years, during which he published his *On Translating Homer: Three Lectures given at Oxford* (1861) and *Essays in Criticism* (1865), in which he referred to Oxford as the 'home of lost causes'. It is in his poem 'Thyrsis', which was first published in his *New Poems* (1867), that the celebrated lines appear:

And that sweet City with her dreaming spires
She needs not June for beauty's heightening.

(*See also* BOAR'S HILL *and* POETRY.)

Arnold, Thomas (*1795–1842*). Came up to Corpus Christi College at the age of sixteen as a scholar from Winchester. His contemporaries at the college included JOHN KEBLE and John Taylor Coleridge, afterwards one of the judges of the Court of Queen's Bench, to whom Arnold said he 'owed more than to any living man'. He obtained a First in Classics in 1814 and in 1815 was elected to a fellowship at Oriel. That year he won the Chancellor's Prize for a Latin essay and two years later the Chancellor's Prize for an English essay (*see* PRIZES AND SCHOLARSHIPS). He remained at Oxford for eight deeply formative years, described as a 'golden time'. He became headmaster of Rugby in 1828 and in 1841 was appointed Regius Professor of Modern History, but he died suddenly of angina pectoris the following year.

ART Oxford's most important collections are those of the University which are housed in the ASHMOLEAN MUSEUM. The Departments of Antiquities, Western Art and Eastern Art all contain outstanding works of art. The Print Room has one of the finest collections of Old Master drawings in the country, notably those by Michelangelo, Raphael, Turner and Ruskin. Among the many outstanding paintings in the museum are Giotto's *Virgin and Child*, Bicci di Lorenzo's *St Nicholas of Bari Rebuking the Storm*, Domenico Ghirlandaio's *Portrait of a Young Man*, Uccello's *Hunt in the Forest*, Piero di Cosimo's *Forest Fire*, Bellini's *St Jerome Reading in a Landscape* and the same artist's *Virgin and Child*, Giorgione's *Virgin and Child with a View of Venice*, Bronzino's *Portrait of Giovanni de' Medici*, Alessandro Allori's *Portrait of a Young Man*, Van Dyck's *Deposition*, Poussin's *Exposition of Moses*, Claude Lorrain's *Landscape with Ascanius Shooting the Stag of Sylvia*, Giovanni Lanfranco's *Christ and the Woman of Samaria*, Chardin's *Still Life*, Watteau's *Le Repos gracieux*, Gainsborough's *Miss Gainsborough Gleaning*, Jacob van Ruisdael's *Landscape near Muiderberg*, Philips de Koninck's *View over Flat Country*, Tiepolo's *Young Woman with a Macaw*, Pompeo Batoni's *David Garrick*, Samuel Palmer's *Valley Thick with Corn* (the collection of Palmer's work in the Ashmolean is one of the best in existence), Constable's *Watermeadows near Salisbury*, Millais's *Return of the Dove to the Ark*, Arthur Hughes's *Home from the Sea*, Holman Hunt's *Early Britons Sheltering a Missionary from the Druids*, Stanley Spencer's *Cows at Cookham*, as well as works by Augustus John, Philip Wilson Steer, Matthew Smith and Walter Sickert. Paintings of the French School include works by Bonnard, Boudin, Cézanne, Corot, Courbet, Fantin-Latour, Manet, Matisse, Picasso, Pissarro (a considerable collection of paintings and drawings by this artist) and Van Gogh. There is also an extensive collection of Dutch still-life paintings.

The Ashmolean possesses a particularly fine collection of small bronzes. The nucleus of the collection of Renaissance bronzes was given to the University by Charles Drury Fortnum. Among later bronzes are works by Honoré Daumier, Auguste Rodin, Edgar Degas, Alfred Gilbert, Alfred Drury and Aristide Maillol. The museum also possesses a fine early 17th-century ivory statuette of *Venus and Cupid* by Georg Petel, which was formerly in the collections of Rubens and George Villiers, 1st Duke of Buckingham.

CHRIST CHURCH PICTURE GALLERY also contains a particularly fine collection of Old Master drawings, a changing selection from which is very well displayed in a specially designed part of the gallery. It includes works by Raphael, Michelangelo, Leonardo, Correggio, Titian, Tintoretto and Veronese, as well as Rubens, Van Dyck, Rembrandt and Claude. The paintings include Annibale Carracci's *Butcher's Shop*, Strozzi's *Judith with the Head of Holofernes*, Tintoretto's *Martyrdom of St Lawrence* and *The Virgin and St John* by van der Goes and Van Dyck's *Continence of Scipio*.

The Colleges all have collections of PORTRAITS. Some of these are outstanding also as works of art, but they are dealt with separately and are not included here. Among the other paintings and works of art in the colleges which are accessible to the public mention may be made of the following:

All Souls Large paintings on board of religious subjects by Isaac Fuller (formerly attributed to Robert Streater) dating from the 1660s. They originally decorated the east end of the chapel roof and now hang above the entrance to the antechapel.

Corpus Christi The east window of the chapel was blocked up to show a copy of Guido Reni's *Annunciation*, ascribed to Pompeo Batoni. This was removed in 1794 by the donor to Marsh Baldon church and later replaced by the *Adoration of the Shepherds*, given to the college in 1804 by Sir Richard Worsley. Sir David Piper says that this painting is 'close to Rubens if not by him'.

Exeter The tapestry in the chapel, *The Adoration of the Magi*, was made by WILLIAM MORRIS to the design of EDWARD BURNE-JONES (1890). Also in the chapel are four 14th-century Italian paintings on wooden panels. Two represent unidentified saints and have been attributed by Berenson to a close follower of Pietro Lorenzetti. Two others represent St Peter (with keys) and St Paul (with sword) and are by Luca di Tommé. They have been dated to 1370.

Jesus A large picture of St Michael overcoming Satan, in the chancel of the chapel, is said to be a copy of an original by Guido Reni. Until about the 1860s it served as an altarpiece.

Keble One of the best-known paintings in any of the colleges is Holman Hunt's *The Light of the World*. It was painted in 1853, first exhibited at the Royal Academy in 1854, and was given to the college in 1873 by Mrs Combe. There is a later version in St Paul's Cathedral. The college also has *The Dead Christ Mourned by His Mother, the Three Marys, St John and St Joseph of Arimathea*, a 16th-century Flemish painting by Willem Key. Both paintings are in the side-chapel.

Magdalen The altarpiece in the chapel is *Christ Carrying the Cross*, formerly attributed to Guido Reni and more recently to Valdés Leal (although Professor Sir Ellis Waterhouse has described that attribution as 'not satisfactory').

Merton In the chapel is an altarpiece, *Crucifixion*, perhaps by Domenico Tintoretto. The college also has a collection of cartoon caricatures by MAX BEERBOHM in its Beerbohm Room.

New College El Greco's *Apostle* (St James the Greater), which hangs in the chapel, was given to the college in 1960 by Mr A.E. Allnatt, who also gave Rubens' *Adoration of the Kings* to King's College, Cambridge. In the antechapel are the 7-foot-high statue in Hoptonwood stone by Epstein (1948) of *Lazarus* risen from the grave, and two paintings of *The Annunciation* by Giovanni Speranza (1473–1528).

Oriel The altarpiece in the chapel (usually locked) of *Christ Carrying the Cross* is by the Flemish painter Bernard van Orley (1491/2–1542).

The Queen's College The altarpiece in the chapel is a copy by James Cranke of Correggio's *Notte*.

St Edmund Hall In the chapel is a striking modern altarpiece – Ceri Richards' *The Supper at Emmaus* (1957–8). The east window of the chapel (inserted in 1865) is a composite window with the Crucifixion as the centrepiece – the earliest example in Oxford of the work of SIR EDWARD BURNE-JONES and WILLIAM MORRIS. Two cartoons for the window, one by each artist, are on display in the antechapel.

St Hilda's The college possesses G.F. Watts's *Una and the Red Cross Knight*. In his biography of George Frederic Watts, RA (1817–1904), 'England's Michelangelo', Wilfrid Blunt wrote that in the winter of 1855–6 Watts took Arthur Prinsep (aged sixteen and brother of Val Prinsep) to Paris. 'Arthur was longing to be rid of his girlish looks; but Watts bribed him to retain them while he made several drawings which were later to serve him for his *Sir Galahad, Aspiration, Hyperion,* and *Una and the Red Cross Knight*.'

St Hugh's The chapel contains an engraved glass panel by Laurence Whistler in memory of Miss Gwyer (Principal 1924–46). He also designed the pair of wrought-iron centenary gates at the Canterbury Road entrance to the Principal's lodgings. In the ground-floor corridor is a full set of engravings of cathedrals of England, drawn and etched by John Buckler and engraved by B. Reeve (1799–1814).

St Peter's The college has a small collection of Russian icons of the 17th–20th centuries which are on loan and are kept in Canal House.

Worcester College Worcester has what is, in the opinion of Sir David Piper, 'one of the most gravely grand (and I think the largest) Ruysdael landscapes in Britain'.

In the TOWN HALL the city has an extensive art collection. Apart from some forty portraits there is a collection of twenty-one watercolours by WILLIAM TURNER OF OXFORD, six pen-and-wash drawings by him and two oil paintings. Also in the town hall are *The Rape of the Sabines* after Pietro da Cortona; *Election in the Guildhall at Oxford*, a 17th-century painting by Egbert van Heemskerck (*see* 'An Oxford City Election in 1687 as depicted by Egbert van Heemskerck' by Harold S. Rogers, *Oxoniensia*, Vol. VIII, 1943, p. 155); *A View of Oxford from the West* and *The Village of Iffley*, engravings by Peter De Wint; paintings by T.F.M. Sheard and William Matthison, well known for his postcard scenes of Oxford; an oil painting of *Norwich Tower* by John Bernay Crome; and an abstract *Crusade* by Stanley Simmonds.

In the MAISON FRANÇAISE a bronze nude, *Flore*, by Aristide Maillol stands in the garden. OXFORD UNIVERSITY PRESS has watercolours by J.M.W. Turner which were engraved for the OXFORD ALMANACKS, including a view of Christ Church from the meadows and a view of Worcester College and Walton Street, on permanent loan to the Ashmolean. Of the religious establishments, the Jesuit CAMPION HALL is, in the words of Sir David Piper, 'much the most sumptuous in its devotional furnishings', which include a painted high relief of *St Ignatius Loyola with Disciples*, ascribed to Juan Martinez Montañés.

The BODLEIAN LIBRARY houses a very fine collection of illuminated manuscripts, as well as illustrated books and drawings of Oxford by J.C. BUCKLER, W.A. DE LA MOTTE and others. Keble College also possesses an outstanding collection of mediaeval illuminated manuscripts. The MUSEUM OF MODERN ART holds frequent exhibitions of modern works. Many of the college Senior Common Rooms possess fine collections of paintings, drawings and other works of art, but these are not open to public inspection and are not, therefore, referred to here.

In sculpture Epstein and Barbara Hepworth are both represented in Oxford. Apart from Epstein's *Lazarus*, his bronze bust *Deirdre* is in the quad of the OXFORD HIGH SCHOOL FOR GIRLS. Barbara Hepworth's *Trezion* was installed beside the punt-dock near The Queen's College Florey Building in 1972; her bronze *Meridian* (1959) is in the quadrangle of the Sacher Building, beyond the garden of New College; and her bronze *Archaean* (1959) is in the garden of St Catherine's College. Somerville College has Wendy Taylor's *Triad* (1971) in mild steel with bronze finish, and Nuffield College has a fountain (1962) by Hubert Dalwood, while the cross and reredos in mild steel in the chapel are by John Hoskins. A bronze sculpture by David Wynne called *Noli me Tangere* (with figures of Christ and Mary Magdalen) stands in the Chaplain's Quadrangle of Magdalen College underneath the Great Tower. It was made in 1963. There is another cast of it in Ely Cathedral. St Benet's has the Stations of the Cross in the chapel carved by the Oxford sculptress Rosamund Fletcher.

The Oxford Art Society was founded in 1891 to encourage the practice of the fine arts in Oxford and holds two exhibitions each year, the summer one showing works by members and the autumn one works both by members and non-members. Oxford Art Society Associates was founded in 1962. The society holds lectures twice a term at the Maison Française on a wide variety of subjects connected with art and also organises visits to art exhibitions and country houses.

(*See also* PORTRAITS, STATUES AND BUSTS, STAINED GLASS, PLATE, RUSKIN SCHOOL OF DRAWING AND FINE ART *and* MUSEUM OF MODERN ART.)

(Piper, D., *The Treasures of Oxford*, London, 1977; Hassall, A.G., and W.O., *Treasures from the Bodleian Library*, Oxford, 1976; *Summary Catalogue of Paintings in the Ashmolean Museum, Oxford*, Oxford, 1980; *Treasures of the Ashmolean Museum*, Oxford, 1985; Byam Shaw, J., *Paintings by Old Masters at Christ Church, Oxford*, Oxford, 1967, and *Drawings by Old Masters at Christ Church, Oxford*, 2 vols, Oxford, 1976; Waterhouse, E., 'Paintings and Painted Glass' in *The History of the University of Oxford; Vol. V: The 18th Century*, Oxford, 1986.)

Ashmole, Elias (*1617–1692*). Born at Lichfield, the son of a well-to-do saddler, Ashmole attended Lichfield Grammar School and became an attorney in 1638. His sympathies lay with the Royalists in the CIVIL WAR and in 1644 he was appointed by the King a commissioner of excise. This appointment brought him to Oxford where he entered Brasenose College to study Physics and Mathematics. In 1647 he married as his second wife, and much against her family's will, a woman twenty years older than himself and the wealthy widow of three husbands. He was now enabled to pursue his intellectual interests, particularly in astrology, alchemy, heraldry and antiquarianism, 'without being forced to take pains for a livelihood in the world'. After the Restoration he was appointed

John Riley's 1689 portrait of Elias Ashmole, whose collection of rarities formed the nucleus of the Ashmolean Museum.

Windsor Herald and Comptroller of the Excise, and in 1672 published his great work *Institution, Laws and Ceremonies of the Order of the Garter*. He had made his first recorded visits to the Tradescants at Lambeth in 1650 and his deep interest in their museum of curiosities, which eventually came into his possession, resulted in the creation of the ASHMOLEAN MUSEUM. On 17 February 1683 he recorded in his diary, 'The last load of my rarities was sent to the barge, and this afternoon I relapsed into the gout.' Before his death the degree of MD was conferred upon him by the University, to which he bequeathed his library as well as the Tradescants' treasures and his own collection of medals.

Ashmolean Museum *Beaumont Street*. Named after ELIAS ASHMOLE, described by ANTHONY WOOD as 'the greatest virtuoso and curioso that ever was known or read of in England before his time'. He was a friend of the John Tradescants, father and son, whose collection of rarities, Tradescant's Ark as it was called, was then considered the best museum of its kind in the world. It was open to the public for a fee, apparently 6*d* a head, in South Lambeth, where in 1634 one visitor spent a whole day 'peruseing, and that superficially' the extraordinary variety of objects which had been assembled by John Tradescant the elder, a professional gardener who had been in the service of the Duke of Buckingham and James I and who had been as far as Russia and Algiers in pursuit of specimens. These included, so the visitor wrote, 'beasts, fowls, fishes, serpents, wormes (reall, although dead and dryed) pretious stones and other Armes, Coines, shells, fethers . . . Curiosities in Carvinge, paintings . . . Medalls of Sondrey sorts, etts'. The collection was gradually increased by Tradescant's son, by exchange with other travellers and by gifts from numerous donors, until it included

not only a fine collection of fauna and flora, shells, weapons, shoes, Chinese lanterns and Red Indian hunting shirts but also such remarkable items as 'a natural dragon above two inches long', 'blood that rained in the Isle of Wight', a 'Brazen-ball to warm the Nunnes hands', the thigh bone of the Hertfordshire Giant, Jack o' Legs, a stuffed dodo, whose remnants can now be seen in the UNIVERSITY MUSEUM, and 'the robe of the King of Virginia', a mantle of deer skin and shells known as 'Powhatan's Mantle' which is still preserved in the Ashmolean. Most of the specimens were listed in the *Musaeum Tradescantium* (1656), the first museum catalogue to be printed in Britain, which was compiled by Elias Ashmole and his friend, Dr Thomas Wharton, in collaboration with the younger Tradescant.

Three years before his death, the younger Tradescant made over his collection to Ashmole by deed of gift; but he evidently regretted this, for he subsequently made a will by which the University of either Oxford or Cambridge was to be made the beneficiary, the choice to be left to Mrs Tradescant, who was to retain the collection in her own possession so long as she lived. When the will was read on Tradescant's death in 1662, Ashmole challenged it and filed a bill in Chancery against the widow. The subsequent quarrels lasted intermittently for ten years, growing more frequent when Ashmole took a lease of the house next door to Mrs Tradescant's. While Ashmole insisted that she was a most improper guardian, selling off certain specimens with reckless disregard of her late husband's wishes, Mrs Tradescant counterclaimed that he was harassing her unmercifully. Ashmole's claim was upheld, and the collection was eventually moved to Ashmole's house after an attempted burglary. Not long afterwards Mrs Tradescant was found drowned in her garden pond.

Ashmole, having added to the collection some of his own coins and other objects, now wrote to the VICE-CHANCELLOR: 'It has long been my Desire to give you some testimony of my Duty and filial Respect, to my honoured mother the University of Oxford, and when Mr Tradescants Collection of Rarities came to my hands, tho I was tempted to part with them for a very considerable Sum of money . . . I firmly resolv'd to deposite them no where but with You.' Ashmole stipulated that a suitable repository should be built to house the collection and in 1686 he drafted 'Statutes, Orders and Rules' in which he insisted upon the need for 'the inspection of Particulars, especially those as are extraordinary in their Fabrick, or useful in Medicine or applyed to Manufacture or Trade'. He also stipulated that if a specimen decayed or had to be destroyed a careful drawing should be made of it first, a requirement that, after his death, was generally ignored. Indeed, in their new home in BROAD STREET (*see* OLD ASHMOLEAN BUILDING), the collection was for much of the 18th century sadly neglected, several of the keepers being somewhat lazy and lax in their duties, one of them leaving town a month after his appointment, taking the key with him, 'being apprehensive his Election would be contested'. It was not, in fact, until the first half of the 19th century that the Ashmolean Museum began to regain its reputation.

By then the University had come to possess a large variety of treasures in addition to those kept at the museum in Broad Street. There were numerous objects of antiquity and works of art at the BODLEIAN, including prints and drawings from the bequest of

Zoological specimens, including the Dodo which appears in Lewis Carroll's Alice's Adventures in Wonderland, *on display in the Old Ashmolean Museum c.1836.*

Francis Douce; there were ancient marbles bequeathed in 1654 by the antiquary John Selden; there were Anglo-Saxon antiquities which had come into the University's possession in 1829; and there was the Arundel Collection of marbles given in 1667 by Lord Henry Howard. Benefactions from the Rev. Francis Randolph and Sir Roger Newdigate made it possible for these treasures to be brought together in a new neo-classical building in BEAUMONT STREET designed by Charles Robert Cockerell. These University Galleries were opened in 1845, the pictures being arranged on the first floor and the sculptures on the ground floor in the Randolph Gallery, named after one of the Ashmolean's principal 18th-century benefactors, the Rev. Dr Francis Randolph. These were soon joined by a magnificent collection of drawings by Raphael, Michelangelo and other masters which had belonged to Sir Thomas Lawrence and were presented by subscribers, including the Earl of Eldon; and, in 1850, by the Fox-Strangways gift of forty early Italian paintings, among them Uccello's *The Hunt*. The Penrose bequest and the Chambers Hall gift of 1855 were followed, in 1881, by thirty-six watercolours by J.M.W. Turner deposited by JOHN RUSKIN. The archaeological holdings were much increased by the accession not only of further Greco-Roman and Anglo-Saxon items but also of Egyptian material purchased in Egypt by the Rev. G.J. Chester. From the late 1880s the Egyptian collections were transformed by finds allocated from Sir Flinders Petrie's excavations. To house the new accessions, and his own bronzes and ceramics, a large extension was added to the north of the University Galleries in 1894, thanks to that most generous of benefactors, C.D.E. Fortnum, and to the initiative of his friend, ARTHUR EVANS, Keeper of the Ashmolean between 1884 and 1908 and afterwards the excavator of Knossos. Meanwhile, the natural history items, including what survived of Tradescant's collection, were transferred to the University Museum together with the collections of the explorer William Burchell and the geologist William Buckland; while the ethnographical specimens, other than those associated with the Tradescants, were taken to the PITT RIVERS MUSEUM.

In 1899 the name Ashmolean Museum was applied to the new extension and this name was soon taken to include the University Galleries as well, the building in Broad Street then becoming known as the Old Ashmolean Building and now housing the MUSEUM OF THE HISTORY OF SCIENCE. In 1908 a statute formally created the Ashmolean Museum of Art and Archaeology, comprising two departments, those of Fine Arts and Antiquities, each with its own keeper. The HEBERDEN COIN ROOM was opened in 1922, and a gallery built for the Cast Collection in 1960. The Oriental Collections were transferred from the INDIAN INSTITUTE in 1962 to the galleries of the new department of Eastern Art. Most of the museum's possessions have been acquired by gift or bequest, but since 1931 annual grants for purchases by the various departments have been made by the University. Grants have also been made in recent years by the National Exchequer through the Victoria and Albert Museum Purchase Grant, by the National Art-Collections Fund, and the Friends of the Ashmolean founded in 1971.

Some idea of the scope of the museum may be obtained by a glance at the index attached to the plans of the galleries. Under 'C', for example, are listed Ceramics, Asian; Ceramics, English; Ceramics, European; Chinese Art; Chinese Coins; Civil War Relics; Civil War Coins; Claude Lorraine: *Ascanius Shooting the Stag of Sylvia*; Clocks and Watches; Coins and Medals; Cretan Antiquities, Cypriot Antiquities; Cycladic Antiquities. Under 'M' are Majolica; Medieval Antiquities; Meissen Porcelain; Metalwork, Islamic; Metalwork, Japanese; Metalwork, Asian; Millais, *Return of the Dove to the Ark*; Miniatures; Minoan and Mycenaean Antiquities;

One of Edmund Clerihew Bentley's rhyming tags known as 'clerihews', as illustrated by G.K. Chesterton.

It was not Napoleon.
who founded the Ashmolean
He hardly had a chance
Living mostly in France

Mummies; Musical Instruments. Among the many noteworthy exhibits may be mentioned the Alfred Jewel – an Anglo-Saxon gem consisting of an enamel plaque set under a large rock crystal with a gold mount, with an inscription reading (in translation), 'Alfred ordered me to be made'; Guy Fawkes's lantern; an early 15th-century iron-bound UNIVERSITY CHEST; the Stradivari violin 'Le Messie'; the Hope collection of engraved portraits; silverwork by Paul Lamerie and other Huguenots; communion plate from the University Church, ST MARY THE VIRGIN; a 13th-century Chinese fig-tree wood figure of the seated Bodhisattva; the Anglo-Saxon Cuddesdon bowl; the Roman Wint Hill bowl; the Greek vase, the 'Shoemaker' pelike; the Egyptian fresco of the daughters of Akhenaten and Nefertiti; and the early 18th-century Indian floral carpet. There are pictures by Giotto, Ghirlandaio, Piero de Cosimo (*Forest Fire*), Holbein, Giovanni Bellini, Giorgione, Titian, Dürer, Tintoretto, Bronzino, Allori, Van Dyck (*The Deposition*), Rubens, Rembrandt, Poussin (*The Exposition of Moses*), Chardin, Watteau, Gainsborough, Tiepolo, Pompeo Batoni (*David Garrick*), Rowlandson (*Radcliffe Square, Oxford*), William Blake, Samuel Palmer, Constable, Cotman, Corot, Manet, Pissarro, Degas, van Gogh, Picasso, Stanley Spencer and several Pre-Raphaelites. (*See also* ART.) The Fine Art, Classical and Archaeological Libraries of the Ashmolean are open to readers whose names have been registered with the librarian. The Eastern Art Library is at the ORIENTAL INSTITUTE.

(MacGregor, A., *Ark to Ashmole*, Oxford, 1983; Piper, D., *Treasures of the Ashmolean Museum*, Oxford, 1985; Ovenell, R.F., *The Ashmolean Museum, 1683–1894*, Oxford, 1986.)

Assessors　The office of Assessor to the Chancellor's Court (*see* COURTS), which dates from 1626 and which from 1753 to 1760 was held by WILLIAM BLACKSTONE, fell into desuetude only in 1979. At one time, the CHANCELLOR could exercise jurisdiction in almost all causes – whether civil, spiritual, or criminal – in which scholars or PRIVILEGED PERSONS resident within the precincts of the University were parties. For this exercise, courts were held every Friday during term. At these courts the VICE-CHANCELLOR was the presiding judge; and, for the better despatch of business, he appointed a Doctor or Bachelor of Civil Law to sit with him as Assessor (for a small stipend of £40 per annum) and to act as judge for him in his absence.

The present-day Assessor works closely with the PROCTORS and, like them, is appointed by all thirty-five colleges in a set cycle. When it was first instituted in 1961, the position was called 'Representative of the Women's Colleges' and was chosen from them; but it was seen that the five graduate colleges also needed representation, and from 1964 the office was named Assessor, the holder being chosen from a women's college or a graduate college in turn. With the inclusion of women in men's colleges (and, to a lesser extent, vice versa), the necessity of limiting the choice to the original five women's colleges or to the graduate colleges was eliminated and the Assessor is now a full member of the proctorial cycle, assisting with the heavy burden of the duties which inevitably fall on the Proctors, especially in terms of University business and committees.

Assize Sermon　Formerly delivered on the appointment of the VICE-CHANCELLOR in ST MARY THE VIRGIN, the University Church, before the judges of the assize. JOHN KEBLE's preaching of this sermon was regarded by JOHN HENRY NEWMAN as the birthday of the OXFORD MOVEMENT. It is now known as the Court Sermon. It is held before the beginning of the Michaelmas Term and attended by the judge of the Crown Court.

Association for the Education of Women in Oxford　*see* ST ANNE'S COLLEGE.

Astronomer's House　A house in NEW COLLEGE LANE which was the home of Edmond Halley, the astronomer. He was born in 1656 and educated at The Queen's College, but left without taking a degree. He spent some eighteen months between 1676 and 1678 on St Helena, where he made the first complete observation of the transit of Mercury. On his return in 1678, at the age of twenty-two, he was elected a Fellow of the Royal Society and in 1703 he was appointed Savilian Professor of Geometry at Oxford. A letter dated March 1705 in the BODLEIAN LIBRARY expresses the hope that 'Mr. Halley will prevail so far as that the university will repair the [astronomer's] house, and the adding an observatory to the top of it will be very convenient and indeed useful to the university, and what Sir Henry Savile did expect from them'. The observatory was added and can still be seen on top of the roof. Halley was made Astronomer Royal in 1721 and died in 1742. He computed the orbits of twenty-four comets and came to the conclusion that those of 1531, 1607 and 1682 were in fact the same comet which appeared every seventy-six years or so. In 1704 he accurately predicted the reappearance in 1758 of the comet named after him. Halley's Comet has reappeared every seventy-six years since – in this century in 1910 and 1985–6.

Aubrey, John　(*1626–1697*). Entered Trinity College as a gentleman-commoner in 1642, but left Oxford during the CIVIL WAR. He often returned, however, declaring that he enjoyed more happiness there than anywhere else. He met the cantankerous ANTHONY WOOD in 1667 and gave him considerable help with his *Historia et Antiquitates Universitatis Oxoniensis*, though they subsequently quarrelled. His *Miscellanies* (1696) was the only work he published in his lifetime, the famous *Brief Lives*, mostly written in 1679–80, not appearing until long after his death. These *Lives* include lively portraits of some of Aubrey's Oxford contemporaries and near-contemporaries, such as RALPH KETTELL. Many of Aubrey's manuscripts were deposited in the BODLEIAN LIBRARY.

Augustinian Friary　The Austin Friars began building their friary sometime in the late 13th century in the parish of ST PETER-IN-THE-EAST. The buildings were extended in the 14th century, but by the time of the Dissolution of the Monasteries they were in a ruinous condition and were demolished soon after 1538. The site passed through various hands until it was acquired by the city in 1587. It was bought from the city in 1610 by Dorothy Wadham for the building of Wadham College.

Austin Rover　*see* ROVER.

B

Bainton Road   Named in about 1906 after the St John's College living of Bainton, Driffield, Yorkshire (now in North Humberside), and acquired by the college in 1703. The road runs from No. 247 WOODSTOCK ROAD to 42 Frenchay Road. It is one of the many roads in NORTH OXFORD built on St John's land and named after its livings in various parts of England. St John's playing fields take up the major part of the south and east sides of the road. The rest is almost entirely residential, with most of the houses built in the 19th century. A road which leads to the side of the S.U. Butec factory is situated on the north-west side. The extension of Bainton Road was taken over by the city in October 1951.

Baker's   Wm Baker & Co. were established around 1800 and occupied premises at No. 1 BROAD STREET on the corner with CORNMARKET. They advertised their business as 'cabinet makers, upholsterers, carpet factors, house decorators and complete furnishers'. The premises were rebuilt in 1915 with a rounded front in classical style by N.W. and G.A. Harrison. Baker's specialised in china and glass, furniture and fabrics. In 1987 the property was converted into a bookshop for DILLONS.

Balliol College   In about 1260, or perhaps a few years before, John de Balliol, Lord of Barnard Castle, was involved in a territorial dispute with the Bishop of Durham. Balliol became impatient and insulted the Bishop, who imposed a penance on him. Tradition has it that he had to submit to a public whipping at Durham Cathedral door and carry out a substantial act of charity. The second part of his penance he discharged by renting a house just outside the Oxford CITY WALL and maintaining in it some poor scholars. The house stood roughly where the present Master's lodgings are. The date of this foundation is traditionally reckoned as 1263. There is actually no evidence for such precision, but it is known that the college was a going concern by June 1266. Whatever the exact date, if the age of a college is to be computed from the date when its members first lived communally on its present site, then Balliol is the oldest college in the University. When John Balliol died in 1269, his widow Dervorguilla took on the role of patroness. She continued to give financial support, put the arrangements on a permanent basis by the formulation of statutes (1282) and gave the scholars a house – New Balliol Hall – sited near where the present chapel stands (1284).

A watercolour drawing by J.M.W. Turner of Balliol College quadrangle, c.1804.

There were at first sixteen scholars or Fellows (the terms were synonymous until much later) receiving an allowance of 8*d* a week each until they proceeded to the degree of Master of Arts. They were not allowed to study in other faculties, and if they wanted to continue at the University they had to make other arrangements, which is why several of them migrated to Merton in the early years. The college was firmly established by the end of the 13th century, but the prohibition of study for higher degrees soon led to difficulty. The problem was solved by Sir Philip de Somervyle, with a benefaction which enabled the number of places to be increased by six. These new places were to be made available to members who had completed the Arts course and wanted to go on to study Theology, Law or Medicine. Somervyle also gave new statutes (1340), but they proved unworkable and were revised by the Bishop of London about twenty-five years later. JOHN WYCLIF was Master at about this time. Although the best remembered early member of the college, Wyclif was by no means its first distinguished alumnus, as Richard Fitzralph (Archbishop of Armagh) and 'Doctor Profundus' Thomas Bradwardine (Archbishop of Canterbury, theologian, philosopher and mathematician) had been Fellows before 1330.

Commoners or 'Sojourners', who were not on the foundation but were associated with the college rather like paying guests, became a regular feature in the 15th century. One of these was William Gray, later Bishop of Ely. He studied and travelled in Europe about 1445, and accumulated a substantial number of manuscript books which he gave or bequeathed to the college. These make up the largest single mediaeval collection to survive in England. George Neville, brother of Warwick the king-maker, was a sojourner a little later than Gray: he was Bishop of Exeter before he was twenty years old and was made Archbishop of York in 1464, but his main claim to immortality is the prodigious two-day feast with which he celebrated one of the upward steps in his career. In the 17th century antiquarians credited the college with several other important 15th-century figures (such as Cardinal Archbishop Morton) but some of their attributions may have been fanciful. Circumstantial corroboration of some cases (Cuthbert Tunstall, an influential bishop, politician and scholar, for example) can be provided, however, and there may be something in the notion that the college was especially favoured by young noblemen in this period.

The close of the 15th century saw Balliol reasonably prosperous on an expanded site with a full complement of collegiate buildings. Richard Foxe, Bishop of Winchester (and Founder of Corpus Christi College), promulgated fresh statutes in 1507. The number of Fellows was reduced to ten; the scholars were established as a clearly junior class literally subservient to the Fellows, each of whom had the right of nomination to a scholar's place; and the college was given the unique privilege, which it still enjoys, of appointing its own VISITOR.

The 16th-century college was staunch in its allegiance to Rome (*see* ROMAN CATHOLICS). It tried to resist when Henry VIII made his demand for acknowledgement of his supremacy over the Pope in 1534, the Master and five Fellows signing and sealing their submission only after adding that they intended 'nothing to prejudice the divine law, the rule of the orthodox faith, or the doctrine of the Holy Mother

Catholic Church'. All other known corporate submissions were made without any qualification at all. Members of the college were able to cling quietly to their Catholic ways through the reigns of Henry VIII and Edward VI without attracting unfavourable attention. On the accession of Mary I in 1553, true colours were revealed and James Brookes, the Master, was promptly appointed Bishop of Gloucester. He was a conspicuous instrument of Mary's persecution as one of the judges who condemned Latimer, Ridley and Cranmer to be burned in BROAD STREET (*see* MARTYRS' MEMORIAL). Catholics were strongly represented in the fellowship until well into the reign of Elizabeth I, and survived even the forced resignation in 1574 of Robert Persons (Fellow 1568–74), subsequently a Jesuit agitator and colleague of EDMUND CAMPION. St Alexander Briant was also briefly associated with Balliol before going abroad: he later returned as a Catholic priest–missionary and, with Campion, was executed at Tyburn for high treason in 1581, having been received into the Society of Jesus while in prison. Thomas Pylcher (Fellow 1577–81) was another who followed the same path, meeting his martyrdom at Dorchester in 1581.

The college grew more prosperous with the passing of controversy and the number of COMMONERS increased considerably. The regulations for this category were put on a more organised footing and, like the scholars, they were required to have tutors, although the arrangements remained a matter of purely private contract. Presiding over this expansion was Edmund Lilly (Master 1580–1609). Laurence Kemis was a Fellow under him, resigning in 1589 for a more adventurous life at sea, and eventually becoming Sir Walter Ralegh's senior captain. George Abbot, later puritan Archbishop of Canterbury, was contemporary with Kemis. His brother Robert Abbot succeeded Lilly as Master: of him it was said that 'as a carefull and skilfull Gardiner he set his nurserie with the best plants, making always choyce of the towardliest young men in all elections, and when he had set them, he tooke such care to water and prune them that in no plat or knot in the famous nurserie of the University of Oxford there appeared more beautifull flowers, or grew sweeter fruit than in Baliol Colledge whilst he was Master'. One of the earliest acts of his brief rule (1610–16) was the opening of the gates to Fellow Commoners – wealthy students admitted to the privileges of high table on payment of substantial fees. John Evelyn, the diarist, came as one of these in 1637. The college was also remarkable in the early 17th century for a succession of Greek members, including Metrophanes Kritopoulos (subsequently Patriarch of Alexandria), and the Cretan refugee Nathanael Konopios, who is said to have introduced coffee-drinking to England (*see* COFFEE HOUSES). The exhibitions and awards which were established at this period had marked regional biases, which had been expressly forbidden in a Visitor's injunction of 1542. The Blundell Foundation (1601) was especially significant in this respect. Under it, a scholar with the right of succession to a fellowship was to be elected from Blundell's School at Tiverton in Devon.

The CIVIL WAR caused an abrupt drop in student numbers and a consequent reduction in revenue. To make matters worse, the college was obliged to 'lend' the King not only most of its ready cash (£210) but also all its domestic PLATE (valued at £334) in 1642–3.

No repayment has ever been made. The college's finances were in a parlous state by 1665. It was in debt to tradesmen for basic supplies and was itself owed large sums by defaulting members. Its main buildings were deteriorating – they had had little attention for 150 years. The coffers were empty, admissions were erratic and the loss of rents from London property after the Great Fire of 1666 was almost the last straw. A fellowship was suppressed – in modern jargon 'a post was suspended' – but the saving was not enough and an appeal was launched. At about this time, perhaps as part of the appeal publicity, Henry Savage, the Master, wrote *Balliofergus*, the first full, documented history of any college to be published. When Thomas Goode became Master in 1672, he set about further fund-raising with great persistence but poor judgment. One of his schemes was a composition with the Blundell Trustees, under which, for a cash advance of £600, the college was committed to double the number of Blundell places in perpetuity. This was to enable the West Country faction to become overwhelming in the next century. Soon after this, exhibitions for the support of graduates of Glasgow University at Balliol were endowed by the estate of John Snell. This scheme was regarded with suspicion for many years, and was the subject of litigation later; but the stream of talented graduates it brought from Glasgow operated to the college's unquestionable advantage, and continues to do so. Roger Mander was even more successful than Goode in attracting benefactors, and by the end of his mastership (1687–1704) numbers had risen to a constant level again, some repairs had been carried out on the buildings and the financial position was much sounder. There were not many members of distinction in the early 18th century, but the mathematicians John Keill and James Stirling (a Snell exhibitioner), and the Astronomer Royal, James Bradley, should be noted. Stirling was one of several members of the college who got into hot water because of their Jacobite leanings. Theophilus Leigh was elected Master in 1726. His principal qualification for the position was that he was the Visitor's nephew. His election was a bizarre and scandalously conducted affair, including such extravagances as an attempt to have the holder of a critical vote declared insane. Despite the manner of his election, his surviving correspondence does not show him in a particularly unfavourable light, and the continued decline of the college during his sixty years in office was due more to inactivity and external factors than corruption or scandal. It is a curious paradox that Balliol saw one of its greatest sons in Leigh's time: Adam Smith resided as a Snell exhibitioner in 1740–6.

In Leigh's old age there was a shortlived revival in academic standards under the influence of Richard Prosser (Fellow 1773–93). Numbers rose somewhat, and the first rounds were fought in what was to be a protracted contest to establish the principle that outsiders could be preferred to scholars in fellowship elections. The organisation and financial control of personal tuition was taken over by the college at this time. Unfortunately, in 1780 it was seriously in debt again, to the tune of more than £2000, despite the suppression of a fellowship in 1776. The energies of John Davey, who succeeded Leigh in 1785, were directed mainly to the business affairs of the college. These were in better order by the end of the next decade, partly as a result of the increased income from ancient estates in Northumberland which turned out to be nicely sited on top of coal-mining developments. On the other hand, the membership slumped and was at a very low ebb by the time JOHN PARSONS was elected Master in 1798.

Parsons consolidated the principle that academic excellence demonstrated in open competition should be the main criterion for advancement in the college. This he did in 1806 by insisting on the election of an outsider to a fellowship in preference to three scholars, persuading the Visitor to crush the protests of the opposition and settle the question for ever. The competitive aspect of the Balliol fellowships gave them distinction, and Parsons was able to attract and recruit Fellow–tutors who turned their talents on their pupils so that they were successful in the Honours examination. This created a greater demand for admission than could be satisfied, with the result that it too became selective and the process of raising academic standards gathered momentum.

Parsons died in 1819, but RICHARD JENKYNS, his right-hand man, was elected Master and continued in the same vein. In 1827 Jenkyns and his colleagues, probably largely at the instigation of C.A. Ogilvie, the senior tutor, resolved to abandon their individual patronage and award scholarships corporately on the basis of an open examination. Within a very few years this led to a regular succession of the cleverest young men in the country coming to Balliol as scholars. Among the earliest elections were A.C. Tait and BENJAMIN JOWETT, both of whom went on to win fellowships and become leading tutors.

Several of the flurries of the OXFORD MOVEMENT were centred on Balliol in Jenkyns's time, but the college survived the strain largely unscathed and its rise was hardly affected. By the middle of the century it was the principal force in the University.

A.W.N. Pugin's design for an undergraduate's bedroom, submitted to Balliol College in 1843.

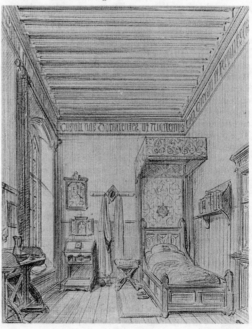

The next fifty years were characterised by an increasing tendency towards liberal views among the Fellows and the diversification of talents and types fostered by them. Under Jowett, who was Master in 1870–93 but effective leader from much earlier, academic brilliance was still encouraged, but so was originality and there was a heavy emphasis on character, leadership, duty and public service. Informal and even close relations between teachers and taught – at vacation reading parties, for example – became a vital component of the Balliol ethos. Several Fellows, like Jowett, were prominent in the debates of 1850–70 on University reform (see ROYAL COMMISSIONS), which the college anticipated in several respects. Some (notably T.H. GREEN) were also to the front in the later campaign to make higher education and degrees available to women. Ladies were allowed to attend college classes from 1884, provided that they were 'attended by some elder person'. A very advanced move was the opening of a college science laboratory in 1853. Jowett also initiated the Sunday concerts in hall which are still a special feature of Balliol life. Athletic prowess too was highly regarded: men like Edmond Warre, who got a Double First, rowed for Oxford against Cambridge three times and then went on to become Head Master of Eton, probably came close to Jowett's ideal.

Only a few of the distinguished Balliol men who came under Jowett's influence can be listed in the space available. Of poets there were MATTHEW ARNOLD, Hilaire Belloc, Arthur Hugh Clough, Gerard Manley Hopkins and Algernon Swinburne; of churchmen, Archbishop Lang, CARDINAL MANNING and Archbishop Frederick Temple; of statesmen, Asquith, LORD CURZON, Grey, Lansdowne and Milner. These were representatives of the Balliol generations of whom Asquith identified the distinguishing characteristic as 'effortless superiority' – a phrase which has dogged members of the college ever since.

The late Victorian period saw the creation of the cosmopolitan tradition which is a very clear characteristic of modern Balliol – there are at the time of writing about thirty nationalities represented in the college. A.L. SMITH and A.D. LINDSAY were successive Masters in 1916–24 and 1924–49. Both were supporters of working-class adult education and Balliol became a regular venue for summer schools in vacations. Previous traditions were continued in the college itself, academic achievement reaching a high point in 1928 when over 40 per cent of the college's candidates in the Final Honour Schools took Firsts. The most far-reaching development between the two world wars was the acquisition and extension of HOLYWELL MANOR for use as a residential annexe. Although intended for a cross-section of the college, it was increasingly favoured by graduates and has evolved into a graduate institution with a character of its own, while remaining an integral part of the college. The increase in the number and proportion of graduate admissions (in 1985 running at between a quarter and a third of all admissions – greater than the proportion for any other traditional college) represents a marked change, equalled only by the admission of women. Balliol was the first ancient college to have a woman Fellow and tutor (1973) and has admitted women as students since 1979.

The range of distinction produced by post-Jowett Balliol has if anything exceeded its previous record.

Leaders of religion once more – Chief Rabbi Israel Brodie, Shogi Effendi (Guardian of the Baha'i Faith), Cardinal Heard and Archbishop William Temple; statesmen too – Lord Beveridge, Edward Heath, Roy Jenkins, Sir Seretse Khama, LORD STOCKTON, Vincent Massey, Lord Samuel; writers – Graham Greene, Aldous Huxley, Anthony Powell, Nevil Shute; and also creative artists in other media – John Schlesinger in film and Laurence Whistler on glass; sportsmen – the Nawab of Pataudi and his son 'Tiger', both famous captains of India at cricket, and Richard Sharp, captain of England at rugby in the year he took his degree; Nobel Laureates – B.S. Blumberg, SIR CYRIL HINSHELWOOD; many Law Lords, cabinet ministers and ambassadors; the well-known gentleman detective – Lord Peter Wimsey; and Fellows of the Royal Society and of the British Academy beyond number.

The tower over the front gate and the range of buildings facing BROAD STREET were built by Alfred Waterhouse in 1867. The buildings (Staircases I–VII) are known as the Brackenbury Buildings after Miss Hannah Brackenbury, whose benefaction made their erection possible. The Brackenbury arms have pride of place immediately over the gate (see HERALDRY).

On passing through the front gate, the visitor enters the front quadrangle. The quadrangular plan was probably established in the 14th century but every part of the quadrangle has been repaired, restored or completely rebuilt several times, and knowledge of its architectural history is sketchy. The only remains of the early buildings are parts of the exterior walls on the north and west sides, beginning at the chapel passage (opposite the front gate) and passing round the quadrangle anticlockwise to the oriel window of the Master's lodgings.

War memorials for the two world wars, in which more than 300 college members fell, line the walls of the chapel passage. The First World War names include two who were awarded the Victoria Cross posthumously – G.N. Walford and J.A. Liddell; a third winner, who survived the war, was A. Carton de Wiart (later General Sir Adrian Carton de Wiart). Raymond Asquith, eldest son of the Prime Minister and perhaps the most brilliant and promising Oxford man of his generation, is commemorated. So is the poet Julian Grenfell. Ronald Poulton is another whose name was a household word in his own time: captain of England's unbeaten Rugby XV in 1914, he was killed in action a year later. From the Second World War German names are included: one of these is that of Adam von Trott, executed in 1944 for his part in the plot to assassinate Hitler.

The chapel is the third on the site. William Butterfield was the architect for the present building (1857). His design has been much attacked, and there was a serious offer to pay for demolition and reconstruction just before the First World War. Inside, most of Butterfield's furnishings and decoration have been replaced and the most interesting features are either recent (for example, the silver-gilt altar of 1927) or survivals from the chapel he demolished (such as the crowned brazen eagle lectern of about 1630, the Jacobean pulpit and the STAINED GLASS). The memorial tablets are mostly post-1860 and do not commemorate actual burials. The stained glass, which is mostly of the 16th and 17th centuries, was reset in 1912.

J.L. Strachan-Davidson, Master of Balliol from 1907 until his death in 1916, photographed with senior members of the college in about 1912.

The upper floor of the building between the chapel and the north-west corner of the quadrangle is the old library. It was purpose-built as a library in two phases. Thomas Chace (Master c.1410–25) was responsible for the first, Robert Abdy (Master c.1477–94) for the second. The windows contain the armorial shields in stained glass of the benefactors who subscribed to the building or were donors of books. The roof and battlements were added in 1792 by James Wyatt, who also refitted the interior. The books were chained until the late 18th century.

The old hall, which is now the main library, lies on the west side of the front quadrangle. It was built at about the same time as the first part of the old library. Major alterations were made by Wyatt about 1792. Conversion for library use was carried out in 1877. South of the library, above the former buttery, is the striking oriel window of the Master's lodgings.

The library passage takes the visitor from the north-west corner of the front quadrangle into the Garden Quadrangle. Flanking the exit are the old gates, which served as the main gates of the college for the 300 or more years before the rebuilding programme of the last century.

The Garden Quadrangle is a garden, but not a quadrangle. In the 18th and 19th centuries the western half of the area was known as the Grove. It has fewer mature trees now than it had then, but those that remain are still an important part of the informal atmosphere which reigns here. It is convenient to make a few remarks about the features of interest in the order in which they appear on a clockwise circuit of the perimeter, starting at the library passage.

The Master's lodgings were rebuilt by Alfred Waterhouse in 1867. Robert Scott was Master of the college at the time, so his arms are prominent on the Broad Street front.

Fisher's Building (Staircases X and XI) was erected at the expense of Henry Fisher by HENRY KEENE in 1767. In the room behind the central window on the first floor, Jowett used to give tutorials in the 1850s. The inscription on the stone beneath the window sill reads 'VERBUM NON AMPLIUS FISHER', but its meaning (literally 'A word no more Fisher') remains a mystery.

The Bristol Building (Staircase XII) is so named because part of the cost was met by the Corporation of Bristol in about 1720. Part of the CATHERINE WHEEL INN was demolished to make way for it. The remainder was demolished in 1826 so that George Basevi could modify and extend the Bristol Buildings northwards. The Junior Common Room block (Staircase XV) was erected by E.P. Warren in 1912, filling the gap between Basevi's Building and Salvin's to the north.

The visitor will not see much of Warren's Building of 1906 (Staircase XXI) from the quadrangle, but its other side has a pleasing design which, together with Salvin's asymmetrical Gothic back-gate complex, makes an interesting façade looking towards BEAUMONT STREET and the TAYLOR INSTITUTION.

The Bulkeley-Johnson Building (Staircases XX and XXII), which comprises two ranges, joined by a bridge at second-floor level, was built by Geoffrey Beard (1968). Principal contributor to the cost of the work was Vivian Bulkeley-Johnson (Balliol 1909–13).

The hall was built by Alfred Waterhouse (1877). In his concept the windows were fully glazed, but the lower sections were blocked up by his son Paul in 1910, when the panelling was installed inside. The gloom resulting from this modification is relieved by the brightly painted heraldic decorations which signify benefactors (mostly subscribers to the hall). The portraits are of Masters and distinguished alumni, including Lord Stockton and King Olav of Norway. The organ is by Willis (1885). An unusual item for a college hall, it was installed at Jowett's personal expense for use in concerts.

The Bernard Sunley Building (the Senior Common Room) was built by Beard (1966); funds were provided by a charitable trust established by the philanthropist Bernard Sunley.

The east side, which was the Master's garden until the mid-19th century, is chiefly notable for the GORDOULI and for mulberry trees, of which there are three in the quadrangle. One of them has been a propped-up but living wreck for at least seventy-five years. There is a tradition that it was planted by Elizabeth I and this legend has been honoured by the planting of two more by royal ladies – Queen Mary in 1921 and Princess Margaret in 1950. It is more likely that the tree was grown from one of the seeds distributed by James I as part of his abortive campaign to foster an English silk industry.

The Fellows' Garden was probably enclosed as at present by Butterfield after completion of the chapel in 1857. An absurd tradition that the object in the middle is the tomb of Dervorguilla the foundress has been current from time to time. In fact, she is buried at Sweetheart Abbey in Galloway, Scotland, and the 'tomb' is a collection of fragments from buildings demolished in the last century.

The corporate designation of the college is The Master and Scholars of Balliol College in the University of Oxford.

The present Master is Dr B.S. Blumberg.

(Davis, H.W.C., *A History of Balliol College*, 1899, revised by R.H.C. Davis and Richard Hunt, Oxford, 1963; Jones, J., *The Archives of Balliol College Oxford*, Chichester, 1984; Mynors, R.A.B., *Catalogue of the Manuscripts of Balliol College Oxford*, Oxford, 1963; Jones, J., *Balliol College: A History 1263–1939*, Oxford, 1988.)

Balsdon, John Percy Vyvian Dacre (*1901– 1977*). A farmer's son, Balsdon was educated at Exeter School and in 1920 went up to Exeter College as Stapledon Scholar. After a time spent teaching at Sedbergh School, he became a tutor at Keble in 1926 and was a Fellow of Exeter from 1927 to 1969. A classical scholar, he also wrote widely and well on Oxford. His *Oxford Life* was published in 1957 (new edition, 1962) and his *Oxford Now and Then* in 1970. (*See also* FICTION.)

Banbury Road Has been known by that name since at least the 14th century. The earliest evidence of the town in north Oxfordshire is a reference to Banesberie in 1086 but it had various spellings before it became Banbury in 1285. It means, literally, Bana or Banna's town. In 1388 there was a highway called Banneburgerwey; in 1859 it had become known as the turnpike road to Banbury. Outside 423 Banbury Road a milestone which marked the Abingdon– Oxford–Banbury turnpike is inscribed 'OXFORD 2, BANBURY 20'. The remains of the toll-house (No. 566), a 19th-century coursed-rubble building, is listed as of special architectural and historic interest.

The present road begins just north of ST GILES' CHURCH. The houses at first had names rather than numbers. On the east side, the road begins north of the junction with KEBLE ROAD. Here the vast University triangle development, built in 1967 by Philip Dowson (Arup Associates), dominates the view. The science blocks replaced a row of mid-19th-century houses – although some of these, in Keble Road and a pair at Nos 44 and 46 Banbury Road, survive. The red-brick Department of Engineering by W.C. Marshall (1914) is on the site of Bates' Nursery. Beyond the junction of NORHAM GARDENS with PARKS ROAD comes WYCLIFFE HALL (Nos 52 and 54) and to the north are Nos 56–62, which form the show-front of the Norham Estate, now saved from demolition (*see* NORTH OXFORD). On the front of the Gothic-style Wykeham House (No. 56) is a statue of WILLIAM OF WYKEHAM, the founder of New College, with the motto 'MANNERS MAKKETH MAN' beneath. It was carved by W. Forsyth of Worcester. The house – the origin of whose name is uncertain – was built for Henry Hatch by John Gibbs in 1865–6 and has the latter date on the frontage. An addition is dated 1894. Hatch was the owner of a drapery and clothing store in Magdalen Street, among other establishments and he opened the Victoria Theatre behind his shop. He never lived in the house but let it to various people, including Prince Leopold, Queen Victoria's youngest son, who lived there while an undergraduate at Christ Church. After fourteen years Hatch sold the lease to George Palmer, of Huntley and Palmer's biscuits, who was MP for Reading. His daughter Emily married E.B. (later Sir Edward) Poulton, the son of a Reading architect, in 1881 and they lived at Wykeham House for the rest of their lives. It was said of Poulton, who later became Hope Professor of Zoology, that he 'married the biscuit and got the tin'. The house, described by Pevsner as 'a yellow brick nightmare castle', is now occupied by the Oxford University Appointments Committee.

Between Nos 56 and 58 is the entrance to the Pauling Human Sciences Centre, a one-storey building in yellow brick, opened in 1981. No. 58, now the Department of Biological Anthropology, was built by John Gibbs in 1865–6 (when it was named Norham House) for William Walsh, a freeman of Oxford. Between Nos 58 and 60 is the entrance to the PITT RIVERS MUSEUM extension, with its howdah-like grey tops on a one-storey red-brick building. No. 60 is also occupied by the Pitt Rivers Museum and by the Donald Baden-Powell Quaternary Research Centre. Nos 60 and 62 are listed Grade II; both were built in 1864, the former by William Wilkinson and the latter by E.G. Bruton. No. 60, once called Shrublands, and illustrated in Wilkinson's book *English Country Houses* (Plate 17), has a stone turret over the porch in front. No. 60 was first leased to T.G. Cousins, the chemist. No. 62 has a beautifully carved Ruskinian doorway above which is inscribed the reference which explains the carving: namely Proverbs 30: xxix. It is by J.H. Pollen, who also worked on the UNIVERSITY MUSEUM. The house, originally known as Ketilby, was built for the Rev. St J. Tyrwhitt, vicar of ST MARY MAGDALEN, in 1858–72. He was an amateur artist who had worked with WILLIAM MORRIS on the debating hall of the UNION SOCIETY, where he painted the ceiling. The house is now inhabited by the Department of Earth Sciences Geodesy annexe and, on the north side, the Robert Hooke Institute of Atmospheric

No. 31 Banbury Road, built for a local tradesman, illustrated in William Wilkinson's book describing 'recently erected' English Country Houses, *1875.*

Research. No. 64, originally Minster House, was designed by E.G. Bruton for J.W. Weaving, an Oxford corn-merchant.

Beyond WOLSEY HALL, on the north corner of Norham Road, is the Cotswold Lodge Hotel (No. 66a), which, to the east, has a modern addition in keeping with the original. Nos 68 and 70 Banbury Road are part of S.L. Seckham's PARK TOWN development and both are listed Grade II. No. 70 was formerly the YWCA hostel now housed at No. 133 WOODSTOCK ROAD. WYCHWOOD SCHOOL (Nos 72 and 74) is a private school for girls. No. 80 was demolished for Murray Court flats and No. 90 is the Godmer School of English. On the north corner of Linton Road is the Parklands Hotel. Cunliffe Close is on the site of GREYCOTES SCHOOL, of which Mrs Cunliffe was founder and headmistress (*see* BARDWELL ROAD). On the north corner of MARSTON FERRY ROAD, approximately where SUMMERTOWN begins, is the Summertown Health Centre.

At No. 180 is the Galaxie Private Hotel. In this area most of the traditional rounded tops of the low, brick walls have been retained. Between Nos 180 and 194 are Diamond Cottages, on the site of the isolated Diamond House (or Hall), notorious in the 18th century as a place where highwaymen lurked. There are drawings of it by Malchair (1767) and by J.H. Grimm (1781) in the BODLEIAN. Diamond Place is the 1971 name for the entrance to the car park and Ferry Centre. To the north are some modern blocks which replaced an attractive row of cottages. Beyond them is the private entrance to the Oxford DELEGACY OF LOCAL EXAMINATIONS. In 1970 this road was named Ewert Place after Professor A. Ewert, a former chairman of the Delegacy. The DEWDROP (or Dew Drop) inn (No. 258), built in 1824, is one of the few remaining original buildings on the east side of Banbury Road in Summertown. It was originally a double house and one part was inhabited by John Badcock, without whom much of the early history of Summertown would be unknown. Badcock, who came here in 1830, called his house 'my humble cott'. The two houses have been an inn since 1888. In 1832 Badcock wrote the *Origin, History and Description of Summertown*. Oxfam House, the headquarters of OXFAM, has occupied the large space between the Dewdrop and Mayfield Road (formerly Diamond Street) since 1964. The attractive Ivy Lodge (No. 274), which was built by John Perkins, was demolished for Oxfam; George Rippon, founder of the *Oxford Times* (*see* NEWSPAPERS), once lived there. Before 1915, on the site of the present North Oxford Garage, was a terrace of poor labourers' cottages, known as Pharaoh's Row after the owner. Members of the Pharaoh family were deacons of the nearby Congregational Church, built in 1893, which became SUMMERTOWN UNITED REFORMED CHURCH in 1972. The old Congregational Chapel was at No. 11 MIDDLE WAY. Just south of the church is No. 294, once TWINING's establishment.

On the north corner of Portland Road is the church hall (*see* SUMMERTOWN) and the war memorial inscribed to the men of Summertown. On the north corner of Hernes Road (named after the former heron or hern lake) is Ritchie Court – a sheltered-housing scheme built in the 1970s on the site of Sunnymeade

31

House School. It is named after Dr W. Ritchie Russell, who was a leading figure and first secretary of the Secure Retirement Co-ownership Association, formed in 1971, whose scheme it is. Between Nos 544 and 548 is the entrance to the City Council's Banbury Road North Recreation Ground, most of which is leased to the Oxford Hawks and Oxford Etceteras hockey clubs and to the North Oxford Tennis Club. Beyond Haslemere Gardens, to the north, is St Frideswide's Farm.

The west side of Banbury Road begins with the OLD PARSONAGE HOTEL. Built on the site of Bethlem, a haven for poor people, it is early 17th century and has the date 1659 over the centre of three stone doorways. It is listed Grade II. A drawing of it made in 1820 by J.C. BUCKLER is in the Bodleian Library. Nos 7–21 are the former Italianate Park Villas by Samuel Lipscomb Seckham, once threatened with redevelopment by the University (see NORTH OXFORD). Nos 7 and 9 (a three-storeyed pair), 11 and 13 (a two-storeyed pair with attics) and 15–19 (three together of two storeys) were all built in about 1855 and are in stucco with arched sash windows. The first four are occupied by the Oxford University Computing Service. All are listed Grade II, as is No. 21, built to the design of SIR THOMAS JACKSON in 1879. This is of red brick with locally made terracotta Corinthian columns and an ornamental frieze. It has a red-tiled hipped roof and cost £8000. It formerly housed the OXFORD HIGH SCHOOL FOR GIRLS, which moved to BELBROUGHTON ROAD, and now houses the Department of Metallurgy and Science of Materials. All this part of the road was once known as St Giles's (Road) East. No. 23 houses the surgeries of twenty-one well-known Oxford consultants and doctors. The ACLAND HOSPITAL's new buildings hide the earlier No. 25, a listed building by Jackson. Nos 27 and 29 are part of St Anne's College, the latter being the Principal's lodgings. Both are by J.J. Stevenson in Queen Anne style (1881), the former being the more elaborate of the two. T.H. Green, the idealist philosopher, lived in one of them. Writing in 1926 in *The Right Place: a Book of Pleasures,* C.E. Montague describes the large houses near Norham Gardens as appearing to suggest that 'the architect's dearest wish was to let no man suffer from any shortage of boxrooms'. He points out how the Venetian Gothic, 'reflecting the immense ascendancy of Ruskin over the educated minds of his time, especially the academic ones, gave way to Queen Anne style houses ... with the style of Ruskin cast off'. The new buildings of St Anne's were erected on the site of No. 31, an 1866 house by Wilkinson, which before demolition was known as Springfield St Mary. No. 31 was built for George Ward, a local tradesman, and is illustrated in Wilkinson's book *English Country Houses* (Plate 19). Nos 35 and 37 (by Frederick Codd, 1865–8) and 39 and 41 (formerly a nurses' home) still survive as St Anne's houses. No. 43, on the north corner of BEVINGTON ROAD, is the Oxford University Department of Engineering Science and Medical Engineering. Nos 45 and 47 are the Wellcome Unit for the History of Medicine; 51 and 53 are the Institute of Social Anthropology (61 is their annexe); 57 and 59, by Codd, are Hertford College annexes, which were threatened with redevelopment in the late 1960s. At No. 61a is LE PETIT BLANC restaurant and 63 is the long-established chemist, Cousins Thomas & Co. There is some delicate ironwork at first-floor level on

No. 65 and a diaper-brick side-elevation to NORTH PARADE on No. 75. No. 77 (see WYCHWOOD SCHOOL) is a listed Grade II villa of 1840, for many years the headmistress's house. Both 77 and 79 are of similar early 19th-century design (listed Grade II) and are two of the few North Oxford houses which have kept their iron railings. Beyond the turn to Canterbury Road, No. 89, slightly back from the road, is now part of St Hugh's. Called The Lawn, it was built about 1830 and later became the home of Professor F. Gotch, Waynflete Professor of Physiology. Beyond the turning to ST MARGARET'S ROAD one comes to No. 101, the headquarters both of the county branch of the British Red Cross Society and the Oxfordshire Rural Community Council. North of the turning to Rawlinson Road, which takes its name from Dr Richard Rawlinson of St John's College, the 18th-century divine, is No. 111, the Swan School of English, and No. 115 is Fairfield – a home for elderly people run by a voluntary association. It has modern extensions on the south and west. No. 117 is the North Oxford Overseas Centre, housing visiting students and their families from all parts of the world. It replaced a unique house designed by an unusual man – Joseph Wright, the distinguished philologist, who, having taught himself to read, became Professor of Comparative Philology and editor of the *English Dialect Dictionary*. No. 121 (designed by T.G. Jackson) became the home of the nuns from Springfield St Mary when they moved from No. 31. They added a chapel but otherwise kept the house much as it was. It now belongs to ST CLARE's whose main premises are further up the road between Staverton and Moreton Roads. An enclosed Carmelite Convent was at No. 153, on the corner of Moreton Road, until 1987, and the Elizabeth (Lady) Nuffield Home for Elderly Ladies (No. 165) is on the north corner of Beechcroft Road. It was given to the Nuffield Foundation by LORD NUFFIELD's wife. Between Thorncliffe and Oakthorpe Roads are a few long-established firms, including (No. 193) that of Lodge Brothers, which opened in ST ALDATE's in 1927.

Between Oakthorpe Road and SOUTH PARADE is the main frontage of the Summertown Shopping Centre. Except for the garage to the south of South Parade, which replaced the Old Vicarage and was made into shops in 1970, the original houses remain and only their ground floors have been converted into shops. With its long line of gables, its unbroken gentle pattern contrasts with the massive uninteresting blocks across the road. Since 1963 there has been a Summertown Traders' Association and now nearly every need is catered for in this area. No. 267 (see SUMMERTOWN), which was built in 1822, was demolished in 1962 when Prama House took its place. No. 269 was the National Farmers' Union but in 1987 was redeveloped for the Anchor Housing Association, whose headquarters are in Oxford, and for RADIO OXFORD, previously (from 1970) at Barclay House, Banbury Road. The next road north is Rogers Street, which was named after Alderman H.S. Rogers, an architect, who became MAYOR in 1937–8. He lived at No. 269. Further north is Hobson Road, which was called Albert Road until 1961, the change of name having been said to be 'Hobson's choice'. James H. Hobson and his wife lived at No. 267 and kept a school for young ladies, known as the Summertown Seminary, from at least as early as 1825.

They were said to be 'kind and useful among the poor in the village'. Jointly with these Hobsons, the road also commemorates Audrey Hobson (*née* Gotch). The wife of Dr F. Hobson of No. 20 ST GILES', she was active in the social services. Nos 275 and 277 are both listed Grade II stone houses, built in the Gothic style in 1831 by an Oxford wine merchant. The windows have Tudor-type stone mullions. On the site of No. 311, popularly known as Ryman's Folly (*see* SUMMERTOWN) are the offices of the General Accident Fire and Life Assurance Corporation Ltd, which were built on the site of Cherwell Motors. Further north, after the turn to Summerhill Road, is No. 333, which is FREEMASONS' HALL. Built in 1823, it has had several extensions since being sold to the Freemasons in 1954 (*see* SUMMERTOWN). Further north, beyond the Banbury Road roundabout on the northern corner of FIVE MILE DRIVE, is Wolvercote Cemetery. Beyond is the post-war OXFORD UNIVERSITY PRESS development of Jordan Hill. It is said to have been so named to signify the Press travelling from JERICHO to Jordan. The city boundary goes through the estate. To the north is the North Oxford Golf Club (*see* GOLF CLUBS).

Banking   The Old Bank in HIGH STREET can trace its origins to 1771 when William Fletcher and Herbert Parsons were in business as bankers. In 1827 the bank was owned by Robinson, Parsons & Co. Herbert Parsons' brother John left his share in the business to Guy Thomson and the business became known as Parsons, Thomson & Co. The HEBERDEN COIN ROOM has a £10 note of 1899 of the Oxford Old Bank signed by Thomson and Parsons. The firm was absorbed by Barclays & Co. Ltd in 1900, the name being changed to Barclays Bank Ltd in 1917. Meanwhile, in 1877, Charles and Alfred Gillett had opened a bank in CORNMARKET in what had formerly been the Shakespeare Hotel. The firm of Gillett & Co., with branches in several towns in the county and in the suburbs of Oxford, amalgamated with Barclays Bank in 1919. Edward Lock, a goldsmith, was also acting as a banker from about the 1770s. The bank of Thomas Walker & Co., also known as the University and City Bank, opened in 1790 at the premises of Edward Lock & Son. Richard Cox and Co. was another bank operating in the late 18th century, and Tubb, Wootten, and Tubb opened in the early 19th century. William Jackson, who owned the *Oxford Journal* (*see* NEWSPAPERS), was also a banker.

The Midland Bank in Oxford was originally a branch of the Birmingham Banking Company, opened in 1883; it later became the Metropolitan Bank and amalgamated with the Midland Bank in 1914. The Midland Bank itself also started in Birmingham in 1836, and opened a branch in Cornmarket in 1912. Lloyds Bank, too, originated in Birmingham. It was formerly a private bank founded by the Quaker family of Lloyd. The Oxford branch was opened in 1900 at No. 11 Cornmarket.

Many mergers have taken place in the 20th century. Martin's Bank, which had a branch at CARFAX, was taken over by Barclays, and the National Provincial merged with the Westminster to become the National Westminster Bank. Oxford Trustee Savings Bank, now the Trustee Savings Bank, took premises in MARKET STREET and the Co-op Bank moved to new premises in NEW ROAD in 1984. Some other banks also appeared. The old banking business of Child & Co.

re-opened in Oxford in 1977 when it established a branch at No. 32 ST GILES' under its ancient sign of the marygold. Child & Co. has had a close banking association with the University since the 17th century. Its first printed banknote was issued in 1729, and the name, date and amount were left to be filled in by hand, in the same way as a cheque today. In the first half of the 19th century the head of the bank was Lady Jersey, a descendant of the Francis Child who owned the business in the 17th century. It was the executors of the 8th Earl of Jersey, the High Steward of Oxford, who sold the business in 1924 to Glyn, Mills & Co., who opened a branch at Carfax in 1932. Both banks are now part of the Royal Bank of Scotland. A branch of Citibank was opened at 129 High Street in 1986. Many of the building societies now also provide some banking services.

Bardwell Road   Named after Bardwell in Suffolk, a St John's College living obtained in 1635. It was originally on the approximate line of part of Greenditch (*see* ST MARGARET'S ROAD). Developed in the 1890s, it is situated off BANBURY ROAD, running eastwards to Chadlington Road beyond the junction of Charlbury Road. Bardwell Court flats are on the south side; so also is the DRAGON SCHOOL (with its lane running through to Norham Road). Their playing fields are at the south-eastern end of the road. A lane which leads to the CHERWELL BOATHOUSE is on the curve of the street as it joins Chadlington Road. GREYCOTES SCHOOL (formerly at 128 Banbury Road, the present site of Cunliffe Close, named after the founder) is now at 1 Bardwell Road, formerly the home of the OXFORD HIGH SCHOOL FOR GIRLS' junior department. WYCHWOOD SCHOOL (on the corner of Banbury Road) has an annexe at 2 Bardwell Road.

Barges   Until recently college barges could be seen moored by the river bank by FOLLY BRIDGE. It was the leading livery companies of the City of London that first owned such barges; and it was not until 1815 that the first Oxford barge was built by King, the boatbuilder, to provide himself with premises for his business, his boatyard having no frontage to the THAMES (*see also* BUMPING RACES). By 1830 colleges were hiring barges from King and from another boatbuilder, Hall, as changing rooms for their boat crews and as grandstands for watching the races during EIGHTS WEEK. In 1846 the OXFORD UNIVERSITY BOAT CLUB bought the Merchant Taylors Company's barge; and after that colleges either purchased livery-company barges or commissioned their own from boatbuilders. Keble College barge is displayed in the MUSEUM OF OXFORD. This, built by SALTER BROS in 1898, remained in use until 1958 when it was pronounced unsound and beached beside the Thames at Iffley Lock. It was salvaged by the museum in 1973. (*See also* ROWING.)

Barton   A large housing estate built on the north-east outskirts of the city, north of the HEADINGTON roundabout and beyond the RING ROAD. Development began in 1946 and by 1977 the estate comprised 1600 houses.

Bate Collection   The most comprehensive collection in England of historic European woodwind, brass and percussion instruments, and of Javanese gamelan.

The six surviving instruments portrayed in this detail of Zoffany's The Sharpe Family *are on loan to the Bate Collection.*

In 1963 Philip Bate gave to the University of Oxford his extensive collection of European orchestral woodwind instruments, which is now housed in the Music Faculty building in ST ALDATE'S. His portrait by Lilla Fox, painted in 1975, hangs in the gallery where the collection is displayed. The collection has been added to by gifts and purchases from Reginald Morley-Pegge, whose son, William, donated his father's extensive library and instruments after his father's death. Among the keyboard instruments is the harpsichord which Haydn is said to have played when in Oxford, on loan from the Taphouse Collection (*see* TAPHOUSE & SON). Other loans include instruments from the collections of Anthony Baines and Jeremy Montagu (both curators) and the six surviving instruments portrayed in Zoffany's painting of *The Sharpe Family*, which is itself on loan to the National Portrait Gallery. A reproduction hangs in the Bate gallery. Over sixty instruments were purchased from Edgar Hunt, including the world-famous Bressan treble recorder. In 1985 the Minister of Forestry in the Republic of Indonesia, H.E. Sudjarwo, presented the Javanese gamelan 'Kyai Madu Laras', the finest playing gamelan in Britain.

Bathurst, Ralph (*1620–1704*). One of fourteen brothers, six of whom were killed fighting for Charles I, and one of whom, Benjamin, was the father of Allen, 1st Earl Bathurst. Ralph was sent to GLOUCESTER HALL, Oxford (*see* also WORCESTER COLLEGE), but soon moved to Trinity College where his grandfather, RALPH

KETTEL, was President. He was appointed a Fellow of the college in 1640. During the CIVIL WAR he studied Medicine, took an MD degree in 1654 and practised as a physician in Oxford, where he was one of the group of men of scientific bent whose meetings in the rooms of DR JOHN WILKINS at Wadham College eventually developed into the Royal Society. Four years after the Restoration he was elected President of Trinity and from 1673–6 was VICE-CHANCELLOR. At Trinity he supervised an ambitious building programme, contributing large sums to its cost, and worked hard to make the college distinguished both academically and socially. His nephew Earl Bathurst, who was an undergraduate at Trinity in his time, said that 'all the young students admired and loved him', though he was acknowledged to maintain 'the most exact discipline', surprising scholars who walked 'in the grove at unreasonable hours, on which occasions he frequently carried a whip'. He left part of his collection of coins and some portraits to the BODLEIAN LIBRARY.

Battels This old word (variously spelt) is still in full and normal use at Oxford, and means the debts (whether for food, drink, lodgings, hospitality, laundry, buttery or other charges) owed by a member of a college to that college: one could not speak of 'University' battels. Originally, perhaps, the application of the word was limited to the food supplied by a college. Its derivation remains obscure, but it has been suggested that it comes from 'little bats', tallies or notched sticks on which accounts were once kept; 'patella', meaning a plate; or is simply an Old English word meaning food. Whatever the derivation, no member of a college is ever in doubt about the meaning of the word. The first example of it in the OXFORD ENGLISH DICTIONARY is ascribed to Exeter College in 1557, and it is also found, in a different gender, in the statutes of 1636 (in both places appearing in Latin).

A cognate term is 'batteler', meaning an undergraduate who ranked below the COMMONERS or Fellow Commoners, but above the SERVITORS. They were distinguished by different scales for CAUTION MONEY, rent and commons. Thus, at The Queen's College, a batteler paid only for his batells (so spelt at Queen's) – that is to say, the victuals with which the college supplied him in addition to his commons, whereas the commoner paid also for his commons, or food supplied at the common table. The status of batteler was abolished there in 1827.

Much detail about battels is preserved in the records of individual colleges. One well-known example is that of SAMUEL JOHNSON at Pembroke, whose full batteling accounts are preserved and are often on display in the college library. They ranged from 7s 11d to 12s 6d per week – not particularly small, despite his relative impecuniosity, though clearly much less than those of, say, Arthur Annesley, a gentleman-commoner of Lincoln, who came up in 1750 and managed to spend no less than £176 5s 0d in a single year, of which £41 15s 6d went on battels. In the 1980s, a resident undergraduate's battels could easily reach £300 or more per term.

Bayswater Bayswater Farm is on the north-eastern outskirts of the city, the land between the farmhouse and the A40 trunk road having been developed as a housing estate. Bayswater Road leads from the HEADINGTON roundabout past the CREMATORIUM and crosses Bayswater Brook running to the north of the RING ROAD.

BBC *see* RADIO OXFORD.

Beale, Dorothea (*1831–1906*). The daughter of a surgeon from Gloucestershire, Dorothea Beale was educated in London and Paris and in 1849 was appointed Mathematics tutor at Queen's College, London, of which she became head teacher in 1854. In 1858 she was chosen out of 150 candidates to become Principal of the Ladies' College, Cheltenham. A shrewd, idealistic yet businesslike pioneer of the higher education of women, she realised that the main reason for the inadequacy of such education was the lack of facilities for the proper training of teachers. A residential training college for women teachers, St Hilda's College, was opened at her instigation at Cheltenham in 1885. And in 1892, in order to take advantage of the education newly available for women at Oxford, Miss Beale purchased for £5000 Cowley House, Oxford, which was opened as St Hilda's hall of residence for women in 1893 (*see* ST HILDA'S COLLEGE).

Beam Hall *Merton Street*. In its eastern half one of the very few remaining Oxford buildings which was a mediaeval ACADEMIC HALL, though through seven centuries it has had various owners, uses and occupiers. Its name is derived from a 13th-century

Dorothea Beale, formerly Principal of the Ladies' College, Cheltenham, founded St Hilda's College in 1893.

owner, Gilbert de Biham, CHANCELLOR of the University, from whom it passed into the hands of ST FRIDESWIDE'S PRIORY in 1262, by which time it was probably already an academic hall. It certainly was one by the mid-15th century, and remained so for the next hundred years, apparently without dependence on any one college – though there is reference to ownership by Merton in the 14th century. Somewhat later it may have housed the first printing press set up in Oxford (*see* PRINTING). At the Dissolution of the Monasteries the building was given to Christ Church, from whom it passed into lay hands. It had apparently ceased to be an academic hall when Corpus Christi College bought it in 1553, in a ruinous condition. It was rebuilt in 1586, from which time it appears to have been used as a residence, as it is today. In the 17th century it was the home of the physician Thomas Willis, Sedleian Professor of Natural Philosophy, and the first to distinguish sugar diabetes. It was during his occupancy that JOHN FELL, ejected from his place at Christ Church, of which he later became Dean, maintained Anglican services in the house during the Commonwealth. The original building (the eastern half of the present larger one) in MERTON STREET was a typical mediaeval house, the main feature of which was the hall, from ground level to rafters, now forming rooms on two floors by the introduction of flooring, possibly in Jacobean times. Thus, consisting simply of a large open hall with a single upper room at the west end, it might possibly have been able to house up to twelve scholars.

Bear Inn *Alfred Street*. Originally sited south-west and north-west of ALFRED STREET with a long frontage to HIGH STREET. Then known as Parne Hall, it was burnt down in 1421. Rebuilt, it became Le Tabard

35

until 1432, then the Bear Inn until 1801. The bear and ragged staff were the emblems of Richard Neville (1428–71), Earl of Warwick. By the mid-16th century the Bear was one of the main and largest taverns in Oxford. ROYAL COMMISSIONS and circuit judges regularly met here. In 1586 Lord Norris and his suite were attacked at the Bear by University scholars as a reprisal against the imprisonment of Magdalen men who had stolen deer from SHOTOVER ROYAL FOREST. The Bear became a coaching inn during the 18th century and was the home of the famous 'Oxford Machine' coach (*see* TRANSPORT). At its closure in 1801 the inn possessed thirty rooms and stabling for thirty horses.

The present Bear began as an ostler's house which was attached to the older premises in 1606. It became an inn, the Jolly Trooper, in 1774 and later the Bear in 1801. The famous tie collection was begun in 1952 by the landlord, Alan Course.

Bear Lane   Named after the BEAR INN, it has been so known since at least 1814. Earlier references must be viewed in the light of the fact that ALFRED STREET was once called Bear Lane. The present lane is a narrow road which runs from ORIEL SQUARE to the junction of BLUE BOAR STREET and Alfred Street, skirting the north side of CHRIST CHURCH. The original Bear inn may have stood at the corner of the HIGH STREET and not where the present inn stands.

Beating the Bounds   The ancient custom of Beating the Bounds dates back to mediaeval times and is still carried on by two churches in Oxford on Ascension Day. At the City Church of ST MICHAEL AT THE NORTH GATE the annual perambulation of the boundaries of the parish takes place after an Ascension Day communion service in the church. The vicar, together with the choir in their red cassocks, undergraduates from Lincoln College in SUBFUSC, and

parishioners, leave the church carrying long canes. They all proceed to the stones which are set in various walls to 'mark' the boundaries. The vicar draws a cross on each stone in chalk and the choir and others then beat the 'marks' or stones with their canes. Now that the parish has absorbed the old parishes of ST MARTIN and ALL SAINTS, the perambulation takes about two hours and some thirty boundary stones are marked. Some of these are now in shops, such as the one in Marks & Spencer's in QUEEN STREET. The original stone is behind a glass door in the store and marked the parish boundaries of St Michael at the North, Gate with St Martin and All Saints; ST ALDATE'S with HOLY TRINITY, and ST EBBE'S with ST PETER-LE-BAILEY. The stone was repositioned in 1978, some 40 feet from its original position, which is marked with a brass cross on the floor of the store. Another stone is on the wall inside the ROEBUCK inn in MARKET STREET. The more easily visible stones are on the walls in NEW INN HALL STREET and at the rear entrance to Boots shop off Market Street. Some are in colleges, including St Peter's Hall, Brasenose and Lincoln. Most have plain crosses, although a few have St Andrews crosses, and a more recent stone on the wall of the car park to the COVERED MARKET bears the special cross of St Michael, which appears on the 13th-century stained glass in the church.

The perambulation finishes at Lincoln College, where the party is entertained to lunch in hall and a special college brew of ivy beer is drunk from pewter tankards. After lunch hot pennies are thrown by undergraduates from the parapet of the buildings in the front quadrangle to the choirboys and girls who scramble for them on the lawn. Cold pennies are also thrown on to the lawn by the watchers in order to confuse the searchers about which pennies are hot and which are cold.

The custom of Beating the Bounds is also observed at the University Church of ST MARY THE VIRGIN. It

Beating the Bounds in Merton Street in the parish of St Peter-in-the-East in 1908.

starts with a sung Eucharist in church at 8.30 a.m. After the service the first mark is beaten in Brasenose College, where the stone is marked with a cross and the letters 'S M V'. The choir then sings one or two verses of an Ascension Day carol or anthem in the front quadrangle. There are other boundary marks on stones on the north wall of the college, on the CLARENDON BUILDING and on the south wall of Hertford College. At All Souls coins are thrown to the choirboys in the north quadrangle and the party is then served breakfast in hall. This always includes cherry cake, as a reminder that part of the college was built on an orchard which once belonged to the parish. After breakfast the party crosses HIGH STREET into University College, where the choir sings again, and also into Oriel College. The last mark is on the south wall of Brasenose and the party then returns to the church, where the choir sings a final verse of the carol or anthem. The Act under which houses in Catte Street were sold to All Souls in 1714 provided that 'it shall be lawful for the parishioners [of St Mary's] every Ascension Day to enter the college through a door to be made in the west side of the college to make their perambulation'.

Beaufort, Lady Margaret (*1443–1509*). Daughter and heiress of the 1st Duke of Somerset. Married at twelve years old to Edmund Tudor, Earl of Richmond, half-brother of Henry VI, widowed not much more than a year later, she then gave birth to a son, the future Henry VII. She married again twice, but lived in retirement during the Wars of the Roses in order to protect her son, who was in danger because of his close relationship with the House of Lancaster. Soon after Henry had secured the crown, Lady Margaret separated from her third husband, the 1st Earl of Derby, to take religious vows. Much influenced by her confessor, John Fisher, later Bishop of Rochester, she used her inheritance to endow the universities rather than the abbey at Westminster as she had originally intended. The Lady Margaret Professorship of Divinity dates from 1502. In 1509, after the deaths of his father and his grandmother, Henry VIII tried to divert the Beaufort fortune to his own coffers, a design fortunately thwarted by Bishop Fisher. In Lady Margaret's funeral oration, Fisher said of her 'All England for her death had cause of weeping', including 'the students of both universities to whom she was a mother'. Lady Margaret Hall is named after her.

Beaumont Palace   Originally known as the King's Houses, Beaumont Palace was built by King Henry I outside the town's North Gate (*see* CITY WALL). It occupied a site at the western end of what is now BEAUMONT STREET. The palace was sufficiently advanced for the King to come here for Easter in 1133. His grandsons Richard Cœur de Lion and John were both born here. By the middle of the 13th century the palace buildings, enclosed by a wall and approached through a large gateway, extended over a wide area. In addition to the King's hall and great chamber, there were chambers for the Queen and for her son, a cloister, two chapels, and quarters for the royal chaplains, kitchens, stabling and store rooms. By the end of the century, however, the palace was no longer used as a royal residence. In 1275 Edward I, who spent part of that summer here, granted the buildings to

Francesco Accorso, an Italian lawyer who had undertaken various diplomatic missions for him. The next year they were granted to Edmund Mortimer, and in 1294 to a relation of the King, Edward of St John. By the beginning of the 14th century the sheriffs were, with royal permission, removing stone and timber for repairs to the CASTLE; and in 1318 the remaining buildings were granted to the Carmelite friars. Part of a late 12th-century arch with nookshafts survives in the garden of No. 300 WOODSTOCK ROAD. There are other fragments from the palace at the Carmelite Friary on BOAR'S HILL. The parts of perpendicular windows in the yard behind No. 28 BEAUMONT STREET may also have come from the palace.

Beaumont Street   Laid out in 1822 and completed in 1833, the street runs westwards from the south end of ST GILES' to Worcester College. It is on the site of BEAUMONT PALACE, which was built in about 1130 for Henry I. With its long terraces of three-storeyed, ashlar-faced houses it makes, in Pevsner's words, 'the finest street ensemble in Oxford'. At the St Giles' end the RANDOLPH HOTEL faces the ASHMOLEAN MUSEUM. The PLAYHOUSE, built in 1938 to the design of Sir Edward Maufe, fits into the scene as part of the south terrace. At the Worcester College end the houses, some with door surrounds, many with balconies and a few with verandahs, are now occupied by professional firms, such as architects, dentists, solicitors, doctors and estate agents. They all belong to St John's College, which laid out the estate. No. 32 was the home of SIR CHARLES OMAN and his family from 1892 to 1895. G.A. KOLKHORST lived at No. 38.

Becket Street   Named after the Church of St Thomas Becket (ST THOMAS THE MARTYR). The original dedication of the church, when it was founded by the canons of OSENEY ABBEY in 1141, was to St Nicholas. Henry VIII ordered that its subsequent name of Becket be blotted out from all service books and that the dedication of the church should revert to St Nicholas. However, by popular desire and custom the name Becket prevailed. Becket was born on 21 December, the feast day of St Thomas the Apostle. On the same side of the street as the church and the vicarage (built in 1893 by C.C. Rolfe) is an entrance to the Post Office Sorting Office.
(Osmond, A., 'Building on the Beaumonts', *Oxoniensia*, xlix, 1984, 301–25.)

Bedels   The office of Bedel (Latin: *bedellus*) is one of the oldest at Oxford, certainly going back to the 13th century. It has greatly shrunk in importance since the reign of Henry VII, when two candidates for the post of Divinity Bedel both called upon royal backing. Yet the four Bedels – Divinity, Law, Medicine and Arts – carrying their staves, still act as attendants to the VICE-CHANCELLOR on ceremonial occasions, at meetings of CONVOCATION and CONGREGATION, and whenever summoned by the Vice-Chancellor. At the degree ceremony (*see* CEREMONIES) it is the Bedel of the Faculty of Arts who marshals the candidates for presentation and superintends the retirement of the Doctors and Masters of Arts from the SHELDONIAN. They then return under his guidance in their new robes to make their bows to the Vice-Chancellor and PROCTORS. One Esquire Bedel, G.V. Cox of New

The Esquire Bedel and Yeoman Bedel taking part in the Encaenia procession in the early 19th century. Four Bedels still act as attendants on ceremonial occasions, although the title Esquire Bedel was abolished in 1856.

College, published a lively and detailed account of his life and experiences in his *Recollections of Oxford* (1868). The title Esquire Bedel was abolished in 1856, but Cox, who was the last holder, was allowed to retain it until his retirement in 1866.

The Bedel of Divinity, who conducts each (University) preacher from his college or society to church and to the pulpit and back, is selected by the Vice-Chancellor. Of the other three, the senior in order of appointment is the Bedel of Law, the next the Bedel of Medicine, and the junior the Bedel of Arts.

Beechlawn Tutorial College *1 Park Town*. Founded in 1947 by Miss J. Keays Young to prepare girls for Oxford and Cambridge entrance. It now offers mainly a two-year A-level course preparing students for entrance to universities and to a wide range of different types of college. In 1986 there were about sixty pupils.

Beerbohm, Sir (Henry) Max(imilian) (*1872–1956*). Entered Merton College from Charterhouse. He soon displayed his great talent both as author and caricaturist, as essayist and parodist, his first essays being published when he was twenty-four under the title *The Works of Max Beerbohm*. His masterpieces, ZULEIKA DOBSON and *Seven Men* appeared in 1911 and 1919. He was made an Honorary DLitt of Oxford in 1942 and an Honorary Fellow of Merton in 1946. His portrait by J.-E. Blanche hangs in the ASHMOLEAN.

Belbroughton Road Named after a St John's College living in Worcestershire which was acquired by the college in 1773. The road, which runs from BANBURY ROAD to Charlbury Road, was developed in the early part of the 20th century. Besides its fifteen houses, the OXFORD HIGH SCHOOL FOR GIRLS is situated at the end of the road. The school moved from Banbury Road to new buildings on this site (once Tuckers' nurseries and allotments) in the 1950s.

Bell *18 Cornmarket Street*. From 1500–72 a building on the site was used as a malthouse. The Bell inn traded from 1700 to 1912. In 1773 it was a small building with a 12-foot frontage. By 1818 the inn contained nine bedrooms, smaller rooms and stabling for ten horses.

BEQUESTS, BENEFACTIONS AND MEMORIAL FUNDS The antiquity of the University and the generosity of its former members, and others, have led to the accumulation of an imposing list of benefactions over the centuries. The relevant chapter of the 1983 edition of *Statutes, Decrees and Regulations* covers 140 pages and lists over 230 separate items under the general heading which includes bequests and memorial funds. Many of such funds have been used to create CHAIRS, PRIZES AND SCHOLARSHIPS, lectureships or fellowships. Others have a more general application. Others, again, are no longer listed.

Any account of bequests to the University must include the exceptional munificence of LORD NUFFIELD, whose benefactions enabled the establishment of the NUFFIELD INSTITUTE FOR MEDICAL RESEARCH in 1935, a scheme for Dominion demonstratorships and clinical assistantships in 1936, the Nuffield Fund for Research in Ophthalmology in 1941, and the Nuffield Chair of Anaesthetics in 1937. He founded NUFFIELD COLLEGE in 1937 (though building could not begin until 1949), and gave generously to several colleges, notably St Peter's, Pembroke and Worcester. In the early 1980s, the University accepted 'with deep gratitude' a benefaction of £1,500,000 from the Nissan Motor Company of Japan as an endowment for the furtherance of Japanese Studies in the University; in *Statutes, Decrees . . .* this benefaction immediately follows much smaller ones of £112.50 to the Napier Memorial Library (*see* LIBRARIES) and a bequest of 'books, music pamphlets, and gramophone records relating to folk music'. Other important benefactors in recent times have included Sir Basil Zaharoff (the Marshal Foch Professorship of French Literature, 1919); ANTONIN BESSE, who founded the graduate college of St Antony's (incorporated in 1963); Drs Cecil and Ida Green, who enabled Green College to be founded in 1979; the Ford Foundation; and Sir Isaac Wolfson. In 1984–5, the Andrew Mellon Foundation gave $1 million to endow a Chair of American Government. The Oxford Centre for Management Studies was renamed Templeton College in 1984 as the result of a benefaction from Mr J.M. Templeton, a former Rhodes Scholar (*see* RHODES SCHOLARSHIPS).

In general, it is almost certainly true to say that the individual colleges have benefited to a far greater extent from benefactors than has the University as a whole – a much more abstract concept. That the University has not been forgotten – and especially some of its more tangible manifestations, such as the science faculties (e.g. £818,000 from the Cancer Research Campaign in 1984–5), the BODLEIAN LIBRARY and the ASHMOLEAN MUSEUM – is sufficiently demonstrated by the variety of the bequests and memorial funds which it has received, by its named chairs and lectureships, scholarships and prizes, and by the richness of its possessions. Each year's benefactors are publicly thanked in the CREWEIAN ORATION at ENCAENIA.

Some of the University's principal bequests and memorial funds are:

Beit Fund. Originated from an annual gift made by Alfred Beit in 1905 and converted into a permanent endowment in 1911. The main charges upon the fund are towards the stipend of the Beit Professor of the History of the British Commonwealth; the payment of the Beit Prize; the establishment of senior research scholarships in the History of the British Commonwealth; and a travel fund for the Beit Professor.

Cooper Fund. Set up in 1982 as a result of a bequest from the late Reginald Fabian Cooper for the furtherance of the study of Philosophy within the University, especially by assisting graduate students of the University who are studying or researching in Philosophy.

Vaughan Cornish Bequest. Accepted in 1957 to encourage and assist postgraduate students of the University engaged in 'the advancement of knowledge relating to the beauty of scenery as determined by nature or the arts in town or country at home or abroad'.

Walter Gordon Fund. Originally founded in 1929, and significantly augmented in 1949 by a gift of £9000 from the O.U. Provident Association, this fund exists for the benefit of needy members of the University, both junior and senior, and especially to help in providing nursing, medical attendance or other aid for senior members of the University who are in need. The Walter Gordon (Undergraduates) Fund is used to further the improvement or maintenance of the health of undergraduate members of the University. The terms of the original will deserve fuller quotation. Walter Gordon bequeathed the residue of his property to the University so that: 'The income thereof may be applied for the benefit relief and assistance of needy Members of the said University as well junior as senior without distinction of Sex Race Nation Creed or Degree NOT by way of remunerative Scholarships or Exhibitions to reward and promote proficiency in learning BUT by generous and judicious relief of distress due to poverty ill-health or other trouble or misfortune not occasioned by repeated misdemeanour or persistent folly affording no reasonable hope of amendment and in particular when debt has been incurred no aid is to be given from this source in cases where advantage has been or is to be taken of the pleas of minority or lapse of time I desire to assist only such needy students as are in the main honest and honourable MOREOVER it is above all my wish to help to provide nursing medical attendance or other aid for senior Members of the University of Oxford who are in need out of health disabled or otherwise have genuine claims on compassion.'

Haverfield Bequest. This Bequest, approval of which dates from 1921, came under the will of Professor F.J. Haverfield (Fellow of Brasenose and Camden Professor of Ancient History). The income is applied to the promotion of the study of Roman Britain, for example by defraying the expenses of excavations, by contributing towards the printing and publication of relevant works and by providing for the delivery of lectures upon the subject.

A.J. Hosier Fund. The sum of £30,000 from the A.J. Hosier Educational Trust enabled the creation in 1978 of a fund for the promotion within the University of agricultural education in the United Kingdom. The first charge on the fund's income is the provision of A.J. Hosier Studentships, tenable at Lincoln College.

Lockey Bequest. Dates from 1941, and enabled the creation of a Lockey Fund 'to be devoted to the interests of science'.

Max Müller Memorial Fund. This fund, originally of £2400, was approved and set up in 1903. Its object is the promotion of learning and research in all matters relating to the history and archaeology, the languages, literature and religions of ancient India.

Osler Memorial Fund. Founded in 1925, the fund enables grants to be made to teachers in the Oxford Medical School to help them to pursue some special study connected with Medicine outside Oxford, and provides for the award of a Bronze Medal every five years to the Oxford medical graduate who shall have made the most valuable contribution to Medicine.

Alexander Allan Paton Memorial Fund. Created in 1947, and consists of the interest in perpetuity on a sum of £10,000 from Miss M.E.B. Paton in memory of her brother Alexander Allan Paton. It enables grants to be made to members of the University *in statu pupillari* to enable them to take part in expeditions organised by the Oxford University Exploration Club.

Pirie-Reid Fund. Set up in 1975, this fund consists of the net income from a trust established by the late Constance Pirie-Reid in memory of her husband. It is used to provide scholarships for the benefit of students in need of university education which would otherwise be denied them for lack of funds. Preference (so far as is possible) is given to candidates domiciled or educated in Scotland, and the fund is used to help those who are already *in statu pupillari*.

J.S. Prendergast Bequest. Accepted in 1964, the bequest provides for the creation of two bursaries to be held by members of the Order of St Benedict belonging to Glenstall Abbey School, County Limerick, while they pursue their studies at ST BENET'S HALL, and to assist 'male persons born in the Republic of Ireland whose parents are citizens of the Republic of Ireland to proceed to the University of Oxford for the purpose of taking their degrees or undergoing postgraduate courses'.

Radhakrishnan Memorial Bequest. This bequest (of £50,000) was accepted in 1975 to enable a lectureship to be set up 'at least in every other year' in the field of Indian Studies. The preference is for the lecturer to come from outside Oxford; the bequest came from the estate of the late Professor Sir Sarvepalli Radhakrishnan.

Cecil Roth Memorial Prize. Established in 1974 as a memorial to Cecil Roth, Reader in Jewish Studies, to encourage and promote Italian Studies within the University.

Voltaire Foundation Fund. Results from a bequest from the late T.D.N. Besterman. The fund is to be applied to the completion or continuation of the publications and research begun by Besterman within the field of Enlightenment and Eighteenth-century Studies, the undertaking of other publications and research projects of a similar nature, the financing of scholarships, lectureships and research in the same field, and the improvement of research collections and facilities in the TAYLOR INSTITUTION with these aims in view. The University decree accepting the benefaction dates from 1983. Two committees are involved: the overall benefaction committee, the Voltaire Foundation Fund Committee; and the management committee, the Directors of the Voltaire Foundation.

Gerald Averay Wainwright Fund. Set up in 1952 to encourage the study 'both by schoolboys and also by more mature students' of the non-classical archaeology and general history of the Near East. An annual prize or prizes totalling up to £200 per annum may be awarded for the best essay of up to 5000 words on the subject submitted by any boy or girl 'at any school of which the head is a member of the Headmasters' Conference or of the Secondary Heads' Association'.

Carlos de Sola Wright Memorial Fund. Established in 1982 by Francisco de Sola as a permanent memorial to Carlos de Sola Wright, formerly of St Antony's College, 'for the furtherance of study or research within the University considered likely to promote the advancement or welfare of the people of Central America'.

Marjory Wardrop Fund. Established in 1910 to perpetuate the memory of Miss Marjory Scott Wardrop by the encouragement of the study of the language, literature and history of Georgia in Transcaucasia, by the purchase or publication of relevant books, the assistance of carefully selected students, or by the public teaching of the subject in Oxford.

Weldon Memorial Prize. Established in 1907 to perpetuate the memory of Professor Walter Frank Raphael Weldon, via a prize (awarded every three years) to whomsoever in the previous six years has published the most noteworthy contribution to Biometric Science, in which either (i) exact statistical methods have been applied to some problem of Biology or (ii) statistical theory has been extended in a direction which increases its applicability to problems of Biology.

Among the benefactions accepted by the University in 1984–5, a characteristic year, were bequests of £750,000 for the study of Mycology; £500,000 for the purchase of Japanese art objects and the study of Japanese art; 200 million yen from the Japan Shipbuilding Industry Foundation for the advancement of understanding of Japan; £25,000 a year from the General Electric Company to establish a Readership in Information Engineering; $137,000 from the Ford Foundation for a lectureship in International Relations; and funds for scholarships for overseas students, a readership in Cellular Cardiology, building grants for the Departments of Pharmacology and Biochemistry from the E.P. Abraham Research Trust, and a fellowship in the Nuffield Department of Pathology and Bacteriology.

The Nuffield Department of Clinical Medicine received some £124,000, including £80,000 from the *Sun* newspaper's 'Tiddlers Save Toddlers' fund.

The Ashmolean received £50,000 from the Victoria and Albert Museum Purchase Grant Fund towards the purchase of a painting by Lanfranco, *Christ and the Woman of Samaria*, and an 8th–9th-century carved red sandstone ceiling boss, Rajasthan; £13,000 from the Museum and Galleries Commission for the creation of a Paper Conservation Studio; benefactions from the National Art-Collections Fund; £4425 from the Friends of the Ashmolean; funds from Christie, Manson and Woods, the Hon. David Astor and the Rothschild Trust Company towards the purchase of Lanfranco's *Christ and the Woman of Samaria*; $108,000 from the J. Paul Getty Trust for computerising descriptions and bibliography of Athenian vases; and gifts of Chinese jade, drawings by John Everett Millais, Jean-Baptiste Perroneau and Stanley Roseman, and a 17th-century silver warming pan.

The Bodleian Library received the William Beckford archive from BLACKWELL'S, papers and records from the Primrose League, as well as various books and manuscripts including a manuscript translation into English verse of Palladius on Agriculture made for HUMFREY, DUKE OF GLOUCESTER, by allocation of the Minister for the Arts.

The Faculty of Music and the BATE COLLECTION of musical instruments received grants for the restoration of an 18th-century organ acquired for the HOLYWELL MUSIC ROOM; £6000 from the National Art-Collections Fund for the purchase of a four-key bassoon by August Grenser of Dresden; a rare Boehm system flute by Eugene Albert of Brussels; and a complete Javanese gamelan (orchestra) from the Republic of Indonesia.

Grants for specific research projects from the research councils and other government agencies totalled £14,836,172, including £4,914,105 from the Medical Research Council and £6,240,983 from the Science and Engineering Research Council. In addition, £7,635,107 was received from charities, industrial firms and other institutions, including £295,805 from the British Heart Foundation; £131,675 from British Petroleum; £808,022 from the Cancer Research Campaign; £107,289 from the Central Electricity Generating Board; £272,840 from the E.P. Abraham Fund; £153,377 from Genetics International USA; £490,812 from the Monsanto Corporation; £116,544 from the Oxford Regional Health Authority; £119,589 from the Rockefeller Foundation; £251,315 from Rolls-Royce; £108,760 from the Royal College of Obstetricians and Gynaecologists; £513,129 from the Royal Society; £217,665 from the United Kingdom Atomic Energy Authority; and £1,068,645 from the Wellcome Trust.

Besse, Antonin (1877–1951). Levantine entrepreneur and perhaps the most remarkable of all college founders, Besse was born in Carcassonne in 1877. Sent to Aden as a young shipping clerk, he built up a great trading empire which extended from the Gulf to the east African coast. Evelyn Waugh first met him in November 1930 at dinner at the Residency in Aden and portrayed him vividly in several novels – as the merchant Youkoumian in *Black Mischief* (1932) and as the financier Mr Baldwin in *Scoop* (1938). Besse gave the University £1¼ million in 1948 to found St Antony's College (the first Warden of which, F.W. Deakin, was involved in Waugh's Balkan adventures in 1944). Besse was given a great welcome with loud clapping for his honorary doctorate at the SHELDONIAN THEATRE – a most unusual distinction. He died a few weeks later, aged seventy-four, a notable benefactor also to eight other Oxford colleges and to the Outward Bound schools.

Betjeman, Sir John *(1906–1984)*. The son of a manufacturer of expensive furnishings, Betjeman left the family home in Highgate to go to the DRAGON SCHOOL, then to Marlborough, whence, in 1925, he went on to Magdalen College. His early years are described in his verse autobiography *Summoned by Bells* (1960). He left Oxford without taking a degree, having failed both to pass a qualifying examination in Divinity and to please his tutors. The first of these was, in Betjeman's own words, 'the Reverend J.M. Thompson, a shy, kind, amusing man, and a distinguished authority on French history. Rumour had it that he had been defrocked for preaching in Magdalen Chapel that the miracles were performed by electricity'. The next was C.S. LEWIS, who, when his former pupil was trying to become a schoolmaster, wrote him a reference 'so double-edged' that Betjeman withdrew it after his first unsuccessful application for a post. But others, in the words of Betjeman's obituary in *The Times*, 'detected the uniqueness of his personality, and he formed friendships that stimulated his enthusiasms – particularly for Victoriana – and his talents, especially for the comic and the poetic, which developed rapidly during his undergraduate career'. Although his Oxford career was undistinguished, he afterwards celebrated in prose and verse his love of the place. 'I had beautiful panelled eighteenth-century rooms on the second floor of New Buildings,' he recalled. 'From my bed I would hear the Magdalen bells "sprinkle the quarters on the morning town". They led the chorus of quarters chiming from Merton and New College'. His affection for Oxford was revealed in his *An Oxford University Chest* (1938). And, throughout his life thereafter, he was ready to give his support to those who fought to preserve its architectural charm (*see, for example,* NORTH OXFORD). Created Poet Laureate in 1972, he was an Honorary Fellow of Magdalen and, appropriately, of Keble College, whose ecclesiastical traditions and architectural style he revered.

Bevington Road   Another of the roads named after a St John's College living. It formerly bore the name of Horse and Jockey Road, and there is a public house of this name in WOODSTOCK ROAD, opposite Bevington Road. In the early 1860s the road was called Jeffreys Lane after the owner of the Globe Nursery to its north. It was once the site of a large pit from which gravel was extracted to repair roads: hence the present dip in the road. A large hoard of Roman coins was discovered here, which suggests that the house on the north-eastern corner had been the site of a Roman dwelling. The first houses here were built in 1825. Those on the south side (designed by Wilkinson and/or Codd) are now in the ownership of St Anne's College, their purchase having been instigated by Lady Ogilvie, Principal of the college from 1953 to 1966. In November 1968 the college asked the Highways Committee of the City Council if the name of the road could be changed to Plumer Road, after a former Principal of St Anne's, but the Committee would not agree. On the north side of Bevington Road is an entrance to St Antony's College.

Bicycles   It has been estimated that there are about 150,000 bicycles in use in Oxford – and 3000 of them are stolen every year. The police have a special Cycles Department at ST ALDATE'S police station, where recovered bicycles are kept in a large store. Professional cycle theft is common and cyclists are now encouraged to have their post code stamped on their bicycles. Many such cycles recovered in London and

A group of cyclists outside the lodge of St Edward's School in the summer of 1897.

elsewhere have been identified as having been stolen in Oxford. The police-station store contains an average of 400 stolen or abandoned bicycles; in 1986 alone the police recovered 1489 machines. Every day nearly fifty people visit the store, which manages to return eight out of ten bikes to their owners. Those which cannot be identified are eventually sold off in job lots, raising about £5500 a year. Bicycles are, of course, used in great numbers by undergraduates to get around Oxford, and some of these are hired for the term. At one time a system was in operation with specially coloured cycles which could be picked up anywhere and left at one's destination to be used by someone else. Too many disappeared altogether for the system to last long and most are now chained and locked. In term time cycles two or three deep line the walls of the colleges in such streets as TURL STREET. In the 19th century there was a University Bicycle Club which held annual races against Cambridge.

Many roads in Oxford are now marked with cycle lanes; by 1985 some 10 miles of cycle lanes had been marked in the city, and cyclists may also use bus lanes. In 1984 the NORTH OXFORD Cycle Route was opened, following a route east of the BANBURY ROAD from CUTTESLOWE to the city centre via Water Eaton Road, King's Cross Road, Charlbury Road and NORHAM GARDENS, using the pedestrian subway under the A40 RING ROAD and the underpass beneath the MARSTON FERRY ROAD. An Advance Stop Line system has been installed by the KING'S ARMS in PARKS ROAD, using two separate sets of traffic lights – one for motorists and one in front for cyclists to allow them to move off ahead of other traffic. The pre-eminence of the bicycle is thus reinforced in the life of Oxford.

Binsey   A small village to the north-west of Oxford which still retains a mediaeval atmosphere. The name is probably derived from Byni's island, which was in the THAMES. It is bounded on all sides by branches of the Thames, but can be reached from the BOTLEY ROAD, or on foot from the towpath or across PORT MEADOW. Round the large village green are a number of farm buildings and cottages, as well as the PERCH inn. The church of ST MARGARET is further up the lane to the north of the green. Binsey belonged to ST FRIDESWIDE'S PRIORY. It is said that ST FRIDESWIDE fled to Binsey to escape marriage to a Mercian king. In pursuit, he marched on Oxford and at the city gates was struck blind. Frideswide's prayers called forth a healing well whose waters cured his blindness. The holy well was known as a treacle well in the mediaeval sense of treacle as a healing fluid. It was a place of pilgrimage in the Middle Ages and the Binsey Treacle Well appears in EDWARD BURNE-JONES'S St Frideswide window in CHRIST CHURCH CATHEDRAL. Lewis Carroll (*see* CHARLES DODGSON) knew the well and referred to it in *Alice's Adventures in Wonderland*, the dormouse at the Mad Hatter's Tea-party telling the story of three children who lived at the bottom of a treacle well. The Rev. Arnold Mallinson, who retired in 1976 as vicar of St Frideswide's and Binsey, writing in *Country Life* about a dog that refused to enter the churchyard, said, 'The sapient hound who . . . refused to enter the churchyard at Binsey near Oxford was not deterred by ghosts, for there are none there, but by perception of the powerful holiness of the place occasioned by the existence of the well of St. Margaret at the west end of the church. . . . Many important persons have been amongst the visitors. They include Henry VIII and Catherine of Aragon, Lewis Carroll and Joyce Cary. Many who have come to scoff have remained to pray or meditate. The only English Pope, Adrian IV, is reputed as a youth to have been incumbent at Binsey. When the Revd. Mr. Prout restored the well in the 19th century he asked Lewis Carroll about it. Carroll advised, "Leave *well* alone." Perhaps he and the dog who would not go into the churchyard were actuated by the same feelings as arrested the progress of Balaam's ass'.

The small village of Binsey is closely associated with Medley, whose manor was once the residence of the ABBOTS OF OSENEY. There is now a boatyard there by Medley Weir and a bridge over the Thames.

Gerard Manley Hopkins, in his poem 'Binsey Poplars', lamented the felling of some poplars at Binsey in 1879 and the loss to the 'sweet especial rural scene', in the following lines:

> My aspens dear, whose airy cages quelled,
> Quelled or quenched in leaves the leaping sun,
> All felled, felled, are all felled.

They were the rare native black poplars. The OXFORD CIVIC SOCIETY has managed to find a number of these trees and has replanted them at Binsey.

Bishop King's Palace   *see* OLD PALACE.

Bishop Kirk School   *Middle Way, Summertown.* Opened as a church-aided school in 1966 for all the parishes in NORTH OXFORD and named after Bishop Kenneth Kirk (BISHOP OF OXFORD 1937–54). It was built to accommodate 260 children aged from seven to eleven years. Extended in 1973, it then became a middle school for 450 children aged nine to thirteen years. Its buildings, designed by Gerald Banks, occupy an open site between MIDDLE WAY and WOODSTOCK ROAD, described in Pevsner as being 'a very attractive environment for a school'. They replaced a villa, The Avenue, at 302 Woodstock Road, erected for his own use in spacious grounds by George Kimber, a tallow-chandler, who was influential in the early development of SUMMERTOWN, the house itself being described as 'a handsome white house, of the first magnitude in Summer-Town; the foundation stone of which was laid by his son Alfred in 1823'. In 1986 there were some 360 pupils in the school.

Bishops of Oxford   The first Bishop of Oxford was appointed in 1542 (*see* ABBOTS OF OSENEY). There have been forty bishops since, excluding Thomas Goldwell, Bishop of St Asaph, who was nominated to succeed Robert King, the first Bishop, but died before he could be installed. Distinguished bishops have included Richard Corbet (1582–1635), the poet who later became Bishop of Norwich; Nathaniel, Lord Crewe (*see* CREWEIAN ORATION); JOHN FELL; Samuel Parker (1640–88); John Hough (1651–1743), President of Magdalen College and later Bishop of Worcester; John Randolph (1749–1813), President of Corpus Christi and later Bishop of London; SAMUEL WILBERFORCE and WILLIAM STUBBS. A complete list of the bishops will be found in Appendix 1. (*See also* CHRIST CHURCH CATHEDRAL.)

Black Boy   *91 Old High Street, Headington.* Village inn dating from 1667. Its name is more usually associated with COFFEE HOUSES. The present tavern, built in 1937, displays over an outside entrance a rare carved wooden black-boy servant which once stood outside a coffee house in Oxford.

Black Horse   *102 St Clement's Street.* The original 17th-century timbered building remains. All parish meetings were held outside the inn till 1914. The Black Horse became a hotel in 1937. (*See also* ST CLEMENT'S.)

Blackbird Leys   The area known by this name in the 18th century is now part of a large estate built in the late 1950s and early 1960s by Oxford City Council. In the 19th century it was sometimes called Blacford Leys (or Lays). There was a sewage farm on the site which attracted many birds, some of them rare and others peculiar to the area. There were also large quantities of wildflowers. Many of the roads are consequently named after the wild birds, flowers and shrubs, and also after well-known Oxford ornithologists and an entomologist. In the south-eastern part of the estate the roads named after the flowers and plants are in alphabetical order and run off the long road called Field Avenue. Some roads have field names (such as Redefield and Longlands). Others (such as Knights Road and Pegasus Road) are so-called because of the connection with the Knights Templars. The remains of the Preceptory which belonged to them are near to Blackbird Leys Farm. Pegasus Road derives its name both from the alleged misdrawing of two knights on one horse and from the famous University Football Club which won the Amateur Cup. Cuddesdon Way, or (originally) Codenshamme Weye, was named in 1960 after the way of the people of Cuddesdon.

Blackfriars, the Priory of the Holy Spirit   *64 St Giles'.* The building next door to PUSEY HOUSE, with an off-centre pediment and wrought-iron gateway, is the House of Studies for the English Province of the Order of Preachers, otherwise known as the Dominicans. It dates from 1929 and is the inspiration of Father Bede Jarrett OP, who, as an undergraduate at Hunter-Blair's Hall in 1904, had looked forward to the day when the Dominicans, who had been suppressed in England since 1538, would once again open a house in Oxford.

The Order, based on the rule of St Augustine, was founded in 1216 by a Spaniard, Domingo de Guzmán, later known as St Dominic. By 1228 it had developed an impressive constitutional structure of government which has remained in its essential pattern to the present day. General Chapters are held every three years and Provincial Chapters every four years. It was at the second General Chapter, held at Bologna in 1221 and presided over by St Dominic, that the decision was taken to send a *conventus* of friars to England under the leadership of Gilbert de Fresnay. Their principal aim was to establish a house at Oxford, as the universities and other centres of learning were important in their campaign of preaching. They landed in Kent at the beginning of August 1221 and, accompanied by the Bishop of Winchester, Peter des Roches, journeyed to Canterbury, where the brilliance of Gilbert de Fresnay's sermon won them the support of Stephan Langton, Archbishop of Canterbury.

They reached Oxford on 15 August, the Feast of the Assumption of Our Lady, and set about building a small chapel in her honour. The site was in the area of the present TOWN HALL. There are the remains of a large archway and a smaller pedestrian archway at the south end of LITTLEGATE STREET. Jordan of Saxony, who succeeded St Dominic as Master of the Order, expressed in a letter from Oxford in 1230 his high hopes for the priory there. These were justified, for Roger Bacon and Richard Fishacre, both Doctors of Theology, were declared by Matthew Paris – no lover of the Dominicans – to have 'none equal to them in Theology and the other sciences'.

To begin with, the Oxford school lectured only in Theology; Philosophy and the Natural Sciences came later. Degrees were conferred within the framework of the University. In 1245 the school moved to a larger site on what was an island in the river near FOLLY BRIDGE. Henry III, Isabella de Vere, Countess of Oxford, and Walter Mauclerc, Bishop of Carlisle, all contributed to this new priory. The Bishop, who was Lord High Treasurer at the time, went so far as to give up all his titles, rank and wealth, and entered the Order as a novice. The success of the friars preachers with the upper classes was bitterly resented by other religious Orders, especially after Henry III inaugurated the custom of appointing a Dominican Royal Confessor.

In 1246 the school was elevated to the status of a STUDIUM GENERALE. The 13th and 14th centuries saw the zenith of the Oxford school. During that period, four of its great theological writers, Robert Kilwardby, William of Macclesfield, Walter Winterbourne and Thomas Jorz, became cardinals. Kilwardby, as Archbishop of Canterbury, crowned Edward I. John of St Giles, the physician and Doctor of Theology, came to Oxford from Paris in 1235. He attended the deathbed of his friend ROBERT GROSSETESTE. The writer and historian Nicholas Trivet (*c.*1258–1328), son of Sir Thomas Trivet, Lord Chief Justice, wrote and studied in Oxford. It seems from a survey that in 1305 there were ninety-six Dominicans in Oxford.

Thomism *v.* Augustinianism was a theological debate that rocked the Church in the latter half of the 13th century. The Order was heavily involved, for Thomas Aquinas, who propounded the Thomist doctrine, was a Dominican. In 1277, four years after his death, many of his propositions were condemned as 'contrary to the true and Catholic faith'. In the same year the Dominican Archbishop of Canterbury, Robert Kilwardby, called a Council at Oxford where he publicly condemned several of the Thomist principles. By that date, however, the Order as a whole had adopted the new teaching and a delegation was sent to England from Rome to put an end to the dissension. Nevertheless, Kilwardby's successor at Canterbury, the Franciscan John Peckham, kept the controversy raging. Discovering that Thomism was fashionable at Oxford, he visited the school in 1285 to upbraid those who argued for it. That his mission failed is evident from the fact that today St Thomas Aquinas is counted as one of the most illustrious of all the Dominican Doctors of Divinity.

The friars' relations with the University became strained in 1303, chiefly over the matter of conferring degrees. The University ruled that an arts degree was a prerequisite for those proceeding to a Doctorate of Divinity. The friars, however, had often been excused from this requirement, as they generally studied arts in their own *studia*. The hardening of the attitude of the University authorities on this and other points caused a quarrel which lasted many years.

In 1396, Roger Dymoke, a Dominican Doctor of Divinity from Oxford, refuted the WYCLIF heresy. After this date, however, the glory of the friar preachers declined, their disputations became feeble for want of stimulus, and they lacked the mental agility to confront the champions of the new religion in the reign of Henry VIII. At the Dissolution of the Monasteries the Oxford community numbered only fifteen. Thomas Cromwell was informed that the 'Blackfriars of Oxford were possessed of well-wooded islands . . .', that they were better off than GREYFRIARS, 'with a newly-built church . . . and a pretty store of plate and [jewels]'. He suggested Oxford needed industrialising, for there 'ys no great thorwfare . . .' and it would be a 'blessyd acte . . .' if the friaries were given to 'thys poor towne' to be turned into fulling mills.

In 1916 Father Bede Jarrett was elected Provincial of the English Province. He set to, at once, to realise his dream of building another Dominican priory in Oxford. Aided by his American friends, and by Mrs Jefferson Tytus in particular, he raised enough money to purchase Nos 62, 63 and 64 ST GILES'. (No. 64 had been the last house of WALTER PATER.) It was beside this house that a site was cleared for a chapel. Both Pope Benedict XV and King Alfonso of Spain were among the subscribers, and Lady Arundel of Wardour agreed to supply the stone, provided Edwin Doran Webb, architect of the Oratory Church in Birmingham, was engaged. The idea was to plan for a community of 100 at an estimated cost of £100,000. Father Bede insisted that it should be a building of quality, for 'one should not put up one's second best in Oxford'.

The chapel cost £23,843 and the priory, which was opened in 1929, £62,854. The statue of the Madonna over the gateway by Thomas Rudge was erected in 1924; the inscription tablet beneath it is by Eric Gill. The statue was criticised at the time for having too small a head and too few clothes. On 20 May 1929, in the presence of many members of the Catholic hierarchy, the chapel was consecrated. It is a wide, simple structure, clearly lit, with Gothic decoration. It reflects Father Bede's idea of a priory church. Enough of the priory had been built for nineteen friars to take up residence, and on the day of the consecration, seated in the choir stalls, they began the solemn recitation of the Divine Office.

The priory was not completed until 1954, twenty years after Father Bede's death. The garden wing and the Bede Jarrett Memorial Tower were built under the direction of the architect Thomas Rayson. Today there are approximately thirty friars in residence, many of whom teach in the University, while several others are preparing for University degrees. Lectures in Theology and Philosophy are given both to the Dominican students and to the general public. Among the many figures associated with this priory are Gervase Mathew (1905–76), polymath, archaeologist and lecturer in Byzantine Studies, and Cornelius Ernst (1924–77), the greatest theologian of the Province in this century.

Blackhall Road Runs from MUSEUM ROAD, skirting the west side of Keble College, into KEBLE ROAD and has borne this name since the late 19th century. It is named after Black Hall (fronting ST GILES') which was in existence as early as 1519. A La Blakehall in the parish of St Giles' was mentioned in a will of 1361. After the Dissolution of the Monasteries, Blackhall was sold to St John's College by REWLEY ABBEY, to which it had been given in 1486 by Joan Gille. Most of the present Blackhall was built in the 17th century but has been much restored. In 1837 it was occupied by a Joseph Parker, who did the restoration work and added a north wing. The hall can be found on a 19th-century reconstructed map of early Oxford at the back of Wood's *City of Oxford*. There is also an engraving in Ingram's *Memorials of Oxford*, Vol. III (1837), p. 14. Wood describes the hall as an 'ancient receptacle for schollers'. Blackhall Farm (with Walton Farm and a house on the site of the ACLAND HOSPITAL) gave the name of The Three Farms to the neighbourhood. On the west side of the road is the back entrance to QUEEN ELIZABETH HOUSE.

Blackstone, Sir William (*1723–1780*). The posthumous son of a London silkman and an orphan at the age of eleven, Blackstone left Charterhouse School for Pembroke College in 1738. His early interests were wide, and included literary effusions and a work on architecture, but the future direction of his energies was indicated by his admission to the Middle Temple in 1741 and his election to a 'legist' All Souls Fellowship two years later. His devotion to All Souls was phenomenal: he held every college office save the wardenship, and was specially concerned with the problem of FOUNDERS' KIN and with the CODRINGTON LIBRARY. He was no less active in University affairs and, though a Tory, he can be counted among its great reformers. Among his achievements were the reform of the VICE-CHANCELLOR'S COURT (1753), of the CLARENDON PRESS (1756–8), the 'dethronement' of the LAUDIAN CODE (1759) and – last but by no means least – the establishment of the teaching of the Common Law in the University. He gave his famous lecture course on the laws of England in All Souls in 1753 and five years later became the first incumbent of the Vinerian Chair of English Law. His admirably written and influential *Commentaries on the Laws of England* were published between 1765 and 1769. He had become Principal of NEW INN HALL in 1761, but his election to Parliament in the same year and his increasing London practice led to his detachment from Oxford and to his resignation from his principalship in 1766 (he had lost his All Souls fellowship by matrimony four years earlier). He was made a Justice of the Common Pleas in 1770 (with the consequent loss of his parliamentary seat) and sat in that court (after a brief interlude in King's Bench) until his death on 14 February 1780 at his house in Wallingford, where he had been Recorder since 1749.

Blackwell, Sir Basil Henry (*1889–1984*). Born in BROAD STREET, where his father Benjamin Henry Blackwell, had established the bookselling business which WILLIAM STUBBS described as 'the literary man's public house' (*see* BLACKWELL'S). Educated at MAGDALEN COLLEGE SCHOOL and Merton College, Blackwell afterwards worked for the OXFORD UNIVERSITY PRESS in London, his father hoping that he would gain experience which would enable him to develop the publishing side of the business. He returned to Oxford in 1913 and devoted himself to publishing until his father's death when he became primarily a bookseller. He was chairman of B.H. Blackwell Ltd from 1922 to 1969. Known throughout the trade as 'the Gaffer', he was said to be one of the best-read men in England. He was knighted in 1956. A Justice of the Peace for the city of Oxford and chairman of the Visiting Justices to Oxford PRISON, he received honours from both the city, which made him an honorary freeman, and the University, which awarded him the honorary degree of DCL at ENCAENIA in 1979. He was also an honorary Fellow of Merton.

Blackwell, Richard *(1918–1980)*. Born at 1 Frenchay Road, the eldest son of SIR BASIL HENRY BLACKWELL, Richard Blackwell was educated at the DRAGON SCHOOL, from which he won a scholarship to Winchester College and from there a scholarship to New College, where he obtained a First in Classical Honour Moderations in 1938. After service in the Royal Navy, in which he was awarded the DSC, he joined his father in the family firm of BLACKWELL'S, whose business he much increased both at home and internationally. He became managing director in 1956, chairman in 1969, and chairman of Basil Blackwell Publisher Ltd in 1976. President of the Booksellers' Association in 1966–8, he was elected a Fellow of St Cross College in 1978.

Blackwell's *50 Broad Street*. Founded in 1879 by Benjamin Henry Blackwell at its present address, Blackwell's has grown to become one of the largest and best-known bookshops in the world. It is still a family firm and a private company, B.H. Blackwell Ltd. Benjamin Blackwell dealt almost exclusively in second-hand books. His first catalogue contained a selection of books about Oxford, including LOGGAN's *Oxonia Illustrata* (1675) at £5. The first edition of Hobbes's *Leviathan* (1651) could also have been purchased for 18s. In 1883 B.H. Blackwell bought the freehold of No. 50 BROAD STREET and moved from HOLYWELL STREET to live over the shop. The business expanded and leases of adjoining premises were acquired to house the increased stock, which by the turn of the century included many new books, fiction, children's books, reference works and foreign books.

Benjamin Blackwell died in 1924 and was succeeded as chairman of the company by his son, Basil (later SIR BASIL BLACKWELL), known to all in the business, and to many outside it, as 'the Gaffer'. It was Basil Blackwell who developed the publishing side of the business. Starting with an annual series of *Oxford Poetry*, he went on in 1919 to publish the magazine *Oxford Outlook*, the editors of which included many names later to become famous in the literary world. Dorothy L. Sayers was his first editorial assistant, and was succeeded by Adrian Mott, who had been at Merton College with Basil Blackwell. Together they formed an associated publishing company, Basil Blackwell and Mott Ltd, which was incorporated in 1922. Some years after the death of Sir Adrian Mott the name of the firm was changed to Basil Blackwell Publisher. The binding part of the publishing business became a separate company in 1962 – Kemp Hall Bindery Ltd. A new factory was built at OSNEY MEAD and the business

A 1926 advertisement by Blackwell's, the Broad Street booksellers, recommends inspection of '240,000 volumes in all branches of literature'.

moved there in 1965, subsequently closing in 1982.

Henry Schollick joined Blackwell's in 1932 and eventually became Vice-President. He was on the council of the Booksellers' Association and was responsible for the development of the Book Tokens Scheme. Basil's friend, financial adviser and founding director of the firm was Harry S. Critchley. He died in 1959 and his son John then guided the firm in financial matters. Basil's son, RICHARD BLACKWELL, joined the firm in 1946, at which point the annual turnover was £165,000. By 1979 it had risen to more than £27 million.

In 1938 the firm had put up a new building at Nos 48 and 49 Broad Street and Bliss Court, having been granted a building lease on the site by Trinity College. However, after the war the business had expanded so much that further steps had to be taken. The children's book department was moved in 1950 to a small three-storey house at 22 Broad Street, where the Children's Bookshop opened. This in turn proved to be too small: in 1974 the Children's Bookshop moved to 6 Broad Street and in 1986 to No. 8. The Paperback Shop in Broad Street was opened in 1964 and in 1988 the Art and Poster shop took over PARKER'S. In 1952 Richard's younger brother Julian joined the firm. He had been educated, like his brother, at Winchester and afterwards at Trinity College. He became responsible for planning and new building operations. The need for more space in Broad Street had become urgent and it was decided, in consultation with Trinity, to expand underground. An enormous terraced chamber was constructed under the south-east corner of Trinity College to the design of Robert Maguire and Keith Murray. This room of 10,000 square feet and 3 miles of shelving found a place in the *Guinness Book of Records* for having the largest display of books for sale in one room anywhere in the world. It was named the Norrington Room after Sir Arthur Norrington, who was then the President of Trinity (*see* NORRINGTON TABLE), and was formally opened in 1966 by Sir William Haley, editor of *The Times*. Above the staircase leading down to the Norrington Room is an amusing mural of Oxford scenes by Edward Bawden, painted in 1973.

Also in 1966 the Art Bookshop was opened by Michael (later Sir Michael) Levey, then Deputy Keeper of the National Gallery, in a building next to the WHITE HORSE inn. This is now the Travel Bookshop. This was followed in 1970 by the Music Shop on a site on the north side of Holywell belonging to Wadham College. It too has a large basement area holding thousands of books on music as well as orchestral scores, sheet music, records and cassettes. It was opened by Sir Adrian Boult.

The greater part of the firm's turnover, however, was now from mail order sales. A large new building was erected in HYTHE BRIDGE STREET to house the Mail Order Division, the Periodicals Division and the Accounts Division. It was designed by the Oxford Architects Partnership with a wall of dark glass to the street and a diagonally set staircase tower of reeded concrete blocks at the REWLEY ROAD end. It was named Beaver House and was opened in 1973. The beaver, 'the Gaffer' said, is 'an animal fond of hard work and aquatic pursuits'. It is the family crest and the official emblem of Blackwell's, as well as being a supporter of the arms of the city (*see* HERALDRY).

Two other branches of the Oxford side of the business are worthy of note – namely, scientific books and rare books. Blackwell Scientific Publications Ltd was formed in 1939 for the publication and sale of medical and scientific research books. Under the direction of Per Saugman, who joined it in 1952 from Denmark, it grew to become one of the most successful of the Blackwell enterprises. It now has subsidiaries in many other countries, such as the Danish firm of Ejnar Munksgaard, the largest academic publishing firm in Scandinavia. In 1972 BSP Ltd moved to new premises at Osney Mead in a building designed by the Oxford Architects Partnership. Blackwell's Antiquarian Book Department was formerly housed in SHIP STREET, but in 1979, the firm's centenary year, it moved to Fyfield Manor, a 14th-century stone house at Fyfield, originally the home of the Golafre family.

RICHARD BLACKWELL, who had succeeded his father as chairman in 1969, died in 1980 at the age of sixty-two, while his father was still alive. The chairmanship was taken over by his brother Julian, and two of Richard's sons, Miles and Nigel, are now directors of the company founded by their great-grandfather. The firm now controls over fifty retail bookshops, mainly in university towns, in the United Kingdom, others overseas, as well as Blackwell North America Inc., and has an annual turnover of more than £100 million.

(Norrington, A.L.P., *Blackwell's 1879–1979. The History of a Family Firm*, Oxford, 1983.)

Blessed Dominic Barberi, Church of *Cowley Road, Littlemore*. Dominic Barberi, an Italian who had established in this country an order of priests known as Passionists, received JOHN HENRY NEWMAN into the Roman Catholic Church at LITTLEMORE on 8 October 1845. The existing church, designed in 1969 by Peter Reynolds, cost £50,000 and seats 350.

Blue Anchor *25 Cornmarket Street*. There has been a building on this site since at least 1205. It was known as the New Inn between 1396 and 1430, then (in royal hands) as the Crown until 1654. In June 1654 Thomas Aldridge became landlord of the new Blue Anchor. ANTHONY WOOD, recorded in 1657: '. . . To see the play at the Blew Anchor, 1s. 8d.' The tavern closed in 1911.

Blue Boar Street This short stretch of narrow road runs from ST ALDATE'S to the junction of BEAR LANE and ALFRED STREET. It was formerly known as Tresham('s) Lane and there is a reference of 1614 to New Lane. Tresham was a Doctor of Divinity and a canon of King Henry VIII's College (Christ Church) in 1532. He was responsible for the construction of the road at the time the college enclosed the road to the south, the former Little Jewry, otherwise known as Jury Lane or Civil School Lane.

In the 17th century a house called the Blewebore stood in the street; ANTHONY WOOD, describing it as Blewboore Inn, says that it was a tenement once owned by Henry III, and it is from this that the modern street-name derives. The Blue Boar Inn was pulled down in 1893 at the time of the building of the Oxford Public Library, now the MUSEUM OF OXFORD, on the corner of St Aldate's.

Blue Pig *Gloucester Green*. A three-storey building of rough stone walls, two west entrances and a large dormer stood as an inn on this site from 1800 to 1935. It was one of five inns serving the county farmers and dealers who used GLOUCESTER GREEN cattle market. Named after the market's pig section, the inn possessed a unique sign – a blue pig in stained glass with a wooden frame. Although the tavern closed in 1931, it was not demolished until 1935.

Blues Although the first VARSITY MATCH against Cambridge was the cricket match in 1827, the association of Oxford with dark blue, as opposed to Cambridge's light blue, started only on the day of the 1836 BOAT RACE. For this race, as for the first race in 1829, Oxford wore black straw hats, dark-blue striped jerseys, and canvas trousers. Cambridge wore white shirts with pink sashes. The popular story goes that just before the race somebody noticed that Cambridge had no distinguishing colours. One R.N. Phillips of Christ's College ran to a nearby shop and purchased a light blue ribbon, which was displayed on his boat. In the next race Cambridge adopted a jersey with light-blue stripes, and the light- and dark-blue colours have been used ever since.

The Blue is the highest sporting achievement at the University and is awarded to certain men's and women's sports clubs whose members meet the criteria set by their respective Blues Committees. Members of certain other sporting clubs are eligible for Half Blues. There is an absolute condition to be met before a Blue or a Half Blue can be awarded:

a sportsman or woman must have competed in the annual Varsity Match against Cambridge. An Olympic gold-medal winner in athletics, for example, who has competed for Oxford all season but is injured and does not turn out against Cambridge, is not eligible for a Blue. Another anomaly is that while each member of the Oxford rowing eight, together with their coxswain, receives a full Blue, as indeed do the Rugby XV, a track and field athlete is awarded a Blue only if a prescribed speed, height or distance is achieved.

The sports for which Blues and Half Blues are awarded are as follows:

Full Blue Sports (Men)

Association Football	Golf
Athletics	Hockey
Basketball	Lawn Tennis
Boat	Rugby Union
Boxing	Squash
Cricket	Swimming
Cross Country	Yacht

Full Blue Sports (Women)

Athletics	Modern Pentathlon
Cross Country	Netball
Hockey	Rowing
Lacrosse	Squash
Lawn Tennis	Swimming

Half Blue Sports (Men)

Archery	Lightweight Rowers
Badminton	Modern Pentathlon
Ballroom Dancing	Orienteering
Canoe and Kayak	Pistol
Croquet	Rackets
Cycling	Real Tennis
Eton Fives	Riding
Fencing	Rifle
Gliding	Rugby Fives
Gymnastics	Rugby League
Ice Hockey	Skiing
Judo	Table Tennis
Karate	Volleyball
Lacrosse	Water Polo

Half Blue Sports (Women)

Archery	Karate
Athletics	Modern Pentathlon
Badminton	Orienteering
Ballroom Dancing	Pistol Shooting
Basketball	Riding
Canoeing	Rowing
Cricket	Sailing
Cross Country	Skiing
Cycling	Squash
Fencing	Swimming
Gymnastics	Table Tennis
Ice Hockey	Volleyball
Judo	Yachting

The dates (before 1930) of the first matches against Cambridge of those sporting clubs still in existence:

1827	Cricket
1829	Boat
1859	Real Tennis
1864	Athletics
1872	Rugby Football
1874	Association Football
1878	Golf
1878	Polo
1880	Cross Country
1881	Lawn Tennis
1890	Hockey
1891	Water Polo
1892	Swimming
*1897	Boxing and Fencing
1900	Ice Hockey
1903	Lacrosse
1912	Sailing
1913	Boxing
1913	Fencing
1922	Winter Sports
1923	Table Tennis
1925	Rugby Fives
1928	Eton Fives
1928	Badminton

* Boxing and fencing were originally one club; they separated in 1913.

(*See also* BOAT RACE, ROWING, VARSITY MATCH *and individual entries for individual Oxford University sports clubs.*)

Boar's Hill A wooded hill, with many big houses in large gardens, on the south side of Oxford. Among the well-known Oxford personalities who have lived on Boar's Hill was the archaeologist SIR ARTHUR EVANS, who in his garden built the 50-foot-high artificial hill known as Jarn Mound to give a view over the surrounding tree-tops to Oxford and the distant countryside. There is a view indicator on top of the Mound. Sir Arthur built a house called Youlbury on the south-west side of Boar's Hill and experimented in acclimatising plants brought back from his archaeological digs. A clump of stone pines in the garden was grown from seed collected by him in the wood that Dante had described in his *Purgatorio* as the 'celestial forest'. Evans also created a wild garden near Jarn Mound. In 1978 a memorial stone was unveiled at the entrance to Jarn Gardens with the inscription:

To
Arthur Evans 1851–1941
who loved Antiquity, Nature, Freedom and Youth
and made this Viewpoint and Wild Garden for all
to enjoy.

Another Boar's Hill resident who created a beautiful woodland garden here was Professor Geoffrey Blackman, Sibthorpian Professor of Rural Economy from 1945 to 1970. He was Keeper of the Groves at St John's College, and his garden at Wood Croft contains many rare species of rhododendron.

Many poets have lived on Boar's Hill, including John Masefield, Robert Graves, Robert Bridges and Edmund Blunden, but it was MATTHEW ARNOLD who made the area famous with his poems 'The Scholar Gipsy' and 'Thyrsis'. Matthew Arnold's Field was bought by the OXFORD PRESERVATION TRUST in 1928. It was from here that he saw 'that sweet city with her dreaming spires', a line which he immortalised in his

The victorious Oxford University Boat Race crew of 1894.

poem 'Thyrsis', written to commemorate his friend, Arthur Hugh Clough, who died in Florence in 1861.

Not far from Jarn Mound is Ripon Hall, formerly a theological college and now part of the Open University. Also on the hill is Warnborough College, the international university college, one of whose houses is Yatscombe, the former home of GILBERT MURRAY.

Boat Race The first Boat Race between crews of Oxford and Cambridge universities was rowed in 1829 over a course at Henley. Oxford (Dark Blues) won. *Jackson's Oxford Journal* (*see* NEWSPAPERS) reported, 'On Wednesday last the grand match between the young gentlemen of Oxford and of Cambridge, in eight-oared boats, and whose crews were picked men, took place on one of the finest and most beautiful parts of the River Thames, called The Reach, near Henley. . . . the stream was crowded with boats of all kinds, filled with rank, fashion, and beauty. . . . The Oxford crew appeared in their blue check dress; the Cambridge in white, with pink silk waistbands. The boats of both parties were very handsome, and wrought in a superior style of workmanship. . . . There was no great distance between them till passing on each side of the island . . . they rowed up to the bridge, amidst the roar and cheers of thousands of voices, and the contest ended in the victory of the Oxford crew by several boats' length. In the evening the concourse of people were delighted with a fine exhibition of the most beautiful fire works we ever saw.'

The second race was not rowed until 1836 and was won by Cambridge (Light Blues). It was over a course of $5\frac{3}{4}$ miles between Westminster and Putney. The present course from Putney to Mortlake was first used in 1845. The start is close to the Star and Garter near Putney Bridge. The Surrey station is the south side of the river and the Middlesex station the north side. After the mile post the crews pass under Hammersmith Bridge, the bend in the river then favouring the crew on the Surrey side. After passing Chiswick Steps and Duke's Meadows, Barnes Bridge is reached after $3\frac{1}{2}$ miles, the bend then being in Middlesex's favour. The finish is between Mortlake Brewery and Chiswick Bridge, a distance of 4 miles 374 yards.

The race became an annual event in 1856. By 1991 there had been 137 races, of which Oxford had won 67 and Cambridge 69. There has been one dead heat – in 1877. As *Punch* said, 'Oxford won, Cambridge too.' The Oxford crew were under the impression that they had won, but the finishing judge, 'Honest' John Phelps, later told the umpire, Joseph Chitty, QC, that he could not separate them. The result aroused a good deal of confusion and controversy and Phelps was accused of saying, 'Dead heat to Oxford by five feet.' The trouble was that he was a long way from the crews and had no post to assist his sight-line. There have been other close results: Oxford won by a canvas in 1952 and 1980.

Sometimes the race has been rowed in appalling weather conditions. Cambridge sank in 1859 and 1978, and Oxford in 1925 and 1951. In 1912 the race was started in half a gale and both crews sank; the race was re-rowed. The average time taken for the course is around 18 minutes, but the fastest time was 16 minutes 45 seconds by Oxford in 1984. The heaviest man ever to row in the race was Chris Heathcote, who rowed for Oxford in the 1990 race; he was 6 foot 5 inches tall and weighed 17 stone 5 lb. The 1987 race was memorable for having the oldest and the youngest men ever to compete in the race. The Oxford President, Donald Macdonald, was aged thirty-two and Cambridge's Matthew Brittin eighteen years seven months.

Boris Rankov achieved another record for Oxford by rowing in six winning boats, first in 1978 as an undergraduate at Corpus Christi College and from 1981 as a graduate at St Hugh's. Oxford also had the first woman cox, Susan Brown of Wadham College, who coxed her crew to victory in 1981 and 1982.

The voice of John Snagge became known to millions of wireless listeners through his commentaries on the race from 1931 to 1980. The race is now televised each year.

(Dodd, Christopher, *The Oxford and Cambridge Boat Race*, London, 1983; Peacock, William, *The Story of the Inter-University Boat Race*, 1900; Ross, Gordon, *The Boat Race: the Story of the First Hundred Years Between Oxford and Cambridge*, London, 1954; Burnell, R.D., *The Oxford and Cambridge Boat Race 1829–1953*, Oxford, 1954, and *One Hundred and Fifty Years of the Oxford and Cambridge Boat Race*, 1979.)

Bocardo Prison   In the 13th century the prison stood at the North Gate of the city. An extra floor was added in 1293 so that felons, women, and minor offenders could be segregated. In 1305 the town authorities were ordered to make a separate prison for

The Bocardo Prison, which stood at the North Gate of the city until it was demolished in 1771. The tower of St Michael at the North Gate can be seen in the background.

females, and in about 1310 prostitutes were kept in a room known as the maidens' chamber in the west tower of the gate. The prison was known as Bocardo by 1391. The name may be derived from a technical logician's term for a syllogism, implying that the prison, like the syllogism, was an awkward trap from which to escape. On the other hand, it may be derived from 'boccard' or 'boggard', meaning a privy and referring to its insanitary state. The prison was altered and repaired in the 16th century, and by the 17th century it is clear that it extended over the North Gate, as it appears in Skelton's engraving of a drawing by J.B. Malchair. Among the Bocardo's most famous prisoners were Archbishop Thomas Cranmer and Bishops Latimer and Ridley, who were kept there before being taken to be burnt at the stake just outside the CITY WALL (*see* MARTYRS' MEMORIAL). The door of Cranmer's cell is preserved in the church of ST MICHAEL AT THE NORTH GATE. The Bocardo was demolished, together with the North Gate, in 1771.

(*See also* CITY GAOL *and* PRISON.)

Bodleian Library   Opened in 1602, the Bodleian is one of the oldest public libraries in Europe, though it was not the first University library in Oxford. The first, largely consisting of the books given to the University by Thomas Cobham, Bishop of Worcester from 1317 to 1327, was housed in a room above the CONGREGATION HOUSE at ST MARY THE VIRGIN. On the Bishop's death, however, the books were pawned by his executors in order to defray the cost of his funeral and his outstanding debts. They were soon afterwards redeemed and deposited in Oriel College, but in about 1337 the Commissary (or VICE-CHANCELLOR) of the University declared the library the property of the University; and the scholars carried off the books by force and returned them to the room at St Mary's.

This room proved inadequate, though, when a large collection of manuscripts was presented to the library by the younger brother of Henry V, HUMFREY, DUKE OF GLOUCESTER, and so a larger room was assigned to them over the DIVINITY SCHOOL, which was then in course of construction. This room was not finished until 1489, more than forty years after Humfrey's death in 1447, but it was given his name and is still known as Duke Humfrey's Library. The elaborate ceiling, restored in 1963, has the arms of the University (*see* HERALDRY) in the panels and the arms of THOMAS BODLEY at the intersections.

Bodley, after whom the Bodleian takes its name, offered to bring back the library to 'its proper use, and to make it fitte, and handsome with seates, and shelves and Deskes' at a time – 1598 – when, in Bodley's words, 'in every part it lay ruined and waste'. For by the middle of the 16th century the contents of Duke Humfrey's Library had been dispersed, partly because of the religious conflicts of the time but also because the University was then so poor and some of the richer colleges now had their own libraries so that a University library seemed less important (*see* LIBRARIES).

For two years the work of refitting Duke Humfrey's Library continued and, having been stocked with books at the expense of both Bodley and of other benefactors, it was officially opened on 8 November 1602. The first librarian, Thomas James of New College, worked closely with Bodley in the selection of books, which, with the help of London booksellers

49

A scholar studying in the Arts End of the Bodleian Library in 1836.

and of agents travelling abroad, came from all over Europe and the Middle East. In 1610 Bodley came to an agreement with the Stationers' Company, which, established in 1403, had obtained its charter in 1577 and which undertook to send a copy of every book registered at Stationers' Hall to the library. This arrangement, confirmed by the government in 1637, led to a steady stream of books being added to the original stock of 2000. But Bodley was not undiscriminating in the books he chose to accept, considering that among the great number of volumes published each year there were many 'idle bookes, & riffe raffes' which ought never to 'com into the Librarie'. Consequently there was a poor selection of English literature and a complete absence of early editions of Jacobean dramatists; and it was not until the library acquired the collections of Robert Burton, Edmond Malone, ANTHONY WOOD and ELIAS ASHMOLE that these lacunae were gradually filled.

The steady influx of books led to the need for more space. The first extension, known as Arts End, was built over the Proscholium (*see* DIVINITY SCHOOL) in 1610–12. This was shelved from floor to ceiling with wall-cases, the folios being chained to the lower shelves, the smaller books being kept on the shelves of the upper gallery. The ceiling was painted with numerous coats of arms in 1612.

While Arts End was being fitted, Bodley was already planning further additions, persuading the University to rebuild 'those ruinous little roomes' which had previously been used for lectures as a two-storeyed quadrangle. To this, so he suggested, should be added a third storey for the 'stowage of Bookes'. These suggestions resulted in the SCHOOLS QUADRANGLE, which was finished in 1624.

The next major extension to the old building was completed in 1637. This was constructed parallel to Arts End at the western end of Duke Humfrey's Library, and, like that of Arts End, its panelled ceiling is decorated with painted shields from the old library at CHRIST CHURCH. Bodley made provision for it in his will; but it takes its name, Selden End, from John Selden (1584–1654), the jurist who was Member of Parliament for the University and who gave 8000 volumes to the University together with his valuable collection of oriental manuscripts. Above, on the second floor, the frieze of some 200 famous men along the south, east and north ranges was painted in about 1620 and revealed in the 1960s.

Gifts continued to be made to the library throughout the 17th century. The benefactions of WILLIAM LAUD, who presented over 1300 manuscripts between 1635 and 1640, and of William Herbert, Earl of Pembroke, whose statue stands in the quadrangle (*see* STATUES) encouraged Greek studies; while those of Christopher, Lord Hatton, and Francis Junius, received between 1675 and 1678, led to a revival of Anglo-Saxon studies. This led in turn to a renewed interest in mediaeval subjects based on the manuscripts of Roger Dodsworth and Sir William Dugdale, which were presented to the library in 1686. Indeed, by the time the Bodleian had accepted the collection bequeathed to it by Thomas Barlow (1607–91), librarian during the Commonwealth and later Bishop of Lincoln, the weight of books placed so great a strain upon the walls that SIR CHRISTOPHER WREN had to be called upon for advice.

With Western manuscripts and books came oriental. Bodley's own purchases had included a large number of oriental books; so had the bequest of Laud;

and so did the collections of Edward Pococke and Robert Huntingdon bought in 1693, the gifts made by William Thurston, a London merchant, in 1661, and the library purchased from Thomas Greaves in 1676. Subsequent additions to the stock have made the Bodleian the principal repository of Hebraica in the country.

Benefactions, including the state papers of Edward Hyde, EARL OF CLARENDON, continued to be made throughout the 18th century, despite the sluggishness of the University as a whole. Gifts came from Alexander Pope, Benjamin Franklin and SAMUEL JOHNSON, and in 1809 the bequest of Richard Gough was rich in topographical and liturgical works. Edmond Malone's collections made the Bodleian the main British library for literature of the Shakespearian period, while the 17,000 printed books from the library of Francis Douce much strengthened it in modern European literature, and the purchase in 1817 of a library in Venice brought to the Bodleian over 2000 further manuscripts and almost 400 Latin and Italian Bibles.

After the ASHMOLEAN had handed over 3700 volumes, and the collections of Elias Ashmole, JOHN AUBREY, Anthony Wood and Martin Lister (?1638–1712), zoologist and sometime physician to Queen Anne, further space both for books and for readers became essential. The problem was partially solved in 1861 when the nearby RADCLIFFE CAMERA was taken over. Yet as the Bodleian's stock continued to grow, the provision of a new building could not long be delayed.

In the 20th century, as well as a large number of outstanding gifts, financial help has been received from such bodies as the Rockefeller and Gulbenkian Foundations; from the Friends of the Bodleian, established in 1925; from Bodley's American Friends, founded in 1957; and from the estate of Kenneth Grahame, who made the Bodleian his heir, bequeathing it the income arising from the copyright of *The Wind in the Willows* in addition to the original holograph manuscript. It was largely due to the Rockefeller Foundation that the building of the NEW BODLEIAN became possible.

Before the New Bodleian was completed in 1939, the Radcliffe Science Library and the libraries of the INDIAN INSTITUTE and of RHODES HOUSE had been absorbed by the Bodleian, though they continued to some extent as separate entities. And after its completion the LAW LIBRARY, another dependent library within the Bodleian group, was opened in 1964. The JOHN JOHNSON COLLECTION was transferred to the Bodleian from the OXFORD UNIVERSITY PRESS in 1968. Soon further expansion of the Bodleian will become essential, by 1987 the library contained almost 5 million books on some 80 miles of shelving. (*See also* LIBRARIES.)

(*The Bodleian Library and its Friends*, Oxford, 1976; Macray, W.D., *Annals of the Bodleian Library*, Oxford, 1890; Craster, Sir Edmund, *History of the Bodleian Library, 1845–1945*, Oxford, 1952; Philip, Ian, *The Bodleian Library in the 17th and 18th Centuries*, Oxford, 1983; *Bodleian Library Record*.)

Bodley, George Frederick (*1827–1907*). The son of a Scottish doctor in practice in Yorkshire, Bodley was descended from the family of THOMAS BODLEY. In 1845 he became a pupil in the office of

GEORGE GILBERT SCOTT, and by 1860 had set up on his own account. His first work was an addition to a church for the brother of JOHN KEBLE, Thomas Keble (1793–1875), author of four of the *Tracts for the Times* (*see* OXFORD MOVEMENT). From 1869 to 1898 Bodley was in partnership with Thomas Garner (1839–1906), with whom he worked at Christ Church, Jesus, Pembroke and Magdalen, and built the Master's lodgings at University College. Bodley's master work at Oxford, however, is the church of St John the Evangelist at COWLEY built for the COWLEY FATHERS. He also designed the stalls in Exeter College chapel, the rood-screen at ST MARGARET'S, ST MARGARET'S ROAD, and, probably, the Gothic fireplace in Magdalen College hall. 'Bodley fills an important position in the history of English ecclesiastical architecture', in the words of the DICTIONARY OF NATIONAL BIOGRAPHY. 'If Pugin, Scott and Street were the pioneers whose work went hand in hand with the Oxford Movement in its early days, Bodley is their counterpart in the last quarter of the nineteenth century.'

Bodley, Sir Thomas (*1545–1613*). Entered Magdalen College in 1558 and became a Fellow of Merton in 1564 and a PROCTOR in 1569. A Greek and Hebrew scholar, in 1576 he obtained a licence to travel to learn modern languages. He thereafter became a distinguished diplomatist, returning to England in 1596 and almost immediately setting about the creation of the great library that bears his name (*see* BODLEIAN LIBRARY). He was buried, as he had requested, in Merton Chapel in which an alabaster and marble monument by Nicholas Stone was erected in his memory in 1615 at a cost of £200.

Nicholas Hilliard's miniature of Sir Thomas Bodley, dated 1598, the year in which Bodley refounded the library which bears his name.

Boffin's Established in 1847 by Alfred Boffin, who advertised the business as 'Pastry Cooks & Confectioners, Fancy Bread & Biscuit Bakers' and ran the Oxford Restaurant from No. 107 HIGH STREET. He also hired out plate and cutlery, and operated the University and City Bakeries in BLUE BOAR STREET. The business was taken over by James Boffin in the 1870s. He supplied 'Wedding Breakfasts and Ball Suppers' and had a cake shop at CARFAX on the corner of ST ALDATE'S and QUEEN STREET, where Marygold House now stands. The Carfax cake shop was a traditional scene of 'high jinks' on the last Saturday of term, with bread rolls and pats of butter flying in all directions across the crowded first-floor restaurant.

Boffin's also had a shop at No. 71 ST GILES'. In the 1920s Boffin's business, which was mainly in cakes, was sold to G.H. Cooper, whose business was mainly in bread, to form Cooper and Boffin Ltd. In 1936 that business went into liquidation and was bought by the brothers J.W. (Billy) and C. Roger Paine, who ran the bakery in SOUTH PARADE. They bought several other small businesses and in 1954 opened an automated bakery plant in OSNEY MEAD. It was sold to Spillers in 1959.

A. & W. Boffin, 'Pastry Cooks & Confectioners, Fancy Bread & Biscuit Bakers', were established in the High Street in 1847.

Bonn Square Formed when the WESTGATE CENTRE was built. The area between QUEEN STREET and NEW ROAD was named Bonn Square after the city of Bonn, with which Oxford is 'twinned'. A Clipsham stone (*see* STONE) in the memorial garden in the square bears the following inscription:

BONN SQUARE
The Lord Mayor of the City of Oxford
Councillor Mrs. Olive Gibbs
and the Chairman of
The Bonn City District Council
Herr Stadtverordneter Reiner Schreiber
named this Square on 5 October 1974

The memorial garden was formed in 1897 out of the churchyard of the church of ST PETER-LE-BAILEY, NEW INN HALL STREET. The Tirah Memorial in the centre was designed by Inigo Thomas and erected in 1900 to commemorate the local officers and men who died in the campaign on the north-west frontier of India.

Boswells *Broad Street*. The business was established in 1738. Francis Boswell had a shop at No. 50 CORNMARKET STREET which sold leather trunks, cases, portmanteaux and travelling goods. The business remained in the Boswell family until the death in 1890 of its last member, a keen botanist

whose studies earned him an honorary degree. The business was then bought by Arthur Pearson, whose descendants still own it. In 1928 the 18th-century house in BROAD STREET where the poet W.B. Yeats lived was pulled down to make way for Boswell House, a six-storey building comprising offices, a restaurant and the department store of H. Boswell & Co. Ltd, which moved there from Cornmarket Street in 1929. It is now Oxford's largest independent department store, together with the OXFORD DRUG CO., the two shops being linked and in the same ownership.

Botanic Garden The Oxford Physic Garden, renamed Botanic Garden in 1840, was founded in 1621 by Henry Danvers, Earl of Danby, and is the oldest physic garden after those in Pisa and Leyden. It was intended for 'the advancement of the faculty of medicine', but from the first botany, medicine and practical gardening were linked in systematic study. It became the centre for the cultivation of plants introduced from abroad, and through seed exchange contributed much to the modern development of horticulture. All the plants are labelled and a guide book is available. Today there is an alpine garden, a fernery, a grass garden, herbaceous borders, a water garden and a collection of historical roses. In the greenhouses are tropical plants, including bananas and rice, collections of ferns, succulents, orchids, insect-eating plants and waterlilies. Oxford has produced its own weed, *Senecio squalidus*, the Oxford RAGWORT, which was the first plant to escape from the Botanic Garden. The first London plane, a hybrid between oriental and American species, was raised in 1665, and one huge London plane at Magdalen College is a direct propagation from the original hybrid. There has always been a strong link with Magdalen, and the Professorship of Botany is attached to the college.

Danby had originally leased from Magdalen 5 acres of land outside the CITY WALLS, which until 1290 had been the JEWS' burial ground. It was low-lying and 4000 loads of 'mucke and dunge' were used to raise the land above the Cherwell flood plain (*see* THAMES). The walls were to be as 'well fair and sufficient as All Soules Colledge walls, Magdalen Colledge Tower, or any of the fairest buildings in Oxford both for truth and beauty'. The gateways, built by Inigo Jones's master-mason, Nicholas Stone, in 1632 are as fine as those in the greatest country houses. Danby appointed John Tradescant as the first Keeper of the Garden but, through failing health, he was unable to take the position. His name is now associated with Oxford through his collection of rarities, which became the basis of the ASHMOLEAN MUSEUM. Jacob Bobart, a local innkeeper, was discovered by Danby to be a competent gardener and was appointed Keeper in 1642. He produced the first catalogue of plants in the garden in 1648, when 1600 were recorded. The garden was laid out in a rough system of botanical classification for medicinal uses and Bobart decided where exotic plants grew best; but it is unlikely that he had any hand in the formal design of the garden as illustrated by DAVID LOGGAN. This was the work of Robert Morison, who was appointed first Professor of Botany in Oxford by Charles II in 1669 and who, during the Commonwealth, had been superintendent of the Duke of Orleans's famous garden at Blois.

The Botanic Garden in 1766, showing the greenhouses on each side of the gateway, which was built by Inigo Jones's master-mason, Nicholas Stone, in 1632.

Bobart's son succeeded his father as Keeper of the Garden and after Morison's death also became Professor of Botany. Professor Daubeny, appointed 1834, not only changed the name of the garden but also the direction of its work, using part of it for experimental purposes in the interest of science and industry, and for the furthering of evolution studies. He gave a party in the garden for the victorious Darwinians after the famous debate between Huxley and Wilberforce over which he had presided at the Oxford British Association meeting in 1860. A garden outside the entrance, designed by Sylvia Crowe, now commemorates Oxford's wartime contribution to the science of antibiotics through the development of penicillin.

Botley   This suburb just outside and to the west of the city existed as a village in ancient times. The name (there is also one in Hampshire) probably comes from the old personal name of *Botta. Leah* (now 'ley') means open space in a wood. Once in the county of Berkshire, Botley has been in Oxfordshire since local government reorganisation in 1974.

Botley Road   The road to Botley was known as Botley Turnpike Road in the 18th century but the alternative name in the 19th century was Seven Bridges Road. Until the early 19th century Oxford had no proper western access road, the way being no more than a track or packway across meadows, and the seven bridges did not exist. However, repairs were carried out and the name Newe Causey adopted. William Morwent, second President of Corpus Christi College, who died in 1558, left £5 for the repair of Botley Way. His predecessor, Claymond, had done much to improve the causeway. In the late 18th century travellers were likely to be held up by footpads and highwaymen. Matters had reached such a state by 1776 that a group of Oxford citizens formed a vigilante committee to stem the robberies. Peter De Wint's famous view of Oxford from the west, dated about 1834, shows bridges and a gravelled roadway fit

for a coach. The Causeway or Causey with the bridges was made under an Act of Parliament in 1766, and at this time part of the castle yard and moat at the Oxford end were taken into the new road. The original Seven Arches bridge in Botley Road was probably 16th century or earlier. It was widened on the south side in 1960 and much rebuilt. The church of ST FRIDESWIDE, west of the bridge and on the south side of Botley Road, was built in 1872 in the Romanesque style; it is a good example of the work of S.G. Teulon.

The present Botley Road runs from the western end of PARK END STREET by the RAILWAY station bridge to Botley. The old LMSR (then London and North-western Railway) passenger station (now a tyre business) is said to have been built in part from woodwork which formed one of the entrances of the Great Exhibition of 1851. The main passenger railway station (British Rail), with access on the north side of Botley Road, was built in 1852 for the Great Western Railway, which had taken over the Oxford and Rugby railway in 1845. The station was rebuilt in the 1950s and again in 1989/90. The building and yards of the old LMSR were built on the site of REWLEY ABBEY and the GWR track runs over the site of OSENEY ABBEY. There are several hotels in the vicinity of the railway station. OSNEY is on the south side of the road and the city recreation ground to the north. The road to BINSEY (Binsey Lane) with its 18th-century PERCH inn, its 18th-century farmhouses and cottages and its 13th-century restored parish church, runs northwards from between 92 and 94 Botley Road. Binsey also has St Margaret's Well, rebuilt in 1874 – the site of the legendary treacle well. On the north side, near Bulstake Close (named after the stream and old bridge of this name – *see* BRIDGES), is Oseney Court (the correct old spelling), a local authority old people's home. On the south side of the road were two old Oxford firms: Stephenson & Co. (ironmongers, builders' merchants and contractors) and Hunt & Broadhurst (manufacturing stationers). Further along on the south side (by one of the bridges) is the long-established veterinary surgery, the Beaumont

Botley Road: from View of Oxford from the West, *an engraving after a watercolour drawing by Peter De Wint (1784–1849).*

Veterinary Hospital (formerly Snodgrass, Eden & Trethewey). The West Oxford Park and Ride site is on the north side a short way from the city boundary.

Bowra, Sir (Cecil) Maurice *(1898–1971)*. The son of an official in the Chinese Customs Service, Bowra won scholarships to Cheltenham College and to New College. After taking a First in LITERAE HUMANIORES, he became a Fellow of Wadham in 1922 and was Warden of the college from 1938 to 1970. A literary scholar of great power and range, his books included *The Greek Experience* (1957) and *Landmarks in Greek Literature* (1966). He received several honorary degrees and was President of the British Academy from 1958 to 1962. Knighted in 1951, he was created a Companion of Honour in 1971. Although he gave as much of his time to Oxford as any man of his generation – being at different times a PROCTOR, a member of the HEBDOMADAL COUNCIL and of the GENERAL BOARD OF FACULTIES, a delegate of the OXFORD UNIVERSITY PRESS and VICE-CHANCELLOR in 1951–4 – his devotion to Wadham was complete. When he became Warden, the college had a long liberal tradition and not much contemporary academic distinction. It was thanks to Bowra that the tradition was maintained and the academic distinction re-established. In presiding over the changes, he never lost sight of the essential fact that a college is the sum of its members, all of whom, whether academically, sportingly or socially inclined, had his understanding, sympathy, praise or abuse whenever he felt that they were needed.

He had an almost legendary reputation for hospitality, wit and an amusingly malicious tongue. Recollections of him by his many younger friends and contemporaries have ensured that he is remembered as perhaps the most remarkable personality of the Oxford of the 1920s and 1930s. 'Immensely generous, Bowra entertained a great deal at Wadham,' wrote Anthony Powell in *Maurice Bowra: A Celebration* (1974). 'The dinner-parties were of six or eight, good college food, lots to drink, almost invariably champagne, much laughter and gossip, always a slight sense of danger. This faint awareness of apprehension was by no means imaginary. . . .' Osbert Lancaster remarked upon 'the warmth and excitement which the Warden's presence immediately generated' in the bleakness of his characterless lodgings; Lady Longford upon her memories of 'incessant thunderous noise and laughter, above which Maurice's voice would rise in a volley of puns and paradoxes, interrupted only by his suddenly pushing back his chair, springing to his feet and marching purposely around the table to fill our glasses yet again. Maurice roared and shouted and his face got red and then purple. . . . It was his pleasure to make his friends helpless with laughter, his own expression meanwhile remaining stern and his speech loud, vehement, emphatic, sometimes menacing.' Examples of his talk are as profuse as those of WILLIAM SPOONER and BENJAMIN JOWETT. 'The Master of Balliol', he once observed, 'has been ill but unfortunately is getting better. Otherwise deaths have been poor for the time of year.'

In his epitaph, his friend John Sparrow imagined him in heaven, having planted himself on the judgement seat:

He'll seize the sceptre and annexe the throne,
Claim the Almighty's thunder for his own,
Trump the Last Trump and the Last Post postpone.

Brasenose College Takes its name from the bronze sanctuary knocker, first recorded in a document of 1279, which used to be attached to the main gate of the mediaeval Brasenose Hall. At that time colleges and ACADEMIC HALLS, like churches, enjoyed special privileges, and once a fugitive from the law entered them he was free from molestation; clutching the door-knocker was deemed to put one on immune territory. The original knocker was taken to Stamford in the 1330s during a migration to find a more peaceable venue for academic studies than that offered by the then turbulent Oxford, torn by North–South divisions within the University (*see* NATIONS) and town–gown disputes (*see* RIOTS). The Brasenose manciple was, it appears, one of the moving spirits in the migration. Edward II, however, did not approve of breakaway universities springing up and the émigrés were forced to return. The Brasenose contingent left the bronze knocker on Brasenose House in Stamford, and there it remained until 1890, when the college bought the house to secure the knocker, which now hangs in the hall, over high table.

Little is known about the mediaeval hall. Legend has it that the 9th-century philosopher John Scotus Erigena studied there; his half-obliterated bust is to be seen, beside that of King Alfred (supposed founder of the whole University), above the steps up to the college hall. Over the centuries many other halls have occupied the site filled by today's Brasenose. Two of these names are remembered over the entrances to rooms in New Quad: BROADGATES, previously called Burwaldescote, which was an academic hall from 1247 to 1469; and Amsterdam. Other halls once on the site include St Thomas's Hall (formerly Staple Hall), Sheld Hall, Ivy Hall, Little University Hall, Salysurry Hall and Little St Edmund Hall.

Brasenose College itself was founded in 1509 by two men from the Lancashire and Cheshire borders: William Smyth (1460–1514), Bishop of Lincoln and a prominent member of the royal councils, and Richard Sutton (d.1524), a successful lawyer and man of business. Almost two centuries after the original brazen nose had last been seen, a new one, probably (but not certainly) meant for the newly founded college, was produced by guesswork. This caricature of a human face is now at the apex of the main gate and stained-glass representations of it are to be seen in the northern oriel window in hall, alongside portraits of the two founders. The college coat of arms consists of the devices of the founders and the diocese of Lincoln, and is thereby one of only three known examples of tierced arms in England, the others belonging to Lincoln College and Corpus Christi College (see HERALDRY).

Bishop Smyth's main endowment to the college was the dissolved Augustinian Priory of Cold Norton in the Cotswolds. The decayed conventual buildings were repaired and used by members of the college as a refuge in times of plague.

Brasenose College takes its name from the bronze sanctuary knocker formerly attached to the gate of the mediaeval Brasenose Hall and now hanging in the college hall over the high table.

Under its first Principal, Matthew Smyth (1512–47; Smyth had also been the last Principal of Brasenose Hall), the college quickly prospered. Generous benefactions in the early years guaranteed its survival; among the names of the donors we find John Cocks, Sir John Port, William Smyth, John Elton, William Porter, John Mordaunt, Alexander Nowell, Edward Darbie, William Clifton, Brian Higden and two women, Elizabeth Morley and Joyce Frankland. College administration was the responsibility of the Principal and six Senior Fellows, and the discrepancy in income between these and the Junior Fellows caused discontent and dissension. Six sons of noblemen were lodged either at their own or at the college's expense, and were educated by a 'creanser' or tutor. The original endowment had provided for no scholarships, but six were founded by John Claymond, President of Corpus Christi, in 1538. By the end of the century there were twenty-six Scholars. The first extant buttery book (dated 1612) shows that between 177 and 200 persons were battelling (*see* BATTELS) each week, of whom twenty-eight were scholars and eighty-seven undergraduates. The endowments also enabled the appointment of twenty-one Fellows, where originally there had been only twelve. Unfortunately, the early years of the college were often marked by financial mismanagement, and in 1643 some Fellows petitioned King Charles I to institute a VISITATION. Most of the abuses flourished under the autocratic rule of Principal Radcliffe (1614–48).

Distinguished members of the college in the 16th century were: John Foxe (1516–87), who celebrated Protestant martyrs in his *Actes and Monuments* (1563; familiarly known as *Foxe's Book of Martyrs*); Nicholas Grimald (1519–62), poet and dramatist, whose Latin play *Christus Redivivus* (1543) is prefaced by an account of the circumstances of its original production at Brasenose; Barnabe Barnes (?1570–1609), dramatist and sonneteer, whose tragedy on the life of Pope Alexander VI, *divils charter* [*sic*], was performed at James I's Court in 1607; Richard Barnfield (1574–1627), one of the 'nest of singing birds' in Elizabethan England, whose work appeared alongside Shakespeare's in *The Passionate Pilgrim* (1599); John Marston (?1575–1634), perhaps the college's greatest literary figure, whose plays include *The Malcontent, The Dutch Courtezan, The Fawn, Sophonisba* and *The Insatiate Countess*; and Robert Burton (1577–1640), author of one of the most extraordinary works in English prose: *The Anatomy of Melancholy* (1621). It has recently been suggested that John Cottom (who took his BA at Brasenose in 1566) was Shakespeare's schoolmaster. Other worthies include Thomas Egerton, Lord Ellesmere (1540–1617), Lord Chancellor of England from 1603 until twelve days before his death (the college's Law Society takes its name from him). The most famous Principal during the 16th century was Alexander Nowell (1507–1602), Dean of St Paul's and one of the great Anglican divines. His portrait in hall is the most important in the college; it is mentioned by Izaak Walton in the first chapter of *The Compleat Angler*, drawing attention to the fishing equipment depicted on it, which, apart from its allegorical significance, indicates that Nowell belonged in the venerable tradition of Anglican anglers. Nowell is also credited with the invention – albeit accidental – of bottled beer.

In the early 17th century the college had a reputation for being something of a Puritan place; that is not to say that it was necessarily anti-monarchical, but that some of its members were opposed to the ecclesiastical establishment. Some joined in the exodus to America: among them Richard Bellingham (?1592–1672), Governor of Massachusetts in 1641, and Richard Mather (1596–1669), grandfather of Cotton Mather, who emigrated to New England in 1635. Lawrence Washington (matriculated 1619), the great-great-grandfather of George Washington, also left for the New World during this wave of emigration.

In 1617 the college was host to the 9-foot-tall wrestler John Middleton ('the Child of Hale'), who came on a visit to his fellow Lancastrians and left an impression of his hand (of which the college possesses copies) – 17 inches long, according to one contemporary. The college owns a life-size portrait of this character. Another Brasenose student was the picaresque writer from the early 17th century John Clavell (1603–42), whose play The Soddered Citizen draws on an intimate knowledge of low life. He was a highwayman and reviews his ill-spent time in Recantation of an ill led Life (1628). The great divine and prose-writer Jeremy Taylor took his DD by royal mandate from Brasenose in 1642.

In 1642, when the CIVIL WAR began and the city was turned into an armed camp, academic life virtually ceased in Brasenose – although the name of the distinguished philosopher and scientist ELIAS ASHMOLE appears in the buttery book, probably as a lodger, in 1644. The fortunes of the colleges were at a very low ebb at this time, and Brasenose was deeply in debt.

In 1647, Brasenose, like other Oxford colleges, experienced the Parliamentary Visitation. Principal Radcliffe was ousted and Daniel Greenwood intruded in his place, along with other Fellows, including the distinguished economist and founder member of the Royal Society, William Petty. Six recalcitrant Fellows elected an alternative Principal, Thomas Yate, but he was unable to assume office until the Restoration in 1660. Greenwood and the Senior Fellow and Bursar John Houghton restored the prosperity of the college, and it remained on a sound financial footing during the next century.

After the Glorious Revolution of 1688 Brasenose, in common with most other colleges, tended to be soundly Jacobite. We catch a glimpse of its allegiance to the Old Pretender in the mention of 'our true English King' in an Ale Verse recited on Shrove Tuesday, 1709. (Ale Verses continue in an almost unbroken tradition to the present day – see CEREMONIES.)

The most colourful Principal in the 18th century was Robert Shippen, an archetypal Jacobite and 'worldly man', who held office from 1710 to 1745. An indication of the tastes and intellectual interests of Principal Yarborough (?1696–1770) is obtained from his library, now housed in Stamford House. In 1786 the Phoenix Common Room was founded, the oldest surviving dining club in Oxford (see CLUBS AND SOCIETIES).

It is often assumed that intellectual life in Oxford was universally torpid in the 18th century, but there were signs of change in the latter part of the century. Dr John Napleton's plea for public examinations (1773) were adopted by the University in 1800, and

Brasenose enjoyed considerable intellectual distinction under Principals William Cleaver (1785–1809) and Frodsham Hodson (1809–22). Under their aegis a brilliant crop of undergraduates flourished, including Reginald Heber (1783–1826), the famous Bishop of Calcutta; Richard Barham (1788–1845), author of The Ingoldsby Legends; and Henry Hart Milman (1791–1868), the great scholar of Biblical history. Brasenose's only Prime Minister, Henry Addington, matriculated in 1774.

Although in the first half of the 19th century the college was sympathetic to the spirit of reform, it adopted an obstructive stance at the time of the first ROYAL COMMISSION into University reform in 1850, mainly because of unfortunate memories of outside interference in the previous 200 years. However, the Ordinance of 1855–7 gave all the Fellows an equal voice in the government of the college. Eight fellowships were suppressed by the Commissioners, and their emoluments used for open scholarships. At the time of the second Royal Commission in 1871 the governing body offered no opposition. As in other colleges, preference in respect of lineage or place of birth was abolished.

It was in the 19th century that Brasenose acquired its reputation as a sporting college. One Principal who actively fostered an athletic tradition was Edward Hartopp Cradock (in office from 1853 to 1886), but to some extent it arose because the social class associated at that time with the college – the greater and lesser landed gentry – was much given to sporting pursuits. Brasenose's best-known sportsmen were Sir Tatton Sykes (1772–1863) and 'Squire' George Osbaldeston (1787–1866), both famous foxhunters; William Webb Ellis (1807–72), said to be the originator of Rugby football; and Walter Bradford Woodgate (1840–1920), the celebrated oarsman. The college rowed head of the river for many years, and at one stage was providing eight members of the University cricket team.

Yet there was no lack of intellectual distinction among the Victorian Fellows and undergraduates. Pride of place must go to WALTER PATER (1839–94), a key figure in the history of the aesthetic movement. Pater's contemporaries and pupils included Falconer Madan (1851–1935), noted bibliographer and Bodley's Librarian; SIR ARTHUR EVANS (1851–1941), excavator of Minoan Crete; Sir Richard Lodge (1855–1936), diplomatic historian and one of the chief influences on the Modern History School at Oxford; and Sir Charles Holmes (1868–1936), director of the National Gallery from 1916 to 1928. The novelist John Buchan (1875–1920) chose Brasenose because of his admiration for Pater; he produced the first history of the college in 1898. Field-Marshal Earl Haig (1861–1928) was an undergraduate from 1880 to 1883.

In 1909, for the 400th anniversary of its foundation, Brasenose produced the magnificently detailed Monographs and a most informative Register. These remain the principal works of reference for any extended study of the college. The Brazen Nose (begun in 1909) is produced annually and contains a wealth of historical material.

Men of note produced by the college in this century include John Middleton Murry (1889–1957), Charles Morgan (1894–1958), William Golding (1911–), Lord Scarman (1911–), Robert Runcie, Archbishop of Canterbury (1921–) and John Mortimer (1923–).

Since the Second World War Brasenose has considerably expanded its numbers: there are now 40 Fellows, 23 lecturers (some of whom are also Fellows of other colleges), 92 graduates and 329 undergraduates. Since 1974 the college has been co-residential. Its recent Principals have been Hugh Last (1948–56), Maurice Platnauer (1956–60), Sir Noel Hall (1960–74), Herbert Hart (1974–8), Barry Nicholas (1978–89) and Lord Windlesham (1989–).

The only building to survive from the period before the college was founded is the mediaeval kitchen south of the hall, its internal proportions partially masked by additions, probably of the 17th century. The magnificent brick barley-sugar chimney is an early 20th-century copy of an original chimney found hidden in a wall in the Hulme Library.

The front (old) quadrangle comprises the Tudor buildings erected at the time of the college's foundation. A replica of the foundation stone is visible in the south-west corner. The quad seems to have taken nine years to complete, the gatehouse tower having been leaded in 1518. The Principal's lodgings occupied the tower and adjacent rooms until 1771, when they were moved to a commodious house on the HIGH STREET, adjacent to ST MARY THE VIRGIN. In 1887–9 THOMAS JACKSON built new lodgings on the site and Principals continued to live there until 1948. In 1956, however, Principal Platnauer returned to the original lodgings (partly to escape from the noise of the High), and there the three subsequent Principals have resided. The small oak door immediately to the south of the tower (previously the entry to the lodgings) is thought to be from the mediaeval

Brasenose Hall. In the 18th century the tower was disfigured by the addition of two sash windows, but the original mullioned design was restored during the 19th century. The tower's two upper storeys are now used for muniments.

The Old Quad is a fine example of early Tudor domestic architecture, substantially unaltered except for the early 17th-century addition of twenty-eight dsplendid dormer windows, lighting the attics which were brought into use when student numbers expanded. In the college archives is a proposal of 1804 to sweep away these dormers and add an extra storey, with battlements, to the whole quad. Fortunately this plan, which would have ruined the proportions of the quad and taken away its very attractive domestic character, was not adopted. With the exception of seven large 18th-century sash windows and three bay windows, the fenestration is original: large windows for studies, small ones for adjoining bedrooms.

Before 1727 the front quad was elaborately planted out as a knot garden, with hedges of box and gravel walks – as can be seen in DAVID LOGGAN's engraving of 1674. It was swept away, a lawn planted and a gigantic lead statue, a replica of Giovanni Bologna's *Samson Killing the Philistine*, familiarly known as 'Cain and Abel', placed in the quad. The statue appears on all the old prints, paintings and photographs but, as vandalism perpetrated on it by undergraduates was a constant problem, it was removed in 1881.

The hall is on the south side of the quad. The almost completely obliterated early 17th-century busts high up in a niche are of the founders. On the roof is an 18th-century lantern with doric columns. Inside the

The front of Brasenose College facing the Radcliffe Camera, drawn by Frederick Mackenzie and engraved for the Oxford Almanack, *1821.*

hall nothing of the original fabric is visible. The panelling was installed in 1684 by the well-known Oxford carpenter Arthur Frogley, the oriel window on the south side in 1683, the plaster ceiling in 1754. The floor was paved in 1763, but the slabs are now covered with floorboards. Originally a brazier stood in the middle of the hall, its smoke escaping through a louvre, but in 1748 the gentleman-commoner Assheton Curzon donated funds for the installation of the marble fireplace which we see today. The portraits in the hall, besides those of the founders, include Lord Ellesmere, Dean Nowell, Lord Mordaunt, Viscount Sidmouth (a painting by the American artist John Singleton Copley on loan from his descendants), the Duchess of Somerset (a 17th-century benefactress), Principal Radcliffe, Principal Yate, John Wordsworth (appointed Bishop of Salisbury in 1885), John Latham (physician to the Prince Regent and donor of an excellent library now housed in the High Street tower), Principal Heberden (*see* HEBERDEN COIN ROOM) and Field-Marshal Earl Haig (both by William Orpen) and Principal Hart (by Derek Hill).

Originally there was a chapel to the west of the hall, but the room was converted to the present Senior Common Room when the larger chapel was built to the south in 1656–66. The panelling in the Senior Common Room dates from 1708 to 1711.

On the north side of the old quad is a magnificent sun-dial, painted in 1719; instructions for using it are to be found on a brass plate to the right of the steps leading up to the Hall. The rooms adjacent to the sun-dial on the first floor were originally the library but became the Bursar's room when the present library was built. They were panelled by Frogley in 1678.

Since the original foundation of the college the building expansion has been to the south, with two important periods of growth: the 17th and the 19th centuries. The library (1658–64) is by John Jackson (*d.*1663), who was also employed as a master-mason at St John's College. Externally it is a curious mixture of Gothic and baroque motifs (there are keystones to traceried windows, and a garlanded frieze over oval windows). Internally there was remodelling by James Wyatt, who was responsible for a plaster ceiling in the main library, an apse and a pair of large black wooden columns as a frame at each end. Originally the lower storey of the building was open to the elements, and members of the college were buried there between 1669 and 1787. In 1807 the cloister was closed in and the area is now occupied by the Graduate Common Room. The small square area south of the hall and west of the library (known as the Deer Park) was originally enclosed by a stone screen with pilasters and oval 'port-holes' matching those in the cloisters. It is clearly visible on Loggan's print, but was pulled down *c.* 1810.

The chapel (1656–66), like the library, is a curious amalgam of Gothic and baroque; it is a case of 'Gothic Survival' rather than 'Gothic Revival'. On the parapet there is an odd mixture of flamboyant baroque urns and Gothic pinnacles, and the west window has an oval-shaped central motif even though the tracery is Gothic. Money for the building derived from Principal Radcliffe, the common chest (*see* UNIVERSITY CHEST), the Principal and Fellows, and donations from old members. This conservatism and hybridisation is partly explained by the use of material from the chapel of St Mary's College for Austin canons in NEW INN HALL STREET (*see* FREWIN HALL). The college had been dissolved by Henry VIII and was purchased by Brasenose in 1580. The original chapel (1428–43) had a fine hammerbeam roof and its dimensions, and those of the freestone window-jambs, determined the plan of the Brasenose chapel. Work was well under way during the Civil War. The most interesting feature is the ceiling (1659) with its plasterwork fan-tracery filling in spaces in the 15th-century wooden original – the whole made more curious and rare by painted decorations added in 1895 during the Aesthetic Movement by Charles Eamer Kempe (whose other painted ceiling in Oxford is in Pembroke College chapel). The west window has painted glass of 1776 by James Pearson, to a design (now in the possession of the college) by J.R. Mortimer. The south window of 1887 in the antechapel is a memorial to Principal Cradock. The organ-case of 1892, designed by SIR THOMAS JACKSON and given by Principal Heberden, houses an instrument recently renewed by means of a benefaction from Maurice Platnauer (Principal 1956–60). The brass lectern was presented in 1731 by Thomas Lee Dummer; the marble altarpiece and altar-rails were erected in 1738–48 and the chandeliers in 1749. The chapel contains interesting monuments to former Fellows, especially to Walter Pater (surrounded by the profiles of Plato, Dante, Leonardo and Michelangelo), and to Principal Albert Watson (d. 1904) – an early work by Eric Gill. There is also a portable 18th-century oak pulpit.

Beyond the chapel is the New Quad (1886–1911). Extension of the college had been intermittently considered for nearly two centuries, and grandiose plans for a complete rebuilding drawn up between 1723 and 1734 by NICHOLAS HAWKSMOOR and in 1807 by Sir John Soane survive. There is also an utterly jejune proposal of 1810 for a High Street front in a cheap-jack version of Strawberry Hill Gothick by Philip Hardwick. In the event nothing was built until the educational boom and the material prosperity of the high Victorian era combined to give the scheme impetus, and the planning of a new quad, covering almost the whole of the southern area of the site (which had gradually been acquired by Brasenose during the 18th century) was entrusted to Sir Thomas Jackson. The west range was completed in 1886 and the High Street front in 1887–1911. In the archives there is a proposal from Jackson to erect a spire reminiscent of St Giles's Cathedral in Edinburgh on the gatehouse tower, but fortunately this monstrous scheme, which would have ruined the graceful homogeneity of the High Street, was not adopted. Instead there was a very full-blown and largely satisfactory exercise in the late Gothic Revival manner (so late that many of the carvings have a distinct Arts and Crafts flavour). The eight oriel windows on the High Street have extremely elaborate foliated designs. The tower itself has blind arcaded tracery and a buttress capped with an ogee-shaped top which cleverly echo the original Tudor gatehouse tower. The planned asymmetry is characteristic of the Victorian Gothic Revival generally and of Jackson in particular. In the south-east corner Jackson built his Principal's lodgings, but these have now been taken over for general college use (including the Junior Common Room and the Stallybrass Law Library). Immediately to the south of the chapel is a group of older buildings, probably of the 17th century, with an interesting bracket of a pair of gold-painted fauns above the entrance to the alleyway between college and St Mary the Virgin. There are two fine panelled rooms in this range of buildings.

West of Jackson's building, on an awkward L-shaped site, is the Platnauer Building (1960) – a four-storey block designed by Powell & Moya, a brilliant and much-commended design which was the prototype of similar buildings at St John's, Cambridge, and the Blue Boar Quad, Christ Church, Oxford.

Approximately half the members of the college now live in a large annexe on New Inn Hall Street: the Frewin Hall complex. This site, acquired by Brasenose in 1580, was completely developed in a two-phase scheme which began in 1975.

The corporate title of the college, commonly known as BNC, is The Principal and Scholars of the King's Hall and College of Brasenose in Oxford.

(Churton, R., *The Lives of William Smyth, Bishop of Lincoln, and Sir Richard Sutton, Knight, Founders of Brasen Nose College*, 1800; Buchan, J., *Brasenose College*, 1898; *Brasenose College Quatercentenary Monographs*, 2 vols, 1909; *Brasenose College Register*, 2 vols, 1909; *Victoria County History of Oxford*, Vol. III: *University of Oxford*, Oxford, 1954, pp. 207–19. Much other miscellaneous information is contained in the volumes of the College magazine, *The Brazen Nose*, from 1909 to the present.)

Brasenose Lane   In the early 13th century this lane, which now runs between TURL STREET and Radcliffe Square, was known as Vicus St Mildridae (St Mildred's Lane) or, popularly, as Mildred Lane. St Mildred's Church was on the site of Lincoln College. The lane still has a gutter or kennel running down the middle in the mediaeval manner. Sometime during the 17th century the lane took the name of Brasenose after Brasenose College, and yet, on a map of 1750, it is shown as Exeter College Lane. Also, it may at one time have been known as Allhallowes Street.

The lane is closed to cars but has always been an informal bicycle park and, in recent years, is often full of motorcycles and scooters at the Turl Street end. Discussions about whether and how to prevent them being parked there have been going on between the city and Exeter and Lincoln Colleges (on either side of the lane) for several decades.

Brewer Street   Runs from ST ALDATE'S to LITTLE-GATE STREET. It has had many names throughout its history, depending upon – as is the case with many ancient thoroughfares – who was living or trading in the street at the time. The old lane ran beneath the old CITY WALL. ANTHONY WOOD speaks of Lumbard Lane, so called 'after Lumbard, a Jew'. Lombard Hall is also mentioned by THOMAS HEARNE, but Hearne (in 1725) says that the street was 'commonly called Brewer's Lane and oftentimes Slaughter Lane'. There is written evidence of Sleyng Lane (1478), Sleyne Lane (1690), Slaughter Lane (1840) and Slaying Lane (1890), all of which reflect the number of butchers gathered here (*see* SHAMBLES). Hearne is quoted as saying: 'The people commonly say 'twas called Slaughter Lane from the scholars being killed there, but that is a mistake. 'Twas so denominated from slaying the cattle there, as being removed from the body of the University'. H.E. SALTER refers to the Latin poem about ST SCHOLASTICA'S DAY when people shout 'Slay, slay.' Hearne also mentions the street being called Friers Street or Lane at a time when the

Dominican and Franciscan friaries flourished there. Herbert Hurst (*Oxford Topography*, 1899), also mentions Lambard's Lane or King Street.

The present name comes from the brewhouse in the street. In the early 1930s there was confusion over whether Brewer should be plural or singular: the street name-plate at the St Aldate's end had an 's' and the one at the St Ebbe's end was without it. The City Council finally adopted the recommendation of the Highways Committee of January, 1932, that it should be Brewer Street. CHRIST CHURCH CATHEDRAL SCHOOL is situated on the south side.

Brewing Throughout the Middle Ages in Oxford much brewing was done in the home as well as in colleges, in the CASTLE, where a new brewhouse was built in 1267, and in such monastic institutions as REWLEY ABBEY, where a building was still in use as a brewhouse in the 18th century. As early as the 13th century, however, professional brewers had begun to make their appearance in the town; and by the time of the Poll Tax of 1381 thirty-two persons were listed as being principally occupied in the trade, which, since the ST SCHOLASTICA'S DAY riots, had been brought under the sole control of the CHANCELLOR rather than, as formerly, being supervised by the MAYOR and Chancellor jointly. Most of these brewers were men of substance. Between 1350 and 1500 ten brewers, vintners and taverners became Mayors of Oxford; and in the 17th century Oliver Smith, a brewer, was Mayor three times. His son, Thomas, also a brewer, was elected to the office in 1638 and 1643; and another son John, a maltster, became Mayor in 1639.

By 1700 high taxes on malt and hops, as well as the rising cost of fuel, had made home brewing uneconomical; ale and beer were thereafter more often than ever obtained from professional brewers, many of whom were also in business in some other trade, such as malting, innkeeping, or as corn chandlers. Not all supplied beer of acceptable standard, and the VICE-CHANCELLOR was called upon from time to time to issue notices such as that promulgated by Vice-Chancellor Bathurst in 1676: 'It hath been observed yt the Common Brewers of this place consulting more yr own private gain than the health and benefit of others, have not of late years made ye beer and ale of equall goodness with that of former times.' It was ordained, therefore, that they 'take particular care yt the said sorts of Beer and Ale ... be made good and wholesome and agreeable to the assize'.

Towards the end of that century and during the next, many smaller brewers went out of business and the great brewing families of Oxford began to emerge. The Swan's Nest Brewery, in existence by 1718, passed in 1780 into the hands of Sir John Treacher, who disposed of it to William Hall (*see* HALL'S BREWERY). And in 1803 Mark and James Morrell acquired from the Tawney family the lease of an important site where beer had been brewed since at least 1597 (*see* MORRELL'S BREWERY). Thereafter the Halls and the Morrells were to dominate Oxford brewing, although in 1840 there were still fourteen breweries in the city.

Originally the University's institutions and AC-ADEMIC HALLS had obtained their beer from town brewers; but by the late Middle Ages several colleges were brewing their own. Merton College had a brewer

as early as 1284, The Queen's College by 1341. All Souls built a new brewhouse, part of which survives, in 1594. Magdalen, St John's, Balliol, Oriel and Brasenose all had brewhouses in the 17th century. Those colleges which did not have their own frequently made arrangements with those that did. Brasenose, for example, obtained permission in 1692 to use St John's brewhouse; and in 1690 New College was granted rights to use the brewing equipment of Queen's. The beer at Trinity was deemed excellent, since the President, RALPH KETTELL, in JOHN AUBREY'S words, 'observed that the Houses that had the smallest beer had the most drunkards, for it forced them to go into the towne to comfort their stomachs. Wherefore Dr Kettell always had in his college excellent beere, not better to be had in Oxon, so that we could not goe to any other place but for the worse, and we had the fewest drunkards of any house in Oxford.' The beer at All Souls was also good but was so strong that in 1609 Archbishop Bancroft, the VISITOR, was shocked at its strength and declared it to be 'astonishing the kind of beer which heretofore you have had in your college, and hath been some cause of your decrements; for redress whereof I do strictly charge you by all the authority I have ... that from henceforth there shall be no other received into your Buttery ... but either small or middle beer, drink of higher rates being fitter for tippling houses'. At least, however, All Souls' beer was wholesome, unlike that of Christ Church in 1729 when the Keeper of the ASHMOLEAN MUSEUM died after drinking 'a pretty deal of bad small beer'. Colleges continued brewing their own beer into the 19th century. Merton was then making its strong 'Arch-deacon' ale, named after E.T. Bigge, college librarian and later Archdeacon of Lindisfarne in the 1840s; Oriel College produced 126 barrels of its own beer in 1866-7; The Queen's College was still brewing its celebrated 'Chancellor' beer in the 1870s and continued brewing until the outbreak of the Second World War. Its timber-framed brewhouse, rebuilt in the 16th century, still stands at the west end of the Fellows' Garden.

(Bond, James, and Rhodes, John, *The Oxfordshire Brewer*, Oxford, 1985; *Victoria County History*, *A History of Oxfordshire*, *Vol. 4*, Oxford, 1979.)

Brickmaking Although Roman bricks were found under the site of the CASTLE during excavations in 1952, very few buildings were constructed of brick in Oxford before the 19th century. ANTHONY WOOD refers to clay being brought from Campus Fields in 1525 for the building of Cardinal College (*see* CHRIST CHURCH) and two mounds on DAVID LOGGAN's map of 1675 of this area south of the old ST CLEMENT'S CHURCH may represent kilns (*see* MAPS). The first college, however, to be built of brick was Keble College in 1868-82. The POPULATION of Oxford grew from 12,000 in around 1800 to 28,000 in 1851 and 46,000 in 1891, and the demand for bricks grew with the enormous increase in housing. Terraces of brick cottages were built in such areas as ST EBBE's, ST CLEMENT's and JERICHO, and large brick-built houses were erected in NORTH OXFORD.

Early Ordnance Survey maps show a brickworks to the north of FIVE MILE DRIVE. This was owned by the Oxford & Berks Brick Co. Ltd, whose bricks mainly went to KINGERLEE LTD for building. The workmen lived in six cottages in Five Mile Drive, then known as

Long Hedge. The clay for the brick kilns was dug from a pit which is now the lake in Linkside Avenue, so named because it was beside the golf links of the North Oxford Golf Club. The brickworks also made a special type of brick called 'sand stocks', which were handmade in wooden moulds on the sandy side of the brickyard. Other brickworks in or close to Oxford were at Cowley Marsh, HEADINGTON, Shotover, and the large brickworks at Chawley on CUMNOR HILL, run by Elizabeth Neale, a farmer, and employing nine labourers in the 1860s and 1870s. Most of the brickworks closed between 1900 and 1940, partly due to competition from the Fletton brick industry in Bedfordshire. Ordinary machine-made bricks cost 30s per thousand in 1906, but one large rival firm was, by 1910, selling 48 million bricks a year at 13s per thousand and sending them by rail all over the country.

(Bond, James, Gosling, Sarah, and Rhodes, John, *Oxfordshire Brickmakers*, Oxford, 1980.)

Bridewell Square A new paved area off ST ALDATE'S, bounded by SPEEDWELL STREET on the south, Cambridge Terrace to the west and CLARK'S ROW to the north. It is on the site of Bridewell Yard, shown on a map of 1850. It can be approached by a tunnel-like path from St Aldate's via the CATHOLIC CHAPLAINCY. To the south is the back of Speedwell House, built in 1972–4 (Olins John Associates), and enclosing the west side is the Oxford Magistrates' Court built in 1966–9 by Douglas Murray, the City Architect (*see* COURTS).

BRIDGES (*See also* FOLLY BRIDGE, HYTHE BRIDGE *and* MAGDALEN BRIDGE.)

Bookbinders' Bridge Crosses the road over a branch of the THAMES into the parish of St Thomas west of the CASTLE. It was probably built by OSENEY ABBEY and presumably took its name from a building nearby where the abbey's books were bound. It was in existence by the end of the 12th century and was replaced by a brick bridge in about 1858.

Bulstake Bridge Takes the BOTLEY ROAD over the Bulstake stream between BOTLEY and New Osney. The original stone arch was built in about 1530 by John Claymond, President of Corpus Christi College. It was rebuilt with a higher arch in 1721 and again reconstructed in 1923–4.

Castle Bridge or **Castle Mill Bridge** Crossed the mill stream south-west of the CASTLE. It was also known as Swan Bridge after the Swan Brewery. In the 17th century it was supported on three stone piers. Widened in wood in 1871, it was replaced by a brick and stone bridge in 1895.

Denchworth Bow Crossed the Shire Lake stream, since silted up, in ST ALDATE'S. It probably took its name from John Denchworth, a leading tradesman in the 14th century.

Donnington Bridge Opened in 1962 to link IFFLEY ROAD with ABINGDON ROAD at New Hinksey.

Little Hythe or **Quakes Bridge** Probably built at the beginning of the 13th century, just to the west of HYTHE BRIDGE. It was rebuilt in the 1870s.

Milham Bridge Crossed the Cherwell (*see* THAMES) south of MAGDALEN BRIDGE. It was probably built by the canons of ST FRIDESWIDE'S in about 1300, and was rebuilt by THOMAS WOLSEY for carrying materials to

the site of his college (*see* CHRIST CHURCH). It was demolished in the CIVIL WAR.

Osney Bridge Takes BOTLEY ROAD over the river towards PARK END STREET. In the early 17th century it had three stone arches. It was widened in about 1777, and a new bridge opened in 1888, after its predecessor had collapsed over two years before while passengers were crossing it – one of them an eleven-year-old child. The new bridge has a single iron span.

Pacey's Bridge Built in about 1770 over the mill stream between Quaking Bridge (*see below*) and HYTHE BRIDGE. It probably took its name after the landlord of the nearby tavern. It was widened in 1856 and rebuilt in 1922.

Preachers' or **Littlegate Bridge** Crossed the TRILL MILL STREAM from Littlegate to Blackfriars. Constructed by the friars in the 13th century, it was rebuilt in 1813.

Quaking Bridge Crosses the mill stream west of the CASTLE. In existence, presumably as a timber bridge, in 1297, it was replaced by an iron bridge in 1835.

Rainbow Bridge Built in the PARKS in 1927 as part of a relief project for the unemployed. It was paid for jointly by the city, the University, the colleges and individual subscribers.

Seven Arches Bridge Built to cross flooded land on the BOTLEY ROAD east of Bulstake Bridge (*see above*) sometime in the 17th century. It was demolished in 1923.

St Frideswide's Bridge Also of seven arches, it was built west of Osney Bridge (*see above*) in about 1674.

Smalle Bridge First mentioned in the 14th century as being west of Bookbinders' Bridge (*see above*). It was known as Lasse Bridge in the 17th century.

Trill Mill Bow Carried the road from ST ALDATE'S into GRANDPONT across TRILL MILL STREAM east of Preachers' Bridge (*see above*).

British Telecom Museum Situated in the Telephone Exchange, SPEEDWELL STREET, the museum was founded in 1962 and records the history and evolution of telecommunications. Amongst the 150 telephones exhibited is Alexander Graham Bell's 'Gallows' telephone of 1875. Other exhibits include telephone kiosks, early manual switchboards and telegraph equipment which pre-dates the invention of the telephone. Several of the exhibits are in working order, and the museum is open to the public by arrangement with the curator.

Broad Street In the 13th century this street was known as Horsemonger Street and was the place where horses were sold. It was later named Canditch after the ditch outside the CITY WALL. It was here that the Protestant martyrs, Bishops Latimer and Ridley and Archbishop Cranmer, were burnt at the stake (*see* MARTYRS' MEMORIAL). A cross in the road surface marks the supposed spot and opposite, on the wall of Balliol College, is a commemorative plaque. Before 1772 there was a forecourt with trees outside Balliol similar to the one in front of St John's College in ST GILES'S. The street is wide in the centre and narrow at each end. In the 19th century carts were parked in the centre and a cab-stand was also sited there; in 1928 the centre was given over to the parking of cars (*see* PARKING).

On the south side of the street at the west end Nos 1–5 were built in 1928 for BOSWELLS department store. No. 6 now houses the OXFORD STORY. A bastion of the

Cabs parked in Broad Street in front of the gate of Trinity College in the 19th century, before the building of the Indian Institute at the east end of the street.

city wall can be seen here. No. 8 is the Children's Bookshop (*see* BLACKWELL'S), one of the many bookshops in Broad Street. Between here and TURL STREET is a range of 18th- and 19th-century houses of varying heights containing small shops. Nos 9 and 10 are by William Wilkinson (1863) in red brick, half-timbered with bargeboards in the gable. These premises were occupied between 1874 and 1895 by HENRY TAUNT, the photographer. THORNTON'S BOOKSHOP is next door, and the old-established tailors, Castell and Son, occupy No. 13, which is late 18th-century. OXFAM opened its first shop at No. 17 in 1948, and the premises were the charity's headquarters until 1954. Blackwell's Paperback Shop is on the corner with Turl Street. On the opposite corner is Exeter College, with the new building by Brett and Pollen erected in 1964 and occupied by Blackwell's Art and Poster Shop. Beyond the buildings of Exeter College are the MUSEUM OF THE HISTORY OF SCIENCE (formerly the OLD ASHMOLEAN), the SHELDONIAN THEATRE, with the row of EMPERORS' HEADS between the railings on the street front. The CLARENDON BUILDING closes this end of the street.

On the opposite side of the street a row of 17th-century houses was demolished in 1936–7 for the building of the NEW BODLEIAN LIBRARY. One of these, No. 46, was once the home of William Fletcher (1739–1826), whose father, James, started bookselling in 1731 in Turl Street. Blackwell's Bookshop occupies Nos 48–51, and the Travel Bookshop is at No. 53. In between is the WHITE HORSE inn. The remainder of the north side of Broad Street is taken up by Trinity College and Balliol. KETTEL HALL is at the east end of Trinity and fronting the street is a row of 17th-century

buildings known as Trinity Cottages, which were reconstructed in 1969.

Broad Walk A broad avenue with CHRIST CHURCH MEADOW on one side and Merton Field on the other. At the west end is Christ Church Memorial Garden, leading to ST ALDATE'S. Broad Walk used to be lined on both sides with elm trees, originally planted by JOHN FELL in 1668. One of Osbert Lancaster's drawings to illustrate the story of ZULEIKA DOBSON shows Broad Walk with these trees. They were killed by Dutch elm disease and cut down in 1976, replaced with alternating oriental plane trees and hybrid plane. The first hybrid plane tree was raised in the BOTANIC GARDEN in 1665. Thomas Sharp, in his OXFORD REPLANNED, proposed a new road to be called Merton Mall along the line of Broad Walk. There is in his book a coloured illustration showing how Broad Walk might have looked if Merton Mall had ever been built.

Broadgates A name acquired by several mediaeval ACADEMIC HALLS. Other such common appellations were White Hall, Black Hall, and Sheld (pied) Hall. It is said that there were, at one time or another, eight halls called Broadgates in mediaeval Oxford. Of these the following can be identified.

Broadgates in Beef Hall Lane. This large hall was one of the eight academic halls surviving at the end of the 16th century. Known originally as Segrene Hall, until the Dissolution of the Monasteries it was owned by ST FRIDESWIDE'S PRIORY. It then passed into the possession of Christ Church and was associated with this college until it was transformed into Pembroke College in 1624, its last Principal becoming Pembroke's first Master. Its earliest known student,

Cardinal Repington, who was made Doctor of Divinity in 1382, was CHANCELLOR of the University in 1397, 1401 and 1402. An 'imperfect catalogue' of Principals of the hall, going back to 1414, was preserved by ANTHONY WOOD. Later figures of note in the hall's history were George Peele ('the Atlas of Poetrie'), who took his BA in 1577, the poet and dramatist Francis Beaumont (entered 1596–7), the great antiquarian William Camden, who migrated from Magdalen in the late 1560s, and the parliamentarian John Pym (1584–1643), who entered Broadgates in 1599, but left in 1602 without taking a degree. A notable figure who spanned the period when Broadgates Hall became Pembroke College was Sir Thomas Browne (1605–82), author of *Religio Medici* and *Urn Burial*.

Broadgates in All Saints. This was a large L-shaped stone building, situated where today the frontage of Brasenose College stands on HIGH STREET. Originally erected as a house by Roger of Burwaldescote, it was an academic hall from about 1247 to 1469, being known as Burwaldscote Hall before its 8-foot wide archway caused it to be referred to as Broadgates in the 14th century. With a total capacity of nearly thirty scholars, it was one of the largest mediaeval halls, and had the rare distinction of being licensed to have a chapel. It was demolished in 1661. In 1736 Brasenose College bought its site.

Broadgates in St Mary's. Situated on part of the present site of University College, this was an academic hall till 1428.

Broadgates to the west of Grandpont. This academic hall, known to have been such in 1370, lay outside the CITY WALL in the area of what is now SPEEDWELL STREET.

Beke's Inn. To the east of St Frideswide's Priory, an academic hall in the 15th century, also referred to as Broadgates, ceded by the priory to the founders of Corpus Christi College in 1517.

Brown's A restaurant in WOODSTOCK ROAD close to ST GILES'. The site was formerly a garage. The restaurant was opened in 1976 by the owners of a similar establishment in Brighton. It is a busy brasserie, popular with students.

Buckland, William *(1784–1856)*. Already a keen student of palaeontology in Devon, where his father was a clergyman, Buckland won a scholarship to Corpus Christi in 1801 and was ordained and appointed a Fellow of the college in 1808. At Oxford he immediately began the geological expeditions, particularly upon Shotover Hill, which were eventually to result in the assembly of the collections which passed to the UNIVERSITY MUSEUM. Buckland succeeded to the chair of mineralogy at Oxford in 1813, and in 1819 was appointed to the newly founded readership in Geology. He became a canon of CHRIST CHURCH CATHEDRAL in 1825. His attempts to reconcile his scientific discoveries with the biblical account of the creation of the world – or, as he put it, 'The Power of Wisdom, and Goodness of God as manifested in the Creation' – were expressed in several contentious works. As Philip Shuttleworth (1782–1842) wrote:

'Some doubts were once expressed about the Flood, Buckland arose, and all was clear as – mud.'

An eccentric, amusing, talkative and cheerful man, Buckland entertained guests at Oxford parties by extracting from the blue bag he usually carried with

William Buckland, the eccentric palaeontologist and Reader in Geology, displaying some of the items in his collection in the geological lecture room.

him everywhere his latest find, which he would describe with 'infinite drollery'. He left Oxford when appointed Dean of Westminster in 1845. At his own request he was buried in a grave hewn from the rock at Islip near Oxford.

His son, Francis Trevelyan Buckland (1826–80) the naturalist, who was born at Christ Church, described in his memoirs the extraordinary household at the corner of Tom Quad, where the family lived surrounded not only by fossils and bones and bits of rock but also by all kinds of animals, including guinea pigs, owls, ferrets, poultry, hawks, a tortoise, a bear and a jackal, which were warned not to disturb the specimens by cards bearing the legend 'PAWS OFF'. Meals served there would include mice in batter, horseflesh and even crocodile. 'Besides the stuffed creatures which shared the hall with the rocking-horse, there were cages full of snakes, and of green frogs,' recalled G.C. Bompas. 'Guinea-pigs were often running over the tables; and occasionally the pony, having trotted down the steps from the garden, would push open the dining-room door, and career round the table, with three laughing children on his back. . . . I was in chapel one Sunday when [an] eagle came in at the eight o'clock service . . . and advanced with its wings nearly spread out. Two or three people left their places to deal with it; Dean Gaisford looked unspeakable things. . . . [Frank] told me one day what he had had for dinner the day before – namely panther chops!' The panther had been buried for a couple of days. 'But,' he said, 'I got them to dig it up and send me some. It was not very *good*.'

Buckler, John Chessell (*1793–1894*). The eldest son of John Buckler (1770–1851), the architect and topographical artist, J.C. Buckler became a pupil in his father's office, where he soon showed that he had inherited his talents as an architectural draughtsman. He was given lessons by the water-colourist Francis Nicholson. He produced numerous sketches and drawings of Oxford street views and Oxford buildings. Some of these were presented to the British Museum, others, done between 1810 and 1830, to the BODLEIAN LIBRARY. The 145 sepia drawings in the Bodleian, some of which are reproduced in the following pages, are remarkable as much for their picturesque quality as for their general architectural accuracy. In 1823 Buckler produced an anonymous work on the architecture of Magdalen College. As an architect his practice was largely limited to restoration. He worked at the University Church, ST MARY THE VIRGIN, on the belfry, pinnacles, spire and statuary, on the gateways of Oriel and Brasenose Colleges, on the CASTLE and ST ANDREW'S, OLD HEADINGTON. He also designed the buildings of MAGDALEN COLLEGE SCHOOL, which were opened in 1851. Buckler died at Cowley St John at the age of one hundred.

Builders *see* MASONS AND BUILDERS.

Bulldog 108 *St Aldate's Street*. Built as a house in 1232, it was reconstructed as Christopher's Inn in 1380. It retained its name, after its original owner, until 1716. It was rebuilt in 1594 by Thomas Smith as 'a freestone house'. Altered in 1716, it became a coaching inn, the New Inn, and in 1754 was a stop on the Gloucester to London 'flying coach service'. It was renamed the Bulldog in 1965 after the University official (*see* BULL-DOGS).

Bulldogs The nickname of the PROCTORS' men or University police presided over by the University marshal (*see* OFFICERS OF THE UNIVERSITY). It is not known when they were first so called (the name is common also to Cambridge), but they are so described in a humorous skit of 1819 (now in the BODLEIAN LIBRARY). In the mid-17th century they appear to have been equipped occasionally with arquebuses, and later with long wooden staves. Formerly they wore beaver hats, at first broad brimmed, then three cornered; later top hats; and more recently bowler hats. The two senior Bulldogs are known as 'cloakmen' because, when they attend on the Proctors at meetings of CONVOCATION or on other ceremonial occasions, they wear long black cloaks and round hats similar to those worn by the BEDELS.

A Bulldog in his bowler hat, satirized in a cartoon from Isis, *1936.*

Bullingdon Club A dining club, with a membership by election of about twenty, meeting once a term. It is no longer connected with the Bullingdon Point-to-point, and in recent years its meetings have not attracted the attention of the PROCTORS. It has no premises.

Bump Suppers Celebrations after the successful conclusion of the BUMPING RACES. A bump supper is given by the college when the college eight finishes Head of the River in either the Summer EIGHTS or TORPIDS, or when it achieves its full quota of bumps – one each night – to finish in the first division. In recent years, with new colleges 'putting on' (entering for the first time), some colleges give bump suppers if their first eight achieves the full quota in any division.

Bumping Races So called because the crews race in procession, each trying to catch and bump the crew ahead, the successful crew changing places with the defeated crew on the following day.

Bumping Races evolved from recreational ROWING at Oxford, probably about 1815 when Brasenose was recorded as the first Head of the River crew. It was the practice for crews to row down to Sandford or Nuneham to dine or picnic. On the return journey several crews would enter Iffley Lock together, and when the lock gate opened the leading crew would emerge and race homewards to FOLLY BRIDGE pursued by the others. What began as a display of high spirits soon became an organised form of racing, which was particularly well suited to the confined waters of the Isis at Oxford (*see* THAMES). The boats of that era were wide and relatively heavy, with fixed wooden thwarts (seats), across which was fixed a gang-plank from bow to stern. The captain, who in those days was invariably the stroke, would take his place on this gang-plank in the bows, and as the gate swung open would push with his oar or a boathook against the gate, walking along the gang-plank until he reached his own seat in the stern, when he would sit down and begin rowing. The crews thus emerged from the lock in processional order, the gap between them depending on the skill and strength of their strokes.

In 1825 more crews appeared than could be accommodated together in the lock, and the races were thereafter started from posts on the bank above the lock, placed, according to W.E. Sherwood (*Oxford Rowing*, 1900) 50 feet apart. However, the practice of rowing down to Sandford and passing back through Iffley Lock before the races continued, probably until 1839. The finish was at the white post below Folly Bridge, to which King's barge was moored (King being the proprietor of the boatyard at that time – *see* BARGES). At the conclusion of each day's racing the flags of the competing crews were run up on King's flagpole and the crews processed past them in salute.

The earliest surviving rules for the Bumping Races date from 1840. According to these, the starting distance between boats was then 100 feet, and 'there should be a night for every boat', so that, in theory, it was possible for the lowest crew to work its way up to the headship. The rules further stipulated that a boat making a bump 'shall immediately draw to one side so as not to impede the boats behind it'. In earlier years the rule had been that all racing ceased as soon as a bump occurred. The details have changed over the years, particularly the duration of the races, which is now only four days, but the principles remain the same. The crews are divided into divisions of twelve crews, starting with the lowest division and finishing with Division 1. The crew which finishes at the top of each division is called the 'sandwich boat', and has the option of starting again at the bottom of the next higher division, which gives it the opportunity to make another bump and so establish itself in that higher division. The crew which finishes at the bottom of each division must start next day at the top of the next lower division. The two lowest men's divisions and the lowest women's division are known as qualifying divisions and, if entries exceed the permitted maximum, new entries together with the crews in these qualifying divisions, take part in time races to determine which shall participate. A bump is scored when a boat (which term includes oars, rudder and crew) touches any part of the boat in front, or when the cox of the leading boat acknowledges a bump by raising his or her hand, or when one boat rows clean past another. A boat which scores a bump ceases to be part of that day's race. In EIGHTS WEEK, but not in TORPIDS, the bumped boat also ceases to be part of the race. The crew finishing at the top of Division 1 earns the title 'Head of the River'.

(*See also* BUMP SUPPERS, ROWING.)

A college crew is noisily welcomed back after a successful row in the Bumping Races of 1892.

Burgesses After several unsuccessful attempts on the part of the University to obtain from Queen Elizabeth I permission to send Burgesses to Parliament, the privilege of sending two was granted by King James I in 1604. Until the abolition of the practice of having University Members of Parliament under the Labour Government of 1945–51, all members of CONVOCATION were electors. Those to hold the office in the past have included Sir Roger Newdigate (1750–80), Robert Peel (1817–29), and W.E. GLADSTONE (1847–65). (For a full list of Burgesses *see* Appendix 4.)

Burne-Jones, Sir Edward Coley (*1833–1898*). Born in Birmingham, he went to Exeter College with the intention of going into the Church. At Exeter he met another undergraduate of Welsh descent, WILLIAM MORRIS. The two friends formed an intimate society with other undergraduates, most of whom had come to the University from Birmingham and many of whom were at Pembroke. They called themselves 'the Brotherhood' and together visited churches, read the works of Tennyson and JOHN RUSKIN, reverenced

Sir Edward Burne-Jones working on the design for the tapestry of The Adoration of the Magi *which was made by William Morris for Exeter College where they had been undergraduates together.*

the Middle Ages and later founded the *Oxford and Cambridge Magazine* (*see* MAGAZINES). They also visited the home of Thomas Combe, collector of Pre-Raphaelite paintings (*see* JERICHO), where they saw the work of Millais, Holman Hunt and Rossetti. On a visit to London, Edward Jones, as he was then known, was introduced to Rossetti, who persuaded him not to return to Oxford but to take up painting instead. He soon displayed a remarkable talent. In 1881 he was awarded an Honorary DCL and he became an Honorary Fellow of Exeter the next year. Examples of his work are to be seen in the UNIVERSITY MUSEUM, in CHRIST CHURCH CATHEDRAL, in the UNION, in the chapels of Magdalen, St Edmund Hall and Manchester College. He designed the Morris tapestry of the Adoration of the Magi in Exeter Chapel and the fine triptych in the chapel of Lady Margaret Hall. His Prioress's Tale cabinet, his first major work in oil-painting, was given to William Morris as a wedding present. Morris's daughter bequeathed it to the ASHMOLEAN MUSEUM.

Bury Knowle Park Bury Knowle House and grounds at HEADINGTON, extending to about 15 acres, were bought by the city in 1931. Bury Knowle Park was part of the estate of Sir Joseph Lock, a wealthy Oxford goldsmith and banker who was MAYOR in 1813 and 1829 and who died in 1844. The house is early 19th century and has a ha-ha separating the formal garden from the park. The house now contains a clinic and the Headington branch library.

Busts *see* STATUES.

—C—

Cadena A café which for more than fifty years occupied premises at Nos 44–46 CORNMARKET STREET. It had tables upstairs round a circular well; there was also a ballroom, and a Palm Court orchestra played for morning coffee and afternoon tea. Bread and cakes from the Cadena Bakery were sold on the premises. W.H. Auden was often to be found here during his time as Oxford Professor of Poetry. The café was closed when Gordon Thoday Ltd pulled down part of the old building in 1970 and built a new shop.

Campion, St Edmund (*1540–1581*). Campion was admitted to St John's College in 1555 by the founder, Thomas White. Two years later he was made a Fellow. As lecturer in rhetoric he was chosen to give the funeral oration for Thomas White in 1566 and, later the same year, to entertain Queen Elizabeth by debating in Latin. She was impressed and promised him her patronage. In 1568 he was ordained Deacon and became PROCTOR. The following year, feeling unable to profess his faith at St Paul's Cross, Campion decided to accept a travelling scholarship from the college and go to Ireland. While in Dublin he wrote *De Homine Academico*, and dedicated his history of Ireland to the CHANCELLOR of Oxford, the Earl of Leicester. From Ireland he went to Douai, and after ten years abroad, in 1580, he returned secretly to England as a Jesuit priest. In June 1581 he distributed copies of his *Decem Rationes*, printed at Stonor Park, from the benches of the University Church, ST MARY THE VIRGIN. In July he was arrested as a Roman Catholic agitator and martyred at the Tower of London the following December. CAMPION HALL is named after him. (*See also* ROMAN CATHOLICS.)

Campion Hall *Brewer Street*. In 1895, when ROMAN CATHOLICS were once again permitted to attend the University, the Jesuits established a small private college, known as Clarke's Hall, in an annexe of St John's College. It was renamed Campion Hall in 1918 after EDMUND CAMPION. The purpose of the college is to fuse religious integrity with academic distinction, and so provide the world with as many priests as necessary, educated to a standard equal to the best of their contemporaries. Today there are some thirty-five priests and student-priests in residence, together with a few laymen.

Campion Hall is the only example in Oxford of the work of Sir Edwin Lutyens. He was commissioned in 1935, after commenting adversely on the plans already drawn up by another architect, which, in his opinion, were 'Queen Anne in front; Mary Anne behind.' FATHER MARTIN D'ARCY asked if Lutyens would, therefore, recommend another architect: 'There is nothing I would rather do myself', was Sir Edwin's reply. He was subsequently sued, unsuccessfully, for unprofessional conduct. The plan he devised is a rectangular building, three storeys high, enclosing the garden of Micklem Hall. Lutyens designed every detail of the interior. The chapel is of particular interest: the roughly rendered plaster, natural oak and barrel-vaulted roof epitomise the discipline of perfect simplicity. Another wing was added to the building in 1958.

As David Piper has observed, 'Of the religious establishments [in Oxford] . . . Campion Hall is much the most sumptuous in its devotional furnishings, most attracted to it in the charismatic reign of Father D'Arcy; they include works by Eric Gill . . . Stations of the Cross by Frank Brangwyn; also a remarkable Spanish late-15C. monstrance, and a gilt and painted high relief of 'St Ignatius Loyola with disciples' ascribed to Juan Martinez Montañés'.

The present Master is the Rev J.A. Munitiz, SJ. (*See also* PRIVATE HALLS.)

Canal Between September 1769 and January 1790 a canal was built from Hawkesbury, near Coventry, to NEW ROAD, Oxford (91 miles at a cost of £307,000). The 27½-mile southern section between Banbury and Oxford included twenty-eight locks and was crossed by forty-one wagon-bridges of stone or brick and by thirty-eight wooden lift-bridges. The canal was built with a 16-foot bottom width to let two 7-foot wide barges pass. The water was 5 feet deep and the 7-foot wide towpath was 1 foot above water-level. The canal's supporters included Sir Roger Newdigate, the University, the City Corporation, the Duke of Marlborough and Lord North (MP for Banbury and Prime Minister). The canal's main purpose was to provide an outlet for Midlands industry, Staffordshire and Warwickshire coal in particular. For Oxford, Midlands coal would be cheaper than the usual sea-coal which was shipped from north-east England to London, transferred on to barges and distributed up the THAMES. Naturally, the sea-coal traders objected to the proposed Oxford Canal. Furthermore, the towns of the north-east coast petitioned Parliament, claiming that any reduction in sea-coal traffic would endanger the Royal Navy's wartime source of manpower – collier sailors. The 1769 Oxford Canal Act therefore prohibited the transfer of Midlands coal from the canal terminal to river barges bound for London. In 1774, with 40 miles of canal open, some Staffordshire coal was sent on to Oxford and the newspaper greeted it, as requiring, 'no stirring, as is necessary for seacoal, but being put on the fire and suffered to lie at rest, makes an exceedingly cheerful fire and burns till the whole is consumed to ashes without further trouble!' The final stretch to New Road was opened on 1 January 1790; the bells of ST THOMAS THE MARTYR rang and the Oxford Militia Band played as a convoy of barges brought over 200 tons of coal, corn and other goods to the canal basin.

The Duke of Marlborough built a cut at WOLVERCOTE linking the canal to the Thames. This enabled coal to travel upriver and be distributed to an area short of fuel. The Duke owned WOLVERCOTE PAPER MILL, which, in 1811, installed a coal-fired steam engine. Subsequently, each week, 100 tons of coal came through Duke's Cut to the mill, a supply which continued until May 1952 when the mill changed over to oil-firing. In Oxford the canal was linked to the Thames in 1796 by Isis Lock, which was built by the felons from the CASTLE gaol; a fine cast-iron bridge carries the towpath over the lock. In 1797 the Canal Company erected an office, Wyaston House, in NEW INN HALL STREET; it remained in the company's possession until 1878 and is now the main entrance to St Peter's College. As the canal office, it was replaced by Canal House, built in 1827–9 to the designs of Richard Tawney; this now provides lodgings for the Master of St Peter's College. A cartouche above the pediment of the Doric portico shows Britannia and, behind her, a narrowboat sailing past the RADCLIFFE CAMERA! Since most of the canal's subscribers had been Oxford colleges, the Canal Committee was largely composed of clergymen and indeed until 1885 the chairman of the Canal Company was ordained. In 1808 canal bye-laws required that the person leading the towing horse must be aged ten or over and the steerer at least eighteen. They also stated that 'No Person or Persons navigating . . . upon the Canal, shall use any horn or noisy instrument by which cattle . . . may be frightened or disturbed . . . No Person or Persons to bathe themselves or send Dogs into the Canal'. Servants of the Canal Company were 'not liable to Prosecution for killing of Fish in the necessary Repairs of the Canal'. Carriers conveyed the smaller lots of merchandise and their premier service was by 'fly-boats' (express boats) that followed a set timetable.

The canal was easily frozen and in 1795 Oxford's coal supply ran out until the boats finally got through in March, after ten weeks of ice. Large ice-breaker boats were pulled by ten or more horses and carried as many men as possible for rocking the boat. In 1839 Henry Ward, a coal merchant, had one of his boats converted to a floating chapel for the boatmen and their families. Donations and subscriptions provided for a minister, a schoolmaster and a schoolmistress. The chapel was moored just above HYTHE BRIDGE. There was school during the week and Sunday School was attended by up to 100 children. However, the boat gradually decayed over the years until one night in 1868 it sank, having 'fulfilled its mission'. A new chapel in HYTHE BRIDGE STREET was opened in 1869.

Although the Grand Junction Canal, which opened in 1780, took a considerable part of the water-transport trade away from Oxford, the Oxford Canal survived this competition with the help of toll remissions. It also survived the coming of the RAILWAY, as several kinds of breakable goods, among them pottery, glass and slate, were more safely carried by water, while the warehouses offered by the Canal Company were better than those available to users of the railway. By the end of the 19th century, however, railway transport had become so much faster and cheaper than water transport that trade on the canal was declining fast. It continued to decline after the First World War and by the 1950s had virtually ceased. In 1937 the canal terminal was sold to LORD NUFFIELD as a site for Nuffield College, and in 1955 the picturesque Banbury to Oxford section was closed to

commercial traffic although a trickle of commercial boats continued to use this stretch after 1955. The canal, which is now used for recreational purposes, ends at HYTHE BRIDGE STREET. Some of the former JERICHO coal wharves became cruiser-hire centres; and under the 1968 Transport Act the Oxford Canal was scheduled as 'a recreation and amenity waterway'. (*See also* THAMES *and* TRANSPORT.)

(H. Compton, *The Oxford Canal* (1976); 'Communications', No. 16, Local History Pack, Central Library, Oxford.)

Canterbury College *see* MONASTIC COLLEGES.

An advertisement for Cape's department store in 1929.

Cape's The firm of F. Cape & Co. Ltd – a department store selling a wide range of haberdashery, drapery, furniture and clothing – was founded in about 1877 by Faithful Cape. Its first premises were at No. 26 ST EBBE'S STREET but in the 1880s the firm expanded to include No. 29 and in 1889 took over Nos 30 and 31, having acquired a seventy-five year lease from the Feoffees of St Martin's. In 1893 the firm was bought by Henry Lewis, who had three sons, all of whom went into the business. One of them, Edmund, became MAYOR of Oxford in 1920. Henry's grandson, Anthony Lewis, ran the business until its closure.

Cape's had a reputation for stocking items which many other shops did not sell, and shoppers were frequently advised to 'try Cape's'. However, increasing competition from the big multiple stores forced the firm to close in 1971. Its premises were demolished, but one of the old mahogany counters, with its bentwood chair and shelving with brass-handled drawers, was saved and is now on display, with other items from the store, in the MUSEUM OF OXFORD. The firm also had a cash railway for catapulting cash to the cash desk, which was later replaced by a pneumatic-tube system.

Many drapery and other businesses like Cape's had staff 'living in' up until the 1930s. The upper floors of Nos 28–32 St Ebbe's Street (which were the main premises when the store closed) were used for the trained, unmarried staff who lived in at Cape's. There were bedrooms, a day room with a piano, and a dining room where all members of staff could have dinner and tea. They worked long hours: until the First World War the shop was open from 9 a.m. until 8 p.m. (10 p.m. on Saturdays), with early closing at 4 p.m. on Thursdays. Later on the shop closed at 1 p.m. for the Thursday half-day holiday. The live-in staff were looked after by a housekeeper and maids, and rules were strict: permission to sleep out had to be obtained in writing from a member of the firm and handed to the housekeeper. There was, however, an active social life, with sports clubs, annual parties at the CADENA and summer outings such as a trip on the THAMES in one of SALTER BROS' launches.

The firm adopted some novel forms of advertising. In 1929 a donkey was led round the streets of Oxford carrying a board which read, 'I am Not going to Cape's Sale – but then, I'm an ass'.

Carfax The ancient heart of Oxford where the four roads from the North, South, East and West Gates of the city met. It was the highest point of the old city. The name is derived from the Latin *quadrifurcus* (four-forked). Carfax was the centre of the mediaeval shopping area; and, in the 13th century, it was also the place where cattle were slaughtered. Petitions were raised against the practice, which was 'proving noisome and injurious to the Health of ye City'. Consequently an ordinance of Edward III forbade the slaughtering of any beast within the CITY WALLS. The SWYNDELSTOCK tavern stood on one corner of Carfax and the City Church of ST MARTIN on the opposite corner. The Butter Bench also stood there and PENNILESS BENCH against St Martin's Church. In 1610 the CARFAX CONDUIT was erected in the centre of Carfax to receive piped spring water from Hinksey Hill.

However, by the 18th century increasing traffic made it necessary to widen many streets and the Oxford Mileways Act of 1771 provided, among many other improvements, for the removal of the conduit from the centre of Carfax and for clearing the houses around St Martin's Church. The conduit was removed in 1789. Penniless Bench had already been removed. Under the Oxford Corporation Act of 1890 the Carfax Improvement Scheme was put in hand and St Martin's, with the exception of its tower, was demolished for street-widening. The tower was restored in 1897. Tower House was built adjoining it in 1896 and the premises now occupied by the Midland Bank in the same year, both designed by H.T. Hare. On the opposite corner is the Lloyds Bank building by Stephen Salter (1900–1).

Carfax Conduit A water conduit built in 1610 by John Clark, a Yorkshire stone-carver, which stood at CARFAX. It was conceived and paid for by Otho Nicholson, a wealthy London courtier, diplomat and lawyer; he was one of the Examiners in the Court of Chancery, a graduate of Christ Church and a scholar skilled in oriental languages. The water came from a cistern on Hinksey Hill, supplied from numerous small springs there, and was conveyed underground in a lead pipe, encased in hollowed elm trunks where it crossed branches of the river. The upper part of the conduit supplied water to a number of colleges and the lower part was for the city. The design is exceedingly elaborate, comprising a 'wealth of images' with 'exquisite carving', and is said to be based on a Renaissance triumphal arch. The initials of Otho Nicholson are carved round the conduit, and included in the design is the figure of the Empress Matilda riding on an ox over a ford.

There is a description of the conduit in RUDOLPH ACKERMANN's *History of the University of Oxford*, and the BODLEIAN LIBRARY has a manuscript description of it after it had been repaired in 1686. The latter states that 'the water which comes from the fountain head or conduit-house near Hinksey aforementioned is conveyed into the body of the carved ox and thereby the city is supplied with good and wholesome water, issuing from his pizzle, which continually pisses into

Carfax Conduit, which was built in 1610, was removed from the centre of Oxford for road-widening in 1789 and now stands in the grounds of Nuneham Park.

the cistern underneath from whence proceeds a leaden pipe out of which runs wine on extraordinary days of rejoycing'. On the Restoration of the monarchy in 1660 the Council agreed that 'a Hogshead of Clarett bee spent by its being putt into the Conduit and running in two pipes Eastwards and Southward'.

Above the foot of each of the conduit's grand arches is one of the supporters of the royal arms of England: an antelope, as supporter in the reign of Henry VIII; a dragon, used in the time of Queen Elizabeth; and a lion and a unicorn, as used under James I. Above the centre of each arch stand figures representing the four cardinal virtues: Justice, Temperance, Fortitude, and Prudence or Wisdom. Eight niches contain the figures of eight 'worthies': King David, Alexander the Great, Godfrey of Bouillon, Ardaticus (or Strapila), the Emperor Charlemagne, Hector of Troy, Julius Caesar, and (flatteringly) King James I. Also in the design are the royal badges of the four kingdoms: the rose for England, the thistle for Scotland, the fleur-de-lis for France (although this is no longer visible), and the harp for Ireland. 'So curious and well contriv'd a structure,' says the writer of the Bodleian manuscript, 'which for usefullness, beauty and neatness is not to be found in the three kingdoms' (France had been lost by then).

The conduit stood at Carfax until 1789 when it was removed so that the road could be widened for coach traffic. It was given to Lord Harcourt and now stands in the grounds of Nuneham Park, near Oxford, its stone figures sadly eroded by the weather. The Nuneham Estate was bought from Viscount Harcourt in 1948 by the University of Oxford.

(*See also* WATER SUPPLY.)

(Cole, Catherine, 'Carfax Conduit', *Oxoniensia*, xxix–xxx, 1964–5, pp. 142–66.)

Carfax Garden   A small garden at CARFAX, which was formerly the churchyard of ST MARTIN'S. Over the stone gateway into the garden is a copper bas-relief of St Martin tearing his cloak to share with a beggar. On the buttress of Carfax Tower (*see* ST MARTIN'S CHURCH) is one of the Peace Stones commemorating the peace with France in 1814.

Carfax Tower   *see* ST MARTIN'S CHURCH.

Cars   *see* MOTOR CARS.

Carroll, Lewis   *see* DODGSON, CHARLES LUTWIDGE.

Castle   One of Oxford's oldest surviving buildings. From the early 10th century Oxford had been fortified by a surrounding earthen rampart; and, in 1071, into the western side of this defence ROBERT D'OILLY built the Castle for William the Conqueror, to enable the Normans to control the upper Thames Valley. The earliest buildings were of earth and timber, and the bailey originally covered 2½ acres. St George's Tower, the first stone building in the Castle and one of the few surviving examples in England of stone military architecture dating from the Conquest, was built at an early date into the bailey wall. Four storeys high and with walls 9 feet thick at ground level, a series of offsets makes it narrower at the top than at the base. It probably served as the keep until the motte and tower were raised. The Normans would have used forced Saxon labour to dig the defensive moat, the material

from which was used to build the rampart and surviving motte – a mound about 250 feet in diameter at the base. The motte was heightened in the 13th century, when a well-chamber was built, and is now 81 feet in diameter at the top and stands 64 feet high. The well-chamber, hexagonal and rib-vaulted, is about 20 feet below the top of the mound and is reached by a descending flight of stone steps. There must originally have been a wooden tower atop the motte, later replaced by a stone keep – probably the 'great tower' which fell down in 1239.

In 1173–4, in the reign of Henry II, further work was done, probably the replacement of the earthen rampart round the bailey by a stone curtain wall with turrets. In 1215 or 1216 King John's captain, Fawkes de Breauté, built a barbican on the east side, and in 1235 a new tower was built, probably to the north of the motte and adjoining the newly built CITY WALL. After the collapse in 1239 of the great tower, a new tower was built in 1253. This was no doubt the decagonal stone keep, the ruins of which were still extant on the motte in the late 17th century. Its footings were uncovered in 1794 by Edward King, a local antiquary. Throughout the 13th and 14th centuries building works and restoration were constantly in progress but, in spite of extensive repairs in 1381–2, by 1388 the Castle was in ruins.

The moat which surrounded the bailey and the mound was supplied with water from the THAMES and was traversed by two bridges, the larger one, 40 paces long in 1480, going south into the town, and the other going west from St George's Tower towards OSNEY. During the reign of Edward II this bridge was demolished and then, in 1324, rebuilt. As all the rubbish of Castle and town was thrown into the moat, despite its being cleaned out periodically, it eventually silted up. Towards the end of the 16th century houses were built on its edge and by the 18th century it had fallen into desuetude.

Robert d'Oilly, who had come to England at the Conquest, founded ST GEORGE'S IN THE CASTLE together with his companion-at-arms, Roger d'Ivri. The crypt and west tower survive. D'Oilly probably also built the Shire Hall, and the Castle Mill was operating in his time (*see* MILLS).

The Castle has not had an eventful history. From the beginning it was used as a royal residence and during the Anarchy it was fortified for the Empress Matilda. There, the chronicler Henry of Huntingdon says, 'In that year [1142] the King [Stephen] besieged the Empress at Oxford from the feast of St Michael to Advent. In the latter season, not long before Christmas Day, the Empress escaped across the frozen Thames, dressed in a white garment, tricking the eyes of the besiegers by her white clothes in the dazzle of the snow'. In King John's reign the barons held the Castle against the King until 1215, when Fawkes de Breauté captured and held it until at least 1223, having withstood a siege by the army of the barons in 1216. In the later revolts of the barons, during the reign of Henry III in 1255–66, the Castle was again attacked and was kept in a state of defence until 1322 during the troubled reign of Edward II. Two earthen mounds were thrown up during one or other of the sieges but nothing of them now remains, Mount Pelham having been levelled in about 1650, and the Jews' Mount in 1790 to make way for the construction of the CANAL. After 1322 the Castle was

An aquatint of 1814 showing St George's Tower of Oxford Castle and the adjacent mill.

not put to military use again until the CIVIL WAR. Garrisoned at first by King Charles's army, it was later taken by the Parliamentarians, who levelled most of the wall-towers and built bulwarks on the mounts. ANTHONY WOOD recorded the subsequent slighting of the Castle: 'notwithstanding, afterwards, though the said works and aedifices were above a yeare in finishing, and cost many hundred pounds, yet . . . [in 1652] they were in four dayes' space in a whimsey quite pulled down and demolished'.

From the earliest times the Castle was used as an administrative centre of the county and as a gaol. The shire courts and assizes were held there from the 13th century until 1577 (*see* COURTS). In that year, after the so-called Black Assize when no fewer than 300 people had died from gaol fever, the Shire Hall or Sessions House was abandoned. Thereafter courts were held in the TOWN HALL. The gaol, which adjoined St George's Tower, was mainly used to house prisoners from Oxfordshire and Berkshire, but also, as recorded in 1236, for the University's 'rebellious scholars'. Over the years prisoners included William de Aylmer, indicted for levying war against Edward II; the Abbot of Eynsham, for forest offences; recusants; debtors; constables who resisted the collection of ship-money; prisoners-of-war from both sides during the Civil War; Quakers; supporters of the Duke of Monmouth; a highwayman; a Frenchman who stole coins from the ASHMOLEAN (possibly the revolutionary Jean Paul Marat). Christ Church acquired the Castle site in 1613 (King James having sold it to speculators in 1611), and leased the gaol to prison keepers. Conditions in the gaol were very poor, and in 1780 John Howard, the prison reformer, wrote an indictment of it in his *State of the Prisons*. In 1785 the County Justices bought the

gaol and redeveloped it as a gaol and house of correction, with a tower on which public executions took place as they had done in the Castle from at least as early as the 16th century. The last public execution was in 1863.

The mound, St George's Tower and the base of the Round Tower are all that survive of the Castle.

(*See also* PRISON.)

Castle Street   Named after Oxford CASTLE. 'Castell Streate' is marked on Ralph Agas's map of 1578. In the Middle Ages the part of the Castle nearest to CARFAX was the bailey, which included QUEEN STREET. A thoroughfare through the Castle grounds went from Castle Street to Quaking Bridge (*see* BRIDGES), which apparently remained open until well into the 19th century. The mound and remains of the Castle are now in NEW ROAD. Before the New Road was cut the street made a roundabout route, but when the WESTGATE CENTRE development was begun in 1969, Castle Street, which had run from the so-called MacFisheries Corner (in Queen Street) to PARADISE SQUARE, was re-sited and it now runs mainly from north to south. By 1970 it was extended to include the east side of the old Paradise Square, joining up with Norfolk Street. It now also runs into OLD GREYFRIARS STREET.

The Westgate buildings take up the whole of the east side of the upper part of the street and the new County Council offices much of the side opposite. A pedestrian subway under the north side of the road connects the two. The Paviers Arms at No. 12 in the old street survived until the WESTGATE redevelopment. A stone doorway on which were the arms of the D'Oilly family was given in 1970 by the city to H.A. Deeley of College Farm, Merton, a descendant of ROBERT D'OILLY, for 're-erection as a porch to his 18-room farmhouse which was rebuilt over 100 years ago following a fire'. Old firms in the past included Butler's corn chandlery (at No. 5), Tyler's (boots and shoes), and Wytham (tripe-dressers).

In 1885 F.J. Codd built Castle Terrace – six dwellings round the corner in Paradise Street, with the PRISON wall behind. This is now SIMON HOUSE, run by the Cyreneans.

Catherine Wheel Inn   Built at the beginning of the 15th century, this was one of the principal inns on the northern side of the city from at least 1526, when it was the property of Balliol College. It was a meeting place for ROMAN CATHOLICS, four of whom – two priests and two laymen – were captured here in 1589 and hanged, drawn and quartered, the first of their faith to be executed in Oxford. Later some of the conspirators in the Gunpowder Plot met here; and it was here that the Cavalier Plot of 1648 was hatched. The unexpired lease was bought back by Balliol in 1714, and about six years later part of the property was demolished for the construction of the Bristol Building (*see* BALLIOL COLLEGE). The remainder of the structure, known as 'Rats Castle', was used as lodgings until 1826, when this also was demolished so that the Bristol Buildings could be extended southwards.

Catholic Chaplaincy   *The Old Palace, St Aldate's.* The OLD PALACE was being used as lodgings by the University when the Newman Trustees bought it in 1917 to house a Catholic centre. Monsignor

Buckler's drawing of old houses in Castle Street in 1825.

Barnes, the first chaplain, restored it, and in 1931 MONSIGNOR RONALD KNOX added a chapel and meeting hall. After the Second World War, more accommodation was required, so Monsignor Elwes purchased a Nissen hut. These additions were demolished in 1959, when Father Hollings engaged Ahrends, Burton & Koralek to design the present complex, which consists of a chapel accommodating 120, a hall with seating for 500, a library, and eight study-bedrooms. Today the chaplaincy caters for approximately 1000 undergraduates, and is the venue for other activities pertaining to the Catholic life of the University.

(*See also* ROMAN CATHOLICS.)

Catte Street Now partly paved, this street runs between the HIGH and BROAD STREETS on the east side of RADCLIFFE SQUARE. All Souls and Hertford Colleges, and the History Faculty Building (formerly the INDIAN INSTITUTE), are to the east and on the west is the church of ST MARY THE VIRGIN, the RADCLIFFE CAMERA and part of the BODLEIAN LIBRARY. Early spellings included Kattestreete (*c.*1210), Catte Street (1402), Cate or Kate (17th century) and Cat Street (18th century). It was once referred to as the street of mouse-catchers, but for 500 years it housed the headquarters of the bookbinders. In the 14th century it was a narrow alley with shops and small tenements on both sides. A hall called St Catherine's (or Cat Hall) stood in the street in the 15th century. It being presumed that Cat was the diminutive of Catherine, the name was made 'respectable' by being turned into St Catherine's Street in the 19th century. The poet Robert Bridges, in the preface to HERBERT SALTER's *Street Names of Oxford* (1921), wrote: 'If the silly modernism St Catherine Street were done away with and the historic Cat restored there is I believe no single

human being whose affairs would be in any way affected.' The Highways Committee of Oxford City Council proposed that the name revert to Cat Street and this was agreed by the Council in December 1930, but with the older spelling of Catte. Until its southern end was restricted to pedestrians in 1973, the road was heavily used by motor traffic on its way from the east to NORTH OXFORD.

Caution Money The money deposited with a college by an undergraduate on his arrival, to stand as a credit against the charges which he incurs and to be repaid when his BATTELS are cleared – or, in case of default, to be used against those charges. We find caution money as early as 1582 at St John's College (40 shillings for each COMMONER), at Lincoln College by 1617 ('four pounds of lawful English money'), and at Corpus Christi (amount unstated) by 1644–5. The amount due might well depend on status: thus, at Pembroke in 1772, caution money was fixed as follows: gentlemen-commoners £24, commoners £12, scholars £10, battlers £6, SERVITORS £4. Earlier in the 18th century, at Pembroke, SAMUEL JOHNSON had paid £7 caution money, which was later deemed exactly to cover his arrears of battels.

As time went by, the importance of caution money in relation to college charges dwindled, and by the 20th century the amount (perhaps £10) might be retained by the college, typically to be used against the cost of acquiring an MA and 'retaining one's name' on the college books. Keeping one's name on the books no longer requires payment, while it costs only £5 for a duly qualified person to supplicate for an MA.

The concept of caution money has now been superseded by a system of pre-payments at colleges to ensure payment of tuition fees and college charges; it would not be unusual in the 1980s for such a pre-payment or deposit to amount to £330 – perhaps one term's battels – which has to be made by an undergraduate on arrival. For non-resident undergraduates the amount would be much smaller – say £55 or £60.

As early as the 15th century the Principals of halls had to deposit annual caution money for the payment of their rent to the CHANCELLOR or his deputy.

Cecil, Lord (Edward Christian) David (Gascoyne) (*1902–1986*). The younger son of the 4th Marquess of Salisbury, Cecil was educated at Eton and Christ Church. He was a Fellow of Wadham College from 1924 to 1930 and of New College from 1936 to 1969. He was Goldsmiths' Professor of English Literature from 1948 to 1969. A perceptive critic of English literature, whose published works were much enjoyed by the general reader, he was also a sympathetic and understanding teacher as well as an outstanding lecturer.

Cemeteries The Jewish burial ground was on the site of what is now the BOTANIC GARDEN. Christians were buried in the parish churchyard, but by 1843 every churchyard in the city was full. In ST ALDATE'S, for example, the ground had to be prodded with an iron rod to find a space. Further burial grounds had become an urgent necessity, and in 1848 new ones were consecrated in OSNEY, HOLYWELL and JERICHO (St Sepulchre's). The latter has a Gothic lodge by E.G. Bruton (*c*.1865). St Sepulchre's contains the graves of many well-known Oxford personalities, including BENJAMIN JOWETT, the Master of Balliol. As conditions became worse over the years there was a growing demand from the public for a general cemetery. In 1889 the Corporation bought 11 acres at ROSE HILL from Christ Church and about 13 acres at CUTTESLOWE from the Dean and Chapter of Westminster. The latter is bounded by BANBURY ROAD on the east and FIVE MILE DRIVE on the south, and is now known as WOLVERCOTE Cemetery. The land for BOTLEY Cemetery, so well known to rail passengers from Paddington to Oxford, covers about 8 acres near Oxford station, and was bought in 1890 from the Earl of Abingdon. HEADINGTON Cemetery was taken over by the city from the parish council in 1928 and extended in 1932. It has a stone chapel by Wilkinson and Moore (1886).

(*See also* CHURCH OF ST CROSS.)

Central Library A public library was established by Oxford City Council in 1854. Its administration was taken over by the County Council in 1974. Besides the usual services provided by this type of institution, this library has important collections relevant to the history of Oxford, Oxfordshire and the part of north Berkshire now in the present county, including photographs, views, school log-books and books on motor-car manufacture. Oxford city ARCHIVES, housed elsewhere, are administered from the Central Library and can be read here.

(*See also* LIBRARIES.)

Central School for Girls (*later* CHENEY GIRLS' GRAMMAR SCHOOL). The Rev. James Hinton, a Baptist minister, founded four Sunday Schools in Oxford – of which this was one – each intended for thirty to forty children. By 1810 they had all become day schools.

This school, which was opened in about 1797, occupied Tubb's Tenement, GLOUCESTER GREEN, from 1812 to 1824; and from 1824 to 1882 was housed in a building in PENSON'S GARDENS, ST EBBE'S, since demolished, in the area now occupied by the WESTGATE CENTRE. (There was also a Penson's Gardens in ST CLEMENT'S.) In 1837 the school became the Oxford United Charity and Sunday School for Girls and by 1854 was known as the Oxford Girls' British School. It received government aid from 1870, though remaining a Voluntary School. In 1873 its name changed to the Penson's Gardens Girls' British School and was referred to as one of the 'Secondary institutions of Oxford': weekly fees were 2*d* for infants and 6*d* for senior girls. In 1882 it moved to the old Wesleyan Chapel in NEW INN HALL STREET, when it became the Central School for Girls. Taken over by the Oxford School Board in 1898, it moved to the south-west end of New Inn Hall Street in 1900 and occupied a purpose-built stone building designed by Leonard Stokes and described by Pevsner as both 'impressive' and 'not really like any other Oxford building'. The 1500-square-yard site was purchased from Balliol College and the building accommodated 270 girls. When the school moved out in 1959, the building was taken over by the COLLEGE OF FURTHER EDUCATION and in 1985 became part of St Peter's College. When the school took over its new premises in Gypsy Lane, HEADINGTON, built to accommodate 360 day girls, it was renamed Cheney County Secondary Girls' School, then Cheney Girls' Grammar School – the title Cheney being taken from CHENEY LANE, which borders the site. In 1972 it was absorbed into CHENEY UPPER SCHOOL.

Ceremonies Oxford's most widely known ceremonies are those which are publicly celebrated – notably ENCAENIA and Degree Days, MATRICULATION and UNIVERSITY SERMONS. Others are scarcely less famous: MAY MORNING and BEATING THE BOUNDS. But there are many other customs and ceremonies peculiar to the colleges – not all of which have survived into the final quarter of the twentieth century – which deserve notice. Trinity College, for example, used to present a masque every Christmas; St John's, which also had a masque at that time of year, 'used to feed upon frumenty in mid-Lent'. At New College, Fellows were at one time summoned to dinner by a choirboy, who went from the chapel door to the garden gate calling '*A manger tous seigneurs*'; the blows of a wooden mallet on the foot of the staircase summoned them to the quarterly college meetings, as was also the case at University College.

At Brasenose, 'Brasenose Ale Verses' are provided at dinner on every Shrove Tuesday; a published volume of them exists for the years 1709 to 1889. Although the college ceased to brew its own ale at that time (*see* BREWING), the verses are still produced, and, unless too scurrilous, may be published in the college's annual magazine. Better known is the Mallard Song, which is sung twice yearly at All Souls College, on All Souls Day and at the Bursar's GAUDY. Reginald Heber of Brasenose recorded in 1801, three years before his election to All Souls, 'I write under the bondage of a very severe cold which I caught by getting out of bed at four in the morning to see the celebration of the famous All Souls Mallard Feast. . . . I had a full view of the *Lord Mallard* and about forty

Fellows in a kind of procession on the Library roof, with immense lighted torches which had a singular effect.' One verse of the Mallard Song, with refrain, may suffice to give the flavour of what Heber heard those Fellows singing:

> The Griffin, Bustard, Turkey, Capon
> Let other hungry mortals gape on,
> And on their bones with stomach fall hard,
> But let All Souls men have their Mallard.

> *Chorus:*

> O by the blood of King Edward,
> O by the blood of King Edward,
> It was a swapping, swapping Mallard.

According to tradition, a mallard had been found in a drain when the foundations of the college were being laid; and writers such as ANTHONY WOOD and THOMAS HEARNE allude to the custom by which on All Souls Day or St Hilary's Day (14 January) the Fellows singing the song used to perambulate the college with sticks and poles in pretended search of it. However, the college historian avers that the earliest reference to the procession dates from 1632 and that the song itself dates from the second half of the 17th century.

The historian of Jesus College, E.G. Hardy, wrote in 1899: 'Up to quite recent years – I do not know whether it was a primaeval institution – a green leek was attached to the tassel of the College cap of every member of the College on the morning of St. David's Day by his servant. With this appendage he was supposed to go to chapel and to lecture, while the more patriotic Welshmen would even display this mark of their nationality in the High. It is to be regretted that this custom has almost disappeared, entirely, I believe, among the Welsh members of the College, though a gallant attempt is from time to time made by some of the foreign element to revive it.' Nothing seems to remain of this custom. There have been other ceremonies celebrated besides May Morning at Magdalen, where two dinners during the year are held in special honour. On 29 May the members of the college celebrate the return of those who were ejected from their fellowships during the Commonwealth. The 'Restoration Cup', engraved with the names of those who suffered, is handed round, and the toast, '*Jus suum cuique*', is given. Five months later, on 29 October, the same cup and the same toast are made use of, this time to commemorate the restoring to Magdalen of the President and Fellows, who were expelled by James II. There are even more famous dinners at The Queen's College, where the Boar's Head Dinner (celebrating the Queen's undergraduate who allegedly thrust his Aristotle down the throat of a wild boar) is still celebrated in late December. The ceremony dates back at least to 1395–6. After the trumpet has sounded for dinner and the Fellows have assembled along the high table, the Boar's Head is carried into the hall. A song composed by an anonymous Queen's man is sung, beginning:

> The Boar's head in hand bear I
> Bedeck'd with bays and rosemary,
> And I pray you, my masters, be merry,
> Quot estis in convivio.

Before the procession entered the hall and after each of the three verses, the refrain used to be sung by the college choir:

> Caput apri defero
> Reddens laudes Domino.

On 1 January, the Circumcision of Christ is celebrated at another feast which survives today – the Needle and Thread Dinner, which owes its name to a pun on the Founder's name, 'aiguilles et fils' sounding rather like (Robert) Eglesfeld. The pun may possibly date back to the Middle Ages, and a needle and thread of wool is duly presented to each person present at the dinner.

Chefs preparing the Boar's Head for the famous dinner at The Queen's College, c.1900.

A.C. Benson, the biographer of WALTER PATER, observed in 1906: 'The [chapel] service at Brasenose retains several peculiar little ceremonies: the candles are lit at celebrations. The Junior Fellows bring in the elements with solemnity from the ante-chapel. When the procession leaves the altar, the dignitaries who carry the alms and the vessels bow at the lectern to the altar, and to the Principal as they pass his stall. The Vice-Principal bows to the altar on leaving his stall, and the Principal as he passes out. These little observances date from Laudian or even pre-Reformation times.' None of these observances is still maintained, though candles are lit at celebrations.

Ceremonies or observances have been, or are still, maintained, however, at most if not all the older colleges at Oxford, where annual dinners in commemoration of founders or benefactors are regularly enjoyed. It is perhaps a tribute to the enduring attraction of such feasts that Pembroke's Salt Dinner, in commemoration of a benefaction from a relatively recent Fellow and Bursar of the college, L.E. Salt, dates only from the middle of the 20th century. Again at Pembroke, Fellows are still admitted by the Master in a brief Latin ceremony. The last word may lie with Thomas Hearne: 'Whereas the University disputations on Ash Wednesday should begin at one o'clock, they did not begin this year (1723) till two or after, which is owing to several colleges having altered their hours of dining from eleven to twelve, occasioned from people's lying in bed longer than they used to do.... It hath been an old custom in Oxford for the scholars of all Houses, on Shrove Tuesday, to go to dinner at ten o'clock (at which time the little bell, called pancake bell, rings or at least should ring at St. Mary's) and to supper at four in the afternoon; and it was always followed in Edmund Hall, so long as I have been in Oxford, till yesterday, when they went to dinner at twelve, and to supper at six; nor were there any fritters at dinner, as there always used to be. When laudable old customs alter, 'tis a sign learning dwindles.'

Certificates and Diplomas Although most graduates study for an advanced DEGREE, the University also offers a restricted range of courses which lead to a certificate or, more commonly, a diploma. The University's Graduate Student Prospectus for 1986–87 listed the following such courses as available;

Diploma in Applied Statistics
Diploma in Celtic Studies
Diploma in Economic Development
Diploma in the History of Art
Diploma in Human Biology
Diploma in Law
Diploma in Slavonic Studies
Diploma in Theology
Certificate in Education

Additionally, the following were open to non-members of the University:

Special Diploma in Educational Studies
Special Diploma in Social Administration
Special Diploma in Social Studies
Certificate in Management Studies
Certificate in Theology

In the case of those courses which were open only to persons who had become matriculated members of the University, applicants must have attained a first or good second-class honours degree, or in the opinion of the board of the faculty or committee concerned be otherwise adequately qualified to undertake the course. Residence for at least three terms (six in the case of Celtic Studies) was required before the examination could be taken or, in the case of the Diploma in Law, the thesis submitted.

Perhaps the best-known of the courses is the Certificate in Education, which is awarded after a one-year course of teacher training for graduates. The emphasis of the course lies upon professional preparation, in close co-operation with associated schools in Oxfordshire. The work is designed for intending secondary-school teachers wishing to specialise in teaching Biology, Chemistry, English, Geography, History, Mathematics, Modern Languages, and Physics. A range of subsidiary courses is also offered.

Chairs The growth in Oxford's professoriate can be shown clearly in numerical terms: in 1800 the University had twenty-one professors; by 1900 this figure had risen to fifty-four; and the *University Calendar* for 1984–5 listed 151 professorships.

The oldest professorship, the Margaret Professorship of Divinity, was founded in 1502 by Margaret, Countess of Richmond, mother of Henry VII, and endowed with an annual stipend of 20 marks; the holder is invariably a canon of Christ Church (and from 1626 to 1638 was Samuel Fell, later Dean of Christ Church). The first five Regius Professorships – of Divinity, Civil Law, Medicine, Hebrew and Greek – were founded by King Henry VIII in 1546, each with an annual stipend of £40, paid in the cases of Divinity, Hebrew and Greek by Christ Church, the other two being paid by the Royal Exchequer. All these chairs except that of Greek received subsequent augmentation by King James I or Charles I. In 1619 were founded the Savilian Professorships of Geometry and Astronomy, by Sir Henry Savile, Warden of Merton. Edmond Halley was Savilian Professor of Geometry from 1704 to 1742. Other relatively early chairs were those of Natural Philosophy (1621), Moral Philosophy (1621), Ancient History (1622), Music (1626), Arabic (1636), Botany (1669) and Poetry (1708), of which mention will be made again. The Regius Professorship of History was founded by King George I in 1724; and in 1758 WILLIAM BLACKSTONE became the first holder of the Vinerian Professorship of Common Law, founded by Charles Viner (1678–1756), the jurist and compiler of a 'valueless encyclopaedia', 'vast and labyrinthine, ill arranged and worse designed'. JOHN RUSKIN was the first to hold the Slade Professorship of Fine Art, founded in accordance with the will of Felix Slade in 1869.

The importance of holding a chair in a collegiate university was for a long time less great than in, for example, the non-collegiate universities of Germany. Thus, for most holders of the Regius Professorship of Greek, the £40 annual stipend mattered little to people who were, or who became, comfortably remunerated canons of Christ Church: DEAN GAISFORD of Christ Church held the chair (without lecturing or teaching) from 1812 to 1855. The University's Historical Register for 1220–1900 comments: 'one of the chief features in the legislation carried out by the University Commissioners under the Act of 1877 was the augmentation of the value of many of the Professorships, by attaching to them Fellowships and other emoluments drawn from the revenues of Colleges, while the endowment of many new chairs was provided from the same source.' Six professorships were founded as a direct result of the 1877 Act.

Reform had been long overdue; even at the time of the ROYAL COMMISSION of 1850, it had been felt that, compared with continental universities, Oxford suffered from a lack of learned men, from deficiencies in the number and endowments of chairs, and from inadequate representation of the professoriate in University government. This case was very forcibly put by Henry Halford Vaughan, Regius Professor of Modern History, in his *Oxford Reform and Oxford Professors* of 1854. Vaughan had been supported by John Conington, first holder of the Corpus Professorship of Latin, but not by BENJAMIN JOWETT, who in 1855 was to become Regius Professor of Greek, and the victim of Christ Church's failure, until 1865, to augment the stipend of £40 a year (doubts over Jowett's religious orthodoxy being one relevant factor). On the other side had stood the influential figure of E.B. PUSEY, Regius Professor of Hebrew from 1828 to 1882, who had maintained, for example, that time devoted by professors to lecturing was time wasted, the proper workshop of the professor being the study. Pusey's real point of issue with Vaughan, however, was to be found in his deep religious beliefs: for, in his opinion, professors subverted religion and morality by seeking novelty rather than truth. Pusey, indeed, had given evidence (of no less than 173 pages) to the Report of the Heads of Houses and Proctors produced in 1853. He expressed there the belief that the German professorial system led to religious infidelity. 'We have', he said, 'abundance of theories about the Professorial system. We have no facts of its having produced any but evil fruits. The training of our youth, the intellectual, moral, religious formation of their minds, their future well-being in this world and the world to come, are not matters upon which to try experiments.' These evils would be brought to Oxford if professors were given charge of instruction. His advocacy was influential at the time. In due course, however, the argument was to be decided in Vaughan's favour, though long after he had resigned his chair in 1858, with decisive results for the course of University history, for the strengthening of its intellectual basis and for the expansion of the professoriate.

To name the most distinguished scholars among those who have held Oxford chairs would be an impossible task, but some of those in the present century whose names are best known are: GILBERT MURRAY, Regius Professor of Greek (1908–36); J.R.R. TOLKIEN, successively Rawlinson and Bosworth Professor of Anglo-Saxon (1925–45) and Merton Professor of English Language and Literature (1945–59); Sir Sarvepalli Radhakrishnan, Professor of Eastern Religions and Ethics (1936–52); Sir Rex Richards, Dr Lee's Professor of Chemistry (1964–74); Sir Edward Abraham, Professor of Chemical Pathology (1964–80); Sir John Beazley Professor of Classical Archaeology and Art (1925–56); Sir Charles Sherrington, Professor of Physiology (1913–35); Sir Alfred (A.J.) Ayer, Wykeham

Professor of Logic (1959–78); LORD DAVID CECIL, Goldsmiths' Professor of English Literature (1948–69); Edgar Wind, Professor of the History of Art (1955–67); SIR CYRIL HINSHELWOOD, Dr Lee's Professor of Chemistry (1937–64); Lord Beloff, Gladstone Professor of Government and Public Administration (1957–74); LORD FLOREY, Professor of Pathology (1935–62); Sir Rudolf Peierls, Wykeham Professor of Physics (1963–74); Lord Dacre of Glanton, Regius Professor of Modern History (1957–80); R.M. Hare, White's Professor of Moral Philosophy (1966–83); Sir Hans Krebs, Professor of Biochemistry (1954–67); LORD CHERWELL, Dr Lee's Professor of Experimental Philosophy (1919–57); Richard Cobb, Professor of Modern History (1973–84); GILBERT RYLE, Waynflete Professor of Metaphysical Philosophy (1945–68); Sir Ronald Syme, Camden Professor of Ancient History (1949–70); DAME HELEN GARDNER, Merton Professor of English Literature (1966–75); Mrs D.M. Hodgkin, Research Professor in Chemical Crystallography (1960–77); R.G. Collingwood, Waynflete Professor of Metaphysical Logic (1935–43); Sir Alister Hardy, Linacre Professor of Zoology (1946–68); and Sir Peter Strawson, Waynflete Professor of Metaphysical Philosophy since 1968.

One professorship has remained untouched by reform. The Professorship of Poetry, founded by Henry Birkhead in 1708, is still tenable for only five (formerly up to ten) years; the stipend is still nominal; and he (or she) is still elected by the votes of CONVOCATION – that is, by all Masters of Arts who present themselves in person to cast their vote. The holders have included Thomas Warton, later Poet Laureate (1718–28), JOHN KEBLE (1831–41), MATTHEW ARNOLD (1857–67), C. Day-Lewis (1951–6), W.H. Auden (1956–61) and Edmund Blunden (1966–8). John Wain was appointed in 1973, Peter Levi in 1984 and Seamus Heaney in 1989.

(*See also* GENERAL BOARD OF THE FACULTIES *and* FACULTIES.)

Chancellor Now the honorific head of the University, elected for life by members of CONVOCATION. The earliest Chancellor of whom we know was Geoffrey de Lucy, who held office before 1216, and the best known of the early Chancellors was ROBERT GROSSETESTE in about 1224. The Chancellor was at first nominated by the Bishop of Lincoln as his deputy or vicar-general; but the Masters, desirous of self-government, sought to assert their independence of the Bishop, gradually acquiring the right to name a man of their choice whose appointment the Bishop then confirmed. There were, however, continuous wrangles between the Masters and the Bishop, Bishop Oliver de Sutton insisting in 1290 that the University had no right to elect but only to nominate a Chancellor. Eventually, after the University had been freed from episcopal control by a papal bull of 1367, the right of election was given to members of Convocation. The Chancellor was normally selected from leading senior graduates and elected by indirect vote (*per modum compromissi*). The first Fellow of a college to be elected was from Merton, Richard de Clyve in 1297. Subsequently Chancellors were often, but not necessarily, chosen from among Senior Fellows; the theologian Thomas Gascoigne, Chancellor in 1444–5, was one exception.

The Chancellor's book contains the first collection of University STATUTES (still in the University's ARCHIVES), the earliest known complete set written soon after 1300. A document of 1427 shows that the insignia of his office included the book of statutes, the University seal and two quires of bulls condemning heresies, together with a brass weights and measures (for grain and liquids), a pair of scales and an anvil and hammer for breaking false measures. The Chancellor had no stipend, but he received certain emoluments, a third of the fines imposed for breaking the peace in the Chancellor's Court (*see* COURTS) and half the profits of the assize of bread and ale, and money from the sale of confiscated arms. The Chancellor was the chief officer of the University, presiding over its assemblies, Convocation and CONGREGATION. He conferred the licence on Bachelors and inceptors. He had substantial judicial powers and could punish offenders by excommunication, imprisonment, expulsion and loss of privileges and fines. He exercised his jurisdiction over all members of the University. In 1244 Henry III gave powers to the Chancellor through his court to hear and decide all suits of scholars. As he was head also of all schools in Oxford, every scholar and master in the town was subject to his jurisdiction. The very wide privileges he enjoyed secured in time almost complete control of the University over the town.

Until the death of Cardinal Pole in 1558 the Chancellor was always an ecclesiastic; ARCHBISHOP SHELDON was the last churchman to hold the office (1667–9). By the late 15th century the Chancellor had, however, become a non-resident magnate. After George Nevill, Archbishop of York, ceased to be Chancellor in 1472, subsequent Chancellors rarely resided in Oxford. Although the Chancellor no longer exercised direct executive power, his influence and the patronage at his disposal remained considerable. Elizabeth I's favourite, the Earl of Leicester, who held the position from 1564 to 1585, was the first Chancellor to nominate the VICE-CHANCELLOR and to use English in writing to the University. After the Restoration real power was vested in the Vice-Chancellor, and the Chancellor's authority became purely formal, being mainly confined to ceremonial occasions, such as presiding over ENCAENIA. By the 18th century he was sometimes installed in office in his own home, representatives of the University waiting on him there, as they did on the Duke of Wellington at Apsley House on 7 February 1834.

Following the death of Harold Macmillan, the EARL OF STOCKTON, an election for a new Chancellor was held in March 1987. The principal candidates were Lord Blake, Provost of The Queen's College, Mr Roy Jenkins and Mr Edward Heath (both Honorary Fellows of Balliol). Of the 40,000 or so Masters of Arts qualified to vote, 8309 did so, by far the highest turn-out recorded. The Conservative vote being split between Mr Heath (2348) and Lord Blake (2674), Mr Jenkins was elected with 3249 votes.

(For a full list of Chancellors *see* Appendix 5.)

Chancellor's Court   *see* COURTS.

Cheney Girls' Grammar School   *see* CENTRAL SCHOOL FOR GIRLS.

Cheney Lane   The old Cheyney Lane was the road to Shotover and Wheatley but under the Mileways

Act of 1771 a turnpike was made through HEADINGTON and Forest Hill which then became the main London and High Wycombe road. It was mentioned in the Enclosure Award of 1805, but the origin of the name is obscure. A certain William Cheyney was MAYOR in King Stephen's reign and was a benefactor of OSENEY ABBEY but it is not thought likely that the lane was named after him. It could mean a lane with a chain at one or both ends. The present MARKET STREET was once called Cheney Lane. Running from the junction of Gipsy Lane and OLD ROAD, Cheney Lane skirts SOUTH PARK and emerges into HEADINGTON ROAD halfway up the hill. Cheney Secondary School is on the north-east, a hostel belonging to the POLYTECHNIC is halfway along, and Granville Court, a large development of flats, is at the south-east end.

Cheney Upper School   *Cheney Lane, Headington.* Cheney Technical School, built in 1954 to the designs of E.G. Chandler, the City Architect, as a mixed school accommodating 450 pupils aged from eleven to eighteen, was a development of the former Secondary Technical School in ST EBBE'S and aimed at 'providing a type of Secondary Education suited to abler children who have a marked practical aptitude', thus standing somewhere between a grammar and a secondary-modern school in its provision of art and craft, technical and commercial as well as GCE courses. In 1959 the Oxford CENTRAL SCHOOL FOR GIRLS moved into buildings designed by E.G. Chandler on an adjacent site in Gipsy Lane, HEADINGTON, and became Cheney Girls' Grammar School. Under comprehensive reorganisation, the two schools merged in 1972–3 to form Cheney Upper School. In 1986 there were 435 boys and 449 girls in the school.

Chequers   *Beaumont Street, Headington Quarry.* An 18th-century village inn with rear garden sunken in a disused quarry. It was extensively altered in 1930 and again in 1979.

Chequers   *131a High Street.* A private house from 1260 until 1434, it was afterwards used by a moneylender, who, in 1460, was conducting his business beneath the sign of the chequer. In 1500 Richard Kent built a tavern, of which oak panelling, a stone fireplace and carved stonework still remain. The earliest reference to the Chequer inn is 1605. By the next century it was used for public exhibitions, such as the fourteen wild animals and large fish shown in 1762. In one of the bars there is a fine example of an English tavern clock of *c*.1760.

Cherwell   Named after the tributary to the river Isis (*see* THAMES), this magazine first appeared on 9 November 1920, edited by George Edinger and with Louis Golding, the future novelist, as its literary editor. The issue contained a short story by Richard Hughes. It was not long before Beverley Nichols, fresh from ISIS, began writing for *Cherwell*. In the magazine's heyday in the 1920s, its eminent contributors included Harold Acton, Christopher Hollis, Peter Quennell, Bryan Guinness, Robert Speaight, Osbert Lancaster, Henry d'Avigdor Goldsmid and Derek Hudson.

No Oxford magazine has had so many different covers; but the most famous and enduring one, originally designed by Evelyn Waugh (who also contributed line-blocks to the paper, but no writing), lasted until the Second World War – a black-and-red design showing University types as puppets. *Cherwell*'s attitude, in contrast to that of *Isis*, was light-hearted, and the imaginary characters dreamed up in the editorial office – Col. Thunderclap-Chutney, Tottie Goldstein, Admiral 'Benbow' Charlton, *et al.* – culminated sensationally in 1933 during the controversy following the Oxford UNION's 'King and Country' debate. A letter written on RANDOLPH HOTEL notepaper and allegedly from 'Dr. Curtius Bohl, Ph.D. Wien' (a *Cherwell* creation), was given pride of place in the *Daily Telegraph* under the banner-heading 'VIENNA REPLIES TO YOUNG OXFORD'.

The magazine fostered many practical jokes and exuberant spectacles. Giles Playfair, editor in 1929, caused a sensation by ascending in a balloon with the celebrated actress Tallulah Bankhead. Michael Barsley, the 1935 editor, effected a *rapprochement* with Cambridge, at a village halfway between the two towns, in defiance of the view of the Master of University College, Sir Michael Sadler, that the provincial universities were more to be favoured. Kenneth Tynan sent out a questionnaire to all colleges asking for details of the sex-life of their students: this caused *Cherwell* to be closed down for the rest of the term.

In succeeding years, before the magazine became a weekly University newspaper with flaring headlines about college scandals, many up-and-coming writers contributed: Marghanita Laski became the first woman editor; the film-writer Paul Dehn graced the editorial chair; John Mortimer, Michael Flanders, William Rees-Mogg, Gerald Kaufman, Tom Driberg, Michael Howard, Gyles Brandreth and Geoffrey Rippon were among the contributors.

(*See also* MAGAZINES.)

Cherwell (river) *see* THAMES.

Cherwell, Frederick Alexander Lindemann, Viscount (*1886–1957*). Born at Baden-Baden, where his American mother was taking the cure, Lindemann was the son of a rich French-Alsatian scientist who had emigrated to Britain. He was educated in Scotland and in Germany, where, in Berlin, he made important contributions to scientific research, demonstrating an extraordinary versatility and developing that haughty manner and those decided opinions for which he later became celebrated. In 1919 he was appointed Dr Lee's Professor of Experimental Philosophy at Oxford. His chair was attached to Wadham College, of which he remained a Fellow until he died, but he preferred to live at Christ Church, where he had also been elected to a studentship. He lived in Meadow Buildings, in spacious rooms which were painted white throughout and furnished hideously. By his appointment to the chair of Experimental Philosophy he became head of the CLARENDON LABORATORY. During the Second World War, 'the Prof.', as he was by then known, became a trusted and influential adviser to the Prime Minister, and was created Baron Cherwell of Oxford in 1941; but in 1945 he returned to Oxford, retiring in 1956, the year in which he became Viscount Cherwell. One-third of the residue of his fortune was left to Wadham, two-thirds to Christ Church.

Cherwell Boat House In 1901, the OXFORD UNIVERSITY BOAT CLUB waterman, Tom Tims, took a lease from St John's College for a landing stage for punts for hire on the upper Cherwell (*see* THAMES) beyond BARDWELL ROAD and built the Cherwell Boat House in 1904, with his initials carved over the centre and those of his daughter, Mrs Sarah Walker, in the foundation stone. She and her husband managed the business and their son, Tom Tims Walker, succeeded them. The separate residence was built in 1908–9.

Pleasure-boating had been introduced on the upper Cherwell twenty years before, and Tims's, as the boat house was called for its first forty years, became a popular place of recreation for the residents of NORTH OXFORD. The Walkers relinquished their third twenty-one-year lease in 1964 and the business was bought by Lieutenant-Commander Perowne, RN (Retd). Perowne set about repairing punts, obtained a wine licence and, with the assistance of his family, established a restaurant. He sold the business in 1968 to Anthony Verdin, an Oxford science graduate.

Verdin secured the freehold of the boat house and with the assistance of Perowne's craftsman, John Mastroddi, re-established the business of boat-building; he is now the only punt-builder in Oxford. (He later established an important separate business of scientific-instrument manufacturing.) The restaurant, while maintaining its modesty, achieved distinction for its excellence – a reputation it has kept over the years (*see* RESTAURANTS). In summer a large, open marquee supplemented its facilities. On the site of the marquee, a new building (with a roof terrace) was erected in 1984 for housing punts.

The Cherwell Boat House has about seventy punts, most of which, during the summer term, are let by block-bookings to colleges. Though the upper Cherwell is comparatively deep and muddy for punting, it is popular because the river is notably beautiful downstream in the University PARKS and upstream is the VICTORIA ARMS, a favourite resort of punters.

(*See also* PUNTING.)

Cherwell Centre *16 Norham Gardens*. A conference centre catering especially for school groups, and for religious and educational conferences. There are nineteen bedrooms. The Holy Child Sisters began educational work in Oxford in 1905 at CHERWELL EDGE, where they had a hostel which was affiliated to the Society of Oxford Home Students, which later became St Anne's College. The Sisters moved from Cherwell Edge to the Cherwell Centre in 1970.

Cherwell Edge *St Cross Road*. Built in 1886–7, on the edge of the SCIENCE AREA and next to the University PARKS, to the designs of J.W. Messenger of the Oxford firm of Pike and Messenger. The most distinguished tenant of the house was JAMES ANTHONY FROUDE, who took it upon his appointment as Regius Professor of Modern History in 1892. He taught and lectured here during his brief tenancy. After his death in 1894 his daughter Margaret continued to live here until 1905, when the house was taken over for use as a convent by the Society of the Holy Child Jesus. In 1908–9 a chapel, designed by Basil Champneys, was added to the south side of the house. The convent also provided lodgings for women undergraduates, mainly from the

Society of Oxford Home Students (*see* ST ANNE'S COLLEGE), for whom a large residential block, also by Basil Champneys, was added to the east side. In 1977 the buildings were occupied by Linacre Collage, which added further extensions and converted the chapel into a library.

Cherwell School *Marston Ferry Road*. It had been intended in the city's development plan to build a new secondary-modern school in NORTH OXFORD in 1948, but until 1961 government policy allowed the building of new secondary schools only to meet the needs of new population and it was not until 1963 that the Cherwell School was opened, with 320 pupils drawn mainly from the five primary schools in North Oxford and from St Barnabas School, JERICHO, which had hitherto retained children to the age of fifteen. In 1973 Cherwell School became a mixed comprehensive, and by 1984 had nearly 700 pupils aged thirteen to eighteen.

Chest *see* UNIVERSITY CHEST.

Chichele, Henry (*c.1362–1443*). Archbishop of Canterbury and benefactor of the University, Chichele was a Fellow of New College from 1387–92. He became Bishop of St David's in 1407 and Archbishop of Canterbury in 1414. Closely involved with the Lancastrian establishment, between 1406 and 1420 he led a number of diplomatic missions to Rome and in connection with the war in France. A firm opponent of Lollardy (*see* LOLLARDS) he was nonetheless from 1421 often in conflict with the papacy. A distinguished ecclesiastical lawyer himself, he saw the need for a clergy educated to serve Church and State, and in 1432 he established the Chichele Loan Chest for the benefit of poor Oxford students. Five years later he gave the land for St Bernard's College, on which St John's College now stands (*see* MONASTIC COLLEGES). In the same year he was buying land to endow and accommodate his most substantial gift to Oxford – All Souls College – established in 1438 (with King Henry VI as co-founder) as a Lancastrian chantry for a Warden and forty graduate Fellows who were also to study for degrees in the higher Faculties of Theology and Law. One of his last acts was to approve the college statutes in their final form on 2 April 1443.

Christ Church The thirteenth of the present Oxford colleges to be founded. The foundation was a complicated process, in which Henry VIII took advantage of the princely munificence of a great clerical subject. CARDINAL THOMAS WOLSEY obtained a Bull from the Pope in 1524 for the dissolution of the Augustinian ST FRIDESWIDE'S PRIORY in the south-east quadrant of the city; the area round the priory was then occupied by houses, hospitia, churches, the Oxford Jewry, and Canterbury College (the house in Oxford of the monks of Christ Church, Canterbury – *see* MONASTIC COLLEGES). Demolition began in 1525, but in the priory church affected only the westernmost bays. Construction of the new Cardinal's College, as it was originally called, was on a grand scale but was not complete by the time of Wolsey's fall from power in 1529. Three sides of the Great Quadrangle were virtually finished, but only the foundations of the chapel which Wolsey intended for its north side were visible, and the plan and elevation of the chapel are

alike unknown. The hall and kitchen were complete by 1529 and have not been fundamentally altered since. The hall was the work of two of the greatest craftsmen of the time: the mason Thomas Redman and the glazier James Nicholson. Wolsey laid down a constitution for his new college of eight canons, a schoolmaster and choirboys, but he left behind neither a library nor a new residence for the head of his college, and he created no link between his college and any particular school.

Henry VIII soon took over the ̄ fabric and endowments of Wolsey's foundation, which he then designated King Henry VIII's College. It led an undistinguished life until 1546, when Henry designated the former priory church as CHRIST CHURCH CATHEDRAL of the new Henrician diocese of Oxford, and as the chapel of the new college of Christ Church. Henry also added further endowments to those of Cardinal College, but gave his new and unique foundation no statutes.

Under Edward VI, Mary I and Elizabeth I, Christ Church shared in the vicissitudes of ecclesiastical faction; under Edward, the continental reformer Peter Martyr Vermigli was nominated to the Regius Chair of Divinity, and took up residence with his wife, both departing with the accession of Mary. In 1561 Elizabeth I supplied the link with a school, hitherto lacking, by setting aside certain awards from Westminster School to be tenable at Christ Church (others were to be taken up at her father's foundation of Trinity College, Cambridge).

In the first century of its existence, the most notable men to attend Christ Church were probably the poet Sir Philip Sidney (1566); Henry Bennet, later Earl of Arlington (1635); the dramatist William Gager; and Richard Hakluyt, the historian of English exploration (1571). Appointments to the deanery and to the

The stairs to the hall of Christ Church were built in 1805 by James Wyatt. The delicate fan tracery dates from c.1640.

canonries were used by the Crown to reward promising churchmen such as Tobie Matthew (Dean 1576), later Archbishop of York. Elizabeth I twice and James I once visited the college during progresses to Oxford. During the CIVIL WAR, Charles I made Christ Church his capital; he himself resided in the deanery, his Parliament assembled in the hall, his privy council met in the canonical lodgings west of the hall, and the cathedral was the scene of the weddings and funerals of members of the Court. The college and the Dean paid heavily for these favours: after Charles's death, the Dean, Samuel Fell, lost his position, and his wife and children were forcibly removed from the deanery by the parliamentary VISITORS, who purged Christ Church of delinquents. Samuel Fell was succeeded as Dean by the Presbyterian Edward Reynolds, and the Independent John Owen, Oliver Cromwell's protégé. Admissions declined under Owen, who put in hand no new building; but Christ Church owed to Cromwell the fact that its lands were not taken away.

Soon after the Restoration, JOHN FELL, who as a boy had been ejected from the deanery twelve years earlier, himself became Dean; he ruled Christ Church firmly, closely supervising the work and conduct of undergraduates, and was the only man who (from 1676) ever combined the positions of Dean and Bishop. He resolved to make Christ Church a place of resort for the governing classes and a prop of the monarchy; among the young men who came thither was James Butler, grandson of the great royalist survivor the 1st Duke of Ormonde. Fell and his canons showed themselves subservient to the monarchy's every wish, in 1684 complying with a royal mandate for the expulsion of John Locke, probably the most distinguished thinker ever to enter Christ Church. John Fell's death in 1686 gave James II the opportunity for an act of folly – the nomination as Dean of the Catholic John Massey. Admissions declined again, as in the 1650s; but the revolution allowed the appointment in 1689 of HENRY ALDRICH, Christ Church's most convivial Dean. Admissions increased steadily, and the number and status of undergraduates required the reconstruction of the buildings of the former Peckwater Inn; Peckwater Quadrangle with its nine staircases was opened in 1707, Staircase IX being assigned to a canonical stall. The quadrangle was named after a mediaeval Oxford family, one of whose members, Robert Peckwater, gave Peckwater Inn to St Frideswide's Priory.

The harmony, musical and metaphorical, which marked Christ Church during the reign of the bonhomous Aldrich disappeared with the arrival of his quarrelsome successor, the Tory (or Jacobite) Francis Atterbury, appointed in 1711. Atterbury and his successors, who from 1724 to 1756 had not been Christ Church undergraduates, held office for relatively short periods; the greatest work carried out in the first part of the 18th century was the construction of the New Library, begun in 1717. A new library had become necessary to house the great collections of books left by successive benefactors – Dean Aldrich, Dr Stratford, the Earl of Orrery, and Archbishop Wake. The future Dean Gregory, as canon–treasurer, supervised the internal decoration of the New Library in the 1750s, and was also responsible for a change in the fenestration of the hall, where the 16th-century glass was replaced, except in the west window, by glass of 18th-century plainness.

The hall already housed the great collection of portraits of Deans and other college members which made, and make, it a portrait gallery of rare importance (see PORTRAITS). The New Library was still incomplete when problems of storage and display once more became urgent with the bequest by General John Guise (d.1765), once an officer in Marlborough's army, who left to the House (see Glossary) the collection of remarkable drawings which he had acquired, as well as Old Masters of various Italian schools (see CHRIST CHURCH PICTURE GALLERY). This vast bequest (contested by the Guise family) was housed in the ground floor of the New Library, which was walled and fenestrated to accommodate it. The completion of the New Library was followed by the conversion to rooms of the Old Library, originally the refectory of St Frideswide's Priory. The other new residential building of the 18th century was Canterbury Quadrangle, which replaced the buildings of the former Canterbury College and was built by the munificence of Richard Robinson, Archbishop of Armagh, later Lord Rokeby. Another considerable benefactor was Dr Matthew Lee, by whose aid was built the Christ Church Anatomy School (1766–7), now usually known as the Lee Building.

The deanery was held with an inferior bishopric until 1768, when William Markham became Dean. Markham had been headmaster of Westminster, and for over a century the connection between Westminster School and the deanery of Christ Church was almost continuous. Markham and his successor Bagot were singled out for honourable mention by Gibbon in 1791 as 'the late Deans' under whom at Christ Church 'learning has been made a duty, a pleasure, and even a fashion, and several young gentlemen do honour to the College in which they have been educated.' But it was Bagot's successor CYRIL JACKSON (1783–1809) who created a legend. The son of a provincial doctor, he loved a lord, and loved to make everyone – whether lord or commoner – work 'like a tiger', as he enjoined the future Prime Minister Sir Robert Peel. Christ Church had already begun to produce MPs in quantity, and Prime Ministers (sixteen between George Grenville in 1762 and Sir Alec Douglas-Home in 1963) naturally followed. The tenure of the premiership of many was brief, though Lord Bath's two days in February 1746 were exceptional; but Lord Liverpool held office for fifteen years and WILLIAM GLADSTONE for fourteen. Among the products of Jackson's Christ Church came a succession of Governors-General, later Viceroys, of India; the first was the Marquis Wellesley, Governor-General from 1797 to 1805, and the last Lord Halifax, Viceroy from 1925–31.

The authoritarian Jackson was seconded by able censors (see Glossary) and tutors, who imitated his gait and dress; but he followed with interest the careers of members, which he furthered through influence over Christ Church men in power. He himself built nothing, but it was in his last year that funds began to be set aside for new buildings to replace the now decaying Fell's Buildings and Chaplains' Quadrangle.

Jackson was one of the prime movers in the creation of a new University examination system at Oxford, and in its early years members of Christ Church took many first-class degrees. This continued under his successors, C.H. Hall (1809–24) and Samuel Smith (1824–31), both Old Westminsters; but THOMAS

J.M.W. Turner's Inside View of the Hall of Christ Church, *one of the largest mediaeval college halls in Oxford, showing the hammerbeam roof and portraits of college members.*

GAISFORD (1831–55), though personally a distinguished Greek scholar and an important curator of the BODLEIAN LIBRARY, set little store by the new University system, having faith rather in college examinations and the college's showing in the class lists became undistinguished. In part this was also a result of a decline in the quality of Westminster School, from which came many Christ Church undergraduates, some of whom stayed on to become tutors.

Gaisford had no time for reform of any kind, but the reformers of the 1830s produced an Act of Parliament which was to have disruptive effects on Christ Church in the time of his successor H.G. LIDDELL (1855–91), who was himself a Carthusian but came from the headship of Westminster: two of the canonries were abolished and all save one of the remaining six were attached to professorships. The body of Students (*see* Glossary), as yet all former undergraduates of Christ Church, found themselves excluded from appointment to canonries which were consequently filled to a greater degree than previously by 'squills' – that is, by those who had never been undergraduates at Christ Church. This made the monopoly of the government of Christ Church by the Dean and canons harder to bear. An agitation begun in 1863 led in 1867 to the Christ Church (Oxford) Act which vested that government in the Dean, canons and students; Liddell himself played little creative part in this result, which was the achievement of T.J. Prout, a Westminster Student and ex-censor with a mountaineer's perseverance.

Liddell cared more for buildings than for government, and in his first years he improved the long-neglected interior of the cathedral. In 1862–5 he also oversaw the construction of Meadow Buildings, a Venetian Gothic construction by T.N. Deane, an associate of JOHN RUSKIN whom the Dean admired. In the 1870s there followed further internal changes in the cathedral necessitating the construction of a belfry tower, which was eventually erected at the east end of the hall.

The belfry was among the many Oxford targets for the wit of the best-known tutor of Liddell's day, C.L. DODGSON, the friend of the Dean's daughter Alice and author of *Alice's Adventures in Wonderland* and *Through the Looking-glass and What Alice Found There* (*see* ALICE). Dodgson found his tutorial work unrewarding; Liddell himself was disappointed in the failure of the House to show to more advantage in the class lists; but he was a good chairman of the new governing body and a successful Dean who left an enduring mark on both college and cathedral. In his day the old system of lecture/classes approached its end, and the tutors of the House covered a wide range of subjects, including the sciences, tuition in Classics being especially successful. Dean Strong (1901–20) was the first Dean to take an active interest in the cathedral choir, which under him began its ascent towards ever higher standards.

Since the Second World War, increases in the number of undergraduates and the decline in the availability of lodgings for them in the city of Oxford have led Christ Church, like other colleges, to erect new residential buildings. Christ Church Picture Gallery (1968) in the Dean's garden has enabled the New Library to be devoted entirely to housing books and readers; there is also a new law library (1976) and a new music room. Additional rooms have been created in Meadow Buildings, in Tom Quad north of the main gate, and to a lesser extent in Peckwater Quadrangle. Works of refurbishment include the redecoration of the first floor of the library (1965) and the refenestration of the hall (1983).

Of the various buildings which compose the architecture of Christ Church, the oldest is the 12th-century collegiate cathedral, originally the conventual church of St Frideswide's Priory. Almost as ancient as the cathedral, and attached to its southern extremity, is the chapter house, part Norman but mainly 13th century, its interior stone walls now clad in a protective covering suggestive of tiles. It contains the diocesan treasury and a place for the display of diocesan silver and for the sale of brochures and postcards. The flanking cloister was rebuilt in about 1499, and the former monastic refectory, constituting its southern boundary, later housed the college library until its removal to the New Library in the 18th century. This nucleus of ancient priory buildings, much restored, is all that escaped demolition when, in 1525, Wolsey set about his ambitious scheme for Cardinal College.

His plan centred upon the great Gothic quadrangle known as Tom Quad, which, measuring 264 by 261 feet, is the largest in Oxford. By 1529, the year of Wolsey's downfall, the south side featuring the Great Hall was finished, and the east and west ranges were well advanced. But it was not until the 1660s that the foundations laid on the north side for Wolsey's college chapel were filled with two-storeyed residences for canons; these were built uniform in appearance with the earlier ranges, which have small doorways with decorated spandrels, and alternating one- and two-

Wren's Tom Tower at Christ Church as it appeared at the beginning of the 19th century.

light windows. At the same time, the terrace was laid out and, in 1670, the central circular basin, 40 feet in diameter, was installed as a reservoir for the college. A representation of Mercury, which had replaced the original fountain in 1695, was removed in 1817 and not until 1928 was the present statue, a lead copy of Giovanni da Bologna's *Mercury*, placed on a pedestal designed by Lutyens. The long formal façade has protruding bays at either end, and increases in height towards the south where it takes up the falling ground. The balustrading here dates from the 17th century, as does Tom Tower, built in 1681–2 above Wolsey's great gateway by CHRISTOPHER WREN. 'I resolved it ought to be Gothic to agree with the Founder's work,' Wren wrote in 1681, and his ogee-capped tower blends convincingly with the early 16th-century masonry. It houses GREAT TOM, the enormous bell which, cast in 1680, replaced the original bell from OSENEY ABBEY. Entrance is through the original door, and in the fan-vaulted ceiling of the gateway, which is flanked by two complex Perpendicular turrets, are forty-eight coats of arms. They commemorate some of the distinguished college benefactors and include those of Wolsey, Henry VIII and Charles II (*see* HERALDRY). In a central niche above the portal is a statue of Wolsey, sculpted in 1719 by Francis Bird and erected here in 1872; and in a corresponding niche on the east side of the tower is an image of Queen Anne by an unknown sculptor, which was set up here in 1706 by Robert Harley, Earl of Oxford. Within the quadrangle, the battlements adorning the ranges were installed in the 1860s by Bodley & Garner, who also added the pinnacles to the hall. This, one of the largest halls in Oxford, is approached up a wide stairway enhanced by the most delicate fan tracery dating from about 1640. The stairs themselves were built in 1805 by James Wyatt and lead to an antechamber containing a statue of Dean Jackson, sculpted in 1820 by Chantrey. The hall is dominated by a great hammerbeam roof, richly carved and gilded and among the notable portraits upon its panelled walls are those of Lewis Carroll (*see* CHARLES LUTWIDGE DODGSON) and JOHN WESLEY, which hang near the entrance (*see* PORTRAITS). The kitchen south of the hall is contemporary with it, but the adjacent buttery was built in 1722 by William Townesend (*see* TOWNESENDS). West of the kitchen is Dr Lee's Gallery, constructed by HENRY KEENE in 1766–7 as the Anatomy School, but now housing Senior Common Rooms. At the southernmost extremity of the college, overlooking the Broad Walk, lies Meadow Buildings, a Gothic range designed in 1863 by T.N. Deane, which displays a tower with steeply stepped gables and a carved portal to the central archway.

At the south-east corner of Tom Quad is the bell-tower built between 1876–9 by Bodley & Garner, who also erected the upper stage of Fell Tower at the north-east corner. This exit provides access to Killcanon, built between 1669 and 1673, and Peckwater Quad. This last was designed by Henry Aldrich in the grand classical manner and constructed between 1705 and 1714. Each of its three sides has fifteen bays, rusticated to first-floor level with huge pilasters above. The central five bays on each side have giant columns and are topped by an enormous pediment. The New Library, which forms the fourth and southern side, was not completed until 1772, although work on it started in 1717. It is a

Cooks at work in the kitchen at Christ Church, c.1813.

monumental baroque building in white and buff-coloured stone, designed by GEORGE CLARKE of All Souls and completely refaced in 1960–2 in Portland and Clipsham stone (*see* STONE). The façade is of seven bays divided by vast smooth Corinthian columns rising from square supports. The ground-floor windows are round-headed; those of the upper storey have straight heads under alternating triangular and segmental pediments. Inside, the upper gallery is strikingly beautiful, with an exquisite stucco ceiling by Thomas Roberts and bookcases in Norwegian oak carved in 1756–63 by G. Shakespear and J. Phillips. The Guise bequest of paintings, originally housed on the ground floor, now hangs, together with other benefactions, in a modern picture gallery. This ingeniously planned building was designed by Powell & Moya in 1964–7 and, faced with coursed rubble, stands unobtrusively at the east end of the deanery garden. Access to it is through Canterbury Quad, completed in 1783 by James Wyatt in a style reminiscent of Peckwater but on a much more modest scale (*see* CHRIST CHURCH PICTURE GALLERY). In total contrast to the 18th-century buildings is the Blue Boar Quad, completed in 1969, again to the designs of Powell & Moya. It consists of a number of identical units separated by narrow bays and featuring square buttresses of Portland stone. The most recent addition to the college is St Aldate's Quad, completed in 1986. It stands on the opposite side of ST ALDATE'S and has been constructed under the supervision of J.G. Fryman of the Architects Design Partnership. It is an attractive two-storey development in buff-coloured brick under slate roofing, with brown timber panels in the upper storey which match the woodwork of the doors and windows.

The Memorial Garden, laid out in 1926 in memory of those members of the House who died in the First World War, is open daily to the public.

After much debate, women were first admitted to Christ Church as undergraduates in 1980. Graduates of the House have increasingly taken up careers in the city of London, but in the House of Commons elected in 1983 there were still more members of Christ Church than of any other Oxbridge college. Distinguished members of the college are legion and include names celebrated in almost every walk of life, except sainthood. But this exception, as Lord Dacre of Glanton (H.R. Trevor-Roper, Student of Christ

Church 1946–57) has pointed out, is 'of course a mere accident of chronology: saints were not made in England after the foundation of Christ Church'.

The corporate title is The Dean and Chapter of the Cathedral Church of Christ in Oxford of the Foundation of King Henry the Eighth.

(Thompson, Rev. Henry L., *Christ Church*, London, 1900; Trevor-Roper, Hugh, *Christ Church, Oxford*, second edition, Oxford, 1973; Hiscock, W.J., *A Christ Church Miscellany*, Oxford, 1946; Bill, E.G.W., and Mason, J.F.A., *Christ Church and Reform*, Oxford, 1970; Bill, E.G.W., *Education at Christ Church, Oxford, 1660–1800*, Oxford, 1987.)

Christ Church Cathedral Unique in being at once a college chapel and the mother church of a diocese, the Cathedral Church of Christ in Oxford is the smallest cathedral in England though the diocese of Oxford is the largest in the country. Domesday Book refers to the canons of ST FRIDESWIDE'S PRIORY, who, in 1122, were required by Henry I to accept the discipline of the Augustinian rule. On this condition they were given a charter and one of the King's chaplains was appointed their first Prior. Some forty years later, in the time of the second Prior, Robert of Cricklade, construction of the present church began; and the sanctuary, choir, the nave and aisled transepts were probably all completed by the end of the 12th century or within the first decade of the 13th.

The building was small but an illusion of height was imparted to it by the double Norman arches on either side of the nave, the main arches rising from the capitals sustaining an upper triforium and lower arches between the pillars supporting a lower triforium. Although learned rather than rich, the canons of the priory continued to improve and enlarge the church in the 13th and 14th centuries, building the spire, one of the oldest in England, adding a Lady Chapel and a chapter house with a lovely five-lancet east window, and, to the north of the Lady Chapel, constructing the Latin Chapel where Latin prayers were said and where the Regius Professor of Divinity lectured in Latin until the mid-19th century. This chapel was completed in about 1320 and dedicated to St Catherine of Alexandra, scenes from whose life are depicted in the east window of the south choir aisle, now the Memorial Chapel of the Oxfordshire and Buckinghamshire Light Infantry. The beautiful vaulted roof of the choir, with its carved bosses and pendants, the stone masterpiece of the building, was apparently finished in about 1500 and may have been the work of William Orchard, who was responsible for the vaulting in the DIVINITY SCHOOL and who was buried in the cathedral in 1504.

At this time Oxford was in the diocese of Lincoln but in 1542 the diocese of Oxford was created, and Robert King, ABBOT OF OSENEY, became the first BISHOP OF OXFORD, his cathedral church being the church of OSENEY ABBEY. In 1545, however, both the chapter of St Frideswide's and that of Oseney were suppressed and replaced by a single corporation of a Dean and eight canons at St Frideswide's, which was now granted the status of a cathedral church, the bishop's throne, or cathedra, being brought here from Oseney.

Twenty-two years before this, in 1523, CARDINAL THOMAS WOLSEY had decided to found a college at Oxford. In 1524 he sought and obtained permission

J.M.W. Turner's watercolour of Christ Church Cathedral from the Dean's Garden, c.1795.

from the Pope to dissolve the priory of St Frideswide, together with other smaller religious houses, and to use the money thus obtained to erect the proposed Cardinal College. Building operations began with the demolition of the three western bays of the nave and preliminary work on a covered cloister, whose unfinished stonework can still be seen in the great quadrangle of the college. But the work was soon halted with the Cardinal's fall from power, and his foundation became known as King Henry VIII's College (*see* CHRIST CHURCH).

The fabric of the cathedral was restored in the 1850s and, much more extensively, by SIR GEORGE GILBERT SCOTT in 1870–6 at a cost of £24,000. Scott's work included the reconstruction of the east end of the sanctuary and the insertion of the rose window and the two round-headed windows in an attempt to re-create the original appearance of the east wall. The stalls in the choir and the splendid iron screen are also Scott's work.

The mediaeval glass in the east window of the small chapel of St Lucy, which was itself built in about 1330, depicts the martyrdom of St Thomas Becket – an unusual survival, since Henry VIII ordered that all memorials to Becket should be destroyed. Here the head only was removed and replaced with plain glass. Also depicted in this window are Christ in Glory, St Martin, St Augustine, St Blaise and St Wilfrid of York holding the head of Oswald, the Christian King of Northumbria who was killed in battle in AD 642. There is further mediaeval glass in three of the four windows on the north side of the Lady Chapel; the east window

here depicts scenes in the life of St Frideswide. The early 17th-century glass at the western end of the north nave aisle, representing the city of Nineveh with Jonah sheltering under a gourd, is by Abraham van Linge, examples of whose work can also be seen in the windows of the north transept and in the east window of St Lucy's Chapel. The glass in the westernmost window on the south side of the Regimental Chapel of St Michael is also early 17th century; it shows Robert King and the tower and a gable end of Oseney Abbey, the oldest surviving representation of the abbey ruins. The windows in the east wall of the Lady Chapel, as well as those in the east wall of the Latin Chapel, in the east wall of the north choir aisle and in the east wall of the south choir aisle were all designed by EDWARD BURNE-JONES. All were executed by Morris and Co. with the exception of that in the Latin Chapel, which was glazed by Powell and Sons in 1859 before WILLIAM MORRIS established his firm in 1861. (*See also* STAINED GLASS.)

Interesting tombs in the cathedral include those of Bishop King in the Regimental Chapel in Purbeck marble; James Zouch (*d.*1503), a canon of the priory, in the north transept below a 16th-century window; and, in the bays between the Latin Chapel and the Lady Chapel, those of an early 14th-century prior, perhaps Alexander Sutton; Elizabeth, wife of Sir William Montacute (*d.*1354), who gave part of CHRIST CHURCH MEADOW to the canons as a chantry endowment; and an early 15th-century recumbent effigy, once supposed to be of Sir George Nowers. Monuments also worthy of remark are of Leopold,

Duke of Albany, by F.J. Williamson (1884); William Goodwin (Dean 1611–20); Robert Burton, author of *The Anatomy of Melancholy*, who came to Christ Church in 1599; Richard Gardiner, installed as a canon in 1629; Viscount Grandison by Jasper Latham (*c*.1670); John Banks by John and Henry Stone (1654); DEAN HENRY ALDRICH by Sir Henry Cheere (1732); Bishop Berkeley (*d*.1753); DR JOHN FELL (*d*.1686); and James Narborough (*d*.1707) by William Townesend. In the Regimental Chapel there is also a bust of EDWARD BOUVERIE PUSEY, who was buried in the cathedral in 1882. In the chapel of St Lucy and the adjoining transept are memorials to soldiers and politicians who died in Oxford when the city was the royalist capital during the CIVIL WAR.

Among the distinguished pieces of furniture in the cathedral may be mentioned the Jacobean pulpit and sounding board, and the throne of the VICE-CHANCELLOR, which is also Jacobean. The reredos is by G.F. BODLEY, who was also responsible for the west porch with its twin entrance, 1872–3. The watching loft in the Lady Chapel, the upper part of which served to watch the St Frideswide's Shrine, is of *c*.1500. The organ, built by Father Bernhard Smith in about 1680, originally stood on a screen under the central tower. Rebuilt in 1848, it was removed to the south transept where it was placed over the choir vestry. After being again rebuilt in 1884, it was removed to its present position and reconstructed in 1922 by Harrison and Harrison, who retained its fine case of 17th-century design. It was again reconstructed, by the Austrian firm of Rieger Orgelbau, in 1979. Organists have included John Taverner (1526–30), the composer of motets and masses, who was accused by Wolsey of heresy but released 'being but a musitian'; William Crotch who became Professor of Music in Oxford in 1797; and Sir Thomas Armstrong, Choragus of the University in 1937–54 (*see* MUSIC).

The cathedral PLATE is displayed on the high altar at the time of great festivals. It includes two chalices with paten covers, two flagons, two candlesticks and an alms dish, all presented by Dean Fell and the chapter in 1660–1; and a chalice and cover, paten and alms dish by John Chartier, 1699–1700.

As well as constituting the cathedral chapter, the Dean and canons, together with the Students of Christ Church, form the governing body of the college. Four of the canons are theological professors in the University (*see* CHAIRS) and one is the Archdeacon of Oxford. There are also twenty-four honorary canons.

(*See also* BISHOPS OF OXFORD (APPENDIX I), CHRIST CHURCH, ST FRIDESWIDE and ST FRIDESWIDE'S PRIORY.)

(Watson, E.W., *The Cathedral Church of Christ in Oxford*, 1935; Warner, S.A., *Oxford Cathedral*, London, 1924.)

Christ Church Cathedral School *1 and 3 Brewer Street*. Established in 1546 for the free education of eight (later fourteen) boy-choristers on King Henry VIII's foundation of Christ Church, and with nineteen fee-paying pupils. In 1867 some thirty boys up to the age of fifteen continued to be given a grammar-school education in the vaults below Christ Church hall, and then in a schoolroom south of the BROAD WALK into ST ALDATE'S. The first boarding-house was established at No. 1, BREWER STREET, where the headmaster has a flat at present; and in 1892 a purpose-built main school building, designed by

H.W. Moore, was erected at 3 Brewer Street. In 1935 a classroom building was added to the eastern side of the school playground; this area occupies the site of former premises of a horse-cab business, the southern wall of which still stands and separates the playground from the Newman Hall of the CATHOLIC CHAPLAINCY. The western side is bounded by CAMPION HALL. The school's sports field is in MERTON FIELD. Today there are sixteen boy-choristers, the school – independent and fee-paying – numbering thirty boarding and seventy day boys between the ages of seven and thirteen. Some forty bursaries are provided for boy-choristers to sing at services in Christ Church, Exeter and Worcester Colleges. Among well-known former pupils are the composer William Walton and the writer James (later Jan) Morris. Miss Dorothy Sayers was born in Oxford, the daughter of the Rev. Henry Sayers, a headmaster of Christ Church School from 1884 to 1897.

Christ Church Meadow A field in the heart of Oxford preserved by Christ Church as an ancient meadow. It is still grazed by cattle and provides a beautiful rural setting for the buildings of Christ Church and Merton. In 1346 its area was stated to be 46 acres. Part of the land now forming the meadow was given by Lady Montacute to maintain her chantry in the Lady Chapel at ST FRIDESWIDE'S PRIORY. The priory became part of Cardinal College, subsequently Christ Church, after the Dissolution of the Monasteries. Christ Church regards ownership of the meadow as a trust and over the years has fought hard to defend it against new roads or other encroachments.

The meadow has always had a tendency to flood and there is a print of people skating on it in 1879. The walk round the meadow has been enjoyed by generations of Oxford residents and visitors. Faber, in his *Oxford Apostles* (1954), gives this picture of the Rev. RICHARD WHATELEY, Principal of ST ALBAN HALL in the 1820s: 'Timid dons shuddered as they saw the great man in his rough clothes, striding with huge steps round Christ Church Meadow, accompanied by a horde of dogs, tossing sticks and stones for their amusement, and shouting logic to some younger companion.'

A walk round the meadow, following the path, can start at Christ Church War Memorial Garden, which is entered from ST ALDATE'S. Laid into the paving at the entrance by the wrought-iron gates is a sword with the inscription from John Bunyan's *Pilgrim's Progress*, 'My sword I give to him that shall succeed me in my pilgrimage.' The garden was laid out in 1925, near to where the TRILL MILL STREAM emerges. The Poplar Walk on the right leads to the THAMES and was planted by DEAN LIDDELL, the father of ALICE, in 1872. The walk continues along the banks of the River Cherwell (*see* THAMES) to BROAD WALK. At the entrance from ROSE LANE was a noticeboard with the inscription:

CHRIST CHURCH MEADOW

The Meadow Keepers and Constables are hereby instructed to prevent the entrance into the Meadow of all beggars, all persons in ragged or very dirty clothes, persons of improper character or who are not decent in appearance and behaviour; and to prevent indecent, rude or disorderly conduct of every description.

Christ Church and Christ Church Meadow seen from across the Cherwell. An engraving after a watercolour by J.M.W. Turner.

To allow no handcarts, wheelbarrows, bath-chairs or perambulators (unless they have previous permission from the Very Reverend the Dean): no hawkers or persons carrying parcels or bundles so as to obstruct the walks.

To prevent the flying of kites, throwing stones, throwing balls, bowling hoops, shooting arrows, firing guns or pistols or playing games attended with danger or inconvenience to passers-by: also fishing in the waters, catching birds, or bird-nesting.

To prevent all persons cutting names on, breaking or injuring the seats, shrubs, plants, trees or turf.

To prevent the fastening of boats or rafts to the iron palisading or river wall, and to prevent encroachments of every kind by the river-side.

The notice has now disintegrated, but there is a similar one on the wall inside the cobbled entrance to the college from St Aldate's.

After the abandonment of Thomas Sharp's plan for a new road along the line of Broad Walk, set out in his report OXFORD REPLANNED, various schemes were put forward for a road across the meadow as a relief road for the HIGH STREET. These aroused a fierce controversy, which raged throughout the 1950s and 1960s. In 1949 the Oxford Chamber of Trade (now the Chamber of Commerce) presented to the City Council *A Plan for the Development of the City of Oxford* by F.J. Minns: in this the Sharp Plan was criticised and a new road running across the meadow was proposed, to be called 'Cathedral Mall'. After a series of traffic surveys, development plans and public inquiries, in 1960 the City Council asked the Minister of Housing and Local Government to conduct an inquiry-at-large into Oxford's road problem. This

was carried out by Sir Frederick Armer, and resulted in the Minister favouring another road across the meadow. The proposal was described by the VICE-CHANCELLOR as 'an act of vandalism'. G.A. Jellicoe, the consultant landscape architect, proposed a sunken road in order to reduce the effect of traffic noise and the visual impact of a road across the meadow. In January 1965 an inquiry into the Oxford Development Plan Review was conducted by A.E. Rochard-Thomas. Many eminent Oxford persons gave evidence, including SIR BASIL BLACKWELL, who described the meadow in the words of MATTHEW ARNOLD as 'one of the last enchantments of the Middle Ages'. The case against the road was stated by Professor C.D. Buchanan (later Sir Colin Buchanan), a past-president of the Town Planning Institute, who said that in his opinion 'the Meadow in its present form and in its entirety constitutes an asset to Oxford of the most remarkable kind. I doubt whether there is another city in the world, still less a city which is a great seat of learning, which provides almost in its centre a comparable scene of pastoral remoteness and simplicity, isolated from motor traffic. Cambridge has nothing to equal this. It is a quite different kind of amenity from anything the University Parks can offer, for they are largely devoted to playing fields. Increasingly these days anyone in search of rural quietude has to go further and further from the cities to find what he seeks, usually having to use motor transport into the bargain. But here, in the heart of Oxford, it is possible to walk straight into such surroundings in a matter of minutes from the busiest part of the city, and to find them on a noble scale. It is not a matter of a minor open space but of a splendid open area with long vistas and wide skies. It is the quiet of the place and the opportunity it provides for contemplation that I would rate most highly. To walk through the Memorial Gardens from St. Aldate's, down the New Walk to the river, round the southern end of the Meadow with its still unmarred views northwards to the towers and spires, then up the placid reach of the Cherwell with its reflections of Magdalen Tower and the glimpses of Magdalen College School cricket field through the trees, and then to reach High Stret either past the Botanic Garden or via the sunny wall of Deadman's Walk and along Merton Grove and Magpie Lane – this is to experience *rus in urbe* at its very best. It is a circuit of singular charm, about a mile and a quarter of easy, level walking, without a jarring feature of any kind whatsoever. This is a rare thing to find in English towns today, and it is the kind of thing which will become more valuable as time goes on. There are no material changes that I would wish to make to the Meadow – the sedgy fields, the few cattle, the rivers, the winding footpaths, the more formal avenues of trees – these all seem to me to form a most felicitous combination to be as zealously safeguarded as any of the more famous features of Oxford.' The inspector's report was published in January 1966 and came out strongly against the proposed road: the meadow was given a reprieve.

Christ Church Picture Gallery In 1764 Christ Church received a splendid benefaction: a collection of 257 paintings and 1734 drawings, the bequest of an old member, General John Guise. Born in Gloucestershire, the General had taken a BA at Christ Church in 1702, had joined the army and fought in Flanders under Marlborough and in the Scottish campaign of 1745. He was a 'great lover of painting', having lived long on the Continent, especially in Italy, collecting pictures and acting as art adviser to Frederick, Prince of Wales.

The gift aroused controversy between Guise's relatives and Christ Church, leading to a lawsuit in Chancery before Christ Church received the full bequest. It also necessitated the conversion of what was to have been an open piazza below the college library into a picture gallery. Henry Keene, the architect who had designed and built the Anatomy School at Christ Church in 1766–7, turned the arches into windows and built six compartments separated by arched walls to house the paintings.

Between 1770 and 1773, £450 was paid to a German picture restorer known as 'Old Bonus', who lived in ORIEL SQUARE, to clean the paintings. He 'profusely applied strong spirit, varnishes, macguilp and actual bodily scrubbing without remorse', causing severe damage to the pictures, which is not entirely eliminated even now.

From 1828 to 1834 another remarkable collection of thirty-seven 14th–15th-century Italian, mainly Florentine, paintings was bequeathed by William Fox-Strangways, 4th Earl of Ilchester, collected when he had been secretary of legation in Florence. In 1897 the Misses Landor and Duke gave twenty-six paintings which had belonged to their great-uncle, and friend of Fox-Strangways, Walter Savage Landor, who had also been in Florence in the 1820s. Pictures were donated by other benefactors too, notably Canon Stratford, Lord Frederick Campbell and Dr Vansittart.

The collections were housed in the lower part of the old library until 1964 when, through the generosity of

Charles, now Lord Forte, the architects Powell and Moya built a modern L-shaped gallery in the east corner of the Deanery garden, supposedly one of the settings of *Alice's Adventures in Wonderland*.

The Guise collection still makes up the main body of the paintings representing the 'taste among the cognoscenti of the period during which it was formed', though also revealing the catholicity of the donors in drawings by Claude and Poussin, and three sketches by Van Dyck, including the virile *Soldier on Horseback*. Outstanding among the paintings, alongside works by Titian, Tintoretto and Paolo Veronese, are Annibale Carracci's *Butcher's Shop*, representing various members of the Carracci family and painted to injure the pride of the artist's brother, Lodovico, who tried to conceal his lowly background; Strozzi's full-blooded *Judith with the Head of Holofernes*; two Flemish portraits found in the old buttery by Horace Walpole in 1760, first thought to be Holbeins but now known to be by Jan Scorel; and a beautiful fragment of the *Lamentation of the Dead Christ*, representing the Virgin and St John, by Van der Goes.

Visitors coming to see the Guise pictures in the 19th century were guided by the library janitor and charwoman, improbably named Mrs Showell. Nowadays, though all the pictures are usually on display, most of the drawings are kept in storage with only a few available for viewing at one time. Various short-term exhibitions are held in the corridor between the main rooms.

Church Cowley Road Previously known as Cemetery Road or New Road, this was cut between Church Cowley and IFFLEY ROAD in the 19th century. The name was officially passed by Oxford City Council in December 1930. The first reference to COWLEY, then with various spellings such as Covelea, Covelie, Couel, Covel, etc., was in 1004. Chirchcovele (Church Cowley) appears in about 1250, also with a variety of spellings. The name was intended to differentiate it from the later Temple Cowley, the first written reference to which is in 1200, with various spellings. The name is probably derived from 'Cufa' meaning a wood or clearing. Temple Cowley takes its name from the Knights Templars. In 1139 Empress Matilda gave all her lands in Cowley to the Knights of the Temple of Jerusalem.

Church House *North Hinksey*. Formerly the vicarage-house for ST LAWRENCE'S CHURCH, NORTH HINKSEY, it was conveyed in 1959 to the Oxford Diocesan Board of Finance, which moved there with the Oxford Diocesan Dilapidations Board from the Diocesan Registry at No. 88 ST ALDATE'S, the Registry itself moving later to No. 16 BEAUMONT STREET. In 1971 a wing designed by Max Surman was added to the building to contain the BISHOP OF OXFORD'S office and other administrative offices. In 1978 another extension was added, to the designs of D.T. Rathbone, containing the Diocesan Education and Diocesan Surveyor's offices. Church House stands in walled grounds between the church of St Lawrence and the A34 dual-carriageway RING ROAD.

Church Streets For many years there were no fewer than six roads in Oxford all called Church Street. 'The foolish appellation Church Street', complained the poet Robert Bridges, 'has directed hundreds astray,' and so to prevent this the City Council in 1955 changed their names after consultation with local residents. The Church Streets were in ST EBBE'S, now PENNYFARTHING PLACE; in COWLEY, now Beauchamp Lane (after a local vicar); in SOUTH HINKSEY, now Vicarage Road; in New HEADINGTON, now Perrin Street (after Canon Perrin); in Old HEADINGTON, now St Andrew's Road (after the church of ST ANDREW); and in SUMMERTOWN, now Rogers Street (after Alderman Rogers).

Churches The first City Church of Oxford was ST MARTIN'S at CARFAX, the first mention of which appeared in 1032. The rebuilt church on the same site was demolished in 1896 for road improvements at Carfax. Its tower, dating from the reign of Edward III and now known as Carfax Tower, still stands. Five Oxford churches are mentioned or implied in Domesday Book (1086): ST MARY THE VIRGIN, the University Church in HIGH STREET; ST MICHAEL AT THE NORTH GATE in CORNMARKET, now the City Church, whose Saxon tower is the oldest building in Oxford; ST FRIDESWIDE'S, the priory church; ST PETER-IN-THE-EAST, now the library of St Edmund Hall; and ST EBBE'S, not specifically mentioned but the church referred to as belonging to Eynsham Abbey. However, two other churches probably existed in 1086; ST GEORGE IN THE CASTLE, of which only the Norman tower and crypt remain; and ST MARY MAGDALEN, MAGDALEN STREET, the Norman chancel arch of which was removed during 19th-century restorations. Eleven more churches were in existence before 1150: ALL SAINTS in High Street, now the library of Lincoln College; ST MILDRED'S, demolished when Lincoln College was built; ST PETER-LE-BAILEY, which stood originally where BONN SQUARE now is, but which was moved to NEW INN HALL STREET in 1874 and is now the chapel of St Peter's College; St Michael at the South Gate, which was demolished for the building of Christ Church; ST ALDATE'S, which has some Norman arcading; St Edward's, which was originally in what is now ALFRED STREET but was closed in the 16th century; Holy Trinity Chapel at the East Gate; ST CLEMENT'S, just outside the East Gate, which was demolished in 1827 and rebuilt on its present site; ST GILES' which was first mentioned in 1133; ST THOMAS THE MARTYR in BECKET STREET; and ST CROSS at HOLYWELL. The 12th-century churches of St John's (now incorporated into Merton College), and St Budoc's in CASTLE STREET, which was pulled down in about 1215, brought the total number of churches within or just outside the CITY WALLS up to twenty-one by the end of the 12th century. Most of the Norman churches which remain contain only traces of Norman architecture. The village church of ST MARY THE VIRGIN, IFFLEY, now within the city, has some of the finest examples of Norman work, particularly the west front. In addition to the parish churches there were the monastic institutions: OSENEY ABBEY, founded 1129; ST FRIDES-WIDE'S PRIORY (1121); GODSTOW ABBEY (1133) and REWLEY ABBEY (1280).

Other 12th-century churches in or close to Oxford include ST MARGARET'S, BINSEY; ST JAMES, COWLEY; ST ANDREW'S, HEADINGTON; and ST LAWRENCE, NORTH HINKSEY. There was a church at WYTHAM in the 12th century, but it was extensively restored in the 15th century and rebuilt in the 19th. ST PETER'S, WOLVER-COTE, has a 14th-century tower, but the church was rebuilt in 1860. ST NICHOLAS, OLD MARSTON, is mostly 15th century.

The 19th-century churches include ST BARNABAS in JERICHO (1869), ST MARGARET'S, ST MARGARET'S ROAD (1883) and ST PHILIP AND ST JAMES (1860) in NORTH OXFORD; ST PAUL'S, WALTON STREET (1835–6) (see ST PAUL'S ARTS CENTRE); ST MARY AND ST JOHN, COWLEY ROAD (1875), ST JOHN THE EVANGELIST, IFFLEY ROAD (1894–6); and ST FRIDESWIDE'S, BOTLEY ROAD (1870–2).

Among the 20th-century churches, mention may be made of ST ANDREW'S, LINTON ROAD (1907); ST MICHAEL AND ALL ANGELS, SUMMERTOWN (1909); ALL SAINTS, LIME WALK (built in 1870, but rebuilt in 1910); and ST LUKE'S, COWLEY ROAD (1937–8).

The Roman Catholic parish church of ST ALOYSIUS in WOODSTOCK ROAD was built in 1873–5 and the modern church of the HOLY ROOD, south of FOLLY BRIDGE, in 1959–61; NEW ROAD BAPTIST CHURCH in 1819; WESLEY MEMORIAL METHODIST CHURCH in New Inn Hall Street in 1878; and ST COLUMBA'S UNITED REFORMED CHURCH in Alfred Street in 1915 (with a new front in 1960).

(*See separate entries for these and other churches; see also* CHRIST CHURCH CATHEDRAL *and* ROMAN CATHOLICS.)

Churchill Hospital *Old Road, Headington.* Built in 1939–40 as an Emergency Medical Services (EMS) Hospital on a 38-acre site, the hospital was originally intended to be staffed by the nearby Wingfield-Morris Hospital (*see* NUFFIELD ORTHOPAEDIC CENTRE). As civilian casualties were not a problem in Oxford, the hospital, named after the Prime Minister, Sir Winston Churchill, was taken over by the United States Medical Services on 3 January 1942. It remained in use as a military hospital until the middle of 1945, when it was placed under the administration of the Management Committee of the RADCLIFFE INFIRMARY.

The wartime prefabricated buildings, constructed to an original design by R. Fielding Dodd (consulting architect also to the Wingfield and LITTLEMORE hospitals), have remained in use to cope with rising admission rates. In 1986 the Churchill with its allied new units, Ritchie Russell House (for the young disabled) and Sir Michael Sobell House (for terminal care), had 370 beds. There were in-patient facilities for chest diseases, haemophilia, certain infectious diseases, gynaecology and urology, together with a renal unit, a Paediatric Assessment Centre, and departments of radiotherapy, physiotherapy and medical genetics.

The hospital stands on the site of a 3rd- or 4th-century Romano-British pottery works, the products of which have been found all over the south of England. The remains of kilns and drying-houses can still be seen.

Cinemas 'One of the few novelties of the fair', wrote the *Oxford Times* journalist in his report on ST GILES' FAIR in 1897, was 'Taylor's cinematograph exhibition, an up-to-date attraction which drew crowded houses, witnessing with manifest delight this marvellous contrivance. . . . The scenes represented included an excellent presentment of the Jubilee procession'. At the 1898 fair, Alf Ball added 'a diagraph showing kinematographic entertainment' to his boxing saloon; but the *Oxford Times* reporter thought that 'two of the items, dealing with the first night of marriage, were not in the best taste'. He preferred Taylor's exhibition, particularly a 'representation of the funeral of Mr Gladstone'. This was the birth of cinema in Oxford. By 1904 cinematograph had 'superseded all kinds of menagerie and freak shows', with six booths 'devoted to the wonders of the flickering film, and their elaborately-decorated fronts and massive organs suggested that their popularity is not confined to Oxford and that they may be recognised as paying concerns'.

Yet in these formative years the moving pictures in Oxford were not only to be seen at the annual fair. In January 1898 a cinematograph was shown at the Oxford Co-operative and Industrial Society's New Year Entertainment for children, and the number of special cinematograph shows rapidly increased during the next decade until, in 1910, the moving pictures found a more permanent home in Oxford. The first cinema, the Oxford Electric Theatre, was opened on 26 November 1910 in CASTLE STREET by Frank Stuart, the proprietor of the East Oxford Theatre. This was quickly followed by the Picture Palace in Jeune Street (1911), the Electra Palace in QUEEN STREET (1911), the Cinematograph Theatre in GEORGE STREET (1912), the Palace Theatre or Picture House in COWLEY ROAD (1912) and the North Oxford Kinema in WALTON STREET (1913). At St Giles' Fair in 1912 the *Oxford Times* reporter noted that Taylor had introduced two 'real cowboys from Western America', Dingle Jack and Rifle Bill, into his cinematograph show in order to attract customers.

The Oxford Electric Theatre, which was built on the site of the old University and City Baths and Wash Houses, closed in 1923, unable to compete with the larger, plusher cinemas built later. It was converted into a works canteen and was demolished in 1968, a casualty of the Westgate development (*see* WESTGATE CENTRE). The Jeune Street Picture Palace closed in 1918 and later became a furniture store, but it was resurrected as a cinema in 1976 by William Heine and Pablo Butcher. They renamed it the Penultimate Picture Palace, erected a large fibre-glass sculpture of Al Jolson's hands by John Buckley on the cinema's façade, kept the original 1911 pay-box, named the toilets Pearl and Dean, and sold home-made confectionery and wholesome food. It became a popular haunt of students.

The Cinematograph Theatre, owned by the Oxford Cinematograph Company and popularly known as the George Street Cinema, was demolished in 1935 and on its site is now a Co-operative shop. The Electra Palace closed in 1958, its site now being occupied by a Marks & Spencer store. The Palace Theatre, at 106 Cowley Road, was built in 1890 as the Assembly Hall. The name was changed to the Empire Music Hall and then to the East Oxford Theatre; and in 1912 it re-opened as the Palace Theatre. 'Animated photos' were shown between the variety turns as early as 1900 by Albany Ward's Velograph Company. The cinema closed in 1938, unable to compete with the new Cowley Road cinema, the Regal, which opened in 1937. The North Oxford Kinema was renamed the Scala in 1920. Its character changed under various managers, the most popular with the JERICHO residents being a Cockney, Ben Jay. He took over in 1925 and introduced a twenty-minute sing-song with a nine-piece orchestra between the films. The University showed its disapproval by placing the cinema out of bounds to undergraduates in 1927, which prompted Jay's departure. J.E. Poyntz took over in June 1930, introducing 'talkies' in October. The cinema stayed in the Poyntz family until 1970,

The Electra Palace Cinema in Queen Street in 1913. The notice in the foyer advises that members of the University are admitted to the 'one shilling seats only' – the most expensive.

when Star Holdings converted it into two auditoria, Studio 1 and Studio X. In 1977 Contemporary Films took over and renamed it the Phoenix, retaining the Poyntz tradition of showing good foreign films.

The next phase in the development of cinema in Oxford came in 1923–37 with four custom-built cinemas and a fifth being adapted from an ice-rink. In 1923 Edwin Hall opened the New Cinema in HEADINGTON, which was quickly developing as a suburb of Oxford. When Hall died in 1960 his son Edward leased the cinema to Unifilms of London, who renamed it the Moulin Rouge. The lease changed hands in 1962, and the cinema eventually gained a reputation as a 'flea-pit', closing and re-opening in the 1970s. In 1980 William Heine, having revived the Picture Palace, revamped the Moulin Rouge (re-opening it as Not The Moulin Rouge), with a spectacular fibre-glass sculpture by John Buckley of a dancing girl's legs on the façade to complement Al Jolson's hands at the Picture Palace.

The Oxford Cinematograph Theatre Company (1922) Ltd opened its second cinema in MAGDALEN STREET in 1924 – the Oxford Cinema, which was advertised as the 'super' Oxford Cinema and was known later as simply 'the Super'. Designed by the theatre architects Frank Matcham and Co. and the local architect J.C. Leed, the auditorium seated 1300 and featured two 30 × 17 foot oil paintings by G. Rushton on the walls, depicting scholars on one side, sportsmen on the other. With its grand marble entrance and lavishly decorated lounge, the cinema was described by the *Oxford Times* as the 'acme of comfort'. On 6 January 1930 it presented Oxford's first full-length 'talkie', *The Broadway Melody*. Eighteen months later the orchestra was dismissed by Union Cinemas, who became lessees in 1931; five years later the services of the organist were no longer required. The cinema, which is still owned by the Oxford Cinematograph Company, was leased to Associated British Cinemas in 1971 and renamed the ABC Magdalen Street. In 1986 the Cannon Group took over and named it the Cannon Magdalen Street.

In 1930 the Oxford ICE RINK was opened in BOTLEY ROAD. It was a vast building which was used as a 'talkie' cinema during the summer months in 1933, seating 2500, and such was its success that, in 1934, it became just a cinema – the Majestic. Five thousand people attended the official opening on 2 April, though not the MAYOR, Miss Tawney, who disapproved of the vulgar choice of film: Mae West in *I'm No Angel*. A bus, the Majestic Special, transported audiences from CARFAX each evening. In 1940 the Majestic closed to accommodate war evacuees and was never again opened as a cinema, becoming a hostel for Pressed Steel until 1949, then a factory for Frank Cooper Ltd in 1950 (*see* COOPER'S 'OXFORD' MARMALADE). In 1967 it was sold to MFI, the furniture company. The Ritz and the Regal were both designed by Robert Cromie for Union Cinemas and opened in 1936 and 1937 respectively. In April 1963 the auditorium at the Ritz was destroyed by fire but the cinema was re-opened in October by Associated British Cinemas as the ABC George Street. It was split into three auditoria in 1975. The Cannon Group took over in 1986 and renamed it the Cannon George Street. The Regal became a bingo hall in 1970.

(Marriott, Paul J., *Early Oxford Picture Palaces*, Oxford, 1978.)

City Archives   *see* ARCHIVES, CITY.

City Burgesses   *see* Appendix 3 *for a list of Members of Parliament for Oxford*.

City Council   *see* GOVERNMENT OF THE CITY.

City Gaol   An elegant low building with a dome erected in the centre of GLOUCESTER GREEN to the designs of Thomas Blackburn and opened in 1789. In 1839 the gaoler was himself imprisoned here for debt. The Gaol Order Book for that year, under the date 19 April, contains the entry: 'Ordered that the whole of the Prisoners under sentence for hard labour . . . be employed on the Tread Wheel except in case of illness or Special Order of the Visitor for the time being'. The gaol was closed in 1878 and demolished.

(*See also* BOCARDO PRISON *and* PRISON.)

City of Oxford Charities   Many charities in Oxford, some dating from the 17th century, were amalgamated in various schemes of the Charity Commissioners from 1863 to 1972, when they were to be administered under the title of the City of Oxford Charities (formerly the Oxford Municipal Charities). The body of trustees consists of twelve co-optative and nine nominative, of whom six represent the City Council, two the University, and one the Oxfordshire Health Authority. The Charities run STONE'S ALMSHOUSES and other almshouses in ST CLEMENT'S. The income of the Charities is used in the upkeep of the almshouses and in making grants to local persons in need, to local charities, and for education.

City of Oxford High School   Opened in 1881 and maintained by the City Council as a grammar school for day boys resident in Oxford, it began with forty-seven pupils. Its motto was *Nemo repente sapit* ('No one suddenly becomes wise'). The school building in GEORGE STREET was designed by SIR THOMAS JACKSON and cost £10,000, the foundation stone being laid by HRH Prince Leopold, the youngest son of Queen Victoria, in 1880. In 1966, when the number of pupils had risen to 360 and the premises had become extremely cramped, the school merged with SOUTHFIELD SCHOOL to become OXFORD SCHOOL. The buildings were taken over by the COLLEGE OF FURTHER EDUCATION from 1966 to 1978, and since 1978 have been occupied by the University Social Studies Faculty Centre. Lawns have replaced the former school playground, bordered on the south side by the remains of the CITY WALL. A tablet at the entrance reads: 'Thomas Hill Green (1836–1882), educationalist, Fellow of Balliol, White's Professor of Moral Philosophy, elected (1876), first University Member of Oxford City Council to help found and establish the High School for Boys (1881–1966), thereby completing the City's "Ladder of Learning" from Elementary School to University – a project dearest to his heart. Thus were united town and gown in common cause.'

T.E. Lawrence, who attended the school from 1896 to 1907, is its most famous former pupil; his portrait in profile, a bronze plaque by Eric Kennington, was unveiled in 1936 by Winston Churchill. John Drinkwater (1882–1937), poet and playwright, was also a pupil.

City Walls Oxford was established in a place with good natural defences: the THAMES and the Cherwell (*see* THAMES) protected the town from the south, west and east. The first-known artificial defences date from the time when the town was brought into the scheme of defended towns devised by Alfred the Great (853–901) and his successor, Edward the Elder (901–924). The enemy at this time was the Vikings, and a network of fortified towns or burghs provided Wessex with defence in depth. The exact construction date of Oxford's first wall is unknown; it was certainly in existence by 919, but could date from as early as the last years of Alfred's reign. The traditional date given is 911. The original walls enclosed a smaller area than their mediaeval successors: while the North and South Gates were probably in their mediaeval positions, it is likely that the original East Gate stood near the church of ST MARY THE VIRGIN and the West Gate in the vicinity of the junction of NEW ROAD and CASTLE STREET. Thus the defences enclosed a town whose plan was rectangular.

Excavations have shown that the late Saxon defences consisted of a ditch, an earth rampart laced with timbers and fronted by a wooden palisade, and a street running round inside the rampart to provide a means of rapid deployment of troops around the perimeter. There was no ditch on the south side of the town because the TRILL MILL STREAM provided adequate protection. The original timber palisade was later replaced by a revetment of coral ragstone. The construction and maintenance of the late Saxon walls was the responsibility of the people who lived in the surrounding countryside.

In 1009 the Danes attacked the town and sacked it. It was probably at this time that the line of the wall was extended as far as the eastern end of the HIGH STREET. A western extension is also possible. The western defences were destroyed in 1071 when the CASTLE was built, and henceforward the Castle supplied the western defence of the town. At this time the West Gate was moved south to the junction of Castle Street and PARADISE STREET. In 1086 Domesday refers to the wall, saying that the burden of its repair then fell on specific houses within the town.

When Stephen attacked Oxford in 1142, the town was well defended with deep water on all sides, an outwork beyond the wall on one side and the Castle and tower on another. The town's first municipal seal, dated 1191, shows a freestanding stone wall, implying that the stone-faced rampart had by then been replaced. Minor realignments were carried out south of ST FRIDESWIDE'S PRIORY and east of the North Gate; major alterations were made when the GREYFRIARS Priory was built across the line of the wall in 1244. The south and east suburbs were protected by outer gates: in ST ALDATE'S a gate-tower stood on the South Bridge (now FOLLY BRIDGE) and there was a drawbridge where MAGDALEN BRIDGE now is.

Although the system of certain houses taking responsibility for the repair of the wall remained until as late as 1251, from 1226 onwards the town was allowed to levy tolls on goods entering the town; the profit from these tolls was then spent on the walls. The towers, known as bastions, were added to the wall from this time. The system of 'murage' was in turn replaced from the late 14th century, when Oxford began to lease off sections of the wall and to grant land adjacent to it, subject to the tenant carrying out repairs. A number of colleges, notably New College and Merton, acquired lengths of the wall in this way and they have been responsible for maintenance ever since. The stretch around New College was once even more impregnable than it still appears, for a unique feature of Oxford's wall was a double section from East Gate to Smith Gate, a postern at the northern end of CATTE STREET. This arrangement was presumably inspired by the plans of concentric castles.

By the 17th century the mediaeval defences were in disrepair. Although they were refurbished during the CIVIL WAR, they were unsuitable to withstand artillery attack and so, between 1642 and 1646, an ambitious new line of earthen defences was built, enclosing not only the mediaeval walled town but also its suburbs. The Civil War defences were subsequently slighted by the Parliamentarians.

Little survives of the Civil War defences, but the mediaeval wall can still be traced. A perambulation can begin at ST MICHAEL AT THE NORTH GATE, whose tower stood adjacent to the Saxon and mediaeval North Gates. Bastions can be seen behind Nos 1 and 15 SHIP STREET. The line can be picked up again at the Hertford College octagon, which represents a drastically-modified tower which stood adjacent to Smith Gate and which was converted into a chapel. Perhaps the finest impression of the wall is gained from the inner portion around New College with its spectacular embattled parapet, wall-walk, and six surviving bastions. The line of the outer wall and one of its bastions is preserved in the low terrace wall which runs to the north, parallel to the New College wall.

The East Gate stood at the eastern end of the High Street. From there the wall continues in a much-modified form around Merton College, but at Corpus Christi College a short section still stands to full height, together with the largest bastion, which may represent one side of a postern. There is no sign of the wall in Christ Church, but the south wall of Pembroke College in BREWER STREET preserves the line and contains original features. Little Gate stood at the junction of ST EBBE'S STREET, LITTLEGATE STREET and Brewer Street. The line can be traced behind Nos 8–10 TURN AGAIN LANE, while parts of the WESTGATE CENTRE have been built on the line.

There was no western wall, because of the presence of the Castle, so the northern circuit begins where Bulwarks Lane and GEORGE STREET Mews join. The north boundary wall of St Peter's College includes the remains of the base of a bastion, and the line of the wall is then preserved in the back boundary wall of the properties which stand on the north side of ST MICHAEL'S STREET.

Civil War The war between the Royalists and the supporters of Parliament which broke out over irreconcilable religious, constitutional and economic differences between King Charles I and the Long Parliament. The Parliament's support came principally from London, the south and east, the King's from the north and west. The King vainly tried to capture London and, after a battle at Edgehill which both sides claimed to have won, the Royalists withdrew to Oxford.

Charles entered Oxford on 29 October 1642 and from that day until June 1646, when he surrendered to

Charles I entered the city in October 1642 and from then until June 1646 Oxford was his military headquarters.

the Scottish army at Newark, Oxford was Charles's military headquarters. During this period four major battles were fought within a 30-mile radius of the city. At the outbreak of the war Oxford had been divided in its loyalties, the University generally supporting the Royalists, the town for the most part favouring the Parliamentarians. Once the King had issued his 'Proclamation for Suppressing the Present Rebellion', on 9 August 1642, the University had begun to prepare its fortifications. Students had formed troops and stones had been stored in Magdalen College tower for use in case an attempt was made to force the gate at MAGDALEN BRIDGE. On 28 August Sir John Byron's royalist troops had entered the city and had stayed there until 8 September. Two days later parliamentary troops had marched into Oxford to take their place. They had proceeded to search some of the colleges for hidden PLATE; had disarmed the members of five colleges; demolished existing fortifications; burned popish pictures and books, and armed the citizens. Parliament's forces had continued to occupy the area until October, when, following the battle of Edgehill, they departed from the city, a trooper from London discharging a parting shot at the image of the Blessed Virgin over the porch of ST MARY THE VIRGIN and striking off her head and that of the infant Jesus in her arms.

On his arrival in Oxford, Charles was greeted with protestations of loyalty not only from the University but also from the MAYOR and the townsmen. Yet, as a precautionary measure, the citizens were disarmed. The King, intending to move on to London along the Thames Valley, left Oxford on 3 November with the bulk of his army. However, Parliamentary opposition at Turnham Green forced him to return to Oxford on 29 November. The King now took up residence at Christ Church and proceeded to hold court there. There also, from June 1643, the newly formed Oxford Parliament met. This consisted initially of forty-four Lords and 118 Commoners. The Lords later met in the Upper Schools, while the Commons gathered in the Great Congregational Hall. The executive committee of the Privy Council was based at Oriel.

The Law and Logic Schools were converted into granaries, and New College cloisters and tower were used as powder magazines. Indeed, buildings all over the University and town were put to different uses. Uniforms were made in the Music and Astronomy Schools; Magdalen College grove became an artillery park; All Souls an arsenal; Christ Church quadrangle a cattle pen; FREWIN HALL a cannon foundry; the tower of Brasenose a food store. Jesus College provided accommodation for 'persons of quality' from Wales; Prince Rupert was lodged at St John's College, having been nominally entered there as an undergraduate during a visit to England in 1636. Pembroke College was reported as holding seventy-nine men, twenty-three women and five children in June 1643, as well as Sir Edward Nicholas, the new Secretary of State. Noblemen, knights and gentry were mostly to be found in the parishes of ALL SAINTS, St Mary's and ST PETER-IN-THE-EAST, while lower household servants were housed in ST EBBE'S. Ordinary soldiers were particularly numerous in the parishes of ST MICHAEL and ST MARY MAGDALEN. Parliamentary prisoners were also held in buildings in these parishes as well as in the churches of ST GILES and ST THOMAS THE MARTYR. Any damage done was paid for by the King. Beyond the CITY WALLS a sword factory was constructed at WOLVERCOTE; and at OSNEY the corn mills underwent alterations necessary for making gunpowder. The royalist troops of about ten foot regiments and three of cavalry were encamped between Oxford and Wolvercote; and drilling took place in the college quadrangles, on PORT MEADOW and in the PARKS.

By 1645, when most of the remaining scholars had been sent home to vacate rooms for further royalist forces, the University had become a military centre rather than a place of learning. 'Lectures and exercises', said ANTHONY WOOD, 'had for the most part ceased.' Extensive fortifications of ditch, rampart, palisade and gates with drawbridges had been erected from St Giles' Church in the north to FOLLY BRIDGE in the south, and from Magdalen Bridge in the east to St Thomas's Church in the west. Barriers were built in the THAMES, whose waters, as well as those of the Cherwell (*see* THAMES), were made to flood the surrounding meadows. To expedite these works, in the summer of 1643 all members of the University between the ages of sixteen and sixty were recruited as labourers for one day a week, or fined 1s. Women were also called upon to help and were liable to fines if they did not appear or send a substitute. In outlying areas trees were uprooted and houses demolished, while a ring of royalist garrisons and strongholds surrounding the city enabled the King to draw supplies and money from the whole area.

To finance these fortifications and to provide for the upkeep of his army, Charles needed constant supplies of money. In July 1642 the University had given him £1360. In December the MINT was established at NEW INN HALL. A further £200 was given by the University on 1 January 1643, followed by £800 from St John's, supposedly in lieu of their plate, though the King took both. In all, plate weighing 2000 lb in gold and silver was melted down and transformed into the new Oxford coinage (*see* PLATE). Yet by June the King had to ask for £2000 from the city, and the same sum from the University.

In addition to these lump sums, regular assessments, worth £1176, were levied each week. Some households were permitted to quarter horses and soldiers in place of the levy; but the colleges had to provide up to £100 per week. And not only was cash required. The townspeople were additionally faced with constant requisitions in the form of horses, cattle and domestic goods. For example, the citizens' brass kitchenware was collected in January 1643 and melted down for ordnance; in 1644 the city's cornmarket, near the North Gate, was pulled down so that the lead roof could be used for bullets, and the timber for military engines; and in December 1643 Charles ordered all surplus food around Oxford to be brought within the city walls.

Queen Henrietta Maria arrived in Oxford on 14 July with money, supplies, ammunition and 2000 men from the north, and took up residence in Merton College. And, while the war dragged on indecisively

The Clarendon Building in Broad Street was partly paid for by profits from the publication of Lord Clarendon's history of the Civil War.

THE

HISTORY

OF THE

REBELLION and CIVIL WARS

IN

ENGLAND,

Begun in the Year 1641.

With the precedent Paſſages, and Actions, that contributed thereunto, and the happy End, and Concluſion thereof by the KING's bleſſed RESTORATION, and RETURN upon the 29ᵗʰ of *May*, in the Year 1660.

Written by the Right Honourable

EDWARD Earl of CLARENDON,

Late Lord High Chancellor of *England*, Privy Counſellor in the Reigns of King CHARLES the Firſt and the Second.

Κτῆμα ἐς ἀεί. *Thucyd.*

Ne quid Falſi dicere audeat, ne quid Veri non audeat. Cicero.

VOLUME THE FIRST.

OXFORD,
Printed at the THEATER, *An. Dom.* MDCCII.

and peace negotiations came to nothing, the life of the Court continued as though its denizens were still in Whitehall. There were musical entertainments and plays; new sonnets and satires were published; new fashions were paraded through the streets and were copied by the citizens' wives; love affairs were conducted by the river bank and beneath the secluded walls of college gardens; fashionable ladies defied the 'terrible gigantique aspect' of RALPH KETTELL, the President of Trinity, and walked into his chapel 'half-dressed like angels'; noble students reappeared in the gleaming armour of the King's Life Guard; duels were so commonplace that Prince Rupert once had to part two furious contestants with a pole-axe; and the King appointed a Master of Revels.

Royalist attempts to march on London failed; and after the Scottish army had entered the war on the side of the Parliamentarians in February 1644, Oxford was in danger of being encircled, with the Earl of Essex's forces in occupation of Reading from 23 May and Edmund Waller's troops encamped at Abingdon. An attack on Oxford was, however, beaten off on 1 August. And on 7 May the next year the King, in excellent heart, left the city with a large part of his army for the summer campaign. 'We have great unanimity among ourselves' his friend, Lord Digby, wrote, expressing Charles's own views, 'and the rebels great distractions.' Yet on 14 June the Royalists were decisively defeated at Naseby; and, after further setbacks, in September the King returned to Oxford, where he was forced to recognise that he had 'neither force enough to resist nor sufficient to escape to any secure place'.

The remaining royalist garrisons had retreated into Oxford, as Sir Thomas Fairfax, who had joined Oliver Cromwell and Richard Browne outside the city, had set up camp at HEADINGTON HILL. In desperation, the Oxford garrison had decided to pull down all houses within 3 miles of Oxford to prevent the enemy using them as billets. They also flooded meadows, burned houses in the suburbs, and garrisoned Wolvercote. But all to no avail. Woodstock fell on 26 April and the next day the King left Oxford with but two companions, one of his chaplains and a groom of his bedchamber. With his long hair trimmed, wearing a false beard and a suit of ordinary clothes, he travelled disguised as his companions' servant, riding by night, sleeping in remote ale-houses as he journeyed north.

Fairfax continued the siege of Oxford, letting no one out of the city except to negotiate. On 11 May he ordered Oxford to surrender. Negotiations continued until 20 June, when the Royalists signed the articles of surrender. The departure of their garrison on 24 June signalled the end of the Civil War in Oxford.

The terms of surrender respected the ancient rights of Oxford and allowed the royalist garrison of 3000 men safe conduct home. Prince Rupert and his brother Maurice were given ten days in which to leave the country, while Fairfax placed guards upon the BODLEIAN LIBRARY to protect it against looting. Oxford was then purged of all strong Royalists and twenty-five clergy were ejected for their religious views.

(*See also* VISITATIONS.)

Clarendon, Edward Hyde, 1st Earl of (*1609–1674*). Through his writings, one of the

University's most notable benefactors. He entered MAGDALEN HALL in 1622, and, having failed to obtain a DEMYSHIP at Magdalen College, took his BA in 1626. A trusted counsellor of Charles I, he devoted himself to raising money for the royalist cause when CIVIL WAR broke out. He was at least partially responsible for obtaining a loan of £10,000 from Oxford, where he lived at All Souls from October 1642 to March 1645. After the Restoration of the monarchy Clarendon was elected CHANCELLOR of the University and interested himself in University reform, advocating the restoration of its ancient discipline, in which he was supported by JOHN FELL. His *Dialogue on Education* suggested, among other proposals, the foundation of an academy of dancing, fencing and riding. His great-grandson left all Clarendon's manuscripts to the University so that this academy might be built. The project was not realised; but in 1868 the money accumulated in the fund was put towards the establishment of the CLARENDON LABORATORY. Already the CLARENDON BUILDING for the OXFORD UNIVERSITY PRESS had been partly paid for by profits from the publication of Clarendon's *The True Historical Narrative of the Rebellion and Wars in England* (three vols, 1702–4), the copyright of which had been presented to the University by his son. There is a portrait of Clarendon after Lely in the BODLEIAN, a statue of him in a niche on the west side of the Clarendon Building and a bust in the Delegates' Room (*see* STATUES).

Clarendon Building *Broad Street.* Built in 1711–13 to the designs of NICHOLAS HAWKSMOOR for the OXFORD UNIVERSITY PRESS, whose printer had previously occupied premises in the SHELDONIAN. It was partly paid for by the profits from the publication of LORD CLARENDON's history of the Great Rebellion, the copyright of which was presented to the University by his son. Although the Press moved to WALTON STREET in 1832, the delegates still meet in a splendid panelled room in the south-west corner. Magnificent wrought-iron gates open on to a tunnel-vaulted passage leading from BROAD STREET into the SCHOOLS quadrangle. The seven lead figures of the Muses on the top of the building are by Sir James Thornhill (1717) (*see* STATUES); the other two (Euterpe and Melpomene) are fibre-glass replicas by Richard Kindersley, given by BLACKWELL's in 1974 to replace the originals which had fallen down.

Clarendon Centre A covered shopping arcade connecting CORNMARKET STREET with SHOE LANE and QUEEN STREET. It was designed by Gordon Benoy and Partners and has a motif of blue tubes and marbled floors. It was constructed in 1983–4.

Clarendon Club *121 High Street.* Founded in 1863 as a social club for Oxford business and professional men. The original premises were in the CLARENDON HOTEL in CORNMARKET, from which the club took its name. In 1882 it moved to new premises in 54 Cornmarket, but the club was obliged to move to new premises in HIGH STREET in 1967. The club's facilities include a bar, a reading room, a snooker room and a dining room. Various sporting and social activities are organised, including an annual dinner and a Punch Night. Membership is by invitation. Until 1967 voting was by the use of a ballot box. Three

black balls in twelve were sufficient to exclude membership, and there are records of several candidates for membership being blackballed. Most of the leading business and professional firms and organisations in the city are represented in the Clarendon Club or the FREWEN CLUB. There are no women members, although there are Ladies' Supper Parties and Ladies' Nights.
(*See also* CLUBS AND SOCIETIES.)

Clarendon Hotel Formerly the Star, one of Oxford's leading coaching inns (*see* TRANSPORT), the Clarendon Hotel stood on the west side of CORNMARKET STREET. The original building was granted to OSENEY ABBEY by one Thomas the Marshall in 1337 and it was then known as Marshall's inn. Its name had been changed to the Star by 1469. Its ancient front was replaced by a new symmetrical façade in 1783; and extensive stabling was added in the early 19th century. In its heyday as a coaching inn many distinguished guests stayed here: Frederick, Prince of Württemberg put up at the Star in 1797 and the exiled Louis XVIII of France in 1808. With the coming of the RAILWAY, however, its prosperity sharply declined. By the 1850s, when there were only three coaches a week to London, many of its rooms lay empty for days on end, as did those of the ANGEL. The estimated value of the Star fell from £15,500 in the 1830s to £6000 in the 1850s, but with the expansion of both the University and the town in the 1860s its fortunes revived.

The Star was acquired by the Clarendon Hotel Company in 1863 and thereafter it was known as one of Oxford's best hotels. The building was bought by Messrs F.W. Woolworth & Co. Ltd in 1939 and demolished in 1954 to make way for their new store.

Clarendon Laboratory *Parks Road.* In 1865 Robert Bellamy Clifton was appointed Professor of Experimental Philosophy. He was largely responsible for persuading the trustees of Edward Hyde, EARL OF CLARENDON, to pay for the erection of a laboratory for Physical Science with the funds accumulated from a bequest made by the Earl's great-grandson. The building, which was erected in 1868, was the first to be built in Europe for the special purpose of experimental instruction in Physics. It was designed by T.N. Deane, but all the fittings and equipment were designed by Clifton himself. He was said to be an excellent teacher, but little research was carried out during his professorship. He held that 'the wish to do research betrays a certain restlessness of mind'. The old Clarendon Laboratory is now part of the Department of Earth Sciences.

Early this century the Drapers' Company gave a grant for the building of the Electrical Laboratory, which was opened in 1910. It is in red brick with stone dressings and was designed by SIR THOMAS JACKSON. Known as the Townsend Building after J.S.E. (later Sir John) Townsend, the first Wykeham Professor of Physics, for whom it was built, it is now part of the Clarendon Laboratory, to which it is joined by a bridge. In 1919 F.A. Lindemann, later LORD CHERWELL, became Professor of Experimental Philosophy and soon attracted a number of gifted physicists to work at the Clarendon, such as G.M.B. Dobson, A.C.G. Egerton and D.A. Jackson, all future Fellows of the Royal Society. It was Lindemann who persuaded ICI and other companies to provide funds for fellowships for scientists who had left Germany and other countries with the rise of Nazism and had come to Britain. Among them were Professor F.E. (later Sir Francis) Simon, the low-temperature physicist, and Kurt Mendelssohn, who first liquefied helium in Britain in the old Clarendon Laboratory on 13 January 1933. A plaque has been fixed to a wall not far from the spot where the original experiment was carried out. This was dedicated by Professor David Shoenberg, the last director of the rival Mond Laboratory at Cambridge. Lindemann regarded low-temperature Physics as a key research topic for the Clarendon, and another of the scientists who came to Britain in the 1930s to work in this field was Dr Nicholas Kurti from Hungary, later to become Professor of Physics.

At the instigation of Lindemann, a new Clarendon Laboratory (now the Lindemann Building) was built in 1938–9. During the Second World War radar research was carried out in the laboratory, as well as work under F.E. Simon on the separation of the uranium isotopes for the Tube Alloys Project, the cover-name for the atomic bomb.

(*See also* LABORATORIES.)

Clarendon Press   *see* OXFORD UNIVERSITY PRESS.

Clark, Sir George Norman   *(1890–1979)*. The son of a prosperous Yorkshire draper and businessman, Clark was educated at Bootham School, York, and at Manchester Grammar School. He won a Brackenbury Scholarship to Balliol, and obtained first-class degrees in both LITERAE HUMANIORES and Modern History. He was elected to a Prize Fellowship at All Souls in 1912. After service in the First World War, he became a Fellow of Oriel and, in 1931, Chichele Professor of Economic History. After some years in Cambridge, he returned to Oxford in 1947 upon his appointment as Provost of Oriel. He was editor of the fifteen-volume *Oxford History of England* (1934–65), published by the OXFORD UNIVERSITY PRESS, and author of *The Seventeenth Century* (1929), among other fine books. He received the honorary degree of DLitt in 1947, was an Honorary Fellow of Balliol as well as of Oriel, and was re-elected to an All Souls fellowship in 1961.

Clarke, George   *(1661–1736)*. Son of Sir William Clarke, Secretary at War, he entered Brasenose in 1675 and was a Fellow of All Souls from 1680 until his death. A lawyer (Judge Advocate-General 1684–1705) and politician (BURGESS for the University 1685 and 1717–36, and Member for other constituencies 1702–11), Clarke was a virtuoso and a competent amateur architect. At All Souls the original designs for the Warden's lodgings in HIGH STREET (1704, and quasi-Palladianised by Daniel Robertson in 1827) and for a double-quadrangle reconstructed college (*c.*1705) were his. From the death of DEAN ALDRICH in 1710 until his own in 1736, he was the architectural arbiter of new collegiate buildings in Oxford, often collaborating closely with NICHOLAS HAWKSMOOR. He was responsible for the design of Christ Church library (1717) and of Worcester College (his part of the design was built in 1753–9), and he had a hand in Hawksmoor's new buildings at The Queen's College (1710) and at All Souls (1716–34). University College's Radcliffe Quadrangle (1717–19) and

Magdalen's New Building (1733) were built to designs which had been subjected to his scrutiny. Clarke was a wealthy bachelor and was generous to a number of Oxford colleges, including Brasenose and Queen's. In spite of a difference with the Fellows, his will included legacies to All Souls, though most of his fortune and his fine library and remarkable collection of architectural drawings were bequeathed to Worcester College.

Clark's Row   A short path which runs from ST ALDATE'S along the end of BRIDEWELL SQUARE into Albion Place, in the vicinity of Cambridge Terrace. No. 7 is a Grade II listed building, probably built in the mid- to late 18th century but since refurbished. In 1939 a house of refuge for girls awaiting admission to a home or penitentiary moved to this building when their original premises in FLOYD'S ROW were demolished. It was then called Skene House, after Miss F.F. Skene, a 19th-century Oxford lady who did much in the field of social welfare. It became a mother-and-baby hostel under the jurisdiction of the City Council's Health Department in the 1950s and 1960s, and closed in 1971. Before slum clearance began in St Aldate's in the 1920s there were as many as twelve small terraced cottages in the short length of the row.

Clubs and Societies   Craftsmen's guilds and religious fraternities flourished in mediaeval times (*see* CRAFT GUILDS). Several guilds were re-established or regulated by the City Council in the 16th century; but the last survivors, lacking the wealth and vitality of the City Companies of London, were dissolved in the 1840s and 1850s. Clubs or societies in something like the modern sense may have begun in Oxford about 1650. William Ellis, the St John's College organist, brought a group of friends together every week to play music at his house in BROAD STREET. The Warden of Wadham College, JOHN WILKINS, similarly organised a regular meeting of scientific virtuosi. Members of this group were among the founders of the Royal Society of London in 1663 and a regular scientific society remained active in Oxford. In 1683 a Philosophical Society was formally established to 'talke of Chymicall matters'.

Senior Common Rooms seem to have begun in the 1660s as clubs for college Fellows and subscription concerts were started in 1665, thirteen years before London. A less serious Banterers' Club was active in 1678, and from 1694 the Red Herring Club founded by Edward Lhuyd, second Keeper of the ASHMOLEAN MUSEUM, kept up a Celtic interest for much of the 18th century.

Little is known about Oxford clubs of the early 18th century. A later Philosophical Club imitated the Freemasons with 'symbolical words and grimaces' unintelligible to outsiders. The Jellybags wrote epigrams. The Nonsense Club, Free Cynics and Arcadians diverted themselves in various ways. The music subscribers built themselves, in 1748, the earliest music room in Europe (*see* HOLYWELL MUSIC ROOM). At Exeter College there was a literary club in the 1730s and there may have been many ephemeral undergraduate societies which have left no trace. Some pursuits, such as bowls and tennis, were run by proprietors of alleys and courts who were often tavern- or innkeepers (and sometimes also stationers or booksellers) and not, as now, by clubs. Dancing and

Members of one of Oxford's innumerable clubs, the Shakespeare Club, in 1906.

fencing, part of the upbringing of every gentleman but outside the academic curriculum, were taught by private masters; ball games such as fives were often played on college courts while plays were brought to Oxford by travelling companies (often paid to go away by the University) and also put on by the scholars for royal visits and other such grand occasions (*see* THEATRE).

Oxford clubs listed in 1762 include fourteen friendly societies, eight learned groups, seven drinking or dining clubs and fourteen others, political, ethnic or sporting. The friendly societies were very recent, the first having been started in 1758 by the innkeeper of the MITRE. Typically Georgian were the Florists, who met regularly from 1768. An exclusive social society of a dozen members, The Club, was founded in 1790. A Mitre Club was active at the inn of that name from 1820 to the 1840s. One Regency club, the UNION, still exists. The Freemasons had their Apollo Lodge from 1819 (*see* FREEMASONS' LODGE); another exclusive group, the Etonians, banded together in 1839. The first regular ROWING races between colleges were in 1815 and the BOAT RACE with Cambridge began in 1829. The boat clubs that held these events are an obscure and fascinating topic. Cricket matches with Cambridge go back to 1827, even before the Boat Race. Bowmen clubbed together in 1830, chess-players in 1855, athletes in 1860, change-ringers in 1872, bicyclists in 1877, polo-players in 1878 and so on. Political societies are not so old: the Canning goes back to 1861, the Conservative to 1869, the Liberal to 1915 and the Labour Club to 1919. All were primarily undergraduate clubs. Their elders started the Ashmolean Society for those with scientific interests in 1828. For antiquaries the Society for Promoting the Study of Gothic Architecture was remarkably fashionable from 1839; it survives as the

Oxfordshire Architectural and Historical Society with an annual publication, OXONIENSIA.

By the end of the 19th century, clubs covered every conceivable interest or whim. Many undergraduate clubs were shortlived, but some survived. Religious societies were particularly strong from the 1870s for a generation, with long-persisting differences between, for instance, the middle-of-the-road Christian Union (OUCU) and the evangelical Inter-collegiate Church Union (OICCU). Since 1884 the Dramatic Society (*see* OUDS) had presented regular productions. From 1936 the Experimental Theatre Club gave scope for the avant-garde and those thrown out in the rivalries of the older club. (*See also* OXFORD UNIVERSITY OPERA CLUB *and* THEATRE.)

There have been innumerable college societies. At Exeter the college archives have records of twenty-two clubs, although there must have been more. At Wadham, as well as all the usual bodies, there was a Book Club from 1822, a Guild of St Andrew from 1887 and a Society for the Study of Social Problems from 1906.

A great range of sporting, political, cultural and social activities is covered by present-day societies. There are, in fact, well over a hundred societies and clubs of different sorts listed in *The Oxford Handbook*, published by the Oxford University Students' Union.

(*See also* BULLINGDON CLUB, CLARENDON CLUB, FREWEN CLUB, GRIDIRON CLUB, VINCENT'S CLUB, *and individual entries for Oxford University sporting clubs.*)

Coach and Horses *35 Broad Street.* Opened in September 1587 as the Prince's Arms. In February 1723 its name was changed to the Dog and Partridge, and finally to the Coach and Horses in 1895, taking this name from an inn (1672–1895) opposite. The NEW BODLEIAN LIBRARY was built on the site in 1936.

Codrington, Christopher *(1668–1710)*. The son of Christopher Codrington, a wealthy plantation owner and Governor-General of the Leeward Islands, entered Christ Church as a gentleman-commoner in 1685 and was a Fellow of All Souls from 1690 until 1697. 'An accomplished, well-bred gent and an universal scholar', he was a wit and a poet who could hold his own in Matthew Prior's company. The soldier–poet–scholar campaigned in the West Indies and in Flanders during the years 1692–7. In 1699 he succeeded to his father's estates and to his position as Governor-General of the Leeward Islands. As an administrator he was not without his detractors, but a complaint against him was dismissed by Parliament in 1702. He had some early military and naval successes against the French, but his failure at Guadeloupe in 1703 brought about his removal from public office. Thereafter he turned to theological and philosophical studies and to his library. He had been a bibliophile since his undergraduate days and he continued to add systematically to his library (much of which was stored in All Souls) after he left Oxford. After his death in 1710 All Souls received by bequest his library of some 12,000 volumes and £10,000 to build and maintain what was to become the CODRINGTON LIBRARY. An estate in Barbados was also left by the bachelor book-collector to establish and support a quasi-monastic foundation on the island. This has developed into Codrington College, now an affiliated institution of the University of the West Indies.

Codrington Library The library of All Souls College, named after its chief benefactor, CHRISTOPHER CODRINGTON, was the successor to a library which dated from the college's foundation in 1438. This old library had reflected the college's academic interests – Theology and Law, and (to a much lesser extent) Medicine. In 1598 a fine plaster ceiling was inserted in the library room and standing presses replaced the old lectern presses; but by the end of the 17th century accommodation for books had become quite inadequate, and Codrington's bequest in 1710 of £10,000 to build and endow a new library must have seemed heaven-sent. NICHOLAS HAWKS-MOOR revised his plans for extensive new building at All Souls, giving pride of place to a great library along the northern boundary of the college site. He made the building reflect in its dimensions and in its 'Gothic' exterior the 15th-century chapel and the new 'Gothic' hall, which together formed the south range of his Great Quadrangle. The foundation stone of the library was laid on 21 June 1716 and the fabric of the 200-foot-long room (the first ground-floor academic library in England) was complete by 1720. The furnishing of the baroque interior was unhurried: the final design of the bookcases was due to James Gibbs (1740); and Thomas Roberts's plaster ceiling (simplified in 1804) dates from ten years later. The books were transferred from the old library in 1751. Thereafter the stock was actively developed over the whole field of learning (at first with WILLIAM BLACKSTONE's energetic participation), but since 1867, when the library was opened to members of the University reading for the Law and History School (and a new reading room was built to accommodate them), the Codrington has specialised in Law and History. Its present (1987) stock of some 120,000 volumes includes over 350 incunabula and much 16th- and 17th-century continental literature; there are special collections in Military History and Strategic Studies. Among its manuscripts are the Jenkins–Luttrell–Wynne papers (late 17th century), the Vaughan Papers (diplomat 1774–1849), and some 450 drawings from the office of SIR CHRISTOPHER WREN.

(Craster, Sir Edmund, *History of All Souls College Library*, ed. E.F. Jacob, London, 1971.)

Coffee Houses When the JEWS (expelled from England during the reign of Edward III) were re-admitted to the country by Cromwell, they brought from the Levant the social custom of coffee-drinking. John Evelyn, who went up to Balliol College in 1637, wrote 'There came in my time to the Coll. one Nathaniel Conopius out of Greece. . . . He was the first I ever saw drink Coffè, which custome came not into England til 30 years after'. In fact the first coffee house in England was opened in Oxford only fourteen years later, in 1651, by Jacob the Jew at the ANGEL inn. Thereafter coffee houses, in which chocolate and wine were also available, became very popular meeting places both for the exchange of news and gossip and for more serious discussion.

Cirques Jobson opened a coffee house at the corner of QUEEN'S LANE and HIGH STREET in 1654, and a more famous one was opened in 1655 by Arthur Tillyard, an apothecary and Royalist, at 90 High Street. Tillyard's (known, like the other coffee houses, by the proprietor's surname) was frequented by CHRISTOPHER WREN, Robert Boyle and Robert Hooke. The Chemical Club, whose members formed the Royal Society when most of them moved to London, met here. In 1660 Short's opened on the site where the SHELDONIAN began to be built four years later. Christ Church kept a library at Short's from 1668, and in 1669 this coffee house moved to the corner of Hell Passage, now known as ST HELEN'S PASSAGE.

In 1677 the VICE-CHANCELLOR forbade coffee houses to open on Sundays – a ban which was for the most part ignored. By 1740 there were some thirteen in Oxford; by 1800 there were about twenty, but thereafter their popularity waned and by 1840 there were very few left.

A coffee house at the corner of HOLYWELL opposite the KING'S ARMS was open by 1754 and possibly earlier.

A coffee house, formerly known as Bagg's, then as Seal's, was established in 1754 on the site on the corner of Holywell Street later occupied by the Indian Institute.

Later in the century it was known as Bagg's, and as Seal's under a different proprietor in the 19th century. From about 1844 until 1882 (when it was demolished) it was a private house. One of the longest-lived coffee houses was built some time after 1671 at the corner of SHIP STREET and TURL STREET. In 1829, more than a century and a half later it was sold, having in the meantime become Dickeson's Hotel. Another coffee house at 104 High Street, opened in 1676 and formerly the Salutation Inn, was known during the 18th century as Hambleton's, Horseman's, and finally, when taken over by John Horseman's son James, as James's. It survived until the early 19th century.

(Aubertin-Potter, N., and Bennett, A., *Oxford Coffee Houses, 1651–1800*, Oxford, 1987.)

Coghill, Nevill Henry Kendal Aylmer (*1899–1980*). The younger son of Sir Egerton Bushe Coghill, 5th Baronet of Castle Townshend, County Cork, Coghill was educated at Haileybury and won a scholarship to Exeter College, of which he was elected a Fellow in 1925. He was an inspiring tutor – W.H. Auden and Richard Burton were among his pupils – but his main interests were mediaeval literature and the production of plays and operas. Some of the most outstanding presentations of the OXFORD UNIVERSITY DRAMATIC SOCIETY and the OXFORD UNIVERSITY OPERA CLUB were due to his inspiration. In 1936 he founded the Experimental Theatre Club (*see* OUDS). The spectacular production of *The Tempest* in Worcester College garden in 1949 was particularly memorable. He made fine translations of Langland as well as of Chaucer, directed Richard Burton and Elizabeth Taylor in *Doctor Faustus* at the PLAYHOUSE in 1966, and was largely responsible for an eminently successful stage version of *The Canterbury Tales* in 1968. A lively and amusing conversationalist, he was a prominent member of the INKLINGS. He was elected Merton Professor of English Literature in 1957.

Cole Group Took its name from G.D.H. Cole (1889–1959), the socialist and writer who was appointed University Reader in Economics in 1925. Cole and his wife Margaret (1893–1980; latterly Dame Margaret Cole) invited undergraduates sympathetic to their views for weekly discussions at their house. Among those the Cole Group attracted were W.H. Auden, Hugh Gaitskell and JOHN BETJEMAN. Cole himself became one of the first Fellows of Nuffield College in 1939; and in 1944 was appointed Chichele Professor of Social and Political Theory.

Colet, John (*c.1467–1519*). The Dean of St Paul's and founder of St Paul's School went to Oxford in about 1483 and, after some seven years of intensive study, took his MA. After travelling on the Continent, he settled in Oxford in 1497 and began a remarkable course of lectures in Latin on St Paul's Epistle to the Romans and, later, on St Paul's First Epistle to the Corinthians. The lectures attracted large attendances and Colet's principles of interpretation, directly opposed to those of scholastic theologians, were widely influential. Erasmus came to Oxford, heard Colet speak and became his friend, acknowledging his mastery of scriptural interpretation and recognising him as a worthy colleague of his fellow Oxford humanists WILLIAM GROCYN, Sir Thomas More and THOMAS LINACRE.

Collections A name now used to describe both the informal college examinations held at the beginning of each term to test an undergraduate's progress in his or her work, and the terminal reports given orally at the end of the term by the tutors. The present usage appears to date from the end of the 18th century: C.K. Sharpe wrote in 1799 that 'we are all in a fuss here about Collections which come on next week', and in 1807 Sir W. Hamilton described Collections as 'public examinations at the end of each term on all the books we have read during the continuance of the term.' Earlier the name referred to certain academic exercises in the University. Collectors, named in the STATUTES as early as 1346 and abolished only in 1822, elected originally by the scholars but later appointed by the PROCTORS, were the masters responsible for arranging the Lenten disputations, one of the exercises necessary for the Bachelor's degree.

College of Further Education *see* FURTHER EDUCATION, COLLEGE OF.

College Stamps Colleges have always used a messenger service for delivering letters locally. In an Act of 1656 it was provided that the Universities of Oxford and Cambridge 'may use their former liberties, rights and privileges of having special carriers to carry and recarry letters, as they formerly did and as if this Act had not been made'. This right was reserved even after the Act had been repealed in 1710.

The charges for letters delivered by college messengers were entered on the member's BATTELS at the end of each term. This involved a good deal of book-keeping, and in order to save the cost of this Keble College decided in 1871 to issue its own stamps for use on letters or messages delivered within the centre of Oxford; the scheme was so successful that seven other Oxford colleges and three Cambridge ones eventually followed Keble's lead. Keble's first stamps were embossed by SPIERS & SON on orange surface-coloured paper. They were roughly perforated and bore the college arms with the words 'Keble * College * Oxon' in an oval. In 1872 another issue was embossed with clean-cut perforation, followed by stamps embossed on magenta-coloured paper. In 1876 a new but similar design by S.P. Spiers appeared, printed by lithography in ultramarine. Each sheet of forty-eight stamps carried the printer's name and address, 'Spiers & Son High St Oxford', at the foot of every stamp. Keble's last stamp appeared in 1882, in a different shade of ultramarine and without the printer's name and address.

It was nearly five years after the first issue before another college followed Keble's example. Merton's first stamps, embossed on blue surface-coloured paper by EMBERLIN & SON, were issued on 1 June 1876. Merton's last issue in 1883 was a mauve stamp printed by lithography and supplied by Emberlin & Son. Hertford's stamps had been delivered to the college in December 1875; the wrapper still exists which contained the original supply, addressed to the college Bursar and bearing one of the stamps. However, these stamps were not issued until 1879. The stamps of Lincoln College were designed, engraved and recess-printed by Allan Wyon of London. They bear the words 'Message' and 'One Penny' round a mitre, and are the only ones to show the purpose of the stamps

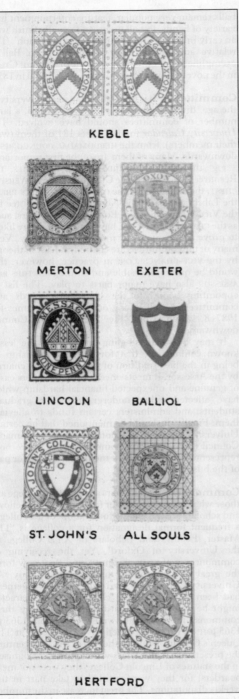

KEBLE

MERTON

EXETER

LINCOLN

BALLIOL

ST. JOHN'S

ALL SOULS

HERTFORD

These stamps were used for local posts by a number of Oxford colleges between 1871 and 1886. They were finally suppressed by the Postmaster-General, although Keble College, which had been the first to introduce college stamps, continued to use franked envelopes until the 1890s.

and their price. All other issued stamps bear the name of the college, the design being based on part of the

college's coat of arms. Lincoln's stamps were issued in 1877, 1878, 1882 and 1884 in different shades of indigo. Exeter College issued its stamps on 11 November 1882, St John's on 19 January 1884 and All Souls on 26 January 1884.

Balliol had its stamps prepared for use in 1885, but the stamps were never issued because on 28 January 1886 the Postmaster-General objected that the system was an infringement of the Post Office's monopoly. The use of college stamps was thus stopped. They had been in use for nearly fifteen years, but examples of them are now rare and they are much sought after by specialist collectors. Several of the envelopes which have survived are addressed to Messrs T. & G. Mallam, a firm of solicitors in HIGH STREET. (Thomas Mallam was a PROCTOR in the VICE-CHANCELLOR'S court. *See* MALLAMS.)

Although Oriel College did not issue stamps there exists a notice issued by the college in October 1885 which shows the use of the system. It reads in part:

MESSAGES

The Messenger will go out with Notes, etc. at the following hours, viz:—

| 10.0 a.m. | 12.0 noon | 7.0 p.m. |
| 11.0 a.m. | 2.0 p.m. | 8.30 p.m. |

Except in emergencies the Messenger will not go beyond the range of the Colleges; but all Notes, etc. for distant parts of Oxford will be stamped in the Lodge, and sent by Post.

Stamps were sometimes cancelled with a pencil stroke or, in the case of Exeter, by various manuscript marks, including an E with a line drawn through it. Keble and Hertford, however, had special cancellers: a cancellation with five dots was used on the early issues of Keble, and Hertford used a cross *patée fitchée*, which is now in the museum at the Royal Philatelic Society in London. Only four examples of this used on cover have been recorded, one of which is in the Royal Collection. Keble, Merton and Hertford also used embossed envelopes and postcards as well as stamps, and Exeter an embossed postcard.

The three Cambridge colleges which issued stamps were Selwyn (1882), Queens' College (1883) and St John's (1884).

(Lister, Raymond, *College Stamps of Oxford and Cambridge*, Cambridge, 1966; Cummings, Hayman, *The College Stamps of Oxford and Cambridge*, 1904.)

Colleges There are thirty-five colleges in the University of Oxford, scattered around the city centre and in NORTH OXFORD. All are self-governing bodies, owning the buildings they occupy, and many of the wealthier colleges have valuable investments and assets not only in Oxford but throughout the country. Each of the colleges has charitable status. All now admit both men and women, with the exception of Somerville and St Hilda's, which (up to 1989) admit women only. The colleges are listed below in the order of their foundation with the title of the head of each college. Although University College and Balliol have the earliest foundations, Merton has the earliest college statutes. Some of the colleges existed at an earlier date in another form; for example, St Edmund Hall was an ACADEMIC HALL in the University in 1238 but did not achieve full college status until 1957; Hertford existed as HART HALL in 1283, became a college in 1740, closed in 1818 and was re-founded in 1874; and St Peter's was founded as a hall in 1929.

College	*Year of Foundation*	*Head of College*
University	1249	Master
Balliol	1263	Master
Merton	1264	Warden
Exeter	1314	Rector
Oriel	1326	Provost
Queen's	1341	Provost
New College	1379	Warden
Lincoln	1427	Rector
All Souls	1438	Warden
Magdalen	1458	President
Brasenose	1509	Principal
Corpus Christi	1517	President
Christ Church	1546	Dean
Trinity	1555	President
St John's	1555	President
Jesus	1571	Principal
Wadham	1612	Warden
Pembroke	1624	Master
Worcester	1714	Provost
Hertford	1740	Principal
Keble	1868	Warden
Lady Margaret Hall	1878	Principal
Somerville	1879	Principal
St Hugh's	1886	Principal
St Hilda's	1893	Principal
St Anne's	1952	Principal
St Antony's	1953	Warden
St Edmund Hall	1957	Principal
Nuffield	1958	Warden
St Peter's	1961	Master
St Catherine's	1963	Master
Linacre	1965	Principal
St Cross	1965	Master
Wolfson	1966	President
Green	1977	Warden

Permanent Private Halls

Campion Hall	1896	Master
St Benet's Hall	1899	Master
Mansfield	1955	Principal
Regent's Park	1957	Principal
Greyfriars	1957	Warden

Collinwood Road United Reformed Church
In 1949 a hall was built to house a growing congregation that had been meeting in a private house since 1945. Its first full-time minister was appointed in 1951. The present church, in red brick and designed by H.D. Bailey, was built in 1959.

Commemoration Balls The term is applied to certain large-scale and expensive balls which have long taken place in colleges each year after the end of Trinity Term. The 'commemoration' referred to is nothing to do with the individual college, but is related to the fact that the dances are held in the week formerly known as the Commemoration, in which take place, notably, ENCAENIA and the service at which the University's benefactors are remembered. The balls have traditionally rotated among the colleges on a three-year cycle (thus giving every undergraduate an opportunity to attend one during a normal University career), but this appears no longer to be observed. The

balls remain very popular, feature entertainment by a variety of bands, last all night, and usually finish with an early breakfast and a 'survivors' photograph'. The relative antiquity of the Commemoration Ball is exemplified by the attendance at one of Verdant Green in the novel of that name which was published in 1853.

Committees It is inevitable that, in a University of the age, diversity and complexity of Oxford, a large number of committees should have evolved. The *University Calendar* for 1987 lists 131 of them (with their members), from the HEBDOMADAL COUNCIL itself downwards. Many of them are of the first importance – e.g. the GENERAL BOARD OF THE FACULTIES, the Resources Committee, the Curators of the UNIVERSITY CHEST, the Delegates of the OXFORD UNIVERSITY PRESS, the Libraries Board, the Nominating Committee for the Vice-Chancellorship. Equally, many others, such as the CRAVEN COMMITTEE, have duties which are likely to prove less arduous, or meet less frequently. Very many of the committees are chaired, at least in theory, by the VICE-CHANCELLOR; in practice, however, this would be quite impossible and so the PROCTORS and ASSESSOR also have major parts to play. The list of appointing bodies to the University boards and committees is itself a long one, with 107 names for 1987–8, again from the Hebdomadal Council downwards.

It may be worth singling out, among the lesser known committees, that for Student Hardship as being in the best tradition of the University: chaired by the Assessor, it meets once a term, considers cases of genuine and unexpected financial hardship which have affected either undergraduates or graduate students, and administers certain funds to alleviate them. Finally, it should be mentioned that on certain University committees (notably the Hebdomadal Council and some joint committees) there are now representatives of the junior members, at least for part of the business transacted.

Commoners Commoners at an Oxford college are those who, unlike the Master (or equivalent), Fellows and scholars are not 'on the foundation' of the college: a frequent formal designation for a college is 'The Master, Fellows and Scholars of XYZ College in the University of Oxford'. Yet the receiving of commoners is of great antiquity, and they now form the great majority of the undergraduate body. At University College already by 1292 an arrangement had been made by which clerks of good character might be admitted to board and lodge ('take their commons') there at their own expense; from 1363 to 1365 JOHN WYCLIF was effectively a commoner at The Queen's College, while by the end of the 15th century the presence of commoners was expressly recognised in the statutes of Lincoln College; they were not mere boarders, for they were entitled to take part in the weekly disputations. The great increase in the number of commoners began in the reign of Elizabeth I, when all students were brought into colleges or ACADEMIC HALLS; Oriel had thirty in 1612 out of a total number of seventy-nine people at the college in that year.

Various terms have been used in the past, including gentlemen-commoners or Fellow Commoners (who would pay high fees for their instruction and, especially in the 17th and 18th centuries, would receive some of the amenities reserved for Fellows).

Nowadays, the main difference between scholars and commoners is found in the shorter gown worn by the latter, though scholars at some colleges may retain a few other privileges. With the disappearance in 1986 of entrance scholarships at Oxford, the distinction seems likely to fade still further.

Commons *see* BATTELS.

Conference of Colleges First met in 1966, convened under the impetus of the Report of the Commission of Enquiry (the FRANKS REPORT). Provisional constitutional arrangements were approved by 1968 and have remained relatively unaltered since that time. The Conference is not a statutory body; its function is to discuss matters of common concern to colleges, including the relationship between the colleges and the University. Two representatives from each college may attend the meetings – normally the head of house and the (senior) Bursar, though other college officers (e.g. senior tutor, or tutor for admissions) will attend if relevant matters are on the agenda. Conference meets at least once a term (on the Thursday of the fifth week), and occasionally twice if the level of business warrants it. Both the HEBDOMADAL COUNCIL and the GENERAL BOARD OF THE FACULTIES receive standing invitations to be represented. The Conference has created and appoints members to two committees: a Standing Committee and a Colleges' Fees Committee. Voting at Conference is normally on the basis of one vote per college. The chairman serves for one year, but is re-eligible.

Congregation The legislative body of the University, now comprising mainly resident Masters of Arts who are members of the academic and administrative staff. Originally it consisted of all Regent Masters, constituting the supreme authority in the early mediaeval University, but by the end of the 13th century the Regent Masters were supplemented by non-Regent Masters to form the Great Congregation or CONVOCATION. Congregation retained the right to legislate in minor matters, to regulate procedure, to interpret statutes and to grant graces.

There was a further body in the mediaeval University known as the Black Congregation (*congregatio nigra*), consisting of Regent Masters of Arts, which met at St Mildred's Church until it was demolished in 1437 and after that at ST MARY THE VIRGIN. It met the day before Convocation to make a preview of the agenda, though it had no power to block a motion. It declined in the late Middle Ages and by 1570 had ceased to exist.

In the 16th century Congregation acquired some of the powers of Convocation, becoming the supreme legislative authority in 1508, but by the LAUDIAN CODE of 1636, which restored the status of Convocation, it was empowered to deliberate on resolutions put forward by the HEBDOMADAL BOARD and to admit to DEGREES. In 1854 it was remodelled to include all resident members of Convocation. It was allowed to conduct its debates in English instead of in Latin and was granted the power of accepting, rejecting and proposing amendments to statutes proposed by the HEBDOMADAL COUNCIL. In 1913 it was remodelled in such a way that it became a genuine organ of the teaching and administrative staff of the University and

colleges, its present structure in the main determined by the statute of 1926. To all intents and purposes Congregation now constitutes the parliament of the University.

There is a vestigial remnant of the pre-1854 Congregation in the so-called Ancient House of Congregation. By an oversight, the old Congregation of Regents was not abolished and retained those functions not transferred to the new Congregation – viz. granting graces, conferring degrees and confirming the appointment of examiners.

Congregation House Built in about 1320 with money supplied by Thomas Cobham, Bishop of Worcester, on the north-east side of the tower of ST MARY THE VIRGIN for meetings of CONGREGATION, with a room above it for the library which Cobham intended to leave to the University. When he died in 1327, however, there was not enough money to complete the library, whose interior was not fitted with shelves and whose windows were not glazed until the beginning of the 15th century (*see* BODLEIAN *and* ST MARY THE VIRGIN). Both the library and the vaulted Congregation House below were remodelled in the Perpendicular style between 1503 and 1510. As well as for meetings, the Congregation House was used for storing the University ARCHIVES. Congregation continued to meet here until the building of the CONVOCATION HOUSE in 1637. By the 19th century it was being used to house the University fire engine, but was restored as a chapel in 1871. Approached through a small vestry, it was subsequently used to contain some of the statues removed from the spire of the church when it was restored in 1892–6 by SIR THOMAS JACKSON (*see* STATUES). The room above is now used for parish meetings.

Conservation Areas All buildings listed as of Architectural or Historic Interest, of which there are some 1400 in Oxford, and all property in Conservation Areas are subject to special planning control. There are fourteen Conservation Areas in Oxford, designated as such under the Civic Amenities Act, 1967 (now the Town and Country Planning Act, 1971), because of their distinct character as a whole. The areas, with the dates of their designation, are NORTH OXFORD Victorian Suburb (1968, extended in 1972, 1975 and 1976), IFFLEY village (1969, extended 1985), Old HEADINGTON (1971, extended in 1976, 1985 and 1986), HEADINGTON QUARRY (1976), Central Area (1971, extended in 1974, 1981 and 1985), Beauchamp Lane (1973), Walton Manor (1975), Bartlemas (1976), OSNEY town (1976), ST CLEMENT'S and IFFLEY ROAD (1977). HEADINGTON HILL (1977), WOLVERCOTE with GODSTOW (1981, extended 1985), Upper Wolvercote with BINSEY (1981) and Temple Cowley (1986).

Convocation The collective name given to the assembly of all Masters of Arts whose names are on the college books. First mentioned in 1274, it was known originally as the Great Congregation (*magna* or *plena congregatio*) to differentiate it from the CONGREGATION of Regent Masters. From the end of the 13th century Congregation had been reinforced by the non-Regent Masters, so replacing the original Congregation of Regents as the highest legislative body and court of appeal in the University. It acted as a final court of appeal, admitted new Masters by inception, granted

101

dispensations and duties, elected the principal OFFICERS OF THE UNIVERSITY, managed the UNIVERSITY CHEST and was concerned with all the major questions of administration. Its meetings took place in ST MARY THE VIRGIN until the CONGREGATION HOUSE was built by Thomas Cobham, Bishop of Worcester, in about 1320.

The powers and authority of Convocation waned in the later Middle Ages as Congregation proved more active and became the supreme legislative authority in 1508. But in 1636 the LAUDIAN CODE restored Convocation's full authority, its chief function being the enactment and repeal of STATUTES. It had also the right to appoint University officers, professors and lecturers, to grant dispensations, to present to benefices and to supervise all major matters relating to University administration. As a result of the University Reform Act of 1854 (*see* ROYAL COMMISSIONS) it lost the right to appoint professors, and subsequently most of its powers passed to Congregation. Its sole functions now are to make elections within its statutory powers – e.g. to the chancellorship and the Professorship of Poetry (voting on such occasions has to be done in person).

Convocation House *Old Schools Quadrangle.* Built in 1634–7 at the same time as Selden End of the BODLEIAN LIBRARY, which is above it. The panelling, stalls and VICE-CHANCELLOR's throne, with its hexagonal canopy, are all of the 17th century. The fan vault was added in 1758–9 by John Townesend (*see* TOWNESEND'S). Convocation House is the parliament house of the University. The national Parliament met here in times of plague in London and also during the CIVIL WAR.

Cooper's 'Oxford' Marmalade In 1874 Mrs Sarah Jane Cooper made 76 lb of marmalade on her

kitchen range from an old family recipe. This was more than the family required, so her husband Frank put the surplus in earthenware jars and sold it to dons and undergraduates from his grocery shop at No. 84 HIGH STREET, where the ANGEL INN used to stand. The product, which is made from Seville oranges, was so successful that in 1900 the firm of Frank Cooper Ltd opened new works in the Victoria Buildings in PARK END STREET. In 1947 production was moved to the old Oxford ICE RINK premises in the BOTLEY ROAD, but in 1967 Cooper's was taken over by Brown & Polson and moved from Oxford. In 1985 the firm was able to move back to Oxford, having obtained the lease of 84 High Street where the famous 'Oxford' marmalade was first made. The premises are now a museum showing the history of the firm of Frank Cooper Ltd, as well as selling its products.

Cornmarket Formerly called North Gate Street because it ran from CARFAX to the North Gate of the city. As its name implies, Cornmarket Street was the street where corn was bought and sold. In 1536 Dr John Claymond, President of Corpus Christi College, had a lead roof supported on stone pillars erected in the middle of the street, 'that thereby in wet seasons sacks of corne might be preserved from the violence of the weather'. It was demolished in 1644 to provide lead for bullets during the CIVIL WAR. Increasing traffic made the sale of corn in the street inconvenient and the corn dealers moved first to the COVERED MARKET and then to the Corn Exchange, which had been built for the purpose. The street is mainly a commercial one, most of its buildings being used in the 19th century as small shops or inns and more recently as large stores, banks or fast-food premises.

On the east side from CARFAX the Lloyds Bank building on the corner with HIGH STREET was built in 1900–1, designed by Stephen Salter. No. 3 is a

The preparation room of Frank Cooper's marmalade and preserve works in 1902.

Cornmarket Street in 1838 by the Oxford drawing master and lithographer William De La Motte.

15th-century building with an 18th-century front, containing the PAINTED ROOM in what was formerly the Crown Tavern. Beyond a building which in 1923–4 was Week's Restaurant is the GOLDEN CROSS inn. Between the Golden Cross and MARKET STREET there was in the 19th century a 'fancy repository at No. 7 called The Civet Cat. This was replaced in 1907 by a stone-fronted building by J.R. Wilkins, built for Arthur Shepherd, the tailor. The Old Roebuck Hotel next to it was demolished in 1935 for the building of the Woolworth store, later occupied by Boots. The development in a Cotswold style on the south corner with Market Street was built in 1938–9, while the small shops on the opposite corner were demolished in 1963 for the erection of the former Marks & Spencer store, by Lewis and Hickey in Portland stone (*see* STONE).

Between Market Street and SHIP STREET there were no fewer than three inns in the 19th century: the BELL, the White Hart and the BLUE ANCHOR. The Edwardian Buol's Restaurant, in a gabled building designed by Stephen Salter, was at No. 21, on the site of the old White Hart inn. Nos 22 and 24 are four-storeyed, early 20th-century buildings, No. 24 having been occupied between 1928 and 1972 by Fuller's Café. No. 28, the much-photographed building on the corner of Ship Street, was restored in 1952 by Thomas Rayson and now looks much as it did in the 18th century and earlier, with timbered upper storey projecting. It was occupied successively by Buckell & Ballard, estate agents, and Harvey Bros, a firm of tea and coffee merchants. In 1986–7 the adjoining building, occupied by the tailors and rainwear specialists ZACHARIAS AND CO. ('Zacs for Macs'), was extensively restored by its owners, Jesus College.

On the opposite corner with Ship Street is the church of ST MICHAEL AT THE NORTH GATE, with its Saxon tower, the oldest building in Oxford. The house which stood next to the church on the south side was demolished in about 1780 and the one which joined the tower on the north side early in the 20th century. It was formerly occupied by Lewis Solomon, a jeweller, and then by Nurse, the furrier. No. 30 (Elliott House) is of ashlar stone in neo-classical style, with a Dutch gable; it was refronted in 1904 to the design of Herbert Quinton. It was the home of the

Elliott family in the second half of the 19th century and in the early 20th. (Edwin Litchfield Elliott was a shoe manufacturer and leather merchant.) The building was bought by ST MICHAEL AND ALL SAINTS CHARITIES in 1985. BOSWELLS department store adjoins the house. In the 19th century Henry Boswell carried on business at No. 50, selling trunks and portmanteaux. BAKER'S occupied the building on the corner with Broad Street, which was erected in 1915 and is now DILLONS.

The ancient North Gate of the city stood across Cornmarket by the tower of St Michael's; above it was the BOCARDO PRISON. ANTHONY WOOD writes of the North Gate in his *City of Oxford*: 'This was the strongest gate of the city; as indeed by good reason it should, having no river before it, as the others hath. It was well strengthened on each side with a strong bulky tower; and backt on with another gate, both formerly well fenced with a port-close or port-cullis to let downe before; as also a military engine erected over it, through which they could cast downe anything obnoxious to the enemy approaching thereto. . . . Besides this there were two great folding doors hung thereon, made strong with barres of iron nailed upon them; as alsoe a massive chaine that crossed the outward gate'. Both the North Gate and Bocardo were demolished in 1771.

No. 35, on the site of the Bocardo, was formerly the premises of the ALDEN PRESS, booksellers and publishers of *Alden's Oxford Guides*. On the opposite corner with ST MICHAEL'S STREET was the PLOUGH INN, whose sign can still be seen over the shop door. Affixed to the building is one of the early fire marks issued by the Sun Insurance Office in about 1720, bearing the number of the fire policy beneath the sun face. The CADENA café was at Nos 44–7. Just south of FREWIN COURT stood the CLARENDON HOTEL and Morris Garages (*see* LORD NUFFIELD *and* MOTOR CARS). These were demolished in 1955 to make way for Clarendon House, the new Woolworth store (the initial 'W' can be seen in the stonework over the entrance to the offices above). The building was designed in 1956–7 by Lord Holford, with a deeply recessed shop-front with walling of squared rubble and infill panels of slate. Woolworth closed in 1983 and the front is now disfigured by the blue tubular hoops marking the entrance to the CLARENDON CENTRE. In *Brideshead Revisited* Evelyn Waugh refers to the old Clarendon Hotel in the 1930s: 'In the Cornmarket a party of tourists stood on the steps of the Clarendon Hotel discussing a road map with their chauffeur, while opposite, through the venerable arch of the Golden Cross, I greeted a group of undergraduates from my college who had breakfasted there and now lingered with their pipes in the creeper-hung courtyard.'

The southern part of Barclays Bank at No. 54 was built around 1875 as the Shakespeare Hotel. Gillett's Bank took over the premises in 1877. The building also housed the office of the Oxford County Court (*see* COURTS) and the University Turkish Baths. The northern half of the bank's premises was built in 1922 to the same design. The CLARENDON CLUB occupied premises above the bank until 1967. Nos 55 and 56 were occupied by the grocery firm of GRIMBLY HUGHES & Co., whose premises were replaced in 1964 by a building with vertical fins designed by D.M.C. Ruddick for Littlewood's, but now occupied by McDonald's. The CROWN INN (not to be confused with the Crown Tavern, which was at No. 3) is down a yard adjoining this building. At the southern end of the street stood ST MARTIN'S CHURCH and the PENNILESS BENCH. The building now on the Carfax corner is the Midland Bank, built in 1896–7 to the design of Henry Hare.

The surface of Cornmarket Street was, like that of other main streets, paved with cobblestones in mediaeval times. There were then no pavements for pedestrians, the cobblestones extending up to the houses. The road sloped down to the middle where there was a gutter or kennel, as in BRASENOSE LANE. Householders were obliged to repair the section of road in front of their house as far as the kennel. A pillory and whipping post stood in the centre of the road opposite Frewin Court. It had three holes, one for the neck and two for the wrists, and was raised on a platform. It was used as a punishment for minor offenders, such as bakers or brewers who adulterated their goods. It was last used in 1810. In the 18th century the street was paved and in the 19th tram-lines were laid (*see* TRANSPORT). After the Second World War the volume of traffic passing along Cornmarket was so heavy that fears were expressed that the vibration was damaging the buildings and an experimental surface of rubber blocks was laid. This proved to be dangerous in wet weather and was taken up in 1955. The street became increasingly congested over the succeeding years and it was accepted that it was no longer necessary for through-traffic to use it. In 1973 a form of pedestrian precinct was adopted: the pavements were widened, the kerbs removed and the street was closed to all vehicles except buses, taxis and vehicles requiring access.

Corpus Christi College   On 30 June 1513 Richard Foxe, the statesman and ecclesiastic, was building a MONASTIC COLLEGE in Oxford for eight monks from St Swithun's, Winchester, where he was Bishop. The site was a rectangle 100 yards long between MERTON STREET and the CITY WALL. It was 80 yards wide, later increased to 90 yards by the addition of a roadway which lay between it and Christ Church. Here had stood Urban Hall, St Christopher Hall, Corner Hall, Ledynporch (or Nevile's Inn) and Bekes Inn, all of

which had been ACADEMIC HALLS but had fallen into decay. The landlords were Merton College, GODSTOW ABBEY and ST FRIDESWIDE'S PRIORY. Foxe acquired the halls and intended that St Swithun's should own them.

Foxe did not in fact found a monastic college like Canterbury College, for his friend Hugh Oldham – a Lancashire yeoman who became adviser to Henry VII's mother – persuaded him to alter his plan and instead to found a secular institution. Oldham had been in bitter dispute with the Abbot of Tavistock, and Holinshed quotes John Hooker for Oldham's phrase: 'shall we build houses and provide livelihood for a company of bussing monks, whose end and fall we ourselves may live to see? No, no, it is more meet a great deal that we should have care to provide the increase of learning, and for such as who by their learning shall do good in the church and common-wealth.' The change almost tripled the personnel, involving larger buildings and an increase in endowment from £160 to £380 a year. Oldham, who also founded Manchester Grammar School, gave £4000.

Corpus has seven portraits of Foxe and others of Oldham and Richard Pate, another benefactor (*d.*1588). Foxe also founded schools at Grantham and Taunton. He often compared Corpus Christi to a beehive. Bees did, in fact, settle above the room of Dr Ludovicus Vives in a new cloister built in 1521; they did not depart until the Parliamentary VISITATION in 1648.

College life began on 5 March 1517 with ten Fellows. By Michaelmas there were twenty residents and by 1522 forty. The front quadrangle was presumably built by March 1517 with twenty sets of rooms, each for one Fellow and his *discipulus*. In the 16th century the President lived in the tower, whence he could see all the entrances. A bastion in the garden probably protected a postern gate to which ran the roadway, acquired from the city. Foxe employed men high in royal service: William Vertue and William East, master-masons, and Humfrey Coke, master-carpenter. The library occupied the south side of the quadrangle and gradually extended eastwards. Its chained humanist books led Erasmus to predict that it would attract more scholars to Oxford than once flocked to Rome. It had 371 books in 1589, of which 310 remain, as well as 498 manuscripts. The muniments (now under the Fellows' building) were kept in the tower in cupboards contemporary with the foundation; modelled on those at Magdalen, these were an advance on the traditional use of chests. There are significant similarities in the plans, perhaps by Vertue, for Corpus Christi College and St Mary's College for Austin Canons (*see* MONASTIC COLLEGES). At Corpus Christi the chapel projects from the south-east corner of the quadrangle, parallel to a 15th-century building used as the kitchen, which abutted the middle of the east range. It is almost a mirror image of St Mary's (built the following year), except for the position of the gate-tower and the absence of a great cloister. The roofs are twins; the craftsmen were the same. St Mary's was apparently rebuilt by Vertue for THOMAS WOLSEY in 1518. Significantly, St Mary's was monastic and did not long survive the Dissolution – FREWIN HALL now stands on the site.

The 1517 statutes of Corpus Christi decreed that the twenty scholars should be natives of the many

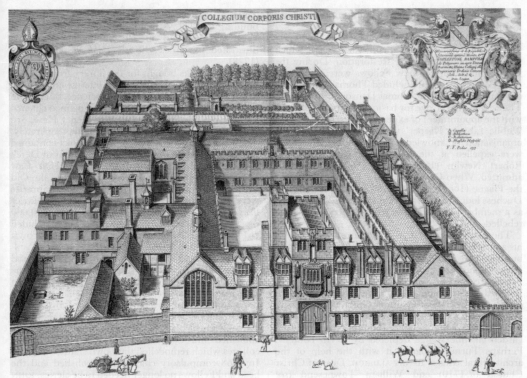

David Loggan's bird's-eye view of Corpus Christi College in 1675. Outside his kennel (left) *stands the fox who commemorated Richard Foxe, the statesman and founder of the college.*

counties where the college estates lay, or of dioceses of which Foxe had been Bishop. Fourteen came from Surrey, Hampshire, Gloucestershire or Worcestershire and Kent, and the dioceses of Durham, Bath and Exeter. Five came from Lincolnshire and Lancashire (the birthplaces of Foxe and Oldham), Bedfordshire, Oxfordshire and Wiltshire, and the twentieth from the kin of William Frost, Foxe's steward, whose bequest included Maplederwell, Hampshire. Scholars were occasionally admitted from other counties but it was not until the time of the Victorian reforms that the territorial nexus was abolished altogether.

Fellows were on probation for two years, and for the first forty years kept fellowships for only five years on average. *Discipuli* were boys generally aged between twelve and seventeen years of age at election, studying at Corpus as junior members of the college in *statu pupillari*. Small emoluments were paid. Some sons of noblemen were permitted to come at their own cost, but none did. Before admission, undergraduates had to be able to write Latin verse. The college had professors of Latin and Greek, and a professor of Theology was allowed by statute but not appointed, although the aim of the college was to produce educated clergymen. On becoming MA each Fellow had to be ordained and at least 250 out of 800 Tudor Corpus men became clerics. The statutes were the first to specify Greek and to define which classical texts were to be read. Foxe also introduced Nicholas Kratzer from Munich to teach Mathematics. The chapel had a precentor and sacristan (both priests), two acolytes (for the organ and bells), and two choirboys, who, if qualified, could become *discipuli* when their voices broke.

The first President, John Claymond (1517–37), Master of St Cross in Winchester and once President of Magdalen, followed Foxe in his presentation of classical texts, many of which contained his manuscript notes. He was a public benefactor, erecting a building for the corn merchants in the CORNMARKET and a causeway in BOTLEY. He bequeathed a sapphire ring for successive Presidents, and is commemorated in a Latin poem and by a brass showing his shrouded skeleton. Claymond's successor, Robert Morwent (1537–53), had also moved from Magdalen as Vice-President in 1517. He survived various official changes of religion, and on his accession brought out of hiding a number of Catholic vestments and ritual objects. One of his successors, William Cole, was forced to flee abroad as a heretic during the reign of Mary Tudor. John Jewel, a Protestant Fellow, also fled. Cole later returned, and on the insistence of Elizabeth I he was made President in 1563. In 1573, John Rainolds, who became famous as a great Puritan preacher, became a lecturer in Greek at the age of twenty-three. In 1593 he was made Dean of Lincoln by Queen Elizabeth, although a year earlier she had 'schooled [him] for his obstinate preciseness'. In 1598 Sir Robert Cecil, prompted by Archbishop Whitgift, persuaded the Queen to transfer the deanery to William Cole, thus, by exchange, enabling John Rainolds to become President of Corpus Christi. During his Presidency (1598–1607) Rainolds was chief of four leading Puritans at the Hampton Court Conference; the translators of the Authorised Version of the Bible met weekly in his lodgings until his death in 1607.

In 1642 Corpus Christi subscribed £400 for Charles I but retained its valuable early PLATE, which was packed away until the Restoration. During the Interregnum fourteen new Fellows were appointed. 'The Cambridge scum' included Thomas Gilson, son of a Suffolk baker, and Thomas Danson, the chaplain. The new faction strove for basic educational reforms, with the appointment of experimental scientists and a 'Public Library Keeper' with a central role in the organisation of knowledge in the BODLEIAN. They were expelled at the Restoration when President Robert Newlin (1640–8 and 1660–87) was re-admitted. When Charles II lived in Oxford to avoid the Plague (1665), the Duke of Monmouth and his Duchess lodged at Corpus and his name was entered as a member. It was erased from the book when he rebelled.

Thomas Turner (1687–1714) spent liberally from his ample fortune on the President's house and other buildings. He had 'the greatest authority among the Heads', and his good taste is apparent. Arthur Frogley, carpenter, panelled the hall. Work in 1979 revealed his skill and that of Jonathan Mayne, the carver (an associate of Grinling Gibbons), especially on the screen and cartouches of arms of donors.

In 1706–12 the Fellows' building replaced the garden chamber range depicted by DAVID LOGGAN. Perhaps Turner designed it with the help of the architectural skills of HENRY ALDRICH, Dean of Christ Church (d. 1710) and William Townesend (see TOWNESENDS), who worked on the chapel and hall. The President's lodgings of 1607 were replaced during this period. Old members subscribed for Townesend to erect the gentlemen-commoners' building in 1737. A fireplace inserted in the hall in 1741 was restored in 1979 following a design illustrated in James Gibbs's *Book of Architecture* (1728).

A list of books bought for the library from 1717 to 1774, giving prices, shows an interest in English history, classical sites and some in science, but little in recent literature. Most of the books remained chained until 1784. The Italian bequest of Henry Hare, 3rd Baron Coleraine (admitted 1712), was kept separately. The bequest of Sir Robert Ensor's books contained material on early socialism in England; that of Derek Hall is commemorated in the Derek Hall Law Library. Junior members were admitted to the Old Library in 1929. The Senior and Junior Libraries were amalgamated in 1962. In 1977 all the lower library was converted for open access, making 10,000 more volumes accessible. The collections included 261 incunables. A book repository at No. 8 PARK TOWN was completed in 1976.

WILLIAM BUCKLAND, the geologist, JOHN KEBLE, and THOMAS ARNOLD of Rugby were admitted during the lengthy presidency of John Cooke (1783–1823). In 1850 President James Norris (1843–72) had conscientious difficulties (overcome by the Bishop of Winchester as VISITOR) about helping the ROYAL COMMISSION, but gentlemen-commoners were abolished and Corpus was one of the only three colleges which remodelled their own statutes in 1855. In 1868 compulsory chapel was abolished and the head and Fellows no longer needed to be clerics. JOHN RUSKIN, when Slade Professor, lived in the Fellows' building from 1871 to 1877, though Norris warned, 'You will, I am afraid, find the Tutors Great Radicals.'

The quadrangle of Corpus Christi, showing the celebrated late 16th-century sun-dial surmounted by the college pelican, which was designed by Charles Turnbull, a Fellow of the college.

The greatest was John Matthias Wilson, 'with his frank out-spokenness and Northern accent', leader of the Liberal Party in Oxford. His presidency (1872–81) was marred by ill-health. Other Fellows included Sir Henry Maine, followed as Regius Professor of Civil Law by Sir Frederick Pollock and Sir Paul Vinogradoff, the Rev. Henry Octavius Coxe (Bodley's librarian) and Henry Nettleship (winner of the first open scholarship in 1857 and Corpus Professor of Latin in 1878). Thomas Fowler (1881–1904) wrote the history of Corpus (1893) and left a letter-book to the presidential archives.

In 1885 SIR THOMAS GRAHAM JACKSON built an annexe at the corner of Merton Street and MAGPIE LANE and in 1928–9 T.H. Hughes designed the Emily Thomas building. Fowler's undergraduates included J.G. Milne (who, in old age, amplified the early history of Corpus and worked in the library and muniments) and P.S. Allen (President 1924–33), who edited the letters of Erasmus. In 1891 the *Pelican Record* (probably the earliest college magazine) began. It recorded the details of college life, with honours, appointments and family details of past members.

Thomas Case (1904–24), like Thomas Turner, designed and paid for his new President's lodgings, skilfully reconciling existing Italian and Gothic features. He 'opposed changes in Church, State and university', supported the exclusion of women from the University, and defeated the abolition of compulsory Greek at a cost of £100, importing secretaries and despatching endless postcards to rally CONGREGATION. Lieutenant-Colonel Aubrey Vere Spencer was Bursar from 1925–46; he was also University Land Agent from 1939 to 1946 and High Sheriff of Oxfordshire in 1959. He skilfully managed the college estates in eleven counties, professionally surveying each farm. He annotated large-scale maps and visited the estates regularly. He also managed domestic expenditure.

In 1926 there were seventy-five undergraduates at Corpus; the ten new sets in the Thomas buildings allowed the upper limit to rise from eighty to ninety in 1928. No sons of noblemen or very rich people or Etonians applied in the 1920s and 1930s; sons of Corpus men and of clergymen and the pupils of schoolmasters who had been at Corpus were, however, numerous. Most became teachers or administrators. Support for Baldwin against the General Strike of 1926 was a matter of course. The rise of unemployment and Fascism led to socialist sympathy in the 1930s, but there was no agitation for changes in the college.

Sir Richard Winn Livingstone (President 1933–50), the educationalist, retired simultaneously with W. Phelps (elected 1906), the senior tutor, and F.B. Pidduck (elected tutor 1921). This led to a break in the customs of the Senior Common Room. F.A. Lepper notes: 'The strict order-of-march into Hall was dropped; Fraenkel was given free rein to talk as much shop as he liked.' Eduard Fraenkel, successor of A.C. Clarke as Corpus Christi Professor of Latin (1935–53), a refugee from Hitler, died in 1970 – the year in which his successor, Sir Roger Mynors, retired; Fraenkel's study was named 'the Fraenkel room'. The ashes of E.A. Lowe (Honorary Fellow 1936), the great palaeographer who died in 1969, were laid in the chapel.

In 1954–5, 21 per cent of the undergraduates at Corpus were scientists, increasing to 24 per cent in 1959–60 and 36 per cent in 1964, compared with 33 per cent in the University as a whole. In 1959 the college elected for the first time two tutorial Fellows in Natural Science and Physics, and in Chemistry. During the 1960s, although oriented towards the humanities, it introduced outstanding people in Medicine, the sciences and Mathematics. This meant greater diversity, but the college's outstanding classical reputation remained, and in 1967 undergraduates gained nine Firsts in Classical Honour Moderations and twelve in Final Honour Schools. The number of those in *statu pupillari* reached a record in 1963–4 with 200, seventy of whom lived in college, eleven in the annexe and four more in a house in Magpie Lane.

It was agreed in 1963 that ten ladies would be allowed to dine at the guest table on two occasions each term – a dramatic proposal with a surprising absence of opposition in a community where the name of no living woman had been permitted to be mentioned in hall. In 1969 Corpus had long been politically inert, but in Michaelmas its Junior Common Room took the lead in withholding grants to any Oxford University sports club which played in South Africa. At the same time the governing body gave leave for denominations other than Anglican to hold services in the chapel. A first tutor in Economics was appointed. In addition to the new President, G.D.G. Hall, there were six new Fellows and two new lecturers, one female. In 1971 the college formed a loose and informal alliance with SOMERVILLE. A majority of the governing body proposed changing the statutes to institute undergraduate female residents, but junior members were disappointed that the necessary two-thirds did not give support. Eventually the Privy Council amended the statutes to let women take the entrance examination in November 1978 and to matriculate in October 1979. In Michaelmas 1979 twenty women were accepted for entry. The first woman elected President of the MIDDLE COMMON ROOM was Miss Z.H. Szymanska in 1979–80.

W.F.R. Hardie (1950–69) was a Scottish philosopher who cautiously criticised any proposal, although he could see the case for any change as clearly as its advocates. He was amused to see the editorial error in the *Victoria County History* which ascribed the presidency of Corpus to his brother instead of to himself. His successor, George Derek Gordon Hall (1969–75), an authority on mediaeval legal history, worked to avoid the worst aspects of student unrest of the late 1960s. Like John Matthias Wilson he came from South Shields and was dogged by ill-health. He died aged fifty-one.

In the early 1950s, at the suggestion of Sir Douglas Veale, Cecil Handyside surveyed the crumbling college buildings and work started on the south façade of the Fellows' buildings. The gentlemen-commoners' building was then restored, although without the reinstatement of the chimneystacks at the ends. Under President Frank Hardie, Dr Harold E. Desche rebuilt the cloister and turned the cellars of the Fellows' buildings into muniment rooms. Refacing of the south elevation of these in 1954 and of the eastern one of the gentlemen-commoners' building was a prelude to a ten-year programme of a proposed £45,000 restoration made possible by the Historic Buildings Scheme. Since 1970 Geoffrey Beard, founder member of the Oxford Architects' Partnership, has worked closely with the Buildings and Furniture Committee and has been responsible for the library extension and the new Senior Common Room. In 1972 the college extended its graduate accommodation by the conversion of No. 68 BANBURY ROAD into a hostel with nine single rooms and three flats; and in 1973 the great external changes were completed with the paving of the front quadrangle – an operation which revealed the probable line of the Saxon defences of Oxford.

The work in the archives by BRIAN TWYNE and Thomas Fowler was continued through the initiative of Percy Stafford Allen (President 1924–33). When J. Grafton Milne (1886), two years his senior, retired to Oxford, Allen suggested that he 'should gather together and arrange the College archives, which were scattered in all parts of the building. . . . So Milne reduced the chaos to something like order'. Proper storage and organisation for the archives was eventually accomplished in connection with the remodelling of the buildings (1960 and 1965), and the transformation of the library by Trevor H. Aston, a librarian who initiated *Past and Present* and the official history of the University.

Sir Kenneth Dover, Professor of Greek at St Andrews University since 1955, became President of Corpus in 1976. He chaired the Dover Committee on admissions and was knighted in 1977. His successor, Sir Keith Thomas, became President in October 1986.

G.B. Grundy listed fifty-five distinguished *alumni* of Corpus Christi. These included fourteen in the home Civil Service, five in the Indian and three in the British service in Africa, four in the church, fourteen in universities, seven in schools and two in literature. Distinguished names: Lord Beloff, Sir Isaiah Berlin, Sir Edmund Chambers, Oliver Elton, H.W. Garrod, Lord Hailey, E.G.V. Knox, Sir Charles Petrie, Sir Ian Richmond, Sir Hubert Llewellyn Smith.

The corporate designation is The President and Scholars of the College of Corpus Christi in the University of Oxford.

(Fowler, Rev. T., *History of Corpus Christi College*, Oxford, 1893; Liddell, J.R., 'The Library of Corpus Christi College, Oxford', *The Library*, March 1938; Milne, J.G., *The Early History of Corpus Christi College*, Oxford, 1946; Hassall, W.O., 'Corpus Christi College', *Victoria County History of Oxfordshire*, Vol. III, Oxford, 1954; Pattenden, P., 'Robert Hegge, An Oxford Antiquary', *Oxoniensia*, Vol. XLV, 1980, pp. 284–99; *The Pelican Record*, 1891–1969, thereafter called *The Pelican*.)

County Hall *New Road*. A castellated building in Norman style by John Plowman, erected in 1841 adjoining the PRISON. It has been described as 'quite the most abominable pseudo-Gothic Assize Court in all England'. A plaque (dated 1875) inside recalls the Black Assize of 1577 (*see* COURTS). The Sessions House or Shire Hall, where the assize was held, was on the site of County Hall; it is shown on a map of 1617 which is in the possession of Christ Church. The court room in County Hall was used for the assizes and the Crown Court until the opening of the new Crown Court building in ST ALDATE'S. Another court room was used by the Bullingdon Magistrates' Court and is still used as the Council Chamber of the Oxfordshire County Council. The subterranean passages and rooms beneath

County Hall now house over $2\frac{1}{2}$ miles of shelving for the County Records Office.

Court Sermon *see* ASSIZE SERMON.

Courts In the Middle Ages the principal courts in Oxford were the assizes, the town courts and the CHANCELLOR of the University's court. Some religious houses and manors also had their own courts. By the reign of Edward I there were two town courts, both called 'Curia Oxon'. The King's court, known as the Monday Court, met on a Monday and was presided over by the bailiffs; it dealt mostly with criminal cases. The MAYOR's court, known as the Friday Court, met on a Friday to deal with such offences as breaches of market regulations and small debts. Both courts were held in the Guildhall (*see* TOWN HALL) until the 19th century and their jurisdiction tended to overlap. The city's earliest title deed to have survived is a grant made in 1229 by King Henry III 'by the grace of God King of England, Lord of Ireland, Duke of Normandy and Aquitaine and Count of Anjou'. The grant is of 'a certain house in the Town of Oxford with its appurtenances which belonged to Moses ben Isaac the Jew [the site of part of the present TOWN HALL] . . . for our courts to be held in that house for ever'.

By a statute of 1414 Justices of the Peace were required to meet four times a year for the trial of more important offences, which sittings came to be known as Quarter Sessions. In the city ARCHIVES are detailed records of the Court of Quarter Sessions for the early 17th century. The justices were also required to deal with persons who were tried for petty offences at Petty Sessions. Both Quarter Sessions and Petty Sessions for the city were held in the Guildhall. The Mayor, who was always a magistrate, presided over the Petty Sessions. Offenders were often put in pillories or stocks, which were sited in CORNMARKET. The city also owned a cage, also kept in Cornmarket, into which offenders could be put, and a whipping post.

More serious offences, as well as civil cases, were tried at assizes. The shire courts and assizes were held in the Shire Hall at the CASTLE until 1577, the year of the Black Assize. In the COUNTY HALL is a plaque, dated 1875, concerning the Black Assize, which reads, 'Near this spot stood the ancient Shire Hall unhappily famous in History as the Scene in July 1577, of the *Black Assize*, when a malignant disease, known as the Gaol Fever, caused the death, within 40 days, of The Lord Chief Baron (Sir Robert Bell), The High Sheriff (Sir Robert D'Oyly of Merton) and about 300 more. The Malady from the stench of the Prisoners developed itself during the Trial of one Rowland Jenkes, a saucy foul-mouthed Bookseller, for scandalous words uttered against the Queen.' After the Black Assize the assizes were held in the town hall until the opening of the County Hall in 1841. Judges of the High Court travelled round the country to assize towns, of which Oxford was one. The judge stayed in the Judge's lodging in ST GILES' HOUSE. At the opening of the assizes the judge would attend a service in ST MARY THE VIRGIN and then proceed to County Hall, where he would be greeted by the High Sheriff with great pomp and a fanfare of trumpets. The opening of the assize was a very impressive ceremony. On 14 July 1833 JOHN KEBLE preached the ASSIZE SERMON in St Mary's (*see* OXFORD MOVEMENT).

Convicted felons were sometimes hanged on gallows in the fields to the north of the city. In the 17th century at least one was hanged from a tree in GLOUCESTER GREEN and another outside Balliol College. The latter had murdered a college servant. According to ANTHONY WOOD he 'died very penitent and hang'd there 2 or 3 in the afternoone. The next day hanged on a gibbet in chaines on this side Shotover'. There were gallows belonging to HOLYWELL MANOR at the east end of HOLYWELL STREET until the 18th century. Later executions took place at the Castle and, until the abolition of capital punishment, within the Prison. George Napier, a Fellow of Corpus Christi and a ROMAN CATHOLIC, was, according to Anthony Wood, 'sent Prisoner to the Castle of Oxford, and, the next sessions after, being convicted of Treason, was on the 9 Nov. 1610 hanged, drawn, and quartered in the Castle yard. The next day his head and quarters were set upon the 4 Gates of the City, and upon that great one belonging to Ch. Ch. [Christ Church] next to St. Aldates Church, to the great terror of the Catholics that were then in and near Oxford'.

Minor offences were tried in the Magistrates' Courts, which sat in the court rooms at the town hall until the building of the Magistrates' Courts in SPEEDWELL STREET and Albion Place in 1966–9. Designed by Douglas Murray, the City Architect, they were opened on 6 December 1969 by Lord Gardiner, who was then Lord Chancellor. The building has five court rooms, including one designed for the Juvenile Court.

Quarter Sessions were abolished by the Courts Act of 1971 at the same time as the assizes, and were replaced by Crown Courts presided over by circuit judges and recorders. The Oxford Circuit was amalgamated with the Midland Circuit in 1972 to become the Midland and Oxford Circuit. Until 1985 the Crown Courts sat in the County Hall and the town hall. They deal now with the more serious crimes formerly dealt with by Quarter Sessions and assizes. New buildings for the Crown Court and the County Court were opened on 4 October 1985 in ST ALDATE'S, opposite the police station, by Lord Hailsham, the Lord Chancellor. They were built by using the façade of the old Morris Motors showrooms, which had been designed by Harry W. Smith and built in 1932, with an extension in dark-brown brick later added to the back (see LORD NUFFIELD and MOTOR CARS). The building houses five courts, four for the Crown Court and one for the County Court.

Civil cases which were not taken in the High Court were tried in the County Court when such courts were set up in 1846. The Oxford County Court, presided over by the County Court judge, sat in County Hall until the new court building in St Aldate's was opened. Minor civil cases, and much of the work of the Family Division of the High Court in divorce and ancillary matters, are tried by the registrar of the County Court, whose offices were formerly at Harcourt House in MARSTON ROAD.

The Probate Division of the High Court, under the registrar, has a District Registry in Oxford in NEW ROAD. The Probate Registry was built in 1863, and designed by Buckeridge. It deals mainly with the grant of probate of wills and letters of administration to the estates of persons dying intestate. The Coroner's Court sits in Oxford, where the City Coroner holds inquests. Of the ecclesiastical courts

the Arches Court of Canterbury has its registry in BEAUMONT STREET, as has the Consistory Court of the Oxford diocese.

The VICE-CHANCELLOR's court is one of Oxford's oldest courts. From earliest times the masters and scholars of the University had their own court. In the 16th and early 17th centuries the Chancellor's Court sat in the Lady Chapel of St Mary the Virgin. A new room for CONVOCATION and the Chancellor's Court was built at the west end of the DIVINITY SCHOOL between 1634 and 1636. The jurisdiction was half-secular, half-ecclesiastical, much of it derived from royal charter. It included the regulation of the market, rent restriction, civil actions for debt, the keeping of the peace and the protection of morals. The Chancellor had power to bind over parties to keep the peace and confiscate weapons, and to imprison offenders. The town was mapped out into six districts, each having a Doctor of Divinity and two Masters of Arts to receive complaints or 'presentments'. The court could deal with all actions, with a few exceptions, where one party was a member of the University. That included not only graduates and scholars, but also college servants and members of certain trades which served the University, such as stationers, cooks and carriers. These men were later known as PRIVILEGED PERSONS because they shared the privileges of the University. As scholars and Privileged Persons were outside the jurisdiction of the town courts, townsmen were forced to appear in the Chancellor's Court to recover debts or answer any charge brought by members of the University. When the Chancellor became a non-resident, the Vice-Chancellor was the judge and the court came to be known as the Vice-Chancellor's Court.

Under the LAUDIAN CODE of 1636 fines included 2s for wandering about the streets, 3s 4d for visiting the houses and shops of townsmen, 6s 8d for frequenting taverns and tobacconists or playing dice, cards or bowls, and 40s for wandering outside one's college or hall after 9 p.m. The University was much concerned with the moral welfare of its members. A certain Lucy Colbrand, a notorious 15th-century procuress and prostitute who had been 'the occasion of litigations, fornications, fights and homicides in the university', was banished from the town. Even as late as 1887 the PROCTORS' manual stated that 'it is one of the most important duties of the Proctors to keep the street clear of prostitutes', and the basement of the CLARENDON BUILDING contained cells for their imprisonment. The court's ecclesiastical jurisdiction originally included the probate of the wills of all its members, but by the 20th century it had become purely a civil court, mostly for cases of debt. By the middle of the 20th century it had virtually ceased to function.

Covered Market *High Street and Market Street.*
On 24 June 1771 John Gwynn, who had designed MAGDALEN BRIDGE, showed his draft plans for a new market to the members of a committee representing both city and University interests, which had been established by the recently passed Oxford Mileways Act. This Act had been drawn up with the intention of making Oxford's roads 'more safe and commodious for traffic' where necessary by rebuilding them, demolishing the surviving city gates, and providing a market for meat, fish, poultry, vegetables and herbs to

replace the untidy and often noisome mediaeval street markets in Fish Street (now ST ALDATE'S) and Butcher Row (now QUEEN STREET).

Gwynn's estimate of the cost of the market, which was to be built between HIGH STREET and Jesus College Lane (now MARKET STREET), was £5647 15s, a sum which he reckoned could be reduced to rather less than £4000 by the sale of surplus property acquired by the committee, principally by the sale of the premises on the High Street frontage. These were accordingly sold to purchasers willing to rebuild to designs approved by the committee. The new premises, four in all and designed by Gwynn, were completed in 1774 and occupied by two firms of mercers, a grocer and a fishmonger.

By then twenty butchers' shops had been built behind the High Street façade (known as Oxford Parade or New Parade) and the market had been officially opened on 1 November 1774. It was announced that it would be open every day, and that on three days a week country butchers, as well as the city butchers who had shops, would be allowed to sell their wares there. By the end of the next year a further eight shops and forty stalls had been built for the other traders mentioned in the 1771 Act. At that time the shops were divided into blocks by wide avenues; they were constructed on stone foundations of timber-framed lath-and-plaster with slate roofs and with surrounding stone colonnades. At the Jesus College Lane end, where the market was bounded by a high wall pierced by three gates, there were stalls for the

Avenue 2 of the Covered Market in 1909. 'Real Oxford Sausages' were a small kind of sausage sometimes also known as 'Oxford Dainties'.

sale of fish, garden produce and small quantities of other goods. The whole was supervised and cleaned by a beadle, who was provided with a house at the north-west corner of the site and wages of 10s a week. He was assisted by the watchman of ST MARTIN'S parish after lead had been stripped from the roofs of the butchers' shops and complaints had been made by traders about the pilfering of their wares.

In the late 1770s traders other than those mentioned in the Oxford Mileways Act were allowed to sell their wares in the market. These included sellers of china and, later, butter-sellers, who had hitherto traded from the Butter Bench on the south-west side of CARFAX, and sellers of fruit who, in 1781, were prohibited from selling any fruit elsewhere in Oxford unless from shops or houses, and then only if it had been grown within the city or bought in the market.

Thereafter the market was gradually improved: new stalls were created, a new avenue constructed, and new sheds built against the market's outer walls. And in the 1830s Charles Fowler, who had designed Hungerford Market in London, was called in to advise on the complete remodelling of the premises. This scheme was abandoned, however, and it was decided to expand rather than to improve. But negotiations with neighbouring property owners were pursued so slowly that, having had to wait two years for his account to be paid, Fowler withdrew, to be replaced by Thomas Wyatt the younger. Under Wyatt's supervision the market was extended beneath an iron roof; and, later on in the century, the rest of the open areas were roofed over, new avenues were built and, in the 1880s and 1890s, extensive reconstruction was undertaken.

As samples of corn were still being displayed at Carfax or in the Roebuck Hotel in CORNMARKET STREET in the early 1850s, it was proposed that the market should also serve as a Corn Exchange. This was first established in January 1855, but it was not a success, as people were 'huddled together and pushed and incommoded in a way which [was] not seen or felt in any place in England assuming the name of a Corn Exchange'. In 1863, therefore, a Corn Exchange building, designed by S.L. Seckham, was opened in the town-hall yard.

The covered market continues to flourish, retaining much of its Victorian atmosphere and appearance.

(For Clerks of the Market *see* OFFICERS OF THE UNIVERSITY.)

(Graham, Malcolm, 'The Building of Oxford Covered Market', *Oxoniensia*, xliv, 1979, pp. 81–91.)

Cowley Meaning 'Cufa's wood' or 'clearing', Cowley is a large district to the south-east of Oxford. Although the name is Saxon, there is evidence of a considerable pottery industry and early dwellings which date from Roman times. These remains were found in the vicinity of the Roman road which ran from Dorchester to Alcester, part of which is now known as Roman Way. The first written version of the name is Covelea, given in 1004. Ley can mean a clearing between woodland and river – in this case between SHOTOVER ROYAL FOREST and the Isis (*see* THAMES).

COWLEY ROAD was always a main way from London to Oxford, crossing the marsh (which was common pasture) as a causeway. It then passed ST BAR-THOLOMEW'S HOSPITAL and continued westwards to

MAGDALEN BRIDGE. In the charters of OSENEY ABBEY and ST FRIDESWIDE'S PRIORY it is called Londonyshe (London) Street. In the 17th century part of the road was known as Berrye Lane (*see also* HOLLOW WAY).

From the 12th century, Chirchecovele (*see* CHURCH COWLEY ROAD) and Tempull (Temple) Cowley grew up round the Preceptory of the Knights Templars. In 1139 Queen Maud, wife of Stephen, had given all her Cowley lands to the Templars. The remains of their fishpond have been discovered in excavations in the area. In 1240 the Templars left the Preceptory for Sandford. Temple Cowley was designated one of the city's CONSERVATION AREAS in 1986 and includes several old houses of note. In Temple Road, No. 48 is restored 17th century, No. 74 early 18th century and No. 76 late 18th century. Later a Middle Cowley was established between the manors of Church and Temple Cowley. ST JAMES'S CHURCH, now in the conservation area of Beauchamp Lane, was built late in the 12th century by Oseney Abbey, probably on the site of an earlier church acquired in 1149.

In Domesday Book nearly fifty tenants are recorded in Cowley – mainly farmworkers. Over the next few centuries there was little increase in population. The stone manor house, built in the 17th century (and demolished in 1957) became, in 1841, Cowley College, a public school 'for middle class boys'. Some of the college's other buildings still remain. It was bought by a military college in 1876, but soon afterwards closed and the site was sold in 1899. For a time the buildings became the premises of William Breese Ltd, mechanical engineers; but they had been vacant for some years by the time William Morris, later LORD NUFFIELD, bought them in 1912, thus

starting the transformation of Cowley. The total number of people who now work in the body and assembly plants of the AUSTIN ROVER group at Cowley is 11,500. The original buildings became the home of the Nuffield Press.

The population of Cowley began to increase by the mid-19th century before the coming of the motor industry. In 1877 the Barracks arrived, followed in 1868 by Cowley's first large industry – the Oxford Steam Plough Company. The Barracks, erected on Bullingdon Green for the 43rd and 52nd Foot Regiments of the Oxfordshire and Buckinghamshire Light Infantry, was a large establishment which included quarters for officers, married and single men, a hospital and a canteen. It had a magnificent stone keep, which was demolished in 1971. It ceased to be the headquarters of the regiment in 1959. The Oxfordshire Steam Ploughing Company was founded by John Allen and in the early 1920s was run by his two sons, Major G.W.G. Allen and Capt J.C. Allen. The firm, which had changed its name to John Allen and Sons (Oxford) Ltd, sold and hired out a wide range of agricultural and industrial machinery.

Although part of Cowley had been absorbed into the city in 1889, it was not until 1928 that nearly all the civil parish of Cowley came into the county borough of Oxford. In 1882 the new parish of Cowley St John had been created for the area which had grown up between ST CLEMENT'S and the old Cowley. The church of ST MARY AND ST JOHN was built in 1882–3 by A.M. Mowbray and the church hall in 1892–3 by Bucknall & Co. By 1901 the population of the civil parish was 11,061 and by 1921 it had risen to 13,181. The old Congregational Chapel (built in 1878) was taken over

The Oxfordshire Steam Ploughing Company, Cowley's first large industry, traded in the 1920s under the name of John Allen and Sons (Oxford) Ltd. Capt J.C. Allen is shown here with five of his sales representatives.

in 1900 by the Church Army Press. The Cowley Poor Law School had been founded in 1831. In 1854 the Board of Guardians built an industrial school in Cowley and in 1865, when the 'House of Industry' left WELLINGTON SQUARE, the workhouse was established in Cowley Road (*see* COWLEY ROAD HOSPITAL).

In Junction Road are buildings of St Kenelm's Anglican Public School by W. Wilkinson (1880). The school itself did not last long, and between 1906 and 1921 the Franciscan Friars were there. It later became Salesian College. Cowley Parish Hall was built in 1931, ST LUKE'S CHURCH in 1938 and the Baptist Church in Crowell Road in 1962–4.

In Salegate Lane is the Roman Catholic church of OUR LADY HELP OF CHRISTIANS. The name Salegate comes from the place near a gate in the lane where hay from the common pasture on Bullingdon Green was sold. Known as Bulesdene in 1179, the Templars had a sheepfold there in the 13th century. It appears as Bullingdon Penn in 1605. It was on this green that Charles I reviewed his troops during the CIVIL WAR. There is the tale of a giant of Bullingdon who stood near there and 'shot over' Shotover Hill. In the 17th century undergraduates used to play games on the Green and in the 18th century also rode there. When Bullingdon Green was enclosed in 1851 the University Club, the Bullingdon, played cricket there until 1881, when they moved to the PARKS. The University Golf Course was at Cowley Marsh from 1875 until 1923, when it moved to SOUTHFIELD. A swimming bath with health centre next door has now been transformed into the modern Temple Cowley swimming pool. Like many places in Cowley, it commands magnificent views of the spires and towers of Oxford. The COWLEY CENTRE was built in 1960–5.

Although described as being 'almost part of Oxford' even in the early 1920s, Cowley has a definite identity of its own; Oxford has even been described as 'Cowley's Latin Quarter'. A councillor once mentioned to a Cowley woman whom she was taking to vote that she lived in Oxford. 'Oh, Oxford,' the woman replied. 'Yes, I went there once.'

Cowley Centre A shopping centre in Between Towns Road, COWLEY, designed by E.G. Chandler, the City Architect, and continued by his successor, Douglas Murray. It was built in 1960–5, with shops arranged round a square and an adjoining multi-storey car park. *See* TEMPLARS SQUARE.

Cowley Fathers The Society of St John the Evangelist, a religious community for men in the Church of England, was founded in Oxford in 1866 by the Rev. Richard Meux Benson (1824–1915), at that time vicar of COWLEY. The Cowley Fathers, as they were popularly known, described themselves as a congregation of mission priests, and became the first stable men's community within the Church of England since the Reformation. In 1868 the three original members of the community moved into the Mission House in Marston Road, Cowley, whose buildings still remain alongside the monastic buildings and G.F. BODLEY's conventual church of ST JOHN THE EVANGELIST. The Lady Chapel was also designed by Bodley, but was altered and extended in 1938 by Sir Ninian Comper. The original buildings are no longer occupied by the community, the mother house now being St Edward's House in Westminster. Since the Cowley Fathers' departure in 1980, the premises have been occupied by ST STEPHEN'S HOUSE, an Anglican theological college in the Catholic tradition.

Not only Father Benson but many other early members of the community were outstanding as spiritual directors and teachers. The community grew notably overseas, with houses in India and South Africa and separate congregations in America and Canada. Other religious communities of the Church of England were nurtured by members of the Cowley Fathers, who played a significant role in the revival of Anglican religious life. Father Benson himself, who owed much to E.B. PUSEY, left an important legacy of spiritual letters and retreat addresses.

Cowley Road Runs from THE PLAIN to Oxford Road in the parish of COWLEY. The road formerly passed north of the old St Clement's Church (since demolished) at The Plain. Part of Cowley Road was known in 1605 as Berrye Lane; earlier it had been Londonyshe (London) Street, or Regia Via, and was the high road to London. The modern urban Cowley Road consists of houses, shops, churches, offices, cafés and public houses. On the north-east side No. 95 is the Elm Tree Tavern designed by H.T. Hare, who also designed Oxford's TOWN HALL. No. 99 is the Roman Catholic Convent of the Poor Sisters of Nazareth, which was founded in 1875. The chapel (1878) is by F.W. Tacker. Originally a home for poor, elderly and infirm people, a wing for children was built later in 1902 by Edward Goldie. Further along the road is the former workhouse, which later became the COWLEY ROAD HOSPITAL. At No. 393 lived the photographer HENRY TAUNT. On the south-west side, No. 106 was built as the East Oxford Constitutional Hall. It later became the Palace Cinema and, in the late 1960s, a soft-furnishings shop. No. 302 is the former Regal Cinema (*see* CINEMAS).

Cowley Road Hospital The buildings known later as Cowley Road Hospital were constructed by an order of the Oxford Poor Law Board of 1861 as a workhouse for 330 inmates in classified categories. The earlier Oxford City Workhouse, built in WELLINGTON SQUARE in 1771, became inadequate for the increasing numbers of poor and infirm in Oxford. Designs for a new workhouse were invited solely from Oxford architects, and the successful candidate was William Fisher of ST CLEMENT'S. The 11-acre site on the northern side of COWLEY ROAD was purchased in two lots from Magdalen and Pembroke Colleges. Its foundation stone was laid on 6 April 1863 and the building, of red and white brick with dressings of Bath stone, was completed in 1865. The workhouse comprised three parallel blocks or ranges. The centre one, topped by a 90-foot tower and a weathervane, housed the resident Master and Matron. The front range accommodated the elderly and the infirm, while the rear building provided kitchens, dining rooms, domestic offices and workshops in which the able-bodied poor were employed. An infirmary, fever wards and a chapel were added soon after the institution opened. Inmates were classified strictly according to age and sex, the infirm and the able-bodied; and separate heavily used casual wards were provided for tramps and vagrants. There were also rudimentary maternity facilities, for the most part dealing with illegitimate births within the workhouse.

Following the Local Government Act of 1929, the workhouse was reclassified as a Public Assistance Institution. During the First World War it was designated as the Cowley Section of the Third Southern General Hospital (whose headquarters were at the Oxford University EXAMINATION SCHOOLS) and provided orthopaedic, surgical and rehabilitative care for wounded servicemen. During the Second World War part of the building was used as an Emergency Medical Services Hospital, though there were still 220 geriatric cases and fifteen maternity beds. After the introduction of the National Health Service, Cowley Road Hospital was transferred by the Public Assistance Authority to the United Oxford Hospitals. There followed an innovative period under the enlightened management of Dr Lionel Cosin, which reduced the average stay of geriatric patients from a year to thirty-five days. This was achieved by the establishment, in 1958, of a halfway house (called Hurdis House after James Hurdis, 1763–1801, Professor of Poetry at Oxford, who lived nearby at Temple Cowley), and a day hospital. These were the first institutions of their kind in Britain. These new, single-storeyed buildings in the workhouse grounds were designed by Richard Llewelyn Davis and used to implement a new, more hopeful trend in geriatric care.

Despite the stigma of its workhouse background, Cowley Road Hospital emerged as a respected agent of community care for the elderly and considerable regret accompanied its closure in 1981 and its subsequent demolition. The remaining geriatric patients were removed to the RADCLIFFE INFIRMARY.

Cowley Road Methodist Church *Cowley Road*.

The church, originally known as Wesley Hall, was opened in 1904 and became Cowley Road Methodist Church in 1934. It is a large Arts and Crafts Gothic building in stone, designed by J. Stephens Salter. Wesleyan Methodism had in fact been established in East Oxford in 1821 and in 1839, the centenary of JOHN WESLEY's conversion, a small Centenary Chapel was opened in Caroline Street. By 1851, this was leased by the Primitive Methodists. In 1984 the church was divided at gallery level and the building completely renovated to a design by J. Alan Bristow. The ancillary premises were sold. The emphasis was on flexibility, with a first-floor dual-purpose sanctuary and ground-floor accommodation fully serving the needs of a busy cosmopolitan neighbourhood.

Craft Companies see CRAFT GUILDS.

CRAFT GUILDS
There were at least fourteen craft guilds or companies in Oxford in the Middle Ages, five of which are known to have survived into the 19th century. The most noteworthy of them were the following:

Bakers' Guild Established in the middle of the 15th century, the guild was split in 1570 when separate whitebakers' and brownbakers' guilds were founded. Both guilds appear to have been dining together at the beginning of the 17th century but neither survived the CIVIL WAR.

Barbers' Guild Incorporated in 1348 to include barber–surgeons, the guild's orders forbade the shaving of men on Sundays, except on market Sundays at harvest time, or if the customer had a

sermon to preach. It was also forbidden to divulge a customer's secrets or such misfortunes as 'stinking breath', to entice a customer from another barber, or to teach the craft to anyone not an apprentice. The guild was re-established in 1675, after having disintegrated during the CIVIL WAR, and opened its membership to wig-makers and trimmers. By 1719 there were over eighty members; but numbers thereafter declined, and at the beginning of the 19th century the guild was little more than a dining club. It was dissolved in 1859.

Brewers' Guild Although there are references to earlier incorporation from the 1450s onwards, the guild was officially incorporated in 1521. The orders were approved by CONGREGATION with the town's agreement; but, as with other guilds, there were subsequent quarrels between the University and the town regarding their respective authority. In 1571 the city granted an incorporation, limiting brewing to members of the guild and empowering officers to search for inferior or over-priced beer and to punish offenders. The University took exception to this, and the VICE-CHANCELLOR, in endeavouring to establish his authority over the trade, had its recalcitrant master imprisoned. The guild did not survive long thereafter, and was certainly extinct by the end of the Civil War.

Butchers' Guild Incorporated in 1536, though butchers had formed some kind of association in Oxford at least as early as 1294. There were further incorporations in 1573 and in 1703, when poulterers were admitted. The guild was extinct before the end of the 18th century, and many years before that the city had assumed direct control of the trade and its operations in Butcher Row (*see* SHAMBLES).

Cooks' Guild Established in the 15th century, the guild was limited to cooks employed by the University. No female cooks were then allowed, though there was one at MAGDALEN HALL in 1552. Ordinances were approved by the University authorities in 1481 and 1616, when they were sealed by the VICE-CHANCELLOR and signed by sixty-eight cooks. The master and wardens of the guild had the right to inspect all cooked products sold within the precincts of the University and to bring offenders before the Vice-Chancellor's Court (*see* COURTS). A cook's sermon was preached on Good Fridays at the church of ST PETER-IN-THE-EAST. No mention of the guild has been found later than 1719.

Cordwainers' Guild There was a guild of corvisers in Oxford at least as early as the reign of Henry I, the cordwainers being admitted later and, from the 16th century, giving their name to the guild. Most of the members' shops were in Northgate Street. The lease of a house next to BOCARDO was bought by the guild in 1592 and a new house built on its site in 1595–6. This house, known as Bocardo House or Shoemaker's Hall, was usually let to the keeper of the prison until the lease was sold in 1633. The Cordwainers' was an extremely exclusive guild until after the middle of the 16th century, with the result that the number of shoemakers in Oxford was small. Cobblers and workers in old leather were not admitted to membership. There were no more than twenty-nine members in 1614, sixty-three in 1640 and eighty-nine in 1660. Membership increased towards the end of the century, but declined again in the 18th and still further in the 19th. The last meeting of the guild was held in 1849.

Glovers' Guild This guild, which had existed since the middle of the 16th century – though condemned by the University as having been upheld illegally by the town – was incorporated in 1562 after inferior imported gloves, 'naughty foreign wares', had been offered for sale in the market. Thereafter, it was ordained, only gloves made in the city or its suburbs were to be offered there. New ordinances were issued in 1604 and 1669; but the guild is not mentioned in the records after 1728. The so-called 'glover's sermon' was, however, preached until 1844 in the church of ALL SAINTS, HIGH STREET, where a glovers' mass had been regularly held until the 1520s.

Mercers' and Woollendrapers' Guild A guild of mercers was in existence in 1348; but it was not until they were incorporated in 1572–3 that the woollen-drapers joined them in a guild which also included linendrapers, haberdashers, milliners, ironmongers, grocers and salters. This guild had a very short life and was evidently defunct by 1625. It was revived, however, after the CIVIL WAR; and by 1691 member-ship had risen to 101. It thereafter fell, rarely being more than seventy in the 18th century and declining to sixty in the early 19th. The guild was dissolved in 1855.

Tailors' Guild There were large numbers of tailors in Oxford in the Middle Ages but, although some kind of association no doubt then existed, the first reference to a guild is in 1454. In 1491 the University undertook to curb the activities of all tailors who were not members of the guild, provided the tailors in turn agreed to observe the statutes controlling ACADEMIC DRESS. Early attempts by the town to gain control of the guild failed; but by the 1530s the town had wrested control from the University. By the beginning of the CIVIL WAR membership had risen to almost 200; it was reduced to less than half that number by the time of the Restoration; and, after a rise in the early 18th century, thereafter fell rapidly. The guild, almost extinct in the early 19th century, was dissolved in 1838.

Weavers' and Fullers' Guild The weavers of Oxford were granted a charter in the reign of Henry I; but by 1439, when their guild was amalgamated with that of the fullers, there were only two members of the weavers' guild left. By the middle of the 16th century the craft of fulling as well as that of weaving had declined; and when the other guilds marched out to meet the King in 1687, there were so few members of the Weavers' and Fullers' Guild that it was decided that they should not form part of the procession. The combined guild is last mentioned in 1725.

Other Guilds There are also brief references in the records to guilds of hosiers, fishmongers, smiths, freemasons and to a joint corporation of joiners, carpenters, slaters and paviours. At ALL SAINTS CHURCH, HIGH STREET, there were annual Masses for the Goldsmiths' Company at Whitsuntide and for the Skinners' Company on Corpus Christi Day.

Craven Committee Elects, or assists in the election, to the Derby Scholarship (established in 1872 for the higher study of Classical Antiquity), the Pelham Studentship (established in 1909 for the encouragement of the original study of Roman History and Archaeology) and the T.W. Greene Prize for Classical Art and Archaeology founded in 1935. The Committee also elects to the Craven Fellowships, though this is not specifically stated in the relevant University statute, which speaks of a 'committee of five persons appointed for the purpose by the Board of the Faculty of Literae Humaniores'. The Committee is chaired by the Lincoln Professor of Art and Archaeology. (*See also* PRIZES AND SCHOLARSHIPS.)

Crematorium The Oxford Crematorium and Garden of Remembrance is situated just beyond Bayswater Brook on the BAYSWATER Road on the eastern outskirts of the city. It was opened in 1939 by the Oxford Crematorium Co., and the grounds were extended in 1968. The chapel is now surrounded by extensive gardens with many rose trees. An additional chapel was built in 1976.

Creweian Benefaction Nathaniel, Lord Crewe was born in 1633. He entered Lincoln College in 1652, was made a Fellow in 1656 and Rector in 1668. He received Charles II in the BODLEIAN LIBRARY with a witty speech, which ANTHONY WOOD described as 'light, vain and silly'. In 1671 he was made BISHOP OF OXFORD, and Bishop of Durham three years later. In 1697 he succeeded to the title of Baron Crewe of Stene. He died in 1721, having left his estates in Northumberland to his trustees for charitable purposes. A sum of £200 per annum was set aside for Oxford University, £10 of which was allocated to enable the CHANCELLOR of the University, the heads of houses, Doctors and Professors and others to partake of champagne and strawberries before proceeding to the SHELDONIAN to listen with members of the University and guests to the CREWEIAN ORATION at ENCAENIA. This bequest has always been known as Lord Crewe's Benefaction. Although traditionally the benefaction has consisted of champagne and strawberries, now-adays it sometimes amounts to Veuve du Vernay and peaches.

Creweian Oration Pronounced, in alternate years, by the Professor of Poetry (*see* CHAIRS) or by the PUBLIC ORATOR at ENCAENIA. It is the record of the outstanding events of the University year which is about to end. The oration (and the CREWEIAN BENEFACTION which precedes it) are derived from Lord Crewe's Trust: Nathaniel, Lord Crewe, BISHOP OF OXFORD, Bishop of Durham, sometime Rector of Lincoln (1668–72) in his will of 24 June 1720 left his estates in Northumberland and Durham to five trustees. Of annual payments therefrom of £1099 a year, £200 was to go to the University. Of this latter sum, £20 was to go to the University Orator and £20 to the Poetry Lecturer, who would be obliged to give the oration referred to above, which was originally in commemoration of benefactors to the University. Crewe died in 1721; the orations seem to have begun in the 1730s. They were given in Latin until 1972, when Roy Fuller, then Professor of Poetry, inaugurated the practice of delivering them in English.

Cricketer's Arms *Iffley Road.* On the corner of Circus Street the public house, owned by Morland of Abingdon, was rebuilt in 1936 with a stone carving in relief of a batsman on the outside wall. It is supposed to represent Sir Donald Bradman, who played on the Christ Church cricket ground just opposite. The Cricketer's Arms has its own cricket team – 'The Cricketer's Cricketers'.

Crown Inn *59a Cornmarket Street.* A private house from 1032–1220, it was known as Drapery Hall until 1364 when it became Spicer's Inn, the first tenant being William le Spicer and his family. The name was changed to the King's Head in 1495. In 1600 it was in royal hands and became the Crown Inn. Much Jacobean panelling remains. The tavern is not to be confused with the old Crown Tavern (1647–1750) opposite at No. 3. This had been an inn since 1370 and in 1604 was occupied by John Davenant, Shakespeare's friend. The Crown at 59a was a large inn in 1666, containing fifteen hearths. The Morrell family acquired it in 1672. It became a coaching house in the 18th century, serving many coaches such as the Pig and Whistle mentioned in *Tom Brown's Schooldays.* (*See* TRANSPORT.)

Cumberlege, Geoffrey Fenwick Jocelyn (*1891–1979*). Educated at Charterhouse and Worcester College, Cumberlege joined the OXFORD UNIVERSITY PRESS after distinguished service in the First World War, in which he won the DSO and the MC. After working successfully for the Press in India, in 1927 he was appointed President of Oxford University Press Inc., New York, which he transformed from a badly organised into a highly efficient business. Returning to England in 1934, he became principal assistant to SIR HUMPHREY MILFORD and in 1945 Publisher to the University, a post which he held with notable credit until 1956, when he was succeeded by John (Gilbert Newton) Brown, later Sir John Brown (*b.*1916). Cumberlege was elected an Honorary Fellow of Worcester College in 1952.

Cumnor Hill The high ground and residential suburb on the western outskirts of Oxford. The road up the hill from BOTLEY was part of the main road from Oxford to Faringdon and Swindon passing Cumnor village at the top of the hill, with its 12th-century church and ancient inn, the Bear and Ragged Staff. The hill was made famous by MATTHEW ARNOLD in his poem 'The Scholar-Gipsy' with lines such as:

And thou hast climbed the hill,
And gained the white brow of the Cumner range;
Turned once to watch, while thick the snowflakes fall,
The line of festal light in Christ Church hall –
Then sought thy straw in some sequestered grange.

Arnold is commemorated in Arnold Way, off Cumnor Hill, and in Matthew Arnold School on the hill. Cumnor Hill is now bypassed, the main road to Swindon leaving the RING ROAD at Botley.

Curzon, George Nathaniel, Marquess Curzon of Kedleston (*1859–1925*). Having won seventeen prizes at Eton, Curzon went up to Balliol College in 1878 and within a few weeks was making speeches at the UNION and playing a leading part in the formation of the Canning Club, a political club, of which he later became secretary. He also became President of the Union. His political activities were at least partly responsible for his obtaining a Second rather than a First in LITERAE HUMANIORES – a result which he greeted with the words, 'Now I shall devote the rest of my life to showing the examiners that they have made a mistake.' His precocity and aloofness led to his undergraduate days being celebrated in lines which he afterwards claimed had done him more harm than any others subsequently written of him:

Lord Curzon, who went up to Balliol in 1878, was installed as Chancellor of the University in 1907.

My name is George Nathaniel Curzon
I am a most superior person . . .
My face is pink, my hair is sleek.
I dine at Blenheim once a week.

In 1883, the year after he came down, Curzon won the Lothian Prize (*see* PRIZES AND SCHOLARSHIPS) and was elected a Fellow of All Souls. After a distinguished political career, and having served as Viceroy of India, he returned to England a disappointed man and was thankful in 1907 to be elected CHANCELLOR of the University. He occupied himself wholeheartedly with the problems of University reform and spent several weeks in Oxford staying at ST GILES' HOUSE. His *Principles and Methods of University Reform* appeared in 1909. Intent upon ensuring reform from within rather than by government intervention, he succeeded in protecting the University from outside interference for several years. (*See* ROYAL COMMISSIONS.)

Cutteslowe A City Council estate north of SUMMERTOWN, built in the 1930s but given an ancient name. In 1004 there was a Cuðues Hlaye; in 1086 Codeslam or Codeslave, which, by about 1142, had become Codeslowe. It had various names through the next two centuries, becoming Coteslowe in 1480, then Cutslow in 1797 and finally Cutslow or Cutteslowe. All the roads were named in July 1932 after people connected with Oxford buildings, mainly architects: Wren Road; Jackson Road; Hawksmoor Road; Scott Road; Wolsey Road and Aldrich Road. Buckler Road is named after J.C. BUCKLER, the architect and artist whose work includes the new front of Jesus College (1854) and the New School Room, Magdalen College (1851); and Bodley Place possibly takes its name from SIR THOMAS BODLEY but more probably from the 19th-century architect G.F. BODLEY, whose work includes ST MARGARET'S CHURCH, the church of ST JOHN THE EVANGELIST for the COWLEY FATHERS (1894–6) and the Master's House, University College. Wyatt Road was built later and named in March 1961 after James Wyatt (1746–1813), architect of Canterbury Quad and of the gateway at Christ Church. (*See also* CUTTESLOWE PARK *and* CUTTESLOWE WALLS.)

Cutteslowe Park The largest of the parks belonging to the city. Comprising some 62 acres, it was originally part of St Frideswide's Farm at Cutslow (as it was then spelt) and is situated on the north side of the RING ROAD. It was laid out in 1951–2 with avenues of chestnut trees and a lake. The old farm buildings are used as the depot for the city parks, and the Council's nurseries, with their extensive greenhouses, are also there. There are facilities for cricket, football, hockey, rugby, tennis (four hard courts), bowls, putting and croquet.

Cutteslowe Walls The Cutteslowe Council Estate lies some 200 yards east of the BANBURY ROAD. Between the estate and the road another estate of middle-class houses was built by the Urban Housing Company; and in order to prevent the workers and children of the council estate from crossing the middle-class estate to the main road, a wall was built across the entry roads between the two estates. As a result of this wall, the Cutteslowe tenants were obliged to make a detour of nearly a mile, which, according to Arthur Wynn writing in the *Communist Review* in August 1935, cost the workers, and the children on their way to school, several extra hours a week.

The City Council had started the Cutteslowe Estate development in May 1931. In 1933 the land between the estate and the Banbury Road had been sold for private development to the Urban Housing Company. The council estate was completed in October 1934. While the building of the £650 private houses was being completed, the company enclosed its land with a barbed-wire fence, but when the Council announced that twenty-eight slum-clearance families were to be housed on the estate, the company decided to erect a wall instead. By December 1934 two 7-foot high walls, topped with revolving spikes, had been built across the two roads connecting Cutteslowe to the Banbury Road.

In 1935 a Communist Party member and TGWU official, Abe Lazarus (popularly known as 'Bill Firestone' after he had led a successful strike at the Firestone Rubber Company), produced a pamphlet, 'The Cutteslowe Wall Paper', for the estate tenants in which they were offered 'our assistance – the assistance of workers experienced at organisation –

experienced in fighting for the working-class'. In a further pamphlet Lazarus invited 'every Oxford citizen to help us to take down the walls on Saturday May 11th at 3.00 pm'. A band, a children's procession and speeches would precede the demolition of the walls, and a victory meeting and 'a play by the Workers' Theatre Movement' would complete the celebrations. Lazarus had received an assurance from Sir Stafford Cripps that the wall had been built illegally – a view which was supported by the chairman of the Highways Committee, who stated at a City Council meeting that the erection of the walls was in breach of the City Bye-Laws and the common law. However, watched by a crowd of over 2000, the militants, shouldering picks, were stopped at the walls by a chain of policemen. The Chief Constable warned them that, should they try to demolish the walls, they would be arrested for assaulting his policemen. Direct action had failed, but the campaign continued in Parliament and in the courts. Though in 1936 a public hearing went against the Council, in 1938 a Parliamentary committee, led by Sir Stafford Cripps, ordered the company to destroy the walls. The company refused, but the walls were demolished on 7 June by the Council. The following day, company men arrived to rebuild the walls but, as each brick was laid, it was knocked down by opposing Council workers. As a temporary compromise, padlocked council gates were erected. Meanwhile the company had applied for a High Court injunction, and in 1939 the court decided in its favour, with an award for damages and costs, and the walls were rebuilt.

During the war years one of the walls was demolished by a tank on manoeuvres, and the other was hit by a motor car; but both were rebuilt despite claims that they hindered air-raid wardens from carrying out their duties efficiently: in times of emergency the wardens were obliged to scramble over. After the war the Urban Housing Company sold its remaining interest in the estate to Wendholm Ltd, and the 1947 Town Planning legislation strengthened compulsory purchase powers. The 1953 Oxford Development Plan contained a proposal to buy the 9-inch strips of land on which the walls had been built. This was approved by the Minister of Town and Country Planning in 1955. Wendholm Ltd sold its two strips of land to the Council for £1000, and on 2 March 1959, watched by a small crowd, councillors and workmen demolished the 'insult to the working class' and a crocodile of council-estate children took the short way to school for the first time.

D

Daily Information A broadsheet founded in 1961 and published daily during the University TERM. It contains details of meetings, entertainments, recitals and other items, as well as advertising. The broadsheet is displayed on the notice-boards of colleges, University departments, language and secretarial schools, and in certain public houses and restaurants. During vacation *Daily Information* is published weekly and becomes *Weekly Information*. The publishers also produce the monthly *What's On In Oxford*, as well as *The Oxford Guide* – information for residents and visitors, which by 1986 had reached its twelfth edition.

Dames' Delight A bathing place on the River Cherwell (*see* THAMES) close to the weir by THE ROLLERS. Originally called the Ladies' Pool, it opened in 1934 for family bathing and a fence screened it from view from the MESOPOTAMIA walk and from the nearby PARSON'S PLEASURE, which is for men only. It closed in 1970 after being damaged by floods.

D'Arcy, Martin (*1888–1976*). From 1933–45 CAMPION HALL was governed by one of its most enlightened Masters – Father Martin D'Arcy SJ. It was he who in 1936 appointed Sir Edwin Lutyens to enlarge the hall, and it was under his inspiration that the building was enriched by a remarkable collection of sacred art, known affectionately as 'the Objets D'Arcy'. Born in 1888, he came up to Oxford from the novitiate at Stonyhurst in 1906 to read Classics. Before going down in 1916 he won the Charles Oldham Prize. In 1918 he won the John Locke Scholarship, and the Green Moral Philosophy Prize in 1923. As an ordained priest, he returned to Oxford in 1927 to lecture in Philosophy. The impact he made was such that it was said of him that he made the words 'Catholic' and 'intellectual' compatible. After retiring as Master in 1945, he became Provincial of the English Province until 1950. He died in 1976. Lord Hailsham, his close friend for many years, gave the panegyric at his requiem at the CATHOLIC CHAPLAINCY. Of his published works, he considered *The Mind and Heart of Love* to be his best.

Davenant Road   *Upper Wolvercote*. Lying between No. 399 BANBURY ROAD and No. 358 WOODSTOCK ROAD, this road contains over fifty houses, almost all of which are different from each other. It is likely that the road takes its name from Sir William Davenant (or D'Avenant), known as the 'Sweet Swan of Isis', who became Poet Laureate in 1638. He was the son of John Davenant, a wealthy vintner who kept a tavern called the Crown Inn near CARFAX, where William was born in 1606. John Davenant died as MAYOR in 1622. He was a friend of Shakespeare who was godfather to William, and William is said to have encouraged the legend that Shakespeare was his father. The first of Davenant's many plays was produced in 1629. He was knighted after fighting in the siege of Gloucester in 1643 and died in 1668.

No. 41 Davenant Road is Rutland House, which is run by the Richmond Fellowship for young people who are recovering from mental breakdown.

Deadman's Walk A path along the outside of the CITY WALL between Merton College and Merton Field. It was the route taken by Jewish funeral processions from ST ALDATE'S to their burial ground in what is now the BOTANIC GARDEN.

De La Motte's drawing of Deadman's Walk, beneath the walls of Merton College, in 1843.

DEGREES Academical degrees date from the second half of the 12th century. Women, however, were not awarded degrees until October 1920, though they had been able to take examinations and to be classified for over a quarter of a century before that date. The degree system has undergone numerous changes; nowadays all undergraduate courses, whether in arts or science, lead to a Bachelor's degree (BA) with Honours, except the course leading to the unclassified degree of Bachelor of Fine Art. The usual length of time required to complete the course for the BA is three years, though for certain courses of study (notably LITERAE HUMANIORES, Biochemistry and Chemistry) it is four years. In order to qualify for a Bachelor's degree the student must pass two examinations: the First Public Examination, usually taken during the first year, and the Second Public

117

Examination at the end of the final year. Candidates may be awarded first-, second- or third-class Honours, or (if their performance does not warrant the award of Honours) a Pass; from 1986, the second class has itself been divided into two categories: 2.1 and 2.2. Candidates who have secured their BA may proceed without further examination to their Master's degree (the MA) after they have passed twenty-one terms from matriculation.

Graduate students may read for one of the higher degrees (or CERTIFICATES AND DIPLOMAS). These degrees comprise:

Master of Studies (MSt) A three-term course of special study followed by an examination. The degree is regarded as being the equivalent in arts subjects of the taught MSc degree.

Master or Bachelor of Philosophy (MPhil, BPhil) This degree is granted after an examination, and normally the submission of a thesis, following six terms of study over the range of arts subjects.

Master of Science (MSc) This degree may be obtained either by following a course of special study, extending usually over a period of twelve months, and passing an examination in certain science-related subjects, or by pursuing a course of research in the Faculties of Anthropology and Geography, Biological Sciences, Clinical Medicine, Mathematics, Physical Sciences, Physiological Sciences or Psychological Studies, culminating in the submission of a thesis. Residence for at least three terms is required in either case. In the case of research students, the thesis must normally be submitted within nine terms from admission.

Master of Letters (MLitt) Confined to arts subjects, including Social Studies, and awarded on the submission of a thesis. It is broadly the equivalent of a research MSc. Residence for a minimum of six terms is required, and the thesis must normally be submitted within nine terms of admission.

Doctor of Philosophy (DPhil) An advanced research degree in arts or science, of the same nature as the research MSc or the MLitt but of a higher standing and presupposing preliminary training in research and evidence of outstanding ability. The examiners of a DPhil thesis must be satisfied that the student has made a significant and substantial contribution in the particular field of learning within which the subject of the thesis falls. It is the normal practice of most Boards of Faculties not to admit directly to the DPhil, admission in the first instance being to read for an MSc or MLitt degree. A qualifying test may be necessary before transfer can take place. Residence for a minimum of six terms is required and the student's thesis must normally be submitted within twelve terms of admission.

Bachelor of Civil Law (BCL) An advanced degree by examination, though students may offer a short thesis in depth *in lieu* of one paper.

Bachelor of Divinity (BD) This degree is open to graduates of Oxford if they have satisfied the Board of the Faculty of Theology that they are well qualified to pursue a course of Christian Theology. Examination is by written and oral examination and thesis.

Bachelor of Music (BMus) This examination is open only to members of Oxford University who have been placed in the first or second class in the Honour School of Music for the BA degree.

There are also superior Doctorates (DD, DCL, DM, DLitt, DSc, DMus, and MCh) which are awarded only to University members of scholarly distinction and of many years' standing. Such degrees are often conferred upon honorands by the CHANCELLOR or VICE-CHANCELLOR at ENCAENIA. Other degrees are formally conferred at a number of Degree

The Vice-Chancellor, Philip Wynter DD, conferring the degrees of Bachelor of Arts in the Sheldonian Theatre in 1842.

Day ceremonies held in the SHELDONIAN THEATRE throughout the year (*see* CEREMONIES). Degrees can also be conferred *in absentia*. (*See also* CERTIFICATES AND DIPLOMAS.)

De La Motte, William (*1775–1863*). Drawing master, landscape painter, water-colourist and lithographer, De La Motte was born in Weymouth of a French refugee family and studied at the Royal Academy under Benjamin West. His career was spent largely in Oxford, where he inherited Malchair's drawing practice, and in the Thames Valley. He illustrated topographical books, especially about Oxford. These included *Original Views of Oxford* (1843) and *Remains of Ancient Splendour in Oxford and its Vicinity* (six drawings, published and sold by J.H. Parker, 1837). He may also have drawn the special Oxford Envelopes (*see* POSTAL SERVICES).

Delegacy of Local Examinations *Ewert Place, Summertown*. Established in 1857 by statute of CONVOCATION to concern itself with 'the examination of candidates who are not members of the University', to 'confer a great benefit on that large class of persons who cannot afford, or who do not require a University education for their children, by undertaking to examine boys, about the time of their leaving school', and 'to give a definite aim to schoolmasters and a greater stimulus to scholars', the Delegacy consisted of twenty senior members of the University, with the VICE-CHANCELLOR as chairman and one of its members as part-time secretary. In the statute, the delegates also 'considered themselves bound to consult the wishes and requirements of the existing schools, and to interfere with them as little as possible'. Boys under the age of fifteen took a junior examination, and those under eighteen a senior. Girls were first admitted to the system in 1867. The Senior Local Examinations were later replaced by the School Certificate and Higher Certificate Examinations, the Junior Local Examination ending in 1945; in 1951 the Ordinary Level of the General Certificate of Education took over from the School Certificate and the Advanced Level from the Higher Certificate. In 1858 there had been twenty-nine subjects available to candidates; in 1982 there were 228. The number of centres at which candidates sat 'Oxford Locals', dispersed over the country, rose from eleven in 1858 to 1047 in 1957 and to 1700 in 1982.

In 1897 the Delegacy built administrative offices, to the designs of T. G. JACKSON (*see also* EXAMINATION SCHOOLS), at No. 12 MERTON STREET, and in 1965, to the designs of J. Lankester, in Ewert Place, SUMMERTOWN.

Demyship The terms 'Demy' and 'demyship' are found only at Magdalen College, where they refer to those who are elsewhere called scholars. Under William of Waynflete's statutes of 1480, the scholars were divided into two classes: the Fellows, forty in number, formed one class; the thirty Demies formed the other. The word itself comes from the provision that the allowance of a Demy was half that of a Fellow, although the original meaning of the word has of course long since become irrelevant (as, for instance, has that of POSTMASTER at Merton). Originally, by the terms of their selection, the Demies were to be chosen from parishes or places in which the college had possessions, or from counties within which such possessions were situated. They had to have reached their twelfth year, and could not retain their demyships after their twenty-fifth year. Gradually, however, the custom grew up whereby Demies, after a tenure prolonged beyond the statutable term, succeeded, as if of right, to vacant fellowships. The terms of the original statute were confirmed by the VISITOR in 1854, and the last Demy of the prolonged system resigned in 1877, aged sixty, having held his demyship for nearly forty-two years.

Dewdrop Inn *258 Banbury Road*. Originally two adjoining cottages built by Nathanial Hanks in 1824 and lived in by him. In 1850 one of the cottages became the Dewdrop: it consisted of a front parlour, a small hall and a passage. Simonds' Brewery purchased the inn in 1888, adding a small shop in front (closed in 1904). The Dewdrop was completely renovated in 1979.

Dictionary of National Biography One of the most valuable and distinguished of all the publications of the OXFORD UNIVERSITY PRESS. The DNB was founded in 1882 by George Smith (1824–1901) of the publishers Smith, Elder & Co., who announced that it would supply 'full, accurate, and concise biographies of all noteworthy inhabitants of the British Islands and the Colonies (exclusive of living persons) from the earliest historical period to the present time'. The first editor was Sir Leslie Stephen (1832–1904), who was succeeded by Sir Sidney Lee (1859–1926). The first volume appeared in 1885 and further instalments were published until the Dictionary was complete in sixty-three volumes in 1900. Three supplementary volumes subsequently appeared. The whole work has been reprinted in twenty-two volumes several times, the Dictionary having been transferred to the Oxford University Press in 1917. Decennial supplements have been published since the appearance of the first supplement covering the years 1901–11. After Lee's retirement the 1912–21 volume was edited by H.W.C. Davis (1874–1928), Fellow of All Souls and, later, Regius Professor of Modern History, and J.R.H. Weaver (1882–1965), President of Trinity; Weaver was sole editor from 1922 to 1930. The 1931–40 volume was edited by L.G. Wickham Legg (1877–1962), Fellow of New College, who also edited the 1941–50 volume in association with E.T. (Sir Edgar) Williams, Fellow of Balliol, Pro-Vice-Chancellor (1968–80) and secretary to the Rhodes Trust (1951–80) (*see* RHODES HOUSE). Williams edited the 1951–60 volumes in conjunction with Helen Palmer and the 1961–70 volume with Christine S. Nicholls. The 1971–80 volume was published in 1986, edited by Robert Blake, Provost of The Queen's College, and C.S. Nicholls. The Dictionary has always been closely associated with Oxford scholarship.

Dillons *William Baker House, Broad Street*. A large bookshop in a building formerly owned by Debenhams on the corner of CORNMARKET STREET and BROAD STREET. The shop was officially opened by the CHANCELLOR, Roy Jenkins, on 19 November 1987. Its warehouse is at OSNEY MEAD.

Diplomas *see* CERTIFICATES AND DIPLOMAS.

Discipline   Discipline has always been an issue of the first importance in the history of the University. The earliest evidence of this is that, by ancient rules dating back to at least 1231, every scholar, under pain of excommunication, had to have his name placed on the roll of a Regent Master. PROCTORS were instituted by 1248; by the 1250s clerks could be tried by the CHANCELLOR for offences short of homicide or theft; and by 1275 the University's oldest statutes prohibit seditious pacts and factions, night prowling, poaching, loitering after curfew, games which led to quarrels, or the temptations of women of ill-fame. Penalties included excommunication, banishment from Oxford and (for slight offences) imprisonment over BOCARDO Gate near the church of ST MICHAEL AT THE NORTH GATE. Fines were also imposed. In 1432, after the 'unrestrained continuance of execrable dissensions' had 'almost blackened' the University's 'charming manners, its famous learning and its sweet reputation', the authorities ordered that whoever was convicted of disturbing this peace should be fined 'according to the quantity and quality of his crime, over and above the usual penalties, viz:

> For threats of personal violence, twelvepence; for carrying of weapons against the statute, two shillings; for drawing weapons of violence, or pushing with the shoulder or striking with the fist, four shillings; for striking with a stone or club, six shillings and eight-pence; for striking with a knife, dagger, sword, axe, or other weapon of war, ten shillings; for carrying a bow and arrows with intent to harm, twenty shillings; for gathering armed men or other persons and conspiring to hinder the execution of justice or to inflict bodily harm on anyone, thirty shillings; for resisting the execution of justice, or going about by night, forty shillings as well as satisfaction to the injured party.'

Fines proving ineffective, however, the birch was commonly used for numerous offences other than riotousness – for playing or talking during lectures, for example, for unprepared lessons and for speaking in English rather than in Latin. In 1411 when the University was divided over whether or not to submit to the VISITATION of Archbishop Arundel and party spirit ran so high that the University was in danger of complete disruption, it was determined that the younger students who had opposed the Archbishop should be 'soundly whipped, to the great satisfaction of Henry IV'.

Sixteenth-century rules concerning collegiate, as opposed to University, discipline are listed most fully and clearly in the statutes of Brasenose College (founded 1509; revised statutes 1522), of which Hastings Rashdall observed '[they] are the first which exhibit the undergraduate completely stripped of all his medieval dignity, tamed and reduced to the school-boy level'. The college gates were closed at 9 p.m.: those arriving later were fined. Indeed, almost every offence was so punishable, with fines varying in amount from a farthing to twopence being imposed for coming late to a lecture, for omitting to wear a surplice in the chapel, for neglecting any ritual observance, for entering the buttery, the pantry or the kitchen without leave, for lingering in the hall after a meal, or for speaking in English in any public place within the precincts of the college. Books were so valuable that a fine of a shilling was imposed upon any student who omitted to close his volume, or to fasten the windows of the library before leaving. The use of offensive language was punished by a fine of eightpence. A scholar who struck another was fined 3s 4d if the offence was committed with the hand or the foot, 6s 8d if with a stick or a stone, and 13s 4d if the blow drew blood; these fines were proportionately heavier if a Fellow was one of the parties concerned. Personal violence to the Principal or the Vice-Principal was punishable by expulsion. In cases where a pecuniary fine seemed unsuitable or insufficient, the Principal and the Reader had power to inflict corporal punishment with a rod. All the students of Brasenose who did not belong to the foundation were under the charge of some Fellow, who was held responsible for the payment of their dues and fines.

Several of the other disciplinary enactments in the college's statutes deserve notice. The use of dice, cards and balls was forbidden except at Christmastide, when games of cards might be played in public in the common hall. Dogs and birds were excluded only in so far as they were likely to prove troublesome to the Fellows and scholars. The inmates of the college were strictly forbidden to disturb the studies or the slumbers of their neighbours by noisy shouts or by instrumental music – a rule still enforced (especially with the advent of hi-fi) today. Within the college and without, in chapel and hall alike, everyone was required to give place to his senior. The Fellows' costume was subject to the control of the Principal and Vice-Principal, and a clause forbidding them to wear

Undergraduates breaking college rules, as depicted in Rowlandson's Varsity Trick – Smuggling In *(1810).*

long hair or to array themselves in costly materials was copied almost verbatim from the statutes of Magdalen College.

Corpus Christi (founded in 1517, not long after Brasenose) also had very detailed rules concerning college discipline. The chief gate under the tower was usually to be kept closed, and the wicket in it was to be closed from 8 p.m. until 6 a.m. in winter, and from 9 p.m. until 5 a.m. in summer. No Fellow was to go out alone, except on academical or scholastic business. Non-graduates were not to go out without permission except to disputations or to ordinary lectures, and permission to walk in the country was not to be granted to parties of less than three. The practice of archery was allowed, as was a game of ball against the garden wall, but other games with wooden balls, dice and cards were strictly prohibited. The Fellows, scholars, disciples and clerks were alike forbidden to keep dogs, ferrets, hawks or even singing birds within or without the college. Long hair, robes of velvet, damask, silk or other costly materials, red, white or green hose, and peaked shoes were declared incompatible with clerical sobriety. There were stringent rules enforcing residence for Fellows and scholars alike.

The severity of these rules, some of which owed their existence to the extreme youth of the matriculants, was inevitably and properly modified over the years (though the statute *de Moribus Conformandis* of 1636 was to govern undergraduate behaviour for some three centuries). By the 19th century books such as *Verdant Green* (*see* FICTION) show relations between undergraduates and Proctors or BULL-DOGS on the one hand or Deans (as college disciplinary officers) on the other as being altogether more relaxed. It was popularly supposed, and often asserted, that sanctuary from Proctors and Bull-dogs could be found on the steps of The Queen's College and on those of St John's (because Proctors had no authority within colleges), but this is a myth handed down from one generation of undergraduates to the next. By the 1920s an undergraduate might keep a car, provided it was identified with a special green light and provided proctorial permission had been granted. However, he still might not attend public race meetings or take part in shooting, coursing or other sports. He might not enter the rooms of a female undergraduate; a woman undergraduate had to be chaperoned if she wished to enter a man's rooms. Rules concerning compulsory attendance at chapel or the obligation to return to college by a certain hour were slow to disappear; even in the 1950s the practice of 'climbing in' to (or out of) college was prevalent. (Some colleges were much easier to climb into than others: entry to Oriel, for example, was particularly simple.)

Today's undergraduate has achieved a degree of freedom from formal rules and regulations that would have been undreamt of a hundred or even fifty years ago. GOWNS are often not worn to lectures or tutorials; the once familiar penalty of 'rustication' (sending out of residence, normally for one or two terms) has effectively vanished, and undergraduates are only rarely 'sent down' – have their course terminated – for anything other than twice failing their First Public Examination. Even the word 'gating' – physical confinement to one's college – a punishment at its zenith in the 19th century – would probably not be understood by most undergraduates of the 1980s.

College discipline, enforced by the Dean or Deans, is nowadays for the most part a matter of ensuring that large numbers of active and energetic young men and women can live in one relatively confined space without causing undue annoyance to one another or to the Fellows and staff of the college. At University level, junior members nowadays play a role in the making of the (by now attenuated) rules that exist and are circulated each year to undergraduates in the Proctors' Memorandum, which, *inter alia*, covers all disciplinary and appeal procedure. Even the ancient practice of SCONCING has largely fallen into desuetude.

(*See also* LAUDIAN CODE.)

Dissenters It was in the first third of the 19th century that the demand for the admission of Dissenters to the University began to be pressed. This, of course, had been impossible so long as all matriculands (*see* MATRICULATION) had to subscribe – as had been the case since 1581 – to the Thirty-Nine Articles. However, towards the end of 1834 the proposal to abolish the necessity of subscribing to the Thirty-Nine Articles found strong support in Oxford and outside, and the heads of houses decided to ask CONVOCATION to substitute a declaration for subscription. The Duke of Wellington, then CHANCELLOR, favoured the proposal: he thought that 'a stiff Declaration' would be generally approved. But opposition was fierce, especially on the part of JOHN HENRY NEWMAN, E.B. PUSEY, and the Tractarians (*see* OXFORD MOVEMENT). Pusey was one of the signatories of a declaration, also signed by Edward Burton, Regius Professor of Divinity, and Godfrey Faussett, Lady Margaret Professor of Divinity, deploring the proposals: 'They wish to state in the first place, that the University of Oxford has always considered Religion to be the foundation of all education; and they cannot themselves be parties to any system of instruction which does not rest upon this foundation.

'They also protest against the notion, that Religion can be taught on the vague and comprehensive principle of admitting persons of every creed.... They also believe in their consciences, that these doctrines are held by the Church of England, as settled at the period of the Reformation; and as on the one hand they cannot allow these doctrines to be suppressed, so on the other they cannot consent that they should be explained or taught in any sense which is not in accordance with the recognized tenets of the Established Church.

'In thus stating it to be their solemn duty to provide for a Christian education, they feel that uniformity of faith upon essential points is absolutely necessary; and that the admission of persons who dissent from the Church of England would lead to the most disastrous consequences; that it would unsettle the minds of the younger members of the University; would raise up and continue a spirit of controversy which is at present unknown; and would tend to reduce Religion to an empty and unmeaning name, or to supplant it by scepticism and infidelity.'

In May 1835 the proposal to abolish the subscription on MATRICULATION was very heavily defeated in Convocation, despite Sir William Hamilton's vigorously worded reasoning on the other side. If the colleges (as opposed to the University) could not be forced to admit Nonconformists, he had argued, then the re-establishment of ACADEMIC HALLS or hostels

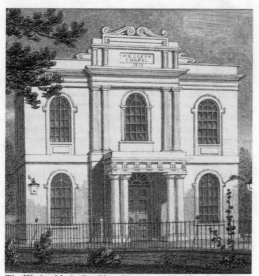

The Wesley Methodist Chapel was opened in New Inn Hall Street in 1818 and demolished in 1969.

under proper conditions would give the Nonconformists the opportunity they needed. He contended that there was no practical objection to the admission of Dissenters on grounds of religion. The Theological Faculty would continue to teach the doctrine of the Establishment, as before, but no one would be compelled to attend its instruction except those who were destined for the Church. The arts course did not attempt to teach Theology, so that no practical difficulty arose. The plea that the removal of tests might fill the high places of the Universities with men indifferent to religion was considered and not allowed.

Hamilton did not at that time carry the day. Yet, despite the setback, change was on its way. The University of Cambridge was already admitting Dissenters, seemingly with no ill-effects. London University, with no religious tests, had been launched in 1826. Although the Oxford University Bill of 1854 did not originally include provisions for the admission of Nonconformists, the House of Commons took the matter into its own hands. A clause removing the test at matriculation was carried against the government by a large majority. A compromise was agreed which abolished tests for matriculation and for the Bachelor's degree, though the tests for the mastership, for a vote in Convocation and for fellowships of colleges survived. All 'governing and teaching functions' at Oxford were retained by the Church of England for a few more years. To Pusey even this partial surrender naturally seemed deplorable. But Convocation appeared to be divided on the subject; the Chancellor, Lord Derby, was half-hearted; and not a single bishop was prepared to fight. On 7 August the measure received the royal assent.

Matters did not rest there. After years of increasing pressure in favour of further changes, in 1871 the University Tests Act passed successfully through Parliament. Except for theological degrees and professorships, every man at Oxford was to be free to take degrees and to hold office without subscribing to any article or formulary of faith. He need not make any declaration of religious belief, attend any form of public worship or belong to any specified church or denomination. The religious services and the religious instruction of Oxford were preserved, but no person was to be compelled to attend any lecture to which he objected on religious grounds. The change, though long expected, was profound. To Pusey and those who thought with him it meant that Oxford was 'lost to the Church of England', that the last barrier was swept away. But there were many more who rejoiced.

There was still no specific provision for Oxford's Nonconformists, and, in the training of students for the Nonconformist ministry, Manchester and Birmingham Universities had taken the lead. Thus, at Birmingham, a Nonconformist college, for the education of men for the Congregational ministry, had been founded by George Mansfield and his sisters. This college, Spring Hill College, was renamed MANSFIELD COLLEGE and removed to Oxford. Its successful establishment here also led to the removal to Oxford of MANCHESTER COLLEGE.

It may reasonably be argued that the admission to Oxford of Dissenters was an essential step towards what happened later in the century through the University Commission of 1877: the establishment in nearly all colleges of the new principle that fellowships restricted to those in Holy Orders were justified only by the need to fulfill religious obligations – in effect to appoint a chaplain. Thus teaching in the University was transformed from a usually temporary appointment for young clergymen waiting for a college living to fall vacant to a separate profession in the hands of professional scholars. The role of the 19th-century Dissenter in creating the 20th-century don is, therefore, central and indisputable.

Certain factions in the University had persistently annoyed and persecuted Nonconformists in the city – in particular Quakers, whose meetings in the 17th century were often broken up by undergraduates jeering and shouting, singing bawdy songs, setting dogs upon the congregation and letting off fireworks. In the 1650s, when meetings were held at the house of a surgeon in NEW INN HALL STREET, Quakers were offered some protection by the VICE-CHANCELLOR, John Owen, who was himself an Independent, and by Thomas Williams, the Baptist MAYOR, who managed to save certain of the sect from whipping after they had interrupted church services and who had saved others from ducking by undergraduates after one of their number had stripped herself naked to walk through the streets, declaring that those in authority would in like manner be stripped by God of their power.

Meetings of Quakers continued to be held in New Inn Hall Street after the Restoration, though penalties imposed upon the Society of Friends were then more severe: several were imprisoned for a variety of offences, including refusing to take the oath of allegiance. The Friends continued to flourish, however, and in 1688 a new meeting house was built on land behind Nos 63–4 ST GILES'; but in the 18th and 19th centuries Quakerism in Oxford declined sharply, and by the 1730s there were believed to be fewer than ten Friends in the whole city. Weekly meetings were discontinued in the 1740s, and in 1867 the meeting house was sold. There was, however, a revival in late Victorian Oxford. The Scottish Presbyterian church in Nelson Street was bought as a new meeting house in 1888. This was sold in 1921, and thereafter meetings

Despite persecution, the Society of Friends flourished in Oxford during the 17th century.

were held in Canal Street, GEORGE STREET and HIGH STREET until, in 1946, when membership had reached 173, a meeting house was opened at No. 43 St Giles', a house which had been purchased by the Society in 1939. In 1955 a new meeting house, designed by Thomas Rayson, was built in the garden behind the property. Membership reached a peak of 290 in 1973, declining to 215 by 1986.

Baptists were also persecuted in the 17th century, when, despite rowdy protests, public baptisms were held at HYTHE BRIDGE and elsewhere. After the Restoration many Baptists, like many Quakers, refused to take the oath of allegiance, and some were fined while others were imprisoned. Their meeting rooms were occasionally invaded and in 1669 the Vice-Chancellor ordered that a number of them who had congregated in a private house should be marched off to listen to a sermon at ST MARY THE VIRGIN. By 1780 the number of Baptists in Oxford had fallen so low that they decided to join the Presbyterians, who had been similarly, though not so harshly, persecuted and who, after their meeting house had been burned down in the RIOTS of 1715, met at a chapel in the NEW ROAD. Following a disappointing start, the combined congregation began to grow in the time of an energetic pastor, James Hinton; but after his death in 1823 the membership fell sharply again. Some members were lost to the Congregationalists, whose church in GEORGE STREET, designed in the Anglo-Norman style by J. Greenshields of Oxford, was attended by SIR JAMES MURRAY, the lexicographer. Others left for the Adullam Chapel in Commercial Road, which was designed by William Fisher and opened in 1832 by the Rev. H.B. Bulteel, the wealthy curate of ST EBBE'S CHURCH whose extreme views, which had led him to allow a chimney sweep to recite his own prayers in the Sunday School, had eventually resulted in his curate's

licence being revoked. Bulteel's powers as a preacher and his reputation as a faith-healer ensured that the chapel was often full, even though it was the largest Nonconformist chapel in Oxford, with seating for 800, compared with the 700 seats at the Congregational Church in George Street.

But after Bulteel left Oxford in 1846, the Baptist congregations at the chapel in Commercial Road declined. Other chapels flourished elsewhere, however – notably in New Hinksey, JERICHO, ST CLEMENT'S, OSNEY, COWLEY, HEADINGTON and NORTH OXFORD. The chapel in Cowley was replaced by a building designed by Peter Reynolds in 1964. The COWLEY ROAD Congregational Church was demolished in 1963, the profits from the sale of the site being assigned to the ecumenical church of the HOLY FAMILY, BLACKBIRD LEYS. There are other Congregational Churches in Oxford Road, Cowley, MARSTON ROAD and in Collinwood Road, Headington.

With the death of JOHN WESLEY, Methodism in Oxford declined for a time; but a new chapel, designed by William Jenkins, was opened in 1818 (demolished in 1969) and this attracted increased congregations. Some years later, however, Wesleyan Reformers and the Primitive Methodists seceded from the main body, the Primitive Methodists building a chapel for themselves in New Street, ST EBBE'S in 1843 (this closed in 1943) and later in 1875 another chapel, designed by J.C. Curtis, in Rectory Road (closed in 1953). Curtis also designed a chapel for the Wesleyan Reformers (United Methodist Free Church) in ST MICHAEL'S STREET in 1872 (closed in 1933). The ROSE HILL METHODIST CHURCH, at Cowley, was enlarged in 1942 and 1958. From the 1870s Wesleyan Methodism began to revive once more: a chapel was built in Cranham Street in 1873 (closed 1918); another in WALTON STREET in 1883 (closed 1946); and two in Headington, one of these in HEADINGTON QUARRY, the other in Lime Walk. The WESLEY MEMORIAL METHODIST CHURCH was opened in 1878; the St Clement's Mission Chapel in Tyndale Road in 1883; and COWLEY ROAD METHODIST CHURCH in 1904.

The church of The First Church of Christ Scientist, Oxford, was built in 1934 behind 34–6 St Giles's. A new church was being built here in 1986. The German-speaking Lutherans, who formerly met at Mansfield College, now have services in St Mary the Virgin. There are Spiritualist churches in Cowley and SUMMERTOWN.

(*See also* COWLEY ROAD METHODIST CHURCH, COLLINWOOD ROAD UNITED REFORMED CHURCH, NEW ROAD BAPTIST CHURCH, ROSE HILL METHODIST CHURCH, ST COLUMBA'S UNITED REFORMED CHURCH, SUMMERTOWN UNITED REFORMED CHURCH, JOHN WESLEY *and* WESLEY MEMORIAL METHODIST CHURCH.)

Divinity School *Old Schools Quadrangle.* Begun about 1420 and completed in the 1480s after both Cardinal Beaufort and Henry V's brother, HUMFREY, DUKE OF GLOUCESTER, had made substantial contributions. The vault, completed in 1483, is regarded as one of the wonders of Oxford. The master-masons Richard Winchcombe and Thomas Elkyn both worked on the building, and William Orchard was responsible for the vault. There are nearly 100 15th-century coats of arms on the bosses, which are identified in *An Inventory of the Historical Monuments in the City of Oxford* (1939). The Gothic north doorway, probably

The Divinity School was begun c.1420, the magnificent vault being completed in 1483.

designed by CHRISTOPHER WREN, was inserted in 1669 to take the place of a window and to allow processions to pass through to the SHELDONIAN THEATRE. The door at the west end leads to the CONVOCATION HOUSE. At the east end is the Proscholium, or vestibule, which is now the entrance to the BODLEIAN. Here are exhibited some of the Bodleian's prized possessions, including the first book printed by Caxton in England and the only known copy of Shakespeare's *Venus and Adonis* (1593).

Dodgson, Charles Lutwidge *(1832–1898)*. After three years at Rugby, Dodgson matriculated in 1850 at Christ Church, where he lived almost uninterruptedly until his death. In 1854 he was placed in the first class in the Final Mathematical School; the next year he became a lecturer in Mathematics, and in 1861 he was ordained Deacon. Intensely shy, his most intimate friends were little girls, of whom he took many photographs. He contributed verse to *The Train*, a periodical edited by Edmund Yates, who chose Lewis Carroll from four suggested pseudonyms proposed by his contributor – Lewis being derived from Lutwidge by way of Ludovicus and Carroll from Charles (Carolus). Under this name Dodgson wrote *Alice's Adventures in Wonderland* (1865) and *Through the Looking-glass and What Alice Found There* (1871) (*see* ALICE). He also wrote on mathematical subjects, his *Euclid and His Modern Rivals* appearing in 1879. It is said that Queen Victoria, having told him how much she had enjoyed *Alice in Wonderland* and that she was looking forward to another work by him, was disconcerted to receive his *Syllabus of Plane Algebraical Geometry*.

D'Oilly, Robert *(d.c.1091)*. Landed in England with William the Conqueror and became one of the greatest Norman landowners in the neighbourhood of Oxford. He built Oxford CASTLE and, with his friend Roger D'Ivri he founded or refounded ST GEORGE'S IN THE CASTLE. He also probably acquired the churches of ST MARY MAGDALEN and ST PETER-IN-THE-EAST. He held land at HOLYWELL, HEADINGTON, OSNEY and elsewhere, and seems to have built or improved GRANDPONT, while Robert d'Oilly the younger *(d.1142)* founded OSENEY ABBEY.

Dolphin and Anchor *St Aldate's Street*. One of Oxford's oldest inns. First recorded as Burwell's Inn in 1292, it was later known as the Pike, then as the Dolphin and finally, from about 1830, as the Dolphin and Anchor, after the dolphin crest of the local waterman's trade association and a nearby Anchor inn. It was used as a Jewish synagogue for some years in the 13th century.

Dragon School The year 1877 found a group of thirty resident graduates, including four heads of colleges and seven professors, on the lookout for someone to undertake the education of their sons. Their choice was A.E. Clarke, a DEMY of Magdalen College and an experienced teacher. A 'Visiting Council' was formed, led by the Dean of Christ Church, H.G. LIDDELL, and lessons began in September 1877 with fourteen pupils in two rooms at Balliol Hall, which stood on the east side of ST GILES' at its northern end.

The name 'Dragon' seems to have originated with the boys of the first entry, who, seeking a corporate identity and a badge to wear, arrived at it by way of familiarity with the George and Dragon on the current coinage and with the name of an active member of the council, the Rev. H.B. George. Home-produced

124

Charles Lutwidge Dodgson, as Lewis Carroll author of Alice's Adventures in Wonderland, *matriculated in 1850 at Christ Church and soon afterwards became a lecturer in Mathematics.*

dragon badges appeared on caps and hatbands and were accepted by Clarke. But though the boys called themselves and were known to other schools as 'the Dragons', the name Dragon School was not officially used until 1921. The school's first official title was the Oxford Preparatory School.

After two years, the first move was made – to No. 17 in the newly developed Crick Road, where the Oxford Preparatory School became well established, despite an unexpected setback in the death of its headmaster. Four years earlier Clarke had appointed to his staff an undergraduate of Hertford College, Charles Cotterill Lynam, who now, recently married, bought the school from Mrs Clarke and, beginning in January 1887, continued as its headmaster for the next thirty-four years. He was the true begetter of the Dragon School and it can be said that he pioneered the emancipation of the preparatory schoolboy from the shackles of Victorian convention.

Lynam – known throughout the school as 'the Skipper' because of his great love of the sea – was the eldest of fourteen children – ten boys and four girls – of Charles Lynam, architect, of Stoke-on-Trent. In his own schooldays he had enjoyed the comparative freedom of King William's College, Isle of Man. He now brought to preparatory schoolmastering a new approach, owing nothing to convention. His boys had less supervision and more freedom – the latter enhanced by the possession and use of bicycles. They played cricket or football on Sunday afternoons – a stumbling block for many Victorian parents. Curriculum and timetable had to cope as best they could with an unusual number of extra half-holidays, or even with a winter week or two given up to skating. But the school acquired, and has maintained, a reputation for high academic standards.

The school's third and last move was made in 1895 to a site then on the edge of Oxford's northern expansion, at the bottom of what would soon be BARDWELL ROAD, adjoining the field on which the boys had for some years played their games. Here was built a school hall with classrooms, designed by Charles Lynam. The transition from makeshift to purpose-built was completed in 1910, when the same architect, still practising at eighty, was called in to build the new school house to take sixty boarders, who now made up half the school's numbers – a balance that was to be maintained. Also inaugurated were various features now well established in the school, such as the handful of girls, introduced by the Skipper's daughter, who now form a steady 3 or 4 per cent of the total; and the strong Old Dragon connection, originally a tribute to the personality of the Skipper, with its annual dinner which was held at the school until increasing numbers moved it to London and lowered the frequency. Then there was *The Draconian*, started by three Dragons in college at Winchester in 1889, taken over by the school and published each term; with its reports of worldwide events written by Old Dragons, it became rather more than a school magazine. Another important innovation was the Skipper's introduction of blue flannel shorts, blazers and open-neck shirts instead of knickerbocker suits and Eton collars.

C. C. Lynam died in 1938. The school, now officially known as the Dragon School, had been handed over in the early 1920s to a younger brother – A.E. Lynam, nicknamed 'Hum' – who had taught the top form for twenty-five years. He preserved the Skipper's ideals, but also imposed an element of orderliness which caused numbers to rise rapidly to well over 300. One of his more important contributions was the school service on Sunday

A self-portrait of 'the Skipper', Charles Cotterill Lynam, who was headmaster of the Dragon School for thirty-four years from 1887.

mornings, devised and developed in accordance with his conviction that religion must be made intelligible and interesting to the young. The third and last of the Lynam dynasty, Hum's son Jocelyn (who was always known as Joc), like his father and uncle joined the staff while still an undergraduate in 1924.

In 1953 the school, whose numbers had increased to over 400 since the war, became an Educational Trust as the Dragon School Trust Ltd, with a Board of Governors; John Christie, Principal of Jesus, was its first chairman. Continuity was thus assured.

In 1956 Hum died, and in 1965 Joc's retirement brought the end of an era. The governors chose as his successor Keith Ingram, who had been on the staff for twelve years, and a colleague, Michael Gover, was presently invited to join him. An increase in numbers bringing the total to over 600 was authorised.

The school's centenary was celebrated in 1977, and two Dragons made a notable contribution by winning, for the second time in the school's history, the top scholarships at both Eton and Winchester in the same year. A considerable development programme was carried through in the late 1970s and early 1980s, by which time, with the acquisition over the years of many of the surrounding houses, the school had successfully colonised their corner of NORTH OXFORD.

Distinguished Old Dragons include Admiral Sir William Wordsworth Fisher (left 1888), Sir Norman Warren Fisher (1892), J.B.S. Haldane (1905), Naomi Mitchison (1911), Nevil S. Norway (Nevile Shute; 1912), Hugh Gaitskell (1919), SIR JOHN BETJEMAN (1920), Sir John Kendrew (1930), Leonard Cheshire (1931), John Mortimer (1937) and Baroness Young (1939).

(Jaques, C.H., *A Dragon Century 1877–1977*, Oxford, 1977.)

Ducker's Oxford has a dozen or more shops selling shoes in the central shopping area around CARFAX, but all are multiple stores. Ducker & Son is one of the few

Ducker & Son, still in business as a shoe shop in Turl Street in 1987, was established in the 1890s.

small shoe shops left, having been in the business of making and selling footwear in Oxford since at least the 1890s. The men's shop is at No. 6 TURL STREET; the women's shop was at 12 Turl Street, but closed in January 1986 and its premises are now occupied by ROWELL & SON.

Durham College *see* MONASTIC COLLEGES.

E

Eagle and Child *49 St Giles'*. An inn since 1650 and named after the family of the Earl of Derby, whose crest was a coronet with eagle and child. The tavern was a favourite haunt of the diarist ANTHONY WOOD in the 17th century and of THE INKLINGS in this century. It is known locally as the Bird and Babe.

Eastgate Hotel *73 High Street*. Occupies the site of an inn known as the Crosse Sword, which, in existence since at least 1605, was demolished in 1772. In about 1840 another inn, the Flying Horse, was built here. This, in turn, was replaced by the Eastgate Hotel, built to the designs of E.P. Warren in 1899–1900. The hotel was enlarged in 1964–5. In 1987 there were thirty-four bedrooms. A cartouche on the first floor of the hotel shows the East Gate as it was before its demolition in 1772.

Educational Studies, University Department of *15 Norham Gardens*. In 1885 the Rev. S.A. Barnett (Wadham), founder of Toynbee Hall, began a series of vacation courses in Oxford in the belief that 'culture spreads by contact' and in the hope of encouraging 'communion between the cultivated and the ignorant'. The success of these courses led in 1892 to the establishment by the University of a Day Training College supervised by a Delegacy for the Training of Elementary Teachers. Its students were members of the University who worked to qualify for the government teacher's certificate while reading for a degree: their headquarters was No. 19 HOLYWELL STREET, where there was a social club, the 'Dominies Club'. In 1896 an examination in the theory, history and practice of education was established by statute. In 1897, as the responsibility of the DELEGACY OF LOCAL EXAMINATIONS, the first course of lectures and tuition began, leading to an examination and the awarding of Diplomas in Education. Rooms were rented at No. 22 ST JOHN STREET to provide a classroom and library, and in the first two years fifty-one men and twenty-one women studied for the diploma. By 1903 the total number of students was 320. In 1902 the University created a readership in Education and a Delegacy for the Training of Secondary Teachers, which took over from the Delegacy of Local Examinations. Of several agencies for the training of women teachers, the most notable, Cherwell Hall, was opened in 1902 at Cowley Grange (now part of St Hilda's College) by the Church Education Corporation. It was linked in 1905 with MILHAM FORD SCHOOL, whose pupils provided the students with teaching practice; and when Cherwell Hall was sold in 1921 staff and students moved to 12 Linton Road (Talbot Lodge). In 1919 a statute was passed creating a University Department for the Training of Teachers, incorporating the Day Training College, under a Director of Training. The Department moved to No.

15 NORHAM GARDENS in 1921, its students then numbering eighty. In 1935 there were nearly 200; and by 1968, nearly 300. In 1936 it became the Department of Education and in 1969 the Department of Educational Studies, when it was amalgamated with the Institute of Education (established in 1951 to provide a professional centre for training and educational research in the area). In 1978 a Committee for Educational Studies and a Board of Studies in Education replaced the existing supervisory delegacies.

Eights, Summer Eights, Eights Week College BUMPING RACES held during the summer term. These races started at least as early as 1815, initially on an informal basis. College crews were often 'put on' or 'taken off' – participated or did not participate – on different days during the races, and it was not uncommon for one college to borrow men from another, or to call on past members to return to their rescue when things were going badly. On occasions, even professional watermen were employed, but this practice was banned in 1824. That was also the year in which the names of the Head of the River crew were first recorded.

College barges and punts on the crowded River Thames in Eights Week, c.1905.

Originally racing continued for as many nights as there were crews, and not always consecutive nights, sometimes beginning in the Lent Term and continuing in the Hilary Term (*see* TERMS). The number of racing days was progressively reduced to nine, then eight, and for many years six – hence, no doubt, the term 'Eights *Week*'. Today racing is held on only four nights, ending on the Saturday of the fifth week of the Hilary Term, when the races also provide the focal point of the University's social season.

(*See also* BUMP SUPPERS, ROWING *and* TORPIDS.)

Electors The members of the boards specially nominated to appoint to all professorial CHAIRS, excepting the regius professorships, readerships and certain other posts in the University.

Elizabeth Restaurant *84 St Aldate's.* Opened shortly after the Second World War as a tea house, it was subsequently taken over by Elizabeth Wood, who opened a restaurant in a panelled room on the first floor with a fine view of Christ Church Memorial Garden. When Antonio Lopez joined her in June 1958 the restaurant also served morning coffee and afternoon tea, and a 10s 6d lunch voucher, which bought five lunches between Mondays and Fridays, was available to students. In 1959 Kenneth Bell bought the business and established the Elizabeth as a restaurant of the highest class with a fine wine cellar. Antonio Lopez stayed on, and when Kenneth Bell moved to Thornbury Castle in 1966 Lopez took over the business. In 1976 two panelled rooms over Nos 82 and 83 ST ALDATE's were leased from the Newman Trust to provide additional facilities.

Elliston & Cavell Ltd Jesse Elliston started business as a draper in 1823 in MAGDALEN STREET and in 1835 went into partnership with James Cavell. Their firm became the largest department store in Oxford. It was taken over by Debenhams in 1953, but the old name was retained until 1973. The part of the present building next to FRIAR'S ENTRY is by H.G.W. Drinkwater and was built in 1894, as was the corner building with turret. The central part was built in Gothic style in 1913 by M.V. Treleaven.

Emberlin & Son A firm of stationers with premises originally at No. 4 MAGDALEN STREET. The firm supplied COLLEGE STAMPS for Keble, Merton, Exeter and St John's Colleges from 1876 to 1884. In 1889 it published the charming 'Wonderland Postage-Stamp Case' containing '12 separate pockets for stamps of different values', invented by Lewis Carroll (*see* CHARLES DODGSON), who provided with it 'Eight or Nine Wise Words about Letter-Writing'. The firm moved in 1940 from premises in BROAD STREET to a shop on the corner of TURL STREET and MARKET STREET, continuing in business until 1970.

Emperors' Heads When CHRISTOPHER WREN built the SHELDONIAN THEATRE, he commissioned William Byrd, the Oxford stonecutter and mason with a yard in HOLYWELL, to carve fourteen stone heads to stand in front of the building in BROAD STREET. Byrd was appointed 'carver to the theatre', and in 1669 the heads were put up on stone columns. No one knows for certain what the heads represent – whether gods, wise men or emperors. One theory is that they are 'termains', or boundary marks, named after the

The Emperors' Heads were commissioned by Christopher Wren from William Byrd and were erected in 1669 in front of the Sheldonian Theatre.

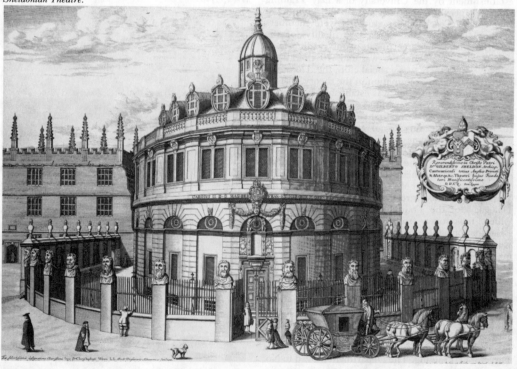

The Chancellor, Viscount Goschen, proceeding past Brasenose College to Encaenia on 22 June 1904.

Roman god of boundaries, Terminus. Originally 'termains' were square pillars surmounted by busts of the god Hermes, which were common in ancient Greece and were known as *Hermae*; by Roman times they were popular as ornaments and the busts were not confined to Hermes. The heads are shown in DAVID LOGGAN's print of the north view of the Sheldonian and in the aquatint of 'The Clarendon Printing House, Theatre & Museum' in RUDOLPH ACKERMANN's *History of the University of Oxford* (1814). They were carved in good Headington freestone (*see* STONE) and lasted for some 200 years. One head was removed to make way for the CLARENDON BUILDING; the remaining thirteen were replaced in 1868 by copies made in poor Headington freestone or Milton-under-Wychwood stone, which wore badly, and by the middle of the 20th century the crumbling stone had turned them into faceless lumps. JOHN BETJEMAN compared them with 'illustrations in a medical textbook on skin diseases'. They have been variously referred to as 'the faceless Caesars' (in ZULEIKA DOBSON), 'the Philosophers', and the 'Twelve Apostles' (although there were thirteen), but are popularly known as the Emperors. After much debate, it was eventually decided to replace them and the Oxford sculptor, Michael Black, was commissioned to carve new heads.

The old heads were taken down in 1970 and the work of replacing them took two years. Michael Black set about finding the original heads and managed to trace and photograph eleven of them to use as models. (Many were found in NORTH OXFORD gardens.) Each head is different and the Emperors wear a variety of beards: Black says they may be taken to represent a history of beards. The thirteen new heads weigh about a ton each and are carved in Clipsham stone. They were put in place in October 1972 with much ceremony and the four similar heads in front of the MUSEUM OF THE HISTORY OF SCIENCE were also replaced soon afterwards. The cost of the new heads was largely paid for by the Oxford Historic Buildings Fund.

Encaenia The name given since the 18th century to the vestigial part of the longer ceremonial known as the ACT – the ritual consummation of the academic year when DEGREES were conferred. By the late Middle Ages, apart from the conferral of degrees, the Act was accompanied by a series of festivities which gave it the appearance of a public fair – especially the often satirical and sometimes bawdy speeches of the TERRAE FILIUS. Fear of political disturbances and subversion led on occasions to the cancellation of the Act. Its secular character promoted ARCHBISHOP SHELDON to move it from the University Church, ST MARY THE VIRGIN, to the SHELDONIAN THEATRE, dedicated (*encaenia* means dedication) in 1669. The Terrae Filius was suppressed in 1713 (though his speech continued occasionally to be published) and the last Act, which occurred in 1733, was made memorable by the concerts which Handel gave in the Sheldonian Theatre.

Henceforth Encaenia, involving the giving of honorary degrees and the recitation of prize compositions (the remnant of the former academic exercises) replaced the Act as the ceremonial high point of the academic year. Technically Encaenia is a meeting of CONVOCATION presided over by the CHANCELLOR and it takes place on the Wednesday in

129

the ninth week of the Trinity Term (*see* TERMS); earlier it was held three weeks from the beginning of what was called the Act Term, in July. Encaenia is preceded by the CREWEIAN BENEFACTION when the Chancellor, the honorands, the doctors and heads of houses are entertained with wine and fruit before listening to the CREWEIAN ORATION. Honorands are presented for their degrees by the PUBLIC ORATOR.

English Language Schools The English Language Schools in Oxford listed here have been recognised by the British Council as meeting the standards required in the scheme it introduced in 1982:

The Eckersley School of English, 14 Friar's Entry (founded 1955 as St Giles' School of English); Godmer House, 90 Banbury Road (founded 1953); The Lake School of English, 14B Park End Street (founded 1978); The Oxford Academy of English, 18 Bardwell Road (founded 1954); Oxford Intensive School of English, Binsey Lane (founded 1973); Oxford Language Centre, 108 Banbury Road (founded 1974); The Swan School of English, 111 Banbury Road (founded 1965).

English classes are also run by the COLLEGE OF FURTHER EDUCATION and WARNBOROUGH COLLEGE.

(*See also* ST CLARE'S.)

Evans, Sir Arthur John (*1851–1941*). Went up to Brasenose College from Harrow and obtained a First in Modern History in 1874. After several years spent abroad he delivered the Ilchester lectures at Oxford in 1884, the year in which he was appointed Keeper of the ASHMOLEAN MUSEUM. He remained Keeper until 1908, having become recognised as a great archaeologist and having made highly important discoveries in Crete. He offered himself as a Liberal candidate for the University of Oxford in 1909 but was induced to withdraw by Lord Lansdowne, Unionist leader in the Lords. A rich man, having inherited two fortunes, he lived at Youlbury, an estate on BOAR'S HILL, which he had acquired in 1893 and the gardens and woodland of which, in consultation with the OXFORD PRESERVATION TRUST, became a 'private open space'. From his house here he went frequently to the Ashmolean, and three days before his death, at the age of ninety, he presented his account of a newly traced Roman road from Oxford to the south coast. There is a portrait of him by Sir William Richmond in the Ashmolean (1907) as well as a crayon drawing by Robin Guthrie (1937), which are both on loan to the Department of Antiquities, and a marble bust by David Evans (1936) on display outside the Hill Music Room.

Examination Schools *High Street*. By the end of the 18th century examinations were being held in some of the rooms on the ground floor of the SCHOOLS QUADRANGLE, which had been given the names of the mediaeval 'schools' demolished when the quadrangle was built. In the early years of the 19th century some were completely given over to examinations and the 'Clerk of the Schools' was responsible for making arrangements. The term 'examination schools' distinguished the schools in the quadrangle used for that purpose.

Examination statutes of 1849 and 1850 produced demands for increased accommodation for written examinations. Simultaneously the BODLEIAN LIBRARY

Sir Arthur Evans, Keeper of the Ashmolean from 1884–1908, painted in the ruins of the Palace of Knossos.

was in need of more space, and in 1859 a committee recommended that the whole of the old Schools Quadrangle should be handed over to the library and 'new examination schools' be provided.

It was over twenty years before this recommendation was put into effect; in the meantime every aspect of the proposal was the subject of controversy in the University. Three architectural competitions were held, each producing a design for the new schools; only the third, in 1875–6, led to the erection of the building, on the site formerly occupied by the ANGEL INN. The successful architect, THOMAS GRAHAM JACKSON was little known outside a small Oxford circle. The contractor was Albert Estcourt of Gloucester. Farmer and Brindley of London were responsible for specialist carving in wood and stone. The hand-over to the VICE-CHANCELLOR took place on 13 May 1882; the first examinations were held in the new building on 19 May.

The HIGH STREET front is immediately recognisable as being based on an Elizabethan or Jacobean country house (Jackson's later quite separate building on the corner of MERTON STREET fills part of the site covered by houses when he designed the Schools). The quadrangle behind, open to Merton Street through tall ornamental iron railings and gates, is more in the Jacobean collegiate style, with a tower resembling the one in the Old Schools Quadrangle. Both here and in the Great Hall, Jackson's deliberate mixing of styles is noticeable. The Great Hall, strikingly lofty, with hammerbeam roof, has on one side a narrow wooden gallery supported by arches and brackets of stone, all heavily carved. The floor is a pavement of variously coloured marbles, incorporating large mosaics, including appropriate creatures from *Aesop's Fables*. Opening out of the marble-paved corridor formed by the quadrangle are rooms intended for *viva voce* examinations. A sumptuous staircase leads to the upper floor, with a balustrade of alabaster incorporating discs of lapis lazuli and coloured marble. The landing above has marble columns supporting a frieze of red-marble inlays. Out of it open the two larger 'writing schools', each intended for 200 candidates. The third, for 120, is reached by another, and more modest, staircase. The atmosphere of a Jacobean mansion pervades these vast, lofty rooms, panelled from floor to ceiling, with their huge, heavily carved wooden doors and doorcases, and with ceilings elaborately decorated with plaster designs. Over the door of each is a title in Latin designating, respectively, the Great North, South and East Schools, in commemoration of the humbler rooms they replaced.

Putting up such a building stretched the University's finances to the limit. The colleges, many times richer than the University, made no contribution. No budget for the project was ever produced and the limit of the cost was the money available. Although £60,000 was raised by a thirty-year mortgage of two of the University's properties, by the time this had been paid off £180,000 had been spent on the project. When the Examination Schools were handed over, the building as designed by Jackson was not complete, either inside or out. Most of his carving scheme on the High Street front was never done, though he did manage to achieve the sculptured panels over the doorway, showing a *viva voce* examination and the MA degree ceremony. In 1906–9 a private benefactor enabled the

carving in the Great Hall to be carried out. The completion of the quadrangle was a drawn-out process, complicated by the demands of the military hospital for which the Schools were used during the First and Second World Wars. It was only in 1978 that the tower received its clock, to which some colleges made a contribution.

Academically, the Examination Schools are a symbol of reform. Architecturally, their importance is that they gave Jackson his entry to the Oxford scene; and in choosing Clipsham stone for them he introduced into Oxford what has since become a popular material (*see* STONE).

As one of the largest and most adaptable buildings at the disposal of the University, the Examination Schools are sometimes the setting for University occasions; they are also the University's portrait gallery. They are much used for lectures. It can hardly be possible to be an undergraduate at Oxford without ever entering the Schools, which is the official place for the display of examination results. Yet – not normally open to visitors – it is one of Oxford's less-appreciated buildings.

Exeter College Founded in 1314 by Walter de Stapeldon, Bishop of Exeter. A Devon man by birth and an Oxford graduate by training, Stapeldon rose from humble origins to high prominence at the court of Edward II, whom he served as Treasurer and by whose enemies he was eventually murdered in 1326. In establishing Stapeldon Hall, as the college was originally known, he was no doubt concerned to provide both for the safety of his soul and for the education of the prospective parish clergy of his diocese. His practical, even austere, attitude towards

An etching after a drawing by T.G. Jackson of his neo-Jacobean Examination Schools, where examinations were first held in 1882.

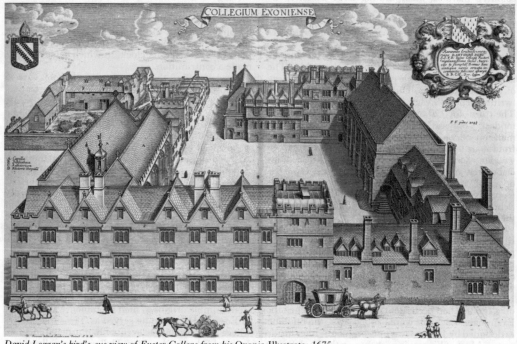

David Loggan's bird's-eye view of Exeter College from his Oxonia Illustrata, *1675.*

his new foundation was reflected both in its endowment and in its statutes, which in conjunction were to set limits to its growth and achievement for the remainder of the Middle Ages. From the start Exeter was poor: in fact, the poorest of the six Oxford colleges which had been founded by 1350. Stapeldon had endowed it only with the tithes of the Cornish church of Gwinear, worth about £20 a year, together with some urban property in Oxford. To these revenues the tithes of Long Wittenham in Berkshire, worth about £30 a year, were added in 1355. The income thus produced was hardly sufficient for the college to pay its way and the early accounts were often in deficit. Its statutes, drafted by Stapeldon in 1316, were similarly restrictive. There were to be thirteen Fellows of the college, one of whom was to be its Rector and another its chaplain. All except the chaplain were to come from the diocese of Exeter (that is, from Devon and Cornwall) and were obliged to study Philosophy. Stapeldon made no provision for the study of Theology and Canon Law (subjects which the University reserved for higher degrees) and allowed a maximum period of residence of some thirteen years, after which each Fellow had to vacate his fellowship. The Rector was to be elected annually.

These regulations were intended to ensure that trained graduates did not linger at the University but returned to their diocese, where there was work to be done. But they also meant that Exeter men could never excel themselves in the University and that the college as a whole forfeited the chance of academic distinction which came to such an establishment as Merton. It remained throughout the Middle Ages a very small society of mainly young men, the seniors teachers and the juniors pupils, but all equal in their fellowships. The only enlargement came in 1404, when Bishop

Stafford of Exeter added two new fellowships to the diocese of Salisbury. Those who wished to go further in an academic career had to migrate, and some of the most eminent Exeter men of the period made their mark only after they had joined a second college. Three men, for example, Henry Kayle, Walter Lyhert and John Hals, later became Provosts of Oriel; and John Trevisa, perhaps the best-known literary alumnus, went on to become a Fellow of The Queen's College, chaplain to the baronial family of Berkeley, and a famous translator of Latin works into English. Lyhert, later Bishop of Norwich, was one of some half dozen Exeter graduates who reached the episcopate. Perhaps the most outstanding of these was William Reed, Bishop of Chichester from 1368 to 1385, and a Fellow of Merton as well as of Exeter. Famous as a mathematician and astronomer, he gave a number of his books to the Exeter library.

By 1405, when the college formally assumed its present name, it had acquired buildings which roughly filled the area of its modern site. The earliest, given by Stapeldon in 1315, was St Stephen's Hall, which was built on the site of the Rector's lodgings. A chapel was built in the 1320s, and a library, thatched with straw, by 1375. Nothing survives of these mediaeval buildings except the three-storey staircase known as Palmer's Tower (after William Palmer, Rector from 1425 to 1432) in the north-east corner of the main quadrangle. Formerly the main entrance to the college, Palmer's Tower gave access to the lane which ran beneath the CITY WALL. Not until the 16th century did the college change its axis and acquire its present TURL STREET frontage.

Throughout this time Exeter's financial standing remained precarious. In the 15th century it was particularly hard hit by the prevailing decline in agrarian prices, and it emerged from recession only in 1479, when some members of the Exeter Cathedral chapter gave the college the Cornish living of Menheniot, worth £20 a year. By this time the college had probably begun to supplement its income by taking in young men to whom it gave board, lodging and some teaching; known as 'sojourners', they formed the nucleus of the later undergraduate body. Among them, probably about 1520, was the man who was to become the college's greatest benefactor after Stapeldon and in effect its second founder: William Petre. Like Stapeldon, Petre rose from a farmstead in rural Devonshire, via an Oxford education and government service, to power and wealth. Beginning as tutor to Anne Boleyn's brother, George, he won the favour of Thomas Cromwell and survived the religious changes of four reigns to end as Queen Elizabeth's trusted counsellor. In 1566, after his retirement from politics, his plans for his old college came to fruition, bringing to its corporate life the most drastic changes since the days of Stapeldon.

Three of those changes were especially important. First, Petre endowed seven new fellowships, to be held by men from the counties in which he or his heirs held lands – originally Devon, Somerset, Dorset, Oxfordshire and Essex. The college could thus draw its senior members from a much wider area than that envisaged by Stapeldon, though still a relatively restricted one. The costs were met by Petre's gift of the four Oxfordshire rectories of Kidlington, Merton, South Newington and Yarnton, which he had purchased from the Crown. Secondly, Petre revised the college's constitution. The rectorship now became a life appointment, rather than an annual one, and the Fellows too were now admitted for life, with certain provisos. In this way the fluctuating group of mainly young men which had supervised Exeter's affairs in the later Middle Ages was replaced by a more permanent body. Under the Rector, a hierarchy of college officers was established, headed by the Sub-Rector, to which post the succession has been continuous since Petre's day. Finally, formal arrangements were made for the tuition of the college's undergraduates. A Dean and Lector were appointed to take charge of teaching; arrangements were made for their payment; and a timetable was drawn up for the day's work.

Petre's munificence thus created the bones of the modern college. He widened its area of recruitment, saw to the teaching and discipline of its undergraduates, and above all endowed it with the moderate wealth which enabled it to survive. He was also generous in other ways. He gave a large number of books to the college, including the magnificent Bohun Psalter, a 14th-century illuminated manuscript made for the last Bohun Earl of Hereford, later owned (and signed) by Elizabeth of York and Catherine of Aragon, and given to Petre by Queen Elizabeth herself. It remains the college's greatest treasure.

During this time of religious upheaval, Exeter continued to be strongly Catholic in its sympathies (see ROMAN CATHOLICS). This was partly because it drew most of its members from the religiously conservative counties of the south-west and partly because Petre's religious sympathies seem finally to have moved in a similarly conservative direction. Several Fellows became prominent defenders of the old faith and two died for it: Ralph Sherwin and John

Cornelius, executed respectively in 1581 and 1594. Sherwin, canonised by Pope Paul VI in 1970, is the only Fellow of the college so far to have been declared a saint. The prevailing ethos changed drastically after 1578, however, when the college was visited by the Queen's commissioners (see VISITATIONS). Several Fellows were then removed and a new Rector appointed, and by the early 17th century the college had turned about and become notable for the Puritan character of its membership.

Then followed Exeter's most prosperous period. It became attractive to benefactors, well ordered, a home for learned men, and a school for lawyers and politicians as well as divines. These larger fortunes were reflected in the college's buildings. The present hall, conventionally Gothic in style, was built in 1618, and so was Staircase V adjoining the hall at its north-east corner. This new staircase was named Peryam's Buildings after John Peryam, an Exeter merchant who gave £560 towards its construction. A new chapel followed in 1623–4 on the opposite side of the main quadrangle. For this expansion Exeter had largely to thank JOHN PRIDEAUX, whose rectorship from 1612 to 1642 was longer than that of any other Rector but one in the college's history. Coming to Oxford from a poor yeoman family in Devonshire, Prideaux rose to be Regius Professor of Divinity, twice VICE-CHANCELLOR of the University, and eventually Bishop of Worcester. His portrait, the first of any Rector of the college, hangs today in the Hall. Combining high intellectual powers with a notable humanity, Prideaux did much for his college. The number of undergraduates in his time (183 in 1612) was not exceeded until the second half of the 19th century, and they came from all parts of England, from Scotland and from the Continent. One of the foremost was Anthony Ashley Cooper, gentleman-

Bath stone in Turl Street outside Exeter College, the front of which was refaced and provided with oriel windows by H.J. Underwood, the Oxford architect, in the 1830s.

commoner in 1637, and later 1st Earl of Shaftesbury, Lord Chancellor to Charles II, and the founder of the Whig Party. Among the rest were many prominent on both sides in the CIVIL WAR – men such as William Strode (1617), one of the Five Members whom Charles I tried to arrest in 1642; John Blakman, one of the regicides who signed the King's death warrant; and Sir Bevil Grenville (1614), killed leading the Royalists at the battle of Lansdown in 1643.

The civil war was a bad time for the college, and the Restoration a worse. The war brought financial difficulties, the surrender of the college PLATE to the King, and the dismissal of ten Fellows by the Parliamentary Visitors in 1648. George Hakewill, the ageing and absent Rector, could do little to mend matters, and under Rector Bury (1666–92) decline became precipitous. Although Bury was a generous benefactor, he mismanaged the college funds, suspended five of the Fellows only to have his decision reversed by the Vice-Chancellor, shut out the VISITOR, the Bishop of Exeter, when he tried to enter the college, and published a theological treatise which was condemned as heretical. Only in its buildings was the college improved at this time. The present range fronting TURL STREET was built in two stages between 1668 and 1703, and in 1708 Peryam's Buildings were extended northwards to form the east range of the present main quadrangle. Much of the money for these projects was raised by Narcissus Marsh (Fellow 1658–73), later Archbishop of Armagh, and one of the few men of distinction in the late 17th-century college.

As in most Oxford colleges, the 18th century saw few notable changes at Exeter. Such minor building works as were put in hand were swept away by the much greater enterprises of the 19th century and have left no visible trace. Of the Fellows, only one was a man of European reputation: Benjamin Kennicott (Fellow 1747–71). Born the son of the parish clerk at Totnes in Devon, Kennicott became the most learned Hebrew scholar of his generation, a man known and respected by SAMUEL JOHNSON. His liking for figs is commemorated by 'Kennicott's fig tree', which still enhances the college garden. His contemporaries were not unlearned (in 1786, 233 books were borrowed from the Fellows' library), but none was so distinguished. Of the undergraduates, most still came from the West Country, studied the Dialectics, Philosophy and Rhetoric which their ancestors had studied, and often returned as clergymen to their native counties. Despite the transformation of the college since the days of the founder, the progression remained one which Stapeldon would have recognised.

In 1800 Exeter was thus an unreformed college in an unreformed University. The developments of the next hundred years, in constitution, membership, syllabus of studies and buildings, were to be the most far reaching and rapid in its history. Reforms such as the foundation of the modern examination system and the increasing range of subjects studied are part of the general history of the University. Within the college, three sets of changes were particularly important. First, the constitution was amended. Under the new statutes of 1856 (the first major revision since Petre's day), fellowships were no longer restricted by geographical area, as they had been under the old statutes, but were thrown open to competition. Ten of the twenty-five fellowships then existing were

abolished, and the revenues thus freed were used to fund scholarships for undergraduates. The fifteen survivors were still expected to take Holy Orders, but in 1881, after a dogged rearguard action, even this limitation was abolished. The college was thus no longer governed by a fairly large body of clergymen, mainly from Devon and Cornwall, but increasingly by a small body of laymen selected according to merit.

Secondly, the period saw much new building. It began modestly with the start of the present BROAD STREET front, running from the east side of the Broad Street gate to the OLD ASHMOLEAN. H.J. Underwood, a local architect, was responsible in the 1830s both for this range and also for the refacing of the Turl Street range, with the addition of the surviving oriel windows. Much more obtrusive was the work of GEORGE GILBERT SCOTT in the 1850s. Between 1856 and 1859 Scott built the present chapel, the library, the Rector's lodgings, the Broad Street gateway and tower, and the range running west from the Tower. The construction of the chapel, its design based on that of the Sainte Chapelle in Paris, entailed the demolition of the fine 17th-century chapel and the adjoining Rector's lodgings: a testimony to the mood of confident expansionism among the Fellows, if not to their aesthetic sensibilities. The resulting mixture of 17th- and 19th-century Gothic had, by 1860, given the college much of its present-day aspect.

Thirdly, the college grew greatly both in numbers and in reputation. Although it did not rank with such intellectually pre-eminent colleges as Oriel or Balliol, it included some remarkable men among its senior members: W.A. Sewell (Fellow 1837–74), the founder of Radley College and said to have been one of the best tutors in Oxford; J.A. FROUDE (1842), the historian and one of the last of the great Devonians to be associated with Exeter; F.T. Palgrave (1847), poet and compiler of the *Golden Treasury*; C.W. Boase, a Fellow for over forty years (1850–95) and the college's historian; and Sir Ray Lankester (1872), the pioneer biologist. These five very different figures, taken at random, suggest the variety of talents which found a home at Exeter. Some of the undergraduates became perhaps better known than the dons. One, Charles Lyell (1816), was to become the father of English geology and probably the only Exeter man to be buried in Westminster Abbey. Others included F.D. Maurice, Christian Socialist and later Professor of Moral Philosophy at Cambridge; R.D. Blackmore, author of *Lorna Doone*; Hubert Parry, the composer; and WILLIAM MORRIS and EDWARD BURNE-JONES, both up in the 1850s. Morris was certainly the first major artist, as well as writer, whom the college had produced. As an undergraduate he lived in rooms standing on the site of the present Rector's garden, soon to be swept away in the building works of the time. He later remembered Exeter with affection and enriched it with his work. The tapestry which he executed to Burne-Jones's design hangs in the chapel; his copy of the Kelmscott Chaucer, one of the finest pieces of 19th-century book production, was given by his widow to the library; and among the miscellaneous relics which came to the college after his death were his pipe, spectacles and ink-pot.

In the University, however, it was not for learning or culture that Exeter was then best known, but for sport. It was among the first colleges to promote ROWING (the Exeter boat appeared in 1824); its

A detail of the tapestry in Exeter College chapel, executed by William Morris to the designs of Edward Burne-Jones.

boat-club records, dating from 1831, are the earliest for any Oxford college; it was the third college to have its own cricket ground (in 1844); and in 1850 it mounted the first athletics meeting in the University. But, like all colleges in the 19th century, it also had a number of thriving literary and debating clubs – a testimony to undergraduate interests, which were markedly more college-centred than those of today.

The 20th-century college has had a less organic and more diversified history. It has continued to retain strong links with the West Country: the Bishop of Exeter remains the Visitor; a substantial minority of undergraduates still come from west of England schools; and the college still holds the living of Menheniot, granted to it in 1479. Building has been confined to the Margary Quadrangle (or 'Back' Quad), where Staircases XII, XIII and XIV, designed by Lionel Brett, were completed in 1964, and to the area behind Staircase IX, where a new building to house a bursary, lecture room, etc., was begun in 1987. The quadrangle is named after I.D. Margary (1896–1976), a distinguished archaeologist and former member of the college who provided a large part of the funds for its construction. The only other change has been to the Rector's lodgings, where much of Scott's exterior work was stripped away in 1946 to make a more classical and less Gothic building. Of the undergraduates, one has perhaps eclipsed all previous alumni in world fame: J.R.R. TOLKIEN, who came up in 1911, took a First in English in 1915 and returned to Oxford in 1918 after three years' war service. He was already a linguist of extraordinary abilities before he arrived in Oxford, learning Gothic and Anglo-Saxon while still at school; and it is in character that his one

traceable entry in the J.C.R. Suggestions Book should be a request for the purchase of 'a good English dictionary'. His early mythological writings took shape in a paper given to the Essay Club in 1920.

Other old members of the college in this century have included Liaquat Ali Khan, President of Pakistan, who came up in 1921; Richard Burton, actor (1944); 'Tubby' Clayton, founder of Toc H (1905); Alan Bennett, playwright (1954); Lord Fisher, Archbishop of Canterbury (1906); Professor Frederick Soddy, chemist and Nobel Prize winner (1919); Professor NEVILL COGHILL, author and scholar (1919); Professor Sir Alister Hardy, zoologist (1914); and Sir Roger Bannister, athlete (1946). Perhaps the best known of the dons has been DACRE BALSDON, whose book *Oxford Life*, published in 1957, has given many people their first impressions of college and University.

The college today has some 290 undergraduates and thirty-five Fellows. In 1987 it was announced that Professor Sir Richard Norman was to succeed Lord Crowther-Hunt as Rector. Lord Crowther's predecessors were W.G. Barr (1972–82) and Sir Kenneth Wheare (1956–72).

The corporate designation is The Rector and Scholars of Exeter College in the University of Oxford.

(Boase, C.W., *Registrum Collegii Exoniensis*, Oxford, 1879, second edition 1894 (the first edition contains documents relating to the college's history which are not given in the second edition); Stride, W.K., *Exeter College*, London, 1900; Buck, Mark, *Politics, Finance and the Church in the Reign of Edward II: Walter Stapeldon, Treasurer of England*, Cambridge, 1983; Butcher, A.F., 'The Economy of Exeter

College, 1400–1500', *Oxoniensia*, xliv, 1979; Southern, R.W., 'Exeter College', *Victoria County History of Oxfordshire*, Vol. III, Oxford, 1954.)

Experimental Theatre Club   *see* OXFORD UNIVERSITY DRAMATIC SOCIETY (OUDS).

External Studies, Department of *Rewley House, 3–7 Wellington Square.* The idea of taking the University to the masses was first voiced in 1850 by a Fellow of Exeter College, the Rev. William Sewell (founder in 1847 of Radley College, Abingdon), but adult extension work did not start until 1878. With Michael Sadler, Student of Christ Church, as secretary, development increased rapidly from 1885; and by 1890 the numbers taking classes had risen to over 20,000. In 1888 Sadler also introduced from the United States the idea of residential summer schools as part of extension work. In 1908 the report *Oxford and the Working Classes* marked the emergence of the Workers' Educational Association from these tutorial classes and extension lectures; and in 1924 the committees for these classes and lectures were combined under the management of the Delegacy for Extra-Mural Studies. Since 1947 international links have developed, especially through summer-school programmes and the provision in 1965 of sixty-seven-bed residential accommodation funded by the Kellogg Foundation. In 1971 the Habakkuk Committee brought the delegacy under the GENERAL BOARD OF FACULTIES as a University department. At present more than two hundred courses are taken annually by over 4000 non-residential students; nearly one hundred courses by about 2500 residential students; and fourteen summer-school courses by about 3500 students, housed for the most part in colleges during the long vacations.

On the present site stood REWLEY ABBEY, founded in 1280 by Edmund, second Earl of Cornwall, to serve as a residence for Cistercian monks studying at the University. At the Dissolution of the Monasteries the buildings were despoiled and abandoned. In 1873 the present buildings were erected for Rewley House, a girls' school, previously St Anne's Rewley in WORCESTER STREET, founded by the Rev. Thomas Chamberlain, vicar of ST THOMAS THE MARTYR, who was also founder in 1863 of ST EDWARD'S SCHOOL. The school moved out in 1903 and the premises were used as a furniture warehouse until 1925, then in 1926 were acquired by the University for 'the establishment of a Centre or House for Extra-Mural Students'. Repaired and adapted to the designs of Thomas Rayson, it opened in 1907. In 1982 the Kellogg Foundation gave $3 million to develop Rewley House as a major centre for continuing education in the United Kingdom: a new library, lecture theatre, dining and common rooms, teaching rooms, offices and improved residents' accommodation to the designs of the Bradley, Burrell partnership opened in 1986. The director in 1988 was R.G. Smethurst.

—F—

FACULTIES There are sixteen faculties in the University. Faculties are listed below with their respective professors. The dates of foundation of CHAIRS established before 1920 are given in parentheses.

Anthropology and Geography *Professor of European Archaeology; Professor of Geography; Professor of Biological Anthropology; Professor of Social Anthropology; Halford Mackinder Professor of Geography.*

The School of Geography (established in 1898) is in MANSFIELD ROAD. The Institute of Archaeology (established 1961) is at Nos 34–6 BEAUMONT STREET. The Department of Biological Anthropology is at No. 58 BANBURY ROAD; the Institute of Social Anthropology (a subject recognised since 1905, as distinguished from Anthropology which had been taught since 1883) at Nos 51–3 and 61 BANBURY ROAD.

Biological Sciences *Professor of Biomathematics; Professor of Genetics; Royal Society's Research Professor in Zoology; Iveagh Professor of Microbiology; Professor of Molecular Biophysics; Professor of Biochemistry (1920); British Heart Foundation Professor of Molecular Cardiology; Sibthorpian Professor of Rural Economy (1796; reorganised 1883); Hope Professor of Zoology (Entomology) (1861); Linacre Professor of Zoology (1854); Sherardian Professor of Botany (original foundation, 1669; Sherard's foundation, 1734); Professor of Animal Development.*

The Institute of Agricultural Economics (established 1913) is in LITTLE CLARENDON STREET; the Department of Agricultural Science in PARKS ROAD. The Sibthorpian Professorship, founded in 1796 by Dr John Sibthorp (1758–96), the Oxford-born botanist, was the first agricultural chair in an English university. But University courses in agriculture were not properly established until 1908. The Departments of Biochemistry, Biomathematics, Botany and Zoology are all in SOUTH PARKS ROAD.

Clinical Medicine *Nuffield Professor of Orthopaedic Surgery; W.A. Handley Professor of Psychiatry; Professor of Geriatric Medicine; Professor of Clinical Biochemistry; Rhodes Professor of Clinical Pharmacology; Regius Professor of Medicine (1546); Professor of Morbid Anatomy; Medical Research Council Clinical Research Professor of Immunology; Action Research Professor of Clinical Neurology; Nuffield Professor of Surgery; Action Research Professor of Paediatrics; Professor of Clinical Biochemistry; Field Marshal Alexander Professor of Cardiovascular Medicine; Nuffield Professor of Anaesthetics; Nuffield Professor of Obstetrics and Gynaecology; Professor of Social and Community Medicine; Nuffield Professor of Clinical Medicine.*

The various Clinical Medicine departments are all at either the RADCLIFFE INFIRMARY or the JOHN RADCLIFFE HOSPITAL, with the exception of the Nuffield Department of Orthopaedic Surgery, which is at the NUFFIELD ORTHOPAEDIC CENTRE, and the Department of Psychiatry, which is at the WARNEFORD HOSPITAL.

English Language and Literature *Thomas Warton Professor of English Literature; Merton Professor of English Literature (1894; first professor, 1904); J.R.R. Tolkien Professor of English Literature and Language; Goldsmiths' Professor of English Literature; Professor of Poetry (1708); Merton Professor of English Language (1885); Rawlinson and Bosworth Professor of Anglo-Saxon (1795).*

The English Faculty library is in the St Cross Building, Manor Road.

Law *Professor of English Law; Professor of Philosophy of Law; Chichele Professor of Public International Law (1859); Professor of Jurisprudence (1869); Regius Professor of Civil Law (1546); Professor of Comparative Law; Vinerian Professor of English Law (1758).*

The LAW LIBRARY is in the St Cross Building, Manor Road.

Literae Humaniores *Professor of the History of Philosophy; Lincoln Professor of Classical Archaeology and Art (1877); Professor of Comparative Philology (1868); Wykeham Professor of Logic (1877); Wykeham Professor of Ancient History (1877); Professor of the Archaeology of the Roman Empire; Regius Professor of Greek (1546); Camden Professor of Ancient History (1622); Corpus Christi Professor of the Latin Language and Literature (1854); Waynflete Professor of Metaphysical Philosophy (1859); Professor of Mathematical Logic; White's Professor of Moral Philosophy (1621); Professor of Ancient History; Professor of Philosophy; Professor of Classical Literature.*

The Philosophy Library and Centre is at No. 10 MERTON STREET.

Mathematical Sciences *Royal Society Research Professor in Mathematics; Sedleian Professor of Natural Philosophy (1621); Professor of Computation; Savilian Professor of Geometry (1619); Professor of Numerical Analysis; Rouse Ball Professor of Mathematics; Waynflete Professor of Pure Mathematics (1892); Professor of Mathematics (Theory of Plasma); Professor of Arithmetic; Wallis Professor of Mathematics; Professor of Mathematical Biology.*

The Mathematical Institute, established in 1953, is at Nos 24–9 ST GILES'.

Mediaeval and Modern European Languages and Literature other than English *Jesus Professor of Celtic (1876); Professor of Russian; Professor of German; Serena Professor of Italian Studies (1918); Professor of General Linguistics; Bywater and Sotheby Professor of Byzantine and Modern Greek Language and Literature (1915); King Alfonso XIII Professor of Spanish Studies; Professor of Romance Languages (1909); Taylor Professor of the German Language and Literature (1907); Marshal Foch*

Professor of French Literature (1918); Professor of French Literature.

The Modern Languages Faculty Library is in the TAYLOR INSTITUTION, ST GILES'.

Modern History *Professor of the History of Science; Professor of the History of Art; Regius Professor of Modern History (1724); Chichele Professor of Mediaeval History (1862); Chichele Professor of Economic History; Harold Vyvyan Harmsworth Professor of American History (1920); Professor of the History of Latin America; Rhodes Professor of American History and Institutions; Beit Professor of the History of the British Commonwealth (1905); Professor of Modern History (1724); Chichele Professor of the History of War (1909); Regius Professor of Ecclesiastical History; George Eastman Visiting Professor (History).*

The Institute of Commonwealth Studies (established in 1945) is at QUEEN ELIZABETH HOUSE, No. 21 ST GILES'; the Department of the History of Art (established in 1961) at No. 35 BEAUMONT STREET. The History Faculty library is in BROAD STREET in the old INDIAN INSTITUTE building.

Music *Professor of Music (1626).*

The Faculty of Music is in ST ALDATE'S.

Oriental Studies *Professor of Egyptology; Regius Professor of Hebrew (1546); Calouste Gulbenkian Professor of Armenian Studies; Boden Professor of Sanskrit (1830); Laudian Professor of Arabic (1636); Spalding Professor of Eastern Religions and Ethics; Professor of Chinese (1875); Visiting Professor of Arabic.*

The Oriental Institute is in PUSEY LANE.

Physical Sciences *Professor of Nuclear Structure; Waynflete Professor of Chemistry (1854); Savilian Professor of Astronomy (1619); Royal Society's Research Professor in Physical Chemistry; Professor of Physical Metallurgy; Royal Society's Research Professor in Theoretical Physics; Wykeham Professor of Physics (1900); Professor of Inorganic Chemistry; Isaac Wolfson Professor of Metallurgy; Coulson Professor of Theoretical Chemistry; Dr Lee's Professor of Experimental Philosophy (1749); Professor of Electrical Engineering; Professor of Elementary Particle Physics; Dr Lee's Professor of Chemistry (1919); Professor of Experimental Physics; Professor of Mechanical Engineering; Professor of Geology (first professor 1818; endowed 1877); Royal Society's Napier Research Professor; Professor of Engineering Science (1907); Professor of the Physics and Chemistry of Minerals; Professor of Information Engineering; Newton-Abraham Visiting Professor (Chemistry); Professor of Electron Spectroscopy; Visiting Professor of Engineering Science.*

The Departments of Engineering Science, of Earth Sciences, and of Metallurgy and Science of Materials are in PARKS ROAD; the Department of Astrophysics in SOUTH PARKS ROAD; the Department of Atmospheric Physics in the CLARENDON LABORATORY, and the Department of Nuclear and Theoretical Physics in KEBLE ROAD.

Physiological Sciences *Waynflete Professor of Physiology (1877); Abraham Professor of Chemical Pathology; Royal Society's Henry Dale Research Professor; Dr Lee's Professor of Anatomy (originally 1885; reconstituted 1907); Burdon Sanderson Professor of Cardiovascular Physiology; Professor of Pharmacology; Professor of Sensorimotor Physiology.*

The Departments of Human Anatomy and of Pharmacology are in SOUTH PARKS ROAD; the Department of Physiology in PARKS ROAD.

Psychological Studies *Watts Professor of Psychology; Professor of Physiological Psychology; Professor of Psychology.*

The Department of Experimental Psychology (established in 1936) is in SOUTH PARKS ROAD.

Social Studies *Montague Burton Professor of International Relations; Chichele Professor of Social and Political Theory; Professor of Social and Administrative Studies; Professor of Economics; Rhodes Professor of Race Relations; Edgeworth Professor of Economics; Professor of Economics; Gladstone Professor of Government and Public Administration (1912); Drummond Professor of Political Economy (1825); Professor of Applied Economics; Modern Russian and East European Studies; Research Professor in Commonwealth Studies; Research Professor in Agricultural Economics; Andrew W. Mellon Professor of American Government.*

The Institute of Economics and Statistics (established in 1947) is in the St Cross Building, Manor Road; the Department of Social and Administrative Studies (established in 1960) at Barnett House, WELLINGTON SQUARE; the Social Studies Faculty Centre in GEORGE STREET.

Theology *Regius Professor of Hebrew (first professor 1535; settled and confirmed 1546); Lady Margaret Professor of Divinity (1502); Oriel Professor of the Interpretation of Holy Scripture (1877); Regius Professor of Moral and Pastoral Theology (1842); Dean Ireland's Professor of Exegesis of Holy Scripture (1847); Nolloth Professor of the Philosophy of the Christian Religion (1920); Regius Professor of Divinity (1546); Regius Professor of Ecclesiastical History (1842).*

The Theology Faculty library is at PUSEY HOUSE, ST GILES'.

(There are in addition three Departments (Archaeology and the History of Art, Educational Studies, and Fine Art) and four Committees (for Japanese Studies, Modern Middle Eastern Studies, Queen Elizabeth House, and Slavonic Studies) which do not rank as faculties. Details of these and of holders of CHAIRS and full lists of Readers and Lecturers, together with the dates of their appointment, will be found in the *Oxford University Calendar*, published annually by the OXFORD UNIVERSITY PRESS.)

Fairs The fair later known as St Frideswide's Fair was held from at least the late 11th century, for its profits formed part of the King's annual revenue from Oxfordshire in the early 12th century. In 1122 it was granted to the Augustinian canons of the refounded ST FRIDESWIDE'S PRIORY, which meant that the priory henceforth controlled the fair and took the profits from it, including tolls and the rent for stalls, and that the fair was held on the priory's land, probably on part of what later became known as CHRIST CHURCH MEADOW. The priory also held a court to deal with all disputes which arose during the fair. The fair was originally held on the eve and feast of the translation of St Benedict and the five following days (that is, from 10 to 16 July), but in 1228 it was moved to the vigil and feast of ST FRIDESWIDE (18 and 19 October) and the five following days.

What little evidence there is suggests that St Frideswide's was principally a cloth fair – a logical

St Clement's Fair, c.1910.

arrangement in the early Middle Ages when Oxford was a cloth-making town. In 1292 the MAYOR's court heard a case about a piece of black russet (a fairly coarse cloth) bought at the fair; in about 1380 Edmund Stonor tried, but failed, to transport many different kinds of cloth to Oxford for sale at the fair; and in about 1420 a Bedfordshire draper complained that four Oxford men, aided and abetted by the Prior of St Frideswide's, had taken linen and woollen cloth worth £20 from him at the fair. In 1423 the wardens of embroidery in London had a warrant to search or inspect all embroidery work, mainly in gold and silver, at four fairs, including St Frideswide's. In the late Middle Ages, however, the fair seems to have become a more general one: in the early 16th century a bookseller sold 185 books at it, and in 1502 Magdalen College bought six razors there. The fair was apparently attended by merchants from outside Oxford: in addition to the Bedfordshire draper already mentioned, a Coventry man was recorded in 1423, and in 1383 the Prior of St Frideswide's claimed that people from 'various countries' (or rather parts of the country) came to the fair.

The priory's privileges during the fair were disputed, first by the town and then by the University. In the 12th century there was a long-running dispute between the townsmen and the priory about the site of their stalls. Later in the Middle Ages the town courts sometimes continued to sit during the fair, although only the Prior's court was supposed to sit then, and sometimes heard cases arising from the fair. In 1344 and 1346 there was a dispute over the collection of toll from those coming to the fair, the Prior claiming that

the town officers had taken toll and other profits worth £1000 – no doubt an exaggeration. The University's intervention was more violent; on at least one occasion in the early 1380s scholars and others – possibly University officers – pulled down merchants' tents and pavilions by cutting their ropes, provoking a riot which completely disrupted the fair. The University was trying to extend to the fair the rights which it had already won over the MARKET, but it was unsuccessful. In 1383 it had to concede to the Prior control of all commercial activity within the priory precinct during the fair.

After the dissolution of St Frideswide's Priory in 1524 the fair passed, with the rest of the Priory's possessions, to Cardinal College, then to Henry VIII's College (*see* CHRIST CHURCH), and then to the King. In 1549 Edward VI granted the fair to the city, which had apparently held a lease on it since 1543. The city moved the fair to the TOWN HALL, its courtyard and the streets round it in 1549. By that time, however, it was in decline. In 1554 its profits were only £13 14*s*; and by the early 17th century they had fallen to only about £1 a year. By then it had become a small affair, attended by a rather motley group of local tradesmen, including, over the years, goldsmiths, grocers, pewterers, mercers, a seal-maker, a girdler, a hosier, a linen-draper, a dish-maker, a basket-maker, a shovel-maker, and the 'Muscovia man'. Despite orders issued by the city in 1600, 1602 and 1605 that tradesmen should attend, in 1608 only two chapmen, a turner and a pedlar woman took stalls. The fair revived slightly in the 1630s, but by 1663 was 'hardly acknowledged to be a fair'. It nevertheless survived, in very attenuated

139

form, until the mid-19th century, 'when it was represented by a couple of cake stalls and a booth with a calf possessing an abnormal number of limbs'.

In 1474 Edward IV granted the Austin or Augustinian friars a fair for all kinds of merchandise, to be held outside their church (on the site of Wadham College) on the vigil and feast of St John before the Latin Gate (5 and 6 May) and the four following days. This Austin Fair was never as important as St Frideswide's, but merchants from as far afield as Leicestershire and London attended in 1499 and 1500, and in 1518, in spite of an outbreak of sweating sickness, the town decided not to cancel it because to do so would cause complaints and murmurs in London. Presumably all kinds of merchandise were sold, but there is evidence only for the sale of saddles in 1498 and 1499, and of books in 1520.

The AUGUSTINIAN FRIARY was dissolved in 1538, and the fair passed, with its site, to the Crown. The city acquired a lease of it in 1549 and in 1587 bought it outright, with the friary site, from its then owner, William Frere. Like St Frideswide's, the Austin Fair declined in the later 16th century, its profits ranging only from £4 to £10. Over the years those attending included pewterers and a goldsmith, but once the fair moved to the town hall after the foundation of Wadham College in 1610 it was attended by only a few hucksters or pedlars. By the 1660s it consisted 'only of trumperies', and seems to have come to an end soon afterwards.

The city's new charter of 1601 granted three fairs, on 3 May, 2 July and 23 October; but they were not held then, and an attempt to hold them in 1684 was defeated by the University, which saw the new fairs as a threat to its control of the market. In the late 18th century and in the 19th, however, a fair was held on 3 May on GLOUCESTER GREEN; it was described in 1783 and 1834 as a fair for toys and small wares. In 1890 it was a fun-fair with 'the usual steam and hand-power round-abouts and some shooting tubes with shots at glass bottles, swings, throwing for coconuts, etc.' It continued to be held until 1915.

Another, very similar, fair was held in ST CLEMENT'S on the Thursday before Michaelmas. In the early 18th century it was intended as a fair for hiring servants, but was said to be in fact 'a very mean thing of no other account but for children's baubles'; it was described as a toy fair in 1783 and 1834. It survived until the 1930s.

(*See also* ST GILES' FAIR.)

Farnell, Lewis Richard (*1856–1934*). Farnell won an open classical scholarship from the City of London School to Exeter College in 1874. Having obtained a First in Classical MODERATIONS in 1875 and in LITERAE HUMANIORES in 1878, he was appointed a Fellow of the college in 1880. He was University lecturer in Classical Archaeology in 1903–14, Rector of Exeter in 1913–28, and a strict VICE-CHANCELLOR in 1920–3. As a prominent figure in University politics, he inaugurated and supported several reforms, frequently placing the University's interests above those of the individual colleges and stressing that a college tutor should combine his tutorial functions with 'original research and literary production'. He himself wrote several books on Greek religion, including the magisterial *Cults of the Greek States* (5 vols, 1896–1906). His interesting autobiography, *An Oxonian Looks Back*, was published in 1934. There is a portrait of him by J.St.H. Lander in the hall at Exeter College.

Farriers Arms *Abingdon Road*. Built in 1776 as a private residence called the Further White House. It was renamed the Farriers Arms in the 19th century after a local farrier in Cold Arbour. It was a small inn of two storeys, comprising a front porch and central hall with a bar on either side. It was modernised in 1930 but demolished in May 1963 for the new Oxford–Abingdon spur road.

Feiling, Sir Keith Grahame (*1884–1977*). The son of a stockbroker, nephew of the novelist Anthony Hope and also closely related to Kenneth Grahame, author of *The Wind in the Willows*, Feiling went up from Marlborough to Balliol College and in 1906 obtained a First in Modern History. He was elected to a prize fellowship at All Souls, and in 1911 to a studentship at Christ Church. He remained a Student for thirty-five years, during which he and SIR JOHN MASTERMAN made the Christ Church History School supreme in the University. He wrote admirable lives of Warren Hastings (1954) and Neville Chamberlain (1946), and a masterly *History of England* (1950). He was appointed Chichele Professor of Modern History in 1946.

Fell, John (*1625–1686*). The son of Samuel Fell, who was appointed Dean of Christ Church in 1638 and, as a committed Royalist, VICE-CHANCELLOR in 1645, John Fell was admitted to Christ Church by his father at the age of eleven. Having served as an officer in the Oxford garrison during the CIVIL WAR, he was dismissed from his studentship in 1648; but, moving to a house opposite Merton College, he, with several other clergy, celebrated the rites of the Anglican church throughout the Commonwealth. Upon the Restoration of the monarchy he was appointed a canon of CHRIST CHURCH CATHEDRAL; soon afterwards Dean of the college; in 1666 Vice-Chancellor; and in 1676 BISHOP OF OXFORD in succession to Henry Compton. In all these offices he was extremely zealous in the fulfilment of his duties: as a canon he attended the college chapel four times a day; as Dean he ejected men whose religious convictions were dubious, and visited the rooms of junior members of the college to examine them in their studies; and as Vice-Chancellor he was a strict enforcer of DISCIPLINE, particularly in the matters of ACADEMIC DRESS and attendance at lectures, which had come to be known as 'wall lectures' because they were addressed, when given at all, to the bare walls of the room. He seems not to have been a popular figure in the college. The well-known verses by the licentious poet and miscellaneous writer Thomas Brown (1663–1704), whom Dr Fell apparently threatened to expel from Christ Church, reflected a common sentiment:

> I do not love thee, Dr Fell,
> The reason why I cannot tell;
> But this I know, and know full well,
> I do not love thee, Dr Fell.

Fell was industrious also in carrying on his father's work of improving and extending the buildings of the college and had much to do with the building of the SHELDONIAN THEATRE as a place where University CEREMONIES could take place instead of within the hallowed walls of ST MARY THE VIRGIN. He was buried in Christ Church Cathedral, where there is a memorial to him with a long inscription recording the events of his life. There is a statue of him in Tom Quad at Christ Church and two portraits in the college hall, one of these by Van Dyck.

(*See also* OXFORD ALMANACKS *and* OXFORD UNIVERSITY PRESS.)

Ferry Hinksey Road Named after a punt ferry which once operated across Bulstake Stream. The road leads to the OSNEY MEAD Industrial Estate. Laurence Binyon's poem *Ferry Hinksey* recalls the peaceful scene before the industrial estate was thought of:

Beyond the ferry water
That fast and silent flowed,
She turned, she gazed a moment,
Then took her onward road

Between the winding willows
To a city white with spires:
It seemed a path of pilgrims
To the home of earth's desires.

Blue shade of golden branches
Spread for her journeying,
Till he that lingered lost her
Among the leaves of Spring.

Ferry Pool The North Oxford Association campaigned for many years for a swimming pool and community centre in NORTH OXFORD and raised over £35,000 towards the cost. The Ferry Pool was opened in August 1976 as part of the Ferry Centre. The heated indoor pool is 25 metres long; there is also a small, shallow pool for children and learners. Access to the complex, which includes squash courts, a community centre and car park, is from MARSTON FERRY ROAD or from Diamond Place in SUMMERTOWN.

Fiction Fiction about Oxford comes in many guises, some of them purporting to be fact. Of the numerous novels from or about Oxford, two have achieved widespread and enduring fame: *Alice's Adventures in Wonderland* (*see* ALICE) and ZULEIKA DOBSON; but others are almost as well known. The few mentioned here are divided into three groups: (a) novels about University (especially undergraduate) life; (b) novels in which Oxford plays a significant but not the only role; (c) detective novels.

(a) A book known almost as well as *Zuleika Dobson* is *The Adventures of Mr Verdant Green* (1853–7) by 'Cuthbert Bede, B.A.' (actually the Rev Edward Bradley of University College, Durham), of which 170,000 copies had been printed by 1883. By 1933 it was estimated that over 250,000 copies had been sold; and it was reprinted in paperback format in the 1980s. *Tom Brown at Oxford* (1861) by Thomas Hughes is a somewhat disappointing sequel to *Tom Brown's Schooldays*, but had gone through three editions and twenty-one reprints by 1914. *Robert Elsmere* (1888) by Mrs Humphry Ward, granddaughter of THOMAS ARNOLD, contains a convincing evocation of the Oxford of WALTER PATER, T.H. GREEN and MARK PATTISON. Evelyn Waugh's highly successful *Brideshead Revisited* (1945) is well known for its portrayal of undergraduate life in the 1920s. *Freshman's Folly*

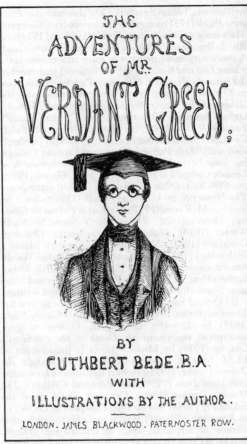

Title page of The Adventures of Mr Verdant Green *(1853–7), one of the most popular novels ever written about university life.*

(1952) by DACRE BALSDON is the lively work of a prolific Oxford pen which later produced the satirical *The Day They Burned Miss Termag* (1961). J.I.M. Stewart's five-volume opus *A Staircase in Surrey* (1974–8) is weightier and more mannered. A notorious spoof was *Sandford of Merton: A Story of Oxford Life* by 'Belinda Blinders' (D.F.T. Coke), published in 1903. This book includes the words 'as the boats began to near the winning-post, [Ralph's] oar was dipping into the water nearly *twice* as often as any other', usually rendered as 'all rowed fast, but none so fast as stroke'. Other interesting Oxford novels are *The Comedy of Age* by Desmond Coke (1906); *Barbara goes to Oxford* by Barbara Burke (1907); *Keddy* by H.N. Dickinson (1907); *A City in the Foreground* by Gerard Hopkins (1921); *Patchwork* by Beverley Nichols (1921); *The Oxford Circus* by Hamish Miles and Raymond Mortimer (1922); *Most Loving Mere Folly* by Paul Bloomfield (1923); *Oxford et Margaret* by Jean Fayard (1924); *Laurel and Straw* by James Saxon Childers (1927); *Neapolitan Ice* by Renée Haynes (1928); and *Storm in Oxford* by Tangye Lean (1932).

(b) Of novels which are partly and significantly (though not wholly) set in Oxford, W.M. Thackeray's *Pendennis* (1848–50) is probably the earliest to become well known; Tobias Smollett's *The Adventures of Peregrine Pickle* (1751) is arguably an antecedent. Compton Mackenzie's *Sinister Street* (2 vols, 1913 and 1914) and Rhoda Broughton's *Belinda* (1883) are still widely read. A more surprising novelist is JOHN HENRY NEWMAN, whose *Loss and Gain* (1848) is a fictional treatment of the author's life; much of the novel's action takes place in Oxford, but the book was condemned by the *Athenæum* for being 'flippant and farcical'. Finally, Oxford figures as Christminster in Thomas Hardy's *Jude the Obscure* (1896); but whether George Eliot's Mr Casaubon in *Middlemarch* (1871–2) should be identified with Mark Pattison, Rector of Lincoln College, has long been disputed (*see The Commonwealth of Lincoln College 1427–1977* by V.H.H. Green (1979), pp. 698–706). Other novels with Oxford settings are *The Hypocrite* by C. Ranger-Gull (1898); *Sonia* by Stephen McKenna (1917); *Harvest in Poland* by Geoffrey Dennis (1928); *Other Man's Sauce* by Keith Winter (1930); *Making Conversation* by Christian Longford (1931); *My Bones will Keep* by Maurice Richardson (1932); and *Lapsing* by Jill Paton Walsh. Among modern novelists, Philip Larkin (*Jill*, 1946), Barbara Pym, A.N. Wilson, Penelope Lively and Margaret Forster have all made good use of Oxford settings.

(c) Oxford has always been a favourite setting for detective stories. Best known is probably *Gaudy Night* (1935) by Dorothy L. Sayers. Others to give widespread enjoyment are *Death at the President's Lodging* (1936) by Michael Innes (a pseudonym of J.I.M. Stewart – *see above*); J.C. MASTERMAN's *An Oxford Tragedy* (1933); Robert Robinson's *Landscape with Dead Dons* (1956); and Edmund Crispin's *The Moving Toyshop* (1946). Crispin's *The Case of the Gilded Fly* (1944) was entitled *Obsequies at Oxford* in its American edition (1945); it includes the definitive account of arrival by train at Oxford via Didcot. Several of Colin Dexter's novels, including *Last Bus to Woodstock* (1975) and *The Dead of Jericho* (1981) have Oxford settings, as do Howard Shaw's *Death of a Don* (1981), Amanda Cross's *The Question of Max* (1976) and Antonia Fraser's *Oxford Blood* (1985).

The section on fiction in Cordeaux and Merry's *Bibliography of Printed Works Relating to the University of Oxford* (1968) lists 209 items, though not all of these are novels; among the better-known authors or scholars who make an appearance (in addition to those mentioned already) are Henry Kingsley, Sir Arthur Quiller-Couch, Hilaire Belloc, G.D.H. Cole, R.A. KNOX (*Let Dons Delight*, 1939), Lord Berners, L.P. Hartley, S.P.B. Mais, and Rachel Trickett. It is not understood why Cambridge has attracted less attention from novelists.

(Batson, Judy G., *Oxford in Fiction: An Annotated Bibliography*, Garland Publishing Inc., New York, 1990.)

Field House Drive The access drive to a large house at the northern end of SUMMERTOWN known in the 19th century as Apsley Paddox. It was built in 1830 for James Sykes, a gunmaker in HIGH STREET. In 1911 it passed to Charles Robertson, a ROMAN CATHOLIC who bought land on which to build a chapel in the 10-acre grounds. The building on the corner of the drive is now the church of ST GREGORY AND ST AUGUSTINE. The house then passed to the Clapperton family, who owned Sandford Paper Mill. They sold it in 1925 to ST EDWARD'S SCHOOL, which used it as a

boarding house and renamed it Field House. A new Field House was built by the school in 1965. The school had two rugby fields in the grounds. The BANBURY ROAD and SQUITCHEY LANE frontages were sold off for housing in 1935. In the 1960s part of the house was converted into flats and a development of town houses in part of the grounds was called the Paddox after the original name of the house.

Final Honour Schools *see* SCHOOLS.

Fires and Fire Services As in all English cities, fire has been a constant hazard in Oxford. The earliest recorded major outbreak, in 1138, was said to have entirely destroyed the town, which was again burnt down by Stephen after he had captured it in 1142 when his rival, Matilda, made her celebrated escape from the CASTLE. Oxford was once more deliberately set on fire during the RIOTS of 1236, after having been badly damaged in an earlier conflagration in 1190, when ST FRIDESWIDE'S PRIORY was among its many victims. That year also saw the destruction of CHRIST CHURCH CATHEDRAL, which was left 'horrible because of the ruins of its walls'. No further catastrophic outbreaks are recorded until 1644, when a fire broke out in GEORGE STREET; a large area in the western part of the city was destroyed and damage was estimated at £300,000. This was during the CIVIL WAR, when several houses in the suburbs were burnt by the Royalists as a defensive measure. There were further, less serious, outbreaks in 1657 and 1671. Thereafter fires were generally localised, such as those that twice almost destroyed GRIMBLY HUGHES in 1857 and 1863; the fire that consumed the Post Office, then at No. 123 HIGH STREET, in 1842; that which severely damaged the New Theatre (*see* APOLLO THEATRE) in 1892; and that at ST MICHAEL AT THE NORTH GATE in 1953.

From at least as early as the 16th century the town authorities had forbidden the use of certain combustible building materials and had required parishes to keep fire-fighting equipment, hooks, ladders and buckets; and the danger of fire was offered as one of the principal reasons why the waterworks should be built at FOLLY BRIDGE in 1694. In 1654 a fire engine had been purchased by the Corporation, which bought two more after the Great Fire of London of 1666 had induced all local authorities to look to the dangers of fire in their own communities. Later, parishes bought their own fire engines and most charged fees for the use of these machines outside their boundaries. The University had its own part-time fire service from the early years of the 19th century until the 1880s. In 1845 nine of Oxford's fifteen fire engines were owned by the University or by individual colleges, the other six by, respectively, the city, the county, OXFORD UNIVERSITY PRESS, the parishes of ST MARY THE VIRGIN and St Michael at the North Gate, and the Sun Insurance Company, whose fire marks can be seen on several Oxford buildings including VANBRUGH HOUSE and Austin Reed's shop in CORNMARKET STREET. Nine years later, however, the city and county fire engines had been disposed of, and only privately owned machines and those belonging to the University and colleges remained. In a fire of 1870, however, two people were killed, and this led to the creation of a volunteer fire brigade, which operated until 1887 in conjunction with a fire-fighting service provided by the police. A headquarters and engine house were built in 1873–4 for the Volunteer Brigade in NEW INN HALL STREET; and a new station was opened in George Street in 1896. The firemen, sixty in number in the 1890s, became professionals in 1940. The next year they became part of the National Fire Service, though they were once more under the control of the Corporation after 1948. The headquarters moved from George Street to REWLEY ROAD in 1971.

Fisher, Herbert Albert Laurens *(1856–1940)*. Fisher went up as a scholar to New College from Winchester in 1884. He was appointed a Fellow of the college in 1888, having obtained a First in both Classical MODERATIONS and LITERAE HUMANIORES. A conscientious tutor, he was also a prolific writer, an authority on Napoleon and the biographer of his brother-in-law, the historian Professor Frederick William Maitland (1856–1906). After a successful term as Vice-Chancellor of Sheffield University, he was asked by Lloyd George to become President of the Board of Education in 1916. He returned to Oxford in 1925 as Warden of New College. His best book, the *History of Europe* (3 vols, 1935) was used, often too indiscriminately, in the preparation of their essays by a whole generation of undergraduates reading History.

Fisher Row Runs from HYTHE BRIDGE STREET southwards to Quaking Bridge (*see* BRIDGES) and St Thomas Street, alongside a branch of the THAMES. Formerly Weyeham or Wareham Bank, it was known as early as the 1660s as Fishers' Row, and as Fisher Row by 1772. There was once a row of 17th-century cottages here, since destroyed. Upper Fisher Row leads north from Hythe Bridge Street.

Five Mile Drive This road was at one time known as Long Hedge; by 1820 it had become Horsemonger (or Horsemanger) Lane, and also Horselow Field. At that time there were few roads connecting the BANBURY and WOODSTOCK ROADS between what is now ST MARGARET'S ROAD and Five Mile Drive. Apart from riding on PORT MEADOW and at WYTHAM, the dull 'Five Mile round' or 'Stingy Drive' was the only alternative to riding beyond the turnpike gates on the outskirts of Oxford where tolls had to be paid (*see* TRANSPORT). The ride was made daily by some members of the University. In the early 19th century walking was one of the main recreations for undergraduates and in about 1820 a few senior members of the University gave money for the creation of a dry footpath along the Woodstock and Banbury Roads. The walk started from ST GILES' CHURCH, continued along the west side of Woodstock Road as far as Upper Wolvercote (*see* WOLVERCOTE), crossing over by the then Horsemonger Lane and then back by the east side of Banbury Road to St Margaret's Road (then Rackham's Lane) and continuing via the Plantation to St Giles' Church. From this came the saying 'walking round the Five Mile'. In fact, it was still being called *the* Five Mile in 1934 and was an unclassified road even in 1935. Part of the raised footpath remains at the north end of Woodstock Road, running along by the wall of what is now Sheriff's Drive. Today Five Mile Drive is lined with prunus and cherry trees.

Florence Park Situated at COWLEY, this park of about 20 acres was given to the city in 1934 by Mr F.E. Moss in memory of his sister Florence.

Florey, Howard Walter, Baron Florey of Adelaide *(1898–1968)*. Born in Australia, where his father, a shoemaker from Oxfordshire, had settled some years before, Florey obtained degrees in Medicine at Adelaide University before winning a RHODES SCHOLARSHIP and entering the Department of Physiology at Oxford. He gained a First in Physiology and, encouraged by Sir Charles Sherrington

Members of the Oxford Volunteer Fire Brigade which was founded in 1870 and operated until 1887.

Dilapidated 17th-century cottages in Fisher Row in 1885, shortly before their demolition.

(1857–1952), Fellow of Magdalen College and Waynflete Professor of Physiology, Florey remained in Oxford to work on a study of the bloodflow in the capillaries of the brain. After further work in Cambridge, America, London and Sheffield, in 1935 he succeeded Georges Dreyer (1873–1934) as Professor of Pathology at Oxford. He immediately set about reorganising the SIR WILLIAM DUNN SCHOOL OF PATHOLOGY, which had been established by Dreyer but had not lived up to its early promise. By the end of the decade the Oxford School of Pathology was one of the most distinguished in any university. The work done in Oxford by Florey and his colleagues and assistants on penicillin therapy was among the most valuable undertaken in the whole history of medicine. A complete account of this work was given by Florey and some of his collaborators in the two-volume *Antibiotics* (1949). In 1945 Florey shared the Nobel Prize for Medicine with his colleague Sir Ernst Boris Chain (1906–79) and Sir Alexander Fleming (1881–1955), who had discovered penicillin in 1928. Florey was appointed Provost of The Queen's College in 1962 and was made a life peer in 1965.

Floyd's Row *off St Aldate's.* Probably named after the Floyd family, one of whom, William, owned tenements in ST ALDATE's in the early 19th century. He was almost certainly the son of John Floyd, cordwainer, who had been one of the city's official leather-searchers from 1783–6.

Folly Bridge Takes the ABINGDON ROAD across the THAMES into ST ALDATE's. It originally formed part of the GRANDPONT causeway, being known then as South Bridge. Like MAGDALEN BRIDGE, it was largely maintained by charity, and bridge-hermits were appointed to collect alms at the wayside chapel of St Nicholas. In about 1530 repairs were paid for by John Claymond, President of Corpus Christi College; his donation was cited in the next century as evidence that maintenance of the bridge was the responsibility of the college. For centuries disputes continued over the respective liabilities of Corpus Christi, the University, the city and the county of Berkshire. Until 1779, halfway across the bridge stood a tower, known successively as Bachelor's Tower, Friar Bacon's Study, the New Gate and the Folly. It was here that Roger Bacon (*c.*1214–94) was said to have studied Astronomy. By 1815 the bridge, called Folly Bridge since the late 17th century, was pronounced irreparable and an Act was obtained for its replacement.

The new bridge was completed in 1827 to the designs of Ebenezer Perry, and a toll-house was built in 1844 by James Gardiner. The bridge was freed of tolls in 1850, the trustees, who had advanced the money for its construction, having recouped their outlay.

(*See also* BRIDGES.)

Founders' Kin At Oxford the founders' kin privilege applied, strictly speaking, to those who could show that they were 'of the kin' of the founder or founders of a college, and who by the original college statutes thereby enjoyed an absolute right of entry to (or a preference when they were in competition for) a fellowship, scholarship or exhibition at that college. The Merton statutes of 1274 contain such a provision, and similar clauses are in the statutes of The Queen's College (1340), New College (1379), All Souls (1438), St John's (1555), Wadham (1612), Pembroke (1624) and Worcester (1714). The foundation statutes of Corpus Christi (1517) enshrine similar privileges, but they are in favour of the kin of a named person other than the founder. Later on, benefactors established 'engrafted' fellowships, scholarships and exhibitions (added to the original statutes) to which their kin or the kin of their nominees had privileged access, and by the middle of the 19th century such arrangements existed at two-thirds of the twenty-four colleges and halls of the University. The value and incidence of kin privileges varied widely from college to college (between 1815 and 1857 over two-thirds of those elected to the valuable All Souls fellowships were of the, by then very tenuous, 'blood of the founder'), and a system which had begun as a charitable impulse (*cf*. I Timothy 5:viii) had largely declined into an anachronistic abuse. This fact, and the essentially inegalitarian nature of the system, made it fair game for the reforming ROYAL COMMISSION of 1850, and the statutes and ordinances which followed the Executive Commission in 1857 and 1858 swept away all kin privileges, sparing only the recently established How Exhibitions at Exeter College (1831) and the Fereday Fellowships at St John's (1854). Both these privileges, which still exist, were of the engrafted variety – as were the post-Commission (and also still extant) Gomm scholarships established at Keble College in 1878 in favour of the kin of the then Marquess of Lothian. Two years later, three scholarships were endowed at Hertford College by its founder, T.C. Baring, limited to his own and his wife's kin. Though too late for the foundation statutes of the college, they are indubitably 'founder's kin' scholarships – and the only ones to survive at Oxford.

(Squibb, G.D., *Founder's Kin: Privilege and Pedigree*, Oxford, 1972.)

Franks Commission Appointed by the HEBDOM-ADAL COUNCIL in February 1964 and chaired by Lord Franks, Provost of Worcester College. Its terms of reference were 'to inquire into and report upon the part which Oxford plays now and should play in the future in the system of higher education in the United Kingdom, having regard to its position as both a national and an international University'. The Commission's report was published in May 1966 and made many recommendations concerning the administration of the University, its size, the financial arrangements between the University and the colleges, admission to the University, its teachers and teaching, and the setting up of a Council of Colleges.

(*University of Oxford. Report of Commission of Inquiry*, 2 vols, Oxford, 1966; Bridges, Lord, 'The Franks Report', *Oxford*, xxi, Dec. 1966, No. 1, p. 47.)

Freeman, Edward Augustus (*1823–1892*). Won a scholarship to Trinity College in 1841 and was elected a probationary Fellow in 1845. He married his former tutor's daughter and, for a time, lived at LITTLEMORE. His first book, *A History of Architecture*, published in 1849, was followed by many more and by numerous articles for the *Saturday Review*, to which he contributed for more than twenty years. His most celebrated works, the *History of the Norman Conquest* (5 vols, 1867–79) and *The Reign of William Rufus* (2 vols, 1882) were followed by an unfinished *History of Sicily* (4 vols, 1891–2). His archaic style and longwindedness make his works difficult to read, while his wayward treatment of his sources and his prejudices render them unreliable. In 1884 Freeman succeeded WILLIAM STUBBS as Regius Professor of Modern History. Violently outspoken and on occasions malevolent, he attacked his enemies, including J.A. FROUDE, with unremitting ruthlessness; yet he was also warmly and devotedly loyal to such friends as J.R. Green (1837–83), author of *A Short History of the English People* (1874) and instigator of the Oxford Historical Society. Freeman was a man of 'very singular manners' and could often be seen walking the streets of Oxford reciting poetry to himself and jumping into the air when he reached his favourite passages. His eldest daughter married SIR ARTHUR EVANS.

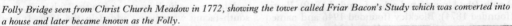
Folly Bridge seen from Christ Church Meadow in 1772, showing the tower called Friar Bacon's Study which was converted into a house and later became known as the Folly.

Freemasons' Hall *333 Banbury Road*. The house on this site, originally called Summerhill, was built in 1823 by John Mobley, a butcher. He sold it the following year to another butcher, who lived there until 1846, when he disposed of it to James Ryman, an art dealer with a shop in HIGH STREET. Ryman bought land adjoining the house and laid out a large garden, extending to 11 acres, with many exotic trees. He died in 1880, leaving the house to his adopted nephew, James Frank Ryman-Hall. When the latter died in 1925, the estate was sold in lots. Most of it was bought by a builder, Noah Capel, who developed the building land up to SQUITCHEY LANE and created two new roads, Summerhill Road and Capel Close. A total of sixty-four houses was built on what had been the garden of Summerhill. Capel resold the house, with 1½ acres of garden, to H.W. Adamson, a tailor in High Street, who in 1954 sold it to the Freemasons. They added a meeting hall with a temple above, designed by Kenneth Stevens & Associates. Further additions were made from time to time, the last extension, to the design of Peter Reynolds, being added in 1986. This is a new temple, named the Rathcreedan Temple after Lord Rathcreedan, who was a Provincial Grand Master. The original temple in the old house is called the Amery Temple after another Provincial Grand Master. The hall is used for dinners, receptions, dances and other functions.

Until 1829 meetings of the masonic lodges were held at the Star Hotel (later the CLARENDON HOTEL). In 1829 the meetings moved to the ANGEL INN, where they continued until the new Masonic Hall opened in ALFRED STREET. Subsequently meetings were held at the Forum near the East Gate in HIGH STREET, until the move to No. 333 BANBURY ROAD.

The lodges which use the Freemasons' Hall are: Alfred (founded 1769, but ceased in 1783 until re-started); Amery (founded 1970 and named after G.D. Amery – *see above*); Annesley (founded 1919); Apollo (the University Lodge, founded 1819); Bertie (founded 1874); Blockley (founded 1946 and named after a former Provincial Grand Master); Carfax (founded 1938); Churchill (founded 1841; Lord John Spencer Churchill was a former Provincial Grand Master); Clarendon (founded 1978; it has a number of members of the CLARENDON CLUB, but is not restricted to such members); Clavis (founded 1974; although attached to Oxfordshire Province, it draws its members – all of them interested in bell-ringing – from the whole country); Culham College (founded 1903, mostly for members of the teaching profession); Isis (founded 1921); Islip (founded 1963); Old Headington (founded 1939); Oxnaford (founded 1948); St Giles (founded 1980).

Freemen *see* PRIVILEGED PERSONS.

Frewen Club *98 St Aldate's*. Founded in 1869 by officers of the 2nd Corps, Oxfordshire Rifle Volunteers, which was recruited from local citizens, with the aim 'to further comradeship among the Volunteers and to encourage relationships with the Townspeople'. The club was named the 2nd Oxfordshire Rifle Volunteer Corps Club and rented rooms in the Three Cups Hotel in QUEEN STREET. It subsequently moved to a club room in CORNMARKET, but in 1876 was reconstituted with forty members as the Oxford Rifle Volunteer Club and took rooms at the present address.

The word 'Rifle' was omitted from the name in 1878. Ten years later the club moved to rooms at 51 Cornmarket, with its entrance in FREWIN COURT. The name was then changed to the Frewen Club – possibly spelt thus because that was the spelling then (and sometimes still) used for the nearby FREWIN HALL. When the lease expired in 1901 the club moved next door to 49–50 Cornmarket, and in 1908 finally returned to its old premises at No. 98 ST ALDATE'S, the freehold of which it was able to purchase in 1973 from Magdalen College; it then carried out an extensive rebuilding programme. The club is run on similar lines to the CLARENDON CLUB, with which it maintains a friendly rivalry.

(*See also* CLUBS AND SOCIETIES.)

Frewin Court A narrow lane off CORNMARKET, which may originally have been built at the end of the 12th century by the ABBOT OF OSENEY. By 1405 it was known as Bodin's Lane, and as Bridewell Lane in the late 16th century. It was renamed Frewin Court in the 19th century after Richard Frewin, Camden Professor of Ancient History, who lived there in 1726. The lane leads to FREWIN HALL and the Oxford UNION.

Frewin Hall *New Inn Hall Street*. Stands on a site, originally occupied by a Norman stone house, which was given in 1453 for the founding of St Mary's College for Augustinian canons (*see* MONASTIC COLLEGES). Erasmus stayed there in 1497. The college was dissolved in 1541, and such of its buildings as remained were acquired by Brasenose College in 1580. In the CIVIL WAR cannon were cast in the chapel. When Brasenose College built its own chapel between 1656 and 1666 some of the materials came from the former chapel of St Mary's College, demolished in the process. Its 15th-century hammerbeam roof was rebuilt in Brasenose Chapel, though today only the wooden brackets supporting the roof are visible.

A house was built on the site in the 16th century, a south-facing wing being added in the 18th. It was altered in 1888 by SIR THOMAS JACKSON. There is a Norman column in its fine undercroft which has recently been restored with help from the Rhodes Trustees (*see* RHODES HOUSE). The attractive garden is one of the last to survive in this part of Oxford. The whole house, together with other properties in the vicinity, was converted in the 1970s to provide accommodation for junior members of Brasenose. The architect for Phase I of the conversion was Fletcher Watson and for Phase II the Architects Design Partnership. Evidence of the former vaulted gatehouse of St Mary's College is plainly visible. (For the derivation of the name acquired by the house *see* FREWIN COURT.)

When he was up at Christ Church in the late 1850s, the Prince of Wales, later Edward VII, lived here. With six other Christ Church undergraduates chosen as his companions he listened politely, though inattentively, in the dining room of New Inn Hall opposite, to lectures in English History given by the Regius Professor of Modern History, Goldwin Smith, who was more interested in academic reform than in teaching and who felt driven to confess that his bored pupil – who could occasionally be seen walking about the town in the gold-tasselled mortar board with which undergraduates of noble birth were then allowed to adorn themselves – might well have acquired more knowledge of history from the novels of Sir Walter Scott. Other occupants of the house have been SIR CHARLES OMAN, and WALTER PATER'S intimate friend C.L. Shadwell, Provost of Oriel and translator of Dante.

(Blair, John, 'Frewin Hall, Oxford: a Norman Mansion and a Monastic College', *Oxoniensia*, xliii, 1978.)

Friar's Entry A pedestrian way between MAG-DALEN STREET and the present GLOUCESTER STREET and GLOUCESTER GREEN. It was in existence in the 17th century and probably earlier. It has had various spellings, including Frier's Entry (1731), and is said to be named after the Carmelite friars who lived in the neighbourhood of Gloucester Green. It would have been on their route to and from the south chapel of the church of ST MARY MAGDALEN, which stands opposite and which was built in 1320 and dedicated to Our Lady of Mount Carmel. Edward II gave BEAUMONT PALACE, on the site of which BEAUMONT STREET is built, to the Carmelites. In a gazetteer of about 1840, William Jewell, bath-chair owner, is shown carrying on business in Friar's Entry. He was one of nine such owners in the space of about one square mile.

Friars Wharf Named after the BLACKFRIARS who had a wharf here in ST EBBE'S beside the THAMES. When the wharf was filled in in the 19th century, a street was built and houses erected on the site. These were demolished in the St Ebbe's redevelopment; but when new houses were built along the Thames frontage in the 1970s the old name was retained.

Frideswide, Saint (*d. c.735*). The patron saint of the city and University of Oxford, about whom little can be said for certain. The earliest account of her dates from the 12th century, and she appears to have been the daughter of a Christian Saxon nobleman who lived in Oxford. Sought as a wife by a Mercian king whom she refused to marry, she fled to woods on the banks of the THAMES where she remained for three years, living with a swineherd and his wife and helping them in their work. Her suitor marched with his army to the gates of Oxford, where he was blinded by lightning in a storm. Frideswide then returned to the town, where she founded a religious house. By the beginning of the 11th century her shrine was established in ST FRIDESWIDE'S PRIORY. In the 13th century the capitals of some of the pillars of CHRIST CHURCH CATHEDRAL were decorated with carvings of foliage – in one of which a woman's head can be seen among the leaves – to commemorate her hiding in the woods. Episodes in her life are shown in the east window of the Latin Chapel. The name Frideswide means 'bond of peace'. Her feast day is 19 October, on which day each year the BISHOP OF OXFORD, together with the Dean and Canons and the whole cathedral body, the VICE-CHANCELLOR and PROCTORS, the LORD MAYOR and Councillors gather for a service in the cathedral, where the site of her shrine is indicated by a brass plate in the floor of the Lady Chapel. The shrine itself was broken up in the 16th century and its fragments inserted in the walls of a well at the west end of the cathedral. They were found there and reassembled in the Lady Chapel by J. Park Harrison in 1889–91. St Frideswide's banner, preserved in a glass case in the cathedral, was made for the Church Congress which met in Oxford in 1924. The saint is shown holding a model of the cathedral in her right hand and surrounded by the arms of various places and institutions connected with the diocese of Oxford, including OSENEY ABBEY.

Froude, James Anthony (*1818–1894*). The son of a Devonshire clergyman, he matriculated from Oriel College in 1835 and in 1842 was elected a Fellow of Exeter. He was obliged to resign his fellowship, however, upon the publication of his novel *The Nemesis of Faith* (1849), which ARCHBISHOP RICHARD WHATELEY condemned as evidence of the evil effects of tractarianism and a copy of which William Sewell (1804–74), Fellow of Exeter who had withdrawn from the OXFORD MOVEMENT, hurled into the fire at a lecture delivered in the Hall of Exeter College. Froude then left Oxford for London, where he became a disciple of Thomas Carlyle. Between 1856 and 1870 he published the twelve volumes of his monumental *History of England from the Fall of Cardinal Wolsey to the Defeat of the Spanish Armada*. Numerous other works followed this, some of them giving grounds for the accusation that he was a man of letters rather than a historian; others, like his *Letters and Memorials of Jane Welsh Carlyle* (1883), being condemned as indiscreet. In 1892 he was, however, offered the Regius Chair of Modern History at Oxford in succession to E.A. FREEMAN, who had been one of his most outspoken critics.

Froude, Richard Hurrell (*1803–1836*). Elder brother of J.A. FROUDE, R.H. Froude entered Oriel College in 1821 and was elected a Fellow of the college in 1826. He was ordained in 1828 and subsequently became an influential early member of the OXFORD MOVEMENT, writing three of the *Tracts for the Times* and advising on others. He contracted consumption before he was thirty and died a few years later at his father's rectory.

Fry, Charles Burgess (*1872–1956*). Perhaps the greatest all-round sportsman Oxford has ever known, Fry won a scholarship to Wadham College from Repton. Representing the University at athletics, cricket and association football, he won three BLUES as a freshman and was captain of all three teams in 1894, having equalled the world's record long jump the year before – allegedly between puffs on a cigar. But for an injury in the last trial fixture he would have won a fourth Blue in rugby football. In 1902 he played for Southampton in the final of the Football Association Cup on a Saturday and scored 82 at Lord's on the following Monday. He went on to play cricket for England as, in the opinion of his Sussex partner Prince Ranjitsinhji, the greatest batsman of his time.

Further Education, Oxford College of *Oxpens Road*. The college, created in 1960, developed from the former College of Technology (*see* POLYTECHNIC) and was located in the COWLEY ROAD until its establishment on the OXPENS ROAD site. In addition to this main 7-acre site, on the former recreation ground by the banks of the Castle Mill Stream and the site of the old cattle market, it has three other branches: its original home, the Cowley Road precinct, of some 2 acres; the 2-acre premises of a comprehensive school at BLACKBIRD LEYS; and East Oxford School. Former premises in NEW INN HALL STREET, REWLEY ROAD, and ST CLEMENT'S have been closed. The intention is to concentrate all facilities at Oxpens in due course. The site there has been steadily developed since 1969, when the first two teaching blocks were completed to cater for Science and Domestic Sciences. In 1973 a further two blocks were opened, for Business Studies, Arts and Languages, Drama, Art and Administration. These buildings were designed by the Oxford City Architect's Department under the direction of Douglas Murray. Construction, Engineering, Mathematics and Computing workshops were completed in 1982. Further Engineering workshops and laboratories are now under construction (1986).

The purpose of the college is to provide a full range of further-education courses, mainly at craft, technician and intermediate professional level, and principally in the Oxford area. The majority of the 11,000 students (1300 of them full-time) are aged between sixteen and twenty-one; there are some 220 full-time and 350 part-time academic staff, with some 100 administrative and technical staff.

G

Gaisford, Thomas (*1779–1855*). Elected a Student of Christ Church in 1800, he became Dean in 1831 and remained in that office until his death twenty-four years later. Appointed Regius Professor of Greek in 1812, he was one of the foremost classical scholars of the age. The Gaisford Prize was founded in commemoration of him (*see* PRIZES AND SCHOLARSHIPS). Gaisford was also a conscientious curator of the BODLEIAN LIBRARY, while, as an influential delegate of the OXFORD UNIVERSITY PRESS, he made a valuable contribution to its success in the first half of the 19th century.

Gaol   *see* CITY GAOL.

Gardens   'Beautiful city! So venerable, so lovely, so unravaged by the fierce intellectual life of our century, so serene! . . . spreading her gardens to the moonlight and whispering from her towers the last enchantments of the Middle Age'. So wrote Matthew Arnold in his *Essays in Criticism* (1865). As with its architecture, Oxford can show a complete history of gardens, from mediaeval to modern, and many of the college gardens have rare historic features given high rating on the English Heritage Register of Historic Parks and Gardens. The meadow walks, quadrangles and gardens were a necessary part of collegiate life and each college appointed its own garden master from among its members. Monastic cloisters can be seen at Christ Church where the original ST FRIDESWIDE'S PRIORY cloisters were incorporated into the college. New College, although built as a college, followed the monastic cloister precedent for covered walks. At Magdalen rooms were later built over the cloisters, forming a cloister quadrangle which today gives a perfect synthesis of ancient building and green space.

At first college gardens were a haphazard arrangement of herb and vegetable plots, orchards and walks,

An engraving from William Williams's Oxonia Depicta *of 1733 showing St John's College garden with the formal 'wilderness' on the right and the stilted elms on the left.*

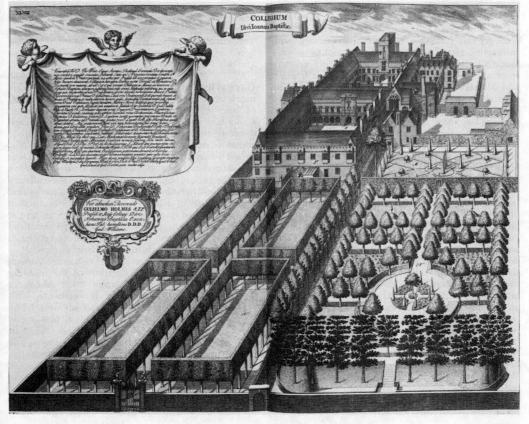

but the Renaissance brought new ideas in garden design as well as in learning. These were first put into practice in Oxford in the gardens laid out for the humanist Warden of All Souls, Robert Hovenden, and are shown in remarkable detail on the Hovenden map (*see* MAPS). Such gardens have now disappeared, having had to be sacrificed when additional buildings were required by colleges within the CITY WALLS. Those colleges built outside the walls, Christ Church, St John's, Trinity and Magdalen, had more scope for making gardens. New College, however, has a spacious garden within the walls, since in 1379 the college was allowed to use the land that had become waste after the Black Death, on condition that it kept the surrounding walls in repair. These are now the best-preserved parts of the walls and today shelter a beautiful modern herbaceous border, with seats provided in the bastions. Although the garden is enclosed by high walls, the Mount – a mound of earth begun in 1594 and 'perfected with stepps of Stone and setts for ye Hedges about ye walke' in 1649 – gave the Fellows an opportunity to look out on to the countryside and a vantage point from which to admire the box scrolls and heraldic parterres set out in the grass, as seen in DAVID LOGGAN's engravings.

When Oxford became the royalist capital during the CIVIL WAR, the quadrangles were turned into parade grounds and the meadow walks banked up to provide fortifications. At Magdalen these walks can still be seen, part of them known as ADDISON'S WALK after Joseph Addison who frequented them, enjoying the 'pleasures of the imagination' while contemplating the rural scenes. Baroque garden design on the European model appeared in the form of parterres, fountains, statues and even a miniature Versailles grille at New College; but full-scale baroque space design with interacting vistas as envisaged in NICHOLAS HAWKS-MOOR's plan was rejected. Eighteenth-century improvements were also resisted by Christ Church and Magdalen, despite the opportunities offered by their riverside settings. The old alleyed walks round the water meadows and the secluded gardens were preferred as more in keeping with ancient founda-tions. Even a sumptuous Red Book with 'before and after' improvement scenes did not tempt the Fellows of Magdalen to employ the services of Humphry Repton, who proposed to create a lake in Addison's Meadow. Worcester College, however, being essen-tially 18th-century in character, does have a landscaped garden. The Provost's lodgings are virtually a Palladian country house opening on to a park. When the college's frontage to the THAMES was cut off by the extension of the Oxford CANAL in 1790, and an unattractive swampy area was left, it was decided to landscape with specimen trees planted on the lawns running down to a lake. At the west end of the monastic side of the quadrangle a garden was made on a banked terrace, raising the ground to the level of an upstairs room, and by means of a curly bargeboard on the gable end and a Regency trellis on the window it was given the appearance of a *cottage orné* in a park. The recent Sainsbury building at the end of an arm of the lake is picturesquely contrived to fit the scene. Naturalising also took place at St John's, Balliol, Wadham and Trinity, whose formal gardens, influen-ced by Dutch topiary, can be seen in Williams's *Oxonia Depicta* of 1733. Formal groves with straight paths were transformed into serpentine walks through flowery shrubberies. New College's 16th-century Mount was also naturalised.

When Oxford's Gothic buildings were erected in the 19th century, evergreens were used extensively to offset the architecture, not only in the college extensions but also in the NORTH OXFORD estate. The St John's rock garden laid out by the Bursar in the 1890s was one of the first of its kind. Miss Annie Rogers of St Hugh's also followed new fashions in her Arts and Crafts gardening for the college. The first strikingly modern college in Oxford, St Catherine's, had its own landscape environment designed as an entity with the building by the architect Arne Jacobsen. Wolfson College, nearer the Cherwell (*see* THAMES), takes advantage of a landscape setting. When further building has been required in the old colleges, little courtyard areas have been made, as in the Goodhart building at University College and in the new accommodation for Lincoln College.

(*See also* BOTANIC GARDEN *and* TREES.)

(Günther, R.T., *Oxford Gardens*, 1912; Batey, M., *Oxford Gardens*, Amersham, 1982; Gray, Ronald, and Frankl, Ernest, *Oxford Gardens*, Cambridge, 1987.)

Gardner, Dame Helen (Louise) (*1908–1986*). Educated at North London Collegiate School and St Hilda's College, she obtained first-class Honours in the School of English Language and Literature. Appointed a Fellow of St Hilda's in 1942, she became a Fellow of Lady Margaret Hall and Merton Professor of English Literature in 1966. She was a delegate of the OXFORD UNIVERSITY PRESS from 1959–63. An authority on T.S. Eliot, John Donne and the Metaphysical Poets, she edited the *New Oxford Book of English Verse* (1972). Described by one of her pupils as 'formidably impressive', she was awarded several honorary degrees and served on numerous academic and other bodies outside Oxford.

Gargoyles and Grotesques In recent years much work has been done in Oxford to restore many of the mediaeval decorations, often amusing, sometimes alarming and occasionally erotic, which decorate the city's buildings. The word gargoyle comes from the Old French *gargouille*, which also meant throat – the English word 'gargle' is of the same derivation – and gargoyles were used to carry rainwater from the gutters behind them away from the walls of a building and to pour it down into the street, sometimes with the help of a lead or iron pipe in the mouth. Grotesques had no such function, though grotesque figures, such as the monkey to be seen above a drainhead at Magdalen College, were sometimes used either to imply or actually to perform a functional purpose.

Magdalen College is particularly rich in grotesques, many of them demons. The front of the building facing HIGH STREET has all manner of carved figures and faces; so has the tower, which is ornamented with demons and mermaids, animals and labourers. The mitred bishop holding up his hand in blessing is William of Waynflete, who founded the college in 1458. On the St Swithun's building further west, just before the corner of LONGWALL STREET, is a favourite subject of mediaeval stone-carvers – a musician puffing laboriously at his pipe, with bloated cheeks and huge staring eyes. Here also are other popular mediaeval characters, Green Men, their faces sur-rounded by foliage and grapes. These figures and

Midgley, Dean and Chaplain (with his labrador). The last of these occasioned this epitaph:

> Beneath this turf the Dean's dog Fred
> Without his master, goes to Earth, stone dead.
> But on the tower, stone Dean and Fred together
> Enjoy the sunshine and endure bad weather.

The likeness of Michael Groser himself is on the north side of the tower overlooking New College, where other splendid examples of his work may be seen. There are imaginary anthropomorphised animals on the chapel wall on the north side of the front quad; more realistic animals, as well as heads, on the southern wall of the college in New College Lane; and, approached from the cloisters, further heads with expressive hands on the bell-tower – those on the south side representing the virtues of Patience, Generosity, Charity, Prayerfulness, Innocent Love, Enthusiastic Joy and Justice; those on the north side (visible only from a part of the college not open to the public) representing the Seven Deadly Sins. Other heads on the bell-tower, including a sinisterly beckoning tempter and his alarmed though gullible victim, can be seen from the gardens of the TURF TAVERN. Yet more examples of Groser's work can be seen inside the front quad of All Souls. The slightly earlier figures on the outside of this college are by E.S. Frith.

Other colleges with interesting grotesques are Corpus Christi; Balliol; St John's, in whose Canterbury Quad (1631–6) are numerous fine carved figures by E.S. Frith, assisted by Michael Black, and Wadham College, on whose gateway tower are the heads of Nicholas Wadham, represented as a rose (part of his family coat of arms) and of his wife, set in a scallop shell (part of the Petre family arms), both carved by Michael Black. There are extremely lively heads, with fingers picking noses or hands holding aching teeth, as well as workers, masons, carpenters and the like, on the High Street front of Brasenose College, which was built in 1891–9 to the designs of SIR THOMAS JACKSON, himself an adept stone-carver and a talented designer of heads for carvers who worked for him. The original gargoyles on the tower of Merton College chapel, whose mouths were stopped up in 1827 when drainpipes were installed, were replaced during the college restoration which began in 1958. The work was carried out by Axtell, Perry and Symm Masonry Ltd of OSNEY MEAD, a firm of masons which, as Symm and Company, had been active in Oxford since the 18th century. Their chief carver was Percy Quick, whose work has already been noted at Magdalen. The charming plaque above the gateway, depicting a bishop (presumably Walter de Merton) praying and St John the Baptist raising his hand in blessing in a romantic woodland setting, is of the late 15th century, though parts have been replaced. The carving of the signs of the zodiac on the roof of the Fitzjames Arch in the far corner of the front quadrangle are also 15th-century work. The grotesque Green Men on the corbels inside the chapel are late 13th century. There are more 13th-century heads of Green Men on ST FRIDESWIDE'S tomb in CHRIST CHURCH CATHEDRAL. In the chapter house at Christ Church are other 13th-century heads carved by John of Gloucester. The grotesques on the pinnacles of Wolsey Tower have been restored by Axtell, Perry and Symm.

The Rev. Graham Midgley, sometime Dean and Chaplain of St Edmund Hall, and his labrador, Fred, carved by Michael Groser on the tower of the college library.

those on the tower were not, however, carved by mediaeval craftsmen, but by Pat Conoley, Percy Quick and Michael Groser between 1977 and 1981, the original stone figures having been almost obliterated. Around the top of the tower are two lines of figures, the lower one containing likenesses of dons and staff of the college, the upper caricaturing members of the firm of masons responsible for the work – the surveyor, his assistant, a draughtsman, the site foreman and carvers. There are further examples of Percy Quick's work on the west end of the chapel. The figures in the triangular quad approached through the arch to the right of the chapel are by Thomas Tyrrell. In the cloisters there is an extraordinary collection of fantastic allegorical statues, twenty-two in all, set on pedestals around three of the sides. These were placed here in 1508–9 and were then brightly painted. In the 17th century one of the Fellows of the college attempted to interpret the meaning of these strange figures in a Latin treatise, *Oedipus Magdaleniensis*. Some were recarved in the 1860s.

As well as at Magdalen, Michael Groser's work can also be enjoyed at St Edmund Hall and at New College. Around the top of the tower of the library of St Edmund Hall, formerly ST PETER-IN-THE-EAST, are the carved heads of men connected with the conversion of the church to its present use in the 1960s, including Dr J.N.D. Kelly, then Principal of the college (with a squash racket); R.E. Alton, Bursar (with money bags); Jeffrey Hackney, Librarian (in barrister's wig); Dr A.B. Emden, Principal of the college, 1929–51 (in spectacles); and the Rev. Graham

Self-portrait of the stonecarver Michael Groser on the north side of St Edmund Hall library tower, overlooking New College.

High up on the wall of the Duke Humfrey Library (*see* BODLEIAN LIBRARY *and* HUMFREY, DUKE OF GLOUCESTER) are an extraordinary array of figures, cats, fish, birds, angels, demons, dwarfs, a salamander, a frog, a peacock and fantastic human heads. Other grotesques line the CATTE STREET front, including a helmeted soldier and a simpleton mocking him. These were all carved in the late 1950s. Some unrecognisable defaced stumps of the earlier carvings remain. From the Fellows' Garden of Exeter College can be seen a likeness of John Sparrow, former Warden of All Souls, on the corner of the Selden end of the library.

Around the base of the 14th-century spire of ST MARY THE VIRGIN are several gargoyles whose drainage channels can be seen by those who climb the steps of the tower. These were carved in Clipsham stone under the direction of Sir Thomas Jackson to replace others of Taynton stone which had worn away, though placed in position less than fifty years before.

(*See also* EMPERORS' HEADS *and* STONE.)

(Blackwood, John, *Oxford's Gargoyles and Grotesques*, Oxford, 1986.)

Gaudy   The word 'gaudy' at Oxford is of considerable antiquity. Derived from the present imperative of the Latin word *gaudere* (to rejoice), it was used at Lincoln College from the reign of Elizabeth I onwards to describe the freshmen's dinner; and by the 17th century it seems to have been used as the designation of a generally commemorative feast at a college. Such gaudies are now widespread among colleges; normally (but not invariably) provided without charge, they give an opportunity for former members to return and spend an evening on a reasonably regular basis. The interval between such gaudy nights inevitably varies, but a period of seven to ten years is not untypical. The form 'gaude' is also found.

General Board of the Faculties   Consists of the VICE-CHANCELLOR and the PROCTORS, the ASSESSOR, a representative of the HEBDOMADAL COUNCIL, and sixteen (eight arts, eight science) members elected by the FACULTIES from among their respective members. Elected members hold office for four years. As one of its chief functions, the General Board is charged with the co-ordination and supervision of the work of the several Boards of Faculties. It receives and makes proposals for the provision of facilities for advanced work and research, and for the maintenance of an adequate staff in all subjects; and it frames statutes and decrees on these matters for consideration by Council and the University. The statutes lay upon the General Board certain further special duties in the same connection, including the transmission to Council of any reports of the Boards of Faculties, with comments and recommendations, the appointment of most University Readers, and the advising of Council upon the regulations concerning such matters as the salaries of teachers, laboratory finances and the duties of professors. It is also comprehensively authorised 'to exercise a general supervision over the studies and examinations of the University'. Applications made to, and proposals contemplated by, Council which affect matters within the sphere of the General Board must be referred to that body, and there are provisions for the steps to be taken in the event of a difference of opinion between the two bodies. The General Board receives block grants to enable it to execute the functions with which it is charged.

The General Board can be summed up as being responsible for the academic administration of the University, and its Vice-Chairman is regarded as one of the University's most important officers. The General Board's committees include two joint ones with junior members; a Computing Council; a Graduate Studies Committee; and an External Studies Committee.

George Street   Known in the 13th century as Irishman's Street, probably after William de Hibernia, bailiff of Northgate Hundred in 1254. The street runs parallel with and outside the CITY WALL on the north side of the old city from MAGDALEN STREET to HYTHE BRIDGE STREET. It was later known as Thames Street, as it led towards the river; but from 1772 it was called George Lane and, by the middle of the 19th century, George Street. On the south side St George's Mansions are on the corner of CORNMARKET. In the 19th century the George Inn was on this corner and subsequently the George Restaurant was on the first floor, until the premises were converted to offices (*see* RESTAURANTS). The GRAPES public house, built in 1894 by H.G.W. Drinkwater, stands opposite the APOLLO THEATRE. Nos 15–19 were occupied from the 1920s until the 1960s by the grocery firm of TWINING'S. In 1872 NEW INN HALL STREET was extended to connect with George Street. On the corner of the two the Royal Champion public house was rebuilt in 1873; the building was demolished in the early 1980s to make way for new shops and offices. Further along is the former CITY OF OXFORD HIGH SCHOOL, designed by T.G.

JACKSON and built in 1878–80. The building was restored in 1978 and is now the University Social Studies Faculty Centre.

On the north side from Worcester Street was the former Municipal Restaurant, closed in 1977, and the WELSH PONY public house. The Corn Exchange and former fire station, built in 1894–6, have been converted to the OLD FIRE STATION ARTS CENTRE. St George the Martyr, which was built in 1849, was demolished in 1934 and the Ritz Cinema built on the site; this is now the Cannon, George Street, comprising three smaller cinemas (see CINEMAS). Opposite New Inn Hall Street is Threeways House, owned and occupied by the OXFORD AND SWINDON CO-OPERATIVE SOCIETY. On the east side of GLOUCESTER STREET in 1878 was The Terrace, timber-framed houses with an ice-house behind. The New Theatre was opened in 1886 when some of these houses were demolished. The present theatre, renamed the Apollo, was built in 1933–4. The former St Mary Magdalen Girls' School, closed in 1926, was behind the theatre. No. 10 was formerly the Oxford premises of the YMCA.

Gibbs, James (*1682–1754*). The Scottish architect of London's St Mary le Strand and St Martin-in-the-Fields also designed the RADCLIFFE CAMERA, which was completed in 1747. His drawings for it were published as *Biblioteca Radcliviana*. Another great work of his in Oxford is the stone screen in the hall of St John's College (1742). Earlier he had given advice on the design of Magdalen College's New Buildings of 1733. He left his books, which included several fine early Italian works on architecture, to the Radcliffe library. Eight volumes of his drawings and one of prints that he collected are now in the ASHMOLEAN MUSEUM. He also gave portraits of himself to St Mary Hall (*see* ORIEL COLLEGE) and to the BODLEIAN LIBRARY (a duplicate of which is in the National Portrait Gallery in London).

Gill & Co. Ltd One of the oldest firms of ironmongers in the country, dating back to the 16th century when the Smythe family were ironmongers in Oxford. Abel Smythe was admitted a freeman in 1537. Thomas Smythe was four times MAYOR between 1585 and 1600, and Oliver Smythe (a brewer) three times between 1619 and 1631. One of the Smythe girls married a Mr Bush and another married a Mr Pitcher, and the firm became Bush and Pitcher. Around 1840 Mr Gill became associated with the business, which became known as Pitcher and Gill and later as Gill and Ward. In 1922 the firms of Barlow & Alden Ltd and Ison, Kidman & Watts amalgamated under the name of Gill & Co. Ltd. The firm had premises at Nos 127–8 HIGH STREET, which were purchased in 1925, but the shop is now down an alley at 128a High Street, where the suggestion to 'try Gills' usually results in a successful purchase.

Gladstone, William Ewart (*1809–1898*). After education at Eton, Gladstone went up to Christ Church in 1828. Among his fellow undergraduates were HENRY GEORGE LIDDELL and HENRY ACLAND. Extremely religious himself, he found the general 'state of religion in Oxford . . . the most painful spectacle it ever fell to my lot to behold'. He was also extremely studious, though not reclusive. He told his mother that the rooms he occupied on the first floor of

the staircase on the north-east side of Canterbury Quad were in the most fashionable part of the college; and he founded an essay society which was known by his initials as 'The Weg'. He was allowed £250 a year by his father, a sum equivalent to perhaps £12,500 today; but he complained that he was unable to live within it, even though his father paid for his horses and private tutoring. In 1830 he became President of the UNION, where he learned his oratorical technique, and the next year obtained a double First in Classics and Mathematics. In 1832 he was elected as Member of Parliament for Newark and, except for very brief periods, sat in the House of Commons for more than sixty years. In the general election of 1847, at that time still a Conservative, he was elected BURGESS for the University, a post to which he was re-elected in 1852, 1853 and again in 1859, although by then he was closely associated with the Liberals and consequently opposed by a Tory, who polled 859 votes against Gladstone's 1050. In the general election of 1865, however, despite the support of BISHOP WILBERFORCE, BENJAMIN JOWETT, JOHN KEBLE, E.B. PUSEY and MARK PATTISON, and a majority of the members of the University who lived in Oxford, he was heavily defeated by the Tory candidate, Sir William Heathcote, in a poll which, under a recently passed Act, lasted for five days and permitted voting by post. He then offered himself successfully as a candidate in South Lancashire. He became Prime Minister in 1868.

On several occasions Gladstone made it clear that he was deeply interested in university reform. He had originally opposed Lord John Russell's appointment of a government commission to enquire into the affairs of Oxford in 1850, believing it should be reformed from within. But after the commission's report, accepting that the University was in dire need of reconstitution, he undertook to prepare a Bill with Jowett's help and wrote well over 300 letters on the subject. The Bill was introduced in 1854, with profound effects on the organisation of the University (*see* ROYAL COMMISSIONS). He remained devoted to the University throughout his life and made frequent visits there, relishing the pleasures to be found within 'its ever congenial walls', talking to the members of the OXFORD MOVEMENT, dining in the halls of various colleges, going for long walks. In 1857 he was awarded an honorary DCL. He was made an Honorary Fellow of All Souls in 1858 and the ten days he spent there in 1890 were accounted among the happiest of his life. He deplored the slackness of ACADEMIC DRESS, the disappearance of the gold tassels from noblemen's caps and the inclusion of women into academic life (though his youngest daughter became Principal of Newnham College, Cambridge), but his enjoyment was infectious. 'I am reading the Lessons,' he told his wife, 'and all sorts of things – such pranks!' In a speech at the Union he said that he would almost like to kiss every stone in the ancient walls of Oxford.

Gloucester Arms *3 Gloucester Place and 21 Friar's Entry*. Since 1825 one of the five GLOUCESTER GREEN market inns. When leased to HALL'S BREWERY in 1896, it contained a tap-room, lounge and large beer cellar. It has been a favourite haunt of theatrical people since Victorian times.

Gloucester College *see* MONASTIC COLLEGES.

Gloucester Green The open area outside the CITY WALL bounded by WORCESTER STREET, GEORGE STREET, GLOUCESTER STREET and, to the north, by BEAUMONT STREET. There was probably housing here in mediaeval times. After the Black Death in 1348 the area was abandoned and became a derelict and decayed area known as Broken Hayes (Hedges). Its present name derives from Gloucester College (*see* MONASTIC COLLEGES).

Apparently the green was surrounded by trees from the 16th century onwards. For a few years from 1631 it served as a public bowling green and throughout the 17th century it was in regular use as a recreation area, though not a salubrious one: ANTHONY WOOD described it as 'a rude, broken and undigested place'. During the CIVIL WAR the site was used for drilling troops, and in 1658 some executions took place on a tree here. By the mid-18th century housing had increased in the vicinity, and in 1789 the green finally vanished when the CITY GAOL was erected in the centre of the site, where it remained until 1878.

From about 1783 until 1915 a Gloucester Green Fair took place each year on 3 May, and between 1835 and 1932 regular cattle markets were held here; a fair was also held on the green on 3 May each year from 1783 to 1915 (*see* FAIRS). After the removal of the cattle market in 1932 to OXPENS ROAD, the west side of Gloucester Green became the city's country bus station in 1935, and the settling room (the room where bargains used to be finalised) was converted into a café. The Oxford Boys' Central School, an un-denominational elementary school founded in 1871, once occupied premises at the south-east corner of the green. New premises, making ingenious use of a triangular site with classrooms leading off a round hall, were built by Leonard Stokes in 1900–1. The school closed in 1934, and the building later served as the bus waiting room. It has two shallow canted bays with mullioned windows, and a pointed doorway. The picturesque front was intended to harmonise with the cottages which formerly surrounded it. Another school, St Mary Magdalen Boys' School, once stood on the west side of the green. Erected in 1841, it was demolished in 1954.

The Cutler Boulter Provident Dispensary, built in 1886 and offering medical assistance to those who could afford regular savings, gave its name to the short stretch of road linking Gloucester Green and Worcester Street.

The Ritz Cinema (*see* CINEMAS) was built in 1935 on the site of St George's Church, which had been erected in 1849 as a chapel-of-ease serving the parish of ST MARY MAGDALEN. Of the various public houses which were situated in Gloucester Green only the WELSH PONY remains, the BLUE PIG having been demolished in the 1930s to make way for a proposed redevelopment of the area.

For many years the green has served as a car and coach park. A proposal to build a multi-storey car park here in 1936 was rejected as the cost of £45,000 was deemed excessive. Redevelopment of the site to the designs of Donald Kendrick commenced in March 1987 and was completed in 1989.

Gloucester Hall An ACADEMIC HALL as late as 1560, it was transformed into Worcester College in 1714. From the late 13th century till the Dissolution of the Monasteries a college existed in the area near the CASTLE, for the education of Benedictine monks, founded originally as a cell of St Peter's Abbey at Gloucester. All the sixty or so Benedictine houses in the south were required to supply monks as scholars

The cattle market in the 1890s at Gloucester Green where regular cattle sales took place between 1835 and 1932.

at the college. The buildings of the college, called Gloucester College (*see* MONASTIC COLLEGES) in recognition of its origin, provided for this collective support: apart from the *aula* (hall) used by all scholars, there were *camerae* (rooms) provided by particular abbeys or priories for the housing of their scholars.

At the Dissolution, the college buildings were let to laymen; the chapel and library were demolished. In 1560 the buildings were bought for St John's College and became an academic hall for its students, Gloucester Hall increasing to eight the academic halls still extant. There is little evidence for the early years of Gloucester Hall, though it seems to have flourished in the latter part of the 16th century. However, from the time of the CIVIL WAR, when part of its buildings was used as an ordnance workshop, it was in a state of almost complete decay. To put it to some use, its penultimate Principal, Benjamin Woodroffe (1692–1711), tried to establish it as a theological college for Greek students. When this failed he suggested that it should be the means whereby a benefactor from Worcestershire, Sir Thomas Cookes, might realise his wish to found a college. Though Woodroffe did not live to see it, Gloucester Hall, having been sold by St John's College, became Worcester College in 1714, with its last Principal as Provost. The memory of Gloucester Hall and Gloucester College is preserved today by the 15th-century buildings incorporated into Worcester College – notably the *camerae* in the south wing of the quad – and by GLOUCESTER GREEN. (*See also* WORCESTER COLLEGE.)

Gloucester Street Runs southwards from BEAUMONT STREET, skirts GLOUCESTER GREEN and ends in GEORGE STREET. It was formerly Pudding Bag Lane. Like the Green, it is named after Gloucester College (*see* MONASTIC COLLEGES), which had connections with Gloucester Abbey. On the west side of the street was the entrance to the car park, which, on Wednesdays, became the site of an open-air market. On the corner of George Street is the OXFORD AND SWINDON CO-OPERATIVE SOCIETY's new department store. With its turret, it is a foretaste of development on the green which is to be along the lines of the so-called 'romantic option'. It is on the site of the head office and car showrooms of the City Motor Company (Oxford) Ltd, which are now on the RING ROAD at WOLVERCOTE. On the east side is Gloucester Place, FRIAR'S ENTRY, Red Lion Square and the premises of Annabelinda, the dress designer.

Godstow The name means God's Place. It is an area to the north-west of Oxford, over the canal and railways and adjacent to PORT MEADOW. This series of fields, often flooded and frozen over in the winter, was mentioned in Domesday Book as being subject to the right of common pasturage in the time of Edward the Confessor. By the late 14th century Godstow Manor, like that of OSENEY, was very prosperous. A detailed survey of the manor's holdings between 1382 and 1386 describes 375 acres of tenants' land dispersed in unregulated acre, half-acre and quarter-acre strips among three fields which lay west of the WOODSTOCK ROAD, between the Woodstock and BANBURY ROADS and to the east of the Banbury Road. At that time GODSTOW ABBEY held courts to which their tenants in

ST GILES', as well as in Walton village, held suit. These courts dealt mainly with agricultural matters.

JOHN WYCLIF once called Oxford 'a vineyard of the Lord', symbolised by the four big monastic houses of OSENEY ABBEY, ST FRIDESWIDE'S, REWLEY and GODSTOW ABBEY dominating the little city. In 1862, CHARLES LUTWIDGE DODGSON (better known as Lewis Carroll) held the little daughter of the Dean of Christ Church spellbound when he related *Alice's Adventures in Wonderland* for the first time on their way by river to Godstow (*see* ALICE). The poet James Hurdis, of Magdalen, also spoke favourably of 'Godstow in summer fair. ... When days are calm and soft winds blow', and as a place in which to find strawberries and cream.

Nowadays Godstow is much visited for the TROUT INN, which has a pretty garden leading to a 15th-century bridge over the river. The ruins of the abbey and nunnery are found by crossing either this bridge or a more modern one constructed when the lock was restored and a new weir built.

Godstow Abbey The Benedictine nunnery dedicated to St Mary and St John the Baptist was founded in about 1133 by a lady who had come originally from Winchester and was living as an anchoress at BINSEY. The church was consecrated in 1179 in the presence of the King, the Archbishop of Canterbury and several other bishops and nobles. It was always an aristocratic institution. Rosamund Clifford, Henry II's mistress, became a nun here; and the King, according to Benedict of Peterborough, bestowed many gifts upon Godstow, which had previously been but a small nunnery. It was also endowed by Walter de Clifford, Rosamund's father.

After her burial in the middle of the church choir before the altar, her tomb was surrounded by silk hangings, lamps and candles. This reverence so shocked ROBERT GROSSETESTE, Bishop of Lincoln, whose huge diocese contained the archdeaconry of Oxford, that, after a visitation of the nunnery, he ordered her tomb to be moved outside the church. Although it was said by Oxford scholars that they could have 'all kinds of good cheer with the nuns to their hearts' desire', the nunnery seems to have been respectable and well disciplined. For a time in the later Middle Ages it was a finishing school for upper-class young ladies. At the Dissolution of the Monasteries it passed to George Owen (*d.*1558) the King's physician, who came to live in part of it. It was fortified in the CIVIL WAR and burned down in 1645. Only a few post-15th-century ruins remain.

Golden Cross *Cornmarket*. The site of the Golden Cross, which lies on the eastern side of CORNMARKET, is described in early records as *in foro*, or in the marketplace. In about 1188 the land was acquired by OSENEY ABBEY, which, apparently, rebuilt it, constructing a fringe of shops on the street front and a house which lay at the back and was approached by an entry. Around 1193 this house, together with the rooms above the shops, was granted by Mauger the vintner for use as an inn. The shops themselves, with the cellars beneath, were retained by the abbey and remained under separate landlords until 1772 when they were bought by New College. During the 13th and 14th centuries the inn had various owners, eventually becoming the property of

155

Sir Robert Tresilian, the judge who sentenced John Ball after the Peasants' Revolt. Following his own execution at Tyburn in 1388, it became forfeit to the Crown and was thereafter acquired by WILLIAM OF WYKEHAM for New College. It was known successively as Mauger's Hall, Gingiver's Inn and the Cross. By the end of the 14th century a post, bearing 'the Signe of the Crosse', stood in the roadway before its door. For this the inn paid a rent or 'landgable' of one shilling a year to the municipal authorities.

At various times during the succeeding centuries the property was rebuilt, added to and generally enlarged. In 1825 New College sold the freehold to a syndicate, which included a solicitor, Henry Walsh, and Thomas Wyatt, a builder. It was probably then that the name was finally altered and the existing gilt sign set up. Thereafter it changed hands several times.

During its long history the Golden Cross has had many notable visitors. In the 14th century it was regularly patronised by Royal Commissioners (see ROYAL COMMISSIONS). In the mid-16th century, during their trial for heresy and before their removal to the BOCARDO PRISON, Archbishop Cranmer and Bishops Latimer and Ridley were confined in chambers above the present dining room; these were known for centuries after as the Martyrs' Rooms (see MARTYRS' MEMORIAL). The inn became extremely fashionable during the 17th and 18th centuries. In June 1679 William Bedloe, accomplice of Titus Oates, stayed with 'about 10 persons with him. He went away Friday the 6th and would have tarried longer but that he was to hang more men next week'. Also appreciative was the diarist, the Rev. James Woodforde, who, as a young man, dined at the Cross on 22 March 1760 and noted, 'We had Clarett, Madeira and Port to drink.' It is probable that during the 16th century the Cross was used for performances by visiting companies of players, possibly including Shakespeare, who is thought to have stayed at the inn. Certainly in the 17th century ANTHONY WOOD recorded, 'Saturday, 17th July 1658; given to see the play att the Cross Inn, 6d.' Comparatively recently, in 1933, Ruth Draper gave a performance in the courtyard.

Nothing remains today of the original building. The courtyard is approached by a 15th-century gateway with moulded wood jambs, a four-centred arch in a square head with leaves carved in the spandrels. The north spandrel has a shield of arms of New College. Of the three ranges which surround the courtyard, the north is 15th century. It is a two-storeyed, plastered, timber-framed structure having a projecting upper floor with original oriel windows. The south range is 17th century. It is three-storeyed, timber-framed with four gabled projecting bays. In the first and second floors are three original oriels with Ipswich windows. In 1986–7 the property underwent extensive renovation and at a cost of some £2.5 million was converted into thirteen new shops, a restaurant and a bar. Golden Cross Way now provides a way for pedestrians to approach the COVERED MARKET from Cornmarket Street. The Golden Cross was meticulously restored and during the work wall-paintings, probably made in the 1550s, were uncovered and have been preserved. The black and white fake Tudor timbering, which had been superimposed in the 19th century on the 17th-century façade of the south range, has been removed and the building restored to its previous appearance. The City Council's Conservation Officer, John Ashdown, has been closely concerned with the project and has described it as 'an exercise in conservation and urban renewal'.

('The Golden Cross, Oxford', W.A. Pantin (Part I) and E. Clive Rouse (Part II: 'The Wall Paintings'), *Oxoniensia*, xx, 1955, pp. 46–89.)

GOLF CLUBS   There are four golf clubs in or close to Oxford:

Frilford Heath Golf Club   *Frilford, Abingdon.* About 7 miles south-west of Oxford. The course was laid out by the course architect, J.H. Taylor, in 1908. A nine-hole course designed by the club's former professional, J.H. Turner, was added in 1928 and has been described by Bernard Darwin as one of the finest nine-hole courses in Great Britain. There are now two eighteen-hole courses, the final nine holes having been designed by C.K. Cotton and introduced for play by 1969.

North Oxford Golf Club   *Banbury Road.* On the northern outskirts of Oxford on the road to Kidlington. The club was founded in 1907. Two fields of 41 acres were leased from Exeter College and Merton College to make a nine-hole course. It was enlarged to an eighteen-hole course in 1910.

Southfield Golf Club   OXFORD UNIVERSITY GOLF CLUB played originally on a course at BOAR'S HILL, later moving to Kennington and then to a course at SOUTHFIELD, which was played across Cowley Marsh. In about 1920 Magdalen College agreed to lease land with a new entrance from Hill Top Road. Further land was leased from Christ Church and play started on the present course of eighteen holes in 1922, the funds being mainly provided by LORD NUFFIELD. The course was laid out by Fred Taylor, the club's first professional. In 1954 the name was changed to Southfield Golf Club Ltd, with six directors appointed from the University and six from the city. The Oxford University Golf Club still uses this course.

Radley College   *near Abingdon.* Five miles south of Oxford. A nine-hole course was opened in 1985, laid out by the course architect Donald Steel. The course is primarily for the school, but the club is open to the public on application, although membership is necessarily limited.

Good Shepherd, Chapel of the   *Bagley Wood Road, Kennington.* Celebrates the start of the pontificate of Pope John XXIII, whose reign had just begun when the chapel was opened in 1965. The site had been acquired in 1958, and while the chapel was being built Mass was celebrated in the Anglican church hall. The chapel was built to the design of a parishioner, Reginald G. Kind.

Gordouli   A song or chant of ritual abuse which is directed over the wall from Balliol to Trinity College at times of celebration and inebriation. The traditional words are:

> Gordouli, Gordouli, Gordouli
> He's got a face like a ham
> Bobby Johnson says so
> And he ought to know.

They seem first to have been shouted in 1896 after Robert Johnson, an exhibitioner at New College and later Deputy Master and Controller of the Royal Mint, had dined with some friends at Balliol and mention had been made of an undergraduate at Trinity whose nickname was 'Gordouli', the name of a firm that manufactured Egyptian cigarettes. Johnson told his friends that he knew 'Gordouli', who had 'a face like a ham'.

'Gordouli' was apparently Arthur Mario Agniola Collier Galletti di Cadilhac, whose father was a colonel in the Italian army and whose mother was a daughter of the first Baron Monkswell. He was extremely good looking, Johnson's face being far more like a ham than his – hence the 'he ought to know' of the cry, which was probably first sung to its present tune in 1898.

A customary response from Trinity, invoking the name of the black world heavyweight champion from 1908 to 1915, was:

Balliol, Balliol
Bring out your black men
[or: Bring out your white men]
Jack Johnson says so
And he ought to know

The rivalry between the two colleges is of long standing. There is a tradition that RALPH BATHURST, President of Trinity from 1664 to 1704, used to throw stones at Balliol College's windows 'with much satisfaction . . . pleased to see a neighbouring and once rich society reduced to a state of desolation while his own flourished beyond all others'.

In 1912 a joint Trinity–Balliol debate took place in Trinity College hall. The motion that 'Balliol exists solely for the innocent amusement of Trinity' was supported by R.A. KNOX and carried by a substantial majority. It seems, however, that a merger of the two colleges may once have been proposed by BENJAMIN JOWETT, who, always anxious to enhance Balliol's reputation, is supposed to have said to R.W. Raper, once a commoner at Balliol and then a Fellow and Bursar of Trinity, 'Balliol and Trinity adjoin. Why should not they be combined into one college, the finest in Oxford?' When Raper appeared interested, Jowett added, 'Of course, as Balliol is the older foundation, the combined College will have to be called Balliol.' After consulting his colleagues at Trinity, Raper returned to Jowett with a further proposal: 'St John's adjoins Balliol on the other side. Why not merge that College also and thus establish the finest foundation in Oxford *and* Cambridge, or indeed in the whole world?' Jowett was manifestly excited by this idea until Raper commented, 'But in that case, Master, surely the three in one would have to be called Trinity?' The project was dropped.

(Knight, G. Norman, 'The Quest for Gordouli', *Balliol College Record*, 1969, and 'A Gordouli Fragment: Balliol's Relations with Trinity', *Balliol College Record*, 1974.)

Government of the City During the Middle Ages Oxford established its independence of the Sheriff and other royal officers, and developed the organs of municipal government which were to last into the 19th century; but from the early 13th century the University came to dominate the town.

The Anglo-Saxon and early Norman town was governed by one or two reeves – royal officers who accounted to the Sheriff of Oxfordshire for the annual rent or 'farm' due from the town to the King. At the same time, however, an alternative form of government was developing from the guild – an association of merchants and other wealthy men, led by two aldermen, which controlled much of the economic life of the town and the privileges of which were confirmed by Henry II in *c*.1155. In 1199 King John granted the BURGESSES the right to account themselves to the Sheriff for the annual 'farm' – a grant which changed the reeves, or bailiffs as they were later called, from royal officers appointed by the King to town officers chosen by the Burgesses. Only in 1257, however, did Oxford obtain the right for the bailiffs to account for the 'farm' directly to the Exchequer, thus removing the town altogether from the Sheriff's control. At the same time, the civic consciousness of the Burgesses was developing. In 1191 they executed a charter to OSENEY ABBEY and sealed it with their common seal, the earliest surviving example of a town seal in England. The merchant guild was then ruled by a single alderman, the powerful and very wealthy John Kepeharm; and by 1205 his son and successor was termed MAYOR and was in charge of town government.

Below the Mayor in the hierarchy of town officers were four aldermen, one in charge of each of the four wards in the town. Their main responsibility was peace-keeping, and their office seems to have developed in the early 13th century and to have been fixed finally by the charter granted to the town in 1255. By that date the aldermen ranked above the bailiffs, who remained responsible for the payment of the 'farm'. Below the bailiffs came the chamberlains, responsible for the day-to-day finances of the town; they were first recorded in *c*.1300. Aldermen held office for life, but the other officers were elected annually, the bailiffs from among the men who had served as chamberlain, the Mayor from among the aldermen. Two councils developed in the Middle Ages. The Mayor's Council, composed of all former bailiffs, developed in the late 13th century; former chamberlains were added in the late 15th century. The common council of twenty-four ordinary (or common) freemen developed from the twenty-four freemen placed in charge of the town's main money chest in 1448.

The charters granted by the kings from Henry II to Edward III and confirmed by their successors gave Oxford other rights besides the control of the fee farm. Oxford's customs and privileges were modelled on those of London and included freedom from toll throughout the country, and the right to settle all disputes in the town COURTS. In 1285 the Burgesses successfully asserted their claim to gallows and a prison, and to hold the assizes of bread and of ale, thereby regulating the sale of those two important commodities.

From the early 13th century, however, the town's privileges were whittled away by the development of the University. The masters and scholars of the University were clerks in Holy Orders, and as such enjoyed special judicial privileges, but the University or Chancellor's Court (*see* COURTS) gradually extended its jurisdiction from the scholars to those who served them.

The University's need for lodgings led to controls over the renting of property in Oxford, and its need for food, clothing and other goods resulted in an increasing control of the market. Moreover members of the University, as clerks, were exempt from lay taxation, and the town had no jurisdiction inside the developing colleges. After the riot of ST SCHOLASTICA'S DAY in 1355, the University gained complete control of the market and of peace-keeping in the town; in addition the Mayor, with the bailiffs, aldermen and other leading citizens (a total of sixty), had to attend an annual Mass at the University Church of ST MARY THE VIRGIN, and to offer 1*d* each in expiation of the riot. The ceremony emphasised for centuries the dominance of the University over the town.

In 1542, when the diocese of Oxford was established, the town was constituted a city. The corporation's charters and privileges, seriously challenged during Henry VIII's reign when the University enjoyed the powerful backing of CARDINAL WOLSEY, were confirmed by Edward VI and Elizabeth I. In 1605 the city acquired a new charter, which survived various challenges and changes in the political upheavals of the 17th century to remain the city's governing charter until Municipal Reform in 1835. The charter confirmed the Corporation's ancient rights derived from the grant of the fee farm (for which the payment was not compounded until 1790) and for the first time defined the make-up and powers of the City Council, enumerated its officers and described election procedures.

Even so, despite a safeguard of city privileges in the Act incorporating the University in 1571, the precise powers of the two corporations over each other remained in bitter dispute. In the 16th and 17th centuries conflicts between city and University affected most aspects of local government and provided continuous trouble for the Crown, the Privy Council, Parliament, or the central courts. The chief conflicts were over control of trade and prices, and the respective jurisdictions of the courts of University and city; but related issues were street-cleansing and repair, policing, poor-relief, alehouse-licensing, building-control, and the taxation of PRIVILEGED PERSONS. In the end, despite crippling litigation costs, neither body made substantial gains: the University's cause reached a brief zenith with its Great Charter of 1636, acquired while ARCHBISHOP LAUD was Chancellor (*see also* LAUDIAN CODE); but the city sought heavy redress in the aftermath of the CIVIL WAR, only to be forced back on to the defensive at the Restoration. The uneasy peace between the two bodies in the 18th century arose from apathy rather than agreement. Even so, throughout the long struggle local government was never entirely disrupted and there were indeed moments of co-operation between the two bodies, as in the redevelopment of THAMES navigation, the appointment of common scavengers, and the relief of plague victims.

As in the Middle Ages, the basis of the city's constitution remained the membership or freedom of the 'guild', and the Council and its officers, strictly speaking, represented not all the inhabitants but the body of freemen. In 1640 there were perhaps 800 freemen out of a population of 10,000. By then the Council structure established in the Middle Ages had been further elaborated by the addition of a body of eight assistants, which, with the Mayor and aldermen, formed an inner council known as the Thirteen. With the bailiffs and chamberlains for the year, and the increasingly powerful town clerk, the Thirteen

effectively ran the city's day-to-day business. In the Council proper the body of twenty-four common councillors was unchanged, but the classes of former bailiffs and former chamberlains expanded rapidly from the later 16th century as men were allowed to compound for, rather than serve, those offices. That practice allowed the numerous successful freemen in the growing city to qualify more speedily for a conciliar rank appropriate to their wealth and status; for until the later 17th century almost all successful citizens, with the exception of Privileged Persons, took their place on the Council. By 1630 the full Council had an unwieldy membership of over 130.

Beneath the apparently unchanging institutional structure of the City Corporation, a major transformation took place during the 17th century. Central government interference, beginning with purges of the Council during and immediately after the Civil War, increased after the Restoration with major purges in the 1660s and 1680s, and the enforced revision of the city's charters in 1664, 1684 and 1688. Although those changes were reversed, the idea of conciliar rank as a natural reflection of successful citizenship was irretrievably lost, and many prominent men (not all of them Nonconformists) now stood aside from city government. At the same time the growth of party politics (Oxford's freemen were entitled to elect two Members of Parliament) frequently transformed elections of mayors or town clerks into fierce contests between the Whig and Tory interests. The status of the freeman was steadily devalued. Hitherto, because the freedom carried substantial burdens as well as privileges, it had tended to be taken up only by masters of trades, but now, particularly in election years, anyone with a claim sought admittance. Political agents spent large sums treating new freemen, many of them very poor, as Oxford developed into a notorious 'rotten borough'.

Such changes inevitably undermined the prestige and influence of the City Council, which for other reasons was becoming ineffective. Its imposition, through the failing CRAFT GUILDS, of out-dated and restrictive economic legislation was increasingly challenged in a period which saw the growth of the great new industrial centres. Moreover, the Corporation, rather like a private club, had drawn its funds largely from its membership – that is, from freemen's admission fees, rents from its own property, and occasional levies on councillors and freemen. By the 17th century its funds were inadequate, and by the mid-18th century its debts were such that it attempted to sell its parliamentary seats to the resident MPs, causing a national political scandal in 1768. Meanwhile the need for expensive solutions to many problems of city life was growing, and with it the modern idea that local government should provide services financed by rates levied on all inhabitants. The old Corporation was manifestly unfit for a new role, so separate governmental institutions were set up by Act of Parliament.

From 1771 until major reorganisation in the late 19th and early 20th centuries, the city's government was shared between the Corporation and a number of statutory bodies on which members of both the city and the University were represented. Exclusive control by the Corporation was restricted to the city waterworks, city estates, city police, and CITY GAOL, and, until Municipal Reform in 1835, the regulation of trading by freemen. Regulation of Privileged Persons remained the prerogative of the University. The reformed council in 1836 comprised a Mayor and Sheriff, ten aldermen and thirty councillors from five electoral wards.

Public services established during the 19th century, such as the gas company, the fire brigade, the tramways service (*see* TRANSPORT) and the public library were all outside direct municipal control. Paving, cleansing, lighting and public improvements were the province of the Paving Commission, established in 1771 on the initiative of the University. The commission, the most important local governmental body in Oxford, was an early example of urban improvement financed by the levying of rates. The Corporation and the University had a statutory right of representation on the commission, which also attracted the energies of prominent citizens such as WILLIAM JACKSON, founder of *Jackson's Oxford Journal* (*see* NEWSPAPERS), for whom a place on a hamstrung City Council was of little interest. The increasingly complex demands of administering a 19th-century city led in 1865 to the replacement of the commission by a Local Board of Health with enhanced powers. The board's composition differed little from that of the commission, comprising the Mayor and VICE-CHANCELLOR, fifteen University members, sixteen from the Corporation, and fourteen elected by parish vestries. The board was cautious in the exercise of its powers, such as that of compulsory purchase, and it faced conflicting pressures from public opinion, which became alarmed at 'immense, unknown, and increasing expenses' on public works while demanding improved roads, drainage and other services. The board administered the public library and, in response to demands for a public cemetery, was constituted a burial board in 1876. The board was abolished and its powers transferred to the Corporation when Oxford became a county borough in 1889. In 1865 the newly established board had raised and spent about £8000 a year; at the time of its abolition it was spending £30,000 and had a debt of £200,000. City and University were each responsible for levying and collecting its own rates.

Under an Act of 1771, poor-relief in Oxford was managed by a Board of Guardians elected by the United Parishes of Oxford. The University and colleges, regarded as extra-parochial, did not pay poor-rates, causing increasing resentment as the burden of poor-relief mounted: in 1843 the overseers of ST MICHAEL's parish distrained on the silver at Exeter and Jesus Colleges in a futile attempt to enforce contribution. In 1854 the University Rating Act imposed poor-rates on the University and colleges, except for Christ Church, which did not contribute until 1862. In 1925 the United Parishes became the civil parish of Oxford, divided into wards for the election of guardians, and the Poor Law Board was abolished in 1930.

The new Council of 1889 included, for the first time, University representatives. Four wards elected twelve city aldermen and thirty-six city councillors; the University formed a separate ward with three aldermen and nine councillors. The new Corporation took over the powers, property and obligations of the old Local Board; the Market Committee and the Police Committee (set up in 1869 to administer a joint University–City police force) became committees of the Council. A series of public improvements instigated in the 1890s earned the council an ill-founded reputation as an interventionist body, and for many years it was cautious and hesitant, criticised in particular for making inadequate provision for a rapidly expanding city in the 1920s and 1930s. A corollary was that Oxford remained one of the lowest-rated boroughs in England in 1939. Expenditure increased greatly after 1945, mainly to provide services for the newly developed areas in the east of the city, and by 1963 expenditure was above the national average. In 1966 University representation was reduced to two aldermen and six councillors. In 1968 the number of city wards, increased to seven in 1929, was further increased to fifteen, the new wards mostly lying east of MAGDALEN BRIDGE. Three councillors are elected for each ward. University representation was ended by local government reorganisation in 1974, when Oxford lost its county borough status and became a district. By special dispensation Oxford kept its title of city, together with its office of Lord Mayor, created in 1962, and its sheriff.

The modern Corporation's responsibilities include local planning, housing, refuse disposal, recreation, environmental health and, as agents of the County Council, local roads and traffic management. The County Council has responsibility for education, social services, libraries, museums, and the fire service, and it is the overall planning authority. The police are controlled by the Thames Valley Police Authority. Health services are administered by the Oxford Regional Health Authority. Water and mains drainage are the responsibility of the Thames Water Authority. The Oxford Gas Co., founded in 1818, was nationalised in 1948 when Oxford came under the Southern Gas Board. The Oxford Electric Co. was founded in 1890. Since nationalisation in 1948, Oxford has formed part of the Southern Electricity Board.

Gowns The gowns worn by the holders of the various DEGREES conferred by the University are described and illustrated in *Academic Dress of the University of Oxford* by D.R. Venables and R.E. Clifford (6th edition, Oxford, 1985). Those who are not Oxford graduates but have been admitted to read for certain Oxford degrees, or students reading for diplomas, may wear an *advanced student's gown*, which is of the same style as that for a COMMONER but reaches to the knee and has streamers on each side hanging the length of the gown.

A *scholar's gown* may be worn by any undergraduate who has been awarded a scholarship to an Oxford college or by an exhibitioner of those colleges which give special permission to holders of exhibitions to wear it. Reaching to the knee, it is of black cotton material with a gathered stiffened yoke behind and short, open sleeves. The *commoner's gown* is also of black material with a turned-over collar. It has no sleeves, but has a streamer on each side with square pleating and hanging the full length of the gown – that is, the length of the jacket of a suit. Undergraduates wear this gown in the presence of the VICE-CHANCELLOR or other high officers of the University in their official capacity, as well as at examinations, MATRICULATION and other University ceremonies. It should also be worn at lectures.

PROCTORS wear a full black gown with royal-blue velvet sleeves and facings, together with a white

Gowns in 1813–14. From the left: *scholar, gentleman-commoner and Bachelor of Arts.*

ermine hood backed with black. The ASSESSOR wears the robe or gown of the degree to which he is entitled; if a Master's gown it has a black button and tassel about 4 inches long attached to the left-hand side of the pleating. The Marshal (*see* OFFICERS OF THE UNIVERSITY) wears a black gown with a shoulder cape and a silver badge on the left sleeve. BEDELS and the University Verger wear long, plain, black gowns with round black bonnets.

(*See also* ACADEMIC DRESS *and* SUBFUSC.)

Grandpont The district to the west of ABINGDON ROAD between FOLLY BRIDGE and HINKSEY Park. The name is derived from a causeway which once stood in this area and consisted of a series of stone bridges across the low-lying lands and the river. It was either built or renovated by ROBERT D'OILLY in the 11th century and served as the main entrance to Oxford from the south. In the early Middle Ages rows of houses stood on either side of the causeway, of which Folly Bridge formed a part; and the chapel of St Nicholas, first recorded in 1365, was on the west side. A survey made in 1279 listed sixty-two houses in this mediaeval suburb. There were also two water mills belonging to Eynsham Abbey. The suburb grew slowly throughout the following centuries, though it was not until the 19th, when most of the causeway apart from Folly Bridge had disappeared, that extensive development took place. This was stimulated by the coming of the RAILWAY and the opening of a station near Folly Bridge. In 1879 the Oxford Building and Investment Company laid out the Grandpont estate, much of it on land reclaimed from marsh, including Marlborough Road and Buckingham Street. The development continued southwards in the 20th century. In 1913 the parish of St Matthew's, Grandpont, was founded out of the southern part of the parish of ST ALDATE's, the church of ST MATTHEW itself having been built in

Marlborough Road in 1891. Grandpont House on the south-east corner of Folly Bridge was built in about 1785 by William Elias Taunton, a rich lawyer who was town clerk from 1756 to 1795. In the latter part of the 19th century it was the home of Alderman Thomas Randall, a hatter and licensing magistrate, who was attacked by a mob in 1872 because of his demands for a reduction in public-house opening hours.

(*See also* ABINGDON ROAD *and* FOLLY BRIDGE.)

Grapes *7 George Street.* The original inn of 1820 was totally rebuilt in the 1890s with a long entrance corridor, lounge and private rooms. It was reconstructed internally in 1973.

Gray, Sir Walter (*1848–1918*). Having proved himself a most conscientious station master at Waddington in Lincolnshire (the railway station nearest the home of a member of the governing body of Keble College), Gray was asked to come to Oxford to be Keble's first steward. He made a fortune speculating in the development of NORTH OXFORD and was MAYOR four times. He lived at The Lodge, No. 304 WOODSTOCK ROAD, a neo-classical house which was built in about 1840 and had previously been occupied by Owen Grimbly (*see* GRIMBLY HUGHES).

Great Clarendon Street Situated in JERICHO, this street runs westwards from No. 35 WALTON STREET and skirts the boundary of the OXFORD UNIVERSITY PRESS. Longer and wider than LITTLE CLARENDON STREET, it contains many houses in the vicinity of the Press which were built in the first half of the 19th century. Grey Coat's (University) School was listed in a gazetteer of about 1840 as being in Clarendon Street.

Great Tom The most revered and the loudest of Oxford's many bells. Together with other bells, known as Austin, Clement, Dounce, Gabriel,

Hautclare and Tom, it was removed in 1546 after the Dissolution of the Monasteries from OSENEY ABBEY to Christ Church, where it was subsequently recast and celebrated in the old round:

Great Tom is cast
And Christ Church bells ring one
Two, three, four, five, six
And Tom comes last.

It has a diameter at the tip of 85 inches and weighs about 7 tons 7¾ cwt. It is rung 101 times every night at 9.05 to signify the original number of scholars at Christ Church.

Greek Orthodox Church *1 Canterbury Road.* The Orthodox Church of the Holy Trinity and the Annunciation, used by both the Greek Orthodox and the Russian Orthodox Churches, was built on land donated by the House of St Gregory and St Macrina. The foundation stone of this small church was blessed in 1972 and the church was consecrated on 11 July 1973 by Archbishop Athenagoras of Thyateira and Great Britain (Ecumenical Patriarchate), Metropolitan Anthony of Sourozh (Patriarchate of Moscow) and Bishop Lavrentije of Western Europe (Serbian Patriarchate).

Green College The latest graduate college to be established in the University, Green College opened in 1979. Its premises are sited at the RADCLIFFE OBSERVATORY. In 1975 a proposal for a new college in Oxford to cater primarily for clinical medical students and their teachers was submitted by the Board of the Faculty of Clinical Medicine to the HEBDOMADAL COUNCIL. The proposal was backed by guarantees from the E.P. Abraham Cephalosporin Trustees, the Rhodes Trustees (*see* RHODES HOUSE), the Radcliffe Trustees and Blackwell Scientific Publications Ltd, and was finally approved by the University after consideration by all relevant bodies, including CONGREGATION. In 1977 Dr and Mrs Cecil Green from Dallas, Texas, paid a four-day visit to Oxford in order to discuss the aims of the college and to consider what was needed for it to become a reality. Dr Green was born in Lancashire but his family emigrated to Canada when he was a child; subsequently he studied at the University of British Columbia and later at the Massachusetts Institute of Technology, before moving to Texas where he founded a company concerned with geophysics, from which the company of which he eventually became chairman, Texas Instruments, Inc., ultimately grew. Dr and Mrs Green agreed to donate a substantial sum in order to establish the college, provided that the building contract was let by the end of 1977. In January 1978 Phase 1 of the building programme began in what was subsequently called Lankester Quadrangle (named after the Surveyor to the University, Jack Lankester, who was the college architect). This was followed by refurbishment of the Observer's House and the conversion of 9–10 Bradmore Road (premises obtained on lease from the University) into a residential annexe. The first thirty students took up residence in 1979 at a time when Phase 2 of the building programme was under way, including rehabilitation of the Observatory and of its associated buildings. This rehabilitation provided a common room for Fellows and students, a library and a music

Green College, the University's latest graduate college, opened in 1979 in the former Radcliffe Observatory.

room on the ground floor, with kitchens and other associated offices; a Fellows' room, a dining room for Fellows, students and other members of the college, and a private dining room were provided on the first floor; and the Tower of the Winds was refurbished to be used for receptions and other functions. In 1980 a residential block, also designed by Jack Lankester, was built on the west side of the garden, with landscaping on the south side of the Observatory. The college was formally opened in 1981.

Since that time the college has grown and developed; in 1985 119 students were in residence. By then the college also had forty Fellows by election, together with a substantial number of non-residential Visiting Fellows, Senior and Junior Research Fellows funded by grants or by endowment, and 150 common-room members. Although the primary aim of establishing the college was to cater for the needs of clinical medical students, it was also proposed that it should bring together graduate students in a number of faculties whose interests overlapped with those of Clinical Medicine, including graduates reading for higher degrees in Social Studies, Biostatistics, Anthropology, Bio-engineering and many other subjects. Other aims included development of a liaison between medicine and industry by appointing Visiting Fellows nominated by industry who would develop programmes requiring collaborative effort; and it was also intended that the college should bring together National Health Service staff who teach clinical students and their academic colleagues. In 1985, fifty of the 119 students were clinical medical students, the others covering a wide range of academic disciplines and interests. Sir John Walton succeeded the founding Warden, Sir Richard Doll, in 1983. In 1991 the Warden was Sir Crispin Tickell.

Green, Thomas Hill (*1836–1882*). A Yorkshire clergyman's son, Green went up to Balliol from Rugby. He gained a First in LITERAE HUMANIORES and was elected a Fellow of the college in 1860 (the first of its Fellows not to be in Holy Orders) and Whyte

Thomas Hill Green, who was appointed Whyte Professor of Moral Philosophy in 1878, was the first Fellow of Balliol not to be in Holy Orders.

Professor of Moral Philosophy in 1878. A highly influential Idealist philosopher of the so-called Neo-Kantian school, Green also played an influential role in the development of the college under the mastership of BENJAMIN JOWETT, and took an active part in Oxford life, speaking at political meetings, contributing to the building of the CITY OF OXFORD HIGH SCHOOL, founding a scholarship there and, as a member of the United Kingdom (Temperance) Alliance, establishing a COFFEE HOUSE in ST CLEMENT'S in 1875. He appears as Henry Gray in Mrs Humphry Ward's *Robert Elsmere* (1888), an evocation of the Oxford of his time.

Greycotes School *1 Bardwell Road.* Founded in 1929 by Mrs Norman Cunliffe as an independent day preparatory school for boys and girls, it began at Cherwell Croft, a Georgian house set in spacious grounds bordered on the BANBURY ROAD between BELBROUGHTON ROAD and MARSTON FERRY ROAD by a long, grey stone wall. Partly as a result of the wartime expansion of Oxford, in 1940 the school numbers grew to sixty children aged from four to twelve, and to 130 in 1944, when it took over No. 108 Banbury Road to accommodate twenty-five boarders. In 1946 another house, No. 158 Banbury Road, previously occupied by women engaged in war work at Morris Radiators, was taken over for forty-one boarders and No. 108 became the junior school. In due course the school occupied six houses in the Banbury Road, and three in Marston Ferry Road – an area, with its playing fields and gardens, of 16 acres. In 1952 a senior department was added when Somerville House was bought, its girls first sitting for GCE O-levels in 1955 and for A-levels in 1957. By the early 1960s there were over 400 pupils, some 100 of whom were boarders. In 1964 the school became a Charitable Trust with a

Board of Governors. In 1966 it reverted to being a day preparatory school and moved in 1970 to No. 1 Bardwell Road when St John's College, owner of Cherwell Croft, developed the site into the present Cunliffe Close. In 1987 there were some 240 children in the school, aged between four and eleven.

Greyfriars *Iffley Road.* In the late summer of 1224 Agnellus of Pisa, a thirty-year-old deacon and friend of St Francis, set sail for England with nine companions. He brought with him a letter from St Francis appointing him Minister Provincial of the Friars Minor in England. Four of them arrived in Oxford towards the end of October. After a week of Dominican hospitality, they rented a house in ST EBBE'S. Their success with the citizens of Oxford was immediate. Their chronicler, Friar Thomas of Eccleston, relates how, in those early days, many 'learned bachelors and many nobles took the habit.' By the following summer they had built their first Greyfriars on land, somewhere between the CITY WALL and CHURCH STREET, given to them by a wealthy merchant, Richard the Miller. By 1233 there were forty friars; in 1317 eighty-four; and in 1377 there were 103. As Friar Thomas put it, 'Sweet Jesus sowed a grain of mustard that afterwards became greater than all the herbs.' They found favour, too, with King Henry III, who gave them land in 1244 on an island in the river known as Paradise Garden; furthermore, they were permitted to pull down part of the south wall of the city in order to facilitate their building operations.

The suppression of the friaries took place in 1538. During the 300 years that the friars had been at Oxford, they had radically changed the structure of the University. They had arrived to discover a collection of small groups of students studying Law and Administration. Tuition had been expensive, and the courses necessarily brief. The friars had introduced a system of education which involved disciplined courses of study for residential students, spanning several years. In a short time they established a reputation for learning, especially in Philosophy and Theology, which rivalled the great universities of mediaeval Europe. Such men as Adam Marsh, Roger Bacon, Johannes Duns Scotus and William of Ockham were among those first Franciscan scholars. After the suppression, almost 400 years were to pass before the Franciscans were able to return. In 1905 the Capuchins, a reformed branch of the Order, opened a friary called St Anselm's in ST JOHN STREET; it was granted the status of a House of Studies by the University in 1910. Nine years later, they moved to the IFFLEY ROAD, naming their new premises Grosseteste House. However, when in 1930 a site became vacant across the road next to the church of ST EDMUND AND ST FRIDESWIDE, the Jesuits decided to hand the church over to the Franciscans; Father Cuthbert Hess then commissioned Gilbert Gardner to design a friary on the adjoining site. The building was completed by September 1931 and given the mediaeval name of Greyfriars. Since 1957, when the University conferred upon it the status of Permanent Private Hall (*see* PRIVATE HALLS), Greyfriars has been receiving students for tuition in most schools. Priority is given to Franciscans, although members of other religious Orders are received. It is a self-governing college, selecting its own students and presenting them for their degrees. The friars also have facilities for visiting students and scholars recognised by the University. As well as the hall, the friars care for the parish.

(*See also* PRIVATE HALLS.)

Greyhound *High Street*. Opened in 1526 as the Cardinal's Hat, it was known as the Greyhound after 1535. It was a coaching house in 1688 (*see* TRANSPORT) and by the 18th century appears in prints as a very large building of four storeys with numerous windows and dormers. The Greyhound was sited on the corner of LONG WALL STREET and HIGH STREET, just outside the East Gate, with its ground floor well below road level. Along its frontage lay the famous gravel walk with elm trees (planted in 1680). The inn had remained in the hands of the White family for over fifty years when James White died in 1772. It was pulled down in 1845 to make way for an extension to Magdalen College.

Gridiron Club Founded in 1884 by Lord Cranbourne as a University club where members belonging to various colleges could dine and entertain their friends. The original premises were in long, low rooms in the HIGH STREET. In 1913, after the demolition of ST MARTIN'S CHURCH at CARFAX, the club moved to new premises over the Midland Bank on that site, the founder (the 4th Marquess of Salisbury) and many old members contributing to the expenses of the change. Since the Second World War the club has been housed successively in premises off GEORGE STREET, over Barclays Bank in CORNMARKET, in and behind QUEEN STREET and, since 1983, over the Royal Blenheim in ST EBBE'S. In 1913 the Prince of Wales, the Crown Prince of Norway and Prince Paul of Serbia were members; others included Aubrey Herbert, RONALD KNOX, Harold Macmillan (later the EARL OF STOCKTON), Lord Boyle and Sir Ian Gilmour. The club is mentioned in numerous memoirs, including Cyril Bailey's of Francis 'Sligger' URQUHART and Evelyn Waugh's life of Knox.

Grimbly Hughes The famous firm of high-class grocers, founded by Owen Grimbly and James Hughes, opened business at No. 56 CORNMARKET in 1840. The shop was destroyed by fire in 1857 and again in 1863. It was rebuilt in 1864 with a Venetian Gothic front, counters of mahogany or marble, and chairs for customers to sit on while they gave their orders or watched their bacon sliced to the thickness they required. It could not, of course, compete with the supermarkets which began to take over Cornmarket in the middle of the 20th century, and was taken over by Jacksons of Piccadilly in 1959. It moved to QUEEN STREET when the premises in Cornmarket Street were demolished in 1961; and the business finally closed in 1963.

Grocyn, William (*c.1446–1519*). Entered New College from Winchester, became a Fellow of the college in 1465 and Divinity Reader at Magdalen in 1481. After a period spent in Italy, where he studied with William Latimer and THOMAS LINACRE, he lived in rooms in Exeter College from 1491 to 1493. He was one of the first scholars, perhaps *the* first, to give public lectures in Greek at the University; and, with Linacre, Thomas More and JOHN COLET, he became a leading disseminator of the new learning, although Erasmus observed that he still read the works of mediaeval

The Cornmarket premises of Grimbly Hughes and Co. were rebuilt in 1864 after a fire destroyed the shop which had opened in 1840.

schoolmen. He bequeathed the residue of his property to Linacre, who was asked to bestow such part of it 'as it shall please hym' for the 'wele' of Grocyn's soul and the souls of his 'fader, moder, benefactors and all Xtian soules'. As well as providing for the poor, Linacre bought books to give to deserving Oxford scholars.

Grosseteste, Robert (*d.1253*). One of the mediaeval University's most influential patrons, Grosseteste, the son of humble parents, was sent to Oxford at the expense of friends. He became CHANCELLOR in about 1224, the year in which he was appointed first Rector of the Franciscans at Oxford, and in 1235 Bishop of Lincoln, in whose diocese Oxford then lay. On his visitations of his diocese he frequently went to Oxford, usually taking the side of the scholars in their differences with the townspeople. In 1238 he offered his protection to those students who had been involved in a fracas at OSENEY ABBEY, where the papal legate was then staying (*see also* RIOTS); and in 1244, after quarrels between the students and the JEWS, he ensured that future disputes about such matters as loans and interest rates, the hiring of accommodation and the cost of provisions should be settled in the presence of the Chancellor or his representatives. Grosseteste was described by Matthew Paris as 'the blamer of prelates, the corrector of monks, the director of priests, the instructor of clerks, the support of scholars, the preacher to the people, the persecutor of the licentious....'

Guildhall *see* TOWN HALL.

Guilds *see* CRAFT GUILDS.

H

Halifax House Originally established in 1946 as the University Graduate Centre, the building was formally opened by the CHANCELLOR, Lord Halifax, and appropriately renamed, in January 1947. The statute giving the house a formal constitution was passed by CONGREGATION in 1950 when the house initiated its move from No. 62 WOODSTOCK ROAD to its present address in SOUTH PARKS ROAD.

Admission to membership of Halifax House is at the discretion of the Halifax House Committee. The main classes of membership are: employees of the University; senior members of the University engaged in advanced study, research, teaching or administration within the University; graduate students engaged in advanced study or research in the University; and visitors temporarily in residence in Oxford for the purpose of advanced study.

Membership of Halifax House is free. It is essentially a social centre where meals are provided in pleasant rooms overlooking the garden and some playing fields. There are large and small reading rooms, a television room and a music room. Exhibitions of works by contemporary artists are arranged by the Art Committee to add to the amenities

of the reading room. A licensed bar is open at lunchtime and in the evening. A substantial cellar has been established by the Wine Committee and tastings are held periodically. There is residential accommodation which members can reserve for their University guests. The gardens have a tennis and a croquet lawn and a variety of social functions is arranged by the committee. Total income in 1985–6 exceeded £100,000.

Halls *see* ACADEMIC HALLS.

Hall's Brewery In 1795 William Hall bought the Swan's Nest Brewery (later the Swan Brewery) from Sir John Treacher, who was MAYOR of Oxford in 1754. The brewery had been in existence since at least 1718. Its name came from its situation near the CASTLE, where there were swans on the river. By 1835 William Hall was in partnership with the old established brewing family of Tawneys and in 1837 Henry Hall became head of the firm. In 1896 the brewery became a private limited company under the name Hall's Oxford Brewery Ltd. In 1897 it took over two other Oxford breweries, the St Clement's Brewery, and the

The drays of Hall's Oxford Brewery at The Plain in the May Day procession of 1912.

Eagle Steam Brewery in PARK END STREET, and in the following year Hanley's City Brewery, whose malthouse was in BECKET STREET where the GPO sorting office is now situated. The Eagle Steam Brewery, whose entrance in Park End Street is through a cast-iron gateway crowned with an eagle, was mainly used for bottling. Hall's had a fleet of over sixty brewery drays pulled by one to three horses. Before the First World War the drays processed around Oxford as part of the annual May Day festivities (*see* MAY MORNING). In 1926 Hall's was taken over by Allsopp and the City Brewery was closed. Its premises now house the Oxford MUSEUM OF MODERN ART. Allsopp was subsequently acquired by Ind Coope, now part of Allied Breweries. Hall's beer is now brewed in Burton-on-Trent, but in 1980 the name was revived when Allied Breweries formed a new company, Hall's Oxford and West Brewery Co. Ltd, with its headquarters at the Eagle Brewery. In 1984 Hall's opened the redeveloped RED LION in GLOUCESTER GREEN with a brewhouse; four beers are brewed on the premises. (*See also* BREWING.)

(Bond, James, and Rhodes, John, *The Oxfordshire Brewer*, Oxford, 1985.)

Hanasters   *see* PRIVILEGED PERSONS.

Harcourt Hill   Named after Viscount Harcourt, who owned the land here. It rises from the RING ROAD at NORTH HINKSEY, past RALEIGH PARK. WESTMINSTER COLLEGE is at the top of the hill and on the other side of the road is a residential area.

Harrod, Sir (Henry) Roy (Forbes)   (*1900–1978*). After winning a scholarship to St Paul's, from which he was moved to Westminster at the request of his mother (the talented sister of the actor Johnston Forbes-Robertson), Harrod was awarded a scholarship at New College and obtained Firsts in LITERAE HUMANIORES and Modern History. He became a Student of Christ Church in 1924 and remained there for over forty years, in 1938 also becoming a Fellow of Nuffield College. One of the most distinguished economists and original philosophers of his time, Harrod was also a highly stimulating tutor. His memoir of LORD CHERWELL, *The Prof*, was published in 1959.

Hart Hall   A mediaeval ACADEMIC HALL which was the first home of Hertford College. The original house, leased in 1283 as an academic hall to scholars by its owner, Elias of Hertford, whose device was a hart's head, stood at the first corner in NEW COLLEGE LANE, as approached from CATTE STREET. In 1312 the founder of Exeter College bought it as accommodation for the scholars of his new college. One of the larger academic halls, Hart Hall remained a dependency of Exeter until the mid-16th century, when, at a time of some strength and under a determined Principal, it became independent, having considerably increased in capacity by new building and the absorption of neighbouring halls. The long course of events that led to its transformation into a college began in 1710, when Dr Richard Newton became its Principal. Against much opposition, notably from Exeter College, he achieved the incorporation of Hart Hall as a college in 1740. However, largely as a result of inadequate endowment, the college failed, and in 1815

was declared to have been dissolved since 1805. In 1815 the buildings were granted in trust to MAGDALEN HALL, which was seeking a new site. In the course of time the strength of Magdalen Hall and a generous benefactor made possible the refoundation in 1874 of Newton's college, to be called Hertford College in recognition of the academic hall from which it had descended.

Hawksmoor, Nicholas   (*1661–1736*). A 'scholar and domestic clerk' of SIR CHRISTOPHER WREN from the age of eighteen, and later an assistant to Sir John Vanbrugh, Hawksmoor worked on several important buildings in Oxford on his own account from 1712 onwards. In that year he produced his designs for the RADCLIFFE CAMERA. His wooden model for this survives; but the library was eventually entrusted to JAMES GIBBS. Hawksmoor's CLARENDON BUILDING was, however, completed in 1713, and three years later work began to his designs at All Souls College, where his North Quadrangle, hall, buttery and CODRINGTON LIBRARY were all finished by 1735. Hawksmoor was also responsible for The Queen's College's screen wall to HIGH STREET, which was executed in 1733–6, with alterations to the cupola, by William Townesend (*see* TOWNESENDS); and he assisted GEORGE CLARKE with the new buildings at Worcester College, which were begun in 1720. His proposed steeple for ALL SAINTS CHURCH, HIGH STREET, and designs for new work at Brasenose and Magdalen Colleges were never realised.

Hayfield Road   So called from Heyfield's or Heathfield's Hutt, which was on the site of the present ANCHOR inn. It was inhabited by one William Heyfield and is shown on Benjamin Cole's 18th-century map of PORT MEADOW, although it was probably there from about 1667. It became an inn in about 1845. It was near the line of this road that Charles I made his escape from Oxford in June 1644, passing the hut and thus making his way, with his troops, to Port Meadow. Today's road, which runs from the northern end of Kingston Road to Frenchay Road, consists of terraced houses, the front doors of which lead directly on to the street. They were built between 1886 and 1888 by the OXFORD INDUSTRIAL AND PROVIDENT LAND AND BUILDING SOCIETY, laid out by Wilkinson and Moore and designed by Moore. The Society was formed in 1860 in order to finance the building of small houses for working people; it was also responsible for developing other parts of Oxford, including areas of SUMMERTOWN, IFFLEY and east Oxford. The CANAL runs behind the gardens on the west side, having been opened as far as Hayfield Road in 1789. The road was included in the NORTH OXFORD Victorian suburb's CONSERVATION AREA in 1976. Until 1985 the street suffered from much through-traffic but the southern end has been blocked off and the road now benefits from being a quiet cul-de-sac.

Head of the River   *see* BUMPING RACES.

Head of the River (inn)   *St Aldate's Street.* Originally a THAMES-side wharf (mentioned in 1628), it became Wharf House in 1827 and the present riverside inn on 27 July 1977. The architects of this, the largest inn in Oxford, were Ronald Lloyd and Ken Smith of Witney. They kept much of the original brickwork with exterior local Headington stone (*see* STONE). It is named after the finish of the annual college eights boat races (*see* EIGHTS WEEK).

Headington Probably named after a Saxon, Hedena, Headington occupies a plateau of high ground to the east of Oxford between 1 and 2 miles from the city centre. In Saxon and Norman times it was a royal manor and the seat of government for the double hundred of Bullingdon, which extended eastwards from ST CLEMENT'S almost to Thame and northwards from Nuneham Courtenay as far as Ambrosden. Since the Oxford Extension Act of 1928, most of the ancient parish has been incorporated within the city boundaries and Headington is now reduced to the status of a suburb.

There have been prehistoric finds in the area. During the Roman period it became an important centre of pottery manufacture. Villas, brickfields and quarries dating from this time have been discovered on and below the slopes of Shotover: a Romano-British kiln found near the CHURCHILL HOSPITAL site in 1971 is exhibited in the MUSEUM OF OXFORD. Lying within the confines of SHOTOVER ROYAL FOREST and Stowood, Headington was later the site of a Saxon palace or hunting lodge belonging to the kings of Mercia. It was a princess of this house, ST FRIDESWIDE, who in the 8th century founded a religious house beside the THAMES in what was then marshland beneath the royal manor on the hill.

There are traditional associations with King Ethelred, whose deed of gift of land and the tithes of the church to ST FRIDESWIDE'S PRIORY was witnessed at Headington in 1004. A large Saxon building, whose foundations have been traced, has been named Ethelred's Palace. The supposed connection is commemorated in the modern Ethelred Court, a cul-de-sac approached via Saxon Way and Dunstan Road.

In Domesday Book it is recorded: 'The King holds Hedintone'; but in the following century the manor was alienated from the Crown by the Empress Matilda, who granted it to a Breton supporter, Hugh de Pluggenait. The manor returned to the Crown in 1280 and formed part of the dowry granted to Edward I's second wife, Queen Margaret; but it soon passed into other hands. The last assertion of royal rights occurred in 1636 when Charles I held a forest court at Headington in an attempt to raise money through the imposition of large fines for breaches of forest laws which had long since lapsed into disuse.

During the CIVIL WAR Headington was occupied in turn by royalist cavalry guarding the eastern approach to Oxford and, after a skirmish on HEADINGTON HILL, by General Fairfax, the parliamentary commander, who moved his headquarters uphill from MARSTON in the summer of 1646. Fairfax gave orders that the villagers should be paid for providing quarters for his troops: previously they had been billeted free 'to the utter undoing of the inhabitants'. He also brought them the spiritual benefit of hearing sermons preached by Puritan divines in the orchard in which his tent was pitched.

From the 17th century Headington was increasingly frequented by undergraduates seeking illicit pleasures out of sight of the PROCTORS. Cock-fighting and bull-baiting proved popular pastimes, and in the 1680s a variety of entertainment was on offer from

Joan of Headington, a well-known alehouse keeper and bawd. Establishments of better repute were kept by Widow Coxe and Mother Gurdon.

Prosperous tradesmen from the city found Headington a more lasting attraction. They bought land and built themselves stone villas in what was still countryside. Headington House, the most handsome of these rural retreats, was erected in 1783 by a printer, WILLIAM JACKSON, proprietor of *Jackson's Oxford Journal* (*see* NEWSPAPERS). On his death it passed to a fishmonger's daughter, and from her to a family of wine merchants. Still standing in large grounds surrounded by high stone walls, it has passed from town to gown and become the home of the philosopher Sir Isaiah Berlin.

Today there are three Headingtons. LONDON ROAD, since 1775 the main route between the capital and Oxford, passes through New Headington – a suburban area whose development dates from 1860. Along its route from the Headington roundabout on the A40 to the top of Headington Hill, the focal point is a shopping centre at the crossroads with Old High Street and Windmill Road known as Headington Carfax. On the right-hand side of the road as one enters the city lie BURY KNOWLE PARK, the OXFORD UNITED (formerly Headington United) football ground, whose relocation on a less cramped site has been under consideration since 1969, and the long frontage of HEADINGTON SCHOOL for Girls. On the crest of Headington Hill, spread along Gipsy Lane, are the buildings of the Oxford POLYTECHNIC (founded as a college of technology in 1955).

To the south of London Road is the other main artery which runs through Headington: OLD ROAD, the former highway between Oxford and London which passed over Shotover Hill and through Wheatley. At the foot of the hill, on the Headington side, extra horses were harnessed to the coaches at Titup Hall, while passengers were expected to dismount and make the ascent on foot. It was in 1669 that a 'flying-coach' first made the journey to London in a single day.

Between Old Road and London Road stands the village of HEADINGTON QUARRY with its own high street, public houses – the Six Bells, the Chequers, the Masons' Arms – and community life. From the quarries here came most of the stone for Oxford's college and University buildings (*see* STONE). Some quarries were owned by the colleges themselves for their own needs, while others also shipped stone down the Thames for building works in Windsor and London. By the time the quarries were exhausted, the village had grown from a collection of masons' huts into a well-established unit. The Gothic Revival church of the HOLY TRINITY, designed by GEORGE GILBERT SCOTT, was erected in 1848. Brickfields were worked until 1914.

Noted also for its mummers and May Day celebrations (*see* MAY MORNING), Headington Quarry achieved fame with its Morris dancers, who inspired Cecil Sharp to collect and record old English folk songs and dances, thus saving them from oblivion. Several Morris dances are Headington Traditional, passed down the generations from fiddler to fiddler in this village.

Headington's other and earlier village, now known as Old Headington, lies secluded between London Road and a stretch of the northern bypass. Approached from Headington Carfax along Old High

Morris dancers outside the Chequers, Headington Quarry, in 1898.

Street, it was designated a CONSERVATION AREA in 1971 and its stone walls and kerbs, its trees and verges of wild flowers and Victorian street-lighting are zealously guarded by the Friends of Old Headington (formed in 1959). The parish church of ST ANDREW, once a royal peculiar, contains a magnificent romanesque chancel arch (*c.* 1160), a window commemorating Simon de Montfort and Vashti, Queen of Persia, and a painted wooden ceiling more suited to a badminton court. Mediaeval wall-paintings uncovered in 1864 have not been preserved.

There are a number of fine stone houses and cottages in Old High Street, St Andrew's Road, Dunstan Road, St Andrew's Lane, Larkins Lane and The Croft. Worthy of special note are Headington House, White Lodge (Regency), Ruskin Hall (formerly The Rookery, home of Sir Michael Sadler), The Grange, The Court, The Manor House (now offices of the Oxfordshire Health Authority), Manor Farm House, Mathers Farm and the White Hart inn. In 1985, in the grounds of Laurel Farm in the heart of the village, the City Council built a high-density brick housing estate, screened by a stone wall.

It is said that while Oxford's air resembles flat beer, Headington's is pure champagne. This may account for the number of hospitals located in the area. The earliest is the WARNEFORD, opened in 1826 as the Radcliffe Lunatic Asylum. There are also the CHURCHILL, the PARK, the SLADE, the NUFFIELD ORTHO-PAEDIC CENTRE, ST LUKE'S and, most prominently, the JOHN RADCLIFFE, its first phase built between 1968 and 1972 and the whole completed in 1979 in the grounds of The Manor House and its farm: a site acquired by the trustees of the Radcliffe Infirmary in 1917.

Other distinguished residents of Headington have included Elizabeth Bowen, the novelist; J.R.R. TOLKIEN at 76 Sandfield Road; and C.S. LEWIS at The Kilns, Kiln Lane.

Headington Hill *see* HEADINGTON ROAD AND HEADINGTON HILL.

Headington Hill Park Bought by the city in 1953 and planted as a woodland garden with over 150 specimen trees and ornamental shrubs. The section at the top of HEADINGTON HILL is occupied by PERGAMON PRESS. It is connected to SOUTH PARK by a wrought-iron bridge over the main road.

Headington Quarry The stone quarries at HEADINGTON are first recorded in 1396–7. They supplied stone for building in Oxford between the 15th century and the middle of the 18th century (*see* STONE). A settlement of quarrymen and tile-makers developed in the area in the 17th century and the name is still kept for that part of Headington which is bounded on the north by LONDON ROAD and on the south by OLD ROAD, and lies between the RING ROAD and Windmill Road. (Edna Mason, 'Headington Quarry *c.* 1820–1860', *Oxoniensia* liv, 1989, p. 363).

Headington Road and Headington Hill In the Middle Ages, after the turn to MARSTON at the foot of the hill, the road, which was steep and dangerous, cut through thickly wooded banks. During the CIVIL WAR the trees were cut down because enemies could easily hide themselves and ambush those journeying on the road below. There are now no visible remains of the siege works built on the hill at that time. The old highway to London turned to the right in the middle of the hill (*see* CHENEY LANE). In the 19th century Wade described the road from Oxford to Headington, which led through a deep hollow way, as having 'on one side of this deep way a fine terrace walk [which] was constructed early in the last century by a general subscription of the University'. The way continued to the top of the hill 'and on fine summer evenings the

Collegians often resort to taste the refreshing cordial sweet air' and look at the views of the city.

The road begins at THE PLAIN, just east of MAGDALEN BRIDGE. At one time there was a turnpike house there (on the site of the fountain of 1899), which controlled two gates. One of these closed the Headington Road and the other the COWLEY and IFFLEY ROADS. The way up the hill was paved in 1725. A milestone, re-set during road improvements into the wall on the north side of Headington Hill, about 20 yards east of the bridge, was inscribed (probably in 1771 when the road was re-aligned) with the words: 'Here endeth Hedington Hiway'.

Headington Road runs from 28 London Place to 1 LONDON ROAD, HEADINGTON, and in the 1950s there was much discussion about the possibility of altering its name by incorporating it into London Road. That part of Headington Road opposite PULLEN'S LANE was officially named Headington Hill in March 1970. The Morrell family, who gave SOUTH PARK (or Morrell Park) to the city of Oxford (which lies to the west of the hill) lived at The Rise, south of Cheney Lane (*see* MORRELL'S BREWERY).

Headington School *Headington Road.* Founded in 1915 (with the motto 'Fight the Good Fight of Faith') by an Oxford group of evangelical Christians, under the chairmanship of Mrs Wingfield Digby, as an independent school to provide 'a sound education for girls to fit them for the demands and opportunities likely to arise after the war'. It was opened by the Bishop of Liverpool, the Rt Rev. F.J. Chavasse, at White Lodge, Osler Road, with ten boarding and eight day girls, and seven members of staff. The first headmistress was Miss A.E.S. MacGregor. In 1917 Miss K.L. Porcher became headmistress and Napier House, PULLEN'S LANE, was acquired (now Cotuit House, Oxford POLYTECHNIC). Brookside, on the LONDON ROAD, taken over in 1916 and later re-named Napier, is now the preparatory department. In 1920 the school numbered seventy girls and Davenport House, together with its 21-acre estate, was bought. This forms the site of the present school, bordered by HEADINGTON ROAD, Headley Way, Cuckoo Lane path and Pullen's Lane. The fine surrounding trees are an attractive feature of the grounds. In 1930 the main teaching and administration block, a handsome neo-Georgian building designed by Gilbert T. Gardner, was opened by HRH Princess Mary, Countess of Harewood; a science-block extension to the east end of this block, in keeping with the main building and designed by I. McRiner of the Falconer Partnership, was completed in 1986. In 1934 Miss M. Moller became headmistress and for twenty-five years saw the school through financial difficulties, the disruptions of the Second World War, and post-war problems. By 1947 there were over 300 pupils. In 1958 part of the school estate was purchased by the City Council for the building of Headley Way. In 1959 Miss P.A. Dunn became headmistress, retiring in 1982: in the sixty-five years from 1917 to 1982 the school had only three headmistresses. In 1961–2 Latimer and Hillstow Houses were built to the designs of G.D. Sykes: Hillstow House became the sixth-form house in 1972 and was renamed Celia Marsh House in recognition of a teacher who served the school from 1934–63. In 1977, the year of the Queen's Silver Jubilee, a classroom block designed by R.B. Gray was opened by Lord Blake, Provost of The Queen's

College. In 1985 there were some 500 girls aged between ten and eighteen in the senior school, about half of them boarders, and some 130 aged from four to ten in the preparatory department. Among well-known former pupils are Elizabeth Harman (Lady Longford), Janet Baker (Baroness Young), Barbara Woodhouse (TV personality), Julia Somerville (TV newscaster) and Hester Burton (children's author).

Health, Public The early medical history of Oxford is almost entirely concerned with epidemics. Charles Creighton mentions a leper hospital, ST BARTHOLOMEW'S HOSPITAL in COWLEY, in the 12th century. Other references are to various temporary pest-houses set up to deal with the frequent epidemics of plague, smallpox, typhus and other pestilences from the 15th century onwards. At times the University would close and the Fellows flee into the country to escape infection. Smallpox inoculation was well established in Oxford by the end of the 18th century, the services of one of the well-known Sutton family, its pioneers, being available for three hours every Saturday in the KING'S ARMS, HOLYWELL STREET, as well as in a residential clinic at Sandford.

Until 1771 Oxford city comprised eleven parishes, each with its own Board of Guardians and workhouse. In 1771 an Act was passed setting up the United Board of Guardians, which immediately built a city workhouse and hospital accommodation for paupers on Rats and Mice Hill, now WELLINGTON SQUARE (*see* COWLEY ROAD HOSPITAL). The RADCLIFFE INFIRMARY was built in 1759–70, and some years later the Oxford Medical Dispensary and Lying-in Charity opened in BROAD STREET, later moving to BEAUMONT STREET. Both infirmary and dispensary were for paying patients or for those who were fortunate enough to obtain free vouchers from subscribers. The Paving Commission was also set up in 1771, with a responsibility, *inter alia*, for the cleansing of the city streets and the removal of nuisances. Gradually it acquired more powers; but a long-running battle which developed between the commissioners and the City Council about various aspects of health responsibility held up much-needed improvements. During the middle of the 19th century increasing numbers of complaints were received from the public about the filthy state of the sewers, cesspools and drains, and therefore of the drinking water. The WATER SUPPLY remained a private concern, supervised by the Council, until the 1860s when the Paving Commission became the Board of Health. During this period the sewers and filth from the slum parishes of ST THOMAS'S, ST EBBE'S and ST ALDATE'S were all discharged into the THAMES about half a mile above the site of the waterworks near FOLLY BRIDGE. Various reports by leading engineers (including Joseph Bazalgette, architect of the Thames Embankment) were commissioned. All recommended that sewage should be discharged into the river well *below* the city at IFFLEY, and that the drinking water should be drawn from the Thames well *above* the city at WOLVERCOTE. Arguments, mainly influenced by the city's unwillingness to spend money and so increase the rates, repeatedly resulted in these proposals being shelved; they were not carried out until the 1880s and then under strong pressure from central government.

Oxford had three cholera epidemics. To deal with the first one in 1832 an efficient and *ad hoc* Board of Health was set up, consisting of doctors, clergymen, parish representatives and city officials. A temporary hospital was established at Pepper Hills, Chalfont Road, a convalescent home at St Bartholomew's in Cowley and a quarantine house in a disused school on a site which is now the eastern end of the OXPENS ROAD. The next two epidemics, in 1849 and 1854, were less efficiently dealt with, largely due to the inadequacies of the Guardians, who by this time had the main responsibility for the control of infections. The first permanent infectious-disease hospital was opened in 1885 at GRANDPONT; it is now the RIVERMEAD REHABILITATION CENTRE. It continued there until a new hospital was opened at the SLADE in 1939. This has now changed its character, and infectious diseases are nursed in a ward at the CHURCHILL HOSPITAL.

(*See also* GOVERNMENT OF THE CITY, WATER SUPPLY and entries under individual hospitals.)

Hearne, Thomas (*1678–1735*).

The son of poor parents, Hearne was educated at the expense of a non-juring Berkshire landowner and entered St Edmund Hall in 1696. After taking his degree, he was appointed assistant keeper at the BODLEIAN LIBRARY, where he spent several years cataloguing the books and coins and amassing a vast and miscellaneous knowledge. He was offered the librarianship of the Royal Society in 1713, but declined it because he did not want to leave Oxford. Denied further advancement by his refusal to take the oaths required of him by the Hanoverian government, he spent the rest of his life studying and writing at St Edmund Hall. In addition to the compilation of numerous other works, including a biography of SIR THOMAS BODLEY, Hearne kept a diary for thirty years. This, contained in 145 volumes, eventually found its way to the Bodleian and was published by the Oxford Historical Society. It provides a unique and jaundiced view of Oxford society in his day. William Lancaster, Provost of The Queen's College, for example, is described as 'old smooth boots', 'the worst vice-chancellor there ever was in Oxon', who 'raised to himself a pillar of infamy'; Dr White Kennett, Vice-Principal of St Edmund Hall and later Bishop of Peterborough, as a man of 'trimming, diabolical principles', whose wife wore the breeches and managed him as his 'haughty insolent temper' deserved.

Hebdomadal Board

Its name derived from *hebdomadalis conventus*, meaning weekly board meeting, this was the principal executive body of the University, first appointed in 1631. It consisted of the heads of houses and was empowered to deliberate on all matters concerning the University and to draw up decrees to be presented to CONGREGATION. It was the most important and powerful body in the University until its reform by the University Commission of 1854 (*see* HEBDOMADAL COUNCIL).

Hebdomadal Council

The governing body of the University, the HEBDOMADAL BOARD, was reconstituted by the University Reform Act of 1854, to make it more representative of the University. It was henceforth to include the CHANCELLOR, the VICE-CHANCELLOR, the PROCTORS, six heads of houses, six professors and six members of CONVOCATION, each of the classes being elected by CONGREGATION. Its present membership consists, in addition to the Chancellor, the Vice-Chancellor and the Proctors, of the ASSESSOR, the vice-chairman of the GENERAL BOARD and eighteen elected members of Congregation. It proposes legislation for Congregation and in general constitutes the University's cabinet, being responsible for the administration of the University and for the management of its finances and property.

(*See also* STATUTES.)

Heberden Coin Room

The University's two main coin collections were kept in the BODLEIAN LIBRARY in the 19th century. They formed a large and varied assemblage of material, but were difficult to consult. The Bodleian Library collection had a long history of its own, reaching back to the gift of ARCHBISHOP LAUD in 1636. It incorporated the distinguished 18th-century cabinets of Browne Willis, the Rev. C. Godwyn, Francis Wise and Thomas Knight. The OLD ASHMOLEAN collection, more modest in size and character, also went back to the 18th century. In 1858 it was removed to the Bodleian. Many of the colleges also had collections, some of considerable size. When ARTHUR EVANS was appointed Keeper of the ASHMOLEAN MUSEUM in 1884, he resolved to try to gather these scattered collections together and to house them in the Ashmolean. 'The juxta-position of the Numismatic Collection with our other antiquities is of vital importance for the sound study of Archaeology in the University', he said in his first report to the VISITORS; but he met with strong opposition from Bodley's librarian, and the Curators refused to hand over their collection. However, in 1907 New College deposited its large collection in the Ashmolean on loan and in the same year H. de la Garde Grissell bequeathed to the Ashmolean his collection of papal coins. It was soon apparent that a strong-room would need to be constructed to house these collections as well as the Bodleian coin cabinets. In 1913 the Curators of the Bodleian resolved that they would be prepared to transfer the coins to the Ashmolean on loan, subject to a secure room and a curator being provided; but the project was shelved owing to the outbreak of the war in the following year. After the war, the transfer of the coins to the Ashmolean was at last authorised and the University collection of some 65,300 coins was 'stacked' in the Ashmolean strong-room. A secure coin room was now even more urgent. The University offered a grant of £1500, but what made a start on the whole project possible was a legacy of £1000 left by Dr Charles Buller Heberden, Principal of Brasenose College, who had died in 1921. He had left the legacy to the VICE-CHANCELLOR to devote to any University purpose he thought fit. The Vice-Chancellor wrote to the

The £10 note of 1899, issued by the Oxford Old Bank and signed by Thomson and Parsons, in the collection of the Heberden Coin Room.

Keeper of the Ashmolean saying that he had 'finally decided to devote the sum to the further equipment of the new Coin-Room in the Ashmolean Museum'. On 24 October 1922 the Heberden Coin Room was publicly opened. Three extensions have subsequently been made, in 1938, 1956 and 1965. It was originally part of the Department of Antiquities, but became an independent department of the Ashmolean in 1961. A steady effort has been made since 1922 to enlarge and systematise the holdings, to such good effect that the accessions since 1922 are by now much the larger part of the entire collection.

The foundation of the present fine numismatic library was laid and the collection augmented by gifts or loans of coins from a number of colleges, including Balliol (1924), Oriel and University (1932), Corpus Christi and Jesus (1933), Keble (1934, including a magnificent collection of Greek and Roman coins formed by Canon Liddon), Magdalen (1936), Christ Church (1940), Merton (1951), Somerville (1954) and St John's (1955–6). Brasenose College has for many years made an annual grant from the Hulme Surplus Fund. The range of Greek coins was extended by the purchase of a large part of SIR CHARLES OMAN's collection in 1947, and purchases from the R.C. Lockett collection. The ancient Greek collection was raised to outstanding importance, however, through the generosity of Dr E.S.G. (later Sir Stanley) Robinson of Christ Church, who was made Honorary Keeper of Greek Coins, after being Keeper of Coins and Medals at the British Museum. The coin room continues to benefit greatly from the generosity of the Robinson Charitable Trust. Many rare Roman coins were bought in 1951 from the L.A. Lawrence collection. The British collection was supplemented by the purchase in 1944 of the Crondall hoard of Anglo-Saxon gold coins as a memorial to Sir Arthur Evans, who on his death in 1941 had bequeathed more than 10,000 coins to the coin room. Other important acquisitions have been made from the collections of E.J. Winstanley (coins of Henry VI) and P. Thorburn (Islamic). Gifts to the coin room have been made by many benefactors, including J.G. Milne (Greek), A.T. Carter (English gold coins), H. Hird (Scottish coins), T.B. Horwood (Indian), R. Laird (Chinese) and many others. In 1934 C.L. Stainer left to the University his collection of the mediaeval issues of the Oxford MINT. The collection of coins now in the Heberden Coin Room amounts to over a quarter of a million items and is the finest collection in Great Britain after that of the British Museum. Although the general public's perception of the coin room is, naturally enough, of a repository in which a large collection is housed, its true character is that of a research institute. Graduate students are trained in numismatic method and can compete for the Barclay Head Prize; more senior scholars from abroad are brought to Oxford with the financial help of the Kraay Travel Fund or as Robinson Visiting Scholars; and international symposia on monetary history are regularly held. An academic staff of five are active in teaching, in the affairs of national learned societies and in publishing articles and books.

(*See also* MINT.)

Helen House *37 Leopold Street*. A small hospice which gives relief care to children with life-threatening illness situated in the grounds of All Saints Convent. It was founded by the Superior General of the Anglican Society of All Saints, Mother Frances Dominica. The idea of Helen House was conceived in 1980 as the result of a friendship between Mother Frances and a small girl called Helen, who suffered severe irreversible brain damage as the result of a brain tumour. Thanks to the generosity of thousands of people, building began in 1981 and the first families were welcomed in November 1982. The children, ranging in age between birth and sixteen years, are normally cared for at home and visit Helen House at intervals; families are welcome to stay in the hospice. No charge is made and funding relies on voluntary sources. The patron is HRH the Duchess of Kent, who takes an active interest in the work. The building, designed by John Bicknell, won an environmental award from the OXFORD PRESERVATION TRUST.

HERALDRY This account covers the arms of the colleges and some of the heraldry visible from the pavements of the main Oxford thoroughfares. It does not cover hatchments and coats of arms in Oxford churches. Those unfamiliar with the terms of heraldry may find useful the following explanations of some of the words that occur below:

addorsed back to back
argent silver
attired usually describing antlers, occasionally used of clothing
barry divided by an even number of bars, otherwise the number is stipulated
bend broad band or stripe from dexter chief to sinister base
brodure a bearing that goes all round and parallel to the boundary of a shield, one-fifth part of the shield in breadth
caboshed the severed head of an animal (usually a stag) without its neck
cadency marks by which junior members of a family difference the arms borne by the head
canton a square, smaller than a quarter, in the upper dexter part of the shield
charnois flesh coloured
chevron bent shield division or charge of inverted V-shape
chief upper third of shield
cotised with narrow bands either side
countercoloured divided by partition, the colours or metals on one being reversed on the other
couped cut off smoothly, as opposed to the jagged *erased*
crosslets crosses with each arm crossed
dancetté or *dancetty* a partition line with a limited number of indentations
engrailed with indented or scalloped edge
estoiles stars with six wavy rays
fesse horizontal *bend* across middle of shield
fitchy having lower limb pointed
flaunches two segments of circles on either side of a shield
flory decorated with fleurs-de-lis
formy of a cross with its limbs diminishing to the centre and with straight outer sides
garb a sheaf of corn
gobony a series of equal rectangles countercoloured
gules red
martlet a bird with feather tufts instead of feet

mullet a spur rowel with five points resembling a star
nebuly a line of regular jig-saw like projections
or gold
ordinary charge of geometrical shape dividing the shield, especially chief, pale, bend, fesse, bar, chevron, cross or saltire
orle a shield-shaped inner band not touching the shield's edges
pale vertical broad band in middle of shield
pall Y-shaped charge, often seen on chasuble vestment or in the arms of the See of Canterbury
patonce a cross with each limb end curved into three points
patty fitchy see definitions of 'fitchy' and 'patonce' above
pheon a charge representing a broad barbed arrow or head of a javelin
saltire a cross placed diagonally on a shield, e.g. St Andrew's cross
seeded related to seeds (as in the centre of a rose)
slipped with a stalk
tau crosses crosses shaped like a capital T
tierced in pale divided into three stripes vertically
tinctures inclusive term for metals, colours or furs. The former are or and argent; the second gules, azure, sable, vert, purpure (purple), sanguine and tenny (orange-brown or chestnut). The main furs are ermine and vair
tressure a diminutive of the orle, consisting of a narrow band one-quarter the width of the brodure

Arms of the City *Argent an ox gules its horns and hooves or passing over a ford of three bars wavy azure and argent.*

Arms of the See of Oxford *Sable a fesse argent between in chief three demi-virgins crowned and vested proper, in base an ox argent in a ford barry wavy azure and argent.*

Arms of the University *Azure, upon a book open proper, leathered gules, garnished or, having on the dexter side seven seals of the last, the words* 'DOMINUS ILLUMINATIO MEA'; *all between three open crowns, two and one, or.*

The arms of the colleges and other foundations of the University are as follows:

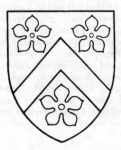

All Souls College *Or, a chevron between three pierced cinquefoils gules.* These are the arms of the founder, HENRY CHICHELE. They can be seen on the wrought-iron gates of the college in RADCLIFFE SQUARE.

The arms which can be seen through the gates on the upper part of the northern tower (that nearer Hertford College) are those of General William Steuart, who contributed £786 towards its building (*or a fess checky azure and argent, over all a bend and an orle flory gules*); the arms on the upper part of the southern tower are those of the 1st Viscount Simon (*gules three lotus flowers in pale proper, between two flaunches gold each charged with a lion gules*). Below these are the arms of Henry Godolphin, Provost of Eton and Fellow of the college, who gave £100 towards the building of the Great Quad in 1718–19 (*gules a two-headed eagle between three fleurs-de-lis argent*); and those of Marshall Brydges (Fellow 1687), who gave £10 at the same time for the same purpose (*argent on a cross sable a leopard's face or*). The 15th-century doorway in the HIGH STREET front bears the college arms and those of Henry VI, who was King at the time of its foundation. The adjoining 16th-century building used to be the Warden's lodging. The arms on the gateway are perhaps those of Kemp (*gules three garbs and a ring or*).

Balliol College *Azure, a lion rampant argent, crowned or, impaling gules, an orle argent.* The arms are those of the founder, John Balliol, impaled by those of his wife, Dervorguilla. John Balliol's arms are *gules, an orle*

171

argent. His wife's are *azure a lion silver crowned or*. These arms are displayed on the college gate, both separately and impaled.

Outside the gateway are the arms of Hannah Brackenbury, a benefactress of the college, who claimed descent from a sister of JOHN WYCLIF. Wyclif's own arms (*silver a chevron sable between three crosslets gules*) can be seen just inside the gateway on an uncoloured shield next to those of John Morton, Archbishop of Canterbury and CHANCELLOR of the University in 1494–1500 (*see of Canterbury impaling Morton viz. quarterly gules and ermine in the first and fourth quarters a goat's head rased argent, its horns or*); A.C. Tait, Archbishop of Canterbury in 1869–82 (*see of Canterbury impaling Tait, viz. quarterly one and four argent a saltire and a chief engrailed gules, two and three argent two ravens suspended by the necks from one arrow sable*); and George Abbot, Archbishop of Canterbury in 1611–1632 (*see of Canterbury impaling gules a chevron charged with a molet between three pears or*).

For the 15th-century armorial glass in the chapel *see* STAINED GLASS.

Brasenose College *Tierced in pale:* (1) *argent, a chevron sable between three roses gules seeded or barbed vert*; (2), *or, an escutcheon of the arms of the see of Lincoln* (*gules, two lions of England in pale or, on a chief azure Our Lady crowned seated on a tombstone issuant from the chief, in her dexter arm the infant Jesus, in her sinister arm a sceptre, all or*) *ensigned with a mitre proper*; (3) *quarterly, first and fourth argent, a chevron between three bugle-horns stringed sable; second and third argent, a chevron between three crosses–crosslet sable*.

The first part of the shield contains the arms of William Smyth, one of the founders of the college; the second part those of his see of Lincoln; the third those of his co-founder, Sir Richard Sutton.

The arms over the main gate of the college are those of the royal House of Tudor and of the see of Lichfield (*per pale gules and argent, a cross potent quadrate*

between four crosses formy countercoloured). Above the gate to the south are the Stuart royal arms. Beyond these, on the wall of the chapel, are the arms of Samuel Radcliffe, Principal of Brasenose (*argent a bend engrailed and in chief a molet sable*). Above the Victorian gateway in the HIGH STREET front are the royal arms between sections of the college arms.

Campion Hall *Argent on a cross sable a plate charged with a wolf's head erased of the second between in pale two billets of the field that in chief charged with a cinquefoil and that in base with a saltire gules and in fesse as many plates each charged with a campion flower leaved and slipped proper on a chief also of the second two branches of palm in saltire enfiled with a celestial crown or.*

Christ Church *Sable, on a cross engrailed argent a lion passant gules between four leopard's faces azure, on a chief or a rose of the third, seeded or, barbed vert, between two Cornish choughs proper.* The arms are those of CARDINAL WOLSEY.

On the ceiling of the gatehouse below Tom Tower are the arms of those who contributed towards the cost of completing it. The four large shields in the middle are those of Thomas Wolsey, Henry VIII, Charles II and James II. The smaller shields are arranged in the four cones of the vault – eleven in each, five shields in the upper row, six in the lower. These are as follows:

South-east Cone
Upper row (1) Donagh MacCarthy, 4th Earl of Clancarty. (2) James Bertie, 1st Earl of Abingdon. (3) Antony Cary, 5th Viscount Falkland. (4) James Howard, 3rd Earl of Suffolk. (5) Edward Hyde, Viscount Cornbury.
Lower row (1) John, 2nd Viscount Scudamore. (2) Sir Nicholas Pelham. (3) Sir Jonathan Trelawney, Bishop successively of Bristol, Exeter and Winchester. (4) Sir Nicholas L'Estrange. (5) Francis Lutterell. (6) Dr Richard Busby, headmaster of Westminster School.

North-east Cone
Upper row (1) James Annesley, Earl of Anglesey. (2) Richard Boyle, Earl of Cork. (3) George, Earl of Berkeley. (4) William Bourke, Earl of Clanricarde. (5) Robert Spencer, Earl of Sunderland.
Lower row (1) Sir Thomas Middleton. (2) Sir Richard Newdigate. (3) Sir Charles Shuckburgh. (4) Sir Justinian Isham. (5) Sir Edward Seymour. (6) Charles Gerard, Earl of Macclesfield.
North-west Cone
Upper row (1) John Dolben, Archbishop of York. (2) Charles Somerset, Marquess of Worcester. (3) Henry Bennet, 1st Earl of Arlington. (4) George Compton, 4th Earl of Northampton. (5) Charles, Viscount Mordaunt, later 3rd Earl of Peterborough.
Lower row (1) Thomas Thynne, 1st Viscount Weymouth. (2) George Morley, Bishop of Winchester. (3) Sir Robert Shirley, later 1st Earl Ferrers. (4) Thomas, Lord Leigh. (5) Hugh, Viscount Cholmondeley. (6) Thomas Needham, 6th Viscount Kilmorey.
South-west Cone
Upper row (1) Thomas Grey, 2nd Earl of Stamford. (2) Thomas Herbert, 8th Earl of Pembroke. (3) James Butler, Earl of Ossory. (4) George Savile, Marquess of Halifax. (5) Heneage Finch, 4th Earl of Nottingham.
Lower row (1) Richard Graham, 1st Viscount Preston. (2) George Booth, 1st Baron Delamer. (3) Henry Yelverton, Lord Grey of Ruthin. (4) Thomas Wood, Bishop of Lichfield. (5) Henry Compton, Bishop of London. (6) Francis, Viscount Newport.

The arms on the inner and outer sides of Tom Tower are those of JOHN FELL (*see of Oxford impaling argent on two bars sable three crosses formy fitchy argent*).

Corpus Christi College *Tierced per pale: (1) Azure, a pelican with wings endorsed vulning* [wounding] *herself* [to feed her young] *or; (2) Argent, thereon an escutcheon charged with the arms of the see of Winchester (i.e. gules, two keys addorsed in bend, the uppermost or, the other argent, a sword interposed between them in bend sinister of the third, pommel and hilt gold; the escutcheon ensigned with a mitre of the last); (3) Sable, a chevron or between three owls argent, on a chief of the second as many roses gules, seeded of the second, barbed vert.*

The first arms are those of Richard Foxe, who was Bishop of Winchester from 1501 to 1529; the second those of his see; the third those of his collaborator, Hugh Oldham, Bishop of Exeter. The owls in these arms are presumably an allusion to his name, which was pronounced 'Owldham'. The arms are displayed over the main gateway of the college.

Exeter College *Argent, two bends nebuly within a bordure sable charged with eight pairs of keys, addorsed and interlaced in the rings, the wards upwards, or.* These are the arms of the college's founder, Walter de Stapledon, Bishop of Exeter.

Over the college gate they are impaled with those of Sir William Petre, Exeter's 16th-century benefactor (*gules on a bend or between two scallops argent a Cornish chough azure between two cinquefoils azure, on a chief or a rose between two demi fleurs-de-lis gules*). Both shields are also displayed separately. Above the gateway are five shields. These are the arms of Sir Jonathan Trelawny (1650–1721), Bishop successively of Bristol, Exeter and Winchester (*argent a chevron sable*); Walter de Stapledon (*a lion in a border gobony*); Sir William Petre; and George Hakewill (1578–1649), Fellow of the college, who built the chapel in 1623–4 (*or a bend between six trefoils slipped*).

Green College *Ermine, between two flaunches vert, on each a mullet argent a pallet engrailed couped sable, entwined by a serpent vert and ensigned by a crown or.*

Greyfriars *Argent in front of the lower limb of a long cross pointed at the foot proper two arms in saltire the dexter charnois the sinister habited in the sleeve of a Franciscan friar the hands upwards and appaumée displaying stigmata proper on a chief azure a paschal*

lamb also proper over all in dexter a crozier erect sable garnished and headed or the head containing a square pierced cross moline and in sinister flank an archiepiscopal staff also erect sable garnished and headed or each limb of the cross terminating in a cross formy.

Hertford College *Gules, a stag's head caboshed argent, attired and between the attires a cross patty fitchy at the foot, or.*

These arms can be seen on the Bridge of Sighs (to the north), which also displays those of Magdalen College (south) as an acknowledgement of the connection between the two colleges, as well as those of Hertford. On the west side of the bridge (that facing CATTE STREET) are also the arms of Lord St Helier, a benefactor, and his wife. On the east side are those of Baring.

Jesus College *Vert, three stags trippant argent attired or.*

The origin of these arms is unknown. They are to be seen above the college gate beside the royal arms of Elizabeth I, and the badge of the Prince of Wales. On the wall near the corner of SHIP STREET are the arms of Sir Leoline Jenkins (*argent three cocks gules*). Jenkins (1623–85) became Principal in 1660 and was a munificent benefactor to the college.

Keble College *Argent, a chevron engrailed gules, on a chief azure three mullets pierced or.*

Lady Margaret Hall *Or, on a chevron between in chief two talbots passant and in base a bell all azure, a portcullis of the field.*

Linacre College *Sable, on open book properedged or bound, gules, the dexter page charged with the Greek letter alpha, the sinister page charged with the Greek letter omega, both sable, the whole between the three escallops argent.*

Lincoln College *Tierced per pale: (1) barry of six argent and azure, in chief three lozenges gules, on the second bar of argent a mullet pierced sable; (2) argent, thereon an escutcheon of the arms of the see of Lincoln (i.e. gules, two lions passant guardant or, on a chief azure the Blessed Virgin Mary ducally crowned seated on a throne issuant from the chief, on her dexter arm the infant Jesus and holding in her sinister hand a sceptre, all gold: the escutcheon ensigned with a mitre azure garnished and stringed or); (3) vert, three stags statant two and one or.*

The first pale displays the arms of the founder, Richard Fleming; the second those of the see of Lincoln; the third those of Thomas Rotherham (Bishop of Lincoln from 1472 to 1480), who re-endowed the college in 1478. On the northern and southern walls of the library (formerly ALL SAINTS CHURCH) are the arms of Nathaniel, Lord Crewe (1633–1722). (*See* BEQUESTS.)

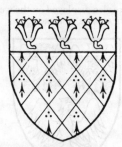

Magdalen College *Lozengy ermine and sable, on a chief of the second three lilies argent slipped and seeded or.*

The arms are those of the founder of the college, William of Waynflete (1395–1486), successively headmaster of Winchester and Eton Colleges, Provost of Eton and Bishop of Winchester. The *chief of lilies* was added to his family arms by Waynflete in allusion to Eton College, which has *lilies argent* in its arms. Waynflete had become the second Provost of Eton in 1443. The lilies and lozenges of the arms are liberally sprinkled over the college; and Waynflete's arms, impaled with those of the see of Winchester, can also be seen, uncoloured, on the front of the college facing HIGH STREET. There is a coloured version across MAGDALEN BRIDGE on the modern Waynflete Building. The High Street front of the college is also embellished with the shield of Henry VI, who was King of England when Magdalen was founded.

Mansfield College *Gules an open book proper inscribed* 'DEUS LOCUTUS EST NOBIS IN FILIO' *in letters sable bound argent edged and clasped or between three cross crosslets or.*

Merton College *Argent, on a saltire gules an escallop or, impaling or, three chevronels party per pale, the first*

and third party azure and gules, the second gules and azure.

The founder of the college, Walter de Merton, Bishop of Rochester, had adopted a form of the arms of his patrons, the Clare family. These are impaled by those of the see of Rochester. The chevronels are as distinctive a feature of Merton's walls as Waynflete's lilies and lozenges are of Magdalen. They can be seen over the main college gate beside a shield which is that of Robert Bullock Marsham, Warden of the College 1826–1880. The arms over the disused gateway are those of Benedict Barnham (1559–98), merchant and benefactor of ST ALBAN HALL. (For the armorial glass in the chapel *see* STAINED GLASS.)

New College *Argent, two chevronels sable between three roses gules, seeded or, barbed vert.* The arms are those of the college founder, WILLIAM OF WYKEHAM. The arms can be seen above the gate in HOLYWELL STREET impaled with those of Winchester diocese. The two shields on either side display the arms of two 19th-century benefactors.

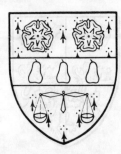

Nuffield College *Ermine on a fesse or between in chief two roses gules barbed and seeded proper and in base a balance of the second three pears sable.*

Oriel College *Gules, three lions passant guardant in pale or within a bordure engrailed argent for difference.*

175

The college bears royal arms since Edward II agreed to become its titular founder. A *difference* is a small alteration used to distinguish a member of a branch of a family from the main bearer of the arms – cf. Ophelia, 'You must wear your rue with a difference' (*Hamlet*, Act IV, scene 5). On the college's HIGH STREET front are the arms of its benefactor, CECIL RHODES, and below them five other shields displaying Rhodes's crest (a griffin's head holding a spray in its beak); the arms of Sir John Holt (1642–1710), Lord Chief Justice (*argent on a bend engrailed sable three fleurs-de-lis argent*); the college arms; the arms of John Robinson (1650–1723), Bishop of London and Fellow of the college from 1675 to 1686 (*see of London impaling vert on a chevron between three stags walking or three cinquefoils gules*); and the arms of Charles Lancelot Shadwell (1840–1919), college archivist and translator of Dante, who was Provost when the building was constructed (*per pale or and azure, on a chevron between three rings four scallops counter-coloured*). Holt, who came down without a degree, was said to have mixed with a very dissipated set when he was at Oriel. He later had to try one of them for felony; and on visiting him in prison and asking about their former companions received the reply, 'Ah, my lord, they are all hanged except myself and your lordship.'

On the main 17th-century gateway in ORIEL SQUARE are the college arms, the Stuart royal arms and those of Anthony Blencowe, Provost from 1574 to 1618. The modern shields over the gateway are, from left to right, those of John Franke, a 15th-century benefactor; John Carpenter (*d.*1476), Bishop of Worcester, who was appointed Provost in 1428; William Smyth, Bishop of Lincoln from 1495 to 1514; and Richard Dudley, a Fellow and benefactor (*d.*1536).

Pembroke College *Per pale azure and gules, three lions rampant, two and one, argent, on a chief per pale argent and or, in the first a rose gules, seeded or, barbed vert, in the second a thistle of Scotland proper.*

The arms are those of William Herbert, Earl of Pembroke, with an augmentation granted by King James I. It has been said that the original grant to the college placed the rose of England on an *argent* shield, and the thistle of Scotland upon *or* 'in order to equalize as far as possible the honours due to the two countries, and probably also as a delicate compliment to King James'. It was a happy coincidence that the arms of Thomas Tesdale, the actual co-founder of the college, contain a thistle or 'teazle' as their principal charge.

The arms of the college can be seen over the main gateway, together with those of William Herbert, Earl of Pembroke; France quartering England, and the arms of Thomas Tesdale; his co-founder, Richard Wightwick; and John Bennet, a benefactor. The arms

of the college are also displayed on the western wall of the annexe to ST ALDATE'S CHURCH.

The Queen's College *Argent, three eagles displayed two and one gules, legged and beaked or, on the breast of the first eagle a pierced mullet of six points of the third as cadency mark.*

The eagles in these arms, which are those of the college's founder, Robert de Eglesfeld, are a 'canting' allusion to his name. The arms are displayed above the entrance to the Provost's lodgings and on the pediments of the college front, together with those of Joseph Williamson, the college's benefactor (*or a chevron engrailed between three trefoils slipped sable*). Also to be seen on the pediments are the arms borne by Queen Anne after the Union of England and Scotland in 1707. Before that date she had borne the Stuart royal arms. As she died in 1714 these post-Union arms are not common. Nor are the Hanoverian arms that superseded them, since little building was done in the University in the 18th century, when, in any case, its Jacobite tendencies were pronounced.

Regent's Park College *Argent on a cross gules an open Bible proper irradiated or the pages inscribed with the words* 'DOMINUS JESUS' *in letters sable on a chief wavy azure a fish or.* The arms are displayed over the doorway of the Principal's lodgings at No. 55 ST GILES'.

St Anne's College arms (see facing page).

St Anne's College *Gules, on a chevron in chief two lions heads erased argent, and in base a sword of the second pummelled and hilted or and enfiled with a wreath of laurel proper, three ravens.* The arms are those of Field-Marshal Viscount Plumer (1857–1932), whose eldest daughter, Eleanor Mary, was Principal of the college from 1941 to 1953.

St Edmund Hall *Or, a cross patonce gules cantoned by four Cornish choughs proper.*

These arms appear for the first time as those of the hall in the Benefactors' Book of *c.*1682. The arms of Abingdon Abbey, which include a cross and four martlets, were presumably a model. They can be seen on the college gates and above the entrance in QUEEN'S LANE.

St Antony's College *Or on a chevron between three tau crosses gules as many pierced mullets of the field.*

The T-cross alludes to St Anthony's crutch. A mullet was used by ANTONIN BESSE as a sort of trademark.

St Hilda's College *Azure on a fesse or between in chief two unicorns' heads couped and in base a coiled serpent argent three estoiles gules.*

The unicorns' heads allude to the foundress, Dorothea Beale, and the serpent to the fossils of Whitby.

St Benet's Hall *Per fesse dancette or and azure, a chief per pale gules and of the second, charged on the dexter with two keys in saltire or and argent, and on the sinister with a cross flory between five martlets of the first.*

St Catherine's College *Sable a saltire ermine between four catherine wheels or.*

St Hugh's College *Azure a saltire ermine between four fleurs-de-lis or.*

177

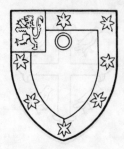

St John's College *Gules, on a bordure sable eight estoiles or; on a canton ermine a lion rampant of the second; on the fesse point an annulet of the third.*

The arms are those of the founder, Sir Thomas White. They are displayed on the northern end of the college's later building facing ST GILES'. Over the gate of the older building are the Stuart royal arms and those of WILLIAM LAUD, who became President of St John's in 1611.

Trinity College *Party per pale or and azure, on a chevron between three griffins' heads erased four fleurs-de-lis, all counterchanged.*

The arms are those of the founder, Sir Thomas Pope, and can be seen on the main college gate, on the garden gates opposite Wadham College and on the chapel tower. On the inner side of the main gate are the arms of the Norths, Earls of Guilford.

St Peter's College *Per pale vert and argent, to the dexter two keys in saltire or surmounted by a triple towered castle argent masoned sable [representing Oxford Bailey] and on the sinister a cross gules surmounted by a mitre or between four martlets sable, the whole within a bordure or.*

University College *Azure, a cross patonce between five martlets or.*

The arms are intended to commemorate Alfred the Great, who, so it was asserted in the 14th century, founded the college. Since heraldry had not been invented in the time of the Saxon Kings, mediaeval heralds devised arms for them based upon coins of Edward the Confessor's reign which were stamped with a cross between four doves. The shield on the college gate has only four martlets. There are ten shields on the HIGH STREET front opposite All Souls. These are those of Percy, Earl of Northumberland; William of Durham; Walter Skirlaw, Bishop successively of Lichfield, Bath and of Durham (*d.*1406) (the six interlaced bastons in this shield are believed to be an allusion to his father's craft of sieve-maker); the royal arms of France quartering England; Thomas Foston, Master of the college in the late 14th century; Percy quartering Lucy; the college arms; the arms of Simon Bennet, a 17th-century benefactor of the college and of JOHN RADCLIFFE, an 18th-century benefactor.

The main 17th-century gate has the arms of the college and of William of Durham; the gate of the 18th-century buildings to the east bears the college arms (with four instead of five martlets) and those of John Radcliffe.

Somerville College *Argent, three mullets gules in chevron reversed between six crosses crosslet fitchy sable.*

Wadham College *Gules, a chevron between three roses argent, seeded or, barbed vert impaling gules, a bend or between two escallops argent.*

The arms are those of Nicholas Wadham impaling those of his wife's family, the Petres. They may be seen between the statues of the Wadhams above the doorway facing the main gate (*see* STATUES).

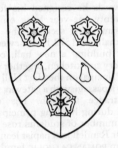

Wolfson College *Per pale gules and or on a chevron between three roses two pears all countercharged the roses barbed and seeded proper.*

Worcester College *Argent, two chevrons between six martlets, three, two and one, gules.*

Other arms which can be seen from the street in the centre of the city are as follows:

Broad Street On the SHELDONIAN THEATRE are the arms of GILBERT SHELDON, Archbishop of Canterbury (*sable a fesse between three sheldrakes argent, on a canton gules a rose or*); those of the see of Canterbury (*azure an archiepiscopal cross surmounted by a pall proper charged with four crosses formy fitchy sable*), the Stuart royal arms and the arms of the University (*see above*).

On the north door of the OLD ASHMOLEAN MUSEUM are the arms of ELIAS ASHMOLE (*quarterly sable and or in the first quarter a fleur-de-lis or*); on the east door are the Stuart royal arms and those of Timothy Halton, VICE-CHANCELLOR 1679–82 (*quarterly azure and gules a lion or*).

On the wall of the NEW BODLEIAN opposite is a row of cartouches containing the arms of various benefactors, CHANCELLORS of the University, antiquaries, bibliophiles and others whose names are associated with the library. From the east, they are Sir Giles Gilbert Scott, architect (1880–1960); Sir Edmund Craster, Bodley's Librarian (1879–1959); Lord Halifax, Chancellor of the University (1881–1959); Viscount Grey, Chancellor (1862–1933); the city of Oxford (*see above*); the Stationers' Company; CECIL RHODES; JOHN RADCLIFFE; HUMFREY, DUKE OF GLOUCESTER; Thomas de Cobham, Bishop of Worcester and benefactor (*d*.1327); WILLIAM LAUD; William Herbert, Earl of Pembroke, Chancellor (1580–1630) (an elaborated version of whose arms can be seen on the base of his statue in the Bodleian quadrangle – *see* STATUES); Sir Kenelm Digby, benefactor (1603–65); Richard Rawlinson, benefactor; Francis Douce, antiquary and benefactor (1757–1834); Oxford University; John Selden, lawyer, orientalist and benefactor (1584–1654); Thomas Tanner, Bishop of St Asaph, antiquary and benefactor (1674–1735); Richard Gough, antiquary and benefactor (1735–1809); Lord Sunderlin, critic, author and benefactor (1741–1812); Thomas, 2nd Earl Brassey (1863–1919), benefactor.

Above the cartouches are the appropriate helms of peers, baronets and knights, commoners and corporations.

Catte Street On the 17th-century door leading to the courtyard of the BODLEIAN are the arms of the University (*see above*), of all the colleges founded by 1631, and of the royal House of Stuart. The latter are often encountered in Oxford as so much building took place here in the 17th century.

High Street Above the small door near the west end of ST MARY THE VIRGIN are two small shields, those of Richard Fitzjames, the 15th-century Warden of Merton (*azure a dolphin argent*) and of Eleanor Draycot (*argent a cross engrailed sable in the quarter an eagle gules*).

On the wall of the National Westminster Bank, above the arms of the bank, are three shields, the arms of the University and of the city (*see above*), and a shield with chevrons, which is presumably a restored version of the arms of New College, which sold the building to the bank in 1875.

Over the doorway of the EXAMINATION SCHOOLS the University arms are displayed. And, further down, at the corner of MERTON STREET on the wall of the University Registry (which was formerly occupied by St Catherine's Society – *see* ST CATHERINE'S COLLEGE) are six uncoloured shields. These bear the arms of BENJAMIN JOWETT (*or a chevron gules between three lions' heads rased sable*); Robert Cecil 3rd Earl of Salisbury (1830–1903), CHANCELLOR of the University (*barry of ten argent and azure six scutcheons sable each charged with a lion argent*); the royal arms; the University arms; and those of George William Kitchin (1827–1912), the first Censor of non-collegiate students (*argent a pile between two crosslets gules, the pile charged with an eagle argent*); and James Bellamy (1819–1909), President of St John's and VICE-CHANCELLOR (*azure on a bend cotised or three crescents gules*).

179

Holywell Street The Merton College shields on Nos 2 (at the corner of Bath Place) and 56 indicate that a large part of this area used to belong to the college. Nos 25–9 are now owned by Manchester College and are decorated with the arms of Manchester and Warrington, Josiah Wedgwood, Richard Frankland and Thomas Bentley.

Merton Street The former History Faculty library is decorated with the arms of the University (*see above*). The arms on the house on the corner of MAGPIE LANE are those of Richard Fox and Hugh Oldham (*see* CORPUS CHRISTI COLLEGE).

Old Schools Quadrangle. The DIVINITY SCHOOL is embellished with nearly a hundred 15th-century coats-of-arms. (For these see the *Royal Commission on Historical Monuments: An Inventory of the Historical Monuments in the City of Oxford* (1939).) Above the door are the arms of SIR THOMAS BODLEY (*argent five martlets in saltire sable on a chief azure three crowns or quartering argent two bars wavy between three honestones sable*).

Pembroke Street The dilapidated gilt achievement (the coat of arms with supporters and motto) on the south side contains one of the very rare examples of the Hanoverian royal arms to be seen in Oxford.

St Aldate's The annexe of ST ALDATE'S CHURCH at the western end bears the shields of the see of Uganda, of Pembroke College, of Simeon for the Simeon Trust (*see* ST ALDATE'S CHURCH), and of the see of Oxford.

In the porch of the TOWN HALL are the arms of the University and of the city (*see above*), and of the 7th Earl of Jersey (1845–1915), who was Lord Lieutenant of Oxfordshire when the town hall was built in 1893–7. These impale those of his wife, the eldest daughter of the 2nd Baron Leigh.

St Giles' The arms on No. 39a are those of SAMUEL WILBERFORCE, BISHOP OF OXFORD from 1845 to 1869 (*see of Oxford impaling argent an eagle sable charged with a mullet argent*).

The shield on No. 55 displays the arms of Regent's Park College (*see above*).

As well as those of Latimer (*gules a cross patonce or, over all a bend azure flory gold*), of Ridley (*argent a bull gules with horns and hoofs or on a base vert surmounting a ford barry wavy argent and azure*) and of Cranmer (*argent on a chevron azure between three pelicans sable three mullets or*), the shields on the MARTYRS' MEMORIAL also include those of the sees of Canterbury, London and Worcester. Latimer was Bishop of Worcester, Ridley Bishop of London, and Cranmer Archbishop of Canterbury. The shields contain various heraldic solecisms: the gold of the see of Worcester's should be silver; the mullets in Cranmer's should be cinquefoils; the swords in the see of London's should be silver not gold; and the bull in Ridley's should be passing through a field of reeds – a play on his name (reed–lea).

(Barnard, F.P., *Arms and Blazons of the Colleges of Oxford*, Oxford, 1929; Stanier, R.S., *Oxford Heraldry for the Man in the Street*, Oxford, [1974].)

Hertford College Hertford derives from two ancient halls of the University, HART HALL and MAGDALEN HALL, whose fortunes became linked in the early 19th century (*see also* ACADEMIC HALLS). The site of Hart Hall was bought around 1283 by Elias de Hertford and conveyed by his son to John de Dokelynton in about 1301. He, in turn, sold it in 1312 to Walter de Stapeldon, Bishop of Exeter, who

intended to found a college for poor students in Oxford. But although in 1314 he installed twelve scholars in Hart Hall, which he renamed Stapeldon Hall, he removed them not long after to the site of the present Exeter College and allowed Hart Hall to resume its old name. Thereafter it remained in the possession of Exeter College and was leased out as an academic hall, which, by 1490, enjoyed the rare distinction of possessing its own library. Hart Hall received its only endowment during the 15th century when Sir John Bignall founded ten exhibitions for ten scholars from Glastonbury Abbey. At the Dissolution the University made a special plea to Thomas Cromwell for the retention of these exhibitions, and they continued to be paid from the Exchequer until the estates passed into private ownership, after which they lapsed. In 1653 Dr Philip Stephens, the Principal nominated by the CHANCELLOR, discovered their existence and forced the proprietors to continue their payment. In 1549–50, Philip Randell, like his predecessors a Fellow of Exeter, became Principal. Shortly afterwards he resigned his fellowship and obtained a twenty-one-year lease on the property while at the same time securing the tenure of the adjacent Blackhall. In 1572 he renewed the tenancy and set about building a new hall, complete with refectory, buttery and kitchen, together with a lodging house for the Principal on the Hart Hall site, linking it to Blackhall by a passage with a gateway which formed the main entrance to both. His establishment prospered and during his long principalship of over fifty years the number of students rose steadily. The rumour that Dr Randell had papist leanings attracted many boys from ROMAN CATHOLIC families; one of the most famous of these was John Donne, poet and divine, who matriculated from Hart Hall at the unusually early age of twelve in order to avoid having to subscribe to the Thirty-Nine Articles. This was in 1584, the year which saw the birth of John Selden, lawyer and politician, who also attended Hart Hall, matriculating from it when he was not yet sixteen. After Randell's death in 1599 he was succeeded by his Vice-Principal, John Eveleigh. Eveleigh did not hold the post for long as he succumbed to plague in 1604; he was followed by Dr Theodore Price of Jesus College, a nominee of the Chancellor, Lord Buckhurst. Dr Price promptly refused to pay rent for the hall to Exeter, but after six years' litigation the next Chancellor, Archbishop Bancroft, decided in favour of the college. Before his resignation in 1622, Dr Price had managed to extend and enlarge the hall – a policy which was continued by his successor, Dr Thomas Iles of Christ Church, who held the principalship until 1633. At the VISITATION of 1646 only four members of Hart Hall made submission; of these, three were given forfeited fellowships in other colleges; the fourth was the cook. Somewhat surprisingly, although the Principal, Dr Philip Parsons of St John's, had taken part in the resistance and did not appear, he was not deprived. But, at his death in 1653, Oliver Cromwell, as Chancellor, nominated in his place the fervent government supporter, Dr Philip Stephens, who in 1654 was appointed to a new Commission of Visitors to make a third purge of the University. His expulsion at the Restoration made way for Timothy Baldwin, Fellow of All Souls, whose resignation three years later left the appointment open to Dr Lamphire. His successor,

The remarkable French Renaissance-style staircase is a dominating feature of Sir Thomas Jackson's quadrangle for Hertford College which was completed in 1890.

Dr Thornton, who became Principal in 1688, was responsible for an extensive programme of new building, which included a monumental gateway in CATTE STREET containing a library above. Despite a benefaction from Emmanuel Pritchard, janitor of the BODLEIAN LIBRARY, and a contribution towards the cost of the library from Dr Hudson, Bodley's Librarian, Dr Thornton became increasingly insolvent, and after his death in 1707 his debts remained outstanding until they were discharged by Dr Richard Newton, who became Principal in 1710.

Dr Newton was strikingly different from any of his predecessors. He at once welcomed the opportunity to put into effect his passionately held educational theories, which he expounded in a publication of 1720 entitled *Scheme of Discipline with Statutes intended to be established by a Royal Charter for the education of youth in Hart Hall in the University of Oxford*. It was his plan that the hall should become a college of the University, and his disciplinarian reforms, somewhat modified, were re-embodied in a publication of 1747, *Statutes of Hertford College*, which set out his aims for the new college which had finally replaced Hart Hall in 1740. Hertford College was intended by Dr Newton to be for the education of clergymen but, while the scholars were in general expected to come from middle-class families, he also accepted gentlemen-commoners provided they were prepared to submit to the same restrictions as the others, and to pay double the fees. In addition, they were required to forgo the customary use of credit which allowed expenses such as ale, the tipping of college servants, etc., to be added to their BATTELS – a system which acted as an efficient curb to youthful extravagance. This proved very popular with parents, and the number of gentlemen-commoners showed a steady increase, thus enabling Dr Newton's establishment to pay its way despite its lack of endowment. The undergraduates were less appreciative: a letter written by N. Amhurst deplored the tyrannical restraints exercised by his Principal and complained of Dr Newton's regime of 'bread and water or what is little better, of small beer and Apple Dumplings'. Dr Newton's first publication had encountered fierce hostility in Oxford, especially from Exeter College, who, as landlords, entered a caveat when his petition for a royal charter was presented in May 1723. However, it was supported by the Attorney-General in consideration of the long and uninterrupted tenure enjoyed by Hart Hall; and the Rector of Exeter College was prepared to withdraw his opposition. However, three of his fellows, led by John Conybeare, remained intractable and persuaded the VISITOR, the Bishop of Exeter, to use his political influence to suppress the petition. Conybeare went so far as to accuse the Rector of locking him out of the muniment room, which, he was convinced, housed documents that would have supported his case. After he himself became Rector, he even insinuated that Dr Newton had purloined Bishop Stapeldon's original grant – an allegation that caused bitter and lasting offence. As Dean of Christ Church he continued to oppose Dr Newton's foundation of a college, justifying himself in a book which he called *Calumny Refuted*. However, when Dr Atwell, Conybeare's last

181

supporter in Exeter, retired in 1737, the Bishop consented to the scheme and Newton, by this time thoroughly embittered, was able to petition for his charter, which he received in November 1740. Sadly, his one would-be benefactor, Thomas Strangways, had died in 1726 and Hertford College started with very little endowment.

Newton died in 1753, and for some years after the college continued to prosper. One of the undergraduates at this time ws Charles James Fox, who entered the college in 1764; he seems to have been very happy there and said of the University, 'I did not expect my life here could be so pleasant as I find it; but I really think, to a man who reads a great deal, there cannot be a more agreeable place.' In 1775, Dr Hodgson of Christ Church became Principal, and from then on the college suffered such a steady decline in numbers that by the time of his death in 1805 there were no students and only two Fellows remaining. No one suitable was anxious to take on the appointment but the Vice-Principal, Hewitt, would have accepted it had not the Dean of Christ Church intervened. He disputed the legality of the revised statutes of 1747, which would have sanctioned Hewitt's appointment, and in the absence of a qualified Principal it was decided to close down Hertford College and hand over the buildings to Magdalen Hall. Hewitt was allowed to carry on the affairs of the college until his fellowship expired in 1818, when he was given a small pension provided from a sum of money reserved from the escheated Hertford property; after his death this sum was used to found the Hertford Scholarship (*see* PRIZES AND SCHOLARSHIPS).

Magdalen Hall, founded by William of Waynflete, had evolved as an independent University hall in part of the buildings originally intended for the grammar school. One of its early scholars was William Tyndale, whose translation of the Bible appeared in 1525. At first the Principal was nominated by Magdalen College from among its own Fellows, but in 1602, at about the time that Thomas Hobbes, philosopher and author of the *Leviathan* (1651), was a student at the hall, the Chancellor appointed Dr James Hussey, Fellow of New College, to the headship. His two portraits hang at present in the upper and lower Senior Common Rooms. Dr Hussey was succeeded by Dr Wilkinson, who, in about 1614, extended the buildings and enormously enlarged the membership. It was during his term of office that Edward Hyde, later EARL OF CLARENDON, having failed to get into Magdalen College, was admitted to the hall in 1622 at the age of thirteen. Parliament later appointed Wilkinson a Commissioner to visit the University, at which time fifty-five members of Magdalen Hall made submission, many of them being rewarded with vacant fellowships and other places in the University. Towards the end of the 17th century, the Fellows of Magdalen College made two unsuccessful attempts to regain control of the hall, but it was not until the beginning of the 19th century that the President of Magdalen College perceived a way by which he could both influence the affairs of the hall and, at the same time, disencumber the college of its now inconvenient neighbour in order to make better use of the site. To this end he managed to obtain from the Crown a grant of the land and buildings escheated from Hertford College, enabling them to be held in trust by the University until their transfer to

Magdalen Hall in 1816. In 1813 Dr Macbride was appointed Principal to supervise the changeover, and Magdalen College undertook to defray all the expenses in this connection, including the repair of the Hertford buildings, the construction of new ones and the eventual redemption of the old rent charge to Exeter College. The removal took place in 1822, two years after a fire had destroyed most of the Magdalen Hall buildings and the mediaeval Catte Street frontage to Hertford College had collapsed.

From 1832 the fortunes of the hall took an upward turn under the Vice-Principalship of William Jacobson, a vigorous reformer, and by the time of the University Commission in 1850 (*see* ROYAL COMMISSIONS), it was generally recognised for its merit and industry. Dr Macbride was succeeded in 1868 by the energetic Dr Michell, who resolved to turn the hall back into a college and revive the old name of Hertford College. He was aided in this enterprise by the generosity of the banker Thomas Charles Baring, who, anticipating some antagonism to his scheme for a foundation restricted to members of the Church of England, took the precaution of lodging the sum of £30,000 with the Chancellor before the Bill was heard. This money was later used for the endowment of five unrestricted fellowships. Countering objections that the hall did not warrant a change of status, Dr Michell pointed out that between 1822 and 1874 it had produced six colonial bishops, four archdeacons, three canons, three Professors and six Fellows of colleges. The Bill, which was passed in 1874, permitted the future acceptance of restricted endowments and named certain Fellows on the old foundation, who, with the Principal and some scholars, were to be incorporated as 'The Principal, Fellows and Scholars of Hertford College'. By 1881 the number of Fellows admitted on the Baring Foundation was complete and included the five original unrestricted fellowships, two fellowships restricted to married members of the Anglican Church and a number (never specifically stated) of fellowships for unmarried members of the Church of England. In addition, Baring endowed thirty scholarships with varying restrictions for undergraduates. The new college was constituted and is governed as a Corporation of Principal and Fellows. The appointment of the Principal is vested in the Chancellor of the University. The position regarding the Baring fellowships was questioned shortly after their foundation when, in 1875, a disappointed Nonconformist candidate took his case to the Queen's Bench and subsequently to the court of appeal. There, it was ruled that the 1871 Universities' Tests Act did not debar the foundation of new colleges of which the endowments might be restricted to members of one particular religion, and the issue has not since been challenged (*see* DISSENTERS).

Dr Michell was succeeded in 1877 by the Rev. Henry Boyd, who was Principal until his death in 1922. During his term of office the college increased in prosperity and the number of students rose steadily. Boyd was assiduous in his attempts to secure the most distinguished classical scholars as Fellows and undergraduates, and was a vigorous champion of all sports in the University, particularly golf. His qualities of leadership were acknowledged in a tribute from the governing board after his death: 'Henry Boyd's personality has throughout been the chief influence in the development of the college. His patience, his quiet determination, his generosity, his humour and knowledge of men gradually and insensibly surmounted difficulties, removed suspicions and established a high standard for the college.'

He was also responsible for much of its architecture, which, designed by SIR THOMAS JACKSON in the late 19th and early 20th centuries, blends harmoniously with the earlier buildings. The oldest of these are in the north-east range, constructed by Philip Randell in the 16th century; they consist of the old hall with two windows of three arched lights, which is now a dining room, and the buttery, which had a third storey added in the late 17th or early 18th century. The buildings to the south-east, adjoining the buttery, were built by Dr Philip Price in the early 17th century, although the top floor was added in the 19th century. At the south-east corner is a plain, four-bay 18th-century house. The south range contains two chapels: Jackson's of 1908 is six bays long with a north-west tower, polygonal from the ground, supporting eight detached columns topped by a dome. The five-light east window is reminiscent of a Venetian window and is embellished with columns and garlands; the two-light windows are unusually long. The old chapel standing to its west was consecrated in 1716. It has three round-headed windows and a large parapet, and is now used as a library. Its predecessor, the Old Library, contains the two earlier collections of Magdalen Hall and Hart Hall and is distinguished for its notable accumulation of geographical literature and archaeological works. Part of the CATTE STREET façade was built by Magdalen College after the old one had fallen down and is the work of E.W. Garbett in 1820–2. His plain, six-bay side-pieces, three storeys high, set off Jackson's ornate centrepiece of 1877. This, executed in the Palladian style sometimes referred to as 'Anglo-Jackson', has an archway with Tuscan pillars and pediment, four upper attached Corinthian columns and three Venetian windows. The past is recalled in the 17th-century wooden gate which was re-set by Jackson in the new place. His north range, also reminiscent of the Palladian style, was constructed two years later. In 1898, when Hertford College bought the corner site off New College, Jackson was invited to develop the new North Quad, three sides of which feature his designs. On the fourth side is a house of late Georgian appearance which was in fact designed in 1929 by T.H. Hughes. The 1521 octagonal Chapel of Our Lady at Smith Gate, known as 'the Round House', was included in the purchase of the site, and, much restored in a general development of 1931, is now the Junior Common Room. The renowned bridge with its ornate centre, which links the two sites, was built by Jackson in 1913–14. The project was strongly opposed by New College, but after the bridge was finally built, it became a much-admired architectural feature and is now one of the most famous landmarks in Oxford, familiarly known as 'the Bridge of Sighs' after the Ponte dei Sospiri in Venice by Antonio Contino (c.1600). The recent Holywell Quad, which incorporates interesting façades of some 17th- and 18th-century houses in HOLYWELL STREET, was completed in two stages in 1976 and 1981, and opened on both occasions by Harold Macmillan (later the EARL OF STOCKTON), Chancellor of the University and Visitor of Hertford College.

During the 1920s one of the undergraduates at Hertford was the author Evelyn Waugh, who did not

The bridge linking the two parts of Hertford College, built by Sir Thomas Jackson in 1913–14, has become known as 'the Bridge of Sighs' after the Ponte dei Sospiri in Venice.

hold his Alma Mater in much esteem. In particular he disliked, and ridiculed in his novels, the History tutor C.R.M.F. Cruttwell, who succeeded Sir W.R. Buchanan-Riddell as Principal in 1930. A contemporary of Waugh's at the college, Eric Whelpton, commented before his death in 1981, 'Cruttwell was notable though an eccentric. He was constantly denigrated by that frightful little sod Evelyn Waugh. I wrote a letter defending Cruttwell and attacking Waugh in *The Times*. I am told that Waugh was very much upset and that I probably hastened his death.'

Many things have changed in Hertford College since the Second World War and some have gone altogether – SCOUTS' boys and coal fires, to mention but two. Since the early 1970s the college's academic performance has been strikingly improved by a deliberate policy of encouraging entry from state schools; and in 1974 Hertford was one of the first five Oxford colleges to admit female undergraduates. In 1987 the total number of undergraduates and postgraduates was 429. There were thirty-four Fellows. The Principal was Sir Geoffrey Warnock, who was Vice-Chancellor from 1981 to 1985. His two immediate predecessors as Principal were Sir Robert Hall (1964–7) and Sir George Lindor Brown (1967–71). Professor Christopher Zeeman was appointed Principal in 1988.

The corporate title of the college is The Principal, Fellows and Scholars of Hertford College in the University of Oxford.

(Goudie, Andrew, ed. *Seven Hundred Years of an Oxford College*, Oxford, 1984; Hamilton, S.G., *Hertford College*, Oxford, 1902.)

High Street Described by Pevsner as 'one of the world's great streets', High Street stretches from CARFAX to MAGDALEN BRIDGE in a great curve. In mediaeval times the street was known as Eastgate Street, being the main street from the East Gate of the city to Carfax. Stalls were set up on market days, even in the middle of the street, the sellers of different goods being allotted their stands in specified parts of the street. Near to Carfax were the permanent shops. Most of these were very narrow, often as little as 6 feet wide, and stood in front of the larger houses. For example, there were five small shops in front of TACKLEY'S INN at 106–7 High Street, and five butcher's shops in the 36-foot frontage of what are now Nos 6–8. Because the houses often had separate leases from the shops in front of them, it was necessary to have narrow passages off the main street to give access, such as the one at No. 119. Some of the larger shops contained a wide range of goods. The inventory of William Clarke, a mercer who died in 1612, shows that his shop in High Street contained – as well as cloths, threads, buttons and ribbons, table napkins, hose and stockings, girdles and garters – such diverse items as groceries, spices, tobacco, nails and screws, chains and padlocks, stationery and basic grammar books, medicines, sucking bottles for babies, and sets of chessmen. The ACADEMIC HALLS for undergraduates were mostly situated behind the shops and the town houses. These houses were on both sides of the street for its whole length, but many were lost when the colleges extended along the street frontages and the EXAMINATION SCHOOLS were built.

On the north side of High Street (often referred to as 'the High'), at the Carfax end, the first building is Lloyds Bank, designed in 1900–1 by Stephen Salter. The bank has remodelled the building and extended it into a shop formerly occupied by Sainsbury's. In an easterly direction from Carfax, No. 5 is Georgian, occupied in the 19th century by GILL & CO., said to be Britain's oldest firm of ironmongers, established in 1530. The façades of Nos 6 and 7 were rebuilt in 1958 to resemble their 18th-century front. WEBBER'S department store (formerly the City Drapery Stores) occupied Nos 9–15 – a long ashlar-fronted building of thirteen bays. No. 9 was rebuilt in Georgian style in 1934 by G.T. Gardner, but Nos 13–16 were built in 1773–4 and are by John Gwynn. On the ground floor

are three entrances to the COVERED MARKET. On the corner of TURL STREET is one of Oxford's oldest inns, the MITRE; its High Street front is partly 1630 and partly 18th century, but its cellars date back to the 13th century.

On the opposite corner of Turl Street is the former ALL SAINTS CHURCH, now the library of Lincoln College, and beyond this is the High Street front of Brasenose College, built by T.G. JACKSON in 1887–1911. East of the entrance to RADCLIFFE SQUARE is the University Church of ST MARY THE VIRGIN and beyond that is the entrance to CATTE STREET, closed to traffic in 1973. All Souls College has a long front to High Street, ending with the Warden's lodging, built in 1704–6 by GEORGE CLARKE and refronted in 1826–7 by Daniel Robertson. To the east is the successor to the famous 18th-century sycamore; Thomas Sharp in his OXFORD REPLANNED described this tree as one of the most important in the world. No. 33 is a 17th-century building, refronted in the 18th century, next to a passage to Drawda Hall, a late 17th-century gabled and timber-framed house named after William of Drogheda, who held the property in the 13th century. No. 34 has an 18th-century front and Nos 35–6 are a timber-framed house of four storeys built before 1600 and refronted in the 18th century. Nos 37–8 are another 16th- or early 17th-century house with two gabled dormers. Beyond this elegant row of houses, all with shops on the ground floor, is The Queen's College, the front quad of which was described by Pevsner as 'the grandest piece of classical architecture in Oxford'.

East of QUEEN'S LANE, Nos 39–41 were completely rebuilt by The Queen's College in 1967–8 behind

Oxford High Street c.1900, with The Queen's College on the right and the famous sycamore tree at the east end of the Warden's lodging of All Souls College.

their early 18th-century stucco and timber-framed front. Nos 42–3 is another timber-framed building, this one dating from the 16th or 17th century. Nos 44–5 were occupied in the late 19th and early 20th centuries by the cabinetmaker Norman Edward Minty, founder of the firm of MINTY, furniture manufacturers, whose range of 'Varsity' furniture was later sold from these premises. The adjoining buildings were rebuilt by St Edmund Hall in 1968 in late 18th-century style. Designed by Marshall Sisson, they provide additional student accommodation, as does the adjoining four-storey building, built in 1975 by Gilbert Howes. No. 48 has an early 18th-century front with an engraved panel in the door indicating that William Morris (LORD NUFFIELD) ran his cycle and motor-cycle business from the premises from 1898 to 1910. Between this house and LONGWALL STREET there were two inns in the 19th century, the Coach and Horses at No. 49A and the Light Horseman at No. 52. The GREYHOUND inn was also on the corner of Longwall Street and High Street until demolished in 1845. Beyond Longwall are Magdalen College and MAGDALEN BRIDGE.

On the south side, and opposite Magdalen College, is the BOTANIC GARDEN, which lies between Magdalen Bridge and ROSE LANE. The houses facing Longwall are now occupied by the Oxford branch of STANFORD UNIVERSITY. A cartouche on the wall of the EASTGATE HOTEL (1899–1900, by E.P. Warren) shows the East Gate as it was before its demolition in 1772. Before the building of the Eastgate Hotel the Flying Horse Inn occupied this corner site on what was then called King Street. On the opposite corner of MERTON STREET are the EXAMINATION SCHOOLS. The RUSKIN SCHOOL OF DRAWING AND FINE ART is at No. 74. No. 84 was the building where COOPER'S 'OXFORD' MARMALADE was first made; the firm has now returned and made the building into a museum as well as a shop. Oxford's most important coaching inn, the ANGEL, was here in the 19th century (see also TRANSPORT). LOGIC LANE is a narrow pedestrian way between High Street and Merton Street belonging to University College, whose buildings front the south side of the street. A plaque on the wall records: 'In a house on this site between 1655 and 1668 lived ROBERT BOYLE. Here he discovered Boyle's Law and made experiments with an AIR PUMP designed by his assistant ROBERT HOOKE, Inventor, Scientist & Architect, who made a microscope and thereby first identified the LIVING CELL.' No. 90 was built in 1612 for John Williams, an apothecary, and contains some fine 17th-century woodwork and plaster ceilings. JOHN RUSKIN's mother lodged in this house while her son was an undergraduate at Christ Church between 1836 and 1840. It was later the offices of the *Oxford Guardian* and the *Oxford University Herald* (see NEWSPAPERS). Nos 92 and 93 were built in 1775 and are occupied by Barclays Old Bank (formerly Parsons, Thompson & Co.). Between MAGPIE LANE (formerly Grove Street) and ORIEL STREET are shops once occupied by Hall Bros and Adamson & Co., both old-established firms of tailors. Nos 102 and 103, timber-framed, were built in about 1714 by William Ives, a wealthy mercer. In the late 19th century the building was occupied by SPIERS & SON. SANDERS of Oxford, the antiquarian bookshop, is at No. 104, formerly the Salutation Inn. Beyond Oriel Street, TACKLEY'S INN was at Nos 106–7, subsequently occupied by James Pen, who described

himself as a chandler and died in 1642. The premises were occupied in the 19th century by BOFFIN'S, the bakers. On the west corner of KING EDWARD STREET are the premises of SHEPHERD AND WOODWARD, tailors, who also own WALTERS in TURL STREET. Next to them, No. 115 was occupied by ROWELL & SON, the firm of jewellers founded in 1797, and before that by Wyatt's, the picture dealers (see OXFORD UNION). The artist John Everett Millais, who married John Ruskin's former wife Effie, once lived here. The premises of the OXFORD UNIVERSITY PRESS are at No. 117. Hall Bros, tailors, occupy the timber-framed building at No. 119, which has a fine bow window. On the corner of ALFRED STREET, at No. 121, is the National Westminster Bank (formerly the London & County Banking Co. Ltd). The premises were built in 1866 in a Gothic style and also house the CLARENDON CLUB.

Between Alfred Street and the Wheatsheaf Yard is a row of shops, including Russell, Acott & Co. (No. 124), the music shop, and a mediaeval timber-framed house with a 17th-century façade and carved bargeboards occupied by the old-established firm of solicitors Thomas Mallam, (see also COLLEGE STAMPS). Thomas Mallam, who founded the firm of MALLAMS in ST MICHAEL'S STREET, practised from these premises from 1832 as both auctioneer and solicitor. Wheatsheaf Yard is a narrow pedestrian passage leading to BLUE BOAR STREET. Down the passage on the left is Gill & Co., opposite which is the Wheatsheaf Inn. Down another passage to the west is KEMP HALL, a timber-framed building of 1637, now occupied by LA SORBONNE Restaurant and formerly the Police Station. At No. 131 are PAYNE & SON, the jewellers, with the sign of a dog and a watch above the shop-front, and then the CHEQUERS inn, down another passage known as Chequers Yard. In the late 19th and early 20th centuries the Vine inn was at No. 133, later occupied by Will R. Rose, the photographers. At No. 137, in a mediaeval timber-framed building that used to be the Fox inn, Savory's has sold pipes, tobacco and cigarettes for over 100 years. The shop has an old balcony inside at first-floor level. From at least 1880 until 1928 the Post Boys' inn was at No. 139, close to Carfax.

Hinksey Park A park of about 11 acres which was laid out by the city in 1934 with an open-air swimming pool. It also contains a large lake used for windsurfing, and a boating pond.

Hinshelwood, Sir Cyril Norman (*1897–1967*). Won a Brackenbury Scholarship to Balliol in 1916; but, before going up in 1919, he worked at the Explosives Supply Factory at Queensferry. In 1920, having had three papers published by the Chemical Society while an undergraduate, he was elected to a research fellowship at Balliol and in 1921 to a fellowship at Trinity. It was in the cellars of the first of these colleges and in the out-houses of the second that much of his early research was done. His first important book, *Kinetics of Chemical Change in Gaseous Systems*, was published in 1926. A highly gifted tutor, a classical scholar, a writer of excellent English prose and a brilliant linguist as well as a great chemist, Hinshelwood was appointed Dr Lee's Professor of Chemistry in 1937 in succession to Frederick Soddy (1877–1956). Hinshelwood left Oxford in 1964 and went to live in the London flat which he had shared with his mother for sixty years.

Historians Few places, if any, have formed the subject of so many books as Oxford, although the great bulk refer to the University rather than to the city as a whole. The desire to prove that Oxford University was older than its rival, Cambridge, was the principal inspiration of its earliest historians, notably John Rous, a 15th-century Oxford scholar, who, as a chantry priest at Warwick, compiled his *Historia Regum Angliae*, which uncritically accepted and built upon current unfounded assertions about Oxford's origins. Rous and his Elizabethan successors constructed a mythical history attributing the town's foundation to a King Mempric in the time of the prophet Samuel and the University's origins to a school at Cricklade established by Greek philosophers accompanying the Trojan Brutus to Britain after the fall of Troy. Such absurdities, and slightly more plausible fabrications concerning the role of King Alfred in Oxford's early history, might be dismissed without comment had they not so tenaciously influenced the historiography of Oxford until modern times.

The first serious historical research on Oxford was carried out by BRIAN TWYNE, keeper of the University ARCHIVES in the early 17th century. Twyne, too, was largely motivated by the desire to prove the greater antiquity of his own University and to document, and if possible to inflate, the privileges of the University at the expense of those of the city. Although his published history, *Antiquitatis Academiae Oxoniensis Apologia* (1608), uncritically recounted the old myths, Twyne's great contribution lay in his manuscript collections from original sources, which, though poorly acknowledged, clearly formed the basis of the works of his illustrious successor, ANTHONY WOOD. Wood's achievement dominates the historiography of both city and University, although satisfactory publication of his minute and careful researches was long delayed. A mutilated Latin translation of his history of the University, *Historia et Antiquitates Universitatis Oxoniensis*, was published in 1674, but it was not until 1792–6 that a worthy edition appeared in English, edited by John Gutch, who in 1786 had separately published Wood's *History and Antiquities of the Colleges and Halls of Oxford* and *Fasti*. Wood's work on the city suffered execrable treatment in an edition by Sir John Peshall, *Ancient and Present State of the City of Oxford* (1773), but was superbly edited as *Wood's City of Oxford* by Andrew Clark (Oxford Historical Society, 1889–99). Wood's biographical studies, the *Athenae Oxonienses*, though published in part in 1691–2, were not reproduced satisfactorily until an edition by Philip Bliss in 1813–20.

Apart from regurgitating Wood's work, 18th-century historians of Oxford achieved little, but early 19th-century works such as R. ACKERMANN's *History of the University of Oxford* (1814), J. Skelton's *Oxonia Antiqua Restaurata* (1823), and JAMES INGRAM's three-volume *Memorials of Oxford* (1832–7) made original contributions to the study of Oxford's topography. Greater progress was made in the later 19th century with the coming together of writers such as J.R. Green, James Parker and Andrew Clark, culminating in the foundation of the Oxford Historical Society in 1884. During the next century the society provided distinguished editions of most of the major sources for the history of Oxford, as well as notable monographs such as James Parker's *Early History of Oxford* (1885), Herbert Hurst's *Oxford Topography* (1899), H.E. SALTER's *Medieval Oxford* (1936) and Salter's monumental *Survey of Oxford* (1960, 1969), edited by W.A. Pantin. Of the many luminaries of the Oxford Historical Society, Salter was pre-eminent; altogether he was involved in as many as thirty-five volumes in that series. Important source material published elsewhere included W.H. Turner's *Records of the City of Oxford* (1880), O. Ogle's *Royal Letters Addressed to Oxford* (1892), J. Griffiths's *Laudian Statutes* (1888) and Strickland Gibson's *Statuta Antiqua* (1931). The eight flawed but important volumes of J. Foster's *Alumni* (1887, 1891) were brilliantly supplanted for the period before 1540 by A.B. Emden's four-volume *Biographical Register of the University* (1957–9, 1974).

From the 1880s there was a flood of general histories, among which may be noted Sir H.C. Maxwell Lyte's *History of the University* (1886), the first critical account of its development; C.W. Boase's readable *Oxford* (1887); Hastings Rashdall's *Universities of Europe in the Middle Ages* (1895), splendidly re-edited by F.M. Powicke and A.B. Emden in 1936; and C.E. Mallet's *History of the University of Oxford* (1924–7). Numerous individual college histories, of uneven quality, were published – notably the series commissioned by Robinson from 1898. Accounts of all the colleges were brought together in *Victoria History of Oxfordshire*, Vol. III (1954), and the full history of the city was critically re-examined for the first time since Wood in Vol. IV of that series (1979). An authoritative study of Oxford's buildings to 1714 was published by the Royal Commission on Historical Monuments in 1939; Pevsner's descriptions of buildings were included in the volume on Oxfordshire (1974) in his *Buildings of England* series; and other major contributions to the study of the city's architecture and topography, notably by W.A. Pantin, were published in OXONIENSIA from its inception in 1936. Two popular histories deserve mention: Ruth Fasnacht's *City of Oxford* (1954) and V.H.H. Green's *Oxford University* (1974). In progress is a large-scale history of the University, of which Vol. I, *Early Oxford Schools* (ed. J.I. Catto), was published in 1984, and Vols III and V, *The Collegiate University* (ed. James McConica) and *The Eighteenth Century* (ed. L.S. Sutherland and L.G. Mitchell), in 1986.

(Cordeaux, E.H., and Merry, D.H., *Bibliography of the University of Oxford*, Oxford, 1968; Oxford Historical Society, *Bibliography of the City of Oxford* (by the same author), Oxford, 1976.)

Hollow Way Recorded as early as 1220 as Holweye, this may have been the 12th-century Wodewye. It was a road or driftway on the level of the surrounding ground, not raised as a causeway. It was originally on the outskirts of SHOTOVER ROYAL FOREST and was used for bringing timber from the forest to Oxford as well as for cattle. The Cowley Award map of 1853 shows some of Hollow Way as HEADINGTON ROAD. Surman's Lane, a continuation of Hollow Way, led to a southerly extension of Hockmore Street. Between Towns Road did not exist until 1853. Today's busy street connects Oxford Road, COWLEY, with the SLADE, and leads to HEADINGTON.

Hollybush Inn *106 Bridge Street, Osney*. The ROYAL OXFORD HOTEL in PARK END STREET stands on the site of the old Hollybush Inn, which was originally a guardhouse (mentioned in 1539) and became the Hollybush in the early 17th century. During the CIVIL WAR it was used as a royalist guardhouse and many songs were composed here, including 'At the Hollybush Guard'. The inn was rebuilt in 1771 as a coaching house for the Cheltenham to Bath run (*see* TRANSPORT). When the RAILWAY came to Oxford, the Railway Hotel was erected in 1851 on the site of the inn. The Hollybush was rebuilt on its present site in OSNEY in 1853. Called the Bush and Railway Inn from 1853–96 it was renamed the Hollybush in 1897 and reconstructed in about 1935.

Hollybush Row   Known as King's Stocke in the 16th century, it took its present name from the famous inn, which was a guardhouse in the CIVIL WAR (*see* HOLLYBUSH INN). THOMAS HEARNE (1726) refers to 'one of the ditches of the Holly Bush at the higher end of Botley Causey'. One of the songs sung by the guard in 1646 is quoted in Squires's *West Oxford*:

> Now no more will we harke
> To the Charms of the Larke
> Or the tunes of the early thrush.
> All the woods shall retire
> And submit to the Quire
> Of the Birds in the Holy Bush.

The birds were not, of course, of the winged variety. The inn (on the north-west corner of PARK END STREET) was the headquarters of the coaches going to and coming from Cheltenham and Bath, and the distances on the milestones west of Oxford start from Hollybush Row and not from CARFAX. The row itself is now only a short stretch from OXPENS ROAD, ending at the traffic lights at the junction of Park End Street and REWLEY ROAD.

Holmes, Sherlock   The great detective, so he told Dr Watson, was bitten on his ankle one morning as he was on his way to his college chapel. Since the recording of that episode, numerous suggestions have been made about which college Holmes attended. T.S. Blakeney, in his *Sherlock Holmes: Fact or Fiction*, went as far as asserting that the detective was not at Oxford at all, but at Cambridge. Dorothy L. Sayers thought so too ('Holmes's College Career' in *Unpopular Opinions*, 1946); so also did Bernard Darwin ('Sherlockiana: The Faith of a Fundamentalist', in *Every Idle Dream*, 1948), who suggested that Holmes was at Magdalen College rather than at Sidney Sussex, as Miss Sayers proposed. But Sir Sidney Roberts, Master of Pembroke College, Cambridge, and President of the Sherlock Holmes Society, deduced in his *Holmes and Watson: A Miscellany* (1953) that Holmes was at Oxford. This was also the opinion of Gavin Brend, who, two years earlier, had set forth his argument in *My Dear Holmes*, as well as of RONALD KNOX, who, in his 'Studies in the Literature of Sherlock Holmes' (*Essays in Satire*, 1928), had not only come down on the side of Oxford but had 'inclined more and more to the opinion that [Holmes] was up at the House [Christ Church]'. The most recent authority on the subject, Nicholas Utechin, has also decided that Holmes was at Oxford, but that he went up as a scholar from Merchant Taylors' School to St John's College in 1869 (*Sherlock Holmes at Oxford*, 1977).

Holy Family, Church of the   *Blackbird Leys Road*. In 1965 a conventional district taken from LITTLEMORE parish was formed for the new BLACKBIRD LEYS housing development and the church was built to serve both Anglicans and Nonconformists (*see* DISSENTERS). In 1973 the district was designated an area of ecumenical experiment, a Church of England minister and a Free Church minister sharing responsibility. The unconventional single-storey church, designed by Colin Shewring, is heart-shaped with a paraboloid roof and curved walls. Constructed of concrete, white brick and engineering brick, its exterior is drab. The oval interior, lit by a narrow band of windows, is simple, with timber-boarded hanging roofs, exposed brickwork, sloped semi-circular seating, and stone font, lectern and circular altar table. Two striking abstract panels of the Apocalypse and of Ezekiel, painted in vivid colours by Kathleen Dodd (1898–1987), contrast emphatically with the unrelieved plainness of the interior.

Holy Rood Church   *Abingdon Road*. Derives its name from the gift by Eric Gill's daughter of a carved stone rood made by her father. The pyramid roof, covering the lantern, can be glimpsed on the right-hand side of the ABINGDON ROAD approaching FOLLY BRIDGE. The need for a church in this area of the HINKSEY parish arose from the number of ROMAN CATHOLIC evacuees who elected to remain in south Oxford after the Second World War. With this in mind, in 1956 Reginald Schomberg – a commoner of New College, a former lieutenant-colonel in the Seaforth Highlanders, an explorer, diplomat and priest – asked Father John Crozier to find a site on which to build. In 1959 an orchard site was purchased from Brasenose College, and the architect Gilbert Flavel was engaged. Built of honey-coloured bricks, the design is hexagonal, rising from a rectangular base and terminating in a four-sided glass lantern. The entrance lobby is dominated by a granite baptismal font. The inscription that encircles it is the work of Kevin Cribb, and so too is the lettering on the high altar. The bronze Pantokrator behind the altar, the corona and the tabernacle, together with the bronze relief of the Madonna and Child, are all the work of Michael Murray. The stained glass is by Charles Ware. The church, which seats 300, was opened in 1961 by Archbishop King.

Holy Rosary   *Yarnell's Hill*. An unknown benefactor gave £200 for the site, and the parishioners started to build the church in 1953. They finished it in 1954, the Marian Year – hence the dedication to Our Lady of the Holy Rosary.

Holy Trinity   *Blackfriars Road*. Built in Early English style to the designs of H.J. Underwood, the church was opened in 1845 to serve a district taken from the southern part of ST EBBE'S parish. Its patrons were alternately the Crown and the BISHOP OF OXFORD until the advowson was bought in 1881 by E.P. Hathaway and vested in the OXFORD CHURCHES TRUST. In 1851 its Sunday congregations numbered some 400 in the morning and 350 in the afternoon, but the eroding effects of the First World War, a declining population, and slum clearance led to the closing of the church in 1954 and its demolition in 1957.

Holy Trinity *Headington Quarry*. Designed by GEORGE GILBERT SCOTT in 15th-century Decorated style and built of Headington stone (*see* STONE), the church consists of a chancel, nave and aisle. The foundation stone was laid in 1848 by the BISHOP OF OXFORD, SAMUEL WILBERFORCE, who consecrated the building in 1849. The present east-window glass, designed by Ninian Comper, depicting Christ in Glory and with the arms of LORD NUFFIELD and the diocese of Oxford, was installed in 1951 as a memorial to those in the parish who fell in the Second World War; the previous glass (*c.*1870) is preserved at the west end of the aisle. The organ by Martin and Coate of Oxford was installed in the old vestry in 1911. Apart from minor repairs, commemorative stained glass and furnishings, and the addition of a new vestry built on to the north-east-corner of the church in 1970, there have been few changes since the church's consecration. The scholar and Christian apologist C.S. LEWIS (1898–1963) was a parishioner from 1930 until his death, and is buried with his brother in one grave in the churchyard. The idea of *The Screwtape Letters* came to him after Holy Communion on 23 July 1940 and he preached in the church on several occasions in succeeding years. Number XII of *Letters to Malcolm* refers to a conversation regarding prayer which he had with the former vicar Canon Ronald Head. A memorial window to the Howe family designed by Sally Scott and based on the Narnia stories was dedicated on 2 July 1991. The parsonage, also in Headington stone, was designed in 1867 by Sir Arthur Blomfield, and the school (1863) by James Brooks, enlarged in 1882 by Frederick Codd.

Holywell Manor, next to St Cross Church, has been in existence since at least the 13th century. It is now an annexe of Balliol College.

Holywell Manor Stands at the junction of MANOR ROAD and ST CROSS ROAD. In the 11th and 12th centuries the manor was held by the rectors of ST PETER-IN-THE-EAST, until it passed to Merton College in 1294. From the early 13th century Merton leased it to tenants, including two Oxford butchers. The manor house, which had been in existence since at least the 13th century, was rebuilt by Merton in 1516. The college leased it in 1531 to Edward Napper. It was during the occupation of the house by his family that it became a refuge for Roman Catholic priests (*see* ROMAN CATH-OLICS). Three members of the Napper family were priests themselves. The family continued to occupy the house, which was enlarged in 1555–72, until the second

half of the 17th century. Thereafter it was occupied intermittently by the bailiffs of the manor. Part of it was demolished in 1761 and the rest was divided into three in 1828. There is a drawing of it in 1820 by J.C. BUCKLER. In 1930 Balliol College took over the tenancy. Little of the early 16th-century house, as rebuilt by Merton, remains, apart from some windows and gables and a buttressed projection facing ST CROSS CHURCH. A quad, designed by Kennedy and Nightingale, was added in 1938 and has a fountain by Peter Lyon. In one of the rooms in the house are wall-paintings by Gilbert Spencer depicting episodes in the life of John of Balliol.

The Holywell Music Room, believed to be the oldest extant concert hall in the world, was opened in 1748.

Holywell Music Room Reputedly the oldest extant concert hall in the world. A subscription for its construction was set up at the beginning of 1742, probably largely at the instigation of the newly elected Professor of Music, William Hayes. The design was by Thomas Camplin, Vice-Principal of St Edmund Hall, and the building measured 65 by 32 feet and was 30 feet high. Completion, however, was delayed owing to lack of finance, and it was not opened until 1748. Its chief function was to house a regular series of choral and instrumental concerts organised by the Musical Society, whose performances had hitherto been given at the King's Head Tavern and in college halls. Local and London professional musicians were engaged, and the concerts continued until 1838, with only a brief interruption between 1789 and 1793. Thereafter the room underwent considerable internal rearrangement and was used for a wide variety of purposes, including lectures, concerts and even auctions, until the lease was acquired by the Oxford University Musical Union in 1901, after which it reverted to purely musical use. It is now administered partly by the Faculty of Music and partly by Wadham College (on whose land it is built), and is heavily used for small-scale musical events. It accommodates up to about 250 people and has excellent acoustics for solo recitals and chamber concerts. The interior was restored to its 18th-century plan in 1959–60, new Green Room facilities were added in 1982–3, and a new chamber organ installed in 1985 (*see* ORGANS; *see also* MUSIC).

Holywell Press Founded at the turn of the century by Harry Burrows and Thomas Doe. The office occupied an old chapel in CATTE STREET until 1921 when it moved to ALFRED STREET. It was then engaged in general printing for the University and commercial work for William Morris (*see* LORD NUFFIELD) in the early days of his bicycle and motor-car manufacture. In 1892 Harry Burrows started University Newspapers, which produced the undergraduate magazine ISIS. Walter Burrows, better known as 'Buzz', the famous *Daily Sketch* cartoonist, took over the firm on the death of his father in 1940. The business, adopting new technology, continues in its traditional role of general printing. In 1989 the company moved from Alfred Street to new premises at Kings Meadow, Ferry Hinksey Road. It has been managed by Peter Burrows since 1969.

Holywell Street A street of charming 17th- and 18th-century houses between BROAD STREET and LONGWALL STREET. It was part of HOLYWELL MANOR, owned by Merton College since the 13th century. House-building started in the 16th century and the street was largely complete by 1675. Through-traffic was excluded in 1975, and there is now a gate across the eastern end. No. 1 was refronted in the late 18th century. No. 2 is an early 17th-century timber-framed house with projecting bays and oriel windows on decorated brackets. No. 3 is also early 17th century, an ashlar stone house with a hood over the door on carved brackets. No. 6 is a remodelled 17th-century house with three dormers. No. 13 has tall gabled dormers with mullioned windows on the upper floors. No. 17 was formerly the King's Head and is a timber-framed house, partly 16th century. Nos 21–3 and adjoining property were demolished for the construction of MANSFIELD ROAD in about 1894. Between Mansfield Road and Broad Street is the HOLYWELL MUSIC ROOM, built in 1742–8 and the earliest of its kind in Europe. No. 35 is a two-storeyed house with three dormers; it is dated 1626 on the brackets to the oriel windows in the timber-framed first floor. No. 36 is a refronted

17th-century property which was the offices and yard of KNOWLES & SON until 1951. BLACKWELL's Music Shop at No. 38 was designed in 1970 by Gillespie, Kidd & Coia to fit into the street scene. It is on the site of the KING's ARMS garage, the hotel itself being on the corner with PARKS ROAD.

On the opposite corner is the former INDIAN INSTITUTE, built in 1883–96 on the site of Seal's COFFEE HOUSE. Hertford's Third or Holywell Quad was created in 1975–81 by infilling and restoration of Nos 51–5. Beyond Bath Place, a house on the site of No. 58 was the home of J.C. BUCKLER. Further along the street are New College's Holywell Buildings, designed by GEORGE GILBERT SCOTT and Basil Champneys and built in 1872–96. Behind them is the best-preserved section of the CITY WALL.

Horse and Jockey *69 Woodstock Road.* Named after stewards responsible for horse-race meetings (1630–1880) on PORT MEADOW, who made their headquarters at the inn. The Horse and Jockey was built about 1750, pulled down in 1880 and rebuilt the same year to the designs of H.G. Drinkwater. The inn was extensively reconstructed in 1968.

Hospital of St John the Baptist In existence by 1180, it was enlarged at the end of the 12th century and moved by royal decree to the old Jew's cemetery near the East Bridge (*see* MAGDALEN BRIDGE) in 1231. Considerable building, including an infirmary, a hall for women and children, and a kitchen and sleeping quarters for the staff, took place between 1232 and 1257. Both priests and sisters of the hospital tended the sick. The hospital owned much property in Oxford and had a large income. In 1456 it was granted to William of Waynflete and its buildings were either demolished or converted for use by Magdalen College.

Steel engraving after a drawing of c.1834 by Peter de Wint of Hythe Bridge (overleaf), a landing place for wood, stone and slate, with the tower of the Castle in the distance.

Humfrey, Duke of Gloucester (*1391–1447*). Educated at Balliol, he later joined his brother Henry V on the French campaigns of the Hundred Years' War, fighting at Agincourt and at the siege of Rouen. He was a great reader and bibliophile, and a generous benefactor to the University library, to which as early as 1411 he started to donate books. He gave no less than 129 volumes in 1439 and contributed to the building of the new library above the DIVINITY SCHOOL, the central part of which is named Duke Humfrey's Library in acknowledgement of his liberality. (*See also* BODLEIAN LIBRARY.)

Hyde *see* CLARENDON, EARL OF.

Hythe Bridge Also formerly known as High Bridge, it takes the road from the RAILWAY and HYTHE BRIDGE STREET into WORCESTER STREET. The first, presumably wooden, bridge was built by OSENEY ABBEY in 1200–10. It was reconstructed in stone in 1383. The present iron bridge was built to the designs of an Oxford engineer, John Galpin, in 1861. By the 16th century the city owned a wharf (hithe – hence the bridge's name) here; this was known as Timber Wharf in 1861. As well as wood, Cotswold stone, hay and slate were unloaded here. (*See also* BRIDGES.)

Hythe Bridge Street Takes its name from the hithe (or wharf) which lay beside the old bridge. *Hithe* is a Saxon word meaning a landing place where barges and other vessels unloaded their wares (as in Rotherhithe and Maidenhithe (now Maidenhead)). There has been a road and bridge here at least since 1233. In the time of Edward I (1285) it was recorded as Brugge de la Hythe; in 1286 as Pontis de Hythe; and in 1262 as Hide Brigge. By the 15th century it was known as Hithe Brigge and at one time as Rewley Lane, the water at Rewley Gate running into a stream under the bridge. The road from Oxford to Witney formerly passed over this bridge and continued by a causeway to BOTLEY. The bridge was rebuilt of stone with three arches in 1383. The present bridge was erected in 1861. The Anabaptists publicly baptised at High Bridge, as it was sometimes called; ANTHONY WOOD observed a baptism there in 1659.

Present premises in the street include BLACKWELL'S, whose headquarters, Beaver House, is a large, glass-curtained block at the station end of the street. Today the bridge connects the WORCESTER STREET car park (on land owned by Nuffield College) and part of the Oxford CANAL at the start of its journey north to WOLVERCOTE and Banbury. The street also straddles the upper and lower parts of FISHER ROW.

Ian Ramsey Centre Established in 1985 at ST CROSS COLLEGE for the study of ethical problems arising from scientific and medical research and practice, and of the underlying philosophical and theological issues. It was named after Professor Ian Ramsey, a former Professor of the Philosophy of Christian Religion in Oxford, and later Bishop of Durham. He died in 1972, but it was a sermon which he had preached in ST MARY THE VIRGIN in June 1964 which eventually led to the formation of the centre. It was funded initially by grants from the Rhodes Trust (*see* RHODES HOUSE) and other sources.

Ice Rink Skating has always been a popular pastime in Oxford, in hard winters in the past sometimes on the frozen River Cherwell (*see* THAMES) or even on the Thames itself, but more often on the flooded parts of meadows such as PORT MEADOW. In the winter of 1763, for example, there was a race on skates along the frozen Thames between IFFLEY and Sandford. In the latter half of the 19th century there was a skating rink behind some racquet courts where the LAW LIBRARY now stands; it is shown on the first edition of the Ordnance Survey Map (1878) and on a map of Oxford drawn in 1883 by W.H. White, who was later to become the first city engineer (*see* MAPS). A new indoor ice rink was opened in 1930 in a building

in BOTLEY ROAD, but its high running costs, coupled with its inadequate seating for spectators and its falling attendances, forced it to close after it had been open for less than four years. The building became a cinema and subsequently the home of COOPER's 'OXFORD' MARMALADE. In 1980 Mary Meagher and her supporters founded the Oxford Ice Skating Trust (OXIST). The trust raised a great deal of money for a new rink in Oxford, and eventually the City Council took over the project. The new rink in the OXPENS ROAD was designed by Nicholas Grimshaw & Partners and was opened in 1984. Its two masts, each 97 feet high, gave rise to the building's being nicknamed 'the Cutty Sark'. The rink is owned and managed by the City Council.

Iffley Stands on a promontory above the THAMES (known at this point as the Isis) some 2 miles to the south-east of the city centre. Evidence of early occupation has been found: a Bronze Age urn, a Romano-British sandstone quern and a Saxon spearhead, all recovered from the the river, are now in the ASHMOLEAN MUSEUM. The manor is recorded in Domesday Book as 'Givetelei'. In mediaeval times numerous different spellings were used, beginning variously with I, Y, E, G, H or Z. The origin of the name is uncertain: 'plovers' clearing' is one suggestion;

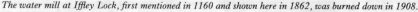

The water mill at Iffley Lock, first mentioned in 1160 and shown here in 1862, was burned down in 1908.

'field of gifts' another. In 1393 the manor of Iffley passed to the Hospital of Donnington, near Newbury in Berkshire, through an endowment from Sir Richard Abberbury, who is commemorated in the modern Abberbury Road and Abberbury Avenue (1937). The Donnington Trust is still the largest landowner in the village. Among other landlords, Lincoln College has been the most important. Until the 1880s the parish embraced parts of COWLEY and LITTLEMORE, and its boundary ran down the west side of IFFLEY ROAD as far as THE PLAIN.

Today Iffley is a small village within the city, beleaguered by suburbia. Encroachment by the city began towards the end of the 18th century and the pace of urbanisation has quickened dramatically since 1971, when the census recorded a village population of still only 425. In 1969 a substantial part of Iffley was designated a CONSERVATION AREA, but the temptation to alleviate Oxford's chronic housing shortage at the expense of Iffley's open spaces has proved too great to resist. Since 1946 the village has been hemmed in to the south and east by the erection of the large council-housing estate of ROSE HILL within the parish boundary. In 1974 a Local Plan by the Council proposed the building of 232 new dwelling houses in the neighbourhood of the village itself. By 1977 new estates and in-filling with modern brick buildings among the old stone houses led to this being described as 'the hardest hit of all Oxford's Conservation Areas'.

The heart of the village has been allowed to retain some of its rural charm. The main road between Oxford and Henley, which once meandered through Iffley, now bypasses it along Henley Avenue and Rose Hill – modern extensions of Iffley Road, which still ends at Iffley Turn. In an attempt to preserve the peace and character of the village, other roads have been blocked and the Turn has become the only means of entrance or exit for motorists. As well as no through-traffic, there is no bus service and only a single shop.

From the Turn, a mediaeval lane, Church Way, runs for half a mile to a giant chestnut tree in a corner of the churchyard. One of the yew trees nearby is said to be a thousand years old, and parts of the mainly 15th-century Old Rectory (recently rescued from dereliction and now divided between the Rectory and Old Parsonage House) date from as early as the 12th century. Mill Lane leads down to the river and past the Iffley Lock, site of a water mill first mentioned in 1160 and burned to the ground in 1908. Two surviving grindstones stand outside Grist Cottage, formerly the toll-house. Upstream is Donnington Bridge (*see* BRIDGES), downstream another modern bridge carrying traffic on the southern bypass; but Iffley Lock, secluded among chestnuts and willows, is still an island of tranquillity unbroken except by passing pleasure cruisers and the clamour of racing in EIGHTS WEEK. The first lock was built in 1632 and rebuilt in 1774; the present one dates from 1924. Before tolls were abolished, it was forbidden to carry dead bodies over the lock because it was believed that this would create a right of way. For this reason funerals on their way to the church from the opposite bank came by boat. As late as 1948 the toll-keeper refused permission for police to pass over the toll-bridge with the body of a drowned man.

As well as the lovely romanesque parish church (*see* ST MARY THE VIRGIN, IFFLEY), the village contains some picturesque stone houses and cottages. Among the most notable are Court Place, The Manor House, Malt House (now Malthouse Cottages), Rivermead, Hawkwell, The Priory, Tudor Cottage, Mrs Sarah Nowell's School and the thatched schoolhouse (now the church hall). Court Place, now a centre of graduate accommodation, was visited in 1784 by DR JOHNSON and Boswell (who duly toasted 'Church and King' after a good dinner) and later inhabited, successively, by the egyptologist Sir Alan Gardiner and the writer Logan Pearsall Smith. In 1940 Richard Addinsell composed the theme of the *Warsaw Concerto* there. Grove House at the Turn was the home of CARDINAL NEWMAN's mother and, more recently, of the novelist Graham Greene. Denton House was once used as a preparatory school, or 'gentlemen's academy', attended by another novelist, Charles Reade. The Tree Hotel, formerly the Tree Inn, commemorates a famous elm tree which stood here for 350 years before succumbing to Dutch elm disease and old age; it was replaced in 1974 by an oak tree. Across the road stood the village stocks, removed and burned on a bonfire at CARFAX to celebrate the fall of Sebastopol. Tree Lane, which runs uphill from the hotel, was a mediaeval sheep run.

Iffley Road The old road to London via Henley. It runs from THE PLAIN to the turn to IFFLEY village at ROSE HILL. On the east side are terraced houses in various architectural styles, together with the church of ST JOHN THE EVANGELIST and ST STEPHEN'S HOUSE (in Marston Street, off the Iffley Road). On the west, close to The Plain, is MAGDALEN COLLEGE SCHOOL, and, further along, Christ Church sports ground, the University Sports Centre with the Iffley Road running track (where in 1954 Roger Bannister ran the

Roger Bannister, who was appointed Master of Pembroke College in 1985, broke all records to become the first man to run a mile in under 4 minutes at the Iffley Road running track on 6 May 1954.

first mile in under 4 minutes) and the UNIVERSITY RUGBY FOOTBALL CLUB ground. Beyond Jackdaw Lane is GREYFRIARS. Donnington Bridge Road connects Iffley Road to Donnington Bridge (*see* BRIDGES) across the THAMES. The ST CLEMENT'S and Iffley Road CONSERVATION AREA was designated in 1977.

Inception   The technical term which describes the prelude to the taking of the degree of Master of Arts. Candidates for the Master's degree were known as inceptors. The last survival of inception was the list of masters headed '*Nomina incipientium . . . secundum ordinem in quo admissi fuerint ad incipiendum disposita*', which continued to be issued until 1913. Inception required participation in certain disputations, described respectively as *in vesperiis* and *in comitiis*, which formed an essential ingredient in the academic exercises which took place at the time of the Act. At the end of such disputations the inceptor became a Master and was licensed to incept in the Faculty of Arts – that is to say, to lecture and to take part in disputations in the University.

Indian Institute   Built of Milton stone (*see* STONE) on the corner of BROAD STREET and HOLYWELL STREET in 1883–5 in 18th-century English Palladian style to the designs of Basil Champneys. It was extended in 1894–6. Among the details which mark its original use are Hindu demi-gods and heads of tigers and of an elephant on the exterior, and a charming golden elephant weathervane. The Institute was founded following a proposal by Sir Monier Monier-Williams, Boden Professor of Sanskrit, in 1875 and built with funds privately collected in India and Britain. His purpose was to provide a meeting place at which Europeans could learn about India, while the West could be studied by Indians. Until 1939 it provided premises for courses for Indian Civil Service probationers at the University. In addition to a library and lecture rooms, it contained a museum, many of whose objects are now in the ASHMOLEAN. In 1968, after a celebrated Oxford controversy in which the University authorities were accused of betraying the donors, the building was appropriated for University offices. The library, based on the collection of Monier-Williams and the Rev. S.C. Malan, was then moved into a specially constructed penthouse on top of the NEW BODLEIAN and is the most extensive open-shelf library on India in Europe. The old Indian Institute now houses the History Faculty library.

Ingram, James   (*1774–1850*). Elected a Fellow of Trinity College in 1803, he was appointed Rawlinson Professor of Anglo-Saxon that same year, Keeper of the University ARCHIVES in 1815, and President of Trinity in 1824. He was, however, more interested in antiquarian research than in the affairs of the college. His celebrated *Memorials of Oxford* was published in three volumes in 1832–7 with a hundred plates by Le Keux (*see also* HISTORIANS).

Inklings, The   A group of friends, centred on C.S. LEWIS, who met from the 1930s to the 1960s to talk and to read aloud their compositions. The members included J.R.R. TOLKIEN; Charles Williams (1886–1945), poet, novelist, theological writer and for many years employed by the OXFORD UNIVERSITY PRESS; NEVILL COGHILL; and H.V.D. Dyson (1896–1975),

W.W. Oless's portrait of Sir Monier Monier-Williams, Boden Professor of Sanskrit, who helped found the Indian Institute in 1875.

Fellow of Merton College. Meetings were frequently held at the EAGLE AND CHILD.

Institutions   Most institutions of the University have separate entries: *see*, for instance, ARCHIVES, ASHMOLEAN MUSEUM, BODLEIAN LIBRARY, BOTANIC GARDEN, MUSEUM OF THE HISTORY OF SCIENCE, OXFORD UNIVERSITY PRESS, SIR WILLIAM DUNN SCHOOL OF PATHOLOGY, UNIVERSITY MUSEUM, PITT RIVERS MUSEUM, SHELDONIAN THEATRE, TAYLOR INSTITUTION and PLAYHOUSE (Oxford University Theatre). Others, such as the Institute of Commonwealth Studies, the School of Geography, and the Departments of the History of Art and of Earth Sciences, are mentioned in the entries on the relevant FACULTIES. Yet others will be found under LABORATORIES or LIBRARIES. Those not mentioned separately are:

The Computing Service, 13 Banbury Road, established in 1978.

The Computing Teaching Centre, 59 George Street, established in 1983.

The Counselling Service, established in 1972 to help members of the University suffering emotional stress.

The Centre for Criminological Research, 12 Bevington Road, established in 1966, as the Penal Research Unit, with a grant from the Nuffield Foundation.

The Department of Educational Studies, 15 Norham Gardens.

The Department of Forestry, South Parks Road, established in 1905 as the University School of Forestry.

The Wellcome Unit for the History of Medicine, 45–7 Banbury Road, established in 1972 (*see* MEDICINE).

The Nissan Institute of Japanese Studies, 1 Church Walk, established in 1981 with a grant from the Nissan Motor Co. Ltd.

The Language Teaching Centre, 41 Wellington Square.

The Latin American Centre, 21 Winchester Road.

The Social Studies Faculty Centre, George Street.

The Department of Surveying and Geodesy, 62 Banbury Road, established in 1938.

The Transport Studies Unit, 11 Bevington Road, established in 1972.

Voltaire Foundation, Taylor Institution, St Giles', founded by Dr Theodore Besterman and bequeathed by him to the University for the use of the Taylor Institution in 1976.

The Oxford Institute for Energy Studies, 29 New Inn Hall Street, founded in 1982.

The Oxford Centre for Postgraduate Hebrew Studies, 45 St Giles', established in 1972.

The Centre for Socio-Legal Studies, Wolfson College, founded in 1972.

(The names of the heads of all institutions and departments, and of their research, teaching and administrative staffs will be found in the *University Calendar* published annually by the Oxford University Press.)

Isis University magazine founded on 27 April 1892 by Mostyn Turtle Piggott and published by HOLY-WELL PRESS. 'We have no politics and fewer principles,' the first editorial declared, 'and should we last until the General Election we shall use our influence for neither side. We shall endeavour to be humorous without being ill-humoured, critical without being captious, militant without being malevolent, independent without being impertinent, and funny (as Mr Albert Chevalier says) without being vulgar.'

The contents, contained in eight pages and issued once a week, were a medley of reports of UNION debates, of sporting events and of theatrical productions, accompanied by jokes and facetious verse. The price was 3*d*, increased in 1893 to 6*d*. In that year there appeared the first of what was to become a regular feature in the magazine: a portrait of a celebrated University figure under the title '*Isis* Idol'. Often in the early days the 'Idol' was a sportsman; then, more usually, a leading personality in the Union, the OUDS or some other undergraduate society. The first of these 'Idols' was the captain of the Rugby XV; subsequent 'Idols' were C.B. FRY, T.E. Lawrence, NEVILL COGHILL, LORD DAVID CECIL and Quintin Hogg. When Lady Longford (Elizabeth Harman, of Lady Margaret Hall) was an 'Idol' in 1930 it was said to be 'almost without precedent' for a woman to be chosen. The early flattering portraits, written by friends of the subjects, later gave way to satirical sketches.

Contributors to the magazine before the First World War included MAX BEERBOHM, Hilaire Belloc (Balliol), John Buchan (Brasenose), A.P. Herbert (New College) and Compton Mackenzie (Magdalen). After its closure in the war, *Isis* was resuscitated in 1919 with Beverley Nichols (Balliol) as editor. Soon afterwards it incorporated a rival magazine, the *Varsity*. Among its contributors in the 1920s were Harold Acton (Christ Church), Claud Cockburn (Keble), Philip Magnus (Wadham), JOHN BETJEMAN (Magdalen), Cecil Day-Lewis (Wadham), Osbert

Lancaster (Lincoln) and Graham Greene (Balliol), then editor of the literary magazine *Oxford Outlook*. At this time its tone tended to be Conservative, even reactionary. Its entire male staff left in the General Strike of 1926 to do what they termed 'National Service'. Evelyn Waugh (Hertford) wrote notes on Union debates for the magazine, while also writing for the CHERWELL, then a more aesthetic publication. Waugh's Sebastian Flyte in *Brideshead Revisited* speaks contemptuously of *Isis*.

Its contents occasionally got the magazine into trouble with University authorities: after an attack on the state of women's colleges by Dilys Powell (Somerville), the deputy editor, Gerald Gardiner (Magdalen), later Lord Chancellor, was sent down, having taken his degree. Jo Grimond (Balliol), later Lord Grimond, who was called to the Bar some ten years later, was editor for a term.

As in the First World War, the magazine was not published during the Second; it reappeared in November 1945. In the later 1940s and early 1950s Kenneth Tynan (Magdalen), Lindsay Anderson (Wadham), Ludovic Kennedy (Christ Church), William Rees-Mogg (Balliol), Alan Brien (Jesus), Shirley Williams (Somerville), Elizabeth Jennings (St Anne's), Ned Sherrin (Exeter), Robert Robinson (Exeter), Christopher Ricks (Balliol), Godfrey Smith (Worcester), Anthony Howard (Christ Church) and James Leasor (Oriel) were among its contributors.

In the late 1950s the magazine became more overtly political; and after the appearance of an article in an anti-nuclear issue in 1958 its two undergraduate writers were sentenced to terms of imprisonment. The editor at the time, Dennis Potter (New College), the future playwright, was removed at the instigation of Holywell Press, which apologised for the magazine's recent display of 'bad manners' and its having become 'definitely left wing'. It remained so under Potter's immediate successors, until in 1960 Holywell Press refused to recognise the traditional right of an editor to appoint his successor; David Dimbleby (Christ Church) was appointed instead. Thereafter the magazine became what Dimbleby described as 'part of the centrist liberal consensus'. Ferdinand Mount (Christ Church), Peter Jay (Christ Church), Richard Ingrams (University College) and Auberon Waugh (Christ Church) were among the new contributors.

In 1963 Holywell Press, concerned by the number of claims made against the magazine by people who maintained that they had been defamed in its pages, decided to sell it. It was purchased by Robert Maxwell of PERGAMON PRESS and for a time, in accordance with its new proprietor's requirements, made an unsuccessful attempt to become a national student publication under the title *Isis National*.

In 1970, as *Isis* once more, it changed hands again and became an independent and undergraduate-owned publication with offices in FREWIN COURT. Isis Publications Ltd was soon in debt and discussions were held with a view to merging with *Cherwell*. But, with some help from Richard Burton (Exeter) and Elizabeth Taylor, it continued to survive. Its issue of 2 May 1986 was No. 1768. Its by now characteristic contents included an interview with Bernie Grant, the 'notorious' leader of Haringey Council, and one with Hugo Young, the political columnist; and articles about a Latin American terrorist group, the financing of higher education, Rupert Murdoch's Wapping

Horse-drawn barge on the Isis at Iffley village. A watercolour painted in the 1830s by Peter De Wint.

printing plant, and pop music, together with reviews of television, films and books. A political and arts review, it is no longer directed at an exclusively Oxford undergraduate audience. (*See also* MAGAZINES.)

(Billen, Andrew, and Skipwith, Mark, eds, *Oxford Type: the Best of Isis*, 1984.)

Isis (inn) *Iffley Lock, Iffley.* Built as a farmhouse with outbuildings in about 1800, it became a riverside

inn in 1842. Noted for its wild and isolated position, it attracted such water colourists as Peter De Wint in the mid-19th century. During the tenancy of the Rose family (1927–79), beer was delivered by ferry punt and in the flood of 1947 Tom Rose had to 'help the chickens up the stairs'. There is a Victorian nine-pin wooden-skittle alley.

Isis (river) *see* THAMES.

J

Jackson, Cyril *(1746–1819)*. The son of a Yorkshire doctor, Jackson matriculated at Christ Church in 1764, and in 1779, having for a time acted as sub-preceptor to those most tiresome of pupils, King George III's two eldest sons – whom he knocked on the head with his silver pencil case until the blood flowed – he was appointed a canon of Christ Church, becoming Dean in 1783. Renowned as a strict disciplinarian, he devoted his great energies to the advancement of the more promising undergraduates entrusted to his care (among whom were Canning and Peel), taking one or other of them with him when he went on holiday, corresponding with them when they went down, and taking a close interest in their political manoeuvres. The Prince Regent pressed him to accept a bishopric; but this was declined and conferred instead upon his brother, WILLIAM JACKSON.

Jackson, Sir Thomas Graham *(1835–1924)*. Architect responsible, between 1876 and 1914, for more buildings in Oxford than any other architect of any period. He left Wadham College in 1858 to become a pupil of SIR GEORGE GILBERT SCOTT, starting his own modest practice in 1862. With the benefit, from 1865, of a non-resident fellowship at Wadham, and on the reputation deriving from a small commission by its Warden, he was invited to compete for the design of the EXAMINATION SCHOOLS in 1875. From this, his finest building, his long and extensive architectural connection with Oxford developed.

Of his other University works, the most noteworthy are: alterations and exterior repairs at the BODLEIAN LIBRARY (1878–84); remodelling the spire of ST MARY THE VIRGIN (1893–6); the Non-Collegiate Students' building adjoining the Examination Schools (1887); the Radcliffe Science Library (1901); the Electrical Laboratory (1908–10); restorations and additions to the RADCLIFFE OBSERVATORY (1899); and the PARKS Cricket Pavilion (1881).

The Examination Schools apart, the buildings that best demonstrate Jackson as an architect are the more substantial among those he designed for colleges. At Hertford most of the present buildings are his (1887–90 and 1903–14): the Palladian façade and most of the quadrangle behind, including a remarkable staircase reminiscent of French châteaux; the chapel; and the Bridge of Sighs connecting the earlier buildings with a second Jackson quadrangle. With the New Quad at Brasenose (1886–9 and 1907–9) he used a style closer to Gothic to create an imposing frontage to HIGH STREET. At Trinity, in the President's lodgings and an adjoining range (1883–7), he designed in a more characteristic 17th-century style.

Jackson's most important non-University buildings (now taken over by the University) are his two High Schools – for boys in GEORGE STREET (1880–1) and for girls in BANBURY ROAD (1879). Among his miscellaneous works are the organ cases in the SHELDONIAN THEATRE and in the chapels of several colleges; 'The King's Mound' – the Tutor's House in MANSFIELD ROAD built for Balliol (1893–5); and CARFAX TOWER, which he restored.

Jackson was responsible for buildings and restorations in many other parts of the country, mostly educational or ecclesiastical. Notwithstanding the baronetcy and other honours conferred upon him, he has an uncertain reputation and but for his Oxford buildings, on which opinions differ, he would probably be little known. He approached design with a determination to borrow freely from various past architectures, the resulting combination being termed by critics 'Anglo-Jackson'. Proclaiming that an architect was essentially an artist, he decorated his buildings lavishly, especially with ornamental carving to his own designs. This view made him one of the leaders in the movement to resist the attempts of the RIBA to require the compulsory registration of architects.

Jackson's scholarly approach to architecture led him to writing on it throughout his long life. His *Recollections*, edited by his son, was published in 1950. A portrait of 'this learned, versatile and lovable man' hangs in Wadham College hall.

Sir Thomas Graham Jackson, architect of the Examination Schools and many other buildings in Oxford, c.1890.

Jackson, William (*1751–1815*). Brother of CYRIL JACKSON, he entered Christ Church in 1768 and won the Chancellor's Prize for Latin Verse (*see* PRIZES AND SCHOLARSHIPS) in 1770. Appointed Regius Professor of Greek in 1783 and a curator of the Clarendon Press (*see* OXFORD UNIVERSITY PRESS), he was made a canon of Christ Church in 1799 and, after his brother had declined a bishopric, was consecrated BISHOP OF OXFORD in 1812. A notoriously self-indulgent man, he died three years later.

'Jackson's Oxford Journal' *see* NEWSPAPERS.

Jack Straw's Lane *Headington*. The name dates from at least 1932, although the road was not officially adopted until 1954. There are various suggestions of why the road is named, but none has any contemporary documented evidence. The name Jack Straw used to be as common as John Smith. It is just possible that Jack Straw, the priest who played a leading role in the Peasants' Revolt of 1381, stayed at a farmhouse here (once the only building in the road), and indeed there is a plaque to that effect in the youth hostel which is still in the lane. On the other hand, the lane may have been named after another Jack Straw – a wealthy and respected citizen who farmed on HEADINGTON HILL in the days when highwaymen took advantage of the Oxfordshire countryside to waylay travellers. He might have resided at what is now Hill Side (No. 69). Over the years many highwaymen were caught, but their leader always escaped. Then when the farmer, Jack Straw, died, in the cellars beneath his farm kitchen were found rolls of silk, gold, silver, spices and other valuable goods which had been stolen from travellers and merchants.

The lane, which runs from MARSTON ROAD to PULLEN'S LANE, is narrow in parts. There was a long-running dispute between the County Council and City Council about a road-widening scheme, and in 1986 the former rescinded the new road line. On the corner of the lane and Marston Road is the church of ST MICHAEL AND ALL ANGELS (1954–6) by Lawrence Dale; inside is a statue of St Michael by Michael Groser.

Jenkyns, Richard (*1782–1854*). The son of a Somerset parson, Jenkyns entered Balliol as a commoner in 1800 and was elected a Fellow as soon as he was twenty, the earliest permissible age. He was Master by 1819 and retained the position for thirty-five years, during which the reforms he instituted raised the reputation of the college to the high position it enjoyed when he appointed BENJAMIN JOWETT a tutor in 1842. Jenkyns' short figure, proud gait, Somerset accent and the oddity of his remarks combined to make him one of early 19th-century Oxford's most remarkable characters, about whom innumerable stories were told. 'He was a gentleman of the old school in whom were represented old manners, old traditions, old prejudices, a Tory and a Churchman, high and dry,' so Jowett said. 'He was a considerable actor, and would put on severe looks to terrify freshmen, but he was really kind-hearted and indulgent to them.' He was VICE-CHANCELLOR from 1824 to 1828 and, as a determined enemy of the OXFORD MOVEMENT, was one of those who condemned the sermons of E.B. PUSEY in 1843.

Jericho Oxford's first suburb, lying in the ancient Walton Manor to the north-west of the CITY WALL in the old Northgate Hundred – an area uninhabited until the 19th century. The name, often used to signify remoteness, is popularly thought to have its origin in the jerry-builders who constructed it, though it was actually taken from Jericho Gardens which lay to the west of the RADCLIFFE INFIRMARY when the hospital opened in 1770. These were mentioned as early as 1688 by ANTHONY WOOD. At that time an inn named Jericho stood near the site of the present public house, JERICHO HOUSE.

The Oxford CANAL, completed in 1790 and connecting the THAMES with the Trent and the Mersey, was the initial focus of commercial activity. This stimulated housing development. In 1825 the Jericho Iron and Brass Foundry was built near Walton Well by William Carter (*see* LUCY'S EAGLE IRON-WORKS). This originated in a smaller enterprise dating back to 1760. The working-class quarter of Jericho then became centred on the new OXFORD UNIVERSITY PRESS building (1826–32, by Daniel Robertson and Edward Blore). The area developed on a simple grid pattern of streets running parallel and at right-angles to the main (then Jericho) street. Bounded by St Sepulchre's cemetery to the north, WALTON STREET to the east, the canal to the west, and the grounds of Worcester College to the south, GREAT CLARENDON STREET formed the nucleus of the development. Most of the housing was terraced.

Jericho was populated principally by general labourers, the majority employed by the printing press until the Second World War. Like the working-class areas of ST CLEMENT'S and ST EBBE'S, Jericho suffered from major cholera epidemics, particularly in 1832, 1849 and 1854, owing to flooding and bad sanitation. Many houses became slums and many residents left for the new housing estates at WOLVERCOTE. In the Victorian era, Jericho was a citadel of the OXFORD MOVEMENT. Local religion centred on Thomas Combe, superintendent of the Clarendon Press (*see* OXFORD UNIVERSITY PRESS) from 1838 to 1877 and benefactor of the area through his provision of schools and the building of ST BARNABAS CHURCH in Canal Street, consecrated in 1869 when the parish of St Barnabas was created out of that of ST PAUL'S. Combe was a friend of Holman Hunt, whose *The Light of the World* in Keble College chapel was painted in the quadrangle of the Clarendon Press. Hunt described Combe and his wife as 'the salt of the earth . . . two of the most unpretending servants of goodness and nobility that their generation knew'. Their collection of Pre-Raphaelite paintings was bequeathed to the ASHMOLEAN MUSEUM, *The Light of the World* was given to Keble. Thomas Hardy's Jude Fawley, the stone-carver hero of *Jude the Obscure*, lodged in Jericho, though in the novel it is called Beersheba.

Besides Jericho Street itself, roads in the area include Blomfield Place, named after the architect of St Barnabas Church; Combe Road, named after Thomas Combe; Cranham Street, which commemorates a St John's College living purchased in 1827 for £4500; Hart Street, which takes its name from the Printer to the University (1883–1915), who had an international reputation in his lifetime and whose rules for compositors and readers became the established code for printing houses in the English-speaking world and is still widely used. His system of management contributed much to the Oxford University Press's development into so large and renowned an institution. Juxon Street commemorates WILLIAM JUXON. Richmond Road was formerly Worcester Terrace, and School Court was built on the site of the former St Barnabas School. It was the Rev. A.R.P. Venables, curate of St Paul's Church and subsequently Bishop of Nassau, who paid for the boys' school (built in 1856) which was situated in Great Clarendon Street; in 1871 it was handed over to St Barnabas Church. Venables Close is named after him. Other roads in the area are Allam Street, Canal Street, Cardigan Street, King Street, Mount Street, Nelson Street, St Barnabas Street, Victor Street, Walton Crescent, Walton Lane and Wellington Street. Jericho might well have suffered the same fate as St Ebbe's and become a clearance area, but the destruction of St Ebbe's aroused such concern that the City Council decided to rehabilitate Jericho where possible. Demolished houses were replaced by small-scale buildings in keeping with the original dwellings. This pioneer scheme of conservation received national and even international acclaim.

Jericho House   *56–7 Walton Street*. Built as an inn about 1650 on land known as Jericho Gardens (*see* JERICHO). In 1818 the inn had three storeys.

Jesus College   Founded in 1571, Jesus is the only Oxford college to date from the Elizabethan period. Its foundation was due to the initiative and generosity of Hugh Price, treasurer of St David's Cathedral. He approached the Queen for her support, which she

gave, while claiming for herself the title of foundress; and Price, who should at least be thought of as co-founder, had to be content with the title of first benefactor. The Letters Patent, dated 27 June 1571, established 'Jesus College within the City and University of Oxford of Queen Elizabeth's foundation', with a Principal, eight Fellows and eight scholars, and a body of eight commissioners to draw up statutes. Price can with some propriety be regarded as a pre-Reformation figure. Born in Brecon in about 1495, he had been educated at OSENEY ABBEY on the western outskirts of Oxford, and must have been one of the last members of the University to attain the degree of Doctor of Canon Law. (Further, if regarded as co-founder, he was almost the last of a long line of ecclesiastical founders of colleges.) Welsh himself, he founded a college which from its inception had close Welsh connections, though there was nothing in the original provisions which laid this down; still continuing in some degree, these connections have become much less close in the last century. Among the original scholars were Lancelot Andrewes of Pembroke College, Cambridge, afterwards Bishop of Winchester, who was one of the translators of the Authorised Version of the Bible; and Thomas Dove, afterwards Bishop of Peterborough. One of the first Fellows was Robert Johnson, founder of Oakham and Uppingham schools.

The college took over the buildings of the defunct White Hall (an ACADEMIC HALL of the University dating back to the 13th century), together with other similar adjacent premises, so that the site has a history of academic use going back three centuries before the foundation of the college itself. The buildings taken

David Loggan's bird's-eye view of Jesus College and its garden, as seen from Turl Street in 1675 before the front was refaced and the gate-tower built in 1854.

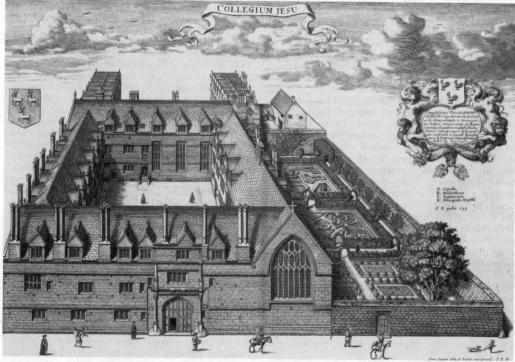

over were gradually replaced, and the oldest parts of the present college are the 16th-century southern part of the TURL STREET front and the adjacent end of the MARKET STREET front. The site, however, was gradually extended, and the construction of the remainder of the first quadrangle proceeded from the second decade of the 17th century.

Initially the college was, and for some time remained, small, poor and without statutes. The first bequest of land – a few small farms in Cardiganshire, which remained college property until the 1950s – produced no revenues at first, but in 1602 Herbert Westphaling, Bishop of Hereford, bequeathed land in Herefordshire, of which the college still owns one farm. As for statutes, the original commissioners of 1571 produced none; nor did the later body nominated in a second promulgation of Letters Patent in 1589, and subsequent moves to secure statutes came to nothing. A third set of Letters Patent in 1622 finally produced statutes in that year. The CHANCELLOR of the University at the time, the Earl of Pembroke (*see* PEMBROKE COLLEGE) was named VISITOR of the college, and the Earls of Pembroke have remained hereditary Visitors to this day.

It was now envisaged that the college should have a Principal, sixteen Fellows and sixteen scholars, but in fact its finances were insufficient to make full provision for that number. Indeed, it is only in relatively recent years that the number of Fellows has regularly exceeded sixteen. The statutes, based largely on those of Brasenose, prescribed in great detail the ordering of college life, with the daily routine beginning with prayers between 5 and 6 a.m. The studies set out included lectures on the logic and, even at this late date, the cosmology of Aristotle, together with disputations in Dialectic, Rhetoric, Physics or Ethics, and also in Theology. Conversation in hall and lecture rooms had to be in Latin, Greek or Hebrew. Scholars were required to show adequate powers of composition in Latin and Greek, and masters were to prepare for the degrees of Bachelor and Doctor of Divinity. The extent to which these requirements continued to be enforced in later times is a matter for conjecture.

In the first half of the 17th century the college was greatly indebted to the energy of three Principals: Griffith Powell (1613–20), Sir Eubule Thelwall (1621–30) and Francis Mansell. Mansell had three periods as Principal: from 1620 to 1621, when he resigned to make way for Thelwall; from 1630 to 1648, when he was ejected by the Parliamentary Visitors (*see* VISITATIONS), and finally from 1660 to his retirement in the following year. It was largely owing to the preparatory work of Powell that the college finally obtained its statutes, and the hall, buttery and kitchen date from his time. The hall retains much of its early appearance, though it originally displayed open rafters; the present ceiling was inserted in 1741. Powell was also diligent, as were his successors, in soliciting much-needed funds in Oxford, London and Wales. Thelwall, who, like some of his predecessors, was a lawyer by training (he was a Master in Chancery), saw the consecration of the chapel (1621; enlarged 1636) and the construction of the Principal's lodgings, the latter built at his own expense. The first quadrangle was now complete, and the second was begun by the construction of a library on its north side, where Staircase XIII now stands. For this, and for the

provision of books, Thelwall raised funds. Of printed books, indeed, the college already had a small collection, as well as an interesting collection of manuscripts (*see below*). Unfortunately, the library seems to have been badly constructed, for in 1630 it had to be dismantled; the books and presses were stored away, and so they remained through the troubled times ahead until the present Fellows' Library (the Old Library) was built in 1679 on the west side of the quadrangle. Under Mansell, however, progress was made towards the construction of the north and south sides of the second quadrangle, until it was brought to a halt by the outbreak of the CIVIL WAR. Meanwhile, by a royal benefaction of 1636, Jesus, together with Exeter and Pembroke Colleges, received an endowment for establishing fellowships for natives of the Channel Islands (intended, it would seem, to counteract Huguenot Calvinist tendencies prevalent there). The changes made in the college statutes in 1857 converted these fellowships into scholarships, which have continued to the present day. A visible memorial remains in the portrait of Charles I by Van Dyck which hangs in the College hall.

Among early members of the college, besides Bishops Andrewes and Dove, were Sir William Vaughan (1597), who was involved in the settlement of Newfoundland; and Morgan Owen (1613), Bishop of Llandaff and friend of ARCHBISHOP LAUD, who in 1637 built the remarkable porch of ST MARY THE VIRGIN and who was subsequently one of the bishops impeached by the Long Parliament. The poet Henry Vaughan seems not to have been a member of the college in the strict sense, despite statements sometimes made to the contrary, but he was possibly associated with it in some way; his twin brother Thomas, who was inclined to alchemy rather than to poetry, certainly became a Fellow in 1642.

The outbreak of the Civil War disrupted the University generally, and proved an unfortunate setback for Jesus College. Rents from distant farms could no longer be collected; the buildings were occupied by royalist troops (among them Lord Herbert, later Marquess of Worcester, and Lord Grandison, who died in college and is commemorated by a memorial in CHRIST CHURCH CATHEDRAL), and the PLATE (86 lb) was surrendered for the royal MINT set up in NEW INN HALL STREET (none of the existing plate pre-dates the Restoration). The college was, like Oxford as a whole, generally royalist in sentiment, and was subjected to a severe inquisition by the Parliamentary Visitors of 1648. Mansell, who had been forced to spend part of the Civil War in his native county of Glamorgan, was ejected; Michael Roberts, a former Fellow, a native of Anglesey and an early graduate of Trinity College, Dublin, was appointed Principal; and out of the sixteen Fellows and sixteen scholars only one Fellow and one scholar submitted to the Visitors and were permitted to remain.

The Commonwealth period was one of dissensions within the college. Mansell returned. The new Fellows made numerous accusations against Roberts and attempted to have him removed; he eventually resigned in 1658, to be succeeded by Francis Howell, though he continued to reside – with the result that there ensued the bizarre situation of three Principals residing simultaneously. The tangled situation was resolved when Mansell (together with four of the

199

A Fellow shows visitors round Jesus College chapel, c.1815.

Fellows extruded in 1648) was restored by the Royal Commissioners of 1660, becoming Principal for the third time. He was now, however, of an advanced age, and retired the following year, to be succeeded by one who is perhaps the college's most distinguished Principal, and also its most notable benefactor: Leoline Jenkins.

While he was Principal, Jenkins, a lawyer, also rose rapidly as a servant of the Crown, and became Judge of the Court of Admiralty, in consequence of which the Court of Admiralty was held in the college hall when it was forced out of London by the Great Plague of 1664–5. He also represented the government abroad, attending the funeral of Henrietta Maria near Paris in 1669, and subsequently resigned the principalship in 1673, becoming Secretary of State in 1680. On his death in 1685 he left the college the greater part of the substantial wealth he had accumulated, receiving the title of 'second founder'. Some of the land so bequeathed has remained in the college's hands. The most important part, however, was on the river frontage in Lambeth, the last remaining portion of which passed to the London County Council in 1940. His settlement of the college tied it more closely to Wales, and in particular, for many years, to the Grammar School of Cowbridge, in Glamorgan, at which he himself had been educated. A feature of his provisions which may seem curious today was that two newly established fellowships required their holders to undertake a chaplaincy in the Fleet (recalling his connection with the Admiralty) or in the 'plantations' (i.e. the colonies).

Jenkins's time saw the second quadrangle all but complete, and in particular the construction at his expense of the Fellows' Library (1679); the books and presses from Thelwall's library, hitherto stowed away, were now brought out and rehoused. All that

remained to be added to the second quadrangle was the north-western corner, which was finished in 1713.

A notable member of the college from this period was William Lloyd (Fellow 1641–8, and from 1660), who was one of the seven bishops tried in 1688 for refusing to read James II's Declaration of Indulgence. Distinguished in the intellectual sphere was Edward Lhuyd (*d*.1709), Keeper of the ASHMOLEAN MUSEUM, who was both an eminent naturalist and one of the most important of Celtic scholars; his *Archaeologia Britannica* (1707) recorded, among other things, his studies of Cornish made at a time when it was still a living language.

From the early 18th century on there is, with few exceptions, little to record for a considerable length of time. In 1713 the college received its second great benefaction under the will of Edmund Meyricke, a former Fellow who had become treasurer of St David's, like Hugh Price before him, and was an ecclesiastical pluralist. This bequest provided for the endowment of scholarships and exhibitions for boys from the six counties of north Wales, thus rendering the college's Welsh connection even closer. It had the desirable effect of making a university education available to a long succession of Welsh boys, frequently from very modest backgrounds; but on the other hand it reinforced the narrowness of the college's membership and outlook and a tendency to isolation in the University. Further, even within Wales the confinement of the benefaction to recipients from the north was to prove unfortunate in a century which began to see a great influx of population into the industrial areas of the south, while the effects of the restrictions were intensified by the fact – outside the college's control – that, although there was a strong drift towards Nonconformity in Wales, the University was confined to Anglicans until 1871 (*see* DISSENTERS).

Meanwhile college life had been briefly enlivened by the scandal of the principalship election of 1712, when one party succeeded in seating its candidate in the Principal's stall in chapel but the other made off with the register. The issue was resolved by an appeal to the Earl of Pembroke as Visitor, whereupon he, being a Whig, confirmed the Whig candidate, John Wynne (later Bishop of St Asaph and then of Bath and Wells).

The University as a whole was at a low ebb in the 18th century, and Jesus College, small in numbers, exhibited a dreary lack of distinction throughout, and indeed well into the 19th century. A grave error was made by the governing body when it opposed the recommendations of the ROYAL COMMISSION of 1854 and insisted on retaining the college's almost completely Welsh character, though restrictions to particular counties within Wales were eliminated. Fortunately this exclusiveness was remedied in the statutes of 1882 which followed the second Royal Commission. Meanwhile, however, the college had shown signs of revival, and had numbered among its members the distinguished historian J.R. Green, a local Oxford boy who came up as a scholar in 1855 but found himself less than happy in the prevailing atmosphere. An equally remarkable member, a few years later, was Sir John Rhys, who, coming from a background of extreme poverty in Wales, was discovered as a self-taught genius by Principal Charles Williams and brought to Oxford. He subsequently became the first Professor of Celtic (a chair ever since attached to the college), Principal from 1895 to 1915, and the most eminent Celtic scholar of his day. Of a later vintage was John Sankey, afterwards Viscount Sankey (Lord Chancellor 1929–35).

To Sir John Rhys's time as Principal belongs the construction of the SHIP STREET block (1907), which included a chemistry laboratory; Jesus was among the colleges which had LABORATORIES of their own, and it continued in use longer than any other, for teaching until 1939 and during the Second World War for governmental research. The years 1907–10 saw the undergraduate career of perhaps the most remarkable of the college's *alumni*: T.E. Lawrence (Lawrence of Arabia), who, coming from an Oxford home (2 Polstead Road), and educated previously at the OXFORD HIGH SCHOOL FOR BOYS, obtained first-class Honours in History in 1910, partly on the strength of a thesis on crusader castles and their influence on military architecture in Western Europe.

The subsequent years have seen an expansion in the numbers both of Fellows and of undergraduate and graduate students, and in the range of subjects covered in college teaching, as well as a continued rise in academic standards. There has also been an increase in accommodation on the existing site, in particular the Old Members' Building, opened by the Prince of Wales in 1971 (for which funds were raised by an appeal among former members to commemorate the college's quatercentenary) and outside the curtilage at Stevens Close in WOODSTOCK ROAD. The college owes this building, which was opened by the Queen in 1976, to the generosity of an old member, A.E. Stevens. Since the disestablishment of the Welsh Church in 1920 several Archbishops of Wales have been Jesus men. (The college's connection is still commemorated by a Welsh service in the chapel on St David's Day.) The most distinguished member of Jesus in recent years has been Harold Wilson (Lord Wilson of Rievaulx), who was an undergraduate from 1934 to 1937. In 1974 Jesus became one of the original group of five of the traditional men's colleges to admit women, both as Fellows and as students (undergraduate and graduate). Since then women have taken part in the whole range of academic studies and played an active part in all aspects of college life.

Since 1984 the Principal has been Dr P.M. North, formerly a Fellow of Keble College and a Law Commissioner; his immediate predecessors were J.T. Christie (1949–67), previously headmaster of Westminster, and Sir John Habakkuk (1967–84), who was previously Professor of Economic History and who from 1973 to 1977 was VICE-CHANCELLOR of the University.

From its early years, Jesus College had a collection of manuscripts amassed by Sir John Prise – like Hugh Price, a Brecon man – who had taken advantage of his opportunities as one of Henry VIII's commissioners for the Dissolution of Monasteries. The manuscripts came mainly from monasteries in and around the Cotswold area (Cirencester, Evesham, etc.), and most were theological, including several containing works by the Venerable Bede. In the 17th century there was a gradual accumulation both of manuscripts and of printed books, in particular an interesting collection of the latter from the library of the philosopher Lord Herbert of Cherbury (1648) and a legal collection from Sir Leoline Jenkins. The library is also strong in scientific works of the period and in politico-religious pamphlets. It has, moreover, received over the years a number of Welsh manuscripts, of which the most important is the *Red Book of Hergest*, a large collection of Welsh literature compiled in the 14th and 15th centuries and given to the college in 1701. The older manuscripts have been deposited in the BODLEIAN

Road-menders at work in Turl Street in front of Jesus College, c.1862.

LIBRARY since 1886. The history of the building of the Fellows' Library has been related above; its appearance is much as it was when first constructed, and it is now mainly of antiquarian interest. The undergraduate library (the Meyricke Library) had its inception in 1865, and there is also a Celtic library.

The corporate designation of the college is The Principal, Fellows and Scholars of Jesus College, within the City and University of Oxford, of Queen Elizabeth's Foundation.

(The standard history of the college to the late 19th century is still that of E.G. Hardy, 1899; more recently there have been the article by J.N.L. Baker in the *Victoria County History of Oxford*, Vol. III, Oxford, 1954, which gives further references, and J.N.L. Baker, *Jesus College, Oxford, 1571–1971*, Oxford, 1971. The history of the Fellows' Library is related by C.J. Fordyce and T.M. Knox in 'The Library of Jesus College, Oxford', *Proceedings and Papers of the Oxford Bibliographical Society*, Vol. V, Part II, 1937.)

Jewel, John (*1522–1571*). Entered Merton College in 1535 and elected Fellow of Corpus Christi in 1542. A lecturer of compelling power, he soon became a prominent figure in the University, being elected PUBLIC ORATOR in *c*.1563; but on the accession of Queen Mary he was deprived of his fellowship because he was a Protestant. He later fled to London and thence to Frankfurt. Returning to England after Mary's death, he was consecrated Bishop of Salisbury in 1560; and in 1566 received the degree of DD by special decree of the University. He accompanied Queen Elizabeth I on her visit to the University that year. At Salisbury he maintained in the episcopal palace a number of pupils intent upon going up to Oxford, where some, including Richard Hooker (*c*.1554–1600), the theologian, were educated at his expense.

Jews Jews first came to England in the wake of William I and settled first in London and then in provincial centres. A group of Jews was settled in Oxford early in the 12th century, and the community developed during the following decades, although always remaining comparatively small. Throughout mediaeval England Jews were restricted mainly to money-lending as a means of livelihood, and they were subject to heavy taxation and not infrequent property confiscation by the Crown: the earliest surviving document relating to Oxford Jews refers to a levy exacted from them in 1141, during the war between Stephen and Matilda.

The expansion of the University in the later 12th century attracted Jews to the city, and many were among the wealthiest in England. They were also scholarly but were prohibited, as Jews, from membership of the University, and their contacts with scholars were through lending money and letting lodgings. Jacob's Hall, facing the present TOWN HALL in ST ALDATE'S, was probably let by a Jew as student accommodation, as was Moyses' Hall, which was to become the property of Oriel College in 1362.

By the end of the 12th century Great Jewry, the street of the Jews, ran from the present CARFAX to FOLLY BRIDGE. Many of the houses were owned by Jews, some of them let to Christians. There were also Jewish houses in Pennyfarthing Lane (now PEMBROKE STREET), Lombard's Lane (now BREWER STREET) and around Wheatsheaf Yard. Jewish investment in house property was an important feature of mediaeval Oxford since the Jews rebuilt the lath-and-plaster dwellings in stone, often extending as well as improving them. Later documented transactions, such as those between Walter de Merton and Jacob of Oxford in the 13th century, show how these residences became part of the newly founded colleges of the University.

Two stone tablets, one on the wall of the town hall and the other at the entrance to the BOTANIC GARDEN, commemorate the mediaeval Jewish community. David of Oxford, a noted financier, owned a house on the town hall site which was, at his death in 1244, expropriated and presented to the Domus Conversorum, the 'home for converted Jews'. Some time after 1190 land outside the East Gate was acquired by the Jews for use as a cemetery. The plaque on the wall of the Botanic Garden gives the date of establishment as 1177, now accepted as too early. On the east side of St Aldate's, just south of the north corner-tower of Christ Church, stood the 13th-century synagogue. The building comprised houses that belonged to Copin of Worcester, an Oxford Jew who had property dealings with ST FRIDESWIDE'S PRIORY.

In general the Oxford Jews' relationships with their Christian neighbours seem to have been friendly. On occasion the latter safeguarded the former's property against confiscation; and Copin of Oxford, a prominent member of the 13th-century community, was cleared of one of the frequent 'coin-clipping' charges by an all-Christian jury.

The 13th century was characterised by extortionate and restrictive measures against Jews in England, culminating in their expulsion by Edward I on 1 November 1290. Oxford Jewry was impoverished and many fled the country. Under Henry III the Jews were urged to apostatise, and in 1221 a Dominican Friary was established in Great Jewry in Oxford, probably for this purpose. Accusations of crimes of violence, fraud and desecration against the Jews increased. In Oxford on Ascension Day, 17 May 1268, Jews were accused of desecrating the processional crucifix. The community was imprisoned and required to pay for its replacement as well as for the construction of a gold-and-marble crucifix, which was inscribed with an account of the alleged incident and erected opposite the synagogue.

During the years leading up to the expulsion, Queen Eleanor appropriated the property of Oxford's Jews as 'death duties' due to the Crown and presented it to her favourite, Henry Owen. By 1290 the Oxford Jewish community numbered fewer than 100, of whom no more than nine remained home-owners; and, following the expulsion, surviving Jewish property, including the synagogue, was presented by King Edward to William Burnell, Provost of Wells, who subsequently bequeathed it to Balliol.

Although unable to take part in University life, through their business and personal contacts the Jews of mediaeval Oxford had had an influence on scholarship, as is evident early in the work of ROBERT GROSSETESTE and of Roger Bacon. Both these scholars studied Jewish exegesis, and the latter was particularly interested in the work of an important Jewish scholar of the 13th century – Moses of Oxford.

In theory no practising Jew lived in England from 1290 until the 17th-century resettlement that followed negotiations between the Dutch rabbi, Manasseh ben Israel, and Oliver Cromwell. Baptism was the solution for many, and during the interim several converts from Judaism are recorded as teaching Hebrew at Oxford. Thus scholarship continued to be influenced by Jewish thought, as well as through the study of surviving books and libraries. In 1312 a teaching post in Hebrew was introduced at the University, and in 1540 a Regius Chair of Hebrew was established, confirming the study of Hebrew as an academic discipline.

Following Jewish resettlement in England, practising Jews became informally involved with the University. SIR THOMAS BODLEY sought the assistance of a Jew to catalogue his collection of Hebrew books; and in 1662 Isaac Abendana arrived from Holland with a letter of introduction to Edward Pococke, taught Hebrew at Oxford and was admitted to read in the BODLEIAN. He became a friend of ANTHONY WOOD and of contemporary theologians.

The earliest record of a post-resettlement Jewish community in Oxford is of a circumcision in 1739; but individuals appeared earlier – for example Jacob the Jew, who opened a coffee house in 1651 (*see* COFFEE HOUSES), and without doubt Jewish pedlars would have visited Oxford as a market town. By 1738 De Blossiers Tovey, Fellow of Merton and Principal of NEW INN HALL, was sufficiently aware of Jews to write his *History and Antiquities of the Jews in England*.

The small community was augmented by Jews teaching Hebrew at the University, but while the number of University members of Jewish origin increased – for example, Emanuel Samuel entered Magdalen in 1782 – no professing Jew could enter the University until the Reform Act of 1854.

The modern Jewish community in the city dates from this time: in 1841 a synagogue was opened for about fifty Jews, mainly second-hand clothes dealers and merchants. A room in PARADISE SQUARE was used as a synagogue from at least 1847; then, in 1871, a building in St Aldate's. From 1878–93 a synagogue was recorded as existing in Worcester Place; and in 1893 a building was erected on the present site in Richmond Road by the local builder, John Jacob Gardner. A new building was dedicated here in 1974. Also in 1893, the present cemetery, a burial plot at WOLVERCOTE, was reserved for Jews.

At the end of the century the community was revitalised by increasing numbers of Jewish students, and the Jewish Society, first known as the Adler Society, was formed. From the late 1930s German refugees and then evacuees from elsewhere in England swelled the community's numbers to about 3000. This figure dropped after the Second World War and in 1986 was less than 300.

While the study of Hebrew at the University has remained in the Department of Oriental Studies, in 1972 the Oxford Centre for Hebrew Studies was founded at Yarnton Manor as an advanced research institute associated with the University. It is committed to the expansion and enrichment of Hebrew and Jewish studies within the University system. It also runs a Yiddish summer school.

(Roth, C., *The Jews of Mediaeval Oxford*, OHS, n.s. ix, 1951; Roth, C., 'Jews in Oxford after 1290', *Oxoniensia*, xv, Oxford, 1950; Loewe, R., 'Jewish scholarship in England', *Three Centuries of Anglo-Jewish History*, ed. V.M. Lipman, Jewish Historical Society of England, 1961; Uriel, Dann, 'Jews in 18th Century Oxford: Further Observations', *Oxoniensia* liv, 1989, p. 345.)

John Johnson, Printer to the University, whose collection of 'everything which would ordinarily go into the waste paper basket' is now held by the Bodleian Library.

John Johnson Collection John Johnson was born in 1882 and educated at MAGDALEN COLLEGE SCHOOL and Exeter College, where he took a First in Classical Moderations and a Second in LITERAE HUMANIORES. Having been selected for the Egyptian Civil Service he stayed on at the University for another year to read Arabic. He spent two years in Egypt as an administrator, then returned to Oxford as assistant to the papyrologists Grenfell and Hunt. His winters were spent in Egypt 'with large gangs of fellahin', as he wrote later, 'digging the rubbish mounds of Graeco-Roman cities in Egypt for the written materials – the waste paper – of those ages. . . . Often I used to look over those dark and crumbling sites and wonder what could be done to treat the background of our own English civilization with the same minute care with which we scholars were treating the ancient'. It was these digs in Egypt which gave him the idea for the formation of his remarkable collection of printed ephemera.

He was asked to join the OXFORD UNIVERSITY PRESS as assistant secretary, and by 1925 he had risen to become Printer to the University. His spare time, however, was spent in accumulating 'everything which would ordinarily go into the waste paper basket after use, everything printed which is not actually a book'. At first these were sorted by putting them under different beds in his house – 'a primitive and not unsatisfactory dodge for keeping the material apart'. Over the years he had accumulated 1000 boxes or cloth folders, 'housing a million and more examples of the ephemera of our lives'. The collection ranges from tram tickets and cigarette cards to Valentines, Christmas cards, banknotes, theatre bills and COLLEGE STAMPS, some sections having been enlarged by the acquisition of other specialised collections.

In 1946 Johnson retired as Printer to the University, but spent the remaining ten years of his life sorting and arranging his vast collection, which was then housed in the Printing House in WALTON STREET, with the assistance of Mrs 'Lil' Thrussell. After Johnson's death it was suggested that the collection should be transferred to the BODLEIAN LIBRARY, and the transfer took place in 1968. Two and a half thousand folio filing boxes were handed over, together with several hundred large folders and several cabinets of drawers. A room, known as the John Johnson Room, has been set aside for the collection in the NEW BODLEIAN, together with a reading room. An exhibition of the collection was held in the library in 1971. The leaflet listing the main subject headings of the collection runs to seven pages, ranging from eight boxes of actors and actresses to four boxes of youth hostels. It includes no less than thirty-two boxes of street ballads, thirty boxes of prospectuses, twenty-three boxes on fashion, and many on Oxford and University societies. Johnson was not a mere hoarder of litter: his collection is now recognised as providing valuable evidence for the historian and it is frequently consulted by writers, journalists and researchers of all kinds.

(*The John Johnson Collection – Catalogue of an Exhibition*, Bodleian Library, 1971.)

John Radcliffe Hospital   *Osler Road and Headley Way, Headington.* Intended, eventually, to replace the RADCLIFFE INFIRMARY in the city centre, this new 642-bed teaching hospital stands on an elevated 75-acre site. The ground was purchased in 1919, with considerable foresight, by the Rev. G.B. Cronshaw, treasurer of the infirmary, assisted by a donation of £15,000 from the British Red Cross Society, specifically to develop tuberculosis facilities. The first two buildings to occupy the site were both pavilion-style hospitals. The Osler, opened in 1926 (forty beds), witnessed the conquest of tuberculosis. It was named in memory of Sir William Osler, Regius Professor of Medicine (1904–19) and founder (1910) of the Oxfordshire branch of the National Association for the Prevention of Tuberculosis; he pioneered the idea that tuberculosis care should be supervised by a general hospital. Sunnyside Convalescent Home (thirty beds) opened in 1930 as a replacement, in a more salubrious environment, for the house in COWLEY donated by Dr Ivy Williams in 1922 for Radcliffe Infirmary convalescents. Like the infirmary, the new hospital was named after DR JOHN RADCLIFFE (1650–1714), an Oxford-trained physician who developed a prosperous royal practice in London.

The John Radcliffe Hospital, designed by Yorke, Rosenberg and Mardall, was to have been built in three phases but financial constraints postponed the start of Phase III. Planning started in 1963 and Phase I, the maternity unit (180 beds and cots), was completed in 1971. Phase II, the main hospital, took six years, cost £30 million and opened in 1979, taking over many of the former infirmary departments. The new hospital provides accident and emergency services; general medical and surgical wards; intensive- and coronary-care units; oral surgery, paediatrics and geriatrics; and incorporates the pharmacy and various para-medical departments, together with the regional specialities of neo-natal surgery, cardiology, cardiac surgery, blood transfusion and a special-care baby unit. Various Oxford University departments are located, wholly or partially, within the hospital, including Obstetrics and Gynaecology; the NUFFIELD INSTITUTE FOR MEDICAL RESEARCH; the Nuffield Departments of Clinical Medicine, Surgery, Anaesthetics and Paediatrics; and the Departments of Morbid Anatomy, Clinical Biochemistry, Cardiology, Orthopaedic Surgery and

Radiology. The academic centre houses the Medical School, School of Nursing and the Regional School of Radiography. There are over 2000 staff, with 120 honorary medical staff and 300 clinical medical students.

Johnson, Samuel   *(1709–1784).* Entered Pembroke College in 1728 with the financial help of his mother, who had recently come into a modest inheritance. He was given a room at the top of the staircase above the main gateway, the shelves of which he filled with books borrowed from the stock of his father, a Lichfield bookseller. These he studied with as much diligence as he could muster; but he admitted to being a lazy and rebellious undergraduate, 'rude and violent', disregarding 'all authority'. Fined for not attending a lecture, he tartly complained that he had been sconced twopence for something not worth a penny; and when asked why he had not attended another lecture he replied with 'much nonchalance' that he had spent the time sliding about on the ice on CHRIST CHURCH MEADOW. Discovered idling in his room by a SERVITOR sent round the college by the Master to ensure that all the undergraduates were working, he chased the unfortunate servant across the quadrangle, clattering a candlestick in a chamber pot. He was often to be found 'lounging' at the college gate entertaining a group of his fellow-undergraduates, declaiming in a tavern, trying out his hand at cricket or playing draughts and drinking ale with friends in the common room. Towards the end of 1729 the money that his mother had given him was all but exhausted. He had had to find 8*s* a week for his board as a commoner, and another 8*s* or so for the rent of his room, for fuel and candles, his tutor's fees, and the wages of the servitor and his bedmaker; and he could afford to spend nothing on his clothes. His shoes were so worn that his naked toes stuck through the broken leather. One day when he went to visit a friend at Christ Church, some other Christ Church men, standing on the pavement of Peckwater Quad, seemed to be laughing at his broken-down appearance. He refused to set foot in the college again and soon afterwards, on 12 December, he left Oxford.

He often returned, however, in later life and always enjoyed his visits. He came back in 1754, staying at Kettel Hall (*see* TRINITY COLLEGE), and making friends with the REV. THOMAS WARTON, later Professor of Poetry. He returned again in 1759, stayed with Dr Robert Vansittart, the future Regius Professor of Civil Law, and clapped his hands till they were sore at the speech made by Dr William King, the VICE-CHANCELLOR, upon the installation of the Jacobite Earl of Westmorland as CHANCELLOR. He was at Oxford in 1769 with his blind friend Miss Anna Williams, and later with James Boswell, with whom he stayed at Pembroke where they were guests of the Master, Dr William Adams (1706–89). It was with Adams's warm support that Johnson was granted the degree of MA. He received the degree of DCL from the University in 1775. He always took great pleasure in extolling the virtues of the University, comparing it favourably with Cambridge. 'He delighted in his own partiality for Oxford,' Mrs Thrale said, 'and one day, at my house, entertained five members of the other University with various instances of the superiority of Oxford, enumerating the gigantic names of many men whom it had produced, with apparent triumph. At last I said to him, "Why there happens to be no less than five Cambridge men in the room now." "I did not (said he) think of that till you told me; but the wolf don't count the sheep." '

Jowett, Benjamin (*1817–1893*). Won an open scholarship in 1835 to Balliol from St Paul's, where the high master, John Sleath, described him as 'the best Latin scholar' whom he had ever sent to the college. He was elected a Fellow of Balliol while still an undergraduate; and, after taking a First in LITERAE HUMANIORES and winning the Chancellor's Prize for a Latin Essay (*see* PRIZES AND SCHOLARSHIPS), he was appointed a tutor. He became involved in the OXFORD MOVEMENT and later in the movement for university reform (*see* ROYAL COMMISSIONS), but he remained a dedicated tutor, a stimulating lecturer and conscientious student of Philosophy and Theology. In 1854 he was a candidate for the mastership of Balliol in succession to RICHARD JENKYNS, but Robert Scott (1811–87), the lexicographer, was chosen instead.

In 1855, however, in the face of opposition from those who objected to the theological views expressed in his *St Paul's Epistles to the Thessalonians, Galatians and Romans* (2 vols, 1855), he was appointed Regius Professor of Greek in succession to THOMAS GAISFORD, though it was not until 1870, when he was fifty-three, that he was elected Master of Balliol. In the intervening years it was said that he had made time to see every undergraduate in the college once a week, despite the amount of work he undertook; and he had done all he could to ensure that clever young men from poor homes were enabled to attend Balliol and other colleges. As Master he presided over a major building programme at Balliol, which he was determined should produce an élite capable of inoculating England. He had, he confessed, 'a general prejudice against all persons who do not succeed in the world'. Having published *The Dialogues of Plato* in four volumes in 1871, he was elected VICE-CHANCELLOR in 1882.

C.M. Ross's 1892 portrait of Benjamin Jowett, who was elected Master of Balliol in 1870.

Jowett energetically encouraged interest in music and the theatre at Oxford, attending performances of the OXFORD UNIVERSITY DRAMATIC SOCIETY and instituting the Balliol Sunday concerts. He also gave his encouragement to the OXFORD UNIVERSITY PRESS. He died at the home of Sir Robert Wright, one of those numerous former pupils to whom he was devoted and who remained deeply attached to him. He was buried in the cemetery of St Sepulchre's. Most of his property was left to his college.

A generous host and, on occasions, a lively conversationalist and anecdotalist, he was prone to bouts of disconcerting silence and to sharp rebuffs. When the President of Corpus Christi said to him, 'Master, I must congratulate you on the appearance of your new volume of Plato. May I send you a few suggestions?' Jowett tersely replied, 'Please don't.' In his autobiography, Augustus Hare wrote that he was 'profoundly grateful to Mr Jowett' but that being 'constantly asked to breakfast alone with him was a terrible ordeal. . . . Sometimes he never spoke at all, and would only walk round the room looking at me with unperceiving absent eyes as I ate my bread and butter, in a way that, for a very nervous boy, was utterly terrifying. Walking with this kind and silent friend was even worse; he scarcely ever spoke, and if, in my shyness, I said something at one milestone, he would make no response at all till we reached the next, when he would say abruptly, "Your last observation was singularly commonplace." '

Jowett Walk Formerly Love Lane, the walk was named after BENJAMIN JOWETT. Love Lane ran from Church Street, HOLYWELL, now ST CROSS ROAD, to the back of Wadham College and then north to SOUTH PARKS ROAD. Only the southern part now exists (as far as MANSFIELD ROAD). On a map of 1897 Love Lane is shown as continuing from Savile Road, now a cul-de-sac. The roadway of Jowett Walk is now gated.

Judge's Lodging   *see* ST GILES' HOUSE.

Juxon, William (*1582–1663*). Entered St John's College as a scholar from Merchant Taylors' School in 1598. He became vicar of ST GILES' in 1609 and, on the recommendation of WILLIAM LAUD, was appointed President of St John's in 1621. Six years later he was elected VICE-CHANCELLOR and in that office was closely involved with the drawing up of the LAUDIAN CODE. He resigned the presidency of his college in 1632 and was consecrated Bishop of London the next year, but he continued to take a deep interest in the affairs of the University and of his college, and was present with Charles I at the opening of the new St John's library, the early stages of whose building he had supervised. He attended the King on the scaffold and was subsequently required to give up his bishopric; but at the Restoration he was chosen to be Archbishop of Canterbury, an office which he held until his death in London. His embalmed body was removed to Oxford, where it lay in state in the DIVINITY SCHOOL until it was buried in the chapel of St John's next to the founder, Sir Thomas White. A few days later, the body of Laud was placed beside his. Juxon left St John's College £7000 for the purchase of lands 'for the increase of the yearly stipends of the fellows and scholars of that college'. He had already given various oriental manuscripts to the BODLEIAN LIBRARY.

K

Keble, John (*1792–1866*). The son of a Gloucestershire clergyman, from whom he received his early education, Keble won a scholarship to Corpus Christi College, where his father had been a Fellow. He obtained a double First in 1811 and was elected a Fellow of Oriel. He was appointed Professor of Poetry in 1831. Five years later he became vicar of Hursley, near Winchester, and for the next thirty years conscientiously occupied himself with parochial duties and writing. His book of sacred verse, *The Christian Year* (1827), appeared in over ninety editions during his lifetime.

Although a shy, retiring and wholly unpretentious man, Keble became one of the acknowledged leaders of the OXFORD MOVEMENT, J.H. NEWMAN going so far as to say that he was the movement's 'true and primary author'. He helped Newman, E.B. PUSEY and Charles Marriott (1811–58, Fellow of Oriel and from 1850 vicar of the University Church of ST MARY THE VIRGIN) with the translations of the works of the Fathers of the Church which became known as the 'Library of the Fathers'. Keble also wrote several of the celebrated *Tracts for the Times*. As a memorial, it was resolved in

Detail of George Richmond's watercolour drawing from life of John Keble, Fellow of Oriel and Professor of Poetry in 1831, as a memorial to whom Keble College was founded in 1868.

the year of his death to build a new college at Oxford where young men of moderate means might receive a university education well grounded in Christian principles (*see* KEBLE COLLEGE).

Keble College Founded in 1868, with money raised by public subscription, as a memorial to JOHN KEBLE, one of the central and most beloved figures of the OXFORD MOVEMENT. At his funeral in 1866 Keble's friends had gathered at Hursley Park, near Winchester, the house of his former pupil, Sir William Heathcote, to consider a memorial. They fixed upon the foundation of a new college in Oxford. But this was by no means the sole impetus for the foundation of a college; there were two further, deeper, forces at work. First, the preceding hundred years had seen a growth of aristocratic exclusiveness at Oxford, rendering undergraduate life expensive for and uncongenial to able men of humble background. This state of affairs was strongly challenged by mid-Victorian social reformers, to whom the existing colleges appeared anachronisms in the world which followed the Industrial Revolution. Second, many of those associated with the Oxford Movement, Keble included, were sympathetic to demands for university reform but feared that the recommendations of the University Commission (*see* ROYAL COMMISSIONS) appointed in 1850 might lead eventually to Oxford's becoming atheistic. Indeed, in the 1840s Keble and E.B. PUSEY supported a scheme of Charles Marriott, a Fellow of Oriel and former Principal of Chichester Theological College, to found a new college in Oxford, open to the less affluent and inculcating the Christian virtues of poverty and obedience; but they were unable to raise the necessary funds either from the government of the day or from other colleges in the University. In 1865 a committee under the chairmanship of W.W. Shirley, Regius Professor of Ecclesiastical History, proposed 'extending the University by founding a college or hall on a large scale, with a view not exclusively, but especially, to the education of persons needing assistance and desirous of admission into the Christian Ministry'. Keble, shortly before his death, saw and approved the recommendations of the Shirley Committee, and the proposal was referred to in the press as 'the Keble Scheme'. It was clear by this time that money for the new institution would have to be raised by public subscription, and Keble's death provided an opportunity for such a wide appeal for funds. In May 1866, a meeting at Lambeth Palace under the chairmanship of the Archbishop of Canterbury resolved 'that a sum of not less than £50,000 be raised for the accomplishment of an object, in which Mr Keble is known to have been deeply interested, namely, the establishment of a college. . . .' The appeal prospered from the start; within two years £35,000 had been raised. The trustees of the Memorial Fund negotiated the

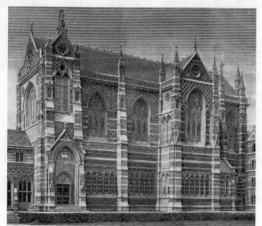

The foundation stone of Keble College chapel, designed by William Butterfield, a convinced follower of the Oxford Movement, was laid in 1873.

purchase from St John's College of a 4½-acre site on PARKS ROAD for £7047. On 25 April 1868, the anniversary of John Keble's birth, the foundation stone of Keble College was laid – the first foundation of an entirely new college in Oxford since that of Wadham in 1612 (Pembroke (1624), Worcester (1714) and Hertford (1740) were refoundations of ancient halls).

The college was intended to be unlike other colleges. It was committed to a certain High Church tradition and to simple, economical living (though the early undergraduates were distinctly middle-class, not poor, and their simple living was usually a matter of virtue, not necessity). It was ruled by a council, largely drawn from outside the college – indeed outside Oxford – instead of by the head of house and the Fellows as the other colleges were. The statutes allowed the college to be moved away from Oxford at the council's will (in deference to John Keble's opinion, obviously shared by some of the founders, that Oxford might not prove to be the best place for a poor scholar's college). This last peculiarity inevitably led, at the time, to Keble's being called a 'gypsy college'.

For their architect, the trustees appropriately chose William Butterfield (1814–1900). A firm follower of the Oxford Movement himself, Butterfield could be relied upon to make the new foundation as unlike the other colleges in appearance as it was in aim. As the architect Norman Shaw once wrote, 'When you come to think of it, what are any of us doing but copying the styles of the past? – except Butterfield and he is paddling in a boat of his own.' The first buildings to go up, in 1868–70, were the ranges on the east and west of the main quadrangle, containing rooms for under-graduates and tutors. The undergraduate rooms were arranged along corridors, with a don's set at the end, a deviation from the usual and more intimate Oxford pattern of staircases with a few rooms off each landing. On the south side two small slate-roofed brick sheds were erected as temporary chapel and hall. Dr Pusey, determined that the college should have at least one impressive feature, paid out of his own pocket for the erection of the entrance gateway and tower on Parks Road.

The grand public rooms did not take long to appear. The foundation stone of the chapel was laid in 1873 by the donor, William Gibbs of Tyntesfield, whose fortune was made from guano. The building, which opened three years later, was optimistically designed to seat far more than the college then admitted. And in a characteristic attempt to keep the college out of the grasp of those whose views might be alien, the council refused to have the chapel consecrated, much to the fury of the then BISHOP OF OXFORD; it remains unconsecrated to this day. In 1895 a side-chapel was built, not by Butterfield, though he was invited to be its architect but declined on the grounds that such an addition was both undesirable and impossible. T.J. Micklethwaite then submitted designs, which were accepted; the result bears out Butterfield's first ground for refusal while disproving his second. The hall and library were opened in 1878, the gift of Anthony and Henry Gibbs, sons of the donor of the chapel. The hall, 127 by 35 feet, is the longest, though not the largest, in Oxford. A posthumous, somewhat ideal-ised, portrait of John Keble by George Richmond was presented to the college by the artist and hung over the high table, where it remains. The library is on the opposite side of the landing of the magnificent staircase, with Senior and Junior Common Rooms placed underneath at ground level (the Junior Common Rooms were recently moved and the space converted to reading rooms). At the library's opening there was already a considerable number of books, including John Keble's library and most of his manuscripts. The library now also houses the best collection of mediaeval illuminated manuscripts in Oxford outside the BODLEIAN, the core of it being the bulk of a collection formed by Sir Thomas Brooke, one of the great bibliophiles of the late 19th century, bequeathed to the college by his brother, Canon C.E. Brooke, in 1913. Of the remaining buildings designed by Butterfield, the smaller (Pusey) quadrangle was built mainly in the 1870s and the Warden's lodgings in 1877. The college had by then grown to quite considerable size, though various raw ends of buildings, some of which remain visible today, testify to ambitions – impressive in a college completely without endowment – to be larger still.

The lack of endowment was intentional. All the money raised by public subscription was put into the buildings; the tutors were to be paid out of their pupils' fees, as in a private school. The lack of funds was to be healthy for the spirit of the college and also to give no opening to meddlesome politicians.

In the early years of the college, when the campaigns of the Oxford Movement were still full of life, important battles were fought over the direction that the new college should take. H.P. Liddon, a well-established theological scholar, was pressed to become the first Warden, but declined and suggested one of his Christ Church pupils, Edward Talbot. There were doubts among the trustees: Talbot was in his mid-twenties and had been a don for only four years. Nonetheless, he was appointed and, much to the irritation of some of the trustees (especially Liddon), he opened the college's doors from the first to ideas other than those favoured by John Keble and the Tractarians. Liddon, himself a second-generation Tractarian, was deeply respectful of the outlook of the first generation; he seems to have seen the aims of the college as the preservation of the past and the production of clergymen committed to the strict observance of Tractarian practices. If he had had his way, Keble would have become in effect a theological college – indeed, a theological college with a static conception of intellectual life. In pursuit of their aims, Liddon, Lord Beauchamp (a prominent lay member of the council) and others of the traditionalist party sought to block what Talbot was trying to achieve in winning academic recognition and respect for the college. Their grievance, as one of them put it, was that Talbot 'had not the church character of Keble at heart so much as its academic well-being'. Talbot stuck to his guns. He insisted on the admission to the college of men reading the widest possible range of subjects. He encouraged the teaching of science, and with several of the tutors contributed to *Lux Mundi*, a publication that welcomed the principle of evolution to theological thinking. Under his direction, the youngest college may at this time have come closer than any other to attaining the Renaissance ideal of a university.

However, by the end of the 19th century much of the fire had gone out of Tractarian controversies, and Keble more than most colleges entered quiet times. During the wardenship of Robert James Wilson (1888–97), chosen by a council anxious to have someone less dangerously progressive than Talbot had been considered, Keble stagnated and at times its financial position was desperate. But under Walter Lock (1897–1920), promoted from a tutorship of the college, the decline was halted; and under James Beresford Kidd (1920–39), the first Warden to have been a Keble undergraduate, some progress began to be discernible. By the 1920s the tutors were exerting an increasing influence on the council's conduct of business, and this was formally recognised in 1930 when the council, while retaining control of finances and ecclesiastical patronage, handed over the internal administration and academic direction of the college to the Warden and tutors, who were now for the first time accorded the status of Fellows.

The second period of rapid expansion and constitutional change came after the Second World War. Harry Carpenter (1939–55), who had been tutor in Theology at the college since 1927, succeeded Kidd as Warden. Carpenter persuaded the council to place the entire control of college business in the hands of the Warden and Fellows and thereby to accept its own dissolution. The new statutes were in due course approved by the University and by the Queen in Council and were promulgated in 1952. This event marked Keble's coming of age, as it brought the college's constitution into line with those of other colleges and thus enabled Keble to assume full rights as a constituent college of the University, freed from the limitations that its previous status as a 'new foundation' had implied. The most fateful provision of the new statutes was the formal abandonment of religious tests. Membership of the Church of England as a condition for admission of undergraduates had been quietly dropped in practice in the 1930s, although the council had still insisted on retaining it for election to a fellowship, which meant that non-Anglican tutors had been ineligible for full membership of the internal governing body. Only the wardenship now remained subject to any limitation, as even in 1952 the council could not stomach that office's falling into lay or non-Anglican hands, and the

retention of the requirement that the Warden be in Holy Orders was made a condition of council's acceptance of the other new statutes. This last surviving restriction, however, was removed in 1969.

In 1956, the raw end which had been left where work on the block west of the chapel had stopped short (the block was to have run the full length of the north wall of the college garden) was finished off by a small addition in the Butterfield idiom, designed by A.B. Knapp-Fisher and T. Rayson; it was the gift of ANTONIN BESSE, founder of St Antony's College and benefactor of many others. In 1965 Keble launched what proved to be a highly successful centenary appeal. The two largest donors were the Adeby Trust and the Hayward Foundation. Two new quadrangles were built, to the design of the firm of Ahrends, Burton and Koralek, and were named after the two men who had endowed the foundations: André de Breyne and Sir Charles Hayward. The buildings are in the style of their time, but they acknowledge the powerful presence of Butterfield's work by using his material – brick – but in colour matching the stone in Butterfield's elevations rather than the brick. In characteristic Oxford way, these new buildings turn a somewhat cold shoulder to the street and present a more friendly, delicate, glazed skin to the interior of the college; and, symbolically, they adopt the general Oxford pattern of rooms off staircases.

The most famous work of art in the college is undoubtedly Holman Hunt's much-reproduced painting *The Light of the World*, which hangs in the side-chapel. It was given to the college in 1873 by Martha Combe (*see* JERICHO). The college so provoked Hunt's ire by charging visitors to see the picture that he painted another version, which he gave to St Paul's Cathedral in London. In all, there are three versions of the picture, but Keble's is the first and the one most fully Hunt's work. Besides George Richmond's oil portrait of John Keble in the hall, the college owns Richmond's fine watercolour portrait of Keble, his portrait bust of Keble, and his oil portraits of Warden Talbot and Archbishop Longley. It also owns W.C. Ross's watercolour portrait of a young J.H. NEWMAN and a fine portrait bust of Newman by Thomas Woolner. In hall, portraits worthy of note are those of Warden Lock by C.W. Furse, Warden Kidd by Henry Lamb, Newman by W.T. Roden, Archbishop Garbett by Peter Greenham, and Warden Nineham by Norman Blamey

Distinguished members of Keble include A.F. Winnington-Ingram (1877), Bishop of London; Cyril Garbett (1895), Archbishop of York; Lakdasa de Mel (1921), Metropolitan of the Church of India, Pakistan, Burma and Ceylon; Baron Helsby (1926), head of the Home Civil Service; Peter Pears (1928), tenor; Sir Thomas Armstrong and Ralph Downes (1916 and 1925 respectively), musicians; Geoffrey Hill (1950), poet; Michael Elliot (1951), theatre producer; Chad Varah (1930), founder of the Samaritans; and Timothy Severin (1959) explorer.

As early as 1913 Keble had become one of the four largest colleges in Oxford, and it is now regularly among the two or three largest. In 1986 it had some 396 undergraduates, 110 graduates and thirty-seven Fellows. The last Warden was C.J.E. Ball; his two immediate predecessors were A.M. Farrer (1959–68) and D.E. Nineham (1969–80). The present warden is Dr George Barclay Richardson.

Holman Hunt's Light of the World, *which was given to Keble College in 1873, hangs in the college chapel.*

(Battiscombe, Georgina, *John Keble*, London, 1963; Lock, Walter, *John Keble*, London, 1894, and in A. Clark, *The Colleges of Oxford*, London, 1892; Talbot, E.S., *Memoirs of Early Life*, London, 1924; Thompson, Paul, *William Butterfield*, London, 1971; Parkes, M.B., *The Medieval Manuscripts of Keble College*, London, 1979.)

Keble Road Named after the college which dominates its south side, Keble Road runs between BANBURY ROAD and PARKS ROAD. On the north side are mainly University departments, including Theoretical Physics, the Radiation Protection Office and the Safety and Fire Office.

Keene, Henry (*1726–1776*). Examples of this architect's work are to be seen all over Oxford. He designed the Provost's lodgings at Worcester College (1773–6) and completed the north range of the college; he was responsible for the Anatomy School (later the Chemical Laboratory) at Christ Church

(1766–7), for the Fisher Building at Balliol, for remodelling the interior of the hall at University College, for the sash windows at the SHELDONIAN THEATRE, and for the first designs for the RADCLIFFE OBSERVATORY. He is also said to have been 'engaged at Magdalen College for about twenty years'. He bought a lease of No. 65 ST GILES' in 1768 and was, no doubt, the architect of the house's new front, which was built soon afterwards.

Kellog Centre for Continuing Education *see* REWLEY HOUSE.

Kemp Hall *129a High Street.* A timber-constructed house with the date 1637 over the doorway, although the building is mediaeval, altered in the 16th and 17th centuries. ANTHONY WOOD states that 'it was in King Henry VIII's raigne the house of Richard Kent, Alderman of Oxon (rather, therefore, Kent's Hall).' It is approached from HIGH STREET by a narrow passage. The overhanging upper storey has oriel windows and there are five gables above. In 1880, and up until *c*.1920, it was the police station; Kelly's Directory for 1894–5 refers to it as the City Police Office with a superintendent, two inspectors, six sergeants and forty-seven constables. It is now occupied by LA SORBONNE restaurant.

Kettell, Ralph (*1563–1643*). Awarded a scholarship to Trinity on the recommendation of the founder's widow, Kettell became President of the college in 1599 and presided over it for the rest of his long life, administering it efficiently, supervising its reconstruction and building KETTELL HALL in BROAD STREET. JOHN AUBREY, who was an undergraduate in Kettell's day and described him in 1642 as having 'a terrible gigantique aspect with his sharp gray eies', said that 'the doctor's fashion was to go up and down the college, and peep in at the keyholes to see whether the boys did follow their books or no. . . . He was irreconcilable to long hair. . . . When he observed the scholars' hair longer than ordinary he would bring a pair of scissors in his muff (which he commonly wore) and woe be to them that sat on the outside of the table. I remember he cut Mr Radford's hair with the knife that clips the bread on the buttery hatch. . . . He was a person of great charity. In his college, where he observed boys that had but a slender [allowance] he would many times put money in at their windows. 'Tis probable this venerable doctor might have lived some years longer, and finished his century, had not those civil wars come on; which much grieved him, that was wont to be absolute in the college, to be affronted and disrespected by rude soldiers.'

Kettell Hall *see* TRINITY COLLEGE.

King Edward Street Known by this name since it was built in 1872, this was one of only two new major streets (NEW ROAD was the other) which were made within the CITY WALL between the Middle Ages and the 1920s. There was no corresponding ancient street. It was cut by Oriel College through its own property – an unusual undertaking, as colleges have more often sought permission to enclose small streets running between their buildings. No. 109 HIGH STREET, on the corner with King Edward Street, was sold to Oriel College for £600 in 1872. It is occupied by SHEPHERD AND WOODWARD. A plaque on a house on the west side of the road indicates that CECIL RHODES lived there.

Kingerlee Ltd *Lamarsh Road*. Firm of builders founded in 1871 by Thomas Henry Kingerlee, who was MAYOR of Oxford in 1898 and 1911. The firm is a family business, with Thomas H. Kingerlee, a descendant of the founder, as managing director. It has built many well-known buildings in Oxford, including the APOLLO THEATRE, the shop premises which were occupied by ELLISTON & CAVELL in MAGDALEN STREET, a number of new buildings at the DRAGON SCHOOL and ST EDWARD'S SCHOOL, several blocks of flats in NORTH OXFORD and CUTTESLOWE, and many additions to the various colleges.

(*See also* MASONS AND BUILDERS.)

King's Arms *40 Holywell Street*. Buildings were erected here in 1268 by Augustinian friars, who owned the site till 1540 (*see* AUGUSTINIAN PRIORY). On 18 September 1607 it opened as the King's Arms (in honour of James I) and contained many lodging rooms, a large stable and back courtyard. In the 17th century the inn was a popular place for plays. Parts of the original inn remain, but in the early 18th century the south frontage and rear wing were rebuilt, containing a staircase and a stone, oak-beamed cellar. The west front was added in the late 18th century. By 1771 the King's Arms had become a coaching inn on the London to Gloucester run (*see* TRANSPORT). Wadham College converted the upper floors into students' rooms in 1962.

Knowles & Son *Holywell House, Osney Mead*. This firm of builders and stonemasons was founded in 1797 by Thomas Knowles, who took over the business of William Townesend with whom he had been associated for many years (*see* TOWNESENDS). The firm was then working on such buildings as Blenheim Palace, the RADCLIFFE CAMERA, and the Abingdon, Henley and Maidenhead bridges. The firm's ledger of 1797 lists twenty-one Oxford colleges and halls as customers. Its stonemason's yard and works were then in HOLYWELL and are shown adjoining New College and the CITY WALL in the 1843 engraving by W. Radclyffe from a drawing by F. Mackenzie. The firm has passed from father to son since its foundation and, although incorporated as Knowles & Son (Oxford) Ltd in 1928, is still owned and run by the great-great-grandson of the founder. The firm has done building work for many Oxford colleges in recent years, including Brasenose, Jesus and Linacre. It moved to OSNEY MEAD in 1966.

(*See also* MASONS AND BUILDERS.)

Knox, Ronald Arbuthnott (*1888–1957*). Educated at SUMMER FIELDS and Eton, Knox came up to Balliol as a scholar in 1906 and obtained a First in Greats in 1910. He won the Hertford Scholarship in 1907, the Ireland and the Craven Scholarships in 1908 and in the same year the Gaisford prize for Greek verse (*see* PRIZES AND SCHOLARSHIPS); in 1910 he won the Chancellor's Prize for Latin Verse. The previous year he had been elected President of the UNION. After graduating he became a Fellow of Trinity and was ordained an Anglican priest in 1912. As college chaplain, he soon established himself as a preacher of

Knowles & Son's stonemasons' yard and works in Holywell in the shadow of New College and the city wall.

renown. He left Oxford in 1914, returning in 1926 as a Catholic priest with the appointment of chaplain to the Catholic undergraduates. He was made a Monsignor in 1936. Several works of literary merit were published by him during this period, notably *Let Dons Delight*. In 1939 he again left Oxford, this time to work on his translation of the Bible which, based on the Vulgate, was a more accurate translation of the original and in a more contemporary idiom. He was made an Honorary Fellow of Trinity in 1941 and of Balliol in 1953. Although gravely ill, he gave the 1957 Romanes Lecture (*see* LECTURES) on 'English Translation'. Two months later, he died at Mells. His biography was written by Evelyn Waugh.

Kolkhorst, George Alfred (*1898–1958*). The son of a successful businessman, Kolkhorst spent much of his early life in Chile and Portugal, and was employed in Spain on government work during the First World War. He went up to Exeter College in 1919 and, having obtained a First in Spanish, was appointed Taylorian Lecturer in Spanish. He became Reader in Spanish in 1931. It is not so much for his scholarship that he is remembered, however, as for his eccentric teaching methods, his caustic wit and his generous hospitality at the Portuguese *quinta* which he had inherited from his father, in his rooms at No. 38

BEAUMONT STREET, and at his country house, Yarnton Manor near Oxford, where distinguished guests might find themselves in the company of undergraduates, uninvited strangers and even village children.

The stories told of Kolkhorst's bizarre eccentricities have made him one of the best-known dons of his time. 'We nicknamed him "Colonel" Kolkhorst,' SIR JOHN BETJEMAN recalled in *My Oxford* (ed. Ann Thwaite, 1977). 'He wore a lump of sugar hung from his neck on a piece of string "to sweeten his conversation", and at some of his parties would be dressed in a suit of white flannel, waistcoat and all. ... We used to stick stamps on his ceiling by licking them and throwing them up on up-turned pennies. After one of his merrier sherry parties, the Colonel accompanied [some undergraduates] to the top of St Mary Magdalen's Tower in the Cornmarket, where they sang hymns and began spitting on the people on the pavement. The Proctors were called ... The Colonel carried a little ear trumpet for "catching clever remarks", but would swiftly put it away and yawn if they were not clever. ... He regarded Spanish as hardly a subject at all, and not worth learning. He thought Cervantes the only outstanding Spanish author, though he liked the Nicaraguan poet Rubén Darío, whose name he would pronounce at sherry parties with a tremendous rolling of 'r's.'

L

Laboratories The earliest laboratories were associated with alchemy, and then with the study of chemistry and the preparation of medicines. Today there are many different kinds of laboratory in Oxford, from the traditional ones for the practical investigation of the numerous branches of Physics and Chemistry which have evolved since the 17th century, to those for the study of computer processing, and even speech, such as the Computer Laboratory established in 1957, and the Phonetics Laboratory in WELLINGTON SQUARE, founded in 1980.

There may have been a laboratory for preparing chemical medicines in the Oxford Physic Garden, now the BOTANIC GARDEN, established in 1621. At about this time, the chemical skills of the town's apothecaries were passed on to members of the University, who then maintained their own laboratories, employed 'operators' to help with their experiments, and gave private courses in chemistry. In the 1650s, the laboratory of John Wilkins, the Warden of Wadham College, was the meeting place of an active circle of chemists which included CHRISTOPHER WREN. Robert Boyle used the laboratory of the leading Oxford apothecary John Cross for 'philosophical' experiments (the site next to University College in the HIGH STREET, where the house once stood, is now occupied by the SHELLEY MEMORIAL). John Locke, too, financed a small laboratory while still a student. This general interest in the sciences eventually led to the founding of Oxford's oldest scientific teaching institution, the original ASHMOLEAN MUSEUM (now the MUSEUM OF THE HISTORY OF SCIENCE), built by the Oxford master-mason Thomas Wood, and opened in 1683. It was erected next to Wren's SHELDONIAN THEATRE, and he may have been consulted about the internal layout of this three-tier structure. The Ashmolean collection – largely of natural and ethnographical specimens – was displayed in an exhibition gallery on the top floor, the middle floor (at entrance level) served as a lecture theatre for the School of Natural History, and the roomy basement (partly below ground) was the first purpose-built teaching chemical laboratory in this country. It remained the main centre of Oxford science for the next century and a half.

Physics (then still called Experimental Philosophy) was transferred with its delicate apparatus in 1832 from the museum to the CLARENDON BUILDING, vacated by the OXFORD UNIVERSITY PRESS for its new premises in WALTON STREET. In 1848 the then Professor of Chemistry, Charles Daubeny, moved into his privately built laboratory adjacent to the Physic Garden opposite Magdalen College; but the museum's basement laboratory was not finally closed down until 1857.

In the second half of the 19th century science education began to develop rapidly at Oxford, helped by the statute of 1850 which established the Honour School of Natural Science. The urgent need for new teaching and research facilities led to the creation of the college laboratories. Some chemistry was already taught in the 18th century at Dr Lee's laboratory at Christ Church, built by HENRY KEENE in 1767 as a School of Anatomy. It was converted into a proper chemical laboratory in 1859, and was not closed down until 1941. Balliol's first chemical laboratory was built in 1853, in the cellars of the Salvin Building, thereby continuing for another ninety years Oxford's honourable tradition of subterranean chemistry. In 1879 Balliol and Trinity established a combined teaching laboratory for their undergraduates, and the original cellar laboratory (now Staircase XVI) was mainly used for research – among others, by Frederick Soddy, awarded the 1921 Nobel Prize for his discovery of isotopes. Two other small laboratories were established at Trinity, both in Dolphin Yard: the Millard Building Laboratory used from 1886 to 1914 for teaching and research in Physics (mainly Mechanics), and – after a hiatus when it was converted into a bath-house by the War Office in the First World War – again from 1929 until 1941 for C.N. (later SIR CYRIL) HINSHELWOOD's kinetics research; and a converted lavatory used by Hinshelwood from 1921 to 1929 for work which won him the 1956 Nobel Prize for Chemistry. The Queen's College converted a stable in 1900 for the teaching of preliminary Chemistry until 1907, and then for research in Organic Chemistry until 1934. Finally, Jesus College built the Sir Leoline Jenkins Laboratory (named after an early Principal of the college) in 1907, which was used until 1944 for Chemistry teaching, and for research in kinetics until 1946. In the early 1900s the teaching in these laboratories was reorganised to make it more effective; the Daubeny Laboratory of Magdalen College concentrated on Analytical Chemistry until its closure in 1923, Christ Church and Queen's on Organic Chemistry, Jesus and the Balliol–Trinity laboratories on Physical Chemistry. These college laboratories were a key element in the development of science in Oxford until the Second World War, especially in the field of Physical Chemistry.

The University's SCIENCE AREA began with the building of the UNIVERSITY MUSEUM between 1855 and 1860 – a masterpiece of Victorian Gothic architecture, if impractical as a scientific institution. The intention was to continue the tradition established by the original Ashmolean Museum of having all the science departments, collections and laboratories in a single building. Indeed, until 1964 the whole Science Area complex was to remain administratively under the heading of the museum. The chemical laboratory, connected to the museum by a corridor, was a replica of the Abbot's Kitchen at Glastonbury Abbey – a typical piece of Victorian archaism expressing the ideals of JOHN RUSKIN, and very inconvenient for the chemists. It was also smaller than the original

Ashmolean basement. In 1878 a large undergraduate teaching laboratory was added, and extensions at various dates, especially in the 1950s, have turned it into the present Inorganic Chemistry Laboratory.

The Dyson Perrins Laboratory of Organic Chemistry was founded in 1916, and yet another benefaction, this time by LORD NUFFIELD, established the Physical Chemistry Laboratory in 1940. Biochemistry has its roots both in Chemistry and in Physiology, and became a separate subject in Oxford in 1920. The Biochemistry Laboratory was opened in 1927, made possible by the Rockefeller Foundation; its eight-storey extension, completed in 1963, dominates the Science Area. The first Physiology Laboratory was founded in 1884, and rehoused in a larger building in 1953. The Professor of Anatomy was initially put in charge of the PITT RIVERS MUSEUM, built at the back of the University Museum in 1885. He was responsible for the whole of Biology, from which have developed the Departments of Physiology, Human Anatomy, and Comparative Anatomy (now Zoology), each with their own laboratories.

The loveliest 20th-century science building is the SIR WILLIAM DUNN SCHOOL OF PATHOLOGY, opened in 1927, which began the expansion of the Science Area eastwards to the end of SOUTH PARKS ROAD. The epoch-making work on penicillin was begun here by LORD FLOREY, Sir Ernst Boris Chain and N.G. Heatley on the eve of the Second World War. The previous Pathology Laboratory became the Department of Pharmacology and, like all laboratories, is forever evolving in step with the latest scientific discoveries, in this case with an Immunotoxicology Unit and an Anatomical Neuropharmacology Unit, established respectively by the Wellcome Trust in 1983 and the Medical Research Council (MRC) in 1985. Other additions to the Science Area have included the Radcliffe Science Library, a handsome building opened in 1903, and an Agricultural Science and Forestry site on PARKS ROAD, established by St John's College in 1907 but with its origins in the professorship of Rural Economy which dates from 1796. Botany, Forestry and the Department of Agricultural Science combined in 1985 to become the Department of Plant Sciences. The Experimental Psychology Laboratory was founded in 1935, and in 1970 was rehoused with Zoology in a striking modern concrete building resembling the superstructure of a passenger liner and designed by Sir Leslie Martin.

Physics, too, had moved from the Clarendon Building to the University Museum in 1860. Twelve years later the subject expanded into its own building, the CLARENDON LABORATORY, which pre-dates its more famous counterpart in Cambridge, the Cavendish Laboratory, by four years. Electricity continued to be taught at the museum until the Electrical Laboratory was established in 1910; it has since been renamed the Townsend Building. H.J.G. Moseley, who had been a student in the Balliol–Trinity Laboratory, returned in 1913 from Manchester to continue his fundamental experiments here on the X-ray spectra of elements, which advanced our knowledge of the atom. He was killed in the First World War. In 1940 a new Clarendon Laboratory (now the Lindemann Building) was built, the old site being taken over by the Department of Geology and Mineralogy, to which was added the Simon Building (named after the Oxford low-temperature physicist Sir Francis Simon)

in 1948. This famous laboratory specialises in atomic and laser physics, high magnetic fields, cryogenics, crystal-growing, and most forms of spectroscopy. The Department of Astrophysics has evolved from the University Observatory, established in 1875. The first proper observatory was constructed in 1772 for the Savilian Professor of Astronomy, Thomas Hornsby, and used by successive professors until the 1830s, although it was never strictly part of the University. The fine tower of the RADCLIFFE OBSERVATORY is now the centrepiece of Green College. After 1914 laboratories also began to be built in the KEBLE ROAD triangle – chiefly the Departments of Engineering Science, Metallurgy and, in the early 1970s, Nuclear Physics, with its characteristic tower housing a coupled Van der Graaff generator for high-energy experiments.

Laboratories in Oxford are continuously advancing in an attempt to keep up with the increasing pace of scientific developments. Computer facilities have expanded dramatically in recent years, as have the clinical laboratories which form part of the Clinical Medical Departments in the RADCLIFFE INFIRMARY and in the JOHN RADCLIFFE HOSPITAL, which have benefited greatly from the Nuffield Benefaction and from the Medical Research Council.

(*See also* SCIENCE AREA.)

Lady Margaret Hall Founded in 1878 as 'a small hall or hostel in connection with the Church of England for the reception of women desirous of availing themselves of the special advantages which Oxford offers for higher education'. The first chairman of its council was Edward Talbot, Warden of Keble and later Bishop of Winchester, while the first Principal, Elizabeth Wordsworth, was the daughter of one bishop and the sister of another. The connection with the Church of England which distinguished Lady Margaret Hall from the other women's hall, Somerville, founded at the same time, remained important, though the last religious restriction (on the principalship) was formally removed in 1968. The hall was named after LADY MARGARET BEAUFORT, mother of Henry VII and a patron of learning. In the words of Elizabeth Wordsworth, 'She was a gentlewoman, a scholar, and a saint, and after being married three times she took a vow of celibacy; what more could be expected of any woman?'

The hall opened in October 1879 in a new grey brick villa leased from St John's College. This soon became too small for the demand and for the expansionist ideas of the Principal. The first purpose-built addition was a red-brick building by Basil Champneys, opened in two stages in 1881 and 1884 and designed in accordance with the requirement of St John's that it should be convertible to two separate houses if women's halls did not prove a success. The freehold of the original site was not acquired until 1923, but in 1893 a broad sweep of land down to the river was bought from St John's. The buildings known as Wordsworth (1896), Talbot (1910), Toynbee (1915, named after Charlotte Toynbee, house treasurer from 1883 to 1921) and Lodge (1926, named after Eleanor Lodge, Vice-Principal of the hall from 1906 to 1921) were all designed by Sir Reginald Blomfield. In 1931 Sir Giles Gilbert Scott designed the Deneke building (named after Margaret Deneke, who raised much money for it) and the adjoining Byzantine chapel (dedicated 1933). In the 1960s a quadrangle was formed by the building of a new library and adjacent ranges, designed by Raymond Erith, across the end of NORHAM GARDENS, and two freestanding buildings by Christophe Grillet were added next to this in 1972. The college gardens cover some 8 acres and stretch down to the CHERWELL (*see* THAMES).

Lady Margaret Hall grew steadily in numbers from 1879, subject until 1957 to the limitation imposed by the University on the number of women undergraduates. Even before this restriction was formally lifted, LMH had been allowed to go some way above its official quota of 150. By 1985 there were about 330 undergraduates and seventy graduate students. The tutorial strength grew more slowly. At first all teaching was provided by tutors from the men's colleges under the supervision of the Association for the Education of Women. The first woman tutor was appointed in 1889 and from the 1890s the AEW took less responsibility for students at LMH; it was wound up in 1920 when women became members of the University. In 1953, when a new charter and statutes made LMH a fully self-governing college, there were still only ten tutors, and only one was a scientist. In 1979 the college began to admit men at all levels; several male tutors were appointed, and a man became the sixth Principal. By 1985 the governing body consisted of the Principal and thirty-four Fellows, including fourteen men. The numbers of men and women undergraduates were then approximately equal, and the balance between those reading arts and sciences was close to that of the University at large.

Distinguished former members of the college include Gertrude Bell, Eglantyne Jebb, Katherine Briggs, Veronica Wedgwood, Mary Warnock, Elizabeth Longford, Antonia Fraser, Benazir Bhutto and Lucy Sutherland. The Principal in 1986 was Duncan Stewart. His immediate predecessors were E.M. Chilver (1971–9), Lucy Sutherland (1945–71), Lynda Grier (1921–45) and Henrietta Jex-Blake (1909–21).

The corporate title is The College of the Lady Margaret in the University of Oxford, commonly known as Lady Margaret Hall.

(Bailey, G., ed., *Lady Margaret Hall: a Short History*, 1923.)

Lamb and Flag *12 St Giles'*. Named after the symbol of St John the Baptist. St John's College bought the property from GODSTOW ABBEY and opened a tavern in around 1695. Parts of the original building still remain.

Laud, William *(1573–1645)*. The son of a Reading clothier, Laud was sent from the free school in his home town to St John's College, where his tutor was John Buckeridge (?1562–1631), who later became President of the college and in 1611 was appointed Bishop of Rochester. Created a Fellow of St John's in 1593, ordained in 1601 and appointed a PROCTOR in 1603, Laud spoke out strongly against the Calvinist leanings in the University, and outspokenly maintained that there could be 'no true church without diocesan bishops' and that Presbyterians were no better than Papists. A sermon he preached on these lines at ST MARY THE VIRGIN resulted in a reproof from the VICE-CHANCELLOR, who condemned its popish flavour. In 1611, however, Laud was appointed President of St John's in succession to Buckeridge despite opposition from the Calvinists, who maintained that there had been irregularities in his election.

Members of Lady Margaret Hall, which was founded in 1878. The first Principal, Miss (later Dame) Elizabeth Wordsworth, is seated in the middle with Gertrude Bell third from the right in the same row.

Ladies of Lady Margaret Hall on the river c.1896, with their college in the background.

After a subsequent attack upon him in a sermon at St Mary's by Robert Abbot (1560–1617), Master of Balliol, Laud seems not to have been sorry to leave Oxford when appointed Dean of Gloucester in 1616. In 1621 he became Bishop of St David's in Wales and, although at the same time granted permission by James I to remain President of St John's, he recognised that the college statutes did not allow it and therefore resigned. Enjoying the regard and favour of James's successor, Charles I, he subsequently became Bishop of Bath and Wells in 1626, in 1628 Bishop of London and in 1633 Archbishop of Canterbury. He had by then already, in 1629, been appointed CHANCELLOR of the University. As Chancellor he immediately made it clear that he intended to bring the University closer to the Church and to restore discipline by such decrees as those concerning examinations and ACADEMIC DRESS. In 1636 his body of statutes, known as the LAUDIAN CODE, was accepted by CONVOCATION. After Laud's impeachment on a charge of high treason by the Commons in the Long Parliament and his execution in 1645, he was buried in All Hallows, Barking; his remains were removed to St John's College in 1663.

Laudian Code WILLIAM LAUD (1573–1645), Archbishop of Canterbury from 1633, was appointed CHANCELLOR of the University in 1629. In his determination to restore discipline in the University he ordered the compilation by special delegates of a body of statutes, known as the Laudian Code, which was accepted by CONVOCATION in 1636. This confirmed the identification of the colleges with the University and required the college heads to meet every Monday on the HEBDOMADAL BOARD, now to be the essential governing body of the University instead of Convocation and CONGREGATION. The statutes also codified an extraordinary variety of miscellaneous rules by which the University was supposed to govern itself. They concerned themselves with all manner of aspects of Oxford life, from ACADEMIC DRESS and the curling and length of hair to the conduct of lectures and the content of sermons, from fashions in dress to the carrying of arms, from gambling and idling to drinking and smoking in inns and the frequenting of harlots. 'It is enacted', characteristic injunctions in Latin ran, 'that neither rope-dancers nor players (who go on the stage for gain's sake), nor sword-matches, or sword players are to be permitted in the University. . . . Scholars of all conditions shall abstain from . . . the games of dibs dice and cards and also ball-play in the private yards and greens of the townsmen. Also, they must refrain from every kind of sport or exercise, whence danger wrong or inconvenience may arise to others, from hunting wild animals with hounds of any kind, ferrets, nets or toils. . . . It is enacted that Scholars (particularly the younger sort and undergraduates) shall not idle and wander about the City, or its suburbs, nor in the streets, or public market, or Carfax (at Peniless Bench as they commonly call it) nor be seen standing or loitering about the townsmen or worksmen shops. . . . Scholars of all conditions shall keep away from eating-houses [and] wine-shops . . . wherein wine or any other drink, or the Nicotian herb, or tobacco, is commonly sold; also that if any person does otherwise, and is not eighteen years old, and not a graduate, he shall be flogged in public.'

'This work', wrote Laud of the Code, 'I hope God will soe blesse as that it may much improve the honour and good government of [the University], a thing very necessary in this life both for Church and

William Laud, shown here in a painting after Van Dyck, was elected a Fellow of St John's in 1593 and was appointed Chancellor of the University in 1629.

Commonwealth.' The Code remained the basis of the University's laws until 1854. (*See also* DISCIPLINE.)

Law Library. Built in 1961–4 at the junction of ST CROSS ROAD with MANOR ROAD, this low building in sand-coloured brick with horizontal bands was designed by Sir Leslie Martin and Colin St John Wilson. In the same St Cross Building are the English Faculty Library and the Institute of Economics and Statistics. The whole building is described by Pevsner as 'monumental' and 'of international calibre'. The wide, open staircase forming the approach to the Law Library 'has the splendour of Persepolis'. The library, which is a part of the BODLEIAN, has space for 450,000 books, most of which are on open shelves. It is probably the largest collection of Common Law material outside the United States, and is the largest law library in the Commonwealth. There are seats for some 300 readers. The main reading room is 70 feet square and 30 feet high; it is a lofty, galleried room lit by evenly diffused natural top-lighting. The reading-room tables are of African walnut. Main benefactors of the building include the Rockefeller Foundation, the Pilgrim Trust, the Government of Pakistan, the Trustees of Henry and Clara Oppenheimer, the Inns of Court and the Law Society.

(*See also* CODRINGTON LIBRARY, *where the Anson Reading Room is specially devoted to Law.*)

Lectures The University statutes list nearly thirty special lectures; but only the following may normally be attended by a person who is not a member of the University:

Sidney Ball Lecture (Social, Economic and Political), founded by Sidney Ball, late Fellow of St John's College, in 1919

Bampton Lecture, see below

Cyril Foster Lecture (International Peace), founded by C.A. Foster in 1958

Halley Lecture (Astronomy and Terrestrial Magnetism), founded by Henry Wilde in 1910 in honour and memory of Edmond Halley, sometime Savilian Professor of Geometry

Ratanbai Katrak Lecture (Religion of Zoroaster), founded in 1922 by Dr Nanabhai Navrosji Katrak in memory of his wife

O'Donnell Lecture (Celtic Studies), founded by C.J. O'Donnell in 1965

Romanes Lecture, see below

Herbert Spencer Lecture, see below

Taylorian Lecture (Modern European Literature), founded by Professors C.H. Firth and Joseph Wright in 1917

Sir Basil Zaharoff Lecture, see below

Of the above one of the oldest, and arguably the most famous, is the *Romanes Lectureship,* created when the University, by decree of CONVOCATION of 24 November 1891, accepted an offer made by the late George John Romanes of Christ Church, late of Gonville and Caius College, Cambridge, who died in 1894, to give an annual sum of £25 for a lecture to be delivered once a year on some subject, approved by the VICE-CHANCELLOR, relating to science, art or literature. The lecturer is called the Romanes Lecturer, and is appointed by the Vice-Chancellor annually in Michaelmas Term, the lecture being delivered in the following Trinity Term. The list of lecturers is of exceptional distinction, and the following gives some idea both of the quality of the lecturers and of the great range of topics upon which they have spoken:

1892	W.E. GLADSTONE	An Academic Sketch
1899	Sir Richard Jebb	Humanism in Education
1907	LORD CURZON	Frontiers
1909	A.J. Balfour	Criticism and Beauty
1910	Theodore Roosevelt	Biological Analogies in History
1914	Sir Joseph J. Thomson	The Atomic Theory
1918	H.H. Asquith	Some Aspects of the Victorian Age
1924	John Masefield	Shakespeare and Spiritual Life
1934	Sir William Rothenstein	Form and Content in English Painting
1935	GILBERT MURRAY	Then and Now: or the Changes of the Last Fifty Years
1943	Julian Huxley	Evolutionary Ethics
1949	Lord Brabazon of Tara	Forty Years of Flight
1952	Sir Lewis Namier	Monarchy and the Party System
1954	Sir Kenneth Clark	Moments of Vision
1956	Sir Thomas Beecham	John Fletcher: a Forgotten Poet and Dramatist
1957	MGR. R.A. KNOX	Translation
1960	Lord Adrian	Factors in Mental Evolution
1966	SIR MAURICE BOWRA	A Case for Humane Learning

1967	Lord Butler	The Difficult Art of Autobiography
1968	Sir Peter Medawar	Science and Literature
1972	Sir Karl Popper	On the Problem of Body and Mind

The most ironic title belongs to a lecture which was never delivered: M. Édouard Herriot's *'Culture allemande et culture française'*, which was to have been given in Trinity Term, 1940.

Much older are the **Bampton Lectures**, which were first given in 1780. In accordance with the will of the Rev. John Bampton, MA, sometime of Trinity College, Canon of Salisbury, 'Eight Divinity Lecture Sermons' are preached in alternate years in Hilary and Trinity Terms 'upon either of the following subjects: to confirm and establish the Christian Faith, and to confute all heretics and schismatics – upon the authority of the writings of the primitive Fathers as to the Faith and Practice of the primitive Church – upon the Divinity of our Lord and Saviour Jesus Christ – upon the Divinity of the Holy Ghost – upon the Articles of the Christian Faith, as comprehended in the Apostles' and Nicene Creeds'.

The Bampton Lecturer, who must be a graduate of a university and a clergyman of the Anglican Communion, is chosen biennially by the heads of colleges; no one can be chosen a second time. In 1952 it was agreed that in those years in which the Bampton Lectures were not delivered 'so much of the income of the Trust Fund as the University of Oxford shall think fit, but not exceeding the amount payable to the Bampton Lecturer in the previous year, shall be applied by way of stipend payable to lecturers who shall be chosen to deliver in the University of Oxford in each of such years a new series of theological lectures in support of the Christian Faith to be called the Sarum Lectures. . . . The only qualifications for candidates for the Sarum Lectureship shall be that they shall be persons of high scholarship who profess the Christian Faith.'

The even tenor of the Bampton Lectures was sharply disturbed in 1832 by Dr Renn Dickson Hampden's lectures, which had the hardly inflammatory title of 'The Scholastic Philosophy Considered in its Relation to Christian Theology'. For (in the words of R.W. Church) 'the conflicts which for a time turned Oxford into a kind of image of what Florence was in the days of Savonarola, with its nicknames, Puseyites and Neomaniacs, and High and Dry . . . began around [this] student of retired habits'. In other words, these Bampton Lectures subsequently came to be identified as among the first shots in the OXFORD MOVEMENT, when Hampden's choice as Regius Professor of Divinity in 1836 aroused widespread dissent at Oxford, and J.H. NEWMAN made his (anonymous) reply to the lectures called 'Elucidations of Dr. Hampden's Theological Statements'. A few years later BISHOP WILBERFORCE was chosen to give the lectures for 1841, but was prevented from doing so by a domestic tragedy. Among others who are well known, Frederick Temple, later Archbishop of Canterbury, lectured in 1884 upon 'The Relations Between Religion and Science'; and in 1899 Dean W.R. Inge lectured on 'Christian Mysticism'. A lecturer better known for his authorship of *Eric, or Little by Little* was Dean F.W. Farrar, who took 'History of Interpretation' as his theme in 1885.

The *Herbert Spencer Lectureship* was founded when, soon after the death in 1904 of Herbert Spencer, the eminent philosopher, the University accepted an offer made to it by Pandit Shyamaji Krishnavarma of Balliol College to provide an endowment in Spencer's memory. The first lecture was given in 1905, and that for 1914 was given by Bertrand Russell. But indisputably the greatest man to give the lecture was Albert Einstein, who in 1933 spoke 'On the Method of Theoretical Physics'. He was followed in 1934 by Dean Inge on 'Liberty and Natural Rights' and in 1935 by Sir William Beveridge on 'The Economic Aspects of Planning under Socialism'. Arnold Toynbee gave the 1952 lecture on 'Democracy in the Atomic Age'; in 1955 J.B.S. Haldane spoke on 'Time in Biology'. The lectureship is now held every three or, more recently, four years, and is given not by a single lecturer but by a panel. The lectures are then published by the OXFORD UNIVERSITY PRESS.

Of other lectures, perhaps the *Sir Basil Zaharoff Lectureship* is the best known. It was founded in 1918 by Sir Basil Zaharoff as part of his benefaction for the promotion of French Studies, and is directed to be on some subject of French art, archaeology, history, literature, science or sociology. The lecturer is nominated in alternate years by the Vice-Chancellor of Oxford University and the Vice-Rector of the University of Paris. The lecturer is appointed annually in Trinity Term and normally delivers his lecture in the Michaelmas Term following. Among the many distinguished scholars or men of letters who have given this lecture, one may single out Sir James George Frazer (1932), Louis Cazamian (1937), Paul Valéry (1938), Enid Starkie (1954), Sir Maurice Bowra (1956) on 'The Simplicity of Racine', and André Maurois (1967) on 'New Directions in French Literature'. The great actor and director Jean-Louis Barrault spoke in 1961 on *'Le Phénomène théâtral'*.

The *Cherwell–Simon Memorial Lectureship* was founded in 1959 by a bequest from 'certain organisations and friends of the late Lord Cherwell and Sir Francis Simon to provide an annual lecture in some branch of Physics of general interest'.

The *Myres Memorial Lectureship* was also established in 1959, thanks to the generosity of certain learned bodies and friends of the late Professor Sir John Myres, to provide a biennial lecture on a subject within the field of Ancient History, European and Near Eastern Archaeology, Ancient Geography, or Ethnology, with special reference to Mediterranean lands.

Not every lecture is given every year; and new Special Lectures are created from time to time. For 1984–5 the *Oxford University Gazette* listed fifteen separately named Special Lectures. Some lectures are given under the auspices of colleges, such as Pembroke's Blackstone Lecture and McCallum Memorial Lecture.

Lewis, Clive Staples (*1898–1963*). Born in Belfast, the son of a solicitor, C.S. Lewis won scholarships to Malvern College and, in 1916, to University College. He came up to Oxford specifically to train in the Officers' Training Corps, and in 1917 was wounded while serving with the Somerset Light Infantry. After the war he went to live with Mrs J.K. Moore, the mother of a friend who had been killed in

Juliet Pannett's chalk drawing of C.S. Lewis, a leading member of the Inklings, who was elected a Fellow of Magdalen College in 1925.

action, and her daughter. He later moved with her to The Kilns, HEADINGTON QUARRY, where she died in 1951 and where he remained until his own death. In 1922, having won the Chancellor's English Essay Prize (*see* PRIZES AND SCHOLARSHIPS) the previous year, he took a First in LITERAE HUMANIORES; and in 1923 also obtained a First in English Language and Literature. He was elected a Fellow of Magdalen in 1925; and it was in his rooms at Magdalen that many of the meetings of THE INKLINGS were held. He later formed the Socratic Club, a Christian discussion group. One of his pupils, JOHN BETJEMAN, who went up to Magdalen in the year of Lewis's election to a fellowship, described him as 'breezy, tweedy, beer-drinking and jolly. He was very popular with extrovert undergraduates'.

Lewis was a highly successful lecturer at Oxford, but he was passed over for the Merton Chair of English Literature in 1946; and, on being appointed in 1954 to a newly established chair in English Medieval and Renaissance Literature at Cambridge, he left Magdalen for Magdalene. He frequently returned to Oxford, however, and never lost touch with the friends he had made there. He married Helen Joy Davidman in 1956 at the Oxford Register Office; and, because she was believed to be dying, they repeated the ceremony in the Anglican form the next year in the CHURCHILL HOSPITAL.

Lewis wrote several critical works, among them *English Literature in the Sixteenth Century* (1954), but he is more generally known for his popular religious and moral books, including *The Screwtape Letters* (1940), for his science-fiction novels, the first of which was *Out of the Silent Planet*; and for his children's books such as *The Lion, the Witch and the Wardrobe*

(1950). After his death at The Kilns, he was buried at HOLY TRINITY, HEADINGTON.

(*See also* NATURE RESERVES.)

LIBRARIES There are about 150 independent academic libraries in Oxford other than the BODLEIAN, varying in size from a single bookcase to that of some modern university collections. They have been built up over the centuries to serve special groups – either to meet wide-ranging interests (such as those of a college) or to cover a limited subject in a department or faculty. There are libraries in thirty-five colleges, five permanent halls, about sixty departments, faculties or institutes. In addition there are about forty libraries in small medical departments and in fifteen institutions not actually under University control, such as Manchester College and PUSEY HOUSE.

With such a miscellaneous collection it is impossible to generalise, but roughly speaking the older libraries contain the sediment left from former curricula with the additions of benefactions and bequests; here it must be emphasised that the loyalty and generosity of former students is generally directed to individual colleges rather than to the University.

College libraries. From the 13th century onwards, collections of chained books were kept for reference. Others were kept for loans, generally for a year at a time. This system continued until the late 16th century, the last annual loans being made at Lincoln College in 1596. Chains were removed between the middle and end of the 18th century, starting with All Souls in 1750 and concluding with Magdalen College in 1799. During the reigns of Henry VIII, Edward VI, Mary I and Elizabeth I, the central authorities forced the University to dispose of books contrary to the religious beliefs of the monarch. Consequently, the Duke Humfrey Reading Room in the Bodleian was empty by 1556; and, since colleges also suffered – a cartload of books was removed from Merton, for instance – their members had to fall back on their own resources. So purchasing in a serious manner began in the reign of Elizabeth I: in 1572, Magdalen College sold some plate to buy the library of Bishop Jewel for £172, the largest sum ever spent on books in Oxford in the 16th century, while in 1597 Corpus Christi began a regular book fund.

Oxford was slow to catch up with the Renaissance revival of learning, and indeed was behind the rest of Europe until later in the 17th century, after the Restoration of Charles II. Though Lincoln took fees from students for book purchasing from 1606, and Trinity had a bequest of £20 a year for books from 1640, regular financial provision did not begin till this time. Simultaneously, attempts were made to fill the gaps inevitably caused by the CIVIL WAR. Each college tried to attract benefactions, evidenced by the many surviving, lavishly bound benefactors' registers in which names were inscribed in the hope that envy might make others follow suit. These volumes were displayed in prominent positions. Incidentally, it was SIR THOMAS BODLEY who first had this idea in about 1604.

The first half of the 18th century saw great activity in Oxford, with new library buildings going up – at Christ Church, The Queen's College and All Souls, for example – and with the donation of magnificent gifts (except at Merton, Magdalen and Trinity). The

The New Library at Christ Church, which forms the southern side of Peckwater Quadrangle, was completed in 1772 to the design of George Clarke.

stream of gifts slowed down during the second half of the century and remained sluggish throughout the early 19th century until a revival not unconnected with the OXFORD MOVEMENT in the 1830s. Then the government-inspired reforms, and the opening of the University to holders of all religious beliefs from the 1870s onwards, is reflected in the growth of college library book-stocks. At the same time the beginning of competitive examinations and the influence of a more Germanic type of research made Fellows use the larger holdings of the central Bodleian rather than the more modest college collections. In the 1870s James Bryce, the historian and politician (then a Fellow of Oriel), advocated a system of subject specialisation for each college; but although Oriel, Balliol and Worcester did make some conscientious efforts, the scheme was wrecked on the perennial rocks of college independence: no college likes giving the freedom of its premises to people from other colleges. Similar schemes continue to be suggested at fairly frequent intervals.

The last hundred years has seen a complete reversal of the original conception of college libraries as being for the use of senior members only; all are now open for first-degree students – but it has been a slow process. Colleges used to maintain small collections of books keyed to the limited unreformed curriculum in a variety of ways: some let seniors borrow on behalf of juniors; Trinity had the first undergraduate library in 1668, and Balliol soon afterwards. Others, like Merton and St John's, opened for a few hours occasionally – the former for only one hour a week. The Queen's College opened the library to all in 1938, while Worcester did not do so until the late 1950s. It is interesting that Thomas James, Bodley's first librarian, had suggested a special room 'for the yonguer sort' as early as 1608, but Sir Thomas exercised his veto on the grounds that an extra member of staff would be required, and he preferred to spend money on books.

In 1868 there was a proposal that *Bibliothekswissenschaft* should be introduced into the curriculum, and that members of the Bodleian staff should be teachers and fellows of All Souls. Although supported by MARK PATTISON, this far-sighted conception never got beyond a few articles in journals.

The opening up of college libraries was much commented on at the first meeting of the Library Association held in Oxford in 1878, when members of the University were closely associated with that body, though this connection did not continue for very long. The real supplier of books for undergraduate needs from the early 19th century onwards was undoubtedly the UNION, which provided reading matter for both work and entertainment. It still does so today, though not to its former extent.

It is now the needs of undergraduate members that are the primary consideration in college libraries. The inevitable demands from researchers for access to the accumulations of older material, and its organisation and preservation, has often to take second place.

Departmental libraries. Oxford departmental libraries go back to the early 17th century. The Savilian chairs of Geometry and Astronomy, founded in 1619, possessed collections of books – as did the Heather Professorship of Music – while books were also kept at the BOTANIC GARDEN during this period. But the real increase in the number of departmental libraries dates from the establishment of that of the Geology Department in 1813. Since then, each department gathers books for current use as it is founded. The libraries of historical interest have usually been deposited in the Bodleian, though there have been regrettable sales in the past, of which the most flagrant was that by the Radcliffe Trustees in 1935 when much valuable scientific material was lost to Oxford.

Faculty libraries. Faculty libraries date from the late 19th century. They are usually not research collections but are designed as borrowing libraries for undergraduates. The TAYLOR INSTITUTION, specialising in modern European languages, acts as the main research library, though the Modern Languages Faculty Library, descendant of the old seminar collections, has aspirations in that direction too. The English Faculty Library has quite extensive holdings of older English literary works, from the 16th century onwards, and is especially strong on the 18th century.

Catalogues. As might be expected, catalogues vary in quality and efficiency. Most colleges have copies of the 1674, 1738 or 1843 published Bodleian catalogues, annotated with the individual library's location symbols. It should be remembered that both Cambridge and Paris took advantage of the pioneer Bodleian catalogues of Thomas James. However, the great defect of this system is that though the right title gets indicated, the correct imprint and date often do not. Every known set of catalogue rules can be found in Oxford, as well as many individual ones. The same goes for classification: there again, all systems are used. Most of the older collections have a fixed location, with three symbols for bay, shelf and number on shelf, but without the disfiguring three white labels on spines seen on so many Cambridge college library shelves.

Staff. Colleges usually have a Fellow acting as librarian, who has control over whatever funds are allocated for library purposes and answers on library matters at college meetings. Few colleges have library committees (though All Souls has one dating back to the mid-18th century), most leaving decisions to the librarian, who acts as a committee of one. Depending on the size of the library, there are one or more assistants to do day-to-day routine work. Young graduates were employed at Christ Church from 1599, and several colleges made like appointments in the next century. Often a literate college servant or choirman was employed, but nowadays most assistants are young graduates who have been through a library school.

Attempts were made several times in the past to arrange more co-operation between college libraries (as proposed by James Bryce in the last century). Nowadays librarians meet once a term to discuss administrative and financial problems common to all, and from time to time to make collective representations to University authorities.

Libraries Board. During the last hundred years several University committees have been appointed to consider the problems of book provision and libraries in Oxford. That chaired by Dr Robert Shackleton, later Bodley's librarian, published a wide-ranging report in 1966. Its most important consequence has possibly been the establishment of the Libraries Board, which has authority, under the GENERAL BOARD OF FACULTIES, to consider all matters relating to the provision and co-ordination of library facilities, and to make financial provision for all libraries under its care; these include all faculty and departmental, but not college, libraries. If this last type participated, they would have to admit any member of the University and they prefer to serve members of their own colleges only. The Board publishes a *Bulletin* which is circulated around Oxford and which often includes news of college and other libraries that do not depend on the Board for financial support.

Union catalogues. Union catalogues of the large collections of manuscripts and printed books scattered around Oxford have been regularly suggested over the last 400 years, and have as regularly failed to reach fruition. Thomas James, Bodley's first librarian, got the post not only because he was a good Puritan propagandist but also because in 1600 he had published a union catalogue of manuscripts in Oxford and Cambridge libraries. A start was made on a union catalogue of printed books in the later 17th century, but then nothing more happened (except for in some special groups, such as Hebrew) until the present century when several starts were made. A conflation of college catalogue entries for books up to 1640 was compiled from the separate catalogues in the 1930s, but the varying standards of the catalogues and their many omissions make it a very imperfect tool, far below the quality of H.M. Adams's great catalogue of continental books 1501–1600 in Cambridge libraries. Dr D.E. Rhodes of the British Library published in 1982 a union catalogue of most of the incunabula in the majority of Oxford libraries, and brief entries for all these are included on the inter-collegiate cards. There is a separate card catalogue of pre-1641 English printed or published books, keyed to the *Short-title Catalogue*. This is more complete than that for foreign books.

A scheme, known as Project LOC, to get all pre-1801 books in the British Library, all Oxford and Cambridge libraries into a machine-readable form began in 1966; but it did not get much beyond pilot experiments, owing to lack of funds. Various specialist union catalogues have been published in recent years, including one of scientific serials. With the increasing use of computers, more are under discussion.

Briefly, it can be said that the services given by Oxford libraries other than the Bodleian to undergraduates and members of particular departments and faculties are efficient and work well. It is the accumulated collections of past centuries – the contents of which are not fully known and cannot be exploited for research workers – whose organisation leaves much to be desired.

The colleges and departments are, however, independent, and their libraries may be used by non-University members only with written permission obtained in advance.

All departments, institutions and units have collections (of various sizes) of books and journals relevant to their subjects, for departmental use only. Excluding college libraries and the CENTRAL LIBRARY, Westgate, Oxford's principal libraries are:

Arts and Social Sciences Libraries ASHMOLEAN; BODLEIAN; INDIAN INSTITUTE; LAW LIBRARY; RHODES HOUSE; CODRINGTON LIBRARY

Archaeology, Institute of, 34–6 Beaumont Street
Commonwealth Studies, Institute of, Queen Elizabeth House, 20–1 St Giles'
Criminological Research, Centre for, 12 Bevington Road
Economics and Statistics, Institute of, St Cross Building, Manor Road
Educational Studies, Department of, 15 Norham Gardens
English Faculty Library, St Cross Building, Manor Road
Ethnology and Prehistory, Department of, Pitt Rivers Museum, South Parks Road
Geography, School of, Mansfield Road
History Faculty Library, Broad Street
History of Art, Department of, 35 Beaumont Street
History of Science, Museum of, Broad Street
Management Studies, Oxford Centre for, Templeton College, Kennington
Modern Languages Faculty Library, Taylor Institution, St Giles'
Music Faculty Library, St Aldate's
Oriental Institute Library, Pusey Lane
Nissan Institute Library, 1 Church Walk
Philosophy Library, 10 Merton Street
Ruskin School of Drawing and Fine Art, 74 High Street
Social Anthropology, Institute of, 51 Banbury Road
Social Studies Library, Social Studies Faculty Centre, George Street
Taylor Institution Library, St Giles'
Theology Faculty and Pusey House Libraries, Pusey House, St Giles'

Science Libraries
Agricultural Economics Unit, Queen Elizabeth House, 20–1 St Giles'
Astrophysics, Department of, South Parks Road
Atmospheric Physics, Department of, Parks Road
Biochemistry, Department of, South Parks Road
Biological Anthropology, Department of, 58 Banbury Road
Biomathematics, Department of, 5 South Parks Road
Cairns Library (Clinical Medicine), John Radcliffe Hospital (branches at Radcliffe Infirmary, Churchill and Slade Hospitals)
Community Medicine and General Practice, Department of, Gibson Laboratory Building, Radcliffe Infirmary
Computing Laboratory, 8–11 Keble Road
Computing Service, 13 Banbury Road
Criminological Research, Centre for, 12 Bevington Road

Dyson Perrins Laboratory (Organic Chemistry), South Parks Road

Earth Sciences: Geology and Mineralogy, Department of, Parks Road; Surveying and Geodesy, Department of, 62 Banbury Road

Engineering Science, Department of, Parks Road

Entomology (Hope Library), University Museum

Ethnology and Prehistory, Department of (Balfour Library, Pitt Rivers Museum), Pooles Road

External Studies, Department for, Rewley House, Wellington Square

Human Anatomy, Department of, South Parks Road

Human Sciences, Pauling Centre for, 58 Banbury Road

Mathematical Institute, 24–9 St Giles'

Metallurgy and Science of Materials, Department of, Parks Road

Nuclear Physics, Department of, Keble Road

Ophthalmology, Nuffield Laboratory of, Walton Street

Oxford Forestry Institute Library, South Parks Road

Pathology, Sir William Dunn School of, South Parks Road

Pharmacology, Department of, South Parks Road

Physical Chemistry Laboratory, South Parks Road

Physiology, Department of, South Parks Road

Plant Sciences, Department of, South Parks Road (combines the libraries of the former Departments of Agricultural Science, Botany and Forestry)

Psychology, Department of Experimental, South Parks Road

Theoretical Chemistry, Department of, South Parks Road

Transport Studies Unit, 11 Bevington Road

Zoology, Department of, South Parks Road: main departmental library; Animal Ecology (Elton Library); Ornithology (Alexander Library, Edward Grey Institute)

Non-University Libraries

MAISON FRANÇAISE, Norham Road

Manchester College Library, Mansfield Road

Oxford Polytechnic Library, Headington Hill and Wheatley

Plunkett Foundation Co-operative Library, 31 St Giles'

(Morgan, Paul, *Oxford Libraries outside the Bodleian; a guide*, second edition, 1980, and Shaw, Dennis F., *Oxford University science libraries; a guide*, 1981, both published by the Bodleian Library.)

Liddell, Henry George (*1811–1898*). The son of an upper-class clergyman, Liddell entered Christ Church from Charterhouse in 1830. After obtaining a Double First he was appointed tutor in 1836 and Censor in 1845, when he was also elected White's Professor of Moral Philosophy. While tutor, in association with his fellow-tutor Robert Scott (1811–87), later Master of Balliol, Liddell published the Greek–English Lexicon with which their names were ever afterwards to be associated. After a time spent as headmaster of Westminster, during which he served on the Oxford University Commission (*see* ROYAL COMMISSIONS), in 1855 he was appointed Dean of Christ Church in succession to THOMAS GAISFORD. The thirty-six years he spent as Dean were remarkable not only for the reforms undertaken at the college but also for the building work there. He was VICE-CHANCELLOR in 1870–4. He was buried outside the southern wall of the sanctuary of CHRIST CHURCH

CATHEDRAL, near to the grave of his daughter Edith, sister of ALICE.

Linacre College   Established by the University in 1962. For some time concern had been felt about the position of graduates of other universities coming to Oxford to read for advanced degrees, many of whom found difficulty in entering fully into the communal life of mainly undergraduate colleges. The move of St Catherine's to its new site left vacant the building in ST ALDATE'S which had been built for the St Catherine's Society in 1936, and it was decided to use this to house a new experimental society solely for men and women graduate students in all faculties. The new society was called Linacre House after THOMAS LINACRE, humanist scholar and medical scientist.

Originally Linacre was conceived of as non-residential, as St Catherine's had been, and like St Catherine's it was, properly speaking, a department of the University, governed by a delegacy under the chairmanship of the VICE-CHANCELLOR. In 1964, however, by which time it was apparent that the new venture was a success, the delegacy was abolished and the day-to-day government of the college was entrusted to the Principal and Fellows under the supervision of the University. In 1986 the college was granted its charter, became fully self-governing, and took its place among the independent colleges of Oxford. There are 200 student members, about half from overseas, and fifty Fellows, who, with a few exceptions, are Professors, Readers and lecturers in the different faculties.

The Worthington building (now the Music Faculty) in St Aldate's had been designed by Sir Hubert Worthington as a centre for St Catherine's Society, and was very well suited for this purpose. It became apparent, however, that graduates increasingly looked for college accommodation, and in 1977 the governing body readily agreed to a proposal to move the college to CHERWELL EDGE. A new main entrance and a large dining hall were accordingly added to the building; and in 1985 a second residential block, known as the Bamborough Building in recognition of the services of the Principal, J.B. Bamborough, and his wife Anne was built on the south side, in a style congruent with the existing buildings, which had been designed by Basil Champneys, and forming a small paved courtyard. The architect for both of these additions was Jack Lankester, the then University Surveyor.

It was announced in November 1987 that Sir Bryan Cartledge, British Ambassador in Moscow, was to succeed Mr John Bamborough as Principal in the summer of 1988.

Linacre, Thomas (*c.1460–1524*). Entered Oxford in about 1480 and was elected a Fellow of All Souls in 1484. A distinguished classical scholar, he was a close friend of William Latimer and WILLIAM GROCYN. After extensive travels in Italy, where he studied Greek and Latin texts and obtained a medical degree at the University of Padua, he returned to Oxford. His many friends there included COLET and his pupils Thomas More and Erasmus, both of whom, as well as THOMAS WOLSEY, became his patients when he established himself as a physician in London. His obtaining Letters Patent from Henry VIII for the institution of a body of physicians empowered to decide who should practise medicine in London and within 7 miles of its centre led to the foundation of the Royal College of Physicians of London. Linacre's benefactions to the University resulted in the foundation of two lectureships in Medicine. These eventually became sinecures, but were reconstituted with the foundation of the Linacre Professorship of Physiology. His name is now associated with the Linacre Professorship of Zoology.

(*See also* LINACRE COLLEGE.)

Lincoln College The College of the Blessed Mary and All Saints, Lincoln, in the University of Oxford was founded in 1427 by Richard Fleming, Bishop of Lincoln. Fleming, who had once unjustifiably been suspected of harbouring heterodox LOLLARD views intended the college to be a small society, a 'little college', its object to train clergy 'in true theology' and so to be able to 'defend the mysteries of Scripture against those ignorant laymen who profaned with swinish snouts its most holy pearls'. He obtained a royal charter (dated 13 October 1427) enabling him to unite the three parishes in Oxford in his gift – ALL SAINTS, ST MICHAEL'S and St Mildred's (the church of which was immediately pulled down) – to provide a foundation for the new college. The college was to enjoy the revenues from these parishes (a very small endowment by comparison with the benefactions enjoyed by other recent foundations, such as New College), from which it was to pay stipends to the chaplains of the churches.

The first few decades of the college's history were precarious. Fleming died in 1431 without making any further significant gifts. There were few buildings and

inadequate money. Lincoln consisted only of a Rector, William Chamberleyn, appointed in 1429, and seven Fellows; but Chamberleyn's two successors, John Beke (1435–60) and John Tristropp (1460–80), were energetic men who managed to attract benefactors whose largesse placed the college on a surer economic footing. Among these, the most notable was John Forest, Dean of Wells and a friend of the founder, who gave funds which enabled Lincoln to construct much of the front quadrangle as well as a library, a chapel, a kitchen and a hall. A parishioner of All Saints, Emily Carr, whose husband John was a Bedel of Theology, gave land in the HIGH STREET (now Nos 113 and 114) and in BEAR LANE on which the college was to erect a building for graduates (1975–7).

Despite the easing of its financial troubles, Lincoln's early days were troubled. Because the charters which legitimised its existence were issued by the Lancastrian King Henry VI, the accession of the Yorkist Edward IV raised the spectre of its possible suppression; but it was able to win the patronage of the Yorkist Chancellor George Neville, Bishop of Exeter, who ratified its charter. Unfortunately, a clerical error led to the omission from the charter of the vital words '*et successoribus*', suggesting that the charter was applicable only to the present Rector and Fellows. An appeal to the VISITOR, Thomas Rotherham, Bishop of Lincoln, remedied this fault, however, and the college was enabled to survive.

The patronage of Thomas Rotherham, whom the college was to describe as its second founder, was a landmark in its history. A vigorous and energetic politician who became Chancellor of England and Archbishop of York, Rotherham was an eager patron

David Loggan's bird's-eye view of Lincoln College in 1675, shortly after the death of Nathaniel, Lord Crewe, Rector of the college from 1668–72.

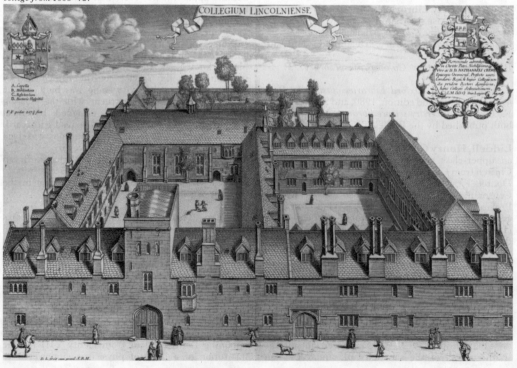

of learning. The Rector called his attention to the college's endemic poverty (by, it was said, preaching a sermon in 1474 in his presence on the text from Psalm 80, verses 14–15: 'Behold and visit this vine, and complete that which thy right hand hath planted' – an indirect allusion to the inadequate funds with which his predecessor, Bishop Fleming, had endowed the society); and he gave it money which allowed the college to complete the front quadrangle and to increase the number of Fellows from seven to twelve. (Earlier a gift from the executors of Bishop Beckington of Bath and Wells had made it possible for the college to infill the south-east corner of the front quad, as his rebus on the walls still demonstrates.) In 1479 Bishop Rotherham gave Lincoln new statutes (by which it was to be governed until 1854) and appropriated to it the churches of Combe, Oxfordshire, and Twyford, Buckinghamshire, so adding to its revenues and more particularly providing a stipend for the Rector (who was henceforth technically the Rector of these two parishes, ensuring for the care of their souls by appointing a chaplain).

These new developments giving Lincoln a settled and respectable position, though it was for long to remain one of the poorer colleges, were made possible by a series of further benefactions which occurred at the end of the 15th and during the first half of the 16th centuries. The full incorporation of the chantry of St Anne (in All Saints Church), which Bishop Rotherham had made possible, brought into the college's possession the Bicester Inn, better known as the MITRE. Bishop William Smyth of Lincoln gave it the rich manor of Bushbury, Wolverhampton; but the college's unwillingness to accede to his request to fund fellowships for his native county led to his turning his attention to other projects, such as the foundation of Lincoln's neighbour Brasenose College. However, a later Tudor benefactor, Edward Darby, Archdeacon of Stow, did provide for the creation of three further fellowships, bringing the total number of Fellows to fifteen (though only for a short period of time did the college maintain fellowships at such a full level). Edmund Audley, Bishop of Salisbury, gave money and made a provision for livery for the Fellows; he was also generous to the library.

The most interesting of all these benefactions was the rich collection of manuscripts given between 1465 and 1474 to the library by the founder's nephew, Robert Fleming, Dean of Lincoln. Largely through gifts, the college had already acquired a useful collection of scholastic Theology, including donations from the founder himself, Dean Forest and Thomas Gascoigne (whose manuscript of the *Dictionarium Theologicum* is still in Lincoln's possession); but Fleming, who had studied in Renaissance Italy, was a scholar of humanist interests who gave the college works of classical and humanistic scholarship, novel to the Oxford of his time. It must be said, however, that in the main the interests and studies of the Fellows of Lincoln remained deeply rooted in traditional learning, more especially in the theologically conservative writings of scholastic theologians.

In the changing world of the Renaissance and Reformation, Lincoln remained an intrinsically conservative society, inimical to the new ideas which were slowly beginning to percolate into 16th-century Oxford. Rector Cottisford (1519–37), who was the Bishop's Commissary (effectively the office of VICE-CHANCELLOR), apprehended preachers from Cambridge of Lutheran persuasion, one of whom is said to have died of sickness from being housed in a cellar normally used to store dry fish beneath the Rector's lodgings. Rector Hugh Weston (1539–56), who was a determined critic of the Edwardian Reformation, disputed in ST MARY THE VIRGIN (in 1554) with Cranmer, Latimer and Ridley (*see* MARTYRS' MEMORIAL) and was made Dean of Westminster by Mary Tudor. But unfortunately his dubious private life – ironical, as one critic commented, in one who so steadfastly championed the cause of celibacy – led to his fall from favour and to the deprivation of all his ecclesiastical offices (he had in fact already resigned the rectorship). Weston's successors were men of Catholic sympathies. Henry Henshaw (1556–8) was expelled by Queen Elizabeth's VISITORS and sought refuge abroad. Francis Babington (1560–3), though transferred by the Queen's powerful favourite, Robert Dudley, Earl of Leicester and CHANCELLOR of the University from 1564 to 1585, from the mastership of Balliol to the rectorship of Lincoln explicitly to forward the government's religious policies, eventually left the country to become a Romanist abroad. Such too was the fate of his successor John Bridgwater (1563–74), who, after a decade as Rector and a secret Romanist, went to France where as Father Aquapontanus he wrote learned Catholic theological works. At least two members of the college, William Filbie and Walter Harte (first holder of one of the first college scholarships, founded by Joan Trappes), were executed as traitors for their religious views in 1582 and 1583 respectively. In 1621 another old member of Lincoln, William Gifford, became Archbishop of Rheims and Primate of France. (*See also* ROMAN CATHOLICS.)

However much Lincoln's inclinations were towards the Catholic faith and the old scholastic learning, it could not resist the pressures for change, more especially for a stronger adherence to Protestantism. Bridgwater's successors to the rectorship, reinforced by Fellows of a distinctly Protestant outlook, ensured that there would be no further deviance from the established faith. In practice Elizabethan England had witnessed a major shift in the social structure of the University, with the effect that from being essentially a society of Catholic priests, so far as its colleges were concerned, it had become a community of Anglican clergymen entrusted with the task of training an increasingly large group of young undergraduates from whom in the future the country could draw a substantial percentage of its clergy, lawyers and politicians. To ensure that such young men were kept under supervision, they were now obliged to become members of a college. Lincoln, like other colleges, grew quickly in size: there were fifty-four undergraduates in 1604; 109 in 1612. The increase in the size of the society and the requirement that Fellows should act as lecturers and tutors made necessary some expansion in accommodation and facilities. In 1608–9, through the beneficence of Sir Thomas Rotherham, the west range of the chapel quadrangle was built; the east range and the magnificent chapel were erected in 1629–31 at the cost of the Visitor, John Williams, Bishop of Lincoln. In 1640 a new cellar was excavated under the hall; and a ball court and a bowling green were created. Among the undergraduates of the time was the future Poet Laureate Sir

William Davenant, while the distinguished churchman and scholar Robert Sanderson, later Bishop of Lincoln, was a Fellow of the college between 1606 and 1619.

Although the life of the society was vigorous and the college was prosperous, between 1620 and 1668 it was much disturbed by friction between the Rector, Paul Hood, a cantankerous and petulant man, and the Fellows, some of whom were good scholars but sometimes indisciplined in conduct. Though often rooted in personal antagonisms, such quarrels were in part associated with the religious controversies of the time, which split the fellowship. The Rector himself, though an object of suspicion to both factions, managed successfully to sit on the fence when in 1642 the CIVIL WAR broke out, emptying the college of its undergraduates and turning Oxford into the headquarters of the royalist army. College rooms were taken as lodgings by cavaliers; Lincoln's silver went to swell the royal MINT (though because of its continued poverty the amount which it contributed, 47 lb 2 oz 5 dwt, was the second smallest amount of all the colleges – *see* PLATE). When the Parliamentarians were victorious, the loyalist Fellows were expelled and replaced by nominees of the parliamentary regime, five of whom were in their turn deprived of their position by the Royal Commissioners appointed at the Restoration of 1660 (*see* VISITATIONS).

Post-Restoration Lincoln – first under the governance of the aged Paul Hood, then under Nathaniel, later Lord Crewe (1668–72) (*see* CREWEIAN BENEFACTION), Thomas Marshall, Dean of Gloucester (1672–85), and Fitzherbert Adams (1685–1719) – was a flourishing community. There was no significant new building, but a room was set aside on the north side of the front quadrangle for a Senior Common Room, a function which it still fulfils; and Rector Fitzherbert Adams further beautified the chapel with some fine carved woodwork and a noble ceiling, bright with the heraldic shields of past benefactors. The library was moved into the former chapel, where it was to remain until 1907. There were some distinguished scholars among the Fellows, notably Thomas Marshall, a pioneer in the study of Philology and languages; and his pupil and friend, George Hickes (Fellow 1664–81), later a prominent non-Juror and Anglo-Saxonist. JOHN RADCLIFFE (Fellow 1670–5), whose relations with the college were later strained, became a wealthy physician, leaving his wealth in a trust from which the University rather than Lincoln College was to benefit. Another Fellow, John Potter (1694–1706), became in 1737 a rather undistinguished Archbishop of Canterbury. The college seemed by and large freer of internal friction than it had been in the first half of the 17th century; but the radical views perpetrated by James Parkinson, critical of Caroline government in church and state, led to his expulsion from his fellowship in 1683.

Lincoln, inconspicuous as it was among the richer, more distinguished societies of Oxford, continued to enjoy a tranquil and modestly fruitful existence in the first half of the 18th century. The election to a fellowship in 1726 of JOHN WESLEY (which he was to hold until marriage obliged his resignation in 1751) brought the college into greater prominence because members of the Holy Club met in his rooms. The other Fellows, sympathetic as they were to Wesley himself, were disturbed by his strong religious convictions and may well have been relieved when, after his journey to Georgia, his visits to Lincoln became increasingly sporadic.

Indeed, as the century wore on Lincoln relapsed into the academic stupor often, if sometimes undeservedly, associated with 18th-century Oxford. In 1792 the election to the rectorship of Edward Tatham aggravated matters in this respect, for Tatham was an aggressive, brusque Yorkshireman, as unpopular with the other heads of colleges as he was with the Fellows of Lincoln. He appeared dictatorial and concerned with the protection of what he conceived to be his

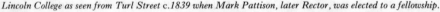

Lincoln College as seen from Turl Street c.1839 when Mark Pattison, later Rector, was elected to a fellowship.

rights. Behind the mask, however, he was a man of considerable intelligence and some insight. A strong opponent of Dissent (*see* DISSENTERS) and a vigorous Tory – he even opposed the conferral of an honorary degree on Edmund Burke – he was also, paradoxically, a critic of the reformed syllabus which introduced the new honours examination because it was still too identified with outmoded concepts of Aristotelian philosophy and too oblivious of the Newtonian ideas with which he had been familiar as an undergraduate at Cambridge. He was, however, a lone and unpopular voice in University and college, married to a termagant wife, and under his long governance – for he did not die until 1834 – the college suffered a severe decline both in its numbers and in its prestige.

From this nadir in its history Lincoln recovered but slowly. Tatham's successor as Rector was a kindly but uninspired cleric, John Radford. Yet even in Radford's time the realisation of the need for change, more especially for promoting better scholarship and improved instructors, began to make its impact on college life. The election of MARK PATTISON to a fellowship in 1839 was a landmark, as a group of liberal-minded and reforming Fellows formed themselves under his lead against the conservative-minded traditionalists. When Rector Radford died in 1851 Pattison was an obvious candidate to succeed him. Yet he lost the election by one vote, after a sudden reversal of one of his would-be supporters – an experience which had a traumatic effect on his introspective personality and which consigned the college, in spite of the compulsory reform of its statutes as a result of the University Reform Act (*see* ROYAL COMMISSIONS), to a decade of reactionary rule.

With the eventual election of Pattison as Rector in 1861, Lincoln entered the modern world, with a greater concern for scholarship and improved standards in general. Its Fellows included many men of real achievement – classical scholars such as Henry Nettleship (1862–71) and Warde Fowler (1872–1921); scientists such as Sir Baldwin Spencer (1886), Walter Garstang (1893–7), and N.V. Sidgwick (1901–52); and the philosopher Samuel Alexander (1882–93), one of the first JEWS to be elected to an Oxford fellowship. The appropriation of the professorships of Classical Archaeology and of Pathology to the college in their turn brought men of great distinction, among them the classical scholars Sir Walter Ramsay (1885–6), Percy Gardner (1887–1925) and Sir John Beazley (1925–56); and the pathologist LORD FLOREY (1935–62), who, with his team of helpers holding research fellowships at Lincoln, was associated with the development of penicillin. Florey's colleague Sir Edward Abraham (1948–80), who ultimately held a professorial fellowship, developed the associated product cephalosporin. Yet Pattison, partly because of his temperament, partly because his views on the nature of a university and college differed from those of his colleagues, proved only an indifferent Rector. On his death, under the long rule of his successor, W.W. Merry (1884–1918), Lincoln reverted in some sense to its inconspicuous place among the Oxford colleges, its revenues so badly affected by the current agricultural depression that it was obliged to cut the number of its tutorial fellowships.

There were, however, encouraging signs – if slow and even superficial – that Lincoln was making progress in the period immediately following the First World War. The success of the Quincentenary Fund made possible the building of a new Rector's lodgings in 1930, to the design of Herbert Reed. And the college numbered some notable figures in its alumni: the poet Edward Thomas was a graduate of a somewhat earlier generation (1898); but in the inter-war years the cartoonist, Sir Osbert Lancaster (1926), the writer of children's books Dr Seuss (T.S. Geisl) (1925), and D. Karaka, the first Indian president of the Oxford Union (1930), were all students here. It was nonetheless patently apparent that the real leap forward in Lincoln's fortunes occurred after, and as a result of, the election of its Bursar Keith Murray (later Lord Murray of Newhaven) to the rectorship in 1944 in succession to J.A.R. Munro. Murray's superb management put the college on a sound financial footing, so enabling his successors as Rector – Sir Walter Oakeshott (1954–72) and Lord Trend (1972–82) – to undertake an extensive and significant building programme, involving the conversion of the Mitre Hotel into college accommodation (1969–70); the transformation by Robert Potter of All Saints Church into the college library (1971–5); the building of the Bear Lane Graduate Building, designed by Geoffrey Beard of the Oxford Architects Partnership (1975–7); and the successful completion of a number of other projects.

Lincoln's numbers certainly expanded, more especially in respect of the admission of graduates, but it has remained essentially a community modest in size: in 1983 there were only 243 undergraduates and eighty-two graduates. Women were admitted in 1979. Its post-war graduates included the novelist John le Carré (David Cornwell) and the politician Lord Donoughue. In spite of the additions which have been made to its buildings, Lincoln is still in many respects a classic example of a small 15th-century college: its hall, though restored in 1891, is substantially the building of 1437, with noble beams and a fine smoke louvre. The chapel is remarkable for the beautiful painted glass of its east window, attributed to the painter van Ling, which Bishop Williams presented to the college, and for the late 17th-century carving which here, as elsewhere in the college, reflects the craftsmanship of a local woodworker, Frogley. The library (formerly All Saints Church) is a beautiful building: many of the church's features – including a number of memorials to past Rectors, reredos and heraldic emblems – have been retained. The room in which John Wesley supposedly lived was panelled and restored by the American Methodists in 1925 (though historical evidence suggests that he resided in another room in the college's Chapel Quad). While many alterations have occurred since its foundation, Lincoln remains one of the least spoilt legacies of mediaeval Oxford.

It was announced in 1987 that Sir Maurice Shock, Vice-Chancellor of Leicester University, was to become Rector of the college in succession to the Rev. V.H.H. Green.

The corporate designation of the college is The Warden or Rector and Scholars of the College of the Blessed Mary and All Saints, Lincoln, in the University of Oxford, commonly called Lincoln College.

(Clark, Andrew, *Lincoln College*, London, 1898; Warner, S.A., *Lincoln College*, London, 1908; Green,

Lord Lindsay was appointed Master of Balliol College in 1924 and Vice-Chancellor of the University in 1935–8.

V.H.H., *Oxford Common Room*, London, 1957, and *The Commonwealth of Lincoln College, 1427–1977*, Oxford, 1979.)

Lindsay, Alexander Dunlop, 1st Baron Lindsay of Birker *(1879–1952)*. Born in Glasgow, the son of the Rev. Thomas Martin Lindsay the historian (1843–1914), Lindsay won a scholarship to University College. He gained Firsts in Classical Moderations and LITERAE HUMANIORES, was President of the UNION in 1902, and in 1906 was elected a Fellow and classical tutor at Balliol. Despite strong opposition, much of it occasioned by his left-wing views, he became Master of the college in 1924. A formidable Master, he was also a highly effective VICE-CHANCELLOR in 1935–8. In 1938 he stood against Quintin Hogg as an anti-Munich Agreement candidate in a by-election in the city of Oxford, reducing the Conservative majority by almost half. Lindsay remained Master of Balliol until 1949, when, at the age of seventy, he became first Principal of the University College of North Staffordshire (later the University College of Keele).

Literae Humaniores The Faculty of Literae Humaniores, the study of the Classics, Philosophy and Ancient History, is the largest classical school in the country. The first examination is called Classical Honour Moderations or 'Mods', and the final school is known as 'Greats'.

The range of subjects can be seen from the professors on the faculty: Professor of the History of Philosophy, Lincoln Professor of Classical Archaeology and Art, Professor of Comparative Philology, Wykeham Professor of Logic, Wykeham Professor of Ancient History, Professor of the Archaeology of the Roman Empire, Regius Professor of Greek, Camden Professor of Ancient History, Corpus Christi

Professor of the Latin Language and Literature, Waynflete Professor of Metaphysical Philosophy, Professor of Mathematical Logic, and White's Professor of Moral Philosophy. There are also Readers in Hellenistic History, Classical Literature, and Mental Philosophy.

Little Clarendon Street Formerly Blackboy Lane, this is a narrow road running from the junction of ST GILES' and WOODSTOCK ROAD westwards to No. 128 WALTON STREET. The name has been used since the latter half of the 19th century. It is now a street of medium-sized shops, University and college buildings. (*See* GREAT CLARENDON STREET *for the derivation of the name.*)

Littlegate Street A continuation of ST EBBE'S STREET. A plaque on the wall marks the site of the Littlegate, sometimes known as Little South Gate, first mentioned in 1244 and one of the seven mediaeval gates of the city. Excavations in 1971 and 1972 uncovered the footings of the west side of the gate and of the 13th-century CITY WALL.

Littlemore A village which is now one of the suburbs of Oxford on the south-east side. The living was at one time held by J.H. NEWMAN. LITTLEMORE HOSPITAL was built in 1846, and on the outskirts of the village is a sewage farm and pumping station.
(*See also* LITTLEMORE PRIORY.)

Littlemore Hospital (Oxfordshire County Asylum) The first plans to establish a pauper lunatic asylum for Oxfordshire were put forward by Joseph Warner Henley, MP, at the Trinity Quarter Sessions in 1840, the opportunity to establish a pauper department in conjunction with the Warneford Asylum (*see* WARNEFORD HOSPITAL) having been turned down by the county magistrates in 1813. A committee was set up to investigate the unsatisfactory facilities for Oxfordshire pauper lunatics, who were housed in private madhouses and in other county asylums. In 1843, a 15-acre site was purchased at LITTLEMORE outside the city boundary. The architect was R.N. Clark of Nottingham; and by 1844, Messrs Plowman and Luck of Oxford were engaged in building a main block of eleven bays with two polygonal corner turrets. This was enlarged rapidly in 1847 and 1852 by H.J. Underwood and J.C. BUCKLER to meet the needs of an increased catchment area. To reduce expenses, Oxfordshire amalgamated with Berkshire and accepted Berkshire pauper lunatics and those of the boroughs of Abingdon, Reading and Windsor. The buildings at Littlemore, however, proved inadequate from the outset.

The first medical superintendent was William Ley (1806–69), who was trained at ST BARTHOLOMEW'S HOSPITAL and at the Middlesex County Asylum, Hanwell, where he was under the personal instruction of Dr John Conolly, popularly regarded as the pioneer of the humane method of treating lunatics in England. Initially Ley's staff was small relative to the number of patients, economy being a guiding principle; but later the staff was increased to include a chaplain and in 1883 a Norman-style chapel was built for the inmates. Religious participation was felt to be highly beneficial in the medical and moral treatment of the insane at this period. The general rules compiled for the government of the asylum in 1846 remained in force, with few amendments, for many years afterwards.

Early reports of the Visiting Commissioners in Lunacy, on their regular inspections, commented favourably on the treatment, diet and care of the Littlemore patients, and expressed approval of William Ley's application of the contemporary ideas of 'moral' management, with limited use of mechanical restraints and coercive measures. By 1848 there were 234 patients, and extensions were embarked upon following criticism of overcrowded dormitories. In 1871 the situation was relieved by the transfer of all the Berkshire patients to the new Berkshire County Asylum; but the pattern throughout the 19th century was an increasing institutionalisation of the insane poor. Once admitted, pauper lunatics tended to be forgotten by their relatives and the continuing involvement of the parish officers who had brought them into the asylum was limited to meeting maintenance costs. In addition, the need for economical running of the asylum meant that the ratio of attendants to patients was insufficient to allow for personal attention to inmates and the regime became custodial rather than caring.

Overcrowding necessitated further building extensions by H.J. Tollit in 1902. During both world wars the hospital was used as a military hospital (the Ashhurst War Hospital), involving considerable movement of patients to other asylums.

Relations with the other Oxford psychiatric hospital, the Warneford, became closer and more cordial when the latter ceased to be a private establishment and became part of the National Health Service, and by 1986 the two hospitals were offering complementary services, with close links and common objectives. By then Littlemore Hospital had 371 beds for acutely and chronically ill patients. There were also psychogeriatric facilities, as well as the Ley Clinic, which treated cases of drug addiction. The out-patient sessions were by then dealing with over 8000 cases a year.

The Ashhurst Clinic takes its name from the Ashhurst family of Waterstock. John Henry Ashhurst was a member of the Committee of Visitors of Littlemore Asylum from 1849 until 1885 and William Henry Ashhurst served on the committee for forty-four years until his death in 1930. The military hospital at Littlemore was known as the Ashhurst War Hospital during both world wars. The clinic was opened in 1956. By 1964 it had fifty-four beds and now serves as a general admission unit.

Littlemore Priory A small Benedictine nunnery founded in LITTLEMORE in about 1120 by Robert of Sandford near his own house. Although there were no more than seven or eight nuns, they were notorious for their dishonesty, violence and sexual incontinence. The priory was suppressed by CARDINAL WOLSEY in 1525. A range of the cloister garth – the chapter house and parlour, and the dormitory above – was converted into a farmhouse, Minchery Farm, and remodelled in about 1600. The building is now used as a country club.

Loggan, David (*1635–?1700*). Born in Danzig (Gdańsk), Loggan came to England sometime before 1653 and by 1665 was living at Nuffield near Oxford. Having made the acquaintance of ANTHONY WOOD, he was appointed engraver to the University in 1669. After his marriage he moved to HOLYWELL and became a naturalised Englishman in 1675. The year before had seen the publication of a work illustrated with such plates as 'Doctor in medicina toga ...'; but this, though often ascribed to Loggan, is not certainly by his hand. His claim to fame rests mainly upon his *Oxonia Illustrata, etc.* of 1675, which contains forty plates providing general views of Oxford, a plan of the city, illustrations of ACADEMIC DRESS and thirty-seven detailed and accurate views of COLLEGES, ACADEMIC HALLS and other buildings. The work was intended as a companion volume to Wood's *Historia et Antiquitates Universitatis Oxoniensis* (1674) and the two books were often presented together to notable visitors to Oxford. Loggan produced a similar work on Cambridge. He also engraved plates for Robert Morison's *Historia Plantarum Oxoniensis* (1680). In 1676 he left Oxford for London, where he died some twenty years later.

Logic Lane Early names for this were Lawdenyslanesine and Horseman Lane (1247); it still retained the latter in 1328. Because there was a horse-mill in the lane in mediaeval times it was also called Horsemul(l) Lane. (There was also a Horsemul Hall at the end of Kibald Street.) The upper part of Logic Lane, beyond the angle of the 17th-century house Kybald Twychen, retained the name Horsemull for a time longer, although it had vanished by 1850. By ANTHONY WOOD's time it had been given its present name of Logick Lane, at least for its southern part, after a school of logicians at the north end of the lane. The ownership of the lane, which runs between HIGH STREET and MERTON STREET, remained in doubt, but in a court judgement of 1904 the soil of the road was awarded to University College.

Lollards The name, from Middle Dutch *lollaert* meaning 'mumbler', given after 1380 to the followers of JOHN WYCLIF and to those sharing his heretical views. Some were Oxford colleagues, led by Nicholas Hereford, Fellow of The Queen's College, and some were simpler men, laity and clerics, 'poor priests' who journeyed about the country preaching in English so that all could understand.

On Ascension Day 1382 Hereford preached an incendiary sermon in English at ST FRIDESWIDE'S, and in the same year Philip Repington, another Lollard, preached the UNIVERSITY SERMON on the feast of Corpus Christi. Archbishop Courtenay, determined to stamp out Lollardy, ordered Robert Rigg, the CHANCELLOR, to publish the decrees of the Blackfriars synod which had condemned Wyclif's writings on transubstantiation, confession, papal jurisdiction, lordship and grace. Rigg claimed, wrongly, that the Archbishop had no authority over the University, and even went in procession to St Frideswide's to hear Repington defend Wyclif's beliefs. After this a synod at Lambeth found the Chancellor and PROCTORS guilty of condoning heresy in Wyclif, Hereford and Repington, and shortly after Hereford and Repington were excommunicated. Repington recanted, as did many of the other Oxford Lollards. Thus died Lollardy in Oxford. Elsewhere, however, the Lollards continued to preach against the worldliness and corruption of the Church, and to encourage the use of the vernacular Bible. They were active until the middle of the 15th century and then gradually declined.

London Place Named after its proximity to the old road to London, this row of some twenty-four terraced houses facing SOUTH PARK lies between No. 76 ST CLEMENT'S and Cherwell Street, near the foot of HEADINGTON HILL. Nos 6–9 are examples of a late Georgian style, not common in Oxford, and, with others in the street, are Grade II listed buildings. The houses nearest the main road were demolished in 1927, so that the terrace is now set back.

London Road *Headington.* Begins at the end of HEADINGTON ROAD and continues to beyond the city boundary at Forest Hill. It includes a local shopping centre on both sides of the road, in the vicinity of Windmill Road and Old High Street. Further east is BURY KNOWLE PARK and beyond that HEADINGTON SCHOOL, a private school for girls. There was a London Waie in Elizabethan times and later the road was a main coachway. In common with some other Oxford roads, it was measured and provided with milestones under the 18th-century Turnpike Acts. Some of the milestones are still in existence. The original Londonyshe Streete, however, followed the line of COWLEY ROAD.

Longwall Street Connects ST CROSS ROAD and HOLYWELL STREET with HIGH STREET. It takes its name from the CITY WALL, which runs parallel with it on the west side within the grounds of New College. The 15th-century wall of Magdalen College runs along the street on the other side, beyond which is a fine view of Magdalen Tower. Behind this wall is Magdalen Grove and deer park. At the junction of Longwall and St Cross Road, Merton College, as Lord of HOLYWELL MANOR, kept a pillory and a gallows where two undergraduates were hanged for highway robbery in the 18th century. On the other side of the street at No. 21 is Morris Garage, built in 1910 in red brick, the central doorway giving access to a covered garage and workshop. In this building in 1912 William Morris built his first motor car (*see* MOTOR CARS). Later, as LORD NUFFIELD, he had an office on the first floor of the building. In 1980 a redevelopment scheme for New College, by John Fryman of the Oxford Architects Partnership, retained the frontage of the garage. Further down the street is New College's Sacher Building (1962 by David Roberts) and, beyond that, Bodicote House (1969), another building for the college, designed by Geoffrey Beard of the Oxford Architects Partnership. Close to High Street is the twin-gabled Longwall House, built in 1856–7, which, together with adjoining buildings down a passage, formed an extension to MAGDALEN COLLEGE SCHOOL.

Lord Mayors *see* MAYORS.

Lucy Faithfull House *Speedwell Street.* Opened in 1978 and designed by the Oxford Architects Partnership. Lucy Faithfull (now Baroness Faithfull), was Director of Social Services in Oxford. The home was run by the Church Army as a hostel for single people, but in 1985 was leased by the Church Army to the Church Housing Association. It offers accommodation for up to eighty-six men who would otherwise be 'on the streets'.

Lucy's Eagle Ironworks *Walton Well Road.* The firm was founded by William Carter, an ironfounder, who opened a shop in HIGH STREET in 1812 as an 'ironmonger, hardwareman, brazier and tinplate worker'. In 1897 the firm became a limited company with the name W. Lucy & Co. Ltd. During the 19th century it made such items as lamp-posts, iron railings and manhole covers; the name Lucy can be seen on many of these in Oxford. It also made agricultural and household equipment, but now specialises in electrical engineering.

(Andrews, P.W.S., and Brunner, Elizabeth, *The Eagle Ironworks, Oxford,* London, 1965.)

The garage in Longwall Street where William Morris built his first motor car in 1912.

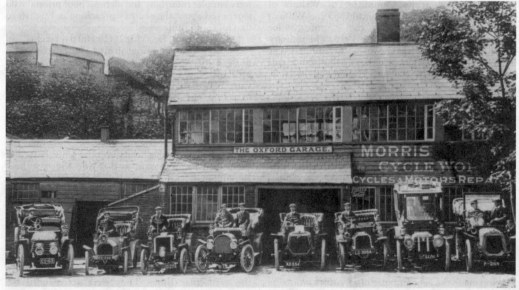

M

Magazines The word 'magazine' derives from a number of different languages, including Arabic. Originally it was connected with explosives, or rather their concentration into a container, just as written articles are condensed into a single publication. As far as Oxford is concerned, the first such publication – not yet called a magazine – was published in 1641 during the CIVIL WAR, two years after Parliament had allowed freedom of the press. It was called *Mercurius Aulicus*, 'a Diurnal Communicating the Intelligence and Affaires of the Court, to the Rest of the Kingdom'. It had as editor (at that time called author) Sir John Berkenhead of Oriel. Its price – 1*d* – could be twenty times as much when sold in London. The *Mercurius* idea caught on, and subtitles such as *Britannicus, Academicus, Rusticus* and *Aquaticus* followed. Only a few years ago, a latter-day *Mercurius* appeared describing the Oxford scene, its author a thinly disguised don.

In 1665 Charles II moved his court to Oxford for fear of plague, and with them came Parliament, and the Grub Street writers, and a local publication called the *Oxford Gazette*. When the court returned to London, the *Gazette* went with it and began a long reign.

Every summer an unofficial part of the ceremony of ENCAENIA was the commentary given by a licensed jester, poking fun at the participants. His official title was TERRAE FILIUS, and one holder of the position, Nicholas Amherst, decided to make his observations into a weekly magazine, which was published in 1721. This caused so much local disapproval that he was sent down and fled to London, and had his effusions printed and distributed in the capital.

The *Student* or *Oxford Monthly Miscellany* (1750–1) was a year-long series of literary pamphlets. The contributors included THOMAS WARTON, Professor of Poetry, and SAMUEL JOHNSON, formerly of Pembroke College. The *Oxford Sausage* (named after a delicacy in the market) ran from 1764 to 1776. It was more a comic anthology of verses, and lampoons on University characters, than a magazine, but it survived through what must have been one of Oxford's dullest periods. It was edited by Thomas Warton. *Olla Podrida*, a publication nicknamed 'The Stewpot', was first published in 1787. It combined a weekly issue called the *Loiterer*, and the two were later described as 'donnish publications of the heaviest and most dismal kind'.

Passing over the shortlived *Undergraduate* (1819) published a few years after a possible contributor, P.B. Shelley (University College), had been sent down, we come to the first use of the title 'magazine' in Oxford. In 1834 the *Oxford Magazine* appeared – no relation to the later thoroughbred. Its aims were high: it was 'not intended to be a receptacle for erotic poetry', ran the editorial, and it too had a limited lifespan. The 1850s saw the foundation of the Oxford UNION's first debating chamber, its walls decorated with Arthurian paintings by young Pre-Raphaelites from Exeter College. One of these, WILLIAM MORRIS, helped to start the *Oxford and Cambridge Magazine* (1856) with an editor from the distinguished Fulford family (Pembroke) and contributions from BURNE-JONES and Rossetti, both Exeter men. In the latter half of the century, the *Rattler* (1867) should be noted, as well as a magazine called the *Twit*. (These days this would be held as a derogatory phrase, but at that time 'to twit' might be a pleasant exercise.)

It is not surprising that the 1880s, which ushered in the era of the Gilbert and Sullivan operettas, should have produced a spate of occasional writing which would suit Oxford. The OXFORD (MAGAZINE) was first issued in 1883, with this theme in its editorial:

> Our zest in this the annals of our noise,
> Our longing for the Oxford that is ours.

It was followed in 1892 by the journal which for generations stood to it *in statu pupillari* – ISIS. Soon this had collected a notable number of contributors. One, MAX BEERBOHM (Merton) wrote for two other publications, the *Clown*, and the *Spirit Lamp* (1893), which included, significantly, writings by Lord Alfred Douglas and Oscar Wilde (Magdalen).

In December 1903, long before Mrs Pankhurst tied herself to the railings, Oxford University beheld its first graduate magazine for women, the *Fritillary*. It was not named after the legendary flowers growing in Magdalen Fields, but after the butterfly, and the first issue, which contained an earnest survey of Oxford, its literature and religions, was likely to offend no one. Although the iron-grey, coffin-like cover was uninviting, the *Fritillary* continued on its way until the early 1930s and it was not entirely sombre. In that first issue, the Butterfly reporter describes how in a mock debate on 24 November 1903 girl speakers dressed up as men, including a foreign visitor called Graf von Musten-fusten-crustenberg-am-Rhein.

Though the First World War took a terrible toll of Oxford men, journalistic inspiration began to spring up again after its end with the *Oxford Outlook* (1919–32), a semi-political survey, partly Union-inspired, and with the CHERWELL. Both have been flowing, in varying degrees, ever since, though as *Cherwell* ex-editor Derek Hudson has pointed out, his paper and the original *Mercurius* are the only two Oxford magazines to have been published in wartime.

There had been an unsuccessful attempt to imitate *Oxford and Cambridge* in 1927, and the revival of the *Outlook* in 1931 was also of short duration, though under the redoubtable editorship of Richard Crossman (New College) and Gilbert Highet, an enterprising Classics don. For many years, 'the Three' (*Oxford (Magazine)*, *Isis* and *Cherwell*) held sway, each representing a different facet of the Oxford scene. In 1939, just before the outbreak of the Second World War, *Oxford Forward*, a progressive weekly, appeared. *Oxford Viewpoint* dates from 1947. Not until

1959 was there a serious challenge to 'the Three', when Richard Ingrams (University College) launched *Mesopotamia*, named after the strip of land made by two sides of the River Cherwell (*see* THAMES), analogous to the Tigris and the Euphrates. Ingrams, later editor of *Private Eye*, engaged several youthful aspirants who later became *Eye* contributors, among them Auberon Waugh, William Rushton and Christopher Booker. It had seeds on a canvas cover so that, when watered, little seedlings could spring up.

In the last two decades, there have been few magazines of note, though photo-copying has made the process of publishing much easier and cheaper. *Tributary* (another river title) began in the 1970s in this way. *Vague* (1978) did not live up to its intention of parodying *Vogue*. The *Jericho Bugle* (but did not Gideon's men blow trumpets?) drew attention to an Oxford suburb and is full of earnest endeavour. *Argo* was once accused in the Oxford Union of being anti-semitic. An echo of the vanished *Fritillary* is *Lilith*, devoted to feminine standpoints.

A glossy termly magazine, *Debate*, first appeared in October 1985, published by, and for, the Oxford Union Society, and distributed free. The last issue appeared in 1988. A hopeful monthly information publication, *Oxon*, announced in 1986 that it could no longer continue publication. The University alumni magazine *Oxford Today* first appeared at Michaelmas 1988. It is sent out once a term to all those members of the University whose addresses have been supplied by Colleges – around 120,000 for the first issue.

(*See also* NEWSPAPERS, OXFORD AND CAMBRIDGE MAGAZINE, OXFORD GAZETTE, OXFORD (MAGAZINE) *and* OXONIENSIA.)

Magdalen Bridge Spans the Cherwell (*see* THAMES) by Magdalen College, taking the road from

A coach passing over Magdalen Bridge towards the tower of Magdalen College, c.1890.

the east across the river from THE PLAIN to the junction of HIGH STREET and LONGWALL STREET. The crossing may be that of the original 'ox ford', although the site has also been identified with FOLLY BRIDGE and, by H.E. SALTER, with HINKSEY ferry. A bridge, formerly known as Pettypont and East Bridge, has stood here since at least 1004. In the Middle Ages the cost of its upkeep was shared between the county and the town, the town meeting its three-quarters share largely by alms and charitable bequests, the maintenance of bridges being then considered a pious duty. Bridge-hermits were also appointed to help travellers with any difficulties they might experience in crossing. The original bridge was of wood, but by the 16th century a stone bridge, some 500 feet long, with about twenty pointed and rounded arches, had been constructed.

At this time the city was still paying for repairs, both by taxation and by the allocation of alms; but William of Waynflete, the founder of Magdalen College, may have paid for restoration of the bridge in the 15th century, and the University certainly did so in 1723. Although a major restoration was then undertaken, less than fifty years later some of the piers had been swept away by floods and the western end had collapsed completely. Condemned as dangerous, it was rebuilt between 1772 and 1778 under the provisions of the Oxford Improvement Act of 1771, to the design of John Gwynn. At the same time a toll-house was built at The Plain, with gates across the roads from HEADINGTON and COWLEY to collect dues for the maintenance of the bridge. Twenty-seven feet wide, with recesses in the middle, the bridge's large semi-circular arches were supplemented by smaller ones over the towpaths. The plain balustrade was designed by John Townesend (*see* TOWNESENDS) after plans for a more elaborate one had been dropped. The bridge was widened in 1835 and again in 1882. Notabilities have frequently been welcomed or taken their official departure at the bridge, as Queen Elizabeth I did on leaving Oxford in 1566.

Magdalen College The college of St Mary Magdalen (which retains its 15th-century pronunciation, 'Maudele'n') owed its conception to William of Waynflete. As Master of Winchester College and Provost of Eton, Waynflete had attracted the attention of Henry VI, who, in 1447, promoted him to the see of Winchester. In the following year Waynflete, following King Henry's example at Cambridge, acquired land in Oxford for the foundation of a college for the study of Theology and Philosophy. The site was on the south side of HIGH STREET, bounded by MERTON STREET and LOGIC LANE, and was occupied by ACADEMIC HALLS, then in decay. Waynflete envisaged an endowed foundation of a President and fifty Fellows, but the disturbed years around 1450 delayed his plans and it was not until ten years later, when he had become Chancellor of England, that these went ahead. In the interval he had found a larger site, between the east wall of the city (*see* CITY WALL) and the River Cherwell (*see* THAMES). This was then occupied by the Hospital of St John the Baptist, founded by King Henry III in the 13th century to tend the sick and for needy travellers, but by 1458 it was occupied by only five brethren. Waynflete secured royal and papal permission to suppress the hospital and transfer its site, buildings and endowment to his new college, which received its foundation charter on

Watercolour drawing of the interior of Magdalen College chapel in 1817. The chapel was originally built in 1474–83, the interior being restored in 1828–35. The altarpiece, Christ carrying the Cross, is attributed to Valdés Leal.

12 June 1458. This named William Tybard as the first President, and six other Fellows. But again ten years of political uncertainty intervened, in which Henry VI was deposed by Edward IV and Waynflete was dismissed from office. Not until 1467 did Edward IV confirm the foundation charter, enabling Waynflete to commence the process of accumulating properties for the endowment, erecting the buildings, drawing up the statutes and appointing the Fellows. All this proved a lengthy and hazardous business, occupying Waynflete until his death in 1486, and accomplished only through his persistence and remarkable longevity. Work on the buildings did not begin until 1474, but then went ahead speedily and by 1480–1 the chapel, hall, founder's tower, and much of the cloisters had been erected at Waynflete's expense. At the same time properties were obtained for the endowment of the college from gifts, the suppression of decayed religious houses (including Sele and Selborne Priories and Brackley Hospital), and the estates of Sir John Fastolf and Lord Cromwell, for whom Waynflete acted as executor. The college's lands, distributed over most of England south of the River Trent, yielded a gross income of £827 by 1488, and by 1536 further endowments had raised this to £1076, making it at that date the wealthiest college in Oxford, though it was later surpassed by Christ Church.

Waynflete's statutes closely followed those of New College. His foundation consisted of a President, forty Fellows, thirty scholars called Demies (*see* DEMYSHIP), eight clerks and sixteen choristers. The thirteen Senior Fellows formed a governing body. Two innovations foreshadowed developments of the next century: the establishment of three readerships, in Theology and Natural and Moral Philosophy, to provide public lectures; and the provision of twenty places for sons of gentlemen (gentlemen-commoners) who would pay for their residence and instruction. Waynflete also erected a grammar school within the college to instruct boys in Latin in preparation for entry to the college. To this the choristers were also attached, and the Master and Usher were a charge on the foundation. Waynflete died on 11 August 1486, aged eighty-eight. Only in his last years did he visit the completed college, bringing 800 books for its library, and the title deeds of its properties; and he was present to welcome Edward IV in 1481 and Richard III in 1483. In 1480 Tybard had been succeeded as President by Richard Mayew, whom Henry VII made royal almoner and chose for the embassy to Spain to arrange the marriage of Prince Arthur and Catherine of Aragon. After the reception of Catherine he was given Flemish tapestries made to commemorate the betrothal, which to this day have remained in the President's lodgings. Both Henry VII and Arthur visited Magdalen, and Mayew was promoted to the bishopric of Hereford. His abiding monument is the Great Tower, commenced in 1492 and completed in 1505. Next year he was forced out of office on grounds of absenteeism and indiscipline, by an appeal to the VISITOR (the Bishop of Winchester, Richard Foxe). To succeed Mayew, Foxe chose William Claymond, one of a galaxy of scholars who were champions of the New Learning, centred on Magdalen in these years. In 1491 WILLIAM GROCYN gave the first lectures on Greek in Oxford, and in the next twenty years Magdalen Fellows promoted into the episcopate included THOMAS WOLSEY, Stokesley, Longland and Lee, all of whom had close connections with JOHN COLET, Thomas More and Erasmus. When Wolsey later founded Cardinal College (*see* CHRIST CHURCH) he drew four of its new Fellows from Magdalen. To Magdalen Henry VIII sent his protégé Reginald Pole (later Cardinal) as a gentleman-commoner, and when Pole moved to Padua to complete his studies, others from Magdalen joined him, notably Thomas Starkey, who became an apologist for the Henrician breach with Rome.

Magdalen's intellectual eminence faded as the Protestant Reformation brought divisions within the college (*see* ROMAN CATHOLICS). Although the college resisted some of the changes ordered in 1549, notably the suppression of the choir and the grammar school, a radical party among the Fellows procured the resignation of the President, Owen Oglethorpe, in 1552 and proceeded to purge the chapel of its mediaeval furnishings and vestments. Under the new regime the college acted as host to Bucer and Peter Martyr, but with the accession of Mary in 1553 Bishop Gardiner of Winchester conducted a VISITATION, ejected nine Fellows, restored Oglethorpe and re-adorned the chapel. Choral music flourished under the distinguished composer John Sheppard as choirmaster. The Elizabethan settlement brought formal doctrinal stability, but religious factions persisted within the college under the new President, Laurence Humphrey. Humphrey, a Calvinist, reimposed puritan austerity in the chapel and the Fellows were reprimanded by the Queen's Council and the Visitor for refusing to wear surplices. But over the period of his office (1561–89) Humphrey gradually conformed. In 1566 he received the Queen on her visit, became VICE-CHANCELLOR in 1571, and enlarged

An engraving after Frederick Mackenzie's drawing of the Great Gateway in the western wall of Magdalen College which was built in 1635 and removed in 1844.

the lodgings to accommodate his family (he was the first married President). His own career flourished, but defects appeared in the management of the college estates and in the discipline of both senior and junior members, notably the gentlemen-commoners for whose education no adequate provision was made. Their numbers were increasing as it became fashionable for the sons of the nobility and gentry to attend university. They were admitted as the private pupils of the President or individual Fellows, and in 1565 there were 132 commoners and their servants at Magdalen, among them THOMAS BODLEY. Not all were sons of the wealthy; among them were poor students supporting themselves as SERVITORS to the MAs. The commoners could be an unruly element; in one incident in 1587 they threw missiles from the tower on to the retinue of Lord Norris as it crossed MAGDALEN BRIDGE in revenge for the imprisonment of a student caught poaching on Norris's estate. In the last two decades of the century, under Nicholas Bond, the college enjoyed a period of financial recuperation and consolidation, remaining a nursery of Puritanism until, with the advent of the Stuarts, its character again changed as it gradually adjusted to the Laudianism of the court (*see* WILLIAM LAUD).

Lying alongside the college, its poor relation MAGDALEN HALL presented a contrast. Over the previous century this jumble of buildings had developed out of the grammar school as a place where poor scholars could be accommodated, and in 1614 a further extension to the old schoolroom was added, which survives as the present Grammar Hall in St John's Quadrangle. Magdalen Hall had always been radical in religious matters since Tyndale had lived there in the 1520s. A century later it matriculated two men of outstanding ability: Thomas Hobbes and

Edward Hyde, later EARL OF CLARENDON, who subsequently moved to Magdalen College.

The college, under royal patronage, moved in another direction. James I brought his son Prince Henry to the city, was entertained at Magdalen and pronounced it 'the most absolute building in Oxford'. Much embellishment had been undertaken for the visit, including a new screen in the hall. The accession of Charles I in 1625 coincided with the election of a new President, Accepted Frewen, whom Charles had already marked out as a preacher to the Court. Despite his name, Frewen was a high churchman, and once more the chapel was transformed to match the new religious climate. The brass lectern, the painted glass by Richard Greenbury in the antechapel, and portions of the black-and-white floor survive from Frewen's restoration. There was no question of where the college's loyalties lay in the CIVIL WAR. In 1642 it lent the King £1000 (half of it advanced by Frewen himself) and when, after the battle of Edgehill, Oxford was garrisoned for the King, Magdalen, which commanded the London road, became part of the defensive works. The tower was used as an observation point and stocked with missiles; troops and artillery were mustered in the grove; and defensive platforms for guns were built in the water walks, part of which (Dover Pier) survives. The college PLATE, the founder's cup alone excepted, was melted down. During the siege of 1646 the college probably formed Prince Rupert's headquarters; but under the parliamentary occupation which followed its character was again changed. The chapel was stripped, its ornaments sold off, and the mediaeval glass destroyed, though two small medallions of Charles I and his Queen still survive *in situ* in the hall. Most of the Fellows, Demies, clerks and choristers refused to acknowledge the new regime and were expelled and replaced with Presbyterians, who indeed numbered among them men of academic ability. A new President, John Wilkinson, was intruded.

The Restoration of the monarchy in 1660 brought with it the return of the expelled Fellows, but relations between them and the Commonwealth Fellows remained tense. The conversion of the old chapel vestry into a Fellows' Common Room, a fashion already set by Merton in 1661 and paralleled in Cambridge colleges, may have contributed to restoring harmonious relations, while the walks and grove were replanted to repair the ravages of the war. Under President Clerke (appointed 1672) the college enjoyed a time of quiet, but his death in 1687 plunged the college abruptly and unforeseeably into the worst crisis of its existence. For the preceding two centuries Magdalen had adjusted to the Crown's demands and benefited from its patronage. Not least it had repeatedly accepted its Presidents on the recommendation of the monarch, though some of these would not have been its first choice and others were technically disqualified under the founder's statutes. Nor, when in 1687 James II used his mandate to recommend one of the Fellows, Anthony Farmer, was this opposed on principle; the objection was to Farmer as a person, and the Fellows petitioned the King to choose an alternative. Only when the King refused did they elect another of their number, John Hough, whom the Visitor promptly admitted as President. Having defied the royal mandate, the Fellows petitioned for pardon and pleaded their oath to elect only a fit person to the office. James now changed tack, agreeing that Farmer was unfit but ordering them to elect the BISHOP OF OXFORD, Samuel Parker. The Fellows insisted that Hough was already President and, even when summoned before James at Christ Church, refused the royal nominee. In October 1687 a Royal Commission visited the college to enforce the King's order, but though the Fellows agreed to obey Parker, they would not acknowledge him to be the lawful President. Twenty-five were thereupon expelled and in their places James nominated others, mainly Roman Catholics. The issue now became whether the King had the right to override the college's statutes and deprive Fellows of their lawful tenure. Opinion was against him, and in October 1688 James admitted defeat, permitting the restoration of Hough and the other Fellows. By December he had fled from England.

The fame which these events brought Magdalen was matched by the admission of a number of extraordinarily gifted Demies in 1689 – a 'golden election' which brought in Joseph Addison; Hugh Boulter, later Archbishop of Armagh; and Henry Sacheverell. All became Fellows in the first decade of the new century, but under a succession of mediocre Presidents the college had little to its credit in the 18th century. Its one notable achievement was the erection of New Buildings, commenced in 1733, from the design of Edward Holdsworth, a Fellow. Unlike many other colleges, Magdalen had made no additions to its mediaeval buildings, and the need was now felt for more commodious accommodation for Fellows and gentlemen-commoners. It was financed by generous subscriptions from the President, Edward Butler, and other Fellows. It was here that Edward Gibbon had an 'elegant apartment' in which he spent the fourteen months (1752–3) which he was later to describe as 'the most idle and unprofitable of my whole life'. His recollection of 'the dull and deep potations' of the Fellows and of his tutor Dr Wilkinson, who 'well remembered that he had a salary to receive and only forgot that he had a duty to perform', have immortalised the college in these years. Gibbon undoubtedly exaggerated both his own idleness and the unstructured nature of the curriculum, and some of the Fellows were men of learning; but there is indeed no sign of intellectual rigour or vitality in the Magdalen of his day.

In 1791, however, the election of MARTIN JOSEPH ROUTH inaugurated the longest presidency in the history of the college: sixty-four years. Routh was a careful and honest scholar in the field of patristic Theology, who kept his head amid the frenzies of the OXFORD MOVEMENT through having a longer perspective and deeper knowledge of the early church than most others in Oxford. Magdalen numbered some prominent Tractarians, for whom J.R. Bloxam, the friend and correspondent of JOHN HENRY NEWMAN, provided a focal point. In other matters Routh was deeply traditional. His dress remained that of the 18th century, as did his view of the purposes of the college. He frustrated a number of grandiose but impractical schemes for extending New Buildings southwards to form a giant quadrangle. This, indeed, had been the original intention in 1730, and it was revived after 1800 as the need to renovate the cloisters became increasingly pressing. A galaxy of architects – Wyatt, Repton, Nash and others – prepared plans, all of which were shelved. But in 1824 the cloister was declared unsafe and demolition began. It was on the insistence of the college architect, J.C. BUCKLER, that work was halted and a rebuilding according to the 'original' design was commenced under J.C. Parkinson. When this was finished the interior of the chapel was remodelled by L.N. Cottingham in the Perpendicular style. Magdalen emerged with the stamp of the

Martin Routh, President of Magdalen College from the age of thirty-five until his death in his hundredth year, pictured in his study in 1854.

Gothic Revival but, partly thanks to Routh, of a distinctly academic quality.

Routh's presidency also saw the removal of Magdalen Hall to the site of Hertford College and, with the demolition of Waynflete's grammar school and the other buildings of the hall in 1844, the way was open for the redevelopment of the westernmost part of the college site. This coincided with the first stirrings of reform among the Fellows, intent on following the lead set by Oriel, Balliol and others in raising academic standards (*see* ROYAL COMMISSIONS). College committees in 1851 and 1854 recommended stricter entrance examinations, the abolition of the gentlemen-commoners and the admission of poor scholars for whom additional accommodation would be built. But virtually all these reforms were blocked by Routh, now in his hundredth year, and the only new building erected was a schoolroom designed by Buckler for the revived college school in the south-west corner of the college.

Reform ultimately came through another Commission in 1857 and an Act of 1877, enabling the college to change the founder's statutes. This did away with territorial restrictions on demyships and fellowships, permitted a proportion of lay Fellows, abolished the President's veto, established new professorships in the sciences and – most significantly of all – allowed the college to admit as many commoners as it chose. At first the increase in these was cautious: they numbered thirty-five in 1870, but then seventy in 1875 and 116 in 1885. From being predominantly a society of graduate foundationers, the college became one of mainly undergraduate commoners. The college was extended and its life

enriched. Between 1879 and 1884 a range of undergraduate rooms was built on the site of Magdalen Hall, forming St Swithun's Quadrangle, followed by the new President's lodgings. Across the road, in buildings adjoining the BOTANIC GARDEN, the science Fellow C.G.B. Daubeny established the first laboratory in Oxford in 1848 (*see* LABORATORIES), while the foundations of the modern tutorial system were being laid under the presidency of Frederick Bulley (1855–85). Magdalen results in the final class lists improved and the college became known both for its aesthetes (in the persons of Oscar Wilde and Lord Alfred Douglas) and its oarsmen. When in 1885 the time came to choose Bulley's successor it was, significantly, a man who had proved an outstanding tutor whom the Fellows elected: Herbert Warren. Warren set about making Magdalen the most prestigious college in the University, and his success was crowned by the admission of the Prince of Wales, later Edward VIII, in 1912. This was a recognition that Warren had achieved for Magdalen the kind of intellectual and moral primacy that BENJAMIN JOWETT had gained earlier for Balliol. Warren took his inspiration from Jowett and sought to inculcate in his undergraduates the ideals of individual excellence, loyalty to the college, and service to the State. Excellence might be achieved on the river, where for a quarter of a century the Magdalen boat was always among the first three in the EIGHTS, or in the number of Firsts in SCHOOLS; service was expressed in the setting up of missions and boys' clubs in Oxford and south London; responsibility and power accrued as Magdalen graduates held high posts in the civil and diplomatic services. Loyalty to the college and to

A milkmaid's misfortune interrupts building repairs in Rowlandson's Original entrance to the Cloisters at Magdalen.

Warren himself was evident in his voluminous correspondence with past pupils, notably during the First World War. A vivid, if rather different, picture of undergraduate life at Magdalen at the turn of the century is given in Compton Mackenzie's novel *Sinister Street* (1913 and 1914). The whole period saw the late Victorian choral tradition personified in three outstanding choirmasters – Sir John Stainer (1859–72), Sir Walter Parratt (1872–82) and John Varley Roberts (1882–1918) – while the MAY MORNING singing from the Great Tower, revived by J.R. Bloxam as a religious as well as a festive occasion, achieved national fame in Holman Hunt's painting *May Morning on Magdalen Tower*, in which Warren, Bloxam and other Fellows are portrayed.

The war brought Warren's Oxford to an end and, although he remained President for a further decade, the reaction against his late-Imperial view of the college built up inexorably among a new generation of Fellows, who came into their own in the 1930s. The tutors now gained control of admissions to the college, and the Tutorial Board regulated the whole pattern of teaching. More emphasis was placed on academic than on social and athletic attainments, and the increasing size of the college led to the building of Longwall Quadrangle and the conversion of Buckler's school building into a college library, opened by the Prince of Wales in 1932. With Sir Charles Sherrington as Waynflete Professor of Physiology, Magdalen attracted a number of able pupils, among them HOWARD FLOREY, who was to discover the therapeutic properties of penicillin. Others who came to Magdalen as undergraduates in the inter-war years were SIR JOHN BETJEMAN, Lord Denning and Sir Peter Medawar.

During the Second World War the depleted college was partially occupied by the RAF, but otherwise escaped unscathed. In 1947 its wartime President, the atomic physicist Sir Henry Tizard, was succeeded by T.S.R. Boase, the art historian. The college adapted itself to the return of servicemen and the post-war expansion of university education by dividing rooms, abandoning compulsory meals in hall, and increasing the number of its tutors. As the period of austerity eased, it erected the Waynflete Building across MAGDALEN BRIDGE for student accommodation. This was completed in 1960. One of the first new buildings in post-war Oxford, it ante-dated the more imaginative architecture of the following years.

In the immediate post-war years, Magdalen Fellows were distinguished in many fields: J.L. Austin and GILBERT RYLE in Philosophy; C.T. Onions and N.R. Ker in Lexicography and Paleography; K.B. McFarlane and A.J.P. Taylor in History; R. Cross and J.H.C. Morris in Law; C.S. LEWIS in English; and C.D. Darlington and J.Z. Young in Botany and Zoology. Under Bernard Rose the choir enhanced its musical reputation. In recent years, under the presidencies of J.H.C. Griffiths (1968–79), K.B. Griffin (1979–88) and A.D. Smith (from 1988), a large-scale programme of restoring the stonework and modernising the domestic facilities of the college has been carried through. This has been financed in great part by generous donations from old members of the college and from charitable trusts. The Great Tower and High Street range, New Buildings, Grammar Hall, and the hall and chapel have all been renovated. A new kitchen has been built in the south-east corner of the college (architects Maguire and Murray), while

accommodation for the increased number of graduates has been found in the Botanic Garden buildings. The college changed its statutes to admit women in 1979.

The range of buildings through which the college is entered from the High Street dates from the 16th century. On entering the first quadrangle (St John's), the visitor faces the 19th-century President's lodgings in yellow stone, with the chapel and Founder's Tower to the right and Grammar Hall and the entrance to St Swithun's Quadrangle on the left. Immediately to the right is a small stone pulpit from which the UNIVERSITY SERMON is preached on St John the Baptist's Day. The small archway adjoining leads to Chaplain's Quadrangle, which contains the remaining portion of the 13th-century Hospital of St John between the arch and the Great Tower. The remainder of this small quadrangle is formed by a 17th-century range to the east and the chapel and hall, with the Senior Common Room below, to the north. It contains a bronze sculpture of Christ and St Mary Magdalen by David Wynne. Returning to St John's Quadrangle, the path leads to the entrance to the chapel beneath the Muniment Tower. The whole of this range, together with the hall and chapel, was commenced in 1474 and completed by 1483, the master-mason in charge being William Orchard, the builder of the DIVINITY SCHOOLS. The west doorway to the chapel has figures of St John the Baptist, Edward IV, St Mary Magdalen, St Swithun, and William of Waynflete. The antechapel contains a number of brasses, including that of the first President, William Tybard, and the tomb and effigy of the father of the founder, Richard Patten, originally in Waynflete Church. The sepia glass, by Richard Greenbury, dates from the 17th century. There are notable wall monuments to Laurence Humphrey, William Langton, John and Thomas Lyttleton, and Herbert Warren, while the remaining mediaeval stalls, with good misericords, are ranged on the northern and southern walls. The organ screen and interior of the chapel are the work of L.N. Cottingham, 1828–35, except for the stained-glass windows of 1857 by Hardman. The altarpiece, Christ carrying the Cross, attributed to Valdés Leal, was presented to the college in 1745 by William Freman. The new organ, installed in 1986, is by Mander in a case designed by Julian Bicknell.

The hall, approached by a staircase at the south-east corner of the cloister, is entered through an early 17th-century screen. To the left, at the top of the stairs, is the buttery. The walls in the hall have early 16th-century linenfold panelling, carried up to the window sills on the north and south and two tiers higher at the west end, where it is finished with a carved frieze and inscription from Colossians III: 11–17. Beneath, nine carved panels, dating from 1541, depict scenes from the life of St Mary Magdalen, with figures of St Mary, St John the Baptist, and Henry VIII. The oriel window has shields and portraits of Charles I and Henrietta Maria, dated 1632. The present roof, of 1903, replaces a plaster vault by Wyatt. Amongst the portraits are those of Cardinal Wolsey, Cardinal Pole, Queen Elizabeth I, Prince Henry, President Routh and President Warren and, more recently, of Presidents Boase and Griffiths. Returning to the cloister, the west side (to the left) is divided by the Founder's Tower, originally the lodgings of the President, to the north of which is the

Old Library, redesigned by Parkinson in 1822–4. The north and east ranges of the cloister were rebuilt at the same time and contain undergraduate rooms. The allegorical figures on the buttresses were erected in 1508–9 and were formerly painted.

Outside the south-east corner of the cloister, along the Cherwell, lies the former kitchen (now Junior Common Room), originally part of St John's Hospital. It has a 15th-century roof and retains its original fireplaces. Adjoining it to the north are bath-houses, built in 1782, known as West's Building. To the north lies New Buildings, commenced in 1733 from designs by Edward Holdsworth. ADDISON'S WALK and the Fellows' Garden can be entered through an iron gate to the right, while to the left lies the grove into which deer were first introduced in the late 17th century. It has recently been replanted after being devastated by Dutch elm disease in 1978. The great plane tree was planted in 1801 by Henry Phillpotts, then a Fellow of the college and later Bishop of Exeter. The wall enclosing the college, along LONGWALL STREET, dates from 1467 when the new site was prepared, and the south-west parts of the college (not open to visitors) are composed of the St Swithun's Quadrangle, built by Bodley and Garner between 1880 and 1884, and Longwall Quadrangle, built by Sir Giles Gilbert Scott in 1928–30, with the college library of 1851.

The corporate designation of the College is The President and Scholars of the College of St Mary Magdalen in the University of Oxford.

(Wilson, H.A., *Magdalen College*, 1899; Bloxam, J.R., ed., *Magdalen College and King James II*, 1886; Denholm Young, N.R., 'Magdalen College', in *Victoria County History of Oxford*, Vol. III, Oxford, 1954, pp. 193–207; 'Magdalen College', in *City of Oxford*, Historical Monuments Commission, 1939, pp. 69–76; Boase, T.S.R., 'An Oxford College and the Gothic Revival', in *Journal of the Warburg & Courtauld Institutes*, Vol. 18, pp. 145–88.)

Magdalen College School *Cowley Place*. When Magdalen College received its first statutes in 1480, the founder, William of Waynflete, began to build a grammar school within the college site, though the teaching of grammar here had almost certainly begun some years earlier in a room below the old chapel of St John's Hospital (between the tower and the present porters' lodge). The school was endowed by the founder with four chaplains, eight clerks and sixteen choristers. Its first recorded Master, John Anwykyll (appointed 1481), his successor John Stanbridge (Master 1488–94), and the latter's former pupil Whittinton were pioneers in teaching boys Latin by means of textbooks in English. In Whittinton's textbook, *Vulgaria*, is found a description of his contemporary, Sir Thomas More, believed to have been a boy at the school: 'Moore is a man of an aungel's wyt and syngler lernyng . . . and as tyme requyreth a man of meruelous myrth and pastimes and sometyme of a sad grauyte as who say, a man for all seasons'. THOMAS WOLSEY was Master in 1498 and among distinguished members in the 16th century were William Tyndale, translator of the Bible and reformer, and William Camden, historian and antiquary.

Following the Reformation, and during the 17th century, the relationship between the college and the school weakened and changed, though the foundation

continued to flourish as an ordinary grammar school with such pupils as Thomas Hobbes (1588–1679), the philosopher; Edward Hyde, LORD CLARENDON, author of the *History of the Rebellion*; and John Milton, father of the poet. Except for the choristers, the school declined during the 18th century. In 1828 the old grammar school building was demolished, except for its northern end and its bell-turret, which remain today. MAGDALEN HALL moved to the disused buildings of Hertford College and the Principal's lodgings became the school until a new schoolroom, designed by JOHN BUCKLER, was opened in 1851 at the corner of LONGWALL and HIGH STREET. Described by Pevsner as a 'very attractive, compact little job', it is now the college library. Under J.E. Millard (a former Magdalen chorister who became Master of the school in 1846 at the age of twenty-three) and his Victorian successors, the school began to revive, until by the end of the century its numbers had risen to 100 boys. In 1894 it moved to a new building, designed by Sir Arthur Blomfield, across MAGDALEN BRIDGE at the junction of Cowley Place and IFFLEY ROAD, although it retained the 1851 schoolroom until 1928. By 1925 the number of boys was 170; by 1939, 190; by 1949, 400; and today, over 500, some 40 of them boarders.

To accommodate increasing numbers, buildings across Cowley Place from the 1894 school house have been added, the principal being a teaching block (1956) and science laboratories (1958) designed by Booth, Ledeboer and Pinchheard; big school and chapel (1966) by Pinchheard and Partners; the laboratory additions and music school (1973) by Ivor Smith and Cailey Hutton; and the quincentenary building for Modern Languages and Mathematics by the Oxford Architects Partnership. The school occupies some 10 acres, with playing fields on two sites of some 24 acres.

After the First World War the school came partially under the Board of Education, and after the Second it became a direct-grant school. With the ending of the direct-grant system in 1976, it became independent.

R.S. Stanier was a notable Master (1944–67) and his wife Maida is a well-known Oxford poet. In this century among the school's very great number of distinguished former pupils have been Noel Chavasse, VC and Bar, and J.F. Russell, VC (both of whom died in 1917); Austin Lane Poole, President of St John's College; Sir Edgeworth David, member of Shackleton's Antarctic expedition; John Johnson, Printer to the University; SIR BASIL BLACKWELL, bookseller; H.A.P. Sawyer, headmaster of Shrewsbury; H.B. Jacks, of Bedales; P.B. Smith, of Bradfield; T.D. Wheare, of Bryanston; and W.H. Ferguson, Warden of ST EDWARD'S SCHOOL, Oxford and Radley; Sir Raymond Unwin, PRIBA; Sir Felix Aylmer, the actor and President of Equity, and his brother, Air Chief Marshal Sir John Whitworth Jones; and Ivor Novello.

(Stanier, R.S., *Magdalen School*, Oxford, 1958.)

Magdalen Hall Originally the grammar school of Magdalen College, built in 1480, it became an independent ACADEMIC HALL in the 16th century. It was situated just outside the CITY WALL in that part of the site of Magdalen College now occupied by Longwall Quad. Throughout almost the whole of its history it was one of the largest and most popular of academic halls. It has William Tyndale among its

16th-century alumni, and in that and the following century was a centre of Puritanism. Cromwell and Fairfax dined there in 1649. Others among its students during this period were Thomas Hobbes (1608); Edward Hyde, 1st EARL OF CLARENDON (1626); Robert Plot, the first curator of the ASHMOLEAN MUSEUM (c.1660); and John Davenport, a Puritan divine who founded the colony of New Haven in New England (c.1617). Following severe damage by fire to its buildings in 1820, Magdalen Hall took over the buildings of the abortive Hertford College on the corner of CATTE STREET and NEW COLLEGE LANE; and when Hertford was successfully refounded in 1874 the mediaeval academic hall as an institution came to an end. Of its original buildings all that remains is a piece built in 1614, now the old Grammar Hall in St John's Quad of Magdalen College; buildings erected in Catte Street on its move there (1818–22) were incorporated by T.G. JACKSON when he designed this façade of Hertford College in 1887–9.

Magdalen Street Runs from ST GILES', near the MARTYRS' MEMORIAL, southwards to CORNMARKET beside ST MARY MAGDALEN CHURCH, whose small tree-shaded churchyard is enclosed by wrought-iron railings. The street was named either after the church or after St Mary Magdalen (or Maudeleyn) Hall, which in ANTHONY WOOD's time was on the north side of the church opposite Balliol College 'ball-court' (*see* MAGDALEN HALL). On the other side of the church is an equally short length of road known as Magdalen Street East, of which part of Balliol College takes up the whole of the east side. Both streets end at the junction of BROAD STREET. Writing in 1821, Wade describes St Giles' as running straight into Cornmarket and does not mention either of the Magdalen streets. (The pronunciation of both streets is usually 'Maudeleyn', like the college.)

Until about 1820 the churchyard was bounded by buildings on the north side; these can be seen in an illustration of 1819 in the *History and Guide of St Mary Magdalen* and in the *Victoria County History*, Vol. IV. Included among the buildings were at least seven public houses. Also in Magdalen Street East are the city's oldest underground public lavatory for women (built 1909) and a long-established bicycle park beside the church. Magdalen Street itself is dominated by the RANDOLPH HOTEL (on the corner of BEAUMONT STREET); Oxenford House with its entrance in FRIAR'S ENTRY, built in 1966 by Fitzroy, Robinson and Partners (on the site was Oxford's first broadcasting studio, 1925); and Debenhams department store. This is on the site of ELLISTON & CAVELL (founded 1823 at Nos 4–12). The street has housed many other old-established firms, including Mary Mattingley (No. 11) and J. Willsher (No. 13), both grocers there in the mid-19th century; William Roddis, cabinetmaker and upholsterer, in existence here at least by 1864 (Nos 14 and 15); and later (at No. 14) Walford and Spokes (silversmiths) and BOFFIN'S (bakers). TAPHOUSE & SON'S music store, established in 1857, was at No. 3; its music replaced that of a noisy public house, the Woodstock Arms, and was therefore welcomed by its neighbours. All these establishments have disappeared but the cinema at No. 18, built by J.C. Leed in 1922 with an Egyptian-style interior, still exists. The cinema is now called the Canon, Magdalen Street (*see* CINEMAS). Only buses and licensed taxis can now enter the street from the north.

Magpie Lane Starting as a narrow path between tall buildings next to No. 94 HIGH STREET, the lane widens as it passes between the back of Oriel College and Corpus Christi College's Jackson building, ending in MERTON STREET. In the 13th century it was known as Grope (Crope or Croppe) Lane from the mediaeval word for a dark and disreputable passage. Later it was Grape Lane. It had other names, including Winkin Lane because Wynkyn de Worde had a printing press there towards the end of the 15th century, although it is not known whether he was ever in Oxford himself. Then in the 17th century the alehouse with the sign of the magpie hanging on its west side gave its name to the lane and this continued for another 200 years. A plan of Oriel College properties in 1814 shows Magpie Lane, but with Group Lane on the line of the present Kybald Street. It shows a break in Oriel College wall, possibly making the crossroads or 'twychen'. By about 1838, however, the lane had become Grove Street. By the late 1920s the name Magpie had been reinstated, though a map of 1935 showed its continuation from Merton Street into the Meadow as The Grove. Behind the front of No. 1 Magpie Lane on the High Street is a 16th-century timber-framed house with overhang.

Maiden's Head *11–12 Turl Street.* A private house existed on this site from about 1300 until an inn, the Maidenhead, opened on 4 May 1607. By 1655 it had become the Globe, but the name reverted to the Maidenhead in the early 18th century. The inn closed in 1911. WALTERS & CO. now stands on the site.

Maison Française Founded in 1945 to encourage closer ties between Britain and France at university level. Originally in a house in BEAUMONT STREET, the

Magpie Lane in 1813, showing the tower of Merton College chapel in the background.

237

Maison Française is now in a new building in Norham Road, designed in a very pale buff brick by Jacques Laurent with Brian Ring, Howard & Partners. The foundation stone was laid on 15 June 1962 by Harold Macmillan, later LORD STOCKTON, CHANCELLOR of the University. It was opened on 18 November 1967 by André Malraux. The bronze statue of a nude girl in front of the building is *Flore* by Aristide Maillol. The building contains a lecture room, also used for recitals and plays, an exhibition room and a library of some 33,500 books and periodicals, and 3000 records. A programme of lectures, colloquia and cultural activities is organised, and there is some accommodation for students and French researchers.

Mallams The oldest firm of estate agents and fine-art auctioneers in Oxford; it claims to have been established in 1788. It was founded by a member of the Mallam family. Thomas Mallam was a solicitor and auctioneer, who from 1832 conducted his business from No. 126 HIGH STREET. The firm later moved to ST MICHAEL'S STREET, where it practised as Mallam, Payne & Dorn, and then as Mallams. The sale room was a prefabricated hut in what is shown in J.C. BUCKLER's drawing as the garden of No. 24. In 1986 a new sale room and offices were opened in a building in St Michael's Street designed by Barnett, Briscoe and Gotch and built by KNOWLES & SON.

Maltby, Alfred, & Son Ltd A firm of bookbinders, established in 1834, and occupying some 19th-century premises in ST MICHAEL'S STREET, within which is incorporated a bastion of the CITY WALL.

Management, Oxford School of Sited at TEMPLETON COLLEGE, the School is to provide a 2-year course leading to the degree of Master of Business Administration (MBA).

Manchester College The 20th century representative of a line of distinguished academies, beginning at Rathmel in Yorkshire in 1686, Manchester College is connected with that historic community of churches which, in 1928, became the General Assembly of Unitarian and Free Christian Churches. However, the college is not and never was Unitarian; neither is its Chapel Unitarian, even though Unitarians worship there together with those of other denominations day by day and Sunday by Sunday. Manchester College has remained faithful to its foundation principle and is open to students 'of every religious denomination, from whom no test or confession of faith' is required. Founded in Manchester in 1786 and established successively at York (1803), Manchester again (1840), London (1853) and Oxford (1889), the college offered theological and general academic courses and continues so to do. Today it is best described as an independent 'liberal arts' college with a ministerial-training component course. There are over 70 students of various religious backgrounds, including a small group of students training for the ministry of the General Assembly. It is in no sense simply a theological college, though it is probably Oxford's oldest established college offering specific ministerial training.

When the University finally admitted Nonconformist students in the late 19th century (*see* DISSENTERS), the college authorities earnestly debated whether they should sanction a move from Gordon Square in Bloomsbury to the possibly demoralising location of Oxford. Fortunately the prospect proved irresistible. A suitable site was bought on the corner of HOLYWELL STREET and MANSFIELD ROAD, opposite New College and next door to Wadham College. Handsome Gothic buildings were erected in 1891–3 to the designs of Thomas Worthington. Seven 17th- and 18th-century houses along Holywell Street and others immediately behind them were bought and now afford accommodation for some sixty students and a small number of senior residents and sabbaticals. In the Gothic complex is a chapel with a splendid set of windows by EDWARD BURNE-JONES and WILLIAM MORRIS. There is a grand organ and the college has a strong musical tradition. A spacious library houses 70,000 volumes and valuable archives.

If Manchester College is not *of* Oxford University, it is undeniably *in* the very centre of it. Its official relationship to the University concerns principally the students in training for the ministry of the General Assembly. In 1965 the college was granted by the University the status of a society or institution for higher study and in 1967 it was authorised to enter names on the Register of Diploma Students. Although, then, it is not incorporated into the University, the college may matriculate a small number of ministerial students for Theology degrees. More students are reading for London University external degrees in English, History, Philosophy and Theology, though the teaching is by the traditional Oxford tutorial method. This is particularly appreciated by that third of the student body from the USA who complete a year of their American degree course at the college. A small number of students from time to time study for the Oxford University Diploma in Social Administration and for diploma courses of the London colleges of music.

Manchester College became the sixth Permanent Private Hall in 1990.

(Smith, B. (ed.), *Truth, Liberty, Religion: Essays Celebrating Two Hundred Years of Manchester College*, Oxford, 1986.)

Manning, Henry Edward (*1808–1892*). Went up to Balliol at the age of nineteen and took a First in Classics. In the Michaelmas Term of 1829 he was President of the UNION SOCIETY, an office in which he was followed a year later by WILLIAM GLADSTONE, who became a lifelong friend. He was elected to a fellowship of Merton College in April 1832 and at Christmas he was ordained. The following year his wedding ceremony was performed by the bride's brother-in-law, SAMUEL WILBERFORCE; but, after only five happy years of marriage, Mrs Manning died. For seventeen years Manning was a much-loved parish priest of Woollavington-cum-Graffham in Sussex. At thirty-four years old he was appointed select preacher at Oxford and such was his popularity that he was consistently able to fill the University Church of ST MARY THE VIRGIN, where, on Guy Fawkes Day 1843, he took the opportunity to preach a strongly anti-papal sermon. Nonetheless, deeply influenced by the writings of J.H. NEWMAN, seven and a half years later he was received into the Roman Catholic Church and, in 1865, succeeded Cardinal Wiseman as Archbishop of Westminster.

Manor Road Named after HOLYWELL MANOR, which stands at the junction of Manor and ST CROSS ROADS and was rebuilt by Merton College in 1516. Balliol College has been tenant since 1930. A workhouse, run by the Train family as contractors, stood near the manor house between 1740–69 and was also used by several other parishes. From 1856–1929 the Sisters of St John the Baptist ran a refuge and training house here for the reform of prostitutes and 'fallen women'. The present-day Manor Road runs eastwards over Holywell Mill Stream to St Catherine's College, which was built on part of the Great Meadow. Manor Place is a short cul-de-sac which runs from 6 Manor Road. On the north side of the road are the headquarters of the Oxford University Air Squadron.

Mansfield College The abolition of religious tests in 1871 brought students from the Free Churches into Oxford colleges, where they could study for arts degrees. Writing in 1890, W.B. Selbie described the situation which had arisen in the early 1880s: 'There was at this time a considerable number of Nonconformists in the University and many of these had come to feel strongly that the Free Churches must have a more vigorous, organized, yet academic, mode of being than they had hitherto possessed, if the faith they represented were to live in Oxford, or their sons were to remain faithful to it.' It was in response to this situation that Mansfield College had its beginnings; it stands today as a tribute to the Free Church theological and historical tradition and as a legacy of those churches and their members to the University and to society. Mansfield has developed and maintained a strong academic record and has, in W.B. Selbie's words, 'become what the University itself claims to be, a place where true religion and sound learning may for ever flourish'.

In 1886 the Congregational Churches made the decision to close their theological college in Birmingham and to move the work and assets of Spring Hill College to Oxford, where a new institution would be developed under the principalship of the Rev. A.M. Fairbairn. The new institution bore the name Mansfield, after the family which had originally founded Spring Hill College in 1838. While instruction was initiated in Michaelmas Term 1886 in rented buildings in HIGH STREET, the new college was being constructed along MANSFIELD ROAD. Basil Champneys was retained as architect and, together with George Faulkner Armitage, designed and constructed the buildings and their furnishings. The buildings were designed in a collegiate Gothic style, which attempted to place the new college within the more traditional Oxford architectural setting.

The chapel provides a lovely combination of oak and stone carving, and fine examples of Victorian stained glass. The arms of the earlier Oxford colleges (*see* HERALDRY) are depicted in the windows, along with the arms of various academic institutions which reflect the Reformed tradition. Numerous historical figures in the history of the Church from biblical times to the 19th century are portrayed in stained glass and stone statuary. The great organ was built by W.G. Vowles of Bristol; it was a favourite of Dr Albert Schweitzer when he was at the college as Dale Lecturer. A smaller instrument, built by Tamburini in Italy, is located in the nave.

The hall and Senior Common Room have retained their original furniture, which was designed and built by Armitage, and these rooms are being refurbished in ways which will retain their late Victorian style. The library has been described as 'one of the most delightful volumes that Champneys designed'. In 1962 a new block of buildings, designed by Thomas Rayson, was completed to provide student accommodation. These buildings complete the south side of the main quad and add to the feeling of openness and spaciousness experienced on entering the college through the ironwork gates.

Mansfield began with a twofold purpose: to provide a centre where Free Church students could gather and worship together; and to provide a Free Church faculty in Theology for research and the training of ministers. The college was non-residential until 1946. Students were accepted to read for University arts degrees and were matriculated through other colleges. The main group, however, were those who had completed an arts degree and who studied Theology in preparation for ordination. In 1955 Mansfield became a Permanent Private Hall (*see* PRIVATE HALLS) within the University and was then allowed to matriculate its own students. Since that time, the development of the college has moved steadily toward becoming a typical undergraduate college with some graduate students in selected fields. Fellows and lecturers have been added to the college in a variety of fields and tuition is now provided in English, Geography, Modern History, Jurisprudence, Mathematics, Philosophy–Politics–Economics, Physics and Engineering Sciences. About 20 per cent of the students continue in a variety of Theology courses, including those preparing for ordination. Students in the college constitute a fine mixture and balance of social, religious, educational, economic, geographic and national backgrounds.

Mansfield has had close ties with the Continent and with North America since its foundation. In the field of Theology there have been ties with Reformed and Lutheran churches and students have represented many traditions, including Anglican, Roman Catholic and Orthodox. New worldwide ties are being developed year by year as academic contacts increase and as relations develop with overseas colleges and universities through student exchange, academics on sabbatical leave and a variety of conferences which meet in the college during vacations.

Distinguished members of the college have included the theologians James Moffatt, T.W. Manson, Nathaniel Micklem, A.M. Hunter, W. Wheeler Robinson, C.H. Dodd, John Marsh and George Caird, and the musicians A.F. Bayly, Erik Routley and Paul Crossley. In addition, J.A. Hadfield, the psychologist, and the Rev. Dr Alex Boraine, the South African politician, have been students at Mansfield.

The present Principal is Mr D.J. Trevelyan.

(*See also* DISSENTERS *and* PRIVATE HALLS.)

Mansfield Road Named after the college (on the west side of the road), the foundations were dug in 1887. On a map of 1889 there was still a dotted line for that part of the road south of Love Lane (now JOWETT WALK) as far as HOLYWELL. The road continues to SOUTH PARKS ROAD in the north. A certain number of CIVIL WAR earthworks survive in the vicinity. In the south-west corner of Mansfield College grounds the line of the works runs north-north-west and is a rampart forming the north-eastern boundary of the garden of Wadham College. On the west side of the road is Manchester College. On the east is the School of Geography, a Grade II listed building by T.G. JACKSON, built in 1898 and with two later additions.

No. 9 nearby is also a Grade II listed building by Jackson but in a 17th-century style and built in 1892–3. Opposite Mansfield College is the Institute of Virology, which was opened on 8 July 1981. A brick building designed by the Architects Design Partnership, it was awarded a Certificate of Merit in 1983 in the Brick Development Association Architectural Awards. The Tinsley Building was named after the first director, Dr Thomas Tinsley, whose portrait by Tristan Humphries hangs in the reception hall.

Maps Several important maps of early Oxford have been reconstructed from documentary and archaeological evidence, the pioneer work being H.E. SALTER's *Mediaeval Oxford* (1936). The earliest surviving map of the city as a whole is a plan by Ralph Agas, published in 1588 but apparently surveyed in 1578. It is on a scale of roughly 1:1650, not very accurately measured, and the buildings are depicted as in a bird's-eye view, but without perspective; the view is from the north, so the south fronts of buildings are obscured. Nevertheless, the map provides a highly detailed picture of the Elizabethan city, which seems to bear out much that is known from documentary sources. The only surviving copy of the original map, in the BODLEIAN LIBRARY, is badly damaged, but the gaps may be filled from a re-engraving commissioned by the University from Robert Whittlesey in 1728.

Agas's map greatly influenced other early maps of the city, not only those published by John Speed from 1611 onwards, which appear to be poor sketches from Agas, but also the important maps of Wenceslaus Hollar (1643) and DAVID LOGGAN (surveyed in 1673, published in 1675), both of which retain the imaginary aerial viewpoint from the north. Hollar, a royalist soldier, presumably prepared his map on site during the royalist occupation of the city, but although he adapted Agas persuasively in some details, notably college buildings, various additions seem to conflict with other available evidence, particularly his treatment of the castle area and the new housing on the northern side of the city. His retentions from Agas should likewise be viewed with caution. Loggan, the University engraver, is known to have used Agas's map, but his additions imply a very careful re-examination of the site: his scale is roughly 1:3250.

Among other early maps of particular aspects of the city are a bird's-eye view of FOLLY BRIDGE and the causeway south of Oxford (*c*.1569, in Brasenose College), a plan of the CASTLE area (*c*.1617, in Christ Church), plans of the CIVIL WAR fortifications, notably that of Bernard de Gomme (1644), and a map of PORT MEADOW by Benjamin Cole (*c*.1695).

A purported 'new and accurate map' of Oxford by William Williams in 1732, while eschewing the bird's-eye view, retains the orientation and roughly the scale of Loggan's map, and is clearly based upon it; but Isaac Taylor's map, surveyed in 1750 and published in 1751, represents a new departure: north is now at the top of the map, and parish boundaries are included in what is clearly a complete and fairly accurate re-survey on a scale of approximately 1:2400. Taylor's map remained for the next century the base for most maps of Oxford, of which the best known are those inset on the Berkshire map of John Rocque (1762) and on the Oxfordshire maps of Thomas Jefferys (1767) and Richard Davis (1797). Also derived from Taylor's map were those in the

numerous guides produced by Oxford booksellers such as James Fletcher, Daniel Prince, and John Cooke; Fletcher's *New Oxford Guide* (1759) was a popular version, running to many editions.

In 1771 John Gwynn, surveyor to the newly formed Paving Commission, alarmed Oxford citizens, who observed him all over town, measuring and making notes on streets and houses. Fears that the whole town was about to be demolished were soon allayed, although there were extensive 'improvements'. Gwynn's large-scale and detailed surveys of the North Gate and East Gate areas, and of MAGDALEN BRIDGE and ST CLEMENT'S in 1773, survive in the British Library; his survey of the area cleared for the new market is in the Oxford city ARCHIVES. All are reproduced in H.E. Salter, *Surveys and Tokens* (Oxford Historical Society, Vol. 75). A map of the whole city (scale 1:2400) was published in 1789 by William Faden, using the plates of Taylor's map altered to incorporate the recent changes. Comparison of the two maps provides a vivid visual record of the extent to which mediaeval Oxford was transformed in the later 18th century. Their value is further enhanced by a survey of 1772 (printed in *Surveys and Tokens*), which proceeds street by street giving the measured width of every house. Maps and survey combined give a picture of Oxford unparalleled in detail.

Existing maps were inadequate for the major sanitary inquiry conducted in 1851, and a new survey was commissioned from Robert Hoggar, to include the new working-class suburbs of ST EBBE'S, ST THOMAS'S, and JERICHO. Hoggar's map (scale 1:6500), published in 1850, ahead of the inquiry, forms a link between the maps of Taylor and his successors and the large-scale maps of the Ordnance Survey of the later 19th century. In importance it ranks with those of his illustrious predecessors Agas, Loggan and Taylor. Hoggar caught the city just as it was about to begin a prolonged period of suburban expansion. Its subsequent growth is charted by the Ordnance Survey, which surveyed Oxford for its 25-inch and 6-inch series in 1876. Those maps, their later revisions and their smaller-scale successors have provided the definitive basis for most of the plans, street maps and tourist guides which have been produced down to the present day. The flood began in the late 19th century, and among the most noteworthy are those printed for local tradesmen; their interest lies less in their cartography than in the accompanying pictorial advertisements showing shops and frontages that have since disappeared. The tradition has continued, less informatively, in the 20th century.

Among maps with particular themes are those depicting colleges, University-licensed lodging houses, boating and rowing, ward boundaries, tramways, drainage and water supply, and epidemics. The well-known Drink Map of 1883, published by the Oxford Band of Hope and Temperance Union, showed seven breweries and 312 licensed houses, accompanied by a scandalised note that 'every twenty second house' was licensed. A *Stadtplan* of Oxford was published by the German High Command in 1940. Purporting to show the city in 1937, it was actually about fifteen years out of date and therefore crucially underestimated the extent of the COWLEY factories. A British map of 1941, in the Bodleian Library, marked road blocks on the city's outskirts and suggested 'strong points' of defence in the event of invasion at BURY KNOWLE PARK, ST EDWARD'S SCHOOL, Pembroke, Christ Church and University College.

Oxford's suburban development can be traced locally from inclosure awards and maps for HEADINGTON (1804), IFFLEY (1815), ST GILES' (1832), COWLEY (1853) and St Thomas's (1853). The gradual building over of much of those areas is recorded in maps and plans deposited with the City Engineer and now kept at the Local History Department of the CENTRAL LIBRARY.

The chief collections of maps relating to Oxford are to be found in the British Library, the Bodleian, the Oxfordshire Record Office, and the Local History Department of the CENTRAL LIBRARY. Of the early maps, those of Agas, Hollar and Loggan are conveniently published with a commentary by H. Hurst in the Oxford Historical Society Vols 38–9.

Market Street From 1330–40 the street was known as Le Cheyne Lane, in 1502 as Cheney Lane and in 1513 as Cheyne Lane; it had a chain at the west end, probably supported on posts. The street led from Lorineria, that part of the CORNMARKET allotted to harness fittings made of metal. Later (1762 and 1821 recordings) it was known as Jesus College Lane. Other early names probably used were Bedford Lane and Adynton's Lane after two families who had property there. The new COVERED MARKET was built in 1772 and opened in 1774, but even as late as 1837 Market Lane, as it was sometimes called, was still also known as Jesus Lane. It is possible too that all or part of it once bore the name of Mildred Lane – that name was certainly given to a continuation of the road on the other side of TURL STREET, the present BRASENOSE LANE. There was a public right of way through St Mildred's Churchyard, leading from School Street to CHENEY LANE. The church was on the site of Lincoln College.

Markets Oxford, like other Anglo-Saxon towns, would have had a market for the sale of food, livestock and other goods from the time of its foundation in the late 9th or early 10th century. Like the later market, it probably centred on CARFAX, extending into QUEEN STREET and CORNMARKET, both of which were much wider in the late Anglo-Saxon period than they afterwards became. By the 13th century the usual market days were Wednesdays and Saturdays, but there was an extra market on Sundays at harvest time when, presumably, there was more to sell.

In 1320 the MAYOR and bailiffs reported that there had been time out of mind fifty-six places or standings for the sale of victuals, situated in the middle of the town where most people congregated. The bakers sold bread from their 'baskets' at Carfax, the butchers meat from THE SHAMBLES at the top of the HIGH STREET outside ALL SAINTS CHURCH. In 1328 some stalls were built at ST MARY THE VIRGIN, but we do not know for whom. No doubt the positions of the different stalls changed from time to time, but a full description of the market in about 1370 is probably fairly typical. It then extended along Cornmarket as far as SHIP STREET and ST MICHAEL'S STREET (that is to say, almost as far as the North Gate), along the High Street as far as St Mary the Virgin, along ST ALDATE'S to about the site of the modern BLUE BOAR LANE, and into the top of Queen Street. On the west side of Cornmarket were, from the south, the standings for the sellers of rushes, brooms, thorns and bushes, and on the east side those for

tanners, 'foreign' poulterers (poulterers who were not freemen of Oxford), and cornsellers. Sellers of hay and grass occupied the middle of the street. On the north side of the High Street, starting from Carfax, were the foreign fishmongers, woollen-drapers, linen-drapers, glovers, whittawers (preparers of white leather), and sellers of pigs and hogs. On the other side of the street were the butchers, the ale-sellers and the sellers of timber and faggots. In the middle of the street were the sellers of coarse bread, earthenware, coals (charcoal) and straw. On the west side of St Aldate's were the vendors of dishes and scullery ware, and on the east side sellers of meal and seeds; the fishmongers and wood-sellers also had stalls or standings in St Aldate's. At the top of Queen Street were the sellers of cheese, eggs, milk, butter, peas and beans, and at Carfax itself were the white-bread bakers. Although they were not said to be so, many of these sellers, particularly those around Carfax, were probably non-freemen – men who had come in from the surrounding countryside to sell their produce.

The street market changed little between the 14th century and its closure on the opening of the COVERED MARKET in 1774. In 1536 John Claymond, President of Corpus Christi College, built a permanent, covered corn market in the centre of the modern Cornmarket. (The market building gave its name to the street, earlier called Northgate Street.) In 1556 the street market was extended along the whole of the modern Queen Street, most of the extra space being occupied by a new butchers' shambles – permanent butchers' shops. By the 17th century the fishmongers, too, had acquired permanent stalls, in St Aldate's outside the southern part of the TOWN HALL site.

Claymond's corn market was pulled down during the CIVIL WAR, in 1644, the lead from the roof being used to make bullets. The butchers' shambles were burnt down in the fire which destroyed much of the western side of the city in the same year. THE SHAMBLES were rebuilt in 1656 and survived until 1773, when they were sold to the Paving Commissioners and demolished. The corn market was not replaced by a permanent structure until 1751, when an open corn market was built on the ground floor of the new town hall. Between 1709 and 1713 a butter bench for the sale of dairy produce was built on the corner of St Aldate's and Queen Street.

Other, shortlived, street markets were recorded from time to time. In the 13th century horses were sold outside the North Gate in BROAD STREET, then called Horsemonger Street. Cattle may have been sold there too, but as the area was outside the town in the Northgate Hundred, whose records have not survived, little is known of it. In the mid-14th century there was apparently a daily market for 'all things needful for a man', called Jaudewynes Market, outside the north wall of the town in Merton College's HOLYWELL MANOR; it was suppressed by the college in about 1362. The meaning of the name is obscure, but may mean fools' or ragamuffins' market. Another shortlived market was held inside the West Gate in a place called Newmarket in the 15th century; this had ceased by 1532. A new market at GLOUCESTER GREEN, granted to the city by the charter of 1601, was not established, but a cattle market was held there for some years after 1755. The cattle market was revived in 1835 and remained at Gloucester Green until 1932, when it moved to the OXPENS on the south-west side of the city. It became a general market and in 1982 moved back to Gloucester Green when the Oxpens site was taken over by the COLLEGE OF FURTHER EDUCATION.

Control of the market was a source of town–gown friction from the late 12th century, the town defending the interests of its freemen and traders, the University anxious to ensure a supply of good, cheap food for its members. One of the conditions of the settlement, in 1214, of the first serious town–gown dispute was that the townsmen should sell food and other essentials to scholars at reasonable prices. In 1280 the University complained to Edward I about the high cost of food in Oxford; and the King fixed the prices of beef, cows, pigs, sheep, geese, hens and eggs. The price and quality of bread and ale were regulated throughout the country by the assizes of bread and of ale, which were enforced by manorial lords or other local authorities. In Oxford these assizes, and that of weights and measures, were gradually transferred from the town to the University. In 1248 Henry III ordered that the CHANCELLOR should be present at the assizes of bread and of ale; in 1324 those assizes and in 1327 that of weights and measures were committed to the Chancellor and the Mayor jointly. After the riot of ST SCHOLASTICA'S DAY in 1355 all assizes were committed to the Chancellor alone. At the same time, control of other foods in the market, the butchers' shambles and the fish stalls passed to the University. Thenceforth the Chancellor's Court (*see* COURTS) dealt with market offences, such as selling goods at too high a price, selling rotten meat or vegetables, and regrating or selling retail, which was forbidden in the market.

Despite complaints from the town, the University controlled every aspect of the market until well into the 19th century. In June 1557, in time of sickness, the VICE-CHANCELLOR, considering the dangers of eating unripe fruit, forbade the bringing of apples or pears into Oxford. Other mid-16th-century orders fixed the prices of goods, including rabbits, capons, geese, pigs, butter, eggs and candles, as well as wine, and forbade the making and selling of 'unwholesome cakebread, stewing of naughty and rotten prunes' as well as the making (presumably by those unqualified to do so) of flans, custard, cheesecakes, apple pies and such like. In about 1600 another set of regulations tried to ensure a good supply of candles by forbidding the sale of tallow to 'foreigners' and insisting that butchers bringing meat into the city should also bring hides, fells and tallow. A few years later bakers were forbidden to sell spice cakes, buns, biscuits or spice breads except at burials, on Good Friday and at Christmas. The prices of most foods were fixed again in 1680, but the Vice-Chancellor's interest in the detailed workings of the market declined in the 18th century as relations with the town improved.

Several of the disputes which marked town–gown relations in the 17th century were over the collection of tolls and rents for market stalls, the University complaining that they were too high, the town that they formed a vital part of its revenue and could not be reduced.

The street market was from its early days a source of nuisances and obstructions. Three butchers were brought before the Mayor's Court in 1304 for soiling the street with 'putrid blood'. In 1310 Edward II forbade the slaughter of animals inside the town, but complaints were renewed in the 1330s, the University

alleging that the smell of rotting entrails caused illness and death. The town protested, but in 1339 slaughtering within the walls was again forbidden. The slaughter houses had moved just outside the wall to BREWER STREET, then called Sleying Lane, by 1478. Sheep being driven through the town caused congestion in 1559. Stalls at Carfax hindered traffic in 1629, and by 1637 the combination of the market and CARFAX CONDUIT placed passers-by in grave danger of being 'thronged to death'. The Oxford Mileways and Improvement Act of 1771 closed the 'very inconvenient' street market, by that date confined to High Street and Queen Street.

(*See also* COVERED MARKET.)

(Ogle, O., 'Oxford Market', *Collectanea*, ii, Oxford Historical Society xvi.)

Marston   A village on the north-east side of Oxford, south of the northern bypass and just inside the RING ROAD. The marshy swamps of the River Cherwell (*see* THAMES) gave Marston – 'Marsh Town' – its name. It is also known as Old Marston to distinguish it from New Marston, a large suburb adjoining it on the south side. Old Marston was held by the Parliamentarians during the siege of Oxford in the CIVIL WAR. The treaty following the siege was signed in the Manor House, Ponds Lane, near ST NICHOLAS CHURCH. The house was owned by the Crokes, 'the most considerable family which ever lived in Marston', and the owner at the time being Unton Croke, serjeant-at-law, JP, and Marston's principal inhabitant. New Marston is separated from the Cherwell by a number of college sports grounds and by the water meadows bordering the river. It is connected to the PARKS by a footpath over Rainbow Bridge, and is linked to SUMMERTOWN by MARSTON FERRY ROAD. The VICTORIA ARMS at Marston Ferry is a popular inn on the Cherwell. It was at Marston in 1819 that the Rev. Jack Russell of Exeter College acquired a milkman's dog called Trump, which was the forerunner of the Jack Russell terriers named after him.

(*See also* ST NICHOLAS CHURCH, OLD MARSTON, and ST MICHAEL AND ALL ANGELS, MARSTON ROAD.)

Marston Ferry Road   So called from the ferry which has crossed the Cherwell (*see* THAMES) at MARSTON since at least 1279. At that time the freehold was held by two fishermen of Oxford, but the exact position of the crossing is not known. The ferry (which later consisted of a line across the river and a punt-type boat pulled along the line by hand and which was in the vicinity of the VICTORIA ARMS public house) is not shown on a map until 1876. By 1879, if not before, the road itself, which begins at BANBURY ROAD in NORTH OXFORD, was a private road called Northern Meadows after the farm of that name, which still exists. It became Marston Ferry Road at the beginning of the 20th century but was then only a short length ending at No. 15 and the Oxford City and County Bowls Club. Until 12 November 1971, when the new road and bridge were opened, connecting the North Oxford section with Cherwell Drive in Marston, the only link between these two parts of Oxford was the ferry. Before the OXFORD HIGH SCHOOL FOR GIRLS was built, people could walk from Charlbury Road to the ferry via the allotments at Tucker's Nurseries. The bridge and new link road were officially opened by the Lord MAYOR of Oxford and the chairman of Oxfordshire County Council, together with five schoolchildren representing the various schools in the road.

There is strong evidence that this was not the first bridge over the river at this point. On 1 May 1646 Thomas Fairfax, the parliamentary commander who occupied a strong military position at HEADINGTON HILL in the CIVIL WAR, flung a temporary bridge across the Cherwell in Marston meadows. The bulk of his forces were quartered on the Marston side, facing the northern lines of the city. In the event, the bridge was not required because the King had offered to surrender and terms were about to be agreed. The treaty was signed in Marston at the serjeant-at-law Unton Croke's house, still known in the 1850s as Cromwell's Castle and now known as Cromwell's House (see MARSTON). During a 19th-century riding of the franchises by the Mayor and Corporation, a boat ferrying a party across the river capsized here. This was said to be caused by unsteady robed passengers: many public houses had been visited en route. The gold mace also fell into the water but was later recovered, less a small piece which was never found.

The modern road, which is 26 feet wide, also has a 6-foot footpath and a 10-foot cycle track, which runs the length of the road and has subways at each end. For part of the way, at the eastern end, the cycle track and road are divided by a tall, earth embankment. Originally intended as a sound barrier, it has been the subject of controversy because cyclists fear for their security, especially in darkness, as it hides them from the view of motorists. The bridge itself, with its 78-foot span, was approved by the Royal Fine Art Commission and was the first modern road-over-river bridge to be built in Oxford north of MAGDALEN BRIDGE. It is carried on piles driven to a depth of about 65 feet.

The Banbury Road end of Marston Ferry Road once contained about fourteen substantial detached houses but in recent years most of these have been demolished and replaced by blocks of flats. On the north side a new road gives access to the FERRY POOL and North Oxford Association Ferry Centre. Also on the north side, beyond the Bowls Club, is the CHERWELL SCHOOL (County Comprehensive). On the south side, beyond No. 15, are the playing fields of the Oxford High School for Girls and Summertown Middle School.

Marston Road Runs from the foot of HEADINGTON HILL to Cherwell Drive and, originally, on to MARSTON village. It now connects the suburb of New Marston to the city via THE PLAIN and MAGDALEN BRIDGE. At its southern end is ST CLEMENT'S CHURCH, HEADINGTON HILL PARK and Harcourt House, formerly the Oxford County Court, and government buildings housing various government departments, such as the District Valuer's offices. On the opposite side of the road are college sports grounds and a lane leading to the MESOPOTAMIA walk.

Martyrs' Memorial When the Roman Catholic Queen Mary came to the throne in 1553 Thomas Cranmer, Archbishop of Canterbury, Nicholas Ridley, Bishop of London, and Hugh Latimer, Bishop of Worcester, were forced to appear before a commission in Oxford to be examined for their alleged Protestant heresies. Before that, in November 1553,

Cranmer had been tried for high treason on two counts. First, that on 10 July he entered the Tower of London with other traitors and there proclaimed Lady Jane Dudley to be Queen; second, that he and other traitors sent men in arms as reinforcements for the Duke of Northumberland against the Queen. Cranmer pleaded not guilty, but later changed his plea and was sentenced to be hanged, drawn and quartered. He was taken to the Tower of London to await execution. However, the execution was delayed because Mary wanted to have Cranmer condemned for the more heinous offence of heresy. In March 1554 he, together with Ridley and Latimer, were taken to Oxford and imprisoned in the BOCARDO.

It was arranged that there should be a disputation, with the Protestant leaders attempting to defend their thesis. They were taken on 14 April to ST MARY THE VIRGIN, where they were told the subjects to be debated – namely the Real Presence at the Mass, Transubstantiation and the Mass as a sacrifice. Cranmer was ordered to submit a written statement of his beliefs. Two days later the disputation began in the DIVINITY SCHOOL and was conducted in Latin. Ridley was required to argue his case the following day, and Latimer the day after. On 20 April all three were brought in turn before the commissioners in St Mary the Virgin, where each was told that he had been proved wrong in the disputation and was offered an opportunity to recant. All refused. They were then told that they had been condemned as heretics. A bill was brought before Parliament to re-enact the statutes for burning heretics, which had been repealed in 1547, but it was defeated in the House of Lords. In the autumn it was decided that heretics should be tried in the courts of the Papal Legate and a new Parliament re-enacted the heresy statutes. Throughout this time Cranmer remained isolated in the Bocardo. In September 1555 he was tried for heresy in St Mary the Virgin before the Pope's commissioners. The trial lasted two days. The proceedings were then sent to Rome, Cranmer being given eighty days in which to appeal. This, coupled with the time taken for documents to travel between Rome and London, helps to explain the long delay between the trial and the sentence's being carried out. Furthermore, it was necessary for the Archbishop to be 'degraded' by being ceremoniously stripped of his vestments. Before then, however, Ridley and Latimer were tried for heresy, excommunicated and burned at the stake on 16 October 1555, after refusing to recant. The burning was in the ditch just outside the northern CITY WALL (a cross let into the roadway in BROAD STREET marks the spot). Cranmer was forced to watch the burning from the parapet of the city wall. At the stake Latimer is reported to have said to Ridley, 'Be of good comfort, Master Ridley; we shall this day light such a candle, by God's grace, in England as I trust shall never be put out.'

Cranmer's time for appealing expired in November. In his absence he was excommunicated by the Pope and ordered to be degraded from Holy Orders. Cranmer had been removed from the Bocardo and lodged in Christ Church through his sister's intervention, but in January 1556 he was returned to the Bocardo. It was there that he wrote out his first recantation. This was a qualified statement and did not go far enough for his accusers. The next day he wrote out another one, and finally an unqualified

243

The Martyrs' Memorial in the 1840s, showing the Taylor Institution on the right and St Mary Magdalen in the background.

submission to the Pope. Two further, more detailed recantations were signed by Cranmer in February, making five in all. Although Foxe states otherwise, there is evidence in 'Bishop Cranmer's Recantacyons' that Cranmer was told three days before his death, and before he had signed his sixth and last recantation, that he was to be burned.

It was a wet morning on Saturday, 21 March 1556, when Cranmer was taken in procession from the Bocardo to St Mary the Virgin. There he was required to stand on a raised platform while Dr Cole, the Provost of Eton, preached the sermon. When he had finished, Dr Cole called on Cranmer to speak and to tell the congregation that he now believed in the true Catholic faith. Cranmer, however, read out a speech which he had secreted in his bosom and in which he repudiated his recantations, saying, 'And forasmuch as my hand offended in writing contrary to my heart, therefore my hand shall first be punished; for if I may come to the fire it shall be first burned.' At the stake Cranmer held his right hand steadily in the fire, crying out, 'I see Heaven open and Jesus on the right hand of God.'

In the 19th century an appeal was launched for a memorial to the martyrs. The memorial, built in 1841–3 in ST GILES' on the site of the Robin Hood Inn and other houses on the north side of ST MARY MAGDALEN CHURCH, was designed by SIR GEORGE GILBERT SCOTT. The design was based on the 13th-century Eleanor Cross at Waltham in Essex – one of the crosses which Edward I erected in memory of Queen Eleanor. The statues of the Protestant martyrs are by Henry Weekes. Cranmer, facing north, is holding his Bible marked 'May, 1541', this being the first year of the circulation of the Bible by royal authority, for which the Archbishop had long pleaded. Ridley's statue faces east and on the west is Latimer, his head bowed and his arms crossed. On the north face of the base an inscription reads: 'To the Glory of

God, and in grateful commemoration of His servants, Thomas Cranmer, Nicholas Ridley, Hugh Latimer, Prelates of the Church of England, who near this spot yielded their bodies to be burned, bearing witness to the sacred truths which they had affirmed and maintained against the errors of the Church of Rome, and rejoicing that to them it was given not only to believe in Christ, but also to suffer for His sake; this monument was erected by public subscription in the year of our Lord God, MDCCCXLI.'

(For the coats of arms on the Martyrs' Memorial, *see* HERALDRY.)

(Wells, J.P., 'The Martyrs' Memorial', *Oxford Magazine*, 1968, pp. 161–4; Loades, D.M., *Oxford Martyrs*, London, 1970; Ridley, Jasper, *Thomas Cranmer*, Oxford, 1962; Foxe's *Book of Martyrs*.)

Masons and Builders Among the mud-walled houses of Saxon Oxford were some timber and a few stone buildings. Large and small cellars have been found dug into the natural gravel on some ten sites. Beneath ALL SAINTS CHURCH, HIGH STREET, a stone house was excavated in 1973–4. At ST PETER-IN-THE-EAST the first church was found in 1968; timber-framed with rubble infilling, it had been built over flimsy stake-built structures. Late Saxon masons used coral rag from the hills of IFFLEY, HEADINGTON or WYTHAM as rubble in the tall tower of ST MICHAEL AT THE NORTH GATE.

In Norman times finer limestone for carved detail was brought from Wheatley, east of Oxford, and from Taynton to the west. Iffley's parish church, ST MARY THE VIRGIN, is a classic example of rich Norman decoration; it dates from the 1120s, not the 1170s as used to be thought, and the beakhead motif comes from the royal abbey at Reading. In the 1150s or 1160s a team of masons from the Severn Valley built the first, eastern arm of CHRIST CHURCH CATHEDRAL. The sophisticated visual trick of the split arcade found at

Gloucester and Pershore and on the Scottish borders at Jedburgh is no doubt a work of the same school. An Oxford craftsman, Elias the Engineer, worked for the Crown throughout southern England in 1187–1203 and kept BEAUMONT PALACE, which he reconstructed in 1195–7. Most Oxford masons' work of the 12th and 13th centuries vanished with the great abbeys and friaries.

The cathedral chapter house, its lavish carving and design matched at Worcester, Chester and Westminster, is probably the work of John of Gloucester, later chief mason to the art-loving Henry III. The aggressive Edward I, Henry's son, brought building skills from Oxford to North Wales for his vast programme of castle-building. As one of his chief carpenters, Henry of Oxford built him a wooden palace and administration block in 1282 at Conwy, where in 1286 he put up the permanent hall roof; and he served on the astounding pontoon bridge to Anglesey in 1282–3.

College archives enrich our knowledge of later mediaeval building in Oxford. William Humberville came from Windsor to tour the south of England looking at libraries with Warden Bloxham, and then built Merton College library in the 1370s. Another, far greater, royal mason, William Wynford, born near Bristol, came from Windsor to build New College in 1380–6 and also its twin foundation at Winchester in 1387–93. A great royal carpenter, the Londoner Hugh Herland, worked with Wynford at New College, but his main roofs there are all lost. (He went on to create the most spectacular of all mediaeval roofs, at Westminster Hall in 1394–1401.) The royal works could not be stripped of men, however, so local masters were brought in with their teams. One was William Brown of Oxford, who built the cloisters and bell-tower of New College, no doubt to Wynford's design. His own work at Oriel, The Queen's and Canterbury Colleges is all lost.

We can now trace only one strand of 15th- and early 16th-century building in the city. At this time the fine-grained, rather soft Headington stone replaced Wheatley; for the finest work, Burford or Taynton was still used (see STONE). The chief mason for All Souls, built in 1438–42, was Richard Chevynton, who spent most of his time at the Burford quarries, sending much of the college ready made; it was assembled on site by Robert Janyns, who may have been a Burford man. The design for All Souls may have been drawn by ARCHBISHOP CHICHELE's chief mason at Canterbury, the Londoner Thomas Mapilton, who died in 1438. Janyns built the fine tower of Merton chapel in 1448–51 before he took up a salaried, but subordinate, post at Eton, coming back to Merton with his son in 1463–4 to carve the elaborate allegory over the gate. It was the son, Henry, who began St George's Chapel at Windsor; and early in the next century the mason who completed St George's, William Vertue, designed Corpus Christi College, while another Londoner, the carpenter Humfrey Coke, designed the hall roof and other woodwork. Neither carried out the work, which was done by local men – the mason–contractor William East of Abingdon and later of Burford, and the carpenter Robert Carow of Oxford. The latter also built the hall roof at Christ Church (under Coke) and the present roof of TACKLEY'S INN. (For the career of a great Oxford-based master-mason, see WILLIAM ORCHARD.)

Oxford's building trade declined after the Dissolution of the Monasteries. For the rest of the 16th century there were only a few middling projects for colleges, as at Jesus and St John's. The handful of Oxford-based masons made foundations and chimneystacks for timber-framed houses, which were contrived and built by the town's carpenters. Joiners flourished, making more furniture and panelled rooms than ever before. But the huge expansion in student numbers of the 1570s and 1580s did not result in any great architectural projects.

Really large-scale building began again in 1610 with Merton Fellows' Quad and Wadham College. Because of the shortage and high prices of Oxford builders, Merton was built by Yorkshire masons and Wadham by Somerset men. These last, under William Arnold, a skilled country-house builder, went home in 1613 when they were finished; but the Yorkshiremen stayed on. The two first partners, John Akroyd and John Bentley, both from Halifax, began the main BODLEIAN quadrangle but both of them died in 1613. Akroyd's son-in-law John Clark and Bentley's brother Michael continued the scheme. Clark also built and carved the remarkable CARFAX CONDUIT before moving on to London to build Lincoln's Inn chapel. One of the original Yorkshiremen from the Merton job, Richard Maude, carried on business in Oxford with various partners until the 1640s. He built much of Jesus, the north range of Canterbury Quad at St John's, and began University College. He may also have begun Oriel, Trinity hall, Exeter hall and chapel, and Lincoln chapel, but all of these are poorly documented. The arcades and elaborate frontispieces at St John's were designed by ARCHBISHOP LAUD's surveyor, Adam Browne, a London joiner. This quad was completed by a newcomer from London, the mason John Jackson, who settled in Oxford; his too is the porch of St Mary the Virgin, executed to the design of Nicholas Stone, and he later designed and built Brasenose chapel and library.

Building in Restoration Oxford was very varied. An Oxford family of masons, the Robinsons, completed Tom Quad at Christ Church in Tudor Gothic style and then worked under CHRISTOPHER WREN at the SHELDONIAN THEATRE in the most up-to-date classical manner. Wren called two major provincial masons to Oxford for two of his college jobs – Thomas Strong of Barrington, Gloucestershire, for a block at Trinity and Anthony Deane of Uffington, Berkshire, for one at The Queen's College. After the Great Fire, Strong moved to London and, with his brother Edward, built much of St Paul's Cathedral under Wren. Later Edward and his son came back to the Cotswolds as contractors, under Vanbrugh and NICHOLAS HAWKSMOOR, for the main block of Blenheim Palace.

Meanwhile, Oxford masons developed a strong tradition. The two main dynasties, PEISLEYS and TOWNESENDS built and sometimes also designed many large schemes in Oxford, as well as the side-wings, bridge and outworks at Blenheim. A Gloucester man, William Byrd, settled in Oxford, did the fine carving at the Sheldonian, made many local monuments, and planned and built the Garden Quad at New College and the chapel at St Edmund Hall before moving on to Winchester as a large contractor on Wren's great unfinished royal palace.

245

The influence of the mason–builder declined in the late 17th century with the emergence of the architect, whether gentleman, scholar or trained professional. The other trades too – joiner, plasterer and so on – no longer made their own designs and deals with the patron. The whole pattern of building was irreversibly changed.

Masterman, Sir John Cecil *(1891–1977).* Disappointing his father, a captain in the Royal Navy, by declining to adopt the naval career for which he had been trained at Osborne and Dartmouth, Masterman won a scholarship to Worcester College in 1909 and obtained a First in Modern History in 1913. After the First World War, during which he was interned in Germany, he was elected a Student of Christ Church and, with KEITH FEILING, did much to make the History School of that college the best in the University. Extremely versatile, he was a novelist, playwright and sportsman – playing lawn tennis and hockey for England and cricket for the MCC – as well as a hard-working tutor. After doing invaluable work as an intelligence officer during the Second World War, he became Provost of Worcester College in 1946 and was VICE-CHANCELLOR from 1957–8. In this office he was largely instrumental in raising £1,750,000 for the Oxford Historic Buildings Fund. After his retirement as Provost in 1961, he continued to devote his time, talents and formidable personality to the various public duties to which his energies and ramified contacts in the political and social world continued to draw him. His book on Oxford, *To Teach the Senators Wisdom,* was published in 1952.

Matriculands *see* MATRICULATION.

Matriculated Tradesmen *see* PRIVILEGED PERSONS.

Matriculation From the Latin *matricula* (a roll), matriculation is the ceremony by which an entrant to a college becomes a member of the University. Although individual college registers were kept at earlier date, matriculation may be traced to a royal statute of 1420 which laid down that all scholars were to be subject to the Principal of a HALL, and which prescribed a ceremony for admission. Within a month of his arrival, every student had to appear personally before the CHANCELLOR and was required to take an oath to observe the statutes for keeping the peace. In 1552 the Chancellor incorporated the statute of 1420 in his register, so providing for the first time in the history of the University a list of all its members. Another statute in 1565 ordered that a register of matriculations should be kept of all scholars and PRIVILEGED PERSONS, who, if sixteen years of age and over, within seven days of their admission to a college or hall had to swear to observe the statutes. The first register, covering the period from 1565 to 1615, gave the name of each scholar, his county of origin, the status of his father and his age. A further statute enacted in 1581 obliged all students of sixteen years and over to subscribe to the Thirty-Nine Articles at matriculation. These two statutes were for long to regulate entry to the University. The LAUDIAN CODE of 1636 obliged all students to be entered at a college or hall, and required the BEDELS to visit each college to obtain the names of newly admitted scholars, who,

within fifteen days, were to be brought by their tutor before the VICE-CHANCELLOR to be matriculated. Students of sixteen and over had then to swear to observe the statutes, take the oath of supremacy and subscribe to the Thirty-Nine Articles. If over twelve years of age, they subscribed to the articles only; if under twelve, their names only were registered. On reaching the age of sixteen they were required to take the oath. The University Reform Act of 1854 abolished oaths or declarations at matriculation. It was not until 1926 that a student had to take RESPONSIONS, or its equivalent, before matriculation. Today every student to be qualified has to be a member of a college and to have fulfilled the University's conditions for entry. Students are presented to the Vice-Chancellor by the senior tutor or Dean of Degrees of their college.

May Morning It has long been the practice on 1 May for undergraduates (and others) to throng HIGH STREET and MAGDALEN BRIDGE in order to listen to choristers sing an invocation to summer, as they are believed to have done for hundreds of years, from the top of Magdalen College Tower at 6 a.m. The custom of singing from the tower may have originated in an inauguration ceremony at the beginning of the 16th century when the building was new. ANTHONY WOOD said that the choristers do 'according to an ancient custom, salute flora at four in the morning with vocal music of several parts'. In the 18th century listeners to the choir were often in danger of being bombarded with rotten eggs and flour by undergraduates in the tower. Holman Hunt's painting *May Morning on Magdalen Tower* helped spread the fame of the festivities.

Morris Dancers still also perform on May Morning. The crowds are usually dense, but in recent years enjoyment of the singing has tended to become subsidiary to such other activities as PUNTING and champagne breakfasts.

Mayors The first Mayor of Oxford, Turchillus, Provost of Oxfordshire, was elected in 1122 or 1123; the first Lord Mayor, Evan Owen Roberts, in 1962. A list of Mayors and Lord Mayors is given in Appendix 2. The mace was made during the mayoralty of John Lambs, tailor, in 1659.

Medicine Oxford has been a centre of medical excellence since the early days of the University, though the Medical School remained small until the 20th century. From the time of Richard I, royal physicians were usually Oxford men, and Oxford physicians influenced very considerably the medical activities of London.

Henry I founded ST BARTHOLOMEW'S HOSPITAL in about 1130; more important was the hospital of St John the Baptist, founded in about 1150, which gained fame for its treatment of war injuries and had an extensive physic garden of many acres. It was incorporated into Magdalen College in 1458. By the beginning of the 13th century, a medical quarter was evolving in Oxford in CATTE STREET, partly because of its vicinity to the physic garden of the hospital and also because the spicers and apothecaries had their houses at the lower end of the HIGH STREET. Later on a School of Medicine was established in Catte Street; this was the residence of the first known medical teacher,

May Morning at Iffley in 1906 when schoolchildren marched in procession round the village.

Nicholas Tingewick (1291–1339), physician to Edward I. A little before this we hear of the first Oxford medical graduate, Simon Moene. One of Tingewick's pupils was John of Gaddesden (*c*.1280–1349), physician to Edward the Black Prince, whose textbook, *Rosa Anglica* (1492) was the first English medical book to be printed; it continued in use for over 200 years. By now many of the early colleges were well established and many had physicians as Fellows, some to look to the health of the college, others to teach, and yet others to study scientific matters not necessarily medical. The Oxford Medical School continued to flourish, but by the 15th century there was much anxiety throughout the country about the control of the growing number of irregular physicians and surgeons. Dr Gilbert Kymer (*d*.1468), physician to HUMFREY, DUKE OF GLOUCESTER, and one of the few medical men to be CHANCELLOR of the University, attempted to resolve this by establishing a faculty of physicians and surgeons in London, with careful rules and regulations. It survived only for a short period, probably due to the opposition of the barber–surgeons, but many of its principles were adopted nearly a century later when THOMAS LINACRE (1460–1524) established the Royal College of Physicians in London in 1518; he also founded lectureships in medicine at Oxford and Cambridge.

There had been changes in the location of the Oxford physicians as All Souls College, founded in 1438, was being built in Catte Street; and fifty years later Magdalen College took over the hospital of St John and destroyed its large physic garden. The result was that most of the physicians and apothecaries moved into the south side of the High Street, where there was more land to plant their own physic gardens.

Oxford was not a healthy place in the 16th century (*see* HEALTH, PUBLIC). There were frequent outbreaks

of bubonic plague, and in 1577 there was the notorious Black Assizes when over 600 people died of typhus. A contemporary account of this was given by a medical Fellow of Oriel College, Dr Thomas Cogan (?1545–1607), who is best remembered for his book, *The Haven of Health* (1584), which was the first book written on students' health with advice on how they should live. When these outbreaks of plague occurred the colleges often used to leave the city, moving to houses in the country – at Woodstock, Abingdon and elsewhere – frequently staying out for the whole year during severe outbreaks. On these occasions huts were erected on PORT MEADOW for the stricken townspeople.

The Regius Professorship of Medicine, which had been established in 1536 by Henry VIII to ensure that adequate standards of education were maintained, was held in the first part of the 17th century by Thomas Clayton (1575–1649), who transformed the Medical School by adopting the seemingly modern technique of finding benefactors to establish a Physic Garden (*see* BOTANIC GARDEN) and to found a readership in Anatomy. He also had a special anatomy book printed for the students. The result was that the number of medical graduates between 1600 and 1650 was double that of the previous fifty years. An added stimulus was the arrival during the CIVIL WAR of King Charles and his entourage, which included William Harvey (1578–1657) and other leading scientists. At this time the young royalist virtuosi formed themselves into a scientific club which met at one of the apothecaries' houses and was probably the origin of the Royal Society, founded in 1660.

From the 16th century, if not before, it had been the custom for Oxford physicians to start to practise in the city, and, if successful, to move on to London; and it is possible to gain some idea of the medical activities at the lower end of High Street in the 17th century.

247

Nos 87–8 High Street was the site of Boster Hall, a mediaeval house which had been rebuilt by a Dr Richard Radcliffe in 1582 and continued as a doctor's house until the end of the 17th century. It was one of the largest houses in the city, with over twenty rooms, and the medical owners also had leases of the ANGEL INN, on the site of today's EXAMINATION SCHOOLS. The evidence suggests that Boster Hall was used as a hospital or nursing home, while the Angel was for visitors or convalescents. Further up the High Street, where the SHELLEY MEMORIAL now stands, were two apothecaries' houses with their own physic gardens. These were used for meetings of the Oxford Scientific Society and Robert Boyle (1627–91), the famous chemist, had his laboratory in one of them. Lastly, 106 High Street, now TACKLEY'S INN, was in the 17th century the house of another apothecary, John Clark; William Petty (1636–1707) lodged here and the society known as the Oxonian Sparkles held its first meetings here.

In the early 18th century there was no hospital accommodation in Oxford apart from the private accommodation in doctors' or apothecaries' houses; but the matter had been discussed for some time and in 1758 it was finally decided to build the RADCLIFFE INFIRMARY. It should be emphasised that the infirmary was in a way more a political gesture than a humanitarian enterprise, and it had not been envisaged by JOHN RADCLIFFE himself, who had left his fortune primarily to build the RADCLIFFE CAMERA, to improve some of the colleges, and to provide travelling fellowships for young doctors. The rest was left to trustees who wanted to demonstrate their disapproval of the Hanoverian government and their support of the Jacobite cause by building an infirmary with Radcliffe's money. There were so many delays, however, that by the time the infirmary was opened, the Court and the University were reconciled.

By now the medical centre of Oxford was BROAD STREET, BEAUMONT STREET and to some extent ST GILES'. In the mid-19th century when SIR HENRY ACLAND returned to Oxford he established himself in a house in Broad Street, which is now part of BLACKWELL'S. Acland did a great deal for the city; he studied the cholera epidemics and showed that the imperfect WATER SUPPLY and sanitation were major factors in these outbreaks. He helped to persuade the University to build the UNIVERSITY MUSEUM, mainly because he felt that all graduates, irrespective of what they were reading, should understand science. He also actively opposed the idea that medical students should spend all their time in Oxford. It was largely due to his enthusiasm that the SCIENCE AREA in the region of PARKS ROAD began to expand, department after department gradually spreading down SOUTH PARKS ROAD. With the development of NORTH OXFORD, the physicians and surgeons began to move there, as it was convenient for both the museum area and for the Radcliffe Infirmary, but general practitioners remained scattered throughout the city. It was not surprising that when Professor William Osler, a distinguished Canadian who had virtually created the famous medical school at Johns Hopkins University, came to Oxford as Regius Professor in 1904, he bought a house in NORHAM GARDENS, which became known as 'The Open Arms' on account of the generous hospitality which his wife provided. Osler brought the Medical School into its modern form, helping to

establish a department of experimental pathology (*see* SIR WILLIAM DUNN SCHOOL OF PATHOLOGY) and attracting the outstanding Charles Sherington to the Chair of Physiology, developing Pharmacology and persuading the OXFORD UNIVERSITY PRESS to undertake the publication of medical books.

In the First World War the Examination Schools became a military hospital. There was also a tented hospital in the gardens of New College for shell-shocked cases and an orthopaedic workshop at the Wingfield Convalescent Home at HEADINGTON for the rehabilitation of soldiers who had lost limbs. Another cause which Sir William Osler adopted was the treatment of tuberculosis and after the war he strongly supported the proposal by the treasurer of the Radcliffe Infirmary, the Rev. G.B. Cronshaw (1872–1929) to purchase the Headington Manor Estate of 120 acres to provide additional accommodation for the hospital. At first the only building on it was the tuberculosis sanitorium, which was named the Osler Pavilion, but for economic reasons the Radcliffe had to try to expand on its old site, even though there was not enough room. However, in 1926 Sir William Morris, later LORD NUFFIELD, purchased the RADCLIFFE OBSERVATORY and land around; he gave the grounds in front of the observatory to the Radcliffe Infirmary and the observatory and its garden to the University for the use of the Medical School. It was his first major charitable gift and, because of his admiration for Sir William Osler, he asked that the Observer's House should be known as 'Osler House'. It was indeed so called when the Director of the Nuffield Institute for Medical Research (which occupied the observatory) lived there, and also when it was the administrative and social centre for the clinical school; but this request has now been forgotten and for Green College it is simply the Observer's House. However, the house on the Headington Manor Estate originally built for the administrator of the hospital and known as 'Manor House Corner' is now the social club for the medical school and is named William Osler House.

The acquisition by the infirmary of the land in front of the Observatory resolved the problem of expansion, so when in 1936 Lord Nuffield made his great benefaction for establishing the Nuffield Postgraduate Scheme, the new buildings could be accommodated on the site. It was only later that it was decided that Manor House Estate should be developed with the building of two JOHN RADCLIFFE HOSPITALS. Owing to the virtual eradication of tuberculosis the Osler Pavilion was no longer needed, but the chest unit at the CHURCHILL HOSPITAL now bears Osler's name.

The Second World War saw many achievements consequent on collaboration between the University Scientific Departments and Oxford physicians. LORD FLOREY's achievement in rendering penicillin available as an outstanding therapeutic agent, Sir Peter Medawar's studies in immunology which enabled organ transplantation to take place, advances in therapy which enabled patients suffering from haemophilia to be treated orthopaedically and by other surgical means, are just a few of a large number of remarkable contributions made to medicine by Oxford research, which is now resulting in remarkable advances in molecular biology.

(*See also* ACLAND HOSPITAL; CHURCHILL HOSPITAL; COWLEY ROAD HOSPITAL; LORD FLOREY; HEALTH, PUBLIC; JOHN RADCLIFFE HOSPITAL; LABORATORIES;

S. Seymour Thomas's 1909 portrait of Sir William Osler, Regius Professor of Medicine.

LITTLEMORE HOSPITAL; NUFFIELD ORTHOPAEDIC CENTRE; OXFORD EYE HOSPITAL; RADCLIFFE INFIRMARY *and* WARNEFORD HOSPITAL.)

Medieval & Renaissance Studies, Centre for

Founded in 1975 as a private institute for the study of the Middle Ages and Renaissance, and to provide an academic training and social centre in Oxford for some fifty overseas students who are not members of the University. The Centre has a library and a stained-glass studio among its facilities. It is housed in St Michael's Hall in SHOE LANE, the former parish hall of the Church of ST MICHAEL AT THE NORTH GATE.

Members of Parliament

For a list of Members of Parliament for Oxford, *see* Appendix 3; for Members of Parliament for the University, *see* BURGESSES *and* Appendix 4.

Merton College

Walter de Merton was of a large family. Although an only son, he had seven sisters, all of whom married, and thirteen first cousins. To provide for this numerous kin was one of the forces that spurred him to establish an educational institution. As his wealth increased, between 1240 and 1277 he acquired fifteen manors or pieces of land and fifteen and a half advowsons. He also made contact with rich and influential persons who assisted his plans by grants of property, support or encouragement.

Merton died, probably in his seventies, on 27 October 1277. Throughout his life he concerned himself deeply with the establishment of his college, reflected on changes to his original intentions and took the advice of 'many wise men'. Collegiate-type institutions existed in the 13th century, especially in the university of Paris. At Oxford, secular students usually lived in ACADEMIC HALLS, often controlled by a Master or group of Masters. These halls could cease to exist or could be refounded, according to the resources and abilities of their Principals. It seems that a logical step was for benefactors to ensure that such halls would be maintained in perpetuity, providing free or subsidised board and lodging. University and Balliol Colleges were of this type: the founders' benefactions were placed in the hands of trustees.

Walter de Merton's first endowment was to be administered by Merton Priory and devoted to the support at Oxford of male members of his family. By 1264 he was planning both an office to administer his legacy at Malden and an institution at Oxford to support twenty Fellows. In the statutes of 1270 is an indication that the founder was considering the amalgamation of administration and accommodation, at Oxford, and by 1274 this had been written into his new statutes.

The college's revolutionary nature was immediately recognised; by 1282 its statutes had been imitated by the Bishop of Ely in his foundation of Peterhouse at Cambridge. The unique features of Merton were, first, the scale and resources of the college: before 1300 more than thirty Fellows were in residence there and many of these were not of the FOUNDER'S KIN; they were supported by estates that brought in considerable sums of money. Second, the physical size of the college, with its hall, its accommodation, its chapel and its library built by the end of the 14th century, was eloquent testimony to the arrival of a new era. Third, and most important, the 1274 statutes gave the college total control of its own assets and administration, with only a right of intervention allowed to the VISITOR, the Archbishop of Canterbury: 'the fully self-governing Oxford college had been born'.

Encouraged to study Medicine and Theology as well as arts, the college fellowship produced in John of Gaddesden the only significant Oxford medical scholar of the Middle Ages, as well as many important theologians, of whom the best known is Thomas Bradwardine (*c.*1323–35). He migrated from Balliol College where he had studied arts, dedicated his *De Causa Dei* to the Fellows of Merton, was consecrated as Archbishop of Canterbury in 1349 but died of the plague in the same year. Many Fellows achieved eminence in the arts. In the 14th century members of the so-called Merton School made a considerable contribution to the study of Mechanics, Geometry and Physics. JOHN WYCLIF was a probationary Fellow of the college in 1356. The careers of former Fellows took them into the service of Church and State. The bishopric of London, for example, was held by Robert Gilbert (Warden 1417–21), John Kempe (Fellow 1395–1407) and Richard Fitzjames (Warden 1483–1507). The Crown employed and rewarded several former members of the college; Henry V was assisted in Normandy by seven Merton alumni: three royal chaplains, one the Dean of the Chapel Royal, another its Repetitor, a sixth the Chancellor of Normandy and the seventh a physician to the King. The numbers of the college Fellows, their quality and their reputation enabled Masters and Doctors to take a high proportion of the University's administrative positions. The college had, like a beacon, 'shone forth to all the inhabitants of this realm'.

A view of Merton College from the Cherwell in the 1820s, with part of the city wall and the bastion on the right and Christ Church on the left.

Archbishops Peckham in 1284 and CHICHELE in 1425, together with other Visitors, attempted to direct the Fellows to an obedience of their statutes. Their injunctions were not always obeyed: Peckham's attempt to prohibit the study of Medicine failed, certainly to the long-term benefit of the college. Chichele's direction that a minimum of forty-four Fellows should be supported was not followed: at the close of the Middle Ages about twenty Fellows could usually be found in residence. The company at this date consisted of the Warden, the Subwarden and Fellows; they were served by chaplains, servants and clerks. The Warden had his own household; the Subwarden and three of the chaplains ate with him. Attached to the college during the mediaeval period were a number of boys of the founder's kin educated at the college's expense: the last of these was admitted in February 1499. In the early years, certain graduates and students were supported in a property in the town. John Wylyot (Subwarden 1346–7) endowed scholarships to support at Merton a number of undergraduates who became known as 'Postmasters'; the Wylyot Bursar administered this benefaction. A few COMMONERS, needy scholars, were chosen annually; other commoners were richer academics who rented college rooms and dined in hall.

The college was supported by income from estates, by rents and feudal payments from various properties and by gifts and legacies from former Fellows and from wellwishers. This income was administered by officials usually elected annually from the fellowship. The Warden's short account detailed the income and expenditure of his household; the Subwarden attended to income and expenditure that mostly related to the chapel and library; the Wylyot Bursar administered the properties left by the founder of the Postmasters' scholarships. The bulk of college income was controlled by three Bursars, each holding office for one-third of the year. The daily task of supplying the Fellows, students, guests and servants with food and drink was entrusted to the Stewards of Hall,

drawn from those Fellows who occupied at that time no senior position: each held office for one week. All these accounts were carefully audited. Merton Fellows were elected as vacancies arose and resources allowed from a wide area. This broad catchment – in contrast, for example, to that allowed to New College – perhaps explains the high quality of the Merton intake. Fellows were required to hold already the BA degree and were expected to complete a probationary year before their full admission to the college. The college attracted applications from such poorer colleges as Balliol, which did not provide proper endowments for advanced work.

Before the Reformation, Warden Fitzjames initiated the college register in 1483, was Chancellor's Commissary on several occasions and later was an influential Bishop of London. Much reconstruction and repair work was carried out at this date. Fitzjames gave books, PLATE, ornaments and money to the college. Warden Rawlins earned hostility for his sale of college property to Corpus Christi, but he was influential at court as King's Almoner and was able to persuade Catherine of Aragon to dine at Merton. With the appointment of John Chamber, who held the post of Warden from 1525 until 1544, the college renewed its close links with the Crown. He had been physician to Henry VII and held the same post at the Court of Henry VIII from 1509 to 1546. His contact with the Court ensured that Merton did not offer opposition to the royal ecclesiastical changes.

The new foundations of Magdalen and Christ Church challenged and eventually exceeded the size and resources of Merton. The neighbouring Corpus Christi claimed the initiative in stimulating the study of Greek and Latin. Allegations, however, that Merton, and especially Warden Fitzjames, were hostile to the new learning seem to have been exaggerated: there may well have been good reasons for the college's reluctance to purchase printed books at this date.

With its support for the study of Theology and its consequent production of many graduates in this field, the college members and former Fellows could hardly escape involvement in the religious changes of the reigns of Edward VI, Mary and Elizabeth (see ROMAN CATHOLICS). Some embraced wholeheartedly the Protestant faith; others held staunchly to the old religion. Among the latter was Richard Smyth, the first Oxford Regius Praelector in Theology, who gave evidence against Cranmer, preached at the burning of Ridley and Latimer, and escaped to the continent after Elizabeth's accession to become Chancellor of the new university at Douai, where he died in 1563. With its loyalty divided, the college came under close scrutiny from the government through its Visitor, the Archbishop of Canterbury.

In 1562, on the resignation of Warden James Gervase, the Visitor declared that there had been an illegal submission of names for a replacement. Archbishop Parker proceeded to appoint John Man, formerly of New College, a staunch Protestant. When he presented himself in the traditional manner before the gates of the college, Man was refused entrance. The Archbishop nevertheless imposed him as Warden and kept in his own hands control of much of the administration of the college, expelling or warning those who opposed his policy. As the Elizabethan Settlement became more firmly established, so the college accepted the new situation and co-operated with it.

The administration of Merton had not been seriously affected by the events associated with the Reformation. Estates and property had been retained to provide an economic basis for later developments: in 1599 the college could spend £1830 on the purchase of another manorial estate, Gamlingay St George in Cambridgeshire, and, in the early years of the next century, resources for the building of a large new quadrangle were available. Nor had these years halted the receipt of further endowments. Bishop Tunstal had decided in 1549–50 to offer to the college the estates entrusted to him by THOMAS LINACRE, humanist and physician, who on his death in 1524 had left lands to his executors for the foundation of medical lectureships at Oxford.

The quality of the personnel of the college during the long reign of Elizabeth contributed to its European reputation. Thomas Bickley (Warden 1569–85) strongly defended Merton against interference by the Visitor, was greatly respected for his work among the sick in Oxford and bequeathed £100 for the endowment of a lectureship in Theology. HENRY SAVILE (Warden 1585–1621) was knighted by James I in 1604, became Provost of Eton in 1596, published editions of Tacitus and Bradwardine, and presided over extensive reconstruction and building work in the college. Savile did not escape censure from the fellowship for his proud and overbearing attitude, but his reputation and position at Court hindered any attempt by the notoriously greedy courtiers of Elizabeth and James to gain control of college property. One estate, that of Malden, was lost, but happily later recovered. Merton Fellows made considerable impact on the scholarly, social and political life of Elizabethan and Jacobean England.

More undergraduates now came into residence, frequently drawn from the gentry. Students no longer looked exclusively to the church for employment, although the continuing conflicts of the late 16th and early 17th centuries ensured a steady demand for degrees in Theology. Courses in Classical Literature and Greek now supplemented the traditional curriculum, and in such Fellows as THOMAS BODLEY and Henry Cuffe Merton produced eminent scholars and teachers of Greek. The Flemish refugee John Drusius, perhaps the most outstanding contemporary scholar of Hebrew, Chaldaic and Syriac, was given rooms and employed at Merton in Elizabeth's reign; he was followed by Bensirius, a refugee from Caen paid to teach Hebrew. Such scholars raised the Fellows' standards and helped moves towards a new translation of the Bible, so eventually giving us the influential Authorised Version. The college continued its interest in the sciences: lectures in Mathematics were given by the new Savilian Professor of Geometry; the Professor of Astronomy, John Bainbridge, imported from Cambridge, settled at Merton, died there in 1643 and was buried with a fine monumental tablet in the chapel.

Savile was followed as Warden by Nathaniel Brent, an ecclesiastical lawyer married to the daughter of the Visitor. He remained in office from 1621 until 1645 and from 1646 to 1651. Brent did not approve of ARCHBISHOP LAUD and accused his VISITATION of the college as threatening to rival in length the siege of Troy. The ordinances Laud imposed on Merton touch many aspects of college life.

When Oxford became the seat of royal government on the outbreak of the CIVIL WAR, the college once more became closely involved in State affairs. Merton supplied plate to support the royal cause and provided accommodation for the Queen. The Warden – Brent – was suspected of support for the rebels and was deposed by the King in 1645, but was probably restored after the surrender of Oxford to the Parliamentarians on 24 June 1646. This short interval, however, gave to Merton the claim to have among its famous Wardens William Harvey, the discoverer of the true circulation of blood. Brent himself headed the Commission sent by Parliament to 'correct' the University, saving some of the less enthusiastic Merton supporters of Parliament, among them the young ANTHONY WOOD, then a Postmaster, from the loss of their college positions. Later interference by parliamentary delegates angered Brent, who resigned the wardenship, dying a year later in 1652. His successor Jonathan Goddard (Warden 1651–60), also served on the new Visitation commission. At the Restoration Goddard was removed; Dr Edward Reynolds, a Presbyterian, followed as Warden until his promotion in 1661 to the bishopric of Norwich, and ejected Fellows were restored.

The installation in 1661 of Warden Thomas Clayton, Regius Professor of Medicine, occasioned another outburst against the authority of the Visitor. Further legal problems had allowed ARCHBISHOP JUXON to nominate Clayton. He was permitted to enter the college only by the wicket-gate and was installed accompanied by just one Fellow. Resistance was maintained but finally Clayton was accepted and retained the position until 1693. This inauspicious start was followed by continuous squabbling between the Warden and the Fellows. Wood accused Clayton of causing much unnecessary expense by requiring the college to cater for the needs of his wife and family, mostly daughters. Despite this unpleasant atmosphere, the college continued to produce notable scholars, especially in Oriental Studies, Theology and Medicine.

Wood died in 1695 and, deprived of his racy attacks on aspects of Merton life and on the cost of supporting daughters produced by Wardens Clayton and Lydall, our knowledge of college life in the first half of the 18th century seems somewhat dull. The college gardens were improved during that time and its accommodation was made more comfortable, but the number of students and Fellows in residence dropped. Warden Holland, in office from 1709 to 1734, attempted with some success to restore the numbers and the academic life of the college. By the middle of the century, the Fellows were reported still to be conducting their variation exercises at a period when most Oxford colleges had ceased to have any interest in corporate scholarly activity. Nevertheless, at a time when a general lethargy hung over the University, when the discoveries of the Enlightenment were better understood in Scotland than in England, and when progressive forces associated with Nonconformist groups were by statute excluded from Oxford and Cambridge (see DISSENTERS), it was difficult for any one college to set itself against such a trend.

The history of Merton at the close of the 18th and throughout the 19th centuries is largely the history of its reaction to those changes that affected the University as a whole: proposals for the reform of the collegiate University together with the broadening of the curriculum (see ROYAL COMMISSIONS), and the debate associated with what came to be known as the OXFORD MOVEMENT. The college generally steered a somewhat conservative course in line with the presence among the fellowship of both liberal and reactionary elements. MARK PATTISON described the Merton common room as belonging to the class he portrayed as 'fashionable, aristocratically inclined men of the world'. Two notable Tractarians, HENRY MANNING and Hope-Scott, were among its 19th-century Fellows and the college accepted then that all but six of its fellowships should be held by clergymen. If Merton was the only college in 1851 without a head in Holy Orders, nevertheless C.S. Roundell (Fellow 1851–74) had failed to obtain there support for an end

to celibacy and the abolition of prize fellowships. It was likely that once events within the University began to move decisively in one direction, the college would not for long be left behind.

Merton was fortunate in that during these eventful years two Wardens only were in charge of its affairs: Robert Bullock Marsham (1826–80) and George Charles Brodrick (1881–1904). Both were aware of the need to come to terms with the call for the reform of the colleges. Marsham supported the demand for new building at Merton, even though the proposals, if fully accepted, would have been an architectural disaster (see below). This would have been the first substantial building at Merton since the early 17th century. The college fund for building, established at £40,000 after the parliamentary Acts of the 1870s and 1880s, was by far the largest of any Oxford college. Following the legislation of 1881, ST ALBAN HALL was fully incorporated into the college. Merton, as one of the wealthier Oxford institutions, played an important role in the transfer of resources from the colleges to the University. The income from four college fellowships was used to endow the chair of the Linacre Professor of Physiology and, in 1885, the Merton Professorship of English Language and Literature was created with a college grant of £500 per year.

Even during the first half of the century, the college continued to produce individuals distinguished by their scholarship and contribution to the affairs of the country, and as the University and college gradually adapted themselves to the needs of Victorian society, so Merton again attracted a distinguished fellowship. Future heads of Balliol, Corpus, Jesus and Keble reached Merton in the 1860s; Mandell Creighton, later Bishop of London and a notable historian, entered in 1862; Lord Randolph Churchill in 1867; and, as an arrival from Balliol, Andrew Lang in 1868. The long fellowship of F.H. Bradley OM (1870–1924) placed the college in the front rank of institutions concerned with the study of Philosophy; the present Bradley Library was established as a result of his generosity (see LIBRARIES). The historian of the

An undergraduate of Merton College, Edgar Everington, entertains his friends in his rooms in 1863.

Stuarts, Samuel Rawson Gardiner, was elected Fellow in 1892, and P.S. Allen, editor of the definitive edition of the letters of Erasmus, in 1908. College life at this date came under the satirical eye of MAX BEERBOHM, a commoner from 1890 to 1894.

Again, it was the pressure of outside events that was to determine much of the college's internal development in the 20th century: two world wars; and the growing demand for higher education at Oxford from students in the United States, the Empire and Commonwealth, from those of lower social classes in Britain, and from women. The college has recorded beneath Fitzjames's Arch those who were killed in two world wars. Others served behind the lines: Bertram Lambert, graduate in Chemistry at Merton in 1903, invented the standard gas-mask. The establishment after CECIL RHODES's death in 1902 of the RHODES SCHOLARSHIPS brought to Oxford students from Germany, the United States and the Empire; some of these were to be received at Merton. The entrance of greater numbers of students from poorer backgrounds had to await a much more significant change in educational provision at a lower level. After the passing and implementing of the 1944 Education Act, a college policy of attempting to choose the best academic candidates regardless of social background brought to Merton many boys from the lower-middle and working classes. The admission of women had to wait until the college had weighed the experiences of other colleges which had braved this experiment.

As the number and variety of those admitted to the college grew, so the contribution of Merton to the life of Britain, and also of other countries, becomes difficult to define. Individuals still made their mark. A.C. Irvine (1922–4), it is said, practised by climbing up and down the walls of the college chapel, and was lost at the summit of Everest in 1924; he is commemorated by a simple memorial in the Grove. The introduction of English Literature into the Oxford curriculum and the endowment of the Merton Professorship in this subject was followed by the growth of an influential group of poets, authors, critics and dramatists within the college. H.W. Garrod, Fellow and honorary Fellow from 1901 to 1960 and editor of the poetry of Keats, was a key figure. T.S. Eliot came from Harvard to Merton in 1914. Edmund Blunden (Fellow 1931–43) and Louis MacNeice (1926–30) were other poets associated with the college. Plays produced by the college drama society provided an opportunity for the revival of little-known works. The tradition of historical scholarship established by Creighton and Gardiner has been continued, especially with an involvement in the history of European countries: F.M. Powicke (Prize Fellow 1908–15) made a considerable revision of the standard history of continental mediaeval universities and Geoffrey Barraclough (Senior Scholar 1932–4 and Fellow 1934–6) introduced many British scholars to the problems of German history. The scientific, mathematical and medical traditions of the college have been maintained with a small but regular output of distinguished work.

As it developed after the Second World War, Merton did not attempt to compete in size with its larger rivals; instead resources were placed to encourage an increase in the provision of research fellowships and scholarships. Foreign scholars are regularly welcomed with specially endowed visiting, temporary fellowships; schoolteachers are allocated studentships so that they can complete research work free from the demands of their schools. Junior fellowships provide an opportunity for successful post-doctoral students to obtain a footing in the academic world, while the generosity of a benefactor and of the college itself has endowed the Harmsworth and Domus Studentships for those seeking support for postgraduate work. In 1964 the college celebrated its septencentenary. Since then other changes have been made in its constitution, notably with the introduction of women in 1979.

The site chosen for Merton College was to limit its development, dictating much of the varied layout of the buildings seen today. To the north, the line of MERTON STREET set a boundary that the college was only occasionally to cross. To the south, the line of the CITY WALL could not be breached; buildings could not be attached to the walls so long as the defences and access to them were required for the protection of the city. Beyond this, the marshy ground was unsuitable for any building work. To the east, other properties and residential halls in the possession of LITTLEMORE PRIORY prevented further expansion, although the college did succeed in leasing these and adjacent land in the 15th century, finally purchasing St Alban Hall in 1548. To the west, the possibility of further development ended abruptly with the conveyance of land to Bishop Foxe in 1515 for the site of Corpus Christi College, an action which probably caused the removal of Warden Rawlins. Attempts by Corpus Christi to acquire more of the narrow strip of open land between the two colleges were thwarted in 1701. Merton, therefore, developed along the south side of Merton Street on a site without considerable depth; space therefore had to be used carefully. Today different types of buildings interconnect, giving the college a very special atmosphere.

From Merton Street, opposite the college entrance, something of its early structure may still be observed. The founder purchased three houses on the south side of the street to accommodate his Fellows. Even after much reconstruction, traces of the individual buildings are still to be seen. The college gateway was erected after licence to crenellate was granted by Henry V in April 1418; it replaced another tenement originally purchased by the founder. Above the outer archway are statues – copies of the original work – of the founder, holding his bishop's crozier and the great seal of his Chancellor's office, and of a King, perhaps Henry III. A stone panel, now reset lower than originally placed, shows the founder kneeling before the book of seven seals from the Revelation of St John, against a landscape which seems to portray John the Baptist in the wilderness: the college chapel is dedicated to St John and the Virgin Mary. The door is of the 15th century. From the front quadrangle, the compact nature of the college buildings can best be observed. To the north is the line of the remoulded houses along Merton Street. To the south is the college hall. First erected in the late 13th century, the present building owes much to reconstructions of the 1790s and the 1870s. The great oak doorway with its scrolled ironwork was probably part of the founder's original structure. To the east, the buildings prescribe the boundary of the original college; beyond this lay St Alban Hall and other properties. Before 1497 this limit was marked first by a southern extension of a house on Merton Street, and, adjoining this to the south, the Warden's lodgings, begun by Warden Sever in the early 15th century. The southern extension was demolished in 1904 and the Warden's lodgings were rebuilt in 1497. This reconstruction by Warden Richard Fitzjames also gave the college the archway that today leads into the Great Quadrangle. This Warden's interest in astrology was well known, and he decorated his arch with the signs of the zodiac, still visible today. Two of the rooms in Fitzjames's building were used to accommodate Charles I's Queen, Henrietta Maria, during the Civil War and so became known as the Queen's Rooms.

The western side of the front quadrangle is dominated by the great east window of the college chapel. At the time of the college's foundation a smaller church, further south than the present chapel, served the parishioners. The acquisition by Walter de Merton of the land, to which belonged the advowson of the church, produced the unusual situation at Oxford where the college became, first, patron, and then rector of a church ministering to both the new college and the older parish. Soon after the foundation, work was begun on an ambitious scheme to erect a new chapel better suited to the character and prestige of the recently established institution. The present choir of the chapel was completed between 1290 and 1294; the glass of the side-windows is contemporary with this work, as is that in the tracery of the east window, but the lower lights are filled with glass mainly of the 15th century (see STAINED GLASS). The transepts were added in the late 14th and 15th centuries; the ceremony of re-dedication in 1425 was celebrated annually by the college (on 6 November). The tower had been completed by 1450. The slow progress was, no doubt, the result of the expense of the building operations. Any attempt to extend the chapel by the addition of a nave and aisles was frustrated by the sale to the founder of Corpus Christi College of the land required for such work.

The chapel received a stream of benefactions from parishioners and former Fellows of the college. The people of the parish, who met in the north transept, entering through the door that leads into Merton Street, provided a small but useful income from offerings and legacies. From the Fellows, many of whom achieved high position in the mediaeval church and state, the college received substantial benefactions. Two new altars in the chapel were built in 1488; the chapel rood-loft was finished and painted by April 1491, and on this a new organ was built at a cost of £28. New stalls were added before 1491; the chapel walls were decorated and many fittings, cloths, books and images were purchased or given. Most expensive were the gowns and copes provided for the Fellows and chaplains: twenty-four copes cost over £218 in 1505.

The Reformation seriously affected the interior of the chapel. During the reign of Edward VI many fittings, the altars, images and the stoup were removed, and paintings and stained glass were covered with whitewash; a communion table was installed. The old service books were replaced by new editions in English. With the accession of the Roman Catholic Queen Mary, the college was able to replace some of the damaged or lost items. Rehabilitation seems to have been slow, perhaps because the Fellows anticipated another move towards Protestantism with the accession of Elizabeth; the chapel's high altar was restored only after the receipt of a special gift of £5 from Robert Morwent, President of Corpus Christi. Following the Elizabethan reintroduction of the Protestant rites, the college chapel was again denuded of its Catholic and papal symbols. After seven years of her reign, the restored altars had been replaced by a communion table, the chapel paintings had been 'deformed' and chapel fittings had been prepared for sale. The organ was removed in 1567 and most of the valuable copes were sold in 1562 to merchants trading with the continental market. The Elizabethan Settlement brought only a temporary respite. Laudians and Puritans struggled for control of the chapel's internal appearance in the 17th century, and the collapse of the south transept roof in 1655 necessitated further rebuilding. SIR CHRISTOPHER WREN added a classical screen, but this was removed in the 1840s when Butterfield 'renovated' the chapel after the fashion of the Gothic Revival, erecting a stall in its place. Hungerford Pollen repainted the inside of the new roof again in the Gothic style. A post-Second World War benefaction has reintroduced two organs.

Today's visitor to the chapel will see the external appearance of the choir and transepts of the mediaeval church much as they were in 1500. Within, some monumental brasses from the later Middle Ages survive; and the fine brass lectern, cast in Tournai and given by the executors of John Martock, Fellow and Subwarden, who died in 1503, is in regular use. Inscriptions, memorial plaques and floor slabs commemorate Fellows of the college, benefactors and their wives and children. Of interest are those recording the achievements of Thomas Bodley, whose bust is surrounded by figures representing four of the liberal arts: Music, Arithmetic, Grammar and Rhetoric, and piles of books, and of Sir Henry Savile, whose monument reflects his interest in Chrysostom, Euclid, Ptolemy and Tacitus, and his association with Merton and Eton. The picture behind the high altar is of the school of Tintoretto, and there are silver candlesticks of the reign of Queen Anne. The war memorial in the chapel floor before the altar is simple and impressive. Wren's screen lay for many years in pieces in the lower library and in a college garret, and has only recently been restored and replaced. All eight bells date from 1680–1.

The arrangement of these buildings around the front quadrangle is also unusual, since the line of the hall is not parallel to the line of the buildings along Merton Street. Perhaps it was considered preferable to construct the hall in line with the original parish church, but front quad lacks the symmetry associated with other Oxford quadrangles. The entrance to the hall, by the porch of 1579, is placed opposite the college gateway – an unusual feature at Oxford though common at Cambridge; few Oxford college halls have porches. A sun-dial of 1629 is on a buttress of the east wall of the chapel. Another, larger sun-dial is provided in the Fellows' Quadrangle.

The narrow passage from the front quadrangle in the south-west leads beneath a short bridge built to give access to the chapel from the Warden's lodgings via the college hall. The space beyond the bridge was until recently enclosed by a storehouse on the south side, so forming a quadrangle known as Patey's Quadrangle, named after a college butler. To the west is the entrance to the small or bachelors' quadrangle, today known as Mob Quad; the origin of the name is

The north front of Merton College in 1772, showing the gateway and chapel with Corpus Christi College beyond.

obscure. In the north-east corner is the 13th-century entrance to the chapel sacristy, built in 1309–11 but much restored in the 19th century. Above this entrance is the college treasury room of the late 13th century – a truly functional building designed to protect the important documents and valuables it formerly contained. There are four small windows and the steep roof is of stone, probably as a precaution against fire.

Mob Quad again shows the eccentric character of buildings at Merton, in that its present form is a result of accident rather than design. The northern and eastern ranges were first built in the early 14th century; the northern occupies approximately the site of the old parish church and perhaps incorporates some of its structure. On the south and the west, ranges were added in 1371–8 with accommodation for Fellows in the lower storey; above this were built two rooms and the college library. So appeared the form of the Oxford quadrangle. The original rooms probably each had four small windows, of which some still survive. The Fellows, four to a room, could sleep in the centre and so each have available a window at which to study. Today, the accommodation beneath the Old Library has been converted into a library for the use of students of English, History, Modern Languages, Classics and Philosophy. The original library owes much to the generosity of William Rede, a former Fellow (*c.*1344–57) and Bishop of Chichester. Until the late 16th century the mediaeval fittings, with the more valuable and rare books chained to lectern desks between the windows, proved adequate. The library acquired its contents from the benefactions of former Fellows. Less valuable textbooks were shared annually among the resident Fellows and stored in their rooms. When, in the late 16th century, the college adopted a deliberate policy of acquiring by purchase large numbers of printed books, the existing shelving proved inadequate. During the wardenship of Sir Henry Savile the interior of the library took its present form. Stalls replaced the older fittings; extra space was provided but books were still chained. Savile's work at Merton and contemporary activity at New College influenced other colleges and also Thomas Bodley. Apart from the insertion of dormer windows in the early 17th century to provide extra light and the placing of late 16th-century German glass in the east window in 1840, the library's appearance has altered little since the death of Elizabeth I, except that a separate room at the far east end has now been incorporated into the library. One stall retains its rod, lock and chains. The entrance to the library is through a door, which may be that purchased from the Carmelite Friary in the 14th century, and continues via a late 16th- or early 17th-century staircase. The greater part of the roof and the wainscotting of the interior walls were completed in the early years of the 16th century; between the presses, the corridors are tiled with mediaeval tiles. Items relating to the history of the college – chests, a desk, globes, a table and the 17th-century benefactors' book are kept in the Old Library. Manuscripts and more valuable printed books are today stored elsewhere. Adjoining the Old Library is a set of rooms, once the librarians', now devoted to the memory of Sir Max Beerbohm and containing books, prints, furniture and other relevant items bequeathed to the college.

Leaving the front quadrangle through Fitzjames's Arch there is a fine view of the Great Quadrangle, known today as Fellows' Quadrangle. This reflects the ambition of Warden Savile, who, himself a Yorkshireman, employed John Akroyd of Halifax and Holt to oversee the work in 1608–10. The kitchen next to the hall had probably been rebuilt earlier; the parapet with its battlements was added later in the century. In 1666 the walls of the eastern wing were in danger of collapse. The iron cramps then inserted to stabilise the structure may still be seen in the wall's second storey. In the centre of the internal wall of the southern wing stands a decorative example of the use of the four orders of columns – Doric, Ionic, Corinthian and Composite; Thomas Bodley may have been stimulated to repeat this feature on a grander scale in his contemporary restoration of the University library, using the same builders as Savile employed.

Work within the college for the next two centuries was largely restricted to repairs and reconstruction. In the 1860s, after the stimulus of the 1854 Repair Act, an ambitious scheme to dismantle the whole of Mob Quad to provide space for a large new quadrangle was discussed. Fortunately the complete plan was never accepted and one block only, Grove Building, from the design of William Butterfield, who had already been employed to work on the chapel, was erected; this building was given its present appearance in 1930. To the north of Merton Street were built new Warden's lodgings in 1908, but changing styles of living have made such a large and grandiose structure unsuitable for today's needs and the college has recently erected new accommodation for its warden at the south-east corner of the street. Twentieth-century needs have also taken the college beyond St Alban Hall, its garden and the eastern line of the city wall. Before and after the Second World War further rooms for undergraduates and postgraduates were built in Rose Lane. Nevertheless, the development of the college along a relatively narrow strip of land between the walls and Merton Street is essentially the result of conditions imposed by the acquisitions of the founder and of gifts from early benefactors of the college.

The corporate designation of the college is the Warden and Scholars of the House or College of Scholars of Merton in the University of Oxford.

The present Warden is Dr J.M. Roberts.

(Henderson, B.W., *Merton College* (College Histories), 1899; Highfield, J.R.L., *The Early Rolls of Merton College, Oxford*, Oxford, 1964 (includes a history of the life of the founder and the establishment of his college); Powicke, F.M., *The Medieval Books of Merton College*, Oxford, 1931 (includes a survey of the organisation and development of the medieval library); Allen, P.S., and Garrod, H.W., *Merton Muniments*, Oxford, 1928 (reproduces and transcribes some of the more important documents from the college archives); Brodrick, G.C., *Memorials of Merton College*, Oxford, 1885 (a history of the college, with biographical details of the Wardens and Fellows, to the middle of the eighteenth century; the information contains many inaccuracies and must be used with caution).)

Merton Street Running from ORIEL SQUARE to HIGH STREET, this mainly cobbled street was known before 1200 as Vicus Sancti Johannis. St John Baptist Church was incorporated into the buildings of Merton

A photograph c.1857 of a carriage in Merton Street waiting outside St Alban Hall which was demolished in 1905–7.

College, from which the street gets its name. From 1661–6, according to ANTHONY WOOD, who lived here (*see below*), it was known as St John Baptist's Street, the name sometimes being corrupted to Joneses Street. Another name for the street in the mid-18th century was Coach and Horses Lane (from the inn situated there), but until about 1776 that applied only to the eastern part leading into the HIGH STREET. The western end was King Street from the early 18th until the late 19th century. Also at one time Hare Hall Street ran from High Street through to the portion of the CITY WALL in Merton College gardens, but it was demolished when the EXAMINATION SCHOOLS were built. The name Coach and Horses survived until about 1838 when Merton Street, which had appeared as early as the Survey of 1772, came into permanent use. In the 1960s the Highways Committee of the City Council threatened to remove the famous cobbles from the street but fortunately the decision was reversed; it is the only street in Oxford (as distinct from parts of RADCLIFFE SQUARE) to retain its old cobbles.

As well as Anthony Wood, who lived at Portionist's or POSTMASTER'S HALL – which still exists, although it has been altered on the exterior and much changed inside – JOHN AUBREY, the English antiquary, lived in Merton Street.

Mesopotamia The name 'Mesopotamia', from the Greek, meaning 'between the rivers', was originally applied to the district between the Rivers Euphrates and Tigris, now part of Iraq. The Oxford version is a narrow strip of land lying between the River Cherwell (*see* THAMES) on one side and a branch of the river on the other. The path along the bank runs between trees for its entire length, making a shady walk in the summer by a stretch of the river which is much used for PUNTING. The whole walk is about three-quarters of a mile long, starting from the entrance to the PARKS by Linacre College, crossing the Cherwell near THE ROLLERS, leaving the Parks at King's Mill Lodge Gate, and thence by King's Mill Lane to MARSTON ROAD.

There is now a path along the other side of the river, running along the edge of Music Meadow, Great Meadow and Long Meadow, past a duck pond to Holywell Ford. A wooden bench by this path bears the inscription 'ORE STABIT FORTIS ARARE PLACET ORE STAT'. Readers whose Latin is not as good as they thought it was may turn to page 268 for a translation.

Middle Common Rooms The common rooms available to graduates studying for further degrees, or doing research, who cannot belong to either a Junior or a Senior Common Room. Their members are not necessarily Oxford graduates and many of them come from overseas.

Middle Way *Summertown.* On a 14th-century map the land in this area between Banbury Way and Woodstock Way is marked 'The Furlong called Twene the Weys'. On the auctioneer's map drawn for the sale of the land in 1821 the road itself, which now runs south–north between SOUTH PARADE and SQUITCHEY LANE, was known as Centre Road. The northern end was known as Oak Lane or Old Oak (1830) from an oak tree planted by Crews Dudley, an Oxford solicitor, to delineate a boundary of land he had bought. Sometimes called Dudley's Oak, it became a large tree and its destruction in 1919 was much regretted. For many years Middle Way was called George Street, and until 1929 some of the houses in it were known as Londsborough Terrace. To avoid confusion with the GEORGE STREET in central Oxford, in 1955 there was a proposal to rename the street Twining, after Alderman Twining, a member of one of Oxford's oldest families, who had served on Oxford City Council for fifty years and was also a local developer and benefactor (*see* TWINING'S). However, a petition signed by sixty-two residents of George Street was presented to the Council protesting at the plan to give the road the name of a local grocer's shop and demanding the reversion to the old Middle Way or Oak Lane. The road, of some ninety houses, now includes many private homes, BISHOP KIRK MIDDLE SCHOOL (on the site of The Avenue, 'a handsome white house' built in 1823), a new block of flats called Martin Court, the offices and meeting hall of the Oxfordshire Federation of Women's Institutes, the Grove House Club, the North Oxford Conservative Club, and the entrance to Alexandra (Tennis) Courts.

Milford, Sir Humphrey Sumner *(1877–1952).* The grandson of C.R. Sumner, Bishop of Winchester, and son of the Rector of East Knoyle, Wiltshire, Milford won scholarships to Winchester and to New College and obtained a First in LITERAE HUMANIORES in 1900. He then joined the OXFORD UNIVERSITY PRESS as assistant to Charles Cannan (1858–1919), who was secretary to the delegates, and in 1913 was appointed to succeed Henry Frowde (1841–1927) as Publisher to the University. He remained with the Press until his retirement in 1945, and during this time OUP expanded dramatically, becoming one of the biggest publishing businesses in England. Milford was responsible for the publication of the *Oxford Dictionary of Quotations* and saw the OXFORD ENGLISH

Humphrey Milford, in whose time as Publisher to the University in 1913–45 the Oxford University Press was greatly expanded.

DICTIONARY to completion. He received the honorary degree of DLitt in 1928 and was knighted in 1936.

Milham Ford School *Harberton Mead.* Begun as a nursery school in the IFFLEY ROAD in 1889 by two sisters, Emma and Jane Moody, it soon moved to the banks of the Cherwell below MAGDALEN BRIDGE (*see* THAMES). As a fee-paying girls' school it was sold in 1904 to the Church Education Corporation, and in 1906 was housed in purpose-built premises opened by Augustine Birrell, then Minister of Education, in Cowley Place (now part of St Hilda's College). Shortly before, in 1902, the Corporation had opened in Cherwell Hall (now St Hilda's College Old Building) a training college for women graduates who used the school for teaching practice, Miss Catherine Dodd combining the roles of Principal of the college and headmistress of the school. Cherwell Hall developed close links with the University Delegacy for the Training of Secondary Teachers (now the University Department of EDUCATIONAL STUDIES). Bought by the city of Oxford in 1923, the school moved in 1938 to buildings designed for it by the City Architect, Douglas Murray, on a spacious, sloping, 16-acre site bounded by JACK STRAW'S LANE, MARSTON ROAD and Harberton Mead; it also then ceased to take boarding pupils. In 1944 it became a maintained grammar school for girls and in 1974 a single-sex girls' comprehensive. In 1966 it had some 600 pupils and by 1985 about 750.

Mills In the Middle Ages there were numerous mills in and around Oxford. Five of these had been in existence since as early as the 11th century. These were the CASTLE Mill, two mills on TRILL MILL STREAM and two at GRANDPONT. In the next centuries other mills were built at HINKSEY, OSNEY, COWLEY, HOLY-WELL, Sandford, BOTLEY, GODSTOW, WOLVERCOTE and elsewhere; and there were constant disputes between the rival owners and operators about the obstruction and diversion of the flow of water, and frequent acts of violence in which weirs and sluices were broken and wheels or buildings damaged. The Castle Mill was a particular cause of resentment, especially after it had come into the hands of the city, which did its best to ensure that all bakers and others over whom it had control should make exclusive use of it.

From the 15th century onwards the number of mills in the area gradually decreased, and by 1660 the only ones still in operation were those at the Castle, at Hinksey, Iffley, Osney, Sandford, Botley and two at Holywell. However, the Castle Mill remained in operation until it was demolished for a road-widening scheme in 1930; one of the remaining mills at Holywell was still working in 1876 but had been converted into a house by 1900; Iffley Mill was burned down in 1908; Botley Mill, which stood next door to the George public house, was demolished in 1923; and Sandford Mill was demolished for housing development in 1985. The larger of the two mills at Osney was gutted by fire in 1946; its shell still overlooks Osney Lock. Part of the surviving building is now used as offices by Osney Marine Engineering and there is also a clubhouse for the nearby marina. WOLVERCOTE PAPER MILL is still in operation.

The 'Oxford' crown piece of 1644, minted in New Inn Hall, showing King Charles I with a detail of the city in the background.

Mint The earliest coins attributed to Oxford, after its establishment as a fortified burgh, are some scarce silver pennies late in the reign of King Alfred (871–99). They carry the town's name, in the spelling 'OHSNAFORDA'. Most of the specimens of this type known today are, however, Danelaw imitations of the prototype, of a lower weight-standard. Thereafter, Oxford is known to have minted coins steadily from the reign of Edward the Elder (899–924) for some 400 years before the mint's closure at the end of the reign of Henry III. Out of some fifty or more royal mints in boroughs throughout England, Oxford was among the seven or eight most active. At least eight moneyers worked there during Athelstan's reign (924–39). The place-name is abbreviated on late Anglo-Saxon coins in a variety of ways, such as Oxnaford, Oxna, Oxenefor. The HEBERDEN COIN ROOM has a specialist collection of coins of the Oxford mint of all reigns, including, for example, a silver penny minted in Oxford during the reign of King Eadgar (944–75). The obverse reads 'EADGAR REX ANG(L)OR V' and the reverse 'MO (netarius) OXNA(ford) VRBIS', Oxford being one of the few places in 10th-century England described as an *urbs*, or city. There were normally about three moneyers working at once in Oxford after the Norman Conquest; one, by the name of Swetman, is mentioned in the Domesday Book, where Oxford is spelt OXENEFORD. Coins continued to be minted at Oxford until the latter part of the reign of Henry III (1216–72), after which the number of the King's mints was drastically reduced. No more coins were minted in Oxford until the CIVIL WAR.

When Charles I occupied Oxford in 1642 he set up a royal mint in NEW INN HALL under Thomas Bushell. Large numbers of silver coins were minted from the silver PLATE contributed by the colleges, as well as a few gold ones. Two of the finest coins, examples of which are in the Heberden Coin Room, are the gold triple unite (£3) of 1643, the largest denomination ever coined in 17th-century England, and the beautiful 'Oxford' crown piece of 1644. The latter was designed by Thomas Rawlins and shows a distant view of Oxford, with Charles I on horseback in the foreground. The Oxford mint produced gold and silver coins up to 1646, the silver in denominations of a pound, half-pound, crown, half-crown, shilling, sixpence, groat, threepence, half-groat, and penny. There were a great many different dies, some of the coins bearing the legend 'RELIG. PROT. LEG. ANG. LIBER. PAR': this refers to the declaration made by Charles I to the privy council at Wellington in 1642 that he would support the Protestant religion, the laws of England, and the liberty of Parliament.

Minty The furniture firm of Minty had its beginnings in 1885 when Norman Edward Minty purchased the shop at No. 45 HIGH STREET, where he himself had served his apprenticeship as a cabinet-maker. In the workshop at the rear he produced his wickerwork frame chair in about 1900 and named it the 'Varsity'. Soon he designed a sectional bookcase which was added to the 'Varsity' range, and these became the forerunners of the present Minty furniture. The adjacent shop at 44 High Street was purchased and showroom space was enlarged by the removal of the workshop to a factory in Cherwell Street, ST CLEMENT'S. In 1965 a new purpose-built factory was opened by the RING ROAD at COWLEY.

Mitre Hotel *High Street.* Situated on the corner of TURL STREET, the Mitre is one of only three ancient Oxford inns which have survived into the 20th century. It dates from around 1300, when Philip de Wormenhale, Bailiff and later MAYOR (1310) of Oxford, having acquired two houses in HIGH STREET and several tenements in Turl Street, turned them into an inn with front and back entrances. After his

The 'Defiance' coach leaving for Henley and London outside the Mitre Inn in the 1830s.

death in 1314 his widow was re-married to William of Bicester, under whose will of 1341 the property was assigned in part endowment of his chantry in ALL SAINTS CHURCH, HIGH STREET. Thus, in the 15th century it passed into the possession of Lincoln College, whose property it remains to the present day. The name 'Mitre' was probably adopted from the connection with the college which used the arms of the see of Lincoln beneath a mitre (see HERALDRY). It was usual for an inn or alehouse to have a sign or distinguishing mark, and that of the Mitre was included in a register containing licences for some 140 inn signs which was kept by the city from 1587 until 1766.

In the 17th century the Mitre was held by a succession of ROMAN CATHOLIC landlords. Mass was sometimes celebrated on its premises, and in 1640 it was reported to be a rendezvous for Papists. As a result, the innkeeper, Charles Green, was dismissed from his common councillor's place as a recusant. Nevertheless, in 1663, during the tenancy of another Catholic sympathiser, a priest, visiting Oxford openly, stayed at the Mitre and laid his hands on the sick. On 21 December 1683 the hostess of the Mitre, Mrs Lazenby, 'fell into fits and died' after having been 'most strangely affrighted by 3 rude persons' (all from All Souls College), who abused her as a 'Popish bitch' and told her she deserved to have her throat cut. Five years later there was a riotous demonstration of anti-Catholic feeling when a mob, incited by the provocative words of the recusant landlord, T. Thorpe, visited every known Roman Catholic dwelling in Oxford and broke the windows, starting with the Mitre (see RIOTS).

During the 17th century the great coachyard inns expanded and by 1671 there were coaches running between London and the Mitre three days a week (see TRANSPORT). In the 19th century, when Oxford was at its zenith as a coaching centre, the Mitre was one of the leading coaching inns. *The City and University Guide* of 1824 states that, 'Close to the front of the Market is "The Mitre" Inn, whence go well-regulated coaches to all parts of the Kingdom. Chaises are also kept at this Inn'. Well into the 20th century there were frequent revivals of coaching: on 21 September 1928 a coach belonging to Captain Bertram W. Mills and Mr Claud Goddard ran from the Berkeley Hotel,

Piccadilly, to the Mitre, where the event was celebrated with a special banquet.

For centuries the Mitre has been a well-known resort for scholars, townspeople and visitors of all kinds. Some have revelled there too well: in 1690, according to ANTHONY WOOD, 'John Foster, M.A. Fellow of All Souls College ... died at the Mitre Inn late at night after immoderate drinking.' But most patrons have fared more happily: when the German traveller C.P. Moritz arrived in Oxford in 1782 'he sat up all night in the Mitre drinking beer with a convivial group of parsons.'

The hotel has undergone many structural changes during its history. The present building dates mainly from around 1630 and contains contemporary panelling and stairs. The rest of the façade is partly 18th century and partly more recent. It is stucco-fronted with canted bay-windows. Of the original building only the 13th-century rib-vaulted stone cellar survives.

Since 1967 the landlords have been the Berni Inns and the Mitre has functioned solely as a restaurant since about that time, the upper floors being used to accommodate members of Lincoln College. Early in 1986 the property underwent considerable renovation.

Moderations Abbreviated as 'Mods', this is now the first of the two public examinations for a Bachelor's degree in some subjects – for instance Greats (see LITERAE HUMANIORES). It was introduced in its modern form in 1850. The master who presided over the scholastic disputations, which in earlier times were a necessary part of the exercises for the Bachelor's degree, was known as a Moderator.

Monastic Colleges Oxford colleges are among the few religious corporations which survived the Reformation. But one small group perished because, unlike the others, they housed communities of monks. These five monastic colleges occupied a distinctive position in the mediaeval University. Founded by the various religious orders which habitually sent students to Oxford – and essentially a product of attempts between the late 13th and early 15th centuries to revive monastic learning – they existed in the interests of DISCIPLINE, convenience and prestige. In them scholars from houses throughout the country could follow a corporate life and observe their rule together, under the watchful eye of a 'Prior of Students'. The colleges, which were built and maintained by the monasteries that provided their students, generally lacked substantial endowments of their own and hence they died a natural death with the Dissolution of the parent houses; the buildings of three were adapted to house new secular colleges, but the other two were demolished, leaving only vestigial remains. A sixth, Corpus Christi, was originally begun for the monks of St Swithun's, Winchester, but in the event it was established as an ordinary secular college.

Gloucester College (re-founded after the Dissolution as GLOUCESTER HALL, now Worcester College) served the Benedictine houses of the southern province. In 1277 the General Chapter ordered the provision of a 'house of studies', to be supported by an annual levy on all the relevant monasteries. A small priory was founded, as a cell of Gloucester Abbey, in 1283. After attempts to annexe this as the common property of the province, it was recognised in 1298 as a federation, the monks from each monastery forming a semi-independent group. The hall, kitchen and chapel were maintained in common, but each house sending monks built its own set of chambers (*camerae*). Thus the site was gradually built up with separate lodgings maintained by different owners, producing a very unconventional layout. The main block (destroyed in the 18th century), with a small central court flanked by hall and chapel, was insignificant beside the long rows of private *camerae*, about half of which still survive. By the Dissolution most of the buildings seem to have been of the 15th or early 16th century. The chapel was finished shortly before 1424, and the *camerae* were built progressively during the next century. On the first floor of the south range is a fine room with a ribbed timber waggon-ceiling, perhaps used as a chapel before the later chapel was finished. The parent monasteries of most of the *camerae* are identified by their carved shields of arms above the doors.

Durham College (re-founded after the Dissolution as Trinity College) existed for Benedictine monks of the northern province. Richard de Hoton, Prior of Durham, bought the site in 1291 and began the buildings. At first the monks (of whom there were only six to ten) were supported by Durham Cathedral Priory, with occasional gifts from its cells. In 1381 the college was endowed from the estate of Thomas Hatfield, Bishop of Durham, and new statutes were made. The buildings, arranged around a conventional quadrangle, were taken over substantially complete by Trinity College, though much rebuilt since. The south range comprised a large gateway built in 1397 and a chapel dedicated in 1409, and in the west range some fragments of the hall, possibly of the 14th century, remain. Only the east range, built in 1417–21 with the library on its first floor, is still largely mediaeval.

Canterbury College (now part of Christ Church), the third Benedictine college, was exclusively for the benefit of monks from Canterbury Cathedral Priory. There was a hall for this purpose on another site from 1331, but in 1362 Archbishop Islip established the college for twelve students. At first this was a hybrid community, part monks and part secular priests; the first Warden was a monk, but he was displaced by a secular in 1365. The seculars were expelled by papal order in 1370, and over the next few decades the college, now purely monastic, grew in size and wealth. An exceptional number of surviving inventories show that it was lavishly equipped with books and vestments. At the Dissolution its buildings, including a hall and chapel, were acquired by Christ Church; they appear on the early maps and engravings, but nothing now remains. All the buildings except the hall and two chambers were rebuilt by Prior Chillenden (1378–1411), but the hall, of *c*.1364–78, had some of the earliest Perpendicular windows in Oxford.

St Bernard's College (re-founded after the Dissolution as St John's) was established by ARCHBISHOP CHICHELE in 1437 for monk-students of the Cistercian Order. Regulations were promulgated in 1449, and it was decreed in 1482 that every monastery of twelve monks was to send one to St Bernard's, and every monastery of twenty-six was to send two. St Bernard's remains largely intact as the front quadrangle of St John's – the finest architectural survival from the

monastic colleges. The fully developed late mediaeval college plan was adopted at the outset, with the hall and chapel forming the north range and the gatehouse in the centre of the west range. The building history of this scheme was long and tortuous. The south range was apparently under construction in 1438, but despite regular fund-raising there seems to have been little progress for several decades. In 1489, the abbot of Fountains complained that 'if the annual contributions duly collected over so long a period had been well and faithfully applied to the aforesaid building, they would have sufficed to build not a college but a great castle'. From 1502 real progress was made, and by 1517 the hall and chapel were finished and the last range of the quadrangle had reached roof level. But there must have been further problems, for in 1546 the east range was still only 'roof high, purposing a library and chambers'. Much of the original stonework detail and several internal partitions and doorcases survive intact. The lower part of the three-stage gate-tower retains its original stone vault. In the north range the chapel has been heavily restored, but the former kitchen (now the hall) has a contemporary timber roof, and below the buttery is a four-bay vaulted cellar, also contemporary. Even the statue of St Bernard remains above the front gate, though equipped with a false beard and hair to serve as St John the Baptist.

The Augustinian canons, with their tradition of contact with the outside world, sent students to Oxford long before they had a college. As early as 1356 it was ordered that scholars should, so far as possible, live together and wear a uniform habit, and a Prior of Students was ordered in 1371 to hold chapters in ST FRIDESWIDE'S PRIORY. These provisions reflect a justified concern for rule and discipline: in 1374 it was complained that students were adopting fashionable footwear against the rule of the Order, and would walk around public places lifting their clothes above their knees to display their shapely legs, glorying in their own flesh rather than in the cross of Christ. The need for a common residence was reinforced by University pressure, and in 1419–21 there were abortive proposals to found a college. In 1435 Thomas Holden gave a large house (now FREWIN HALL) standing in open grounds, which had long been the home of wealthy burgesses, as the site for a new college, *St Mary's College*. The basement of a magnificent 12th-century town house was incorporated into the Augustinian buildings, and still survives. A chapel (probably a temporary one) was dedicated in 1443, but progress on the permanent buildings was as slow at St Mary's as at St Bernard's. In 1446 Henry VI urged the canons to make provision 'for the building of the said college, that it go forth in haste effectually ... that your students for more increase of science tarry not so shamefully as it is said it doth, notwithstanding ye have great help of secular benefactors'. Statutes were issued in 1448; but, despite numerous contributions, the building-works languished for nearly seventy years. In 1518 CARDINAL WOLSEY took them in hand, and the college seems to have been complete by its dissolution in 1540. During the next forty years, when it became briefly a charity school and finally a private house again, most of the buildings disappeared. The site of the chapel, probably Wolsey's work, was excavated in 1977, and its fine hammerbeam roof survives, re-used, in Brasenose College. Fragments of the gatehouse and a timber-framed lodging range are

The entrance to Morrell's Lion Brewery in St Thomas' Street c.1895.

also still extant. In the late 16th century a timber-framed house with decorated plaster ceilings was built over the Norman undercroft. As a private house it went through successive enlargements and was the home of several notables (including Edward VII, as Prince of Wales, and the historian SIR CHARLES OMAN). It has now returned to a kind of collegiate use as an annexe of Brasenose College.

(Blair, John, 'Monastic Colleges in Oxford', *Archaeological Journal*, 135, 1978, 263–5; Pantin, W.A., 'Gloucester College', *Oxoniensia*, XI–XII, 1946–7; Colvin, H.M., 'The Building of St. Bernard's College', *Oxoniensia*, XXIV, 1959; Blair, John, 'Frewin Hall, Oxford: A Norman Mansion and a Monastic College', *Oxoniensia*, xliii, 1978.)

Morrell Avenue Built on the south side of SOUTH PARK in 1929–31, with council houses (of a higher standard than normal) on each side of the avenue going up the hill to HEADINGTON. The avenue was named after the Morrell family who lived at Headington Hill Hall (*see* MORRELL'S BREWERY).

Morrell's Brewery Mark Morrell and his son James became partners of the old-established brewing family of Tawney's in the late 18th century. The brewery in St Thomas' Street was established in 1782 on a site which had been used for brewing for some 200 years; it stretched along the bank of Wareham Stream, a backwater of the THAMES. When James Morrell died in 1855 the business passed to his son, also named James. Since 1943 it has been run as a private limited company under the control of the Morrell family. The entrance to the Lion Brewery in

St Thomas' Street is through a late 19th-century cast-iron gateway, flanked on either side by a pair of rampant lions. The brewery owns 140 public houses in the Oxford area. Headington Hill Hall, the largest private house in Oxford, was acquired by the first James Morrell in 1831 and remained in the family until 1953.

Another member of the family, also James Morrell (1739–1807), founded the solicitors' firm of Morrell, Peel & Gamlen in ST GILES'. Philip Morrell, MP for Oxfordshire, and his wife Lady Ottoline, entertained many of the leading literary figures of the day at Garsington Manor, just outside Oxford.

(Bond, James, and Rhodes, John, *The Oxfordshire Brewer*, Oxford, 1985.)

Morris, William (*1834–1896*). The son of a City bill-broker, Morris was educated both at Marlborough and privately before matriculating at Exeter College in 1852. At Oxford he became an intimate friend of EDWARD BURNE-JONES, with whom he formed that undergraduate circle known as The Brotherhood. He had originally intended to take Holy Orders, but on going down decided instead to train as an architect and so became an articled pupil in the BEAUMONT STREET office of G.E. STREET, who had recently been appointed architect to the diocese by SAMUEL WILBERFORCE. Persuaded that he should be a painter rather than an architect, Morris left Street's office to share a studio in London with Burne-Jones. Poet as well as artist, he was one of the founders of the *Oxford and Cambridge Magazine* (*see* MAGAZINES), to which he was a contributor of prose and poetry. With Burne-Jones, Rossetti, Arthur Hughes, John

William Morris (third from right) *and Sir Edward Burne-Jones with members of their families in 1874.*

Hungerford Pollen, Valentine Prinsep and Spencer Stanhope, he also helped to decorate the UNION. After 1861, when he established his firm of manufacturers and decorators, he rarely returned to Oxford. He was elected an Honorary Fellow of Exeter in 1883, but declined to have his name put forward for the Professorship of Poetry.

Morris, William Richard *see* NUFFIELD, VISCOUNT.

Motor Cars In 1910 the thirty-three-year-old William Richard Morris (*see* VISCOUNT NUFFIELD), who had started his working life at the age of fifteen in a bicycle shop in Oxford, had then built his own cycles and motor cycles, and progressed to sell and service cars, planned production of a car to bear his name. This car would be reliable, easy, and inexpensive to maintain – qualities then lacking in many cars of low to medium power and price, as he knew from his own experience. In October 1912, WRM Motors Ltd of LONGWALL STREET announced the 'Morris–Oxford light car'. As with many cars of the time, it was assembled from proprietary parts: a four cylinder White and Poppe engine, axles and steering from Wrigley's of Birmingham, frames by Redpath, Brown, with Sankey wheels, Dunlop tyres and Powell and Hanmer acetylene lights. The two-seater body was painted grey; leather upholstery was standard. At £175, the Morris–Oxford cost £40 more than the two-seater Ford, £25 less than the Turner Ten. The *Motor* declared that the new car was 'in every sense a high grade production', and it was so enthusiastically received that Morris needed larger premises. He rented (and then bought) a former military training college at Temple Cowley, which earlier had been

Hurst's Grammar School, where his father had been educated. Bodies made in Coventry came by rail to Oxford station, then by horse and cart to COWLEY. Later, the works would have its own goods station: Morris–Cowley. Initially, Morris's father kept the books. His brother-in-law worked in the loft, painting wheels, later becoming Transport Manager, a position he held until his death in 1941.

The first production model left Cowley on 28 March 1913. Morris had hoped to display his car at the 1912 Motor Show, but none was ready. The engine manufacturer had hired draughtsmen from other firms to help, one of whom, to save paper, produced half-size drawings for the cylinder block – and forgot to mention this. Morris was determined to make some sales at the show and so took along a blueprint of his car to show prospective buyers. One London dealer, Gordon Stewart, was so impressed that he agreed to buy 400 cars; Morris was in business. By the end of 1914, he had sold 1300 cars.

During the First World War, Morris Motors, as the company became, produced hand-grenades, parts for mines and shell cases, but still assembled 1344 cars between January 1915 and December 1918. In the post-war slump, however, car sales declined drastically and Morris's bank overdraft increased from £48,120 in September 1920 to £84,315 by the following January. He had calculated on making £15 clear profit on each car, but he now had so many unsold vehicles that he had no space to store more. Accordingly, and against much cautious advice, he cut the price of the £525 Morris–Cowley (a cheaper version of the Oxford) by £100 and more expensive models by lesser sums. The result was dramatic. With sales soaring from seventy-four in January 1921 to 400 in March, profit on each car increased to £50 due to cheaper costs consequent upon the purchase of components in larger quantities. Later that year, Morris cut his prices again by as much as £85. By the time production of the famous bull-nose 13·9 h.p. Morris–Oxford and the cheaper 11·9 h.p. Cowley ceased in 1926, Morris Motors had sold 154,244 cars, and was the most important volume producer in the British motor industry, which then numbered 198 separate makes of car.

As his car sales increased, Morris began to buy up his component makers to guarantee sufficient supplies, at his price, to his specification. In 1922 he took over Hotchkiss in Coventry, who built engines. Previously he had asked them to produce 500–600 engines a week, but the most they could make was less than 300. A Hotchkiss director had suggested that if Morris was not satisfied, he should buy the works. This he did, and improved efficiency so much that within a year he had his 600 engines a week; and within two years earnings from the reorganised factory had paid for the capital cost of the company.

In 1923 Morris bought Wrigley; the purchase of SU Carburettors followed three years later. By then Morris Motors employed 4000 people at Cowley, where the factory now occupied 80 acres, producing 1000 cars a week. In 1926 Morris also joined with the Edward G. Budd Manufacturing Company of Philadelphia and the merchant bankers J. Henry Schroeder & Co. to form the Pressed Steel Company, next door to his Cowley factory. This company produced all-steel car bodies, using huge power-presses to stamp out individual body panels, which were then welded into a complete – and very strong – car body. The Morris interest was withdrawn in 1930; five years later the American company also withdrew from the enterprise and shares were offered to the public. As an independent company, Pressed Steel now built bodies for other car manufacturers, although Morris Motors remained one of their major customers.

Morris bought Wolseley Motors in 1927. This had started by making sheep-shearing machines. Herbert Austin, Morris's great rival as car maker, had once worked for the company. Ten years later, Morris took over Riley. MG (after Morris Garages) had started producing sports versions of Morris cars in the Longwall premises, but soon became a manufacturer in its own right and then moved to Abingdon. Success in racing made MG famous. By the mid-1930s Morris was producing cars that varied in size from 8 h.p. to 25 h.p. and commercial vehicles capable of carrying from one up to 7 tons in weight. This range was rather too wide for maximum profitability and Morris called in Leonard Lord from Austin to rationalise production. 'Specialisation' was now the theme. Each factory, in what became the Nuffield Organisation – Morris was created Viscount Nuffield in 1938 – concentrated on its own particular products. Earlier in the 1930s the Austin Motor Co. had proposed a merger with Morris Motors, but Morris, a sturdy individualist, declined, sensing that the offer held greater advantages for Austin than for him. A similar amalgamation was again proposed and declined in 1948, but finally took place at the third time of asking in 1952 – the year after Morris Motors produced their two-millionth car. Lord Nuffield was first chairman of the new company, the British Motor Corporation. After six months he retired to become honorary president and Lord became chairman.

In 1965 BMC acquired the ordinary shares of the Pressed Steel Company and announced a major restructuring of its car body manufacturing activities.

William Morris, Lord Nuffield, congratulates staff at Morris Motors Ltd on the production of the millionth Morris car in 1939.

Cowley became the headquarters of Pressed Steel Fisher Ltd, which comprised the six car-body manufacturing plants of the corporation. Subsequently, BMC became British Motor Holdings and merged with Leyland Motors to form the British Leyland Motor Corporation. In yet another reorganisation, the Cowley factory became part of the Austin Morris group and the headquarters of body and assembly, the largest division within the group. In 1975 British Leyland Motor Corporation ran into financial difficulties and, through the National Enterprise Board, the Government acquired about 95 per cent of the company's equity. Three years later the name became Austin Morris BL Ltd. In 1980 the Cowley factory was renamed the Light Medium Cars division, BL Cars Ltd. Two years later, the Austin Rover Group Ltd was launched as Britain's largest car manufacturer. In 1986 it was announced that the company had lost over £200 million in the first six months of that year, but it was announced on the Stock Exchange towards the end of 1987 that the company, now called the Rover Group, was expected to make a profit that year. (*See also* ROVER *and* NUFFIELD, VISCOUNT.)

Murray, (George) Gilbert (Aimé) (*1866–1957*). Born in Australia to parents of Irish descent, Murray was sent to school in England and in 1885 entered St John's College from Merchant Taylors'. In his first year at Oxford he won both the Hertford and Ireland Scholarships (*see* PRIZES AND SCHOLARSHIPS), and after gaining a First in LITERAE HUMANIORES was elected a Fellow of New College in 1888. Described by Sir Richard Jebb, Regius Professor of Greek at Cambridge, as 'the most accomplished Greek scholar of his day', Murray soon left Oxford for the chair of Greek at Glasgow; but he returned to his fellowship at New College in 1905 and in 1908 was appointed Regius Professor of Greek at Oxford. His translations of Ancient Greek dramatists had by then brought

them to a wide audience on the contemporary stage. His work as an internationalist kept him in Geneva for such long periods between the wars that in 1923 the VICE-CHANCELLOR felt obliged to ask him whether he should continue to hold the chair, which he nevertheless retained until 1936. Murray died at his home on BOAR'S HILL at the age of ninety-one.

Murray, Sir James Augustus Henry (*1837–1915*). The son of a Scottish clothier, Murray became an assistant master at Hawick grammar school at the age of seventeen and later taught at Mill Hill School, where he began work on the *New English Dictionary*, afterwards known as the OXFORD ENGLISH DICTIONARY, which was to occupy so much of the rest of his life. In 1885 he came to live in Oxford, where in his garden at Sunnyside, BANBURY ROAD, he erected a corrugated-iron building to house the slips on which the quotations for the Dictionary were written; these were eventually found to weigh three tons. By 1897, fifteen years after the publication of the first volume, it had become recognised, as a speaker put it at the 'Dictionary Dinner' held at The Queen's College that year, that it would have been a 'national calamity' if any other editor for the Dictionary had been chosen. During the course of his labours Murray received honorary degrees from nine universities, including Oxford in 1914. He was Romanes Lecturer at the University in 1900 (*see* LECTURES). A man of commanding height, formal manner, stiff bearing and with a full white beard, the father of twelve children, Murray was a familiar and formidable figure in the Oxford of his day. He died after a long illness during which he insisted upon continuing his work. He was buried in WOLVERCOTE Cemetery.

Museum of Modern Art Founded in 1966 by a group of Oxford art enthusiasts, under the chairmanship of architect Trevor Green. Their original

Sir James Murray, who came to live in Oxford in 1885 and thereafter devoted most of his life to the project, working with his team on the New English Dictionary.

intention was to open a museum housing a permanent collection of post-1945 art but, realising that this would not be financially feasible, they decided to use their first premises in KING EDWARD STREET as a space for a series of changing exhibitions. When HALL'S BREWERY vacated its 19th-century storehouse at No. 30 PEMBROKE STREET, the city of Oxford purchased the property and, in 1970, leased the front section to the museum. When offered further exhibition space within the building, an appeal was launched and the new extension, including the John Piper Gallery, was opened in 1981, thus doubling the size of the museum. Further improvements were completed in 1986, including a reference library and the restoration of the Pembroke Street façade to a design by Professor A. MacMillan of Gillespie, Kidd and Coia. The museum has an international reputation for initiating and mounting major exhibitions of the work of contemporary artists. It is also a local centre for workshops, lectures and seminars on all aspects of the visual arts.

Museum of Oxford *St Aldate's.* Opened in 1975 in the former premises of the public library adjoining the TOWN HALL, the museum illustrates the history of the city and University from early times to the present day. Beginning with displays devoted to the geology and prehistory of the Oxford area (*see* PREHISTORIC OXFORD), to Roman potteries and the Saxon town, it continues with exhibits relating to the Norman CASTLE, the growth of the town and the development of the University, the Reformation, Elizabethan and Stuart Oxford, the CIVIL WAR, the city and University in the 18th century, and the eventual transformation of a county town into a modern industrial city.

Among the varied exhibits are part of the Fitzjames gateway of Merton College; the mace of the MAYOR'S sergeant (1606); part of the 17th-century screenwork from the old Exeter College chapel; the two original clock jacks from the church tower of ST MARTIN'S, known as the CARFAX 'quarter boys'. Jan de Wyck's painting of the siege of Oxford during the Civil War; Keble College barge; a circular staircase made at Dean's Ironworks, Temple Street, in about 1897; examples of Oxford STONE, Oxford PRINTING, street signs and trade tokens. Several of the exhibits came from the private museum of William Fletcher, an antiquary who lived at No. 46 BROAD STREET. The museum also shows reconstructions of an Elizabethan inn parlour, part of a gentleman-commoner's room at Christ Church of the late 1770s, a Victorian kitchen in JERICHO and a drawing room in NORTH OXFORD, a classroom of about 1915, and part of CAPE'S Cash Drapery, ST EBBE'S STREET.

Museum of the History of Science *Broad Street.* In 1924 the upper floor of the OLD ASHMOLEAN BUILDING was assigned to the Lewis Evans collection of scientific instruments. This collection had been presented to the University by Lewis Evans and established with the help of various livery companies of the City of London, notably the Goldsmiths' and the Fishmongers'. To this collection were later added others, among them those presented in 1957 by J.A. Billmeir and in 1966 by C.F.C. Beeson, as well as numerous purchases by the museum. The museum, which was established by statute in 1935, now occupies the whole of the Old Ashmolean Building,

the principal exhibits being displayed in the basement, ground floor and upper galleries, and in the Beeson Room, which takes its name from the Beeson collection of clocks and watches displayed here together with timepieces from the Barnett and Iliffe collections.

Other exhibits include an unrivalled collection of early astronomical and mathematical instruments, among them armillary spheres, orreries, globes, astrolabes, equatoria, quadrants, sun-dials, instruments of navigation and telescopes; an almost complete series of early microscopes, and other optical instruments and photographic apparatus; air-pumps, frictional electrical machines, early X-ray apparatus, and other instruments of physics, many deposited by the colleges of the University; early chemical apparatus, including an important collection of early 19th-century chemical glassware from the Daubeny Laboratory, Oxford; surgical and dental instruments, anatomical preparations and *materia medica*, a large number of drug-jars and other items relating to the history of pharmacy; several exhibits of special interest for the history of science in Oxford – for example, equipment used in the production of penicillin at Oxford from 1939 to 1943 and H.G.J. Moseley's X-ray spectrometers.

The museum also possesses a unique reference library of early and modern works concerning the history of scientific instruments and related subjects, miscellaneous manuscripts, correspondence and other papers of historical scientific interest, a collection of portraits of scientists and scientific prints, and an extensive series of photographic and other records of relevant material in museums and collections throughout the world.

Museum Road Named after the UNIVERSITY MUSEUM, the road runs westwards from PARKS ROAD, past the junction with BLACKHALL ROAD and continues, as a path and then a passage, to ST GILES', past the LAMB AND FLAG. In the 1870s and 1880s it was known as Museum Terrace, with Museum Villas on the north side; by 1897 it had all become Museum Road. Houses on the north side at the east end were demolished around 1970 for a new Keble College building.

Music *The study of music in the University.* Music as a theoretical science, being one of the liberal arts and grouped with Arithmetic, Geometry and Astronomy into the Quadrivium, formed at least a nominal part of the mediaeval and Renaissance curriculum of the University, with Boethius's *De Musica* as the standard work of authority. The degree of BMus is known to have been held by one Robert Wydow as early as 1478, and the first recorded DMus is that of Robert Fayrfax in 1511. As codified in the LAUDIAN CODE of 1636, music degrees were awarded on submission and performance of a vocal work together with evidence of so many years' study or practice in the art – seven years for the BMus and a further five for the DMus. These degrees were usually taken externally, mostly by practising organist–composers from London and elsewhere, and no formal training for them was given in the University. Notable early recipients of the BMus include John Bull (1586), John Dowland (1588), Thomas Morley (1588) and Thomas Weelkes (1602).

In 1622 William Heather, a Gentleman of the Chapel Royal, took his BMus and DMus degrees

The Oxford University Press band c.1884.

simultaneously (an unusual event), and in 1627 endowed a music lectureship together with the post of Choragus, whose duty was to stimulate the practice of music in the University. The lectureship, an annual appointment, proved to be of little importance, but the office of Choragus – first held by Richard Nicholson – became an influential one and its holder was soon known as the Professor of Music (though not officially until 1856). By the 18th century the two posts seem to have been held together, and this continued until the separate post of Choragus was re-established in 1848; it still exists, although now without responsibilities. Heather's endowment stipulated that a weekly practice should be held by the Choragus in the Music School (now part of the Old Library Quadrangle of the BODLEIAN LIBRARY), and he gave music books and instruments for the purpose. The weekly meetings, though interrupted by the CIVIL WAR, were an important feature of 17th-century Oxford musical life, particularly under the professorships of John Wilson (1656–61) and Edward Lowe (1662–82), and the music library grew appreciably throughout the century; it now forms part of the Bodleian's music collections.

The 18th century, dominated by the professorships of William Hayes (1742–77) and his son Philip (1777–97), saw no new developments on the academic side. William Crotch, Professor from 1797 to 1847, gave a course of lectures on the History of Music in 1800–4, but did not repeat them. He soon moved to London, and started the tradition of having a largely non-residential Professor – a situation which persisted into the early part of the 20th century.

The beginnings of academic reform came under the professorship of Sir Frederick Gore Ouseley (1855–89). He instituted a new syllabus for the BMus and DMus in 1862, which included written examinations in harmony, counterpoint, history and general musical knowledge, in addition to the traditional submission of a composition, performance of which ceased to be an obligation (for the BMus in 1878 and

for the DMus in 1891). Sir John Stainer, Professor from 1889 to 1900 and unusual in being a resident one, pioneered exploration into some of Oxford libraries' musical treasures with his *Early Bodleian Music*, and with W. Henry Hadow (1859–1937), Classics Fellow of Worcester College and editor of the first edition of *The Oxford History of Music* (1901–5), instituted some courses of lectures in Music History. Music degrees, however, were still most commonly taken externally; not until after the First World War was regular tuition offered or residence made compulsory. It then became the regular practice for aspiring musicians, particularly college organ-scholars (a late 19th-century innovation) to take the BMus in conjunction with the BA in another Pass or Honours School.

The Faculty of Music, with an establishment consisting of the Heather Professor and lecturers, finally came into existence in 1944. Its premises were for many years in HOLYWELL STREET next to the HOLYWELL MUSIC ROOM, but in 1981 it moved to the former Linacre College building in ST ALDATE'S. The BA Honours School in music started in 1950, the BMus becoming a postgraduate degree in composition, with research work leading to the degrees of MLitt and DPhil. The DMus has now become almost exclusively an honorary degree, recent recipients of which have included Dame Janet Baker (1975), Sir Geraint Evans (1985), Olivier Messiaen (1978), Andrés Segovia (1972) and Sir Michael Tippett (1967). Twentieth-century professors have included Sir Hubert Parry (1900–8), Sir Hugh Allen (1918–46), Sir Jack Westrup (1946–71), Joseph Kerman (1971–4) and Denis Arnold (1975–86), while among composers on the faculty have been Egon Wellesz, Edmund Rubbra, Kenneth Leighton and Robert Sherlaw Johnson. Other 20th-century composers who have studied or lived in Oxford include Sir Lennox Berkeley, Geoffrey Bush, Bryan Kelly, Gordon Crosse, Bernard Naylor, Nigel Osborne, Sir William Walton, and Christopher Headington.

Music in college chapels and Christ Church Cathedral. New College, Magdalen and Christ Church were all founded with large-scale choral establishments and still retain their choirs of boys and men, which rank among the finest in the country. In addition to choral services on most days of full term, their work includes regular recitals, broadcasts and recordings. The boys are educated at associated schools, while the men, who at one time were all professional lay-clerks, are now undergraduate choral scholars at Magdalen and a mixture of choral scholars and lay-clerks at New College and Christ Church. Several other colleges, such as Queen's and St John's, also had choral provision made on the foundation, although on a more modest scale. Nowadays such colleges mostly have mixed student choirs, although Exeter and Worcester still have a boys' treble line. Only Christ Church, as the CATHEDRAL choir, maintains choral services outside the University terms. The three choral foundations, together with Queen's, have college Fellows as organists, and undergraduate organ-scholars as assistants. In other colleges the organ-scholars themselves preside over the chapel music.

Secular music-making. City waits are recorded from mediaeval times and survived into the 19th century. They seem to have numbered about six and many were also innkeepers. A similar group of 'University Musicians' existed for official functions. Evidence of regular music-making goes back to the 17th century when, besides the weekly meetings in the Music School, there were gatherings in taverns and at the lodgings of people like William Ellis, organist of St John's, and Narcissus Marsh, Fellow of Exeter. Professional musicians often took part, especially during the Commonwealth when choral services were forbidden. Out of one such group which met at the King's Head tavern in the early 18th century developed what became known simply as the 'Musical Society at Oxford'. It was principally for their performances that the Holywell Music Room was opened in 1748. A regular professional band was assembled and subscription series of vocal and instrumental concerts were instituted, often featuring celebrated London musicians. They continued until 1838, when lack of support brought about their demise.

Music was also an important feature of the festivities surrounding royal visits to the city, such as that of James I in 1605. It featured prominently too in the late 17th-century ACT celebrations in the SHELDONIAN THEATRE (of which the present-day ENCAENIA is the only survival), and John Blow among composers who wrote Act music. For the 1733 revival of the Act, Handel came to give a series of concerts, including the première of his oratorio *Athalia* as well as performances of *Deborah*, *Esther* and *Acis and Galatea*, while apparently declining to take an honorary DMus. In 1791, however, Haydn visited the city to receive his DMus, and directed works in the Sheldonian, including his 'OXFORD' SYMPHONY No. 92.

Music-making in Oxford today. The present network of music societies and organisations started to develop in the 19th century. An Oxford University Amateur Musical Society flourished around the middle of the century, and in 1872 came the foundation of the Oxford University Musical Club,

followed in 1884 by the Oxford University Musical Union. The two amalgamated in 1916 as the Oxford University Musical Club and Union, which was renamed the Oxford University Musical Society in 1983. Their weekly concerts, at one time partly professional, are now almost always given by members. Other 19th-century University societies included the Glee and Madrigal Society and even (in 1888) a Banjo Club! The OXFORD UNIVERSITY OPERA CLUB was founded in 1926. The orchestra formed for its post-war productions evolved into the Oxford University Orchestra in 1954. Of university-based choirs the Kodaly Choir and the SCHOLA CANTORUM OF OXFORD were founded by László Heltay in 1957 and 1960, respectively.

Many other societies catering for everyone from folk and jazz to avant-garde enthusiasts have sprung into existence, although often they expire within a short time. Since the early 1970s the Allegri String Quartet has been 'in residence' for a period each term, giving a series of recitals and open rehearsals. The earliest recorded existence of a college musical society is that of a St John's Musical Club in 1817. Christ Church and Queen's had societies in the first half of the 19th century, the latter becoming the Eglesfield Musical Society in 1883. The oldest regular college concerts still in existence are the Sunday evening concerts of the Balliol College Musical Society, founded in 1885 by John Farmer and now past their 1500th concert. The majority are given by professionals and many eminent artists have appeared. Since their inception no admission charge has been made. Nearly every college now has its own musical society, organising concerts and recitals, and generally fostering musical activity among its members.

A parallel growth has taken place in city and joint city–University musical circles. The earliest amateur choral society was the Oxford Choral Society (founded 1819), which in 1890 merged with the Oxford Philharmonic Society (founded 1866). The resulting Oxford Choral and Philharmonic Society in turn merged in 1910 with the OXFORD BACH CHOIR (founded 1896). Other long-established choirs are the OXFORD HARMONIC SOCIETY (founded 1921) and the OXFORD WELSH MALE VOICE CHOIR (founded 1928). Operettas and musicals are catered for by the Oxford Operatic Society. Among a number of amateur orchestras the oldest is the OXFORD SYMPHONY ORCHESTRA (founded 1902). Series of professional concerts are promoted by the Oxford Chamber Music Society (founded as the Oxford Ladies' Musical Society in 1898 and renamed in 1970), the OXFORD SUBSCRIPTION CONCERTS (from 1920), and more recently by the local professional orchestra the OXFORD PRO MUSICA (from 1965) and the Music at Oxford organisation (from 1982).

Artists of international stature have long been visitors to the city, ranging from Liszt, Jenny Lind and Paderewski in the 19th century to Brendel, von Karajan, Menuhin, Rostropovich, Rubinstein and Segovia in recent years. Festivals combining local and other resources have been a feature since the 18th century, and the more notable ones in the 20th century have included commemorations of Bach (1914), the Heather Professorship (1926), Haydn (1932), Bach and Handel (1935), Parry (1948) and Handel (from 1985, annually in July). In addition, the English Bach Festival was held in Oxford from 1963 until the late

1970s, offering a sumptuous range of concerts of both baroque and contemporary music. The Oxford Music Festival is an annual, partly competitive, event which was started in 1974.

Oxford is also an important centre for brass bands. The oldest is the City of Oxford Silver Band, founded as the Headington Temperance Band in 1887, and adopting its present title in 1952. The Austin Rover Band is the current name of the famous band founded as the Morris Motors Band in 1933, while Hall's Oxford Concert Brass is a comparative newcomer, starting as the Oxford Concert Brass in 1972 and renamed on being sponsored by the local brewery in 1979. All three are well known outside the city for their tours, broadcasts and competition successes.

Apart from the Holywell Music Room, which seats no more than 250, Oxford has no proper concert hall, so the Sheldonian Theatre and TOWN HALL have to accommodate most large-scale events, although neither is very satisfactory for the purpose. The University Church of ST MARY THE VIRGIN, the cathedral and college halls and chapels are also widely used for concerts. The APOLLO THEATRE hosts the regular visits of professional opera and ballet companies in addition to serving as the principal venue for rock concerts and other popular entertainments. The present-day musical life of the city is characterised by a vast over-supply of amateur performances, particularly from college-based societies, which are too often over-ambitious and under-rehearsed. Although they provide undergraduates with invaluable experience in conducting, performing and general concert organisation, their number does result in severe competition for audiences. In turn this threatens the financial viability of top-class professional concerts in the city.

The Music Trade. The oldest retail music shop is the HIGH STREET firm of Russell Acott, a 1951 amalgamation of two 19th-century businesses, James Russell & Co. (founded 1811) and Sydney Acott, both of whom also published a little music. For many years the firm of TAPHOUSE & SON in MAGDALEN STREET (founded in 1857) was prominent in the city's musical life, acting as a ticket agency and offering concert management services in addition to their retail activities. They ceased business in 1984 shortly after a move to the WESTGATE CENTRE. BLACKWELL'S has a separate Music Shop in Holywell Street, as well as a large music mail-order department based in HYTHE BRIDGE STREET. In the music department of the OXFORD UNIVERSITY PRESS the city has one of the country's largest publishers of music and music books.

Music and Instrument Collections. Outstanding collections of manuscript and printed music are to be found in the Bodleian Library (around 450,000 items), while Christ Church has the rich music collection assembled by HENRY ALDRICH and Richard Goodson at the end of the 17th century. The Faculty of Music has its own library for music students, and houses a fine collection of musicians' portraits dating back to the 17th century, most of which were formerly in the old Music School. The public CENTRAL LIBRARY in Westgate also has a well-stocked collection of music and recordings.

Oxford has three important collections of musical instruments: the Hill collection of string instruments in the ASHMOLEAN MUSEUM (including Stradivarius's 'le Messie' violin), the BATE COLLECTION of historical musical instruments in the Faculty of Music, and the mainly ethnological collections in the PITT RIVERS MUSEUM.

Mesopotamia The inscription referred to on page 257 can be read as:

'O/RE ST/A/BIT/ FOR/TIS A/RARE/ PLACE/T O/RE ST/AT'

—N—

Nations The groups, regional or racial in origin, into which the students of the mediaeval University were divided. The English were considered Northern English if they came from north of the River Nene, Southern English if from the other side of it. In the frequent disturbances that erupted in the University, the Welsh and Irish usually, but not always, allied themselves with the Southern, the Scots being even more unpredictable, although more often than not supporting the Southern. (*See* RIOTS.)

Nature Reserves, The Berkshire, Buckingham-shire and Oxfordshire Naturalists' Trust (BBONT) has several nature reserves in and around Oxford. The Henry Stephen/C.S. Lewis Reserve of about $7\frac{1}{2}$ acres (3 ha.) off Lewis Close at Risinghurst was bought in 1969. It was here that C.S. LEWIS and J.R.R. TOLKIEN conceived the worlds of Narnia and Middle Earth. There is a large pond rich in aquatic flora and fauna, including dragonflies and damselflies. Moorhens and little grebes nest here regularly. The reserve extends up the hill into woodland behind the pond. BBONT manages a large reserve of 82 acres (33 ha.) at Iffley Meadows, off Donnington Bridge Road. This ancient wet meadow, liable to flooding, belongs to Oxford City Council. Fritillaries and many other plants are found here, as well as in the quarter acre at Iffley Island, also managed by the Trust. By agreement with the City Council, the Trust manages a Site of Special Scientific Interest extending to about 1 acre (0.4 ha.) known as Bullingdon Fen (Lye Valley). This is a peat fen near the CHURCHILL HOSPITAL at HEADINGTON, where many rare plants have been recorded. A reserve which is very good for woodland birds and butterflies, as well as plants, is The Spinney (28 acres – 11.2 ha.) at Shotover, close to the SHOTOVER COUNTRY PARK. This reserve is open to BBONT permit-holders only.

Three nature reserves close to the city are the reserve of 3.85 acres (1.5 ha.) at Matthew Arnold Field, BOAR'S HILL, which is managed by BBONT for the OXFORD PRESERVATION TRUST; Chilswell Valley or Happy Valley, which is just off the RING ROAD at SOUTH HINKSEY and was given to the City Council in 1938; and Sydlings Copse (42 acres – 16.8 ha.) to the east of Oxford. The latter is a varied reserve with many birds and mammals and some 400 species of plant. About $24\frac{1}{2}$ acres were bought by BBONT from Brasenose College in 1977 and $17\frac{1}{2}$ acres are managed under an agreement with Christ Church. The reserve is a Site of Special Scientific Interest and is open to members of BBONT, whose headquarters are at No. 3 CHURCH COWLEY ROAD.

The Trust has many other reserves in Oxfordshire, as well as in the other two counties, the largest being the Warburg Reserve (257 acres – 102.8 ha.) near Henley-on-Thames. The City Council has also designated Rock Edge, a small disused quarry in Headington, as a nature reserve.

(*See also* WYTHAM; PARKS, UNIVERSITY; PORT MEADOW; *and* RALEIGH PARK.)

New Bodleian Library *Broad Street and Parks Road.* The report of a University Commission published in 1931 led to the building of a new library in Bladon stone with Clipsham dressings (*see* STONE) to allow the BODLEIAN to expand. The New Bodleian, designed by Sir Giles Gilbert Scott, was completed in 1940 and was opened by George VI after an embarrassing ceremony during which the silver key broke in the lock. The Rockefeller Foundation contributed three-fifths of the £1 million that the library cost. It contains administrative rooms, reading rooms and an eleven-floor book-stack, which is connected to the old library by an underground conveyor belt and can accommodate 5 million volumes. On a south-facing extension on the roof is the library of the INDIAN INSTITUTE, which was built in 1966–8 to the designs of Robert Potter. (For a description of the shields on the façade *see* HERALDRY.)

New College *Holywell Street* and *New College Lane.* St Mary College of Winchester in Oxford, better known since 1400 as New College to distinguish it from the other college of St Mary (now Oriel College), was founded on 26 November 1379 by WILLIAM OF WYKEHAM, Bishop of Winchester and Lord Chancellor of England. The decline in the University population following the Black Death had severely reduced the number of educated clergy in the parishes, and Wykeham's foundation was intended to provide for the Church's need. Six colleges had already been founded in Oxford: University, Balliol, Merton, Exeter, Oriel and The Queen's College, but most of these existed principally for graduates studying Theology; undergraduates lived mainly in ACADEMIC HALLS rented and run by Regent Masters, the teaching members of the University. New College was exceptional in its size and composition. The statutes provided for a Warden and seventy scholars, also called Fellows, who would range from under-graduates straight from school to Regent Masters. There were also to be ten chaplains, three clerks and sixteen choristers, who would say Masses for the soul of the founder.

The college had three especially significant features. First, provision was made for the teaching of undergraduates within the college. While there may have been precedents for this, New College provided for many more Fellows than any other college and Wykeham's endowments ensured that the practice continued. Second, in order to supply his Oxford college with students properly grounded in Latin grammar, in 1382 Wykeham founded a second college, at Winchester, which would send its boys to New College when they were ready. Only scholars of Winchester could become Fellows of New College.

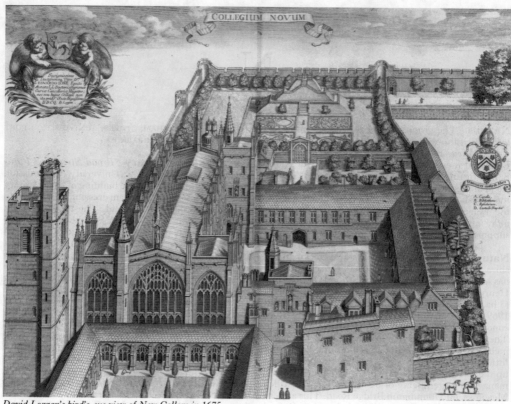

COLLEGIUM NOVUM

David Loggan's bird's-eye view of New College in 1675.

Third, and most important, the college was designed as a quadrangle, which contained in an integrated whole the principal buildings essential to the communal life envisaged by the founder: chapel, hall, library, muniment tower, bursary, Warden's lodgings and Fellows' chambers. This became the pattern for many subsequent foundations. Wykeham himself had supervised the building of new royal lodgings at Windsor Castle and may have been responsible for the overall design of his two foundations (Winchester College was devised upon a similar, but modified, plan to New College); but more probably his masons, William Wynford and Henry Yevele, and his carpenter, Hugh Herland, were the designers, with Wynford playing the leading role.

Wykeham had begun buying land in Oxford as early as 1369, but he made his most substantial purchases ten years later, acquiring a complex of small plots in the north-east corner of the CITY WALL, an area reduced by plague to being, in the words of a local jury, 'full of filth, dirt, and stinking carcasses . . . a place as 'twere desolate and not included or by any occupied'. Here the foundation stone of New College was laid on 5 March 1380; and on 14 April 1386 the Warden and Fellows entered their quarters. The chapel, hall and muniment tower were probably not finished until later. The cloisters, built on land acquired in 1389–90, were begun in 1390 and completed in 1400; and the bell-tower was erected between 1396 and 1403.

The entrance to the college lay through the great gate at the end of NEW COLLEGE LANE. Over this rose the tower of the Warden's lodgings. To the left of the entrance, forming the tall north range of the quadrangle, lay the chapel and hall, placed back to back. West of the chapel were the cloisters and the bell-tower. Facing the entrance were the stairs leading to the hall, the muniment tower, and the first-floor library, which occupied most of the eastern side. Finally, on the south, lay the Fellows' chambers. There was no attempt to create symmetry in the design: rather the opposite, since chapel, hall, muniment tower and Warden's lodgings dominated the single-storeyed ranges on the east and south. While the form of each building was determined by its function, account was taken of aesthetic effect.

The T-shaped form of the chapel, with the antechapel at right-angles to the nave, was wholly original. (The chapel at Merton College is similar in plan, but the transepts there were not built until 1424.) The design allowed the entire community to worship in the nave, while private Masses could be said at smaller altars in the antechapel, where disputations and elections were also held. The stone fabric of the chapel heralded the Perpendicular style, especially in the huge west window. But the decoration, particularly on the exterior, is restrained, at any rate by comparison with the later DIVINITY SCHOOL. Little of the interior now survives in its original form. The roof was probably a tiebeam construction, similar to that in the hall and quite different from the present, taller hammerbeam roof put in by SIR GEORGE GILBERT SCOTT. Sixty-two of the original misericords remain in the Fellow's stalls, some of them presenting rich images of 14th-century Oxford life: a doctor lecturing, Wykeham receiving visitors, scholars fighting with daggers. Virtually all the rest of the woodwork in the chapel belongs to the 19th century, as do the figures on the reredos. Much of the original glass survives in the windows of the antechapel, although some of it has been rearranged. But the great Tree of Jesse in the west window was removed to York in the 18th century; and the present windows in the nave were installed in the same century.

The cloisters and bell-tower, to the west of the chapel, were not part of the original design, but were added ten years or so later when Wykeham had acquired more land. Consequently, their plan does not fit comfortably with the older buildings, since an untidy space is left outside the west wall of the chapel. But the cloisters have suffered little from later 'improvements' and the design of Herland's arched roof can still be seen.

The hall was raised above ground level, with rooms beneath it. Like the chapel it has been greatly altered in succeeding centuries, but to better effect. The linenfold panelling was bequeathed by Archbishop Warham in the 1530s. The roof was renewed by Scott in 1865, but his tiebeam design is probably close to the original roof by Hugh Herland. The glass in the high two-light windows belongs to the 19th century.

The design of the Fellows' chambers, on the south side of the Great Quadrangle, was crucial to Wykeham's purpose. Within the two-storeyed range (a further storey was built in the late 17th century) the living-quarters were arranged on the staircase pattern. Each staircase had two sets on the ground floor, each housing four Fellows, and two on the first floor, each housing three. A set had one large 'common chamber', in which all the inhabitants slept, and three or four small rooms which served as individual studies. So that the lives of the young men could be fully and continuously supervised, Wykeham ordered in his statutes that seniors and juniors should share this accommodation. (There were eleven ground-floor and nine first-floor sets, which exactly provided for seventy Fellows.) Close to the living quarters was the Long Room, a mediaeval latrine described in the 17th century (inaccurately) as a 'Stupendous Piece of *Building*, it being so long and deep, that it has never been emptied since the foundation of the college'.

The heads of older Oxford colleges lived in chambers with the Fellows. Wykeham determined that the Warden of New College should be provided with separate and specifically designed lodgings. From these he could observe events in the lane approaching the main gate, in the Great Quadrangle, and, through a squint, in the antechapel. In the lodgings the Warden would live in suitable style and entertain visitors. Accordingly the lodgings contained a spacious hall for meals, a kitchen, bedchambers and study.

In the first century and a half of its history, New College justified the founder's generosity and vision. Former Fellows included HENRY CHICHELE (Fellow 1387–?93), Archbishop of Canterbury and founder of All Souls College; William Warham (Fellow 1473–88), Archbishop of Canterbury and Lord Chancellor of England; WILLIAM GROCYN (Fellow 1465–81), Lecturer in Greek, friend of Thomas More and Erasmus, and the most learned humanist of his generation in England. The influence of Wykeham's

foundation was reflected in the statutes and buildings of All Souls and Magdalen in Oxford, and of King's College in Cambridge.

The impact of the Protestant Reformation was first felt in the college in 1528, when the Warden, Dr London, deprived John Quinbey of his fellowship for heresy. Quinbey was later imprisoned in the bell-tower, where he died, 'half starved with cold and lack of food'. Although London himself sometimes found it difficult to keep his footing on the narrow road between religious orthodoxy and obedience to the commands of Henry VIII, he presided over the abolition of the teaching of Canon Law and the destruction of many of the college's precious manuscripts; the works of Duns Scotus were seen blowing round the quadrangle. But the college remained a bulwark of the Catholic faith, in spite of the election of its first married Warden, Ralph Skinner, in 1551. Several distinguished Catholic apologists became Fellows under Henry VIII: John Harpsfield (Fellow 1532–51), later Regius Professor of Greek and Archdeacon of London; his brother Nicholas (Fellow 1534–53), author of the first *Life of Thomas More* (written c.1557 but unpublished until 1932) and of a history of the English church; Thomas Harding (Fellow 1534–54), defender of the Roman cause under Elizabeth; and Nicholas Saunders (Fellow 1546–61), whose *De Visibili Monarchia Ecclesiae* was the Catholic response to Foxe's *Book of Martyrs* (1563). After Elizabeth's accession there was a drastic and prolonged purge of Catholic Fellows. Some, like the Harpsfields and Harding, had already moved from their fellowships to higher posts, which they now had to quit. But others had stayed in the college and had been reinforced under Mary. In the first two years of Elizabeth's reign four men left the college 'voluntarily' and five others were expelled; eleven more were deprived of their fellowships in 1562. By the end of the first decade of the reign some thirty-eight Fellows had been extruded for their religious beliefs. The altars in the chapel were removed in 1560; some of the mediaeval glass was destroyed in 1564; the niches of the reredos were plastered over in 1566; and finally the rood-screen was dismantled in 1571–2. The destruction of the old religion was slow but thorough, the effects upon the college of this process profoundly damaging. From having been the centre of humanist learning in Oxford until the reign of Henry VIII, New College became almost an intellectual backwater. Although it produced a few notable scholars like Thomas James (1591–1602), first librarian of the BODLEIAN, and Robert Pinke, Warden from 1617 to 1642, the intellectual and religious leadership in Oxford passed to other colleges. (*See also* ROMAN CATHOLICS.)

Some significant changes were made to the buildings of the college in the 15th and 16th centuries – partly the result of demands on space; partly in consequence of a desire for greater privacy. The bursary, situated between the muniment tower and the archway to what is now the Garden Quadrangle, was soon found to be too small for the business of the college and an additional room, the Chequer, was built on to the back of the eastern range in 1449. Then, as now, the pressure of books upon the shelves of the library became acute and an additional law library was built above the Chequer in 1480–1. By the 16th century the Chequer had become the resort of Senior

An engraving after Frederick Mackenzie's drawing of New College from the garden in 1834, from James Ingram's Memorials *of Oxford.*

Fellows and formed, contrary to the spirit of the statutes, the nucleus of a separate Senior Common Room, of which it is still a part. The hall was transformed by Archbishop Warham's bequest of money for the linenfold panelling, screen and screens-passage, which were made between 1533 and 1535: carvings above the doors leading off the screens-passage show choristers carrying beer and bread. The Warden's lodgings were extended, probably by Dr London, to provide more rooms for the entertainment of visitors. Two chambers were built above the Warden's study, which lies between the tower of the lodgings and the antechapel. A gallery was built at the level of the first storey above the Warden's kitchen, which abutted on to New College Lane; probably this formed a 'guest suite'. The Fellows were also providing themselves with extra space and some privacy by constructing cocklofts above their chambers: these were attic rooms in the roof, lit by gable windows facing away from the quadrangle. Finally, the garden was given its ornamental appearance in the 16th century. In the reign of Henry VIII 500 loads of earth were used to level the ground and to make terraced walks, and under Elizabeth the existing mound was formed as a decorative feature (*see* GARDENS).

The CIVIL WAR did less damage to the college than might have been expected. After the battle of Edgehill in 1642 Oxford became the headquarters of the royalist cause and New College cloisters were converted into the main arsenal for the King's army. Academic life was virtually suspended and the younger Fellows engaged in drill in the Great Quadrangle. After the war three sets of VISITORS were appointed by Parliament to supervise the conduct of University business and to expel men hostile to the government. As they had been under Elizabeth, the Fellows of New College were thoroughly hostile to the regime. Only one of the seventy Fellows submitted to the VISITATION, the rest insisting that the statutes forbade them to recognise any Visitor who was not a member of the University. In the end fifty Fellows, four chaplains, twelve choristers and thirteen servants were ejected; fifty-five new Fellows in all were installed; and a new Warden, George Marshall, a Cambridge MA, was appointed by the Visitors, contrary to the statutes, which laid down that the Warden must be a Fellow or ex-Fellow of the college.

But with the Restoration of Charles II in 1660, New College returned, relatively undamaged, to its former state. Marshall had died in 1658 and in his place the college had elected a former Fellow, Michael Woodward, a man of little scholarly eminence but an excellent manager. Several of the Fellows intruded by the republican regimes were removed and some deprived men were brought back. Woodward toured the college estates investigating the condition of the property and the conduct of tenants. The revenue was quickly restored to around £3300 per annum, the level reached in the pre-war decade. This made New College the third richest college in Oxford, after Christ Church and Magdalen. But if the Restoration of the King was accompanied by a return of the prosperity of the 1630s, other less desirable features of pre-war days came back as well. The Fellows had long been accustomed to living away from Oxford while enjoying the benefits of the college. Many of them had gained their fellowships by claiming to be FOUNDER'S KIN. Some effectively sold their fellowships by offering to resign in return for a suitable inducement from the parents of the man at the top of the roll of those waiting to come from Winchester. The college came to be less a place of education than a club whose members competed among themselves for the benefices to which the governing body had the right of presentation. ANTHONY WOOD complained that the Fellows were 'much given to drinking and gaming and vain brutish pleasure. They degenerate in learning'. The 18th-century diary of James Woodforde, who entered the college in 1759, shows its author preoccupied with cricket, bowls, billiards, music, food and wine: 'I carried off my drinking exceedingly well indeed', he remarks in a typical entry.

Although intellectual life was almost inert in the 17th and 18th centuries, the Fellows were vigorous builders. Before the Civil War the cocklofts of the seniors had been converted into a row of gabled studies above the first-floor chambers. In 1674–5 the eastern, western and southern ranges were raised in height by extending the cocklofts and hiding them behind a castellated parapet, giving the quadrangle its present form. This did not satisfy the desire of the Junior Fellows for more spacious accommodation. Partly to satisfy them and partly to provide for fee-paying gentleman-commoners, the college commissioned William Byrd to design a new quadrangle on the site of the western part of the garden. After he had presented a number of plans, the Fellows accepted a scheme for an open courtyard flanked by two wings on the north and south. These were built between 1681 and 1684. Twenty years later the demand for extra accommodation was again raised, and was satisfied by two additional wings in the Garden Quadrangle, extending Byrd's building to the east, but stepped back from it. The first, by Richard Piddington, was begun in 1700; the second, by William Townesend (see TOWNESEND'S), in 1707. Although the Garden Quadrangle was built in three stages by three different men, its parts are harmonious. The castellation of the whole parapet, carried over from the Great Quadrangle, helps to provide unity; and the buildings were drawn together by the installation of a wrought-iron screen and gate across the entrance to the garden. By the early 18th century the garden itself was laid out into formal parterres, with the mound and its terraces as the central feature.

The 18th century also saw major changes in the chapel. In 1736–40 William Price of Hatton Garden 'restored' the windows on the south side of the nave. Then, in 1765, William Peckitt of York was commissioned to repair the glass on the north side and in the west window. Peckitt removed the glass from the west window and sold it to York Minster, where it can still be seen. He replaced it, at great cost, with a window of his own design. This was so generally disliked that the Fellows decided in 1777 to remove the glass and use it for replacing the windows in the north-east of the nave. A new west window of painted glass was then commissioned, to be designed by Sir Joshua Reynolds and executed by Thomas Jervais. The new window depicts the Nativity, with shepherds on each side and four cardinal virtues, together with Faith, Hope and Charity beneath (see STAINED GLASS). Between 1789 and 1794 the interior of the chapel was substantially changed by James Wyatt, who had already advised upon changes in the upper library (now known as the Wyatt Library, although the work was eventually executed by James Pears). In the chapel he made a plaster vault in the roof, replaced the reredos with a plaster imitation of the original, built new stalls for the Fellows and a new screen for the organ – the latter forming an arch through which the Reynolds' window could be seen.

The spirit of 'improvement' began to affect the University of Oxford early in the 19th century. A new honours examination was established in 1800, with more rigorous standards; and the number of undergraduates began to rise after 1810. But New College remained for long aloof from these developments. Its membership continued to be the seventy Fellows laid down by the original statutes, although it did admit a few COMMONERS who were not on the foundation. It preserved its privilege of exempting its members from the University examinations. Philip Shuttleworth, Warden from 1822 to 1840, fought hard against the 'uninspiring indolence' of the Fellows. He persuaded them to surrender the college's right to set separate examinations and secured some improvement in standards. But in 1850 the state of the college was little different from what it had been in the 18th century: its members were drawn entirely from Winchester, where education was at a low ebb; nearly half the Fellows were founder's kin, elected by right of birth rather than merit; the Senior Fellows were mostly absentees, and even when present did no teaching. The pressure for reform came mainly from outside, with the appointment in 1850 of a University Commission, with powers to inquire and to recommend reforms (see ROYAL COMMISSIONS). This was followed in 1854 by a second Commission, which had the power to draw up new statutes for the University and the colleges. The Fellows of New College responded by refusing to provide the first Commissioners with a copy of the statutes and then by appealing to the Visitor, the Bishop of Winchester. The Bishop advised the college to accept certain reforms, but these were overtaken by the similar proposals of the 1854 Commission. In 1857 the reforms were agreed and incorporated in new ordinances. The foundation was to consist of forty Fellows, who were graduates, and thirty scholars, who were undergraduates. The Fellows would be elected after examination and only half the fellowships were restricted to men from Winchester. The privileges of founder's kin were abolished. In the next decade further changes followed, to culminate in the new statutes of 1873. Fellows were allowed to marry in 1867, so that it became possible to make a career in University teaching; commoners were admitted on a large scale, so that undergraduate numbers rose from ninety-five in 1873 to 225 in 1884, after which the college grew more slowly, to reach 301 in 1913. By 1884 New College had come to be in essence very much the institution that it is today. Although the changes had been triggered by the outside pressures of the parliamentary Commissions, the principal responsibility lay with reforming Fellows of the college, in particular with E.C. Wickham (Fellow 1852–74), founder of inter-collegiate lectures, son-in-law of WILLIAM GLADSTONE and headmaster of Wellington; Hereford B. George (Fellow 1856–1910), the first married Fellow, tutor in Law and History; and Alfred Robinson (Fellow 1864–95), Senior Bursar from 1875. W.A. SPOONER, who became Warden in 1903, provided quiet support. J.E. Sewell, Warden throughout the reforming period, from 1860 to 1903, devoted himself to research on the history of the college and accepted the changes which others brought about.

The great additional intake of undergraduates had to be accommodated, and in 1870 Sir George Gilbert Scott was appointed architect. Houses on the south side of HOLYWELL STREET were demolished to provide a site and in 1872 building began on the first phase: four staircases to the west of the Holywell entrance. There followed successively the tower in the centre of

Cooks at work in the kitchen of New College c.1890.

the range and two further staircases to the west of it. Scott had originally intended his building to have only three storeys, but he added an additional one to provide further accommodation at the insistence of Robinson and Wickham: in consequence the building looms heavily over its neighbours. When more rooms were needed, the college chose Basil Champneys, who designed a tutor's house and three further staircases in the area called 'Pandy', short for Pandemonium (the origins of this name are unknown). His building is in a domestic Tudor style, which contrasts with Scott's Gothic, and is of only three storeys. Finally, in 1896, Champneys completed the Holywell range with the Robinson Tower over the entrance.

While undergraduate accommodation was being built, Scott was also engaged on 'improvements' elsewhere. In 1865 he completed the restoration of the hall, removing the 18th-century plaster ceiling and installing a tiebeam roof on the probable pattern of the original. But his main energies and the greatest expense were devoted to the chapel. He produced plans in 1877 and the work was carried out, after his death the following year, by his sons. Against Scott's preference for a roof similar to that in hall, the Fellows insisted on the construction of a hammerbeam roof, on the ground that it was 'more ecclesiastical in character'. A new case was built for the Willis organ which had been installed in 1874, together with new stalls in the nave. The existing woodwork in the chapel is therefore almost entirely of Scott's design. Wyatt's plaster reredos was replaced by one in stone, whose niches were filled with sculptures by J.L. Pearson.

By the beginning of the 20th century New College was distinguished in many fields. Its eight was always in the first three on the river between 1883 and 1906 (*see* BUMPING RACES). Its members – either Fellows or undergraduates – included H.A.L. FISHER, later Minister of Education and Warden from 1925 to 1940; GILBERT MURRAY (Fellow 1888–9 and 1905–8); Leonard Woolley (1899); Alfred Lord Milner (Fellow

1876–81); J.S. and J.B.S. Haldane (Fellows 1901–c.13 and 1919–22 respectively); and John Galsworthy (1885/6). Between the two wars, under Fisher's wardenship, the college achieved a degree of distinction that it had not known since the 15th century – perhaps not even then. Among the Fellows were Julian Huxley (1919–25), G.H. Hardy (1920–31), H.W.B. Joseph (1891–1932), David Ogg (1914–56), Isaiah Berlin (1938–50) and DAVID CECIL (1929–69). Six undergraduates later became Cabinet ministers: Hugh Gaitskell (1924), Richard Crossman (later Fellow 1930–7), David Eccles (1923), Frank Pakenham (1924), Hugh Molson (1922) and Douglas Jay (1926). Six more – Lords Simonds (1906), Cohen (1906), Oaksey (1899), Tucker (c.1907), Radcliffe (1919) and Wilberforce (1935) – became Law Lords. Other men of distinction included George Woodcock (1931), Secretary-General of the TUC; Gerald Ellison (1930), Bishop of London; John Hackett (1929), Commander-in-Chief of the British Army of the Rhine; Lord Harlech (1936), Ambassador in Washington and chairman of Harlech Television.

There have been fewer changes and less building in the sixty or so years after 1918 than in the sixty before it. Teaching and research in the natural sciences has much increased, with the consequence that the academic life of many Fellows and undergraduates is centred in the University SCIENCE AREA rather than in the college. The number of graduate students rose from forty-seven in 1950 to eighty-three in 1974. And in 1979, the year of its sixth centenary, New College first admitted women research students and undergraduates. The first building of substance to be completed after 1918 was the new library, designed by Hubert Worthington in 1938 and placed between the city wall and the New Buildings. In 1963 the Sacher Building (named after benefactors of the college, Mr and Mrs Harry Sacher, and designed by David Roberts) was built on LONGWALL to house graduate students. Two new buildings have been erected to accommodate undergraduates: Bodicote House, on Longwall, in 1969 (financed by the sale of college lands in the parish of Bodicote and designed by Geoffrey Beard), and the Longwall Building in 1981 (by J.G. Fryman) on the site of the old Morris Garage (*see* MOTOR CARS).

An account of New College is fittingly completed with some words on its MUSIC. The founder provided for ten chaplains, three clerks and sixteen choristers, and the seven canonical hours and seven Masses were sung daily from the beginning. Instruction was given to the choristers from at least 1394 by the *informator choristarum*. The first mention of an organ is made in 1449, when payment was made for repairs; another was donated by William and Joan Porte in 1458. Since then the college has had a succession of organs, notably Dallam's (1662–3), Green's (*c.*1794), Willis's (1874), and the present instrument by Grant, Degens and Bradbeer (1968). Among its distinguished organists have been Philip Hayes (1776–97), thought to be 'the largest man in England'; Hugh Allen (1901–19); William Harris (1919–29); and John Dykes Bower (1929–33). While the chapel was the centre of musical life in the college, there were glee clubs in the 19th century for the performance of English music and from then until today the college has maintained a strong tradition of performing secular, as well as sacred, music.

Harvey McGregor became Warden in 1985. His immediate predecessors were Arthur Hafford Cooke (1976–85), William Goodenough Hayter (1958–76) and Alic Halford Smith (1944–58).

The college's corporate title is The Warden and Scholars of St Mary's College of Winchester in Oxford, commonly called New College in Oxford.

(Buxton, John, and Williams, Penry (eds), *New College, Oxford 1379–1979*, Oxford, 1979; Rashdall, H., and Rait, R.S., *New College*, Oxford, 1901; Smith, A.H., *New College and its Buildings*, Oxford, 1952; Steer, Francis, *The Archives of New College*, Chichester, 1974; Buxton, John, *New College, Oxford: a Note on the Garden*, Oxford, 1979; Woodforde, C., *The Stained Glass of New College, Oxford*, Oxford, 1951; Hayter, Sir William, *William of Wykeham, Patron of the Arts*, London, 1970.)

New College Lane Named after the college, the lane runs from CATTE STREET under the bridge of Hertford College until, after two right-angled bends, it joins QUEEN'S LANE by the lodgings of the Provost of The Queen's College. The lane also leads to the west gate of New College. Some modern maps show the lane continuing further east still. It has borne this name since at least 1648, but in 1722 it ran right through from Cat (*sic*) Street to HIGH STREET. By 1889 it was described as the lane that 'went from Catherine Street to the main entrance of New College'. In ANTHONY WOOD's time (1661–6) it was sometimes called St John's Street. ST HELEN'S PASSAGE (Hell Passage), leading to the TURF TAVERN, is found on the north side next to the house where Edmond Halley, discoverer of the comet (*see* ASTRONOMER'S HOUSE), lived. Halley's house is a Grade II listed building, as are Nos 5 and 8, the latter pair making up a group with Nos 6 and 7. A small gate leading into the grounds of New College at the Queen's Lane end of New College Lane is known as 'the non licet gate'. When the Lord Mayor and members of Oxford City Council undertake their traditional periodic inspection of the CITY WALLS within the bounds of the college, the college must open this gate when a representative of the city knocks on it. The city party, robed, then enters through the gate before climbing the walls to inspect them.

New College School *Savile Road.* When William of Wykeham founded New College in 1379, he also provided for sixteen choristers to be housed and educated within its walls: initially 'chaplains, clerks and choristers lived very thick together in dark gloomy chambers beneath the hall'. Little is known of the school's early history until the historian ANTHONY WOOD, an eleven-year-old chorister in 1643, describes life in the college during the CIVIL WAR. By the end of the 17th century choristers were being drawn from the city of Oxford, and New College School is listed as one of its grammar schools, taking 'not only clerks and choristers of the said House, but the sons of oppidans and others'. Wood states that in 1694 the school 'flourishes much under the tuition of James Badger, for there are about one hundred commoners besides choristers', requiring a removal of the school 'to the old Congregation House at St Mary's'. In the 19th century the school numbered some sixty boys, who were taught at NEW COLLEGE LANE and boarded at No. 19 HOLYWELL STREET. In 1903 it moved to its present premises, the headmaster's house being built to the designs of Nicholson and Corlette. In 1959 Upper School (classrooms and assembly hall) was built to the designs of Bridgewater and Shepheard; in 1972 the music school, science laboratories, and art-and-crafts studios were built to the designs of Geoffrey Beard, as were the new library (1981) and the computer laboratory (1985). There are at present 140 boys aged between seven and thirteen; 120 are day boys and twenty are day or boarding choristers. In addition to Anthony Wood, Sir Keith Falkner (President of the Royal College of Music), Ralph Holmes (violinist) and Ian Partridge (tenor) were former pupils.

New Inn Hall Stood on a site in the street to which it gave its name, now occupied by a former Oxford city school and parts of St Peter's College. The name New Inn Hall was given to an existing ACADEMIC HALL, then called Trillock's Inn, when this was extensively rebuilt in the late 15th century. At the time of the founding of New College in 1379, WILLIAM OF WYKEHAM had bought Trillock's Inn for use as an academic hall; and it retained this status, though with varying fortunes, till 1887, when it was absorbed by Balliol College. In the 17th century, as a former haven for Puritans, it was deserted, and in the CIVIL WAR Charles I used it as a MINT for the coinage being made from college silver. Though its 18th-century Principals included some eminent lawyers, the principalship had by then become little more than a sinecure. In spite of efforts made then to revive the teaching of Law in New Inn Hall, for which it had had a reputation, it was reported in the early 19th century that there had been no students there for a hundred years. However, under Dr J.A. Cramer, Principal from 1831 to 1847, its fortunes revived. At his own expense he built accommodation for students which was later rebuilt to become the Hannington Hall of St Peter's College. It was in the dining hall of New Inn Hall that the lectures were given which the future Edward VII attended when he was living in FREWIN HALL opposite.

New Inn Hall Street Connects BONN SQUARE with GEORGE STREET. One of Oxford's oldest streets, it was originally L-shaped and ran inside the CITY WALL, connecting Northgate Street (CORNMARKET) with the Bailey (QUEEN STREET). The street was known as North Bailey by 1399, and from *c.*1550 to 1800 as the Lane of the Seven Deadly Sins – the name derived either from an inn sign or from seven poor cottages which stood here. The present name comes from NEW INN HALL, now part of St Peter's College. In 1872 the street was extended through the old city wall to George Street, but it was not until 1899 that the section leading to Cornmarket Street was renamed ST MICHAEL'S STREET.

At the south end on the west side No. 1, adjoining Bonn Square, is a timber-framed house with a large, early 17th-century, stone chimney stack. When the NEW ROAD BAPTIST CHURCH property was redeveloped, this was restored and the 18th-century front of No. 5 was retained. It incorporated a mediaeval stone chimney from New Inn Hall, which was built on the site of Trillock's Inn (*c.*1460). Adjoining this block the former CENTRAL SCHOOL FOR GIRLS (later Cheney Girls' Grammar School) was converted in 1986 to provide further accommodation for St Peter's College, which now incorporates Hannington Hall, built in 1832, and the church of ST-PETER-LE-BAILEY, built in 1874. The latter is by Basil Champneys and replaced the old church in Bonn Square. It is now the college chapel. Adjoining it is Wyaston House, a fine Georgian house which was built for the Oxford Canal Company, then became the rectory for St-Peter-le-Bailey and now forms an entrance to St Peter's College. North of the college is the WESLEY MEMORIAL METHODIST CHURCH. The engine house of the Oxford Volunteer Fire Brigade, now demolished, was between the church and George Street.

On the east side of the street all the buildings between St Michael's Street and SHOE LANE belong to Brasenose College. They include FREWIN HALL and the adjoining quad. On the old Methodist Meeting House is a plaque recording that JOHN WESLEY preached there on 14 July 1783. Adjoining is the 16th-century gateway of the former St Mary's College – a college of Augustine canons founded in 1436. Several old houses, including cottages 6, 7 and 8 Frewin in a courtyard, are included in the Frewin Hall development. On No. 50 is a plaque recording the fact that ST EDWARD'S SCHOOL was founded in 1863 in Mackworth Hall, which stood on the site. Also let into the wall further along is a stone marking the boundaries of St Michael's and St Peter's parishes, with the date 1933 (*see* BEATING THE BOUNDS). St Michael's Infants' School on the corner of Shoe Lane was demolished in 1979 when Brasenose College redeveloped this side of Shoe Lane. The development was designed by John Fryman of the Architects Design Partnership. On the opposite side of Shoe Lane, North Bailey House (1974–5 by Collins, Stonebridge & Bradley) replaced Newspaper House (1880), where the *Oxford Mail* and *Oxford Times* were printed until 1972 (*see* NEWSPAPERS).

New Road One of only two new major roads built in central Oxford between the time of William the Conqueror and 1872. (The other was KING EDWARD STREET.) It was cut in 1770–6 through the CASTLE precincts and the base of the castle mound, which still towers above the road opposite Nuffield College.

There were suggestions at the time that the entire mound might be removed to allow the road to run straight from CARFAX to BOTLEY ROAD. There is a picture of the New Road, drawn before the Assize Courts (*see* COURTS) were built in 1841, in JAMES INGRAM's *Memorials*, Vol. III (1837). F. King, writing in about 1830, said that 'toll was demanded of all vehicles going through the castle ground; the road there was ... much used before the New road was cut. One had to go down Castle Street some distance before turning to the right over a castle bridge now destroyed and round either through Titmouse Lane [TIDMARSH LANE] or Hollybush Row to Botley causeway'. The castle bridge over the fosse was said to be about 27 yards long.

The wharves of the CANAL beside New Road, built on land once in the northern precincts of the castle, were opened on New Year's Day 1790. This meant the end of the castle moat, which in the past had been up to 10 yards wide in places. According to Squires, the first canal boats were greeted by the band of the Oxford militia and crowds of cheering people. The site of the canal basin was sold in 1937 to Nuffield College and the Canal House is now part of St Peter's College.

The QUEEN STREET end of the road is now known as BONN SQUARE and the NEW ROAD BAPTIST CHURCH (built in 1819 by John Hudson) is actually in the square. The church of ST PETER-LE-BAILEY (now part of St Peter's College) once stood on the north side of what is now the square. In 1849 the church opened a parochial school for boys and girls, described in Gardner's *Directory* of 1852 as 'a very neat red brick building'. By 1866 it had 105 girls and seventy-five boys. Because of the increase in the amount of traffic in New Road by 1898, the school moved round the corner into NEW INN HALL STREET.

On the north side of the road No. 11, on the eastern corner of Bulwarks Lane, is used by 'UB 40', an organisation for unemployed young people, named for the serial number on the DHSS form for unemployment benefit. On the other corner of Bulwarks Lane is the Probate Court (now Registry), which was stone-built in a 13th-century style in 1864 by Charles Buckeridge. A shed for bins built in front of it had to be constructed in matching stone in accordance with planning conditions. Next to it is the central Conservative Club. On the south side is the 19th-century COUNTY HALL, which also housed the Assize Courts, built on the site of the Great Hall and north walls of the castle. A two-storey link building designed by Albert E. Smith, County Architect, has arched windows mirroring those of County Hall. It joins the new office block at the corner of CASTLE STREET and was opened by the Queen in 1976. Further down the road, beyond the PRISON (1805), on the corner of Tidmarsh Lane are the County Offices, erected in 1912 for £8421 and occupied by the County Director of Education. When the foundations were being dug, water from the old castle moat seeped into them with the result that the building had to be constructed on timber piles. New offices, now used by the Education Department, were built some fifty years later between these offices and the Castle mound. In 1964 the Oxford Development Plan included the demolition of the New Road Baptist Church and the erection of a roundabout at MacFisheries corner (*see* ST EBBE'S), but this scheme was not implemented.

New Road Baptist Church *Bonn Square*. The Baptist tradition in Oxford goes back at least to 1646 when the Parliamentarians entered the city (*see* CIVIL WAR). Many of the soldiers were Baptists and soon made their presence felt. There is a record of the attendance of Oxford representatives at the Berkshire Baptist Association at Tetsworth on 17 March 1653 and this is generally held to be the foundation date of New Road Baptist Church. From 1661 Baptists met in the home of Richard Tidmarsh, their first minister, on the bank of the river which flows under Pacey's Bridge in PARK END STREET (*see* BRIDGES). A commemorative plaque is to be found on the bridge. There has been a Baptist church on the present site since 1721, following the wrecking of both the Baptist and Presbyterian Meeting Houses during the 1715 Jacobite RIOTS in the city. The two congregations came together under a joint covenant, although since the late 18th century all the ministers have been Baptists. The church was rebuilt and enlarged several times in the 19th century, reflecting its growth and increasing importance in the city centre. The present frontage was added in 1819. A major programme of renewal was completed in 1982 under the direction of the Oxford architect Peter Reynolds. Four floors of new halls and rooms have been created, with a foyer leading up to the church coffee-house situated in a 17th-century building overlooking BONN SQUARE. The church interior retains the traditional atmosphere of Nonconformity, though it now also offers a small but pleasing concert auditorium. Of special note are the striking cross of African woods by Heather Harms and the etched glass doors by Meinrad Craighead, symbolising the strategic missionary location of the church at the city centre.

Newdigate Prize Perhaps the most widely known of University prizes. Before 1806, unnamed prizes for English verse composition were awarded at the University; but in that year Sir Roger Newdigate of University College established an annual prize in his name for 'a copy of English verse of fifty lines and no more in recommendation of the study of the ancient Greek and Roman remains of Architecture, Sculpture and Painting', written by a member of the University within four years of matriculation. After 1827 restrictions on length and subject were removed, though since the late 19th century there has been a limit of 300 lines, the use of heroic couplets has no longer been obligatory, and any form of verse other than dramatic composition has been allowed. The entries are judged by the Professor of Poetry (*see* CHAIRS) and a panel of judges, and part of the winning entry is read out by the author at ENCAENIA. Until 1939 the set subject was most commonly a person, place or event of historical significance; since 1947 it has more often been of an abstract or philosophical nature. In its first 100 years, the prize was only twice not awarded (1849 and 1903), and again only twice (1915 and 1926) between 1906 and 1939; between 1947 and 1984, however, it has not been awarded on twelve occasions. The prize was suspended in 1917 and 1918, and from 1940 to 1946.

Among the most notable prizemen in the 19th century were JOHN RUSKIN (1839), MATTHEW ARNOLD (1843), Oscar Wilde (1878), Laurence Binyon (1890) and John Buchan (1898). More recently, Jon Stallworthy (1958), John Fuller (1960), James Fenton (1968) and Andrew Motion (1975) have continued to show distinction as poets. Among other winners of the prize have been R.S. Hawker (1827); F.W. Faber (1836); J.A. Symonds (1860); J.W. Mackail (1881); Arthur Waugh (1888), father of Alec and Evelyn; H.W. Garrod (1901); Julian Huxley (1908); James Laver (1921); John Bayley (1950); and Donald Hall (1952). Three prizemen later became Professors of Poetry in the University: H.H. Milman (1812), T.L. Claughton (1829) and Matthew Arnold (1843).

The prize has been won five times by women (1927, 1928, 1929, 1930 and 1937); of these, Phyllis Hartnoll (1929) also twice won the SACRED POEM PRIZE. (The Newdigate cannot be won twice by the same person, although those qualified may enter more than once.) It is reported that Rachel Burton, daughter of a canon of Christ Church, won the prize under a male pseudonym in the 1830s. The best-known line produced by the prize is 'A rose-red city – "half as old as Time"' by J.W. Burgon (1845), the set subject being *Petra*; and perhaps the best-known of disappointed entrants is A.E. Housman (1879). One-third of the prizewinners have come from three colleges: Balliol, Christ Church and New College. (*See also* PRIZES AND SCHOLARSHIPS.)

Newman, Cardinal John Henry *(1801–1890)*. A snapdragon on the wall of Trinity College was described by Newman as 'the emblem of my own perpetual residence unto death in my University.' And yet, on his conversion to Roman Catholicism, he

John Henry Newman, one of the leaders of the Oxford Movement and vicar of St Mary the Virgin from 1828–43, was received into the Roman Catholic church in 1845.

The masthead of Jackson's Oxford Journal, *Oxford's first newspaper, which was originally published as the* Oxford Flying Weekly Journal *in 1746 and which survived until 1909.*

left Oxford, not to return for thirty-three years, until, at the age of seventy-nine, he was elected the first Honorary Fellow of Trinity. He matriculated at Trinity in 1816 and was elected a scholar in 1818. Despite his poor second in Classics and the failure of his name to appear at all on the Mathematical side, he was, by 1827, a Fellow and Public Tutor of Oriel College, and also curate of ST CLEMENT'S. In 1828 he was instituted vicar of ST MARY THE VIRGIN, a position which he held until 1843. Lord Coleridge remarked that, during the last years of his incumbency, 'scarcely a man of note in the University, old or young, did not habitually attend the service and listen to the sermons.' He was one of the leaders of the OXFORD MOVEMENT, responsible for several *Tracts for the Times*. After the tumult caused in 1841 by *Tract XC*, Newman retired with a few friends to LITTLEMORE. Here, in a set of converted stables, he was received into the Roman Catholic Church by Blessed Dominic Barberi (*see* CHURCH OF BLESSED DOMINIC BARBERI), in the autumn of 1845. He was created a cardinal in 1879. His many publications are still widely read, among the best known being *Apologia pro Vita sua* (1864) and *The Dream of Gerontius* (1865).

Newspapers The first Oxford newspaper (apart from the OXFORD GAZETTE), the *Oxford Flying Weekly Journal and Cirencester Gazette*, published from 1746 to 1748, was printed first in ST CLEMENT'S and later in HIGH STREET. William Jackson, who published it with Robert Walker of London, started another weekly newspaper, originally to promote the Tory cause in the county election of 1753. This paper, for a short time called *News, Boys, News, or the Electioneering Journal*, and then renamed *Jackson's Oxford Journal*, had, in the period April–September 1839, the largest circulation of the three Oxford newspapers of the time, selling 57,000 copies compared with the *Oxford City and County Chronicle*'s sales of 33,000 and the *Oxford University, City and County Herald*'s 29,000. *Jackson's* survived until 1909, having been sold on

Jackson's death in 1795 and again in 1816 when it was bought by its printers, Grosvenor and Hall, and published at their printing office in CARFAX. William Hall became sole proprietor in 1824 and the Hall family owned the paper for more than seventy years until it was bought in 1899 by the Oxford Times Company. Renamed the *Oxford Journal Illustrated* in 1909, with sixteen pages copiously illustrated with photographs, it cost only 1d; in 1753 the four-page *Jackson's* had cost 2d. It continued to appear weekly until 1928 when the daily *Oxford Evening Times*, owned by the Company, incorporated in a weekly supplement the kind of material formerly produced in the *Oxford Journal Illustrated*.

Jackson's Oxford Journal was Oxford's only newspaper for fifty-three years, until in 1806 Henry Slatter and Joseph Munday started the *Oxford University and City Herald*. A four-page weekly, it cost 6d. By 1833 the paper was published at Slatter's bookshop in High Street and at an office in QUEEN STREET. Two years later it incorporated the *Oxford Conservative*, a paper of similar political persuasion. The name was changed twice in the ensuing years – in 1838 to the *Oxford University, City and County Herald*, and in 1852 to the *Oxford University Herald*. In that year Joseph Vincent became the owner, and published it at 90 High Street. It was still in the possession of his family when it was discontinued in 1892.

Liberal political opinion was served by the *Oxford City and County Chronicle*, a four-page weekly newspaper first published in 1837 and costing 5d. The publisher and printer was Henry Cooke, the office at 127 High Street. By 1869 the office had moved to No. 1 ST ALDATE'S and the paper had twice been renamed – in 1842 as the *Oxford Chronicle and Reading Gazette* and in 1845 as the *Oxford Chronicle and Berks. and Bucks. Gazette*. Under this name it survived until 1929, when the Oxford Times Company bought it and amalgamated it with the *Oxford Times*.

The next newspaper to begin publication was the *Oxford Times and Midland Counties Advertiser* in 1862. This eight-page, allegedly apolitical weekly cost 2*d*. Owing to financial problems it had to be sold in 1867 to a company who also bought the Conservative *Banbury Herald* and amalgamated the two. The resultant paper, not a success, was bought the next year and thenceforth edited by George Rippon, who, in 1881, became managing director of the newly formed Oxford Times Company. The *Oxford Times* continued to have a Conservative bias until 1929, when the Liberal *Oxford Chronicle* was amalgamated with it and it became a non-political newspaper.

In 1928 Frank Gray, director of the *Oxford Chronicle* and a former Liberal MP for Oxford, interested Sir Charles Starmer, head of Westminster Press, in the idea of a daily evening newspaper. The *Oxford Mail*, eight pages and costing 1*d*, was first published in November that year by the Counties Press, NEW INN HALL STREET. Simultaneously, the Oxford Times Company started publishing the *Oxford Evening Times*, a paper of the same size and price. In March 1929 the proprietors of the two newspapers agreed to publish together Oxford's only daily evening paper, the *Oxford Mail*, at Newspaper House, New Inn Hall Street, and the only weekly, the *Oxford Times*. The controlling company was the Oxford Mail and Times Co., now Oxford and County Newspapers, which has acquired several other newspapers in the county, including the free paper, the *Oxford Star*; the company is a division of the Westminster Press.

In 1972 the division moved from its cramped site in central Oxford to a new headquarters in the OSNEY MEAD estate, in a Civic Trust Award-winning building designed by Arup Associates (1970–2). For the six months to June 1986 the daily circulation (Monday to Friday) of the *Oxford Mail* was 39,464 and on Saturdays 34,429. The *Oxford Times*'s circulation for the same period was 31,641.

Nixon's Free Grammar School, opened in 1659 in the court of the Guildhall, was closed in 1894.

Nixon's Free Grammar School First mooted by the City Council in 1576, the idea of a school for the sons of freemen (*see* PRIVILEGED PERSONS) was realised in 1658 when Alderman John Nixon, MAYOR of Oxford in 1636, 1646 and 1654, offered £30 per annum to pay a master's stipend if the city provided a suitable schoolroom. By 1659 a building had been erected in the court of the Guildhall (*see* TOWN HALL) and Nixon's bequest was increased by £205 for the education, for not more than seven years, of forty poor freemen's sons between the ages of nine and ten. The school, unusually, aimed at providing an intermediate education, neither elementary nor solely classical, as well as religious instruction. Nixon's wife Joan, the foundress, actively interested herself in dealing with problems of truancy, hygiene and the apprenticing of boys. During the 18th and early 19th centuries the numbers and curriculum fluctuated, until in 1862 Charity Trustees were appointed with power to elect staff and pupils. Despite opposition by the Oxford freemen, adverse reports by the government inspector led to the closure of the school in 1894.

Non-collegiate Students *see* ST CATHERINE'S COLLEGE.

Nonconformists *see* DISSENTERS.

Norham Gardens *see* NORTH OXFORD.

Norrington Table A table of finals results first proposed by Sir Arthur Norrington, a former President of Trinity College (1954–70) and VICE-CHANCELLOR (1960–2), and first published in 1964. Each first-class degree is now awarded five points, each upper Second three points, lower Seconds two points and third-class degrees one point. The table has been widely criticised by dons, who emphasise that examination success is only one indication of a college's performance. Schoolteachers and applicants for admission, however, study the table closely. The results for 1986 are given below in Table 1. The 1986 table was computed in a way slightly different from its predecessors: for the first time, upper and lower second-class degrees were differentiated. Table 3 shows which colleges did best in particular subjects over the ten years from 1976 to 1985. Table 4 shows the colleges in order of achievement from 1964 to 1986. Table 5 lists in alphabetical order the results over that period. Table 6 gives the results of 1990.

Table 1: NORRINGTON TABLE 1986

Position (last year's in brackets)	College	Pts	1st (%)	2:1 (%)	2:2 (%)	3rd (%)	Poss. max	(%)
1 (1)	St John's	363	33.0	48.1	14.2	4.7	530	68.5
2 (6)	Merton	220	30.8	52.3	10.8	6.1	325	67.7
3 (5)	Corpus Christi	155	30.4	47.8	19.6	2.2	230	67.4
4 (2)	Exeter	278	30.1	48.2	18.1	3.6	415	67.0
5 (17)	Lincoln	213	23.1	58.5	18.4	—	325	65.5
6 (7)	University	322	27.0	46.0	22.0	5.0	500	64.4
7 (19)	Brasenose	276	21.1	48.9	24.4	5.6	450	61.3
8 (12)	Hertford	280	18.5	52.2	26.1	3.2	460	60.9
9 (9)	Balliol	318	20.9	44.8	29.5	4.8	525	60.6
10 (18)	Christ Church	333	17.1	50.5	30.6	1.8	555	60.0
11 (19)	Trinity	200	16.4	50.8	31.3	1.5	335	59.7
12 (3)	New College	335	14.2	59.3	21.2	5.3	565	59.3
13 (4)	Magdalen	301	11.6	64.1	17.5	6.8	515	58.4
14 (8)	St Edmund Hall	288	16.2	49.5	27.3	7.0	495	58.2

continued overleaf

Table 1: NORRINGTON TABLE 1986 continued

Position (last year's in brackets)	College	Pts	1st (%)	2:1 (%)	2:2 (%)	3rd (%)	Poss. max	(%)
15 (24)	Worcester	263	17.4	40.2	35.9	6.5	460	57.2
16 (16)	Wadham	310	14.7	49.5	26.6	9.2	545	56.9
17 (15)	Keble	340	14.2	50.8	25.0	10.0	600	56.7
18 (14)	Oriel	223	11.2	53.8	26.3	8.7	400	55.8
19 (28)	St Anne's	299	12.0	46.3	36.1	5.6	540	55.4
19 (22)	St Catherine's	349	15.1	41.3	34.1	9.5	630	55.4
21 (10)	Lady Margaret Hall	279	11.9	48.5	31.7	7.9	505	55.2
22 (11)	Jesus	239	13.8	42.5	34.5	9.2	435	54.9
23 (12)	Queen's	231	10.5	47.6	31.4	10.5	430	53.7
24 (21)	St Peter's	228	13.0	38.8	38.8	9.4	425	53.6
25 (23)	Pembroke	219	7.1	53.6	25.0	14.3	420	52.1
26 (26)	St Hugh's	267	7.7	42.3	41.3	8.7	520	51.3
27 (25)	St Hilda's	240	3.2	49.5	41.0	6.3	475	50.5
28 (27)	Somerville	260	3.8	46.7	39.0	10.5	525	49.5

Table 2: NORRINGTON TABLE 1987

Position (last year's in brackets)	College	Pts	1st (%)	2:1 (%)	2:2 (%)	3rd (%)	Poss. max	(%)
1 (6)	University	330	23	60	17	1	505	65.3
2 (1)	St John's	316	22	55	19	3	495	63.8
3 (10)	Christ Church	384	28	62	27	4	605	63.5
4 (15)	Worcester	265	18	47	15	4	420	63.1
5 (16)	Wadham	333	22	58	23	3	530	62.8
6 (2)	Merton	232	18	34	18	4	370	62.7
7 (13)	Magdalen	338	21	64	19	5	540	62.6
8 (22)	Jesus	261	17	44	21	2	420	62.1
9 (17)	Keble	357	24	57	30	6	585	61.0
10 (12)	New College	313	19	54	25	6	520	60.2
10 (23)	Queen's	256	17	42	19	7	425	60.2
12 (4)	Exeter	246	14	43	22	3	410	60.0
13 (8)	Hertford	308	18	54	24	8	520	59.2
14 (25)	Pembroke	239	14	41	20	6	405	59.0
15 (3)	Corpus Christi	170	7	34	16	1	290	58.6
16 (18)	Oriel	261	11	53	21	5	450	58.0
17 (9)	Balliol	263	14	45	26	6	455	57.8
18 (5)	Lincoln	222	10	42	21	4	385	57.7
19 (14)	St Edmund Hall	279	13	54	21	10	490	56.9
20 (21)	Lady Margaret Hall	306	12	58	34	4	540	56.7
20 (11)	Trinity	187	7	37	19	3	330	56.7
22 (7)	Brasenose	270	11	49	30	8	490	55.1
23 (19)	St Catherine's	350	14	60	45	10	645	54.3
24 (28)	Somerville	266	7	51	37	4	495	53.7
25 (26)	St Hugh's	265	9	47	35	9	500	53.0
26 (27)	St Hilda's	270	7	52	35	9	515	52.4
27 (19)	St Anne's	301	8	58	38	11	575	52.3
28 (24)	St Peter's	207	5	38	29	10	410	50.5

Table 3: PERFORMANCE BY SUBJECT 1976–85

	Top	2nd	3rd
PPE	Magdalen	Balliol	Brasenose
English	University	Merton	St Catherine's
History	Merton	St John's	Jesus
Modern Languages	University	Worcester	St Hugh's
Law	Hertford	Magdalen	Keble
Maths	St Edmund Hall	Merton	Keble
Chemistry	St John's	University	Keble
Physics	University	St Catherine's	St John's
Classics	Corpus	University	Oriel
Engineering	St John's	Hertford	Balliol

Table 4: ORDER OF SUCCESS 1964–86

1	Balliol	15	Exeter
2	Merton	16	Hertford
3	Corpus Christi	17	Worcester
4	St John's	18	Lincoln
5	University	19	Lady Margaret Hall
6	Magdalen	20	St Edmund Hall
7	Wadham	21	Brasenose
8	New College	22	Oriel
9	Jesus	23	St Hugh's
10	St Anne's	24	Pembroke
11	St Catherine's	25	Keble
12	St Hilda's	26	Christ Church
13	Somerville	27	Trinity
14	Queen's	28	St Peter's

Table 5: RESULTS 1964–86

	64	65	66	67	68	69	70	71	72	73	74	75	76	77	78	79	80	81	82	83	84	85	86
Balliol	3	9	1	1	8	2	4	7	9	5	3	3	5	5	15	4	6	8	6	4	14	9	9
Brasenose	16	22	22	18	22	26	24	12	19	15	21	17	26	18	16	21	27	24	9	9	10	19	7
Christ Church	24	20	28	27	24	24	23	27	24	18	19	20	12	19	16	10	26	21	26	16	22	18	10
Corpus Christi	8	4	13	2	2	1	2	11	1	1	1	4	1	4	10	3	11	6	16	22	17	5	3
Exeter	15	21	21	12	11	16	6	6	20	13	20	18	23	10	28	27	24	10	23	8	15	2	4
Hertford	26	27	27	24	26	25	27	28	21	27	12	6	6	19	5	2	5	8	7	7	12	8	
Jesus	20	5	12	4	10	19	22	16	22	13	15	5	9	10	21	6	9	18	9	2	11	11	22
Keble	27	28	24	21	27	28	26	26	25	22	14	22	24	7	13	26	8	21	13	10	19	15	17
Lady Margaret Hall	4	2	17	6	18	17	18	17	7	17	25	27	21	13	16	14	21	26	13	24	24	10	21
Lincoln	17	12	4	16	3	23	21	3	15	16	27	25	27	22	24	17	7	15	12	6	17	17	5
Magdalen	6	6	3	3	21	3	5	13	26	4	9	20	2	3	9	9	4	17	24	20	5	4	13
Merton	11	15	9	5	13	4	1	1	1	3	2	2	4	2	1	3	2	10	3	22	14	6	6
New College	14	18	11	19	12	15	12	9	4	8	4	11	18	13	6	19	3	9	2	11	8	3	12
Oriel	12	19	23	22	28	27	9	25	18	20	28	23	14	21	11	14	28	20	6	19	9	14	18
Pembroke	13	10	19	26	25	20	11	22	23	25	26	19	17	17	27	20	25	18	16	26	2	23	25
Queen's	5	14	5	11	5	18	7	5	13	24	23	9	20	25	11	22	15	15	16	13	22	12	23
St Anne's	2	1	6	15	19	11	8	4	14	2	6	11	9	8	14	12	14	23	28	23	26	28	19
St Catherine's	28	23	18	23	15	9	3	8	16	21	12	13	4	16	8	12	12	4	3	3	12	22	19
St Edmund Hall	25	24	26	7	20	10	16	19	17	19	15	28	24	15	4	10	22	12	21	16	12	8	14
St Hilda's	10	3	8	8	9	10	14	5	7	11	10	7	25	19	18	23	14	13	18	26	25	27	
St Hugh's	18	13	7	20	14	12	19	15	11	11	18	14	13	27	26	24	19	26	27	25	28	26	26
St John's	9	8	20	13	6	6	15	10	6	5	5	26	11	6	24	5	4	1	4	1	1	1	1
St Peter's	22	25	25	28	23	22	28	23	27	26	17	16	22	28	23	18	15	28	25	27	20	21	24
Somerville	1	7	2	9	1	14	20	18	12	10	7	8	9	20	14	15	25	20	21	21	27	28	
Trinity	21	26	15	24	17	21	25	24	28	28	23	23	28	23	22	25	20	7	16	14	15	19	11
University	22	17	16	10	7	13	14	21	8	23	7	1	1	1	7	1	2	1	5	4	7	6	
Wadham	7	11	14	17	4	5	17	2	3	9	10	6	15	24	3	6	17	13	4	11	3	16	16
Worcester	19	16	10	14	16	7	13	20	10	12	22	15	15	12	7	23	13	12	11	28	25	24	15

Table 6: RESULTS 1991

Position	College	Students	Points	%	1	2:1	2:2	3
						Degree results		
1	(4) St John's	112	386	68.9	36	57	16	3
2	(5) Balliol	114	380	66.7	33	57	20	4
3	(14) Wadham	128	418	65.3	29	76	22	1
4	(9) Magdalen	93	299	64.3	23	47	20	3
5	(10) University	115	366	63.7	28	57	25	5
6	(1) Merton	78	248	63.6	17	46	10	5
7	(12) Keble	124	391	63.0	29	60	31	4
8	(3) Corpus Christi	65	204	62.8	8	50	7	—
9	(2) Queen's	97	303	62.4	19	53	24	1
10	(16) Hertford	96	298	62.1	19	53	20	4
11	(6) Jesus	110	341	62.0	20	64	23	3
12	(11) Exeter	92	282	61.3	16	54	18	4
13	(8) Lincoln	79	242	61.3	17	37	21	4
14	(23) Oriel	89	270	60.7	16	46	25	2
15	(13) Brasenose	111	330	59.4	17	62	27	5
16	(15) St Catherine's	138	407	58.9	21	72	41	4
17	(17) Christ Church	122	359	58.8	17	69	31	5
18	(7) New	126	367	58.2	19	67	31	9
19	(22) Trinity	75	218	58.1	11	40	19	5
20	(21) Lady Margaret Hall	113	325	57.5	16	58	32	7
21	(20) Worcester	108	304	56.3	12	59	30	7
22	(19) Pembroke	83	231	55.7	9	44	24	6
23	(25) St Hilda's	116	315	54.3	5	71	37	3
24	(24) St Edmund Hall	105	283	53.9	8	60	26	11
25	(28) Somerville	94	253	53.8	7	50	31	6
26	(27) St Peter's	92	246	53.5	7	50	26	9
27	(18) St Anne's	133	354	53.2	8	71	47	7
28	(26) St Hugh's	115	298	51.8	8	54	43	10

(Previous positions in brackets)

North Hinksey A village on the south side of the city. It was at Hinksey that, in 1874, JOHN RUSKIN had teams of undergraduates engaged in road-mending with the idea of improving the countryside and reminding undergraduates of 'the pleasures of useful muscular work'. Oscar Wilde was among the undergraduates who helped Ruskin with this work.

Undergraduates at work in North Hinksey on road-mending, an activity encouraged by John Ruskin, Slade Professor of Fine Art, not only to improve the countryside but also to provide the students with the 'pleasures of useful muscular work'. The road was not a success.

The original ford from which Oxford derives its name is thought by some historians to have been at North Hinksey. A deed of 1352 describes a piece of land lying to the west of OSNEY in Bullstake Mead as having on its south side 'the ford called Oxford, hard by the bridge which leads towards North Hincksey' (Margaret Gelling, *Place Names of Oxfordshire*, Cambridge, 1953).

(*See also* CHURCH OF ST LAWRENCE.)

North Oxford Throughout its history this Victorian development has been admired and ridiculed, romanticised and threatened. Much of it is now a CONSERVATION AREA, but during the 1960s, at the time when the original ninety-nine year leases (allowed by Act of Parliament in 1855) were running out, many of its finest examples of Victorian architecture were in danger of demolition for redevelopment. The exact boundaries of North Oxford are vague, but it was originally an area running north from ST GILES' to approximately Marston Ferry, Staverton and Frenchay Roads south of SUMMERTOWN, including PARK TOWN and Norham Manor, and even the eastern parts of Walton Manor (*see* WALTON MANOR ESTATE). A map in the City Planning Department shows the approximate boundaries of the 'North Oxford Victorian Suburb' as designated by the Council on 6 July 1976. Many of the roads are named after St John's College livings or property, the college being owners of most of the land. These roads are BAINTON, BARDWELL, BELBROUGHTON, BEVINGTON, Bradmore, Chadlington, Chalfont, Charlbury, Crick, Farndon, Fyfield, Garford, Kingston, Leckford, Linton, Northmoor, Polstead and Warnborough.

Before North Oxford was developed there was open country between St Giles' and the little settlements of WOLVERCOTE and Summertown, except for a few scattered houses, mostly around NORTH PARADE. In the 14th and 15th centuries the whole of North Oxford was called Walton Field, and part of it was in the manor of HEADINGTON. It is often supposed that the development of North Oxford began when dons were permitted to marry, but this is not so: the abolition of the celibacy rule for college Fellows did not come until the ROYAL COMMISSION of 1877. The first houses had been built and inhabited well before that time by wealthy merchants and traders. It is true that some professors and many University coaches had taken up residence there before 1877, but it was not until after this date that the dons came flooding in. Although now often living side by side, there was still much snobbery, and town and gown rarely mixed socially, prejudices such as those expressed in 1826 by T. Little in *Confessions of an Oxonian* not having been entirely overcome: 'pastry cooks who had made fortunes cheating members of the University' should 'not pollute the magnificent entrances to the most beautiful of cities in the Kingdom'. Others, like JOHN RUSKIN, extolled the architecture and could not understand why (in 1876) visitors wished to see Magdalen walks rather than view the newly built KING EDWARD STREET, or stroll under the 'rapturous sanctities of Keble'. 'Finally', Ruskin asked, 'in the name of all that's human and progressive, why not [walk] up and down the elongated suburb of the married fellows on the cock-horse road to Banbury.' The Rev. W. Tuckwell, in his *Oxford Reminiscences* (1900) was less complimentary. Writing of 'the interminable streets of

William Wilkinson's design for a characteristic North Oxford house, 13 Norham Gardens, 1867.

Villadom, converging insatiably protuberant upon distant Wolvercot and Summertown', he could not 'frame to pronounce them Oxford'. 'Nine tenths of these denizens', he was told, were 'married Professors, Tutors, Fellows; men who formerly lived in College, resident and celibate and pastoral'. Tuckwell was probably the first of the early 20th-century commentators on North Oxford, who, almost without exception, ridiculed the architecture of the Victorians. Some seventy years had to pass before the area's villas came to be admired again. In a guide book of 1915, Butterfield was thought to be 'the worst architect in history'; and just as people derided the Albert Memorial in London, so they denounced Keble and North Oxford.

St John's College had bought the NORHAM GARDENS estate, part of Norham Manor, as early as the 16th century, but the first wave of development did not come until about 1833. By about 1850, according to Holman Hunt, 'the University taste for modern Gothic was established beyond recall'. William Wilkinson (1819–1901), who lived locally, was commissioned by St John's to lay out the estate. His roads were wider and less formal than those of PARK TOWN. Most of the houses were designed by him or by Frederick Codd, an architect as well as a speculative builder. Other architects were E.G. Bruton, Charles Buckeridge and John Gibbs. Most of the houses, which were of red and yellow brick, tall and gabled in the High Victorian manner, were built between 1860 and 1880. Quite a few were semi-detached. In his *English Country Houses* (1875), a practical treatise on house-building, William Wilkinson published views and plans. They include No. 31 BANBURY ROAD (The Firs), since demolished; No. 60 Banbury Road, with its turret over the porch; and No. 113 WOODSTOCK ROAD (demolished for Butler Close). St John's, though selling the leases, controlled the designs and the size of the plots. By 1860 the building boom had begun in earnest; and a guide-book of that year said that the houses were occupied at great speed. One of the attractions was that the land was above flood-level and much of it on gravel. By the mid-1870s most of the area south of Linton Road had been developed, most houses being provided with a spacious garden. Later houses were of red brick with facings of Bath stone. Front gardens had low brick walls with iron railings on the rounded brick tops, and wrought-iron gates. It was, and is, the gardens, trees and flowering shrubs, especially in spring and early summer, which delight the visitor to North Oxford.

Oxford soon became a place where people having no connections with town or gown wished to come to live. Instead of housing large Victorian families, the majority of houses have, since 1945, been converted into flats or college rooms, or have been occupied by institutions. Some, like Wykeham House, are offices. SIR JOHN BETJEMAN, who was at the DRAGON SCHOOL in the First World War remembers North Oxford with nostalgia in *Summoned by Bells* (1960).

Take me Centaur bike, down Linton Road
Gliding by newly-planted almond trees
Where young dons with wives in tussore clad
Were building in the morning of their lives
Houses for future Dragons . . .
And show me thy road, Crick, in the early Spring
Laurel and privet and laburnum ropes

And gabled-gothic houses gathered round
Thy mothering spire, St. Philip and St. James
Here by low-brick semi-private walls
. . . I glimpsed, behind lace curtains, silver hair
Of sundry old Professors. . . .

In his *Oxford University Chest* (1938) Betjeman writes, 'Each house learns something from Christ Church Cathedral and the Parks' Museum. Each house repeats its special way. Ever changing, never the same'.

It was to Sir John Betjeman that Councillor Ann Spokes turned in August 1962 when, the southern parts of Victorian North Oxford being threatened with demolition and redevelopment, she had started a campaign to preserve them, since none of the North Oxford houses was then scheduled under the Town and Country Planning Act. St John's College had announced in March of that year that it was preparing a development plan for the area. The author of the plan, the architect Lionel Brett, had said, 'My personal view of North Oxford is that it is one of the most beautiful sites it is possible to imagine for modern buildings. . . .' Betjeman, always a lover of North Oxford and all things Victorian even when it was unfashionable to be so, replied to Councillor Spokes by return of post, deploring the 'slow invasion' of North Oxford and said that he saw the 'salvation of the Norham Estate as very important'. He wrote to the Royal Fine Art Commission, while Councillor Spokes pressed the Ministry of Housing and Local Government to list the houses. By July 1964 the Ministry had published addenda to the list, including five houses as Grade II, though one of them, 31 Banbury Road, had already been demolished for St Anne's College. The others in Banbury Road to be listed were Nos 27 (by SIR THOMAS JACKSON), 29, 60 (by Wilkinson) and 62 (by E.G. Bruton).

In 1966 outline planning permission was sought by the University to build a new museum on the sites of 54–64 Banbury Road and 1–11 Bradmore Road. Sir William Holford's plan of May 1963 had been commissioned in response to a University report which said that by 1981 one million square feet of office space would be needed for an expanded science area. Holford had replied that the University could find 1000 square feet of floor space by demolishing 56–64 Banbury Road, and some more space by demolishing Park Villas (7–9, 11–13 and 15–19 Banbury Road). In June 1966 the Planning Committee recommended approval of the plan for the museum, but this was referred back by the full Council by twenty-six votes to eighteen. Although still reserved as a site for the museum, the proposed development did not take place because the requisite funds could not be raised. A smaller building was planned at the rear of the houses, which have now been preserved. The Conservation Area was instituted in 1968 (omitting these houses) but it was extended later. If Nos 56–64 had been demolished, the show-front of the Norham Estate would have been lost and other University departments would have followed, thus disastrously affecting the character of North Oxford.

The entrance to the Norham Manor Estate starts at the lodge of the UNIVERSITY PARKS (c.1865 by Deane). Norham Gardens curves round, ending at Lady Margaret Hall, and Fyfield Road leads off, at right-angles, to the north. The estate has an air of what Pevsner calls 'leafy sobriety' now that the trees have grown to maturity. In Norham Gardens itself most of the odd-numbered houses on the south, with views over the University Parks, are by Wilkinson, Buckeridge or Codd (Wilkinson's pupil). Nos 17 and 19 were formerly ST STEPHEN'S HOUSE and are now Norham St Edmund. Nos 2–8 on the north side are also by Codd. No. 16 is now the CHERWELL CENTRE. Nos 15, 28 and 30 are occupied by the University Department of Educational Studies. No. 13 has a plaque on it indicating that Sir William Osler, the physician and medical historian, lived there from 1907–19. In Bradmore Road, where most of the houses are by Codd, Mrs Humphry Ward lived at No. 2 in 1872/3 and then No. 5 (now No. 17) in 1880. Also in that road, again at No. 2, lived WALTER PATER in the 1880s.

Norham Road has been eaten into at the west end by buildings which do not offend the eye – the extension to WOLSEY HALL and the MAISON FRANÇAISE, for which eight houses were demolished. To the east, in the 1970s Norham End was demolished and flats built in its place. Also at the east end of the road is Benson Place, a modern terraced development (1967, by Brett and Pollen), built on the site of WYCHWOOD SCHOOL sports ground. Opposite is the Norham Gardens Lawn Tennis Club, one of the oldest in the country, where the first men's championship doubles was held in 1877 (the present club was founded in 1929); it is now no longer in Norham Gardens because extensions to Lady Margaret Hall have blocked access from that road. Crick Road, now mainly converted into flats, Fyfield Road (with the University Department of Education at No. 15 on the Norham Gardens' corner) and Norham Road were all built in 1872–80. Further north, beyond Bardwell Road, is Linton Road. No. 2 was by H.W. Moore (1894), Wilkinson's nephew, and No. 7 by A.H. Moberly (1910). In Northmoor Road was the home of J.R.R. TOLKIEN, from the 1920s to the 1940s first at No. 22, then at No. 20. No. 2 was built in the Dutch style by E.W. Alfrey and is listed Grade II. In Charlbury Road, where most of the houses are post-1900, is Blackhall Farm (No. 21). On the west side of Woodstock Road are ST MARGARET'S ROAD, Rawlinson Road (1886–9) and Staverton Road (1898–1906). Most of these houses, first inhabited by married dons, were by H.W. Moore. Farndon Road (1870–80) might have been the site for a railway station in 1851 if the plan had materialised. Warnborough Road was built from 1870 onwards. Leckford Road, with its view of the church of ST PHILIP AND ST JAMES, was completed by the end of the 1870s. Polstead Road (built 1887–94), in which was the childhood home of T.E. Lawrence, Chalfont Road (1889–99) and Frenchay Road (1895–6) contain many houses by H.W. Moore. The furthest north parts of St John's Estate were MARSTON FERRY ROAD (and just beyond it up the Banbury Road) and Bainton Road, in which the plots and house sizes are smaller than in the roads developed earlier. Cottages in Kingston Road (most of which were designed in 1870 by C.C. Rolfe) are Grade II listed buildings. This road, officially named in the 1870s, was almost on a line of the route taken by Charles I when he made his escape from Oxford in June 1644, on his way to Heyfields (or Heathfield's Hutt) and beyond (see HAYFIELD ROAD).

The name North Oxford is now generally used loosely to mean all that part of Oxford north of the MARTYRS' MEMORIAL. It can also be used as an adjective. The supplement to the *Oxford English Dictionary* offers these examples: 'She had … a Sybil Dunlop moonstone on a long silver chain. A bit North Oxfordy? Well, she was North Oxford!' (Naomi Mitchison, *We Have Been Warned*, 1935); and 'Why you should have to drag Coleridge in, only your staunch North Oxford spirit can explain' (Angus Wilson, *Such Darling Dodos*, 1950).

North Parade Runs from Nos 75–7 BANBURY ROAD into Winchester Road. Although officially named North Parade Avenue it is usually known by all the local residents simply as North Parade. The use of the word 'Avenue', said the headmistress of a local school in 1936, 'merely excites ridicule and no one ever calls the street by that name.' Before the building of the church of ST PHILIP AND ST JAMES the Parade was a cul-de-sac built at the time of the enclosure of ST GILES'. There is a myth, which many people would like to believe, that North Parade was so called because it formed the north patrolling ground of the Royalists during the siege of Oxford (*see* CIVIL WAR), and that SOUTH PARADE in SUMMERTOWN formed the south patrolling ground of the Parliamentarians. However, there is no written evidence for this: the favourite exercise grounds were PORT MEADOW and the 'New Parks'. North Parade has for many years been a street of popular small shops mainly serving the local neighbourhood.

Novels *see* FICTION.

Nuffield, William Richard Morris, Viscount (*1877–1963*). The first and last Viscount Nuffield, created 1938, motor manufacturer and benefactor, was born in Worcester, one of seven children. The family moved to HEADINGTON, where he attended the village school. He had hoped to qualify as a surgeon, but his father's ill-health made this impossible and at the age of fifteen he started work in a local bicycle shop. When refused a shilling a week rise, he resigned, and in 1893, on £4 capital, opened his own bicycle shop at the back of his father's house in James Street, Cowley St John. From selling bicycles Morris soon progressed to building them – using parts which he often cycled to Birmingham to buy. In 1904 he married Elizabeth Maud Anstey, and also started Morris Garage (later Morris Garages), running taxis and selling cars from premises in LONGWALL STREET, Nos 36 and 37 QUEEN STREET, and behind the CLARENDON HOTEL. In 1913 he announced production of the first Morris cars. In the 1921 slump, faced with ruin, he cut prices by up to £100 a car, and two years later his company's annual turnover was £6 million.

In 1926, surprised to find that so few British businessmen spoke Spanish, Morris gave £10,000 to help fund a chair of Spanish Studies at Oxford. Ten years later he gave £2 million to the University for establishing a school of medical research (*see* NUFFIELD INSTITUTE FOR MEDICAL RESEARCH). In 1943 he gave £10 million to form the Nuffield Foundation as a charitable trust, a gift described as 'the largest and most notable in the history of the nation'. This trust was principally designed to benefit medical research, hospitals and education. The managing trustees were instructed to have particular regard to: (1) the advancement of health and the prevention and relief of sickness, especially by medical research; (2) the advancement of social well-being, particularly by scientific research; (3) the care and comfort of the aged poor; and (4) the advancement of education. The Foundation is administered from Nuffield Lodge, Regent's Park, London.

By the time Lord Nuffield was eighty, he had given away £27 million, much of it in medical benefactions and to found chairs at Oxford. He always remained essentially the same – a modest man, spare, fit, and a heavy smoker, with a dry sense of humour. 'Giving away is pleasant,' he said once. 'But the worry, which comes from giving, is very great . . .'

(*See also* MOTOR CARS, NUFFIELD COLLEGE *and* NUFFIELD ORTHOPAEDIC CENTRE.)

Nuffield College

On 8 July 1937 VISCOUNT NUFFIELD visited the CHANCELLOR of the University (Lord Halifax) and offered to found a College on the CANAL wharf, which he had recently bought, on NEW ROAD opposite the CASTLE mound. One of his reasons was that he wished to improve the western approach to the city. He first suggested a college of Engineering and Accountancy, but changed his mind when he learned from the VICE-CHANCELLOR (A.D. LINDSAY) that what the University most needed was a graduate college primarily concerned with Social Studies. Lord Nuffield gave the site and £900,000 for the erection of a College and for its endowment. In October 1937 the University formally accepted the offer and Nuffield College came into being. Its trust deed and statutes contained features not normally found in other Oxford or Cambridge colleges.

Lord Nuffield laid it down that the college was for 'post-graduate work, especially in connection with the study by co-operation between academic and non-academic persons of social (including economic and political) problems. . . .' There would be no under-graduates, only graduates, usually working for a higher degree (*see* DEGREES). It would not cover science and the whole range of University disciplines but would concentrate principally on the Social Sciences. The co-operation of non-academic persons, defined in the statutes as persons competent to assist those engaged in the college and University in research by giving the fruits of their experience in practical affairs, is furthered by some dozen visiting Fellows from politics and government, industry and commerce, and public affairs in general. The other feature of the college, very much an innovation at the time, was its admittance of both men and women. The first half-dozen years of the college were marred by bad relations between the University and Lord Nuffield. He disliked the first design for the buildings and was unhappy about what he considered to be the slow development of its academic work. At that stage the college was in effect a department of the University and it was not until 1958 that it secured the independence which is a fundamental feature of the Oxford college system. But by the time he died in 1963 Lord Nuffield was happy with the college he had founded, for he bequeathed it almost the whole of his remaining wealth, including his house, Nuffield Place.

Sir Harold Butler was the first Warden, but was absent on government duties for most of his period of office. It was not until Sir Henry Clay became Warden in October 1944 that the college began to take shape. A number of permanent Fellows were appointed, and the first graduate students were selected in 1945–6. The fact that the official Fellows are not obliged to teach undergraduates makes the college attractive to those who wish to concentrate on their research and writing. By limiting the number of its students to between fifty and sixty, the college has been able to be highly selective. As soon as sufficient building became available, each student was provided with living accommodation in college or, if married, with a study. The college offers a number of one- or two-year research fellowships, mainly for those who have recently finished or are well advanced with their doctorates. These and the studentships are available in its range of studies – usually spelt out as Economics; Politics; Sociology; Social Psychology; Recent Economic, Social or Political History; Industrial

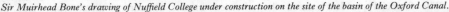

Sir Muirhead Bone's drawing of Nuffield College under construction on the site of the basin of the Oxford Canal.

Relations; Management Studies; Public and Social Administration; and International and Public Law.

In October 1985 Nuffield College had a Warden (Michael Brock), twenty-six permanent Fellows, sixteen Research Fellows and sixty-eight students. There were fifteen visiting Fellows not allocated rooms but who could stay in the college whenever they visited it. The permanent fellowships were divided almost equally between the three main fields of the college's interests; Economics, Politics and Sociology. The college also provides facilities for ten or so visiting scholars each year.

The University chose Austen St B. Harrison, FRIBA, aged forty-seven, recently architect to the government of Palestine (where all his work had been), to design Nuffield College. He recruited Thomas Barnes and Pearce Hubbard as partners to assist him. They started work in the summer of 1938 and their first design was approved by the University in January 1939. Lord Nuffield was not shown it until June, having been abroad for much of the time. On 15 August 1939 he told the Vice-Chancellor that he thought the design to be un-English and out of keeping with the best tradition of Oxford architecture, and that he would not allow his name to be associated with it. Harrison thereupon submitted an alternative design which was accepted by Lord Nuffield in March 1940. By then, however, the war was well under way and there was no chance of construction being started.

Work on the college could not begin until 1948, and the foundation stone was laid by the Chancellor of the University on 21 April 1949. Even then, so strict was the government's control of building that work could proceed only at the rate of a staircase a year. In 1955, however, it became possible to start on the hall, common rooms and library tower. These were substantially completed by 6 June 1958, when the Duke of Edinburgh presented the Royal Charter at the first luncheon served in hall. The cost of building had risen very markedly and it was no longer possible to provide out of the money available the full extent of the building originally envisaged. In any case, the plan included substantial accommodation for University departments. The financial problem caused the college to modify the plan considerably: the hall was reduced in size, building of a formal chapel was deferred, and development of the western side of WORCESTER STREET was abandoned, at least for the time being. The chapel tower was developed to provide a library book-stack. In 1956 the Nuffield Foundation, on Lord Nuffield's recommendation, made a grant of £200,000 to enable the lower quad to be completed. The present buildings were finished in 1960.

They comprise an upper and a lower quadrangle. The upper contains the hall, library and administrative offices of the college; the lower contains the residential accommodation and studies for Fellows and students. The tower provides an open-access book-stack of ten floors, holding some 70,000 books. There is also a reading room. In place of the chapel originally designed on traditional lines there is a small upper chapel on L Staircase. This owes a great deal to John Piper, who advised the college. The pews and altar are in black and white wood, the windows were designed by John Piper and executed by Patrick Reyntiens, who were also responsible for the windows in Coventry Cathedral. The reredos and the cross are the work of John Hoskins. The stone used is blue Clipsham quarried in Rutland (see STONE), the roofing being of Colley Weston stone tiles from North Oxfordshire. The tower is 100 feet high to the parapet, the flèche adding another 60 feet. It was the first tower to be built in Oxford for two centuries.

The furniture in hall was designed by Edward Barnsley, the chairs being made by him, the tables and benches by R.H. Fyson of Lechlade. Over the fireplace in the hall, carved out of a single block of stone by David Kindersley of Cambridge, is the founder's coat of arms. The hall also contains a portrait of Lord Nuffield, painted by Sir Arthur Cope, RA, and presented to him by the staff and workpeople at his COWLEY works; originally it hung in Nuffield Place. In the corridor outside the hall there are drawings of three previous Wardens: Sir Henry Clay (1944–9), A. Loveday (1949–54) and Sir Norman Chester (1954–78), and of the first official Fellow, Dame Margery Perham (Fellow 1939–63 and Honorary Fellow 1963), and of G.D.H. Cole (Fellow 1939), one of the earliest Fellows of the college. There is also a drawing of Sir Norman Chester by David Hockney in the corridor outside the library reading room.

At an early stage in the building, the college decided to set aside a fixed sum for the commissioning of the works of contemporary artists, taking the view that these were an essential part of any new building. Among the fruits of that important decision are the large painting *Late Summer Parkland with a Lake*, by Ivon Hitchens, in the Senior Common Room; a mural, *The Seasons*, by Derek Greaves and Edward Middleditch, in the library reading room; and a bronze fountain by Hubert Dalwood in the upper quad. Unfortunately, Dalwood's original conception, a fine spray or curtain of water from small holes in the half bowl, has been abandoned, leaving the sculpture with no obvious purpose. The sculpture on the wall at the foot of the tower is *Apparition* by F.I. Kormis.

The present Warden is Sir David Cox.

Nuffield Institute for Medical Research

Headley Way, Headington. Established in 1936 with an endowment from LORD NUFFIELD. It was originally housed in the RADCLIFFE OBSERVATORY and in buildings nearby, but moved to a new building in the grounds of the JOHN RADCLIFFE HOSPITAL in 1970. Its work is directed by the Board of the Faculty of Clinical Medicine (*see* FACULTIES).

Nuffield Orthopaedic Centre

Windmill Road, Headington. This nationally famous hospital developed, with several modifications of name and function, from an eight-bedded 'house of recovery'. The Wingfield Home opened in 1872 for convalescent cases, chiefly from the RADCLIFFE INFIRMARY. It was built on an 18-acre site to the design of William Wilkinson, the Oxford architect. The Rev. John Rigaud, Fellow of Magdalen College and an indefatigable worker for charitable causes, raised considerable funds locally following the receipt of £1500 from Mrs Hannah Wingfield to found a convalescent home. The resident steward and housekeeper maintained close links with the infirmary and, for a time, provided lodgings in the home for the Headington district nurse. By 1908 there were thirteen convalescent beds at the Wingfield.

In October 1914 the home changed its function to become a twenty-bedded military hospital under the

E.H. Shepard's cartoon of Lord Nuffield lavishing money upon the University appeared in Punch *in 1936, the year in which he gave £2 million for establishing a school of medical research.*

Third Southern General Hospital. By 1918 the gift of additional buildings, including a small operating theatre, from Miss K.J.D. Feilden of High Walls, PULLEN'S LANE, commandant of the Wingfield Military Hospital, allowed an increase in the number of its beds to 100. At the end of the war the hospital was transferred to the Ministry of Pensions and in 1922 it was handed over to the new Wingfield Committee.

Gathorne Robert Girdlestone (1881–1950), the first British Professor of Orthopaedic Surgery, was appointed Honorary Consultant to the Wingfield in 1920. Aware of its potential for the orthopaedic treatment of war casualties, Girdlestone quickly realised the usefulness of the Wingfield's resources for his own subject of special interest – the care of crippled children suffering from joint or bone tuberculosis, paralysis or congenital deformities. Under his leadership, by 1924 the Wingfield had developed into a 125-bedded open-air hospital, with three private wards and seventeen associated orthopaedic out-patient clinics in Oxfordshire, Berkshire and Buckinghamshire. Following the gift of £70,000 from Sir William Morris, VISCOUNT NUFFIELD, in 1931, it was renamed the Wingfield–Morris Orthopaedic Hospital and was rebuilt and modernised under the architectural supervision of R. Fielding Dodd to accommodate 140 patients. Further Nuffield bequests established the Nuffield Department of Orthopaedic Surgery in 1937, with Girdlestone as its first Professor. His plans to enlarge the hospital came to fruition when the Second World War necessitated the provision of 600 extra orthopaedic beds, some of which were located, initially, in the new CHURCHILL HOSPITAL.

The Wingfield–Morris gave up its voluntary status in 1948, becoming part of the National Health Service. Although the incidence of tuberculosis had decreased, beds were needed increasingly for polio-myelitis and orthopaedics, and for patients with degenerative conditions affecting mobility. Girdle-stone's achievement in pioneering a regional service, and his brilliant work with crippled children, led to a suggestion, which he declined, to rename the hospital the Nuffield–Girdlestone Hospital. In 1950 the hospital became known as the Nuffield Orthopaedic Centre, in recognition of its most generous benefactor. Its present international reputation owes much to the inspiration of Girdlestone and to the resources of Lord Nuffield. In 1986 it had 196 beds, with eighteen at the Mary Marlborough Lodge, the associated Disabled Living Research Unit, which was named after the Duchess of Marlborough, chairwoman of the hospital committee from 1936 to 1961.

287

Observatory Street Named after the nearby RADCLIFFE OBSERVATORY, the street runs between WOODSTOCK ROAD (Belsyre Court) and No. 111 WALTON STREET.

Officers of the University The University officers are: CHANCELLOR, High Steward, VICE-CHANCELLOR, Pro-Vice-Chancellors, Vice-Chairman of the GENERAL BOARD OF THE FACULTIES, PROCTORS (and Pro-Proctors), ASSESSOR, Deputy Steward, PUBLIC ORATOR, Bodley's Librarian (*see* BODLEIAN LIBRARY), Keeper of the Archives (*see* ARCHIVES, UNIVERSITY), Director of the ASHMOLEAN MUSEUM, Clerks of the Market, REGISTRAR of the University, Counsel to the University, University Auditor, BEDELS, Clerk of the Schools, Marshal, Verger.

Many of the above have separate entries. Those who do not are noticed here.

The *High Steward*, whose office is held for life, is appointed by the Chancellor. His special duty was to hear and 'determine criminal causes of the gravest kind, such as treason and felony, at the mandate of the Chancellor, and according to the laws of the land and the privileges of the University whenever the accused is a scholar or privileged person'. The *Deputy Steward* is appointed similarly. The privilege of having such causes tried by an officer of the University was first granted by Henry IV in 1406; the first holder is recorded in 1453. The offices are now purely honorary, and the last records of cases being heard before the Steward or his Deputy date from 1634. The High Steward is ex-officio VISITOR of Wolfson College and nominates the chairman of the Disciplinary Court.

Keeper of the Archives. His office was instituted in 1634; it is his duty to take charge of and to arrange all the muniments and papers concerning either the estates, possessions, rights and privileges of the University, or the endowments of professorships, and all the registers and records of the University.

Clerks of the Market. Control of the market, in order to secure fair dealing for students in provisions of all kinds, was granted to the Chancellor by King Edward III in 1355. Two Clerks of the Market are appointed, who must be Principals of halls, Masters of Arts, or Bachelors of Divinity, Medicine or Law. The Clerks, who receive a small stipend, are invited to the annual Corn Rent Dinner of Estates Bursars, at which the latest price of corn is formally reported; there are now no duties.

Counsel to the University. Under Statute I.ix, the Counsel to the University is qualified for membership of CONGREGATION. His duties are not laid down by statute, but are implied by his title. Since 1971 the office has been held by Sir Frank Layfield QC.

University Auditor. A named partner in the firm of accountants which audits the University's books, he comes to the University once a year to report on and discuss the accounts with a Committee of the Curators and the secretary to the UNIVERSITY CHEST.

Clerk of the Schools. The full-time officer who runs the management of the EXAMINATION SCHOOLS, including their use for lectures and examinations. He is responsible to the Curators of the Schools.

Marshal. The head of the University police, or BULLDOGS. As such he reports to the Proctors. The policing of the SCIENCE AREA is a particularly major and responsible task.

Verger. The Verger's main duties are to attend at all sermons preached before the University and all meetings of Congregation, CONVOCATION and HEBDOMADAL COUNCIL; to provide for the ringing of the bell on the occasion of all such sermons or meetings; and to provide for the cleaning and the arrangement of books and furniture in the University Church of ST MARY THE VIRGIN.

(*See also* UNIVERSITY APPOINTMENTS COMMITTEE.)

Old Ashmolean Building *Broad Street*. One of the finest examples of 17th-century architecture in Oxford, the Old Ashmolean was built in 1679–83 and was probably designed by Thomas Wood, the Oxford master-mason (*c*.1643–95), who was, perhaps, inspired by the plan of a similar building which SIR CHRISTOPHER WREN was to have built for the Royal Society in London. The building was opened by James, Duke of York, later James II, whose cipher and crown can be seen on the north front. He and his wife and daughter were 'entertained first with rarities in

The Old Ashmolean in Broad Street, which was built in 1679–83, now houses the Museum of the History of Science.

Old Palace, also known as Bishop King's Palace, St Aldate's in 1821 before its early 17th-century façade was reconstructed.

the upper room, and afterwards with a sumptuous banquet there at the charge of ye University. Then they went downe to the Elaboratory, where they saw some experiments to their great satisfaction'. The building had cost £4500 – a huge sum that so depleted the University's purse that the purchase of books for the BODLEIAN LIBRARY had to be suspended for some years. This, and a distaste for the 'new philosophy', led to several of those 'Doctors and Masters' who had been invited to the Musaeum Ashmoleanum three days later declining to visit it and dismissing its collections as mere baubles.

The ground floor was divided by two rows of fluted Ionic columns in 1833 and the steps on the north side, removed in 1733, were restored in 1958. The museum was built to house the collection of natural curiosities inherited by ELIAS ASHMOLE from John Tradescant the Younger (*see* ASHMOLEAN MUSEUM), the School of Natural History and the first chemical laboratory in England. The first curator was Robert Plot (1640–96), Professor of Chemistry and author of the *Natural History of Oxfordshire* (1676), who wrote to a friend in February 1683, 'Fryday next I goe for London to fetch down Mr Ashmole's Collections towards furnishing this House, when I guess I shall spend about a month in Catalogueing and boxing them up.' They were eventually packed into twenty-six big boxes which were sent to Oxford by barge; and the catalogues, compiled by Plot and his assistant Edward Lhuyd, who succeeded him as keeper in 1690, ultimately appeared in Latin. After Lhuyd's time, the museum's reputation declined and a German visitor at the beginning of the 18th century was horrified by the way the public was permitted to behave, 'even the women' being allowed up for sixpence and then running 'here and there and grabbing at everything and taking no rebuff from the Sub-Custos'. The building now houses the MUSEUM OF THE HISTORY OF SCIENCE.

Old Fire Station Arts Centre The former Oxford Playhouse Company, Meadow Players, leased from the City Council the old Oxford city fire station premises in GLOUCESTER GREEN to use as offices, wardrobe and properties storage, and for scenery painting. When the company closed and vacated the premises in 1973, the Oxford Area Arts Council was formed to take over the building and to operate it as a centre for performance and participation arts, dance, drama and musical performances, arts-and-crafts workshops and fairs, exhibitions, lectures and recitals. The responsibility for the performing arts was transferred to the ST PAUL'S ARTS CENTRE in 1985. At the beginning of 1987 the Old Fire Station Arts Centre was closed, but was reopened by the City Council that same year.

Old Gatehouse *2 Botley Road.* Named after the old gated toll-house pulled down in 1850 to make way for the new RAILWAY station. In the same year the present building was erected as a toll-house. It became an inn in 1869. Additions were made to the north side in 1902 to the designs of J.R. Williams.

Old Greyfriars Street A newly constructed street south of the WESTGATE CENTRE crossing the site where the Greyfriars or Franciscan Friars Minor resided when they came to Oxford in 1224 and settled in ST EBBE'S. (The house in which they later lived, also called Greyfriars, is still in existence in PARADISE STREET.) The Greyfriars eventually moved to IFFLEY ROAD but the name was kept in St Ebbe's and it was therefore suggested, when the new road came into existence in 1969, that the word 'Old' be added to the name to indicate the earlier connection with the Greyfriars.

Old Palace *96–7 St Aldate's.* Also known as Bishop King's Palace, after Robert King, first BISHOP OF OXFORD, though there is no evidence that he, or indeed any other bishop, ever lived here. In the Middle Ages the site was occupied by a Dominican guest-house. Originally two houses, the larger part was built in the 1620s by Thomas Smith, a brewer, the smaller, once called Hither Friars, slightly earlier. The smaller property was acquired by the Smith family in 1621 and the two were soon afterwards united, making the house one of the biggest in Oxford. It is presumed that as a Member of Parliament and MAYOR of Oxford, Thomas Smith would, on occasions, have entertained Charles I while he was living across the road at Christ Church during the CIVIL WAR. The ST ALDATE's façade was reconstructed by Russell Cox in the 1950s and the property enlarged in 1970–1 to designs by Ahrends, Burton and Koralek. The Palace now houses the CATHOLIC CHAPLAINCY.

Old Parsonage Hotel   *3 Banbury Road*. Stands on the site of a hospital founded in the 11th century for the care of the poor and infirm of the parish of ST GILES'. Rent was paid to the adjacent church in the form of candles made in the hospital. The Norman building was still in existence in 1390 when one John Ocle bequeathed elevenpence to each poor person living here. It was rebuilt in the early 17th century as a house for the priest who had lived in the hospital until its closure. One of the doorways is dated 1659. Undergraduates who have lived here include Oscar Wilde (Magdalen), RONALD KNOX (Balliol) and Compton Mackenzie (Magdalen). The building is now a hotel with thirty-five bedrooms. The interior contains some original work, including fireplaces and early 18th-century panelling.

Old Road   Part of the old road from Oxford to London which left by ST CLEMENT's and passed over Shotover Hill.

Old Schools Quadrangle   see SCHOOLS QUAD-RANGLE.

Old Tom   *101 St Aldate's*. On 25 March 1681 Andrew Harvey opened an inn called the Unicorn and Jacob's Well. The name was retained until 1865 when it was changed to Great Tom after the bell-tower of Christ Church (*see* GREAT TOM), which stands almost opposite. The present name was first used in 1878.

Oman, Sir Charles William Chadwick (*1860–1946*). Won a scholarship from Winchester to New College, obtained a First in LITERAE HUMANIORES in 1882 and in Modern History in 1883, and was elected to a fellowship at All Souls. In 1884, for an essay on 'The Art of War in the Middle Ages', for History (*see* PRIZES AND SCHOLARSHIPS). The subject was more fully developed in his *History of the Art of War in the Middle Ages* (1898), one of numerous books which he wrote on all kinds of subjects, including numismatics. He was himself a keen collector of coins. The seven huge volumes of his magisterial *History of the Peninsular War* occupied him for almost thirty years, for many of which he occupied the Chichele Chair of Modern History, to which he was appointed in 1905. His remarkable memory, wide knowledge and friendly manner made him a delightful companion. A strong Conservative, he was BURGESS for the University of Oxford from 1919 to 1935. A tall and striking

The eighty-year-old Sir Charles Oman, who was appointed Chichele Professor of Modern History in 1905.

figure in his grey morning coat, he was sometimes referred to as the uncrowned King of Oxford. For some time he lived at FREWIN HALL. His *Memories of Victorian Oxford* appeared in 1941. A most charming portrait of Oxford before the First World War was provided by his daughter, Carola, in *An Oxford Childhood* (1976).

Orchard, William   (*d.1504*). Architect and 'free-mason of Oxford', he was engaged in 1475 by William of Waynflete, Bishop of Winchester, Lord Chancellor of England and founder of Magdalen College, as master-mason for the chapel and cloister of Magdalen, which were completed by 1478 and on which he did further work in 1479. It is probable that it was he who, in 1480, was made responsible for the superb vault of the DIVINITY SCHOOL, which was finished in 1483 and in which his initials can be seen on one of the bosses. He lived all his life in Oxford and was buried in the church of ST FRIDESWIDE's PRIORY, now CHRIST CHURCH CATHEDRAL, the vaulting of the choir of which is so similar in style and technique to that of the Divinity School that it is very likely that he was responsible for this too.

Organs   There are records of the existence of organs in the colleges and churches from mediaeval times, and 17th-century instruments by the Dallam family are known to have been in Magdalen, New College and the Music School, and by Bernard ('Father')

Smith in the SHELDONIAN THEATRE, ST MARY THE VIRGIN and CHRIST CHURCH CATHEDRAL. Among 18th-century work were organs by Renatus Harris in the Sheldonian and in Trinity, and by Byfield in the HOLYWELL MUSIC ROOM and in Jesus College. No pipework from these instruments survives in Oxford apart from some Dallam pipes stored at New College. The Magdalen Dallam instrument, however, was moved to Tewkesbury Abbey in 1736 and partially survives there. Smith's original case at Christ Church is incorporated in the present organ, and some Smith pipe shades in the new St Mary's instrument. The 1725 Harris case from the Sheldonian now houses the Pembroke organ. Such pre-1800 organs as now exist in the city are of 20th-century importation. Merton and Mansfield have 18th-century one-manual chamber organs in addition to their main instruments. A 1761 one-manual Snetzler, formerly a subsidiary organ in Magdalen, is now in All Saints Convent, while since 1985 the Holywell Music Room has had a handsome two-manual organ built in 1790 by John Donaldson of Newcastle, which was formerly in Belvedere House, Dublin. The previous Music Room instrument, a one-manual 18th-century house organ from the Low Countries, is now housed in the Faculty of Music rehearsal hall.

A number of 19th-century organs have survived in more or less original condition, including three by Henry Willis in Wadham (two manuals, 1862), Balliol hall (three manuals, 1885) and the TOWN HALL (four manuals, 1897), the last having some particularly fine reedwork. A substantial amount of William Hill pipework remains at ST GILES' CHURCH (three manuals, 1875 with later additions), and to a lesser extent in the former ST PHILIP AND ST JAMES organ (two manuals, rebuilt by J.W. Walker, 1864) which was moved to ALL SAINTS, LIME WALK, HEADINGTON, in 1986. Other substantial 19th- and 20th-century instruments of non-classical design include Balliol chapel (three manuals, Harrison, 1937), Hertford (three manuals, Hunter rebuild, c.1930), Mansfield (three manuals, Vowles, 1890), ST CLEMENT'S CHURCH, MARSTON ROAD (four manuals, Nicholson), ST EDWARD'S SCHOOL (three manuals, the former Magdalen instrument by Gray & Davison/Harrison/Hill, Norman & Beard 1855–1964, rebuilt for St Edward's by Deane, 1986), ST MARY AND ST JOHN (three manuals, Norman & Beard, 1914), ST MARY MAGDALEN (three manuals, Jardine, 1962), Sheldonian Theatre (three manuals, Harrison, 1963) and WESLEY MEMORIAL METHODIST CHURCH (three manuals, Nicholson, 1878 and 1892/ Willis, 1950). The first organ to return to classical principles was the fine Frobenius in The Queen's College (two manuals, 1965). This has been followed by Merton (two manuals, J.W. Walker, 1968), New College (three manuals, Grant, Degens & Bradbeer, 1969), Brasenose (three manuals, Collins, 1972), ST JOHN THE EVANGELIST (one manual, Nicholson, 1978), Christ Church (four manuals, Rieger, 1979), St Hugh's (one manual, Tamburini, 1980), Magdalen (two manuals, Mander, 1986), St Mary the Virgin (three manuals, Metzler, 1986) and St Peter's College (two manuals, Neil Richerby, 1987).

Oriel College On 24 April 1324, the Rector of ST MARY THE VIRGIN, Adam de Brome, obtained from King Edward II licence to found 'a certain college of scholars studying various disciplines in honour of the Virgin' and to endow it to the value of £30 a year. Brome was a chancery clerk engaged in the King's confidential business; his intentions are uncertain, but he had already been involved in University affairs and, though founding his statutes on those of Merton (1274), he specifically directed the Fellows to study in the higher faculties; presumably they were to be educated for service in both Church and State. By January 1326 he had revised and expanded his plan, with Edward II himself as founder: the King's foundation charter was accompanied by the gift of St Mary's, and de Brome became the first Provost. Meanwhile, the Bishop of Lincoln, Henry Burghersh, who seems to have been associated with the gift, issued further statutes with himself as VISITOR, and these appear to have been subsequently observed rather than the King's. It has usually been assumed that this was due to the impending fall of Edward II, but it is more likely to have been a simple internal development making the original statutes more specific. The college's charter was confirmed by Edward III. The earliest home of the ten Fellows thus established was to be TACKLEY'S INN, but by 1329 they had received through royal grant a large house near the end of Shidyerd Street, now ORIEL STREET. This was La Oriole, which stood on the site of the present front quadrangle and was so called from its *oratoriolum*, or projecting upper window. The more spacious site was to be the kernel of the college, which gradually expanded northward to the HIGH STREET with piecemeal acquisitions of property throughout the 14th century.

The college established by Adam de Brome was one of several founded in the shadow of government, though the first to boast a royal founder. It was a small institution with an income at first of about £30 a year, rising to £60 by 1350 and £180 a century later. Neither de Brome's kin nor his countrymen found a foothold in Oriel, one of the least regional of colleges: a slight early bias towards Derbyshire and Nottinghamshire may be due to the second Provost, William of Leverton (1332–48). The Provost and ten (occasionally more) Fellows studied Theology, Canon Law and, increasingly, Arts; and rooms were also let to other masters not on the foundation who paid rent, among them the future Archbishop Thomas Arundel, in the 1360s, and the scholar and churchman Thomas Gascoigne. They added substantially to the college's wealth and reputation, attracting benefactors like John Frank, Master of the Rolls. Frank endowed four fellowships about 1441 for south-westerners, and by 1529 the total fellowship had reached eighteen. The ancestor of the front quadrangle, on the same site though smaller, was built probably in the century after 1350; the first chapel, built on the north side by the Arundels about 1376, was succeeded about 1420 by another on the south, of which one doorway remains. There was a library, of which a book-list was drawn up probably before 1375; but the books left at St Mary's by Bishop Cobham were seized by the University about 1337 and, in spite of litigation, were never returned (*see* BODLEIAN LIBRARY). As its early manuscript collection shows, pre-Reformation Oriel was a society of young logicians and theologians who played their part in the controversies and other disturbances of the age. A document of 1411 records the proceedings of Archbishop Arundel against the Fellows who resisted his VISITATION of Oxford: it

J.M.W. Turner's watercolour drawing of Oriel College quadrangle c.1801, showing the hall porch with its pierced parapet tracing the words 'REGNANTE CAROLO' *to commemorate Charles I, in whose reign the quad was completed.*

reveals riotous young Fellows coming in late with strangers and offering violence to the Provost, while others' resistance to Church authority brought them under suspicion of Lollardy (*see* LOLLARDS). Oriel's lack of a regional bias brought the sporadic rivalries of northerners and southerners into college, which may explain the disputed elections to the provostship in 1385, 1402, 1417 and 1422 (*see* NATIONS). One of the Fellows of the 1420s, Reynold Pecock, displayed an idiosyncratic approach to the defence of orthodoxy through English tracts which would ultimately lead to his condemnation and disgrace. His critic Gascoigne's presence in college must have led to lively polemic, while the promotion to bishoprics of three successive Provosts, John Carpenter (1428–35), Walter Lyhert (1435–46) and John Hals (1446–9) ensured the college powerful patrons.

By 1500 the original endowment of St Mary's with the appropriation of Aberford, Yorkshire, had been expanded with the further appropriations of ST BARTHOLOMEW'S HOSPITAL (Bartlemas) to the east of Oxford (1328), and Coleby, Lincolnshire (1346), and the manors of Wadley (1440) and Littleworth (1478) in Berkshire. At the same time, undergraduates were indirectly being integrated into Oriel, as elsewhere, through the practice of Fellows becoming Principals of ACADEMIC HALLS where they were instructed. By the convention of certain halls being rented successively by Fellows of particular colleges, their members were informally attached to a college. Oriel's dependent halls were ST MARY HALL on the High Street, the manse of the vicar of St Mary's, which retained its separate identity until 1902; Bedel Hall, south of St Mary Hall,

and by about 1503 annexed to it; and Martin Hall, where the present chapel now is. By 1502 Oriel owned them all. According to the antiquary Miles Windsor, Thomas More was one of the undergraduates of St Mary Hall. Bishop Carpenter left money in 1451 for undergraduate benefit, the St Anthony Exhibitions for scholars to live in Bedel Hall. But it was only after the Reformation that undergraduates were admitted as members of the college, either as Fellow Commoners, ordinary commoners or bible-clerks (*see* COMMONERS *and* SERVITORS). From the beginning of the 16th century more is known of the internal affairs of Oriel from the Dean's register. It throws light on the college's stance in the great religious question which faced the whole of Oxford after 1530 (*see* ROMAN CATHOLICS), and confirms the strong Catholic tradition which lasted up to the provostship of Roger Marbeek – a Provost of advanced views but brief tenure (1565–6). Two former Fellows, Edward Powell and George Crofts, were executed for refusing the Oath of Supremacy (1539–40), though Provost Ware (1530–8) was said to have held reformed opinions. In the middle of the century a strong Catholic influence was exercised by the Dean, Morgan Phillips, whose pupil William (later Cardinal) Allen abandoned his fellowship to found the English College at Douai (1568). During the 1570s several Fellows joined him there.

The transformation of the college to its recognisably modern form began during the long provostship of Anthony Blencowe (1574–1618), who gradually brought it to accept the new religious order. A practising civil lawyer, he strengthened the college's legal independence by obtaining a charter of incorporation (1603). The admission of undergraduates, among them Sir Walter Ralegh about 1572, strained its limited space. One result was evidently the development in 1590–8 of the garden (which became the second quadrangle) for recreation, with a raised terrace and a ball-court. Another result was the plan to rebuild entirely the front quadrangle. Blencowe himself left the largest contribution to the funds, from which, in 1620–2 and 1637–42, the present quadrangle was formed; and the fund-raising was carried on by his successors William Lewis (1618–21), who began the building, and John Tolson (1621–44), who completed it. This ambitious undertaking was one of the largest architectural projects to be realised in pre-Restoration Oxford, and was the largest in Oriel's history. It is a variation on the quadrangle of Wadham (c.1611) and designed to incorporate a new hall and chapel on the east. Comparison with Bereblock's woodcut of 1566 suggests that the quadrangle was larger than its predecessor, and with its three storeys must have provided considerably more room. The undergraduate occupants were still to some extent pupils of particular Fellows, who even seem to have sub-let them their rooms, and until the early 18th century they continued to share sets. In Blencowe's time they evidently received instruction which combined old-fashioned and perhaps antiquarian learning with a puritan spirit: an example is *Day's Dyall*, the lectures of the Dean, John Day, given in the chapel in 1612–13. Among the undergraduates were two notable future parliamentarians, Sir Robert Harley (1597–9) and William Prynne (1615–21). Where the Fellows' sympathies lay during the CIVIL WAR is, however, unclear. Like other colleges, Oriel suffered a severe decline in income and had to suspend elections to fellowships and reduce commons by half, as well as surrender most of her PLATE. The Fellows were certainly regarded with suspicion by the Visitors appointed by Parliament in 1647, returning evasive answers to their demand for the college's muniments. Under the guidance of Provost Saunders (1644–53) and Robert Say, Dean in 1647 and Provost 1653–91, they managed to retain their independence at the cost of seven Fellows expelled by the Visitors, their places being filled up, as Dean Fell put it, by 'the dregs of the neighbour University'.

During the late 17th and 18th centuries Oriel's development was mainly domestic. The college's estates, which had been augmented in the 16th century with lands at Shenington in Oxfordshire and Swainswick in Somerset now provided a fair income, poorer than Merton or Corpus Christi but apparently richer than Balliol or University College. In 1667 there were twenty-five undergraduates, a number which grew slowly during the 18th century, in the care of the Provost and eighteen Fellows. Only a minority of the Fellows were tutors, and many were only seasonally resident. The fellowship was unusually open, with only the four Frank Fellows restricted to particular counties; the majority were recruited from the University at large, and were elected, at least as early as 1696, after a written examination and disputation. In this way men of ability such as John Robinson of Brasenose (elected 1675) were brought in. Subsequently Bishop of London, Ambassador to Warsaw and Stockholm, and an authority on Sweden, Robinson was a notable

benefactor of the college, endowing an exhibition and erecting the Robinson Building in 1720, which he adorned with a runic inscription. Oriel was beset with the rivalry of parties which rent the University after 1688. Provost Carter (1708–27), in particular, was a strong Whig, and exerted his influence to strengthen the Whig interest in successive fellowship elections, as THOMAS HEARNE relates and Carter's own memorandum book confirms. The majority of Fellows, notably Richard Dyer the botanist, were Tories or at least resentful of the Provost's interference; and after one particularly outrageous episode in 1723, when a Fellow was elected with only three votes, there was an appeal to the Bishop of Lincoln as Visitor. Complex litigation followed in which the Bishop supported the Provost, but was overturned by the Court of Common Pleas determining that Edward II's statutes of January 1326 and not those of Burghersh were valid: thus returning the visitorship from the Bishop to the Crown. Six Fellows whose election the Provost had refused to recognise were admitted by the Senior Fellow and the Dean (1726). The Provost died of apoplexy soon afterwards, leaving, however, a benefaction with which the Carter Building was put up in the garden. By his death the political allegiances he had promoted were becoming irrelevant; but his defeat vindicated the tradition that learning alone was the criterion for fellowship. The next half-century was a period of peace, or torpor. Although only Gilbert White the naturalist (Fellow 1744–93) is remembered from this period, Fellows such as Edward Bentham (1731–55), whose 'learned and lively conversation' was admired by SAMUEL JOHNSON, and undergraduates like John Bowle (1743–50), the first critical editor of *Don Quixote*, show that intellectual life continued.

The greatest period of Oriel history began with the reforming provostship of John Eveleigh (1781–1814) and is notable for both the Noetic and the Tractarian movements, the focus of each of which was in Oriel: for the first time, reminiscences like those of Tom Mozley and the *Memoirs* of MARK PATTISON bring college characters to life. Eveleigh's first achievement was the building of the enlightened new library and common room which housed Lord Leigh's benefaction of books (1791) and completed the second quadrangle, once the garden. Eveleigh was a leading figure in the reform of the University examinations in 1800 which established the Honour Schools of LITERAE HUMANIORES and Mathematics (*see also* SCHOOLS). Together with Edward Copleston, who eventually succeeded him (1814–28), he placed Oriel fellowship elections entirely on the basis of academic merit. This was not a complete innovation in a college where the majority of Fellows had been elected after examination from the University at large; but Eveleigh and Copleston made an Oriel fellowship the mark of intellectual distinction most sought after in the University. Their chosen instrument was the tutorship, the small body of three or four Fellows who undertook the education of the undergraduates. As he explained in a counterblast to the utilitarian *Edinburgh Review* (1809), Copleston aimed at a liberal, enlightened education through the traditional study of Aristotle; and the Oriel tutors, through college lectures and intense personal attention to the minds of their pupils, were to encourage the competitive spirit of 'emulation'. A remarkable body of Fellows applied

The front of Oriel College from a drawing by De La Motte showing the dome of the Radcliffe Camera with the spire of St Mary the Virgin in the background.

the system, including the logician RICHARD WHATELY and the future headmaster of Rugby THOMAS ARNOLD. Together they formed the 'Noetics', a body united in free-thinking method rather than any particular belief; the common room, it was said of their time, 'stank of logic'. Naturally such argumentative men generated their own opponents, in part from the Oriel undergraduates who, like the Fellows, were now a carefully selected intellectual élite. The OXFORD MOVEMENT was the child of the Noetics in sharing their strong commitment to tutorial education and their willingness to contemplate great changes in the Church, but in contrast it looked back to the tradition of the Fathers. In Oriel, where its root could be found in Whately's contemporary JOHN KEBLE's 'great and intelligent dislike' of the Evangelicals, it found powerful protagonists in HURRELL FROUDE and, above all, in JOHN HENRY NEWMAN (Fellow 1822–45). Newman's and his friends' use of the tutorship as a means of religious influence early brought them into conflict with the new Provost, Edward Hawkins (1828–82), who, in removing them from that office, precipitated its gradual decline from uniqueness. But during these years many of the best of Oxford scholars held fellowships at Oriel: besides Hurrell Froude, there were Charles Marriott (1833–58), R.W. Church (1838–53), Arthur Hugh Clough (1842–9) and MATTHEW ARNOLD (1845–50).

By 1850, as other colleges developed their tutorial systems, the pre-eminence of Oriel was abating. The ROYAL COMMISSIONS of 1850 and 1877 brought the permanent tutorial Fellow into existence, though formally the old limited body of tutors survived at Oriel until 1938. In the later years of Provost Hawkins the fellowship grew steadily more liberal, and after he finally retired to his Rochester canonry in 1874 (retaining only the title) the Fellows led by the Dean, D.B. Monro (Provost 1882–1905), secured new statutes which relaxed their obligation to take Holy Orders and permitted them to marry. At the same time St Mary Hall, under the principalship of an Oriel Fellow, D.P. Chase, was destined by the second Royal Commission to full union with Oriel; this was effected in 1902, and following the large bequest of CECIL RHODES, the High Street front of the hall was rebuilt as the Rhodes Building by Basil Champneys (1909–11). The new building, though in questionable taste, enabled a larger body of undergraduates to reside in college. Monro was also the leader of a tutorial body which joined participation in the European world of learning with the old tradition of the pastoral tutorship. Himself a leading philological scholar and original Fellow of the British Academy, he presided over a fellowship in which brilliant minds like that of John Cook Wilson (Fellow 1874–89) were inclined to put tutorial teaching before publication. The succession of Regius Professors of Modern History, beginning with William Stubbs (1866–84), added another dimension of wide-ranging secular scholarship. In the 20th century the tradition was maintained, notably in the provostship of Sir David Ross (1929–47); through his agency Oriel was able to provide a home for some of the most brilliant continental scholars to take refuge in England from Nazi persecution.

Equally characteristic of Oriel in the age of Monro and his successors have been its links with the overseas English-speaking world. One of the earliest was formed by the career of C.H. Pearson (Fellow 1854–74), who played a great part in Australian education and government; and many more were forged through Cecil Rhodes, who had been a mature student from 1873 to 1881 and whose legacy to the college proved to be not only the endowment necessary for the Rhodes Building but a lively and permanent Commonwealth and American connection. With the provostship of Sir Zelman Cowen, former Governor-General of Australia (Fellow 1947–50; elected 1982) this relationship reached maturity. College life in the 20th century has changed in many respects. The agricultural depression diminished Oriel's income from estates, and a number of fellowships were temporarily suppressed between 1881 and 1914. Many of the estates were eventually sold in 1922, and until 1985 the college's endowments were almost wholly derived from investments and urban property. At the same time the number of undergraduate and graduate students has increased, reaching 354 in 1984, including nearly a hundred graduates. Women have been admitted since 1984. Among 20th century alumni there have been scholars, scientists and public men beyond number, and Oriel has also been distinguished in sporting achievement, notably in holding the headship of the river (*see* BUMPING RACES) consecutively for longer than any other college. To house the greater numbers, the college has transformed its properties across Oriel Street into a fourth quadrangle, preserving their variegated character and joining them to the main site by a tunnel. Incorporated in the new quadrangle is the original home of the college, Tackley's Inn.

The visitor to Oriel enters through the front gate from ORIEL SQUARE, and immediately confronts the scene recorded by DAVID LOGGAN in 1675, the work of the early 17th-century rebuilding. The most prominent feature is the hall porch opposite, with its pierced parapet tracing the words 'REGNANTE CAROLO' to commemorate the reign of Charles I in which the

'The Oriel Fathers' – from the left: *Manning, Pusey, Newman, Keble and Wilberforce – mostly Fellows of the college in the 1830s and 1840s.*

quadrangle was finished. The statues above represent the founder, Edward II, and either James I or Charles I, surmounted by the Virgin, patron of the college (*see* STATUES). The quadrangle is a notable achievement of early 17th-century architecture, though its architect is unknown. The east side is a remarkable feat of symmetry, uniting in one façade the hall, aligned on a north–south axis, with the chapel at right-angles to it. The latter, contemporaneous with the quadrangle, is a barrel-vaulted construction, lengthened into the antechapel in 1884; the panelling and marble floor are original. Only a small fragment of mediaeval glass survives in the north-west window of the antechapel, but there is a remarkable painted window by William Peckitt, *The Presentation in the Temple* (1767). Above the altar is Bernard van Orley's *Carrying of the Cross*. The hall is not large, but contains a fine hammerbeam roof with louvre above the original central hearth, now demolished. It is adorned with portraits, notably of Whately, Keble and Newman. The second quadrangle is reached through a passage in the north side. It retains the appearance of the garden it originally was, though now dominated by the magnificent neo-classical library, with common room beneath, designed by James Wyatt (1788–92); the common rooms were the first in Oxford to be built for the purpose. The library houses the fine collection of Lord Leigh. This building completes the transformation begun by the Robinson Building on the east side and the Carter Building on the west. Separate blocks until the early 19th century, they imitate the gabling of the front quadrangle. A further passage leads to St Mary's Quadrangle, a happy jumble of buildings from a 15th-century wall in the south-west to the 20th-

century Rhodes Building. Notable among them are the hall of St Mary Hall, now the Junior Common Room, built in 1640, with the chapel (now the Junior Library) above; and the strange timber-framed building on the east put up in 1743. The fourth quadrangle, still taking shape, is approached by a passage in Oriel Street, or by the tunnel. It is dominated by the 17th-century tennis court which fills the centre; on its south side is a house of the same date, Kylyngworth, and on the east a number of houses largely of the 18th century, which now open inwards to the quadrangle.

Sir Zelman Cowen's two predecessors as Provost were Kenneth Charlton Turpin (1957–80) and Sir Michael Meredith Swann (Baron Swann) (1980–1); his successor was Professor Ernest Nicholson.

The corporate designation of the college is The Provost and Scholars of the House of the Blessed Mary the Virgin in Oxford, commonly called Oriel College, of the Foundation of Edward the Second of famous memory, sometime King of England.

(Shadwell, C.L., and Salter, H.E., eds, *Oriel College Records*, Oxford, 1926; Richards, G.C., and Salter, H.E., eds, *The Dean's Register of Oriel*, Oxford, 1926; Richards, G.C., and Shadwell, C.L., eds, *The Provosts and Fellows of Oriel College, Oxford*, Oxford, 1922; Mozley, T., *Reminiscences Chiefly of Oriel College and The Oxford Movement*, London, 1882; Rannie, W.D., *Oriel College*, London, 1900; Emden, C.S., *Oriel Papers*, Oxford, 1948.)

Oriel Square Formerly known as Canterbury Square, the Canterbury Gate of Christ Church being at the south-west corner. The name was changed after the Second World War at the request of Oriel College which maintained that it had originally been known as Oriel Square. Certainly ORIEL STREET ran right down to the corner of MERTON STREET until the late 19th century. In addition to Oriel itself and the eastern part of Christ Church, the square contains several 18th-century houses owned by Oriel College.

Oriel Street   In about 1220 this street was known as Shidyerdestret and there is a recorded use of Sidyerd Street in 1238, which probably refers to a palisade. In 1337 Shidierd is recorded and a 1342 cartulary of ST FRIDESWIDE'S PRIORY mentions Shidyard Street. It was also spelt Schydiard or Shydyard. According to THOMAS HEARNE in 1728 it was Sched (or Writers') Row. This is possibly because books which had been printed in MAGPIE LANE were sold here at the sign of the St John the Evangelist's Head. By 1762 it had become St Mary (or St Mary's) Hall Lane. (ST MARY HALL was incorporated with Oriel College as late as 1902.) A map of 1814 shows the lane running in a southerly direction through what is now ORIEL SQUARE as far as the lodgings of the President of Corpus Christi College, just as Shidyard Street did before it. Hunsingore's Inn was where Corpus now is. Today Oriel Street runs from No. 102 HIGH STREET into Oriel Square. By JAMES INGRAM's time (mid-19th century) the name Oriel Lane was being used as an alternative to St Mary Hall Lane. The word derives from La Oriole (the French form of *oratoriolum*), the name of a house which belonged to Edward III and was given to the college in 1329. It was sometimes spelt Oryell and comes from a building with a large projecting window. Coaches used to drive down Oriel Lane, which has always been a narrow street, taking the back way to the yard of the ANGEL INN in the High Street. The Rev. W. Tuckwell, writing in 1900, says that Oriel Street was Skimmery Hall Lane until 1838. A large covered REAL TENNIS court is situated behind the stuccoed houses facing the college. Oriel College built a tunnel under the street which was completed in August 1986.

Oriental Institute   *Pusey Lane*. Situated in what is really a mews off PUSEY STREET, the Oriental Institute building was erected in 1958–60 to the design of Easton & Robertson, Cusdin Preston & Smith. It houses the lecture and teaching rooms, administrative offices and library of the Faculty of Oriental Studies. The institute was founded in 1960 by University statute. The library, which occupies most of the ground floor and part of the basement, was created in 1961 from a number of separate, specialised collections, including the private libraries of past professors, notably in the fields of Arabic and Sanskrit studies. The Nissan Institute is financed from a benefaction made in 1979 to the University by the Nissan Motor Company Ltd; its library is in Church Walk.

Oseney Abbey   Founded as an Augustinian priory by ROBERT D'OILLY's son, also Robert d'Oilly, in 1129. Legend has it that he was persuaded to do so by his wife Edith, who had seen a flock of magpies flying across a meadow and had been persuaded that they were restless souls from purgatory. Within a century of its foundation, the buildings of the priory, which was raised to the rank of abbey in about 1154, spread over an extensive area to the south of the present RAILWAY station. The abbey became a popular centre

The remains of the mediaeval Augustinian Priory, Oseney Abbey, in the 17th century.

for councils in the 13th century: one held here in 1222 established St George's Day as a lesser holy day. Its canons were of good reputation and on friendly terms with both town and University.

In 1238 the abbey was the scene of a violent fracas involving the papal legate who had come to Oxford 'to reform the Corruptions of the Place'. A deputation of scholars went to welcome him, according to an account of the affair provided by John Ayliffe, 'presuming a good Reception of themselves. But as soon as they came to the Abbey-Gate, they were rudely saluted by the Porter, in his loud Italian voice, demanding their Business; who reply'd, they came in Duty to attend the Legate; but he, in contumelious Language, refus'd them Admittance at the Door, which they forcing open went in, the Legate's Retinue at the same time repelling them with Staves; but at length falling together by the Ears, many Blows ensued on both sides: Whilst some of the Scholars ran home for Arms, there happen'd a poor *Irish* scholar to wait at the gate for Alms, on whom the chief Cook (being the Legate's Brother) threw scalding Water; which a *Welshman* perceiving, shot the cook dead through the body, which caused an uproar throughout the House. The Legate hearing this Tumult ran into the Belfry, and locking the Door, stay'd there till Midnight, but the Scholars in no wise pacified, fought them in every Corner, exclaiming against him as Usurer, Simoniack, and one guilty of extortion etc. The Cardinal, in the Silence of the Night, coming out of his Fort, convey'd himself over the river to the King at *Wallingford*, who, on this Outrage, sent troops to protect the Legate's Attendants.' The University was placed under an interdict; the scholars were required to find sureties for their good behaviour; and their goods were forfeited and taken over by the MAYOR and bailiffs in the King's name.

The fine church of the abbey was 332 feet long and contained nave with double north and south aisles, presbytery, choir, the Lady Chapel, five other chapels behind the high altar, as well as a central and west tower. It became the cathedral of the new diocese of Oxford in 1542. Its last abbot, Robert King, was the first BISHOP OF OXFORD (see ABBOTS OF OSENEY).

After the see was moved to ST FRIDESWIDE'S in 1546, the dismantling of the abbey church began. Furnishings, bells and lead were first removed; then, following the lease of the site to a clothier, iron, glass and woodwork were removed, and most of the old buildings were demolished. An explosion in a powder-house in 1643 caused further damage, and a few years later the remaining west tower was pulled down. All that can be seen of the once splendid church today is one small 15th-century building by the BOTLEY ROAD.

Osney In existence as early as 1200, the village to the west of Oxford had various spellings from Osanig to Osseney. Ousen-eye means 'island in the Ouse', which was a possible early name for the THAMES. The spelling Osney seems to have come into use from the 1920s. The discovery of a burial urn of the latter part of the 5th century indicates an early settlement of the area. In 1315 the Keeper of the King's Horses was attacked by some Abingdon men at Oseney. Two new mills built by the ABBOT OF OSENEY in about 1350 were blamed for the flooding of the CASTLE mills. In 1381 the ninety residents of the village included clothiers, tailors and leather-workers. In 1418 a jury decided that the manors of North and South Oseney were outside the liberty of the town of Oxford and therefore not entitled to its privileges. From about this time the settlement was urban rather than rural. In 1546, at a time of widespread unemployment, there was a scheme to set up a cloth factory in Oseney to employ 2000 people. Oseney Lock was opened in 1790. One Edward Edge had contracted to build it for £750; but the officials at the county gaol made a lower tender which was accepted. It was accordingly built by prisoners and a Mrs Hill was put in charge of the lock in 1793 for a wage of 3s 6d a week. The modern Mill Street runs from No. 3 BOTLEY ROAD, southwards to an old cemetery, alongside the main railway line. For some years Pickford's had a depository, the large sign of which was plainly visible on a building which towers over the gravestones. At one time the graveyard looked so neglected that Professor Arthur Goodhart, Master of University College, gave a sum of money to the City Council to improve it.

In the 19th century a substantial suburb known as Oseney Town grew up on an island west of the original Ousen-eye. The attractive terraced houses which make up today's Osney Town are part of a CONSERVATION AREA. It consists of streets named after points of the compass, together with Bridge Street (which runs from Botley Road, near Osney Bridge, to the weir), Swan Street and Doyley Road. The streets were first laid out in 1851 by G.P. Hester, Town Clerk of Oxford, and the land was divided into forty lots of meadow land suitable for building. Much of the ground was raised above flood level but the surrounding land constantly suffered from flooding,

as a result of which the place was sometimes known as Frog's Island. The first houses were occupied by the end of 1852. No. 4 West Street was built in 1853 by Lawrence Wyatt (1800–87), who was a member of the Oxford Local Board. On Nos 2–5 Bridge Street is a plaque with the date 1853. The West Oxford Democrats Club on the corner of North and East Streets was built in 1881 by J.C. Tanner.

Osney Mead Formerly a meadow at the end of FERRY HINKSEY ROAD, the land was developed as an industrial estate after a public inquiry in 1961. It now houses several well-known firms, including ALDEN PRESS, Axtel, Perry and Symm Masonry (stonemasons), Blackwell Scientific Publications (see BLACKWELL'S), KNOWLES & SON (builders), OXFORD INSTRUMENTS GROUP, and the *Oxford Mail* and *Oxford Times* (see NEWSPAPERS).

Other Place, The Cambridge.

Our Lady Help of Christians, Church of *Hollow Way, Cowley.* In 1920 the Salesian Fathers took over the Cowley parish from the Franciscans. Although they had enlarged the church in Crescent Road, the population growth over the years necessitated a new building. The present church, on the corner of Salegate Lane and Hollow Way, was designed by Patrick Sheahan in 1962. It is built of fawn-coloured bricks with stone dressings. Over the main entrance there is a statue of the Madonna against a panel of blue mosaic, and on the north side of the church is a small bell-turret. The plan, which is cruciform, accommodates 350. The Salesians, an educational Order founded in 1859 by St John Bosco, had at one time both a junior and a secondary school in the area. Until 1986 the Fathers had a novitiate and house of studies in Crescent Road. This is being replaced by a presbytery, now under construction next door to the church, which will house the few Salesians remaining in Oxford.

Oxfam During the Second World War the Ministry of Economic Warfare in the United Kingdom was putting pressure on Hitler's Germany by preventing, as far as possible, the import of food supplies into mainland Europe which, in 1941–2, was under his control. At that stage a number of famine relief committees were set up throughout the United Kingdom, anxious to mitigate the suffering and hardship of the civilian populations, particularly the children, then under the control of Germany. One of these committees was based in Oxford and was known as the Oxford Committee for Famine Relief. It was formed at a meeting held in the library of the University Church of ST MARY THE VIRGIN on 4 October 1942, the chair being taken by Canon T.R. Milford, then vicar of St Mary's. A local businessman, Mr C. Jackson-Cole, agreed quite early in the life of the committee to act as honorary secretary and he served in this capacity until he died in 1979. He was particularly concerned to link the skills and organising ability of business with the appeal and needs of the charity world. The Oxford Committee for Famine Relief proved to be the first of a number of charitable ventures in which he was involved throughout the rest of his life.

The committee was engaged, with its counterparts in some 200 other towns, in publicising the conditions applying in occupied Europe, particularly Greece, and in pressurising the government to allow the import of food consignments controlled and distributed by the International Red Cross. This activity continued until the opportunity to collect and distribute clothing and food supplies in Europe became available a few years later. Collection and distribution schemes continued in the post-war period in various parts of Europe, including Germany, and by about 1948–9 most of these famine-relief committees had reached the conclusion that their work was finished and they wound themselves up. In Oxford the honorary secretary was of the opinion that there was a need for an additional national body to fill the gaps as far as needs in the poorer parts of the world were concerned. He carried the majority of the committee with him in the ensuing debate and the work of the Oxford Committee for Famine Relief, centred primarily on the collection of clothing, was then expanded beyond Europe. It extended to the Middle East after the formation of Israel in 1948 and the creation of the Palestine refugee problem; to Korea, with assistance to refugees stemming from the war in that country; to refugees from Hungary in 1956, and so on.

Oxfam's first permanent shop was opened in 1948 at No. 17 BROAD STREET, which also served as the administrative centre in the early years of the charity. The shop is still open but has now been joined by another 800 or so, scattered around most towns and cities in the United Kingdom and providing the charity with its biggest single source of income.

In the 1950s, when the charity began to grow rapidly, it was compelled to spill over into a number of offices in the centre of Oxford but all these activities were brought together under one roof when the present headquarters were built in SUMMERTOWN in 1962.

The name change was not achieved until about 1958–9, following the registration of the committee as a charitable company limited by guarantee. Thus 'Oxfam' began to be used generally in the committee's appeals, information activities and fundraising. Over the years this five-letter word has become known worldwide and by 1985 the charity was one of the leading charities in the United Kingdom, with an income of over £50 million.

Oxford Almanacks The promotion of a learned press worthy of a great University was the work of JOHN FELL, who, with three colleagues, leased the control of PRINTING from the University in 1671. One of his first publications was the Oxford Almanack for 1674. Unlike the popular almanacs of the time, this was a large sheet decorated with an elaborate allegorical engraving. Classical and Norse deities symbolise Time and the calendar is inscribed on a tower rising from the sea which represents the might of Britain. It was not only a grandiose and scholarly advertisement but a source of finance for academic publishing. No Almanack appeared the next year, but since 1676 the Oxford Almanack has been published annually. In addition to the calendar, the large sheets give information such as tides, lists of monarchs and University officers, and they are decorated with a variety of subjects which illustrate the changing interests of the University. For 156 years the pictures and calendar were printed from a single copper plate;

The Oxford Almanack for 1683. Time is symbolized by the group on the right, with a horoscope derived from Raphael's School of Athens *and the* Sun God *after Giulio Bonasone. Oxford, in the background, shows Wren's Tom Tower (left), built in 1682.*

for the first fifty years they were engraved by Michael Burghers, the Engraver to the University.

Most of the Almanacks were designed by HENRY ALDRICH, who became Dean of Christ Church in 1689. He had a large collection of engravings after Italian and French masters on which he drew for his 'inventions', copying or adapting details from them and in one case reproducing the entire composition – Poussin's *Dance to the Music of Time*. Details from Emblem Books and astrological diagrams were also used. The subjects were usually allegories on Time and there were allusions to the University and to contemporary politics. Some were thought to be subversive and the engraving for 1706 was debated in the House of Lords on suspicion of reflecting Jacobite sympathy in the University. The intellectual wit and scholarly invention, as well as the imputed political meaning, made the Almanacks immensely popular. Some were printed on silk scarves.

GEORGE CLARKE, a Fellow of All Souls, was responsible for the Almanacks after Dean Aldrich's death in 1710. As well as allegorical subjects, he illustrated designs for architectural developments in Oxford, some of which were not built. Drawings for 1720 and 1721 were commissioned from Sir James Thornhill. The University was growing and for the next thirty years George Vertue drew and engraved designs for new college buildings, some of which were designed by Clarke. Vertue's antiquarian interests are shown by his portrayal of college founders and benefactors. Allegory appeared again in 1755, the year after the controversial Oxford parliamentary election. It was officially explained by the press as 'Science or Learning conducting Mankind from Sloth, Ignorance, and Sensuality . . .' but a pamphleteer saw in it a High Church attack on the immorality of a Fellow and the Whig politics of Exeter College. Ten years later the University's loyalty to the Crown was demonstrated in allegories recording the achievements of the nation since the accession of George III. Since then, with few exceptions, the Almanacks have illustrated topographical subjects. The first, in 1768 and 1769, were by J.B. Malchair, an Oxford drawing master, then for twenty years watercolours by Michael Angelo Rooker were engraved by his father, Edward Rooker. Other well known artists were commissioned and in 1799 the delegates bought two watercolours from J.M.W. Turner for £21 and later eight more, but there were complaints of inaccurate drawing and only nine were reproduced. James Basire, Engraver to the Society of Antiquaries, engraved Turner's and Edward Dayes's watercolours, and Joseph Skelton was the engraver from 1815 to 1831.

In 1832 steel engraving replaced copper engraving and the calendar was printed from type. Eight landscapes were contributed by Peter De Wint, and J.H. Le Keux painted and engraved the Almanacks from 1856 to 1870, some illustrating old buildings and others the new University buildings which were taking their place. Since 1871 a variety of reproductive processes have been used, including Woodbury Type and autotype, early forms of photographic reproduction, and wood engraving and etching. Collotype was first used in 1894 and colour collotype in 1911. This and the following Almanacks reproduce originals of earlier engravings. Between 1906 and 1951 fifteen drawings and watercolours by Sir Muirhead Bone illustrated landscape and architectural subjects and scenes such as ST GILES' FAIR. Since 1947 the Almanacks have been printed by offset lithography, most of them in colour, and the subjects have included some of the new University and college buildings.

Oxford and Cambridge Magazine   A periodical containing stories, poems, essays and reviews which appeared in twelve monthly numbers in 1856. It was largely paid for by WILLIAM MORRIS, who anonymously contributed to it. EDWARD BURNE-JONES was another Oxford contributor. Several of the pieces from Cambridge were supplied by Henry Lushington (1812–55), Tennyson's friend and early admirer. D.G. Rossetti's 'Burden of Nineveh' first appeared in the magazine. (*See also* MAGAZINES.)

Oxford and Cambridge Schools Examination Board   *Elsfield Way*. Founded in 1873 in response to a recommendation by the recently formed Headmasters' Conference to provide external examinations and award certificates to candidates at public schools, a 'joint board' was formed with two offices, one in Oxford and one in Cambridge, its governing body consisting of delegates from both Universities. Until 1944 at Cambridge and 1947 at Oxford, administration was conducted by part-time secretaries who were Fellows of colleges; since then there have been a full-time secretary and staff for each office (or 'side') working together in the organisation of single examinations for each subject. A 'School Certificate' was instituted in 1905 and a 'Higher Certificate' in 1918, these being absorbed into the General Certificate of Ordinary and Advanced Examinations in 1951. From 1888 the Oxford office had no permanent home; from 1935 it was situated at No. 74 HIGH STREET and the moderation of examinations was conducted in the University EXAMINATION SCHOOLS. In 1964 it leased the Territorial Army Drill

Hall at Elsfield Way, NORTH OXFORD, for all its functions.

Oxford and County Secretarial College   Popularly known as the 'Ox and Cow', the college was founded in 1936 by Ernest Hall, who died in 1983. It is now carried on from No. 34 ST GILES' by his son Peter, and has about 200 students, who are taught the use of word processors and similar computer-related subjects in addition to shorthand and typing.

Oxford and Swindon Co-operative Society   The Oxford Co-operative and Industrial Society Ltd was formed in 1872. Its first premises were at No. 39 GEORGE STREET and it has remained in the street ever since. At first trading was in the evenings and on Saturday afternoons only, the committee members acting as salesmen. Business flourished and the committee decided to open the shop all day – 8 a.m. to 7 p.m., Monday to Friday, with 'late-night shopping' on Saturdays until 10 p.m. Many small branches were opened during the 19th century. Among the assets of the Clifton Hampden Society, which was taken over in 1897, was a donkey used to deliver purchases to customers; it was replaced by a pony and trap.

In 1938 the society changed its name to the Oxford and District Co-operative Society Ltd. Its range of services was constantly being expanded: a milk round had been started in 1929, and in 1943 a café and restaurant were opened in HIGH STREET and named the Angel after the ANGEL INN and the first coffee house in England, which had stood on the site (*see* COFFEE HOUSES). A new bakery was opened in the BOTLEY ROAD in 1955, and the society's first supermarket at LONDON ROAD, HEADINGTON, in 1957. In the same year the department store at Nos 13–15 QUEEN STREET was opened, extended the following year by the purchase of the old Electra Cinema (*see* CINEMAS). In 1969 the society merged with the Swindon Society to become the Oxford and Swindon Co-operative Society.

In 1975 Marks & Spencer exchanged their store in CORNMARKET STREET for the Co-operative Society's store in QUEEN STREET, which they have since rebuilt and greatly enlarged. In 1985–6 the Co-op redeveloped the old Marks & Spencer store in Cornmarket by creating several smaller shops, but retaining the basement food hall and a small part of the ground floor. At the same time they modernised their Threeways House in George Street and rebuilt that part of the island site which faces GLOUCESTER GREEN. This is now their main store in Oxford and their headquarters.

Oxford Bach Choir   Founded in 1896 by Basil Harwood with the intention of promoting performances of Bach's works, following the example of the Bach Choir of London, which had been founded some twenty years earlier. In 1901 Hugh (later Sir Hugh) Allen became conductor and by 1902 it was usually performing together with the longer-established Oxford Choral and Philharmonic Society, the two finally merging in 1910. From 1902 also the choir was partnered by what became known as 'Dr Allen's Orchestra' (in 1919 renamed the Oxford Orchestral Society and now the OXFORD SYMPHONY ORCHESTRA), which continued to be the choir's regular orchestra until 1971, since when professional orchestras have been engaged. During Allen's twenty-five-year reign

299

the choir developed a wide repertoire, and it gave one of the first complete performances of Vaughan Williams's *Sea Symphony* in 1911. With a mixed town-and-gown membership, which at times has been up to 400 strong, it has given many generations of undergraduates their first experience of singing the great choral masterpieces. In 1926 Allen was succeeded by William Harris, and later conductors have included Thomas Armstrong, Sydney Watson, Simon Preston and Christopher Robinson.

Oxford Bags Flannel trousers with very wide bottoms fashionable among undergraduates at the University in the 1920s.

Oxford Bath Also known as a hip-bath or a sitz-bath (from the German *sitzen*, to sit). An oval portable bath with an inclined semi-circular back.

Oxford Blues The Royal Horse Guards were called the Oxford Blues in 1690 after their commander the Earl of Oxford and their blue uniform. The nickname was later shortened to the Blues and was incorporated in the regiment's title of the Royal Horse Guards (the Blues). The regiment was amalgamated with the Royal Dragoons in 1969 to form the Blues and Royals (Royal Horse Guards and 1st Dragoons).

Oxford Chair A mid-19th-century upholstered easy chair with open padded arms on turned supports and a seat projecting beyond the supports.

Oxford Churches Trust In 1853 a fund was formed, later known as the Oxford Fund, to augment, for the benefit of evangelical incumbents, Oxford livings in the Crown's gift. The first church to benefit

Loose flannel trousers with wide bottoms, known as Oxford Bags, were commonly worn by undergraduates in the 1920s.

was ST CLEMENT'S. In 1864 the group bought the advowsons of ST EBBE'S, ST PETER-LE-BAILEY, and St Clement's, and vested them in five trustees, later known as the Oxford Trust. In 1881 HOLY TRINITY, BLACKFRIARS ROAD, was acquired for the Trust and in 1914 St Matthew, GRANDPONT.

Oxford Civic Society Founded in 1969 with the objects of encouraging the citizens of Oxford to express their views on their city, and of conveying their opinions on town planning and services to the authorities. The society co-operates with local amenity societies and community groups in order to preserve the best in the environment from piecemeal planning, traffic, noise and pollution. The society organises public meetings and lectures and publishes a newsletter.

Oxford Clay A deposit of stiff blue clay underlying the coral rag of the Middle Oolite in the Midlands, especially Oxfordshire.

Oxford Corners A printing term to denote ruled border lines enclosing the print on a page which cross and extend beyond each other at the corners in the manner of an OXFORD FRAME.

Oxford Drug Co. *Cornmarket.* The original ironmongery, paints and medicines business was bought in 1882 by Frederick Pearson from Alderman Stanley Lowe, a former MAYOR of Oxford. Before electric light was introduced, the Oxford Drug Co. supplied most of the oil to light the lamps in undergraduates' rooms. The present premises in CORNMARKET STREET were built in 1912 and necessitated large sections of the CITY WALL being taken out. A secret passageway to the church of ST MICHAEL AT THE NORTH GATE was also uncovered. In 1959 a wide opening was made in the wall between the chemist's shop and BOSWELLS so that the two shops, which are in the same ownership, could be opened into one. There is a toy department in the basement of the Oxford Drug Co.

Oxford English Dictionary The name given in a reprint of 1933 to what had originally been known as *A New English Dictionary on Historical Principles.* The historical method which was adopted involved tracing over 400,000 words for their earliest appearances and giving nearly 2 million quotations as examples of their use, these quotations being collected by more than 800 voluntary researchers. Work began in 1858 under the editorship of Herbert Coleridge (1830–61) and F.J. Furnivall (1825–1910), who collected materials over a period of twenty years. The philologist JAMES AUGUSTUS HENRY MURRAY (1837–1915), was appointed editor in 1873 and the first part of the dictionary, *A–Ant*, was published six years later. Murray continued as chief editor until his death and was succeeded by Henry Bradley (1845–1923), whose review of the first volume had revealed his remarkable knowledge of English philology. Bradley came to live in Oxford in 1896 and thereafter (having become a Fellow of Magdalen) most of his time was devoted to the Dictionary. Other editors were William Alexander Craigie, later Sir William Craigie (1867–1957), who was appointed Rawlinson and Bosworth Professor of Anglo-Saxon in 1916, and Charles Talbut Onions (1873–1965), who left Birmingham to work on the

Dictionary in Oxford, where, except for one brief period, he spent the rest of his long life.

Although Murray had estimated that the Dictionary would be completed within twelve years of the appearance of the first volume, it was not in fact finished until 1928. The supplement of 1933 was followed by another supplement, edited by Robert William Burchfield, Fellow of St Peter's College, who began work on it in 1957. This has appeared in four volumes – 1972, 1976, 1982 and 1986 – and contains words which came into use when the main Dictionary was being prepared or after its publication. The Second Edition of the Dictionary, with the supplement and additional words, was published in 1989. With the aid of computers it took 5 years to prepare.

The Shorter Oxford English Dictionary is an abridgement in two volumes of the larger work, officially authorised by the delegates of the OXFORD UNIVERSITY PRESS. The *Concise Oxford Dictionary of Current English Based on the Oxford English Dictionary and its Supplements* is also published by the Clarendon Press (*see* OXFORD UNIVERSITY PRESS). This has been several times revised for new editions since its first appearance in 1911 and is constantly reprinted with corrections and additions.

Oxford Eye Hospital *Walton Street*. Patients with eye disorders or injuries were originally treated at the RADCLIFFE INFIRMARY by the honorary physicians and surgeons. Robert Walter Doyne (1857–1916), founder of the Eye Hospital, was a general practitioner with a particular interest in eye problems. He opened the first Oxford District Eye Dispensary in May 1885 in temporary premises in a builders' yard next to the TAYLOR INSTITUTION. Five hundred patients were seen there in five months; thirty-four of these were admitted as in-patients to temporary premises at No. 68 GREAT CLARENDON STREET.

In November 1885 the MAYOR of Oxford, Alderman Robert Buckell, appealed publicly in support of the infant Eye Hospital, which for five months had accommodated in-patients at Nos 35–6 WELLINGTON SQUARE, with out-patient facilities at 22 Wellington Square. The hospital was formally opened in December 1886. By 1894 it had outgrown its premises and, with funds raised by voluntary subscription, rented the former fever block of the Radcliffe Infirmary, vacated at the opening of the new City Isolation Hospital at Cold Arbour (*see* RIVERMEAD REHABILITATION CENTRE). The altered buildings were officially inaugurated as the Oxford Eye Hospital by the Earl of Jersey on 6 March 1895. Separated from the Radcliffe Infirmary by a fence until 1948, the hospital maintained its individuality and partial independence, issuing its own annual reports and having its own management committee.

There were six building adaptations, starting with the addition of an upper storey in 1903 and culminating in major modernisation following a rebuilding appeal in 1945. The Eye Hospital was continually under pressure: out-patient attendances doubled between 1939 and 1945, and improved facilities were required for eye-surgery and orthoptics. The entire hospital was evacuated to the CHURCHILL HOSPITAL in 1949 during rebuilding. In July 1950 Sir William Morris, VISCOUNT NUFFIELD, performed the re-opening ceremony, celebrating the transformation of the former fever block into an efficient specialist hospital, acting as the Regional Ophthalmic Centre

for Berkshire, Buckinghamshire and Oxfordshire.

The Margaret Ogilvie Readership in Ophthalmology was established in the University in 1902 and, on 17 June, Doyne was appointed as the first Reader. The hospital provides postgraduate and undergraduate teaching for the Diploma in Ophthalmology. It supplies scientific and clinical material for the University Department of Ophthalmology, and training schools for ophthalmic nurses and orthoptists. By 1986, its centenary year, the Oxford Eye Hospital had again outgrown its facilities and new resources were urgently required.

Oxford Frame A frame for pictures or texts in which the horizontal and vertical members form a cross at each corner, thus:

Such frames were much used for hymn boards in churches when the design of church furniture was influenced by the ideals of the OXFORD MOVEMENT, from which the name of the frame may well have been derived. They were also often used for framing photographs of college groups and teams.

Oxford Gazette The first newspaper to be printed in England, it made its appearance on Tuesday, 14 November 1665, when the royal Court was at Oxford because of the Great Plague and a regular news-sheet was sorely missed by its denizens. Its founder was the celebrated journalist Henry Muddiman (*b*.1629), but after a few numbers the editorship came under the control of Sir Joseph Williamson (1633–1701), the influential statesman and diplomatist. After the return of the Court to London, the *Oxford Gazette* became the *London Gazette*, which Pepys described as 'very pretty, full of news and no folly in it'. As a record of official appointments, notices of bankruptcy and other such announcements, it still exists and is issued by Her Majesty's Stationery Office.

(*See also* MAGAZINES *and* NEWSPAPERS.)

Oxford Group The connection of the Oxford Group with Oxford is slight. Dr Frank Buchman (1878–1961), an American evangelical Lutheran minister, came, it is said, with two Cambridge undergraduates to Oxford in 1921 and began to hold house-parties at Oxford to campaign for the renaissance of the practice of the 'truths of simple Christianity'. This fact, together with the application of the word Oxford by the South Africans to a team from the group which visited that country, led to the establishment of the name – perhaps helped by a reminiscence of, or even confusion with, the OXFORD MOVEMENT. In 1938 the Oxford Group became better known as Moral Rearmament, and the term has by now fallen into desuetude.

Oxford Harmonic Society Choral society, founded in 1921 as the Iffley Glee Club and assuming its present title in 1924. Its membership of about 120 is drawn from both city and University, and over the years it has revived many neglected works besides performing the standard repertoire. Among its conductors have been Reginald Jacques, Sydney Watson, George Thewlis, Peter Ward Jones and Philip Cave.

Oxford High School for Girls *Belbroughton Road.* Founded in 1875 as the eighth school to be established by the Girls' Public Day School Trust, its first home was in ST GILES' HOUSE, No. 16 ST GILES', where there were twenty-nine pupils. In 1880 it moved to No. 21 BANBURY ROAD, which had been built for the school to the designs of SIR THOMAS JACKSON. (The building, with its distinctive cupola and decorated terracotta façade-columns, is at present used by the University Department of Metallurgy.) By 1888 there were 240 girls on the school roll, and by 1951, 468. In 1945 it became a direct-grant school, and in 1957 moved to its present building, designed by Stanley Ramsay, in the quadrangle of which there is a bust in bronze, *Deirdre*, by Epstein. The lower school has some fifty girls from nine to eleven years old, and the upper school some 500 aged between eleven and eighteen years, a high proportion of whom leave to go on to university or other further education. In 1976 it became an independent day school for girls. Among its former headmistresses is Dame Mary Warnock, and former pupils who have achieved distinction are the writer Rose Macaulay, the economic historian Eileen Power, the scholar Helen Darbishire, the actresses Margaret Rawlings and Maggie Smith, and the poet Elizabeth Jennings.

Oxford Historical Society *see* HISTORIANS.

Oxford Industrial and Provident Land and Building Society Ltd Oxford's building society was founded in 1860 and registered under the Industrial and Provident Societies Acts in 1871. The society laid out eight building estates in plots some 20 feet wide in Oxford between 1871 and 1892. A typical estate was that between the WOODSTOCK and BANBURY ROADS in SUMMERTOWN. The houses in Oakthorpe Road and Stratfield Road were all on this estate, as well as those along the Banbury Road north of Oakthorpe Road, which are now all shops. The society's offices were first in GEORGE STREET, and later in NEW INN HALL STREET. In 1962 the society moved to No. 154 COWLEY ROAD and changed its name to the Oxford Provident Building Society; it then registered under the Building Societies Acts. In 1974 it was taken over by the Rugby and Warwick Building Society, which, in the same year, became the Heart of England Building Society.

Oxford Instruments Group The business was founded in 1959 by Martin Wood (now Sir Martin Wood), who started the Oxford Instruments Company in a shed at the bottom of his garden in NORTH OXFORD. He was a research officer in the CLARENDON LABORATORY. The business started with some unique technology in magnet design and had the technical and academic support of the University. It grew steadily and expanded, and is now involved in the development, manufacture and marketing of high-technology products in the field of scientific, medical and industrial equipment. The group became a public limited company (plc) in 1983. It has premises on OSNEY MEAD industrial estate and elsewhere, and the companies in the group include Oxford Instruments

(superconducting magnet and cryogenic systems), Oxford Magnet Technology (magnet systems for NMR (Nuclear Magnetic Resonance) whole-body scanners), Oxford Medical Systems (health-care equipment based on ambulatory patient-monitoring) and Oxford Automation (monitoring and control systems for industry).

Oxford **(magazine)** When in 1930 Lionel Curtis proposed the formation of an OXFORD SOCIETY he envisaged as its organ an elaborate and expensive journal which would be read in influential circles and help to secure endowments to preserve Oxford's historic buildings and its standing in the academic world. In the event, only the *University Report* was issued to members in the first two years, but in 1934 it was decided that a magazine more in accordance with Curtis's notions and, as he had proposed, to be called *Oxford*, should be published three times a year. The first volume contained short articles by such distinguished contributors as John Buchan, Philip Guedalla and H.A.L. FISHER and two hitherto unpublished drawings by Muirhead Bone.

During the war the magazine was much reduced in extent and frequency, only one a year appearing between 1941 and 1949, when publication resumed at twice-yearly frequency. Notes from all colleges appear in the May number and extracts from the University Report and VICE-CHANCELLOR's Oration in the December number. The original cover, designed by the Printer to the University, depicted the University crest on an ochre background, and this was superseded in 1963 by a dark-blue cover with drawings of Oxford scenes. Since 1977 it has had a plain blue cover with a simpler crest.

Oxford goes to all members of the Oxford Society and to academic libraries throughout the world. It has not been on sale to the public since 1968. Its contents include profiles of distinguished senior members of the University, notes on colleges, appointments to professorships, reports of the functions of branches, articles on such subjects as undergraduate admissions and 'Forty-Six Years Ago in Keble', and book reviews.

Oxford Mail *see* NEWSPAPERS.

Oxford Mixture A very dark-grey woollen cloth.

Oxford Movement A religious movement originating in Oxford in 1833, which had as its major objectives a return by the Anglican communion to a 'Catholic' Church, not Roman Catholic, faithful in doctrine and ethos to the pure Church of the Early Fathers, and, concomitantly, a disavowal of Erastianism, or the undue influence of the State in Church affairs. The Movement, whose adherents were often known as Tractarians or Puseyites, was at its height between 1833 and 1845. The most famous of the figures connected with it are JOHN HENRY NEWMAN, his mentors JOHN KEBLE and RICHARD HURRELL FROUDE, EDWARD BOUVERIE PUSEY, Isaac Williams, W.G. Ward of Balliol, and the Movement's distinguished historian, R.W. Church; but there can be no doubt that the moral and intellectual leadership of the Movement belonged to Newman. Immense as was the Movement's significance in England's religious history, its political implications as an ecclesiastical wing of the

Conservatives' resistance to the Liberals in an age of reform should not be forgotten.

Newman himself always regarded the Oxford Movement's birthday as 14 July 1833, when John Keble preached the ASSIZE SERMON in the University Church of ST MARY THE VIRGIN. This was later published under the title of *National Apostasy*. The subject of Keble's attack was the suppression of ten Irish bishoprics, regarded as symptomatic of the government's willingness to take high-handed liberties with the relations between Church and State. Shortly afterwards a meeting took place at the parsonage of Hugh James Rose (the only Cambridge figure connected with the Movement) at Hadleigh in Suffolk; and from this fateful meeting (at which neither Keble nor Newman was present) resulted the *Tracts for the Times*. The first of these *Tracts*, of which there were to be ninety in all, was dated 9 September 1833. It was published anonymously, though Newman's authorship did not go unknown for long. Its once famous opening words were:

'FELLOW-LABOURERS, – I am but one of yourselves – a Presbyter; and therefore I conceal my name, lest I should take too much on myself by speaking in my own person. Yet speak I must; for the times are very evil, yet no one speaks against them.

'Is not this so? Do not we "look one upon another", yet perform nothing? Do we not all confess the peril into which the Church is come, yet sit still each in his own retirement, as if mountains and seas cut off brother from brother? Therefore suffer me, while I try to draw you forth from these pleasant retreats, which it has been our blessedness hitherto to enjoy, to contemplate the condition and prospects of our Holy Mother in a practical way; so that one and all may unlearn that idle habit, which has grown upon us, of owning the state of things to be bad, yet doing nothing to remedy it.'

Newman went on to argue the principle of the apostolic succession of the bishops and the validity only of that priesthood upon which the hands of true bishops had been laid. Many other *Tracts* followed, often devoted to the true and essential nature of the Christian Church, its authority, its doctrine, its faults, its services, its liturgy. The first forty-six *Tracts* were collected and published in 1834; in 1835 the accession of E.B. Pusey, Professor of Hebrew at Oxford, greatly strengthened the Movement, with, as Church puts it, 'the vision before him of a revived and instructed Church, earnest in purpose and strict in life, and of a great Christian University roused and quickened to a sense of its powers and responsibilities'.

It was not long before the Tractarians had incensed the Evangelicals, the orthodox, and the Liberals alike. THOMAS ARNOLD's notorious article in the *Edinburgh Review* in 1836, 'The Oxford Malignants', showed them up as the most unpopular and suspected body of men in the Church. Yet only a short time earlier, in May 1835, the emphatic rejection by CONVOCATION of the proposal to abolish compulsory subscription to matriculands (*see* MATRICULATION) to the Thirty-Nine Articles could be argued as a substantial success.

Arnold's bitter article had been prompted in part by the fierce opposition of Newman, Keble, Pusey and others to the appointment of Dr Renn Hampden in 1836 as Regius Professor of Divinity, because they objected, *inter alia*, to the content of the eight Bampton Lectures (*see* LECTURES) which he had delivered to the University four years earlier (they even, unsuccessfully, petitioned the King to annul the appointment). Such personal animosities became an unhappy feature of the Movement, with, for example, E.B. Pusey being suspended in 1843 from preaching within the University for two years and Newman's supporter, W.G. Ward, being deprived of his degree (a step of doubtful legality) in 1845.

In his history, Church characterises the period from 1835 to 1840 – despite the death of Hurrell Froude in 1836 – as the years of its growth, in numbers and influence. But by the end of the decade the first signs were appearing of what was to come. In 1839 Newman's examination of the Monophysite heresy and schism of the 5th century led him to ask whether he, also, was not in heresy, whereas the Church of Rome had remained unwavering through the centuries; the result was to be the notorious *Tract XC*, in which he sought to determine how far the Articles of the Church of England could be reconciled to the Roman Catholic Church. Reaction was immediate and severe, and *Tract XC* had to be the last of the series. Newman himself moved to LITTLEMORE and, with what now seems inevitability, embarked upon the road to Rome which he finally reached in October 1845. Others followed him, though Keble and Pusey stood firm. Historians normally mark Newman's conversion as the Movement's climax (or catastrophe). Yet it continued, though with its field at least as much out of Oxford as in it, and Anglo-Catholicism is, of course, not dead today. But the Puseyites had not successfully combated materialism, rationalism, latitudinarianism – or Erastianism. As MARK PATTISON observed, 'If any Oxford man had gone to sleep in 1846 and had woke up again in 1850 he would have found himself in a totally new world. . . . In 1846 Oxford was fiercely debating its eternal Church question. . . . In 1850 . . . theology was totally banished from Common Room and even from private conversation. Very free opinions on all subjects were rife.'

(May, J. Lewis, *The Oxford Movement*, London, 1933; Hutchinson, W.G., ed., *The Oxford Movement*, n.d.; Harrison, T. Dilworth, *Every Man's Story of the Oxford Movement*, London, 1932; Griffin, John R., *The Oxford Movement: a Revision*, London, 1984; Faber, Geoffrey, *Oxford Apostles: a Character Study of the Oxford Movement*, London, 1933; Church, R.W., *The Oxford Movement: Twelve Years, 1833–1845*, 1891; Ward, Wilfrid, *William George Ward and the Oxford Movement*, 1889.)

Oxford Oolite A limestone composed of rounded grains. Oxford Oolite is the middle division of the Oolitic system.

Oxford Playhouse *see* PLAYHOUSE.

Oxford Preservation Trust Founded in 1927 after H.A.L. FISHER, Warden of New College, and Sir Michael Sadler, Master of University College, had organised a series of meetings to set up a body to 'so guide the development of Oxford, as to preserve and increase the beauty of the City and its surrounding neighbourhood.' From 1928 to 1972 the Trust's offices were at No. 3 CORNMARKET STREET, and the PAINTED ROOM was used for its meetings. Since 1972 the headquarters of the Trust in Oxford has been at No. 10 TURN AGAIN LANE (formerly Charles Street), where it bought and restored a row of 17th-century houses which in 1970 had been scheduled for demolition by the city.

The objects of the Trust include the protection of ancient buildings from demolition or disfigurement, the encouragement of a high standard for all new buildings, the preservation of unspoilt country within walking distance of the city, the planting of trees, and the provision of public open spaces for recreation. One of its first actions was to purchase land at BOAR'S HILL in order to preserve the view of Oxford and its 'dreaming spires'. Matthew Arnold Field belongs to the Trust, as does the old golf course at Boar's Hill. More recently it has helped to restore the wild garden established at Jarn Mound on Boar's Hill by SIR ARTHUR EVANS, a keen supporter of the Trust's work. Land was also bought at MARSTON to preserve the open nature of the Cherwell Valley (*see* THAMES), and this has been added to by generous gifts from donors. In 1931 the Trust bought some 56 acres of land at SOUTH PARK, which twenty years later were presented to the city as a permanent open space. Similarly, in 1952 over 180 acres of land at Shotover, which the Trust had acquired by purchase over the years, were given to the city as permanent open space (*see* SHOTOVER COUNTRY PARK). The land had been bought partly with money donated by Sir Michael Sadler, and one of the fields is named in memory of his daughter Mary. The Trust has also given trees for Oxford's housing estates and in the late 1930s planted the fastigiate hornbeams along the northern section of the RING ROAD, known as Sunderland Avenue.

The Trust was active in initiating discussions which led to the approval in principle of a Green Belt for Oxford. It does not, however, seek to oppose all development in the Green Belt: in 1968 it was awarded a Civic Trust Commendation for the building of a group of houses in the Green Belt at Wood Eaton, near Oxford, which has helped to maintain a viable community in this village. The Trust has also been represented at many public inquiries in Oxford – including that into the proposed extension of the M40 from Oxford to Birmingham, when the Trust opposed the route on the ground of the damage which it would inflict on the Green Belt and on Otmoor. It also opposed the proposed road across CHRIST CHURCH MEADOW. In 1960 it published its own Report on 'The New St Ebbe's and Oxford Roads.' In 1977 the Trust started a scheme of environmental awards to encourage architectural work which enhances the environment, whether it be new building, the restoration, extension or conversion of old buildings, or landscaping. The awards, made annually, take the form of plaques or certificates, and work in the city which has received a plaque includes HELEN HOUSE; the court building in ST ALDATE'S (*see* COURTS); the HEAD OF THE RIVER (HALL'S BREWERY); Emden House (twenty-four retirement flats in Barton Lane, designed by the Oxford Architects Partnership); the restoration of the Great Tower of Magdalen College and the Saxon tower of ST MICHAEL AT THE NORTH GATE; and the landscaping of ST EBBE's Riverside Park. In 1973 the Trust published an account of its work since 1927 which ended with the words: 'Sir Julian Huxley wrote, "Oxford shares with Venice the distinction of being, each in its own different way, the world's most beautiful small city." The purpose of the Oxford Preservation Trust is to treasure and develop this inheritance.'

Oxford Pro Musica Professional orchestra established as a result of a concert in 1965 organised by the American trumpeter and musicologist Don Smithers and the Oxford trumpeter John King, who has been the orchestra's manager since its inception. Varying in size from small chamber groups to a full symphony orchestra, it plays for local choral societies in addition to promoting its own concert seasons and managing visiting artists and ensembles. It has its own associated chorus.

Oxford Replanned In May 1945 Oxford City Council instructed Thomas Sharp, a town-planning consultant, to prepare a report on the planning and development of the city. His report was published by the Architectural Press in 1948 in a lavishly illustrated book, *Oxford Replanned*. His recommendations were not adopted, partly because of the large number of buildings in the centre of Oxford which would need to be demolished and the cost of carrying out the plan. His most controversial proposal was a new road (to be called Merton Mall), roughly on the line of BROAD WALK, which was intended to relieve the HIGH STREET of some of its traffic. The City Council, however, decided to await the effect on the High of the construction of the Oxford RING ROAD.

Oxford Road The main road through Temple Cowley connecting COWLEY ROAD with Garsington Road.

Oxford School *Glanville Road*. The school, which in 1986 numbered 560 boys aged between eleven and eighteen, was the result of the amalgamation in 1966 of the CITY OF OXFORD HIGH SCHOOL with SOUTHFIELD SCHOOL. Buildings erected between 1964 and 1966 were added to the existing Southfield School, those in brick to the design of Douglas Murray, the City Architect, and those in concrete by the Department of Education and Science Architects' Department; the playing fields were extended to some 20 acres. In 1973, with the end of eleven-plus selection, the school became a comprehensive boys' upper school. A bronze bas-relief plaque by Eric Kennington of T.E. Lawrence, from the City of Oxford High School, hangs in the entrance hall.

Oxford Shirting A plain-weave shirting of good-quality yarns that has two warp ends weaving as one. Fancy-weave effects can be incorporated and dyed yarns are used to form stripes. Typical cotton particulars were 30s × 12s, 88 × 56.

Oxford Shoe A style of shoe laced over the instep.

Oxford Society A worldwide association of present and former members of the University, formed to forward the interests of the University and to keep its members in touch with each other. This is achieved through an international branch organisation and the magazine OXFORD.

On 1 December 1930 Lionel Curtis, a Fellow of All Souls, alarmed at the incapacity of Treasury grants to keep pace with rising costs, presented to HEBDOMADAL COUNCIL a memorandum urging the necessity of raising money to preserve Oxford's heritage of buildings and to secure endowments for its continuation as a centre of intellectual excellence. He thought the University's own graduates should first be organised to this end through the formation of a worldwide Oxford Society with its own magazine, to be called *Oxford*. Hebdomadal Council, after much consideration, accepted the idea in principle but stressed that such a society would in no sense be a fund-raising body and, instead of an expensive magazine, suggested a news-sheet with addresses of members and items of interest about them, together with the publication of the *University Report*. This was approved by Council. The Society was formally launched at a dinner at Lord Astor's London house on 9 June 1932. Among the twenty-nine very distinguished men present were the CHANCELLOR (Viscount Grey of Fallodon), the VICE-CHANCELLOR, the Archbishops of Canterbury and York, and the Marquess of Salisbury. The Vice-Chancellor spoke of the proposed society and invited those present to constitute themselves its nucleus. This was agreed, a provisional executive committee nominated, and a letter from the Chancellor, with a supporting leader, appeared in *The Times*. This was followed by an individual letter to all graduates whose addresses were known. The Warden of RHODES HOUSE made premises available for temporary offices and the Rhodes Trust made a loan of £500.

The early office was run by voluntary help under a Balliol don, Kenneth Bell, until in June 1933 the Hon. J.F.A. Browne (Magdalen), later Lord Kilmaine, was appointed the first permanent secretary. By this time the office had set up about 150 local committees all over Great Britain and the University had given rent-free offices and made an annual grant for the first three years. During his seven years as secretary, Lord Kilmaine set up a network of branches throughout the United Kingdom and appointed representatives in all the most important centres of the English-speaking world; but in 1940, with his enlistment, the work of the society had perforce to come almost to a standstill. During the war the office was manned by part-time and voluntary workers under the direction of the President of St John's and the Principal of Brasenose, W.T.S. STALLYBRASS. After the war Kilmaine resigned to become secretary of the Pilgrim Trust and his place was taken by George Docker (Lincoln). Kilmaine became chairman on the death of Stallybrass. By 1959, when Docker left to become assistant registrar at the Australian National University, Canberra, and Daphne Lennie (St Hugh's) succeeded him as secretary, the branch system was firmly established and the office records had been brought up to date.

The society was beset by financial difficulties from the outset. Curtis had envisaged all freshmen joining on coming into residence, but this necessitated the co-operation of the colleges. The concept of an Oxford Society had been formed by Hebdomadal Council and a small body of influential Oxford men outside the University; colleges themselves had heard little about it and Lord Grey's announcement in *The Times*, followed by a great deal of international publicity, had appeared at the beginning of the long vacation. When in Michaelmas Term the colleges received a late and formal request to allow their undergraduates to pay their subscriptions in instalments through college BATTELS, a number of them felt that they should have been consulted earlier and refused to co-operate. It took Lord Kilmaine a great many years to retrieve this situation. Life subscriptions had been based on the

expectation of almost universal membership and were not economically viable in these changed circumstances. By June 1939 the committee had already decided to raise an endowment fund of £25,000 and ask for extra voluntary subscriptions. This had to be deferred until after the war but, despite its success, from the 1950s onwards continuous increases in subscriptions had to be made to keep up with inflation. By 1981, though membership was increasing and the branch network was flourishing, the financial situation was grave and rescued only by a massive appeal to existing life members.

Had Lionel Curtis's grandiose schemes been accepted *in toto*, who knows what great financial benefit might not have accrued to the University and the city? As it is, the University keeps contact with its old members by the society's widespread branch organisation and the publication of *Oxford*. The society rendered considerable service to the University over the BODLEIAN appeal in 1937 and the Historic Buildings Appeal in 1957. It gives grants to undergraduates and with University and college help in recruitment, it should be able to do much more in future.

Oxford Story *6 Broad Street*. An exhibition centre by Heritage Projects Ltd, where visitors are taken through a kaleidoscope of visual images and sounds illustrating the history of the University. A bastion of the CITY WALL can also be seen here.

Oxford Subscription Concerts These were started in 1920 as the successors to the Public Classical Concerts run by the Oxford University Musical Club from 1891 to 1914. Their aim was to provide a series of professional chamber and orchestral concerts, and in particular to bring to Oxford full symphony orchestras, which otherwise were not heard in the city. For many years orchestras such as the Hallé, the London Philharmonic and the Royal Philharmonic, under conductors like Barbirolli, Boult and Beecham, were regular visitors. In addition, up to the 1950s one concert each season was given by the Oxford Orchestral Society with professional strengthening. Until the late 1950s the concerts were usually held on Thursday afternoons, an apparently convenient time in view of the local half-day closing. In recent years the cost of large professional orchestras has become prohibitive, especially as there is no sizeable concert hall, and in consequence the concerts have tended to be given by smaller ensembles and solo artists, although they have included such eminent names as the Beaux Arts Trio, Emil Gilels, Heinz Holliger and Paul Tortelier.

'Oxford' Symphony Haydn's Symphony No. 92 is the 'Oxford' Symphony. It was composed in 1788 and performed in 1791 when the composer was in Oxford to receive the honorary degree of Doctor of Music.

Oxford Symphony Orchestra An amateur orchestra was first established in 1882 as the Oxford Orchestral Association by Alfred Gibson and was conducted from its second concert by C.H. Lloyd. It seems to have been disbanded in about 1898. In 1902 Hugh Allen assembled a new orchestra to play for the OXFORD BACH CHOIR's concerts. This soon became known as Dr Allen's Orchestra, and it began also to play in the Public Classical Concerts run by the Oxford University Musical Club until 1914. It changed its name to the Oxford Orchestral Society in 1919 and to the Oxford Symphony Orchestra in 1974. It played a prominent role in the various major music festivals held in the first half of the century, as well as contributing regularly for many years to the OXFORD SUBSCRIPTION CONCERTS. It remained the Bach Choir's principal partner until 1971, and continues to play for other local choral societies, in addition to mounting its own regular concerts.

Oxford Times *see* NEWSPAPERS.

Oxford Union *see* UNION SOCIETY.

Oxford United Football Club In 1896 the village of HEADINGTON formed its own football club, Headington United. It was a village team until 1929, when Headington became incorporated in the city of Oxford. In 1949 the club turned professional and joined the Southern League. After only moderate success, the former Wolverhampton Wanderers footballer Arthur Turner was appointed manager in 1959; and in 1960 the club was renamed Oxford United. Turner and his team captain Ron Atkinson (affectionately known as 'the Tank' on the terraces and later to become manager of Manchester United) were the inspiration behind the first major successes of the club. The club was elected to the Football League (Division 4) in 1962; became the only 4th-division side to reach the quarter finals of the FA Cup in 1964; was promoted to Division 3 in 1965; became Division 3 champions in 1968 and was promoted to Division 2. The following season Turner became general manager but was dismissed in 1972. The club was relegated to Division 3 in 1976. Several years of boardroom wrangles, financial problems and uninspired performances on the field almost closed it, but in 1982, on the point of bankruptcy, it was rescued by the Headington millionaire-publisher Robert Maxwell, who became chairman and appointed the former Birmingham City manager Jim Smith as team manager. Arguments with the City Council for refusing to give the club planning permission to build a new stadium away from the residential Manor Park site, which it had occupied since 1921, led to the announcement of plans by Maxwell to merge Oxford United and Reading Town. The new team, to be called the Thames Valley Royals, was to play on a site between Oxford and Reading, but the supporters of both clubs marched together through Oxford in a demonstration against the proposal. The idea was dropped and immediately the second successful era in the club's history began. In 1984 Oxford became Division 3 champions for a second time; and, after only one year in Division 2, in which the team won the championship, the club was promoted to Division 1. In 1986 it won its first major knock-out competition trophy – the Milk (League) Cup, by beating Queen's Park Rangers 3–0 at Wembley Stadium.

Oxford University Amateur Boxing Club
Boxing became a regulated sport in the University in the 19th century when there was a combined boxing and fencing club. This was divided into two in 1913. As the OU Boxing Club, it was disbanded for a time in

the 1960s and then reformed in 1968–9 by R.L. Nairac, who captained the team for two years and who was later murdered by the IRA while serving in the Special Air Service. Other celebrated BLUES include Eric Lubbock (now Lord Avebury), Lord James Alexander Douglas-Hamilton, the Hon. Colin Moynihan and Kris Kristofferson.

Oxford University Association Football Club Founded on 9 November 1871, then comprising thirty-five members from various colleges. In 1872 the club entered the FA Challenge Cup and lost 0–2 in the final to Wanderers, an amateur club which won the Cup five times before its dissolution in about 1880. But in 1874 the University Club won the Cup by beating the Royal Engineers 2–0. Also in 1874, the first two Varsity Matches were played: on 30 March Oxford won 1–0; and on 28 November Cambridge won 2–0. So far 102 Varsity Matches have been played, of which Oxford has won thirty-seven and Cambridge forty-three, the rest having been drawn. In recent years the match has been played at Wembley and it is now sponsored by St Quintin, Chartered Surveyors.

From 1872 to 1970 over forty Oxford players have won full or amateur international caps. One of these, C. Wreford-Brown, became Vice-President of the Football Association (1941–51). The formation of the Pegasus Football Club in 1948 gave a great boost to University football, especially as Pegasus won the FA Amateur Cup in 1951 and 1953. The founder of the club, Sir Harold Thompson, FRS, who was president of the OUAFC, became chairman of the Football Association (1976–81). Membership of the Pegasus Club is open to members of the Cambridge Falcon Football Club and the Oxford Centaurs Club, these being the Universities' second teams. Oxford BLUES are also members of Centaurs. Another amateur club, now defunct, was the Corinthian Football Club, most of whose members were Oxford or Cambridge Blues. This club was founded towards the end of the 19th century and had several early successes in the FA Challenge Cup and during a revival in its fortunes in 1920–35. It played its last match in the 1950s.

Oxford University Athletic Club Founded in 1860. One of its affiliates, Exeter College Athletic Club, staged an athletic meeting in 1850 and claims to be the oldest athletic club in the world.

Official world records have been ratified only since 1913; before that there were 'amateur bests on record'. Of these, OUAC claimed world best performances in three field events and for the 880 yards. The earliest was the first 6-foot high-jump, achieved by the Hon. Marshall Brooks (Brasenose) on 17 March 1876. Brooks, who was also an England Rugby International, cleared 6 feet and one-eighth of an inch with a cat jump. The first track world best was set on the old IFFLEY ROAD track when in 1888 Francis J.K. Cross (New College) ran 880 yards in 1 minute 54.4 seconds.

In 1893 the most famous of sports all-rounders, C.B. FRY (Wadham), equalled the world long-jump record set by the American Charles S. Racker two years earlier, clearing 23 feet 6½ inches (7.24 metres). In 1905 the American shot-putter Wesley W. Coe (Hertford) became the first man to beat the 15-metre barrier with a put of 49 feet 6 inches at Portland, Oregon, for the United States national title.

A drawing of c.1880 of the Oxford University Boat Club's new boat house, built on land belonging to University College to which the building has now reverted.

The first Oxford athlete to become an official world-record holder was G.R.L. Anderson (Trinity), who ran the 440-yards hurdles in 56.8 seconds in 1910. After this eleven other OUAC members set world athletic records, including the milers Norman Taber (St John's) – 4 minutes 12.6 seconds in 1915; Dr Jack Lovelock (New Zealand) – 4 minutes 07.6 seconds in 1933; and the first man in the world to run a mile in less than 4 minutes – Sir Roger Bannister of Exeter and Merton Colleges (and now Master of Pembroke), with a time of 3 minutes 59.4 seconds on the Iffley Road track on 6 May 1954.

Two other individual world-record holders over Olympic distances were Tom Hampson (St Catherine's), who won the 1932 Olympic 800-metre title in 1 minute 49.7 seconds, and Christopher Chataway (Magdalen), who set a 5000-metre world record in 13 minutes 51.6 seconds in 1954 against the Russian Vladimir Kuts. Apart from Hampson, the OUAC Olympic champions are Arnold Strode-Jackson (Brasenose) in the 1500 metres in Stockholm in 1912; Bevil Rudd (Trinity) in the 400 metres in Antwerp in 1920; Jack Lovelock (Exeter) in the 1500 metres in Berlin in 1936; and David Hemery (St Catherine's), whose 48.1 seconds for the 1968 Olympic gold medal in world-record time in hurdles is arguably one of the best British feats of all time.

Oxford University Boat Club The most important function of this club, which was founded on 23 April 1839, is to produce crews for the annual BOAT RACE with Cambridge. For many years Oxbridge rowing was the foundation of the British Olympic teams but, although the Boat Race was as keenly contested as ever, the Universities suffered a decline in standard in the 1950s. Since that time, however, they have re-established themselves, regularly producing crews which are among the fastest in the country and

providing members for the national rowing team. In the five years to 1984 Oxford oarsmen won six Olympic and world-championship rowing medals, representing their respective countries.

The other function of the OUBC is to organise ROWING within the University. At any time, up to a quarter of the University may be involved in the sport, with most of the interest centred on the BUMPING RACES at the end of Trinity Term.

(*See also* OXFORD UNIVERSITY WOMEN'S BOAT CLUB.)

Oxford University Cricket Club Founded at an uncertain date between 1800 and 1805. It was at first known as the Magdalen Club until properly constituted as the OUCC in 1862. The first Varsity Match was played in June 1827 at Lord's. Early home matches were played on Cowley Marsh, and it was not until 1881 that the club moved to its present ground in the University PARKS, which is thought by many to be the most beautiful first-class cricket ground in the world. By the 1870s the side was a match for any in the country – the 1884 side, probably one of the best ever, beat the Australians (at the Christ Church ground where the tourists often played since a 'gate' cannot be taken in the Parks).

Many fine players were in the side in the 1890s, among them P.F. (Plum) Warner (Oriel), R.E. Foster (University College), who scored 287 on his Test debut in 1903, and C.B. FRY (Wadham). In more recent years famous names have included D.R. Jardine (New College), M.P. Donnelly (Worcester), D.B. Carr (Worcester), M.C. Cowdrey (Brasenose), M.J.K. Smith (St Edmund Hall), the Nawab of Pataudi (both senior and junior, both Balliol) and Imran Khan (Keble). A total of thirty-nine Oxford men have played Test cricket and fifteen of these have captained their country. In the Varsity Matches played between

307

Alan Mackinnon, a founder member of OUDS, as Prince Hal in Henry IV, Part I, *the first production ever staged by the Society which was then permitted to perform Shakespeare only.*

1827 and 1986 Oxford have won forty-six, Cambridge fifty-four, and forty-two have been drawn.

    (Bolton, Geoffrey, *History of the Oxford University Cricket Club*, 1962.)

Oxford University Dramatic Society (OUDS) Religious plays and pageants were performed by members of the University during the mediaeval period, and by the mid-16th century play-acting was a fairly frequent activity; several monarchs watched dramatic performances during their visits to Oxford. During the 17th century visiting professional companies provided a distraction to undergraduates which incurred the disapproval of the authorities, and the Licensing Act of 1737 banned any dramatic performance in Oxford University or within 5 miles of the city. A century later, groups of undergraduates began to perform one-act farces in their colleges for their own amusement, and in 1879 a Philothespian Society was formed in Christ Church, drawing its members from the whole University. Its first notable member, Arthur Bourchier (afterwards a noted actor–manager), played Shylock in an 1883 production of *The Merchant of Venice*, which won the approval of BENJAMIN JOWETT, the then VICE-

CHANCELLOR, and led to the formation of an Oxford University Dramatic Society in October 1884.

    In its early years the OUDS was permitted to perform Shakespeare only; female parts were taken by local lady amateurs, and the production was usually directed by Alan Mackinnon, a founder member of the society who had left the University but returned each year to produce. The overall standard was rarely above that of country-house amateur dramatics, but a number of notable actors came to the fore, among them Henry Irving junior (son of the great Irving) and Nigel Playfair. However, the chief activity of the OUDS in the early 1900s was not the producing of plays but the management of its club-rooms in GEORGE STREET, opposite the New Theatre where OUDS productions were then staged (*see* APOLLO THEATRE). At this period the OUDS was a socially exclusive organisation rivalling the Grid, the Bullingdon, and other dining and drinking clubs (*see* CLUBS AND SOCIETIES).

    Between the wars it was the custom to invite professional producers to direct OUDS shows, and the results were frequently remarkable. J.B. Fagan, the first director of the Oxford PLAYHOUSE (which was then situated at the junction of the WOODSTOCK and BANBURY ROADS), staged a 1924 *Hamlet* with Gyles Isham in the title role (and Emlyn Williams as stand-in prompter) which attracted much praise. Robert Speaight appeared in a memorable 1925 *Peer Gynt*, and as Falstaff in *Henry IV, Part 2* the next year, reducing the critic James Agate to tears by the excellence of his performance. Other OUDS stars in the inter-war years who became professionally involved with the theatre included Valentine Dyall, George Devine, Terence Rattigan, and Raymond Massey; and the casts of OUDS shows also included at various times JOHN BETJEMAN, Osbert Lancaster and Peter Fleming. Professional directors continued to mount shows until 1939 – particularly memorable was Max Reinhardt's 1933 *A Midsummer Night's Dream*, staged on the slopes of HEADINGTON HILL – but the most notable director of this period was NEVILL COGHILL, whose first production for the society was a 1935 *Hamlet*. Coghill continued to direct for the OUDS at intervals until the 1960s, and made a particular mark with his 1949 version of *The Tempest*, staged alongside – and on – Worcester College lake. In 1936 Coghill founded the Experimental Theatre Club (ETC), intended to be a more adventurous group than the OUDS and to give equal opportunities to women undergraduates, who were not yet allowed to become full members of the OUDS.

    The OUDS entered a second 'golden age' immediately after the Second World War, with such members as John Schlesinger, Tony Richardson, Michael Codron, Robert Robinson, Shirley Catlin (the future politician Shirley Williams), Peter Parker, Ronald Eyre, Lindsay Anderson and Kenneth Tynan. From 1945 Coghill led a movement to build or acquire a University Theatre, and in January 1961 the University took over ownership of the Oxford Playhouse in BEAUMONT STREET, this building having housed OUDS productions since just before the Second World War.

    The ownership of the Playhouse certainly stimulated University theatrical activities, with many college as well as OUDS and ETC productions being staged there; but this was not accompanied by any official study of the theatre or dramatic training. Drama does not appear in any University curriculum, and the professionalism of the Playhouse and its technical equipment has often highlighted the amateurism of the acting and direction. Since the early 1960s the OUDS and ETC have helped to train a number of notable performers, among them Diana Quick (first woman President of the OUDS in 1968), Michael Palin and Terry Jones of *Monty Python's Flying Circus*, and Rowan Atkinson; but the overall standard of performance has never been consistently high and University theatre remains a pleasant hobby for most of its participants rather than an opportunity for serious professional training.

(*See also* THEATRE.)

Oxford University Golf Club Founded in 1875, as was Cambridge University Golf Club. The first Varsity Match was played at Wimbledon Common in 1878: Cambridge has won fifty-four matches and Oxford thirty-six; five have been drawn. Early home matches were played at COWLEY, HEADINGTON, NORTH HINKSEY and Radley, but in 1923 OUGC moved to the new SOUTHFIELD course and this location, shared with Oxford City Golf Club, has been its permanent home since (*see* GOLF CLUBS). Championships won by OUGC members include the French Open: C.J.H. Tolley (twice), the only amateur to win it; British Amateur: H.G. Hutchinson (twice), Sir Ernest Holderness (twice), Tolley (twice), A.G. Barry, R.H. Wethered and R. Sweeny; English Amateur: J.J.F. Pennink (twice), G.H. Micklem (twice) and A.G.B. Helm; Welsh Amateur: A.A. Duncan (four times). OUGC has been represented thirty times in the Walker Cup and sixty-two times in the Home Internationals.

Oxford University Lawn Tennis Club In existence before 1879, the year the club held its first doubles championships. The first Varsity Match between Oxford and Cambridge, held in 1881, took place at the Prince's Club and was won by Oxford. Over the years the matches have had many venues, including Prince's, Wimbledon, Hurlingham, Queen's and Eastbourne. Since 1946 Cambridge has won thirty times and Oxford ten.

Oxford University Opera Club The Opera Club was formally constituted in May 1926 after an initial venture in December 1925, when the first stage performance in the country of Monteverdi's *Orfeo* was given in an edition newly prepared by a Balliol undergraduate, Jack Westrup, and conducted by William Harris, organist of New College. This pioneering spirit has characterised the club's productions throughout its history, the emphasis having been on reviving neglected operas, or more occasionally commissioning new works. Among operas specially written for the club have been Egon Wellesz's *Incognita* (1951), Robert Sherlaw Johnson's *The Lambton Worm* (1978) and two by undergraduates. In addition to a variety of smaller activities there has usually been one major production each year, apart from the period around the Second World War. Westrup, on returning to Oxford as Heather Professor in 1947, revived the club and conducted its productions for sixteen years, often also preparing the English translations himself. Although the majority of the work of these productions is undertaken by club members, professional singers are normally engaged for most of the main roles.

Oxford University Press This ancient institution traces its origins back to the late 15th century – or did so in 1978 when it chose to celebrate the quincentenary of PRINTING in Oxford. But, although printing did begin in Oxford in 1478, it had no particular connection with the University, which could hardly claim to have a press of its own for another 200 years.

In the 17th century ARCHBISHOP LAUD had a clear idea of what a University press ought to do. It should be printing for posterity the manuscripts mouldering in Oxford libraries, and in particular the early manuscripts of the Eastern churches, many of which had been presented to the University by Laud himself. What may be regarded as the first meeting of a Board of Delegates of the Press, which in years to come was to be the governing body, was summoned in 1633 in order to select a manuscript from the BODLEIAN LIBRARY for printing. That done, the board did not meet again for many years. Laud obtained for the University in 1636 the privilege of printing all manner of books, including Bibles. Cambridge, in fact, had enjoyed the same privilege since 1534, sharing it with the Company of Stationers and the Royal Printer. Neither Oxford nor Cambridge exercised the Bible privilege, however, fearing the wrath of the all-powerful Stationers.

The SHELDONIAN THEATRE, opened in 1669, was a milestone in the pre-history of the University Press. In a letter of endowment to the VICE-CHANCELLOR, ARCHBISHOP SHELDON concluded that whatever money might be left over after paying for the upkeep and

Sir John Everett Millais's painting of Thomas Combe, patron of the Pre-Raphaelites and partner in the University Press from the 1830s to the 1870s.

repairs should be 'imployed for the best advantage and encouragement of the Learned Press'. So the printers acquired a permanent home, and the Dean of Christ Church, DR FELL, took a very close interest in it. Fell was a man of vast energies and there followed now the great florescence of early Oxford printing associated with his name and with the imprint of the Sheldonian Theatre. But it hardly qualified as the work of the University Press. By 1672 the University had leased the privilege of printing to what amounted to a private company; Bishop Fell was chairman and managing director. The famous Fell types, and all the equipment he acquired for the printing house during the period of his ascendancy, were eventually presented to the University on his death in 1686.

The 18th century was sadly unproductive. LORD CLARENDON's *History of the Rebellion* was published between 1702 and 1704, and the Press began to emerge as one of the most prolific Bible printers when the great monopolist John Baskett leased the Bible privilege from the University in 1713. A new printing house was built and named the CLARENDON BUILDING. But a fiery young lawyer and delegate, WILLIAM BLACKSTONE, took a critical look at the Press in 1757: he described it as 'languishing in a lazy obscurity'. Blackstone's reforms mostly affected the printing house, but he did briefly galvanise the Board of Delegates, ensuring that they met at regular intervals, bore in mind the spirit of Laud and Fell, and their own primary obligation of publishing books.

The Press had long been divided into two parts – the Learned or Classical Press and the Bible Press. In the first half of the 19th century the latter became a thriving business. Tens of thousands of Bibles and prayer books poured from the privileged presses. Competition was intense. The biggest customer, the British and Foreign Bible Society, was constantly forcing the price down. Profit margins were cut, there was much hard bargaining, and it seems that a general anxiety often prevailed. The good fortune could not last. The Press more than held its own, however, and the first half of the 19th century was a time of unparalleled prosperity. For most of the period the printing house was run by 'partners' – master-printers with shares in the business. The Press had established itself as a joint stock company, with forty-eight shares of which the University as 'owner partner' held half. The most famous of the partners was Thomas Combe (*see* JERICHO). The University's share of the Bible profits in 1850 brought in £60,000, out of which it was decided to build a natural history museum. Earlier the Press had made substantial contributions to the building of what became the ASHMOLEAN MUSEUM.

The Press itself had moved again, in 1830, when the building in WALTON STREET was opened. The Bible Press occupied the south wing and the Learned Press the north wing. No provision was made for a publishing office. One or two Delegates were scholars with European reputations, like THOMAS GAISFORD, who brought some distinction to the Clarendon Press, but the number of books published for the University – as opposed to those privately printed by the University Press – was few.

Gradually, however, the Board of Delegates began to build up a publishing business. Schoolbooks were greatly in demand as a result of educational reforms, and the Delegates saw their opportunity. G.W. Kitchin (1827–1912) became the first secretary of the Board of Delegates. He promoted the Clarendon Press Series of textbooks, which so increased the business of the Press that it was decided to get help from professionals in London. Alexander Macmillan, already an eminent publisher, was chosen to serve the Press's interests there and to handle the commercial side of the business. From 1863 to 1880 he was the Oxford publisher based in London. From then on the Oxford publisher was the outward image of the OUP, whose name appeared on innumerable title pages. Alexander Macmillan was succeeded by Henry Frowde, SIR HUMPHREY MILFORD, GEOFFREY CUMBERLEGE, and Sir John Brown. The post was abolished in 1977 when the businesses in London were moved to Oxford for administrative convenience.

The dominant figure in Oxford during the early period of growth was the Rev. Professor Bartholomew Price, who was appointed secretary (and therefore chief executive) by the Delegates in 1868. A Delegate himself, and Master of Pembroke, he was active in the Press's affairs for over thirty years. He and Macmillan established the Clarendon Press as a major publishing house. Charles Cannan, a classicist and Aristotelian scholar, succeeded Price as secretary in 1897 and remained in the job until his death in 1917. A man of rare sharpness of mind, his achievement was great. The new OXFORD ENGLISH DICTIONARY had already been taken over by the Press; it moved forward at a snail's pace and at enormous expense. Cannan saw that the big Dictionary could be milched in order to make smaller, cheaper dictionaries like the *Concise Oxford*. As Bible sales diminished, dictionaries gradually came to take their place. In 1900 Cannan launched the *Oxford Book of English Verse*, edited by Arthur Quiller-Couch – the first of many 'Oxford Books'. The establishment of the Oxford English School opened up a new market, supplementing the editions of classical texts. Cannan wanted to build 'the First Press in the world'.

An office in New York had opened in 1896, and in the decade before the First World War there was much activity in the setting up of branches throughout the world. New York was followed by Canada (1904), Australia (1908) and India (1912). At one time or another there have been branches in Paris, Nairobi, Ibadan, Cape Town, Tokyo, Pakistan, Kuala Lumpur – and in other centres too numerous to mention. The object has been first and foremost to sell Oxford books – a formidable task in, say, India or Addis Ababa. Eventually, especially after World War II, branches were encouraged to publish books of more local interest to own areas, and also more academic titles; the New York branch was given a distinct constitution and now, trading under the name OUP(USA), is one of the largest academic publishers in the US.

Humphrey Milford became publisher after a long grooming from Cannan. In charge from 1912 to 1947, he had a rare gift for seizing opportunities: whatever he might casually dabble in, it seemed, turned astonishingly into a major project. The Press became a large medical publisher as a result of one of his initiatives; it became a highly successful publisher of children's books; almost in a fit of absent-mindedness, Milford made OUP the second largest music publisher in the country. Most notably, he undertook a few tentative probes into the overseas market, and in due course the department called 'Overseas Education' had successfully captured a substantial part of the market for English primers and textbooks. Milford had enormous confidence in his subordinates and readily gave them a free hand.

A pattern of expansion which showed itself towards the end of the 19th century has continued to this day – and ever more vigorously, despite the set-backs of two wars. One of the largest and fastest-growing departments is now called 'Oxford English' (formerly 'English Language Teaching', and, before that, Milford's seedling 'Overseas Education'). The department is supplying a contemporary worldwide demand for English learning books larger even than that for Bibles in the 19th century.

In all its widespread manifestations, however, the OUP remains a department of the University, controlled by the body of senior scholars who serve as Delegates of the Press. There are no shareholders, but the Press is expected to be self-financing and therefore needs to compete in the world of commercial publishing.

On 5 May 1989 the OUP formally closed its printing house in WALTON STREET, thus ending a long tradition of PRINTING, once the city's biggest industry.

(Sutcliffe, Peter, *The Oxford University Press: an Informal History,* Oxford, 1978; Barker, Nicolas, *The Oxford University Press and the Spread of Learning 1478–1978,* Oxford, 1978; Madan, Falconer, *A Brief Account of the University Press at Oxford,* 1908; Carter, Harry, *A History of the Oxford University Press to 1780,* Oxford, 1975.)

Oxford University Rugby Football Club

Founded in 1869, fifteen months before the foundation of the Rugby Football Union. A lease was taken, and a pavilion built on the IFFLEY ROAD ground in 1899. The ground was purchased in the 1920s and with the pavilion and stands, is now held in trust by the Stanley's Trustees. The Trust is named after Major Stanley, who, though he himself never played well, if indeed at all, exerted a long-term influence on both Oxford and English rugby. The trustees include eight Old BLUES who were also internationals, and two Old Blues who were Presidents of the English Rugby Union. The Trust organises an invitation XV to play against the University at Iffley Road each November. It is called the Major Stanley's XV and continues the tradition begun by him. Most of the international players from the Home Counties have played in this match. The Iffley Road ground has stand accommodation for nearly 2000 spectators.

Rugby Blues are awarded to those who play in the annual VARSITY MATCH at Twickenham every December. Oxford Blues have made immense contributions to British rugby, and have often included international players from Australia, New Zealand and South Africa. Among the famous players who began their first-class rugby career at Iffley Road are Obolensky and Poulton Palmer.

In addition to the Blues XV there are Greyhounds and Whippets teams, the latter consisting of undergraduates in their first year at Oxford. All three University sides draw players from the college clubs, of which there are twenty-eight. The colleges organise a league competition before Christmas and a knock-out competition, called Cuppers, in the spring term. The Blues fixtures before Christmas are against first-class club sides as preparation for the Varsity Match; and in most years there is an international tour in one of the vacations.

Oxford University Sports Centre *Iffley Road.*

While most of the thirty-five Oxford colleges have their own sports facilities, nearly all University sports clubs also use the facilities provided by the University Sports Centre and the University PARKS. The Sports Centre's facilities were mainly provided through benefactions from the Rhodes Trust (*see* RHODES HOUSE) and include a modern gymnasium, together with ancillary rooms for weight-training, fencing and judo; a squash complex; an all-weather synthetic track; and an indoor cricket school which can be converted for small-bore pistol and rifle shooting. The spectators' stand was designed by D. Armstrong Smith (1962) and the gymnasium by Jack Lankester (1966), the University Surveyor.

Oxford University Swimming Club The first

recorded swimming Varsity Match was held in 1892 and was won by Cambridge, a result more often than not repeated since. In the 1970s the Oxford club was placed second in the British Universities Championships four times and won the title in 1977 by a record margin. During this period Nigel Smith (St Catherine's) won three successive 100-metres butterfly titles.

Oxford University Women's Boat Club

Founded in May 1926 when the women's colleges boat clubs joined forces to produce a united eight. The first contest against Cambridge was held at Oxford in 1927, the crews first racing half a mile upstream and then rowing downstream in a 'style competition'. Oxford won the race but the umpires disagreed regarding style. BLUES were awarded. The Principals of the women's colleges disapproved, ruling that 'style competitions may be continued if desired, but racing is not sanctioned'. This set-back was overcome by racing outside Oxford during the vacation. In 1936 Miss F.E. Francombe (Oxford Home Students), stroke of the first Oxford women's eight and coach from 1931 to 1936, presented a cup for the winning crew.

The OUWBC was disbanded in 1953 because of insufficient financial support, but was reformed in 1964. The annual Women's Boat Race was thereafter held alternately on the Isis (*see* THAMES) and Cam until 1978, when it moved to Henley.

(*See also* OXFORD UNIVERSITY BOAT CLUB.)

Oxford University Yacht Club This, the oldest

university sailing club in England, was founded in 1884 when undergraduates who sailed their own boats at PORT MEADOW clubbed together to organise racing. In 1923 the club purchased four 14-foot clinker-built dinghies, designed for it by Morgan Giles, the leading small-boat designer of the day. These have been followed by many others of different designs, those in use in 1986 being Laser II racing dinghies; they are sailed on Farmoor Reservoir, which opened in 1986.

Team racing has long been the predominant form of competition. The Varsity Match started in 1912, since when Oxford has won thirty-one out of the sixty-nine matches, with four ties and one match abandoned. The club gained full BLUE status in 1967 and has raced successfully abroad as well as in England.

Oxford Welsh Male Voice Choir The choir

came into being as a result of Welsh emigration to the COWLEY car factories in the inter-war years. It was founded in 1928 as the Cowley Male Voice Choir, but changed its name to the Oxford Welsh Glee Singers in 1931 and to its present one in 1978. It achieved considerable renown through its radio broadcasts in the 1940s and 1950s, as well as for its competitive successes. Although Welshmen now form only a minority of the membership, the national flavour is retained in the choir's repertoire.

Oxford Wycombe Chair   A plain chair with a cane seat, the back rails projecting beyond the uprights. The design, as executed by the chair-makers of High Wycombe, may have been suggested by the OXFORD FRAME.

Oxfordshire and Buckinghamshire Light Infantry Regimental Museum   *TA Centre, Slade Park, Headington*. The 43rd Regiment of Foot since 1881, the Oxfordshire and Buckinghamshire Light Infantry became the 1st Green Jackets in 1957 and – with the former 52nd Regiment of Foot, the 60th (2nd Green Jackets, King's Royal Rifle Corps) and the Rifle Brigade – is now incorporated in the Royal Green Jackets. The museum contains the county's militaria, a medal collection, uniforms, badges, pictures and regimental silver.

Oxoniensia   A journal dealing with the archaeology, history and architecture of Oxford and its neighbourhood, published annually by the Oxford Architectural and Historical Society since 1936.

Oxpens Road   Oxpens (or Ox-Pens) was a farm in the area but the road did not exist by that name before 1850; until then it had been known as Nun's Walk. Squires (*In West Oxford*, 1928) says that it was sometimes described as Oxmead Wall and 'even now the fields to the south are known as the Ox-Pens'. The stone wall of Ox-Pens field formed the boundary line of the south side of Osney Lane, the east end of which lies at the north end of the present Oxpens Road. Squires told of a 'cowman employed at the Ox-pens farm [who] was frequently at Evensong [in the nearby church of ST THOMAS THE MARTYR] and often fell asleep from weariness, as his working day lasted from 4 a.m. to 6 p.m.; the smell of his boots kept everyone at a distance, but he was a sample of the old St Thomas's "saints".'

Situated in St Thomas's parish, the road runs from the junction of HOLLYBUSH ROW and Osney Lane to Norfolk Street, ST EBBE'S, at its junction with THAMES STREET. In 1866–7 Christ Church built a large residential block, which was originally called 'Model Buildings', on the north-west side of the road. Later known as Christ Church Old Buildings, Pevsner describes it as 'depressing'. The cattle market used to be situated on the east side of the street but the site has now been incorporated in the COLLEGE OF FURTHER EDUCATION, the buildings of which were begun in 1968 and now take up most of that side of the road. On the west side there was a field which was used by travelling circuses and fairs but in 1984 this became the site of the ICE RINK and car parks.

─── P ───

Pageant, 1907 The Oxford Historical Pageant was performed in CHRIST CHURCH MEADOW in the week of 27 June to 3 July 1907. There were fifteen 'dramatic scenes with words' and an interlude of masques. Among the events depicted were the 'Beginnings of the University', ST SCHOLASTICA'S DAY, the 'Expulsion of the Fellows of Magdalen College in 1687' and the 'Visit of George III in 1785'. Characters represented included ST FRIDESWIDE, Friar Bacon, Henry VIII and CARDINAL WOLSEY, SIR THOMAS BODLEY, ARCHBISHOP LAUD, JOHN RADCLIFFE and SAMUEL JOHNSON. The writers of the dialogue, descriptive pieces and poems included Laurence Housman, Robert Bridges, Laurence Binyon, SIR CHARLES OMAN, Sir Walter Ralegh and Stanley Weyman.

Painted Room Discovered in 1927 at No. 3 CORNMARKET by E.W. Attwood, whose firm of tailors, Messrs Hookham, occupied the premises. The room was part of the CROWN INN where Shakespeare often stayed with his friends, John Davenant, the innkeeper who was MAYOR of Oxford, and his attractive wife, 'a very beautiful woman, and of a very good witt, and of conversation extremely agreable'. Shakespeare, says JOHN AUBREY, 'was wont to go into Warwickshire once a yeare, and did in his journey lye at this house in Oxon, where he was exceedingly respected'. Shakespeare was godfather to the Davenants' son William, who was baptised on 3 March 1606 in ST MARTIN'S CHURCH at CARFAX. William (later Sir William Davenant) became a playwright himself and was made Poet Laureate in 1638.

The brickwork of the fireplace in the Painted Room dates from 1350, and the letters 'I.H.S.' above the fireplace from about 1450. The room contains 16th-century mural paintings which had been covered by substantial oak panels put in in about 1630, and later by canvas and wallpaper. The murals on the north and east walls contain an elaborate design of linked arabesques with fruit and flowers in the lower border and mottoes round the top border. Part of the wording reads 'Serve god Devoutlye . . . Feare god above anythynge'. The oak panels have now been put on rollers so that they can be slid back to reveal the painted walls.

The Painted Room was used for meetings of the OXFORD PRESERVATION TRUST and is open to the public. The building formerly belonged to New College, but now belongs to the city of Oxford.

Palm's Delicatessen *Covered Market.* Opened in 1954 by Mr and Mrs E. Palm, who came to England in 1938 from Czechoslovakia and moved to Oxford the following year. The first shop in the COVERED MARKET consisted of two stalls, the business moving later to its present shop in the middle of the market. Mrs Loisl Palm ran the delicatessen, offering advice on continental as well as West Indian, Asian or African food, while her husband dealt with the wholesalers and looked after the business side. The Palms established their delicatessen at a time when such shops were rare outside London: they were the first shop in Oxford to stock such items as avocado pears, sweet potatoes and yams, and had a wide range of continental foodstuffs and items not usually found in shops in the city. They retired in the early 1970s, but the delicatessen is still in the Covered Market under the same name.

Paradise Square This part of ST EBBE'S has been so much redeveloped in recent years, with car parks taking the place of attractive domestic buildings, that the square's name seems inappropriate. At one time it was known as West-Gate Street, but the name Paradise Square was certainly in existence in ANTHONY WOOD's time (1661); he says that the name came from an orchard called Paradyse, and it is known that the Greyfriars' property had an orchard called Paradise in at least 1540. (The word 'paradise' derives from the Persian for garden.) There is also a Paradise Garden shown in a sketch map of 1605. In 1886 a report of the Oxford Architectural and Historical Society mentions a Paradise Place, describing it as 'an uninviting yard'. The Rectory of ST EBBE'S CHURCH is one of the few older buildings left in the square. It was designed by G.E. STREET in 1852 and finished in 1855, but was altered at the back in 1869. (*See also* PARADISE STREET.)

Paradise Street Running from PARADISE SQUARE to Quaking Bridge (*see* BRIDGES), the street contains several buildings of note. Both Greyfriars and Blackfriars lived in the area. The site of Greyfriars Church and cloisters (*c.*1246–1538) lies under the WESTGATE CENTRE and the multi-storey car park. Giving character to the south side of the street is Greyfriars, a late 17th-century house of which the inside was refitted *c.*1700 and the whole beautifully conserved in 1985. An excellent drawing by BUCKLER (now in the BODLEIAN) shows Greyfriars and its doorway with a distinctive floral shell-hood over the door. Also in the street is the picturesque Jolly Farmers public house, SIMON HOUSE (for homeless men) and, further to the north, Telephone House. This was originally called Hume House after the developers, Hume Properties. It was built to the designs of Donald Rowswell and Partners in 1964–6 on the site of the Old Swan Bakery. The building was taken over by the Post Office in 1966.

Park End Street A continuation of NEW ROAD running westwards to No. 2 BOTLEY ROAD, completed in about 1770. By the 1930s it housed offices and warehouses and also so many garages that it became known as the 'Street of Wheels'. Even in 1968 nine garages still remained. The establishment of Archer,

Cowley & Co., removals and storage, at Nos 36–9 (south side), is one of the oldest in the street. The buildings were erected in 1894–1909 and the firm retains an archive of tributes made by satisfied customers, including John Masefield (who was moved from BOAR'S HILL to Cirencester) and two Masters of University College. Further along on the same side, on the corner of HOLLYBUSH ROW, are the premises of HALL'S BREWERY. Further west is the old factory of COOPER'S 'OXFORD' MARMALADE, which became offices for the Oxfordshire County Council in 1951. The 1964 Development Plan had foreseen its destruction to make way for an inner relief-road, but this never came about. Opposite, on the corner of REWLEY ROAD (on the site of REWLEY ABBEY) is the Old London Midland Scottish Railway (formerly LNWR) station, now occupied by a tyre firm. The building incorporates parts of the 1851 Great Exhibition. The ROYAL OXFORD HOTEL is on the corner of HYTHE BRIDGE STREET. Pacey's Bridge (see BRIDGES) is near the west end of the street. The road is now one-way from east to west with a length of bus lane on the south side.

Park Hospital for Children *Old Road, Headington.* Originally Highfield Park, the home of the Moss family. The house, with its 28-acre grounds adjoining the WARNEFORD HOSPITAL, was acquired by the Warneford in 1933 and came into service as a psychiatric convalescent home in 1936. When Dr R.G. McInnes succeeded Dr Alexander Neill as medical superintendent of the Warneford in 1938, Highfield Park House was converted into the Park Hospital for Functional Nervous Disorders, with twenty-six beds. Most cases were referred from out-patient clinics for nervous diseases held at the RADCLIFFE INFIRMARY.

In the mid-1940s, the first out-patient psychiatric services for the Warneford were provided at the Park Hospital and continued to be held there until the latter was converted into a children's psychiatric hospital in 1958. In 1986 the Park was a thirty-bedded hospital for children, incorporating the National Centre for children with epilepsy and a modern four-bedded mother-and-baby unit.

Park Town This quarter of NORTH OXFORD, a 'new and salubrious' Oxford development, was originally made up of four separately named groups of houses: Park Town, Park Terrace, Park Crescent and Clarendon Villas. They became officially and collectively known as Park Town in June 1938. The area was laid out in 1853 by Samuel Lipscomb Seckham, who was chosen as the architect after a competition had been held. All the houses are now listed Grade II, forming a group with Nos 68 and 70 BANBURY ROAD. To the west of Park Crescent (laid out 1853–5), on the south and north, are Italianate houses with Welsh slate roofs and sash windows. The crescent is made up of two curved rows of three-storeyed stuccoed houses with basements, one on the south and one on the north. Park Terrace (1855) at the east end is made up of three-storeyed houses with basements, all of brick, yellow in front and red at the back. It is given character by a central archway and by the whole curved terrace's being about 4 feet above the roadway. In the centre are gardens of trees and shrubs originally planned by W. Baxter, curator of the BOTANICAL GARDEN from 1813 until 1848. Some of the attractive iron railings round

the crescent survived the Second World War (when most of North Oxford's railings were removed in an attempt to help the war-effort) because they formed the edges of basement wells. New railings have been erected in recent years to enclose the central green areas. The pillar-box (1865) at the west end of the crescent garden is of the hexagonal type known as Penfold (see POSTAL SERVICES). There are public lavatories concealed by bushes on an island at the western end beside the Banbury Road. In 1849 the Oxford Board of Guardians purchased land here on which they proposed to build a workhouse, but this plan was not implemented. Early residents in the houses included J.C. Cavell, linen draper (see ELLISTON & CAVELL LTD), William Baker, cabinet-maker, whose family shop at the corner of BROAD STREET and CORNMARKET was built in 1915 (see BAKER'S), and William Matthison, the artist, who lived at No. 9 Park Terrace from 1903 until his death in 1926. Seckham himself lived here at Carlton Lodge (now No. 5).

Parker's Bookshop in BROAD STREET founded by James Fletcher, who came to Oxford from Salisbury and leased from the city a bookshop at the Broad Street end of TURL STREET in 1731. By 1769 the firm was known as J. and J. Fletcher. James Fletcher the Younger took into partnership his son-in-law W. Hanwell and by 1798 the firm had become Fletcher and Hanwell. Hanwell took Joseph Parker into partnership in 1797. He is described by the Rev. W. Tuckwell in his *Reminiscences* as modelling himself on the style and appearance of 'that formidable person', Dr Coplestone, the Provost of Oriel. (Sackville Parker, his great-uncle, had already established a bookshop at No. 88 HIGH STREET. Dr Johnson visited him there in 1784, reporting, 'I have been to see my old friend Sack Parker. I find he has married his maid; he has done right. She has lived with him many years in great confidence.' Sackville Parker died in 1796.) In 1805 Joseph entered into partnership with the University to found the Bible Press. He retired in 1832, leaving the bookselling business to his nephew, John Henry Parker. The latter's son, James, was taken into the business in 1855. After alterations to join the Turl Street and Broad Street premises into one, the bookshop was re-opened in January 1914, having been the Parker family home for many years and previously the Fletcher bookshop.

BLACKWELL'S acquired a substantial interest in the business in 1938 and in 1973 acquired the majority of the shares in Parker and Son Ltd. In 1964 the site on the corner of Turl Street and Broad Street was redeveloped by Exeter College, incorporating a new split-level bookshop for Parker's in the Thomas Wood Building designed by Brett & Pollen. The new shop was opened by Harold Macmillan, later EARL OF STOCKTON, the CHANCELLOR of the University. In 1988 it became Blackwell's Art and Poster Shop.

(Paintin, H., 'Some Famous Oxford Booksellers', *Oxford Chronicle*, 30 January 1914; Whiteman, A., 'Parker & Son, Oxford, the History of a Bookshop', *Oxford Magazine*, 1962, pp. 383–4.)

Parking When most of the buildings in ST EBBE'S were demolished the area was covered in car parks. In October 1974 Oxford's first central multi-storey car park was opened in St Ebbe's as part of the Westgate development (*see* WESTGATE CENTRE); it was said to be the most advanced multi-storey in Europe. Built in brown brick and designed by Vernon Gibbs & Associates, it has capacity for 1025 cars. The motorist takes a ticket at the barrier on entering; on returning to the car park, the ticket is fed into a machine which indicates the amount payable. When this is paid into the machine another ticket is issued, which the motorist feeds into a machine at the exit to raise the barrier. In case of difficulty the motorist can speak into the ticket machine to call the controller, whose office is in a many-faceted spherical control-tower. There is a fountain in the courtyard which throws a jet of water some 15 feet into the air.

Oxford's parking problems were alleviated by the Park and Ride system. Car parks are sited at points on or near the RING ROAD and from them a frequent bus service carries passengers to and from the city centre for a cheap return fare. Parking is free. The first Park and Ride was set up in 1973 on the south side of the city at Red Bridge on the ABINGDON ROAD and after a tentative start the system is now widely used. The park on the north side (opened in 1976) is at the Pear Tree roundabout and that on the west side (opened in 1974) is at Seacourt on the BOTLEY ROAD. The east park (Thornhill Park and Ride), opened in December 1985, is close to the HEADINGTON roundabout.

The main car parks in the centre of Oxford, apart from St Ebbe's, are WORCESTER STREET (188 cars) on land belonging to Nuffield College, which was formerly part of the CANAL wharf, and GLOUCESTER GREEN. Oxford has never had parking meters. In 1970 parking discs were introduced for street parking: the motorist carried a card which was set to the time the car was parked and was displayed so that it was visible from outside the car and allowed two hours' parking. The difficulty was that most visitors did not have a parking disc, and the system was abandoned in 1980 in favour of a park-and-display system – a parking ticket being displayed on the windscreen. The main on-street parks are in ST GILES' and BROAD STREET.

Parks, University The land which now constitutes the University Parks (always now referred to in the plural) was held in 1086, according to Domesday Book, by ROBERT D'OILLY. It was referred to as 'thirty acres of meadow near the wall, and a mill' – that is Holywell Mill. HOLYWELL MANOR was given to Merton College by Henry III in 1266. Sir John Peshall, writing in 1773, said, 'Before I take my leave of this Manor I should speak of a neat Terras Walk made round part of a large field, called the Park, adjoining to the north-east end of the city, extending about a mile, which serves for a pleasant and whole-some walk.' During the CIVIL WAR the Parks became the exercise ground for the royalist troops, and it has been said by some writers that they got their name because at that time the area was used as an artillery park. In fact, the Parks are an amalgamation of an old and a new park. They were a popular place for walks: Charles II exercised his King Charles spaniels here when staying in Oxford in 1685; Mrs Gamlen, writing of the Parks in her memoirs in 1860, said, 'Of course we went for walks. Sometimes in the Parks, then a grass field with a cart track across it from East to West, approached from St. Giles by a footpath between hedges, where Keble Road now is.' In those days the Parks included the whole of what is now the SCIENCE AREA.

In 1853 the University bought part of the land from Merton College and during the following eleven years acquired the whole area of 91 acres. It stretches from North Lodge, built about 1865 in an area formerly called 'Rome', down a wide path bordered by trees past Lady Margaret Gate to the lily pond constructed in 1925 beside the River Cherwell (*see* THAMES). From the pond a path runs in a south-easterly direction by the side of the Cherwell to High Bridge or Rainbow Bridge, over the Cherwell, and continues along a stretch of the river popular for PUNTING and then in a westerly direction past South Lodge by Linacre College, skirting the Science Area to Keble Gate in PARKS ROAD. The land on the east side of the Cherwell was acquired in 1886 and the meadow to the north-east of Rainbow Bridge in 1934. From South Lodge the MESOPOTAMIA Walk forms the southern boundary of the Parks, passing PARSON'S PLEASURE and THE ROLLERS, and extending to King's Mill Gate. The walk crosses the Cherwell by a concrete bridge built in 1950 to replace an old wooden one. In 1944 Mr and Mrs H.N. Spalding gave the University 18¾ acres between Mesopotamia and New Marston to form a nature reserve.

The cricket pavilion, designed by T.G. JACKSON, was built in 1880 and the cricket ground, opened in 1881, is used by OXFORD UNIVERSITY CRICKET CLUB for first-class cricket matches in term. Other games are now played in the Parks, including tennis, croquet, hockey and rugby. The Parks are closed to the public at dusk each day and on one complete day in the year, usually ST GILES' FAIR day, in order to prevent the acquisition of a public right of way.

In 1928–9 an avenue of many different varieties of thorn trees was planted across the middle of the Parks from north to south, and much new planting has been carried out in recent years, partly to replace trees uprooted by gales, elms lost through Dutch elm disease, and trees which have come to the end of their life. An avenue of different varieties of maple has been planted on either side of the path leading to Rainbow Bridge. The Parks are under the supervision of the Curators of the University Parks, whose general policy has been to provide 'specimens of as many interesting trees as possible without sacrificing the appearance of spaciousness and without detracting from the natural beauty of the indigenous by an excess of the exotic'. (*See also* TREES.)

Parks Road Takes its name from the University PARKS and runs from BROAD STREET to NORHAM GARDENS. In the 1830s it was known as Park Street and then as the Parks Road. In the early 1870s there was a dispute between the University, Wadham College and the Local Board concerning that part of the road running from BROAD STREET to Museum Terrace (now MUSEUM ROAD) in the north. Despite the college and University's opposition to the increase in heavy traffic, the road became a public highway, but in order to prevent vibrations, which might harm the valuable laboratory instruments in the vicinity, heavily laden carriages or carts and wagons without springs were forbidden. Today the road is still important for LABORATORIES, including those for Chemical Crystallography and those connected with the Department of Physics (*see* CLARENDON LABORATORY), the Department of Geology and Mineralogy, the Department of Agricultural Science (built 1907), the Department of

Physiology, the Department of Metallurgy and the Science of Materials and, at the northern end, the Department of Engineering Science. On the east side (from Broad Street) are the KING'S ARMS public house, Wadham College, the garden entrance to RHODES HOUSE, the Radcliffe Science Library (1933–4), the UNIVERSITY MUSEUM (1855), and the PITT RIVERS MUSEUM (1885–6) with the Department of Ethnology and Pre-History. At the northern end, on the east side, is the North Lodge of the Parks, built in 1862 to designs by H.W. Moore. On the west side is the NEW BODLEIAN LIBRARY, on the top floor of which is the INDIAN INSTITUTE library (moved from its original building) and further north is Keble College.

Parliamentary Visitation (1647) *see* VISITATIONS *and* VISITORS.

Parsons, John (*1761–1819*). The son of the butler of Corpus Christi College, Parsons was born in the parish of ST ALDATE'S and attended MAGDALEN COLLEGE SCHOOL. From there he went to Wadham College and was elected a Fellow of Balliol in 1785. In 1798 he became Master, and from that time the reputation of Balliol and of the University as a whole began to revive in consequence of the reforms instituted by Parsons and by some of his fellow heads, including Dr Eveleigh, Provost of Oriel. Parsons was VICE-CHANCELLOR from 1807 to 1810, and for many years was the dominant figure on the HEBDOMADAL BOARD. His appointment as Bishop of Peterborough in 1813 was said to be a recognition of his services in reforming the examination system at Oxford.

Parson's Pleasure   A bathing place for men on the River Cherwell (*see* THAMES) close to THE ROLLERS. In the 17th century it was known as Patten's Pleasure and was used by undergraduates for swimming. ANTHONY WOOD mentions that on 18 June 1666 a Mr Oliver Craven of Trinity College was drowned at Patten's Pleasure, and on 9 July 1689 an undergraduate of

Brasenose was also drowned there. In 1692 Wood refers to 'Patten's Pleasure neare New Park'. It was known as Loggerhead in the 19th century and received its present name only in this century. The name may derive from the early use of the bathing place by parsons, but it is more likely to be a corruption of Patten's Pleasure. Charlie Cox looked after the bathing place for some seventy-five years until his death in around 1917. The spot is screened off on all sides except the river frontage. It has always been used by men for bathing and sunbathing in the nude. Until recently it was customary for ladies to disembark from their punts before reaching Parson's Pleasure and to walk round to the Rollers to pick up the punt again.

(*See also* DAMES' DELIGHT.)

Pater, Walter Horatio   (*1839–1894*). Went up to The Queen's College at the age of nineteen and graduated with second-class Honours in 1862. When he was about twenty-four and a member of Old Mortality (the essay society which flourished in Oxford from 1859–65) he met and became a friend of Swinburne, and later was on friendly terms with other poets and artists of the Pre-Raphaelite Brotherhood. In 1864 he became a non-clerical Fellow of Brasenose College, living in college until 1869 when he bought No. 2 Bradmore Road, where his two sisters made their home with him. From 1886 the ménage was in Kensington, but moved back to Oxford in 1893 when Pater bought No. 64 ST GILES', the house in which he died a year later. Edmund Gosse wrote of him that in all these years 'his real home was in his rooms at Brasenose', and, of his work, that 'he was the most studied of the English prose-writers of his time'. His *Studies in the History of the Renaissance*, published in 1873, includes essays on Botticelli, Leonardo and Winckelmann, and was the work by which he first became known. Among later publications are *Marius the Epicurean* (1885), *Imaginary Portraits* (1887) and *Plato and Platonism* (1893). In the centre of the

Parks Road c.1813, before the demolition of the wall and rails in front of Wadham College.

The Rollers at Parson's Pleasure on the Cherwell, for centuries a popular bathing place for 'men only'.

memorial plaque in Brasenose antechapel the critic and humanist is depicted surrounded by Leonardo da Vinci, Michelangelo, Dante and Plato.

Pathology, Sir William Dunn School of *South Parks Road.* Pathology was at first taught at Oxford as part of general medical instruction. Gradually, however, it became a separate subject, together with Anatomy and Physiology. When SIR HENRY ACLAND became Lee's Reader of Anatomy in 1845, Pathology was taught in Christ Church Anatomy School, both by Acland himself and by his assistant, the great microscopist, Lionel Beale (1828–1906).

In 1860, when the UNIVERSITY MUSEUM was opened, a large collection of pathological rarities was transferred from Christ Church to the medical department of the museum where Acland had a laboratory for research in practical Pathology and, later, in Bacteriology. At the same time, George Rolleston, who was appointed Linacre Professor of Anatomy and Physiology in 1860, included pathological instruction in his lectures. In 1899, after the purchase of a very large collection of pathological specimens from Holland, a benefactor offered the University £5000 for the building of a Department of Pathology; the University added another £5000 and in 1901 the new department was opened. There was, however, an annual grant of only £150 a year and no money to pay for a chair. Following the appointment in 1904 of William Osler (1849–1919) as Regius Professor of Medicine, funds were obtained for a chair to which in 1907 was appointed the thirty-four-year-old Danish experimental pathologist Georges Dreyer (1873–1934).

At the beginning of 1922 it was suggested that the trustees of the late Sir William Dunn (who had already made a grant for a Department and Chair of Biochemistry at Cambridge) might make Oxford a grant for the establishment of a more extensive Department of Pathology. And, despite objection from anti-vivisectionists and from those who protested against nearly 3 acres of the University PARKS being taken over for this new department, a decree accepting £100,000 was passed by CONGREGATION on 21 November 1922. The architect chosen was E.P. Warren who worked closely with Professor Dreyer and on 9 May 1923 the foundation stone was laid. The building was completed at the end of 1926 and the formal opening took place on 11 March 1927. It is a testament to the careful and detailed planning that Professor Dreyer carried out that, although there have been great changes in experimental pathology since his day, the building, to which a wing was subsequently added, has continued to be perfectly functional and effective.

Dreyer was succeeded by Professor Howard Walter Florey, later LORD FLOREY. In 1987 the head of the department was Henry Harris, who was also Regius Professor of Medicine.

(*See also* LABORATORIES *and* MEDICINE.)

Pattison, Mark (*1813–1884*). The eldest of the twelve children of an evangelical Yorkshire clergyman, Pattison went up to Oriel College in 1832. Having read diligently but too widely to obtain the first-class degree he had hoped for, he also failed to obtain the fellowship at Oriel upon which he had set his heart; but in 1839 he was elected a Fellow of Lincoln. He was ordained in 1841, having fallen under the influence of E.B. PUSEY and J.H. NEWMAN. For a time he lived in Newman's house in ST ALDATE'S and helped in the translations of the works of the Fathers of the Holy Catholic Church. He was appointed a college tutor in 1843 and an examiner in the School of LITERAE HUMANIORES in 1848; and, although he had been extremely shy and often unhappy as a young man, he now began to enjoy University life, proving himself an effective lecturer, an inspiring teacher of rare ability and conscientiousness, and a highly astute examiner. His religious writings were combined with articles of a general literary character.

Pattison's retiring and studious nature, which induced him to abandon the Senior Common Room

Mark Pattison, who was appointed Rector of Lincoln in 1861, was a leading advocate of university reform.

for his study of an evening, and his occasionally sharp tongue and habitually stiff manner in the presence of those whom he found uncongenial, resulted in his being passed over when the election of a new Rector of Lincoln took place in 1851. He was, however, elected Rector ten years later. This did not, though, prevent him from continuing as an examiner, as a delegate of the OXFORD UNIVERSITY PRESS and of the BODLEIAN LIBRARY, or from contributing articles, reviews and biographical articles to numerous magazines, newspapers and encyclopaedias. His distinguished life of Isaac Casaubon appeared in 1875. He was deeply interested in university reform (his *Oxford Studies* was published in 1855 and his *Suggestions on Academical Organisation* in 1868), but declined to become VICE-CHANCELLOR in 1878 and was not as active a Rector of Lincoln as had been hoped. He was, however, on occasions an extremely intimidating man, capable of crumpling up and hurling an incompetent essay into a nervous undergraduate's face and being as alarmingly silent and dismissive as BENJAMIN JOWETT. One unfortunate undergraduate summoned to go for a walk with him 'essayed a literary opening to the conversation by volunteering "The irony of Sophocles is greater than the irony of Euripides". Pattison seemed lost in thought over the statement, and made no answer until the two turned at Iffley to come back. Then he said, "Quote." Quotations not being forthcoming, the return and the parting took place in silence.'

Pattison remained a highly stimulating lecturer, however, and in the company of the young and with women his formal manner was relaxed. In 1861 he married Emilia Frances Strong, a writer on art twenty-seven years his junior, who subsequently became the wife of Sir Charles Wentworth Dilke. It has been suggested that their relationship inspired that of Casaubon and Dorothea in George Eliot's *Middlemarch* (*see* FICTION). Pattison's sister was the philanthropist Dorothy Wyndlow Pattison (1832–78).

Payne & Son (Goldsmiths) Ltd This firm of jewellers, silversmiths and goldsmiths was founded in Wallingford in 1790 by John Payne of London. The Oxford shop was opened in 1888 at No. 131 HIGH STREET, where it still is. The business is still owned and personally directed by members of the Payne family. The firm was in the forefront of the art-nouveau movement and has a worldwide reputation for modern and antique silver.

Peisleys One of 18th-century Oxford's most celebrated families of MASONS AND BUILDERS (*see also* TOWNESENDS). Bartholomew Peisley the first (*c.*1620–94) built the Senior Common Room at St John's College and completed the library and chapel of St Edmund Hall. His son, Bartholomew Peisley the second (*c.*1654–1715), who was apprenticed to his father in 1669, worked on many of the buildings in Oxford which were erected in his time, including, apparently, Trinity College chapel and STONE'S ALMSHOUSES. He may also have built ST GILES' HOUSE. His son, Bartholomew Peisley the third (*c.*1683–1727), was taken into apprenticeship in 1698 and subsequently often worked in partnership with William Townesend. He and Townesend built the Radcliffe Quadrangle at University College and the CODRINGTON LIBRARY at All Souls College to the designs of NICHOLAS HAWKSMOOR. Writing in August 1727 THOMAS HEARNE observed of Bartholomew Peisley the third: 'Yesterday died of a Feavor, or rather (as I hear) of the Gout in the Stomack, after 4 or 5 days Illness, Mr. Peisley, a noted wealthy mason, that lived in New-Inn Hall Lane in Oxford, leaving a Wife (a very pretty Woman) and three Children, & his wife is big again. He was about 44 or 45 years of age, & he and one Townesend carried (as it were) all the business in masonry before them, both in Oxford and the Parts about it. This Mr. Peisley was looked upon as a very courteous well behaved man'. He was buried in the churchyard of ST GILES' CHURCH. His widow subsequently married the President of Trinity College. The Peisleys were probably quarry-owners, as well as masons and builders, and certainly supplied Headington Stone for St Paul's Cathedral (*see* STONE *and also* VANBRUGH HOUSE).

Pembroke College Founded in 1624 by James I by incorporation on the same site as the much older BROADGATES HALL. The college owes its name to William Herbert, 3rd Earl of Pembroke, then CHANCELLOR of the University. Its original endowment, however, came from neither Pembroke nor the King. How direct was the involvement of the King is far from certain, and the Earl of Pembroke was destined to die suddenly at the age of fifty in 1630 before making the generous benefaction to the college which, it seems, he had promised; the splendid piece of PLATE which he actually gave was doubtless melted down in the CIVIL WAR. The Letters Patent granted on 29 June 1624 by James I refer to the foundation as being 'at the cost and charges of Thomas Tesdale and Richard Wightwick', and indeed it was they who were the actual founders of the college.

Thomas Tesdale of Glympton and Abingdon, a wealthy maltster, had died in 1610, leaving in his will a sum of no less than £5000, the annual revenue from which was to be used for the maintenance in Balliol College of seven Fellows and six scholars from Abingdon School. However, the Master and Fellows of Balliol may initially have decided that they were unable to accept the bequest upon the conditions (which involved FOUNDER'S KIN and local connection) prescribed in Tesdale's will. Yet it remains strange that, when Richard Wightwick of East Ilsley, a former member of Balliol, offered to add three Fellows and four scholars, also from Abingdon School, to the Tesdale foundation, the senior Tesdale trustee, George Abbot (a former Fellow of Balliol and by now Archbishop of Canterbury) was persuaded by the Mayor and Corporation of Abingdon, as governors of the school, to found a new college rather than to allow the planned benefactions to Balliol to proceed. The theory that the King himself, always interested in academic affairs, wanted to be known to posterity as the founder of an Oxford college and thus vetoed

the Balliol plan, cannot be proved – nor entirely discounted. Certainly a Master of Balliol was expressing considerable resentment on the subject less than forty years later.

Thus the last Principal of Broadgates Hall, Thomas Clayton (ironically himself a Balliol man), became the first Master of Pembroke College and, at the inauguration ceremony in August 1624, the first of four Latin speeches was delivered by Thomas (later Sir Thomas) Browne (1605–82), author of *Religio Medici* and *Urn Burial*; its text still survives. Browne was to display little later interest in Oxford or his college. Pembroke's first statutes (1624, amended 1628) appear to be similar to those of other colleges, but in fact they differ in one important respect: no salary for the Master or for anyone else is mentioned, since the Tesdale and Wightwick benefactions were for individuals rather than for the college. Indeed, it was some time before the original endowments were supplemented from other sources – including Charles I, who provided the college in 1636 with two important endowments. The Chancellor of the University was to be the VISITOR, as he still is; but the statutes have, of course, been very substantially modified or altered over the years.

So soon did the Civil War break out after Pembroke's foundation that the loss of its plate to the King's cause was probably less of a sacrifice than it must have been for the older foundations; the King's

Michael Burghers' engraving of Pembroke College in 1700, showing the college as it would have appeared in Samuel Johnson's day.

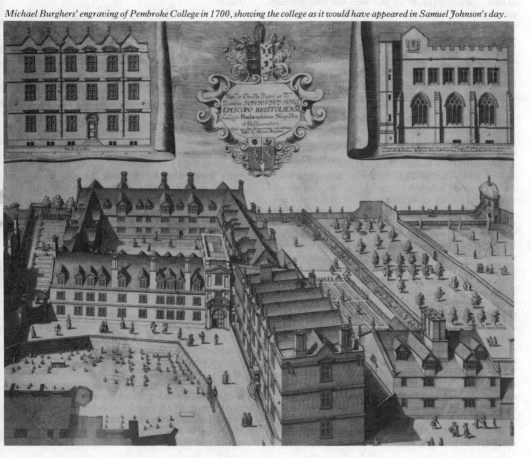

letter of thanks is preserved in the archives. In the war itself, Pembroke was strongly royalist and provided a complement of officers for the King's army. However, an accident a little later on caused it to be affected with peculiar thoroughness by the Parliamentary VISITA-TION of Oxford. Clayton died shortly after the surrender of Oxford in 1646. Though a parliamentary committee had ordered that no University appoint-ments should be made, the Fellows of Pembroke hastily elected Henry Wightwick as Master. On 26 August Parliament retorted by appointing Henry Langley, one of the Parliamentary Visitors and himself a Pembroke man, in his place. On 8 October the order was read in Pembroke. Most of the members submitted to the authority of the Visitors and the new Master, Langley; but some, including the Master, Wightwick, were expelled. Others later made their peace; yet others seem not to have returned until the expulsion of Langley at the Restoration in 1660. Under Langley, Pembroke became, on the whole, strongly puritan, and after the short rule of the restored Wightwick, Dr John Hall (Master 1664–1709) a Puritan but a Conformist, carried on the tradition.

The 18th century passed as placidly for Pembroke as for the University generally, and its most notable events were the building and consecration of the chapel (see below) and the brief residence of the college's indisputably most famous old member, SAMUEL JOHNSON (1728–9). But with the 19th century came reform. In the early 1830s JOHN KEBLE remarked that: 'As light dawneth in a cellar from a decayed mackerel, even so it is bruited that in Pembroke, the cellar and dusthole of the university, there are those who send forth sparks of reform.' This undoubtedly refers to Francis Jeune, but there had been signs of change even earlier. The effects of the new system of public examinations had been shown in the resolution of 1818 not to raise any scholar to a fellowship 'who shall have brought discredit upon the Society by having been refused a "Testamur" at the public examination'. (In 1821 an exception was made if he should subsequently obtain a place in the first or upper part of the second class.) Jeune was tutor and Fellow from 1828 to 1837 (when he helped to reject Fellows and scholars who were not *sufficientes doctrina*), but his enduring work for the University and college followed his (disputed) election as Master in 1843. The transformation which he effected in the college was as remarkable as it has proved enduring. Matriculations increased sharply, to the point where they were, at one stage, the third largest in the University; the college buildings were doubled in size; a new hall was completed (1848) on a munificent scale; and sweeping changes in the statutes, designed to reduce or eliminate the crippling ties which bound the college to certain schools and localities, and which compelled Fellows to take Orders, were at last, and not without a hitch over the college's Channel Island endowments, effected in 1857 (though it is worth noting that even after the 1877 ROYAL COMMISSION Pembroke, with the deanery of Christ Church, had the only necessarily clerical headship of an Oxford college, since it could not afford to dispense with the canonry of Gloucester annexed to the Master's office).

So important did Dr Jeune, and the college, rightly consider these changes, that a petition was presented to the House of Commons in 1854, couched in the following remarkable terms:

'The humble Petition of the Master, Fellows, and Scholars of Pembroke College, in the University of Oxford, sheweth . . .

'That the Statutes passed for the Government of the College by Commissioners appointed by the Crown limited the choice of the Fellows and Scholars of the College on the original foundations partly to persons of the kindred of Thomas Tesdale, with a preference to those educated in Abingdon School, and to persons of the name or kindred of Richard Wightwick, wherever educated; and partly to youths educated in Abingdon School, without reference to their parentage.

'That experience has shewn that neither from particular localities or families, nor from schools with small endowments situated in poor places, and not possessing the means of local extension, can be expected a supply of Scholars likely to do credit to the College or to advance the main objects for which Colleges were founded.

'That on Fellows of Colleges devolve chiefly in our time the education of the students of the University, and that to the efficiency of Collegiate instruction a fair proportion of students of talent and attainments is as indispensable as a succession of Fellows of superior merit; but that such students can scarcely be secured without open Scholarships of adequate value.

'That the Statutes specially require, and the Country expects, that young men not on the foundation shall be educated in Pembroke College; that the number of such students has greatly increased there of late years; that they amount at present to an average of twenty; and that the college has recently erected, at great cost, a new Hall and apartments for such students.

'That two engrafted foundations very scantily endowed, but comparatively open, principally enable the College to discharge its educational functions.

'That if richer Colleges, where the restrictions on the election to Fellowships and Scholarships are only local, shall be enabled, by the wisdom of Parliament, to open their foundations, and to attract to themselves the ablest men as Fellows and Scholars, it is only just that a poor College from which the same educational duties are required shall be relieved of all its shackles, for otherwise every improvement in other Societies will place it in a situation positively and relatively worse, till at last it must lose public confidence and see itself deserted.

'That such must inevitably be the case with Pembroke College if, other Colleges being set at liberty, it is to continue limited in its choice of Fellows and Scholars to the few boys educated in an obscure school, to the kindred of Founders, and to confined localities; if it is not permitted to avail itself of the talents and energies of all the Fellows by extending to them all equal privileges and emolu-ments; if it cannot by reducing the number of its Fellowships render them sufficiently valuable to attract to itself a fair share of superior men; and if it is precluded from making provision for the election of its Fellows and Scholars according to personal merit and fitness.

The front of Pembroke College in 1838, with the graveyard of St Aldate's shown beneath Tom Tower on the left.

'That it cannot reasonably be hoped that any of these beneficial objects can be attained in case the improvements which may be desired by the College shall be liable to the veto of two-thirds of a body external to the College, and looking naturally to the advantage of individuals and the small school in its patronage rather than to the interests of the College or the great University of which the College forms a part, or the promotion of religion, learning, and science generally, the great ends for which Colleges and Universities are founded and endowed.

'That no improvements deserving of consideration can be effected in Pembroke College without touching in a greater or lesser degree those of its foundations which are connected with Abingdon School.

'Your petitioners therefore earnestly intreat your Honourable House not to place them under the controul of a small municipal corporation, but to release them from all such foreign intervention in the election of Fellows and Scholars as they are now subject to, and to enable them generally, by the removal of restrictions, to discharge their high duties with efficiency and honour. . . .'

Such a statement could hardly be improved upon today; and it was scarcely surprising that the last-minute hitch mentioned above led Jeune to note indignantly that 'the College has thus lost the credit of effecting its own reforms'.

The changes thus begun made possible the provision of far more adequate college teaching than had been available before. Already (1845) the college had added a Mathematics lecturer to its teaching staff; now a lecturer in Philology and one in Law and History were provided, and in 1863 a fund was opened to pay for 'professional or private instruction for such

undergraduates as are fitted to receive it'. A few months later Jeune resigned on obtaining the deanery of Lincoln, and Pembroke lost its place in the forefront of reform.

The evolution of the college over the last century into a modern college has been as unspectacular as it has from most other colleges. The statutes have been further revised; the undergraduate body has increased very greatly in size (from perhaps eighty to 300); there is a substantial graduate body (sixty to seventy members); and a fellowship of forty compared with ten in the late 19th century. The most important visible changes have lain in the physical additions and alterations which have come about on the college's limited site since the Second World War, and it is to Pembroke's architectural development that we now turn.

The college lies on an almost rectangular site, with natural boundaries: ST ALDATE'S to the east, BREWER STREET (with a section of the old CITY WALL) to the south, ST EBBE'S to the west, and PEMBROKE STREET (and Pembroke Square) to the north. The architecture of the Old Quadrangle, lying between Brewer Street and Pembroke Square, now dates from 1829 to 1838, though it conceals the building of 1626 to about 1670; DAVID LOGGAN's engraving of 1675, showing a tower in the *middle* of the north face, is simply incorrect. A more accurate depiction of the college as it would have been known by Dr Johnson, for example, is shown by Michael Burghers' engraving of 1700, specially commissioned by the then Master, John Hall. This hardly justifies the notorious comment of the dyspeptic German traveller, von Uffenbach, who visited Oxford in 1710 but dismissed Pembroke out of hand: 'a very indifferent and confused building, and

321

one of the poorest Colleges in Oxford', though it has to be admitted that Pevsner (1974) has described the college as 'complicated and confusing as one walks around', and it is best comprehended with a plan.

Work had begun on the front quadrangle soon after Pembroke had received its royal charter in 1624, although existing houses on the site remained in use. Broadgates Hall, at the north-west corner of the quadrangle, was then the college dining hall, used also for lectures; 'Cambery's Lodgings', purchased in 1625, was to be demolished to make way for the new Master's house, and the two gabled houses in the foreground of the Burghers engraving, which occupied the sites of the mediaeval ACADEMIC HALLS called Polton Hall and Michael Hall (by 1700 confusingly referred to as 'Beef and Dunstan' halls), were to remain in use until 1844, when they were demolished to make way for the present range. They provided the worst, and the cheapest, accommodation in college, the garrets probably occupied by SERVITORS and battlers (see BATTELS), poor students working their way through college, and part of the ground floor, approximately where the Fellows' Staircase now stands, providing the 'common house of easement' of the college. By contrast, the walled gardens, in what is now Chapel Quad, were one of Pembroke's chief attractions, with lawns, a ball-court, a bowling green, and a pagoda-like summerhouse built in 1698 and not demolished until 1869; here Dr Johnson used to play draughts with his fellow undergraduates. (At the time in question, incidentally, the college library and chapel were both housed in the south aisle of ST ALDATE'S CHURCH, known as Docklinton's Aisle and rented for 6s 8d per annum from the churchwardens.) The original Broadgates Hall (the oldest part of the college) at the north-west end of the Old Quadrangle, after undergoing successive metamorphoses – it was for a long time the library – is now the main Senior Common Room.

When Pembroke was extended westwards in the 18th century, the chapel was built (1728–32); its restoration by C.E. Kempe (1884) in a neo-Renaissance style won high praise at the time. The substantial building (now consisting of a Fellows' Staircase and two large staircases for undergraduates) which directly fronts it, was the result of the mastership of Francis Jeune; it was built in 1844–6. The quadrangle known as the Chapel Quad, and 'the great asset of Pembroke, spacious and attractive all round in the variety of its ranges' (Pevsner), was completed by John Hayward's large Victorian-Gothic hall on the west side (1848).

North of Chapel Quad is the Besse Building (1956), named after ANTONIN BESSE, symmetrical, three-storeyed, of ashlar with mullioned windows; and, even more importantly, in 1966–7 a range of old houses in Pembroke Street, nobly given to the college by a benefactor, Mr Reginald Graham, and well restored by C.P. Cleverly, was effectively linked to the Besse Building by a brick building now called Staircase XII (1967), thus creating the North Quadrangle, and taking Beef Lane into the college. The complex design of the whole contains three major features as yet unmentioned: Wolsey's Almshouses, lying between the Old Quadrangle and St Aldate's, was acquired from Christ Church in 1888 and converted for use as the Master's lodgings in 1927; it is claimed that the open timber roof was brought thither by THOMAS WOLSEY from OSENEY ABBEY. The Almshouses themselves were begun by Wolsey c.1525, but the architecture has been cursorily dismissed: 'most of it is of 1834 by Underwood, anyway' (Peter Howell, according to Pevsner). Finally, two recent buildings: the McGowin Library (1974), located between the lodgings and the Old Quadrangle, was the product of yet another munificent benefaction from old members – in this case the McGowin family of Alabama; and the Macmillan Building, on the extreme west side of college bordering St Ebbe's and parallel to the hall, was named after the college's Visitor, Harold Macmillan (later LORD STOCKTON) in 1976. In both cases the architect was Sir Leslie Martin. A new high table was designed for the college by Latrobe Bateman in 1984.

For a college which, until recently, has been small and which has never counted itself among the better endowed, Pembroke has attracted its fair share of leading men. Viscount Harcourt (later Lord Chancellor) matriculated in 1677. Mention has already been made of Sir Thomas Browne and Dr Samuel Johnson. When Johnson referred to Pembroke as a 'nest of singing birds', he may have had chiefly in mind the poet William Shenstone (1732). The eminent jurist Sir William Blackstone entered the college as a commoner in 1738, and became the first Vinerian Professor of Common Law in 1758. A little later, in 1744, John Moore came to Pembroke at the age of fifteen and stayed there for nine years; he was to become Archbishop of Canterbury in 1783. An alumnus who has gained more enduring renown was James Lewis Smithson (1753–1829), who claimed to be the natural son of the 1st Duke of Northumberland. He had the reputation while at Pembroke – where he matriculated strangely late in 1782 – of 'excelling all others in the University in chemical science'. Smithson's craving for posthumous fame, however, was expressed by him in these words: 'The best blood of England flows in my veins: on my father's side I am a Northumberland; on my mother's I am related to Kings. But it avails me not. My name shall live in the memory of man when the titles of the Northumberlands and Percys are extinct and forgotten.' He accordingly bequeathed the reversion of his substantial property to the United States government, to found an institution at Washington 'for the increase and diffusion of knowledge among men.' The property came to the United States in 1838, and in 1846 was founded the Smithsonian Institute (as he had directed it should be called), including a library, art gallery and museum.

Briefer mention may be made of Thomas Beddoes (1820), author of *Death's Jest-Book* (1850); of the eccentric and precocious John Henderson (1781), 'a forgotten genius', who was fluent in Persian, Arabic, Hebrew, Greek, Latin, Spanish, Italian, French and German, and expert in Divinity, Law, Metaphysics, Chemistry, Mathematics and Medicine (yet he was only thirty-one when he died in 1788); and of John Lemprière (1786), undergraduate author of the well-known *Classical Dictionary* (1788). In the 19th century we have already mentioned Francis Jeune (1822), but the college's alumni otherwise left little mark on Church or State; a Fellow, Henry Chandler (1867–98), left to the library his remarkable collection of Aristoteliana. Twentieth-century members of the college especially well known are the politicians

Senator William Fulbright (1925) and M.R.D. Heseltine (1951), and, in the world of theatre, Lord (Bernard) Miles of Blackfriars (1926). The present Master of Pembroke is Sir Roger Bannister (elected 1984; took office 1985); his predecessors were Sir George Pickering (1969–74) and Sir Geoffrey Arthur (1975–84).

In March 1987 work began on the Sir Geoffrey Arthur Building, a three-storey block, designed by Maguire and Murray of Thame, looking across the river to Oxpens (*see* OXPENS ROAD). Now completed, it is the second largest residential development by a college since the Second World War. Estimated to have cost about £4 million, it provides accommodation for nearly a hundred undergraduates and post-graduates.

The corporate designation of the college is The Master, Fellows and Scholars of Pembroke College in the University of Oxford.

(Macleane, Douglas, *History of Pembroke College, Oxford*, Oxford, 1897 (much the most detailed history of all aspects), and *Pembroke College*, London, 1900 (essentially a shorter version of the above); Sutherland, Lucy S., 'Pembroke College', *Victoria County History of Oxford*, Vol. III, Oxford, 1954 (useful detailed material); Royal Commission on Historical Monuments, *City of Oxford*, London, 1939, pp. 95–6 (state of the buildings).)

Pembroke Street   For seven centuries, until about 1838, the street was known as Pennyferthing Lane (or Street) after a family who lived there, the spellings varying from Pinke-farthing to Pinyferthy. A William Penyverthing was Provost of Oxfordshire in about 1240. The name has recently been re-used for the small square alongside the WESTGATE CENTRE leading off ST EBBE'S – PENNYFARTHING PLACE. Today's Pembroke Street, which runs between ST ALDATE'S and St Ebbe's, derives its name from the college, which was formerly BROADGATES HALL. The street contains many Grade II listed 17th- and 18th-century houses (some considerably altered), with Nos 11–28 and 36–9 forming separate groups. Some belong to Pembroke College. Inside No. 38 there is some 17th-century panelling, the design of which is said to be unique in Oxford. Nos 13–14 were built in 1641 but have been altered since. On the north side, No. 40 is the rectory of the church of ST ALDATE. At the St Ebbe's end, at No. 30 next to the back entrance of Marks and Spencer's QUEEN STREET store, is the MUSEUM OF MODERN ART. Oxford's first automatic telephone exchange was built in Pembroke Street in 1926 and on 11 December that year Oxford's 1600 telephone subscribers could dial their own local calls for the first time. By the time the exchange moved to SPEEDWELL STREET in 1959 there were 11,330 subscribers.

Penniless Bench   A bench at CARFAX which was built by the churchwardens of ST MARTIN'S CHURCH in 1545 and which became the semi-official meeting place of the City Council, who 'at the time of the ringing of the bell for the sermon come together to the pennylesse bench, or thereabouts, and staye there until the comyng of the Mayor'. This first bench was a lean-to on the east wall of the church, with a leaded roof. It was doubtless used by beggars and so got its name. The first anniversary of the Gunpowder Plot was commemorated at Carfax and the Council

minutes for 4 November 1606 contain this entry: 'Upon the fifth day of this instant November being the day that is to be solemnized for the miraculous deliverie of his Majestye, the Queene, the prince and whole state of this realme from the late trayterous practize intended, there shall bee some fiftye or three score musketts discharged uppon the leads after the Sermon and Communion ended, with a bonfyer at Carfaxe and some bread and beare for the poore and some ten or twenty shillings to bee allowed for wine to bee drancke at Penylesse bench, so that there bee not above foure poundes in all to bee spent'.

In 1667 the bench was rebuilt by the city in stone against the east wall of the church with an arcade of four round-headed arches supported on pillars. It is shown in an insert in Benjamin Cole's map of PORT MEADOW (*c.*1720). It was used as a butter bench on market days, but in 1747 it was described as 'a great nuisance, a harbour for idle and disorderly people', and the Council ordered it to be removed – which seems to have been done by 1750.

St Martin's Church at Carfax c.1720 showing Penniless Bench, which was reconstructed in 1667 against the east wall of the church.

Pennyfarthing Place   A new cul-de-sac in ST EBBE'S created by the closure of the last of Oxford's CHURCH STREETS. The name, originally of a mediaeval street (now PEMBROKE STREET), was revived at the time of the building of the WESTGATE CENTRE and was derived from an old family resident there, one of whom was William Penyverthing. He was Provost of Oxfordshire during the reign of Henry III, in about 1240. There was also a Nicholas Pennyfader, who was an inhabitant of the area probably in the reign of Edward I. Pinke-farthing Street is also to be found in early records, Pyneferthyng Strete in a will of 1349 and, in 1451, Pingferthing Strete. The lane off Pennyfarthing Place to the south-west was to be called Pennyfarthing or Penny Lane but later (because of its unfortunate connection with the phrase 'to spend a penny') it was changed to Roger Bacon Lane (*see also* ABINGDON ROAD).

Penson's Gardens   One of the old streets in ST EBBE'S, the houses of which were demolished after the Second World War to make way for car parks (*see* PARKING). It was named after the market garden owned by Nathaniel Penson, a leading 18th-century gardener. HENRY TAUNT, the Victorian photographer, was born here.

Perch   *Binsey*. A 17th-century thatched village inn beside the THAMES. It contained oak beams, flagged floors and stone hearths until the building was severely damaged in a fire 11 June 1977. Although St Margaret's Well, beside BINSEY church, was visited by pilgrims from the 12th to the 18th century, no inn on this site can be traced before the 17th century.

Pergamon Press   *Headington Hill Hall.* Founded in 1948 as Butterworth-Springer Ltd, a joint Anglo–German enterprise. It acquired its present title in 1951 following a change in share-ownership. The name derives from a town in Asia Minor famed for its ancient Altar of Pergamon. The company's logo is a reproduction of a Greek coin bearing the head of Athena, goddess of wisdom. Before its sale in 1991, Pergamon Press was part of Maxwell Communication Corporation plc, which, with national newspapers, magazines, cable television, printing, packaging and software companies, is one of the world's largest global communication corporations, employing over 25,000 people.

Permanent Private Halls   *see* PRIVATE HALLS.

Petit Blanc   *61a Banbury Road.* William Day's Victoria Nursery was at No. 63 BANBURY ROAD in 1835. It was then taken over in about 1884 by John Gee, who built the iron-and-glass conservatory in 1897, designed by H.W. Moore. Gee's was a flower shop and greengrocer's until 1984 when the conservatory was bought by the owners of BROWN'S restaurant in WOODSTOCK ROAD and converted into a restaurant called Gee's. In December 1985 the restaurant was bought by Raymond Blanc, owner of Le Manoir aux Quat' Saisons at Great Milton, who moved his smaller restaurant, Le Petit Blanc, from SUMMERTOWN to Banbury Road and renamed Gee's 'Le Petit Blanc'. In 1988 the restaurant was sold and reverted to its original name of Gee's.

Phaidon Press Ltd   Dr Bela Horovitz founded Phaidon Verlag in 1923 in Vienna. Threatened by the Nazi invasion of Austria in 1938, he saved his publishing firm by transferring it to England with the help of Sir Stanley Unwin. In Oxford during the war, at No. 14 ST GILES', and then in London, Horovitz pioneered the publishing of high-quality popular art books, the most famous being Sir Ernst Gombrich's *The Story of Art.* Since his death in 1955 the firm, which moved back to Oxford in 1975, has continued the tradition of well-produced books on the fine arts and art history. Phaidon Press is named after a speaker in one of Plato's dialogues, and its logo is the Greek letter *phi.* The firm moved from ST EBBE'S to Jordan Hill Road in 1988, and, after its sale in 1990, to SUMMERTOWN. It has subsequently moved to London.

Pitt Rivers Museum   *Parks Road.* One of the great ethnological museums of the world. It takes its name from Lieutenant-General Augustus Henry Lane Fox Pitt Rivers (1827–1900), who was born Lane Fox and assumed the additional name Pitt-Rivers (though he did not himself use the hyphen) in 1880 on inheriting the estates of his great uncle, George Pitt, 2nd Baron Rivers. Educated at Sandhurst, he was commissioned in the Grenadier Guards in 1845, served with distinction in the Crimean War and remained on the active list until 1896. Having shown a talent for experimental research, he was employed in investigations into the use and improvement of the rifle in the early years of its introduction into the army, and had soon formed a collection of

Henry Balfour, curator of the Pitt Rivers Museum for forty-eight years from 1891, with the first students to take the diploma course in Anthropology.

firearms which gradually developed into more varied and extensive collections of specimens illustrating changes from simple to complex types. In time the rooms of his house in London became filled with all manner of weapons, looms, costumes, musical instruments, magical and religious symbols, and other specimens, and he was forced to the conclusion that another home must be found for them. They were accordingly moved in 1874 to the Bethnal Green branch of the South Kensington Museum, from there in 1878 to the main museum; and in 1883 they were offered to the University of Oxford on condition that a special building should be constructed to house them and that a suitably qualified person should be appointed to give lectures upon them.

The offer was accepted: a building designed by T.N. Deane and Son was erected to the east of the UNIVERSITY MUSEUM and Edward Burnett Tylor was appointed the first lecturer in Anthropology in Britain. In 1891, at Tylor's suggestion, Henry Balfour, a graduate in Zoology, was appointed curator of the Pitt Rivers Museum. He held the post for forty-eight years, during which he greatly enhanced the museum's reputation and increased its collections. On his death in 1939 he was succeeded by T.K. Penniman, in whose time the collections were listed on index cards, and its library, known as the Balfour Library in honour of the late curator, whose collection of books and pamphlets had been its largest single accession, was housed in part of the premises vacated by the Department of Geology on their move to a new building. The Balfour Library contains nearly 30,000 books as well as periodicals, pamphlets, offprints and a collection of 60,000 photographs, and is quickly outgrowing the space available.

Indeed, the buildings of the museum as a whole are now quite inadequate, although Penniman's successor, B.E.B. Fagg, who was appointed in 1964, added to them by obtaining permission to use various vacant premises in the area. A much larger museum has accordingly been approved by the University and a site allocated on the east side of BANBURY ROAD extending eastwards to Bradmore Road. It had been hoped that a circular building could be constructed and designs were prepared by Pier Luigi Nervi in collaboration with Powell and Moya, but this plan had to be abandoned on grounds of cost, and Oxford, in the words of H.M. Colvin, 'was deprived of a spectacular architectural concept which would have delighted many besides anthropologists'. A new plan conceived by Schuyler Jones, the present curator, envisaged rectangular modular units. Phase I of this new development opened in 1986. Known as the Balfour Building, it has two galleries showing musical instruments and exhibits of hunter–gatherer cultures.

As well as being a museum open to the general public, the Pitt Rivers is, as its founder would have wished, a teaching establishment and is part of the University Department of Ethnology and Prehistory. A diploma in Anthropology was introduced in 1907, and from 1939 students at the School of Geography have been able to take Ethnology as an optional subject. The department also teaches for the degree in Human Sciences and has its own research students for higher degrees in Ethnology and Prehistoric Archaeology.

Accessions by gift, purchase, loan and transfer from other University departments and institutions, including most of the ethnological exhibits of the ASHMOLEAN have increased the museum's collections to their present size from the 14,000 in the General's original gift. The museum 'takes the world for its province', in the words of Beatrice Blackwood, and for its period, from the earliest times to the present day, excluding the products of modern industry. The

visitor will, therefore, be regaled with an extraordinary variety of objects, from one of the world's finest collections of musical instruments to fire-making appliances, a totem pole 40 feet high, the largest collection of votive offerings and amulets in existence, model ships, pipes, masks, games, fans, beadwork, belts and numerous other objects offering a unique cross-cultural view of material culture and technology on a worldwide scale.

Plain, The Originally the site of the mediaeval church and churchyard of St Clement, which was demolished in 1830. Thereafter the area acquired its unusual name, meaning an open area surrounded by buildings. In the Middle Ages beside the church was St Edmund's Well, where miracles are said to have occurred. The Bishop of Lincoln forbade the veneration of the well in 1290 and again in 1304. MAGDALEN BRIDGE leads straight on to the roughly triangular area of The Plain, from which diverge St Clement's Street, COWLEY ROAD and IFFLEY ROAD. Magdalen College's Waynflete Building, built in 1960–1 to the designs of Booth, Ledeboer & Pinckheard, faces The Plain on the north-west side. On the opposite side, at the junction with Cowley Place, is MAGDALEN COLLEGE SCHOOL. The middle is a traffic island on which stands the VICTORIA FOUNTAIN. On one of the surrounding lamp-posts is the inscription: 'Peace was proclaimed in the city of Oxford June 27, 1814', commemorating the short-lived peace during Napoleon's sojourn on Elba. The Cape of Good Hope public house, on the corner of Cowley and Iffley Roads, was rebuilt in 1892 to the designs of H.G.W. Drinkwater.

Plantation Road Runs from No. 91 WOODSTOCK ROAD to No. 174 Kingston Road. At one time a plantation, it had already been laid out as building plots by the 1832 enclosure award. A few houses, including No. 75, had been built before then. Originally two separate lanes, the road gave access to development on the back land known as Cabbage Hill,

The St Clement's toll-gate at The Plain, photographed c.1868, was demolished to make way for the Victoria Fountain.

which lay between Woodstock and Kingston Roads. The part nearest Woodstock Road is still today much narrower than the western end. The Gardeners' Arms public house dates from the late 1830s; No. 73 was built in about 1850, and St John's Villas (Nos 53–5) in the 1870s. A block of seven cottages on the south side of the road was built by the Oxford Cottage Improvement Company in 1888. A map of 1850 shows the road with the plantations laid out to the north. In the 1930s Mrs Sarah Hall sold pork pies and dough-cakes from her bakery at No. 28. The road is now almost exclusively residential.

Plate Silver and silver-gilt plate, formerly and sometimes still used in Oxford churches and college halls and common rooms can be seen displayed in the ASHMOLEAN MUSEUM, in CHRIST CHURCH CATHEDRAL chapter house, in the TOWN HALL plate room, in New College chapel, in the tower of ST MICHAEL AT THE NORTH GATE (where the church plate of three old city parishes is on show) and at the MUSEUM OF OXFORD. Spectacular displays of early college silver have been arranged from time to time; more ordinary items such as Georgian tankards or Victorian cutlery were in regular use until twenty or thirty years ago but are now too valuable to use and too much part of college tradition to sell. Many pieces are exactly documented by inscriptions or coats of arms engraved on them or by bills and inventories in college archives.

The earliest Oxford plate seems to be various base-metal (lead and pewter) chalices and patens at the Ashmolean and Christ Church, dating from the 12th and 13th centuries, found on local sites; of course this excludes prehistoric gold artefacts excavated from ancient archaeological sites. After these the oldest piece of precious plate in Oxford is at All Souls; it is the lid, which covered a shell or nautilus, made by a Court goldsmith in Paris at the end of the 13th century. It appears in a college list of 1556 but the story of how it arrived in Oxford is lost, as is the cup itself. It is now on deposit in the British Museum.

A few late-mediaeval specimens, four or five of the 14th century and about thirty of the 15th and early 16th centuries, remain. These include the 'Wassail' horn of The Queen's College, supposedly given by the founder, who died in 1349. At New College the founder's pastoral staff, with splendid cast figures and enamel panels, all gilt or gold, and the city's silver seal-matrix at the town hall both date from the 1370s. The New College Treasury contains some Pre-Reformation plate, including the Hill Salt, considered to be the finest of all mediaeval salts, the Monkey Salt, and three coconut cups, as well as the Founder's jewel, mitre and rings. All Souls has five mazers, turned-wood bowls with silver-gilt rims and mounts, on loan to the Ashmolean, and a famous 'Giant' or 'Huntsman' salt bequeathed to the college in 1799. Exeter, New College and Oriel have coconut cups and Corpus has the founder's pastoral staff, chalice and owl spoons. Christ Church and St Edmund Hall have pastoral staffs, both recently given and only partly mediaeval. Very little of this early plate is on show, but two mediaeval silver patens and a fine gilt chalice from parishes around Oxford can be seen in the Christ Church display.

There is not much surviving plate of late 16th-century date. Christ Church has a gilt paten, given, perhaps, by Queen Elizabeth; and the display there also contains silver communion cups from the churches of ST CLEMENT'S and ST CROSS. The display at St Michael at the North Gate has the communion cup of that church and another from the destroyed ST MARTIN AT CARFAX. The Ashmolean has the ancient bedels' staves of the University faculties.

From the early 17th century the University's own communion plate for use at the University Church of ST MARY THE VIRGIN is on show at the Ashmolean. A gilt communion cup from ST PETER-IN-THE-EAST is at Christ Church. In the display at St Michael at the North Gate are a silver wine-cup given to that church by a city alderman, a gilt standing-cup from ALL SAINTS, HIGH STREET, and a silver ewer-flagon from St Martin at Carfax. Almost all secular plate, private and college, and some chapel and church plate was looted during the CIVIL WAR or taken and melted down for coinage in Charles I's mint in NEW INN HALL. An interesting minor item that survived is a miniature silver staff-of-office of one of the city constables (in the Museum of Oxford).

The great period of Oxford plate begins in the 1660s with the splendid cathedral altar plate at Christ Church. The Ashmolean has a fine tankard given to the University in 1669 by its CHANCELLOR, the Duke of Ormond, for the current senior PROCTOR, and a pair of flagons of the 1690s. This display has many choice things of the 18th century and a notable collection of Huguenot silversmiths' work; none of this has an Oxford connection. The town hall has some splendid items, most notable among them the great city mace. St Michael at the North Gate has flagons of the 1670s from that church and from All Saints. Besides the Cathedral and Diocesan church plate at Christ Church there are some opulent examples of secular college plate of 18th- and early 19th-century date, the display being continued with fine Victorian and modern church plate.

Plater College *Pullen's Lane.* A young Jesuit, Father Charles Plater, revealed in a diary of 1909 his dream of founding an English Roman Catholic college in line with the Catholic social movement on the Continent: a place where Catholics could study the social implications of the Gospel and learn how best to apply them in a changing society. With this end in view, the Catholic Social Guild was formed in Manchester. As secretary, Father Plater worked through the Guild, organising tutorials in various towns. It was not until his death in 1921, however, that his dream was fulfilled: as a memorial to him, the Catholic Social Guild founded the Catholic Workers' College in WALTON WELL ROAD, Oxford. Father Leo O'Hea, SJ, opened it with three students in two rooms and very little money. Nevertheless, the venture was a success. The University was sympathetic and gave the students permission to attend lectures and to take the University diploma examinations in Economics and Political Science. In 1955 the college moved to a mansion on BOAR'S HILL; and in 1965, because the Guild was no longer effective, a new governing body was appointed by the trustees, the Cardinal Archbishop of Westminster and the Archbishops of Birmingham, Cardiff and Liverpool. It was then that the college adopted its present title. The site off LONDON ROAD, HEADINGTON, was bought in 1975 and Broadbent, Reid and New of London were employed to erect the four two-storey residential blocks and the main building. There are eight tutors and approximately eighty students. Although the study-courses have developed and multiplied over the years, the aims of the college remain the same as those envisaged by Father Plater and endorsed by Pope John XXIII – namely to enable people to 'humanize and Christianize the trends of contemporary civilisation.'

(*See also* ROMAN CATHOLICS.)

Playhouse The first Oxford Playhouse was in the Red Barn – a former big-game museum at the ST GILES' end of the WOODSTOCK ROAD. On Monday 22 October 1923, J.B. Fagan, director of the weekly repertory company the Oxford Players, opened the theatre with his production of George Bernard Shaw's *Heartbreak House*. Leading the company was Tyrone Guthrie, with Flora Robson making her professional début. Shaw, who attended the last night of his play, congratulated Fagan on bringing 'high-brow' theatre to Oxford. Ibsen, Wilde and Sheridan were among later productions in the 1923 season. John Gielgud appeared in the 1924 season, which also opened with a Shaw play, *Captain Brassbound's Conversion*. The success of the 1925 season was Fagan's production of Chekhov's *The Cherry Orchard*, which transferred to the Lyric, Hammersmith, and then to the Royalty Theatre in the West End. But towards the end of the 1920s the Oxford audience began to turn away from the theatre. Though Fagan struggled to keep his company going in 1929 with Robert Donat and Flora Robson in the cast of *Iphigenia in Tauris*, he finally conceded defeat on 7 December 1929. Fagan resigned, the theatre closed and the Red Barn re-opened as a miniature-golf course.

Soon afterwards, however, three actors, Arthur Brough, Stanford Holme and Edward Wilkinson, under the auspices of Sir Ben Greet, formed the Oxford Repertory Company and reclaimed the Red Barn as a theatre in 1930. The plan was to 'amuse and not to educate', and their first production was the Ben Travers' farce *Rookery Nook*. But, despite appearances by Margaret Rutherford, Valentine Dyall and Greet himself in their programme of predominantly light entertainment, the company always struggled against empty seats and, after the last performance of the 1934 spring season, Holme announced the theatre's closure. The audience immediately responded with a £400 collection to keep the company afloat and a new season of plays duly opened in the autumn. Eric Dance joined the company and, in 1936, he became Holme's co-director and producer. Despite the theatre's history of financial struggle, Dance went ahead with his plan to build a new theatre for the company and, after an appeal for funds had reached the necessary sum of £25,000, work began on building the present Oxford Playhouse in BEAUMONT STREET. The last production at the Red Barn, Wilde's *The Importance of Being Earnest*, was on 12 March 1938.

The land for the Beaumont Street Playhouse was leased from St John's College. There were local objections to the theatre, but the architectural complaints were largely overcome by employing Sir Edward Maufe to design the façade. The first production in the new Playhouse, J.B. Fagan's *And So To Bed*, was exactly fifteen years after the first Red Barn opening – 22 October 1938. During the war, the company added a series of popular revues to their repertoire but the two men who had brought the theatre to Beaumont Street were no longer with it: Holme left in 1939 and Dance died as a prisoner-of-war in New Guinea. Though the company survived – and sometimes thrived – through the 1940s, the 1950s began with financial problems and dwindling audiences. On 4 April 1956 the company gave its last performance. Later that year, however, Frank Hauser began an eighteen-year reign with his company, Meadow Players, of which he was the artistic director. In his opening season, 1956–7, he staged five world premières and three British premières of European plays. He maintained a high standard of producing new and classical works, introducing many European playwrights to British audiences and employing some of the best actors of the day, including Sybil Thorndike, Leo McKern and Dirk Bogarde.

In 1961 the University purchased the lease of the theatre, which was in urgent need of repair and modernisation; this work was carried out in 1962 under the administration of Elizabeth Sweeting. The use of the theatre was now shared between Meadow Players (who were also touring with their productions around the country and overseas) and the various University and city drama groups. Being unable to continue an artistic policy of employing the best performers in high-quality productions because of financial constraints, Hauser closed Meadow Players in 1974. Gordon McDougall now took over Hauser's role and the Arts Council grant, and formed Anvil Productions, the new Oxford Playhouse Company. His opening production was Gogol's *The Government Inspector*. McDougall and his co-director, Nicolas Kent, commissioned a new generation of playwrights and produced a mixture of popular comedies, classics, musicals and modern dramas. While the company was out on tour, the Playhouse played host to other touring companies, notably the popular dance troupes, the Ballet Rambert and the London Contemporary Dance Theatre. The National Theatre visited and several notable West End productions opened at the Playhouse, including Sir Alec Guinness in *Habeas Corpus*. In 1984 McDougall and Kent left and Richard Williams became artistic director of the company. Meanwhile, the Playhouse launched an appeal for funds to pay off debts and, not for the first time in its history, faced the prospect of finally closing its doors. A new Board of Management formed to replace the curators was unable to prevent closure in May 1987, when the cost of satisfying new fire regulations could not be met. In 1990 the lease was transferred from the university to the Oxford Playhouse Trust, an independent charitable company, which announced a fund-raising campaign, to be followed by the re-opening of the theatre in 1991.

Plough Inn *38 Cornmarket Street*. From 1195 OSENEY ABBEY owned two houses on this site. The Plough opened here on 26 September 1656 and was periodically enlarged until 1700. A leaded window on the first-floor frontage bears the date 1665. The inn was reconstructed in the 19th century, and closed in 1924 when it became first a bazaar and later Austin Reed's. George Benham, a circus clown known as the 'modern Grimaldi', was tenant here in 1891–1902.

Poetry The aspects considered here are divided into four groups (which, of course, overlap): (a) poets associated with Oxford; (b) poetry written by undergraduates; (c) poetry specifically about Oxford; (d) light verse.

(a) There is a long list of distinguished poets who spent part of their youth at Oxford. Any representative selection of earlier names would have to include

The Plough Inn on the corner of Cornmarket Street and St Michael Street opened in 1656. The premises were in 1988 in the occupation of Austin Reed.

Sir Philip Sidney, Sir Walter Raleigh, John Donne, Richard Lovelace, John Wilmot, Earl of Rochester, SAMUEL JOHNSON, P.B. Shelley (sent down for atheism, *see* SHELLEY MEMORIAL), MATTHEW ARNOLD, Arthur Hugh Clough, Gerard Manley Hopkins, Algernon Charles Swinburne, W.S. Landor, WILLIAM MORRIS, Oscar Wilde, Lionel Johnson, Hilaire Belloc, A.E. Housman and James Elroy Flecker; and this century has seen Edward Thomas, Edmund Blunden, Robert Graves, Roy Campbell, W.H. Auden and Louis MacNeice, JOHN BETJEMAN and Philip Larkin, Robert Bridges and T.S. Eliot, Stephen Spender, Bernard Spencer, Sidney Keyes, and C. Day-Lewis, Keith Douglas, John Heath-Stubbs, Kingsley Amis, John Wain and Elizabeth Jennings, Geoffrey Hill, Adrian Mitchell, Peter Levi, Jon Stallworthy, John Fuller, James Fenton and Craig Raine, Anne Ridler, George MacBeth, Anthony Thwaite and Andrew Motion. The list could be easily extended.

(b) Oxford undergraduate poetry has a long tradition of achieving publication, even if the main interest it arouses in later years lies in reading the early poetical works of those who became famous in other spheres. Volumes of *Oxford Poetry* were published annually by BLACKWELL's from 1914 to 1919, 1920 to 1932, 1936, 1937, and 1947 to 1952; and by Oscar Mellor at the Fantasy Press, Eynsham, from 1953 to 1960. In them may be found poems by G.N. CLARK, G. Elton, BASIL BLACKWELL, Aldous Huxley, Dorothy L. Sayers, L.A.G. Strong, G.D.H. Cole, Philip Guedalla, A.P. Herbert, Vera Brittain, J.B.S. Haldane, L.P.

Hartley, RONALD KNOX, Winifred Holtby, Richard Hughes, Harold Acton, Anthony Asquith, LORD DAVID CECIL, Graham Greene, Christopher Hollis, A.L. Rowse and the Earl of Longford. One volume includes the splendid but arguably outdated lines by Anon. of Balliol:

> But murmur of the cosmic drum
> throbs through the study of Lit. Hum.
> And he who takes a first in Greats
> masters the secret of the Fates

which were for many years pinned up in THORNTON'S BOOKSHOP.

(c) Oxford has long been a favourite subject for poets (*see* Antonia Fraser's *Oxford and Oxfordshire in Verse*, 1982), with even Wordsworth, in a sonnet dated 30 May 1820, singing:

> I slight my own beloved Cam, to range
> Where silver Isis leads my stripling feet

and Keats writing (in a letter) even more ecstatically: 'This Oxford, I have no doubt, is the finest City in the world.' Dryden, like Wordsworth a Cambridge man, had earlier written (in his Prologue to the University of Oxford *Miscellanies*, 1684):

> If his ambition may these hopes pursue,
> Who with religion loves your arts and you,
> Oxford to him a dearer name shall be,
> Than his own mother-university.
> Thebes did his green, unknowing, youth engage,
> He chooses Athens in his riper age.

And in 1749 Samuel Johnson wrote in *The Vanity of Human Wishes*:

> When first the College Rolls receive his Name,
> The young Enthusiast quits his Ease for Fame;
> Through all his Veins the Fever of Renown,
> Burns from the strong Contagion of the Gown;
> O'er *Bodley's* Dome his future Labours spread,
> And *Bacon's* Mansion trembles o'er his head. ...

Long before their time, Chaucer's Clerk had been one of the pilgrims on their way to Canterbury:

> A CLERK ther was of Oxenford also,
> That un-to logik hadde longe y-go.
> As lene was his hors as is a rake,
> And he nas nat right fat, I undertake;
> But loked holwe, and ther-to soberly.
> Ful thredbar was his overest courtepy;
> For he had geten him yet no benefyce,
> Ne was so worldly for to have offyce.
> For him was lever have at his beddes heed
> Twenty bokes, clad in blak or reed,
> Of Aristotle and his philosophye,
> Than robes riche, or fithele, or gay sautrye.

In *The Minstrelsy of Isis* (ed. J.B. Firth, 1908), a substantial anthology of 'Poems relating to Oxford' is assembled. Unhappily, few of the illustrious names earlier mentioned actually wrote about Oxford, nor did even Joseph Addison ever sing about the walk that now bears his name at Magdalen (*see* ADDISON'S WALK). Most of the verse anthologised can safely be allowed to remain unread; but two poems in it above all are, and may long remain, Oxford's most famous: 'The Scholar Gipsy' and 'Thyrsis' by MATTHEW ARNOLD, the latter commemorating Arthur Hugh Clough (1819–61; Balliol). Oscar Wilde expressed his affection for Oxford in 'The Burden of Itys'; and in the 20th century, John Betjeman's autobiographical *Summoned by Bells* (1960) has won deserved popularity. Keith Douglas, W.H. Auden and Louis MacNeice have all written poems on Oxford; yet it may be that Sir Arthur Quiller-Couch, in 'Alma Mater' (1896), has best summed up Oxford's enchantment for those willing to be enchanted:

Know you her secret none can utter
  Her of the Book, the tripled Crown?
Still on the spire the pigeons flutter,
  Still by the gateway flits the gown:
Still in the street, from corbel and gutter
  Faces of stone look down. . . .

Know you the secret none discover?
  Tell it when *you* go down.

(d) Oxford's tradition of epigrammatic, satirical and humorous verse goes back a long way, identifiably to the last decade of the 17th century. *The Oxford Sausage* ('Select poetical pieces written by the most celebrated wits of the University of Oxford') was first published in 1764 (*see* MAGAZINES). Better known nowadays and more accessible is *The Masque of B-ll—l* (1881), with its famous lines on BENJAMIN JOWETT, then Master of Balliol:

First come I; my name is J–W–TT.
There's no knowledge but I know it.
I am Master of this College,
What I don't know isn't knowledge.

(Several variants exist; *see Balliol Rhymes*, 1955.) The Oxford Magazine (*see* MAGAZINES) published much light verse on University topics, especially from the pen of A.D. Godley (1856–1925), who not infrequently composed, with equal facility, in Latin; his four volumes of published verse and two volumes of posthumous *Reliquiae* attest to his fluency. If much of his output is of essentially ephemeral interest, the following brief extract from 'Ad Lectionem Suam' (1895) may yet give a poignant flavour of his wit:

When Autumn's winds denude the grove,
  I seek my Lecture, where it lurks
'Mid the unpublished portion of
  My works,

And ponder, while its sheets I scan,
  How many years away have slipt
Since first I penned that ancient manuscript. . . .

Though Truth enlarge her widening range,
  And Knowledge be with time increased,
While thou, my Lecture! dost not change
  The least,

But fixed immutable amidst
  The advent of a newer lore,
Maintainest calmly what thou didst
  Before.

Lewis Carroll (*see* CHARLES DODGSON) spent his entire adult life as undergraduate and Student of Christ Church; of later writers of light verse, Hilaire Belloc left several pieces about Oxford (e.g. 'Lines to a Don', and 'Balliol Men'), and John Betjeman wrote attractively about NORTH OXFORD ('May-Day Song for North Oxford'). SIR MAX BEERBOHM has left only one unmemorable squib on his old University; ruder and funnier by far were D.H. Lawrence's lines on the Oxford accent (from 'Pansies', 1929). Finally,

Kingsley Amis's 'Their Oxford' (*Collected Poems*, 1979) attractively mixes the serious with the ironical:

In my day there were giants on the scene,
Men big enough to be worth laughing at:
Coghill and Bowra, Lewis and Tolkien.
Lost confidence and envy finished that.

A far cry from the Oxford of Gerard Manley Hopkins: 'Cuckoo-echoing, bell-swarmed, lark-charmed, rook-racked, river-rounded' ('Duns Scotus' Oxford', from *Poems, 1876–1889*).

(*See also* BOAR'S HILL (*Matthew Arnold*); BINSEY (*Gerard Manley Hopkins*); NORTH HINKSEY (*Matthew Arnold*); NEWDIGATE PRIZE *and* CHAIRS (*Professors of Poetry*).)

Polytechnic *Gypsy Lane, Headington*. In 1865 the Oxford School of Art was established in the TAYLOR INSTITUTION with 126 students, rising to 284 within a year. The school increasingly included the teaching of technical subjects, until in 1891 it became the Oxford City Technical School, founded by the City Council in response to the Technical Instruction Act (1889) and housed on the site of the former Bluecote School for Boys in Church Street, ST EBBE'S. Built to the designs of H.W. Moore, it opened in 1894. The appointment in 1928 of J.H. Brookes as Vice-Principal led to the introduction of architectural courses and later to a School of Architecture; he continued to exert a decisive influence on technical training when in 1934 he was appointed Principal of the newly named Schools of Technology, Art and Commerce, which were spread over a number of premises in the city and were attended by over 200 day students and over 1000 evening-class students. A plan to concentrate the scattered departments under one roof as the City Technical College was abandoned on the outbreak of war in 1939; and it was not until 1949 that the present site on HEADINGTON HILL was purchased in response to increasing post-war demand for technical training. Despite initial opposition by the City Council, public pressure under the leadership of K.C. (later Sir Kenneth) Wheare, chairman of the governors of the Schools of Technology, Art and Commerce from 1944 to 1949, led to the laying of the foundation stone of the College of Technology, Art and Commerce in 1954 by LORD NUFFIELD, a former student. The college was divided into five schools: Art, Architecture and Building, Commerce, Engineering, and Science. It opened in 1955 and in 1956 became the Oxford College of Technology, though it was not until 1963 that, with some 800 full-time and some 6000 part-time students, it was officially opened by HRH the Duke of Edinburgh. In 1958 Cotuit Hall, PULLEN'S LANE, built in 1890–1 to the designs of H.W. Moore, was bought to accommodate some ninety resident students.

Following the Robbins Report on Higher Education in 1963, the establishment in 1964 of the Council for National Academic Awards, and in 1965 the DES White Paper on Polytechnics, the Oxford Polytechnic came into being in 1970 with some 2400 full-time and 2500 part-time students divided among four faculties: Architecture, Planning and Estate Management; Educational Studies; Modern Studies; Technology. Each catered for degree and diploma courses, less advanced courses being taken at the newly instituted Oxford COLLEGE OF FURTHER EDUCATION in OXPENS ROAD. In 1973 the first multi-disciplinary modular course in Higher Education to be validated by the Council for National Academic Awards was pioneered by the Polytechnic – a credit-accumulation system allowing the student to combine a wide choice of subjects with considerable flexibility.

The Polytechnic buildings, on an 11-acre site bordered by HEADINGTON ROAD, Gypsy Lane and CHENEY UPPER SCHOOL, were designed by the Oxford City Architects Department up to 1976, and since then by the Oxfordshire County Council Architects Department. Between 1970 and 1974 Cheney Hall, CHENEY LANE, providing residential accommodation for some 400 students, was built to the designs of Douglas Murray, the City Architect; and in 1978 Morrell Hall, John Garne Way, housing some ninety students and currently being expanded, was built to the designs of Mervyn Bennett.

In 1974 the Oxfordshire County Council took control of the Polytechnic and also assumed responsibility for the Lady Spencer-Churchill College of Education, amalgamated with the Polytechnic in 1976. The Lady Spencer-Churchill College for the training of women teachers began life in 1948 with 140 students as Bletchley Park College, Buckinghamshire, in the buildings used during wartime by MI5 and the *Enigma* code-breaking team. Closed as an Emergency College in 1950, it re-opened immediately with fifty students as a permanent teacher-training college under Buckinghamshire County Council, joining with Culham College, Westminster College and the University Department of Education to form the Oxford University Institute of Education. It moved in 1965 to 65 acres of Holton Park, Wheatley, where 350 students are accommodated in buildings designed by the Buckinghamshire County Council Architecture Department and opened by Lord Avon in 1966.

In 1986 the Polytechnic had over 4000 full-time and sandwich-course students, over 1100 part-time students, and some 850 members of teaching and non-teaching staff.

Population The earliest estimate of the population of Oxford has to be based on the figures given in Domesday Book for the number of houses in the town in 1086. Those figures are ambiguous, but there seem to have been 1018 houses, which, assuming four or five persons per house, would give a population of *c*.4500. It must be stressed, though, that this figure can be only an approximation. The population fell immediately after the Norman Conquest, but recovered in the early 12th century. Documentary and archaeological evidence for the subdivision of properties and the development of suburbs indicates that the population rose quite rapidly in the later 12th and the first half of the 13th. The survey known as the Hundred Rolls, made in 1297, suggests a total of *c*.1400 properties, including nearly 200 shops and other non-residential buildings, which would imply a population of at least 5500. The figure should probably be raised by a few hundred to allow for those members of the University living in colleges or halls (*see* ACADEMIC HALLS) which held more than the four or five people assumed per household. The total membership of the University *c*.1300 has been estimated at about 2000, not all of whom would have lived in colleges or halls.

Soon after 1279 the population of Oxford, like that of the whole country, began to decline, and it was drastically reduced by the Black Death between November 1348 and June 1349. No accurate records were kept, but a study of the town's register of wills, of the lists of small brewers (over 200 in 1348), and of the presentations to town churches indicates that between a third and a half of the town's population died or moved away. Part of this population loss was made good almost at once by immigration from the surrounding countryside, but in 1377, after the second outbreak of plague in 1361, only 2357 men and women over fourteen years of age paid poll-tax. That figure should probably be increased by half, to *c*.3500 to allow for children under fourteen and for the comparatively few adults who evaded the tax. Numbers in the University also declined in the later 14th century, probably reaching *c*.1500.

Falling rents and other economic indicators suggest that the population dropped further in the later Middle Ages. For a subsidy in 1524 only 533 people were assessed, including employees of the University and colleges, but not scholars. It seems reasonable to regard that figure as representing two-thirds of the adult male population, excluding the relatively few scholars; therefore the total population of Oxford in the early 16th century was probably below 3000. Similar multipliers applied to mid-16th-century tax-returns suggest that there had been little change, but thereafter there was rapid expansion, confirmed by many indicators such as parish registers and apprenticeship enrolments. Between the 1580s and 1630s recorded baptisms and burials in four sample parishes increased by 80 per cent, and expansion was probably even greater in suburban parishes for which comparable figures are not available. It is clear from register and other evidence that by the 1630s Oxford's population was very similar to that of the 1660s, for which fairly reliable estimates may be made. In 1667 a total of 8566 persons were assessed for poll-tax, including over 2000 members of the University. How many citizens were exempt through poverty is uncertain, but it is probably safe to estimate a total population of around 10,000. By extrapolation, therefore, Oxford's population in the 1630s may be estimated at about 10,000, having risen from perhaps 5000 in the 1580s. Much of that spectacular growth, since parish registers show little sign of natural population increase, may be attributed to immigration, stimulated largely by the growth of the University. As the University lost impetus in the late 17th century, Oxford's population became fairly stable, and a survey of 1750 enumerated 1814 houses in the city and 8292 inhabitants, excluding the occupants of colleges. Parish registers of the later 18th century show the preponderance of baptisms over burials, reflecting the national growth of population. In 1801 the total population of Oxford was nearly 12,000.

Decennial totals of population from 1801 are given below, arranged to take account of boundary changes. Between 1811 and 1831 Oxford's population grew by 50 per cent, matching the rapid urban expansion found elsewhere in the country. Much of the increase was due to immigration from the surrounding countryside, as large numbers moved into the city in search of employment. There were, however, no industries in Oxford capable of supporting such numbers and the city's rate of growth fell behind that of the burgeoning industrial towns, despite the absorption in 1837 of ST CLEMENT'S parish with its

2000 people. Significantly, the town's growth had outstripped that of a moribund University, which in 1861 comprised only a twentieth of the total population, compared with a tenth in 1801. In the later 19th century, however, a reformed and reinvigorated University grew rapidly, drawing the city along with it.

The bald statistics of population obscure the fact that the rate of growth varied greatly from area to area within the city. The central parishes lost population steadily by migration after 1821, nearly all the growth taking place in the outer parishes, notably ST EBBE'S, ST THOMAS'S, ST GILES' and St Clement's. In the 1870s, for instance, the inner area suffered a net loss of almost 1900, whereas the outer area grew by 4700. That the decline of population in the city centre was not even more rapid was due to the late and slow development in Oxford of middle-class suburbs, such as NORTH OXFORD, and the colleges' continuing residential role has served to maintain a level of population found in the centre of few towns elsewhere.

The growth of the motor industry led to very rapid population growth in the 1920s and 1930s (*see* MOTOR CARS). Between 1921 and 1937 *c*.10,300 insured workers moved to Oxford, and nearly half the city's male insured workers above the age of twenty-one were immigrants. Although South Wales provided many immigrants, fewer than is usually supposed came from the depressed areas of the north, while 43 per cent came from within 50 miles of Oxford. Since 1945 the city's population has remained fairly static, and it has been official policy to discourage significant expansion. Educational establishments have become prominent once more, and in 1981 were estimated to comprise slightly more than a fifth of the total population.

Year	Persons	Increase	
1801	11,921		
1811	13,257	1336 (11%)	1801–81: population of municipal borough
1821	16,446	3189 (24%)	
1831	20,710	4264 (26%)	
1841	24,258	3548 (17%)	Boundary extended 1837
1851	27,843	3585 (15%)	
1861	28,601	758 (3%)	1861–1911: University on vacation
1871	31,404	2803 (10%)	
1881	35,264	3860 (12%)	
1891	45,742	–	1891–1921: population of parliamentary borough
1901	49,285	3543 (8%)	
1911	52,979	3694 (8%)	
1921	57,036	–	1921–81: population of county borough
1931	80,539	23,503 (41%)	
1941	107,000	26,461 (33%)	Estimated
1951	98,684	– 8316 (– 8%)	University on vacation
1961	106,291	7607 (8%)	Boundary extended 1957
1971	108,805	2514 (2%)	
1981	93,500	– 15,305 (– 14%)	University, Polytechnic, etc., on vacation. Estimated total population 116,200

Port Meadow The flat expanse of land on the north-west side of Oxford, known as Port Meadow, is mentioned in Domesday Book (1086) as the place where 'all the burgesses (or Freemen) of Oxford have a pasture outside the city wall in common, which pays 6s. 8d.'. It is said that an American academic visiting Oxford, on asking if he could be shown the city's oldest monument, was taken to see Port Meadow.

A poster advertising the flying ground which opened on Port Meadow shortly before the First World War.

Originally Portmaneit (or Burgess Island) the name Port Meadow was in use by 1285. It may then have been as much as 500 acres in extent, including what is now WOLVERCOTE Common, Wolvercote Green, BINSEY Green, and other land adjoining. On Benjamin Cole's map of Port Meadow (*c*.1720) the area is stated to be about 439 acres. When registered as common land in 1970 it comprised about 342 acres. A Bronze Age burial mound known as Round Hill situated on the east side of the meadow is marked on Cole's map, and there is a charge in Sheriff James Hunt's accounts for 1842 for 'turning over the round hill, to see what was under it, and making its shape correspond with its name'.

Freemen (*see* PRIVILEGED PERSONS) have the right to graze horses and cattle on the meadow (it has been grazed for over 1000 years). Until 1970, when some 200 freemen registered their grazing rights, there were periodic disputes between the freemen and the city over the ownership of the meadow and the rights of the freemen to pasture. In each century from the 16th, attempts by the Corporation of Oxford to encroach on the meadow or to enclose the land were resisted by the freemen. Until 1982 the City Council operated a rubbish dump on the east side of the meadow and hundreds of lorries crossed the land every week to the tip. In 1985 a public inquiry was held into alleged encroachments on to the meadow by the Medley Boat Station, and a dispute arose over the proposed erection by the City Council of bollards to mark a track across it from WALTON WELL ROAD to the boat station. It was Sheriff Hunt who in 1841 built the

331

bridge at Walton Well Ford known as Sheriff's Bridge. From this entrance one can cross the meadow to Medley, where there is a bridge across the THAMES and a footpath leading to the PERCH inn at Binsey. Another entrance to the meadow is by ARISTOTLE LANE.

Since at least 1562 inter-commoning rights have been held by the Wolvercote Commoners. Pasturing is now controlled by regular drives across the meadow by the Sheriff of Oxford; this has become an annual event, and in 1981 a pound was built at the northern end to help the Sheriff to impound the animals. Freemen and commoners with grazing rights can then retrieve their horses and cattle for a nominal fee while those owners with no grazing rights are fined. The pound in GLOUCESTER GREEN was used for this purpose in the 16th century. Sheep are not allowed on the meadow, but geese used to be kept on Wolvercote Common and escorted to the river each day by goose girls or boys. Some of these bred with wild geese to produce the hybrid known as Port Meadow Special.

Horse-racing was a popular pastime on Port Meadow and Wolvercote Common from the 17th to the 19th centuries. Cole's map shows a pear-shaped racecourse at the Wolvercote end, with the starting post marked. Zacharias Conrad von Uffenbach (1683–1734), a collector of manuscripts and books who spent two months in Oxford in 1710, described in his *Travels* a visit to the races: 'In the afternoon of 16 September a race meeting was held about a mile and a half away from the City. This happens every year in Oxfordshire. We took a boat up the Thames, which flows past the fields in which the races are held. This meadow is two and a half miles in circumference and much more suited for a race-course than the one at Epsom, though it is somewhat marshy. Many booths had been set up, where beer was sold, each of which had its sign, a hat, a glove and suchlike. Nearly all the people from the town were there and also many strangers, some riding, some driving, some in boats. The horses which were to run were six in number and had to race twice round the whole course – five English miles, which took inside ten minutes.' Racing was discontinued around 1848, but was revived on Wolvercote Common in 1980 as the Sheriff's Races.

Skating is another popular activity in winter, when the lower, southern end of the meadow floods and freezes. The meadow is also used by the public for riding, walking, bird-watching and other recreations. The river at the northern end has a gravel bed and Wolvercote Bathing Place is near the pound. Port Meadow has been designated as a Site of Special Scientific Interest, never having been ploughed. Floating sweet-grass, much enjoyed by cattle and horses, and water mint thrive on the low-lying southern part, while Oxford RAGWORT spreads on the higher land on the northern part. Allotments have been in use since 1943 on Wolvercote Common. There was an airfield on the northern part of the meadow during the First World War.

(Cordeaux, E.H., and Merry, D.H., 'Port Meadow Races', *Oxoniensia*, Vol. XIII, 1948, p. 55; Atkinson, R.J.C., 'Archaeological Sites on Port Meadow, Oxford', *Oxoniensia*, Vol. VII, 1942, p. 24.)

Portraits Portraits in Oxford are almost exclusively the property of the University and colleges, although a small number belong to the city and are housed in the TOWN HALL. For the most part they are hung in college halls and common rooms, on staircases or in corridors, in libraries or committee rooms – a part of the long history of the institutions to which they belong. Their display is archival and iconographical rather than aesthetic. Nonetheless there are among them works of art-historical significance, and sometimes of beauty. The city, University and college portraits were excellently catalogued in three volumes by Mrs Reginald Lane Poole, but the last volume appeared in 1925 and there have been many additions since that time, particularly commissions from contemporary artists, some of them controversial.

The portraits which belong to the University rather than to the colleges may be seen in the BODLEIAN LIBRARY, the SHELDONIAN THEATRE, the ASHMOLEAN MUSEUM and the EXAMINATION SCHOOLS. By the beginning of the 18th century the Bodleian had accumulated portraits sufficient in number and variety for a catalogue to be compiled by THOMAS HEARNE and printed in 1708. In the adjacent OLD ASHMOLEAN (now the MUSEUM OF THE HISTORY OF SCIENCE) were the portraits of members of the Tradescant family which were part of ELIAS ASHMOLE's gift to the University in 1683. Other portraits filtered in throughout the 18th and early 19th centuries, and when the University Galleries (the present Ashmolean) were built in 1845, a sorting out took place whereby some portraits were transferred to the new building from the Bodleian and elsewhere. A further sorting took place when the Examination Schools, which offered a great amount of wall space, went up in 1882. These allocations are still effective.

The Bodleian portraits, good, indifferent and bad, are a fascinating collection of notabilities – some 400, not necessarily connected with Oxford but almost all connected with learning – which came in by haphazard gift: Chaucer, Luther, Froben and Erasmus, Paracelsus, Montaigne, Sarpi, Grotius and Galileo among them. Artistically or art-historically, many of them are generally undistinguished, but there are a number of exceptions, notably the anonymous portrait on panel of William Cecil, Lord Burghley, incongruously mounted on a mule, and the fine, recently cleaned Kneller of Nathaniel, Lord Crewe. The portrait of Flora Macdonald by Allan Ramsay deposited in the Ashmolean in 1859, although not a good example of the artist, is considered to be the most authentic likeness of her.

Elias Ashmole inherited the 'curiosities' which formed the nucleus of the Old Ashmolean, together with the Tradescant portraits, from John Tradescant the Younger of Lambeth. These portraits, which are now hung in the Founder's Room in the present Ashmolean, are attractive and puzzling. They are apparently the work of several hands and present an intriguing and important problem of identification to students of early 17th-century portraiture in England. The problem is unresolved. They are associated with a family of Flemish painters, by name de Critz, who were related to the Tradescants by cousinship. In the same room hangs a fine portrait of Ashmole himself by John Riley. This is not the place to attempt to list or discuss the numerous portraits of the European schools of painting which form part of the Ashmolean's main collection but only those which relate to Oxford city, county or University, and in this respect there must be mention of the Grand Tour

Bryan Organ's portrait of Harold Macmillan, later the Earl of Stockton, Chancellor 1960–86, was commissioned by the University and hangs in the University Offices.

portrait of William Fermor of Tusmore Park painted by Anton Mengs in Rome in 1757, and the portrait of Thomas Combe, the secretary of the OXFORD UNIVERSITY PRESS and patron of the young Pre-Raphaelites, painted by Millais at the Combes' house in WALTON STREET in 1849. These are usually on display, but in a museum of the size and the scale of activity of the Ashmolean it is impossible to guarantee that they will be at all times.

The portraits in the Examination Schools are, generally speaking, those which are too large to be accommodated elsewhere. They include one of the best versions of Sir Thomas Lawrence's state portrait of George IV, originally commissioned by the University when he was Regent to mark his visit to Oxford with the Allied Sovereigns in 1814; and a portrait of Chichester Fortescue, Lord Carlingford, by Tissot. The Schools are not open to the public.

The college collections have developed rather more systematically than those belonging to the University. Many of the portraits have come by gift, but an equal, if not larger, number have been commissioned by the colleges to record the features of persons on their governing bodies or of distinguished old members. It is the almost invariable custom for a head of house to be painted either in office or on retirement. The tendency now is for him to be painted in office before he (or she) has 'gone off'. So, to mention only the 19th century and only some of the more celebrated heads of that time (not necessarily painted by the more celebrated artists), at Balliol there is the Master, BENJAMIN JOWETT, by G.F. Watts; at New College the Warden, W.A. SPOONER, by Hugh Rivière; at Lincoln the Rector, MARK PATTISON, by Alexander Mac-donald; at Magdalen the President, Martin Joseph Routh, who died in office at the age of ninety-nine, by Karl Hartmann. Portraits of heads of houses were painted reasonably consistently after about the last quarter of the 18th century, but before then one cannot depend on there being a portrait at all. Portraits of founders are even scarcer and are necessarily posthumous. They are of small merit, with one or two

exceptions – notably the portrait of Bishop Richard Foxe at Corpus Christi, traditionally ascribed to Joannes Corvus and datable to the 1520s, which has a compelling quality despite some restorations, and the portrait at Jesus of Queen Elizabeth I, who, though not the founder, granted the college its charter in 1572.

Naturally the college collections vary in extent and character. Some have surprising treasures – Jesus with its portrait of Canon David Jenkins standing in New College cloisters, painted by Holman Hunt in 1852; Balliol with its Swinburne on the Northumbrian seashore by William Bell Scott, 1860; Jesus, again, with its Lawrence of John Nash; Keble with its poignant portrait of JOHN HENRY NEWMAN by a little-known artist, William T. Roden; or St Hugh's with its conversation piece of the library in the 1930s, with lady dons who might have stepped straight from the pages of Dorothy L. Sayers's *Gaudy Night*. For the most part, however, these collections are, like the National Portrait Gallery, an assemblage of likenesses first, a collection of works of art second; they are historical data. How a particular artist was chosen for a particular sitter is rarely recorded. It was always a matter of chance and often of intrigue and dispute.

If one is to single out one college collection it must be that of Christ Church. The long, high hall is crowded with portraits, sometimes two deep. There are distinguished artists – Lely, Kneller, Reynolds, Mengs, Romney, Gainsborough, Hoppner, Lawrence, Millais, Orchardson, Orpen – and dis-tinguished sitters – among them Richard Busby; John Locke; Robert Harley, Earl of Oxford; Charles Boyle, Earl of Orrery; JOHN WESLEY; George Canning; Lewis Carroll (*see* CHARLES DODGSON); WILLIAM GLADSTONE; Anthony Eden. The Mengs of the diplomat Louis de Visme, and the early Lawrence of William Eden, Baron Auckland, are important examples of these artists. And above the dais Graham Sutherland's Dean Simpson looks down curiously at high table. Every college has this same mixture of eminent subjects and eminent artists, but none has quite the sweep of Christ Church.

Group portraits such as that of the ladies of St Hugh's by Henry Lamb are rare, but at Worcester there is Sir William Rothenstein's record of five members of the Senior Common Room at dessert, and at Trinity a group by June Mendoza of five members of the college who in the 1970s had achieved the distinction of the Order of Merit. At Pembroke there is an old-fashioned problem picture of 1914 by Sidney P. Hall – a conversation piece if you like, not demonstrably a group portrait (although it is possible that the heads are portraits), but close enough to be mentioned in this context. It shows a viva voce examination in the Schools and is grimly entitled 'We pause for an answer'.

In the years from 1930 to the present day numerous portraits have been commissioned. Mrs Lane Poole would have raised her eyebrows at some of them. This has been a time when accepted standards of composition and technique, of dignified portrayal and of an air of pride and loyalty have been questioned in official portraiture, as similar standards have been questioned in every other profession. There is no doubt that some recent college portraits do not fit happily in hall. Their tonality is too light, their informality too insistent. One can only list some of the best or more unusual of them: Paul Brason's *Michael Maclagan* (Trinity), William Coldstream's *Dr van Heyningen* (St Cross), Margaret Foreman's *Sir Richard Southern* (St John's), Patrick George's *Enid Starkie* (Somerville), Lawrence Gowing's *A.D. Lindsay* (Balliol), Peter Greenham's *Miss Julia Mann* (St Hilda's) and *Dame Joan Evans* (St Hugh's), Derek Hill's *Christopher Hill* (Balliol) and *Sir Isaiah Berlin* (Wolfson), Rodrigo Moynihan's *Anthony Kenny* (Balliol), Bryan Organ's *Lord Stockton* (UNIVERSITY OFFICES) and *Sir Rex Richards* (Merton), Graham Sutherland's *Lord Goodman* (University College), Lawrence Toynbee's *Sir William Hayter* (New College), John Ward's *Sir George Pickering* (Pembroke), Carel Weight's *Dame Kathleen Kenyon* (St Hugh's). Among portraits included in an exhibition of Oxford portraits since 1945 held at the Ashmolean in 1983, in addition to several of the above, were those of Geoffrey Warnock, Principal of Hertford College and VICE-CHANCELLOR, by David Hockney, and of E.A. Barber, Rector of Exeter, by Annigoni.

Oxford University and its colleges have always regarded themselves as families, the larger family being the whole University, the smaller each individual college. It is therefore wholly in the spirit of Oxford that there are portraits of others than the heads and Fellows of the colleges or of those old members who have become renowned. There are also portraits of servants respected and beloved. 'Servant' is now an unfashionable word; in Oxford it has long been a word to be proud of. At Christ Church there is a portrait by Riley of a scullion of the college, probably William Forde, a cook; at New College an anonymous and touching portrait of Thomas Hodges, servant to the chaplains, tankard in hand, of the mid-18th century; at Wadham 'Mother George' (*c*.1691); and at Balliol, in the buttery, a portrait by Catherine Pritchard, an undergraduate, a speaking likeness of Bert Blagrove, a porter for forty years who died as recently as 1986.

There are other small pockets of portraits within the University – in the Science Libraries, for instance, and in the Faculty of Music, where there is an anonymous

likeness of Henry Lawes, who died in 1662, given by himself to the Music School of his day.

College halls are frequently open to visitors and the porters in the lodge can give the times of opening. Portraits elsewhere in the colleges are usually in rooms which are in constant daily use – the Senior Common Rooms and the corridors leading to them, the bursaries and the small dining rooms. Here there are often portrait drawings which are too small or too intimate to hang in hall. These areas are necessarily private.

Post Boys *140 High Street.* By 1533 there were private houses on this site, but by 1778 an inn existed known as the Post Boy or Jolly Post Boy. In 1836 it was a small three-storey timbered inn with leaded windows and a single carved gable. (The Red Lion, next door at No. 139, was architecturally almost identical.) The Post Boys closed in 1935.

Postal Services In 1635 Thomas Witherings, the postmaster appointed by Charles I to run a postal service for the public, was instructed to operate the main post road from London to Bristol through Oxford. Before 1635 there was no official postal service for the general public. Although private letters were often carried in the mails, the postal service was officially for government mail and Royal Mail only. When the service was reorganised after the disruption caused by the CIVIL WAR, the main post road from London to Bristol ran through Reading and Newbury rather than Oxford. All mail then had to go through London, but in 1709 a branch of the cross-post from Exeter to Chester via Bristol was extended to Oxford via Bath and Wantage. Many of the early postmasters were innkeepers. In 1673, for example, the landlord of the Cross Keys Inn in QUEEN STREET was appointed postmaster. (POSTMASTERS' HALL in MERTON STREET has no connection with the Post Office.) Letters were carried by 'post boys' riding horses between post stages, usually inns, the innkeeper being required to provide fresh horses. Letters were put into bags for each post town and all the bags put into a larger bag which was sealed. Each postmaster removed his bag, resealed the 'Great Maile' bag and sent it on to the next post stage. Postage rates depended on the distance the letter was carried and on the number of sheets of paper. Up to 80 miles (e.g. from Oxford to London), the rate was 2*d* in the 17th century and 3*d* from 1711 to 1765. By 1812 it had risen to 8*d*. For two sheets of paper the charge was double. By 1740 the post set out for London from the post office in Oxford every day, except Saturday, and to other places on certain days each week – for example, to Witney, Burford and Stow 'or anywhere that Way' at 2 p.m. on Sundays, Tuesdays, Wednesdays and Fridays.

In 1784 John Palmer of Bath revolutionised the postal services with his inauguration of mail coaches. The mail coaches and horses were hired; they carried a limited number of passengers and an armed guard, and ran to a strict schedule. The horses were changed at the coaching inns, and if a passenger was not ready on time he was left behind. The coaches had a difficult time in winter, many becoming stuck in the snow and the mail being taken on by the armed guard on horseback. An advertisement in *Jackson's Oxford Journal* (*see* NEWSPAPERS) for 1829 shows that Royal Mail coaches were leaving the ANGEL INN in HIGH

STREET for London at 11.30 each night, one coach travelling via Henley and the other via High Wycombe (*see also* TRANSPORT). Oxford RAILWAY station was opened in 1844 and the era of the mail coaches soon came to an end. Penny posts began to be established in many areas outside the big cities in the early 19th century. The majority of letters were left at the post town until called for, unless there was a local postal service. Under this system letters were delivered for a penny to and from a post town and the receiving offices in villages within the area of the local penny post. It is likely that there was an unofficial local service for the area around Oxford in the late 18th and early 19th century, but it did not become official until about 1829. Receiving offices are known to have existed at Gosford and Eynsham, but no record of them in any other village has yet been found.

In 1859 the Oxford UNION SOCIETY was given permission to overprint its initials on 1*d* stamps of this period as a precaution against pilfering. The overprint consists of the initials 'O.U.S.' between two wavy lines running up and down the stamp, reading either upwards or downwards. This is the only instance in which the Post Office has permitted an overprint for private use on the face of postage stamps. It continued in use for some ten years until permission was withdrawn in 1870.

With the expansion of postal services, pressure grew for a central post office. In 1842 the post office was at 123 High Street, but when this was destroyed by fire an office was provided at the southern end of the TOWN HALL. In 1865 it was enlarged by an extension beneath NIXON'S FREE GRAMMAR SCHOOL, and in 1879 a new post-office building, designed by E.G. Rivers, was built in ST ALDATE'S and is still in use as the GPO. When the foundation stone was laid, the postmaster gave some facts concerning the postal service in 1879: the staff at Oxford was then 121, of whom eighty-seven were attached to the chief office; the number of letters, newspapers, etc., which had to be sorted and delivered was 240,000 a week, of which just over a third were delivered in Oxford and its neighbourhood. He said that there were many people then living who could remember all the letters for Oxford being delivered by one letter carrier; now there were twenty-three and in 1879 there were four deliveries and six collections of letters a day in Oxford. By the end of the century there were eighteen sub-offices, the busiest of which is now in ST MICHAEL'S STREET. The sorting office is in BECKET STREET.

Pillar-boxes were first introduced in 1853. The first ones in Oxford were erected near the church of ST MARY MAGDALEN and at the junction of LONGWALL STREET and High Street. A fine example of one of the early Penfold types is still in service in PARK TOWN.

(*See also* COLLEGE STAMPS, POSTMARKS *and* TRANSPORT.)

Postmarks The first Oxford postmark was a straight-line 'OXFORD' and its earliest recorded use was in 1705. There are over twenty-five variations of this hand-stamp, which was in use for practically the whole of the 18th century. In 1719–20 letters on the cross-post between Exeter and Chester received the hand-stamp 'OXON.X' at Oxford. A curved 'OXFORD' hand-stamp was in use from 1793, but only lasted for about six years. Mileage marks were introduced in 1784 to show the mileage to London in

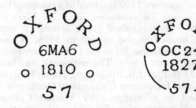

 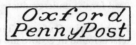

Some early mileage marks and other postmarks.

order to facilitate the calculation of the postage rate. The earliest recorded Oxford one, showing 57 miles from Oxford to London, is of 1785. The figures '57' appear before the word 'OXFORD' in a straight line thus: '57 OXFORD'. Mileage marks were stopped in 1797 because so many of them were inaccurate, but they were re-introduced in 1801 with the mileage shown in a box below the word 'OXFORD'. The first circular postmark was also the first one to include the date; it was issued in 1809. It had a curved 'OXFORD' at the top, the mileage of 57 at the bottom and the date in the centre. Various hand-stamps were in use at the post office before 1840 and examples of these can be found on mail of this period – for example the small three-lined 'PAID/AT/OXFORD' and 'MISSENT/ TO/OXFORD'. The former is also known in two lines in a box and the latter in two lines in script-lettering. In 1834 Oxford was issued with an official penny-post hand-stamp, which was in use until 1840 when the uniform penny post throughout the country was established. At the same time as the introduction of the Penny Black postage stamp on 6 May 1840, 1*d* and 2*d* wrappers and envelopes were issued. The design was by William Mulready, RA. They were intended to carry a letter of up to $\frac{1}{2}$ oz or 1 oz, respectively, without further charge. The design was greeted with ridicule and many caricatures of the 'Mulready' appeared. A rare example shows the famous 'dreaming spires' of Oxford, with a boat race on the river, an archery contest in the adjoining meadow and figures in their academic gowns and hoods.

Oxford's postal number is 603. The first stamps were cancelled with a Maltese cross, but an obliterator with the number 603 was used to cancel stamps between 1844 and 1855. In that year the first of a series of Duplex cancellers came into use, the 603 cancelling the stamp and the other half of the duplex containing the date-stamp in a circle. Over sixty different dies have been recorded in use during the 19th century, but they were replaced around the turn of the century by the double-circle cancellation with thick arcs. In June 1871 the Oxford post office was issued with a numeral canceller, incorrectly numbered 613. Six months later, for some inexplicable reason, another hand-stamp was issued to Oxford, again with the wrong number. The error was not corrected for over two years.

(Chambers, E.R., *The Postmarks of Oxford 1705–1978*, 1983.)

335

Postmasters *see* MERTON COLLEGE.

Postmasters' Hall *5 Merton Street.* Owned by Merton College since 1290 and used as a grammar hall till 1380, it was the ACADEMIC HALL for Merton's 'portionists' – impoverished young scholars – until they were housed in the college in 1575. It then became a private house, let in the 17th century to the father of ANTHONY WOOD. The antiquary was born here in 1632 and, in this, his lifelong home, he wrote the *Historia et Antiquitates Universitatis Oxoniensis*. It is still used as a residence by Merton College. 'Postmasters', a corruption of 'portionists', is the term used for the undergraduate scholars of Merton.

Prehistoric Oxford The earliest man-made artefacts found in Oxford are so old that they date from the period when the landscape of the Thames Valley and its gravel terraces was still being created. A number of palaeolithic finds are known from Oxford, but these objects were originally manufactured elsewhere; they were swept down to Oxford by the swirling waters which created the Summertown–Radley gravel terrace on which the later town developed. At WOLVERCOTE, however, eighty-three flint hand-axes and about 100 other flakes and tools, which date to the late Acheulian period, were found in the so-called Wolvercote Channel. These large hand-axes were skilfully made with plano-convex sections and ogee or acute points which demonstrate a clear Micoquian connection. It is believed that these artefacts must have been made in the immediate vicinity of the find spot, which is now the flooded brick-pit adjacent to Lakeside. The artefacts were found in association with faunal remains.

Once the topography of the region had been established, the site which was later to become Oxford had the same natural advantages as other centres for prehistoric settlement in the Thames Valley, such as Stanton Harcourt, Abingdon and Dorchester-on-Thames. All shared the common attributes of being situated where the THAMES was joined by a tributary river and where the floodplain and the well-drained higher gravel terrace offered a variety of soil types for agricultural exploitation, ranging from well-watered meadowland to arable.

The character of prehistoric Oxford is, however, more difficult to ascertain than elsewhere in the Thames Valley, because the existence of modern buildings over much of the ground surface means that the technique of aerial photography, which is the major means of locating prehistoric sites in the region, is impossible. There are a few open spaces, such as the University PARKS, Oxford City Football Ground and PORT MEADOW, where in dry summers the differential growth of the grass over underlying man-made features reveals the density of prehistoric settlement. Elsewhere, the only evidence for settlement is provided by stray finds which have come to light during excavations in advance of development and during building works.

There are no known Mesolithic sites in Oxford itself, although they are known from the Corallian hills which surround the city. Linear crop-marks which could be the ditches of a Neolithic cursus have been seen in the University Parks, while a relative concentration of Neolithic finds from the area around later Christ Church suggests that there may have been

substantial occupation in the vicinity. The pattern of human activity becomes somewhat clearer only in the Beaker period and in the Bronze Age. There is evidence for a Late Beaker settlement with occupation material and indications of early arable cultivation on the former floodplain of the Thames in St Thomas's. This material was accompanied by a child burial, for which a radiocarbon determination indicates a date of 1320 BC. The evidence was sealed by a later alluvial deposit and suggests that ground conditions on the floodplains were much drier in the Bronze Age than by the middle Iron Age. Other Beaker graves have come from SUMMERTOWN and Polstead Road. A number of Bronze Age funerary monuments are known. On Port Meadow, also on the floodplain, there are six 'ring ditches', probably barrows, including that known as Round Hill, excavated in 1842 by Sheriff Hunt and by T.E. Lawrence when a boy at the CITY OF OXFORD HIGH SCHOOL. On the higher gravel terrace, air photography has revealed three further ring ditches in the University Parks, and in the nearby SCIENCE AREA a double-ditched barrow has been partially excavated. Hoards of Late Bronze Age metalwork are known from Burgess Meadow and Leopold Street. Interestingly, these hoards contain pieces made from the same mould. Finds from the river suggest that the ford over the Thames at NORTH HINKSEY was already in use by this time.

On Port Meadow there are three small farmsteads of middle Iron Age date (*c*.350–50 BC), around which a number of paddocks were grouped. There are also several small enclosures in the University Parks which are probably Iron Age, although their date has not been tested by excavation. Such farmsteads could, however, date to the early Roman period and the late prehistoric settlement pattern of Oxford probably continued relatively undisturbed by the Roman Conquest.

Prideaux, John *(1578–1650).* The son of poor parents, he was sent to Exeter College at the expense of a rich woman who lived in their Devon village of Hartford. At Exeter he is said 'to have lived in very mean conditions and to have gotten his livelihood by doing servile offices in the kitchen; yet all this while he minded his book and what leisure he could obtain from the Business of the Scullery, he would improve it all in study'. By his diligence he obtained his degree and in 1601 he was elected a Fellow of Exeter, whose reputation then stood high under the rectorship of Thomas Holland (*d.*1612), the Regius Professor of Divinity. Prideaux succeeded Holland as Rector in 1612, and became Regius Professor of Divinity in 1615. Exeter continued to flourish and so did Prideaux's career. He became VICE-CHANCELLOR in 1619, when he was obliged to use his authority to settle the fierce quarrels at Jesus College, where the election of Francis Mansell (1579–1665) as Principal had been disputed by some of the Fellows, three of whom Mansell expelled and a fourth of whom was dismissed with Prideaux's support. Prideaux was consecrated Bishop of Worcester in 1641. There is a portrait of him in Exeter College hall, a copy of an original at Lacock Abbey.

Printing An exposition of the Apostles' Creed attributed to St Jerome but written by Rufinus of Aquileia and printed by Theodoric Rood from

Cologne is believed to be Oxford's first printed book. Printing the date of the completion of his work, Rood omitted a decade and printed M.cccc.lxviij (1468), which would have made him England's first printer by eight years; but the correct date is now known to be 1478. For the next eight years or so Rood printed in the University and for its members, but his press was neither owned nor supported by the University. Oxford's second press, at which on much the same terms John Scolar printed in 1517 and 1518, and Charles Kyrforth in 1519–20, may have been an offshoot of the London press of Wynkyn de Worde, who came to England from Cologne with England's first printer, William Caxton.

Thereafter for over fifty years there was no printing in Oxford and next to none anywhere else in England outside London. Under the stern control of Henry VIII and his heirs, and in the ferment of the Reformation, English books were censored and printing was permitted only by royal licence. From 1585, apparently with the consent of Queen Elizabeth, Joseph Barnes printed on his own account for the University (*see* OXFORD UNIVERSITY PRESS). He was followed by a succession of Printers to the University and of other printers in the city. University and city together controlled local entry into the printing trade; University printers, like other tradesmen serving the University, were academically enrolled (matriculated) and printed under academic privilege (*see* PRIVILEGED PERSONS). Other master-printers were permitted to set up in business only as freemen or hanasters (locally spelt 'hannisters') of the city and members of a guild, until the Municipal Reform Act of 1835 made entry into the trade comparatively free.

The small number of town printers in Oxford in the 18th century was due to the difficulty of making a living from any single department of the book trade, or even from several at once, rather than to academic and municipal restrictions. Book-tradesmen survived by practising several trades at once, and by no means all of these were connected in any way with books. By the early 19th century this versatility was developed and recorded; Henry Alden (*see* ALDEN), for example, whose business later became the ALDEN PRESS, was joint publisher of an Oxford weekly newspaper, bookseller, stationer, bookbinder, printer, and publisher of books and local magazines; he also sold music, hardware, tea, cloth, and patent medicines. Government restrictions on printing, embodied in the Licensing Act of 1662, had lapsed in 1695 and left English provincial printing free to develop as best it could. The University Press apart, that was not very far; in the last five years of the 17th century the University printed some eighty-six books and the other sixteen printers in Oxford hardly more than thirty.

Up to the end of the 18th century, the equipment and techniques of printing in the Western world had changed little. The text was set by hand in metal type and printed on a wooden hand-press. Copperplate engraving was almost as old as typographic printing, and lithography was comparatively new. By the end of the 19th century printing, type-founding, paper-making, illustration reproduction, and bookbinding were all mechanised to some extent. The single shops in which books and periodicals had been printed not far from CARFAX were being replaced by factories, some of them combining several shops and others on the outskirts of the city. The variety of printed product, the volume of production and the complexity of the printed image were vastly increased.

Printing was Oxford's leading manufacture in 1851 and continued to be so in 1911, accounting for about 4 per cent of the men employed – a higher proportion than in other English towns of the same size. Even in 1971, when the COWLEY motor works was employing several times as many as all Oxford's printers together, the number of men working at printing and bookbinding had risen to 5 per cent of the workforce in a greatly increased population.

(*See also* OXFORD UNIVERSITY PRESS.)

Prison In 1785 the county justices bought the old gaol in the CASTLE and redeveloped it behind a curtain wall as a gaol and house of correction, under the supervision of George Moneypenny. It was said to have had a 'very castellated appearance'. There were two wings – one on each side of the keeper's house – one containing debtors, the other felons. The condemned cell was in the Castle's St George's Tower. The early prisoners were employed on building and roadworks. A house of correction for the county, with separate wings for men and women, was constructed behind the keeper's house in 1788. Alterations were carried out in 1819 and 1820, and exercise yards to the designs of Thomas Hooper were added. After a new governor's house was built by Benjamin Ferrey in 1848, the whole prison was enlarged in the 1850s to designs by H.J. Underwood; when completed it held 218 male and twenty-four female felons, and 133 male and twenty-five female debtors. As in the CITY GAOL, prisoners were exhausted by the use of the treadmill and the crank. By 1945 the prison was already badly overcrowded.

Oxford's is now a local prison serving the magistrates' courts of Oxfordshire and Buckinghamshire, which commit prisoners for trial at two crown courts, located in Oxford and Aylesbury, which in turn send sentenced men to the prison. The population of the establishment is therefore a combination of male adults and young offenders, some of whom are convicted and some unconvicted. The establishment is designed to hold 130 prisoners but the average daily population is in the order of 230 prisoners.

(*See also* BOCARDO PRISON.)

Private Halls Established as the result of a recommendation of the 1850 University Commission (*see* ROYAL COMMISSIONS), as a means of providing less expensive residence at the University. Under a statute passed in 1855, any MA over twenty-eight years old could become a 'Licensed Master', permitted to open a 'Private Hall' under certain conditions. On the basis of this, and a modifying statute of 1882, and until the present statute was passed in 1918, thirteen private halls in total were in existence at various times, all taking their names from the licensed Principal, and lasting under that guise for periods from one year (Butler's Hall, 1857) to twenty-nine years (Charsley's Hall, 1862–91), with mixed academic results. The essential feature of their status was that a private hall was a private venture of its Master, which came to an end when he died or surrendered his licence. In the closing years of the 19th century two private halls were established, for which in course of time it became clear that this concept was inappropriate. These were Clarke's Hall (1896–1901) and Hunter-Blair's Hall (1899–1908). Their names concealed the fact that they were the property respectively of the English Province of the Order of Jesuits and of the Benedictine Abbey of Ampleforth, established by these religious houses as academic communities in Oxford for their members. In the first two decades of the present century the first hall survived three changes of Master (and hence of name) and the other saw two such changes. The hall known successively as Clarke's (1896–1901), Pope's (1901–17) and Plater's (1917–18) gained many academic distinctions – examination results and University PRIZES AND SCHOLARSHIPS. There was therefore general support for the statute of 1918 that provided for the establishment of 'Permanent Private Halls'. By then these two were the only surviving private halls; they became respectively CAMPION HALL and ST BENET'S HALL.

The 1918 statute includes among its provisions that a Permanent Private Hall shall be situated not more than 2½ miles from CARFAX; that it shall not be run for profit; that the Master must be an MA of the University; and that CONGREGATION must approve the grant of a licence and the name of the hall. Students at the hall have the same privileges and obligations in relation to the University as if they were members of a college. The University prescribes the maximum numbers studying for University degrees, etc., for each hall.

There are at present five Permanent Private Halls established under the statute, the dates of their licence and prescribed maximum numbers being: CAMPION HALL (1918; 6); ST BENET'S HALL (1918; 28); MANSFIELD COLLEGE (1955; 105); GREYFRIARS (1957; 17); and REGENT'S PARK COLLEGE (1957; 47); MANCHESTER COLLEGE (1990; 60).

Privileged Persons Persons who were granted the privileges of the University but were not students. Before the Municipal Reform Act of 1835, the University dominated the city not only culturally but also economically, and not only by its purchasing strength but also by the authority it had wielded over trade ever since the charter granted after ST SCHOLASTICA'S DAY. Certain occupations were for many years reserved for Privileged Persons – tradesmen sworn to the service of the University. These persons might be freemen; but, whether freemen or not, their privileged status allowed them to carry on trade in the town. Many of them were booksellers or bookbinders; others were University or college servants. By the 1520s a fifth of the town's taxable inhabitants were Privileged Persons. As such they were exempt from the city's jurisdiction. The University could admit anybody it chose to its privileges, regardless of apprenticeship or nationality. Enrolment as a University supplier took the form of MATRICULATION, for which an oath of allegiance to the monarchy and to the Established Church was required (hence the term 'matriculated tradesmen'). Privileged Persons apart, nobody was supposed to enter into business practice as master or journeyman within the city boundaries unless he was 'free' of the city and its CRAFT GUILDS. A citizen could be made free by act of Council or by patrimony, but most were sworn free after serving an apprenticeship of seven years from the age of about fourteen. Oxford freemen were also known as 'hanasters' or 'hannisters'.

Privileges Thanks to royal support and intervention from the earliest days, the University and its scholars enjoyed long-lasting and important privileges throughout the Middle Ages. The CHANCELLOR was afforded considerable authority and jurisdiction at the expense of the local burgesses (notably by Edward I in 1304–5). Scholars were protected from undue noise, unfair pricing policies, the use of false weights and measures, and from violence. The appointment of the High Steward (see OFFICERS OF THE UNIVERSITY) in 1406 by Henry IV was another important step, for it was to be his special function to ensure to the University members the continued enjoyment of their existing privileges. Such privileges were more than welcome during the long periods when town and gown were almost permanently at loggerheads – as evidenced most notoriously in the affray of ST SCHOLASTICA'S DAY in 1355 – but they gradually evaporated as the need for them lessened. Similarly, the roles played by the High Steward and the Clerks of the Market (see OFFICERS OF THE UNIVERSITY) have long since become wholly ceremonial (and even the office known as ASSESSOR to the Chancellor's Court (see COURTS) has fallen into desuetude since 1978–9). PROCTORS have the ancient privilege of sitting at the judge's right hand during the assizes.

Little, if anything, now remains of scholars' privileges (except indeed that of being admitted to the University), though the word itself is often still to be found in statutes and elsewhere: thus a degree on a Master 'incorporating' from, say, Cambridge will be conferred in these words: '*ego admitto te ad eundem gradum statum dignitatem et privilegia hic apud nos Oxonienses, quibus ornatus es apud tuos Cantabrigienses*'.

PRIZES AND SCHOLARSHIPS In the course of an academic year, the University announces approximately eighty prizes and forty scholarships (or, often, studentships) to be competed or applied for. Most of these are derived from benefactions (see BEQUESTS, BENEFACTIONS AND MEMORIAL FUNDS) and many are of considerable antiquity. Although by now prizes or scholarships have been established in all the main subjects, there inevitably remains a bias towards the Classics (with about fifteen separate awards in all at graduate or undergraduate level) and, to a lesser extent, towards Theology, History and Law. Recent years have seen an increase in the number of awards – especially studentships – available to graduate students (often with their financial circumstances as a major criterion), in line with their increasing importance in the University as a whole, and a gradually declining emphasis on the concept of special competitive examinations to determine the award-winner. A number of scholarships or prizes have undergone significant modifications in their terms of reference over the years; others have disappeared, while new ones have come to take their place. The value of the awards varies very greatly. It is normal, but not invariable, for limitations to be placed on the eligibility of candidates in respect of time (for instance, the number of terms from MATRICULATION) and on the frequency with which a given award can be held by one individual (normally once; occasionally twice). One of the least tied of the prizes is that for an English poem on a sacred subject (see SACRED POEM

PRIZE), for which any MA may compete, which may be awarded twice to the same person and which had the value in 1987 of £1100. This prize, which is offered only once every three years, was founded in 1848 'by an unknown benefactor'.

Inside the University some of the scholarships and prizes carry, or used to carry, special prestige. Such are the Ireland Scholarship (founded 1825 by John Ireland of Oriel, Dean of Westminster) and the Craven Scholarships (Classics, founded in 1647 by John, Lord Craven of Ryton); the Vinerian Law Scholarships (1758); the Eldon Law Scholarships (1830); the Hertford Scholarship (Latin Language and Literature, 1834); and the John Locke Scholarship in Mental Philosophy (1898); the Chancellor's Prizes (1768) for Latin Verse, Latin Prose and English Essay; the Gaisford Prizes (1856) for Greek Verse (now no more) and Greek Prose; the Mathematical Prizes (1831); and the Arnold Historical Essay Prizes (1850); but the lists could readily be extended. However, probably only one prize is at all well known outside the University: the NEWDIGATE.

Changes in availability and applicability render comparisons between generations partially invalid, but the records show that a few undergraduates, notably in the Classics, have succeeded in winning all or almost all of the University scholarships and prizes open to them; two are on record as having won eight (or equivalent to eight) awards, and another has won seven; while GILBERT MURRAY's six awards in the 1880s were equivalent to seven in the 1960s. Only three undergraduates, all from Balliol, are on record as having won all four Classical Composition Prizes. The record of the brothers C.G.R. Leach (Balliol, all four prizes) and J.H.C. Leach (Brasenose, three prizes and a *proxime accessit* (*see* GLOSSARY)) between 1953 and 1956 will now presumably stand for all time, since the abolition of the Gaisford Greek Verse Prize.

In general, it seems fair to say that recent trends have tended to lessen the importance of winning scholarships and prizes: the fact that tuition fees of almost all undergraduates are paid by Local Education Authorities has rendered their financial aspect less relevant, while the value of many of the awards has tended not to keep pace with inflation (the Ireland Scholarship, for example, was worth up to £200 to its winner in 1955; thirty years later its value was only £300, as opposed to the roughly £2000 which would be necessary to match the 1955 sum). The increasing range of options now open to undergraduates, with the resulting diffusion of interest, may have contributed to the same end, while the element of intense competition resulting from examinations which had to be specially entered (normally with a tutor's express permission) has also declined as more awards are made as a result of application rather than examination, or, in some instances, because of the candidate's performance in the SCHOOLS. Again, the taking of a higher degree is now a more important factor in the career of a prospective academic than the winning of a prize (*see* DEGREES).

Yet even so, and even if many of those who appear in the lists of prizewinners subsequently made little or no mark elsewhere, it is also the case that many who *did* later distinguish themselves, in a variety of fields, drew attention to their promise at an early stage by success as undergraduates. Some who deserve notice are George Canning (Chancellor's Latin Verse, 1789);

F.E. Smith, Lord Birkenhead (Vinerian Law Scholarship, 1896); G.N. CURZON, Lord Curzon of Kedleston (Lothian Prize for History, 1883, with an essay on 'Justinian', and Arnold Historical Essay Prize, 1884, on 'Sir Thomas More'); JOHN KEBLE (Chancellor's Latin Essay, 1812, and Chancellor's English Essay with 'On Translation from Dead Languages', 1812); THOMAS ARNOLD (Chancellor's Latin Essay, 1817, and Chancellor's English Essay, 1815, on 'The Effects of Distant Colonization on the Parent State'); Aldous Huxley (Stanhope Historical Essay, 1916, on 'The Development of Political Satire in England from the Restoration to the Revolution'); H.H. Asquith (Craven Scholar, 1874) and Raymond Asquith (Craven Scholar, 1898); Oliver (Lord) Franks and Sir Isaiah Berlin (John Locke Scholarship, 1927 and 1931, respectively); Victor Gollancz (Chancellor's Latin Essay, 1913); John Addington Symonds (Chancellor's English Essay, 1863, on 'The Renaissance'); Lord Wilson of Rievaulx (as J.H. Wilson, Gladstone Memorial Prize, 1936, on 'The State and the Railways in Great Britain, 1823–63', and the Junior and Senior George Webb Medley Scholarships for Economics, 1936 and 1937); SIR MAURICE BOWRA, Warden of Wadham and VICE-CHANCELLOR of the University (Conington Prize for Classics, 1930).

An early multiple prizewinner was Roundell Palmer, 1st Earl of Selborne, and later Lord Chancellor, whose successes numbered the Chancellor's Latin Verse (1831) and Latin Essay (1835), besides the Ireland Scholarship (1832), the Eldon Law Scholarship (1834), and the Newdigate (1832). RONALD KNOX enjoyed a rather similar career, winning the Hertford (1907), the Ireland and Craven (1908), Gaisford Greek Verse (1908) and Chancellor's Latin Verse (1910). MARTIN D'ARCY won both the John Locke Scholarship (1918) and the Green Moral Philosophy Prize (1923). This prize, which was founded in 1882 and is awarded triennially, was also won by R.M. Hare (1950). More recently, C.J. (now Sir Jeremy) Morse, chairman of Lloyds Bank, also won five University scholarships or prizes in the early 1950s (Hertford, 1951; Craven, 1951; Chancellor's Latin Prose and Verse, 1951; and Gaisford Greek Prose, 1952).

The following articles on individual awards are in alphabetical order:

The Chancellor's Prizes Founded in 1768 by the Earl of Lichfield, CHANCELLOR of the University, and worth £100 each in 1987. These prizes, numbered among the University's oldest, have enjoyed a number of distinguished winners, including (Latin Verse) Edwin Palmer (1844) and John Conington (1847), both to become Corpus Professors of Latin; A.D. Godley (1877); GILBERT MURRAY (1886); R.A. KNOX (1910); Sir Denys Page (1928); and John Sparrow (1929). The prize was also won in 1851 by the poet Charles Stuart Calverley (then called Blayds), who, according to tradition, once hurled a stone through the Master's window while showing some people round the Garden Quad at Balliol. 'That,' he said, 'is the Master's window. And now, unless I am much mistaken, you will see the Master himself.' They did, and Calverley was sent down.

The Latin Prose (before 1822 known as the Latin Essay) winners include JOHN KEBLE (1812), THOMAS ARNOLD (1817), E.B. PUSEY (1824), Robert Scott, who became HENRY LIDDELL's collaborator (1834), BENJA-MIN JOWETT (1841, on 'The Etruscans'), once again E. Palmer (1847), and J. Conington (1849). D.B. Monro won in 1859 and A.D. Godley, later PUBLIC ORATOR, in 1879. Winners in this century include Sir Ronald Syme (1926) and Gilbert Highet (1934).

The English Essay was won by Henry Addington, 1st Viscount Sidmouth, and Prime Minister 1801–4, in 1779. Reginald Heber, divine and hymn-writer, succeeded in 1805, John Keble in 1812 and Thomas Arnold in 1815. J.A. FROUDE won in 1842, J. Conington in 1848, and A.C. Bradley ('Utopias') in 1875. Hastings Rashdall foreshadowed his life's work by winning in 1883 on 'The Universities of the Middle Ages'; C.S. LEWIS won in 1921 ('Optimism') and Professor George Steiner in 1952 ('Malice').

Eldon Law Scholarship Founded in 1830 as a testimonial to John, 1st Earl of Eldon. It can be held for up to three years by award-holders, who must be of graduate status and intend to practise Law, and was worth £1450 a year in 1987. Past winners include J. Conington (1849), Raymond Asquith (1902), Patrick Shaw-Stewart (1910), Cyril (later Lord) Radcliffe (1923), D.S. Dannreuther (1926), John Sparrow (1929), Lord Blake (1938), and Sir Patrick Neill, Warden of All Souls and VICE-CHANCELLOR of the University (1951).

Gaisford Prizes for Greek Verse and Prose Founded in 1856 in memory of THOMAS GAISFORD, DD, Dean of Christ Church and Regius Professor of Greek. The Greek Verse Prize was discontinued in 1975, and the Prose Prize is now awarded on performance in Classical Honour Moderations. The compositions of two winners achieved a fame which even today is not quite vanished: Sir John Beazley's Greek Prose award in 1907 ('The Zoological Gardens', written in the style of Herodotus) and R.A. KNOX's Theocritean hexameters of 1908 from R. Browning's 'Pippa Passes'. Other winners of the Verse Prize include A.D. Godley (1878), GILBERT MURRAY (1886), Edgar Lobel (1911), Sir Ronald Syme (1927) and Sir Denys Page (1928). The Greek Prose Prize has been won by Gilbert Murray (1887), Sir Ronald Syme (1926) and the philosopher J.L. Austin (1931).

Hertford Scholarship (Latin Language and Literature) Founded in 1834 after the dissolution of the old Society of Hertford College. Its worth in 1987 was £480. It is taken in conjunction with the two de Paravicini Scholarships, founded in 1926 in memory of Baron Francis de Paravicini and worth £275 each in 1987. Both awards are now prizes, and are awarded for performance in Classical Honour Moderations. Winners of the Hertford include BENJAMIN JOWETT (1837), GILBERT MURRAY (1885), Cyril Bailey (1891), Sir R.W. Livingstone (1900), Sir J.D. Beazley (1905), R.A. KNOX (1907), Sir Roger Mynors (1924) and Hugh Trevor-Roper, Lord Dacre (1934). Sir Denys Page (1928) and Anthony Chenevix-Trench (1939), later Headmaster of Eton, won the *de Paravicini*.

Ireland and Craven Scholarships Dean Ireland's scholarship was founded in 1825 'for the promotion of Classical learning and taste'; it became linked with the much older Craven Scholarships (1647) in 1886. Perhaps the most remarkable incident in the history of the Ireland Scholarship occurred in 1831, when it was won by Thomas Brancker, then still a schoolboy at Shrewsbury School. Among the vanquished were no lesser rivals than Robert Scott, another Salopian (who himself won in 1833), and WILLIAM GLADSTONE, who wrote to his father: 'This has contributed amazingly to strengthen a prevalent impression that the Shrewsbury system is radically a false one.... However, we who are beaten are not fair judges.'

The records of the Craven Scholarship become relatively complete only after 1776, and even after that the early award-holders are dominated by 'Founder's kindred or name', though the above-mentioned Robert Scott won in 1830. After 1886 the examinations for the Ireland and Craven Scholarships were merged, and one or other, or both, scholarships have been won by many of the country's leading classicists or scholars: in the case of the Ireland, we find E. Palmer (1843), J. Conington (1844), GILBERT MURRAY (1885), J.D. Beazley (1904), R.A. KNOX (1908), E.R. Dodds (1914), T.B.L. Webster (1924), Lord Dacre (1934), and Professors Sir Kenneth Dover (1946), Hugh Lloyd-Jones (1947), Robin Nisbet (1949) and Martin West (1957). Among winners of the Craven only are Cyril Bailey (1891), A.W. Pickard-Cambridge (1893), Edgar Lobel (1909), J.D. Denniston (1909), Sir Denys Page (1928) and Gilbert Highet (1930). A notable absentee is A.E. Housman, though one of the winners while he was at Oxford (A.C. Clark, who won the Ireland in 1879) was to become a distinguished Latinist. In 1987, the values of the Ireland and the three Craven Scholarships were respectively £300 and £150 each.

John Locke Prize Originally the John Locke Scholarship, it was worth £400 in 1987. It was founded in 1898 by Henry Wilde, FRS. In addition to such well-known names as Oliver Franks (1927) and Isaiah Berlin (1931), the winners include such philosophers as C.E.M. Joad (1914), J.O. Urmson (1938) and Sir P.F. Strawson (1946). (*See also* CRAVEN COMMITTEE.)

Proctors The disciplinary and administrative officers of the University, elected in rotation annually by the colleges. Their office can be traced as far back as 1248 and may even go back to a much earlier date, when they were described as 'taxors' or 'rectors'. Originally they were the principal executive officers of the University, responsible for its good order both as regards studies and conduct. More especially they represented the interests of the Regent Masters and it was their function to ensure that the townspeople did not charge exorbitant rents or prices. At first they were chosen by the regional groupings or NATIONS into which the University was divided, the Senior Proctor representing the southerners, the Junior the northerners. Although rivalry between the two nations caused constant dissension, sometimes developing into RIOTS, the Proctors were essentially representatives of the University and did not themselves seek to represent the rival regional interests. In general, though not continuously, the Proctors were Fellows of colleges; from 1285 to 1340 over half the Proctors were Fellows of Merton. In 1534 Henry VIII summarily took over the appointments to the proctorship and in 1541, alleging that unsuitable men had been selected, he ordered that the Proctors should henceforth be elected by the CHANCELLOR, the VICE-CHANCELLOR, heads of houses and Doctors. Later, from 1574, Proctors were elected by CONVOCATION, but subsequent intrigues led the

A Proctor, one of the disciplinary officers of the University, demands to know a young man's name and college.

King in 1628 to impose an order of election by which colleges in a prearranged order elected the Proctors from among their numbers. In a period of twenty-three years the biggest colleges, such as Christ Church and Magdalen, were to have five or six Proctors, the smaller only one. This proctorial cycle was incorporated in the LAUDIAN CODE of 1636 but subsequently has been modified in 1859 and in 1889 by the inclusion of the Non-Collegiate Society (later St Catherine's) and Keble in simple rotation, each electing body choosing a Proctor every eleven years. A later amendment was devised to accommodate the interests of the then women's colleges. A new cycle was devised which included an ASSESSOR, similarly elected, to serve with the two Proctors. The Proctors, like the Assessor, are elected by members of the governing bodies of colleges who are on the roll of Convocation, acting with members of the college who are members of CONGREGATION. Candidates must be Masters of Arts of more than four and less than sixteen years standing, the Senior Proctor being the one who has taken his Master's degree first. At his installation, the Proctor is presented with the insignia of his office and the keys.

The Proctors' obligations and powers were, and remain, very wide. Originally they were responsible for calling meetings of Masters of Arts, for arranging the liturgical functions of the University, reflected still in their right to sing the Latin litany at the start of each term and in their presence at University funerals. They were responsible for administering oaths. They supervised exercises for degrees and the conduct of examinations, as they still do. They sat, then as now, on all University boards and committees. They had the right to veto any motion put forward in Congregation or Convocation – a right they exercised, for instance, in 1845 when they vetoed the motion to condemn J.H. NEWMAN's *Tract XC*. Their best-known duty was the imposition of DISCIPLINE, at first not merely on students but on all culpable offenders,

which might include townspeople as well as members of the University. They kept a register of homicides and prostitutes (whom they were empowered to expel from the city). In the exercise of their duties they were accompanied by the University Marshal (*see* OFFICERS OF THE UNIVERSITY) and University police or BULL-DOGS. Their disciplinary powers are now confined to students, those *in statu pupillari*.

In spite of some diminution in their functions, the Proctors are among the most prominent and important of the University's officials, entrusted with the safekeeping of the Chancellor's seal and the seal of the University, and they are always obliged to witness the affixing by the REGISTRAR of the latter.

Professors   *see* CHAIRS *and* FACULTIES.

Provisions of Oxford   Promulgated by the so-called 'Mad Parliament' which met at Oxford in 1258 and intended to limit the power of King Henry III. The epithet 'mad' was probably given to the Parliament because of a misreading of the word *insigne* (famous) as *insane* in a contemporary account. The Parliament met at the Dominican friary in ST EBBE'S. During the subsequent baronial revolt, the town was sometimes in the King's hands, at others in those of his enemies. In 1263 Simon de Montfort and his principal supporters met here at the outset of their campaign, but for most of that year and the next King Henry III was in possession of the town. In 1264 and again in 1266 the whole knight service of England was summoned to Oxford to support the King against his enemies.

Public Health   *see* HEALTH, PUBLIC.

Public Orator   A University official, elected by CONGREGATION from among the members of CON-VOCATION. He presents those to be admitted to honorary degrees (*see* DEGREES) and makes an oration on each of them. He may also be required to compose letters and addresses at the direction of the HEBDO-MADAL COUNCIL and to make speeches at the reception of members of royal families. His office appears to date from 1564, when he was appointed on the expectation of a visit from Elizabeth I. When the Queen did visit Oxford in 1566 the Public Orator, Kingsmill, traced the country's history in a speech of inordinate length. Sir Isaac Wake similarly addressed James I on his visit to Oxford in 1605.

Pullen's Lane   Runs between the top of HEAD-INGTON HILL and JACK STRAW'S LANE. It is named after the Rev. Josiah Pullen (1631–1714), who was Vice-President of MAGDALEN HALL and vicar of ST PETER-IN-THE EAST, where he is buried. He used to walk daily to the top of Headington Hill and at the turning-point in the walk, where he stopped to admire the view over Oxford, he planted an elm tree in about 1680. This tree, known as Joe Pullen's tree, grew to a great size but was destroyed by fire on 13 October 1909. A tablet in the wall of Davenport House on the east side of the lane records the event. There are portraits of Josiah Pullen in the BODLEIAN LIBRARY and in Hertford College.

On the west side of the lane, at the top of Headington Hill, is Headington Hill Hall, built in 1861 for the Morrell family (*see* MORRELL'S BREWERY) and designed by John Thomas. It is now owned by Oxford City Council and leased to the PERGAMON PRESS. Other properties along the lane include Pullen's Gate (formerly Brockleaze); The Barn, a 17th-century barn converted into a dwelling house for Dr H.M. Harris by Thomas Rayson; High Wall, built in 1910 for Miss K.J.D. Feilden by Walter Cave and possessing a beautiful garden, laid out by H.A. Peto; Pullen's End (formerly Torbrex); Pollock House (formerly The Vineyard), built about 1889 by H.W. Moore for Professor Sydney Vines, Sherardian Professor of Botany; Langley Lodge (1895) now occupied by RYE ST ANTONY SCHOOL; Fairfield (formerly The Pullens) now PLATER COLLEGE; and Cotuit Hall, a students' residence of Oxford POLYTECHNIC. A plaque in the wall of Headington Hill Hall, opposite that referring to Joe Pullen's tree, records that the lime and plane trees nearby were planted by his wife and family in memory of Dr H.M. Harris of Wembley, Middlesex, and The Barn, Pullen's Lane, a 'Beloved Physician. 1894–1976'. The lane is a private road maintained by the residents. There were once white gates at both ends of the lane, but only the white posts remain at the junction with Jack Straw's Lane.

(Harris, H.M., *Between the White Gates*, Oxford, 1975, limited edition of 100 copies.)

After the decline of work-punts in the 1860s, punting became one of Oxford's most popular leisure activities.

Punting The punt is a native THAMES craft, square-ended and built with a durable frame like a ladder. The two sides are joined at the bottom by cross-pieces called 'treads' or, in Oxford only, 'rounds' – names for steps of a ladder. The ends of a punt are 'huffs' and the upwards slope to them 'swims'. The stern of a smaller, narrower punt is strengthened with decking called a 'till' or, in Oxford, a 'box'. The word 'punt', of Gallic origin, appeared in written English about AD 1000 and was used for any small craft. In the 19th century the Bengali word 'dinghy' largely replaced this usage, 'punt' being increasingly restricted to the description of the Thames craft.

Punts were work-craft with oak frames and renewable softwood bottoms, of different sizes for different tasks: for barge-work, ferrying, dredging, fishing or light river-transport. They were capacious, simple to build, and especially suitable for the Thames when locks were less efficient and the river was therefore shallower.

A punt is handled with a pole, its foot shod with a forged or cast metal 'shoe'. Heavy work-punts were 'walked'; the pole was dropped at the bow, the open end, if the punt was decked, and the punter walked down the punt, shoving on the pole. The waterman's term for 'to punt' was in fact 'to shove'. Punt-poles at Oxford are 16 feet long, though on the lower Thames they are usually 14–15 feet. Recently aluminium has been replacing wood for poles, although it is not possible to taper aluminium poles for balance as it is with wood.

After 1860, as the use of work-punts declined and the population of the Thames Valley increased, riverside residents had varnished mahogany pleasure punts built on the lines of fishing punts. Besides a till, a fishing punt had a watertight box for live bait across its width – the 'wet well'. Mahogany sides with straighter grain cut thinner than oak made pleasure punts lighter, and they could easily be 'pricked', or punted with the leading foot stationary. In order to face the passenger or 'sitter', the punter then usually punted stern first, from the end opposite the box, against which a cushion or mattress was placed for the sitter. Today's 'saloon' design of pleasure punt, with four sitters placed facing inwards, was not introduced until after 1880; this craft is a little less than 3 feet wide, usually 24–7 feet long, and sometimes called a 3-foot punt. Elsewhere on the Thames (and when after 1900 punts were first introduced to Cambridge), saloon punts were punted bow first; but at Oxford the custom of punting stern first did not change – the punter stood in the open end – and it has become a tradition.

The present punt-hiring locations in Oxford are the CHERWELL BOAT HOUSE on the upper Cherwell (*see* THAMES), where Oxford's only punt-building is continued; Howard's at MAGDALEN BRIDGE on the Lower Cherwell; and Hubbucks' at FOLLY BRIDGE on the Isis (*see* THAMES). As expected above a weir, as at PARSON'S PLEASURE, the upper Cherwell is comparatively deep and muddy, but popular because of its proximity to the fashionable NORTH OXFORD residential area and its beautiful riverside. The lower Cherwell is shallower and gravelly, and a reasonably good punting bottom extends for its length to the new mouth; the stream to the old mouth is narrow, shallow and muddy. From Folly Bridge to the college boat-houses, the Isis is good for punting, though there is mud close to the CHRIST CHURCH MEADOW bank. Further downstream there are a few deeps, notably at the new Cherwell mouth and in the Gut. The finest punting bottom in the vicinity of Oxford is along PORT MEADOW bank.

In the 19th century punts were principally hired in the locality of Folly Bridge and some in Medley Weir Stream. There were also many private owners. Punting on the Cherwell, today the principal river for it, developed from about 1890. The Cherwell Boat House, established in 1901 by Tom Tims the University waterman, was known as Tims's until relinquished by the family in 1964; punt-hiring at Magdalen Bridge was established in 1911 on a former site for watering horses; at Folly Bridge, Hubbucks' and the Riverside Boating Co. alone remain of many.

Abel Beesley, University Waterman and for many years champion professional punter on the Thames, on his punt between Hythe Bridge and Pacey's Bridge c.1895.

From 1947 punts became increasingly popular for hearing carols sung from Magdalen Tower on MAY MORNING. However, from the 1950s vandalism had been increasing and, since 1964, all punt-hirers have prohibited the use of punts on May Morning. In 1953 the Charon Club was founded to hold an annual punt relay-race against the Cambridge University Dampers Club; girls jumping from punt to punt acted as relay batons. Again, increasing damage to punts caused punt-hirers in 1973 to prohibit the use of punts for this or any other racing. However, MORRELL'S BREWERY has recently donated a shield for a college dongola regatta, the punts being propelled with paddles by mixed crews of six.

The only University punting championship was held in 1905, along Port Meadow bank. Punt-racing is a recognised sport governed by the Thames Punting Club, but local to the lower Thames. Punts 35 feet long and 14 inches wide are used for singles racing, and 30 feet long and 2 feet wide for doubles racing. At both Oxford and Cambridge there are about 160 punts for hire. College Junior Common Rooms usually hire punts by block bookings for the Trinity Term and a few own their own. Elsewhere, a small number are found for hire at Henley, Hampton, Bath, Stratford-upon-Avon and Knaresborough.

The punting stroke begins with a throw or drop to the river bottom, made with the forward hand in a single, unbroken movement. The punter stands facing either side, but the forward foot is placed firmly against the side, and it does not move from that position. The angles of the drop, forward and lateral, decide the steering and are determined by the lower hand immediately before the drop. (The angles and direction of the pole are much the same as those for a single canoe paddle; there is a technical similarity in the strokes.) The hands then rise, grip the pole close together, and pull towards the centre of the chest; from there, with the body turning, the hands move away parallel to the water and the rear foot moves below them (the 'after-shove'). At the end of the

shove, the hands relax before recovering the pole in three movements, the rear hand throwing it over the forward before the latter tilts it up. In a stationary or slowly moving punt, a 'half-shove' must be used, with the pole dropped at an angle of 45 degrees. The half-shove is also useful for beginners and for idle punting.

(Rivington, R.T., *Punts & Punting*, 1982, and *Punting: Its History & Techniques*, 1983.)

Pusey, Edward Bouverie (*1800–1882*). The grandson of the 1st Viscount Folkestone and son of Philip Bouverie (who changed his name to Pusey on inheriting that family's estate in the Berkshire village of the same name), E.B. Pusey was sent to Eton in 1812 and entered Christ Church in 1819. After taking a First in Classics, in 1822 he was appointed a Fellow of Oriel College, where he became a close friend of JOHN KEBLE and JOHN HENRY NEWMAN, both also Fellows of the college. At the instigation of Charles Lloyd (1784–1829), Professor of Divinity and BISHOP OF OXFORD from 1827, Pusey spent almost two years in Germany studying the country's language and theological literature, as well as oriental languages, returning to Oxford in 1827 and soon afterwards publishing his *Historical Enquiry into the Probable Causes of the Rationalist Character lately predominant*

An 'Ape' cartoon of E.B. Pusey, Fellow of Oriel, one of the leaders of the Oxford Movement.

in the Theology of Germany. In the following year he was ordained, and in November appointed to succeed Alexander Nicoll (1793–1828) as Regius Professor of Hebrew. For the next six years or so he was engaged upon completing Nicoll's work of cataloguing the Arabic manuscripts in the BODLEIAN LIBRARY.

Although a Liberal in politics and a supporter of Peel's re-election as BURGESS for the University (*see* ROMAN CATHOLICS), Pusey lent his great authority to opposing liberalism in the Church. By the middle of the 1830s he was one of the leaders of the OXFORD MOVEMENT, and was able, in Newman's words, 'to give a name, a power, and a personality to what was without him a sort of mob'. He now began his edition of translations of the works of the Fathers of the Holy Catholic Church and began also to exercise profound influence in Oxford as a preacher in CHRIST CHURCH CATHEDRAL, ST MARY THE VIRGIN and elsewhere. One of his more controversial sermons, however, resulted in his being suspended for two years as a preacher before the University – a suspension which led to a protest to the VICE-CHANCELLOR from WILLIAM GLADSTONE. After the publication of the report of the ROYAL COMMISSION in 1852, Pusey became identified with the conservative opponents of what were seen as damaging reforms of University institutions; and in 1854 he was elected to the new HEBDOMADAL COUNCIL. Pusey's young wife died of consumption not long after their marriage and he was survived by only one of their four children.

(*See also* OXFORD MOVEMENT *and* PUSEY HOUSE.)

Pusey House Situated in ST GILES', Pusey House was founded in 1884 in memory of EDWARD BOUVERIE PUSEY. It was originally known formally as the Dr Pusey Memorial Library. One of its central concerns was the housing of Dr Pusey's large theological library, to which many additions have subsequently been made of books, manuscript collections associated with the OXFORD MOVEMENT and Catholic revival in Anglicanism, and a very important collection of 19th-century pamphlets. The library formed the centre of a 'house of sacred learning', whose Principal and priest–librarians were also to afford pastoral care and theological instruction to members of the University.

The first building was 61 St Giles', and the houses on either side were subsequently acquired. Two 18th-century rooms survive internally (the Pamphlet Room and the Van Heyningen Room). Early in the 20th century a bequest of more than £70,000 from John William Cudworth (*d*.1904), a Leeds solicitor and a Quaker convert to Anglicanism through the ministry of St Saviour's, Dr Pusey's church in Leeds, enabled the present buildings to be erected. They were designed in late Gothic style by Temple Moore. The first range, erected between 1912 and 1914, comprised the Chapel of the Resurrection and half of the library, followed by the rest of the library and the St Giles' front (1918). In 1924–6 the south range was completed in the same style, with John Coleridge as architect. The chapel follows a monastic arrangement – a large chapel used mainly for Sunday worship being divided from a smaller chapel at the east end by a solid stone screen surmounted by painted rood with a rood-screen altar at its foot. The eastern chapel was adorned in 1935–6 by an east window and altar with canopy designed by Sir Ninian Comper. Since 1982 the buildings have been shared with St Cross College, which has refurbished a number of the rooms and created a new hall on the ground floor of the south range.

There have been eight Principals of Pusey House since its foundation, a number of whom have been outstanding as theological scholars and spiritual directors. Charles Gore (Principal 1884–93) caused an early furore by contributing to the volume of Oxford theological essays *Lux Mundi* (1889) an essay recognising the limitation in Jesus's knowledge, thus signalling an acceptance of biblical critical ideas by the heirs of the Tractarians (*see* OXFORD MOVEMENT). Darwell Stone (Principal 1909–34) was a notable liturgical scholar. The house continues its work of theological scholarship and pastoral ministry to the University within the Catholic tradition of Anglicanism.

Pusey Street Connects ST JOHN STREET to ST GILES'. It was known as Alfred Street, St Giles', until 1925. In August that year consent to the name Pusey (*see* EDWARD BOUVERIE PUSEY *and also* PUSEY HOUSE) was given by the City Council and was applied to both the street and the lane. Pusey Place, however, which connects St John Street with Pusey Lane, was known as Alfred Place as late as April 1948, when the change was suggested by St John's College. (Pusey Lane runs southwards off Pusey Street.) No. 5 Pusey Street is a Grade II listed building. On the north side of the street is a well-designed raised ramp specially built to enable a disabled member of staff to have access in a wheelchair to the Department of Bio-mathematics (founded 1967).

Q

Quarry High Street *Headington Quarry.* Shown as Quarry Pitts on a map of 1605. The street runs from Quarry Road to Green Road, HEADINGTON. In the 1930s it was known as High Street, HEADINGTON QUARRY, but was officially named Quarry High Street in 1942.

In the 17th century Headington stone was popular for building because of its softness and ease of cutting. However, by the late 18th century it had been realised that it tended to crumble with time, and by the 19th century it was mainly used for interior work; in the 20th century, by which time the quarries had anyway become almost exhausted, much of the interior work done in it was replaced by Clipsham and Portland stone. The harder variety of Headington stone was used for road kerbs until the early 1950s.

(*See also* STONE.)

Queen Elizabeth House *21 St Giles'.* Established by Royal Charter in 1954 as a centre for political, economic, social, administrative, historical, legal and other studies affecting developing countries, both within and outside the Commonwealth. A gift by the late Sir Ernest Oppenheimer enabled the centre to be established. In 1985, its annual grant from the Overseas Development Administration having been withdrawn the previous year, the centre was merged with the Institute of Commonwealth Studies and the Institute of Agricultural Economics, which in 1986 were housed in Dartington House in LITTLE CLARENDON STREET. At the time of going to press, all three bodies were due to be moved to the 17th-century Black Hall in ST GILES', to which was added in 1961 a new building in light brick, designed by R.E. Enthoven. Queen Elizabeth House is now a department of the University and the director of this new organisation is Professor Robert Cassen.

Queen Street The street running from CARFAX to BONN SQUARE in the west. In the 13th century it was known as the Bailey because of its proximity to the CASTLE bailey. Cattle were slaughtered there and the meat sold from stalls set up in the middle of the street. In consequence, the street came to be known as Butcher Row. The slaughtering of animals in the street was later forbidden; but meat continued to be sold from the permanent stalls until the SHAMBLES, as they were called, were removed by authority of the Oxford Mileways Act, 1771. The butchers then moved to the new COVERED MARKET. The street was renamed Queen Street after Queen Charlotte, wife of George III, who visited Oxford with her husband in 1785.

Most of the houses in the street were gabled and timber-framed until the late 19th century. Many of the buildings have now been demolished and replaced by modern stores – notably Marks & Spencer's, built in 1975–8 on the south side, to the design of Lewis &

Hickey. At No. 17 was the Electra Cinema (*see* CINEMAS), and further old buildings were demolished for the extension to the City Chambers, built in 1961. At No. 23 in the 19th century was the Balloon Inn, later the Air Balloon Inn. On the north side was the King's Head Inn, with Coach and Horses Yard behind it. Nos 36–7 is a gabled and half-timbered building of 1912 by Herbert Quinton, which until 1932 was the showroom for Morris Garages Ltd. Queen Street, now one of Oxford's principal shopping streets, was in 1970 made into a pedestrian precinct, open only to buses, taxis and vehicles requiring access.

Queen's College Licence to found a college or hall (both terms were used before 1584) was granted by Edward III in January 1340/1 to Robert Eglesfeld, a King's clerk and chaplain to Queen Philippa. Third son of the family who were lords of Eaglesfield, a Cumberland village, Robert inherited no family property but profited by his opportunities in the King's service not only to acquire money and lands himself but, more important, to induce other people, including his royal master and mistress, to take an interest in his foundation. Robert purchased, between 1340 and his death in 1349, a number of tenements in the parish of ST PETER-IN-THE-EAST as a site for his college, and also gave the manor of Renwick in Cumberland. The King, at the instance of Queen Philippa, gave the rectory of Brough, Westmorland, and the wardenship of the hospital of God's House, Southampton, which carried with it a large and potentially valuable estate. Other friends of the founder, notably Robert Achard, John de Handlo, William Muskham and Lady Isabel Parvyng gave further livings and estates, so that, on paper, there was a respectable endowment; but for over fifty years the new college had to struggle with legal complexities and intransigent tenants, and its existence was precarious. To poverty, most likely, must be attributed the fact that no attempt was made to develop the whole site purchased by the founder; the college contented itself with adapting some old houses which stood on the rectangle of land immediately south of the east–west section of QUEEN'S LANE. Extensive plots to the east and west of this rectangle were sold to WILLIAM OF WYKEHAM, founder of New College, in the late 14th century, while the row of tenements fronting the HIGH STREET, which Queen's acquired piecemeal between 1345 and 1497, was not incorporated into the college site until the 18th-century rebuilding.

Queen's was the sixth Oxford college to be founded, and Eglesfeld provided, in February 1340/1, an elaborate body of statutes, which in theory (and in many instances in practice) governed the college until 1858. He planned on a large scale, and sought to regulate the development of his institution and the lives of its three categories of members – Fellows,

An aquatint after Rowlandson of Queen's College from the High Street, dominated by William Townesend's entrance screen and cupola of 1730–5 based on the Luxembourg Palace in Paris.

chaplains and 'poor boys' – down to the smallest details. Patronage was to belong to successive Queens Consort, though Eglesfeld attached no positive rights to patronage: Queens were to be the *nutrices* of his college, but not governors. The VISITOR was to be the Archbishop of York. The foundation was to consist initially of a Provost and twelve Fellows or Scholars (the terms were used indiscriminately until the mid-19th century), poor boys, and, when the expense could be afforded, up to thirteen chaplains. The Provost and Fellows were to be MAs and in priests' orders. One out of every seven Fellows might study Canon Law but the rest were to be theologians. Each Fellow was to have ten marks a year, inclusive of his daily allowance for commons, while the Provost's stipend 'beyond the Fellow's portion' was to be on a sliding scale, increasing as the number of Fellows should increase. Eglesfeld envisaged the number of Fellows rising to forty, but four or five were all that the college could support for many years. The poor boys – who probably numbered four, on average, at any one time during the mediaeval period – were to be educated at the college's expense, and any of them staying in the college long enough to attain the status of MA were to be given a preference in the elections for fellowships. Detailed regulations were made relating to academic study, DISCIPLINE, dress, meals, internal economy and the rendering of accounts. Exhaustive as the statutes seem, there were lacunae and ambiguities which quickly made their appearance. The principal ambiguity related to the election of Fellows, after the initial twelve who had

been chosen by Eglesfeld himself. He began with a statement that 'no race or deserving nation' was to be excluded, and emphasised the need to choose men who were 'distinguished in moral character, poor in means, and apt for the study of theology'. Presumably he had acted on those principles when selecting the first Provost and Fellows, for they were chosen from all the colleges then existing in Oxford (six from Merton alone) and between them represented ten dioceses. But the founder went on to say that a 'preference' was to be given to natives of Cumberland and Westmorland, especially those who were of his own blood, and, next, to natives of places where the college held property. Similar preferences were inserted in the rules relating to the choice of poor boys.

After the founder's death a controversy arose, which came to a head in the provostship of Henry Whitfeld (1361–77). A 'free election' party, to which Whitfeld himself, a Devonshire man, belonged, evidently wished to continue the practice of choosing Fellows from other Oxford colleges on merit, while a 'two counties' party wished to give an absolute, not merely a *ceteris paribus*, preference to northerners. In 1379 a decree of the King's chancery sensibly stipulated that some Fellows should be elected out of each of the categories mentioned in the statutes, but by the 16th century the 'two counties' party was strong enough to ignore this and the statutes themselves, and to bring into being a very narrowly defined foundation. A boy would come on to the foundation as a 'poor boy' from one of the two counties or as FOUNDER'S KIN, and would proceed to the status of BA;

if he chose to stay in the college to take the MA he would be a 'bachelor on the foundation', and, after taking the MA, a 'master on the foundation'. As such a Master, or even as a Bachelor, he might be given one of the chaplaincies or other college offices to tide him over until his turn came round, by seniority, to be elected a Fellow. Eventually, when he became a Senior Fellow, he would stand a chance of being elected Provost. The worst feature of this system – the exclusion from the society at any given time of the great majority of available men of talent – meant that for some centuries the Provosts and Fellows of Queen's (with some notable exceptions) were worthy and respectable rather than clever. Some mitigation was afforded by the practice of admitting *commensales* – scholars who paid for rooms in college and shared the common table with the Fellows. The most famous of these lodgers (though his period of residence was before the narrowing of the foundation) was JOHN WYCLIF, who lived in Queen's from 1363 to 1381. Later *commensales* included Cardinal Henry Beaufort; Richard Courtney, Bishop of Norwich; and Richard Fleming, first founder of Lincoln College – each of whom later held office as CHANCELLOR of the University. An ancient tradition that Henry of Monmouth, later Henry V, lived and studied in Queen's under the care of his uncle, Cardinal Beaufort, is unsupported by documentary evidence.

In the later mediaeval period the college settled down to a peaceful and uneventful existence, which lasted until the mid-16th century. Unable to compete with the grander establishments of Wykeham and Waynflete, the Provosts and Fellows of Queen's nonetheless steadily increased their endowments, partly by purchase, partly by soliciting gifts. By the beginning of Henry VIII's reign the college could support a Provost, six to nine Fellows, one or two chaplains, and an unknown number of poor boys, and its external gross income had risen from about £80 to about £200 per year. The admission of COMMONERS and battelers (*see* BATTELS), who paid fully or partly for their maintenance and who, not being on the foundation, did not have to come from the 'two counties', began about this time, though the numbers at first were small. The religious and political upheavals of the later 16th century left little mark on Queen's, though one former Fellow, John Bost (1565–*c.*74) suffered martyrdom for the Catholic cause, while another, Bernard Gilpin (1550–4) acquired fame, as the 'Apostle of the North', on the other side (*see* ROMAN CATHOLICS). In the years 1540 to 1581, however, the college had its own troubles, which seem to have owed more to strong ale and weak discipline than to the heady vapours of Renaissance or Reformation. Four Fellows were expelled in 1542–4 for contumelious and scandalous behaviour, and in 1565 Provost Lancelot Shawe was expelled by the Visitor after having been convicted of squandering college property, making leases to his friends, neglecting academic duties and 'being greatly overseen with drink'. His immediate successors were not much better, except perhaps in the matter of drink, but the election of Henry Robinson to the provostship in 1581 brought a change. Robinson, with the help of Sir Francis Walsingham, secured a new charter and statute of incorporation from Elizabeth I in 1584 – a move which enabled nearly all the college leases to be called in and renewed on terms more favourable to the

college. He began a programme of repairing college buildings, which went on until the 1640s, tightened up discipline, and instituted a 'common chest' or fund for the purchase of lands and livings. The moral and intellectual atmosphere changed under the strong puritanical influence exercised by Robinson (who resigned in 1599 to become Bishop of Carlisle) and his immediate successors, Barnabas Potter (Provost 1616–26, later also Bishop of Carlisle) and his nephew Christopher Potter (Provost 1626–46). They saw the college as a nursery for 'painful and studious preachers' who would go forth and serve the church, but the education of the laity was not neglected: the number of commoners rose from about seventy in 1581 to 194 in 1612, making Queen's for some years the largest collegiate body in the University.

The rise of the college, in influence and in prosperity, was only slightly hampered by the CIVIL WAR and its aftermath, even though the Provosts and Fellows were royalists almost to a man: two Fellows, Guy Carleton and Michael Hudson, served in arms for the King, and another, Richard Rallinson, had a hand in designing the Oxford fortifications. The 'loan' of the college silver and a gift of £800 in money to the King were made without resentment: early in his reign Charles had generously given the college six Hampshire livings. That the college did not suffer much for having been on the losing side was due principally to the careful management and political astuteness of Gerard Langbaine, Provost from 1646 to 1658. Langbaine was also an eminent scholar, and was succeeded as Provost by another distinguished scholar, Thomas Barlow (1658–77), later Bishop of Lincoln. Under these two, and their successor Timothy Halton (1677–1704), Queen's had a most successful period; among its alumni were Edmond Halley (1673), discoverer of the comet (*see* ASTRONOMER'S HOUSE); William Wycherley (*c.*1660), the playwright; and Henry Compton (1654), who, as Bishop of London, took a prominent part in the Glorious Revolution of 1688. As far as the college's affairs were concerned, the most noteworthy of its members were John Michel (1676) and Sir Joseph Williamson (Fellow 1657; Secretary of State 1674–9). By his will Michel provided for the establishment in the college of a new foundation for Fellows and scholars, separate and distinct from the old foundation, and expressly meant for the benefit of persons who did *not* come from the north. Williamson at his own expense (£1700) put up a new residential building at the north-east corner of the college site – the only college building in the design of which SIR CHRISTOPHER WREN was concerned – and in his will left the college £6000 for further building work. In 1692–6 Provost Halton built the new library, providing nearly £2000 out of the total cost of £5247 himself, and thereby enabling the college to house the large collection of books bequeathed by Thomas Barlow. Halton probably thought no more large buildings necessary, but his successor, William Lancaster (1704–17), was more ambitious and committed the college to a scheme for demolishing the old college in its entirety and replacing it with the splendid structure which exists today.

Academically the later 18th and early 19th centuries, in Queen's as in other colleges, have been condemned by posterity as a dull and stagnant period; this was certainly the view of two of the most

J.C. Buckler's drawing of Queen's College library, which was built from 1692–5. Its fine plaster ceiling is by James Hands.

intelligent persons ever to have come up to Queen's: Jeremy Bentham (1760), and Francis Jeffrey, founder of the *Edinburgh Review* (1791). However, for less critical people, Oxford at this time must have been a pleasant place, and the inadequacies of the old syllabus and forms of instruction did not hamper the production of learned men in various fields. Queen's seems to have specialised in turning out antiquarian and topographical scholars and writers, of whom may be mentioned Thomas Tanner (1689), Richard Burn (1729), William Nicolson (1679), Edmund Gibson (1686), William Gilpin (1740), Thomas Pennant (1744) and Samuel Meyrick (1800). When the winds of reform began to blow, Queen's was in most respects in the same position as other colleges, but the closed foundation constituted a special 'abuse'. The people of Cumberland and Westmorland strove to preserve their monopoly: the monster petition against reform, sent to the college in 1838, was signed by virtually every literate person in the two counties, from the Bishop of Carlisle and William Wordsworth downwards; but the 'open college' party, ably led by William Thomson, who subsequently became Provost (1855) and later Archbishop of York, won the day. In the new statutes made by the Oxford Commissioners in 1858 (*see* ROYAL COMMISSIONS), the old foundation and the Michel foundation were merged, and all fellowships were thrown open to competition; the two counties retained only a number of closed exhibitions. Despite this, the college for over a century retained firm links not only with Cumberland and Westmorland but also with Yorkshire, the latter by virtue of the closed exhibitions for boys from Yorkshire schools which had been established in the

late 18th century under the will of Lady Elizabeth Hastings. In recent years, because of factors outside college control, these links have weakened, and Queen's draws its undergraduate members from as wide a range of schools and localities, British and foreign, as any other college. Another link with the pre-1858 college to have been broken recently is the tradition of electing Provosts from among the Senior Fellows: when John Walter Jones (Provost 1948–62) retired, he was succeeded by Sir Howard (later Lord) Florey, formerly a professorial Fellow of Lincoln; on Lord Florey's death, in 1968, he was succeeded by Robert Norman William (now Lord) Blake, who had been a scholar of Magdalen and a Student of Christ Church. With the election of John Moffatt in 1987 to succeed Lord Blake, the college returned to pre-1962 practice. Despite the fact that Queen's, after the days of the bustling William Thomson, has never been in the forefront of 'reform' movements, it has not been able to avoid changes, most of which have been due to the ever-increasing involvement of Oxford with the public educational system. The mid-Victorian Fellows, if they could come alive, would be hard put to it to find more than a few features of college life with which they were familiar: a trumpet is still blown as a summons to dinner, as it has been since Eglesfeld's time; a few picturesque customs have survived in connection with the principal GAUDIES; the college still prints Eglesfeld's arms on its writing paper and employs the common seals of 1584 on its formal documents (*see* HERALDRY). But despite the many substantial changes of the last century, the college still retains considerable freedom of action, while a strong corporate spirit, shared by the great majority of its members, senior and junior alike, probably constitutes its principal safeguard for the future.

Although the corporate designation of the college is The Provost and Scholars of the Queen's College in the University of Oxford, no Provost or Fellow referred to it as *The* Queen's College before the 1890s, when the Provost, John Richard Magrath, chose to adopt that title in preference to the older Queen's College. His introduction of the definite article was not welcomed by the University, which still refers to Queen's College in some, though not all, of its official publications.

The visitor entering the college from the High Street finds himself in the front quadrangle, called by Pevsner 'the grandest piece of classical architecture in Oxford'. It was for long supposed to have been designed by NICHOLAS HAWKSMOOR, who produced several sketches and plans now in the college archives. Hawksmoor, however, does not seem to have been paid for his designs, which differ in many respects from what was actually built, and he cannot be shown to have exercised any supervision over the building work. The only other candidate who need be considered is William Townesend, the eminent Oxford mason–architect who had a hand in most of the new buildings put up in Oxford between about 1701 and his death in 1739 (*see* TOWNESENDS). Townesend built the whole of the front quadrangle, apart from some of the east range, and was paid £160 for his 'own time in drawing and directing the work'. Pevsner thought that Queen's would not have been satisfied with a mere 'mason-entrepreneur' for 'the most monumental job in Oxford at that moment', but H.M. Colvin, in *A Biographical Dictionary of English*

Architects 1660–1840 (1978), pointing out that Townesend undoubtedly altered Hawksmoor's proposal for the design of the cupola over the entrance screen, thinks that the design of the whole quadrangle may be his. It may be that credit should be shared, and that Townesend's rôle was to put some of Hawksmoor's – and possibly other people's – proposals into forms which were practicable to build and within the college's means.

The first part to be built was the west range, containing *inter alia* the Senior Common Rooms, buttery, cellar and (former) Provost's lodging. It was built between 1709 and 1716, the total cost being £4323. The pediments on the east and south elevations were carved by one Garratt. The joinery contractor was Jeremiah Franklin, but all the interior of the range, with the roof, was destroyed in a fire in 1778, following which the building was restored by George Shakespear of London, to the designs of Kenton Couse. A second fire, in 1886, destroyed again some of the rooms at the south end of the range, but on this occasion the worst damage was that done to college archives in the bursary, though fortunately the older archives were not affected. Townesend began work on the north range, consisting of the hall and chapel, in January 1714. The hall was finished by May 1715, the chapel sufficiently complete to be consecrated in November 1719. Townesend designed most of the interior work himself, including the ceilings, the chapel screen and the fine marble reredos (which has been mutilated at some time since). Names of other artists are scarce; Sir James Thornhill painted the circular *Ascension* in the chapel apse and is supposed (on flimsy evidence) to have designed the carving in the timpanum over the central passageway. This carving, much patched-up over the years, has recently been replaced by a new composition – following the general design of the old but not a mere copy – executed by Michael Groser. Of the chapel glass, only the east window and the semicircular tops of the other windows were new: they were made by Joshua Price. The other windows were taken from the old chapel, and include eight which had been made by Abraham van Ling in 1636. The adaptation of these to fit windows of a different size and shape was not altogether successful. The chapel ironwork, which is of high quality, was probably made by William Cowdry, who died in 1772. The total cost of hall and chapel was about £5000.

William Townesend's last piece of work for the college was the entrance screen and cupola, said by Provost Lancaster to have been designed on the pattern of the Luxembourg, Paris. This work, done between 1730 and 1735, included the streetward end and a single half-staircase of the east range; it cost £2800. The rest of the east range was completed in stages, between 1757 and 1765, as and when money came in from various sources, by John Townesend, William's successor, in association with William and Edward King and Robert Tawney. The statue of Queen Caroline (who had given £1000 to the building fund) was made by Sir Henry Cheere, who also made the three statues on top of the pediment of the east range. The east range altogether cost about £5750, and Cheere received £265. It was originally planned to have further statues above the central pediments of the east and west ranges, but apparently funds would not allow this.

Turning to the back quadrangle, the library, which occupies the west side, was built between 1692 and 1696. As in the case of the front quadrangle, the name of the designer is not known. HENRY ALDRICH, Dean of Christ Church and designer of ALL SAINTS CHURCH, HIGH STREET, is strongly favoured, but Halton, an accomplished man, may have been his own designer. John Townesend, father of William, was the builder. Originally the library had an open arcade on the east side, and a staircase in an annexe on the south side; when the front quadrangle was built, this annexe was demolished and a new connecting piece built, the staircase being turned round to give access not only to the library but to the common-room gallery in the new west range. In 1843–5, following the bequest of £30,000 by Robert Mason for the purchase of books, the open arcade was closed in and a new ground-floor reading room built to the design of C.R. Cockerell. Cockerell's reading room is merely functional, but Halton's upper library is the most sumptuous room in the college, perhaps (for its date) in Oxford. Most of the plasterwork in the ceiling was done by James Hands, who was paid £84 'for fretwork', but the beautiful stucco frieze was made by John Vanderstein, the sculptor who also made the eight statues of benefactors which stand in niches on the outside of the west wall, and four statues of philosophers (now removed) which stood on the pediments. The rococo decorations in the three large panels were commissioned from Thomas Roberts in 1756. The outstanding carving on the bookcases, and especially the manuscript cupboards, is attributed by Pevsner to Thomas Minn. Minn and his son, also named Thomas, held the joinery contract for the whole building, and did other work about the college, but it is not clear that they, or either of them, executed the fancier work in person.

The remaining ranges of the back quadrangle have a distinctly severe character, which was accentuated in the 1930s when a cheerfully untidy Victorian layout of shrubs, trees and creepers was removed and the present arrangement of funeral urns, stone paths and stone-edged lawns was constructed. These ranges were built between 1707 and 1721, by John and William Townesend successively, though the east range conceals the remains of Wren's Williamson Building of 1672, which was heightened by one storey and provided with new façades, back and front, to bring it into line with the other ranges. Provost Lancaster paid half the cost of the north range; in all he contributed over £5000 towards the rebuilding programme, and ranks with Halton and Williamson among the college's most generous benefactors.

All the buildings so far mentioned were built mainly in Headington stone, with Burford stone used in special places, such as cornices, pilaster-bases and pediments, and Bladon stone used for pavings (*see* STONE). Over the years there have been restorations and repairs, in the course of which Axminster, Bath, Portland and (more recently) Clipsham stones have been used, and there is not much of the original exterior surfaces left. Queen's was, however, lucky to escape both the Gothick and the Gothic revivals, the latter of which in particular did much damage to Oxford. There was a moment of danger in 1876, when J.P. Seddon was asked to produce proposals for 'beautifying' the chapel, but fortunately the least expensive of his designs would have cost £25,000, which the college was unable to afford. Unpleasing, though innocuous, whitewash was resorted to, which saw the chapel safely through until High Church fervour subsided. The only major change came when the organ, by Thomas Frobenius, was built in 1962–4.

Queen's made no extensions to its buildings in the 19th century, but in 1908 Nos 33–8 High Street were purchased from Magdalen and their upper floors turned into residential accommodation for the college, the ground floors becoming lock-up shops. The name 'Drawda Hall' was bestowed upon No. 33, to commemorate William of Drogheda, a 13th-century canonist who had occupied a house hereabouts, while the garden behind it has become known (for reasons which are obscure) as 'the nuns' garden'. In 1957–9 a new Provost's lodging, designed in a neo-Georgian style by Raymond Erith, was built at the north-west corner of the college site, and at the same time the former brewhouse, which had been famous in its day for the strong 'Chancellor' ale produced there, was converted into a carpenter's shop and a range of garages (see BREWING). The reversion of the former Provost's lodging in the front quadrangle to the society made several handsome rooms available, one of which has become a new Senior Common Room, and part of the large cellar was turned into a beer cellar: not the least attractive feature of the college to many of its members. In 1967–9 a new quadrangle,

the Queen's Lane Quadrangle, was built to the design of Marshall Sisson behind the preserved or reconstructed frontages of Nos 39–43 High Street. This has proved a most valuable addition: maintenance costs have been small, and the new accommodation has been popular with those, mainly undergraduates, for whom it was designed. Somewhat less valuable, in those and in other respects, has been the Florey Building – an 'irregular polygon' propped up on stilts, built in 1968–71 to the design of James Stirling on a site in ST CLEMENT'S.

The present Provost is Dr J. Moffatt.

(Magrath, J.R., *The Queen's College*, 2 vols, Oxford, 1921; Royal Commission on Historical Monuments, *An Inventory of the Historical Monuments in the City of Oxford*, London, 1939; Hodgkin, R.H., in *Victoria County History of Oxford*, Vol. III, Oxford, 1954, pp. 132–43, and *Six Centuries of an Oxford College*, Oxford, 1949.)

Queen's Lane Named after the college, this was originally Torald Street. However, the line was slightly different and probably it went right through from the HIGH STREET to HOLYWELL. On a 1762 map it is also shown as Edmund Hall Lane, and in 1821 this name was still in existence, while Queen's Lane only began at the corner of it.

R

Radcliffe, John *(1652–1714)*. Entered University College in 1665 and became a Fellow of Lincoln in 1670. Having taken a degree in Medicine in 1675, he established himself as a physician in Oxford. He had limited medical knowledge and his medical equipment, so he confessed, contained nothing but a skeleton, a herbal and a few phials; but he soon became a successful and prosperous physician, renowned for his instinctive diagnoses. He moved to London in 1684 and was soon making 20 guineas a day, not so much by his skill as a doctor, so it was said, as by his entertaining conversation for which his richer patients were ready to pay fees when they were in perfectly satisfactory health. He became physician to William III, and by 1707 was worth £80,000, despite the high-handed rudeness with which he treated many of his patients. He left most of his fortune to the University and to University College, to whose chapel he had already given an east window and large benefactions of money, including £1100 for exhibitions.

(*See also* RADCLIFFE INFIRMARY, RADCLIFFE OBSERVATORY *and* RADCLIFFE CAMERA.)

Radcliffe Camera *Radcliffe Square*. After JOHN RADCLIFFE's death in 1714 it took over twenty years of negotiations to clear the site for the building of the library for which he had left £40,000 in his will. During this time the architects consulted included NICHOLAS HAWKSMOOR and JAMES GIBBS. The rotunda form was proposed by Hawksmoor, but it was Gibbs who was eventually preferred. Building began in 1737 and was completed in 1748. At the opening ceremony in 1749, the VICE-CHANCELLOR and Principal of ST MARY HALL, Dr William King, made a highly tendentious Latin speech in the SHELDONIAN THEATRE in favour of the Jacobites. The Camera, which is believed to be the first round library in the country, was originally intended to be a science library, but the books in its reading rooms and galleries are now mainly devoted to the arts. The plasterwork in the splendid domed upper room is by the mastercraftsmen Joseph Artari, Charles Stanley and Thomas Roberts, an Oxford plasterer who was responsible also for the lovely stuccowork in the upper library at Christ Church, in the Senior Common Room at St John's and the library ceiling at The Queen's College.

Henry Le Keux's engraving after Frederick Mackenzie's drawing of the Upper Reading Room of the Radcliffe Camera – which was built to the designs of James Gibbs in 1737–48 – highlights the splendid plasterwork.

Radcliffe Infirmary *Woodstock Road.* The first proposals to build a 'county hospital' for Oxford, then a city with a POPULATION of about 8000, were made in 1758 at a meeting of the trustees of the will of DR JOHN RADCLIFFE, who released £4000 from the Radcliffe estate towards founding a hospital. Coggins Piece, a 5-acre site in the open fields of ST GILES', was donated by Thomas Rowney (Tory Member of Parliament for Oxford 1722–59), and the foundation stone was laid on 27 August 1761. The original architect, Stiff Leadbetter, surveyor to St Paul's Cathedral and designer of the Gloucester County Hospital, died in 1766 and the task was completed under John Sanderson of London. The change of architect, together with drainage problems, caused significant delays.

The new hospital depended on voluntary subscriptions for its running costs, while the right to act as governors and to recommend deserving patients was conferred upon subscribers of £3 annually or donors of sums exceeding £30. At meetings of governors and subscribers in July and September 1770, the infirmary's lay and medical staff were elected. On 18 October 1770 seven patients were admitted to the two original wards, Lichfield (female) and Marlborough (male), the first named after the 3rd Earl of Lichfield, then CHANCELLOR of the University, the second after the 4th Duke of Marlborough, one of the original supporters of the infirmary who met in 1770 to issue an advertisement appealing for subscriptions. Two others, Rowney and Frewin, were in use by 1771. The original infirmary (now the central administrative block facing WOODSTOCK ROAD) accommodated sixty-eight patients in these four wards and its early staff comprised six honorary physicians and surgeons, an apothecary, a matron, six nurses, three servants and a porter. Living conditions were spartan, with patients assisting with ward-cleaning and household chores, as was usual in hospitals at that time. Local tradesmen supplied provisions, fuel and hardware; these supplies were supplemented by produce grown in the 3-acre infirmary garden. Discipline was strict and both staff and patients were discharged summarily for misconduct. A year later, three additional wards opened (Mordaunt, Bagot and Drake, named after various Radcliffe Trustees). Out-patients were seen on a twice-weekly basis from 1835; and, from 1845, the separation of medical and surgical cases on a ward basis was introduced. From the early days of the hospital, the medical and surgical staff were progressive; electrical treatment was available and John Grosvenor, honorary surgeon 1770–1817, introduced the use of massage in the treatment of injuries. Similarly, the first operation under ether anaesthesia was carried out at the Radcliffe by Charles Parker (1810–48) on 4 March 1847, little more than two months after the first operative use of ether in London.

In the second half of the 19th century there was a considerable increase in building on the infirmary site. An out-patients' department was added in 1863 (and replaced in 1913 by a larger one). A year later a hospital chapel was erected. This was designed by Sir Arthur Blomfield as a gift from Thomas Combe, superintendent of the Clarendon Press (*see* OXFORD UNIVERSITY PRESS). The Victoria and Alexandra block for women was built in 1871; and fever wards and the first separate children's block (Leopold) followed in 1876–7, replacing the small children's ward established in 1867. There were by now 166 beds distributed in seventeen wards. Gradually, separate specialties acquired their own premises outside the main hospital: in 1885 fever cases were transferred to

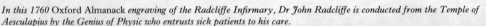

In this 1760 Oxford Almanack *engraving of the Radcliffe Infirmary, Dr John Radcliffe is conducted from the Temple of Aesculapius by the Genius of Physic who entrusts sick patients to his care.*

the new City Isolation Hospital at Cold Arbour (*see* RIVERMEAD REHABILITATION CENTRE); and, in 1886, separate premises were utilised for eye disorders treated formerly in the general wards (*see* OXFORD EYE HOSPITAL). Maternity care, previously limited to home confinements and the services of various Oxford lying-in charities, was first provided by the Radcliffe at Marcon's Hall, SOUTH PARKS ROAD (near Keble College), in 1918. This unit expanded rapidly when it was re-sited in a new maternity wing (fronting WALTON STREET), which was financed by LORD NUFFIELD, designed by Stanley Hamp and opened by the Duchess of York (later Queen Elizabeth the Queen Mother) in October 1931. The first pathologist was appointed to the Radcliffe in 1903, to be followed by a dermatologist and an ENT surgeon in 1906. A separate X-ray department was set up in 1907; specialists in orthopaedics and mental disorders were introduced in 1918, and an obstetrician a year later. Shortly after the First World War, a Midwives' Training School and a Preliminary Training School for Nurses were set up.

From its establishment until it obtained a royal charter in 1885, the Radcliffe Infirmary was a University institution, governed, and largely staffed, by University officers. The training of students in Physic and Surgery, therefore, formed an integral part of its duties. In 1772, the Chancellor, the Earl of Lichfield, endowed at the Radcliffe the Lichfield Clinical Professorship, the first British academic post specifically designed to provide clinical instruction in the wards. From 1847, the greatest influence in the development of the Radcliffe was SIR HENRY WENT-WORTH ACLAND. While physician to the infirmary (1847–79), he pioneered the use of diagnostic instruments (including the first microscope in 1848), established a clinical-pathology laboratory in 1862, and increased the range of training for medical students, with bedside instruction and frequent lectures. Another Regius Professor of Medicine, Sir William Osler, consulting physician to the Radcliffe Infirmary from 1905 to 1919, continued Acland's work by active participation in clinical teaching and by introducing postgraduate demonstrations. Under Osler's influence, the new three-storey block, designed by Edward Warren to harmonise with the adjoining original façade of the infirmary, on opening in 1913, incorporated not only a new out-patients' department but also facilities for X-ray, electro-therapy and radiology. The building was financed by a bequest of £63,000 from John Briscoe, honorary surgeon at the Radcliffe in 1865–81.

It was, however, the unprecedented generosity of Lord Nuffield which effected the most profound changes to the resources and potential of the Radcliffe and associated hospitals, enabling the University to establish a full Clinical School. In 1936, Lord Nuffield gave £2 million to the University. This benefaction led to the endowment of five original Nuffield professorships: in Medicine, Surgery, Obstetrics and Gynaecology, Therapeutics, and Anaesthetics. These were followed shortly by chairs in Orthopaedic Surgery (*see* NUFFIELD ORTHOPAEDIC CENTRE), in Social Medicine, and in Plastic Surgery. This magnificent endowment transformed the Radcliffe from a good provincial teaching hospital to one of the leading medical centres in the country.

The Second World War had a profound effect on the Radcliffe. It had to be prepared to deal with large numbers of military and civilian casualties and to provide a whole range of specialist services for the temporary hospitals set up around Oxford. The burns unit at the Radcliffe developed into the first comprehensive accident service in Great Britain. Here Professor Sir Hugh Cairns (1896–1952) carried out research into head injury and campaigned for the compulsory wearing of crash helmets by army dispatch riders. Of all the Radcliffe's contributions to medical advances, undoubtedly the most famous started on 27 January 1941, when an infirmary patient became the first person to receive an intravenous injection of penicillin. A plaque in the entrance hall commemorates this outstanding event. Research by PROFESSOR HOWARD FLOREY and his colleagues at the SIR WILLIAM DUNN SCHOOL OF PATHOLOGY upon the penicillin-producing mould, first recognised by Sir Alexander Fleming in 1928, made it possible for Dr Charles Fletcher, a member of Professor Witts's Department of Medicine, to initiate a clinical trial of penicillin under the supervision of Lady Florey. On the wards of the Radcliffe Infirmary, penicillin was demonstrated to be a uniquely effective drug, capable of curing a wide range of infections.

By the end of the war there were 630 beds at the Radcliffe, including those in four prefabricated, hutted wards. With the departure of the United States Medical Services, the administration of the CHURCHILL HOSPITAL was transferred to the Radcliffe Committee of Management. From 1948 to 1974 these two hospitals, together with the Eye Hospital, the Osler, Sunnyside, COWLEY ROAD HOSPITAL, the SLADE HOSPITAL and Cold Arbour Isolation Hospital, formed a group of teaching hospitals known as the United Oxford Hospitals.

By the 1960s the Radcliffe Infirmary site was over-developed and crowded; so, from 1963, plans were initiated to transfer some of its functions to the now vital Osler Road site in HEADINGTON. The first transfer was the Maternity Department, which set up in Headington in 1971. Others followed steadily. But the original infirmary site has continued in use and, in 1986, continues to provide a total of 282 beds for neurology, neuro-surgery, special medicine, endocrinology, plastic surgery, ENT conditions, geriatric medicine and one children's ward.

Radcliffe Observatory *Woodstock Road.* Built for the University with a grant from the trustees of the estate of JOHN RADCLIFFE. HENRY KEENE prepared the original design but after his death the work was completed in 1794 by James Wyatt. Sir Nikolaus Pevsner believed it to be 'architecturally the finest observatory of Europe'. The building is surmounted by a version of the Tower of the Winds, the octagonal horologium in Athens built *c.*100–50 BC by Andronicus of Cyrrhus for measuring time. The reliefs of the winds on Wyatt's tower were carved in 1792–4 by John Bacon the Elder, who was also responsible for the lead group above of Hercules and Atlas supporting the globe, a prominent Oxford landmark. The reliefs of the signs of the zodiac above the windows of the first floor are of Coade stone and were made by J.F. Rossi. Inside there are three main rooms, one above the other.

When it ceased to be used as an observatory in 1935, the building was occupied by various medical

The Radcliffe Observatory, finished in 1794 to the designs of Henry Keene and James Wyatt, ceased to be used as an observatory in 1935 and is now occupied by Green College.

BBC presence in Oxford was a small, unmanned interview studio at No. 12 BEAUMONT STREET, now part of the Oxford PLAYHOUSE Company offices.

Ragwort *Senecio squalidus*, the Oxford ragwort, is part of the Compositae or daisy family. The stem is about 1 foot long and the plant produces yellow flowers from June to September. It looks rather like a bigger version of groundsel. It is not a British native plant, but was introduced from the Continent. In 1699 a specimen was growing in the BOTANIC GARDEN; it spread on to the walls and by 1877 it had reached the railway line. It is at home in a volcanic, cindery soil and, the rails being laid on clinker, it soon spread along the railways, the seeds, each with soft hairs, being carried along by the rush of wind from the trains. It was commonly found on bombed sites and is now abundant on waste ground and walls in Oxford and elsewhere. It was also common on PORT MEADOW.

(Keble Martin, W., *The Concise British Flora in Colour*, London, 1965, plate 47.)

Railway In 1837 an Oxford railway was proposed. Its route was to leave the Great Western Railway (GWR) at Didcot and enter Oxford alongside COWLEY ROAD (then a muddy lane through fields), terminating near MAGDALEN BRIDGE. However, the major landowner, Christ Church, strongly opposed this route. There was also opposition from the City Corporation, which was concerned about paying for the rebuilding of FOLLY BRIDGE and afraid that the line, 'if carried into

At the heart of Radcliffe Square stands the Radcliffe Camera, now part of the Bodleian Library to which it is connected by an underground passage and conveyor belt.

departments of the University, serving them both as offices and as laboratories for medical research. It was purchased in 1930 from the Radcliffe trustees by LORD NUFFIELD, who donated it to the University. When the NUFFIELD INSTITUTE FOR MEDICAL RESEARCH moved to the John Radcliffe Hospital in 1976, the building became vacant and was taken over by its present occupant, Green College.

Radcliffe Square The square, often referred to as 'the heart of Oxford', surrounds the RADCLIFFE CAMERA with the BODLEIAN LIBRARY to the north, Brasenose College and BRASENOSE LANE to the west, the University Church of ST MARY THE VIRGIN to the south, and All Souls College beyond CATTE STREET to the east. This area 'is unique in the world,' Sir Nikolaus Pevsner wrote, 'or, if that seems a hazardous statement, it is certainly unparalleled at Cambridge. ... It is the closeness and compactness, the absence of anything that is merely a foil that is only true of Oxford'. The large pebbles, rammed into gravel in accordance with the instructions of the Paving Commissioners appointed under the 1771 Oxford Mileways Act, were condemned at the time as being ruinous to shoes. Beneath the pavement and grass of the square are the book-packed vaults of the Bodleian. The defeat of Napoleon was celebrated in the square in 1814 by a dinner given to 4000 poor people.

Radio Oxford Opened on 29 October 1970 at premises in the BANBURY ROAD, SUMMERTOWN. It was one of twelve local radio stations opened by the BBC as part of its regional radio-broadcasting development, started in 1967 with an initial eight stations. The editorial area is Oxfordshire and West Buckinghamshire. Before the station opened, the only permanent

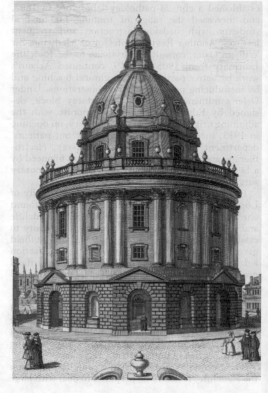

effect must lessen, in a very great degree, the amount of . . . Folly Bridge tolls, and the sum of £8,750 . . . now due and only secured upon the said toll, is likely to be entirely lost'. An alternative route was proposed, running alongside ABINGDON ROAD and terminating at GRANDPONT, near Folly Bridge. However, a combination of powerful interests swayed the House of Lords to turn down successive Bills for the Oxford Railway in 1837, 1838 and 1840. This opposition was headed by the two landowners who together owned over half the land. The Oxford Canal Company (*see* CANAL) organised opposition to the proposed railway to protect its own business interests. The University objected to the railway out of fear for the morals of its students: the CHANCELLOR of the University, the Duke of Wellington, at first opposed all railways because they might encourage the lower orders to 'move about'. More practically, the University argued that railway embankments would hinder drainage and increase flooding. Nevertheless, by 1842 many Oxford inhabitants were taking the one-and-a-half hour stagecoach to the new GWR station at Steventon, 10 miles south of Oxford. These included 'young gentlemen' (undergraduates) on their way to Ascot races. In spite of this, the University dropped its opposition to the Oxford Railway upon receiving certain concessions from the railway company. Thus, the successful enabling Act (1843) stated that University authorities 'shall . . . have free Access to every Depot or Station . . . and to every Booking Office, Ticket Office or Place for Passengers . . . and shall then and there be entitled to demand and take and have, without any unreasonable Delay . . . such Information as it may be in the Power of any Officer or Servant of the Company to give with reference to any Passenger . . . who shall be a Member of the said University or suspected of being such.' The Act also stated that if the University authorities 'shall . . . notify to the proper Officers, Bookkeeper, or Servant of the said Company that any Person or Persons about to travel in or upon the said Railway is a Member of the University not having taken the Degree of Master of Arts or Bachelor in Civil Law, and require such Officer . . . to decline to take such Member of the University as a Passenger upon the said Railway, the proper Officer shall immediately thereupon, and for the space of 24 hours . . . refuse to convey such Member of the said University . . . notwithstanding such Member may have paid his Fare.' The Act also stated that junior members of the University were to be carried only to approved stations and not to places like Ascot. When the Warden of Wadham still objected to the railway, it was not as a representative of the University but as the chairman of the Oxford Canal Company. The Oxford Railway, having passed under the aegis of the GWR, was completed in the summer of 1844. The broad-gauge track crossed the Abingdon Turnpike Road on the flat as the planned road-bridge was not ready because the landowner had erected a house to win compensation – the 'house' was made from brown paper stretched over timbers. The line was opened on 14 June 1844 and it was reported that 'the greatest bustle and excitement prevailed around the station and neighbourhood, and thousands of persons paid a visit to the line'. The line of that railway is now Marlborough Road and the wooden station was at the bottom of Western (that is, Great Western) Road. Tickets to London cost 15s, 10s and 6s

'Jove hurling Vulcan out of Heaven'; Dr Lightfoot, Vice-Chancellor in 1865, casts a Great Western Railway worker out of Oxford.

for each class, compared to the 5s stagecoach fare. The journey took two hours twenty minutes.

In 1850 the Banbury line was opened, its ballast being excavated from fields between the original line to Grandpont and the new one north. The resulting crater was filled by underground springs, thus forming Hinksey Lake, which the city bought for use as a reservoir. In 1851 the London and North Western Railway (LNWR) reached Oxford from Bletchley, providing connections to Euston, Birmingham and Cambridge. Its REWLEY ROAD terminus was on the old site of REWLEY ABBEY. A swing-bridge carried the line over the Sheepwash Channel, a branch of the THAMES leading to the Oxford Canal; the bridge had to be opened to allow barges to pass through. The LNWR station was erected by Fox, Henderson Ltd, who also built Joseph Paxton's Crystal Palace in the same year; both buildings were constructed with cast-iron, bolt-together sections. The station's roof was a ridge-and-furrow design borrowed from Paxton; until 1888 it was glazed longitudinally, but rebuilding left the glazing panels running laterally. In 1852 the line to Banbury was extended to Birmingham and a new GWR station was opened next door to the Rewley Road station. The Grandpont station was closed to passengers, although it remained a goods depot until 1872. With the opening of lines to Worcester (1853), Wolverhampton (1854) and High Wycombe (1864; closed to passengers 1963), the increase in traffic

355

meant that the GWR station needed improvements including new lavatories, advertised as 'based on the latest scientific principles'. After 1910 the station remained unaltered for sixty years. In 1970 the station – most of its wooden structure now in an advanced state of decay – was demolished. The pre-fabricated structure of 1971 left only the old plat-forms and the 1910 roof-extension girders on the north end of the up platform. A new station costing £3,000,000 and designed by BR architects was opened in June 1990.

In 1922 the LNWR was taken over by the London, Midland and Scottish Railway (LMS). In 1948 all railways were nationalised and in 1951 Rewley Road station was closed and its passengers had to use the former GWR station. The former LMS line was closed to passengers in 1967. The swing-bridge over the river is permanently open for barges and is a scheduled Ancient Monument. The old station is now a motorists' tyre and exhaust centre. The platform and train-shed have been removed, leaving a truncated structure which is a Grade II listed building.

(*See also* TRANSPORT.)

('Communications', No. 27, Local History Pack, Central Library, Oxford; Munby, Julian, 'Historic Features of Oxford Station Yard', *Oxford Preservation Trust Newsletter*.)

Raleigh Park   A park of about 27 acres at NORTH HINKSEY between WESTMINSTER COLLEGE and the RING ROAD. It was given to the city in 1924 by Raymond ffennell of WYTHAM Abbey. The park is on rising ground giving views over the city.

Randolph Hotel   *Beaumont Street.* Takes its name from the Randolph Gallery which stood opposite and which, in turn, took its name from the Rev. Dr Francis Randolph, one of the principal benefactors of the ASHMOLEAN MUSEUM in the 18th century. It is a Grade II listed building of 1863–6 by William Wilkinson, architect of the Norham Manor Estate. Describing the opening ceremony, *Jackson's Oxford Journal* (*see* NEWSPAPERS) of 17 February 1866 reported: 'Entering by the portico in Beaumont Street, the visitor notices the mosaic flooring of the hall, the conservatory in the rear, and a massive staircase of Portland stone, leading to the various landings and corridors. The railing is of iron, with ornamental pillars and timber coping, the stairs being of a width recalling the baronial mansions of older time, and doubly carpeted.'

The iron porch and ballroom were added in 1889 by H.W. Moore. The hotel underwent major alterations in 1923 by Colcutt and Hemp, who improved the interior by adding the two bays on either side of the main entrance and extra vaulting over the doorway. A further extension was built in 1952 by J. Hopgood. The hotel retains its original façade of yellow brick with stone dressings, as seen by Henry James in 1872 when he stayed here on his first visit to England. It was from here that his characters in *A Passionate Pilgrim and Other Tales* (1875) set out to visit the colleges.

A brochure printed in about 1910 recommends the Randolph as a 'first-class Hotel for families and gentlemen. . . . It contains many handsome suites of rooms with very charming prospects. It is fitted with an American elevator, and is supplied throughout with Electric Lighting. An omnibus meets all the most important trains. Carriages and horses can be obtained from the Randolph Stables adjoining the Hotel; there is also a large garage attached.' At that time a suite of rooms cost from 21s to 42s a night, a single bedroom from 3s to 6s. The table d'hôte dinner at seven o'clock was 5s.

There are now 109 bedrooms, all with bathrooms, and two suites known as Balliol and Trinity. There are also large rooms for conferences and seminars. The bar contains several specially commissioned and delightful paintings by Sir Osbert Lancaster illustrating scenes from MAX BEERBOHM'S ZULEIKA DOBSON. There are other paintings of the same series in the Spires Restaurant. The Randolph is one of the 800 or so hotels owned and managed by Forte Ltd. Major internal alterations were carried out in 1989.

Real Tennis   Real tennis has been played in Oxford for more than 500 years (the earliest mention is in 1450). This racket and ball game is one of the oldest court games in the world, and its name is derived from the old French word *réal* or royal. It is played by two or four people in a four-walled court, divided by a net as in lawn tennis, but the walls are in play. Features of the court are the penthouses, dedans, tambour, grille and chase lines. During the 16th century 'ball courts' or *sphaeristeria* are recorded at Queen's, Lincoln and Christ Church (in BLUE BOAR STREET). There were also two at Smith's Gate (where Hertford College now stands) and others off ALFRED STREET, ORIEL STREET and MERTON STREET. In 1508 four citizens were fined sixpence each for keeping unlicensed courts. In 1643 during the CIVIL WAR Charles I sought and obtained permission from Parliament for material for a tennis suit to be sent from London so that he could play the game in Oxford.

The Christ Church court, rebuilt in 1670 as a 'fair and stately' court, went out of use in the 1830s, and today only two courts remain. One of these, Oriel's, has not been used for tennis since the 1850s. By 1857 it had become the Theatre Royal and later suffered conversion into billiard rooms, lecture rooms and a bicycle store. In 1990 it was converted into under-graduate accommodation. The Merton court, rebuilt in 1798, is the second oldest court still in play in England (the oldest being that at Hampton Court, built in 1529 and used by Henry VIII). It is the head-quarters of a flourishing club, the Oxford University Tennis Club, employing two professionals. The former world champion, Chris Ronaldson, learned the game on this court.

There have been University real tennis matches against Cambridge since 1858.

(*See also* THEATRE.)

Recognised Student   The category of Recognised Student is unique at Oxford. Such students are members neither of a college nor of the University. Normally of senior-student status, they are placed under an academic adviser and pay fees only to the University or for the LIBRARIES and lectures which they may use or attend. There are very few Recognised Students at any one time, and no one may retain the status for longer than three terms. Admission to this category is by the relevant faculty board.

Regent's Park College   Founded in Stepney, London, in 1810 to prepare men (exclusively in those days) for the Baptist ministry in Great Britain and overseas – a direct result of the Baptist Education Society which had been formed in 1804. Its pioneers came mainly from the Particular Baptists and throughout its history the college has been encouraged and supported by the Particular Baptist Fund. In 1856 the college moved from Stepney to Holford House in Regent's Park. The Principal of the time, Joseph Angus, believed the move essential for closer links with London University, while the new premises provided space for an enlarged college of up to forty students. In 1901 it became a Divinity School of London University.

The college continued to grow and its educational standards to rise. In 1920 Henry Wheeler Robinson, later to achieve worldwide acclaim as an Old Testament scholar, became its Principal. In 1927, under his leadership, the move to Oxford began. The site, which fronted on to ST GILES' on the east and adjoined PUSEY STREET to the south, was first suggested by a research student, Ernest Payne, later to become senior tutor of the college, general secretary of the Baptist Union, and Vice-President of the World Council of Churches.

From 1927 to 1940 education continued both in London and Oxford, those at Oxford sharing the buildings of Mansfield College. The north and west wings were completed by 1939 just before the outbreak of war put an end to all private building. In these buildings the college repaid Mansfield's hospitality by housing its students while its own buildings were requisitioned by the Admiralty.

Since the war growth has been continuous. The biggest step forward was in 1957 when the college was incorporated as one of the five Permanent Private Halls of the University. This led to the admission of lay as well as ministerial students to read a variety of subjects for degrees at Oxford, although emphasis remained on Theology and ministerial training, all academic members of the staff being members of the University Faculty of Theology. Women had long been admitted as candidates for the ministry, but when the majority of the Oxford colleges became co-residential, Regent's also admitted women students to read Theology and other subjects as lay students.

In this period the buildings have been enlarged. The Balding Block, comprising twelve single study-bedrooms was added as a wing to the north side of the quadrangle; the south wing adjoining Pusey Street was completed; Angus and Gould Houses, offering thirteen flats for married students, were built parallel to the Balding Block. In 1985 work began on the south-east corner which was to lead to the completion of the quadrangle in 1986, offering more accommodation for married students and their families, with added teaching rooms.

Today the college community numbers about ninety, of whom fifteen are training for the ministry in a new way which involves their spending part of their time in college and part in pastoral charge of churches. About one-third of the rest of the student body is training for the Baptist ministry in the more customary full-time way. A considerable number of undergraduates read Theology with a view to teaching and other work, while six are admitted each year to read other arts subjects. Usually another fifteen postgraduate students from Britain and many parts of the world are reading for advanced degrees.

Preference is given to Baptists but the college is fully ecumenical and from time to time has members of many denominations of the Christian church.

This small college plays a full part in the life of the University. In recent years it has provided a President of the Oxford UNION, several BLUES in a number of sports, and has achieved a creditable number of first-class degrees. Many leaders of the worldwide Baptist community have received their training here and the number of applicants, both ministerial and lay, shows a healthy upward trend. The Principal's house is at No. 55 St Giles'. The college arms (*see* HERALDRY) are displayed on the façade. The Rev P.S. Fiddes, MA, D.Phil, is the present Principal.

(*See also* PRIVATE HALLS.)

Registrar The first person to be found in the University records acting as Registrar, or public scribe, of the University is John Manyngham, who signed a letter in 1448; a 15th-century statute (the precise date is uncertain) required him to be a Master of Arts, a notary public, and versed in rhetoric. An unbroken list of those holding the office runs from 1508. As time has gone by, the office has grown greatly in importance, and the Registrar of the University might, by a rough analogy, now be equated with the head of the Civil Service. A permanent official, he is the chief executive officer of the University and secretary of HEBDOMADAL COUNCIL, CONGREGATION and CONVOCATION. He is responsible for communications which express the general policy of the University (as opposed to that of the colleges), and for the conduct of correspondence with public bodies; his duties are set out by statute (Title IX, Section VII). He has a substantial staff, mostly now located at the UNIVERSITY OFFICES in WELLINGTON SQUARE. Although the role of the Registrar is essentially and necessarily a University rather than a collegiate one, the Registrar will invariably hold a professional fellowship at a college. He is appointed by Hebdomadal Council.

Responsions The name of a University examination derived from the University exercises for a degree, once oral, which required a student to respond or dispute on logical questions. The old scholastic exercises known as Responsions, which had fallen into desuetude, were replaced in 1808 by an elementary examination (in Greek, Latin, Logic and Geometry) which had to be passed by students before their degree, generally in the second year. In 1849 the rules for Responsions were revised and the standards raised. In 1850 a new examination between Responsions and Final Schools, known as the First Public Examination or, in some faculties as MODERATIONS, was introduced. As a result Responsions, known colloquially as 'Smalls', was downgraded. After a heated debate in 1920 Greek ceased to be a compulsory subject in the examination. From 1926 Responsions, or an equivalent, was a requirement for entry to the University and had to be taken before MATRICULATION. The four Regent Masters who presided over the disputations and later over the examination were known as Masters of the Schools. The examination was abolished in 1960.

Restaurants In the 19th and early 20th centuries Oxford's best restaurants included those at the RANDOLPH HOTEL, the MITRE, Buol's Restaurant at

No. 21 CORNMARKET STREET (opened here in 1901, having moved from No. 15 BROAD STREET where it had been established in the 1890s), the Swiss Café in Broad Street, and the restaurant of the George Hotel on the corner of Cornmarket and GEORGE STREET. The George Restaurant was still one of the best restaurants in Oxford from the 1920s to the 1940s. SIR JOHN BETJEMAN, who went up to Magdalen College in 1925, said that 'aesthetes never dined in hall but went instead to the George restaurant ... where there was a band consisting of three ladies and where punkahs, suspended from the ceiling, swayed to and fro, dispelling the smoke of Egyptian and Balkan cigarettes. Mr Ehrsham, the perfect Swiss hotelier, and his wife kept order, and knew how much credit to allow us.' The novelist Angus Wilson, who went up to Merton College in 1932 with an income of some £300 a year, soon discovered 'that the best food was at the George – it served that sort of good semi-French cuisine that still existed in the best English provincial restaurants before the war, before ignorant and pretentious "international" menus based on deep freezes had led to our present sad state of affairs'.

The following restaurants (which have separate entries) have all established a name for themselves in recent years and have all at some time appeared in the Consumer Association's *Good Food Guide*: BROWN'S, CHERWELL BOATHOUSE, ELIZABETH, SARACENO (now closed), SORBONNE.

Rewley Abbey Founded in 1280 by Edmund, Earl of Cornwall, nephew of Henry III, as a retreat and place of study for Cistercian monks. Rewley is derived from *rois-lieu*, meaning King's place. Its site was on a branch of the THAMES opposite Gloucester College (*see* MONASTIC COLLEGES). The riverside abbey church was dedicated in 1281. There were never more than about fifteen monks here and it was not an important abbey, but it contrived to make itself extremely unpopular with the townsmen of Oxford, who attacked it twice, in 1300 and 1316. After the Dissolution of the Monasteries, its site was granted to George Owen, Henry VIII's physician, who was also granted GODSTOW ABBEY. Owen later offered it to the King for his endowment of Christ Church. By the 18th century most of the buildings had been pulled down, the rest converted into a private house with outbuildings. Nearly all that survived, however, was demolished in about 1850 – when the site was sold to the London and North Western Railway (later the LMSR). The only fragment that can now be seen is part of the precinct wall and a 15th-century doorway north of BLACKWELL'S building in HYTHE BRIDGE STREET.

Rewley House Became the thirty-sixth college of the University on 1 March 1990.

(*See also* EXTERNAL STUDIES, DEPARTMENT OF.)

Rewley Road Takes its name from REWLEY ABBEY. It is in St Thomas's parish and runs northwards from PARK END STREET, past the western end of HYTHE BRIDGE STREET. There was a Rewley (or Ruley) Lane in 1538. ANTHONY WOOD describes a 'hollow way from Rewley to Hythe Bridge'. The name is either an anglicised form of the French *réal-lieu*, meaning a royal place, or *rois-lieu* or *regali loco* meaning King's place. Until recently, at the point to the north-west of Hythe Bridge Street where the last remnant of the abbey still stands, the road was dominated by coal wharves and coal merchants' premises. On the west is the line of the old LMS railway, the abbey having been demolished when the station was built in 1851. The County Fire Station now dominates the road at the northern end and on an adjoining site to the east, near the back of BLACKWELL'S building, are the offices of the County Council Public Protection Department.

Rhodes, Cecil John (*1853–1902*). The fifth son of the vicar of Bishop's Stortford in Hertfordshire, Rhodes was sent to the grammar school in the town and then, disappointing his father by having no disposition to become a clergyman himself, he was sent out to join an elder brother who was growing cotton in Natal. Having made some money in South Africa he was able to return to England to go up to Oxford as he had long wanted to do. He failed to gain admittance to University College, but he then sought an interview with Edward Hawkins (1789–1882), Provost of Oriel, who accepted him. Rhodes accordingly went to live in lodgings at No. 18 HIGH STREET. Early in 1874 he fell ill after rowing and a doctor whom he consulted decided he had not 'six months to live'. He returned to South Africa where his health improved sufficiently for him to return to Oxford during term time, living first at No. 116 High Street, then at No. 6 KING EDWARD STREET, and eventually obtained his degree at the age of twenty-eight. Having made a huge fortune in southern Africa, where Rhodesia was named after him, he was able to found the RHODES SCHOLARSHIPS and to leave £100,000 to Oriel College. (*See also* RHODES HOUSE.)

Rhodes House Built firstly as a permanent memorial to CECIL RHODES, secondly as a contribution to Oxford as a centre of education and learning, and

Cecil Rhodes as an undergraduate at Oriel College c.1877.

thirdly to provide accommodation for the offices of the Rhodes Trust in Oxford, the trustees of which administer the RHODES SCHOLARSHIPS. The building in SOUTH PARKS ROAD was erected in 1926–9 to the design of Sir Herbert Baker on land which was bought from Wadham College. The main building is of squared rubble in the style of a Cotswold manor house and in the shape of an H, with a classical copper-domed rotunda between the wings on the north entrance front. Over the cast-bronze entrance door is carved a ship of state, with the British lion on one sail and the American eagle on the other. On the top of the dome of the rotunda is a bronze Zimbabwe bird, similar to those set round the ramparts of the ruined city of Zimbabwe. Inside the dome is the memorial to Rhodes Scholars killed in the First and Second World Wars. Inscribed round the dome is a quotation from Aristotle which greatly influenced Rhodes's life and which may be roughly translated as follows: 'Man's highest good proves to be activity of the soul in accordance with its special excellence; and in so far as excellences vary, in accordance with that which is the best and most complete: and that in a full life'. In the centre of the ceiling are symbols of national elements in the British Commonwealth of Nations, and in the centre of the floor is a circular slab quarried from the Matopo mountains near Rhodes's grave.

The vestibule beyond the rotunda commemorates Sir George Parkin, the first general secretary of the Rhodes Trust. Over the door is a carved representation of the Matopos with the words 'Non Omnis Moriar' ('I shall not wholly die'), taken from the ode of Horace beginning 'I have fashioned a monument more lasting than bronze'. The main room on the ground floor is the Milner Hall, named after Lord Milner, who was associated with Rhodes in South Africa and was one of the first Rhodes trustees. Over the dais is a portrait of Cecil Rhodes. The other rooms on the ground floor are the Jameson Room, named after Sir Leander Starr Jameson, a lifelong friend of Rhodes and another of the original trustees named in his will, and the Beit Room, after Alfred Beit, Rhodes's partner, friend and adviser. In the passage is a tapestry, *The Romance of the Rose*, by WILLIAM MORRIS, bequeathed by the architect Sir Herbert Baker.

The west wing contains, on the upper floor, the Rhodes House library, a department of the BODLEIAN LIBRARY specialising in the history and current affairs – political, economic and social – of the British Commonwealth and former British colonial territories, of the United States of America, of sub-Saharan Africa, and of islands such as St Helena. (Books on Burma and India are in the INDIAN INSTITUTE library.) Rhodes House library contains over 300,000 books, most of which are kept in a large closed book-stack in the basement. The library also has a large collection of manuscript material relating to the history of British colonial administration, as well as the Rhodes papers, the Anti-Slavery Society's archives, the Fabian Colonial Bureau, and the papers of the Brookes of Sarawak, among other collections. The east wing contains the Warden's residence and the offices of the Rhodes Trust. The present Warden and Secretary to the Rhodes Trust is Dr Anthony Kenny, formerly Master of Balliol. He succeeded Dr R.A. Fletcher in 1989. The previous Warden was Sir Edgar Williams.

Along the high parapet on the south front of the building is a Latin inscription meaning 'This house stands for ever as a reminder of the name and example of Cecil John Rhodes to the Oxford he loved'. In the south wall are stones carved with the heraldry and symbolism of the British and American nations. Rhodes House has a beautiful garden which adjoins the Fellows' Garden of Wadham College. An opening was made in the stone wall dividing the two gardens in 1983 for the garden party attended by the Queen and Prince Philip to celebrate the eightieth anniversary of the foundation of the scholarships.

(*Cecil Rhodes and Rhodes House*, eleventh edition, Oxford, 1982.)

Rhodes Scholarships CECIL RHODES was a fervent believer in the British Empire and in the ability of the English-speaking people to work towards the establishment of justice, liberty and peace in the world. In order to promote his ideas through education, he left his considerable fortune to found scholarships for male students, 'tenable at any College in the University of Oxford for three consecutive academical years'. He set out in his long will his reasons for establishing the scholarships, considering 'that the education of young Colonists at one of the Universities in the United Kingdom is of great advantage to them for giving breadth to their views for their instruction in life and manners and for instilling into their minds the advantage to the Colonies as well as to the United Kingdom for the retention of the unity of the Empire'. He said that he also desired 'to encourage and foster an appreciation of the advantages which I implicitly believe will result from the union of the English-speaking peoples throughout the world'. He directed his trustees that in the election of a student to a scholarship regard should be had to '(i) his literary and scholastic attainments (ii) his fondness of and success in many outdoor sports such as cricket football and the like (iii) his qualities of manhood truth courage devotion to duty sympathy for the protection of the weak kindliness unselfishness and fellowship and (iv) his exhibition during school days of moral force of character and of instincts to lead and take an interest in his schoolmates. As mere suggestions for the guidance of those who will have the choice of students for the Scholarships I record that . . . my ideal qualified student would combine these four qualifications in the proportions of three-tenths for the first two-tenths for the second three-tenths for the third and two-tenths for the fourth qualification. . . . No student shall be qualified or disqualified for election to a Scholarship on account of his race or religious opinions'.

There was, however, a sexual disqualification in that the scholarships were limited to male students. When Rhodes died there were very few female students at Oxford, which was then virtually a single-sex university. Now that men and women are on an equal footing in the colleges the scholarships have been opened to unmarried men and women between the ages of nineteen and twenty-five. Rhodes Scholars will usually have spent at least two years at a university in their own country. The scholarship is now for two years, with an extension for a third year in certain circumstances. Scholars can marry at the end of their first year at Oxford. There are about 100 selection committees throughout the world and

Scholars are selected on their academic record, confidential testimonials and a personal interview.

The first Rhodes Scholars came to Oxford in 1903. The distribution has had to be varied over the years with the many constitutional and territorial changes since then, and the present distribution is as follows: United States of America – 32 each year; Canada – 11; South Africa – 9; Australia – 7; Zambia and Zimbabwe – 3 (shared); New Zealand – 2; India – 3; Bermuda, Jamaica, Hong Kong, Singapore, Kenya, Pakistan, Malaysia, Nigeria and the British Caribbean – 1 each. In a codicil to his will, Rhodes included Germany within the scholarships in the hope that 'an understanding between the three strongest Powers will render war impossible and educational relations make the strongest tie'. The German scholarships were suspended in 1916, revived in 1929 at the rate of two each year instead of the original five, and lapsed again in 1939. In 1969 the two annual scholarships were resumed for West Germany.

Among those who have held Rhodes scholarships have been Sir Zelman Cowen (former Governor-General of Australia; New College 1945–7); Norman Manley (former Prime Minister of Jamaica; Jesus College 1914–15, 1919–20); Lord Florey (Nobel Prizewinner; Magdalen 1922–4); James Fulbright (founder of the Fulbright Scholarships in America; Pembroke 1925–8); Robert Penn Warren (writer; Christ Church 1928–31); Dean Rusk (former US Secretary of State; St John's 1931–4); Dominic Mintoff (former Prime Minister of Malta; Hertford 1939–41); Dr Edward de Bono (writer; Christ Church 1955–7); Kris Kristofferson (actor; Merton 1958–60).

(Elton, Lord, *The First Fifty Years of the Rhodes Trust and the Rhodes Scholarships 1903–1953*, Oxford, 1955.)

Ring Road Oxford's first ring road was the road or lane running on the inner side of the mound of earth which, with its stone wall, formed the city's defences. The road is now represented by ST MICHAEL'S STREET and SHIP STREET on the north and ST EBBE'S and NEW INN HALL STREET on the west. On the other sides the ring road has since been built over.

The first section of Oxford's modern ring road, the northern bypass, was constructed in the mid-1930s as unemployment relief work. It ran from the HEADINGTON roundabout to the BANBURY ROAD roundabout. It was a three-lane road and the scene of many fatal accidents, as a result of which it was eventually made into a double-carriageway road in 1971, with a flyover at MARSTON. It is part of the A40 trunk road. The section of the southern bypass from BOTLEY to SOUTH HINKSEY was opened in 1938 and the section from South Hinksey to Heyford Hill in 1965. The first section was made into a double-carriageway road in 1973 and is now part of the A34 trunk road. The section of the eastern bypass from Headington to ROSE HILL was opened in 1959 and the link from Rose Hill to Heyford Hill in 1966. The link in the ring road known as the western bypass, was opened in 1962 from the Pear Tree roundabout to a flyover at the BOTLEY ROAD. The road is 15.8 miles in length, and in order to travel right round it the motorist would have to pass nine roundabouts, and travel under seven bridges as well as the overhead conveyor line for cars at the COWLEY works. The construction of the ring road has saved CHRIST CHURCH MEADOW from having

an inner relief-road across it by removing most of the heavy through traffic from the centre of Oxford.

Riots Relations between town and gown in Oxford were for long extremely uneasy, and violence frequently erupted. The first notable disturbance occurred in 1209 when two clerks were hanged by townsmen after a student had killed a woman, either intentionally or accidentally. To escape further revenge, many scholars fled to Cambridge, where a university may already have been founded. At this time King John was in dispute with the church, and it seems that the townsmen felt confident of his support; but when the quarrel with the Pope was settled they were obliged to apologise to the papal legate for their behaviour and to grant privileges to the scholars. At the same time those scholars who had previously come to terms with the citizens without the Church's blessing were suspended from teaching for three years.

There was further trouble in 1228 when townsmen assaulted and wounded several scholars; in 1236 when the town was set on fire; in 1238 when there was a fracas at OSNEY where the papal legate was staying, the legate himself being forced to flee to Wallingford and his brother being shot dead (*see* OSNEY ABBEY); and in 1248 when a clerk was killed in a vicious riot. Indeed, throughout the 13th century there were repeated outbreaks of violence in which both students and townsmen lost their lives. Although the scholars were ordered by Henry III to move to Northampton in 1263 for giving comfort and support to the baronial cause, the Crown usually took the side of the University against the town and often granted the University further privileges after a bout of uproar had subsided. In 1272, after a particularly violent

Illustration of a fracas in Cuthbert Bede's The Adventures of Mr Verdant Green *(1853–7): 'Science was more than a match for brute force'.*

dispute, the town was ordered by the King to make amends to the University, and in 1275 the MAYOR and bailiffs were commanded to observe the University's privileges. In 1290 the town complained about the autocratic rule of the University's CHANCELLOR, yet his authority over all crimes in which scholars were involved, except murder and mayhem, was confirmed by King Edward I and the University's rights and privileges were reaffirmed. This naturally exacerbated relations between town and gown, and led to increased complaints by the scholars of the citizens' excessive charges for food and wine and other supplies, of the high rents demanded for accommodation, of the rubbish dumped outside the schools, of the butchers using the thoroughfares as slaughterhouses. In 1298 the quarrels erupted into a violent disturbance near CARFAX, where the bailiff was attacked by students who knocked him down, trampled on him and took away his mace. The next day other townsmen were beaten and kicked, one was killed and a burgess was said to have been dragged into ST MARY THE VIRGIN and assaulted before the high altar. On Monday there was further rioting, when 'full three thousand clerks with bows and arrows, swords and bucklers' were alleged to have attacked all the citizens they came across 'and injured more than fifty and many were wounded to death'. 'After this uproar the bailiff would have pursued and taken the felons,' so the Oxford city burgesses claimed in an address to Edward I, 'but the Chancellor would not suffer them to be imprisoned, and threatened that the town would be burnt and the burgesses slain, if he arrested them'.

Some years later, in 1334, the Masters and scholars once more decided to abandon Oxford for a more accommodating town – this time Stamford in Lincolnshire. But the King ordered them to go back and once again the rights and privileges of the University were confirmed and even extended. In 1355 there was a fearful outburst of rioting and slaughter on ST SCHOLASTICA'S DAY.

The students did not only fight with the citizens, they fought among themselves, particularly when one of the so-called NATIONS quarrelled with another. In about 1258 the Northern and Welsh scholars allied themselves against the Southern and, after a fight in which several were wounded and some killed, defeated them. The English had their revenge, however, in 1389 when they rampaged through 'divers streets and lanes', according to ANTHONY WOOD, 'crying out "War, war, war, sle, sle, sle the Welsh doggys and her whelyps, and ho so loketh out of his howse, he shall in good soute be dead etc." and certain persons they slew and others they grievously wounded, and some of the Welshmen who bowed their knees to abjure the Town, they the Northern Scholars led to the gates, causing them first to piss on them, and then to kiss the place on which they had pissed. But being not content with that, they, while the said Welshmen stooped to kiss it, would knock their heads against the gates in such an inhuman manner, that they would force blood out of the noses of some, and tears from the eyes of others.'

Although relations between town and University gradually improved after St Scholastica's Day 1355, and although not repeated on the same horrifying scale, riots continued to be common throughout and beyond the Middle Ages. In the 1570s an alderman complained of the many 'riots and misdemeanours' in the town. It was particularly unruly during the CIVIL WAR, when there were large numbers of Welsh soldiers in Oxford, as well as Welsh and Irish women; in 1641, townsmen attacked a PROCTOR while he was arresting a 'lewd woman' at the time of curfew and 'rang their great bell at Carfax . . . as at the great slaughter'. After a subsequent disturbance in February 1646 a general curfew had to be ordered. There were also disturbances in 1658, when scholars pelted the Mayor and his attendants as they were proclaiming Richard Cromwell Protector; there were riots in 1679 at the time of the Popish Plot; and in 1688, after the recusant landlord of the MITRE had announced that he would like to see the whole town in ashes and to wash his hands in the blood of the Earl of Abingdon, a leading Tory prominent in Oxford politics, the mob roared through the streets smashing the windows of Catholic houses. Soon afterwards, in the 1690s, there were bread riots in the town. In 1757 corn was seized by the mob; and corn mills were attacked in 1766. As late as 1867 there were riots in protest at the increased price of bread. Outbreaks of violence became common in Oxford after it became a centre of Jacobitism. In 1715, after a dinner had been held to celebrate King George I's birthday, Nonconformist chapels and Quaker meeting houses were sacked; houses of DISSENTERS were pillaged; a Presbyterian pulpit was burned at Carfax and an effigy of a Presbyterian minister consumed in the flames. Indeed, Dissenters were liable to be roughly treated in Oxford throughout the 18th century and well into the next. In 1825 a Primitive Methodist preacher was forced to hold his tongue when pelted with rotten eggs by undergraduates; while, four years later, antagonism to a Nonconformist preacher in ST GILES' provoked another riot.

Politics provoked riots less often than religion. There were violent disturbances in 1748 and after the election of 1754. Yet at the height of the Chartist disturbances in the 1840s, Oxford remained relatively quiet. The Chartist meetings held in Oxford were not well attended, and, though petitions attracted fairly large numbers of signatures, committed support for Chartism was not strong.

Throughout the 19th century there were periodic outbreaks of violence in Oxford, particularly during and after the Guy Fawkes Night celebrations on 5 November. In November 1867, for example, hundreds of special constables had to be summoned, and even a company of Grenadier Guards from Windsor marched in, after fights had broken out between men of the town and the members of an audience, mostly undergraduates, who had left the TOWN HALL after a concert. The Grenadier Guards were also ordered in, together with the County Constabulary, the University Police, members of the Militia and the City Rifle Corps, during a subsequent riot over the price of bread. The Vice-Chancellor called upon the Mayor, who addressed the crowds from the town hall, while all undergraduates were required not to stir beyond their college gates. The disturbances died down when the bakers agreed to reduce the price of the quartern loaf by a penny.

In August 1872 there were even more serious disturbances when the government decreed a restriction in the opening hours of public houses by the Intoxicating Liquor Licensing Act. An angry crowd marched from Carfax upon Grandpont House, the home of Alderman Randall, who had opposed the special licences commonly granted to innkeepers during ST GILES' FAIR. Broken up there by charges of police, the demonstrators returned towards the centre of the city, smashing the windows of various well-known teetotallers on their way. The violence was repeated the next evening and again the following week when windows and street lamps were smashed in St Giles' and another attack made upon Grandpont House. After a fireplug in Carfax had been turned on so that water could be played at full force upon the crowds, the rioters eventually withdrew soon after two o'clock in the morning.

Twentieth-century riots have been mild by comparison, though on Guy Fawkes Night, even in recent years, streets have been blockaded by revellers and cars carried off to be dumped in side streets.

Rivermead Rehabilitation Centre *Abingdon Road.* This centre received its name in 1956, when it was taken over by Dr Lionel Cosin to combine the dual function of a geriatric unit and a rehabilitation department for young disabled patients. The buildings originated in 1885 as the City Isolation Hospital, Cold Arbour. They were erected by KINGERLEE LTD for the Oxford Local Health Board and were intended for infectious and fever cases formerly nursed at the RADCLIFFE INFIRMARY. A series of detached, red-brick Victorian buildings in the Pavilion style continues in full use (including the lodge and the present administration block).

From 1885 to 1939 the hospital provided isolation facilities for smallpox, diphtheria, scarlet fever, scabies, whooping cough and for a limited number of tuberculous patients. In 1939 a replacement hospital was opened at the SLADE, HEADINGTON; but due to the pressure on beds with the outbreak of the Second World War, Cold Arbour was not abandoned, as originally intended; it continued to provide terminal tuberculosis care and facilities for dermatology and parasitology. From 1954 to 1956 the hospital changed its function, becoming a psycho-geriatric centre linked with the COWLEY ROAD HOSPITAL and the psychiatric hospital at LITTLEMORE.

From 1963 the former isolation hospital emerged as one of the leading rehabilitation centres in the country. Its excellence stemmed from its modern methods and the expertise of its large staff, which more than compensated for the difficulties of its antiquated buildings. In recent years a fine range of purpose-built facilities for physiotherapy, occupational and hydrotherapy, and comprehensive industrial workshops for rehabilitation have been added. Rivermead specialises in the assessment and rehabilitation of young stroke victims, neuromuscular and neurological disorders and cases of head injury, chiefly from road accidents. In 1986 there were fifty-five beds, and its annual turnover of 250–300 patients has enabled it to resist a recent threat of compulsory closure.

Roebuck *8 Market Street.* Private houses from 1230–1330, the buildings thereafter became Cary Hall or Inn after the Cary family who owned property here. Thomas Coventree owned the site from 1420 to 1452 and renamed the tavern Coventry Hall or Inn. The inn kept its name until 1610 when it became the Roebuck from the arms of Jesus College. At this time

MARKET STREET was called Jesus College Lane. By 1740 the tavern had become a large coaching inn on the London to Gloucester run, with yard and main entrance in CORNMARKET STREET (*see* TRANSPORT). The Mazeppa coach frequently staged from the Roebuck. With no frontage on Market Street, access was gained by using a long archway. But in 1865 the Roebuck's coaching office, Chaundy's cigar depot and the Little Cross inn were demolished and the Roebuck Vaults erected. Pulled down in 1924, it was rebuilt in 1938. Subsequently there have been many changes in the name: Roebuck Vaults (1938–44), Roebuck Tap (1944–50), Roebuck Restaurant (1950–61) and the Roebuck from 1961. The main Cornmarket frontage was closed in 1925.

(*See also* BEATING THE BOUNDS.)

Rollers, The Between PARSON'S PLEASURE and the bridge over the River Cherwell (*see* THAMES) to MESOPOTAMIA, the level of the river drops at a weir. To enable punts to negotiate the change in level, a series of metal rollers was constructed on an incline. Punters and their passengers disembark and either drag and push the punt up the Rollers to the higher level or roll it down to the lower (*see also* PUNTING).

Roman Catholics The fortunes of Roman Catholics in the University after the Reformation, and before the Catholic Emancipation Act of 1829 and the final removal of the obligation to subscribe to the Thirty-Nine Articles in 1871, were mixed, often depending on the religious convictions of the monarchy. Thus, under Henry VIII the fate of the MONASTIC COLLEGES was effectively sealed by the Dissolution of the great abbeys. The friars' houses met similar fates, the houses of the Austin Friars being eventually absorbed into Wadham (*see* AUGUSTINIAN PRIORY). The houses of the Franciscans and Dominicans were also dissolved.

Following the accession of Edward VI in 1547, the University underwent a formal VISITATION, and the religious injunctions of the VISITORS were extremely radical. Symbols of Roman idolatry, altars, superstitious pictures, images, bells and vestments were prohibited. Thus was Protestantism firmly established; for while the views of many at the University may have remained essentially Roman Catholic, papists were undoubtedly placed on the defensive. Even LIBRARIES were purged of popish manuscripts and books. This policy was soon (if briefly) to be reversed, for following the accession to the throne of the Catholic Mary Tudor in 1553, vessels and vestments were brought out from their hiding places, while there was a flow of Protestant dons to the Continent. The University became the scene of the historic collision with the leading Protestant protagonists who were ultimately to be humiliated and burned at the stake. Ridley, Latimer and Cranmer met their fates in 1555 and 1556 (*see* MARTYRS' MEMORIAL).

When Elizabeth became Queen in 1558, matters were once again reversed, with the outward symbols of Romanism being destroyed or concealed. Protestant exiles were restored to fellowships and some Romanists were deprived of their positions – although it seems that their numbers may have been less than a dozen. Gradually, Oxford became a bastion of Protestantism, with only occasional infiltration by

Romanism. From 1581, all those who matriculated over the age of sixteen had to subscribe to the Thirty-Nine Articles, and all tutors were required to purge themselves of suspicion of popery if they wished to retain their pupils. The orthodoxy of those intending to take degrees was investigated carefully, while unattached students residing in Oxford were suspected generally of Romanist opinions, since subscription to the Articles could be avoided if one refrained from entering a college or a hall (*see* ACADEMIC HALLS). Yet throughout the 16th century there were dons and undergraduates who still adhered to Rome, often reappearing as priests on the Continent. EDMUND CAMPION was perhaps Oxford's most celebrated Catholic martyr. Initially a scholar of St John's, he acted as PROCTOR in 1568–9, but after that he left the University and yielded to the opinions which were driving him to Rome. After returning to England, Campion was captured and martyred in December 1581. In general, however, Protestant opinions were steadily making their way at this time, with CONVOCATION in 1584 preventing the circulation of Romanist prints, while in 1591 the CHANCELLOR called on the University to suppress 'all Jesuits, Seminaries, and Recusants'. In 1629 the Speaker of the House of Commons required the University to report all persons who had contravened the Articles of Religion; and in 1679 the heads of houses were told to make returns of any in their colleges whom they suspected to be papists.

The accession in 1685 of the Roman Catholic James II put the University's loyalty to the monarchy severely to the test. The Master of University College, Obadiah Walker, opened a chapel in a private room in 1686 for public Mass. John Massey, as Dean of Christ Church, opened an oratory and made a Jesuit his chaplain. These moves aroused widespread and vocal resentment in the University. And there was the notorious dissension between the King and the Fellows of Magdalen in 1687 which did so much to alienate the University from the King and to strengthen its alliance with the Church of England. The 18th century was a quieter period. In 1753 Edward Gibbon was removed from the University because of his brief flirtation with Roman Catholicism, but his removal was demanded not by his college, Magdalen (where he remained on the books), but by his father. However, in 1772 the University was still insisting on the need to guard against 'the two great factions of papists and puritans', in connection with a movement at the time for relief from the obligation to subscribe to the Thirty-Nine Articles.

As late as 1817 the University, by rejecting George Canning as BURGESS, showed that it would tolerate no friend of Catholic emancipation. Again, in 1829 Sir Robert Peel's letter, resigning his seat as Burgess, was read to Convocation, which had just been discussing its annual, if futile, protest against the idea of Roman Catholic emancipation. In the contest which followed Peel lost his seat, entirely because he believed that there should be some satisfactory adjustment to the Catholic question; it is surprising indeed, in the light of later events, to find JOHN HENRY NEWMAN exerting himself to secure Peel's defeat on such an issue. Yet in 1829 Catholic emancipation did finally reach the statute book, and, for all the opposition to Romanism brought out by the OXFORD MOVEMENT, the necessity to subscribe to the Thirty-Nine Articles was at last

abolished in 1871. It was not, however, until 1895 that the Roman Catholic hierarchy's policy of forbidding Roman Catholics to attend the University was reversed. In 1986, St John's, the college of Edmund Campion, elected its first Roman Catholic President in Professor William Hayes; and the University's PRIVATE HALLS now include CAMPION HALL, the Jesuit academic community; GREYFRIARS for Franciscans; and ST BENET'S HALL for Benedictines. BLACKFRIARS, the Priory of the Holy Spirit, was completed in 1954 for the Dominicans. PLATER COLLEGE was opened in HEADINGTON in the 1970s.

The priests who ministered to members of the University in the 16th and 17th centuries also worked among people in the town. Mass was celebrated in various taverns in Oxford, among them the STAR and the MITRE, and in certain private houses, including Richard Owen's house at GODSTOW, in HOLYWELL MANOR and in the house of the Napper family at Temple Cowley, where priests were sheltered. George Napper, one of three members of his family who were priests, was captured and executed in 1610.

In the previous century several other Roman Catholics had suffered at the hands of the authorities in Oxford. Rowland Jenks, a stationer, was tried at the Black Assize of 1577 (*see* COURTS) and condemned to lose his ears for distributing popish books; and a few years later, in 1589, two priests and two laymen who had been arrested at the CATHERINE WHEEL INN, were hanged, drawn and quartered. Yet priests continued to say Mass in the town and by the 1620s they were said to have 'uncommon liberty'. At the beginning of the CIVIL WAR papist books and pictures were burned in the streets, though when Oxford became the royalist headquarters Mass was said without interruption and after the Restoration – following a period of persecution during the interregnum – priests were once more to be found openly practising their religion and saying Mass. This new tolerant attitude was, however, strongly condemned by many of Oxford's firmly Protestant citizens. When it was reported, for example, that the Roman Catholic Master of MAGDALEN COLLEGE SCHOOL had made no less than sixty converts, he was driven out of the city; in 1678, after the Rev. Titus Oates had caused a national panic by his Popish Plot to assassinate King Charles II and massacre Protestants, there were anti-Catholic RIOTS in the city, effigies of the Pope were burned, and the houses of known papists were searched for arms; the next year Oates was given the freedom of the city; and in 1688 there were further anti-Catholic riots before the Glorious Revolution put an end to the reign of the Roman Catholic King James II.

After the accession of William III and Mary II, the numbers of Roman Catholics in Oxford sharply declined. By the beginning of the 18th century there were evidently no more than fourteen of their faith in the whole city; and at the end of that century, when the Jesuits built the church of ST IGNATIUS, there were still only about sixty. By 1859 the congregation of this chapel had risen to no more than 118, but after the opening of the church of ST ALOYSIUS in 1875 there was an increase in the number of conversions. This church had a congregation of almost 900 by the end of the 19th century. To serve the growing number of Roman Catholics in Oxford, the construction of St Aloysius was followed by that of ST EDMUND AND ST FRIDESWIDE in the IFFLEY ROAD in 1911; by ST GREGORY AND

ST AUGUSTINE in WOODSTOCK ROAD, also in 1911; by Corpus Christi Church in Margaret Road, Headington, in 1936; by ST ANTHONY OF PADUA in JACK STRAW'S LANE in 1948; by the church of the HOLY ROOD, ABINGDON ROAD, in 1961; by the Church of OUR LADY HELP OF CHRISTIANS in Hollow Way, COWLEY, in 1962; and by the church of the SACRED HEART, BLACKBIRD LEYS, in 1966.

Rose Hill *Iffley.* A continuation of Henley Avenue, beginning in the vicinity of CHURCH COWLEY ROAD and ending at Oxford Road, LITTLEMORE. The house Rose Hill, which gave its name to the area, was first inhabited by Dr John Ireland, an eccentric apothecary and medical practitioner, in about 1830. The name was also given to the adjoining estate of Oxford city council houses (built in the 1940s and 1950s) through which runs the boundary line with South Oxfordshire District. The Rev. William Tuckwell, in his *Reminiscences of Oxford* of 1900, writes of 'the Rose Hill heights' as having been known to MATTHEW ARNOLD in the 1840s. *Jackson's Oxford Journal* (*see* NEWSPAPERS) of 27 January 1872 has a news item on 'The Rose Hill Road': 'Some slight relief will, we hope, be afforded to a few of the Oxford unemployed by the cutting of the new road from the bottom of Rose Hill at a turn leading to the Cemetery to the Iffley Road, thus cutting off a very dangerous corner. The City will contribute £500 on the condition that this sum is allocated to the provision of work on the road for the Oxford unemployed.' At that time Rose Hill would have been outside the city boundary. Although the road was known as Rose Hill in 1853 it was not officially named by the City Council until December 1930. At the foot of the hill is a war memorial of the Oxfordshire and Buckinghamshire Light Infantry, designed by Sir Edwin Lutyens in 1923. It is a tall obelisk on a moulded plinth and contains the names of the dead of both world wars. There is a milestone outside No. 37. A highway stone at the foot of the hill on the south-west side is inscribed 'Ifily Hy Way 1635', indicating that this was the old main road to London via Henley.

Rose Hill Methodist Church *Rose Hill.* Iffley Wesleyan Methodist Church, as it was then known, was founded in 1835 by Henry Leake, whose father had previously been one of the trustees of the original WESLEY MEMORIAL METHODIST CHURCH. The original building is still in use, making it the oldest Methodist church in Oxford. Considerable enlargements were made in 1940–2 and in 1958, producing a dual-purpose sanctuary but still retaining the external appearance of a village church, which it was until the 1930s. The graveyard, an unusual feature of a Methodist church, was used between 1842 and 1963. The organ, which was originally installed in the parish church, was presented to the church in 1895 by R.J. Campbell (later Chancellor of Winchester Cathedral), who worshipped here when an undergraduate.

Rose Lane A narrow way running beside the BOTANIC GARDEN and leading from No. 61 HIGH STREET to the gate which leads to DEADMAN'S WALK and BROAD WALK. In the 17th century it was known as Trinity (or Trinitie) Lane and was shown as such on maps of 1762 and 1772. ANTHONY WOOD speaks of Teckew or St Frideswide's Gate, opposite Magdalen Hall; Teckew

Gate seems to have been between Trinity Lane and the city ditch. Most of the few houses in the lane belong to Merton College. Nos 1 and 2 are a pair (Meadow Cottages) in one building; probably 17th–18th century in origin but restored, they are listed Grade II.

Rose Place A lane off ST ALDATE'S created in 1862–4 by culverting the TRILL MILL STREAM. At the St Aldate's end is the OLD PALACE.

Rotunda Museum of Antique Dolls' Houses *Grove House, Iffley Turn.* Mrs Graham Greene's collection of over forty dolls' houses made between 1700 and 1900 with their period carpets, furniture, dinner services, silver, books and families.

Routh, Martin Joseph (*1755–1854*). Elected to a fellowship at Magdalen College in 1775, Routh became successively college librarian, junior Dean of arts, senior PROCTOR, and, at the age of only thirty-five, President – an office which he held with unimpaired mental faculties until his death in his hundredth year. It is said of him that 'a lover of old ways, he always clung to his wig [now preserved in the college library] and to the fashion in dress of his younger days', and declined to acknowledge the existence of railways: 'Railway, Sir? Railway? I know nothing about railways'. When asked for a maxim to sum up the benefit of his many years' scholarship, he replied 'Always verify your references.' 'It was as a *spectacle* that he excited popular interest,' wrote Tuckwell in his *Reminiscences of Oxford* (1900). 'To see him shuffle into Chapel from his lodgings a Sunday crowd assembled. . . . After 1836 he was rarely visible in the streets, but presided at College Examinations, and dined in Hall on Gaudy days, occupying the large State Chair, never profaned by meaner loins, constructed from the immemorial Magdalen elm, which, much older than the College, fell with a terrific crash in 1789. In front of his lodgings stood a scarcely less venerable acacia tree, split from the root originally, and divagating in three mighty stems, of late years carefully propped. Once while he was at his country home, word was sent to him that a heavy gale had blown his acacia tree down: he returned a peremptory message that it should be put up again. Put up it was. . . . Mrs. Routh was as noticeable as her husband. She was born in the year of his election to the Presidency, 1791; so that between "her dear man," as she called him and herself – "that crathy old woman," as *he* occasionally called *her* – were nearly forty years. But she had become rapidly and prematurely old: with strongly marked features, a large moustache, and a profusion of grey hair, she paraded the streets, a spectral figure, in a little chaise drawn by a donkey and attended by a hunchback lad named Cox.' Routh is buried in the college chapel.

Rover The motor-car manufacturing company founded by William Morris (later LORD NUFFIELD) has had many changes of name in its history. In 1952 Morris Motors merged with the Austin Motor Co. to become the British Motor Corporation (BMC). In 1966 the Jaguar company joined the group, which changed its name to British Motor Holdings. Leyland Motors also acquired the Rover Company, and in 1967 the name was changed again to British Leyland

Motor Corporation. In 1975 this became Leyland Cars (BL UK Ltd) and in 1978 the name was changed yet again to Austin Morris BL Ltd. In 1986 it decided to adopt the name of one of its most successful products, the Rover car, and the name was changed to Rover Group, the car section being named Austin Rover.

(*See also* MOTOR CARS.)

Rowell & Son Ltd   *Turl Street*. A firm of gold- and silversmiths, jewellers and clockmakers established in 1797. George Rowell served as a watchmaker and came to Oxford from Newcastle-upon-Tyne in 1791. In the early 19th century the firm of Rowell & Son carried on business as clock- and watchmakers at No. 36 BROAD STREET. In 1885 Richard Sydenham Rowell, a silversmith, bought the larger premises at No. 115 HIGH STREET, which had been occupied by Wyatt & Son, the picture dealers. There is an 18th-century watch by Rowell in the ASHMOLEAN MUSEUM; and a grandfather clock made by Rowell in 1841 stands in their new shop premises in TURL STREET. The firm moved there in 1986, when the business was sold after the death of the major shareholder; it is now carried on by four of the company's long-time employees.

Rowing   Rowing has no doubt been practised for thousands of years, and where there were rowing boats there must surely have been boat races in various forms. The THAMES became navigable below Oxford during the reign of James I, and was indeed – as it still is – a Queen's highway for transportation. T.F. Dibdin, who was at Oxford from 1793–1801, recalled that, 'Boating, hunting, shooting and fishing – these formed in time of yore the chief amusements of the Oxford scholars.' G.V. Cox commented that in 1805 'boating had not yet become a systematic pursuit at Oxford. Men went down indeed to Nuneham for occasional parties in six-oared boats, but these boats belonged to the boat people'. From 1815 onwards, however, there are records of the college BUMPING RACES, so we know that rowing as an organised competitive sport at Oxford can be dated from the second decade of the 19th century.

The first 'away fixture' came in 1828 when Christ Church made a wager match to race from Westminster to Putney against the gentlemen of the Leander Club – at a cost to the Oxonians of 200 sovereigns. In the following year, 1829, came the first University BOAT RACE against Cambridge; it took place at Henley-on-Thames, ending in victory for Oxford by several lengths. In those days the captain was always the stroke of the crew, and Oxford in honour of their stroke and captain, T. Staniforth of Christ Church, wore dark-blue striped jerseys. When Cambridge adopted light blue in 1836 the tradition of BLUES was established, and for many years it was in fact the prerogative of the Boat Club to adjudicate on whether other sports could award Blues.

In 1831, there being no race against Cambridge, Oxford arranged a match against Leander, also held at Henley. The Londoners, as was their wont, insisted on a stake of £200 a side, and this was the last occasion on which a University crew is known to have raced for a wager. After a desperate struggle Leander won by two lengths. According to a report in *Bell's Life*, 'The exertions at the conclusion of the contest became lamentably apparent. Captain Shaw nearly fainted and had to be carried ashore. Mr. Bayford was obliged to retire to bed immediately; so was also one of the Oxford gentlemen.'

Though Cambridge had formed a University Boat Club in 1828, Oxford did not do so until 1839, when the college strokes and representatives of those colleges which had no boats on the river in the Bumping Races met together on 23 April at King's Boat House and formed the OXFORD UNIVERSITY BOAT CLUB, with the object of providing 'an organized system by means of which a crew might be kept in constant practice, or might with the greater ease be got up, for the defence of the University. . . .' The OUBC also took over responsibility for arranging racing dates and rules.

In the same year Henley Regatta was founded, as a direct result of the public interest generated by the two matches which had taken place on the Henley waters between Oxford and Cambridge in 1829 and between

Henry Taunt's photograph of the New College Eight alongside the college barge, c.1902

Oxford and Leander in 1831. Bearing in mind that there were neither trains nor cars at that time, so that all boats had to be transported either by water or by horse and cart, it is not surprising that the new regatta relied heavily on the support of Oxonians for its survival. At the first regatta Oxford provided three of the four entries (Etonian Club, Oxford, and Brasenose and Wadham Colleges) in the Grand Challenge Cup, which was the only open event offered. But the winners, by half a length over the Etonians, were Trinity College, Cambridge.

Undoubtedly Oxford's most famous victory at Henley came in 1843. Negotiations for a boat race against Cambridge at Easter having broken down, Oxford entered their University crew at Henley. The Grand Challenge Cup in those days was, indeed, a 'challenge' event, in which the 'winner' became the 'holder' in the following year, required to defend only against the winner of the 'challenge' rounds. Oxford, having defeated the Etonian Club and Trinity, Cambridge, in the heats, were to race against the holders, Cambridge Subscription Rooms, in the final, when their stroke, Fletcher Menzies, was taken ill. No substitutes were permitted so Oxford declared their intention of rowing with seven men; Cambridge objected, but Lord Camoys, as acting Steward of the regatta, declared that there was no rule against seven men. The Subscription Rooms' crew led briefly, but Oxford soon pulled back, forged ahead, and won handsomely. So great was the enthusiasm of the Oxford supporters, led, according to the Rev. W.E. Sherwood (*Oxford Rowing*, 1900) by 'a small, decorous, shy man in spectacles, who probably never pulled an oar in his life', that they proceeded to dismantle the toll-gate on Henley Bridge and threw it into the river. 'Fortunately no harm came of it,' Sherwood recorded, 'but a few broken heads and black eyes, and the local authorities, making allowance for the provocation, were lenient at the next petty sessions.' One must assume that 'the provocation' was the presence of an unpopular toll-gate.

Some idea of the size of the racing boats of that era may be gleaned from the fact that when their racing days were over some of them were converted into passenger boats, two stern rowlocks being removed to make way for seats, over which an awning was provided. Thus altered they could carry some twenty passengers.

In November 1867 the University was invited to race an eight-oar crew against Harvard University, the conditions being that the race should be over a straight course free from obstructions and that the teams should row without coxswains. Protracted negotiations followed concerning coxswains and possible venues, which included Lake Windermere and the River Ouse at King's Lynn, but at length Oxford's first international race was arranged to be rowed in coxed fours over the Boat Race course from Putney to Mortlake, on Friday, 27 August 1869. Harvard led by nearly a length at Hammersmith, but Oxford, with the bend in their favour, drew level at Chiswick Eyot and then forged ahead to win by some three to four lengths.

The main college events at Oxford besides the Bumping Races are the University Pairs, Fours and Sculls, instituted respectively in 1839, 1840 and 1841. Until 1851 these were all side-by-side races, starting above Iffley Lock and finishing below FOLLY BRIDGE;

but the difficulty in negotiating the Gut if the crews were racing level, and unfair advantage of the towpath station, led in 1851 to another Oxford innovation – the 'time' or 'signal' race, which still operates today. Starting from posts set some 50 yards apart, the crews race to equally spaced posts, equipped with signal arms, at the finish. As each crew passes its own finishing post the signal arm is dropped, and the interval between the signals provides the verdict.

Rowing is by no means confined to the University. Oxford Royal Regatta dates from about 1846, earning the title 'Royal' when the Prince of Wales became patron while at Oxford in about 1880. The regatta today is organised by the City of Oxford Rowing Club, which was founded in 1968 from two much older clubs – Neptune Rowing Club and Hannington Rowing Club. The oldest surviving city rowing club is the Falcon, which was founded by members of Holywell Church in 1869 for the purpose of pleasure-boating. Remarkably in that era, Falcon admitted active women members, including the daughters of several of the local boat-builders, 'who well knew how to ply an oar'.

The most recently formed club is Oxsrad Rowing Club (Oxford and District Sports and Recreation Association for the Disabled), founded in 1984 by Dr Richard Yonge, an ex-President of the University Boat Club. Oxsrad is based at Falcon Rowing Club and organises an annual regatta for the disabled.

(*See also* BOAT RACE, BUMPING RACES, BUMP SUPPERS, EIGHTS, OXFORD UNIVERSITY BOAT CLUB *and* TORPIDS.)

Royal Commissions It was widely acknowledged in the early 19th century that the University was in need of reform. Its curriculum was still severely limited; the cost of its education was high; it still declined to open its doors to DISSENTERS, JEWS and ROMAN CATHOLICS; Fellows were more likely to be elected because of their family connections than because of their learning; and as late as 1851 out of a total of 542 there were 349 in Holy Orders and the head of only one college, Merton, was not ordained. Many Fellows undertook so little teaching that an undergraduate anxious to get a good degree, or indeed any degree at all, was normally obliged to employ a private tutor, as Charles Larkyns does in Cuthbert Bede's novel *Verdant Green* (1853–7); professors found it difficult to obtain rooms in which to lecture or laboratories in which to instruct students or undertake research. Despite the strong objections of such Conservative members of CONVOCATION as those who had refused to vote for Robert Peel in 1829 when he offered himself for re-election as BURGESS for the University, having announced his support of Roman Catholic emancipation, certain limited reforms were put in hand by the University itself. Yet these reforms were condemned by Liberals as quite inadequate; and by the middle of the 1840s, after the OXFORD MOVEMENT had for a decade involved the University in other controversies, Oxford seemed as ill-equipped as ever to play its appropriate part in a rapidly changing world. The election of the Duke of Wellington, the enemy of parliamentary reform, as CHANCELLOR in 1834 had seemed a sure protection against university reform; and three years later a demand by Lord Radnor for a Royal Commission to investigate the misuse of college endowments and the misinterpretation of college statutes was rejected. Although the

Duke of Wellington proved a more astute critic of university abuses than some of his supporters had expected, and although Oxford came under increasingly vituperative attack as being characterised, in the words of the *Edinburgh Review*, by an 'utter absence of all spirit for investigation of every sort', it was not until 1850, after repeated demands by James Heywood, a Nonconformist Member of Parliament, that the Prime Minister, Lord John Russell, agreed to the establishment of a Royal Commission.

The HEBDOMADAL BOARD as a body, and several heads of colleges individually, refused to co-operate. But the Commission was eventually appointed; and the sentiments of its more liberal members – who included H.G. LIDDELL, Professor of Moral Philosophy, Francis Jeune, the Master of Pembroke, and Samuel Hinds, the Bishop of Norwich – found expression in a report which threw a harsh light on many of the abuses of which the University's critics had long complained. Indeed, in its findings that Oxford did not cater as it should for poor students, that many Fellows were inadequate, and that the requirement that most should be in Holy Orders was anachronistic, the report was condemned as 'revolutionary'. The consequent University Reform Act of 1854, largely the work of W.E. GLADSTONE, assisted by BENJAMIN JOWETT and others, provided the University with a new constitution, a remodelled CONGREGATION, and a HEBDOMADAL COUNCIL instead of the former Board; it also provided for more fellowships to be open to laymen, for restrictions on the non-residence of Fellows, for the revision of college statutes and for the creation of new Honours Schools. It paved the way, too, for the appointment of liberal-minded men to influential positions in the University: Liddell became Dean of Christ Church in 1855; MARK PATTISON was chosen as Rector of Lincoln in 1861; and Benjamin Jowett, appointed Professor of Greek in 1855, became Master of Balliol in 1870.

Reform did not, however, proceed unchecked. Conservative opinion successfully opposed, for instance, the rescinding of religious tests until 1871, and Greek remained compulsory until 1919. Extreme Liberals were persistently excluded from the Hebdomadal Council, and when voting took place in Convocation numerous Masters of Arts travelled to Oxford to rally to the Conservative cause. In 1866 the Tory WILLIAM STUBBS became Regius Professor of Modern History, succeeding the Liberal Goldwin Smith; and in 1868 another Tory, William Bright, became Regius Professor of Ecclesiastical History. Gladstone had already lost his seat as Burgess for the University, coming at the bottom of the poll.

This rallying of Oxford's Conservative forces resulted in renewed demands for University reform. In 1870 a Liberal government drew up a bill which was to be passed by Parliament, proposing the abolition of religious tests for all degrees except those in Divinity and for University posts. And in 1871 another Royal Commission was set up under the chairmanship of the Duke of Cleveland. Its report, published in 1874, eventually resulted in the University Reform Act of 1877, which further improved teaching in the University, promoted research, created new laboratories and established a Common University Fund to ensure that the richer colleges – far better endowed as they were than the University as a whole – should contribute to the common good. Demands for further reform and for a government enquiry by Royal Commission were successfully resisted by Conservatives, with the help of the Chancellor, LORD CURZON, until the outbreak of the First World War put an end to them.

But after the war the University found itself in financial difficulties, exacerbated by an agricultural depression which had led to a fall in college revenues. It was agreed, therefore, that the VICE-CHANCELLOR should be authorised to apply for a government grant, provided an investigation was undertaken into the University's revenues and expenses. There was widespread resistance to the proposal, which, it was felt, would seriously compromise the independence of the University; but opposition was finally overcome and an initial grant of £30,000 was accepted. At the same time another Royal Commission was appointed under the chairmanship of H.H. Asquith, resulting in renewed criticisms of the idea of reform. 'Reform a university!' exclaimed Lord Hugh Cecil, who had been elected Burgess for the University in 1910. 'You may as well reform a cheese. There is a certain flavour about a university as there is about a cheese, springing from its antiquity, which may very easily be lost by mishandling.' The report of the Commission led, however, to the University Reform Act of 1923, by which faculties were reorganised, the duties of professors defined, dons permitted to retire with pensions, and entrance to the University made dependent upon examination – either RESPONSIONS or its equivalent – rather than upon the separate college examinations of the past.

(*See also* FRANKS COMMISSION.)

Royal Oak *42–4 Woodstock Road.* Originally a 17th-century coaching inn containing coachmen's and grooms' cottages on the north side (*see* TRANSPORT). Wallpaper from 1720 was discovered in about 1950.

Royal Oxford Hotel *Park End Street.* Built in 1934 on the site of the old HOLLYBUSH INN under a building lease granted to HALL'S BREWERY on land owned by the Dean and Chapter of CHRIST CHURCH CATHEDRAL. The hotel is now one of J. Lyons and Co. Ltd's Embassy Hotels. There are twenty-five bedrooms.

Ruskin, John (*1819–1900*). The son of a well-to-do wine merchant and of an evangelical Puritan of such strong convictions that she was said to turn her husband's pictures to face the wall on Sundays, Ruskin was educated at first by his mother, then by tutors and at a day school in Camberwell before going up to Christ Church as a gentleman-commoner in 1836. His mother took lodgings in the HIGH STREET and his father came there every weekend. The son was rarely parted from either of them – except during the brief period of his marriage to Ephemia ('Effie') Chalmers Gray – and the three were almost always together when they travelled in England and abroad. At Oxford Ruskin displayed those talents as artist and writer which were to bring him fame, though he was never a 'pure scholar'. After two unsuccessful submissions in 1837 and 1838, he won the NEWDIGATE PRIZE in 1839 with his poem on 'Salsetta and Elephanta'. He graduated MA in 1843, having already started work on his *Modern Painters* and having developed those ideas which were to find expression in

John Ruskin, founder of the Ruskin School of Drawing and Fine Art, with his friend Sir Henry Acland, photographed by Acland's daughter in 1893.

The Seven Lamps of Architecture (1849) and *The Stones of Venice* (1851–3). Ruskins's friendship with SIR HENRY ACLAND was an important factor in the creation of the UNIVERSITY MUSEUM. In 1870 he was appointed to the chair of Fine Arts endowed by Felix Slade (1790–1868), the virtuoso and art benefactor. He later founded the RUSKIN SCHOOL OF DRAWING AND FINE ART, to which he presented several important works and in which he himself taught. His professorial lectures were always crowded, the numbers wishing to attend his first being so great that it had to be given in the SHELDONIAN THEATRE. In April 1871 he was appointed an Honorary Fellow of Corpus Christi College, where his rooms became 'an intellectual centre of the highest kind'.

Ruskin College Established in 1899 by two American non-collegiate students and named after JOHN RUSKIN, the artist and social reformer. At first located in ST GILES' and known as Ruskin Hall until 1903, when it settled in its permanent site in WALTON STREET, it was set up as a new type of educational institution. The main innovation was to provide residential education for working men (and women from 1919), but the scheme went beyond that to include extension classes throughout Britain as well as correspondence courses. Moreover, several local Ruskin Halls were established in Birmingham, Liverpool, Manchester and Stockport. Particularly significant was the close connection with the organised labour movement, notably the trade unions and the co-operative societies. A number of Oxford University dons were closely associated with the college from the start, and these early supporters included Professor York Powell, Edward Caird and Sidney Ball.

Since a major purpose of the college was to provide education for future leaders of the Labour movement,

the courses were mainly in the Social Sciences. One consequence of this approach was the help it gave towards the development of the study of Political Science within the University. At first the funds came largely from private and philanthropic sources, but increasingly more came from the trade unions – a development which, during the first ten years, coincided with a period of growing trade-union activity. Consequently some students and ex-students suggested that the college should be in the hands of the Labour movement and fully separated from the University. Fearing that the college might be taken over by the University, they further recommended that there should be no philanthropists or Oxford dons on the executive committee. In the ensuing argument the Principal, Dennis Hird, was dismissed; the students went on strike; and a number of them left to form the Central Labour College.

The college's response to these events of 1909 was to meet part of the dissident students' demands by changing the constitution. Thenceforth, the executive committee was to be composed of representatives of working-class organisations which supported the college financially. At the same time the college came closer to the University in that certain of its students could sit the University's Diploma in Economics and Political Science. By this time the college's work was centred on Oxford: throughout the rest of the country the local Ruskin Halls and the local classes were discontinued, though the correspondence courses continued until they were taken over by the Trades Union Congress in 1964.

Apart from its closure during the two world wars, that remained the pattern of the college's work for the next half-century. Students came for one or two years and sat the University diplomas (a second being that in Public and Social Administration). In the inter-war years the numbers were small; as few as thirty might attend during the years of economic depression. Few people were willing to give up jobs for a risky future, and trade unions did not have the funds to supply many scholarships or other financial support. Many of the students could get grants for only one year and thus could not complete the two-year course and sit the diploma examinations. However, a few who did so were able to go on to other educational work to obtain degrees or to go into teaching.

After the Second World War the demand for places grew enormously and new premises were urgently required. They were provided by The Rookery in Old HEADINGTON, an 18th-century house, latterly occupied by Sir Michael Sadler (1861–1943), the educational pioneer and art patron, which was acquired when Lionel Elvin was Principal (1945–50). During the principalship of his successor, H.D. Hughes (1950–79), the college underwent dramatic developments. New buildings were erected or acquired on both sites and the total number of students reached some 180; from the late 1960s the college developed its own diploma courses, parallel to those of the University; and it began to house other facilities and activities, usually separately organised and separately financed, including the Trade Union Research Unit and the Trade Union International Research and Education Group.

By the 1970s and 1980s much of the financial support for Ruskin College came from the Department of Education and Science (which also provided grants to most students) and from the Department of Health and Social Security (for the course for social workers). Under J.D. Hughes, Principal from 1979, new developments included a tripartite educational experiment with the Workers' Educational Association and the Open University, aimed at local students, as well as a separate scheme also 'outside the walls', together with the WEA, specifically for trade-union students. Its main work remained the courses provided for the 180 full-time students.

Dr Stephen Yeo is the present Principal.

(Pollins, Harold, *The History of Ruskin College*, Ruskin College Library, Occasional Publication, No. 3, 1984.)

Ruskin School of Drawing and Fine Art

74 High Street. Founded by JOHN RUSKIN in 1871 while he was Slade Professor of Fine Art (1870–9), it occupied part of the ASHMOLEAN MUSEUM until moving to its present premises in 1975. Governed by a Board of Trustees representative of University bodies and acting through the Ruskin Master of Drawing, it offered a certificate course in Fine Art until 1978, since when it has prepared members of the University for the three-year Bachelor of Fine Art degree course. Each year some seventeen students are admitted.

Russian Orthodox Church   see GREEK ORTHODOX CHURCH.

Rye St Antony School   *Pullen's Lane, Headington.*

An independent Roman Catholic girls' school founded in 1930 by two teachers, Elizabeth Rendall and Ivy King, following their conversion to Roman Catholicism, it took its name from the church of St Antony in Rye, Sussex. Starting life at No. 86 Hamilton Road with eight young day pupils, it moved in 1931 to No. 84 WOODSTOCK ROAD, where it began to take boarders and to expand. At the outbreak of war in 1939 the school moved to Langley Lodge, PULLEN'S LANE, while the Woodstock Road premises were occupied for the duration of the war by the city of Oxford. By 1944 there were forty-two boarders and seventeen day girls, and to provide for increasing numbers the school bought the Croft and the Cottage in Pullen's Lane. In 1960 Miss Rendall died and in 1963 the school became an Educational Trust with a board of governors. In 1966 an assembly hall, the Elizabeth Rendall building designed by Peter Bosanquet and John Perryman Associates was completed, the school by this time numbering 108 boarders and forty-seven day girls between the ages of eight and eighteen. In 1970 a heated open-air swimming pool was added. By 1972 there were 189 pupils and the school was organised in four groups for social and competitive purposes – Hendred, Holywell, Stonor and Binsey, named for Catholic historical association in the Oxford area. At the Golden Jubilee of the school in 1980 Miss King (headmistress 1959–76) was awarded the Papal Medal Pro Ecclesia et Pontifice for her services to Catholic education. In 1986 King House, for junior boarders, and a science building were opened, both designed by the Barnett, Briscoe and Gotch partnership. In 1986 there were some 200 boarders, all Roman Catholics, and 100 day girls of various denominations. (*See also* ROMAN CATHOLICS.)

Ryle, Gilbert   (*1900–1976*).

Won a classical scholarship to The Queen's College from Brighton College and obtained Firsts in LITERAE HUMANIORES and in the newly established School of Philosophy, Politics and Economics in 1924. The following year he was elected a Student of Christ Church. He later became a Fellow of Magdalen and Waynflete Professor of Metaphysical Philosophy. One of the most influential and original philosophers of his generation, he played a prominent part in making Oxford a leading centre of Philosophy after the Second World War. The new degree of Bachelor of Philosophy was introduced at his instigation. He died unmarried and chose to leave a large part of his fortune to Hertford College because it was so less well endowed than those colleges of which he had been a Fellow.

Sacred Heart, Church of *Blackbird Leys*. Because of the expansion of the population of COWLEY a separate parish for ROMAN CATHOLICS was founded here in 1966. The church was originally built as a multi-purpose structure to serve as both church and hall. The architect, Charles MacCallum, has now separated the building. The church is square in plan and seats 150. The altar is of Clipsham stone (*see* STONE), inlaid with marble and travertine on a brick base. Tabernacle and font are in cast bronze and are the work of Jacqueline Steiger.

Sacred Poem Prize Founded in 1848 by an unknown benefactor, the prize is awarded triennially for a poem of between sixty and three hundred lines on a prescribed subject written by any graduate member of the University; it cannot be won more than twice by the same person. Its current value is £1100. There have been only three winners of both the Sacred Poem and NEWDIGATE Prizes: Frank Taylor (Newdigate 1894) who won in 1905 ('Esther'); John Fuller (1960) who won in 1977 ('Bel and the Dragon'); and, most notably, Phyllis Hartnoll (1929) who won in 1947 ('St Luke') and again in 1965 ('The Mammon of Unrighteousness'). Only two other entrants have won the Sacred Poem Prize twice: Charles Box in 1932 ('The Shunamite Woman') and in 1938 ('Naaman'); and Viola Mary Caird in 1962 ('The Death of Ahab') and in 1974 ('Thou shalt see my back parts but my face shall not be seen'). On five consecutive occasions (1962, 1965, 1968, 1971 and 1974) the winner was a member of St Hugh's College. The Rev. Adam Fox, Professor of Poetry (1938–43) won the prize in 1929 ('Babylon'). The prize was not awarded in 1881, 1899, 1935 and 1959, and was suspended in 1917, 1920, 1941 and 1944.

Sadler's Balloon Ascents James Sadler was born in Oxford on 27 March 1753. While working as a laboratory technician in the Department of Chemistry at the University he began experimenting with small gas-filled balloons. In 1784 he constructed a hydrogen-filled balloon, 36 feet in circumference, which was launched at Oxford on 9 February 'before a great concourse of people' and was picked up in Kent. Later that year he constructed a much larger balloon, 170 feet in circumference, which he inflated over a contained fire on 4 October 1784. The balloon was then untethered and in the early morning James Sadler 'ascended into the Atmosphere'. He came down about 6 miles from Oxford, between Islip and Woodeaton, after the balloon had risen to an estimated height of 3600 feet.

Sadler's second flight was on 4 November 1784 from the BOTANIC GARDEN, then known as the Physic Garden. This was in a hydrogen balloon and was watched by thousands of spectators. He landed some twenty minutes later near Aylesbury. Sadler gave up ballooning for twenty-five years, but made an ascent from Merton Field on 7 July 1810, followed by many subsequent flights. He died on 27 March 1828 and is buried in the churchyard of ST PETER-IN-THE-EAST. In the church, now the library of St Edmund Hall, is a plaque which reads:

To the Memory
of
James Sadler
of this City
1753–1828

The First English Aeronaut
He made his earliest Ascent,
At Oxford October 4 1784

The bicentenary of this event was celebrated on 4 October 1984 when a balloonist took off from Merton Field and the Lord Mayor unveiled a plaque set into the wall by DEADMAN'S WALK reading:

James Sadler, son of an Oxford pastry cook, the first Englishman to make an aerial voyage in a hot-air balloon, ascends from Merton Field on 7 July 1810.

James Sadler
1753–1828
First English Aeronaut
who in a fire balloon made a successful ascent
from near this place – 4 October 1784
to land near Woodeaton

St Alban Hall One of the mediaeval ACADEMIC
HALLS to survive into the 19th century. After leasing it
for over a hundred years from the nuns of LITTLEMORE
PRIORY, Merton College bought the property in 1549
as a means of meeting the problem of housing
the growing number of fee-paying undergraduate
COMMONERS in a college of ancient foundation. In
the following half-century it had its best days, as one of
the largest surviving academic halls, the early 17th-
century dramatist Philip Massinger being among its
members. In the 19th century it reached its lowest
point, at one time being empty of members. In spite
of the defiant views of its Principal, the University
Commission of 1877 (*see* ROYAL COMMISSIONS) recommended its incorporation into Merton College,
which took place in 1881. The OXFORD ALMANACK of
1851 shows the buildings that were demolished in
1904 to provide space for the building of St Alban's
Quad of Merton College.

St Alban the Martyr, Church of *Charles Street*.
In 1889 the original brick Mission Church of St Alban
was built to the designs of A.M. Mowbray as a
daughter-church of ST MARY AND ST JOHN to serve the
needs of the expanding population of East Oxford. By
1910 there were times when 200 communicants
crowded into a building designed for 120, and by 1912
the church had been enlarged by the addition of a
temporary corrugated-iron extension to the north
aisle; the population of St Alban's district at this time
numbered some 3000. A larger church, to cost an
estimated £5000, was proposed, and a house in Percy
Street, with its own chapel, was bought in 1913 for
£610 as a curate's house and church hall. It was not,
however, until 1928 that the BISHOP OF OXFORD laid the
foundation stone of the present building (designed by
T. Lawrence Dale), which was dedicated in 1933. The
architect's plans for a church to seat 390 were never
fully realised, nor were the hopes of forming an
independent St Alban's parish. From 1933 to 1982 the
church was served by priests-in-charge; since then by
the curate of its mother-church.

An unassuming, single-storey brick building, the
church has a small bell-turret at the west end; over the
south porch is a bas-relief by J.H. Brookes, Principal of
the College of Technology (*see* POLYTECHNIC), and the
hinges on the main doors are in the shape of Roman
swords in allusion to St Alban's service as a Roman
soldier before his conversion to Christianity and later
martyrdom. Of the many ornaments expressing Christian iconography and the High Anglican temper of the
church's foundation, the incised slate Stations of the
Cross by Eric Gill are the most remarkable. They were
executed between 1938 and 1941 at a cost, through the
artist's generosity, of only 7 guineas each; there is only
one other identical set, to be found in Westminster
Cathedral. A marble pulpit complements the double-
cube marble altar, and a reredos mural (1946) by Peter
Greenham (now RA), hidden since 1949 behind a
curtain, depicts St Alban's vision of the Resurrection.
The painting was commissioned for £160 by the Rev.

Kenrick Joyce, priest-in-charge 1943–6, whose son,
the Rev. John Joyce, was priest-in-charge 1977–80.
An extension at the south-east corner of the church for
a parish room and offices has been added to serve
community needs.

St Aldate, Church of *St Aldate's*. First recorded
early in the 12th century, the church is probably older
than this, perhaps taking its name from Eldad, a
Welsh churchman of the 5th century who died in
battle resisting the Saxons under Hengist. ANTHONY
WOOD wrote that the church 'seemeth to me to have
been very ancient, if we regard to whom it was
dedicated and whose name it bears'. (The only other
church dedicated to St Aldate is in Gloucester.) The
church has been known as St Ald's, St Toll's, St
Olave's and often as St Old's. Some authorities
suggest that the name is a corruption of 'old gate'; but
the city gate nearest to the church was South Gate, and
the now demolished Church of St Michael at the
South Gate was closer to the gate than St Aldate's.
The advowson was shared by Abingdon Abbey and ST
FRIDESWIDE'S PRIORY until it passed to the Crown at
the Dissolution of the Monasteries. In 1629 it was
granted to Pembroke College by Charles I. In 1859 it
was sold by the college to Samuel Hanson, who vested
it in Simeon's Trust, an evangelical body, the present
patron. The living was a poor one in a poor parish, and
the rectors were non-resident until the arrival of
Henry Swabey in 1850. His successor, 'the good and
mild and loving' A.M.W. Christopher, Rector from
1859 to 1905 and founder of St Matthew, GRANDPONT,
established St Aldate's as a centre of evangelical
influence in town and University and was the
originator of the Inter-collegiate Christian Union.
Among his successors were C.M. Chavasse (1922–8),
first Principal of St Peter's Hall (now College), and
later Bishop of Rochester; F.E. Lunt (1943–51), later
Bishop of Stepney; J.E. Fison (curate 1937–40), later
Bishop of Salisbury; and Canon O.K. de Berry
(1952–74), who established the church bookshop
nearby, created Commonwealth House, a hostel for
overseas students, and built the Catacombs Youth
Centre in LITTLEGATE STREET.

The 12th-century church remains visible only in
the Norman arcading of the north chancel aisle. A
14th-century crypt lies below the east end of the south
aisle. From about 1530 until 1843 an upper storey
above the south aisle housed the library of BROADGATES
HALL (later Pembroke College). In the 19th century
the church was extensively rebuilt and enlarged: in
1832 the interior was remodelled to the designs of H.J.
Underwood, and in 1862 the Rector's cousin, J.T.
Christopher, carried out further alterations, adding
north and south chapels, and the east window, the
glass of which is in memory of A.M.W. Christopher
and contains the figures of Bishop Hannington, early
missionary to Uganda; St Paul; Christ; Philip the
Evangelist; and Henry Martyn, pioneer missionary to
Iran. After the spire was taken down in 1865, the new
tower and spire were built in 1873 to the designs of
J.T. Christopher. Among its many possessions, the
church has a 15th-century font with a 17th-century
cover; a chained Book of Homilies; and an organ
(1925) given by LORD NUFFIELD.

St Aldate's Probably Oxford's oldest street, it led
from the THAMES to the highest part of the early

settlement at CARFAX. Until 1300 that part of the street between Carfax and the South Gate of the city contained many houses occupied by JEWS and was known as Jewry or Great Jewry. By 1342 the street was known as Fish Street. At its northern end was the permanent fish market, with stalls against the old TOWN HALL building. These stretched right across the street on market days. The South Gate of the city was situated between Christ Church and BREWER STREET and was demolished around 1613. The mediaeval church of St Michael at the South Gate was demolished in 1525 to make way for the building of Christ Church. The southern part of the street was known variously as Southbridge Street (c. 1225), Grandpont (1282), Fisher Street (1433) and Bridge Street (1751). By 1772 the whole street was called Fish Street, but it was renamed St Aldate's in the 19th century after the church of ST ALDATE, the name possibly being a corruption of 'old gate'.

On the east side of the street the town hall stands close to Carfax. Before the present town hall was built, NIXON'S FREE GRAMMAR SCHOOL was in the courtyard behind the old town hall. The MUSEUM OF OXFORD is on the corner of BLUE BOAR STREET in that part of the town-hall building which used to house the CENTRAL LIBRARY. The 17th-century timber-framed building with two gables on the opposite corner of Blue Boar Street was formerly the Unicorn inn (closed in 1670), behind which in 1635 there was a REAL TENNIS court. The building was also used for the performance of plays (see THEATRE). When the Unicorn closed as an inn, the building was used for many years as a University lodging house, among its occupants being the poet Hilaire Belloc. Further down the street Wren's Tom Tower stands over the main entrance to Christ Church. The Memorial Garden leading to CHRIST CHURCH MEADOW and BROAD WALK adjoins the college, and on the south side is the MUSIC Faculty and the BATE COLLECTION, a site formerly occupied by St Catherine's and Linacre Colleges. Beyond FLOYD'S ROW is the police station. Among buildings which have been demolished to make way for these developments are the Green Dragon, Wheatsheaf and Plough inns and the Kemp Hall Bindery. Part of SALTER BROS' boatyard at the north end of FOLLY BRIDGE has now been converted into a public house, the HEAD OF THE RIVER.

On the west side of St Aldate's, just north of Folly Bridge, is the Old Toll House built in 1844 and in use until 1850 when the debt incurred in building the bridge had been paid off. A hotel was to be built between the bridge and Thames Street. Plans were drawn up and pile-driving started but the developers went into liquidation. After lying vacant for some years, the site is now occupied by housing. The old Morris Garages building opposite the police station was converted into the new Crown Courts building, opened in 1986 (see COURTS). No. 83, opposite the Memorial Garden, is ALICE's Shop – the old Sheep's Shop in Lewis Carroll's *Through the Looking-glass and What Alice Found There* (1871) (see also CHARLES DODGSON). Above it is the ELIZABETH RESTAURANT. Beyond CLARK'S ROW is the building of the Oxford University CATHOLIC CHAPLAINCY, designed by Ahrends, Burton and Koralek in 1972, and the Newman Rooms. At Nos 86–7, next to ROSE PLACE, is BISHOP KING'S PALACE, named after Bishop Robert King, the last ABBOT OF OSENEY and the first BISHOP OF OXFORD.

When a 17th-century house at No. 89 was demolished in 1985 the Oxford Archaeological Unit discovered in the excavations two leather shoes of a type known to date from the 9th century, thus providing evidence that Oxford was a settlement long before it was mentioned in the Anglo-Saxon Chronicle of 911 AD. The shoes were discovered preserved in wet clay, in a ditch outside the south CITY WALL, which may have served as a mill stream for ST FRIDESWIDE'S PRIORY. In 1986 Christ Church built a block for student accommodation behind the demolished house. Beyond the narrow Brewer Street, on the line of the city wall, is Pembroke College, next to St Aldate's Church. North of PEMBROKE STREET the FREWIN CLUB is at No. 98 and the General Post Office, built in 1878, is opposite Blue Boar Street. The Information Office is opposite the town hall.

St Aloysius, Church of *25 Woodstock Road.* In 1870, the Jesuits, tired of repairing their chapel in ST CLEMENT'S, longed for 'a fine handsome church' where they could perform the liturgy 'in a grand and imposing style'. With bequests from Lord Bute, Baroness Weld and JOHN HENRY NEWMAN, a site near ST GILES' was purchased, and Joseph Hansom, designer of the Hansom cab, was engaged as architect. His first design was rejected for being too like New College chapel. The second, in the Victorian-Gothic style, suffered a set-back after work had begun: a change of plan necessitated demolishing the half-built walls of the apse and the materials being sold before work could be resumed. However, eighteen months later, in November 1875, the building was ready for the ceremony of dedication, memorable for CARDINAL MANNING's sermon berating the University for abandoning Aristotle. The church is built of yellow brick with stone quoins and a slate roof. It is approached from the road through a stone arch, leading on to a small courtyard. The east façade, pierced by a large rose window, has a stair-turret on the southern corner. The interior is long and narrow, with seating for 400. A holy-water font between the arches that separate the narthex from the nave is a memorial to Gerard Manley Hopkins, priest at St Aloysius in 1878–9. Arcades along the north and south aisles are decorated with slim shafts of red and green marble, which soar up past the lancet windows of the clerestory to join the dark green of the painted barrel-vault. A gilded crucifix of Christ in Majesty, the work of Arthur Pollen, hangs from a central point above the marble altar-rails. To the left is the pulpit with carved figures; a memorial to Father Parkinson, a convert from Anglican Orders, and parish priest in 1876–87. Marble panels, which used to decorate the walls of the nave, were painted over in 1954, as they were thought to distract from the altar and the apse with its imposing double row of saints, angel frieze, pinnacled tabernacle and twenty circles, containing carved reliefs of Fathers of the Church. The murals at the rear of the church were completed in 1979. In 1981, when the Jesuits handed St Aloysius over to the Birmingham Diocese, the chapels lost much that was of interest, notably the collection of relics bequeathed by Hartwell de la Garde Grissell of Oxford in 1907. The Relic Chapel is now the baptistry. The parish includes care of those Catholics in the RADCLIFFE INFIRMARY and Oxford PRISON.

St Andrew, Church of *Old Headington*. The village of HEADINGTON was a royal domain in Anglo-Saxon times: from it by AD 912 the fortified borough of Oxford had been established to guard the crossing of the THAMES. A timber-built chapel of the Saxon kings was replaced in the mid-12th century after Henry I had granted to ST FRIDESWIDE'S PRIORY in 1122 the building of a stone church. The work was undertaken at the expense of Hugh de Pluggenait, Lord of the Manor from 1142 to 1201, a Breton knight in the service of Queen Matilda, in thanksgiving for one of his relatives who had had his eyesight, hearing and right arm miraculously restored at ST FRIDES-WIDE's shrine. At the Dissolution of the Monasteries the church passed to Cardinal College (later Christ Church) and by 1547 had been sold to John Brome, Lord of the Manor. It was in the possession of successive Lords of the Manor until Mrs Martha Rawlinson, who had acquired the advowson in 1879, gave it to Keble College, the present patron, in 1927.

The fine chancel arch of *c*.1160 remains from the original building. In the 13th century a south aisle was built to form a Lady Chapel. By 1500 the tower had been completed, probably with the advice of WILLIAM ORCHARD, the master-mason who designed the nave-vaulting of St Frideswide's Priory Church (now CHRIST CHURCH CATHEDRAL), owner of property and quarries in Headington. Renovations to the tower were carried out in 1679 and 1972; and its six bells were rehung in 1967. The oldest (mid-15th-century) bell bears the inscription '*Sancta Margareta Ora Pro Nobis*'; two more bells were added in 1974.

Despite some work being undertaken during the 18th century, by 1862 the church was in serious need of repair. In 1864 the necessary restoration was carried out, including the extension westwards of the nave, under the direction of J.C. BUCKLER, at a cost of £3000. In 1881 a north aisle and vestry were added, to the designs of William Wilkinson at a further cost of £2300. Between 1977 and 1979 further restoration work was completed.

The organ, by J.W. Walker and Sons, installed in 1967, is from Merton College chapel. The east window (1891), by Henry Holiday, depicts the Adoration of the Magi and commemorates E.F.G. Tyndale, vicar from 1870 to 1889. In the baptistry a small window records the inauguration in 1961 of the 'Fish' (Good Neighbour) scheme, which began in the parish and has spread beyond it. In the churchyard a loyal supporter of Charles I has the following tombstone inscription:

> Here lyeth John,
> Who to the King did belong,
> He liv'd to be old
> And yet dyed Young.

In Memory of John Young who dyed Nov. 19, 1688 aged 100 years.

St Andrew, Church of *Linton Road*. Following vigorous demands from as early as 1881 for an evangelical church in NORTH OXFORD, in 1905 a parish was taken from part of ST PHILIP AND ST JAMES and of ST JOHN THE BAPTIST, ROGERS STREET, the patronage being vested in the Council of WYCLIFFE HALL. A temporary iron church was built in 1905; and St George's Chapel, which was due to be demolished, was offered free, to be re-erected in its place. The offer was rejected and despite some opposition to the proposed plans – one local correspondent claiming that a 'Norman church will look elephantine dumped down amidst twentieth-century North Oxford villas' and that a 'more cheerful style of architecture' was needed 'where there is not ornate ritual to add warmth and colour, and perhaps beauty' to the 'comparative simplicity of the services' – the present Norman-style church seating 650 was built in 1906–7 to the designs of A.R.G. Fenning. Pevsner described it as 'rock-faced, large, and rather mechanical-looking'. The site at the north-east corner of Linton Road and Northmoor Road was given by St John's College and £5000 towards the cost of the building was raised by the Rev. the Hon. W. Talbot Rice (rector, 1893–1902, of ST PETER-LE-BAILEY (now St Peter's College chapel)), who suggested the dedication to St Andrew.

The church consists of a wide clerestoried nave, with aisles, and an apsidal chancel containing seven windows designed to provide a gradation of light from the central east window of blue outwards through ruby, orange, green and clear windows, altered in 1928 to provide more light at the centre by moving the ruby windows to the extremities. In addition, there are north and south porches at the west end of the nave, a south-east vestry, a two-storey south-west porch and corresponding north-west offices (1959), a chapel (1964) at the east end of the north aisle, and in the west gallery an organ (1975) by Reeves of Stoke-on-Trent, which replaced one built (*c*.1914) by Lindsey Garrard of Lechlade. A tower, proposed in the original plans, has not been built. A former incumbent, F.J. Taylor (vicar 1954–5), later Principal of Wycliffe Hall, became Bishop of Sheffield.

St Anne's College Traces its direct ancestry to the body that initiated higher education for women in Oxford. In 1878 the Association for the Education of Women in Oxford (AEW) was founded, largely on the initiative of a group of liberal-minded dons. Behind this move there were several pressures: the mounting national campaign for women's intellectual rights; the needs of newly developing girls' schools; the eagerness of dons' wives and daughters to share in the intellectual life of the University. In October 1879, Lady Margaret Hall and Somerville College opened as halls of residence for women, while still remaining under the academic control of the AEW. This left, as the largest group of women students, those living in private homes. The question of how they were to be designated was the subject of mild controversy: 'Unattached Students' was deemed to have undesirable implications; in the *Calendar* for 1890–1 the term 'Home Students' first appears; finally, in 1898 the title 'Society of Oxford Home Students' was formally adopted. Much later, the story is told that, when this title had to be latinised, the VICE-CHANCELLOR, Dr Blakiston, a veteran opponent of degrees for women, took his revenge by saddling the Society with the clumsiest Latin rendering: *Societas Mulierum Oxoniae Privatim Studentium* (*Soc. mul.Ox.priv.stud.*).

The Society of Home Students owed much to the group of distinguished men who supported its early development. Professor T.H. Green was the first honorary secretary of the AEW while his wife was associated with Home Students for forty-two years. Arthur Sidgwick lectured to the women on a wide range of topics. Professor Nettleship's library, given

373

by his widow, became the core of the society's library (known in early days as the Nettlebed). Professor Geldart's library later formed the foundation of St Anne's unusually good law library. H.A.L. FISHER and GILBERT MURRAY were strong supporters. Arthur Johnson of All Souls, a vivid and pugnacious Oxford character, worked in partnership with his wife for 'the cause' and backed her up all through the long period, from 1883 to 1921, when, first as lady secretary of the AEW and then as Principal of the Home Students, she ran the rapidly expanding society.

Mrs Bertha Johnson conducted the affairs of the Home Students from her NORTH OXFORD home, in the midst of bringing up a family and organising her household. She combined intense femininity with a passionate belief that women should cultivate their intellectual powers to the full. The concept of 'Home Students' – young women living in cultured homes while pursuing their studies under the best possible guidance, exactly fitted her ideal and she advocated this pattern, as against collegiate life for women, right to the end. Equally, she was sceptical about degrees for women: the BA degree, she declared, was a boot made to suit men. These – to us surprising – views probably constituted one factor in the slowness with which the women's position developed in Oxford. Nonetheless, Mrs Johnson was a powerful campaigner, though there was nothing strident in her methods. The male stronghold must be stormed by female propriety as well as determination: *chi va piano, va sano*, she said.

A corporate society almost independent of buildings recalls the mediaeval students who could migrate at will. Mrs Johnson harangued her flock over cups of tea in her own house and it was not until 1910 that a small common room was opened in SHIP STREET, purchased by Mrs Johnson and friends. In true Oxford style administration received no attention at all and the finances of the society were ludicrous. Mrs Johnson's post was honorary and she hoped that 'a lady resident in Oxford . . . willing to undertake the work as a service' would succeed her. By 1899 she was allowed £6 per annum for a Secretary–Vice-Principal but all other costs were met from her pocket. Students paid separately for classes and tutorials. A great variety pressed in. Many names represent important Oxford families: Price, Sidgwick, Murray, Butler, Lane-Poole. Foreign students rapidly appeared, and the first Annual Report stresses the importance of North American and European students. The educational policy of the society was open and experimental: this had academic dangers but has left a valuable trait in the college's character. By *c*.1910 there were about 100 students, of whom fifteen or sixteen were North Americans. In 1908 a hostel for Catholic students was founded at CHERWELL EDGE, to be followed by Springfield St Mary (Anglican) on the BANBURY ROAD.

The style of the early Home Students was a mixture of relentless determination and delicate caution. They trooped earnestly to lectures, sitting in a bunch as inconspicuously as possible. Chaperones attended everywhere and North Oxford ladies were hard-worked. The college still possesses three cartoons from S.P. Hall's *Oxford Sketches: Photographs of a series of One Hundred Caricatures produced in 1864 to 1866* parodying these early lectures. A high idealism was embodied in the Beaver crest, adopted in 1913. The Butler sisters promoted this, explaining that the

A skit by S.P. Hall on the lectures for women which were instituted in Oxford in the 1860s, several years before the foundation in 1878 of the Association for the Education of Women in Oxford, which later became St Anne's College.

beaver was communally minded and served others but returned to her own little lodge, 'remaining at heart a Home Student'. Two complacent Beavers still preside over the main door of the college. The Butlers carried forward the tradition of Mrs Johnson: R.F.B., who assisted her from 1906, was later Modern History tutor and Vice-Principal, then Dean of Degrees until 1942, and remained closely associated until her death in 1983; C.V.B. was Economics tutor from 1914 to 1945 and in her involvement with the city social services and Barnett House kept alive the 'service' aspect of the society. A.M.A.H. Rogers, a daughter of Professor Thorold Rogers, who in 1873 won a Worcester award before her sex was revealed, was the first secretary to the Home Students governing body and a leading campaigner in the fight for women's degrees, recorded in her *Degrees by Degrees* (1938).

Informality had gone so far that for nearly thirty years women had been attending University lectures and for nearly twenty they had been taking University examinations, under the aegis of the unofficial AEW, when, in 1908, the University decided to shut its eyes no longer. An official Delegacy for Women Students was set up in 1910 and one of its first acts was to create a governing body for the Home Students, with Professor Geldart as chairman and a grant of £25 per annum for administration. The First World War brought development to a standstill, but below the surface change was eroding attitudes. So it was that, after years of bitter conflict, the revolution was accomplished with swiftness and calm. In February 1920, Professor Geldart proposed the Titulus xxiii, granting degrees to women. After the victory he was seen shaking hands with Miss Rogers, who summed up the outcome of battle thus: 'We were in the wilderness for more than forty years, but when we entered the promised land we came in peacefully, not with shouts and blowing of rams' horns; and Jericho opened its gates and welcomed us with smiles.'

The inter-war years constitute the first stage in the transition from Society of Home Students to St Anne's College. Mrs Johnson still presided over its inception, when numbers shot up and in 1920 250 Home Students had to be matriculated all at once. At the age of seventy-three she interviewed every applicant, arranged their courses and supervised their living arrangements, but when she resigned in 1921 her highly personal style – 'a benevolent autocracy of a vivid and somewhat unconventional style' – ended. Her successor Christine Burrows might be described as halfway between the amateur lady and the modern professional woman. The society began to take institutional shape. In 1921 both the AEW and the Delegacy for Women Students were abolished and the governing body of the Society became a delegacy directly under the University, chaired by the Vice-Chancellor or his representative. Finance was the most crucial problem: in 1921 the society's capital assets were about £2000 and its annual income, apart from student fees, just over £500. Voluntary effort had carried it far, but its dedicated Principal and band of tutors had to live. In 1922 the University began to make grants towards administrative salaries. Through a general appeal for the Women's Colleges, a tutorial fund was set up, but for the bulk of their income tutors still relied on 'piece-work', teaching up to twenty to thirty hours a week in their own homes. They had no corporate status until 1926 when a Tutors' Meeting was officially constituted with the right to appoint four members to the delegacy.

An urgent need was for a *locus* more adequate than the little Ship Street house. In 1921 the University acquired Holywell House (No. 1 Jowett Walk), largely paid for by the windfall of accumulated dues and fees from the women claiming degrees. The Home Students were allotted part of this. So the Nettleship library was transferred from the attics of the CLARENDON BUILDING, the Junior Common Room got the large music room, Principal and tutors established themselves in the bedrooms and administration was crammed into the back quarters. At the same time the system of 'hostesses' was developed. Mrs Johnson had relied on dons' families to set the moral tone. As numbers increased, other North Oxford ladies had to be recruited, but never as 'landladies'. They were handpicked and carefully drilled in their moral and disciplinary roles, playing a vital part in this period.

When Grace Hadow succeeded Christine Burrows in 1929 – the jubilee year – the first hints of a major benefaction were in the air. In 1932 Mrs Hartland bought from St John's College the freehold of a site between the Banbury Road and WOODSTOCK ROAD. With hindsight it is clear that this gift to the society was of crucial importance, yet at the time her plan to build was received with some misgiving. Did the society want buildings? Would this change its character? In the event, Sir Giles Gilbert Scott was commissioned to design a building to be erected in stages, of which the library and lecture rooms were completed in 1937. In the same period Mrs Musgrave left to the society the remainder of the lease on her home at No. 1 SOUTH PARKS ROAD. This was its administrative, tutorial and social home from 1936 to 1952. Another indication of a growing institutionalism is seen in the increasing solidarity of the tutorial body. In 1929 it successfully claimed a share in the appointment of the Principal and in 1930 the delegates agreed that for tutorial appointments one tutor at least should sit on the selection committee. But financial problems were the price paid for a more formal structure. The Cassel Trust gave support and by the 1930s the University grant towards salaries had risen to £100 per annum, but the Home Students still survived only by devoted, underpaid labour and the voluntary efforts which scraped together an Endowment Fund of £1000. Over a long period from the First to the Second World War, the society owed much to the financial skill of Alderman Mrs Pritchard.

Grace Hadow was the professional woman with a wide interest in public and social affairs. She was full of plans for maintaining the open and outward-looking traditions of the Home Students, but the outbreak of war in 1939 and her sudden death in 1940 cut these off. Four tutors served on the Selection Committee which recommended the appointment of the Hon. Eleanor Plumer as Principal in 1941. Eleanor Plumer was in every sense the field-marshal's daughter: she had soon organised a unique college war-effort in Hartland House, where a sub-unit of the Morris motor car company worked in shifts. For Home Students one effect of the war was the gradual disappearance of hostesses. Miss Plumer persuaded the delegates that the only possible solution was for the society to run its own hostels, and the first of a number of these was opened at 11 Bradmore Road in 1945. Some mourned the demise of the true 'home student' but more were already demanding a less misleading name. Thus in 1942 the name was officially changed to St Anne's Society.

Miss Plumer's unique contribution to St Anne's was in the field of University politics. Grace Hadow had been the second woman to sit on HEBDOMADAL COUNCIL; Eleanor Plumer was a member for a number of years. From this stance she viewed the position of St Anne's and set out to gain collegiate status for it. The society now owned property and was becoming a residential institution, yet its finances were still controlled by the UNIVERSITY CHEST. Miss Plumer's tactics – exemplifying the Plumer motto *Consulto et audacter* – were highly successful. On 29 April 1952, Queen Elizabeth II gave consent to the Charter of Incorporation which had already been approved by the University Congregation. The Council of St Anne's College assembled for the first time on 2 June, when nine tutors were elected to fellowships. For an interim period five 'outside' members fulfilled a tactful role in advising the new college until, in 1959, St Anne's, with the other women's colleges, achieved full collegiate status and became totally self-governing. The college was permitted to adopt the Plumer coat of arms (*see* HERALDRY).

One factor which had furthered the claim to collegiate status was the large bequest which had come to St Anne's on Mrs Hartland's death in 1945. By 1950 it was possible to start on the second stage of Scott's plan. In 1952 the college moved from 1 South Parks

Road and for the first time had its library, administration, teaching rooms and common rooms gathered on to one site. But the students still lived in hostels and private homes scattered around North Oxford and there was no common table. At this point a combination of good luck and statesmanship sent St Anne's sweeping forward. Because the society had acquired a toe-hold on its land in 1935, St John's was ready to assist the young college by selling at a generous price the freehold of the whole of BEVINGTON ROAD, with 58–60 Woodstock Road. This was largely paid for from a fund in honour of Miss Plumer raised by old students and friends. Again, because in the 1950s the University Grants Committee (UGC) was following a policy of encouraging residence, it was willing to step in with grants, first for a dining hall and then towards acquiring, converting and furnishing the houses on the periphery of the site from 27 to 41 Banbury Road and 48 to 60 Woodstock Road, together with the conversion of Bevington Road. That St Anne's became so late in the day proprietor of so excellent a site was largely due to a combination of St John's friendship and UGC support.

By this time the first election of a Principal by the college itself had taken place. Lady Ogilvie succeeded Miss Plumer in 1953, to become not only a great 'building principal' but the welder together of new and old in diverse ways. Overnight, it seemed, the college lawn was created out of two kitchen gardens, masquerading with its fine, mature trees as centuries old. The Queen opened the dining hall (architect Gerald Banks) in 1960. Springfield St Mary, after serving the society faithfully for many years, departed up the Banbury Road in 1961, leaving the college in possession of its three houses. In 1962 the UGC

commented on 'the high proportion of students now in residence'. Lady Ogilvie had a gift for attracting benefactors: in 1960 she reported a large gift from Sir Isaac Wolfson for the first purpose-built student residence. Messrs Howell, Killick & Partridge were appointed architects and invited to prepare a complete site plan. The Wolfson block was opened in 1964 and the Rayne, gift of the Max Rayne Foundation, in 1968. Another of an Oxford college's characteristic buildings, the Founder's Gatehouse, was raised by a Founders' Fund collected by devoted old students, together with the last UGC grant. It was opened in 1966 by those two remaining survivors of the old 'shoe-string' days, Ruth and Violet Butler. By the early 1970s the honeymoon period for building was over and St Anne's regretfully – but, as it proved, wisely – put on one side the architects' imaginative site plan and settled down in its unique combination of Victorian houses and modern buildings. Students appear to find advantages in the combination.

There were still pockets of amateurism to be cleared out when Nancy Trenaman (Principal 1966–84) brought the administration up to date, but the new professionalism was still combined with openness to experiment and human warmth. Lady Ogilvie opened the first nursery for college children in 1963. The first schoolmistress student in Oxford (a sixth-form teacher seconded on study leave) was elected at St Anne's in 1958. St Anne's was one of the first colleges to organise a MIDDLE COMMON ROOM (1961) and from 1967 to 1984 combined with Balliol to run a joint postgraduate house at HOLYWELL MANOR. Music (fostered by Mary Ogilvie and Nancy Trenaman) is a distinctive feature: St Anne's now has one of the best music-practice rooms in Oxford and its own Balfour

St Anne's College dining hall was built in 1959 to the designs of Gerald Banks.

Memorial Concerts. The library, which has expanded to fill two-thirds of the first floor in Hartland House, is enriched by some unique benefactions and the college has received generous gifts and bequests of scholarship endowments, pictures, silver, etc.

At its inception the governing body was heavily weighted on the humanities side. This has been steadily rectified. The greatest advance was made when it was agreed that a large proportion of the Centenary Fund should be invested in new fellowships, particularly in science, rather than in buildings. The first two new science Fellows were elected in 1978 when the Wallis Chair of Mathematics was also allocated to the college. Like her three predecessors, Mrs Trenaman sat on Hebdomadal Council for a considerable period: she also chaired for a time both the CONFERENCE OF COLLEGES and the University Chest. Two recommendations of the FRANKS COMMISSION had important consequences for St Anne's. All through its history the society/college had been dogged by financial difficulties. Only the generosity of outside bodies and benefactors had provided its buildings, and its endowment fund was infinitesimal. Under the Franks-inspired College Contributions Scheme, St Anne's was assisted by the richer colleges to build up a more adequate endowment fund. Secondly, Franks recommended an increase in the number of women students. The old limitation on women had been abolished in 1957 and from that date onwards St Anne's had expanded steadily in numbers. By 1979 (the centenary year) there were 389 undergraduates and ninety-eight graduate students, making St Anne's at that moment the largest college. Since then, under present government policies, numbers have been somewhat reduced.

By the time of its centenary, St Anne's had taken one more important experimental step. In 1969 it was already debating the question of becoming a mixed college. In 1976 it changed its statutes to admit men to the governing body; in 1978 the entrance examination was opened to men. In its centenary year St Anne's started out as a mixed college with one-third of its students men. By 1985, the college, under Dr Claire Palley, a constitutional lawyer elected in 1983, accommodated 50 per cent men. Mrs Ruth Deech was elected Principal in 1991.

Distinguished alumnae include Ivy Williams (1896–9), the first woman to be called to the Bar in this country; Hannah Holborn Grey (1950–1), President of the University of Chicago; Dame Cicely Saunders (1938–9 and 1944–5); Baroness Young of Farnworth (1944–7); Elizabeth Jennings (1944–7); and Naomi Mitchison (1914–18).

The corporate designation is The Principal and Fellows of St Anne's College in the University of Oxford.

(*Saint Anne's College: A History*, Part I: *The Society of Oxford Home-Students: Retrospects and Recollections (1879–1921)*, ed. R.F. Butler, M.H. Pritchard (privately printed); Part II: *A History of St. Anne's, formerly The Society of Oxford Home Students (1921–1946)*, by R.F. Butler (privately printed); *Supplement 1946–1953*, by M.D.R. Leys (privately printed); Parts I and II were reprinted, with the Supplement, as one volume in 1957. Reeves, Marjorie, *St. Anne's College, Oxford: An Informal History* (privately printed, 1979); Rogers, A.M.A.H., *Degrees by Degrees*, Oxford, 1938.)

St Anthony of Padua, Church of *115 Headley Way*. This yellow brick church with its green felt roof was designed in 1960. The author of *The Lord of the Rings*, J.R.R. TOLKIEN, was not only a faithful parishioner but also a generous benefactor, and when he died in 1973 his requiem was held here. The corner site was acquired in 1959 by Father Albert Adams, a parish priest of prodigious determination. When the hall in JACK STRAWS' LANE (used as a Mass centre since 1948) became inadequate, Jennings, Horner & Lynch were commissioned to design a church to seat 280 at a cost of £25,000. The entrance is through a door set in a screen of coloured glass. The chancel is rectangular. The figure of Christ the King behind the altar by George Wagstaff was commissioned in 1975 by the present incumbent, Monsignor Wilfrid Doran. St Anthony of Padua, the saint who retrieves lost objects, was a friend of St Francis and may have been chosen as patron as a tribute to the Franciscans, who first served the neighbourhood in 1906.

St Antony's College The college occupies the buildings of the Victorian Holy Trinity Convent (1868) and the contrasting Hilda Besse Building (1970) in the WOODSTOCK ROAD, but has a modest claim to earlier history as a site of the first habitations in the University area. Hutton's *Dissertation on the Antiquities of Oxford* (1630) declares that BEVINGTON ROAD, which bounds the college to the south, represented the 'traces of the Roman settlement nearest to Oxford in this direction' and HENRY TAUNT noted the probability that bricks excavated during the construction of the convent were Roman. Close to the prehistoric Portway, the land which the college occupies has been in recorded ownership from 1279, when an inquisition of King Edward I noted that Hugo de Plessis held it from the King for one knight's fee. Briefly owned by the city in the 16th century, it was purchased by St John's College with the life interest of the widow of the founder, Sir Thomas White. It was a market garden when Mother Marian Rebecca Hughes (1817–1912), the first woman since the Reformation to take a nun's vows within the Church of England, purchased the leasehold in 1864 for the religious order she founded, the Society of the Holy and Undivided Trinity. From her own means she commissioned a local architect, Charles Buckeridge, to build (between 1866 and 1868) the fine set of Gothic Revival buildings which the convent occupied until the Second World War. The chapel (now the college library), to a design by John Loughborough Pearson (1817–97), was not added until 1891–4. The undercroft was the nuns' refectory and continued in that use by the college until its new hall was opened in 1970 (architects: Howell, Killick, Partridge & Amis); now a periodicals annexe of the library, it was named the Gulbenkian Room in that year to commemorate a benefaction from the Calouste Gulbenkian Trust.

The college's creation also derived from one who made his fortune in the Middle East – ANTONIN BESSE, whose life is narrated by a late Fellow of the college. Provisional arrangements for establishing the new college were passed by the University CONGREGATION on 21 September 1948. It was made a New Foundation on 30 May 1950 and opened its doors to its first Fellows and students in Michaelmas Term that year. It became a full college of the University by a statute of 21 May 1965. Although initially restricted to men, admission was extended to women by a Supplementary Charter of 2 October 1962, thereby making St Antony's the first Oxford college to change its statutes to admit both sexes. Its first Warden, Sir William Deakin, was succeeded in 1968 by Professor (later Sir) Raymond Carr, who, on retirement in 1987, was succeeded by Professor Ralph (later Sir Ralph) Dahrendorf. The founder's widow, Madame Hilda Besse, added to her husband's endowment, and among other benefactions are those of the Ford Foundation in 1966 and the Volkswagen Foundation in 1973.

All Fellows and a majority of students are engaged in research or courses related to the nine areas of the world in which the college specialises (organised within regional centres) or to international relations. The Nissan Institute for Japanese Studies is wholly financed by the University from a major benefaction from the Nissan Company, while the Latin American Centre and the Middle Eastern Centre enjoy substantial University backing. The Centre for Indian Studies has support from the government of India. The Asian Studies Centre, the Chinese Studies Centre, the Russian and East European Centre and the West European Centre are, on the other hand, almost solely college-financed. Race relations and African studies have been developed by the permanent attachment to the college of the Rhodes Chair of Race Relations. The other associated professorships are of the History of Latin America and of Modern Japanese Studies and the directorship of QUEEN ELIZABETH HOUSE. In Michaelmas Term 1987 there were thirty-three Fellows on the governing body and 201 junior members (embracing thirty-nine nationalities); in addition the college has numerous visiting scholars on short-term attachment (at any one time some twenty funded Visiting Fellows and around thirty Senior Associate Members, mostly from overseas).

The corporate title of the college is The Warden and Fellows of St Antony's College in the University of Oxford.

(Footman, David, *Antonin Besse of Aden: The Founder of St Antony's College*, London, 1986; Saint, Andrew, and Kaser, Michael, *St Antony's College, Oxford: A History of its Buildings and Site*, Oxford, 1973; *St Antony's College Record 1983–85*, Oxford, published triennially.)

St Barnabas, Church of   *Cardigan Street, Jericho.* Thomas Combe, son of a Leicestershire bookseller, joined the CLARENDON PRESS in 1837; in 1869, by which date he was the superintendent, he paid for the church of St Barnabas to be built in Cardigan Street to serve the needs of the growing population in that area, its mother-church being ST PAUL'S, WALTON STREET, of which Combe was churchwarden. An Anglo-Catholic, he was, with his wife Martha, an early patron of the Pre-Raphaelite Brotherhood. He chose as architect Sir Arthur Blomfield, a son of the Bishop of London, of whom he required a building of 'strength, solidity, and thoroughly sound construction', capable of accommodating a thousand worshippers. Blomfield designed his church in the style of a Romanesque basilica with campanile, like the cathedral on the Venetian island of Torcello. The builder was Joseph Castle of Oxford and the site was given by William Ward, a leading Tractarian (*see* OXFORD MOVEMENT). Consecrated in 1869 by BISHOP WILBERFORCE, the church cost £6500, and the lofty campanile, 132 feet high, erected in 1872, £800. The steep roof of the campanile was replaced in 1893 by one of lower pitch.

The Church of St Barnabas, Jericho, was paid for by Thomas Combe of the Clarendon Press, designed by Sir Arthur Blomfield, and consecrated in 1869.

The north chapel, also by Blomfield, was added in 1888. The richness of the interior of the church, with its golden sanctuary, canopied altar and nave murals, is in striking and calculated contrast to the simplicity of the exterior. Thomas Hardy, who assisted Blomfield in designing the chapel of the RADCLIFFE INFIRMARY, described the church of St Barnabas in *Jude the Obscure* as 'the church of ceremonies' and gave it the name 'St Silas'.

In his diary for May 1876, the Rev. Francis Kilvert describes an Ascension Day service, 'with a procession, incense-bearers and a great gilt cross, the thurifers and acolytes being in short white surplices over scarlet cassocks and the last priest in the procession wearing a biretta and a chasuble stiff with gold. . . . The poor humble Roman Church hard by is quite plain, simple and Low Church in its ritual compared with St. Barnabas in its festal dress on high days and holidays.' The tradition of High Anglican worship continues today.

St Bartholomew's Chapel *Cowley Road.* The chapel was part of ST BARTHOLOMEW'S HOSPITAL, founded by Henry I in 1126–8, which was 'assigned for the receiving and sustaining of infirm leprous folk and appointed a convent of twelve brethren and one chaplain'. In 1327 the hospital was granted by Edward III to Oriel College as a rural retreat 'that he might gratify his scholars of Oriel Hall the use of wholesome air in times of pestilential sickness'. The chapel suffered depredation during the siege of Oxford in 1643, 'not only its roof (being of lead) taken away and employed towards the making of bullets for the soldiery, but also by the parliamenteers put to base uses and almost ruinated to the ground'. The chapel and almshouses (which stand nearby to the north) were largely rebuilt in 1649 by Oriel, the college giving the oak chancel screen in 1651. To the west of the chapel is the 16th-century St Bartholomew's Farm, part of the hospital group of buildings.

St Bartholomew's Hospital Founded by Henry I near Cowley Marsh for twelve lepers to be cared for by a chaplain. The hospital was granted to Oriel College in 1328, and from 1536 was used as a city almshouse. The buildings were restored in 1600 and 1635 and reconstructed in 1649 after they had been severely damaged in the CIVIL WAR. By the late 18th century, however, most of the almsmen were living elsewhere, since the stipend was too little to pay for their keep as residents in the hospital. In 1770 only four men were in receipt of pensions of 7s a week. Two years later the charity was incorporated in Oxford City Charities. Inside some of the 17th-century features remain, but the exterior has been rebuilt.

(*See* ST BARTHOLOMEW'S CHAPEL.)

St Benet's Hall *38 St Giles'.* In 1895, Pope Leo XIII rescinded the Papal Instruction of 1867 and so gave English ROMAN CATHOLICS the freedom once more to attend the universities. Two years later the Abbot and Community of Ampleforth Monastery decided that, after an absence of three centuries, the time had come for the Benedictines to return to Oxford. However, as no member of the Community held an Oxford MA, they were unable, under University law, to open a PRIVATE HALL. Their first house, No. 103 WOODSTOCK ROAD, was rented. Here three young monks, under their Superior, Dom

Edmund Matthews, studied for their degrees while continuing to live according to the Rule of St Benedict. In 1899, with the advent of Dom Oswald Hunter-Blair, an MA of Magdalen College, they were able under his mastership to become a Private Hall. Following mediaeval custom, it was known by the name of the Master, the name changing to Parker's Hall in 1909, when Dom Anselm Parker succeeded Dom Oswald. This confusing state of affairs ended in 1918 when the University introduced the status of Permanent Private Hall. St Benet's Hall (*Aula Sancti Benedicti*) then became the institution's official designation, with the Abbot and Community of Ampleforth as the governing body. By this time they had moved to larger premises in BEAUMONT STREET, renting Nos 8 and 9 from St John's College. Here they remained for eighteen years, until in 1922 the Ursuline nuns vacated Nos 38 and 39 ST GILES' and the Benedictines were at last able to purchase a freehold. And so it is that the members of this ancient monastic Order, which once owned three Oxford colleges (GLOUCESTER, DURHAM and CANTERBURY – *see* MONASTIC COLLEGES) are today established on the north-west side of St Giles'.

The two houses were built as private residences in the reign of William IV; together they form one eight-bay dwelling of five storeys with an iron balcony across the first floor. The simple chapel, built in 1911 in the garden of No. 39, contains Stations of the Cross carved by the Oxford sculptress Rosamund Fletcher. In the library is a fine bronze head of Yehudi Menuhin by Kostek Wojnarowski. Of the thirty-six or so students in residence today, half are monks, many with degrees, who are reading Theology at the University; the rest are laymen. Notable among the many graduates of St Benet's are Dom Edmund Matthews, the first Benedictine to take an Oxford degree since the Reformation (1899); the Provincial of the English Dominicans and founder of BLACKFRIARS, Father Bede Jarrett (1906); the Cardinal Archbishop of Westminster, Basil Hume (1947); and the Master of Balliol College, Anthony Kenny (1961). Dom Henry Wansborough OSB succeeded Dom Fabian Cowper as Master in 1991.

St Bernard's College *see* MONASTIC COLLEGES.

St Bernard's Road Originally St John's Road (after the college) but changed, with effect from October 1961, to St Bernard's, the name of the college from which St John's developed. The change was made on the recommendation of the governing body of the college. It had been requested by residents of the road as early as February 1946 because of continual confusion with ST JOHN STREET further to the south. The road was formerly (1829) Horse and Jockey Road (or Lane) after the inn of that name. In about 1870 there was still in the vicinity a cliff of gravel with a rough and winding lane and a row of white poplars: this was the route taken by Charles I, his cavaliers and 6000 troops during his escape from Oxford on 3 June 1644. It was accomplished at night in silence and not one resident gave the secret away.

St Catherine's College Originated in October 1868 with the MATRICULATION of eighteen undergraduates as '*Scholares nulli Collegio vel Aulae ascripti*'. Popularly termed 'unattached students',

such matriculates were spared the considerable expense of membership of and residence in a college. The introduction of this category of student had been suggested first by the ROYAL COMMISSION of 1850 in order to open the University to 'a much larger and poorer class' of the population. The necessary University statute was passed in June 1867, based on the recommendations of the University Extension Committee of 1866, which also drew up the regulation for a Delegacy, composed of the VICE-CHANCELLOR, the PROCTORS and two stipendiaries, to license lodgings for the new students.

In 1870 the two stipendiaries, the Rev. G.W. Kitchin and the Rev. G.S. Ward, assumed the titles of Censors and took on responsibility for the organisation and supervision of teaching. The delegacy was allocated a room in the OLD CLARENDON BUILDING, where a library was founded with gifts of books from WILLIAM GLADSTONE, Dr Liddon and DR PUSEY. A number of colleges, including Oriel, The Queen's College and University, opened their Pass lectures to the 'unattached students', and Balliol its Honours lectures. In the next few years the numbers of men matriculating as 'unattached students' increased rapidly, so that, by 1872, 330 had been admitted (although of these seventy-nine had migrated from colleges – a practice strongly discouraged after 1877). To attract applicants of ability to the delegacy, awards were established, the first exhibitions being endowed in 1871 by the Grocers' Company.

A students' social club was founded in April 1869. Named the Clarendon University Club, it met for two years at No. 23 CORNMARKET before moving to No. 35 HOLYWELL where it held a weekly debate. In 1874 a more ambitious venture, St Catharine's Club, was started, taking its name from St Catharine's Hall, a house opposite the Old Clarendon Building, where members could meet for lunch and dinner. The club ran until 1881 or 1882 when it went bankrupt, but the name St Catharine's was retained for societies and it was as 'St Catharine's' that the 'unattached students' began to participate in inter-collegiate activities. In 1871 the University made available a chapel in the CONVOCATION HOUSE in ST MARY'S THE VIRGIN where weekly services were held until 1883.

Despite this steady growth the delegacy suffered poor academic results. Between 1868 and 1874, 37 per cent of the 'unattached students' migrated to colleges and 14 per cent left Oxford without a degree. This disappointment prompted the University to reorganise the delegacy by statute in 1881. The Rev. G.W. Kitchin was named as sole Censor and it was stated that tutors and lecturers would be appointed. The University undertook to provide funding for salaries and for new buildings, while the undergraduates were to be required to attend lectures and to pay fees for them. A great boon was the opening in 1887 of almost all Honours lectures to the entire membership of the University.

In 1884 the designation 'unattached student', which had always been unpopular, was abandoned in favour of the more accurate term, 'non-collegiate student'. The number of delegates was increased from five to twelve and in 1888 the delegacy moved to more adequate accommodation in the HIGH STREET, to a building, which is now the RUSKIN SCHOOL OF ART, beside the EXAMINATION SCHOOLS. Designed by T.G. JACKSON, it contained an office, a library, two lecture rooms and rooms for the use of the Censor and the tutors.

Kitchin resigned as Censor in 1883 on his appointment as Dean of Winchester and was succeeded by Dr W.W. Jackson. He was in turn succeeded in 1887 by the Rev. Dr R.W.M. Pope, who proceeded to hold office for thirty-two years, presiding over the steady development of the delegacy. The numbers of non-collegiate students continued to increase, especially after the introduction of the graduate degrees of BLitt and BSc in 1895 and after the foundation of the independent theological colleges, Mansfield and Manchester. Sports and societies flourished. A BARGE was purchased from Wadham in 1908 and a sportsground was acquired at New Marston. In 1914 the colours of maroon and French grey were adopted as standard. Debating, musical and historical societies were established and in 1896 *The Non-Collegiate Students' Magazine* was started, superseded in 1919 by *St Catherine's Magazine*.

The chief concern of Dr Pope's successor as Censor, J.B. Baker (nicknamed 'The Jibber'), was to improve the position and morale of the delegacy by banning the practice of migration to colleges and by seeking a second change of name, to 'St Catherine's Society', which CONGREGATION accepted in 1931. (The spelling of the patron's name had been resolved in 1919 when the Finance Committee of the Clubs had rejected the older form, 'St Catharine's'.) In 1936 the society, which had long outgrown its site on the High Street, moved to new buildings in ST ALDATE'S, designed by Sir Hubert Worthington and opened by the CHANCELLOR, Lord Halifax. (These buildings now house the Faculty of Music.) A dining hall was opened and a Senior Common Room established. The continued expansion of the society was shown when in 1948 it admitted the second-largest number of freshmen in the University and reached an all-time peak of 350 undergraduates in residence.

The removal to St Aldate's and the expansion of the society had been overseen by the Rev. V.J.K. Brook, who served as Censor from 1930 to 1952. Under his successor Alan Bullock (later Lord Bullock of Leafield), a more ambitious programme was adopted. The first plans for development, accepted by the delegates in December 1953, raised the number of tutorial posts from three to ten and, with the financing of the University Grants Commission, provided limited teaching accommodation in BREWER STREET, where a law library was also established. The desire to provide accommodation for undergraduates pointed the need for further expansion and led to the decision of the delegates on 21 April 1956 to transform St Catherine's Society into a college.

It was an opportune moment, for the University was anxious to increase the number of college places it could offer, particularly in the science subjects, and HEBDOMADAL COUNCIL and Congregation were readily persuaded to give their consent. It was evident to all that the 1944 Education Act had removed much of the original purpose of St Catherine's as a non-collegiate society by providing the means for every undergraduate to afford residence in a college.

A site was found quickly. In March 1957 the Censor reported that Merton College had offered to sell 6 acres in Holywell Great Meadow to the University and that the City Council had given permission for the erection of college buildings on the site. St Catherine's had acquired, in the Censor's words, 'a lovely setting . . . unexpectedly close to the historic centre of the University'. Hebdomadal Council made provision for the new college in the University building programme for 1960 to 1963 and secured pledges from the UGC of £45,000 for the purchase of the site and £250,000 for the construction of undergraduate rooms. The specification was made that these were not to be of a noticeably higher standard than at other universities, which was eventually to limit expenditure to £840 per unit and to constrain the architect to modify his original designs.

The UGC grants were, however, but a fraction of the £2 million that the Censor estimated were required for the foundation of the college. He had since 1957 been actively appealing to industry and was fortunate to secure the assistance of A.H. Wilson, a director of Courtaulds, and Sir Hugh Beaver, the managing director of Arthur Guinness & Co. and the President of the Federation of British Industries. They promoted an appeal to the City with such success that on 8 July 1958 the Censor could announce to CONVOCATION that £675,000 had been pledged in addition to the sums contributed by the UGC.

The same meeting established a committee of Council, the Committee on St Catherine's College, to supervise the various steps towards bringing the college into existence. Uniting representatives of the delegates, the University and the city, it concerned itself not merely with fund-raising but with the design and building of the college, the appointment of the fellowship and the fixing of student numbers. One of the committee's first decisions was to establish a timetable for the transitional period. It was agreed that the effective date of the appointment of the Master and Fellows of the new college should be 1 October 1960 and that October 1961 should be the target date for the partial occupation of the new building and the dissolution of the society.

In order to realise these objectives, the success of the appeal was crucial. With the aid of the Rockefeller Foundation a headquarters was established in 1958 at No. 42 BANBURY ROAD in a condemned Victorian house which was also to serve as a planning office. Thousands of brochures were circulated to old members and they produced a sufficient response for the Censor to announce in November 1959 that contributions had reached £1,460,000. Over 200 firms had made donations, including the Shell Petroleum Company, Rolls-Royce and the Ford Motor Company. The Isaac Wolfson Foundation had pledged £100,000 for a library.

Thereafter progress was slow and by 1961 was causing concern; yet the magnanimity of an old member, Dr Rudolph A. Light, transformed the college's position. His donation of 20,000 shares in the Upjohn pharmaceutical firm, valued at more than £350,000, provided an essential supplement to the endowment and permitted the completion of the building programme. Two other generous gifts were of £100,000 from the Sunley Foundation towards the lecture-room block and of $250,000 from the Ford Foundation for the establishment of fellowships.

The appointment of the Danish architect, Arne Jacobsen, aroused controversy for it was taken by many as a tacit condemnation of the British profession. However, the University had been particularly impressed by Jacobsen's expertise in all aspects of design, and in its invitation it asked him to 'undertake as much as possible of the landscape design and the design of the fittings and furniture'. At the same time he was requested to retain the traditional features of staircases and quadrangles. Jacobsen's design was completed by autumn 1959 and was enthusiastically approved by the society and the University. It was made public at a press conference in London in October 1960, when it aroused generous and favourable comment. The *Guardian* described the future St Catherine's as 'Oxford's most classical building' and the *Daily Mail* wrote that it was 'the college to house the cold logic of nuclear youth'.

The contract for the site works was let in the summer of 1960 and on 4 November 1960 the Queen came to Holywell Great Meadow, accompanied by the Chancellor, Harold Macmillan (later EARL OF STOCK-TON), to lay the foundation stone. By June 1961 the piling was finished and preparations had been made for building. The contract was let by tender to Messrs Marshall-Andrew & Co. Although delays occurred, the college was able to open in October 1962 (a year later than the Committee on St Catherine's College had envisaged). Twenty-eight undergraduates, three Fellows and the Master were provided with rooms. By the end of the academic year, 150 undergraduates had taken up residence and the Junior and Senior Common Rooms had been brought into use.

In the following academic year attention turned to the layout of the gardens and the completion of the library and the lecture-room block. The Duke of Edinburgh, who had in March 1962 consented to become VISITOR to the college, made a tour of the site in May 1964, and on 16 October 1964 the college was officially opened by the Chancellor. The governing body resolved to retain the colours of St Catherine's Society and adopted a motto, '*Nova et Vetera*', and a coat of arms (*see* HERALDRY).

It had been the delegates' intention that the postgraduate members of the society would remain non-collegiate members of the University and would separate from St Catherine's to form a new body, Linacre House, which would occupy the St Aldate's site. Yet, as it turned out, a large number migrated to the new college, which began the 1963–4 year with 326 men reading for first degrees and ninety registered for postgraduate degrees and diplomas.

Subsequent years saw student numbers increase steadily, to the extent that in Michaelmas 1978 St Catherine's became the University's largest college. The academic year 1984–5 began with 511 under-graduates and postgraduates registered for degrees at the college. The fellowship also grew with elections to all categories and by Michaelmas 1984 there were forty-eight tutorial positions at the college.

Although some hoped and others feared that St Catherine's would abandon Oxford traditions for modernity, the college has been careful to remain within the conventions of University life. While preserving its special interest in the sciences, St Catherine's has offered the complete range of undergraduate courses (except LITERAE HUMANIORES). Academic results have steadily improved with the percentage of Firsts and Seconds increasing. In Trinity Term 1981 the impressive record of twenty-seven Firsts was set. St Catherine's students have won BLUES in most sports and won the University Athletics

Cuppers in 1967, 1970 and 1971, the Soccer Cuppers in 1973 and the Tennis Cuppers in 1983. In Michaelmas 1974 the college was one of the first five in the University to become co-educational.

A number of new buildings have been added since the college's opening. The squash courts and the music house, both brought into use in 1965, formed part of Jacobsen's original design; but the punt-house, built to the west of the main complex, was a later commission in 1970. It proved to be Jacobsen's last piece of work for St Catherine's. The college entrance was resited and redesigned by Philip Dowson in 1975, using money raised by the 1968 Centenary Appeal to alumni. The newest additions are the Mary Sunley Building and the Alan Bullock Building, on the east and west sides of the college entrance. Designed by Professor Knud Holscher, Jacobsen's erstwhile assistant, they were opened in 1982 and 1983. A block of graduate flats was also built off-site in Bath Street, ST CLEMENT'S in 1973.

In recent years the college has been very active in the promotion of its relations with alumni and has established a new College Committee, composed of equal numbers of Fellows and alumni. It is to this committee that St Catherine's looks for the success of its recently inaugurated development appeal, which will, it is hoped, match the success of earlier appeals.

Lord Bullock, the Founding Master, retired on 30 September 1980, and was succeeded in 1981 by Sir Patrick Nairne, who came to the college on retirement from the Civil Service. In March 1987 it was announced that he was to be succeeded by Dr Brian Smith, a Fellow of the college.

St Catherine's has since its opening attracted comment as one of Oxford's outstanding modern buildings. It is characterised by its strong geometry and consistent design, typical of the Scandinavian mood of the 1960s. The chief buildings form a rectangle 600 feet long. To the east and west lie two identical residential blocks, containing tutors' and students' rooms on three floors. Between them are the hall, the Wolfson Library and the Bernard Sunley Building (the lecture-theatre block), all identical in width. On either side of the hall branch the college offices and Senior Common Room to the west and the Junior Common Room to the east. The Great Quad is dominated by its circular lawn, planted with two cedar trees out of axis. Between the library and the Bernard Sunley Building, enclosed by low walls, is the Middle Common Room Garden, which contains an 80-foot concrete bell-tower. Outside the parallelepiped lie the squash courts, the amphitheatre and the music house to the south, the Master's lodgings and the circular bicycle sheds to the west and the Mary Sunley Building and the Alan Bullock Building to the north. Also to the north and across the approach road which leads from Manor Road over Napper's Bridge lie the punt-house, the college tennis courts and the car parks. There is no chapel, as members are able to use the nearby 13th-century church of ST CROSS. The college's playing fields at New Marston can be reached by footpaths which cross the University PARKS.

St Catherine's is built of exposed concrete beams filled in with plate glass and sand-coloured bricks of a special 2-inch size. The library is in part clad in bronze, and bronze louvres shield the upper-storey windows of the Bernard Sunley Building.

On the west side of the college runs a moat crossed by a drawbridge which leads into the porters' lodge, from which the Great Quad may be entered. A fountain towards the northern end of the moats was donated by Lord Bullock on his retirement. On the front lawn to the south of the drawbridge stands an abstract sculpture by Barbara Hepworth.

The hall, the largest in Oxford and built with the financial support of the Esso Petroleum Company, provides accommodation for 365 dining members. Its floor is of Westmorland slate and its furniture of oak. The hall is distinguished by its atmospheric wall- and table-lighting and by six modern tapestries, designed by Tom Phillips, an alumnus of the college, and executed by Edinburgh Weavers.

The strict geometry of the buildings is imaginatively softened throughout by the gardens. Designed by Jacobsen, they intersperse the buildings in a way unmatched in any other Oxford college. The framework is a formal series of yew hedges, which shelter smaller gardens, each with block plantings of shrubs and areas of grass with small trees. The gardens aim for two climaxes: May–June and October. May and June see the flowering of the formal iris beds, the climbing and bush roses and the water garden, while October is served by a wide range of berrying plants and autumn-colouring trees. In the lower garden, beside the tributary of the Cherwell (see THAMES), shaded and private areas are created by groups of willow and swamp cypress, while the vestibule gardens which lead to the hall illustrate the contrast of desert plants on the west side and half-hardy or tender stove plants on the east. The offices and SCR enclose the Helen Gaskin Memorial Garden, designed in 1983 by Joyce Lowrie, and containing a water garden and plantings in Chinese glazed pots. To the south of the music house is a rock garden.

Among distinguished alumni of the college are Sir Glyn Jones, Governor-General of Malawi, 1964; Dr Eric Williams, historian and first Prime Minister of Trinidad and Tobago; the Most Rev. Lord Blanch, Archbishop of York; Sir Grantley Adams, Premier of Barbados and of the West Indian Federation; Eric Partridge, writer and philologist; Dr John Vane, winner of the Nobel Prize for Medicine, 1982; David Hemery, Olympic 400-metre gold medallist, 1968; J. Paul Getty, industrialist.

The corporate title is St Catherine's College in the University of Oxford.

(Trotman, R.R., and Garrett, E.J.K., *The Non-Collegiate Students and St Catherine's Society, 1868–1962*, with an Epilogue by Lord Bullock, Oxford, 1962.)

St Clare's *139 Banbury Road.* Established in 1953 as a language-study centre. It developed as a tutorial college for A-levels and University of London external degrees and in 1977 began offering the International Baccalaureate, founded in Geneva and now examined in Britain, which has become its main course for sixth-form students. It continues to offer English-language teaching and a Liberal Arts programme for American university students.

St Clement, Church of *Marston Road.* One of the Royal Chapels given to ST FRIDESWIDE'S PRIORY by Henry I in 1122, St Clement's passed at the

Cattle being driven towards the toll-gate on Magdalen Bridge past the old Church of St Clement c.1820.

Dissolution of the Monasteries to Christ Church and then to the Crown. In 1864 the living passed to the OXFORD CHURCHES TRUST, the evangelical tradition continuing to the present time. The former parish church stood on THE PLAIN. THOMAS HEARNE, the antiquary, described it as 'a very pretty little church', and Sir John Peshall in 1773 as having a nave of some 40 feet in length, a chancel of some 20 feet, and a width of some 20 feet; 'on the north and west sides are galleries. Over the latter is a small capp'd tiled tower containing three bells.' The tower was replaced in 1816 by a square tower of plaster and lath costing £80. From 1771 to 1869, close to the west end of the old church, stood a turnpike toll-house. When increasing population in the parish required a larger building, the present site in Hacklingcroft Meadow was given in 1824 by Sir Joseph Lock. The three bells were taken from the old church to the new: one of them, cast in the 13th century, is the oldest bell in Oxford. In 1950 the last traces of the old churchyard disappeared when the present roundabout was constructed on The Plain.

The present church, built in 1826 at a cost of £6500 raised by public subscription (both JOHN KEBLE and E.B. PUSEY were contributors), was designed by Daniel Robertson and was the first church in Oxford since the Reformation to be built on a new site. Said to have been inspired by ST MARY THE VIRGIN, IFFLEY, it was an attempt at romanesque revival following 'the old churches called Saxon or Ancient Norman . . . laudable, especially as such a building must be much less costly than one in the more florid and ornamental style'. Another view, however, described its appearance as 'the boiled rabbit'.

Pews, pulpit, lectern (all of 1871) and font follow the Georgian–Norman style, echoing the heavy romanesque columns and curves. The axis of the building is north-east–south-west, with clear windows on the south side; on the north side, four of the stained-glass windows came from ST MARTIN'S, CARFAX, demolished

in 1896, their captions composing a rhyme: In Faith, Love; In Faith, Obey; In Faith, Endure; In Faith, Pray. The east window (c.1847) is by J.H. Russell; and tracery by E.G. Bruton was inserted in the windows in 1876.

Among former incumbents of the old church were Humphrey Prideaux (Rector 1679–83), later Dean of Norwich, and John Conybeare (Rector 1724–34), later Rector of Exeter College and Bishop of Bristol. JOHN HENRY NEWMAN (curate 1824–6) was appointed as 'a kind of guarantee to the subscribers that every exertion shall be made, when the church is built, to recover the parish from meeting-houses, and on the other hand ale-houses, into which [people] have been driven for want of convenient Sunday worship'.

St Clement's This parish became part of the city of Oxford in 1835 at the time of the Municipal Corporations Act. Before that date it was part of Bullingdon Hundred. The number of houses then in the parish was about 400, having increased from seventy in 1771. The ancient village had lain outside the East Gate of the city, the River CHERWELL (*see* THAMES) from MAGDALEN BRIDGE to King's Mill forming the boundary. St Clement's was separated from HEADINGTON by HEADINGTON HILL as far as PULLEN'S LANE and then the dividing line ran along Gipsy Lane and Divinity Road to COWLEY ROAD. It is low-lying clay ground at Magdalen Bridge but rises at the Headington side to a height of over 300 feet on gravel. Most of the early St Clement's formed part of the land which, by Ethelred's charter, was given to ST FRIDESWIDE'S PRIORY in 1004. St Clement's Chapel was given to St Frideswide's in 1122 and was probably in existence earlier. However, at this time it was known as Bruggeset (Bridset or Bridgeset) or Bolshipton (with various spellings, a shippon being a shed for cattle). The name St Clement did not come into use for the district until the 17th century. The

Bolshipton House stood opposite the BLACK HORSE inn. The Bolles were farmers in the district in the 13th century when St Clement's was still largely rural in character. The house was destroyed in 1643 to make way for the fortifications of the Parliamentarians in the CIVIL WAR. St Clement's suffered more than most in the war because houses were demolished and orchards dug up to create fortifications and bulwarks. Almost a whole street was destroyed and, in addition, houses on the fringe of the defences were pulled down so that the enemy could not take cover in them. However, by 1675 there were more houses than before the war because tradesmen found it a convenient place from which to sell their wares to the city market yet escape the regulations and fees of the city freemen (see PRIVILEGED PERSONS). In 1683 the city traders tried to prevent this unfair competition and asked for St Clement's to come within the city franchises. But, with the help of the BISHOP OF OXFORD and the University, the St Clement's tradesmen fought successfully against this. The University thought that prices would rise if freemen had the monopoly.

John Knibb (1650–1722), clockmaker, started his business in St Clement's; and by the 18th century the area had become crowded with a wide variety of traders and shopkeepers. Many college servants were also housed here. Jackson first published the *Oxford Flying Weekly Journal* (which preceded *Jackson's Oxford Journal* (*see* NEWSPAPERS)) in St Clement's in 1746. The early 17th-century Black Horse inn, built on the site of the Green Croft (No. 102 St Clement's), is almost the only building to have survived from the time of the Civil War demolitions. It is said that PARKER's bookshop began as an open-air stall in front of the inn. The court of the Lords of the Manor of Headington was convened here in earlier days and there were stocks on the cobbles outside. Members of the University frequented the area from the 17th century and sometimes attended the bull- and bear-baiting. In 1781 a man was gored by a bull tethered for baiting. As late as 1826 there was a University bull-baiting club. A FAIR was held outside the Black Horse for toys and other small items on the Thursday before Michaelmas in the 18th and 19th centuries. Later it became a Michaelmas pleasure fair, which continued annually until the 1930s.

There was widespread poverty in St Clement's and, since its only supply of water came from the Cherwell, into which sewers discharged and which lay stagnant at times, the cholera epidemic of 1832 spread quickly here. St Clement's suffered a third of all deaths in Oxford. Although clear drinking water was brought from Headington to pumps at the end of each street in 1849, there was no proper drainage until after 1854 (*see* HEALTH, PUBLIC, *and also* WATER SUPPLY). Poverty was worst in University vacations and it is said that many did not go to church as they could not afford decent clothes. The parish had its own workhouse. More and more poor people moved into the area as they lost their homes when they were demolished to make way for college buildings.

St Clement's lay on the main road to London and on the routes for the carriage of STONE from Headington and wood from SHOTOVER ROYAL FOREST (St Clement's people had forest rights until the early 19th century). The road was continually in need of repair and the poor St Clement's parishioners had to pay for it. However, money for improvements was given by others, including Dr Claymond, the first President of Corpus Christi College, and CARDINAL WOLSEY, building materials for Cardinal College (now Christ Church) being conveyed along the road. The new IFFLEY ROAD was cut through the most built-up part of St Clement's after the Mileways Act of 1771. This necessitated the demolition of many houses and there was naturally strong opposition to the development, but to no avail. Two hundred years later, however, the residents successfully opposed a new relief-road through the area. In 1829 St Clement's old church on THE PLAIN, its 'little whitened tower, adorned with pinnacles', was taken down, a new church having been built further east (*see* ST CLEMENT'S CHURCH).

Among the fourteen or so streets in the area are Dawson Street, Boulter Street, Bath Street and Little Brewery Street. Thomas Dawson of Reading, the son of an Oxford alderman, left land in trust to the church in 1521. Edward Boulter, the heir of his great-uncle, Sir John Cutler, Bart., gave money in 1736 to build almshouses in St Clement's for 'six poor, neat, honest men'. In 1786 a house was added for an apothecary; and the earliest dispensary in Oxford was situated here at the Cutler-Boulter Almshouses. The dispensary remained here until 1884 when, on the buildings being demolished, it moved to GLOUCESTER GREEN. The baths, after which Bath Street takes its name, were erected in 1827 with a reading room attached. In 1886 they were converted into Turkish baths. Little Brewery Street is on the site of St Clement's Brewery, which was established in 1826.

St Clement's, the main street of the area, which still retains some older buildings, was beginning to look run down in recent years with deserted shops and decaying buildings. It has now taken on a new lease of life. On the south side there still remains the Black Horse inn, STONE'S ALMSHOUSES and the Port Mahon inn (No. 82). This inn, 18th-century in parts, is named after the Minorcan port which was captured by the British in 1708. On the north, in front of the Florey Building and on the site of a wartime municipal restaurant, is the new Anchor House, a sheltered housing scheme opened in 1985 with shops on the frontage. On the other side of the entrance to the municipal car-park is a mid-18th-century house, once threatened with demolition, which has been well restored by the Oxfordshire Buildings Trust. On the north side is St Clement's Mission Hall (No. 57a) by H.W. Moore (1887–9).

St Columba's United Reformed Church *Alfred Street*. From 1908 onwards there was continuing concern for the spiritual welfare of presbyterian undergraduates, which eventually led to the establishment of a joint chaplaincy, shared by the Church of Scotland, the United Free Church of Scotland and the Presbyterian Church of England. The church itself was built in 1915 to a design by T. Phillips Figgis which allowed for a rectangular chancel and a nave. The vestibule, added in 1960, was designed by E. Brian Smith. In 1929 a congregation of the Presbyterian Church of England was established and St Columba's has continued to serve as a University chaplaincy. Following the union of the Presbyterian and Congregationalist Churches in 1972 it took its present name.

Among the notable people associated with St Columba's are John Buchan (1875–1940), Sir

Maurice Powicke (1879–1963), sometime Regius Professor of Modern History, and M.N. Tod (1878–1974), Fellow of Oriel and an eminent classicist. The latter, a man of great modesty and beautiful handwriting inspired the lines:

'My name is Marcus Niebuhr Tod,
I have the autograph of God.'
And so the Reader in Greek Epigraphy
Has a specimen of the Divine calligraphy.

St Cross, Church of *Holywell*. In existence from c.1100, St Cross was in its early years a chapel for ST PETER-IN-THE-EAST, both of them passing to Merton College in 1266. The inhabitants of HOLYWELL were baptised and buried in St Cross but paid their dues to the vicar of St Peter's; the church was last described as a chapel in 1738. After 1770 the living was an endowed perpetual curacy, and in 1957 the benefice and parish were united with St Peter's, the united benefice in 1966 being joined to that of the University Church of ST MARY THE VIRGIN.

St Cross was served chiefly, though not exclusively, by Fellows or other members of Merton; the number of services and the kind of ministry offered by incumbents fluctuated in the 18th century, but from 1849 St Cross was served by High Church curates. By 1854 Communion was being celebrated every Sunday. Despite protests from some parishioners in the 1850s against ritualistic practices, in 1860 the BISHOP OF OXFORD, SAMUEL WILBERFORCE, commended the religious state of the parish. In 1876 the Guild of the Holy Cross was formed to foster brotherhood among parishioners and to counter the 'sectarian spirit' reported earlier (1854); it met regularly until 1907. The number of Easter communicants rose from 145 in 1866 to 278 in 1887; in 1915 Communion was celebrated daily; in 1916 Choral Eucharist was introduced; and from 1936 the Sacrament was reserved.

When first built in the late 11th or early 12th century, St Cross probably consisted simply of a nave and chancel, the chancel arch surviving from the original building. North and south aisles were added in the 13th century, as well as the west tower, rebuilt in 1464, perhaps after collapsing. The south porch was added in 1592 and the north wall rebuilt in 1685. In 1837–8 the north aisle was rebuilt; in 1843–4 the south aisle was also rebuilt, to the designs of J.M. Derick. Repairs were made to the tower in 1874; and in 1876 a vestry was added to the north of the chancel. The east window glass (1874) is by John Hardman, and in 1901 a window at the east end of the south aisle was given in memory of Sir John Stainer (1840–1901), the composer, a former churchwarden, whose grave is in the cemetery. In 1923 a Lady Chapel was made at the east end of the south aisle, a figure of the Virgin being placed in a nearby niche close to the 19th-century stone pulpit, south of the chancel arch. The nave, with painted roof, measures some 60 feet in length and 24 feet in width, the north and south aisles each being 15 feet wide. The chancel, with canted roof painted in 1885, is 30 feet in length, the chancel arch being 10 feet wide.

Near the entrance door in the south aisle is a memorial (1974) to members of St Catherine's College who fell in the two world wars; and on the south wall of the tower is a 19th-century painted sun-dial, perhaps replacing one made in 1667. Within the church an interesting brass wall-tablet depicts Eliza Franklin (*d.*1622 in childbed), wife of the innkeeper of the KING'S ARMS, lying in bed with her four children, three of them in shrouds and one in swaddling clothes. The church possesses a chalice of 1569, an alms-dish of 1683, and a fine 18th-century wooden parish chest from St Peter-in-the-East. The north wall of the churchyard has windows in it which are remains of the chapel (1863) designed by James Castle for the Clewer Sisterhood, occupants of HOLYWELL MANOR from 1862.

The cemetery adjacent to the churchyard is of interest in having many well-known Oxford figures buried there, among whom are SIR HENRY ACLAND (1815–1900), Regius Professor of Medicine: WALTER PATER (1839–94), art critic; Hastings Rashdall (1858–1924), historian; Kenneth Grahame (1859–1932), author of *The Wind in the Willows* (1908); Charles Williams (1886–1945), poet, novelist and INKLING; an associate of the Inklings, H.V.D. Dyson (1896–1975), Fellow of Merton College; Sir Hugh Cairns (1896–1952), Nuffield Professor of Surgery; SIR MAURICE BOWRA (1898–1971), Warden of Wadham College; Lord Redcliffe-Maud (1906–82), Master of University College; and Kenneth Tynan (1927–80), theatre critic.

St Cross College One of the University's younger graduate colleges, it was founded in 1965, at the same time as Iffley (now Wolfson) College, at a time when the University was particularly concerned to provide full college affiliations for those among the greatly increased numbers of academic staff and postgraduate students who did not have them. St Cross spent its first seventeen years in temporary accommodation on a site made available to the University by Merton College, just south of the mainly mediaeval ST CROSS CHURCH and its churchyard. The principal permanent building here is a former parish schoolhouse, built in 1858, which the college used as a library and meeting room, while its common-room-cum-dining-room, kitchen and offices were located in a large and moderately commodious single-storey wooden hut.

It was originally envisaged that, if funds were forthcoming, the college would erect permanent buildings on this site, which extended to about three-quarters of an acre. These plans did not materialise, however, and the empty space developed only into an attractive garden, well set off by the north wall of Magdalen College's deer park and the fine large trees beyond. In 1981, after four years of intricate negotiation involving St Cross, the University and the governors of the Dr Pusey Memorial Fund, the college moved to its present site on the west side of ST GILES', which had previously been wholly occupied by PUSEY HOUSE, its chapel and library (the latter also incorporating the Theology Faculty's library). The 999-year lease of the site to St Cross excluded the chapel and safeguarded the arrangements for the Theology Library, while the role of Pusey House in Oxford continued as before.

While retaining its original site for possible future use, St Cross thus acquired distinguished and highly appropriate buildings in a fine central location. Pusey House is mainly the work of the architect Temple Moore, with additions by Leslie Moore. The style is determinedly Gothic, and though the charming and imaginative quadrangle is occasionally taken by visitors to be mediaeval, the buildings all belong to the period 1911–26. Discreet additions and alterations, mainly internal, on behalf of St Cross are the work of Geoffrey Beard and the Oxford Architects Partnership. They include the much admired Saugman Hall, created as a dining room where a cloister and a clutter of store rooms previously existed. Beyond the existing Richard Blackwell Quadrangle, a large open garden area, reached via an elegant arched passageway (the Four Colleges Arch), offers magnificent scope for the gradual creation of a second quadrangle: the first stages of this are already being planned. The named features just mentioned commemorate important benefactions to the college, crucially important to its development thus far, including the move to St Giles'. Per Saugman of Blackwell Scientific Publications (*see* BLACKWELL'S) and RICHARD BLACKWELL (both Fellows of the college) were instrumental in arranging for the large Blackwell benefaction to the college. The Richard Blackwell Quadrangle was partly financed by Blackwell's (B.H. BLACKWELL and Blackwell Scientific Publications) and partly by the Pilgrim Trust and the OXFORD PRESERVATION TRUST.

In 1986 St Cross was still technically a department of the University, but it is expected to move to fully independent collegiate status within the next few years. The college has developed special relationships with several academic institutions in Oxford, providing or enhancing their formal links with the University – for example, the Oxford Centre for Postgraduate Hebrew Studies and the recently established Oxford Centre for Islamic Studies. Another is the IAN RAMSEY CENTRE, located within the college, whose work concerns the ethical problems arising from scientific and medical research.

It was announced in March 1987 that the Master, Dr Godfrey Stafford, who had succeeded the founding Master, W.E. van Heyningen, in 1979, was to be succeeded by Dr Richard Repp, Fellow of Linacre College and University lecturer in Turkish History.

St Cross Road Runs from HOLYWELL STREET to SOUTH PARKS ROAD. It takes its name from the parish church built in the form of a cross (or *crux athelana*). This was once a chapel-of-ease for the church of ST PETER-IN-THE-EAST. 'Although the original name was St. Cross, as being dedicated to the Holy Cross,' wrote THOMAS HEARNE, 'yet it became to be called Holy-well before the reign of King Edward I and was known at that time more by that name than by the original one.' There is a large graveyard adjoining the churchyard in which lie buried many Oxford worthies. On the west side of the road is Holywell Cottage (late 17th century). On the east side, down Mill Lane, is Holywell Ford, which was built for himself in 1888 by C.C. Rolfe, and HOLYWELL MANOR, rebuilt by Merton College in 1516 and reconditioned in 1931. Balliol College have been tenants of the manor since 1930. Most of the land in the area was at one time owned by Merton College. On the curve of the east side of the road is the new St Cross building by Sir Leslie Martin and Colin St John Wilson (built 1961–4), which houses the LAW LIBRARY, the English Faculty Library and the Institute of Economics and Statistics. New College playing fields are at the north-east end of the road and beyond them is Linacre College, formerly CHERWELL EDGE. A modern building, the Martin

Building, opposite Holywell Manor is by Sir Leslie Martin and houses graduates of both Balliol and St Anne's Colleges. Sir Leslie Martin is also the architect of the massive concrete Zoology and Psychology Building on the north-west corner of South Parks Road, which was finished in 1970. St Cross College owns the Old School and Master's house, built in 1857 by Buckeridge, situated on the east side at the western end. The main buildings of the college are now in ST GILES'. The lane which runs between St Cross and the wall of Magdalen College passes allotments and the Oxford City Lawn Tennis Club.

St Ebbe's This parish, to the south of the city centre, was united with that of St Budoc in about 1265. It extended beyond the town wall as far as the north bank of the THAMES. St Ebbe, to whom the church was dedicated in about 1005, was a 7th-century saint, daughter of the King of Northumbria. By 1279 property built in St Ebbe's was inhabited by the poorer townsfolk. From the 13th century the area was occupied by the BLACKFRIARS and GREYFRIARS, who built two large churches and priories. Greyfriars Abbey was erected next to the present ST EBBE'S CHURCH. Perrings' furniture shop in LITTLEGATE STREET was built over some of the foundations of the abbey. At the time this shop was built, bases of the abbey pillars and some walls 9 feet thick were discovered. It was because of the association of the friars with St Ebbe's that the modern inhabitants and the district itself came to be known as the Friars, and until recently there was an annual party at which former residents of the Friars came together for a reunion.

Between 1642 and 1644, when Oxford housed the King and his Court and became the royalist capital, some of the less important servants of the King lodged in St Ebbe's. Many people died of a plague in the summer of 1643 (*see* HEALTH, PUBLIC); and a serious FIRE in October 1644 further reduced the number of residents. After the CIVIL WAR, when there were extensive market gardens in the area, the population increased again. Foremost among the employers was Thomas Wrench (*d*.1714). He owned Paradise Gardens (*see* PARADISE SQUARE), which had formerly been the orchard of Greyfriars and was reputed to be the best kitchen garden in England. His successor, Thomas Tagg, paid his workmen high wages. It was not until the district was developed in the 19th century that the gardens ceased to exist. The name PENSON'S GARDENS (both here and in ST CLEMENT'S) recalls another leading family of gardeners of the 18th century. Even at that time the area continued to house many of the poorest citizens and became a large working-class district in the 19th century. St Ebbe's kept its public water pump until the 1820s. The area was transformed by the passing of an Act of Parliament in 1818 which allowed the manufacture of 'inflammable air' for lighting. That year the Friars district of St Ebbe's was chosen as the site for the gasworks. This building and that of its extension put a blight on the area for the next 125 years, during which the acrid smell from the gasworks and the intermittent flooding of the houses made St Ebbe's an unpleasant place in which to live. Gas Street, a road of long terraces of small brick houses, took its name from the works. The City Council in 1961, wishing to extinguish a name they thought unpleasant, renamed that part of it which survived the redevelopment Preachers Lane (reviving an old name in the vicinity). The name-plate reads: 'Preachers lane, formerly Gas Street'. Although in 1832 St Ebbe's did not suffer as much as St Clement's, in a subsequent cholera outbreak in 1849 thirty people died. A survey in 1848 had reported that many alleys and yards off Church Street showed 'a degree of neglect and filth rarely witnessed'.

In 1871 there was a riot among the poor because of the mishandling of the Bridgewater Charity which had been set up in 1859 to buy coal for five poor families. The Woodington Charity, set up in 1879, also gave coal to eight old people. These and other charities in the parish were combined in 1884 and became St Ebbe's Parochial Charities. Much charity work was undertaken in the area, members of the University playing their part, as in the foundation of the Balliol Boys' Club. A branch of the Co-operative Society was opened in 1876. In 1881 a Baptist chapel was built in Albert Street, but closed in 1972. So much housing was built between 1811 and 1851 in the vicinity of the gasworks that, when the Gaslight and Coke Company wished to expand, it was necessary for them to build bridges over the Thames and erect the new works in 1882 on the south bank. By 1928 the gasworks employed 300 people, labourers working as long as a forty-seven-hour week and stokers up to fifty-six hours. One of the bridges is now used as a cycle track from South Oxford. The last of the vast gasometers towering above the St Ebbe's skyline was demolished in 1968.

The destruction of St Ebbe's itself began in earnest in the 1950s and car parks replaced the houses until redevelopment began. Building was held up while road plans were discussed. In 1941 there had been a plan for a riverside road through St Ebbe's, and from 1948 onwards there were interminable plans, enquiries, surveys and ministerial pronouncements. The Queen visited St Ebbe's in 1968 when she viewed the excavations under the old Church Street (*see* THAMES STREET). The names Friars, Paradise and Gas remind one of the old St Ebbe's, little of which remains.

In the early 1970s the WESTGATE CENTRE was built on the site of the old Castle Street and Church Street (*see* CASTLE STREET and PENNYFARTHING PLACE). These years also saw the end of MacFisheries Corner, at the junction of QUEEN STREET, NEW ROAD and the former CASTLE STREET, which was so called after the fish shop on the corner. The Salvation Army Citadel on the west side of Castle Street was demolished but a new one (by John Fryman) was erected in 1970–1 in Albion Place. St Ebbe's now has many other new buildings. The New Centre for the Deaf was restored in 1968, retaining not only 17th-century parts but also a mediaeval gateway found in a wall during restoration. LUCY FAITHFULL HOUSE (by Philip del Nevo of Oxford Architects Partnership, 1978) is nearby; and opposite, in Albion Place, are offices now occupied by Central Independent Television, the holders of the IBA franchise for the area which includes Oxfordshire. Some of the old streets have disappeared, such as Albert Terrace, Belvidere Street, Bridge Street (which crossed the TRILL MILL STREAM), Bridport Street, Cambridge Terrace, Commercial Road (formerly Row), Friars Street, New Street, Orchard Street, Pike Street (revived in 1986), Union Street and most of Wood Street. Abbey Place survives only as the name of a car park. A short length of Albert Street, Cambridge Terrace, Littlegate and Norfolk Streets still survive, as do the names of Blackfriars Road and Trinity Street, which, with FRIARS WHARF and Preachers Lane built some years ago, now form some of the roads in a new (1978 onwards) housing development beside the river south of Thames Street. Sadler Walk and Dale Close (not to be confused with the former Sadler Street and Dale Street) are among other new roads in that area.

St Ebbe's Church *Pennyfarthing Place*. The present church stands on the site of one dedicated in about 1005 to Ebbe, a 7th-century saint, the daughter of Aethelfrith, King of Northumbria, and sister of the Northumbrian kings Oswald and Oswy. Becoming a nun, she founded a nunnery at Ebchester, on the Derwent, and was later Abbess of a 'double' monastery, containing both monks and nuns, at Coldingham (St Abb's Head) on the coast of Berwickshire. Until the Dissolution of the Monasteries, when it passed to the Crown, the church formed part of Eynsham Abbey. In 1864 the advowson was sold to the Earl of Shaftesbury, passing later to the OXFORD CHURCHES TRUST to ensure the continuance of an evangelical ministry, which continues at the present time. Part of the tower fell down in 1648 and the whole church was repaired in 1696. Despite further repairs, by 1813 its condition had become dangerous and it was demolished. Rebuilt and enlarged in Early English style to the designs of William Fisher, it was reopened in 1816 and further enlarged in 1862 and 1868 by G.E. STREET, the diocesan architect, who added a south aisle, created a north aisle by arcading, and rebuilt the top stage of the tower. In 1904–5 the tower was heightened, and a 12th-century doorway with fine beakhead ornamentation taken from the south wall in 1813 and preserved in the church was inserted in the west wall, A.M. Mowbray being the architect. When in 1961 the church of ST PETER-LE-BAILEY ceased to be parochial and became the chapel of St Peter's Hall (now College), the benefice was united with St Ebbe's. The Rector of St Ebbe's from 1736 to 1742, Nathaniel Bliss, later became Astronomer Royal; and Thomas Valpy French (Rector 1875–7) resigned to become the first Bishop of Lahore. Roger Bacon (*d.*1294) is buried in the parish, his fellow Franciscans having come to Oxford in 1224 and built their church and friary outside the CITY WALL, close to St Ebbe's.

The original rectory-house recorded in 1324 and 1352 was ruinous by about 1520 and demolished in 1790. In 1854–5 a house was built in PARADISE SQUARE to the designs of G.E. Street, enlarged in 1869. It is now the office of the Chief Environmental Health Officer. It was replaced in 1971 by a new rectory-house built in Roger Bacon Lane, PENNYFARTHING PLACE, to the design of K.C. White and Partners. The adjoining parish centre was completed in 1974.

St Ebbe's Street Running southwards from QUEEN STREET to LITTLEGATE STREET, it was known as Little Bailey in the 17th century when it ran at right-angles to the Great Bailey. It is recorded as St Ebbe's Lane in the Survey of 1772. It may also have been known as Milk Street, although ANTHONY WOOD says there is no written record of this. There were tenements in the

Performers on stilts outside St Ebbe's Church in 1835 after it had been rebuilt in the Early English style by William Fisher.

street as early as 1302, and next to one belonging to the HOSPITAL OF ST JOHN THE BAPTIST was Carole Hall, owned by John de Derham and later by Richard le Noreys. In more recent times the northern half of the street has been occupied entirely by shops, the most famous of which was CAPE'S at Nos 28–32. Today, the firm which has been longest in the street is Ivor Fields, which moved here in February 1962. On the corner of PEMBROKE STREET on the site of St Ebbe's Cash Drapery Stores, is a branch of Barclays Bank by Martin and Lumley (1976). Fenwicks store was built in 1972. The northern part of St Ebbe's is now paved and has benches down the middle.

St Edmund and St Frideswide, Church of

Iffley Road. The weathercock on the copper spire of this Franciscan church is a familiar landmark. The church stands on the corner of Jackdaw Lane and IFFLEY ROAD, not far from the University rugby ground. It was designed for the Jesuits by a Brigittine priest – Fr Benedict Williamson – and Peart Foss in 1910 in order to serve the expanding ROMAN CATHOLIC population in the locality. It is in the romanesque style, faced with knapped flints and stone dressings. The cost of £4671 was met by an anonymous donor. The titular saints are well chosen: St Edmund Rich (1180–1242) was born at Abingdon, became Professor of Philosophy at Oxford in 1219 and was elected Archbishop of Canterbury in 1234; ST FRIDESWIDE, a Saxon princess who became a nun, is patron saint of the city. The Franciscans acquired the church in 1930, and built GREYFRIARS next to it. The main entrance, through the west door, opens into a vestibule partitioned from the main body of the interior by a glass screen. Stairs lead to the choir loft above. An open-timbered roof covers the wide nave which leads through a chancel arch to the sanctuary steps. The high altar is a simple stone table. Behind it a window depicts Blessed Agnellus holding the letter of obedience from St Francis, with the University in the background. On either side the wall is pierced by grilles to the monks' choir. Arcaded aisles on the north and south side of the church terminate in chapels decorated with grey marble. The Stations of the Cross were designed by Fr Benedict Williamson. The six-branch 18th-century candlesticks come from the Jesuit chapel in ST CLEMENT'S. A relic which spans the centuries is incorporated in the credence table in the Chapel of the Mother of the Good Shepherd – a capital from the mediaeval Greyfriars at ST EBBE'S, which was found at the beginning of the century by workmen demolishing houses built of rubble from the suppressed friary.

St Edmund Hall

Queen's Lane. Although a college in the strict sense only since 1957, St Edmund Hall's history goes back to the 13th century, for it is the sole survivor of the mediaeval ACADEMIC HALLS that provided undergraduates with accommodation and tuition before the colleges began to do so. It can claim to be 'the oldest academical society for the education of undergraduates' (A.B. Emden) in any university. It takes its name from St Edmund of Abingdon, Archbishop of Canterbury (1234–40), who traditionally resided and taught in a house at the western end of the present front quadrangle when he was a Regent Master in the arts, probably in the 1190s. Mediaeval halls were not incorporated and had no initial endowment or individual statutes; the hall has, therefore, no date of foundation. But early in the 13th century the site of the front quadrangle was owned by John de Bermingham, Rector of IFFLEY, whose relatives in 1261–2 sold part of it to Thomas of Malmesbury, perpetual vicar of COWLEY. The Berminghams and Malmesbury are likely to have kept a student hall. In 1271–2 Thomas granted his part of the site to OSENEY ABBEY, which owned it until the Dissolution in 1539. The name *Aula sancti Edmundi* first survives by chance in an Oseney rent-roll for 1317–18; it may be considerably older. The list of sixty known Principals begins with William Boys (*c*.1315). The front quadrangle reached its present extent *c*.1469 when Oseney purchased from Magdalen College some land that the Principals had been renting.

The Dissolution brought the hall into danger of extinction. In the early decades of the 16th century it had come into a close relationship with its neighbour The Queen's College, of which a number of its Principals were also Fellows, and *c*.1531 Queen's had obtained a lease of the hall from Oseney Abbey. Nevertheless, in 1546 the Crown sold the hall to property speculators, ultimately to the Londoner William Burnell; and the principalship came into the hands of Ralph Rudde, who had recently been expelled from his fellowship at Queen's. Rudde used his office as a base for vexing the Provost of Queen's, William Denysson. Fortunately, in 1553 Denysson managed to buy the freehold of the hall from Burnell, and when Rudde died in 1557 he transferred the freehold to his college. In 1559 Denysson himself received from the CONVOCATION of the University authority to name the Principal, but soon afterwards the right to elect was vested in The Queen's College, which was placed under the obligation that 'henceforth for ever [it] will preserve the ... Hall and will preserve it to literary uses'. Not until 1564 was a new Principal appointed, but the future and the separate identity of the hall were assured under

The east range of the front quadrangle of St Edmund Hall was built 1680–90 by Stephen Penton.

the aegis of The Queen's College. There was no considerable development as regards its position until the period of University reform in the later 19th century.

As a hall, St Edmund Hall both before and after the Reformation had no Fellows. Subject to the Aularian Statutes of the University, which prevailed from the late 15th century until 1937, the Principals exercised full control; they commonly held an ecclesiastical benefice at a distance from Oxford as well as the principalship. From the late 16th century they were usually assisted by Vice-Principals. The academic teaching of undergraduates was provided by graduates who served as tutors, and after the hall acquired a chapel in 1680–2 there were sometimes chaplains. The buying of provisions was the responsibility of a manciple. Undergraduate numbers fluctuated but were small. The year 1552 saw them as low as six, but early in the 17th century they were up to nearly forty and after the Restoration of 1660 they reached about sixty-five. In 1850 they were down to twenty-five, and in 1913 they were about forty.

In academic respects, before its 20th-century transformation, the hall had three high points. The first was in the mid-15th century after the appointment as Principal of John Thamys (1438). There were additions to the site, notably by the annexing of White Hall and then St Hugh's Hall. The latter was used as a dependent grammar hall until the 1480s, when the school that William of Waynflete attached to Magdalen College appears to have ended its *raison d'être*. The second came with the Restoration of 1660 and the principalships of Thomas Tullie (1658–76), Stephen Penton (1676–84) and John Mill (1685–1707). A well-known Vice-Principal of this period was White Kennett (1691–5), later Bishop of Peterborough. From Tullie's time the hall was particularly favoured by Wiltshire and other West Country families, and a number of its members entered Parliament – for example John (later Lord) Methuen (1665), who in 1703 negotiated the Methuen Treaty with Portugal after which port superseded Burgundy as a favourite wine in England. Two of Tullie's undergraduates, Sir Thomas Littleton (1665) and Sir Richard (later Baron) Onslow (1671), became Speakers of the House of Commons. The antiquary THOMAS HEARNE, who matriculated in 1696, remains the most distinguished scholar to have been an undergraduate of the hall. During the period of evangelical ascendancy in the early 19th century – before the academic revival of the colleges inaugurated by Balliol and Oriel took general effect – the hall for a third time achieved academic prominence: Isaac Crouch (Vice-Principal 1783–1807) in particular was recognised to have impressed upon it 'a novel character for erudition no less than seriousness', a character to which its holding of evangelical scholarly literature still testifies. Among the Principals of the 17th to the 19th centuries there stand out as scholars and writers John Aglionby (1601–10), who took part in the preparation of the Authorised Version of the Bible; the New Testament textual scholar John Mill (1685–1707); Thomas Shaw (1740–51), whose travels in Barbary and the Levant won him European fame; and Edward Moore (1864–1913), the authority on Dante.

From the 15th until the 19th century a feature of the hall's history was its connection with current religious movements of one kind or another. In the early 15th century it was a stronghold of Lollardy (see LOLLARDS). One Principal, William Taylor (c.1405), became a Lollard preacher and in 1423 was burnt at the stake at Smithfield as a relapsed heretic. Another, Peter Payne (1411), in 1413 fled to Prague, where he died in 1455 after an active sojourn with the Hussites; in 1432 he had represented the moderate Taborites at the Council of Basle. The late 17th century found the hall a nursery of two well-known Non-Jurors – men who, from loyalty to the Stuarts, refused to take oaths to their successors after 1688: John Kettlewell, the devotional writer, who matriculated in 1670, and Thomas Hearne, who would not take an oath to the Hanoverians. The year 1768 saw the Vice-Principal, John Higson, expressing alarm at the presence in the hall of young men 'who talked of regeneration, inspiration and drawing nigh unto God'. When the tolerant Principal George Dixon (1760–87) declined to take action, Higson reported them to the VICE-CHANCELLOR of the University who, with four ASSESSORS, held an inquiry in the dining hall and expelled six students. This event occasioned a celebrated exchange between Boswell and SAMUEL JOHNSON: 'I talked [Boswell wrote] of the recent expulsion of six students from the University of Oxford, who were methodists, and would not desist from publickly praying and exhorting. JOHNSON. "Sir, that expulsion was extremely just and proper. What have they to do at an University, who are not willing to be taught, but will presume to teach? Where is religion to be learnt, but at an University? Sir, they were examined, and found to be mighty ignorant fellows." BOSWELL. "But, was it not hard, Sir, to expel them, for I am told they were good beings?". JOHNSON. "I believe they might be good beings; but they were not fit to be in the University of Oxford. A cow is a very good animal in the field; but we turn her out of a garden."' There ensued vehement pamphlet-warfare that lasted into the 19th century. Despite the expulsion, St Edmund Hall was soon to become for more than half a century a fervent centre of Oxford evangelicalism. At a time when the Principals were content to leave the running of the hall pretty much to the Vice-Principals, three successive Vice-Principals – Isaac Crouch who was Dixon's last appointee to the office, Daniel Wilson (1807–12), later Bishop of Calcutta, and John Hill (1812–51) kept the evangelical tradition alive. But thereafter, with the principalships of John Barrow (1854–61) and John Branthwaite (1861–4), the hall became Tractarian (see OXFORD MOVEMENT), especially with the advent of the theologian and preacher H.P. Liddon as Vice-Principal (1859–62) after evangelical attacks had forced him to leave Cuddesdon Theological College.

It fell to the next Principal, Edward Moore (appointed 1864), to ensure the survival of the hall as the repercussions of the later 19th-century reform of the University became apparent. The appointment of the Oxford University Commissioners of 1850 (see ROYAL COMMISSIONS) had already led to the canvassing of the suggestion that 'the appointment to the Principalship may be adjusted with a view of hereafter throwing the post open to the University, and also of securing to the Hall its proper independence'; in 1855 the suggestion was, however, strenuously resisted by William Thompson, the Bursar of The Queen's College. By 1870 the introduction by the University of an 'unattached students' system deprived the few remaining halls of a main justification – their cheapness as places of University education – and Moore viewed the future with pessimism when in 1871 a new Royal Commission was set up. The Statutory Commissioners of 1877 confirmed his fears by providing for the suppression of the other halls and, with the agreement of The Queen's College, for the reduction of St Edmund Hall, when its principalship next became vacant, to being a dependency of The Queen's College with only twenty-four exhibitioners. In 1903 Moore announced that he intended to resign. Queen's sought to persuade the University to enact an amending statute effecting not now a partial but a total absorption of the hall. University opinion rallied in its defence as the last surviving hall which, under Moore, had shown vigorous life. Moore postponed his resignation for ten years, and from 1907 the hall found a champion in LORD CURZON, who, as CHANCELLOR of the University, was ex officio its VISITOR. In 1912 a University statute, approved in 1913 by a royal Order in Council, provided 'for the continuance of the Hall as a place of education, religion and learning separate from The Queen's College, while preserving the right of the College to appoint the Principal of the Hall'. Moore could safely resign.

Between the First World War and 1957 the hall underwent a gradual transformation from its circumstances as a hall to its present status as a college. A small beginning was made in 1926, when a body of six trustees, including the Principal, was empowered to hold property on its behalf. More thorough changes came through the vision, skill and determination of A.B. Emden (Principal 1929–51). A distinguished mediaevalist and historian of universities, he was resolved that the hall's by now unique character should be preserved. It should expand and be reconstituted to meet modern needs, but remain the oldest surviving hall rather than becoming the youngest of the colleges. In 1934 The Queen's College expressed willingness to relax the control that it had exercised since 1557. In due course the freehold of the site and buildings was vested in the Official Trustee of Charity Lands, as Custodian Trustee. The statute of the University, approved by the King in Council on 21 December 1937, by which the hall's new constitution was laid down, vested all real and personal property belonging to the hall, with the exception of the site and buildings, in the University as Custodian Trustee. It raised to ten the trustees as established in 1926 and gave them, in conjunction with the Principal, enlarged powers as managing trustees. They also became the body of electors to the principalship. The hall received statutes of its own. On the academic side of its life, the Vice-Principal and tutors were accorded the title of Fellows, and in matters of internal administration and educational policy they had a claim to be consulted and to consent. Nevertheless, in accordance with Emden's vision for the hall, the Principal retained his prerogatives and authority: as the statute expressed it, 'The Principal shall have charge of the Hall, subject to the superintendence of the Trustees and the collaboration of the Fellows.'

Emden was without doubt one of the outstanding heads of house in 20th-century Oxford. But his very success in building up undergraduate numbers, in expanding the buildings, in providing for a wide range of subjects to be taught at the hall, and in appointing tutors of high personal and academic quality, made it inevitable that the hall would transcend his vision for it and become a fully collegiate institution that could satisfy the aspirations of all who taught and studied there. His successor as Principal, the patristic scholar, J.N.D. Kelly (1951–79), speedily and successfully brought about the necessary change. In 1957 Queen Elizabeth II approved the grant to the hall of its charter of incorporation as a college, which HRH the Duke of Edinburgh presented to it on 6 June 1958. A wholly new body of statutes, further revised in 1974, came into force. Thus, since 1957, the hall as a corporate body has stood in possession of its own site, buildings and other property, and has begun the task of accumulating endowments. Subject to its statutes it has control of its affairs through a governing body in which, as in other colleges, the Principal is *primus inter pares* with the Fellows. But from respect for a history extending over eight centuries it has kept the name St Edmund Hall.

Its buildings are best approached in the light of its history. Apart from the church of ST PETER-IN-THE-EAST, which it has used since 1970 as an undergraduate library, and from a small portion of the mediaeval CITY WALL, the old buildings are all in the front quadrangle, which is among the most attractive in Oxford. The only visible remains of the mediaeval hall is a large mid-15th-century fireplace in the middle of the north range, which was part of the reconstruction in John Thamys's day. (The shaft, though not the head, of the well in the middle of the quadrangle is also mediaeval.) The part of the north range to the east of the sun-dial was built during the principalship of Thomas Bowsfield (1581–1601); that to the west was built *c.*1741 by Thomas Shaw. Shaw intended to replace the ruinous mediaeval buildings there in correct but dull Palladian style, but fortunately funds did not allow, and he faithfully copied Bowsfield's work. The Old Dining Hall and the rooms above represent Thomas Tullie's first step towards his improvement of the hall; begun in 1659 they are one of the few Oxford buildings from the Interregnum. His predecessor, Adam Airey (1631–58), had already (*c.*1635) built the adjacent quarters that are now the porters' lodge and part of the Principal's lodgings. The cottage in the south-east corner of the quadrangle is a little earlier still. Most of the east range is taken up by the chapel and Old Library built by Stephen Penton at the culmination of the hall's late 17th-century prosperity. Members of the hall had hitherto worshipped in St Peter-in-the-East. In 1680 Penton began the chapel in classical style which BISHOP FELL of Oxford dedicated in 1682 as 'St. Edmund's Chapel in the University of Oxford'. The mason of the building, which was completed within ten years, was Bartholomew Peisley (*see* PEISLEYS *and* VANBRUGH HOUSE). The panelling and other woodwork are by the Oxford joiner, Arthur Frogley. The east window was reconstructed in 1865; the glass is by BURNE-JONES and MORRIS. The altarpiece, of the Supper at Emmaus, was painted in 1957–8 by Ceri Richards. Over the antechapel Penton built the hall's first library, announced from the outside by the sculpted piles of books supporting the pediment of the chapel door. It was the first Oxford library to be built with shelves along the walls, and the last to be furnished with chains. It was extended in 1931. The south range of

the quadrangle is the latest. The portion of the Principal's lodgings at the west end was built in 1826, and the adjacent rooms were added a hundred years later. Until 1934 the remainder of the south side was a shrubbery; in that year, as a tablet commemorates, the range was completed to mark the 700th anniversary of St Edmund's consecration as Archbishop of Canterbury; the architect was R. Fielding Dodd. Architecturally diverse though it is, the quadrangle composes splendidly into a visual whole, and its small scale perpetuates the friendliness that has always been a mark of the hall's life.

The buildings to the east – a new dining hall and extensive residential accommodation – are the result of the hall's post-1945 development. A.B. Emden had the foresight to begin the leasing of properties on the HIGH STREET so that the hall was no longer constrained by its 15th-century dimensions, and in 1948 a share in the Besse Benefaction to the University made possible a large increase in the number of student rooms along the High Street (*see* ANTONIN BESSE). Under Emden's successor J.N.D. Kelly the hall purchased further properties there in 1956. The main development, mostly completed in 1968–70, was an achievement of Kelly's middle years as Principal. The architect was Gilbert Howes, of Kenneth Stevens and Associates, who planned the highly successful, economical and pleasing use of a somewhat restricted site. In 1979 the Hall acquired extensive property in Norham Gardens, including the architecturally interesting house known as Gunfield. In 1986 the Isis Hotel in IFFLEY ROAD was converted into further accommodation for junior members.

Kelly was succeeded as Principal by the engineer Sir Ieuan Maddock (1979–82); the present Principal is the philosopher J.C.B. Gosling. Since 1978 the hall – Teddy Hall as it is familiarly known – has admitted women to membership. As a result of its 20th-century transformation it has become numerically one of the larger Oxford colleges, with (at the time of writing) some forty Fellows, eighty-five graduate students, and 340 undergraduates. Unique by reason of its history, it combines the maturity and confidence of long, rich experience as a hall with the modernity and adaptability of its new life as a college.

The corporate designation is The Principal, Fellows and Scholars of St Edmund Hall in the University of Oxford.

(Emden, A.B., *An Oxford Hall in Medieval Times*, second edition, Oxford, 1968; *An Account of the Chapel and Library Building, St. Edmund Hall, Oxford*, Oxford, 1932; and 'St. Edmund Hall', in *The Victoria History of Oxford*, Vol. III, Oxford, 1954, pp. 319–35; Ollard, S.L., *The Six Students of St. Edmund Hall Expelled from the University of Oxford in 1768*, London and Oxford, 1911; *Royal Commission on Historical Monuments, England: An Inventory of the Historical Monuments in the City of Oxford*, London, 1939, pp. 100–3; Sherwood, J., and Pevsner, N., *The Buildings of England: Oxfordshire*, Harmondsworth, 1974, pp. 191–4.)

St Edward's School *Woodstock Road.* An independent boarding school (of St Edward, King and Martyr) for boys aged thirteen to eighteen, founded in 1863 by the Rev. Thomas Chamberlain, a Tractarian (*see* OXFORD MOVEMENT), the vicar of ST THOMAS THE MARTYR, Becket Street, his curate, the Rev. Frederick

Fryer, becoming its first headmaster. The school was moved from its original premises in NEW INN HALL STREET in 1873, under the Rev. A.B. Simeon, from 1870 to 1892 its second headmaster, to its present 110-acre site. Its buildings occupy an area bounded by the WOODSTOCK ROAD, Oakthorpe Road and SOUTH PARADE, and are linked by a subway (1928) under the Woodstock Road to playing fields and some further buildings extending to the Oxford CANAL: there are uninterrupted views across PORT MEADOW to WYTHAM woods. The school has its boat-house (1927) at GODSTOW, and cricket pavilion (1933) on the playing fields, both presented by the Old Boys.

From 1884 the headmasters have been known as Wardens. Under the Rev. W.H. Ferguson (Warden 1913–25, and Warden of Radley College 1925–37), the number of boys rose from 100 to 250, under the Rev. H.E. Kendall (Warden 1925–54) to over 450, and under the Hon. F.F. Fisher (Warden 1954–66, and Master of Wellington College 1966–80) to over 500. Divided among eight Houses, there are at present some 460 boarders, 100 day boys and since 1983 a dozen sixth-form day girls. Since 1863 there have been over 8500 names on the school roll. From 1921 to 1927 the school was a member of the Woodard Society.

The main buildings are formed around a spacious quadrangle and are in red brick, except for the chapel (1877), which is in stone; its situation in the north-east corner of the quadrangle befits its symbolic position as the cornerstone of the school. The original school building (1873) contains the Warden's house, the dining hall and Apsley House, and occupies the north side of the quad; the Lodge (1879) is on the west side; Big School (1881) on the east side. All these were designed by William Wilkinson. The high-roofed chapel has a raised apsidal chancel with nine lancet windows containing stained glass (1893–97) by C.E. Kempe. The altar crucifix was brought by Simeon from Oberammergau. The chapel tower in the south-west corner of the building has an exterior niche containing a statue of St Edward; the 100-foot-high tower makes its contribution to Oxford's 'dreaming spires'. A Calvary for those who fell in 1914–18 stands in a small quad by the south wall of the chapel and nearby are buried, among others, the first Warden, Simeon, and his wife.

Across the quadrangle, on the south side, stand Macnamara's House (1882), designed by H.W. Moore, and Tilly's House (1925), by H.S. Rogers; to the south-east a classroom block (1931) and Cowell's and Segar's Houses (1936), by Brook Kitchin; to the north-east of Big School, the Memorial Library (1954), by Fielding Dodd and Stevens; and by the playing fields, Sing's and Field Houses (1965), by Matthew, Johnson-Marshall and Partners. Extensions and renovations to all these have taken place in recent years. Latterly, the New Hall (1975), for assemblies, plays and concerts; the New Library (1976), a conversion of Big School; the indoor sports complex, opened in his name in 1982 by Sir Douglas Bader; and Corfe House (1983) have all been designed by the Falconer partnership.

Known until 1892 as the Confraternity of St Edward's, the St Edward's Society (Old Boys) has numbered among its distinguished members the writer Kenneth Grahame (1868–75), the actor Lord Olivier (1921–4), the pioneer of flying Sir Geoffrey de Havilland (1898–9), the RAF heroes Sir Douglas Bader (1923–8) and Guy Gibson VC (1932–6), the

A.B. Simeon (seated centre), *Warden of St Edward's School, surrounded by the school's staff, 1876.*

poet and biographer Robert Gittings (1927–30), Tom (Sir Thomas) Hopkinson of *Picture Post* (1919–23), the Cabinet Minister Sir John Davies (1929–34), the Rt Rev. R.C. Mortimer, Bishop of Exeter (1916–21), *The Times* cricket correspondent John Woodcock (1940–5) and J.S. Woodhouse, headmaster of Rugby from 1967 to 1981 and of Lancing since 1981 (1946–51). Before beginning a distinguished career in the public service, (Sir) George Mallaby was an assistant master (1924–35).

(Hill, R.D., *A History of St Edward's School, 1863–1963*, 1963.)

St Francis of Assisi, Church of *Hollow Way, Cowley.* Designed by Lawrence Dale as a simple rectangular hall without aisles or tower, the church was built in 1930–1, on a site given by Morris Motors, to serve as a chapel-of-ease for ST JAMES, COWLEY, the foundation stone being laid by Sir William Morris (*see* LORD NUFFIELD). In 1962 it became a permanent church dedicated to St Francis of Assisi. At the east end a 'chancel' area with altar and hanging cross of abstract design (by A. Hawkesley) is convertible into a chapel when folding panels are closed to divide it from the main 'nave' area of the hall. Scenes from the life of St Francis are depicted on the roof beams, colourfully painted by members of the Oxford School of Arts and Crafts (later, Schools of Technology, Art and Commerce – *see* POLYTECHNIC).

St Frideswide *see* FRIDESWIDE, SAINT.

St Frideswide, Church of *Botley Road.* Between 1851 and 1861, OSNEY town (or New Osney) was built in the parish of ST THOMAS, west of the THAMES. In response to the vigorous presence of the Baptist church in the new district, Christ Church, patrons of St Thomas's, together with the High Anglican vicar of the parish, Thomas Chamberlain, pressed for the establishment of a church. The foundation stone of St Frideswide's was laid in 1870 and the consecration performed by the BISHOP OF OXFORD in 1872. The architect, S.S. Teulon, of Huguenot descent, had planned a 54-foot tower with a 40-foot spire to complete the present building but financial problems prevented their realisation. Later plans for the completion of tower and spire by H.G.W. Drinkwater in 1876 and J.O. Scott in 1888 were also unfulfilled.

Built in an approximately Early English style with Franco-Flemish elements and described in Pevsner as 'typical Teulon in its ruthlessness', its exterior appearance is of sturdy strength, in rough-hewn stone, heavily buttressed, with a squat octagonal tower. Its interior consists of an aisleless nave narrowing to an apsidal chancel, the overall length being 105 feet, and seating some 300 people. The vestry, the short north transept (later a Lady Chapel) and south transept, housing the organ (1879 by A. Hunter of Kensington), were later additions by H.G.W. Drinkwater, who in 1875 also designed the vicarage-house on the south side of the church.

Among the stained-glass windows are five in the nave brought from St Thomas's Convent (founded by Thomas Chamberlain in 1847) when demolished in 1958; and placed on the walls of the nave in 1955 are fourteen wooden roof-angels from the chapel of St Mary's Home, LITTLEMORE, and which may have originated in the Oxford Female Penitentiary

(established 1832) in HOLYWELL MANOR. Also in the nave is the Alice Door, carved by Alice Liddell, daughter of DR LIDDELL, Dean of Christ Church (*see* ALICE), for the mission church of St Frideswide, Poplar, built in 1890 and closed in 1953 following wartime bomb damage.

Vicars of St Frideswide's have often been colourful characters: G.L. Kemp (1872–96), an Oxford boxing BLUE, floored 'an intruder in the belfry with a blow to the chin'; A.J. Miller (1896–1905), father of seven, was 'frequently seen with a child on his shoulder (either his own or someone else's) like an amiable St Christopher'; W.A. Spence (1905–14) introduced a tabernacle into the Lady Chapel without the Bishop's permission and resigned to become a Roman Catholic; G.H. Tremenheere (1914–22) alienated his choir by insisting on teetotalism and the singing of Gregorian plainsong; C. Overy (1922–33) collected unusual musical instruments and rigorously followed religious observance; and, best known, Arnold Mallinson (1933–76), antiquary and notable numismatist, was inundated with gifts of stuffed owls in glass cases when he appealed for one to frighten bats lodging in ST MARGARET'S, BINSEY, of which he became Perpetual Curate in 1950. The benefice was united with that of ST THOMAS THE MARTYR in 1979.

St Frideswide's Priory Founded at the beginning of the 12th century by Gwymund, a royal chaplain, by the south wall of the town on the site of an earlier collegiate church which Gwymund had acquired from the diocese of Salisbury. The Augustinian canons of the priory were later granted permission to build over the wall; and in 1183, when the church seems to have been rebuilt, the relics of ST FRIDESWIDE – who had founded a religious house on the site in 703 – were translated here. Ten years later, however, both church and priory buildings were destroyed by fire. Reconstruction was completed by the early 13th century; and in the early 15th a guest-house was added on the instructions of the Bishop of Lincoln. Towards the end of the 15th century new and commodious lodgings were provided for the prior, and the cloister was rebuilt. The priory was extremely prosperous and owned large estates, though its canons did not enjoy a good reputation. After the Dissolution of the Monasteries the priory buildings were either demolished by CARDINAL WOLSEY or converted to use for his Cardinal College, later known as Christ Church. In 1546 the church became the cathedral of the diocese of Oxford which was created from part of the huge diocese of Lincoln in 1542.

(*See also* CHRIST CHURCH CATHEDRAL.)

St George's Chapel *George Street.* Consecrated in 1850 to serve as a chapel-of-ease for the poorer part of the parish of ST MARY MAGDALEN. Built to the designs of P. Harrison at a cost of £5500, it was described as 'chaste and handsome in the Decorated Gothic style'. The chapel attracted congregations of over 250 in 1854 but fewer than half that number in 1869. Despite increased congregations in the 1880s, it was closed c.1918 and demolished in 1935, being replaced by the Ritz (now Cannon) cinema (*see* CINEMAS).

St George's in the Castle Before embarking with William the Conqueror, ROBERT D'OILLY and Roger d'Ivri agreed to share all their spoils equally between them. And three years after d'Oilly had built Oxford CASTLE in 1071 the two friends together founded or refounded a college for secular canons within the castle walls. The canons, one of whom for a time was Geoffrey of Monmouth (d.1154), quickly earned a reputation for piety and learning. For a time the chapel was the church of a parish whose boundaries stretched beyond the castle walls, but some time in the 13th century, because of its inconvenient site, St George's lost its parish to ST THOMAS'S. In 1149 the church was granted to OSENEY ABBEY which agreed to maintain two priests to serve it and which, towards the end of the 15th century, founded a new college with five chaplains. At the Dissolution of the Monasteries the church passed to Christ Church, but by 1611 was no longer in use. The early Norman rubble west tower survives, as does the low, groin-vaulted crypt, which was extensively reconstructed in the late 18th century and again in the mid-19th.

St Giles' By the War Memorial at the north end of St Giles', the BANBURY ROAD and the WOODSTOCK ROAD merge to create the widest street in Oxford. It extends from ST GILES' CHURCH in the north to the MARTYRS' MEMORIAL in the south and is lined on both sides by London plane trees. There are lamp standards down the centre of the street, with PARKING for cars under the trees. The whole of the street may have been built up by 1279, but the north end remained rural, many of the houses being used as farmhouses. Cattle and sheep used to be driven along St Giles' to market in Oxford and early MAPS show a pond in the middle of the road where the War Memorial now stands. ST GILES' FAIR has been held in the street in September for centuries. The many 18th-century houses, built as residences and offices for professional men and University professors, make St Giles' one of the most attractive and unspoilt streets in the city.

Passing along the east side going north from Balliol College by the Martyrs' Memorial, No. 1 is a three-storey, 18th-century listed stone building owned and occupied by Morrell, Peel & Gamlen, Oxford's oldest firm of solicitors, founded before 1765. Adjoining is the Dolphin Building and the rear entrance to Trinity College. St John's College has a long frontage to St Giles'. Opposite the main entrance is a forecourt with a low stone wall on three sides called The Terrace. No. 9, later the college estate office, was for many years in the 19th century the offices of the solicitors, Dayman & Walsh. The President's Drive is at the north end of the college. By the LAMB AND FLAG inn is Lamb and Flag Passage, cobbled and leading past an ancient chestnut tree to MUSEUM ROAD. No. 13 St Giles' is a narrow four-storey house and Nos 14 and 15 are occupied as offices. No. 16 is ST GILES' HOUSE (formerly the Judge's Lodging). The OXFORD HIGH SCHOOL FOR GIRLS opened here in 1875 before transferring to No. 38 in 1878. Nos 17–20 are the town houses belonging to St John's College. No. 21 is Black Hall, now part of QUEEN ELIZABETH HOUSE, and No. 22 is a white stuccoed house with three dormers, next to the new Mathematical Institute. No. 30, on the corner of KEBLE ROAD, is early 17th century and was formerly the Pheasant Inn, now occupied by Wenn, Townsend & Co., chartered accountants. Behind the War Memorial and in front of St Giles' churchyard

is a bronze sun-dial by Karl König, erected in 1985 to commemorate the Oxford–Bonn link.

Passing south along the west side from LITTLE CLARENDON STREET, the building on the corner is occupied, above the shop, by the Plunkett Foundation for Co-operative Studies, founded in 1919 by Sir Horace Curzon Plunkett for the study and development of co-operation throughout the world. Nos 32–3 is occupied by the bank of Child & Co. The stone building with wrought-iron balcony (Nos 34–6) is occupied by the OXFORD AND COUNTY SECRETARIAL COLLEGE, the RN and RM, Army and RAF Careers Information Office, and the Christian Science Reading Room respectively. At the rear is a new building for First Church of Christ, Scientist. No. 37 is a late 18th-century house. No. 38, formerly the home of the Oxford High School for Girls, was later St Ursula's Convent School and is now ST BENET'S HALL. Nos 38 and 39 were built about 1830 and advertised as residences for persons of the first distinction. No. 39a has above the door the arms of SAMUEL WILBERFORCE, BISHOP OF OXFORD 1845–69, who lived here. Parts of No. 40 are early 17th century. A white house set back from the road with a lawn in front, it appears in one of Osbert Lancaster's illustrations for ZULEIKA DOBSON in the RANDOLPH HOTEL. It was the home of the Bywater-Ward family. No. 41 is an ashlar stone house built about 1700 and occupied by the Mathematical Institute's Centre for Mathematical Biology. No. 42, with a wrought-iron balcony, is occupied as professional offices. No. 43 is dated 1660, but was subsequently altered, and is occupied by the Religious Society of Friends (Quakers). Beyond Wellington Place is the EAGLE AND CHILD inn. Next to No. 54 is a passage known in the 19th century as Drewett's yard, while No. 54 itself is a 16th- to 17th-century cottage of two storeys with two dormers, occupied by REGENT'S PARK COLLEGE. No. 55, a late 18th-century house, is the Principal's lodgings of the college with a fine coloured coat of arms above the door (see HERALDRY). Beyond PUSEY STREET (formerly Alfred Street) is the chapel of PUSEY HOUSE and St Cross College. No. 64 is BLACKFRIARS, the Dominican Priory of the Holy Spirit. Nos 66 and 67 is a 19th-century Gothic house built in 1869 by George Wyatt, an ironmonger whose shop was at No. 66. Beyond that lie the TAYLOR INSTITUTION and BEAUMONT STREET.

St Giles, Church of *St Giles'*. Probably built as a private church by Edwin, son of Godegose, between 1123 and 1133, it soon became parochial, the parish extending as far as the River Cherwell (see THAMES) to the east, the present bypass to the north, and the present WALTON STREET to the west, an area then of open land except for Walton village. When NORTH OXFORD was built in the 19th century the parish was divided by the creation of the parishes of SUMMER-TOWN (1834), ST PAUL'S (1837), and ST PHILIP AND ST JAMES (1863). In 1139 Edwin granted the church to GODSTOW ABBEY; at the Dissolution of the Monasteries it passed to the Crown, then to Henry VIII's physician, George Owen, Lord of Walton manor; finally, after further changes of ownership, to St John's College, the present patrons, in 1573. Until the middle of the 19th century the vicars were all Fellows of St John's, living in college, the best known being WILLIAM JUXON (vicar 1610–15), distinguished for his 'edifying way of preaching', who succeeded WILLIAM

A watercolour of c.1812 by William Turner of Oxford showing sheep being driven down St Giles' with the church of St Mary Magdalen in the background.

LAUD as President of the college, and, like Laud, later became Archbishop of Canterbury, in 1660. In its exposed position, St Giles' was much damaged during the siege of Oxford in the CIVIL WAR and was still in 'great decay' in 1659. In 1643 its furniture was burnt by parliamentary troops captured at Cirencester by Prince Rupert and being held prisoner in the church; in 1645 John Goad (vicar 1644–6) held services while parliamentary cannon bombarded the city defences.

After the turbulence of the 17th century there was tranquillity during the 18th; and though affected by the OXFORD MOVEMENT, particularly in its interior decoration, St Giles' did not become High Church, its services showing 'cheerful simplicity and good taste', in contrast to the 'objectionable practices' and 'Romanising tendencies' of the Tractarians elsewhere. Later, on his retirement, C.C. Inge (vicar 1913–37) wrote of 'the central type of churchmanship with which our church has been for so long identified'.

Although some work was carried out in the 18th century, high box pews being installed, and in 1767 a gallery being built at the west end, the church remained in poor repair until restoration work under the influence of the Oxford Movement was carried out: in 1838 the south aisle was re-roofed, the gallery removed, and the chancel arch and south porch were restored; in 1851 the south wall of the south chapel was rebuilt and the north aisle and chapel re-roofed; in 1860 the chancel was redecorated with 'ornament of pseudo-Gothic character'; and in 1877 its floor repaved. In 1919 'the extremely bad glass' of the later 19th century was replaced; the chancel had its decoration removed and its 13th-century roof revealed. In 1941 the south chapel was revived with an altar and furnishings; in 1967 oak pews from ST PETER-IN-THE-EAST were placed in the nave.

There was no vicarage-house for the church until No. 1 NORHAM GARDENS, built to the designs of William Wilkinson in 1864–5, was bought in 1914.

The benefice was united with that of ST MARGARET, ST MARGARET'S ROAD, in 1985.

Although little is known of him, St Giles was so popular a saint in the Middle Ages that over 150 churches were dedicated to him in Britain alone. He was, perhaps, a hermit who lived near Arles during the 9th century. He was regarded as a patron saint of the poor and crippled. His emblem of an arrow is derived from a legend that he emerged from a thicket, pierced through the chest, and holding in his arms a hind that hunters had tried to shoot. The hunters' hounds stood motionless, as though rooted in their tracks before him.

St Giles' Fair Evolved in the second half of the 18th century from the St Giles' parish wake, which is first recorded in 1624 and became known as St Giles' Feast. In the 1780s it was a toy fair and by the beginning of the next century had become a general fair for children. By the 1830s, however, its booths and side-shows catered more for adults; and as the century progressed, as well as entertainment, it provided opportunities to buy clothing and crockery, baskets and tools and various other commodities, including, in 1892, sewing machines. Toll was exacted by St John's College as Lord of Walton Manor. Towards the end of the century it was more than once proposed that the fair should be suppressed on the grounds that it had become too rowdy and licentious, but after more efficient policing was promised and obtained, these attempts at suppression were abandoned. The Corporation took over sole control of the fair in 1930. From the 19th century it has been customary to hold the fair on the Monday and Tuesday following the first Sunday after St Giles' Day, 1 September. Apart from the war years, the fair has been, and still is, a regular annual event. The whole of the street is closed for it.

Writing in 1937, JOHN BETJEMAN observed, 'It is about the biggest fair in England. The whole of St

Booths erected in St Giles' for the fair of 1868.

Giles' and even Magdalen Street by Elliston and Cavell's right up to and beyond the War Memorial, at the meeting of the Woodstock and Banbury roads, is thick with freak shows, roundabouts, cake-walks, the whip, and the witching waves. Every sort of fairman finds it worth his while to come to St Giles'. Old roundabouts worked by hand that revolve slow enough to suit the very young or the very old, ageing palmists and sinister, alluring houris excite the wonder and the passions of red-faced ploughmen.... Beyond St Giles' the University is silent and dark. Even the lights of the multiple stores in the Cornmarket seem feeble.... And in the alleys between the booths you can hear people talking with an Oxfordshire accent, a change from the Oxford one.'

(*See also* FAIRS.)

St Giles' House *16 St Giles'*. Built in 1702 for Thomas Rowney on land belonging to St John's College. Thomas Rowney, whose portrait hangs in the TOWN HALL, was Member of Parliament for Oxford and High Sheriff of Oxfordshire in 1691. He was succeeded as MP by his son Thomas, who also lived in the house. He was a benefactor of the RADCLIFFE INFIRMARY and one of the wards is named after him. He died in 1759. During the latter part of the 18th century the house was occupied by the Duke of Marlborough. From 1852 to 1965 it was the Judge's Lodgings (*see* COURTS), and was used by the Judge when staying in Oxford during the Assizes. It is now used by St John's College, to which it belongs, for teaching, entertainment and other purposes.

The house is described by Pevsner as 'the best house of its date in Oxford'. It is not known who the architect was, but it could have been designed and built by Bartholomew Peisley (*see* PEISLEYS), the master-mason who lived at VANBRUGH HOUSE. It has a seven-bay ashlar façade. On the front are gate-piers topped with urns and at the back is a decorated hood over the doorway to the garden. There was formerly a similar one over the front door. In the walled garden is a garden house or temple which supports a scale model of JAMES GIBBS's design for a stone dome for the RADCLIFFE CAMERA. Inside there is a fine plaster ceiling over a beautiful early 18th-century staircase with twisted balusters.

St Gregory and St Augustine, Church of *322 Woodstock Road*. Before 1900, ROMAN CATHOLICS who lived to the north of Oxford had to travel a long way to attend Mass, ST ALOYSIUS being at the southern end of WOODSTOCK ROAD. It was to relieve these Catholics that Charles Robertson, a convert to Catholicism, bought an acre of land from the Duke of Marlborough on which to build a church. Ernest Newton, a disciple of the Arts and Crafts movement, designed the present structure in 1912 as the parish hall. However, as the large church planned for the site was never built, this unassuming building, which can accommodate only 130 worshippers, became the parish church. Set back from the road on raised ground, it has a rustic charm, unspoilt, even by the large wrought-iron lettering and unsympathetic panel of coloured glass on the west façade. The simple fenestration, the white pebble-dash walls and the grey-tiled roof, present a homogeneous elevation. The interior, reached through a porch on the south side, is light, harmonious and domestic. A screen separates the body of the church from the vestibule; the floor is parquet, and the roof is barrel-vaulted, painted white, with tiebeams that anchor it to a wood cornice. Attention is focused on the altar by a baldacchino.

St Helen's Passage A narrow pedestrian alleyway off NEW COLLEGE LANE, leading to the TURF TAVERN and Bath Place. It winds to avoid extensions to Nos 6–7

New College Lane and passes the Holywell Quad of Hertford College. The passage was formerly known as Hell Passage, possibly a reference to a disreputable gaming house, or perhaps to the dark conditions under the CITY WALL.

St Hilda's College was opened in this house beside Milham Ford in 1893.

St Hilda's College   Founded in 1893 by DOROTHEA BEALE (1831–1906), Principal of Cheltenham Ladies' College, whose purpose it was to provide a hall of residence in Oxford where ladies from Cheltenham could take advantage of educational opportunities newly available to women in the University. After the failure of plans to build a new college on a site in BANBURY ROAD, Miss Beale bought Cowley House in Cowley Place which today forms the nucleus of the Old Hall building of the college. It had a beautiful situation beside Milham Ford, looking across branches of the Cherwell river (*see* THAMES) both towards Magdalen College Tower and MAGDALEN BRIDGE and, to the south-west, towards CHRIST CHURCH MEADOW. The house itself had been built in 1775–93 and, though altered in later years, it still contained several of the original features, including an Adam-style staircase brought from a country house of the Bertie family in Oxfordshire and some elaborate fireplaces. Nineteenth-century alterations included a north wing, outer hall and porch decorated with sculptured capitals, all still visible today.

The house which came to be known as St Hilda's Hall was opened by WILLIAM STUBBS on 6 November 1893; when it was said that the education of the students was 'to be conducted according to the principles of the Church of England without restrictions upon the liberty of other denominations'. Miss Beale's ideas went further: 'I want none to go [to this hall] for the sake of a pleasant life . . . none merely for self-culture. . . . But that they may do better service for the glory of Our Creator and the relief of man's estate'. She had used the name St Hilda because she thought of the Saint of Whitby as the first great educator of women in England and because, as abbess in her religious houses, St Hilda had 'laid chief stress on peace and love'. The college motto became '*Non frustra vixi*' and Miss Beale chose as first Principal in 1893 Mrs Esther Burrows (Principal until 1910), who

had previously been in charge of boarders at Cheltenham. Miss Beale intended to keep the new foundation closely associated with the school and firmly under her own control. This, by skilful manoeuvres, she succeeded in doing until her death. She did not solicit or accept other major financial benefactions. 'We did not want any contributions to the general fund of St Hilda's', she had written in 1893, 'but we should not refuse assistance in the form of scholarships, exhibitions or loans for those who need help – and especially we should be grateful for contributions to the library.'

In 1897 St Hilda's Hall was incorporated and a council of ten members was constituted of whom four were from Cheltenham Ladies' College. In 1896 St Hilda's Hall was recognised by the Council of the Association for the Higher Education of Women in Oxford (*see* ST ANNE'S COLLEGE). Miss Beale now wished to assure its finances and at the same time ensure its association with Cheltenham. She therefore obtained in 1901 the dissolution of the earlier incorporation and replaced it with the amalgamation of St Hilda's Hall, Oxford, with St Hilda's College, Cheltenham (a teachers' training college which she herself had founded). The joint foundation was called St Hilda's Incorporated College. St Hilda's Hall finances were in the hands of the incorporated college, though its Oxford administration remained in the hands of the Hall's council. Miss Beale sold the freehold of St Hilda's Hall on generous terms to the joint foundation, to which she left £1000 in her will. When the Delegacy for Women Students was formed in Oxford in 1910, St Hilda's was one of the five women's societies it recognised. Further developments in women's education were halted by the First World War. When progress was resumed in the post-war years, St Hilda's with other women's colleges benefited from new attitudes towards women's position in society. Higher education for women was seen as a social need; many thought women should have the same right as men to university education and recognition. In 1920 an act of CONVOCATION admitted women 'to the privileges of the statute' (Number XXIII), giving them the right to membership of the University. This meant that when, six years later, HEBDOMADAL COUNCIL recommended changes in the constitutions of the women's colleges, St Hilda's association with the incorporated college at Cheltenham had to be dissolved, and on 13 March 1926 a royal charter was granted with statutes annexed for the government of the hall under the name of St Hilda's College, Oxford. Some association with Cheltenham Ladies' College remained, with Cheltenham members (though not *ex officio*) still on the council and in the Old Students Association (founded 1906). There were also closed scholarships for students from Cheltenham. These were abolished after 1955 when rules for college entrance were changed.

After the First World War, with an increase in the number of students, St Hilda's began to develop a new post-Beale identity. This was strengthened when Miss Julia de Lacy Mann became Principal following the death of Miss Winifred Horsbrugh Moberly, Principal 1919–28. Miss Mann's long incumbency (1928–55), the stability and wisdom she brought to her job, and her gifts to the college, encouraged its growth and development and helped it to establish its independent character.

Problems connected with the peculiar circumstances of its foundation and earlier dependence on Cheltenham Ladies' College continued to affect its governing body, especially in discussions between the Old Students Association, the Association of Senior Members and the college council. This situation was eventually resolved after the Second World War when college government was brought into line with that of other colleges of the University. In 1955 St Hilda's received from the Queen a supplemental charter and revised statutes by which the Principal and Fellows at last became the governing body of the college. Further changes in the statutes were made when, together with other women's colleges, St Hilda's was admitted to the status of a college of the University.

The college has always been poor. It had no original benefactor. Miss Beale's generosity was limited because St Hilda's was only one of her educational foundations and the residual legatee to her £55,000 estate was Cheltenham Ladies' College. St Hilda's buildings were not custom-built but were added to and altered piecemeal over the years, building always being started with insufficient funds. Attractive but unsuitable building had to be adapted to a residential college whose numbers grew steadily. In 1897–8 a south wing was added to the hall to provide a dining room and accommodation for twenty-eight residential students. In 1909, as a result of Miss Beale's bequest, additions were built to the south wing of the hall to provide a basement library and rooms for a tutor and students.

In 1921, to meet the post-war increase in women students, intake was increased from forty-nine to seventy and the college bought (for £17,500) nearby Cowley Grange, a house originally built for the Vernon Harcourt family which had been adapted for use as a teachers' training college. It came to be called St Hilda's South. Its gardens had been in mediaeval times the site of St Edmund's Well, famous for its healing properties. All traces of this had disappeared, as did the Harcourts' REAL TENNIS court. Structural alterations (costing £13,000) were carried out, including a dining room (in existence and use today), kitchens and new rooms to provide accommodation for 100 students. The college with its two main buildings, South and what was now called Old Hall, had for a time two libraries and two porters' lodges (though these were replaced later by new buildings). Both houses faced the River Cherwell and, though difficult of access from that front and from the high walls to the road, were still considered to be sufficiently vulnerable to male intrusion for grilles to be fitted to windows of rooms on the ground floors. Helped by a grant from Dame Elizabeth Wordsworth, funds were raised to build a chapel in 1925 and the first custom-built part of the college was erected in 1934 north of Old Hall to the designs of Sir Edwin Cooper. This was called the Burrows Building after the first two Principals, Esther Burrows and her daughter, Christine Burrows (1910–19). It contained a fine oak-panelled and galleried library with accommodation rooms above. The stock room under the library was transformed into an enlarged reading room in 1978. After the acquisition in 1958 of the Milham Ford site which linked Old Hall and South properties, it was possible to build the Wolfson Block (1964), the architect of which, Robert Potter, also restored the 18th-century front. The Sacher Block (1971) and

the Garden Building (1971) were designed by Alison and Peter Smithson.

Further rooms, including a kitchen and bar for the Junior Common Room, were added to the Old Hall complex in 1974. All these new buildings were made possible by generous benefactions from Isaac Wolfson, from Mrs A.L. Baker and the three Marks sisters, Mrs Blond, Mrs Marks Kennedy and especially Mrs Miriam Sacher. Christ Church also helped with grants, and funds were raised in a strenuous campaign mounted by St Hilda's from 1952 onwards. In the early 1970s the college's endowment was strengthened by capital grants made to the college, as to a number of other poorer colleges of the University, under a scheme set up in the wake of the FRANKS COMMISSION, by which richer colleges were 'taxed' to provide help for the poorer foundations. Valuable help also came from the endowment by Miss Pauline Chan of Hong Kong, Honorary Fellow of the college, of a fellowship in Physics (1982); and from generous grants from the EPA Cephalosporin Fund which made possible the endowment of a fellowship in Botany and a junior research fellowship in Biological and Chemical Sciences.

Miss Beale had been eager that her foundation should educate women who would spread education to further generations – an aim amply fulfilled by succeeding generations of students, many of whom became teachers in schools and colleges all over the world. Miss Beale had had a special interest in History and St Hilda's produced some notable History teachers and scholars, including Agnes Sandys (Vice-Principal 1928–33), Kathleen Major (Principal 1955–65), Beryl Smalley (Vice-Principal 1957–69) and Rosalind Hill, all outstanding Mediaeval History scholars. Julia de Lacy Mann (Principal 1928–55) was a noted economic historian. Distinction was not only in History. DAME HELEN GARDNER, Merton Professor of English Literature 1966–75, was an authority of world repute on T.S. Eliot, D.H. Lawrence and Shakespeare. Distinguished writers included D.K. Broster, Cecil Woodham-Smith and Barbara Pym. Other noted daughters in many fields include Dr Doris M. Odlum (1909–13), a pioneer psychiatrist and doctor; Kathleen Gibberd, journalist; Hermione Lee, literary critic; Yvonne Furneaux, actress; Florence Elliott, educationalist; and Mrs K.S. Chatterjee, Indian social worker.

Being situated by the Cherwell, the college had from the beginning its own boats and boat club; and PUNTING was always a popular pastime.

The college library was begun by its founder in 1898 with money she had earned by a contribution to the *Spectator* which she used to buy copies of BENJAMIN JOWETT's *Plato* and R.H. Hutton's *Essays*. Miss Beale wrote, 'I specially desire a good library of poetry, philosophy and theology.' Her wish was fulfilled, at least in the first two subjects. The library has a strong History section and specialises today in Biochemistry and Engineering. Special collections include the Maconchy music MSS; papers of the Capper family (1887–1943), correspondence and documents dealing with the early struggles for women's education in Oxford. The library also has a 15th-century Dutch Book of Hours and a miscellaneous collection of 16th- and 17th-century Italian and French books.

In 1986 St Hilda's had twenty-four Fellows, and about 400 undergraduate and graduate students. Over the years the college has drawn students from, and established links with, many different countries. A high proportion of the graduate student body is from overseas, especially from the USA, but with strong representation from India, Hong Kong and China. At the senior level, the college offers a Rhodes Fellowship to women scholars from overseas (*see* RHODES SCHOLARSHIPS), and (as a result of a generous donation from Mr R.C. Lee) a visiting research fellowship to a woman scientist from the Peoples' Republic of China. The college is one of only two single-sex colleges remaining in the University; in 1986 it still did not admit male students or Fellows as members of the college, though it employed a number of male lecturers.

The corporate title of the college is The Principal and Fellows of St Hilda's College in the University of Oxford. Miss Elizabeth Llewellyn Smith, CB, is the present Principal.

(Burrows, Christine M.E., 'St Hilda's College', in *Victoria County History of Oxford*, Vol. III, Oxford, 1954; Hampshire, G.M., *St Hilda's College, Oxford Memorabilia*, Oxford, 1980; *St Hilda's College Register 1893–1964*, 1971; Brittain, V., *The Women at Oxford*, London, 1960.)

St Hugh's College   Founded in 1886 as a society for women students by Elizabeth Wordsworth, the first Principal of Lady Margaret Hall and great-niece of the poet. Until 1916 it existed in various houses in NORHAM GARDENS and Norham Road, but in 1913 a site was acquired between the BANBURY and WOODSTOCK ROADS on which the first custom-built college for women was completed in 1916. It was designed by H.T. Buckland and W. Haywood. Of its character Pevsner writes: 'Symmetrical, neo-Georgian. All red brick except for two lodges which are of stone. In axis with the lodges is the doorway to the building, with a big, decorated scrolly pediment. The building is large

and has its true façade to the s., i.e. to the garden. It has two projecting wings there and many pretty bow-windows on the ground floor. . . .' The south front opens on to a stone-flagged terrace planted with a variety of alpines and shrubs, the work of Miss Annie Rogers, a formidable fighter for women's education who was the college's first *custos hortulorum* and an early member of the college council. She was a classicist of distinction and an amateur gardener, an eager follower of Gertrude Jekyll. She is commemorated by a sun-dial which is between two cypresses where the terrace ends and the open gardens begin.

These gardens are among the most extensive and beautiful in Oxford, consisting of 14 acres of ground, the main lawn and wooded areas fronting the college being now designated a garden of historic interest. One part of it, The Dell, a Victorian fernery, was the original shrubbery of The Mount, the house demolished when the college was built. A nut walk and a wilderness of the same date run along the southernmost edge of the main garden. A magnolia tree strikingly placed on the front lawn was planted for the armistice after the First World War in 1918.

The main building of the college was extended in 1928 in the original style, and in 1936 the library wing was a further addition. The library itself is a powerful and characteristic example of 1930s design, especially in its interior furnishings, the mouldings of the ceiling and woodwork. Two new buildings were added after the Second World War, both designed by David Roberts of Cambridge. One, the Kenyon Building, is a strong, fortress-like design jutting into the garden and so devised that all the windows face south. The Wolfson Building, a lower curved connecting link between the library block and the Kenyon block, has the same orientation.

The existence of a number of large 19th-century houses on the perimeter of the college site is a distinctive feature of St Hugh's. These include two

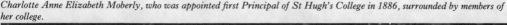

Charlotte Anne Elizabeth Moberly, who was appointed first Principal of St Hugh's College in 1886, surrounded by members of her college.

listed buildings – The Shrubbery (72 Woodstock Road), now the Principal's lodgings, and The Lawn (89 Banbury Road), which houses undergraduates. Both of these were built in the 1830s before Victorian NORTH OXFORD had developed. The lawn was clearly (and disastrously) altered and 'improved' in an early 20th-century manner. Bow windows, not the original sash, have also been built into the extension of The Shrubbery, dated 1900, which was designed to show off a genuine Tudor ceiling brought from a demolished house at Carfax. The other houses on the site represent a characteristic range of North Oxford mock-Gothic architecture. No. 82 Woodstock Road, which today houses the law library and lecture room as well as undergraduate studies, belonged originally to GILBERT MURRAY and was his home for many years.

Inside the main college building are four public rooms besides the library: the Mordan Hall, a large auditorium with a stage at one end, which was the original library; the dining hall below it; and the Wordsworth Room, a recent extension which is used as a buttery and a general-purpose room. Upstairs on the first floor is the chapel, notable for its original and striking decor of dark green, pink, white and gold-leaf, which was designed by the artist Laurence Whistler. A glass panel of the Old English poem 'The Dream of the Rood' incorporating a background of the spires of Oxford was engraved by the same artist to commemorate Miss Barbara Gwyer, the third Principal of the college. The chapel also contains an oblong plaque, the lettering engraved by Reynolds Stone, to the memory of Miss Cecilia Ady, the distinguished Renaissance Italian historian, originally a tutor of the college and later a Senior Research Fellow. A new chamber organ was built in 1979 by Tamburini in Crema in Italy, and was installed and dedicated in 1980. The chapel can no longer be described in Pevsner's dismissive phrase as 'just a square vaulted room'.

The college possesses a valuable and unusual collection of rare books, and a number of interesting original paintings. The books include rare topographical and literary works published in France in the 18th century, from the library of Eleanor Jourdain the second Principal; valuable ornithological books which were the gift of the Duchess of Bedford; and a collection of works on the OXFORD MOVEMENT, a bequest from the library of Dean Richard Church. A series of early 19th-century engravings of English cathedrals by JOHN BUCKLER hang on the ground-floor walls. Paintings in the Mordan Hall, the dining hall and the Senior Common Room include a remarkable conversation piece, *Principal and Four Fellows*, by Henry Lamb and portaits by Robert Lutyens, Carel Weight and Peter Greenham (*see* PORTRAITS). In the Senior Common Room hangs a pencil drawing of the college's first benefactress, Clara Evelyn Mordan, in her youth, wearing a wreath of white roses.

St Hugh's was founded as St Hugh's Hall, and was incorporated in 1911 under the Companies (Consolidation) Act as St Hugh's College. In November 1910 it had been recognised by decree of CONVOCATION. In 1920 its members, like those of the other women's colleges, were admitted to degrees of the University. In 1926 it was incorporated by Royal Charter and in 1959 the college was admitted to all the rights and privileges of other colleges in the University of Oxford. Its first Principal was Annie Moberly (1886–1915), daughter of the Bishop of Salisbury. The title St Hugh's, after the great mediaeval bishop of that name, was chosen by Elizabeth Wordsworth its founder, whose father was

Detail of Henry Lamb's conversation piece of 1936, Principal and Four Fellows, *the Principal* (second from the right) *being B.E. Gwyer of St Hugh's College and the Fellows* (from the left) *E.E.S. Procter, E.E. Wardale, E.A. Francis and C.M. Ady.*

the Bishop of Lincoln. Eleanor Jourdain followed Miss Moberly (1915–24), Barbara Gwyer succeeded her (1924–46); Evelyn Procter, previously tutor in Modern History, was the next Principal (1946–62), followed by Dame Kathleen Kenyon, the archaeologist (1962–73). The present Principal, appointed in 1991, is Derek Wood, QC, who succeeded Rachel Trickett.

Among many distinguished senior members of the college are Dame Mary Cartwright (1919), formerly Mistress of Girton; the Rt Hon. Mrs Barbara Castle (1929); and the late Mary Renault, the novelist (1925). Other literary figures educated at St Hugh's include Margaret Lane, novelist and biographer (1925); the biographers Margaret Laing (1953) and Janet Morgan (1964), the poet Alison Brackenbury (1971) and the novelist Brigid Brophy (1947). Professors Elizabeth Anscombe, Alison Fairlie and Kathleen Coburn are all senior members of the college, as is the conductor and musicologist Jane Glover. Among its Honorary Fellows are Dame Peggy Ashcroft and Mrs Helen Suzman. In 1977 the college amended its statutes to admit men tutors, of whom there are now eleven, and has now also amended its charter to admit men undergraduates and graduates. It remains an Anglican foundation but there is no religious test on any member or officer of the college except the chaplain.

The corporate designation of the college is The Principal and Fellows of St Hugh's College in the University of Oxford.

(Griffin, P., *St Hugh's: One Hundred Years of Women's Education in Oxford*, London, 1986.)

St Ignatius, Church of *St Clement's*. Until 1875 this 18th-century Jesuit chapel was the only ROMAN CATHOLIC church in Oxford; and as such was one of the focal points of the religious debate that rocked the nation in the 19th century. Although derelict, it still stands behind iron railings on the east side of ST CLEMENT'S. The classical street façade with its handsome stone finials dates from 1909, when the chapel was enlarged to incorporate a school. In 1795 a Jesuit priest from Waterperry, Father Charles Lesley, conscious of the fact that there were some sixty Catholics in Oxford without a church, decided to build them one. The £1000 needed for the cost of the simple stone building came partly from his own pocket; the remainder he borrowed from friends. In those days St Clement's was a rough, poverty-stricken neighbourhood where it was a struggle to raise even £10 a year bench rates. On Sundays two PROCTORS would stand outside on the look-out for undergraduates, for whom the chapel was out of bounds. After Mass the congregation would breakfast at the Port Mahon, a nearby public house.

It was from St Ignatius that Father Dominic Barberi (*see* CHURCH OF BLESSED DOMINIC BARBERI) borrowed chalice and vestments one October evening in 1845 in order to celebrate Mass at LITTLEMORE the morning after CARDINAL NEWMAN'S reception into the Catholic Church; and it was here that Newman came, four days later, to attend his first public Mass. As the religious controversies continued to gather force, and the Tractarians (*see* OXFORD MOVEMENT) began building churches like ST BARNABAS, Father James Corry, SJ, the parish priest of St Ignatius in 1871, felt it imperative for his Superiors to do the same. Protesting about the inadequacy of his own church for

his sermons, he declared, 'Even if I were a storm, what can I do in a tea-kettle?' He went on to plead that he 'pointed, painted and repaired the venerable chapel' and that he would 'dance with delight if some day, it would tumble down before my eyes'. In 1875 ST ALOYSIUS was built. The new parish was so successful that before long a caricature attacking proselytism was widely publicised. It depicted three Jesuits fishing for mortar-boarded and coroneted souls in a pond, and carried the caption, 'Members of the Romish Church are requested not to trespass in Protestant waters and on no account to tamper with the Gold Fish.' The last Mass was said in St Ignatius in 1911, after which it became St Joseph's School. Until recently it housed the Oxford Lithoplate Graphics Co.

St James, Church of *Beauchamp Lane, Cowley*. The east boundary of this ancient parish lies along Roman Way, in Roman times part of the road linking the camps of Dorchester and Alcester (Wendlebury); during the Saxon period the district became known as Cufa's Lea, hence COWLEY. After the Conquest, as part of the estates of Bishop Odo of Bayeux, the Cowley area passed into the possession of ROBERT D'OILLY and Roger d'Ivri, who joined him in building ST GEORGE'S IN THE CASTLE. In the mid-12th century OSENEY ABBEY took possession of St George's and the Cowley area, at which time the church of St James was built: its chancel arch, with painted pillars, the font (now on a modern plinth), and the north and south doorways, all date from this period. In the 15th century the church tower was built and the nave lengthened. At the Dissolution of the Monasteries, Christ Church became the patrons until the advowson passed to the Board of Patronage.

By 1849 St James's had become increasingly dilapidated and inadequate for a growing parish population; but it was not until 1864 that rebuilding work began, to the designs of G.E. STREET, the diocesan architect. The north wall was pulled down, a north aisle added, galleries and pews removed, and the roof raised to the level of the tower. Street also designed the pulpit, stalls and reredos, the latter a memorial to John Randolph (*see below*). Wall tablets were removed and placed on the walls inside the tower; one of them is to Francis Wastie, Sheriff of Oxfordshire in 1770, and his daughter. During the renovations, services were held in a 'certain Barn belonging to the Rev. Richard Meux Benson situate at Temple Cowley'; Benson, who had become vicar in 1854, built a temporary iron church in Stockmore Street in 1859 and formed the new parish of Cowley St John in 1868.

Following his incumbency there was 'a period of bitter strife between the parishioners and their parson', the scrupulous James Coley (vicar 1870–5), who in 1875 refused to conduct a burial service for one Frederick Merritt, a 'notorious evil liver'. When he locked the church in face of protests, a large crowd, including forty navvies armed with picks, forced an entry, the burial service later being performed by another priest. A parody of a couplet by SAMUEL JOHNSON appeared in *Punch* magazine:

See Coley, scarcely wise, and hardly just,
Over unburied Merritt raise a dust.

Coley's successor from 1875 to 1928 was 'the pugilistic parson' George Moore, a curate from ST MARY MAGDALEN and a former University boxer, who in the first ten years of his incumbency was twice summoned for assault in his own churchyard, where he lies buried. In 1896 the fine organ from ST MARTIN'S, CARFAX, was installed by him in the church for £150. He was followed by M.H. Beauchamp (vicar 1928), who inspired the building of ST FRANCIS OF ASSISI and ST LUKE as chapels-of-ease to St James's. When in 1959 the vicarage-house was sold, St Luke's House became the vicarage; the vicar served St Luke's Church, and his curate St James's. When Beauchamp retired as Vicar, his curate, A.G. Whye, became Vicar and Beauchamp stayed on as curate. The tradition of High Churchmanship established by Benson still continues.

Among former incumbents to achieve distinction were Richard Robinson (1737), later Archbishop of Armagh; William Sharp (1747), Regius Professor of Greek and Latin at Oxford and Principal of Hertford College; Edward Smallwell (1748), BISHOP OF OXFORD; John Randolph (1780), who was successively Regius Professor of Divinity at Oxford, and Bishop of Oxford, Bangor and London; Samuel Slade (1798), Bishop of Gloucester; William Carey (1800), Bishop of Exeter; W.H. Coleridge (1815), nephew of the poet, who was the first Bishop of Barbados and British Guiana, and who 'greatly hastened the emancipation of the slaves throughout his diocese'; Thomas Short (1816), Bishop of Sodor and Man; and C.T. Longley (1823), later Archbishop of Canterbury and convenor of the first Lambeth Conference in 1867.

St John Street An old street of this name is now MERTON STREET. The new St John Street, which runs from WELLINGTON SQUARE to BEAUMONT STREET and was presumably named after the college, was begun in about 1825 and completed by about 1835. The unified terraces, in a simple style, are made up of three-storeyed houses with cellars built in brick but with Bath stone fronts (*see* STONE), moulded cornices and parapets. They are listed Grade II and many are used as lodgings for undergraduates or as guest-houses for visitors to Oxford. A tale is told by William Bayzand, janitor at the RADCLIFFE CAMERA and a former coachman, of a meeting he had (probably in the 1830s) at the corner of St John Street with three retired tailors of Beaumont Street. The tailors said they were going to rename St John Street, where Bayzand lived, Whipcord Terrace, because of the number of coachmen who lived there. Bayzand replied that he was going to rename Beaumont Street, Threadneedle Street. WILLIAM TURNER OF OXFORD lived in St John Street from 1812 until 1862. In Beaumont Place, off St John Street, are the Oxford offices of the British Council, designed by John Fryman of the Architects Design Partnership, 1966–7.

St John the Baptist, Church of *Rogers Street* (*formerly Church Street*). Built in 1832 to serve the growing population of ST GILES' parish, the church was endowed by its patron, St John's College, and by 1854 drew congregations of 300 on Sundays. By 1904 the church had become too small for the numbers it attracted, and ST MICHAEL AND ALL ANGELS, Lonsdale Road, was built, St John the Baptist being closed in 1909, demolished in 1924, and the site sold in 1970. Dudley Court flats were erected on the site. Designed by H.J. Underwood in Early English style, the church comprised an aisleless nave, a shallow chancel, and

north and south transepts. In 1857 the chancel was extended eastwards to the designs of G.E. STREET and a vestry added to the north-east. In 1875 the east end was extended, and a north aisle added. W.W. Jones, (vicar 1864–74) later became Archbishop of Cape Town.

St John the Evangelist, Church of *Iffley Road*. Built in 1894–6 to the designs of G.F. BODLEY as the conventual church of the Society of St John the Evangelist (the COWLEY FATHERS), it is at present part of ST STEPHEN'S HOUSE and attended by some local worshippers as a public rather than parish church. An impressive building, with a tower (1902) originally intended to be higher, it is connected to the monastic house by cloisters at its east end. The fine, decorated ceiling, painted by Brother Maynard, of nave and chancel is lofty; the east-window glass (*c.*1900) by C.E. Kempe depicts the Tree of Life with monastic saints branching from it; the reredos and tester above the high altar are by Ninian Comper. In the chancel arch is a rood from Oberammergau presented in 1933 by the 2nd Viscount Halifax, a leading Anglo-Catholic, to celebrate the centenary of the OXFORD MOVEMENT. The organ, in a case designed by Bodley, is by Nicholsons of Worcester, installed in 1978 to the specification of James Dalton, organist at The Queen's College. The Stations of the Cross, in painted panels by E.A.F. Prynne (1919), commemorate the fallen of the First World War.

St John the Evangelist, Church of *Vicarage Road, New Hinksey*. Designed by Bucknall and Comper, the present church was built in 1900. It replaced an earlier chapel-of-ease (1870, E.G. Bruton), built for the parish of ST LAURENCE, SOUTH HINKSEY, to serve the needs of New Hinksey as the city suburbs expanded southwards. Comper's original design was to include an ornate screen between nave and chancel, topped by a gallery containing a central organ with a rood above it; only the nave and four-bay aisles were completed, a fifth bay, also designed by Comper, being added as a chancel in 1937 but without an east window. Four fine Perpendicular-style windows in the north aisle, and three in the south aisle, all large and clear-glazed with bottle-end panes, provide the building with a light and airy interior; colour is supplied by handsome, decorated roof-panels. Entry to the church is by the west door. There is a chapel at the end of the north aisle, and the vestry at the east end of the south aisle has above it the organ. On the altar in the south aisle is a wooden crucifix brought from Oberammergau in 1872 and placed in the Oratory of the Holy Rood (closed in 1882), of which E.B. PUSEY was founder and Warden. Passing to the Superintendent, Miss Mary Milner, it was bequeathed by her to the vicar of St John the Evangelist, W.B. Lander, in 1922. The patron of the living is the BISHOP OF OXFORD. The Tudor-style red-brick vicarage (1887–8) was designed by H.W. Moore.

St John's College Originally St Bernard's College (*see* MONASTIC COLLEGES), founded by ARCHBISHOP CHICHELE in 1437 as a house for Cistercian students in Oxford. Its buildings, the present front quad, were based on the traditional New College plan but built piecemeal due to lack of funds. The west and south

St John's College from the garden c.1783, with the Laudian Library to the right and buildings of Trinity College to the left.

ranges were probably complete by the time the tower was built in the 1470s. The hall and chapel followed later, the latter being consecrated in 1530, but the east range was never finished.

In 1539 St Bernard's College was dissolved, although it remained as an ACADEMIC HALL. In 1546 Henry VIII granted it to Christ Church, from whom it was bought nine years later by Sir Thomas White (1492–1567), founder of St John's. The son of a Reading clothier, he became a Merchant Taylor, Master of his Company and Alderman of London, in which capacity he supported Mary I against Lady Jane Grey and was elected Lord Mayor shortly after the former's accession.

The college was founded on 29th May 1555 and dedicated to St John the Baptist, the patron saint of tailors. The main statutes were promulgated in 1558. The VISITOR was to be the Bishop of Winchester, and there were to be fifty Fellows, six of FOUNDER'S KIN, two each from Bristol, Coventry and Reading (chosen by the respective corporations), one from Tonbridge (chosen at first by the Skinners' Company and then by the Vestry), and the rest eventually from the Merchant Taylors' School, which White had helped found. It was thus a completely close foundation. One Fellow was to study Medicine, twelve Civil and Common Law and the remainder Theology. There were lecturers in Rhetoric, Greek and Dialectic, and later in Law and Natural Philosophy. The President and ten Senior Fellows formed the governing body, although while he lived the founder retained control.

It was thus a college of the Counter-Reformation. The founder provided it with elaborate vestments, later condemned as popish but now treasured, and a number of early members went over to Rome, notably EDMUND CAMPION, Cuthbert Mayne and John Roberts, all recently canonised. The second President, William Eley, who had disputed against Cranmer before his execution (*see* MARTYRS' MEMORIAL), was deprived in 1563 for his allegiance to Rome, and his successor and co-religionist soon resigned. Perhaps to ensure loyalty to the Church of England the next President was imported from Cambridge, but

in Tobie Matthew (President 1572–7, and later Archbishop of York), the college at last found a satisfactory Oxonian head.

Sir Thomas White endowed St John's with seven local manors and three livings, and left the means to purchase the two manors of Walton comprising much of modern NORTH OXFORD. With them came the ancient deeds of Walton Oseney and Walton Godstow, the patronage and great tithes of ST GILES' CHURCH and the basis of St John's riches today. In 1576 the terrace outside the west front was bought, and in 1583 Bagley Wood. Nevertheless the college was poor for many years; the choir had to be abandoned in 1577, and expenditure frequently exceeded revenue.

The buildings of St Bernard's were used almost unchanged by St John's. The founder built the present kitchen to the north of the hall and completed the east range, the northern half as the President's lodgings. In 1573, to make more space, attics were added to the south and west ranges, and in 1596 the Old Library was built to the east of the quad, some of the stone and timber coming from the ancient BEAUMONT PALACE. Before the founder's death the President's garden and much of the grove had been enclosed, and in 1604, after the enclosure of the rest, John Lamb was appointed the first *custos sylvarum*, although he was a working gardener not a Fellow.

The most notable of the early members of the college was John Case (Fellow 1564–74), theologian, philosopher, poet, political theorist and anatomist, whose commentary on Aristotle of 1585 was the first work to be published by the OXFORD UNIVERSITY PRESS. Sir William Paddy, MP (commoner 1570–1634) was physician to James I and one of the college's greatest benefactors. In 1605 the King visited St John's (he fell asleep during the comedy put on for him); and, perhaps through Paddy's influence, its members received royal patronage. John Buckeridge (President 1606–11), Laud's tutor, preached against the Presbyterians at the Hampton Court Conference and later received a bishopric.

403

The college's greatest alumnus was ARCHBISHOP LAUD, Reading Fellow 1589–1610, President 1611–21 and second founder. He secured many livings, to make seventeen in all by 1640, and undertook extensive building works. In 1613 the Cook's Buildings were begun in the new three-storey style but his greatest contribution to the college was the Canterbury Quad. The Tudor Gothic of the Old Library was used as the basis of the design, but the arcaded loggias, pedimented frontispieces and Mannerist detailing, designed by the London craftsman–architect Adam Browne, make it the first classical quad in Oxford. It is dominated by fine STATUES of Charles I and Henrietta Maria by Le Sueur. Built at a cost to the Archbishop of more than £3000, it provided a Mathematical Library, additions to the lodgings and rooms for COMMONERS. The stonework was restored in 1887 with the approval of the SPAB.

St John's retains many Laudian relics, including his diary, the manuscript 'History of the Archbishop's Troubles and Trial' written in the Tower, his ivory-and-ebony walking stick and the cap he wore to the scaffold. Through him the college acquired many connections with the Court. The future Archbishop WILLIAM JUXON (President 1621–33) became Bishop of London on Laud's recommendation and later Lord Treasurer, although even at this eminence he and his patron could still inspect the college kitchen book. The Elector Palatine and his brother Prince Rupert were honorary members of St John's; Thomas Turner, Dean of Canterbury (Fellow 1610–29), attended Charles I in captivity; Sir Francis Winde-banke (1599–1602) became Secretary of State in 1632; and Sir William Killigrew (1622–4) commanded one of the great troops guarding the King's person. The height of the college's influence in the University came in 1636 when, to celebrate the opening of the Canterbury Quad, Charles I and Henrietta Maria were entertained by the CHANCELLOR (Laud) and the VICE-CHANCELLOR (President Baylie). They viewed the buildings, dined in the Laudian Library and saw a play in hall. The evening cost the Archbishop nearly as much as the buildings.

In 1603 the first Librarian had been appointed. Some important books had come from the founder and his friends, including monastic manuscripts and many Caxtons. Paddy gave 156 works, mostly medical but also including James I's own Prayer Book, and Laud forty manuscripts (many Oriental) and 100 books, his annotated Vulgate of 1566 being presented in 1729. A second folio Shakespeare was given in 1637, while 1500 volumes came in 1745 as a result of the will of Nathaniel Crynes, former Coventry Fellow. More modern treasures include a number of Jane Austen's letters (her father was a member of the college) and manuscripts and printed books of A.E. Housman.

Early literary alumni included James Shirley (1612–15), the poet and dramatist. Of a slightly earlier generation, Richard Baylie (Fellow 1601–33) succeeded Juxon as President, but much of his term of office was clouded by the CIVIL WAR. Many Cavaliers lodged in the college while the Court was in Oxford and St John's men were often invited to dine with the King, but the college PLATE had to be given up in 1642 and estates in enemy areas were sequestered. During the siege of Oxford earth was banked up against the garden walls, corn was stored in the Laudian Library, arms and powder were bought and members fought in the trenches. John Goad, Fellow and vicar of St Giles', conducted services in his church under fire, and a cannon ball shot into the tower of the college is still preserved.

But all was in vain, and in 1646 Fairfax entered Oxford, ironically on St John's Day. In January 1648 President Baylie was deprived by the Parliamentary Commission (see VISITATIONS). In April, the Chancellor at the head of a troop of dragoons ordered him to submit, but he refused to desert the King and the founder's statutes, and so a successor was intruded by force in June. Of forty-four Fellows, commoners and servants brought before the Visitors in May only four submitted, the rest being ejected by troops.

The new President, Francis Cheynell, the Margaret Professor, was deposed in 1650 for being too moderate and was replaced by Thankful Owen, Fellow of Lincoln, who leased much of the college property to his friends and relations. A former commoner, Sir Bulstrode Whitelocke (1620–3), rose to eminence under the new regime and tried to protect the college as much as possible. One man to come up during these years was Edward Bernard (Fellow 1655–74), Savilian Professor of Astronomy and one of the greatest scholars of the age.

On 29 May 1660 Charles II entered London, and by the beginning of August Owen had been evicted along with three Fellows. President Baylie returned, followed by ten Fellows, so that seven of the ten Seniors were former exiles. Since this time there has hung in the library the famous and much revered portrait of the Martyr-King with the penitential psalms written in the lines of the hair and face.

At first there was little money, as the intruders had left debts of £1000, but just before his death Juxon gave £7000 and Tobias Rustat, Yeoman of the Robes to Charles II, £1000. After an impressive public funeral, the Archbishop was buried in the chapel. Soon afterwards, quietly in accordance with his wishes, Laud was laid beside him and the founder. The previous year the President had begun the Baylie Chapel to the north with a ceiling of late Gothic fan tracery. The common room was built to the north of this in 1676.

With the Restoration, close relations with the government resumed, and indeed every Stuart monarch except Mary II visited the college at some time or another. In 1675 the Medical Fellow, John Speed, drank Admiral van Tromp under the table, no doubt with the approval of the new President, Peter Mews (Fellow 1637–45), whose only published work is An Ex-ale-tation of Ale (1671). A captain in the Civil War, when he was wounded, and then a royalist agent in Holland, Mews was at Breda negotiating peace with the Dutch when he was elected at the request of Charles II in 1667. Described as 'an old honest Cavalier', he was preferred in 1673 but as Bishop of Winchester from 1684 to 1706 later became Visitor of his college. During the Exclusion Parliament at Oxford, St John's was the royalist headquarters. True to its principles it raised a company of foot to fight Monmouth, and Mews stayed there when he came to restore the Fellows of Magdalen.

Its most famous son since Laud was Jethro Tull (1691–6), the great agricultural reformer. William Sherard, the botanist and founder of the Sherardian Professorship, was a Fellow from 1677 until, absent for many years in the Levant, he was finally deprived in 1703 upon becoming Consul for the Turkey Company at Smyrna. Sir William Dawes, Bart. (1687–90) was Archbishop of York from 1714 to 1724. One commoner, Sir John Williams, Bart., managed to spend over £2000 in his four years at St John's, a far cry from the children of the founder's former poor apprentices.

The traditional High Tory politics of the college continued into the next century under William Delaune (President 1698–1728). Although he accepted the accession of George I, he was a Jacobite and friend of Atterbury and Sacheverell, and during his presidency a preacher's text was announced in chapel as 'James III and VIII'. Richard Rawlinson (1708–55), a member of an old college family, was a Non-Juring Bishop and a great antiquary who left much to St John's; his heart is in the Baylie Chapel. George Lee, 3rd Earl of Lichfield (1736–72) became Tory Chancellor of the University in 1762 and founded the Lichfield Clinical Professorship. Dillenius, the noted botanist and first Sherardian Professor, was a commoner from 1735 to 1747. James Dawkins (matriculated 1740) was an archaeologist and Jacobite, whose visit to Palmyra was described by Dr Johnson as 'the only great instance of the enjoyment of wealth'.

However, not all St John's men were Tories, and for twenty years from 1728 the President was the Whig, William Holmes. In his time the first catalogue was made of the contents of the lodgings, listing not only portraits but also other works of art including a Breughel flowerpiece and a Mortlake tapestry of the Supper at Emmaus of 1626. In 1731 the hall chimneypiece was installed; it now contains a reproduction in scagliola by Lamberto Gorri of Raphael's *St John the Baptist*, brought back from Italy by a Fellow in 1759. The screen, designed by JAMES GIBBS, was erected in 1743. A fire engine was bought in 1740 and fire insurance taken out forty years later, at an annual premium of £6. In 1713 GLOUCESTER HALL was sold to become Worcester College.

There was much planting in the groves in 1712–16, with pleached elms in the southern half, and arbours, a wilderness and the present raised walk to the north. In 1770–8 they were thrown into one and completely remodelled by the Fellows themselves with the advice of a local nurseryman, Robert Penson (*see* GARDENS *and* TREES). The result was a very successful application of the landscape manner to an area of only 4 acres, although with flowering plants from the start. SAMUEL JOHNSON often sat there, and George III, who with Queen Charlotte visited the college in 1785 and presented their portraits, declared that 'his dominions did not contain another specimen of gardening skill to match it'. In 1794 money bequeathed by President Holmes was used to erect the buildings which bear his name; they were built in a plain Gothick style by James Pears. In general, however, the second half of the 18th century was a quiet time at St John's, as it was elsewhere in Oxford, perhaps the most notable occasions being when Mrs Siddons read plays in the lodgings. In 1798 the college was armed in readiness for the expected French invasion.

With the 19th century St John's returned to its earlier political views, and was thus proud in 1834 to entertain the Duke of Wellington upon his installation as Chancellor, the guests at dinner in hall including Lord Eldon and the Duke of Cumberland. Philip Wynter (President 1828–71), the last head of the college to be buried in the chapel, was one of the leaders of the Conservative Party in the University and as Vice-Chancellor condemned E.B. PUSEY. By 1847 fourteen livings had been acquired since the Restoration.

Steel engraving after a watercolour drawing by Charles Wild of the inner quadrangle of St John's College c.1813.

Change came, however, even to St John's. In 1802 COLLECTIONS at the end of term were introduced, originally an examination in hall before the President and Seniors. In 1811 came the first book prize and in 1829 Bachelor Fellows were dispensed from residence as they were no longer taught. The first gas-light arrived in 1820. In 1838 the Laudian Library was gothicised and the seven original presses removed, although most have now been rescued. In 1845 the chapel was given a new interior by Edward Blore using oak from the college manor of Eaton. Only the lectern and marble pavements survive from before. The east window and a stone reredos, both by C.E. Kempe, were installed in 1892.

When the ROYAL COMMISSION was appointed in 1850 St John's as a close foundation was especially open to Liberal suspicion, which was reciprocated: the Fellows refused to supply the Commissioners even with a copy of the statutes. The college tried to remain as closed as possible, which its excellent academic record justified, but by holding out to the very last they lost all closed fellowships, the Ordinance of 1861 providing for eighteen Life Fellows and thirty-three scholars.

Among the members at this time was H.L. Mansel, Wayneflete Professor of Moral and Metaphysical Philosophy 1854–64, later Regius Professor of Ecclesiastical History and finally Dean of St Paul's. A.E. Housman came up in 1877, followed by GILBERT MURRAY in 1884. The future Viscount Cave, Home Secretary, Lord Chancellor and Chancellor of the University 1925–8, was a commoner in 1874–81. The Norfolk Squire James Bellamy (President 1871–1909), who had taught the great Lord Salisbury, was the leader of the Conservative Party in Oxford, which met in the lodgings at election time. A steadfast opponent of all change, he fought the proposals of the University of Oxford Commission of 1877–9; but in the end new statutes came in 1881, by which the President could be a layman, and there were to be eighteen Fellows, including a chaplain (and the Laudian Professor of Arabic and the Professor of Civil Engineering *ex officio*), and not fewer than twenty-eight scholars, twenty-two from the founder's schools. Despite this, old St John's died hard. In 1898 there were still no married Fellows and a majority of the governing body was from before the new statutes. The last Fellow holding under the founder's statutes survived until 1930, and not until the following year was the first lay President elected. Up to then the college had had only four heads in the previous 136 years; one died in office at eighty-six, another retired at ninety.

Towards the end of the 19th century St John's was in financial difficulties, and in 1888 the emoluments of all members were reduced by more than a fifth (although President Bellamy made up the deficit for most of the scholars out of his own pocket). However, at the same time the college was offering building plots on its Walton estate, and it is from this that it derives its position today as one of the richest of the Oxford colleges. Most of the roads on the estate are named after college livings, among them Kingston, Crick and JOHN BETJEMAN's Belbroughton.

Gradually the North Quad was developed beyond the kitchen and common room. The Gothic range

Sir Muirhead Bone's chalk drawing of the Canterbury Quadrangle of St John's College in 1936. Most of the figures are portraits of members of the college.

facing St Giles' was started by George Gilbert Scott the Younger in 1881 and finished by E.P. Warren in 1900. The Rawlinson Buildings, commemorating the great benefactor, were designed in a less impressive manner by N.W. Harrison in 1909 with identical additions in 1933 by Sir Edward Maufe (1904–7). In 1935 Middleton Hall on St Giles' was taken into the college to provide extra accommodation, while the next year a statue of St John the Baptist by Eric Gill was placed in an empty niche on the east face of the tower. In 1948 the Dolphin Building and Quad were built by Maufe to the south of the college on the site of the old Dolphin Inn.

Ten years later, however, the Beehive, so called from its low octagonal towers, was built to the designs of the Architects' Co-Partnership, the first important collegiate building in the modern style in Oxford. In 1975 the large new Sir Thomas White Quad was built to the north. One of the most successful modern college buildings in Oxford, it was designed by Sir Philip Dowson of Arups and provides nine staircases, squash courts and rooms for the Junior Common Room and MIDDLE COMMON ROOM. That same year rooms in the Canterbury Quad were incorporated into the library, forming the Paddy and Holdsworth Rooms, the former named after the great benefactor, the latter after a recent Vinerian Professor. In 1966, ST GILES' HOUSE, one of the finest 18th-century houses in Oxford, was converted to provide facilities for music and entertaining.

The rock garden created by H.J. Bidder (Fellow 1871–1923) and R.J. Farrer, the distinguished botanist, flower-painter and author, was one of the first in the country; it was reconstructed in 1986. Under Professor Geoffrey Blackman (Keeper of the Groves 1946–70) the gardens were further developed, notably by the importation of soil from Bagley Wood to enable ericaceous plants to be grown.

St John's has changed as much as any college in the last seventy years. At Easter 1919 the librarian wrote, referring to a consultative committee, 'Next term we expect an Undergraduate Soviet and a strike of scouts.' Today the Junior Common Room acts as a students' union with access to the governing body, and SCOUTS in the old sense have disappeared. As well as about 325 undergraduates there are about 100 graduates in the Middle Common Room and some fifty Fellows, almost all laymen. Women were admitted for the first time in 1979. The most recent well-known alumni have been literary figures: Robert Graves (1919–25), Philip Larkin (1940–3) and Kingsley Amis (1941–2, 1945–9). At one time in the 1960s the Prime Minister of Canada, Lester Bowles Pearson (1921–3), the Foreign Secretary, now Lord Stewart (1925–9) and the American Secretary of State, Dean Rusk (1932–4) were all St John's men. The historian Sir Richard Southern was elected in 1969 to succeed John Mabbott, President since 1963, and under him the college rose to high academic distinction, now frequently heading the NORRINGTON TABLE. He retired in 1981 and was succeeded by Sir John Kendrew, winner of the Nobel Prize for Chemistry in 1963 and the first scientist to be President of St John's. Professor William Hayes, Bursar of the college and head of the CLARENDON LABORATORY, succeeded Sir John in 1987.

The corporate designation of the college is The President and Scholars of Saint John Baptist College in the University of Oxford.

(Hutton, W.H., *S. John Baptist College*, London, 1898; Costin, W.C., *The History of St. John's College, Oxford 1598–1860*, Oxford, 1958; Stevenson, W.H., and Salter, H.E., *The Early History of St. John's College, Oxford*, Oxford, 1939; Colvin, H.M., 'St. John's College: Its History and Architecture', in *Transactions of the Ancient Monuments Society*, 1981.)

St John's Home   Founded in 1873 for people with 'lingering sickness' or other incurable diseases. The home was built on land given by the Rev. R.M. Benson, first Superior of the Society of St John the Evangelist. The foundation stone was laid by Prince Leopold, who was then an undergraduate at Christ Church. The house, which stands in 3 acres of garden in St Mary's Road, was taken over in 1881 by the Anglican Society of All Saints Sisters of the Poor, who occupy one-half of the large house and run the other half as a home for about forty elderly residents. The chapel was designed by Sir Ninian Comper and has a fine stone rood-screen and beautifully carved choir stalls.

St Laurence, Church of   *South Hinksey*. The 13th-century church of St Laurence was originally a chapel sharing its incumbent with Wootton, both chapelries being in the parish of Cumnor; the advowson, first mentioned in 1401, was possessed by Abingdon Abbey, passing in 1723 to the Earl of Abingdon when the two chapelries were removed from the parish of Cumnor. In 1885 the chapelries were separated from each other; and in 1909 the patronage passed to the BISHOP OF OXFORD. When the church of ST JOHN THE EVANGELIST, NEW HINKSEY, was built, the title of the parish with its two churches became 'South with New Hinksey'.

The church consists of a nave measuring some 43 feet in length and 15 feet in width, and seats ninety; the chancel, rebuilt in the 18th century, is some 18 feet in length and 15 feet in width, its narrow, pointed arch being only 6 feet wide. The separation of chancel from nave is pronounced. Over the chancel arch a wooden rood-screen with rood above (the work of Sir Charles Nicholson replacing an earlier screen since decayed or destroyed) was given anonymously in 1932; in 1936 a wooden pulpit and prayer desk were added. A wall-tablet on the south wall of the chancel commemorates Halsall Segar (vicar 1881–90), his wife and their two sons. Entry to the church is by a central door in the north wall. A large round stone font by the door is probably the oldest feature in the church. The mediaeval roof was renewed in 1959. In 1966 a stained-glass window by F.W. Skeat, depicting St Laurence, was placed in the south-east of the nave in memory of George Frank Cooper and Janet Cooper.

The west tower, 39 feet high and 12 feet square at its base, has only one of its original three bells, the 5 cwt treble, cast in the early 15th century and bearing the inscription '*Vox Augustini sonet in aure Dei*' ('The voice of Augustine sounds in the ear of God'). The second, a cracked bell weighing 7 cwt, was probably cast by John Danyell in the 15th century and bears the inscription '*Sancta Margareta ora pro nobis*' ('Saint Margaret pray for us'). The tenor bell (8 cwt), cast in the 16th century and again in 1640, was also cracked; it was sold in 1968, melted down and made into two bells to complete the peal for ST LAWRENCE, NORTH

HINKSEY. The church possesses a silver chalice of *c*.1570–80 and a paten of 1636.

St Lawrence, Church of *North Hinksey*.

This small, ancient church was perhaps originally a chapel and monk's cell maintained by Abingdon Abbey for the use of travellers crossing Hinksey Ford to and from Oxford. The present Norman building (*c*.1100) replaced an earlier Saxon one. Its low, raftered roof emphasizes its antiquity. The nave, 45 feet by 18 feet, has a 12th-century doorway with fine Norman stonework, and its original deep-set windows in the north wall. The chancel, 24 feet by 15 feet, was entered by a narrow archway of 8 feet in height until replaced by the present rounded romanesque arch designed by J.M. Derick, who carried out other restoration work *c*.1840 in two Oxford churches, ST CROSS and ST GILES', and also to St Andrew's, Sandford-on-Thames. The east-window glass was given by S.A. Bloxham in 1930, and depicts Christ meeting St Mary Magdalen in the garden. At the west end of the nave is a musicians' gallery, now occupied by the organ. The 14th-century font has an octagonal bowl with a different design on each face. The short, Early English west tower, about 12 feet square, has a tiled pyramidal roof, and a west lancet window, perhaps of the 13th century. After the CIVIL WAR the tower was reported to be in ruins. Of the four 17th-century bells, the oldest is inscribed 'William Yare made me 1614': they were rehung, with two more bells, in 1972. Among the church's possessions are a silver chalice and cover (1582) and a paten (1681). Of several Finmore family memorials in the chancel is one to William (1646) and his son (1677), believed to be the work of the Oxford stonemason WILLIAM BYRD. There is an ancient stone cross in the churchyard set on a square base with three steps but lacking the crucifix which once crowned it.

The advowson, first mentioned in 1401 and formerly in the hands of the Rector of Cumnor, passed to the Earl of Abingdon and was acquired in 1910 by the BISHOP OF OXFORD.

St Luke, Church of *London Road, Cowley*.

Built by KINGERLEE LTD to the designs of H.S. Rogers in 1937–8, the church and its site were given by LORD NUFFIELD and consecrated by the BISHOP OF OXFORD (K.E. Kirk) on St Luke's Day, 1938. Its dedication to St Luke is a memorial to Lord Nuffield's generosity towards hospitals and medical research. It is a large church with a yellow-brick exterior; the north-west tower has a low spire and a bronze cross rising to a total height of 94 feet, with electrically operated bells, the tenor weighing 25 cwt and inscribed:

> May every tongue beneath the sky
> Send forth so sweet a sound as I
> And praise the Lord continually.

The interior is plain and light, with white walls and pillars, sturdy wooden pews, pulpit and screen of English oak, and clear-glazed windows; the nave and chancel are 126 feet long, with lofty aisles. Described by Pevsner as 'rather lifeless', the effect is of unity rather than variety, of solidity rather than grace. 'Space, proportion and repose were the guiding principles' in a design which does not conform to any traditional style. Above the screen is a rood with attendant life-size figures of St Mary and St John, and above the high altar are five coloured stone figures: ST

FRIDESWIDE, patron saint of Oxford; St Luke, patron of the church; Christ; St James, patron of COWLEY parish church; and St Francis of Assisi, patron of Cowley district church. The font is of stone from the Forest of Dean. The organ, built to a specification by Dr (later Sir Thomas) Armstrong, is by Harrison and Harrison of Durham. The church was awarded the Bronze Medal of the RIBA for the building of the most outstanding merit erected in Berkshire, Buckinghamshire and Oxfordshire during the period 1936–46.

St Luke's Nursing Home

Opened in 1957 as a nursing home in Linton Road. In 1982 St Luke's moved to new and larger premises in Latimer Road, HEADINGTON. These provide for both long- and short-stay patients, with residential nursing care, and there are flats for the elderly and disabled.

St Margaret, Church of *Binsey*.

Standing about half a mile north-west of the village at the end of an avenue of chestnut trees, the chapel of St Margaret was built (*c*.730) originally of 'watlyn and rough-hewn timber' standing next to St Margaret's Well (*see* BINSEY). Confirmed as belonging to ST FRIDESWIDE'S PRIORY in 1122, it passed to Christ Church, the present patron, at the Dissolution of the Monasteries. In his *Memorials of Oxford*, the REV. JAMES INGRAM, President of Trinity, stated that 'the church was originally a small oratory, with some buildings adjoining for the use of the nuns, whither they used to retire for recreation and sometimes to send their refractory members.' He also refers to the chancel, in which there is 'a piscina and niche, in which a costly statue of St. Frideswide is said to have been placed, to which the superstitious people paid such frequent adoration, that the stone pavement around was worn hollow by their knees'. By 1558 the chapel had a graveyard, bodies before then being taken by river to Oxford for burial. From 1919 to 1950 the living was held in plurality with WYTHAM, and has been since then with ST FRIDESWIDE'S CHURCH, Osney.

Less than 50 feet long and 20 feet wide, it has a simple barn-beamed roof (14th–15th century) and a small central bellcote (13th century) rebuilt in 1721 to its original design. In 1833 the east end 'being much decayed, was rebuilt by the Dean and Chapter of Christ Church as nearly as possible on the same model', and in 1875 the whole building was further restored. There is a plain cylindrical font (12th–13th century) on a modern base. An alabaster monument on the south wall commemorates Richard Tawney (*d*.1756) and his sons, Sir Richard (1720–91) and Edward (1735–1800), both of whom were three times MAYOR of Oxford. Unheated and lit only by oil-lamps and candles, it is still in regular use for worship.

St Margaret, Church of *St Margaret's Road*.

In 1875 a mission room in Hayfield Road was established to serve the needs of the neighbourhood as Oxford expanded northwards. It was succeeded by St Margaret's Church, built between 1883 and 1893 to the designs of H.G.W. Drinkwater, in the Decorated style of 1300–30, to serve as a chapel-of-ease to ST PHILIP AND ST JAMES. In 1896 it became an independent parish, until it was reconstituted in 1976 as a shared parish with St Philip and St James (closed in 1982). In 1985 the benefice was united with that of ST GILES'.

When the foundation stone, bearing the inscription *'Una pretiosa margarita 1883'* ('one pearl of great price') was laid by J.A. Shaw Stewart, a former Bursar of Keble College, in a cavity beneath the stone were placed for posterity a bottle containing a copy of the *Gospeller*, the *Morning Post*, the Order of Service, and some silver coins of the year. The consecration by BISHOP STUBBS took place in 1893. In 1899 G.F. BODLEY, who also designed the pulpit and the rood-screen, began a tower in the south-west corner, but only its porch was completed. His partner, Cecil Hare, designed the reredos, aumbry, baptistery screen and the font, the latter a gift from the City Church of ALL SAINTS. The east window and other window-glass (1900–35) are by F.C. Eden. In 1908 a parsonage house by H.G.W. Drinkwater was built next to the church.

St Margaret's Road Because the city gallows stood in this road in the 17th century, it was then known as Gallows Baulk. The University gallows were in HOLYWELL. The road was also known as Greenditch after the 4 foot wide by 3 foot deep trench where those who had committed capital crimes were sent from the city sessions to their execution. For some years in the 19th century the road was called Rackham's Lane and then, in the 1880s, St Margaret's Road after the church at the end on the corner of Kingston Road.

Most of the houses in the road were built between 1879 and 1886, many by H.W. Moore. St Hugh's College takes up all the south side of that part of the road between BANBURY and WOODSTOCK ROADS. In the Second World War a brick air-raid warden's post, manned mainly by the retired gentry of NORTH OXFORD, stood near the college gates at the Banbury Road end. In 1944 twenty-two residents petitioned the Council to change the name of that section of the road from the Banbury and Woodstock Roads to St Margaret's Road East. Others suggested St Hugh's Road, but the governing body of the college was against this.

St Martin's, Church of The original church, probably a private one, was granted to Abingdon Abbey in 1032 by King Cnut. Standing at CARFAX it later became the Town Church of Oxford, the MAYOR and Corporation having special seats allocated to them. At the Dissolution of the Monasteries the advowson passed from Abingdon Abbey to the Crown. The mediaeval church was later declared unsafe and in 1820 was demolished, except for the 13th-century west tower. A new church, designed by Harris and Plowman and supposedly modelled on Gloucester Cathedral, was built in its place. It was a very high rectangular building with no separate chancel. In 1896 this church also was demolished to make way for the Carfax improvement scheme. Sir William Davenant, Shakespeare's godson, was christened at the 14th-century font in St Martin's Church and it is possible that Shakespeare was at the christening. The font was removed to ALL SAINTS CHURCH, HIGH STREET, and subsequently to the City Church of ST MICHAEL AT THE NORTH GATE. The benefice was united in 1896 with All Saints and is now, with the remainder of the church property and its charities, part of the United Benefice of St Michael with All Saints and St Martin's.

St Martin's Church, built to the designs of Daniel Harris and John Plowman in 1820–2, was demolished (save for its tower) in 1896 for the improvement of Carfax.

Only the tower was retained, restored by T.G. JACKSON, who added a stair-turret and buttresses. The 17th-century clock and replicas of the two quarter-boys (figures of men holding clubs) were moved on to the east side of the tower in 1898 and fitted with two quarter jack-bells. The originals of the two quarter-boys can be seen in the MUSEUM OF OXFORD. The replicas, two men in quaint Roman costumes with gold-coloured helmets, are on either side of the two bells, the larger one on the right. At each quarter-hour they strike the bells with their hammers. In 1938 a new electric master clock was installed. Below the clock is the city's motto on its arms, *'Fortis est Veritas'* (*see* HERALDRY).

The Oxford Information Office was situated on the ground floor of the tower until increasing numbers of visitors necessitated its removal to ST ALDATE'S. The tower was cleaned and restored in 1984–5 and is open to visitors. A fine view of the centre of Oxford looking down HIGH STREET can be had from the top.

St Mary and St John, Church of *Cowley Road.* The parish of Cowley St John, formed in 1868, owes its origin to the Rev. R.M. Benson, who had built a temporary iron church in Stockmore Street in 1859 to serve the needs of the rapidly developing district. Benson, living in the Mission House of the Society of St John the Evangelist (*see* COWLEY FATHERS), which he had founded, in Marston Street (now ST STEPHEN'S HOUSE), was vicar of the parish from 1870 to 1886. In 1875 the foundation stone of St Mary and St John was laid. Designed by A.M. Mowbray in early Decorated style, it was built of Charlbury stone, the chancel being completed in 1879 and dedicated to Archbishop Longley of Canterbury, a former vicar of ST JAMES, COWLEY. The church was consecrated in 1883 when the nave and side-aisles were completed. In 1893 the tower and south porch were built, and in 1911–12 vestries were added to the east end. A spire, originally designed for the tower, was never added. The nave, seating 700 and with a lofty barrel-vaulted wooden roof, measures 63 feet in length and with its side-aisles 60 feet in width; the chancel is 36 feet long and 21 feet wide. North and south aisles are given a buttressed and cloistered effect by the half-arches springing from the outer walls to the nave arches. It was Benson's intention that the ornamentation of the interior should convey a divine message in every detail: in the nave and aisles the masonry was left uncarved, in the hope of its being decorated when money was raised and to 'exhibit a view of the Old Testament History in the capitals of the pillars and the corbels of the windows', twelve scenes eventually being carved and making a pictorial progress from the Fall of the Angels and the Fall of Man to Isaiah's Vision of a Redeemer. Of nine Orders of the Heavenly Host to be carved on the roof corbels, five were completed, but the idea of portraying the principal events of Christ's earthly life in the eight clerestory windows was never realised. Benson's successor, William Scott (vicar 1886–1910), succeeded in turn by his brother A.C. Scott (vicar 1910–23), began to fill the aisle windows with glass depicting holy men and women whose lives manifested 'the glory of the hidden kingdom', all but one being designed by Burlison and Grylls; all six windows in the south aisle were completed and are, as intended, of male saints, to be complemented by six female saints in the north aisle windows. Of these only two were achieved – St Anne, and later, in 1949, ST FRIDESWIDE, by Lawrence Lee.

The chancel, like the rest of the church, expresses the iconography of High Anglican worship in its ornamentation, in particular the east window (1891–2) representing the Adoration of the Lamb, and the richly carved reredos, a thank-offering for peace in 1918. A Martin's organ was housed in the Lady Chapel from 1886 to 1913, when it was removed to the north chapel loft until sold in 1940. The present organ, built by Norman and Beard in 1914, was bought from ST MICHAEL AT THE NORTH GATE in 1939 and renovated in 1979. The south transept window (1892), by Bucknall and Comper, was much admired when installed for being 'quite in the manner of ancient stained glass'; the north transept window (1913), also by Comper, is in memory of Mary Scott, wife of the second vicar. The Stations of the Cross were carved at Oberammergau and were presented by individual gift in 1911–13.

The vicarage-house was built in 1901 to the designs of Comper, and the adjacent parish room in 1892–3 to those of Bucknall and Co. Apart from R.M. Benson, the best-known incumbent was F. Underhill (vicar 1923–5), later Bishop of Bath and Wells. The traditions of the OXFORD MOVEMENT, from which the church of St Mary and St John sprang, continue in it today.

St Mary Hall Began as an ACADEMIC HALL in the rectory of the University Church of ST MARY THE VIRGIN, which stood on the corner of HIGH STREET and the present ORIEL STREET. The rectory had been the first home of the scholars of what became Oriel College at its foundation in 1324, but with their acquisition soon after of a house – La Oriole – at the corner of the present MERTON and ORIEL STREETS, it was let in 1327 to a master, and became an academic hall. St Mary Hall retained throughout its long subsequent history the name of the church to which its original building had belonged – a support to its distinctiveness from Oriel College, to which it was closely linked and which normally supplied its Principal. To its first building was added in 1455 Bedel Hall to the south. Much demolition and building involving St Mary Hall took place from the 15th century onwards, the

most recent being the erection early this century of the Rhodes Building of Oriel, part of which is on the site of the old rectory. The present St Mary's Quad of the college contains parts of 17th-, 18th- and 19th-century buildings of St Mary Hall, and a fragment of Bedel Hall.

In the mid-16th century St Mary Hall became a more distinct and separate society, a development symbolised by the blocking up of the door between it and Oriel. Its numbers remained high, at times exceeding those of Oriel itself; with sixty undergraduates in 1875 it was the largest of the surviving academic halls. Although destined for extinction by the 1877 University Commission (*see* ROYAL COMMISSIONS), St Mary Hall lasted until 1902, when the death of its Principal since 1857, D.P. Chase, provided for the University the opportunity to close it – the last of the mediaeval academic halls to be dissolved.

St Mary Magdalen, Church of *Magdalen Street.* A short distance north of the former North Gate of the mediaeval walled city, the present church stands on the site of an earlier Saxon church attached to ST FRIDESWIDE'S PRIORY. In 1074 it became part of the endowment for the college of secular canons serving the CHAPEL OF ST GEORGE in ROBERT D'OILLY'S Oxford CASTLE; in 1149 the endowment passed to OSENEY ABBEY. Soon after the Dissolution of the Monasteries, the Diocese of Oxford was established with Christ Church as its cathedral, and St Mary Magdalen (until then in the Diocese of Lincoln) returned to its original patrons. Only the foundations remain of the Norman church, and little of what St Hugh, Bishop of Lincoln from 1186 to 1200, rebuilt in 1194 when he added north and south aisles, the latter being dedicated to the recently canonised St Thomas of Canterbury (martyred in 1170). In the late 13th century, part of the north aisle was restored by Dervorguilla de Balliol as a chapel for her newly founded college nearby. The south chapel was built in 1320 by Carmelite friars living near GLOUCESTER GREEN, to which the narrow thoroughfare, FRIAR'S ENTRY, still leads from the church. The original 13th-century tower was rebuilt in the early 16th century. Parts of the present graveyard to the north and south of the church were occupied until the early 19th century by shops and dwelling-houses, including (*c*.1530) MAGDALEN HALL, an ACADEMIC HALL for poor scholars from Wales. In 1841, with £8000 left over from the building of the MARTYRS' MEMORIAL, its designer, GEORGE GILBERT SCOTT, enlarged and rebuilt the chancel and north aisle (the Martyrs' Aisle) as part of the Memorial. In 1874 the tower and bells were restored, and in 1913 statues of the Virgin Mary, Elijah, Richard I, and St Hugh of Lincoln were placed in the empty niches on the outside wall of the south chapel. Extensive restoration and cleaning of the stonework was carried out in 1985–6. The high-altar reredos (1894) shows saints associated with the church; St Mary Magdalen, ST FRIDESWIDE, St Catherine, the Virgin Mary, St George, St Hugh, St Thomas of Canterbury and St Simon Stock (the English Carmelite). There is also a modern plaque to JOHN AUBREY (1626–97), biographer and antiquary, who is buried in the church. The octagonal font dates from the late 14th century. An unusual feature of this High Church building is that its width (85 feet) is greater than its length (80 feet).

Steel engraving by William Radclyffe after Frederick Mackenzie's sepia drawing of the church of St Mary Magdalen c.1840.

The church was a royalist centre during the Commonwealth and was the first Oxford church to restore the Book of Common Prayer in 1660, a month before the return of Charles II; it still celebrates annually the Feast of King Charles Martyr on 30 January. However, in the 18th century the church was the only one in Oxford to be greatly affected by Wesleyanism and experienced a period of evangelical fervour, JOHN WESLEY himself writing that one of its curates preached 'with amazing success, both towns-men and gownsmen flocking in crowds to hear him' until he was removed by the Bishop after complaints from parishioners that his teaching was 'very stupid, low and bad stuff'. One early 19th-century vicar, C.L. Atterbury (1815–23), showed greater enthusiasm for stagecoaches than doctrine, and timed his Sunday morning sermons to enable him to watch the arrival of his favourite coach at the ANGEL INN at 1.00 p.m. (*see also* TRANSPORT). However, Jacob Ley (vicar 1844–57) was an outstandingly conscientious parish priest, a 'house-going parson', and responsible for the building of St George's Chapel. Cecil Deedes (vicar 1872–6) followed Tractarian practices during his incumbency (*see* OXFORD MOVEMENT); and in the 20th century extreme Anglo-Catholicism was firmly established, particularly by B.S. Hack (vicar 1922–47) and J.C. Stephenson (vicar 1948–59), author of *Merrily on High*. R. Holloway (vicar 1984–6) became Bishop of Edinburgh in 1986.

The mediaeval vicarage on the north side of the churchyard was demolished in about 1820, and in 1924 No. 53 BROAD STREET was acquired. When this house was sold to Trinity College in 1950, No. 15 BEAUMONT STREET was bought in its place.

St Mary the Virgin, Church of (University Church) Largely rebuilt in the late 15th and early 16th centuries, the University Church dominates much of the HIGH STREET. The existing church is the last of a series of buildings, the earliest of which dated from at least the 11th century, for Domesday Book records that Earl Aubrey of Northumbria, who had resigned his earldom by 1086, had held St Mary's Church and two houses which belonged to it. The two houses were presumably part of the endowment of the church and suggest that it was already of some importance. There may well have been a church on the site from the time of the foundation of Oxford as a borough in the late 9th or early 10th century, for St Mary's stands on the site of what was almost certainly the original East Gate of the borough and might have been a gate church or chapel, like ST MICHAEL AT THE NORTH GATE. Nothing is known of the structure of the early church or churches, although fragments of 11th- or 12th-century work were apparently found behind panelling in the chancel during restoration work in about 1900 and a few others were found during the 19th-century restorations. Most fragments of the mediaeval church found in the 19th century were of the late 12th or 13th century, and may have come from a rebuilding at that date, for the church seems to have been reconsecrated in about 1189. That rebuilding was perhaps initiated by two eminent 12th-century rectors. John of Oxford (rector *c.*1160) was the son of a wealthy Oxford merchant and served Henry II as judge and ambassador, taking the King's part in his quarrel with Becket; he became Bishop of Norwich in 1175. His successor, John of Bridport, was physician to Richard I.

By 1189 the University was developing, centred in the streets around St Mary's. There was a 'school' or lecture room next to the church in 1190, and by the 13th century many Masters and scholars, as well as tradesmen associated with the University, including parchment-makers and bookbinders, lived in the parish. They were probably attracted by its position, within the walled town but away from the main, crowded, commercial centre around CARFAX. Thus St Mary's was associated with the University from an early date; and, at a time when there were no specialised University buildings, the church was used for meetings, examinations and ceremonies, as well as for the sessions of the Chancellor's Court (*see* COURTS).

In the early 14th century the University built the old CONGREGATION HOUSE on the east side of the church tower for meetings of CONGREGATION, but CONVOCATION still met in the church, the different faculties meeting separately in different parts of the building – theologians in the Congregation House, canonists in St Anne's Chapel, jurists in St Thomas's Chapel, and the PROCTORS with the Regents in the Lady Chapel; final decisions were taken by the whole Convocation meeting in the chancel. Students studying for a Bachelor's degree had to dispute and debate in the porch and in the room called the parvise above it; later in their careers, Masters of Arts who wished to take the further degree of Bachelor of Divinity had to preach a Latin sermon in St Mary's. In addition to these examination sermons, a Latin sermon was preached each Sunday in term by a BD or DD (*see* UNIVERSITY SERMON). There is no evidence of where the Chancellor's Court sat in the Middle Ages, but in the 16th century and the early 17th it sat in the Lady Chapel. St Mary's was also used as a place of safe-keeping for the University chests, its treasury, in which were stored the University's money and valuables, and also the 'pledges' given by under-graduates as security for loans from the chests specially endowed for that purpose (*see* UNIVERSITY CHEST). It was to St Mary's that, from 1357, the MAYOR and bailiffs and sixty leading burgesses had to go in humiliating procession every year on ST SCHOLASTICA'S DAY to offer 1*d* each in atonement for the riot on that day in 1355.

Despite the use the University made of St Mary's, it had no official rights in the church. The advowson, or right to present a priest to the rectory, had passed before 1086 from Earl Aubrey of Northumbria to William I, and it remained in the hands of the Crown until 1326 when Edward II granted it to Oriel College, which had been founded two years earlier by the rector of St Mary's, Adam de Brome, a royal clerk. Oriel at once impropriated the rectory – that is, it took over most of the income, including the tithes, which had belonged to the rector, and which amounted to the comparatively large sum of £15 6*s* 8*d* because the parish included the agricultural hamlet of LITTLEMORE, 3 miles east of Oxford. Since 1326 Oriel has appointed vicars to serve the church.

By 1326 part of the surviving church had been built. The north tower had been begun in the later 13th century, possibly under the direction of Richard the mason of Abingdon, to whom the parish leased a house in 1275 to be held rent-free as long as he was in charge of the works on the church. The spire was completed early in the 14th century. In about 1320 the University, with money given by Thomas Cobham, Bishop of Worcester, built the old Congregation House with a room above it for a library. In 1328 Adam de Brome built a Lady Chapel on the north side of the nave; it is now known as the de Brome Chapel and contains a reconstructed altar tomb, of which only the lid is actually 14th-century, which is traditionally ascribed to Adam de Brome himself.

Thomas Cobham had intended that the room above the Congregation House should be used to house the books he planned to leave to the University, but he died in 1327, before the work was finished, leaving insufficient money either to complete the building or to endow the library. Oriel College, having paid some of the bishop's debts, took possession of both the building and the books, and a long dispute with the University ensued, in the course of which some Masters of Arts, acting on behalf of the University, forcibly removed the books from Oriel and broke into the upper room, which was being used as a timber store. The dispute was finally settled in 1410, and the University then completed the building by glazing the windows and fitting up the interior as a library for Cobham's books. The University library remained there until the completion of Duke Humfrey's library in 1480 (*see* BODLEIAN LIBRARY).

Oriel College, as rectors, were responsible for the upkeep of the chancel of St Mary's, and in about 1462 Walter Lyhert, a former Provost of Oriel, then Bishop of Norwich, completely rebuilt the chancel, which had apparently been ruinous for some years. In 1487 the University launched an appeal to rebuild the nave, which was said to have become so dilapidated that it no longer kept out the rain, and was indeed in danger of collapse. In their determination to build a church worthy of the University and suitable for CEREMONIES, the University demolished the whole of the earlier nave, including four chapels, and rebuilt it as a single, rectangular nave with north and south aisles, but no separate chapels apart from the surviving de Brome Chapel. The former St Anne's Chapel, on the

The baroque south porch of St Mary the Virgin was probably built to the designs of Nicholas Stone. The heads of the Virgin and Child, shot off by a parliamentary soldier in 1642, were restored twenty years later.

north-east of the nave, became little more than a passage to the library and Congregation House. Contributors to the building fund included Henry VII, who gave forty oaks from SHOTOVER ROYAL FOREST. The nave was finished by 1503, and between then and 1510 the north walls of the de Brome Chapel and the Congregation House and library were remodelled to match the Perpendicular style of the rest of the church.

The Reformation affected St Mary's as it did other parish churches. In the reign of Edward VI PLATE and vestments were sold and altars and statues destroyed. Under Mary most were restored: a statue of St Thomas was repaired, and copes, crosses, candlesticks and Mass books bought; St Mary's also witnessed the trials of Bishops Cranmer, Latimer and Ridley in 1554, 1555 and 1556 (see MARTYRS' MEMORIAL). The finials of the stalls in the chancel are said to have been flattened to support the platform on which the formal disputations with the three bishops were held in 1554; and in the nave the pillar opposite the pulpit was damaged by the erection of a scaffold or platform for the final trial and sentencing of Cranmer in 1556.

Religious controversy continued to dog St Mary's in Elizabeth's reign. There was such a shortage of Protestant preachers in Oxford in the 1560s that the Puritan High Sheriff, Richard Taverner, preached in St Mary's. In 1581 copies of the recusant EDMUND CAMPION's *Decem Rationes* were distributed in the church at the beginning of the University ACT. About 1582 the vicar, Stephen Rousham, became a ROMAN CATHOLIC and fled to the Continent; he was executed at Gloucester in 1587 on his second mission to England. Controversy of a different kind touched the church with the burial there in 1560 of Amy Robsart, wife of Elizabeth's favourite, the Earl of Leicester. Elizabeth herself visited the church for special University ceremonies, including Latin disputations, in 1566 and 1592.

In the 17th century came the reforms of the 'High Church' party. ARCHBISHOP LAUD, who was CHAN-CELLOR of the University from 1629 to 1641, had been accused of preaching popery in St Mary's in 1606. Laud's chaplain, Dr Morgan Owen, rebuilt the south porch of St Mary's in baroque style, apparently to designs by Nicholas Stone. The statue of the Virgin and Child above the arch on the porch was cited as evidence of Laud's popery at his trial; and in 1642 the heads of both figures were shot away by a parliamentary soldier; they were restored in 1662. Apart from this damage, St Mary's suffered less than other Oxford churches during the CIVIL WAR and Interregnum. It was not used for billeting soldiers or guarding prisoners, and although vicars were expelled in 1648 and 1649, their successors were regularly appointed by Oriel College. Changes were doubtless made in the furnishings of the church, and the floors must have been much disturbed by the many burials which took place there during the sieges of Oxford in 1644 and 1645.

It was to repair the damage of those years that RALPH BATHURST, President of Trinity College and VICE-CHANCELLOR 1673–6, paid for repaving parts of the nave and chancel in black and white marble, the wainscoting of the east wall of the chancel (thus presumably hiding the lower part of the mutilated mediaeval reredos), and the erection of a solid oak screen between nave and chancel. The University gave an organ by Father Smith, paved the remainder of the nave in stone, and supplied new pews. One final alteration was made to the interior of the church in 1733 when the Adam de Brome Chapel was wainscotted and the arches between it and the nave were blocked.

By the 18th century the University's use of the church had been considerably reduced. The building of a new CONVOCATION HOUSE and room for the Chancellor's Court at the west end of the DIVINITY SCHOOL between 1634 and 1636 removed both court and Convocation from St Mary's; and after the completion of the SHELDONIAN THEATRE in 1669 University ceremonies such as the Act also moved from St Mary's. The weekly University Sermon was, and has remained, the only regular institutional connection between the church and the University. The church thus played a lesser role in University life in the 18th than in earlier centuries. Between them, Oriel, the University and the parish carried out the necessary repairs to the fabric, including, in 1790, rebuilding the large west window in 15th-century style. The parochial services were comparatively well attended; but on the whole the attitude of the parish was probably that of an early 18th-century vicar who was praised for opposing faction, schism and 'everything which had the least tendency to innovation'. Among the Masters of Arts who delivered the University Sermons, however, was JOHN WESLEY, who preached there for the last time on 24 August 1744. The sermon caused a stir and the Vice-Chancellor sent for Wesley's notes to check for signs of heresy. Wesley commented, 'Perhaps few men of note would have given a sermon of mine a reading if I had put it into their hands, but by this means it came to be read, probably more than once, by every man of eminence in the university.'

Wesley's reforms were to be made, in the end, outside the Church of England. In the 19th century Oxford, and St Mary's in particular, was for a time at the centre of national religious life. On 14 July 1833 JOHN KEBLE preached the ASSIZE SERMON in St Mary's on 'National Apostasy', a call for the defence of the Church which was sparked off by plans to suppress some Irish bishoprics. The sermon has since been regarded as the start of the OXFORD MOVEMENT, in which JOHN HENRY NEWMAN (vicar of St Mary's 1828–43) played a leading role. His best-known contribution is *Tract XC*, which put forward a Catholic interpretation of the Thirty-Nine Articles, but his influence in the University was exercised far more through his ministry at St Mary's than through his *Tracts*. He started to hold morning and evening prayer daily and Communion services weekly, at a time when in many churches Communion was celebrated only three or four times a year. He was encouraged by the number of weekly communicants among the Masters of Arts, and his Sunday afternoon sermons, 'high poems as of an inspired singer or the outpourings of a prophet, rapt yet self-possessed', attracted large numbers of undergraduates – a fact which actually worried Newman, who felt that undergraduates were the responsibility of college chaplains and that his mission as vicar of St Mary's should be to the senior members of the University. He spoke, too, in 1840, of his difficulties with the parishioners, with whom he felt he did not get on. At the same time opposition to the Tractarians and their

'Romanising' tendencies was growing, and some college chaplains went so far as to alter the times of compulsory chapel services so that they would clash with Newman's sermons. Newman's own growing doubts on the catholicity of the Anglican church caused him to move from Oxford to LITTLEMORE (still part of St Mary's parish) in 1842, and in 1843 he resigned St Mary's, preaching his last sermon, on 'The Parting of Friends', at Littlemore.

Just before Newman became vicar, the interior of the nave was rearranged under the direction of the young Oxford builder and architect Thomas Plowman, and on the initiative of the vicar, Edward Hawkins, later Provost of Oriel. The moveable pulpit of Dr Bathurst's reordering, which had usually been placed at the east end of the nave, was replaced by a Gothic stone pulpit in the mediaeval position, against the second pillar from the east in the south arcade. The pews were rearranged to face it as far as possible. The 17th- and 18th-century monuments were removed from the pillars of the nave arcades, north and west galleries were built, and Dr Bathurst's wooden screen was replaced by a solid stone one in Perpendicular style.

Plowman's work survived for a century, until changing ideas about the ordering of churches, themselves in part the result of the Oxford Movement, led, in 1930, to a new arrangement. The pews were moved to face east, the wall blocking off the de Brome Chapel was demolished, most of the north gallery was removed, and the screen between the nave and chancel was pierced by two extra arches, opening up the chancel to the nave. The exterior of the church, notably the tower and spire, were restored by SIR GEORGE GILBERT SCOTT in 1856–7 and by SIR THOMAS JACKSON between 1892 and 1896. The work, although it involved much refacing, the rebuilding of the top 48 feet of the spire, and the replacing of most of the statues around it, did not really alter the appearance of the church. The interior of the chancel was restored in 1928, and in 1933 statues of St Mary Magdalen, ST FRIDESWIDE, St Catherine, the Virgin and Child, St John the Baptist, St Hugh and St Edmund of Abingdon were placed in the niches of the mediaeval reredos. In 1986 a new organ, made by the Swiss craftsman Metzler, was installed at a cost of £185,000.

(Ffoulkes, E.S., *A History of the Church of St. Mary the Virgin*, 1892; Jackson, T.G., *The Church of St Mary the Virgin*, 1897.)

St Mary the Virgin *Iffley*. The beautifully preserved little Norman church of St Mary the Virgin dates from the second half of the 12th century, although the site on which it stands may have belonged to an even earlier church. It was probably built by the St Remy family, who held the manor of IFFLEY during the reign of Henry II (1154–89); certainly it was in the gift of Juliana de St Remy, who bestowed the patronage upon Kenilworth Priory. By 1279 this had passed to the Archdeacon of Oxford, who held it for nearly 700 years until, in 1965, he conferred it upon the Dean and Chapter of CHRIST CHURCH CATHEDRAL, with whom it now rests.

St Mary's is constructed in ragstone with simple stone dressings, but it displays in its principal doorways and windows much of the elaborate decoration characteristic of the late 12th century. From this period date the chancel, nave and central tower; the north, south and west doorways; the north and south windows adjacent to the west gable and the three recessed windows contained in it. The gable itself, forming the third storey of the picturesque west front, was rebuilt in the 19th century. Altered in the 17th century when the roof of the nave was lowered, it was restored in 1823 by Robert Bliss, and in 1844 the nave roof was returned to its original pitch by R.C. Hussey. The small blind window at the summit of the gable is Victorian and its zigzag embellishment, echoing that of the Norman windows below it, is reiterated in the central rose window in the second storey. This was inserted in the 1850s by J.C. BUCKLER, and follows the outline of a Norman circular window blocked up during the 15th century. The 19th-century restorations blend harmoniously with the magnificent Norman doorway. This is flanked by two tall blind arches and is deeply recessed, displaying six orders of richly carved decoration including zigzag and beakhead, surmounted by a semi-circular hood bearing symbols of the Evangelists and the signs of the zodiac. The south doorway, formerly sheltered by a porch, is less weathered and even richer in its adornment. In the east end of the south wall is a filled-in arch which may have been a window offering a view of the altar to Annora, a 13th-century noble anchoress who lived in a cell by the church. Alternatively, it may have been a priest's door into a Norman apse. The tower is in three stages, with shallow clasping buttresses. The top stage, restored in 1975 and with carvings by Michael Groser, has two arched, recessed openings on each side, the south-west arch being heavily ornamented. To the north-west is a stair-turret with a fluted stone roof opening into the nave.

Inside, the tower arches are richly carved, their western faces displaying octagonal shafts of black Purbeck marble or slate. The aisleless nave contains a contemporary font, large and square, resting on four stone columns, three spiral and one, dating from the 13th century, plain. Also dating from the 13th century is the sanctuary, an extension of the Norman chancel, which houses in its south wall an aumbry, piscina and sedilia. On its north wall is a circular Agnus Dei, presumed to be the head of a mediaeval cross now standing in the churchyard crowned by an 1857 top. The blind arcade across the east wall is Victorian. In each corner of the choir are floral and other emblems carved between the clustered shafts leading to the vaulting. One touching representation is that of a nesting bird. The Norman windows in the choir were altered in the 14th century by the introduction of some simple Decorated tracery. The pulpit, by Sir Ninian Comper, was made in 1907. Most of the stained glass is Victorian, although some fragments in one of the south windows reveal the arms of John de la Pole, Duke of Suffolk (*c*.1475). The 1923 east window is by Christopher Webb. Of the original twelve consecration crosses, four can still be seen on the walls of the tower and nave.

In the churchyard an ancient yew overhangs the mediaeval cross, and to the west of the church is an unidentified octagonal font-bowl of great age. St Mary's was restored between 1975 and 1984 at a cost of £107,000.

St Mary's Church *Bayswater Road*. The origins of the church are found in services conducted first in the study of Bayswater Farm, and then in 1934 in a Nissen hut to serve the new housing estate of Sandhills by the vicar of Forest Hill, in whose parish they lay. When the Barton estate was completed in 1948, the Society of King Charles Martyr purchased the hut used by the foreman of works as a place of worship, which was then presented to the church of ST ANDREW, HEADINGTON. In 1954 the Conventional District of Bayswater was formed to serve both the Barton and Sandhills estates; in 1958 St Mary's Church was consecrated, and granted full parish status in 1983. Built to the designs of N.F. Cachemaille-Day, with brick exterior and simple interior of clear windows and white walls, it has an apsidal east chapel with contemporary stained glass portraying King Charles I and ARCHBISHOP LAUD flanking the Virgin Mary.

St Mary's College *see* MONASTIC COLLEGES.

St Matthew, Church of *Marlborough Road*. Built as a chapel-of-ease of ST ALDATE'S, the foundation stone of this church was laid by WILLIAM STUBBS, BISHOP OF OXFORD, in 1890. In 1913 it became the centre of a district chapelry taken from St Aldate's. The patronage was vested in Simeon's Trustees but passed in 1914 to the OXFORD CHURCHES TRUST.

Designed by Messrs Christopher and White of London in 15th-century Gothic style, it has an 80-foot nave, 30 feet wide, with five bays; its aisles are 15 feet wide. The single-bay chancel, 25 feet in length, is separated from the nave by a slender, open, wooden screen, a memorial to those who lost their lives in the First World War. The lofty, barrel-vaulted roof of undecorated wood is open-beamed; the large windows, all diamond-paned, are of clear or mauve-coloured glass, the only stained glass being a single light (1929) in a north window of Christ calling Matthew from the receipt of custom. The organ is in the north-east corner, the vestry in the south-east. The pulpit, from ST PETER-LE-BAILEY (now St Peter's College chapel) was installed in 1932. The external entrance porch at the south-west corner of the building has some 'nice details' (Pevsner) and a single-bell turret. In the chancel are wall-tablets to Canon A.M.W. Christopher (Rector of St Aldate's for forty-six years) who died in 1913 aged ninety-three, and to D.A.S. Hunt, chaplain of Oxford PRISON and founder of the 1st Oxford Boys' Brigade Company. A tablet on the south-aisle wall commemorates J.A. Paintin, aged twenty-nine, lost in the *Titanic* disaster. The church stands adjacent to the north-west corner of the Oxford City Football Club ground.

In 1934 a small wooden mission church, St Luke's, was opened in Canning Crescent to serve the new district of Weir's Lane, its pulpit and communion table coming from St Matthew's. This was still in use in 1986.

St Michael and All Angels, Church of *Lonsdale Road*. When the church of ST JOHN THE BAPTIST, Rogers Street, was closed in 1909, the church of St Michael and All Angels, designed in Early English style by A.M. Mowbray and built in 1908–9, was opened to replace it, only the chancel, north-east vestry and one bay of the nave being completed. A further three bays were intended for the church, which was designed to hold a congregation of 1000.

The present length of the nave is some 50 feet, with a chancel, rising dramatically on nine steps, of some 40 feet: with a nave of some 35 feet in width and north and south transepts of some 30 feet each in width, the church is as wide as it is long. The east window is a memorial to the fallen of the First World War; in the south (Lady) Chapel, the east window (1934) is dedicated to Canon C.J. Burrough (vicar 1908–14); above the north-east vestry, the organ (1884) is by Henry Willis, and was presented by Mrs Maclaren, founder of SUMMER FIELDS in memory of her husband. In 1931 a gilded statue of the Virgin and Child was placed by the Lady Chapel; and in 1947 a rood was suspended in the chancel arch. The exterior walls of the church are of stone, apart from the flat west front which is of brick and emphasises the unfinished design of the building. There is no tower, but the lofty roof has a central belfry. At the entrance to the churchyard is a large lych-gate (1935) placed in memory of members of the Pepper family. The present vicarage (1924) replaced the previous one built in 1879 at the corner of BANBURY ROAD and SOUTH PARADE. The church hall, at the corner of Banbury Road and Portland Road, was built of materials from the church of St John the Baptist, Rogers Street, when it was demolished.

In 1976 the living passed from the patronage of St John's College to that of the Patronage Board. In the same year an Anglican Team Ministry was formed with ST PETER'S, WOLVERCOTE, and in 1982 this became an Ecumenical Team Ministry with the SUMMERTOWN UNITED REFORMED CHURCH. A former incumbent, R.M. Hay (vicar 1915–23), was later Bishop of Buckingham.

St Michael and All Angels, Church of *Marston Road*. Following the laying of the foundation stone by Lord Bicester, Lord Lieutenant of Oxfordshire, the church was consecrated in 1955 as a chapel-of-ease to ST ANDREW'S, HEADINGTON. It was the first church in the Oxford diocese to be consecrated after the Second World War and replaced a mission church in Ferry Road which had been established (*c*.1919) to serve outlying areas of the parish of ST NICHOLAS, Old Marston. In 1963 the parish of St Michael and All Angels was formed from parts of the parishes of MARSTON, HEADINGTON and ST CLEMENT'S, the patron being the BISHOP OF OXFORD. In 1967 a vicarage was built in JACK STRAW'S LANE (No. 8).

Built to the designs of T. Lawrence Dale (author of *Towards a Plan for Oxford City*, 1944) and described in Pevsner as being of a 'vaguely Italian Renaissance' appearance, the church has a sand-lime brick exterior with a low tower at the east end, a south-east vestry, and a slender campanile at the west end containing a bell given by the church of St Peter and St Paul, Wantage. Over the west door is a bas-relief in stone depicting Adam, the Serpent of Man's Fall, and the Dove with its olive branch to symbolise reconciliation and the hope of regeneration: from this entrance, the view up the nave is of the reredos mural of the Resurrection, crowned by the window above it of Christ in Majesty. Within, the west end has been reformed to provide a church room, with organ gallery above it, the organ being given in memory of J.H. Mortimer (vicar of St Nicholas, Old Marston, 1905–51) by his sister. The nave, now 60 feet to the chancel steps, has narrow north and south aisles, both of four-bay round-headed arches; the overall width of the building is also 60 feet. From west to east the four north aisle pillars are inset with neat bas-reliefs in stone, depicting in order the Expulsion, Abraham and Isaac, Jacob and the Angel, and the Fiery Furnace; these are complemented by the south aisle pillars with bas-reliefs of the Annunciation, the Nativity, Gethsemane and the Resurrection. They are the group-work of John Bunting, Michael Groser and Leon Underwood. At the west end of the north aisle is a fine modern font in stone, and at the east end of the south aisle a life-size statue in stone of St Michael by Michael Groser, in memory of Kenneth Kirk (Bishop of Oxford 1937–54). Also at the west end of the north aisle is a stained-glass window (1937), formerly in the mission church, entitled Faith, to the memory of Ada Louise Jackson, 'poetess, reciter, philanthropist, author of the Gordon League Ballads': previously an exterior window, it is now darkened by the addition of a kitchen beyond.

The lofty chancel (24 feet long and 20 feet wide) has a wooden hanging rood flanked by the Virgin and St John, and a plain brick altar with a reredos mural (18 feet high and 10 feet wide) painted in egg-tempera by Leon Underwood, assisted by Eric Wood, and contemporary with the church. Six diaphanously draped angels proclaim the Resurrection on their trumpets. Designed to dominate the church dramatically, its faded colours and dated figures now fail fully to realise the artist's intentions, and the mural is concealed by a curtain. At the east end of the north aisle another, smaller reredos mural by Leon Underwood, also behind a curtain and also faded, depicts the Annunciation.

Above the main mural is an elliptical east window, also by Underwood, of the Risen Christ above Oxford, its University buildings seen from south of CHRIST CHURCH MEADOW in the curving embrace of Isis and Cherwell (see THAMES) – a panoramic view in allusion, perhaps, to the architect's proposed route for an inner relief for the city.

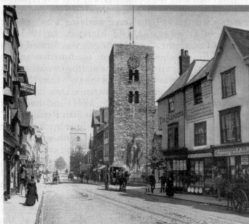

The Saxon tower of St Michael at the North Gate, built c.1050, is the oldest building in Oxford.

St Michael at the North Gate *Cornmarket*. One of the oldest churches in Oxford. Its Saxon tower was probably built around 1050 and stood at the ancient North Gate of the city. It is the oldest building in

Oxford. The doors and windows on the north side were part of the original tower and it seems therefore that, although the tower stood at the North Gate, it was not a defensive wall tower. The CITY WALL was extended north at this point to provide a churchyard and the doorway at first-floor level on the north side of the tower may have opened on to the ramparts. In any case the tower would have made a useful look-out in the defence of the northern part of the city wall. A blocked doorway has recently been discovered at first-floor level in the tower on the south side which may have led to the original Saxon church. There is no trace left of this church, but it may well have stood on the corner of SHIP STREET and CORNMARKET. The tower was later connected on its west side to a building above the North Gate known as the BOCARDO PRISON. The door of the room in the Bocardo in which Cranmer was held before being burned at the stake is now in the church tower.

The church is recorded in Domesday Book (1086) with the entry: 'The Priests of St. Michael's have two houses paying 52 pence.' The advowson was granted to ST FRIDESWIDE'S PRIORY in 1122, and in 1339 it passed to the Bishop of Lincoln. The church has been closely associated with Lincoln College since the college's foundation in 1427, when St Michael's was appropriated to the college, which henceforth until the 19th century appointed a chaplain, often a Fellow, to look after the parish. Lincoln College is still the patron of the living. The chancel was built in the 13th century, with twin lancet windows on the south side and a close-set triplet of lancets on the east side. These narrow slits in the wall at the east end of the church contain the oldest STAINED GLASS in Oxford, dating from 1290. The figure in the piece of glass at the top is the church's patron saint, St Michael the Archangel, carrying a shield with a unique cross which the church has adopted as its symbol. The piece below that contains the figure of the Virgin Mary and Child. On the left or north side is St Nicholas, and on the right or south side is St Edmund of Abingdon, Archbishop of Canterbury. The piscina on the right of the altar also dates from this period. The sedilia, or clergy seats, on the south side of the chancel have stone-vaulted carving and date from the 15th century.

The church was extended by chantry chapels built at different periods. In 1263 Denise (or, in Latin, Dionysia) Burewald, a rich widow, gave the church a rent so that the priests could say Mass for her soul in a chantry chapel, and in 1279 she left the church a property in Ship Street for the same purpose. The part of the south chapel nearest the chancel was probably built about 1280. In the 14th century another chantry chapel was built to the west of the 13th century one. The connection between the two can be seen on the outside of the south wall. Inside is a piscina. The Decorated window in the south wall has modern glass. The two chapels were later formed into one to make the south chapel, which is also called the Welsh Aisle either after the many Welshmen from Jesus College who used to worship there or its proximity to Jesus College.

The north chapel and north transept were also added in the 14th century. The north chapel or Lady Chapel has a late 15th-century east window. It had its own accounts and its own Wardens, who were called 'Custodians of the Altar and lights in the Chapel of the Blessed Mary the Virgin in the Church of the Blessed

Michael in the North at Oxford'. The chapel was partly rebuilt in 1833. The reredos, which is 15th century, has figures by Harold Youngman inserted in the niches in 1939. In the centre is the Virgin and Child; on the left or north side ST FRIDESWIDE; and on the right or south side St Mildred (Abbess of Minster in Kent, c.660–725 AD). She was the patron of the neighbouring parish to the east which was incorporated with St Michael's when St Mildred's Church was demolished to make way for Lincoln College. Late in the 15th century the north and south arcades of the nave were built, replacing the irregular openings into the chantry chapels. About the same time the north aisle was added and the south porch was rebuilt on the site of an earlier porch, but retaining its 13th-century outer door. An arch was also cut into the Saxon tower to open it to the church; this caused a weakness in the tower which had to be strengthened by buttresses built outside some four and a half centuries later. There are some interesting fragments of 15th-century glass in the Lily Window of the north aisle. The twin figures at the sides are combinations of the cherubim in the vision of the Prophet Ezekiel and the seraphim seen by Isaiah, each with a wheel at their feet. In the centre is a figure of Christ crucified on a lily plant, originally part of an Annunciation.

Among the monuments in the south chapel the earliest is one to Ralph Flexney and his wife. He was a wealthy fishmonger and chandler who lived at 26–8 Cornmarket. He was MAYOR of Oxford in 1578 and Member of Parliament for the city. Another is to Anna Lloyd (1615), widow of a Principal of Jesus College, and her daughter Jane, who died aged seventeen. The dates are in the form of a chronogram in which some of the letters of the text are picked out to form the date in Roman figures.

The pulpit from which JOHN WESLEY preached the Michaelmas sermon in 1726 is partly 15th century. The font is a late-14th-century one, which was originally in ST MARTIN'S CHURCH. The church contains a fine 17th-century oak chest, ironbound with three locks and four handles. Three different members of the congregation held a key; and the chest, which contained parish documents, could be opened only if all three were present. The church plate includes a beautiful silver chalice of 1562, one of the oldest in the diocese, another of 1611, and a flagon and plate, both of 1672. These and other treasures of the church, including a sheela-na-gig, a very early erotic female stone figure (possibly late 11th century or early 12th century) are on display in the treasury in the tower. St Michael's possesses the ninth oldest set of churchwardens' accounts in the country. They date back to 1404 and contain many interesting comments on the life of the church. During the CIVIL WAR, for example, soldiers were billeted in the church, and the accounts contain such details as 'For cleansing the Church and perfewminge it after the soldiers was lodged in it a week – 10s. 6d.'

In 1853–4 a major restoration of the church was carried out by G.E. STREET. The chancel was largely rebuilt, its floor level raised and the altar put on a step. The 15th-century chancel arch was replaced by a higher, more pointed one, and a low screen was substituted for the rood-screen. These alterations were strongly opposed by the Rev. Frederick Metcalfe, who was vicar for thirty-six years from 1849 to 1885. He has been described as 'an irascible egotist',

and was firmly against all change. In 1937, in memory of King George V, the 15th-century niche on the south side of the chancel arch was filled with a figure of St George, carved by Harold Youngman, and on the opposite side a figure of St Michael. These were gilded and painted in 1960. The figure of St Catherine was inserted in the niche in the east end of the south chapel in 1946.

When ALL SAINTS, the former City Church in the HIGH STREET, was closed in order to be converted to the library for Lincoln College, the benefice was united with St Michael's, which thus became the City Church. St Michael's has always had a close association with the business houses in the city, many of which are in its parish. A curious survival from the Middle Ages is the Sunday Pence. This was a payment by the larger houses in the parish of one penny for each of the fifty-two Sundays in the year and twopence for the great festivals. The maintenance and repair of the church and its fittings, as well as the augmentation of the stipends of its clergy and the salaries of its staff, is now largely undertaken by ST MICHAEL'S AND ALL SAINTS CHARITIES.

The churchyard used to be surrounded by a high wall with a 17th-century gateway, which can be seen in early prints. The wall was removed in 1878, and replaced by iron railings, which were removed for scrap during the Second World War. In 1956 the south forecourt was leased to the city for ninety-nine years as a public open space and seats for the public were provided. Some alterations were made to the tower over the years. In 1678–9 a cupola was added, but was removed in 1701 as it was considered to be dangerous. In the latter part of the 19th century the 16th-century parapet of the tower was replaced by a plain one, and the belfry windows were opened.

In 1953 the church was severely damaged by a fire, which started in the organ. It was thought to be the work of an arsonist. The roof was destroyed and much damage was caused to the interior and the church furnishings. The church was unusable for nearly a year, but many of the furnishings were saved by parishioners and others, who also removed for safety during the height of the fire the pieces of 13th-century glass from the east window. The restoration after the fire was carried out by G.R.S. Flavel. The choir was moved to a position in front of the organ in the north transept, and a new round-arched, barrel-vault roof was designed by Flavel for the chancel. The fragments of 13th-century stained glass rescued from the fire were reset in a grisaille pattern in the east window copied from contemporary windows at Fawkham in Kent. The cost of the work was paid for by a grant from the Pilgrim Trust. The whole church was cleaned and made lighter, and the first service in the restored church took place on Michaelmas Day 1954. The following Sunday the vicar took as his text the words of the prophet Haggai, 'The glory of this latter house shall be greater than of the former, saith the Lord of Hosts; and in this place will I give peace.' The Great Fire is graphically described by the vicar, Canon R.R. Martin (vicar 1927–61) in his history of *The Church and Parish of St. Michael at the North Gate, Oxford*, which he finished a few hours before he died. It was published after his death and takes the history of the church up to the induction of his successor, Canon N.M. ('Mac') Ramm, a chaplain to the Queen, in 1961.

Two great projects at the church have been initiated by Canon Ramm during his incumbency. The first was the church centre. The church hall used to be in St Michael's Hall in SHOE LANE; it was sold in 1978 and a new church centre was built, designed by G.R.S. Flavel, who had carried out the restoration of the church after the 1953 fire. This was built on to the church in the churchyard on the north side and was opened in June 1974. It incorporates a parish meeting room with kitchen; a large basement room below, named the Ann Alworth Room after a woman who died in 1721 leaving £400 for the education of poor children; a vicar's vestry, and offices for the clergy and the church secretary and staff. Doors connect the church centre with the north chapel. Part of the old city wall can be seen in an enclosure in the Ann Alworth Room.

The second project was the opening-up of the tower. The work was started in January 1986 to the designs of Peter Bosanquet and John Perryman Associates. On the ground floor is a library, also used during services as a 'crying room' where parents can take their children who might otherwise disturb the service. On the first floor above is the treasury where the church treasures, including rare silver and early documents and prints, are on view. Above is the clock room where the mechanism of the church clock, built in 1877 and now restored, is on display. The lower and upper bell galleries house the church bells, a peal of six. The oldest bells, the third to sixth, were cast in 1668 by Richard Keene at the Woodstock bell foundry; the first in 1708 by Abraham Rudhall. Visitors can climb the tower through the bell galleries to the roof, from which there is a fine view of Oxford.

The tower was opened on 24 June 1986 by HRH the Duke of Gloucester.

(Martin, R.R., *The Church and Parish of St. Michael at the North Gate, Oxford*, Oxford, 1967; Green, Vivian, *St. Michael at the North Gate*, Oxford, 1987.)

St Michael's and All Saints Charities A charter of 1612 under the Great Seal of James I required the feoffees of the parish of ST MICHAEL AT THE NORTH GATE to employ the money resulting from the letting of various properties in Oxford for the care and upkeep of St Michael's Church. The five properties mentioned were let at rents totalling just over £6 per annum. St Michael's Oxford Parochial Charity was regulated by a scheme of the Charity Commissioners dated 24 July 1885, which was amended by a scheme dated 3 July 1961 when the charity was renamed St Michael's Ecclesiastical Charity.

The Church of ST MARTIN at CARFAX was closed in accordance with the Oxford Corporation Act 1890, and subsequently demolished, except for the tower. The benefice was united with All Saints in 1890 and all charitable funds vested in the feoffees of All Saints. That charity was regulated by a scheme of the Charity Commissioners dated 2 May 1941 under the name of the Church Houses Charity. It was administered in two branches called respectively the Church Branch and the Poor's Branch. When the church of ALL SAINTS was closed and transferred to Lincoln College for use as the college library the benefice was united with St Michael at the North Gate. The two charities are now regulated by a scheme of the Charity Commissioners dated 7th May 1980 and are commonly known as St Michael's and All Saints Charities. They are administered in two branches known as the Church Branch and the Relief Branch (formerly All Saints' Poor's Branch) respectively.

The Church Branch has an income from five properties in the centre of Oxford, which is used for the maintenance of the church and its fittings and organ, as well as augmenting the stipends of its clergy. The income of the Relief Branch is mainly used in making grants to local charities concerned with helping persons resident in Oxford.

St Michael's Street Originally called Wood Street (1405), it became known as Bocardo Lane (1548) after the BOCARDO PRISON which was at the east end by the North Gate of the city. The street is shown as Woode Street on the Agas map of 1578 (*see* MAPS). No houses are shown on the north side of the street on this map except one next to the Bocardo. By the middle of the 17th century it was called New Inn Lane, of which it was part. A drawing by J.C. BUCKLER in the BODLEIAN LIBRARY shows New Inn Lane as it appeared in 1824. The new auction room of MALLAMS designed by Barnett, Briscoe & Gotch was built in 1986 in the walled garden shown on the left of the drawing. The Saxon tower of ST MICHAEL AT THE NORTH GATE appears at the end of the street. New Inn Lane, called NEW INN HALL STREET in the 19th century, was extended into GEORGE STREET in 1872; the section to CORNMARKET kept the name New Inn Hall Street until 1899 when it was renamed St Michael's Street after St Michael's Church.

The buildings on the north side were built just inside the CITY WALL and have always belonged to the City Council. Parts of the old wall can be seen in the gardens or basements of some of the buildings, including No. 20 VANBRUGH HOUSE. The Northgate Hall (1870 by J.C. Curtis) is on the east side of Vanbrugh House. No. 24 is a late 17th-century house of ashlar stone, three storeys high with twin pedimented, shaped gables; it is used as the vicarage for St Michael's Church. Next to it is Mallams. Nos 28–32 are the 19th-century premises of ALFRED MALTBY & SON. On the south side of the street is the garden of the Oxford UNION and opposite Maltby's a new building providing study rooms for Brasenose College, designed by the Architects Design Partnership and built by KNOWLES & SON. At the other end of the street, at No. 1, were the Shamrock Tea Rooms, now the Nosebag Restaurant.

St Nicholas, Church of *Old Marston*. The present church dates from 1122 when Henry I granted the chapel of Marston to the Austin canons of ST FRIDESWIDE'S PRIORY. The church passed to Cardinal College (later Christ Church) at the suppression of the priory in 1524; the living was sold in 1547 to Sir John Brome, Lord of HEADINGTON Manor. Thereafter presentation to the living was made by a variety of patrons and is now in the gift of the BISHOP OF OXFORD. The nave and chancel, of Headington-quarried STONE, are 13th-century transitional Norman, heavy-pillared and with pointed arches. The 15th-century tower was used as an observation post in the siege of Oxford during the CIVIL WAR, from which royalist artillery was visible in the 'gun parks' (now the University PARKS),

J.C. Buckler's drawing of St Michael's Street looking east in 1824.

Marston being a Cromwellian stronghold. In 1883 restoration work was carried out to the designs of H.G.W. Drinkwater.

The church possesses a rare chalice of 1479, one of the earliest still in use in England. The wooden pulpit and altar-table are Jacobean. In the chancel is a fine alabaster wall-monument to Richard Croke (1623–83). In the 13th-century south porch is a tablet to LORD FLOREY, Provost of The Queen's College and pioneer in the development of penicillin. At the entrance to the churchyard is a lych-gate (1927) dedicated to the memory of H.A. Cumberlege (vicar 1899–1904); and in the churchyard is buried, with his wife, Vincent Harlow, CMG, Fellow of Balliol and distinguished historian of the Commonwealth, in whose memory the gallery in the church was installed in 1962, a previous gallery having been removed in 1883. The church hall is in the former village school, built in 1851. G.D. Savage (vicar 1952–7) was later Bishop of Southwell.

St Nicholas House *Marston Street.* Charles Sydney Gibbes, tutor to the haemophiliac son of Nicholas II, Tsar of All the Russias, was converted to the Russian Orthodox Church and ordained priest in the name of Nicholas. After the Russian Revolution he moved to China and, during the Second World War, to Oxford, where he bought this house and established in it Oxford's first Russian Orthodox chapel (*see* GREEK ORTHODOX CHURCH). He died in 1963 and in 1967 his adopted son, the Russian-born George Gibbes, moved in and restored the house. He made it into a memorial to the Russian Imperial family, full of relics of old Russia and of Tsar Nicholas II and his children, including the Tsarevich and the Tsar's youngest daughter, Anastasia, almost all of which have been removed to Luton Hoo.

St Paul's Arts Centre The Oxford Area Arts Council launched an appeal for funds in 1976 to buy the freehold of ST PAUL'S CHURCH from the Church Commissioners and to convert it into a performing-arts centre. The building was bought in 1979, thus saving it from demolition, and urgent structural repairs were completed in 1981. Meanwhile, a second appeal was launched to convert the interior into a performance space. At an overall cost of £280,000, the centre was opened in August 1985 with a production of Molière's *The Bourgeois Gentleman*, performed by the Actors Touring Company. The centre was closed at the beginning of 1987.

(*See also* OLD FIRE STATION ARTS CENTRE *and* THEATRE.)

St Paul's Church *Walton Street.* A rectangular stone building in Greek–classical style erected in 1835–6 to the designs of H.J. Underwood (*see* EXETER COLLEGE and BOTANIC GARDENS) on land given by the Radcliffe Trust, its west portico of four (now considerably weathered) Ionic fluted columns faces GREAT CLARENDON STREET and the OXFORD UNIVERSITY PRESS building. In 1853 an apsidal chancel by E.G. Bruton was added, its painted ceiling attributed to W. Holman Hunt; and in 1908 the mediaeval-style interior was remodelled by F.C. Eden, who also designed the east window (1910). Other windows (1888–94) are by C.E. Kempe. Thomas Combe, superintendent at the University Press, the benefactor of ST BARNABAS, JERICHO, was a churchwarden at St Paul's, and under A. Hackman (vicar 1844–71) and W.B. Duggan (vicar 1871–1904) the church became a centre for High Anglicanism. (Duggan was a founder of the OXFORD HIGH SCHOOL FOR GIRLS in 1875.) In 1869 the parish was reduced in size by the creation of the parish of St Barnabas, with which it was united in

419

1963. Closed in 1969, the church was saved from demolition when acquired by the Oxford Area Arts Council for conversion to a 200–300 seat theatre/concert hall and exhibition gallery for professional work as well as local community and student use, opening in 1985.

St Peter-in-the-East, Church of *Queen's Lane.*
In a foreword to a short guide to the church of St Peter-in-the-East, published in about 1950, JOHN BETJEMAN wrote: 'Like so much that is worth seeing, St. Peter's in the East is hidden away. It is in a peaceful walled enclosure made by St. Edmund Hall, Queen's College, and New College, down a little lane which is like what Oxford used to be before the petrol age. ... The church itself is like a village church set down unexpectedly in a town.' This description remains true today, except that the church is now the library of St Edmund Hall. An earlier guide to the church (1923) has this: 'The parish is richer in noble buildings than probably any other in Europe, having within its boundaries Magdalen, New College, the Queen's College, Hertford, St. Edmund Hall, part of University College, Merton, Corpus Christi and Oriel Colleges.'

Standing not far from the East Gate of the city, and known as St Peter-in-the-East to distinguish it from ST PETER-LE-BAILEY, NEW INN HALL STREET, near the West Gate of the city, the church was first recorded in 1086, when it was held by ROBERT D'OILLY, and, according to ANTHONY WOOD, was 'the first church of stone that appeared in these parts'. It replaced an earlier 10th-century timber building. In 1266 the advowson was granted to Merton College by

Henry III, the college holding it until the closure of the church in 1965. In mediaeval times the living was the wealthiest in Oxford, its income deriving partly from its daughter-churches of ST PETER, WOLVERCOTE, and ST CROSS, HOLYWELL. In 1891 the benefice was united with St John the Baptist (now the chapel of Merton College); then, in 1957, with St Cross; and in 1966 with the University Church of ST MARY THE VIRGIN. The oldest part of St Peter's is the early 12th-century crypt, attributed to St Grymbald. Measuring 36 feet in length, 21 feet in width, and 10 feet in height, it has a nave of five bays, eight sturdy romanesque columns supporting the floor of the chancel above. The 12th-century chancel is of two rib-vaulted bays, the east vaulting being decorated with a chain-motif. The east window, originally Norman and now Perpendicular, has some 16th-century glass depicting the Four Evangelists. At the north-east and south-east exterior corners of the chancel there are distinctive, buttressing stair-turrets topped by conical spirelets. The crypt is entered by steps down to a door in its south wall but formerly had several entrances within the church. In the early 13th century the present chancel arch perhaps replaced an earlier triple arch, and a north aisle and north Lady Chapel (*see below*, St Edmund Rich) were added. The Norman nave was extended 25 feet westward in the early 14th century; the tower was built at its north-west corner; and the north aisle rebuilt. The south door, entered from a two-storey 15th-century porch, has an impressive beakhead and zigzag arch.

A circular Norman font, carved with figures of the Twelve Apostles, was removed and disappeared, to be

A man cleaning the tombstone of Thomas Hearne c.1823 in the graveyard of the church of St Peter-in-the-East, now the library of St Edmund Hall.

replaced in 1807 by an unusual carved wooden font attributed to Grinling Gibbons, and now in Parham House, Sussex, representing Adam and Eve beneath the Forbidden Tree, with the Serpent encircling its trunk, and is similar to one presented to St James's Church, Piccadilly, in 1685; its cover represents the clustering fruit and leaves of the True Vine. An organ was first recorded in 1488 but ceased to be mentioned between 1623 and 1685; in 1725 the organ from the SHELDONIAN THEATRE was installed, despite protests that it was a 'relic of popery'. In 1845 a new organ was bought for £240, and sold to Begbroke parish church in 1875; in 1878 another new organ, by Messrs Hill and Son, was installed for £786, to be moved in 1970 to Bicester parish church. Of St Peter's organists the best known was A.R. Reinagle, composer of the tune to 'How Sweet the Name of Jesus Sounds'.

In 1970 the eight bells of St Peter's (five cast in 1700, one in 1753, and two in 1891) were moved to St Denys Church, Stanford-in-the-Vale; pews installed in 1905 went to ST GILES'S; the main altar was removed to St Mary the Virgin.

From c.1200 there were some seventy incumbents of St Peter's, the first recorded being John of Bridport; Josiah Pullen (vicar 1668–1714), for fifty-seven years Principal of MAGDALEN HALL (now Hertford College) is commemorated by PULLEN'S LANE, HEADINGTON; Edmond Hobhouse (vicar 1843–58), who was responsible for the restoration of the exterior of the church in 1844, became the first Bishop of Nelson, New Zealand; and J.R. King (vicar 1867–1907) has a fine alabaster wall-tablet to his memory.

Among others associated with St Peter's are Jacob Bobart (1599–1679), Keeper of the Oxford Physick Garden (later BOTANIC GARDEN), whose ornate wall-monument is on the south-west exterior wall of the building; THOMAS HEARNE (1678–1735), the antiquary, buried in the churchyard; and most notably St Edmund Rich of Abingdon (c.1175–1240), Archbishop of Canterbury (1233), patron of St Edmund Hall, who perhaps founded the Lady Chapel in St Peter's. A wall-tablet in the church and headstone in the churchyard commemorate James Sadler (d.1828), the first English aeronaut (1784) (see SADLER'S BALLOON ASCENTS). Also celebrated, in the form of stone grotesques on the tower (1970) are those members of St Edmund Hall principally associated with the conversion of the church into the college library: two Principals, A.B. Emden and the Rev. J.N.D. Kelly, and three Fellows, the Rev. E.G. Midgley, chaplain; R.E. Alton, bursar; and J. Hackney, librarian. The carver, Michael Groser, completes the collection with a self-portrait on the north wall of the tower (see GARGOYLES AND GROTESQUES).

The extensive and sympathetic restoration of the church and its sensitive conversion into a library, under the supervision of John Allen of Kenneth Stevens Partners, begun on 3 March 1969, was completed on 30 December 1970, at a cost of some £55,000. The library incorporates the Bishop Williams and Bishop Allen Libraries; its benefactors were the Pilgrim Trust and Dr A.B. Emden.

The tower was converted into a book-store with a Fellow's room above; the nave, chancel and Lady Chapel were furnished with reading-desks, the north aisle and west end of the nave with stacks for books;

the room above the porch became the librarian's study. The nave roof was vividly redecorated. The exceptionally interesting, varied and numerous wall-monuments were restored to the highest standards and continue to be a feature of the interior of the building, which is described by Pevsner as 'without any doubt the most interesting church of Oxford'.

St Peter-le-Bailey *New Inn Hall Street*. Originally as St Peter-at-the-Castle and later as St Peter-in-the-West, the church stood at the corner of the present QUEEN STREET and NEW INN HALL STREET. It was granted to ST FRIDESWIDE'S PRIORY in 1122, the advowson passing to the Crown at the Dissolution of the Monasteries until it was sold in 1864 to the Rector, Henry Linton, who vested it in the OXFORD CHURCHES TRUST. Described in the late 17th century as 'of a most ancient standing' and in 1724 as 'a very old little church and odd', it was destroyed in 1726 by the collapse of its tower. Rebuilt by 1740 (its tower being completed by 1765) it remained until 1874 when it was demolished for road-widening and rebuilt further north in New Inn Hall Street.

The parish, like many others, was subject to fluctuations of religious fashion from the Reformation until recent times. In 1584 a parishioner was accused of encouraging his boy to break the windows and slates of the church; by 1593 the parishioners had adopted the puritan practice of sitting for Communion; and in 1634 two parishioners were proceeded against for several offences, among them that of failing to stand for the Gloria and Creed, and failing to bow at the name of Jesus. At the Restoration, royalist prayers and traditional observances were reintroduced; and in the 1840s ritualism was reasserted under Tractarian influence (*see* OXFORD MOVEMENT). After Henry Linton became Rector in 1856, however, a succession of evangelical rectors was assured, and congregations increased considerably.

St Peter-le-Bailey, Church of (*now St Peter's College Chapel*). When the earlier church (*see* ST PETER-LE-BAILEY, NEW INN HALL STREET) had been demolished, the present building was erected in 1874 to the designs of Basil Champneys. In 1877 the Rector, Henry Linton, bought a 'fine, plain Georgian house' (Pevsner) nearby as the rectory for the parish which had hitherto been without one. This is now part of St Peter's College. The church continued to provide a centre for vigorous evangelism, F.J. Chavasse (Rector 1879–99 and founder in 1929 of St Peter's Hall), reporting a full church with 300 communicants. In 1927 his son C.M. Chavasse became Rector and in 1929 the first Master of St Peter's Hall. In 1935 the living was conveyed to St Peter's Hall until the union of the parish with ST EBBE'S in 1961, when the church was closed and became the chapel of St Peter's College.

The pulpit and reredos (by F.E. Howard) were given in memory of F.J. Chavasse (later Principal of WYCLIFFE HALL and Bishop of Liverpool) and his wife. The large plaster monument in his memory on the north wall is a replica of the front of his tomb in Liverpool Cathedral. The vivid Expressionist glass (1964) in the east window is by John Hayward, replacing that by Henry Holiday, the figures of which are now in the west window. The organ is by Henry Willis, 1875, enlarged by C. Martin in 1882 and 1889.

A man sticking bills beneath a 'Stick No Bills' notice on the wall of St Peter-le-Bailey, New Inn Hall Street.

St Peter's Church *Wolvercote*. Rebuilt in 1860 to the designs of Charles Buckeridge. It replaced a Perpendicular church, of which only the tower remains. An earlier Norman chapel, perhaps built by Roger d'Ivri *c*.1077, probably stood on the site, and before that possibly a Saxon chapel: a Saxon font in the church may be from the original building. The church at WOLVERCOTE was a chapel-of-ease, like Holywell, to ST PETER-IN-THE-EAST until declared a vicarage in its own right in 1866. Until 1414 it was neither consecrated nor permitted to have its own burial ground, the dead having to be taken two miles for burial at St Peter-in-the-East. In the north aisle there is a notable monument to Sir John Walter (*d*.1630), Attorney-General and later Chief Baron of the Exchequer. His second son, David (*d*.1679), who was Lieutenant-General of the Ordnance under Charles II, has a fine wall-monument bust by John Bushnell. In the south aisle there is a window with stained glass by Patrick Reyntiens to a design by John Piper (1976). (*See also* ST PETER-IN-THE-EAST.)

St Peter's College The youngest undergraduate college in the University. It was founded under the inspiration of F.J. Chavasse, Bishop of Liverpool (1846–1928), and opened as a Permanent Private Hall in 1929 (*see* PRIVATE HALLS). Chavasse had unsuccessfully attempted to acquire its site for WYCLIFFE HALL as early as the 1890s, when he was Principal of that theological college. The founder's son, C.M. Chavasse (1884–1962), later Bishop of Rochester, was the first Master, holding the position from 1929–39.

St Peter's has been called 'the Low-Church answer to Keble' and there is more than a grain of truth in this.

During the 1920s the evangelicals in the Church of England became extremely worried about the ascendancy of the Anglo-Catholics. St Peter's Hall, together with the public schools Stowe, Canford and Monkton Combe, founded at around the same time, reflected this strongly Protestant evangelical impulse. One of the leading promoters, the Rev. Percy Warrington, was a remarkable ecclesiastical entrepreneur, whose financial methods did not always bear close scrutiny. There is an epic account of his relations with C.M. Chavasse in E.H.F. Smith's *St. Peter's: The Founding of an Oxford College*. The greatest benefactor of the college was LORD NUFFIELD, who redeemed the mortgages on its buildings in the financial collapse of the 1930s. Even in its early years the hall was never narrowly sectarian, but it was certainly religious in ethos and a high proportion of its original members entered the church. As a full college there could naturally be no question of religious tests, and the hall's original aim especially to assist students of limited means was rendered obsolete by the spread of government student grants after the Second World War. Its early character, therefore, has largely been subsumed in its wider development since the 1940s, during which time it has grown to become a normal college in the University.

After the Second World War, the University created a new intermediate status for societies which were recognised as being on their way to becoming full colleges. St Peter's Hall was therefore technically a 'new foundation' from 1947 until it obtained a royal charter and its first statutes as a college in 1961. Remaining one of the smaller colleges, in 1985–6 St Peter's had about twenty-six Fellows, forty graduate students and 260 undergraduates.

Its buildings reflect the brief but varied course of its history. The trust which set up the hall acquired a restricted but extremely central and hence desirable site in central Oxford, in NEW INN HALL STREET (which runs parallel to the CORNMARKET between GEORGE STREET and QUEEN STREET). They obtained possession of Hannington Hall, named after Bishop James Hannington (1847–85), in New Inn Hall Street, which had been built in 1832 (designed by Thomas Greenshields), though it has been much altered subsequently. This was owned by the Hannington Trust, an offshoot of the Church Missionary Society, which had acquired the building after the extinction of NEW INN HALL, which had existed on that site from mediaeval times until the later 19th century. St Peter's also acquired the use, though not the ownership, of the parish church of ST PETER-LE-BAILEY (designed by Basil Champneys in 1874), and until the 1960s successive Masters were also the vicars of this parish, which has since been reamalgamated with ST EBBE'S. Hence the college has a sizeable Victorian parish church as its chapel, an unsuitably large building for normal college use, and a potential liability in terms of upkeep.

The oldest building acquired by the trust and now owned by the college is Linton House, also facing on to New Inn Hall Street, which was originally built in 1797 as the headquarters of the newly formed Oxford Canal Company (the architect's name is unknown). Some time after the Canal Company had moved to another building situated above the canal basin, its previous office building was acquired as a parsonage house for St Peter-le-Bailey by the Rev. H. Linton, after whom it is named. In spite of various alterations, its east and west façades present a handsome, characteristically late-Georgian appearance. Canal House to the west of the main site (designed by Richard Tawney, 1828) is – apart from the ASHMOLEAN MUSEUM – one of the few classical-revival buildings in Oxford. It has an unusually massive portico and pediment with Doric columns at its northern end (cf. ST PAUL'S CHURCH, Walton Street). The present elevation is not that of the original building, since an upper floor was added in the 1840s. The house is best seen from NEW ROAD or, ideally, from the CASTLE Mound. It was acquired by St Peter's in the 1960s and is used as the Master's lodgings with 4 tutors' rooms on the lower ground floor. An unusual feature is that the ground floor on the Bulwarks Lane side of the house is the first floor on the New Road side (facing the old law courts (see COURTS), the PRISON and the Castle).

The earliest specially built part of St Peter's consists of the staircases now numbered I–III, dating from the early 1930s. These were designed in a deliberately traditional 'free late-seventeenth-century' style (Pevsner) of brick with some stone dressings. They are solidly constructed and have worn well. Originally the architect (R. Fielding Dodd, advised by Sir Herbert Baker) envisaged a complete quadrangular development in this style, but also taking in Linton House and the church of St Peter-le-Bailey. In fact this was never to be achieved. The other pre-war staircase, No. IV, the Morris Building, paid for by Lord Nuffield in memory of his mother, Emily Morris, lay in the extreme north-western corner of the site and was completely detached from the other buildings. An additional staircase, named Besse, was added to the 1930s range in an almost identical style as late as 1952 (architect Kenneth Stevens), through money donated by the multi-millionaire ANTONIN BESSE, who gave a large sum to the University for the benefit of the poorer colleges, as well as money to found St Antony's.

The next major building dates from the late 1960s, the Matthews Building, which is named after another of the college's benefactors (completed 1971, architect Kenneth Stevens). This is a large rectangular-shaped residential block with the Junior Common Room and the bar on the ground floor. Aesthetically it is not particularly pleasing, but it did come nearer to the cost levels allowed by the University Grants Committee for student accommodation in other universities than most Oxford or Cambridge buildings of the 1950s–1970s. By contrast, the Latner Building (1972, architect Kenneth Stevens and Partners), named after a Canadian benefactor, is of off-white concrete, impressed to look like imitation timber, and is pleasing in appearance. This joins the Matthews Building to Linton House and thus completes, although in a totally different style, the Fielding Dodd quadrangle scheme.

Most recently the college has acquired the site and buildings of what was originally the CENTRAL SCHOOL FOR GIRLS, also in New Inn Hall Street (architect Leonard Stokes, built 1899–1901), latterly part of the COLLEGE OF FURTHER EDUCATION, which has now been concentrated on the OXPENS site. The main part of the school has already been converted for residential and teaching use, and renamed the Chavasse Building in honour of the founder and his son, the first Master. The other existing building on the school site, the so-called Cookery or Pastry School, whose original purpose is therefore self-explanatory, has also been converted to provide a Music Room and a Graduate Common Room. In 1987 the college was also in the process of building a further substantial residential block on the western side of this site, parallel with the ancient foot right of way called Bulwarks Lane, which divides Canal House, its garden and the college car park from the rest of St Peter's.

During what is by Oxford standards a very short life span, St Peter's has included among its old members an ex-President of Ghana, Edward Akufo Addo (1933–6); an ex-Speaker of the US House of Representatives, Carl Albert (1931–4); and the ex-Archbishop of New Zealand, now the Governor-General, Sir Paul Reeves (1959–61). There are also other notable historical figures connected with this site, before the existence of St Peter's. Famous figures of the past connected with New Inn Hall include SIR WILLIAM BLACKSTONE; Sir Robert Chambers (1737–1803), friend of SAMUEL JOHNSON, who used to stay with him here; Alfred Marshall (1842–1924), the eminent Victorian economist who lectured there for Balliol in the 1880s; and in the remoter past, John Trilleck, Bishop of Hereford from 1344 to 1360, after whom the hall was first named. An earlier civil lawyer of distinction connected with New Inn Hall was Alberico Gentile, of Italian origin (1552–1608). During the CIVIL WAR, 1642–6, the Royal MINT of Charles I was on this site, but no more than occasional coins have ever been found there.

The corporate title is The Master, Fellows and Scholars of the College of St Peter-le-Bailey in the University of Oxford. Professor John Penrose Barron succeeded Dr Gerald Aylmer as Master in 1991.

(Smith, E.H.F., *St. Peter's: The Founding of an Oxford College*, Gerrards Cross, 1978.)

St Philip and St James, Church of *Woodstock Road*. In 1853, St John's College was asked for a site for a large church to serve the growing population of the district north of ST GILES'. In 1860 the foundation stone was laid by the BISHOP OF OXFORD, SAMUEL WILBERFORCE, and in 1862 the church was consecrated by him. Designed by G.E. STREET, it is only one of two cruciform churches by him which have central towers; its commanding steeple was completed in 1866. In 1919 an apse by Sir Charles Nicholson was added to form a sanctuary for the Lady Chapel. Pevsner points out that the interior makes 'a statement of principle – the maximum visibility of the altar, not of the parson or the pulpit'. In *An Oxford University Chest* (1938), JOHN BETJEMAN characterises the church as 'the cathedral, as it were, of laburnum-shaded North Oxford' and as 'once the home of Broad Churchism but now on the high side. Fr. Ronald Knox wrote a limerick about its incumbent:

> "There once was a man who said: I
> Am a moderate churchman; for why?
>   St. Philip you know
>   Was inclined to be low
> But St. James was excessively high." '

Popularly known as 'Phil and Jim', in 1976 it was constituted as a single parish with ST MARGARET'S, services being shared until 1980; the church was closed in 1982. In 1988 the building became a study and conference centre run by the Oxford Centre for Mission Studies. A vicarage-house (No. 68 WOODSTOCK ROAD) was built to the designs of H.G.W. Drinkwater in 1886–7, and bought by St Antony's College in 1957.

St Pius X, Chapel of *Wootton*. The Amey family donated land in 1953 for this chapel to be built and so relieve the pressure on the chapel of ST THOMAS MORE. It was completed in 1954 and dedicated to Pius X, whose canonisation ceremonies were being celebrated in Rome at the time.

St Scholastica's Day On Tuesday, 10 February 1355 the troubled relations and often violent antagonisms between town and gown in Oxford (*see* RIOTS) culminated in the worst rioting that the city has known. On that day several students and priests were drinking in the SWYNDELSTOCK tavern when they fell to arguing with the innkeeper about the quality of his wine. After 'snappish words' had passed between them, and the innkeeper had replied to their complaints with 'stubborn and saucy language', a quart pot of wine was thrown at his head. Immediately numbers of townsmen came to his assistance and some of them, 'seeking all occasion of conflict with the Scholars and taking this abuse for a ground to proceed upon', had the town bell of ST MARTIN'S rung to summon the citizens to arms. As the citizens came out into the streets with bows and arrows, the CHANCELLOR also appeared, but was soon forced to retreat as the University bell at ST MARY THE VIRGIN rang out to call the students to the fight.

The next day, when the MAYOR rode to Woodstock to explain the town's grievances to the King and to seek his support, the townsmen sought the help of the villagers beyond the city walls and, in alliance with them, attacked the students in Beaumont Fields. 'One Scholar they killed,' so ANTHONY WOOD wrote, 'some they wounded mortally, others grievously and used the rest basely. All of which being done without any mercy, caused an horrible outcry in the town and . . . divers Scholars issued out armed with bows and arrows in their own defence. . . . Then entered the Town by the west gate about two thousand countrymen . . . of which the Scholars having notice, and being unable to resist so great and fierce a company, they withdrew themselves to their lodgings. The countrymen advanced crying, "Slea, Slea. . . . Havock, Havock. . . . Smyt fast, give gode knocks!" . . . They broke open five Inns, or Hostles of Scholars with fire and sword . . . and such Scholars as they found in the said Halls or Inns they killed or maimed. Their books and all their goods they spoiled, plundered and carried away. All their victuals, wine and other drink they poured out; their bread fish etc. they trod under foot. After this the night came on and the conflict ceased for that day.'

The next day, Thursday, the attacks on the ACADEMIC HALLS were resumed, the townsmen killing and wounding more of the scholars, scalping some chaplains, so it was said, and, having mortally wounded others, 'carrying their entrails in their hands in a most lamentable manner'.

As soon as the disturbances had been quelled, the rioters were severely punished. Several leading citizens were sent to prison; heavy fines were exacted; and the Mayor and bailiffs were ordered to attend a Mass for the souls of the dead every St Scholastica's Day thereafter and to swear an annual oath to observe the University's privileges, which were extended by a new charter dated 27 June 1355.

Protestations against this oath were made from time to time, yet it continued to be exacted for centuries, as did the ceremony of penance in St Mary's, though this was modified at the Reformation. The ceremony was abandoned during the CIVIL WAR but was resumed after the Restoration; and, although in 1681 only the Mayor and twenty citizens attended it, after an alderman had condemned it as 'a great relic of popery', it was decided the next year that attendance in full strength was advisable in the interests of the city's charters. The ceremony was not finally abolished until 1825.

St Stephen's House *Marston Street*. Founded in 1876 by Edward King, Regius Professor of Pastoral Theology, and other leading Oxford churchmen, it was given its name by one of them, Henry Scott-Holland, in commemoration of his friend Stephen Fremantle, who had died in 1874. A Tractarian theological college (*see* OXFORD MOVEMENT) with missionary emphasis, it was originally at 5 Park Street (later PARKS ROAD), a site now occupied by the NEW BODLEIAN LIBRARY. (Its nickname, Canon King's Arms, combined its founder's name with that of the public house opposite.) Closed during the First World War, it moved on reopening in 1919 to 17 NORHAM GARDENS, later occupying also Nos 19, 26, 28 and 30 at various times. In 1980 it moved to the buildings vacated by the Society of St John the Evangelist, the monastic brotherhood known as the COWLEY FATHERS. The original house (1868), now named Benson, contains the founder's chapel at the top of the building; the main community building, King, designed in 1901 by G.F. BODLEY, contains the later (now House) chapel, also by Bodley, with its transeptal altar and white baldacchino designed by Comper (1938); and in the former orchard, Moberly

Close (1980), designed by Philip del Nevo of the Oxford Architects' Partnership and named after the first Principal of St Stephen's House, accommodates staff and married students. The main community building is linked by cloisters to the conventual church of ST JOHN THE EVANGELIST, IFFLEY ROAD.

St Stephen's House has some sixty students at present. Among its many distinguished former members between 1876 and 1976 in diocesan, missionary, academic and liturgical fields have been Glyn Simon (1926) and G.O. Williams (1936), both Archbishops of Wales; Richard Brook (1905), Bishop of Edmundsbury and Ipswich; Eric Kemp (1936), Bishop of Chichester; Charles Plumb (1891), Bishop of St Andrew's; four suffragan bishops in England and twelve overseas bishops; J.N.D. Kelly (1933), Principal of St Edmund Hall, and the historian, T.M. Parker (1927). Christopher Butler (1925) and Gordon Wheeler (1933) later became distinguished Roman Catholic prelates.

St Thomas More, Chapel of *Boar's Hill*. The children from St Mary and St Joseph's School, Poplar, were evacuated to HINKSEY, Kennington, BOTLEY and Wootton at the beginning of the Second World War. In order to relieve the hard-pressed parish of Hinksey, the Newdigate family made a bequest of this former coach-house to the parish in 1945.

St Thomas the Martyr, Church of *Becket Street*. This ancient church took its name from the then recently murdered Archbishop Becket and began as a chapel built by the canons of OSENEY ABBEY towards the end of the 12th century, the consecration probably being performed by Bishop Hugh of Lincoln, in whose diocese it lay. The consecration cross, still visible on the north-east buttress of the church, is the only one of its date in Oxford. As a benefactor of the abbey, Becket, Chancellor of England, no doubt visited Oseney when staying with Henry II at BEAUMONT PALACE. At the Dissolution of the Monasteries, St Thomas's passed to Christ Church, its present patrons.

From 1616 to 1640 the incumbent was Robert Burton, who built the south porch in 1621. He was a Student of Christ Church for some thirty years and author of the *Anatomy of Melancholy* (1621), the only book, so SAMUEL JOHNSON said, that could get him out of bed two hours before his usual time. In 1642 parliamentary troops captured at Cirencester were held prisoner in the church (*see* ST GILES'), burning seats and breaking windows. During the CIVIL WAR all the mediaeval stained glass in the church was destroyed.

Church attendance steadily declined in the 18th century, until by 1802 the number of communicants had fallen to ten; by 1814 nine-tenths of the parish were said to be non-churchgoers. Under John Jones (curate 1823–42) a marked improvement took place: in addition to increased numbers and the restoration of the church fabric, in 1839 H. Ward, a coal merchant, provided a houseboat, known as the Boatman's Floating Chapel, for Sunday afternoon services for families working on the river and canal. When it sank in 1868, the chapel of St Nicholas was built on the north side of HYTHE BRIDGE STREET and was used until 1892. It is recorded that on the night

before he died in 1875, A.R. Mowbray, founder of the firm of ecclesiastical publishers and suppliers, was teaching canal boatmen in the chapel. In 1860 a second chapel-of-ease for St Thomas's was dedicated to ST FRIDESWIDE. This was replaced in 1871–3 by ST FRIDESWIDE'S CHURCH, built to serve the needs of New Osney.

Thomas Chamberlain (vicar 1842–92 and founder in 1863 of ST EDWARD'S SCHOOL), introduced Tractarian ritual to the extent that opponents of the OXFORD MOVEMENT described St Thomas's as 'the headquarters of the ultra-devotees of the Pusey party' and in 1869 referred to its 'long-established celebrity as the most consistent development of the ritual of Oxford popery'. In 1846, through the generosity of his curate, A.P. Forbes, later Bishop of Brechin, Chamberlain undertook extensive restoration work; and in 1847 founded the Community of St Thomas Martyr, a sisterhood which remained in being until 1958, devoting itself in various ways to the poor of the parish. The slum parish was described by the Rev. A.B. Simeon (*see* ST EDWARD'S SCHOOL) in a memoir of Chamberlain as lying 'at the very gates of wealthy Christ Church (like Lazarus of old), a parish full of sores – neglected, poor, God-forsaken, the haunt of thieves and harlots'.

Of the convent buildings (begun in 1886), designed by C.C. Rolfe and now demolished, there remains only an archway, near Coombe House (1702), formerly a small school for boys, which stands at the south-east corner of the churchyard. A large granite cross in the churchyard marks the spot where Thomas Chamberlain lies buried, in the chasuble he had worn on Whit Sunday, 1854, a vestment used at that time in only one other English parish.

Congregations at St Thomas's had risen by 1851 to 500 in the morning, and 750 in the evening; in addition, by 1866 each of its two chapels-of-ease was attended by some 120 worshippers.

Among others associated with the church are C.H.O. Daniel, DD (1837–1919), Provost of Worcester College, renowned scholar–printer and benefactor of St Thomas's; T.H. Birley, DD (vicar 1896–1908), later Bishop of Zanzibar; William Tylock (1504–78), four times MAYOR of Oxford, whose memorial is on the north wall of the chancel; William Washbrook (1864–1923), who formed the Oxford Diocesan Guild of Bellringers in 1881, the early 18th-century bells in the church tower being rehung in his memory, with two additional treble bells; Ann Kendal, whose will in 1714 left £4 for a Christmas sermon, still paid annually; and B.S. Hack (vicar 1908–22), later vicar of ST MARY MAGDALEN, who maintained the Tractarian tradition and large congregations.

The most ancient part of the church is the chancel, dating from the 12th century; it has a priest's door (*c.*1250), with its original ironwork, in the south wall. The chancel arch (1846–7) by J.P. Harrison replaced a 12th-century Norman arch destroyed in 1825 when the floor level was raised to bring it above flood-level. In 1846 H.J. Underwood rebuilt the north aisle and moved the vestry to its west end. In 1897 the church was re-roofed. The east window is 14th century, while both the nave and the Perpendicular west tower date from the 15th century, when the church was extended westwards.

There are several notable features of the interior: the chancel ceiling, decorated by C.E. Kempe; a fine

425

brass chandelier (1705); stained glass by O'Connor, particularly that in the east window (1853), now obscured by a neo-classical reredos; and the east window of the north aisle, depicting Eucharistic Sacrifice, by Clayton and Bell (1860), based on a suggestion by G.E. STREET. This window was described in 1886 as 'an illustration of the licence which is allowed to the clergy in inculcating the pernicious doctrines of a ritualizing Romanism by the process of teaching through the eye' and was later (c.1870) the subject of an unsuccessful appeal to the Privy Council. The organ is by Martin's of Oxford, 1893.

The former vicarage, built to the designs of C.C. Rolfe in 1893 on the north side of the churchyard, is at present leased to the publications division of Mowbray's.

The benefice was united with that of St Frideswide in 1979.

Salter, Herbert Edward (*1863–1951*). The son of a Harley Street doctor, Salter gained scholarships to Winchester and New College. Having obtained a First in both LITERAE HUMANIORES and Theology, he was ordained in 1888 and became vicar of Shirburn in 1899. At Shirburn, whence he rode his bicycle two or three times a week to the LIBRARIES of Oxford, he embarked upon the historical research which was thereafter to occupy so much of his time. He edited thirty-four volumes for the Oxford Historical Society (*see* HISTORIANS), contributed to the *Victoria County History of Oxford*, and compiled numerous historical works including *Oxford Balliol Deeds* (1913), *Medieval Archives of the University of Oxford* (1917–19), *Munimenta Civitatis Oxonie* (1917), *Oriel College Records* (1926), *Oxford City Properties* (1926) and *Medieval Oxford* (1936). His unpublished transcripts were presented to the BODLEIAN LIBRARY. Acknowledged as the leading authority on the history of Oxford since ANTHONY WOOD, he was awarded the

honorary degree of Doctor of Letters by the University in 1933.

Salter Bros *Folly Bridge.* Established in 1858 by John and Stephen Salter. The firm's passenger steamers began operating on the THAMES in 1886. Advertised as 'Delightful summer trips through 90 miles of Thames scenery', the journey between Oxford and Kingston, through Wallingford, Henley and Windsor, took two days each way, but passengers could join or leave the boat at any of the locks or regular stopping places *en route*. Now with diesel engines they carry passengers between FOLLY BRIDGE and Abingdon. They also have services between Reading and Henley, Marlow and Windsor, and Windsor and Staines. Boats were built for the colleges, and many of the college BARGES were built by the firm, including the Keble College barge, part of which is now in the MUSEUM OF OXFORD. The boat used by Oxford in the 1976 BOAT RACE was also built in Salter Bros' yard. During the First World War the firm built oil-fired and coal-fired steam pinnaces, harbour launches, cutters and whalers, as well as fast hydroplanes for the Royal Navy; during the Second World War a large number of landing and support craft were built, many of which took part in the D-Day landing. The company has since expanded its activities into glass-fibre luxury cruisers and steel narrow boats operating on the CANAL for holiday hire. The firm also exports boats to many countries throughout the world, as well as hiring out boats of all kinds.

In 1915 the business was formed as a private limited company, but has always been run by members of the Salter family. Frank Salter was assisted by his nephews Hubert and Arnold, and more recently the firm has been run by Arthur and his son John. Sir Arthur Salter (later Lord Salter) was also a director.

A lifeboat being launched at Salters' Boatyard at Folly Bridge c.1900.

Salvation Army The headquarters were in CASTLE STREET in a building opened in 1888. This was demolished in 1970 for the building of the new County Council offices. The new hostel in Cambridge Terrace, ST EBBE'S, was built in 1970–1 and designed by John Fryman.

Sanders *104 High Street*. An antiquarian bookshop specialising in old prints and watercolours. During the 16th and 17th centuries the Salutation Inn was on this site, which belongs to Oriel College. According to ANTHONY WOOD, 'In the latter end of this year [1658] Davis (David) Mell, the most eminent violinist of London, being in Oxon … did give a very handsome entertainment in the Tavern called "The Salutation", in St. Mary's Parish, Oxon, owned by Thomas Wood.' Sanders possesses a token issued by Thomas Wood in 1652. The design shows a racket, a reference to the REAL TENNIS court at Oriel College. The tavern later became a COFFEE HOUSE kept by James Horseman. Sanders is one of the oldest bookshops in Oxford, but has carried on business since the early part of the 19th century under a variety of names, including Richards, George and Chaundy. HENRY TAUNT, the photographer, worked there as a boy around 1854. The first book known to have been published from 104 High Street, in 1920, was *The Recreation of His Age* by Nicholas Bacon, the last book of the Daniel Press. Leslie Chaundy had bought the library of C.H.O. Daniel, Provost of Worcester College, bibliophile and printer, who died in 1919. The covers of early catalogues issued by Frank Sanders were illustrated by Edmund Hort New (1871–1931), whose best-known work is his *New Loggan Guide to Oxford Colleges*, which he illustrated and which was published by BASIL BLACKWELL in 1933. When Sanders retired the business was carried on by Lord John Kerr, followed by Kyril Bonfiglioli, and now by R.W. Mills and Christopher Lennox Boyd.

Saraceno Restaurant *Magdalen Street*. Opened in 1968 in the basement of Oxenford House. The restaurant was designed by Enzo Apicella in blue and white ceramics on split levels with decor based on Saracen ships. It was Oxford's leading Italian restaurant. On one wall were signed photographs of some of the well-known people who had dined there, including King Hussein of Jordan, the prima ballerina Margot Fonteyn and many stars of stage, screen and television. The restaurant closed in 1990.

Savile, Sir Henry (*1549–1622*). A member of an old Yorkshire family, Savile matriculated at Brasenose College and, after 'establishing some reputation as a mathematician and a Greek scholar', was elected a Fellow of Merton in 1565. Having given lectures in mathematics in Oxford and served as the Queen's Greek tutor, he was appointed Warden of Merton in 1585. A strict disciplinarian, he much improved the standard of the college. He was an intimate friend of SIR THOMAS BODLEY, whom he assisted in the foundation of the BODLEIAN LIBRARY. In emulation of his friend's generosity to the University, he founded the Savilian Chairs of Geometry and Astronomy (*see* CHAIRS). He died in 1622 at Eton College, whose Provost he had become (after much importunate lobbying on his own behalf) twenty-six years earlier.

Schola Cantorum of Oxford University-based chamber choir founded as the Collegium Musicum Oxoniense by the Hungarian émigré conductor László Heltay in 1960. It immediately set new standards for such choirs in Oxford, and in the course of its first decades won several competitions at home and abroad, including the BBC's *Let the People Sing* contest in 1974–5. It assumed its present name in 1964 when Heltay gave up the conductorship on leaving Oxford. His successors have included John Byrt, Andrew Parrott, Nicholas Cleobury and James Wood, and the choir continues to tour and broadcast regularly.

Schools Academic study at Oxford is organised under eighteen FACULTIES. But the subjects for the Bachelor of Arts degree course, known as Final Honour Schools, cover a much wider field, and in 1986–7 were as follows:

Ancient and Modern History
Biochemistry
Biology, Pure and Applied
Botany
Chemistry
Classics and Modern Languages
Engineering Science
Engineering Science and Economics
Engineering Science, Economics and Management
English Language and Literature
English and Modern Languages
Experimental Psychology
Geography
Geology
Human Sciences
Jurisprudence
Literae Humaniores
Mathematics
Mathematics and Computation
Mathematics and Philosophy
Metallurgy and Science of Materials
Metallurgy, Economics and Management
Modern History
Modern History and Economics
Modern History and Modern Languages
Modern Languages
Music
Oriental Studies
Philosophy and Modern Languages
Philosophy, Politics and Economics (PPE)
Philosophy and Theology
Physics
Physics and Philosophy
Physiological Sciences (also Medicine)
Psychology, Philosophy and Physiology (PPP)
Theology
Zoology

There is also a Bachelor of Fine Art course.

These Schools naturally vary very greatly both in their antiquity and in the number of undergraduates which they attract. The first class lists to be issued in the modern style, with the introduction of proper examinations, were for LITERAE HUMANIORES (more familiarly known as 'Greats') and Mathematics in Michaelmas Term 1807. The next subjects to be examined were Natural Science, and Law and Modern History (all in 1853). By the turn of the century, Theology, Oriental Languages and English Language had been added, and women (from 1893) were being classified, though not yet admitted to degree status; indeed, in 1899 ten women and no men were placed in the first class in English. (Women were first matriculated, thus becoming eligible to take degrees, in Michaelmas Term 1920, and received their first degrees on 14 October 1920; they included, on that day, Dorothy L. Sayers of Somerville.)

After the abolition of the fourth class in the early 1960s, classification in Final Honour Schools was limited to First, Second or Third, with the great bulk of candidates receiving Seconds. From 1986, however, the second class was itself subdivided into two sections.

(The word 'Schools' is also used as an abbreviation for the EXAMINATION SCHOOLS. *See also* DEGREES, NORRINGTON TABLE *and* SCHOOLS QUADRANGLE.)

Schools Quadrangle   Conceived by THOMAS BODLEY and built in 1613–24 (*see* BODLEIAN LIBRARY). The master-masons were John Akroyd and John Bentley. Over the doors are painted the schools to which they led: Geometry, Arithmetic, Languages, Metaphysics, Logic, Astronomy, Rhetoric, Law (Jurisprudence), Music, Natural Philosophy, Grammar, History, Moral Philosophy and Medicine. On the east side is the Tower of the Five Orders (Doric, Tuscan, Ionic, Corinthian and Composite). At the top on the elaborate parapet are the Stuart arms and below them, under the canopy, a statue of James I. The University ARCHIVES are kept on the fourth floor.

Science Area   Most of the University's science buildings are grouped in SOUTH PARKS ROAD or PARKS ROAD in what is known as the Science Area. Originally part of the PARKS, a corner bounded by Parks Road on one side and South Parks Road on the other now houses a large number of science departments and LABORATORIES in a variety of architectural styles. Others are in the triangle formed by KEBLE ROAD, BANBURY ROAD and Parks Road. The UNIVERSITY MUSEUM and PITT RIVERS MUSEUM are also in the Science Area.

Sconcing   An ancient means whereby undergraduates in effect disciplined each other for such 'offences' as mentioning a woman's name in hall, by compelling the 'offender' to drink a large tankard of ale without taking breath, under pain of paying for the other's beer in the event of failure. The sconce is still occasionally found on such occasions as BUMP SUPPERS, when, at Pembroke College, for instance, application must be made in Latin to the Dean or Bursar for permission for a sconce to be imposed. If the Latin is correct, the request will be granted. The combination of a Bump Supper and a correctly latinised application is not, however, one of especially frequent occurrence, even at Pembroke.

Scott, Sir George Gilbert   (*1811–1878*). Having won the competition to design the MARTYRS' MEMORIAL at the age of twenty-nine, Scott obtained numerous other commissions to construct and restore further buildings in Oxford. He worked at Exeter on the college chapel, library, Rector's lodgings and the new BROAD STREET range; on the hall at Merton; on the HOLYWELL STREET buildings for New College; on the Founder's Tower at Magdalen; on the library at University College; and on the RADCLIFFE INFIRMARY. He restored All Souls College chapel in 1872–6, CHRIST CHURCH CATHEDRAL in 1870–6, New College chapel in 1877–81 (the work being completed after his death by his sons) and University College chapel in 1862. He worked at ST MARY MAGDALEN in 1842 and repaired the spire (1856) and porch (1864–5) of the University Church (*see* ST MARY THE VIRGIN). He built HOLY TRINITY, HEADINGTON QUARRY, in 1849.

The Tower of the Five Orders overlooks the Schools Quadrangle which was built in 1613–24.

College menservants, now very few in number, have been known as scouts since the beginning of the 18th century.

Scout The word dates back to the opening years of the 18th century, but is of obscure origin in its Oxford meaning of a college manservant. Scouts traditionally have been assigned to individual staircases, where they would often remain for very many years. Nowadays, the term has been broadened to include women (who are in the main bedmakers and cleaners), since the scout's former duties have become, over the years, greatly attenuated. Even as recently as the 1950s such duties would regularly include (*inter alia*) waking up the undergraduates, laying their fires, putting out their sherry glasses and tea things (and washing them up in the pantry which was often attached to the better sets of rooms), buying their travel tickets, giving them usually sensible advice on a wide range of subjects, and of course being on hand at the degree ceremony (*see* CEREMONIES) to hand over the BA gown and be suitably rewarded. Scouts would also wait in hall and, in days when year-round employment was not the norm, might well work in boarding houses – or even LORD NUFFIELD's Morris Motors – in the vacations. For many undergraduates, their scout and their tutor were far more familiar figures than, say, the Master or Bursar; and the former undergraduate, returning to a GAUDY, would often be more likely to enquire after the well-being of his scout than of any other single person. The near passing of the traditional scout – few of whom nowadays are men – is one of the many casualties of the past quarter-century.

Servitors Servitors, sizars or Bible clerks were from early times the lowest order of undergraduate. In return for reduced fees, they would perform such menial tasks as calling Fellows or other under-graduates before morning prayers, waiting at table and lighting fires. They were liable to be treated contemptuously by their fellow students. Being a servitor was not, however, a bar to future success; Benjamin Kennicott, who matriculated as a servitor at Wadham in 1744 (at the late age of twenty-five), was by 1761 receiving a pension of £200 per annum from George III, and was thus enabled to pursue his great work of examining and collating the Hebrew manu-scripts of the Old Testament. William Lancaster,

Provost of The Queen's College from 1704 to 1717, had been a servitor there; and the (undistinguished) Provost of Oriel from 1691 to 1708, Dr George Royse, had been one at St Edmund Hall. Samuel Wesley senior, was a servitor at Exeter in 1683. Most successful of all was Dr John Potter, (?1674–1747), who matriculated in 1688 as a servitor at University College, and successively became a Fellow of Lincoln, Regius Professor of Divinity (in 1707) and finally Archbishop of Canterbury (1737). William Stubbs, the historian who became BISHOP OF OXFORD in 1888 was admitted to Christ Church as a servitor in 1844. Perhaps the last relics were the four Bible clerks maintained at All Souls up to the third decade of the present century.

Shambles At least as early as the 13th century there were butchers' shops on both sides of the west end of the HIGH STREET, which was known as Butchers' Street in about 1218. The shops apparently had stalls in front of them. They had been relegated to the south side of the street by the end of the 15th century, no doubt as a result of complaints about the nuisance of butchering raised in all towns throughout the Middle Ages. Certainly at that time, in response to complaints from Oxford townspeople, the slaughtering of animals commonly took place beyond the CITY WALLS in BREWER STREET (known also as Slaying Lane). In 1556 butchers' shambles were also built in QUEEN STREET which was then known as Butcher Row. They soon became as much a nuisance there as they were elsewhere, the butchers emptying their 'blood and filth' into the street gutters, as well as into the town ditch, as late as the middle of the 17th century. The Queen Street shambles were burned down in 1644 but rebuilt in the middle of the street in 1656 where they remained until demolished in 1773. Thereafter all Oxford's butchers were moved into the COVERED MARKET.

Sheldon, Gilbert (*1598–1677*). Warden of All Souls and Archbishop of Canterbury, matriculated at Oxford in 1614, graduated BA from Trinity College three years later, and was elected to a fellowship at All Souls in November 1622. He soon afterwards became domestic chaplain to Lord Keeper Coventry, to whose interest he owed his early preferment and his introduction at court. In March 1636 he was elected Warden of All Souls, and for the next dozen years took an active part in college and University affairs. His closeness to the King and to Hyde in the 1640s did not commend him to the Parliamentary Visitors (*see* VISITATIONS) and his resistance to their pretensions led to his ejection from the wardenship in April 1648. Imprisoned until the end of the year, he lived in rural retirement until his reinstatement as Warden in March 1660. At the Restoration his star was in the ascendant: he was consecrated Bishop of London in October 1660 (resigning All Souls), and succeeded WILLIAM JUXON as Archbishop of Canterbury (and as *ex officio* VISITOR of All Souls) in August 1663. His connection with Oxford was confirmed by his election to the office of CHANCELLOR in 1667. At that time the theatre (now the SHELDONIAN THEATRE) which he gave to Oxford for its ceremonies and press, had been three years in the building. Designed by CHRISTOPHER WREN and costing its donor over £12,000, it was opened in July 1669. Sheldon resigned the chancellorship at the end of that month – a resignation that ended his formal connection with the University, though as Primate he continued to be Visitor of Merton and All Souls Colleges until his death on 9 November 1677.

Sheldonian Theatre *Broad Street*. Commissioned by the CHANCELLOR, GILBERT SHELDON, Archbishop of Canterbury, the Sheldonian Theatre was intended to serve as a place for the 'enactment of university business' and ceremonies which had previously taken place in the University Church, ST MARY THE VIRGIN. Sheldon provided about £14,500 for the building, the architect chosen being his young friend CHRISTOPHER WREN, at that time Savilian Professor of Astronomy, whose first work of architecture this was. 'It is classical of course, as no previous Oxford building had been, so for Oxford it may be called revolutionary,' Sir Nikolaus Pevsner commented. 'But nationally speaking this façade [facing the DIVINITY SCHOOL] has nothing of the purity of Inigo Jones's masterpieces. In fact it is, as a young amateur's job, just a little confused.' Partly inspired by engravings of the open-air Theatre of Marcellus in Rome, the theatre was completed in 1669, Thomas Robinson having been the master-mason, and William Bird the principal stone-carver. The stone used in the lower half of the south front and in some details of the north was of a high quality; but, as money became short, cheaper Headington stone had to be introduced. This did not last well, and the theatre had to be extensively restored in 1959–60 (*see* STONE).

The roof construction, which allows for a ceiling span of 70 feet by 80 feet without supporting crossbeams, was suggested by ideas advanced by Wren's friend, the mathematician John Wallis (1616–1703), who had been appointed Savilian Professor of Geometry in 1649. Wren presented the design to the Royal Society in 1663, the year in which work on the building began. The roof originally had dormer windows: the present octagonal cupola, which affords splendid views of the city, was designed by Edward Blore and erected in 1838.

Inside the building tiered seats accommodate up to 2000 people. The columns of the gallery are painted to resemble marble; and the allegorical ceiling paintings, executed by Robert Streeter, sergeant painter to Charles I, represent Truth, surrounded by Justice, Law, Music, Geometry, Drama, Architecture and Astronomy, triumphing over Envy, Hatred and Malice. Richard Cleer and his assistants are responsible for the woodwork below, including the fine Chancellor's throne and the two orators' pulpits from which the Chancellor's PRIZES are recited at ENCAENIA and from which the CREWEIAN ORATION is delivered. The case of the organ in the south gallery was designed by SIR THOMAS JACKSON and erected in 1877.

Stairs lead to a large room over the ceiling in which the OXFORD UNIVERSITY PRESS was first set up. Books printed by the Press, before it was moved to the CLARENDON BUILDING, bore on their title page the words '*E Teatro Sheldoniano*' with a vignette of the building. As well as Encaenia, the degree ceremony is held here (*see* CEREMONIES), voting by CONVOCATION takes place and concerts are occasionally given.

(*See also* HERALDRY.)

Shelley Memorial Percy Bysshe Shelley was born in 1792 in Sussex, the eldest son of the Member of Parliament for Horsham. After leaving Eton he went to University College. He was rebellious and atheistic and in March 1811 was expelled for circulating a pamphlet, *The Necessity of Atheism*,

The interior of the Sheldonian Theatre c.1843. Beneath Robert Streeter's ceiling painting are the two orators' pulpits from which the Chancellor's Prizes are recited at Encaenia.

which he had written with his friend Thomas Jefferson Hogg. Shelley eloped to Scotland where he married the sixteen-year-old Harriet Westbrook. The marriage did not last and Shelley went abroad with Mary Godwin, whom he married in 1816 after Harriet Westbrook had drowned herself in the Serpentine. Creditors and ill-health forced him to move to Italy permanently, and in August 1822 he was drowned in the Bay of Lerici when his yacht was sunk in a storm on his returning from visiting Byron.

The memorial to Shelley in University College was designed by Edward Onslow Ford in 1894 and the architecture with the dome over the monument by Basil Champneys. The naked figure of Shelley after drowning lies on a slab of Connemara marble, supported by two winged lions in bronze. In front is a bronze figure of the Muse of Poetry. The monument was originally intended for the Protestant cemetery in Rome, but was presented to the college by Lady Shelley.

Shepherd and Woodward The men's and boys' outfitters in the HIGH STREET originate from the business of a journeyman-tailor, Arthur Brockington. He sold his fourteen-year-old business in 1877 to Arthur Shepherd, who opened a shop at No. 62 CORNMARKET STREET. Arthur Shepherd's two sons ran the business from 1895 to 1897, when one son emigrated. Ernest Shepherd carried on the business until 1927 when he amalgamated with another tailor, Wilton Woodward, and moved the business to its present site at 109–14 High Street on the corner of KING EDWARD STREET. Dennis Venables, the father of the present owners and the author of a booklet on ACADEMIC DRESS, was apprenticed to the business at that time and left in 1930 to open his own shop. After war service he purchased Ernest Shepherd's share of the business and was joined by his two sons, John in 1957 and Peter in 1963. The company opened a branch shop at SUMMERTOWN in 1967 and purchased the old established business of WALTERS in TURL STREET, as well as Bodgers of Cambridge, in 1985.

Ship Street Runs from ST MICHAEL AT THE NORTH GATE in CORNMARKET STREET to TURL STREET and has had many names. In 1385 it was known as Somenors (Somnore or Summer) Lane after a man who rented the Blue Anchor inn here. (The Somnore family became important in the reign of Henry VIII.) Because the lane branched northwards towards Balliol College, in the 16th century it was also called Lawrence Lane after Lawrence Hall, which stood on the east side of the churchyard. Originally, the hall was called Stapull-ledyn because of its lead steeple or turret. From 1679 it was known as both St Michael's Lane (see ST MICHAEL'S STREET) and Jesus Lane. It continued into Exeter Lane before Exeter College Chapel was built. Before 1623 the road wound on through CATTE STREET, ending at the CITY WALL near the East Gate. According to H.E. SALTER, WILLIAM OF WYKEHAM bought that eastern part which ran through New College to the East Gate, while Exeter bought most of the remainder in the 17th century. The continuation of the road would have gone through the Rector's lodgings and garden before winding on to the south of the SHELDONIAN THEATRE. In the 13th century it was also called Dewy's Lane from the family of de Ou, de Ewe or Dewy. As there was a sheep market

nearby the name of the early alehouse may have originally been Sheep and not Ship. The name Ship Lane came into use in the late 1760s, continuing until at least 1838, but it had become Ship Street by 1850.

Nearly all the houses in the street are listed Grade II and survive unspoiled by modern redevelopment. The city wall runs at the back of those on the north side and there is a bastion 26 feet high behind Nos 1–3. Most of the houses seem to have been constructed with highly elaborate timber decorations. Nos 8 and 9, and 11 and 12 (with 18th-century fronts) are of the 17th century, while Nos 1–5 and 10 are of the early 18th. Nos 6, 13, 14, 15 and 16 are 17th century but were remodelled in the 18th century. On the south side is No. 26, a three-storeyed stone rubble house, formerly part of ZACHARIAS AND CO., which has recently been restored by Jesus College. It has 17th-century gables on the north side. St Anne's College started its life in Ship Street and its magazine is still called *The Ship*.

Shoe Lane An ancient lane off NEW INN HALL STREET known in about 1225 as Sewy's Lane. It now leads to the CLARENDON CENTRE.

Shotover Country Park A remnant of the former SHOTOVER ROYAL FOREST. It is now owned by Oxford City Council and is used for informal public recreation. The mixture of woodland, heath, marshland, scrub and grassland is very popular with local residents for walking and picnicking. There are splendid views from the hillside to the south, across the Thames Valley, and the tree-topped Wittenham Clumps may be seen with the escarpment of the Berkshire Downs in the distance. Other popular activities include riding, orienteering, running, kite-flying and walking the nature trails.

Shotover Royal Forest Formerly to be found to the south-east of Oxford. At its most extensive the forest was about 15 square miles in area, with its boundary adjoining the city at MAGDALEN BRIDGE. Royal forests were established in Saxon times and their main function was to provide hunting facilities exclusively for the monarch. There are many records of the King's table at Windsor being supplied with Shotover venison. Boar were also hunted and there is a legend that a scholar of The Queen's College was walking in Shotover Forest reading Aristotle when a wild boar attacked him. The student rammed the volume down the boar's throat, uttering the words '*Graecum est*' and the boar expired. As well as providing excellent hunting, Shotover was also a source of revenue to the crown. Grazing (*agistment*) and feeding pigs on acorns (*pannage*) by local people all had to be paid for. Forest courts (*swainmotes*) provided substantial amounts of revenue. In the 17th century there is a record of a certain William Willoughby being fined £2020 for 'felling 50 oaks valued at 20s each and for grubbing up their roots valued at 5s each'.

Another source of revenue was payments made for quarrying within the forest. Ochre was quarried until the 1930s, and the pigment used for many purposes. Poor-quality ochre was used as a dye for painting wagons – traditionally the body of Oxfordshire wagons was yellow with the bed and wheels red. Finer-quality ochre was used for paint pigments and was ground at Wheatley Mill nearby. The Cuddesdon Charter of 956 is the first endowment of Ethelwold's reconstituted Abingdon Abbey. His famous *Benedictional* contains a picture of Christ entering Jerusalem on an animal painted with mineral ochre, which may have come from Shotover.

Shotover was disafforested, or made no longer subject to Forest Laws, in 1660, following a period when Sir Timothy Tyrell, as Keeper of Shotover Forest, had let the forest deteriorate. This period of waste and decline had been compounded by ravages during the CIVIL WAR, when Shotover's oaks were used for both fortifications and fuel. Following disafforestation, much of Shotover was purchased by individuals and organisations who were encouraged to replace woodland by agriculture. However, some relatively untouched fragments of the forest still remain.

(*See also* SHOTOVER COUNTRY PARK.)

Simon House *Paradise Street.* Started as a night shelter in Mill Street, OSNEY, in 1967. In 1981 it moved to its present building, a new hostel designed by J. Alan Bristow and Partners and owned by Cherwell Housing Trust. It is run by the Oxford Cyrenians. The hostel has sixty beds and, as a 'dry house', it specialises in looking after alcoholics and the homeless. It is named after Simon the Cyrenian, who carried Christ's cross to the place of his crucifixion (Mark 15:xxi).

Sir William Dunn School of Pathology *see* PATHOLOGY, SIR WILLIAM DUNN SCHOOL OF.

Sizars *see* SERVITORS.

Slade, The Runs from No. 333 HOLLOW WAY to OLD ROAD, HEADINGTON. Although Slade can mean a valley, there appears to be no written record of when and why it was so called. In the road is the SLADE HOSPITAL and the fire (sub-)station which was opened in 1957. Slade Park nearby was a wartime development of temporary housing split up into nine avenues; it was not pulled down until 1961. Since about 1974, 320 new houses have been built on Slade Park.

Slade Hospital *Headington.* Built on a 13-acre site by the city of Oxford, to replace the old city isolation hospital at Cold Arbour (*see* RIVERMEAD REHABILITATION CENTRE), the Slade (eighty beds) opened on 3 February 1939 for the treatment of infectious diseases. Its establishment was due to the initiative of Dr Geoffrey Commeline Williams, Medical Officer of Health for Oxford, 1930–47. With the decreased demand for isolation facilities, the Slade accommodated other specialities such as dermatology; and in 1986 two-thirds of its buildings were taken over and adapted for the use of mentally handicapped patients formerly cared for in other Oxfordshire hospitals. The role of the Slade is to act as the 'core hospital' for a new range of services for the mentally handicapped, grouped in small residential units, within the community. This is in accordance with the national policy to phase out the use of large hospitals and institutions in the long-term care of mental defectives.

Smith, Arthur Lionel (*1850–1924*). Won an exhibition from Christ's Hospital to Balliol in 1868.

Having obtained Firsts in Classical MODERATIONS and LITERAE HUMANIORES, and having won the Lothian Prize for an essay on Erasmus (*see* PRIZES AND SCHOLARSHIPS), he was elected Fellow of Trinity in 1874. Two years later he left Oxford to read for the Bar, but returned in 1879 as a tutor in Modern History at Balliol and was elected a Fellow of the college in 1882. A keen oarsman, hockey player, skater and bicyclist, he did much to encourage sport in the University and maintained that he was responsible for the interest that the Master, BENJAMIN JOWETT, took in athletic activities. He was also deeply involved in the work of the University Extension Delegacy and of the Workers' Educational Association. In 1916 he succeeded James Leigh Strachan-Davidson (1843–1916) as Master of Balliol.

Somerville College Founded in 1879 as an undenominational alternative to Lady Margaret Hall. The two colleges share a common origin in the committee set up in 1878 to establish a 'Ladies' Hall' for the accommodation of students coming from a distance to take advantage of the lectures and teaching provided by the Association for Promoting the Higher Education of Women (the AEW) (*see* ST ANNE'S COLLEGE). The committee – senior members of the University and their womenfolk – split on the question of religious observance, and two halls came into being – Lady Margaret Hall as a Church of England foundation, Somerville, under the presidency of Dr Percival (later Bishop of Hereford), offering freedom from any religious test or obligation.

The Somerville founders – Liberals with a strong commitment to the principle of equality of opportunity in education – had access to a wide range of talent and support from outside the Anglican

Mary Somerville, the great scientist after whom the college was named, portrayed by James Swinton, 1844.

432

establishment. Their choice of a name for the new hall was itself a kind of manifesto. Mary Somerville (1780–1872) was internationally regarded as one of the greatest women scientists of the age. Twice married, and the mother of a family, she was almost completely self-taught. She published her first book at the age of fifty-one, and spent the day before her death, forty-one years later, revising a paper on quaternions. She was cultivated, accomplished and sociable. In religion she tended towards Unitarian views, while remaining a member of the established church; in politics she was a Liberal, a supporter of women's suffrage and an advocate of women's education. On her death her family gave her books to the College for Women at Hitchin (later Girton College, Cambridge); they now befriended the new hall at Oxford, allowed it to adopt their arms and motto, and over the years presented it with many family mementos.

On 13 October 1879 the first twelve students arrived at Walton House, a property leased from St John's and equipped with furniture largely donated by friends. The first Principal, Madeleine Shaw Lefevre (1879–89), sister of a Liberal Member of Parliament and niece of a former Speaker of the House of Commons, was equally at ease in the political world of the founders and in the conservative social world of NORTH OXFORD; she did much to allay the apprehension with which the hall was regarded in many quarters. Among her most notable conquests was JOHN RUSKIN, who presented the hall with books and pictures and with a gift of precious stones, the 'Ruskin jewels', which were to form the basis of the Principal's regalia on formal occasions.

The Walton House site proved a convenient one, and in 1881 the freehold was acquired for £7000 and the hall incorporated as an association not intended for profit under the Companies Acts of 1862 and 1867. In 1896 membership was thrown open to past students at the reduced rate of 5s a year. The original constitution of Somerville, as of the other women's societies, was that of a joint-stock limited liability company.

In its gradual advance towards acceptance by the University, Somerville shared in the broader history of women in Oxford. The first Honours examinations were opened to them in 1894. In 1910 their presence in the University was officially recognised by the establishment of a Delegacy for the Supervision of Women Students. In 1896 an attempt to open degrees to women was soundly – but on the whole un-rancorously – defeated; in 1920 a statute admitting them to full membership of the University was passed almost without debate. During these years Somerville took the lead in a number of important respects. In 1882 it was the first of the women's halls to establish internal tuition to supplement the teaching provided by the AEW. In 1894 it became the first to adopt the title of college, believing that this 'would not only improve the educational status of Somerville in the eyes of the public, but would be understood as implying the desire of the Governing Body to raise it above the level of a Hall of Residence'. With the establishment in 1903 of the Mary Somerville Research Fellowship it was the first to offer opportunities for research. The Somerville Council and the second Principal, Agnes Maitland (1889–1906), were prominent in the unsuccessful campaign for degrees in 1895–6; the ease with which the statute was passed in 1920 owed much to the diplomatic

skills and academic reputation of her successor Miss (later Dame) Emily Penrose (1907–26).

Within the college, the advance to self-government was slow. The Principal was not a member of the committee of 1879–81, although she attended its meetings. Her election to the new council in 1881 was personal, not *ex officio*. Tutors had no representation until 1903, and until 1921 – when the articles of association were amended to permit the creation of not less than six or more than nine official Fellows with membership of council – there were never more than two of them. With the admission of women to degrees it was felt desirable to place the women's societies on a more regular constitutional footing, and in 1924 a committee of council recommended that the existing incorporation of the whole body of Somerville members be replaced by that of the Principal and Council of Somerville College. The new body, established by royal charter, came into being on 7 June 1926 with a council including, besides the Principal and Fellows, a nominee of HEBDOMADAL COUNCIL, six representatives of the Association of Senior Members, and four Life Members appointed by special provision in recognition of their past services. For the next twenty-five years, while responsibility for the day-to-day running of the college increasingly devolved on a committee of the Principal and Fellows, Somerville was able to draw on the experience and support of this larger body. In 1951, with the encouragement of the 'outside' members of council, the statutes were amended to restrict membership of the governing body to the Principal and Fellows. (An exception was made for GILBERT MURRAY, the last surviving Life Member and one of Somerville's greatest champions, who continued to chair the college's library committee until his death in 1957.) The other women's colleges quickly followed suit, and a University statute of October 1959 admitted all five as full colleges of the University. When the office of PROCTOR was opened to women in 1977 the last obstacle to equality was swept away.

Somerville's building programme reflected this constitutional development. The site acquired in 1881 stretched from WALTON STREET, where the main entrance and lodge were situated, to St Giles' Road West (now the WOODSTOCK ROAD); it was bounded on the north side by the RADCLIFFE INFIRMARY and on the south by property belonging to University College. The original house, built in 1826, was enlarged in 1881 and again in 1895. In 1886 work began on a new building at the north-west end of the garden, to provide accommodation for eighteen students, with their own dining room and drawing room, in deliberate imitation of the Newnham, Cambridge, plan of separate halls each preserving a family atmosphere. By the turn of the century Somerville could accommodate seventy-six students within its walls, but still lacked any distinctively collegiate buildings. It was characteristic that the first such building should be a library. An appeal for funds was launched to mark the college's coming-of-age, and the official opening by John Morley in 1904, in the presence of the VICE-CHANCELLOR and Proctors, gave outward expression to Somerville's collegiate aspirations. At the request of the librarian Margery Fry later Principal – 1926–31), the poet Robert Bridges composed a masque, *Demeter*, for the occasion. Within three years the new library received two of the

433

greatest of its many subsequent benefactions: the library of John Stuart Mill, presented by his step-daughter Helen Taylor, and the books, pictures and papers of the writer and Egyptologist Amelia Edwards.

The next major project – the building of a hall large enough to accommodate the whole college – was financed by the issue of debenture shares at $3\frac{1}{2}$ per cent, largely subscribed by old members. The architect was Edmund Fisher, brother of the then President of the college, H.A.L. FISHER, and the opening ceremony on 4 October 1913 was performed by the Vice-Chancellor, Dr Heberden, himself twice President of the Council. The building was named after Agnes Maitland in posthumous tribute to her ambitions for the college. Two years later it was in use as a hospital ward.

In April 1915 the college buildings were requisitioned by the War Office for use as a military hospital, an opening being made in the north wall to enable stretchers to be carried straight through to the operating theatre in the Radcliffe Infirmary next door. Students returning for the summer term found themselves rehoused, by courtesy of the Provost and Fellows, in the Rhodes Block and St Mary Quadrangle of Oriel, which was to be Somerville's home for the next four years. Somerville retained affectionate memories of its wartime quarters in 'Skimmery', and in 1919 presented a clock to the Oriel Junior Common Room in token of gratitude. Despite this early experience of co-residence, the two colleges have in recent years shown reluctance in adopting it as a policy. Oriel was the last of the men's colleges to admit women to membership; Somerville has yet to admit men.

Under Miss Penrose it was the college's policy to insist that Somerville students observe University regulations with regard to residence and preliminary examinations, as well as proving their quality in the Final Honours Schools. By 1920 it had some 300 past students qualified to claim their BA. After the first women's degree ceremony a dinner was held in hall at which toasts were drunk in lemonade to celebrate what the OXFORD MAGAZINE described as 'a victory won by courtesy, patience and merit alone'. But 1927 brought a severe setback to the fortunes of all the women's colleges, when, in response to a petition of senior members, CONGREGATION voted by 229 votes to 164 to place a permanent limit on the number of women in the University. A move to force an actual reduction in the number of women – which would have meant bankruptcy for their colleges – was averted, but numbers were frozen at the 1927 figure of c.780 and a quota (in Somerville's case, 150) was allotted to each college. With minor modifications during and after the war, the freeze persisted for nearly thirty years. It kept the women's colleges – which had no endowment – poor, and it deprived many able girls of the chance of an Oxford education. When University restrictions on numbers were removed in 1956, Somerville moved into a phase of rapid expansion. The mid-1960s saw a spate of building activity, the Graduate House, Vaughan and Wolfson buildings transforming the appearance of the college, which had not changed much since the mid-1930s. In 1967 Barbara Craig took over from Dame Janet Vaughan a college of 270 undergraduates and nearly 100 graduates.

The special quality of Somerville derives largely from its non-denominational status. It has never been an irreligious college, but it probably owes more to Quaker and Unitarian tradition than to Anglicanism, and it has tended to attract students of non-Christian faiths and of none. It is, in the broadest sense, Nonconformist. One of the most controversial episodes in the college's history was the decision of council in 1932 to accept from an anonymous old member the gift of an ecumenical, unconsecrated, chapel.

Somerville's reputation has always been firmly grounded in academic excellence, and in popular undergraduate mythology it was soon designated the 'blue-stocking' college. Though arts subjects have tended to predominate, the college has never forgotten that it is named after a scientist, and in Dame Janet Vaughan it had for twenty-two crucial years a distinguished scientist as Principal. Dorothy Hodgkin, an undergraduate of the college from 1928–32 and subsequently Fellow and tutor in Chemistry, was awarded the Nobel Prize for Chemistry in 1964 in recognition of her work on the

A day in the life of a lady at Somerville College, as envisaged by the Illustrated London News *in 1880.*

discovery of the three-dimensional structure of penicillin, vitamin B_{12} and insulin. In Somerville's domestic annals she also made history as the first serving Fellow of the college to have a baby.

To academic distinction Somerville has added an impressive record for public service. The first list of women magistrates included seven Somervillians. The college's civil servants include Baroness Sharp of Hornsey (1922–6), and its diplomats the present Principal, Daphne Park. A Somervillian, Eleanor Rathbone (1893–6), was the first woman graduate to be elected to Parliament – appropriately as an Independent representing the Combined Universities. The college has produced three Labour MPs – one of whom, Shirley Williams (1948–51), went on to help found the Social Democratic Party – and (1943–7) a Conservative Prime Minister. At the centenary celebrations which followed close upon the 1979 General Election, Baroness White said of Margaret Thatcher's achievement: 'It could have happened to a member of another college, but I fear that most Somervillians feel that it was right that it should be one of us.' A college whose political complexion is generally regarded as being to the left has taken ironic pleasure in Mrs Thatcher's career, as exemplifying the equally Somervillian characteristic of nonconformity.

She was not, however, the college's first Prime Minister. Indira Gandhi was a student at Somerville in 1937–8 and an Honorary Fellow from 1966 until her assassination in 1984. The college's links with India date from the arrival as a student in 1889 of Cornelia Sorabji, the passionate defender and reformer of the legal status of women and children in India. Mrs Radhabai Subbarayan, whose arrival in college in 1912 as a married woman caused a considerable stir among her contemporaries (her husband was an undergraduate at Wadham, and the rules were waived to enable them to have tea together in her rooms from time to time, without a chaperone), went on to become the first woman member of the Indian Central Legislative Assembly.

Somerville's literary tradition goes back to its first secretary, the novelist Mrs Humphry Ward. In the 1920s the popular press identified as 'the Somerville School of Novelists' a group of writers who had been roughly contemporary during and just after the First World War. They included Vera Brittain (1914–15 and 1919–21), Margaret Kennedy (1915–19), Sylvia Thompson (1920–3) and Winifred Holtby (1917–18 and 1919–21), the royalties of whose posthumous bestseller *South Riding* (1936) were bequeathed to the college as an endowment for scholarships. But some of Somerville's best-known novelists fall outside this group: Rose Macaulay (1900–3), Dorothy L. Sayers (1912–15) and Iris Murdoch (1938–42). The most celebrated literary portrayal of life in a women's college, in Dorothy L. Sayers's *Gaudy Night* (1935), was thought by some to be too near the bone, and the book has always aroused mixed feelings in Somerville itself. The words of Winifred Holtby, on the other hand, are often cited with satisfaction: 'Somervillians are . . . intractable, convivial . . . inclined to be innovators, even rebels. They probably give more trouble to their spiritual pastors and masters than students of the other [women's] colleges put together. They are certainly inclined to look more untidy – to embrace curious creeds and odd political allegiances

. . . and to make unorthodox but distinguished careers for themselves in after life.'

Miss Daphne Park, CMG (created Baroness Park in 1990) was Principal from 1980–89. Her two predecessors were Mrs Barbara Craig (1967–80) and Dame Janet Vaughan (1945–67). The present Principal is Miss Catherine Pestell, CMG.

The corporate title of the college is The Principal and Fellows of Somerville College in the University of Oxford.

(Byrne, Muriel St Clare, and Mansfield, Catherine Hope, *Somerville College 1879–1921*, Oxford, 1922; Farnell, Vera, *A Somervillian Looks Back*, Oxford, privately printed, 1948; de Villiers, Anne, Fox, Hazel, and Adams, Pauline, *Somerville College, Oxford: a Century in Pictures, 1879–1979*, Oxford, 1978.)

Since 1966 La Sorbonne restaurant has occupied this 17th-century building in an alley off High Street.

Sorbonne Restaurant   *130a High Street*. Opened in 1966 in a timbered building down an alley off HIGH STREET, La Sorbonne is Oxford's best-known French restaurant. Some twenty years before its *chef–patron* André Chavagnon took over, the restaurant was known as the Stowaway and was an eating place popular with students. Raymond Blanc was a chef at La Sorbonne before opening the Quat'Saisons restaurant in SUMMERTOWN.

Southfield   A large area of open land lying between the WARNEFORD, PARK and CHURCHILL HOSPITALS in HEADINGTON to the north and east, Southfield Road to the west and COWLEY to the south. It has had this name at least since mediaeval times. Most of the land is now a golf course (*see* GOLF CLUBS), but there are several college sports grounds on the southern edge. Once part of Donnington Hospital's enclosure allotments – the area in the vicinity of Divinity Road and the present Southfield Road – was laid out and developed by the OXFORD INDUSTRIAL AND PROVIDENT BUILDING SOCIETY in 1891. Southfield Road appears on registers from 1894. SOUTHFIELD SCHOOL is situated to the south in Glanville Road.

Southfield School *Glanville Road*. Established in 1934 when the Oxford Municipal Secondary School, opened in 1895, and the Oxford Selective Central School for Boys, opened in 1900, were combined. It was the first secondary school to be built by the Oxford Education Committee. Its brick buildings, standing on a sloping 16-acre site between the Southfield Golf Course (*see* GOLF COURSES) and Barracks Lane, were designed by H.F. Hurcombe to accommodate 370 boys. One specimen of each native British tree was planted in the grounds. The school was merged with the CITY OF OXFORD HIGH SCHOOL in 1966 to form OXFORD SCHOOL.

South Hinksey A village 1½ miles south of Oxford, separated from it by the Hinksey Stream, and approached from the southern bypass RING ROAD. With the neighbouring NORTH HINKSEY it was made famous by MATTHEW ARNOLD's lines from 'Thyrsis':

How changed is here each spot man makes or fills!
In the two Hinkseys nothing keeps the same;
The village street its haunted mansion lacks,
And from the sign is gone Sibylla's name,
And from the roofs the twisted chimney-stacks.

The Cross Keys Inn once stood on the other side of the road from the present one and in the mid-19th century was kept by Sybela Curr. The name 'Cross Keys' comes from the coat of arms of the archbishop of York. John Piers, Archbishop of York 1589–95, was born in a house opposite.

In ancient times it was known as Hengistesige, from Hengist, the Saxon founder of the Kingdom of Kent. It lies about one mile south-east of NORTH HINKSEY. ST LAURENCE CHURCH (not to be confused with ST LAWRENCE CHURCH at North Hinksey) is 13th century. At one time there was a mill of considerable importance at South Hinksey. Known as Langford Mill, it was granted to the Abbey of Abingdon by William de Seacourt in the early 12th century.

South Parade *Summertown*. Runs from No. 265 BANBURY ROAD to No. 254 WOODSTOCK ROAD. In the 19th century it was originally known as Double Ditch and also, on a map of 1829, as Prospect Road. In 1832 it was called Union Street, but this name was never adopted officially. In 1930, when SUMMERTOWN became part of the city, Double Ditch was renamed South Parade, supposedly on the suggestion of a German professor said to be an authority on Oxford history: it is said that the street was the patrolling area of the Parliamentarians during the siege of Oxford in the CIVIL WAR (*see also* NORTH PARADE). It is a street of mixed shops and houses. Beyond the junction to MIDDLE WAY at the western end there is a County Council Branch Library, and opposite is an entrance to ST EDWARD'S SCHOOL.

South Park A park of some 50 acres on a slope between HEADINGTON HILL and MORRELL AVENUE. Separated from HEADINGTON HILL PARK by the main road up Headington Hill, it belonged to the Morrell family (*see* MORRELL'S BREWERY). It was acquired in 1932 by the OXFORD PRESERVATION TRUST with the help of the Pilgrim Trust and of David and Joanna Randall McIver, as a stone at the foot of Headington Hill, with lettering by Eric Gill, records. The Trust gave the land to the city in 1959 to be preserved as an open space for the benefit of the public.

South Parks Road Dominated by buildings housing University departments in scientific subjects, the road's north side forms the heart of the University SCIENCE AREA. On the north-west corner is the Radcliffe Science Library (*see* LIBRARIES), the buildings of which were erected in 1901 and 1933–4. The earlier one was by SIR THOMAS JACKSON, and Pevsner suggests that the later buildings, by Sir Hubert Worthington, were influenced by the Paris Exhibition of 1925. Next to the library, the Inorganic Chemistry main building is by Lanchester and Lodge (1954–60). To the west of it is a laboratory of 1878. The Pharmacology building, by Gollins, Melvin Ward and Partners, was erected in 1959–61. The Anatomy building is again by Lanchester and Lodge (1954–60), who also designed the 1940–1 extension to the Dyson Perrins Laboratory (Organic Chemistry), the earlier part of which was by Paul Waterhouse (1913–16). Lanchester and Lodge were additionally responsible for the Physical Chemistry building, which was erected in 1939–40 and which has a later block by Ramsey, Murray White and Ward (1958–9). The Department of Forestry and the Commonwealth (formerly Imperial) Forestry Institute (which moved here from Parks Road in 1950) share with Botany a twin block by Worthington. The SIR WILLIAM DUNN SCHOOL OF PATHOLOGY, at the eastern end of the road near the south lodge and next to an entrance to the University PARKS, is by E.P. Warren (1926). Behind it is a new (1967–9) block by Sir Leslie Martin. Pevsner sums up his description of these buildings by saying that none is of real distinction and that 'the squared-rubble, squared-up Georgian brigade will never be a credit to Oxford'.

At the south-east end of the street, on the corner as it winds round into ST CROSS ROAD, is the massive Zoology and Psychology building by Sir Leslie Martin (1965–70). On the opposite corner is Linacre College (formerly CHERWELL EDGE). RHODES HOUSE is at the south-western end of the road. HALIFAX HOUSE is also on the south side, and still standing on this side are a number of other large houses which were built for senior members of the University in the 1860s and 1870s. Before this the site had been the farmland of HOLYWELL parish.

In the 19th century the road was known as South Park Road. No. 2 is Park Grange, on whose site had stood a gibbet. A set of gibbet irons, found when the foundations of the house were dug, can be seen in the ASHMOLEAN MUSEUM.

Speedwell Street In the Middle Ages this was a narrow lane which led to the mill of Philip the Miller. In the early 14th century the BLACKFRIARS took over the mill, which was in use until 1500 and which gave the street the name of Mill Lane; it was so called until at least 1639. However, in a deed of 1427 the name Buterwyke is mentioned as an alternative. This was derived from a University beadle who lived in a house on the south side of the lane, after whom a new development (Butterwyke Place) further west along the present street has since been named. The street was also later known as Water Lane, and in the time of ANTHONY WOOD it was called Preachers' Lane because it led to the land of the Blackfriars or friar preachers.

Today Speedwell Street runs from No. 79 ST ALDATE'S to THAMES STREET in the vicinity of the modern Preachers' Lane. The British Telecom telephone exchange on the south side was opened in April

An illustration from Cuthbert Bede's The Adventures of Verdant Green *showing Spiers & Son's shop in High Street in the mid-19th century.*

1959 (the previous exchange had been in PEMBROKE STREET). Building had begun in 1954 after many years of argument between the City Council and the Post Office about a possible site in St Aldate's. Forty-five families had to be rehoused when the site was cleared, and in 1956 a tunnel 45 feet deep for telephone cables was constructed under the ground. On the north side of the street are modern office buildings which back on to Bridewell Square. The Magistrates' Courts (also in Albion Place), by Douglas Murray, the City Architect, were completed in 1969.

Spiers & Son   Richard Spiers opened a shop at Nos 102 and 103 HIGH STREET in 1835, selling stationery and fancy goods. It became known popularly as Spiers of Oxford. The firm supplied COLLEGE STAMPS to Keble, Hertford, and All Souls Colleges. The stamps were designed by S.P. Spiers and the issues of Keble and Hertford in 1876 and 1879 respectively bore the name of the firm at the foot of each stamp. Spiers & Son closed in 1889.

Spooner, William Archibald   (*1844–1930*). The son of a barrister and nephew of A.C. Tait, Archbishop of Canterbury (1868–82), Spooner won a scholarship in 1862 from Oswestry School to New College, with which he was to be associated for the rest of his life. He was elected Fellow in 1867, Dean in 1876 and Warden in 1903 as successor to James Edwards Sewell, who had been head of the college for over forty years. Spooner was a highly effective and popular Warden, but took little part in University affairs, declining to become VICE-CHANCELLOR. Although a gifted and lucid conversationalist, he gave us the word 'spoonerism', first recorded in 1900 and defined in the *Oxford English Dictionary* as 'an accidental transposition of the initial sounds, or other parts, of two or more words'. Examples given in dictionaries of quotations include 'Kinquering Congs their titles take' (when announcing a hymn in New College chapel); and (on dismissing an undergraduate) 'You have deliberately tasted two worms and you can leave Oxford by the town drain.' Many spoonerisms, however, are now known to be apocryphal. Better authenticated are Spooner's question to an undergraduate he came across in the quad – 'Now let me see. Was it you or your brother who was killed in the war?' – and his invitation to a young don: 'Do come to dinner tonight. We have that new Fellow, Casson, coming.' 'But, Warden, I *am* Casson.' 'Oh, well. Never mind. Come anyway.'

Sporting One's Oak   A slang term dating from the 18th century. It refers to the practice of closing one's outer door in order to show that one is engaged – presumably working – and thus unable to receive visitors. It used to be that such outer doors were almost invariably provided for the rooms of dons and undergraduates, and a feature was, and is, that they have no exterior handle. Although the object of these doors, or 'oaks', was to prevent unwanted friends from coming in, they were also occasionally used to prevent an unpopular member of the college from getting out, since it was sometimes possible to screw them to the door frames. With the expansion of the colleges, the provision of 'oaks' has fallen into desuetude and the term is now scarcely heard except among those few people, mainly dons, who still have them.

Squitchey Lane   Known in 1832 as Green Way and in 1859 as Victoria Road, the street appeared on the maps of 1896 and 1897 as Squitchey Lane. By 1906 it had been decided that Green Lane would be a more respectable name, but the change proved unpopular and eventually Squitchey Lane became its official appellation when the Council adopted the road in 1937. Because of its muddy state people thought the name was a corruption of 'squelchy', though it is more likely that 'Squitchey' derives from the piece of land on the lane's south-west side, which, because of the squitch and couchgrass growing there, was known as late as 1929 as Couchy or Squitchey Piece.

Stadium   *Sandy Lane, Blackbird Leys*. Opened in 1939 by Lord Denham. Since then speedway and

A 'Spy' cartoon of the shortsighted and eccentric William Archibald Spooner, from 1903 Warden of New College with which he was associated for the rest of his life.

greyhound-racing meetings have been held there regularly. The current speedway team known as the Oxford Cheetahs held the British League title in 1985 and again in 1986. Their captain, Hans Neilsen, was the 1986 World Champion and the No. 2, Simon Wigg, the 1985 Long Track Champion. The team also held the Midland Cup and the Marlborough Cup in 1986, a record in the speedway world. In greyhound-racing a locally trained dog won the English Derby, which is the major national trophy. The Oxford Stadium was completely modernised in 1986 by Northern Sports (Oxford) Limited, with additional leisure facilities, including squash courts, gym, sauna and snooker.

Stained Glass Oxford is the best place in the country to study the development of stained and painted glass, and the wealth of examples from the 17th and 18th centuries is of special interest. But there is nothing earlier than the late 13th century; windows of c.1180–1280 are best seen at Canterbury.

The church of ST MICHAEL AT THE NORTH GATE has, now in the east window, figures of the Virgin and Child and three saints, dating from c.1280. Merton College chapel has, in its side-windows, a complete, if restored, ensemble of the 1290s. A wealthy Fellow gave the glass and he appears twice in every window, kneeling on either side of Apostles and Martyrs. The figures and their decorative canopies form a band halfway up the windows. Above and below is a simple trellis pattern of vine, oak, maple, ivy, lily and battlement. The main east window has some fine coats of arms and an Annunciation in the tracery, of about 1300. The upper half of the Lucy Chapel window in CHRIST CHURCH CATHEDRAL is brilliant work of about 1330 with small grotesques and larger story-scenes of SS Martin, Thomas, Cuthbert and Blaise. On the other side of the cathedral, three north windows of the Latin Chapel have various female saints, including a scholarly ST FRIDESWIDE with sceptre and book, and a central Annunciation. The general arrangement, a band of canopied figures with trellis pattern above and below, is like that at Merton – but this may be because the Victorian restorers thought that it should be.

New College chapel was glazed in about 1385; out of twenty windows, seven remain, all now in the antechapel. There are two main rows of figures under fantastic canopies, supposedly the work of a master-glazier, Thomas of Oxford, and his assistants. They are female saints, apostles, prophets and Old Testament figures; four Crucifixions in the four east windows of the antechapel show the positions of former altars. Angels fill the tracery, giving a third rank of figures, quite unlike the Merton glass of a century earlier. The glass was reset and somewhat restored in 1899. Despite the very simple architectural design, the glass gives an overwhelming jewelled effect.

All Souls chapel, with still plainer tracery, was glazed in about 1441; here, too, mediaeval glass survives only in the antechapel. The four east windows have a lower row of female saints with apostles above. These are original to the chapel and were made by John Glazier of Oxford, who is considered to be the son or grandson of the Thomas who made the New College windows. Three windows on the north and west have smaller figures of the Latin doctors and English kings and bishops under rather fussy canopies. These fine panels were made for the Old Library; they have been attributed to a royal glazier, John Prudde of Westminster.

The mediaeval libraries at Balliol and Merton have some good 15th-century glass, perhaps moved from the chapels. The churches of ST EBBE, St Michael at the North Gate and ST PETER-IN-THE-EAST (now St Edmund Hall library) also have 15th-century panels. Some sections of Merton chapel east window, perhaps made for the transepts, are the finest work of the century to survive in Oxford.

The Queen's College chapel has excellent glass dating from 1518 in the two western windows on each side, moved from the old antechapel – English and other saints, bishops and an Annunciation. Balliol chapel has a series of small scenes from the Passion and from St Catherine's life, of 1529 but all rearranged and reset to fit later windows. Christ Church Cathedral chapter house has some fine panels of early 16th-century date. A room by the hall at Trinity has some mixed glass of the 14th, 15th and 16th centuries, perhaps the pickings of a Georgian antiquary rather than survival. There does not seem to be any domestic glass remaining from mediaeval Oxford houses or inns. The Dissolution of the Monasteries crippled stained-glass workshops in the 1530s and 40s.

Much continental glass was retrieved and brought over during the upheavals of the Revolutionary and Napoleonic Wars. The BODLEIAN LIBRARY has many assorted panels from the collection of Alderman William Fletcher, a Regency banker and antiquary; and there is more at Yarnton Church, where he was buried. Merton library has twelve small panels of 1598, scenes of the Passion with merchants' names and marks, pillaged from a South German guildhall; they were put up in 1844. Trinity hall has the cream of a collection from Switzerland – nine panels dated from 1527 to 1595, given in 1877. A Nativity and a Pentecost, 16th-century Belgian work, were bought at a Bond Street upholsterer's and inserted in Wadham chapel in 1836.

Local plumber–glaziers entirely lacked the skills needed to produce fine coloured and painted windows when large-scale college building began again in 1609. In 1613 an Oxford man, Robert Rudland, tried his hand at a set of prophets in the north windows of Wadham chapel, then just built. When he put up his ill-drawn figures in 1614, the college paid him off at once and looked around again. In 1616 an unknown, perhaps French or Flemish, master made the splendid apostles for the south windows; he could get the very best glass and had an eye for pure colours. Christ Church Cathedral chapter house has some coats of arms and inscriptions of similar quality and date; they may have been made for the Audit House, where the canons met.

In 1621 a young North German master-glazier from Emden, Bernard van Ling, was hired by Wadham to produce the chapel east window, completed in 1623. He had spent four years in Paris and was found negotiating for work on St Paul's Cathedral by a friend of the college. Wadham gave him a room and built him annealing ovens, while a book in the college library provided many of the designs, which are scenes from the Passion arranged in two rows of five. This elder van Ling also glazed Lincoln College chapel of 1629–30 and, in London, Lincoln's Inn chapel of 1623–4 (both built by Oxford-based MASONS who had originally come from Yorkshire). At Lincoln College there are prophets on the north and apostles on the south, while the east window has a lower row of Old Testament scenes which prefigure the Nativity, Baptism, Last Supper, Crucifixion, Resurrection and Ascension above.

In 1632 Richard Greenbury, a London gold-smith–artist, produced the sepia-tinted windows of Magdalen antechapel with figures of forty-eight (mostly obscure) saints. Of about 1620–30, and by unknown glaziers, the east window of St Peter-in-the-East has four large Evangelists and a south window at ST MARY MAGDALEN has scenes of Tobias.

Abraham van Ling, presumably a brother or cousin of Berendt, was the leading Oxford glass-painter of the 1630s. In 1631 he made the Jonah window in Christ Church Cathedral, now at the west end of the north aisle – a fine example of Abraham's taste for bold colours and broad landscapes. Also in the cathedral is a memorial window by one of the van Lings to the first BISHOP OF OXFORD, using one of the Lincoln's Inn designs again. Of another ten windows which they provided for the cathedral, only fragments survived Cromwellian puritans and Victorian restorers.

Abraham van Ling reglazed The Queen's College chapel in 1635 and made several new windows for Balliol in 1637. At both much survives, rearranged in later windows. In 1641 he made eight magnificent windows for University College chapel; they remained in store throughout the CIVIL WAR and Commonwealth and were put up only in the 1660s, perhaps not in the order first planned. The design of each window goes right across the full width, ignoring the division into lights. There are six Old Testament scenes – two of Adam and Eve, an Abraham, a Jonah, a Jacob and an Elijah – balanced by only two from the New Testament – Christ with Martha and Mary and Christ driving out money-changers from the Temple.

At Oriel College in 1638 one of the Fellows, John Rouse, who was also Bodley's Librarian, had some coats of arms and five fine portrait roundels put up in his rooms. Perhaps a local painter rather than a plumber–glazier made them; they are now in the Provost's lodgings.

Puritan colleges like Exeter kept their chapel windows plain. After 1642 the Civil War and parliamentarian regime left no chance of work for glass-painters and presumably the van Lings left for the Continent, like many Court artists.

For more than a century after 1660, when the Restoration of the Stuarts allowed fine decoration in churches, York remained almost the sole nursery of glass-painting in England. Henry Gyles (1640–1709), his pupil William Price (d. 1722), Price's brother Joshua (d.1717), Joshua's son William junior (d.1765) and William Peckitt (1731–95) were the successive masters; all are well represented in Oxford, despite the hazard and cost of moving glass 150 miles by land or 400 by water. Gyles's Nativity of 1682–7, given by JOHN RADCLIFFE for the east window of University College chapel, was dismantled in 1862 and parts remain in store. The elder William Price's version of a Raphael Nativity, set in the east window of Christ Church Cathedral in 1696 has been dismembered and several other large windows of this time have been destroyed. In The Queen's College chapel, Joshua Price made the east window in 1717–18 and filled the other windows with the 16th- and 17th-century glass from the old chapel, making various repairs and replacements. In New College chapel the south windows were 'repaired' by William Price in 1735–40; he replaced the old with garish new glass. Peckett reglazed the north windows in 1735–40;

he also remade the north windows in 1765–74, some of his designs being the work of the Italian artist Biagio Rebecca. The college tried to back out of the contract when the first examples could be seen but, surprisingly, these windows survived the Victorian age of restoration. At Oriel a Presentation in the Temple made by Peckett for the east window in 1767 is now in the south-west window of the chapel.

From 1770 London became the principal centre of glass-painting. James Pearson made an east window for Brasenose chapel in 1776 with Christ and the Evangelists designed by J.R. Mortimer; it has been moved to become the west window. Sir Joshua Reynolds himself was commissioned by New College in 1778 to design the chapel west window; he was working on a family portrait at Blenheim Palace. Always a keen businessman, he exhibited the designs in London, where they were much acclaimed, and also sold engravings of the designs in large numbers. The actual window of the Seven Virtues below a large Nativity was carried out by Thomas Jervais of London in 1778–85; it has seemed insipid to 19th and 20th century taste. Glass-painting remained popular and Francis Eginton established a factory in Birmingham where, in 1794, he made a Last Judgement as a west window for Magdalen chapel.

There is very little stained glass of the early 19th century in Oxford but a vast amount of the late 19th century. In the 1830s and 1840s a local workshop, Russell's of ST CLEMENT'S, produced stilted little scenes in medallions, now in the east window of ST CLEMENT'S CHURCH. Most of the later glass is fairly routine work by large London firms – Powell's and Clayton & Bell. Hardman of Birmingham made the main chapel windows for Magdalen, gaudy and provincial, in 1857–60; and Clayton & Bell those for All Souls, pedantically following the lines of the remaining mediaeval glass, in 1874–9.

The earliest Pre-Raphaelite glass is EDWARD BURNE-JONES's Latin Chapel east window of 1859 in Christ Church Cathedral, colourful and crowded. The art firm Morris & Co. (see WILLIAM MORRIS) made small cheerful windows for St Edmund Hall chapel and large sentimental ones for Christ Church Cathedral, installing three minor east windows and one west one in 1871–5, during GEORGE GILBERT SCOTT's restoration. This firm also glazed Mansfield College chapel in 1893–8 using designs by Burne-Jones, some new and some made thirty years before for a Northamptonshire church. Two Georgian college chapels were drastically re-decorated in Victorian days: at Worcester in 1864–5 Henry Holiday designed bold, dark, colourful scenes for the windows; and at Pembroke in 1884–5 C.E. Kempe used a South German style of the early 16th century.

In the 20th century several halls have been glazed with the arms of benefactors or celebrated old members, mostly in Edwardian times. In the 1960s John Piper and Patrick Reyntiens were commissioned to make five abstract windows for the attic chapel at Nuffield College; Hayward made an expressionist east window for St Peter's College. In the suburbs, ST PETER'S CHURCH, WOLVERCOTE, has a 1976 window of waving hands by John Piper.

Details of all the figures in the important pre-1714 stained glass in the colleges and churches are given in the Royal Commission's *Inventory of the Historical Monuments in the City of Oxford*.

Stallybrass, William Teulon Swan (*1883–1948*). The son of William Swan Sonnenschein, he assumed the surname of his great-grandfather, the Rev. Edward Stallybrass, although still generally known for the rest of his life as 'Sonners'. He won a scholarship to Christ Church from Westminster; and, after practising for a short time as a barrister, became a Fellow of Brasenose and tutor in jurisprudence in 1911. On returning to Brasenose after the First World War, he set about raising its standards in every way he could, both academically and athletically, and found time to get to know all the undergraduates of his college as BENJAMIN JOWETT had done at Balliol. He was a keen cricketer himself and as an undergraduate had represented Oxford in cross-country running against Cambridge. He became Principal of Brasenose in 1936, having established his reputation as an authority on and a great teacher of law. He became VICE-CHANCELLOR in 1947 but was killed the next year when, returning by a night train from London, he opened his carriage door and fell on to the track.

Stanford University In 1984 Stanford University in California took from Magdalen College the lease of Nos 65–70 HIGH STREET as a centre for fifty-two undergraduates from Stanford University. The course of study in Oxford is accounted part of their degree course at Stanford. There is no formal link with Oxford University. The buildings, which are 18th century, are timber-framed and inside are some panelling of about 1730.

Stanton Ballard Charitable Trust Established by trust deed in 1986 by Hubert Stanton Ballard, formerly senior partner of the Oxford firm of estate agents, Buckell & Ballard, who died on 19 June 1986, leaving half the residue of his estate to his charitable trust. The main beneficiaries are local Oxford charities.

Star Inn *see* CLARENDON HOTEL.

Statues and Busts At the mention of sculptured portraits in Oxford one's first image is of full-length figures which perform an integral function in an architectural design or setting: Nicholas and Dorothy Wadham in stone (John Blackshaw, *c.*1613) on the outer doorway of the hall at Wadham; James I in stone, halfway up the Tower of the Five Orders (1613–36) looking on to the SCHOOLS QUADRANGLE; Charles I and Henrietta Maria in bronze (Le Sueur, 1634) in the Canterbury Quad at St John's; LORD CLARENDON in lead (Francis Bird, 1721) looking west down BROAD STREET from his niche on the CLARENDON BUILDING; a stately JOHN RADCLIFFE in marble (Rysbrack, 1744) presiding over the RADCLIFFE CAMERA; Queen Caroline in marble (Sir Henry Cheere, 1735) looking towards Magdalen from her cupola over the gateway at Queen's; Queen Mary II and Queen Anne in stone (unattributed; Queen Anne, 1709) looking across HIGH STREET from the east and west gateways of University College. All the Queens have lost their sceptres. Le Sueur had been brought over from France by Charles I in the 1620s and the King thought highly of him. In addition to the figures at St John's there is a bust of Charles I in the BODLEIAN LIBRARY (Duke Humfrey) and the free-standing figure

of the Earl of Pembroke in the Schools Quadrangle which was brought to this site from Wilton House.

SIR CHRISTOPHER WREN, whose contribution to architecture in Oxford was, in the SHELDONIAN THEATRE and Tom Tower, Christ Church, of the first importance, is commemorated by two remarkably fine busts. The first, in marble (Edward Pierce, 1673), now in the ASHMOLEAN MUSEUM, is one of the earliest and one of the most successful essays in the baroque style in English sculpture, the more surprising in that Pierce, who worked for Wren as a mason-contractor, had never been abroad. The second (Rysbrack, 1726), at Queen's, is based on a death-mask and was, perhaps understandably, taken at one time for a bust of Voltaire.

Statues (in the context of Oxford perhaps 'sculptured figures', is a more appropriate term), portrait busts and medallions, unlike paintings, are not easy to place. They are extremely heavy to move. Busts can easily be knocked over despite their weight; and they demand a spacious setting which they rarely get. Medallions can be set in a chapel wall, and busts, if the sitter is deemed worthy, in a chapel lobby, but in an Oxford College the library is usually the most fitting place. Ranged along the top of bookcases, set back in a window bay, placed on either side of wide doorways, sculpture comes into its own – and the often classical presentation of the sitter induces, or should induce, a mood of serious application to work. It is therefore proper to consider Oxford sculpture in relation to its setting rather than in its chronological sequence. There are three venues of particular interest: the libraries of All Souls and Christ Church and the hall of the EXAMINATION SCHOOLS. The CODRINGTON LIBRARY at All Souls, completed around 1750, is vast. Twenty-six bronzed plaster busts (John Cheere) alternate with urns around the upper cornice. Henry Cheere's marble CHRISTOPHER CODRINGTON in Roman dress (1734) stands below with, at the far end, Bacon the Elder's grandiloquent SIR WILLIAM BLACKSTONE holding a rolled Magna Carta (1784). The effect is one of great dignity. The busts and the Codrington statue are in their planned positions. The assemblage in the library lobby at Christ Church came about in a different way. In 1958 the college commissioned Epstein to make a half-length figure of Dean Lowe in bronze. This was placed in the centre of the hallway leading to the stairs which mount to the Upper Library. It was then decided to place against the walls busts from other parts of the college, so creating a kind of Pantheon of Sculpture. George I and George II (both Rysbrack and both undated), George III (Bacon the Elder, 1770), George IV (Chantrey, 1828) and Queen Victoria (Brock, 1901), associate with Richard Frewin (Roubiliac, 1777), Richard Busby (? Rysbrack), Archbishop Robinson (Bacon the Elder, 1770), Archbishop William Markham (Bacon the Younger, 1770) and others. There is enough space and enough light to create a feeling of exhilaration on a good day. In CHRIST CHURCH PICTURE GALLERY there are three small bronzes: Elizabeth Frink's Sir William Walton (1970) and David Wynne's Lord Home (1966) and Lord Salisbury (1967).

In the lobby leading to the library of University College, in a space hewn out of the wall for it, stands a remarkable and colossal marble group of the Law Lord brothers, John Scott, Earl of Eldon, and William Scott, Lord Stowell, looking at first blink like

Henry Cheere's 1734 statue of Christopher Codrington in the library at All Souls, of which he was chief benefactor, stands beneath an array of busts.

Donatello prophets. It is the work of Musgrave Lewthwaite Watson, a sculptor of promise who died in 1847 before it was completed, and it was described by Rupert Gunnis as 'undoubtedly one of the most important portrait groups of the nineteenth century'. The commission had originally been given to Chantrey, who had scarcely begun to work on it when he died in 1841. In 1842 Lady Chantrey gave to the University a collection of some 150 plaster models for his busts and statues. These have been housed for many years in the reserve collection of the Ashmolean Museum where, in 1986, they were undergoing a lengthy process of restoration.

The entrance hall of the Examination Schools has a small collection of busts, which can perhaps best be described as leftovers. Among them, however, are Flaxman's Lord North (1806), H.R. Hope Pinker's BENJAMIN JOWETT (1892) and F.J. Williamson's Prince Leopold, Duke of Albany (1884).

Scattered throughout the college and University buildings there are far more sculptural *jeux d'esprits* or pious platitudes than it is possible to mention. The over-serious Pre-Raphaelite Thomas Woolner is well represented in the UNIVERSITY MUSEUM, at Keble (CARDINAL NEWMAN, 1866), and above all in his WILLIAM GLADSTONE (1866), on a tall marble plinth with Homeric subjects in relief, now in the Ashmolean but originally in the Bodleian. Onslow Ford, apart from his superb SHELLEY MEMORIAL, has a bust of Briton Rivière at Oriel and a small wall-monument to Benjamin Jowett in Balliol chapel. In the 20th century portrait-sculpture has perhaps seemed less relevant to contemporary architecture than in the past, but since

the Second World War it has experienced something of a revival and there have been additions to the Oxford collections. Epstein, as well as Dean Lowe at Christ Church, has Einstein at St Catherine's and A.D. LINDSAY at Balliol. Oscar Nemon has a bronze head of Queen Elizabeth II at Christ Church, and busts of ANTONIN BESSE and Madame Besse at St Anthony's. But the most original piece is surely John Doubleday's MAURICE BOWRA in bronze in the garden at Wadham, in which the head and body evaporate into an empty chair. (See also ART.)

Statutes The principal authority for the University's constitutional and legislative history. If, as has been claimed, the earliest forms of the University's constitution are based on those of Paris, no historical proof of this can be given; yet some sort of academic organisation was in place before the end of the 12th century, as was seen at the visit of Giraldus Cambrensis in about 1187. The earliest collection of statutes was discovered only in the first quarter of the 20th century, on two leaves of a 13th-century manuscript; it consists mainly of proclamations dealing with the preservation of the peace, and the most interesting statute, requiring every scholar to be on the roll of some master, is apparently earlier than 1231. Apart from this, the ancient statutes are preserved in four manuscripts dating from the early 14th to the late 15th centuries (the CHANCELLOR'S Books, and the Books of the Senior and Junior PROCTORS).

The University long governed itself almost entirely by statutes of its own making; but they grew into a

441

confused mass, often inconsistent or at variance with the usages of the University. This was put to rights under the chancellorship (1630–41) of ARCHBISHOP LAUD, who promulgated the so-called LAUDIAN CODE, drawn up at his instigation by special delegates (notably BRIAN TWYNE) and accepted by CONVOCATION in 1636 as the code of laws by which the University was henceforward to be governed. The Laudian statutes effectively survived until the passing of the Oxford University Act in 1854, which, with its numerous and wide-ranging reforms (including, vitally, the abolition of religious tests at MATRICULA-TION, and the partial opening of fellowships to laymen) paved the way for the University as it is now constituted. Further important statutory reforms, especially in the areas of creating professorships and making the colleges contribute more generously to University purposes, resulted from the Universities of Oxford and Cambridge Act of 1877.

The initiation of a statute (or decree) is the statutory prerogative of the HEBDOMADAL COUNCIL, and a member of Council introduces the measure in CONGREGA-TION (though in matters within the sphere of the GENERAL BOARD OF THE FACULTIES, a measure framed by it may be introduced by a member of either body). The statutes themselves are published regularly, though no longer annually, as was the case up to 1983, and appear in English: originally they were in Latin, and Latin was preserved for certain statutes up to 1969. It is not possible here to do more than list the fifteen titles of the present statutes, dating from 1969–70, which are augmented by numerous decrees and regulations. In the broadest sense, general legislation is embodied in the statutes and temporary or particular legislation in decrees, though important issues can and do fall to be presented in the form of decrees.

Title I:	Of Interpretation
Title II:	Of the Congregation of the University
Title III:	Of Convocation
Title IV:	Of the Hebdomadal Council
Title V:	Of the General Board of the Faculties
Title VI:	Of the faculties, faculty boards, and departments
Title VII:	Of the colleges and other societies of the University
Title VIII:	Of other University bodies
Title IX:	Of the OFFICERS OF THE UNIVERSITY
Title X:	Of the conditions of service of persons employed by the University
Title XI:	Of matriculation, residence, degrees, diplomas, certificates, and examinations
Title XII:	Of college contributions and payments to colleges
Title XIII:	Of University DISCIPLINE
Title XIV:	Of other matters which require to be governed by statute
Title XV:	Of statutes amending trusts

The University statutes are, of course, wholly separate and different from those governing the individual colleges (which also were required, like the University, to promulgate revised statutes after 1854, and, with varying degrees of zeal, eventually did so).

Stockton, Maurice Harold Macmillan, 1st Earl of *(1894–1986).* The grandson of the founder of the publishing firm and third son of one of its directors, Macmillan won a scholarship from SUMMER FIELDS to Eton and from there an exhibition to Balliol College, where, after a few happy terms, in 1914 he took a First in Classical Moderations. But war broke out before he could take his finals. During service with the Grenadier Guards he was wounded three times, the last wound being responsible for the pain which he suffered thereafter as well as for his shuffling walk. After the war he did not return to Oxford, which he said had become 'a city of ghosts': of the eight scholars and exhibitioners who had come up with him in 1912 only himself and one other were left. He remained in the army until 1920, and then went into the family business before embarking upon a political career. In 1958 he was awarded the honorary degree of DCL, and three years later, in 1960, after becoming Prime Minister, he was appointed CHANCELLOR, in preference to Lord Franks (*see* FRANKS COMMISSION), after what he himself described to his biographer, Alistair Horne, as 'the most corrupt election' ever held at Oxford. MAURICE BOWRA was 'very anti', he added; 'Balliol was solid for me, ran a buffet with drinks all day long.... The voters were bullied and booed ... a lot of my friends took MAs just to vote, a special train was run from London.' He said much the same to Peter Levi, the Professor of Poetry, and went on, 'Of course you and I are the only two people who were properly elected with no bloody interference from the Hebdomadal Council.'

Once elected, Macmillan proved himself a highly effective Chancellor, obviously enjoying his role and keeping himself fully informed of all University affairs. Sir Nigel Fisher commented that he often seemed prouder of being Chancellor than Prime Minister; and when it was suggested, in his eighty-eighth year, that he might consider retiring, he replied that he would give way only to an older and wiser man.

Stone The stone commonly used in the construction of buildings in mediaeval Oxford was coral rag – a limestone containing beds of petrified corals – which was quarried in the surrounding hills, at HEADINGTON, HINKSEY, WYTHAM and elsewhere. This stone is still to be seen in the CITY WALL, in the tower of ST MICHAEL AT THE NORTH GATE and in the tower of the CASTLE. With the Renaissance, however, and the emergence of a classical style demanding a softer stone which could be sawn into the required shapes, freestone – previously used only for such details as dressings, quoins and cornices – was required for the whole building. The demand was first met by quarries at Taynton; but, as increasing quantities of this stone were needed, beds of it were worked at Headington. It was not for years that the disadvantages of Headington freestone became apparent, when surfaces began to peel and became pitted and scarred – defects accelerated by sulphurous air-pollution. The widespread restoration that became necessary have made Headington freestone difficult to find in Oxford, though the lower, rusticated storey of the RADCLIFFE CAMERA offers an uncharacteristic example which has weathered well.

Headington hardstone is far more durable. This came into use in the 14th and 15th centuries for larger buildings for which coral rag was considered unsuitable. The earliest supplies came from Wheatley before the stone began to be quarried at Headington towards the end of the 14th century. Examples of it can be seen in New College cloisters, where the original tool marks are still distinctly visible, and in the plinths of Exeter and Lincoln Colleges.

Wheatley stone is difficult to distinguish from Headington. It was widely used in squared, coursed blocks, with dressings of Taynton stone, from the late 13th to the 15th century. The masons of Merton College employed it in 1290–1377 and those of New College for the front quad there in about 1380.

Taynton stone is a freestone quarried near Burford which was used extensively for dressings in the Middle Ages and for which the demand increased so much thereafter that quarries in other villages were opened and enlarged. Stone from all these villages was known as Taynton. It is still used for repairs, most recently for internal work at the NEW BODLEIAN LIBRARY.

Most of the quarries supplying Taynton stone were, however, closed down during the early 20th century. One of them, at Milton-under-Wychwood, had been supplying large quantities of stone for Oxford buildings in the middle of the 19th century. This quarry had also been worked in the Middle Ages but had been closed in the intervening period; its reopening proved a disastrous mistake for, although it was some time before its poor quality was recognised, Milton stone was a bad building material – as evidenced at Mansfield College and the INDIAN INSTITUTE, where extensive repairs have been necessary.

In the second half of the 18th century Bath stone became much favoured by Oxford architects. The biggest quarries for this were in the region of Box between Bath and Corsham, and from these came the most celebrated of Bath stones, Box Ground. The Regency terraces of BEAUMONT STREET and ST JOHN STREET demonstrate what an attractive stone this is, though unfortunately it tends to hold dirt and soot on north-facing walls and in time becomes very dark and sometimes even black. Box Ground was used for the BROAD STREET frontage of Balliol, the façades of Jesus and Exeter Colleges on opposite sides of TURL STREET, and the ashlar front of the UNIVERSITY MUSEUM.

Clipsham stone, from the Inferior Oolite Lincolnshire limestone of Rutland, was introduced to Oxford by SIR THOMAS JACKSON in 1876 and soon became the most popular of Oxford stones. It was used for the new EMPERORS' HEADS. It is hard and durable and its large blocks, such as those used at Wadham College, are often attractively blue-hearted. In more modern buildings, Clipsham stone has been used in conjunction with the less expensive Bladon stone, quarried near Woodstock. This combination can be seen at RHODES HOUSE and at the Department of Geology.

Other stones of the Clipsham type are quarried from the same strata at Ketton in Rutland, Weldon in Northamptonshire and Ancaster in Lincolnshire. These freestones are more commonly seen at Cambridge. But Debenhams shop, now DILLONS, on the corner of Broad Street and CORNMARKET has columns of Ancaster stone, and a pinkish variety was used for the north wing of the Rawlinson Building at St John's College (1909), while Weldon stone has recently been used at Green College (1978–9).

The stones mentioned above account for nearly all those used in construction at Oxford, but a few others are occasionally encountered. Yellow Guiting, an Inferior Oolite freestone from the Cotswolds, was used for the ST GILES' front of Balliol College, and White Guiting, quarried in the same area, for the restoration of the south face of the New Building at Magdalen College. A white oolitic freestone from Painswick, near Stroud, was used in the chapel of Magdalen, where pea grit from the Cheltenham area was also used in the buttresses.

Portland stone, a very white stone which quickly discolours and was extensively used in London, was employed in conjunction with Bath stone for the ASHMOLEAN, whose plinth, formerly of Palaeozoic sandstone which decayed where it came into contact with the overlying limestone, was replaced by Portland roach. Portland stone was also used for the columns, pilasters and entablature of the Bath stone TAYLOR INSTITUTION, and for the former Marks and Spencer building in Cornmarket.

Since Britain joined the European Economic Community, freestones have been imported from France, as they were in the Middle Ages. A number of stones from the strata of the Jurassic of Lorraine have been used at Magdalen for the restoration of the chapel and for the New Building. Another French stone, Besacre, can be seen in the restoration work of the old ALL SAINTS CHURCH in the HIGH STREET (now Lincoln College library), while the Eocene St Maximin stone was used at St John's College for the Sir Thomas White Building of 1974–5.

(*See also* MASONS AND BUILDERS.)

(Arkell, W.J., *Oxford Stone*, London, 1947.)

Stone's Almshouses Situated in ST CLEMENT'S, the almshouses were founded in 1700 by the Rev. William Stone, Principal of what is now St Peter's College. The inscription on the cartouche on the front of the building facing St Clement's Street reads, 'This Hospital for ye Poor & Sick was Founded by The Reverend Mr. Will Stone Principal of New Inne Hall In Hopes of thy Assistance A.D. 1700.' The almshouses were built by Bartholomew Peisley (*see* PEISLEYS), and there is a drawing of them by J.C. BUCKLER in the BODLEIAN LIBRARY. At either end are blocks designed in a similar style by Thomas Rayson, with gable ends to the street. Those on the left, known as Parsons' Almshouses, were built in 1960 in exchange for almshouses in Kybald Street, founded by the family of John Parsons in 1816; those on the right, known as Mary Duncan Almshouses, were built in 1964 with the aid of an anonymous donation. The almshouses are now owned and managed by the trustees of the CITY OF OXFORD CHARITIES. They provide accommodation for twenty-two residents and a matron.

Street, George Edmund (*1824–1881*). The Essex-born son of a solicitor, at the age of seventeen he was accepted as a pupil by a Winchester architect. In 1840 he became an assistant in the firm of ecclesiological architects, Scott and Moffat, of which GEORGE GILBERT SCOTT was principal. In this practice he gained wide and valuable experience, and in 1849 he set up his own practice. About this time he was introduced to SAMUEL WILBERFORCE, BISHOP OF OXFORD, who appointed him architect to the diocese, a position in which he was required to supervise all work on ecclesiastical buildings. After travelling abroad to study churches in France and Germany, in 1852 he opened his office in BEAUMONT STREET, where among his assistants were Philip Webb and WILLIAM MORRIS. He was friendly with many of the Pre-Raphaelites and with other artists. Although he left Oxford in 1855 to practise in London, Street still retained the post of diocesan architect and was responsible for much church restoration. The small amount of his original work in Oxford is represented by St Ebbe's rectory (*see* ST EBBE'S CHURCH) and school, and by ST PHILIP AND ST JAMES, a church in the Gothic style from which he never deviated.

Stubbs, William (*1825–1901*). The son of a solicitor's impoverished widow, Stubbs attended Ripon Grammar School, where he came to the notice of Charles Thomas Longley, Bishop of Ripon and afterwards Archbishop of Canterbury, who persuaded THOMAS GAISFORD, Dean of Christ Church, to accept him into the college as a SERVITOR. At Christ Church he took a First in LITERAE HUMANIORES; but, since custom did not permit servitors to become Students of the college, he was offered and accepted a fellowship at Trinity. He was ordained in 1848 and left Oxford for parochial duties in Essex, where he remained until 1866. Although he had become by then a most distinguished historian, he was not elected as Chichele Professor of Modern History in 1862, Montagu Burrows being chosen instead. The following year he was again passed over when Walter Waddington Shirley became Professor of Ecclesiastical History; and it was not until the retirement of Goldwin Smith (1866) that he was given a chair at Oxford as Regius Professor of History. The first Regius Professor to be an ex-officio Fellow of Oriel College, Stubbs moved into KETTELL HALL, BROAD STREET.

Stubbs's lectures were never well attended; but his published work, which included his monumental *Constitutional History of England* (1873–8), was both enormous in volume and highly influential. He was consecrated Bishop of Chester in 1884 and Bishop of Oxford in 1888. He vainly endeavoured to persuade the Ecclesiastical Commissioners to sell the Bishop's house at Cuddesdon and to buy instead a house in Oxford. He took a close interest in university life, being a curator of the BODLEIAN LIBRARY, a Delegate to the OXFORD UNIVERSITY PRESS and a member of the Board of Modern History. The Bodleian possesses a portrait of him by Sir Hubert von Herkomer (1885).

Subfusc From the Latin *suffuscus*, dark brown. Clothing which members of the University are required to wear at degree and MATRICULATION ceremonies and at examinations. For male junior members the PROCTORS stipulate a dark suit, dark socks and shoes, a white shirt with white collar and white bow tie; and for women a white blouse, black tie, dark skirt or trousers, black stockings or tights, dark shoes or boots and, if required, a dark overcoat.

(*See also* ACADEMIC DRESS *and* GOWNS.)

Summer Eights   *see* EIGHTS.

Summer Fields   *Summerfield Road.* An independent Anglican boarding school for boys aged eight to thirteen, Summer Fields was established in 1864 by Mrs Archibald Maclaren (daughter of David Talboys, the radical Oxford printer and bookseller) and her husband, founder of the Oxford University gymnasium and superintendent of army gymnastics; they were actively encouraged by Alexander Macmillan, founder of the publishing house. The school motto is *Mens sana in corpore sano.* (In 1903 Summer Fields at St Leonard's, Sussex, was opened as a sister-school for boys whose parents wanted them to breathe sea rather than Thames Valley air.) The tradition of strenuous classical learning begun by Mrs Maclaren was continued by her sons-in-law, the Rev. Charles Williams, DD, and the Rev. Hugh Alington. The school remained in family hands until 1939. Since 1955 it has been a Charitable Trust with a board of governors. By 1904 the numbers had risen to 125 boys; during the 1930s they declined (to eighty boys in

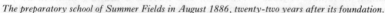

The preparatory school of Summer Fields in August 1886, twenty-two years after its foundation.

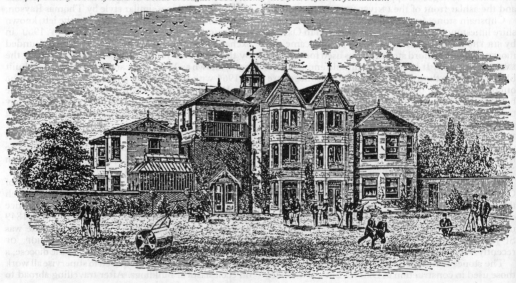

1939), but then steadily increased to 170 in 1964 and to 230 in 1984. Of 3318 boys who left the school between 1864 and 1984, 1296 went to Eton (393 as scholars), 217 to Winchester (64 scholars), 264 to Harrow (24 scholars), 218 to Radley (67 scholars), 142 to Wellington (14 scholars), 125 to Marlborough (29 scholars) and 956 to other schools (133 scholars).

The original house, built in 1820, pre-dates SUMMERTOWN, and from it the present buildings have developed with considerable expansion and modernisation in recent years. The site has 30 acres of gardens and playing fields, with 35 acres of farmland bordered by the River Cherwell (see THAMES). Of the long list of titles and distinctions for public service and in the arts, including two VCs and one GC, only a selection can be made here: Harold Macmillan, later EARL OF STOCKTON (1903–6); Field-Marshal Earl Wavell (1893–6); RONALD KNOX (1896–1900); Bernard Darwin (1887–9); Julian Grenfell (1898–1901); Hugh Dalton (1898–1901); Lord Redcliffe-Maud (1916–19); Lord Caccia (1916–19); Lord Cobham (1918–22); Lieutenant-General Lord Norrie (1905–7); G.O. (now Sir George) Allen (1912–15); Julian Amery (1928–32); Sir Nicholas Henderson (1930–3); Christopher Hollis (1911–14); Anthony Asquith (1913–16); John Lehmann (1917–21); Julian Slade (1939–43); Victor Pasmore (1918–23); and Ben and Nigel Nicolson (1923–8 and 1926–30 respectively). The writer L.A.G. Strong taught at the school from 1917 to 1930, as did a future Poet Laureate, C. Day-Lewis (in 1928), who commemorated the *'rus in urbe'* situation of the school in his poem 'First School', which ends:

Haycastles in the meadow,
Happiness in the air.
Oh, all the fields were summer then,
And there was time to spare.

(Usborne, Richard, ed., *A Century of Summer Fields*, 1964.)

Summertown A suburb lying across BANBURY ROAD some 2 miles north of CARFAX. House-building started here after the sale in 1820–1 of freehold farmland – forty-five lots to the east of Banbury Road and seventy-two to the west. On both sides the larger plots were bought by Oxford businessmen for investment. Houses varied from some dozen Regency-type villas with large gardens, all built before 1840, to cottages, many ill-built like 'a poor hut down in the fields'. Individuality and variety have since remained characteristic of Summertown. By 1832 the area had 112 houses and a population of 562. Building in that year of ST JOHN THE BAPTIST CHURCH off MIDDLE WAY with a new access road (Rogers Street, formerly CHURCH STREET) helped Summertown to become a self-contained village., The church, designed by Henry Jones Underwood and extended by GEORGE EDMUND STREET in 1858 and 1873, was demolished in 1924 and its fabric used in the construction of the church hall near the new parish church of ST MICHAEL AND ALL ANGELS. A Congregational chapel, opened in Middle Way in 1842, was transferred in 1893 to Banbury Road, where it is now the SUMMERTOWN UNITED REFORMED CHURCH.

Both church and chapel started schools, the Congregational one small and shortlived. The church

school, opened in 1848, continued in changing circumstances and in 1965 became identified with the new BISHOP KIRK SCHOOL in Middle Way. Summertown was popular for transient schools for girls, but one for boys begun in 1864 still flourishes as SUMMER FIELDS. Northern House, built in 1822 in SOUTH PARADE, became in 1840 the first home of the Diocesan Training School for Teachers, which in 1851 moved to larger premises and so became the nucleus of Culham Church of England Training College for Schoolmasters. Northern House is today a special school managed by the County Council.

By 1881 houses had increased to 282 and Summertown's population totalled 704. East of Banbury Road new roads had been adapted from farm lanes; to the west, as well as Rogers Street, Hobson Road and Grove Street had been added by the middle of the century. Middle Way had already existed as a farm track. With increasing pressure on housing in Oxford, the city began to look towards Summertown and in 1889 the northern municipal boundary was extended to include what was then the whole parish of Summertown: in the south a line from Moreton Road to ARISTOTLE LANE; in the north the line of Hernes Road and SQUITCHEY LANE, and from the Cherwell (see THAMES) to the CANAL. (The ecclesiastical parish boundaries have been adjusted five times since then.) Banbury Road and WOODSTOCK ROAD were tidied up. Contaminated wells were closed and 'the Oxford water' laid on; drainage and sewerage works were undertaken; roads were paved and surfaced where there had been 'much mud'; and street gas-lighting was extended. Developers immediately became interested.

South of South Parade the only buildings were ST EDWARD'S SCHOOL, built in 1873 on a 5-acre site at the corner with Woodstock Road and, on one acre at the Banbury Road corner, the vicarage of 1878; the latter, designed by J.D. Sedding, was replaced in 1924 by a more modest house next to St Michael and All Angels. In 1893, on the remaining 58 acres, five new roads were made with provision for over 300 houses laid out in plots by the OXFORD INDUSTRIAL AND PROVIDENT LAND AND BUILDING SOCIETY. These included thirty-one two- and three-storey family houses on the west frontage of Banbury Road, which were built over the course of fourteen years, gradually and individually to be changed into Summertown's shopping parade. New houses rather than shops continued on the opposite side of Banbury Road, south of the 1822–30 development.

In 1895 Francis Twining (see TWINING'S) bought 50 acres further north on the east side of Banbury Road, which, together with the Banbury Road frontage, gave space for some 350 houses and still allowed Twining to present the land for the new parish church. To serve Summertown's increasing population, the Roman Catholic church of ST GREGORY AND ST AUGUSTINE was opened in 1912 in Woodstock Road. The last of this stage of Summertown development was the sale in 1925 of the 11-acre estate between Hobson Road and Squitchey Lane, across the Middle Way to Banbury Road. It centred on the house called Summerhill (No. 333 Banbury Road), built in 1823 and much altered to become the home of the Ryman family, who lived there for eighty-five years. It is now the FREEMASONS' HALL. The estate was advertised as 'suitable for medium sized residences for which there is a keen demand'. The demand was met by the provision of two new roads and sixty-four houses.

Except for the building trade, there was little in Summertown that could be called industry. The notable exception was the establishment in 1919 of the Osberton Radiators factory on the south side of Osberton Road, taken over by Morris Motors in 1929 (*see* MOTOR CARS) and moved to a large site between Woodstock Road and the canal. Also in 1919, Oliver & Gurden's 'Famous Oxford Cakes' set up a bakery at the south-west end of Middle Way. It proved very successful, employing 150 local staff, selling its goods all over southern England and exporting as well. It was sold in 1961 and closed in 1975. The factory is now used as stores for BLACKWELL'S, the booksellers. The city was still in need of building land and again acquired it by a boundary extension in 1928. Nothing north of the 1889 line, however, has ever been regarded as part of Summertown. It was no longer a village but comfortably settled into its role as a middle-class residential area until the development upheaval of the 1960s, when the city wanted office space as well as housing. The first clearance was at the corner of South Parade and Banbury Road – the large house called Southlawn, built in 1822 in spacious gardens at No. 267 Banbury Road, was replaced in 1962 by a block named Prama House, containing a supermarket and shops with offices above. This pattern was followed between 1964 and 1971 by the clearance on the east side of Banbury Road of a garage and all thirty of the original small houses (some of which had also been used as shops). The sole survivor was the pair of semi-detached cottages built in 1824 at No. 258, which in 1888 had become the DEWDROP INN. Four more blocks of shops and offices were built extending south to Diamond Place. On the other side of the road the garage that replaced the old vicarage was also converted into shops and offices. In the same period purpose-built flats were put up to accommodate displaced householders, often replacing a single large house and garden. A branch library was established in South Parade (with the loss of six cottages) in 1961, and in 1971 a community building, (the Ferry Centre), the FERRY POOL, and a public car park filled old allotment garden space.

Summertown now houses BBC Local Radio (RADIO OXFORD), and the international headquarters of OXFAM. All high-street banks are represented, and so are building societies, estate agents, insurance companies, schools – state and private – and offices of all varieties, as well as the DELEGACY OF LOCAL EXAMINATIONS – the first overspill of the University into Summertown.

Many well-known Oxford business names have been connected with Summertown. James Ryman of Summerhill had an art-dealer's shop at No. 23 HIGH STREET, over which his name remained for 105 years (1863–1968), and his nephew James Ryman-Hall, who succeeded him, was deeply involved in local politics. It was in 1835 in St John Baptist Church that Sarah Elliston married John Cavell; their names thus united were familiar from 1835 until 1973, when their Magdalen Street store of ELLISTON & CAVELL was renamed Debenhams. Equally well known was Owen Grimbly, founding partner of GRIMBLY HUGHES, grocers in CORNMARKET from 1852 until the business was sold in 1959 and closed in 1963. Grimbly lived at the Lodge in Middle Way for fifty years until his death in 1901. He was succeeded there for a two-year

tenancy by SIR WALTER GRAY, who was MAYOR of Oxford in 1889 and three times subsequently. T.H. Kingerlee (*see* KINGERLEE LTD) followed him in 1898 and 1911. His firm built to his design the new Congregational Church in Banbury Road in 1893. Among other residents of Summertown were Francis Twining, the successful grocer and land speculator, who was a city councillor for fifty years, and was elected Mayor in 1905 (*see* TWINING'S); and E.J. Brooks, his successor as Mayor, who gave his name to a well-known firm of land agents.

(Fasnacht, Ruth, *Summertown since 1820*, Oxford, 1977; Badcock, John, *The Making of a Regency Village*, Oxford, 1983.)

Summertown United Reformed Church
Banbury Road, Summertown. The modern Congregationalist movement in Oxford began in 1830 with a breakaway from NEW ROAD BAPTIST CHURCH led by William Cousins and Samuel Collingwood. Services started in SUMMERTOWN in 1838, apparently to counter the growing influence of the Tractarians (*see* OXFORD MOVEMENT). In 1840 a chapel was opened in MIDDLE WAY and, despite the fact that Summertown was still a village, had a large congregation. In 1894 the new church was opened in BANBURY ROAD. Its congregation was said to average 200 at the turn of the century, and it received many new members when GEORGE STREET Congregationalist Church closed in 1933. The building is Gothic, mainly in brick but with some stone, and was built by a local Congregationalist builder, T.H. Kingerlee (*see* KINGERLEE LTD). In 1972 the Congregationalist and Presbyterian Churches were united to form the United Reformed Church.

In the latter part of his life, C.H. Dodd (1884–1973) was a member of the congregation. An eminent New Testament scholar, he directed the translation of the *New English Bible* and inspired the following limerick:

> I think it extremely odd
> That a little Professor named Dodd
> Should spell, if you please,
> His name with three D's
> When one is sufficient for God.

A young member of the congregation once concluded his reading from the *New English Bible* with the words, 'Thanks be to Dodd.'

Sunnymead
The north-eastern part of SUMMERTOWN, comprising Hernes Road, Hernes Crescent, Islip Road, Harpes Road and Water Eaton Road. The estate was developed in the late 19th and early 20th centuries by Owen Grimbly of GRIMBLY HUGHES, the Oxford grocers. Sunnymead House, No. 380 BANBURY ROAD, was a large Victorian neo-Gothic house which later became a private school and was demolished in 1972 for the building of Ritchie Court (Oxford Architects Partnership), a block of flats for retired people.

Swimming
Bathing and swimming in the THAMES and Cherwell (*see* THAMES) have always been popular pastimes in the summer. Until the second half of the 20th century there were few swimming pools in Oxford. Most young 'Dragons' at the DRAGON SCHOOL and the boys of SUMMER FIELDS learned to swim in the

Cherwell, having to pass the clothes test by swimming the river in sports kit. Men could swim in the nude at PARSON'S PLEASURE, and a family bathing place for women was at DAMES' DELIGHT. There were several other official swimming or bathing places, the first public one authorised by the City Council at Fiddler's Island, near PORT MEADOW, in 1852. Another, at Tumbling Bay, was recommended in 1853 and extended in 1866. Long Bridges bathing place was open at least from 1909. Between Lucerne Road and Lonsdale Road are many river gardens, some with boat houses, with frontages to the Cherwell where the owners and their friends swam from the landing stages.

MERTON STREET indoor swimming baths were opened in 1869. Between 1924 and 1938 they were leased by the city from the University for teaching schoolchildren to swim. HINKSEY PARK open-air

swimming pool was laid out by the city in 1934. When use of the Merton Street baths ceased, the TEMPLE COWLEY SWIMMING POOL was opened in 1938; it was enlarged and reconstructed in 1985–6. The indoor FERRY POOL was opened in 1976. Most of the larger schools in Oxford now have private pools, as have many private houses. The first hotel to have its own was the Moat House at the WOLVERCOTE roundabout, the pool and sports complex being opened in 1986.

Swyndelstock A tavern sited on the corner of QUEEN STREET and ST ALDATE'S. First mentioned in 1279, it was named after the wooden swinging part of a flail used for beating flax. It was the scene of the outbreak of the ST SCHOLASTICA'S DAY riot in 1355 (*see also* RIOTS). It became the Mermaid in the late 17th century but was pulled down in 1708.

Tackley's Inn *106 and 107 High Street*. Built about 1320 by Roger le Mareschal, who held the living of Tackley, near Woodstock. In 1324 it was acquired from him by Adam de Brome as a home for the scholars of 'the House of the Blessed Mary in Oxford', otherwise Oriel College, who still own both buildings, which originally formed one large tenement. It is, in the words of Dr W.A. Pantin, 'one of the very few examples of a medieval academic hall still surviving sufficiently for us to be able to trace its plan and arrangement. It contains what is probably the finest domestic crypt or vaulted cellar in Oxford, a good 15th-century roof, and a good, though mutilated, 14th-century window'. A row of 5 shops faced the HIGH STREET over the vaulted cellar, which, with the refectory hall at the back used by the scholars, is all that remains of the original building. The roof beams of the latter were replaced, probably in the early 16th century. Part of the cellar and the entire refectory hall are now incorporated in the offices of Abbey National at No. 107; the refectory hall was also used as the restaurant of the Tackley Hall Hotel.

In 1438 the building was divided in two, the eastern part being known as The Tavern, while the western part was leased to Richard Buckely and became known as Buckely Hall – a grammar hall recognised by the University. When this closed, the hall and shops in front were leased in 1549 to Garbrand Harkes, a protestant refugee from Holland, who set up business as a bookseller and used the cellar as a wine shop. This use continued until around the end of the 17th century, when the premises seem to have become a COFFEE HOUSE, occupied by William Puffett.

(Pantin, W.A., 'Tackley's Inn, Oxford', *Oxoniensia*, vii, 1942; Woodhouse, Marcus, *Medieval Hall from the 14th century to the present*.)

Taphouse & Son The music shop of C. Taphouse & Son Ltd was at No. 3 MAGDALEN STREET until 1982 when the premises were taken over by Debenhams, who had had shop premises on both sides of it. The firm then moved to a new shop in the WESTGATE CENTRE, but the business closed down in 1984. It had been established in 1857 and had shops in PARK END STREET and BROAD STREET before moving to Magdalen Street in 1859. Known to generations of music lovers in Oxford, Taphouse's was the main ticket agency for theatres and concerts.

Taunt, Henry (*1842–1922*). Born in Penson's Gardens, his interest in photography was stimulated when he joined the staff of the Oxford photographer Edward Bracher in 1856. Taunt was given the outdoor work and, when Bracher sold his business to Wheeler and Day in 1863, Taunt stayed on as photographic manager. Some five years later he set up in business on his own, publishing a shilling series of photographic views of Oxford and its neighbourhood, described in the press as 'amongst the best specimens of the photographic art that we have ever seen'. The success of these views enabled Taunt to open a new shop at No. 33 CORNMARKET. His reputation was such that he became official photographer to the Oxford Architectural and Historical Society in 1871, and in the following year published *A New Map of the River Thames*. The book was an immediate success and ran

Henry Taunt, the Oxford photographer, with his horse and dog c.1910.

William Radclyffe's engraving after Frederick Mackenzie's drawing of the Taylor Institution, completed in 1844, with the Ashmolean Museum behind.

to several editions. In 1874 he moved to larger premises at Nos 9–10 BROAD STREET, but when the lease ran out in 1894 he moved to No. 41, later 34, HIGH STREET. His houseboat, which he also used for his photography business, was a familiar sight on the THAMES. In 1906 he gave up his High Street premises and conducted the business solely from his house in COWLEY ROAD, which he called Rivera and in the grounds of which he had set up a photographic and printing works. They included a large handicraft room where thousands of his glass negatives were stored. He died at Rivera on 4 November 1922. Many of his early photographs of Oxford scenes have been reproduced in illustrated books, most notably in Malcolm Graham's *Henry Taunt of Oxford* (1973).

Taylor-Burton Rooms An extension to the PLAYHOUSE built in GLOUCESTER STREET. In 1966 Richard Burton and Elizabeth Taylor performed Marlowe's *Doctor Faustus* at the theatre in support of a fund to provide scenery workshop space and student rehearsal rooms on the theatre premises. In 1970 a further donation by Burton and Taylor enabled the theatre to build the extension, which was completed in September 1974. The top-floor rehearsal room is now used as a student studio theatre.

Taylor Institution The Taylorian, as it is commonly known, was established in 1845 with a bequest from Sir Robert Taylor. Born in 1714, Taylor was originally a sculptor but later practised as an architect. He built additions to the Bank of England and Lincoln's Inn, and became Surveyor to the Admiralty, Greenwich Hospital and the Board of Works. He was knighted in 1783 when he was Sheriff of London. When he died in 1788 he left the residue of his estate to the University of Oxford for the purchase of freehold land for the erection of a building and 'for establishing a foundation for the teaching and improving the European languages'. The reason for this bequest is not known and in fact his son, Michael

Angelo Taylor, disputed it. The result was that the bequest did not pass to the University until Michael Angelo's death in 1834, when the University agreed to accept a sum of £65,000 in settlement.

The University had also received a legacy from Dr Francis Randolph, Principal of ST ALBAN HALL, for the erection of a building to hold the Pomfret statues and other works of art belonging to the University. Dr Randolph had died in 1796, but it was not until 1839 that the University was ready to build. An architectural competition set up for the design of a building to house both institutions was won by Charles Robert Cockerell, the son of Samuel Pepys Cockerell who had been Sir Robert Taylor's pupil. Cockerell designed a building in the Greek classical manner in conformity with the rules of the competition. The Randolph or University Galleries were to occupy the main part of the building facing BEAUMONT STREET and the Taylor Institution the right-hand wing on the corner of ST GILES'. The building was completed in 1844. The east wing, facing St Giles', has four giant Ionic columns carrying female statues, designed by W.G. Nicholl, representing France, Italy, Germany and Spain, whose languages are the main ones studied in the Taylorian. The arms of Sir Robert Taylor are in the centre. The whole of the original cost of the Taylorian building was met from accumulated income from the Taylor bequest. An extension along St Giles' was built by T.H. Hughes in 1932 in keeping with the original. The words 'Institutio Tayloriana' are carved on the stone of Cockerell's building facing St Giles', and the simple word 'Taylorian' on the newer extension.

The building houses the lecture theatre and offices as well as the main Taylorian Library, which contains over 260,000 volumes in the principal European languages; in addition, there are large collections of books on the language, literature and history of various Slavonic countries, and a collection of Icelandic and Scandinavian books. The Taylorian also accommodates the Modern Languages Faculty Library, founded in 1961.

449

Telephone Exchange *Speedwell Street*. Built in 1954–7 by the Ministry of Works. In 1986 a new digital telephone exchange was opened in the building. Called the Digital Main Switching Unit (DMSU), it is the computer-controlled link between local exchanges and British Telecom's digital national trunk network. The offices, in Telephone House, PARADISE STREET, were built in 1965–6 by Donald Rowswell & Partners of Croydon.

Templars Square Formerly called the COWLEY CENTRE it was renamed Templars Square in 1989 after the Knights Templar, who gave their name to TEMPLE COWLEY. In 1989 the old Cowley Centre was refurbished and covered over with a glass roof.

Temple Cowley Swimming Pool Opened in 1938 and rebuilt in 1985–6 at a cost of £3 million. The new complex has three separate pools. The main pool is 25 metres long and 18 metres wide, with eight swimming lanes; alongside is a children's pool; and there is a diving pool, 3.8 metres deep. The complex also includes a sauna suite, lounge, fitness room, and a large multi-purpose room for keep-fit classes, aerobics, gymnastics, meetings and lectures.

Templeton College Incorporated in 1965 as the Oxford Centre for Management Studies. It was renamed Templeton College in 1984 after receiving a benefaction from John M. Templeton, a former Rhodes Scholar (*see* RHODES SCHOLARSHIPS). The college buildings are on a 37-acre site at Kennington on the lower slopes of Hinksey Hill.

Tennis Courts *see* REAL TENNIS.

Terms, University Originally there were four terms in the academic year at Oxford University, confirmed in the LAUDIAN CODE. The first, or Michaelmas Term was from 10 October to 17 December; the second, or Hilary Term was from 14 January to the eve of Palm Sunday; the third, or Easter Term was from the 10th day after Easter to the Thursday before Whit Sunday; and the fourth, or Trinity Term was from the Wednesday after Trinity Sunday to the Saturday after the ACT. The Easter Term was dropped in 1918 and there are now three terms. Michaelmas Term begins on and includes 1 October and ends on and includes 17 December; Hilary Term begins on and includes 7 January and ends on and includes 25 March or the Saturday before Palm Sunday, whichever is the earlier; and Trinity Term begins on and includes 20 April or the Wednesday after Easter, whichever is the later, and ends on and includes 6 July.

Each term consists of a period of eight weeks, beginning on a Sunday, and known as Full Term, during which lectures are given. Each week of Full Term is referred to as First Week, Second Week, and so on. Long Vacation runs from the end of Trinity Term to the start of Michaelmas Term. The Law Terms for sittings of the COURTS are also named Michaelmas, Hilary and Trinity. (Hilary Term is named after St Hilary (*c*.315–*c*.368), who was Bishop of Poitiers. His feast day is 13 (formerly 14) January.)

Terrae Filius For a long time this licensed buffoon was an integral part of the University's degree

CEREMONIES. Appointed by the PROCTORS, he 'delighted contemporaries' in C.E. Mallet's words, 'with solemn fooling at least as early as Shakespearian days'. Names are known from 1591 to 1763 (when the last appointment was made) and fifteen of their speeches are preserved; it was not unknown for them to be expelled or to have to make public apology. Lancelot Addison, for example, a Queen's College BATTELER apologised on his knees in CONGREGATION in 1658 on account of '*pudenda illa obscaenitate*'. A proposed speech of 1713 was prevented and publicly burned.

Many years – 1707–12, 1714–33, for example – seemingly went by without any public celebration of the ACT (*see also* ENCAENIA). Writing in 1733, Thomas Hearne says that Terrae Filius made 'an ingenious witty satyrical speech, most of it in English, in which he exposed vice and immorality, and discovered the flagrant crimes of many loose Academicians, particularly the abominable Acts of some Heads of Houses'. Most notorious in this area, though not himself formally Terrae Filius, was Nicholas Amhurst, elected a scholar of St John's in 1716, who in due course was sent down. In 1721 he began to publish, under the pseudonym of Terrae Filius, the scurrilous biweekly papers which later appeared as a *Secret History of the University of Oxford*. He was imprisoned in 1737, and died in poverty at Twickenham in 1742 (*see* MAGAZINES).

Thames The river Thames is the reason for Oxford's existence on its particular site, and indeed gave it its name. Centuries before Chaucer's clerk came there to study 'Aristotle and his philosophie', the peasants of the broad valley drove their cattle from one flat meadow to another across shallows in a meandering stream and called the crossing-place Oxenford, so recorded in the Anglo-Saxon Chronicle of 912. The river's name is, of course, even older. Julius Caesar called it TAMESIS, which must have been the Latin approximation to the Celtic name said to derive from two words: *tam* for 'broad' and *wys* meaning 'water'. Uniquely among rivers it now has two names: for most of its length it is the Thames; round about Oxford only it is called the Isis, a pseudo-classical name which was used by John Leland, writing about 1535, and which appeared officially in a statute of George II in 1751.

At the time of the Norman Conquest the river above and around the position where Oxford now stands was a network of narrow streams, which in a dry season were reduced to a trickle and in wet weather overflowed to flood the surrounding flats; and from the earliest times fishermen and millers constructed dams to trap fish or to build up a head of water from weirs to drive their wheels. The principal navigable stream in those times followed the Pot stream upriver past Walton Ford and GODSTOW. (Not until 1790 with the opening of Osney Lock was the present navigation stream along the old Osney mill stream established.) At first the building of the flash-locks and weirs must have been an aid to the passage of small craft, deepening and stabilising the river's flow. On payment of a toll the miller would open his sluice and 'flash' the boat downstream, or let it be hauled upstream. By the 12th century important religious foundations, including ST FRIDESWIDE'S PRIORY and OSENEY ABBEY, had been established and Oxford had become a place of pilgrimage. In 1249 University

Henry Taunt's photograph of a coach and six on the frozen Thames in February 1895, with college barges in the background.

College was founded, to be followed by several others in rapid succession. By the reign of Henry III Oxford was a walled city (*see* CITY WALL). Since roads were impassable in bad weather or for heavy loads, food, merchandise and building materials for the greatly increasing POPULATION had to be carried by river, and the great number of locks and weirs were felt to be a serious impediment to navigation.

Through several centuries numerous Acts were passed to establish and improve conditions for river traffic both on the upper Thames to Oxford and from Oxford down to London. In 1197 a charter of Richard invested the care of the river in the Mayor and Corporation of the City of London, and ordered the removal of all weirs on the Thames. But this seems to have been ineffective above Staines. In 1274 the Sheriff of Oxfordshire and Berkshire was ordered to widen the river, narrowed by weirs, to allow barges to travel between London and Oxford, but complaints about weirs and high tolls demanded by millers continued in the 14th century. However, the river above Oxford was passable, and in the 16th century loads of hay, wood, stone and slate reached the wharf owned by the city at HYTHE BRIDGE. Payments for the use of the wharf went to maintain the river and its banks.

An Act of 1605, superseded by another of 1623, established the Oxford–Burcot Commission, with powers to tax both the city and the University to make the river navigable between the two points. The commission built pound-locks at Culham, Sandford and IFFLEY, and constructed a wharf and wet-dock at FOLLY BRIDGE. Progress was slow; the city delayed paying its tax; but eventually the first barge reached Oxford in 1635 (*see also* TRANSPORT).

In 1757 a new body, the Thames Navigation Commission, was set up and for the first time controlled the whole river west of Staines. It bought all locks, weirs and tolls belonging to the Oxford–Burcot Commission. Osney Lock and Godstow Cut were opened in 1790, and the new navigable channel established through Osney. In 1824 Folly Bridge, which had long been an impediment to barges, was rebuilt with a new navigation arch, the old tower, or 'folly', was removed and a new navigation channel was dug. The flash-lock there was replaced by a pound-lock, but by 1829 the wharf was no longer used. It was sold to John Salter and in 1858 became the site of SALTER BROS boatyard. The pound-lock was removed only in 1884. Finally, in 1866, jurisdiction over the whole river from Cricklade to Teddington Lock passed from the Corporation of London to a new body, the Thames Conservancy Board, which was henceforth responsible for all activities on the river.

Already, with the coming of the RAILWAY in 1844, the nature of these activities had changed irrevocably. The river was no longer needed for the transport of goods. The Oxford CANAL, opened in 1790 and intended to connect Oxford with the industrial north, fell out of use and now ends at a brick wall beside Hythe Bridge. Better roads carried passengers and goods between London and Oxford. The present MAGDALEN BRIDGE was completed in 1779. The Isis was given over to sport and pleasure. ROWING had always been popular at the University and no doubt there had always been light-hearted boat races – or rather, because the river is too narrow for an ordinary race, boat chases: a sort of game of tag in which one boat tried to catch up and 'bump' another (*see* BUMPING RACES). The first organised race, starting above Iffley, seems to have taken place in 1815 between only two colleges – Brasenose and Jesus, though in *Vanity Fair* Thackeray has Bute Crawley stroking the Christ Church boat in what must have been the 1790s. In following years more and more colleges took part. The course was set between Iffley Lock to a point just below Folly Bridge; and, by an unwritten law, college boats merely training on this stretch took precedence of all other craft, as young Mr Verdant Green, in Cuthbert Bede's novel, discovered when his small 'tub' was almost run down by the University eight at practice. The two annual series of bumping races (TORPIDS, for aspiring oarsmen, in Hilary Term and EIGHTS WEEK in May) became the chief athletic events, and Eights Week certainly became the chief social event, of the Oxford year, the racing being watched from the college BARGES at the edge of CHRIST CHURCH MEADOW and by enthusiasts running along the towpath on the other side, shouting encouragement. Perhaps the enthusiasm of today is not as intense as it must have been about 1911, when even the enchantments of ZULEIKA DOBSON could not succeed in deflecting the Judas eight from their immediate aim to bump Univ. and earn a BUMP SUPPER with the further hope of a succession of bumps to bring them to Head of the River. Upstream from Folly Bridge there was less strenuous boating. In 1862 CHARLES DODGSON and a fellow don from Christ Church rowed with the three young daughters of DEAN HENRY LIDDELL to Godstow for a picnic, and this crew was there rewarded by the first unfolding of the dream story of *Alice's Adventures in Wonderland* (*see* ALICE).

Oxford's other river, the Cherwell, has its source in the cellar of a farmhouse in Northamptonshire and joins the Isis below Christ Church Meadow. It has never been used for commerce; history seems to have passed it by except for a brief period during the CIVIL WAR when the New Cut was made to strengthen Oxford's defences on the London side. It is too narrow and shallow for serious rowing and has been reserved for more individual pleasures. Above Magdalen Bridge a dammed-up pool forms the bathing place called PARSON'S PLEASURE. Beyond the little bridge in the University PARKS is a boat-house where punts and canoes can be hired for a leisurely passage upstream or an even more leisurely afternoon moored beneath the willows in some backwater (*see* CHERWELL BOAT HOUSE and PUNTING). In the 1920s one could find the nests of reed-buntings, sedge-warblers, reed-warblers and white-throats, watch kingfishers or water-rats and voles about their tiny affairs along the banks. Only perhaps on MAY MORNING, or the morning after a COMMEMORATION BALL, did the louder human voices of picnic parties disturb the peace. But soon came the portable gramophone and now the transistor radio to drown birdsong, and in summer there are more and more punts out, often forming a procession along the stream. Only in late autumn until early spring does the Cherwell return to its lost peace.

Thames Street Formerly a much narrower road than it now is, and also originally a cul-de-sac, ending at Clay Cross coal wharf. It has been in existence at least since 1850. After the street had been transformed into a wide thoroughfare connecting ST ALDATE'S to OXPENS ROAD in 1968, the first person to travel along it after the opening was the Queen. When told of this by the chairman of the City Planning Committee, Her Majesty replied, 'I am glad it served some useful purpose.' Now that QUEEN STREET and CORNMARKET are closed to through-traffic, Thames Street is the main east–west route through the city. On the corner of St Aldate's is the old South Oxford School, built in 1910 by W.H. Castle. On the south side there was for

some years a derelict area on which were built the foundations of a proposed hotel; but this was never completed, housing being erected instead.

Theatre In the early 16th century the performance of plays in Oxford had become a part of student life. It is recorded that on the occasion of the Queen's visit in 1566 a wall gave way during the performance of a play in Christ Church, killing several people. The University, however, was beginning to take the view that the production of plays distracted students from their studies and in 1584 a University statute prohibited such performances within the city. 'Plays and interludes' were, however, traditionally put on during the ceremony of the ACT. Although the staging of plays during term time was not allowed, Shakespeare's company, the King's Players, came to Oxford six times between 1604 and 1613. Plays were usually performed in inns or their courtyards; the KING'S ARMS in HOLYWELL STREET became the most popular place in the 17th century. After the Restoration the TOWN HALL and its courtyard were also frequently used for both amateur and professional performances, as well as the many tennis courts, some of which had been roofed in (*see* REAL TENNIS).

In 1799 Henry Thornton set up a theatre in the real tennis court at Merton College, transferring the theatre to the tennis court at Christ Church in 1807. His son-in-law, Richard Barnett, opened a theatre in 1833 in the tennis court at St Mary Hall, next to Oriel College. He abandoned this in 1836 for a purpose-built theatre in Red Lion Yard at the rear of the site of the present theatre. The staging of plays during term time was still forbidden; but attitudes were changing and in 1880 BENJAMIN JOWETT decided, after seeing a play performed by members of his college, Balliol, that the Victoria Theatre should be closed and a new theatre built for the performance of plays by professionals, amateurs and members of the University. A company was formed to raise the finance and in 1886 the New Theatre opened with a performance of *Twelfth Night* given by the OXFORD UNIVERSITY DRAMATIC SOCIETY (OUDS). The present theatre on the same site is the APOLLO, Oxford's largest theatre, with seating for more than 1850. The University theatre is the PLAYHOUSE in BEAUMONT STREET, with seating for about 670. The TAYLOR–BURTON ROOMS adjoining it – a valuable addition, with offices, workshops and the Burton Room, seating fifty. The Pegasus Theatre in Magdalen Road was opened in 1974. It is the home of the Oxford Youth Theatre and has seating for 120. The OLD FIRE STATION ARTS CENTRE in GEORGE STREET, used for scenery painting, etc., by the Playhouse, was converted for use for theatrical performances in 1973, and a subsequent venture for the performing arts was the ST PAUL'S ARTS CENTRE in WALTON STREET, opened in August 1985 with seating for 200–300. St Catherine's College has an open-air amphitheatre where plays are performed in the summer. The OUDS used the Playhouse for most of its major productions, but has held some notable ones in the summer in college gardens.

The gardens also provide settings for the performances of Shakespeare every summer by the City of Oxford Theatre Guild; these were started in 1955 by the Oxford Council for Drama and Music, an association of local dramatic societies and individual members interested in drama (renamed the City of Oxford Theatre Guild some ten years later). Their first production of open-air Shakespeare was *The*

Merry Wives of Windsor, performed in 1955 in the garden of Worcester College. The Oxford Operatic Society has been in existence under one name or another since 1907. The City of Oxford Amateur Dramatic Club was founded in 1907 and in the 1920s split into two separate societies – the City of Oxford Amateur Dramatic Society and the City of Oxford Operatic Society. In 1929 the two amalgamated again and became known as the City of Oxford Dramatic and Operatic Society. From that date performances were usually given in the old Oxford Playhouse in WOODSTOCK ROAD, and the society continued until the outbreak of the Second World War. Reformed in 1946, it presented shows in the Town Hall until 1950, when it moved to the Oxford Playhouse. The society continued to present major productions at the Playhouse, except for two years when there was a move to the Apollo Theatre. It has also presented shows at ST EDWARD'S SCHOOL theatre.

There are several University societies apart from OUDS. The best known of these are the OXFORD UNIVERSITY OPERA CLUB and the Oxford University Experimental Theatre Club (ETC) (*see* OXFORD UNIVERSITY DRAMATIC SOCIETY). Most colleges also have their own dramatic societies.

One of the best-known plays set in Oxford is *Charley's Aunt*, a farce by Brandon Thomas which was first performed in 1892 and was at one time running simultaneously in forty-eight theatres in twenty-two languages.

The year 1991 saw the re-opening of the Playhouse and the opening of a new 180-seat auditorium at the Old Fire Station Studio Theatre in George Street.

(Ranger, Paul, 'The Theatres of Oxford: Forty Years of Family Management', *Oxoniensia* liv, 1989, pp. 393–8.)

Thornton's Bookshop Founded in September 1835 by Joseph Thornton, who started business in a small shop in MAGDALEN STREET. In 1840 he moved to No. 51 HIGH STREET and in 1853 back to Magdalen Street. Ten years later, the business was again moved, this time to No. 10 BROAD STREET, and finally, in 1870, to No. 11. The business passed from father to son until 1983 when, then owned by John Thornton, it was amalgamated with another Oxford bookshop, Holdan Books, specialists in European languages.

During the first 150 years of its existence, the clientele of Thornton's consisted mainly of members of the University and of other educational institutions throughout the British Isles and all parts of the world. A feature of the firm's activities since the 1890s has been the circulation of catalogues. Until the amalgamation with Holdan Books its premises remained much as they had been in the early part of the century, but extensive alterations were carried out between 1983 and 1985 to meet fire regulations. The whole of the firm's refurbished premises are now open again.

Tidmarsh Lane The present lane runs from New Road to Quaking Bridge (*see* BRIDGES), although in ANTHONY WOOD's time it may have continued further north into Worcester Place. It takes its name from Richard Tidmarsh, one of the first leaders of the Baptists in Oxford, described in 1681 as the 'Preaching Anabaptist Tanner' (*see* DISSENTERS). His house, where he lived for almost twenty years, was on the west side of the lane in the part which was pulled down in 1770 to make way for NEW ROAD. Tidmarsh came to Oxford in 1644 when he was apprenticed to John Walter, a tanner. It is noteworthy that the clerk who wrote his apprenticeship indentures spelled the name 'Titmouse', having presumably misheard the pronunciation of a surname not usual in Oxford at that time. Tidmarsh was in fact often spelled Titmarsh. It may have been because of later mishearings that the road came in time to be called Titmouse Lane, as it remained until 1953. In 1672 Richard Tidmarsh's house was licensed as a meeting house for the Anabaptists. In 1653 he was elected a city councillor and was later a chamberlain on the MAYOR's Council. He then became a bailiff before leaving Oxford in 1690. The lane itself was probably used by Baptist worshippers until the RIOTS of 1715. Baptisms were certainly held in the nearby THAMES, although the exact spot is not recorded. The REV. H.E. SALTER, Oxford's first authority on Oxford street-names, said in 1936 that he hoped the lane would be changed back to its old name of Tidmarsh. However, it was not altered until 1953 after the then Minister of the NEW ROAD BAPTIST CHURCH had asked that the original name be restored on the occasion of the 300th anniversary of the Baptist Church as a tribute to 'the pioneer of religious freedom in Oxford, a city which was slow to recognise Dissenters'. The change was not universally welcomed by Oxford people, who had associated the former name with the 'bird', though others approved of it, pointing out that 'titmouse' also meant a petty, insignificant person or thing. An architect with a poor knowledge of natural history wrote to the *Oxford Mail* (*see* NEWSPAPERS) in about 1969 suggesting that the original Titmouse had been 'renamed Tidmarsh by the Puritans presumably because of an aversion to rodents'. In 1983 a councillor for the ward caused confusion by suggesting that the city fathers had made a mistake thirty years earlier and had named the road for the wrong Tidmarsh. He withdrew his protest, however, when assured that Tidmarsh had been both a tanner and a Baptist.

The most distinguished building in the lane is the 1956 University Surveyor's Office by Jack Lankester, Surveyor to the University, and N. Riley. It was originally a malthouse and has been well converted, retaining the old hoist. Opposite are modern concrete offices of the County Council designed by Albert Smith, the County Architect.

Tolkien, John Ronald Reuel (*1892–1973*). Born in South Africa, the son of a bank manager whose forebears had emigrated from Germany, Tolkien was educated at King Edward VI's School, Birmingham, and, as an exhibitioner, at Exeter College. While in hospital recovering from trench fever during the First World War, he began to write the stories which were later to appear in the posthumously published *The Silmarillion*. On his return to Oxford he worked for a time on the *New English Dictionary* (*see* OXFORD ENGLISH DICTIONARY); and, after a time spent as Reader in English Language at the University of Leeds, he was appointed Rawlinson and Bosworth Professor of Anglo-Saxon at Oxford, where, with C.S. LEWIS, he did much to improve the study of language in the English faculty. His deeply influential lecture 'Beowulf: the Monsters and the Critics' was delivered in 1936, the year in which his celebrated book *The Hobbit*, based on an invented mythology, was accepted for publication. Published in 1937, it was illustrated by Tolkien himself and his original drawings and paintings for the book can now be seen in the BODLEIAN

LIBRARY. *The Hobbit* was followed by *The Lord of the Rings* (1954–5 in three volumes: *The Fellowship of the Ring, The Two Towers* and *The Return of the Ring*) which Tolkien read aloud in instalments to Lewis and other members of THE INKLINGS. In 1945 he was appointed Merton Professor of English Language and Literature. By 1968 the importunities of the numerous admirers of his remarkable fiction drove him from Oxford to a house in Bournemouth, where he lived in seclusion until 1971 when, on the death of his wife, he returned to Oxford to rooms in Merton College, of which he was elected an Honorary Fellow.

Torpids College BUMPING RACES held in the Hilary Term. The word 'torpid' originally referred to college second eights, and is believed to have arisen because the early races for these eights were not taken very seriously, and the crews were considered torpid or lethargic (*see* EIGHTS). Races for these crews are thought to have started as early as 1827, but on an informal basis, with the crews being permitted to compete in the Summer Eights provided too many crews were not involved. In that case the Torpids held their own races, either after the conclusion of Eights or on rest days during the Eights. The results of the Torpids are recorded from 1838 onwards, but the names of the Head of the River crew were first recorded in 1852 when Torpids were separated from the Summer Eights and removed to the Hilary Term. From that date Torpids came to be regarded as 'feeders' for the Summer Eights, and were taken more seriously. Eligibility to row in Torpids was at first restricted to oarsmen who had not rowed in their college first eight or in a University crew or trials, and boats were restricted to heavy gig eights. Restrictions have been removed progressively, until today the only oarsmen debarred from Torpids are heavyweights currently rowing for the OXFORD UNIVERSITY BOAT CLUB. The maximum permitted entry is 122 crews, rowing in ten divisions, including women's divisions.

In February 1987 Alexandra Horne, a member of the previous year's winning Oxford women's BOAT RACE crew, became the first woman to row in the men's first division of Torpids. Her crew, Pembroke College, rose to third place by bumping Christ Church, leaving Oriel as head crew and Keble in second place. These remained the placings after the last race, Oriel successfully defending headship for the sixteenth consecutive year. Oriel lost the headship to Christ Church in 1991 after 19 years as Head of the River. In the women's first division Somerville, also the leader of the Summer Eights, bumped Osler House to go to the top for the first time.

(*See also* ROWING *and* THAMES.)

Town Hall Before 1229 Council meetings were held in a room in a house in QUEEN STREET, opposite ST MARTIN'S CHURCH, called the Old Yeld Hall. In 1229 King Henry III sold to the burgesses a house on the east side of ST ALDATE'S for use as a court room. The house belonged to Moses ben Isaac, a wealthy Jew, and was on the site of part of the present town hall. It was substantially repaired or rebuilt later in the 13th century. Around 1550 the freehold was acquired of an adjoining house to the south which had belonged to the Domus Conversorum in London – a house for converted Jews. This house became the lower Guildhall. Various alterations and improvements

were carried out to both houses in the 16th and 17th centuries. The old Guildhall was taken down in 1751 and a new town hall built, designed by Isaac Ware in the classical style. This building incorporated the General Post Office in the lower part on the south side, facing St Aldate's. An entrance led to a courtyard at the rear, with NIXON'S FREE GRAMMAR SCHOOL at the back of the post office, and the corn exchange to the rear of that.

The 18th-century town hall was replaced by the present one, the foundation stone of which was laid on 6 July 1893. The architect was Henry T. Hare. This large building, partly in a Jacobean style, was opened by the Prince of Wales, later King Edward VII, on 12 May 1897. The façade is symmetrical, except for the south turret, with a balcony over the entrance from which the results of parliamentary elections are announced to the crowd waiting in St Aldate's. The external sculpture is by Aumonier. At the south end on the corner with BLUE BOAR STREET was the public library. When the new library was built in the WESTGATE CENTRE, this part of the building became the MUSEUM OF OXFORD.

Beneath the town hall is a 14th- or 15th-century vaulted cellar or crypt, where the fine collection of city PLATE is kept. The building incorporated a court room which was used as the magistrates' court until the new Courts were opened (*see* COURTS). This main court room was also used for Quarter Sessions, and later as the Crown Court, until the new Crown Court building was opened in 1985. A grand staircase leads to the main hall, full of sculptured motifs and richly decorated with shields and cherubs on the balcony round three sides and with the original Henry Willis organ behind the platform at the far end. On entering the main hall and facing the organ, the arms on the balcony clockwise from the left are the city arms (*see* HERALDRY), those of the County of Oxfordshire, the Royal County of Berkshire, JOHN RADCLIFFE, ST EDWARD'S SCHOOL, LORD NUFFIELD, ROBERT GROSSE-TESTE (on the right of the stage), the Diocese of Lincoln, REWLEY ABBEY, OSENEY ABBEY, the Diocese of Oxford, the University of Oxford, and (above the entrance doors) the royal arms. The arms above the balcony (clockwise from the left) are the Stuart arms (1707–14), those of Hanover (1714–1801), Hanover (1801–37), Wales, England (on the right of the stage), England and France (1340–1405), England and France (1405–1603), Stuart (1603–88 and 1702–7), William and Mary (1688–1702), and (opposite the stage) Scotland and Ireland.

The Assembly Room on the St Aldate's side contains a large painting of *The Rape of the Sabines* by Pietro Berretini (Pietro da Cortona, 1596–1669), which was presented to the city by the Duke of Marlborough in 1901. Among the large portraits in this room are those of Queen Anne; the 3rd Duke of Marlborough; the 11th Viscount Valentia, MP for Oxford from 1895 to 1917; the 1st Earl of Abingdon; Lord Nuffield by Frank Eastman, 1955; James Langston (1796–1863), MP for Oxford; Thomas Rowney (*see* ST GILES' HOUSE); Sir John Walter, MP; James Herbert, MP; and Sir John Treacher, four times Mayor of Oxford. In the corridor to the Council Chamber is a collection of some twenty to thirty paintings by WILLIAM TURNER OF OXFORD, which were given to the city in June 1931 by Sir Michael Sadler, Master of University College, in memory of his wife. Also in this corridor are twelve small carved heads of

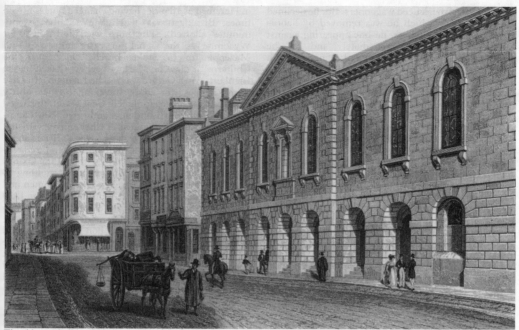

The old town hall in 1835, forerunner of the present building, which was opened in 1897.

the City Council in 1897, the year in which the town hall was opened. They are Alderman Robert Buckell (Mayor), Aldermen J. Saunders, John Seary, George Cooper, Thomas Green, Charles Underhill, James Jenkin, Robert Downing, and WALTER GRAY, and Councillors Thomas Taphouse, Thomas Lucas and Frederick Ansell. The panelled Council Chamber has signs of the zodiac in the plaster ceiling, and contains portraits of mayors, aldermen and benefactors, some of the 17th century. Also off this corridor are the Lord Mayor's Parlour and Committee Room No. 1, both fine panelled rooms.

Townesends A family of MASONS and architects who worked on many buildings in Oxford in the 18th century. In 1720 THOMAS HEARNE wrote: 'Yesterday Mr [John] Townesend, the mason, father to [William] Townesend who hath a hand in all the buildings in Oxford and gets a vast deal of money that way, was elected Mayor of Oxford. This old Townesend is commonly called "Old Pincher" from his pinching his workmen.' John Townesend the first (1648–1728) was mason of The Queen's College from 1688 until his retirement in 1712 and may have designed buildings for the college as well as worked on them as mason. He was buried in ST GILES' churchyard. His son, William, who died in 1739, worked at the RADCLIFFE CAMERA, CONVOCATION HOUSE, the BOTANICAL GARDEN, MAGDALEN BRIDGE, the CLARENDON BUILDING and at Magdalen, Corpus Christi, Oriel, All Souls, St John's, University, Trinity, Worcester, Christ Church and New College. He may also have been responsible for designs in several of these colleges. A sculptor as well as a mason, he carved busts in ST MARY THE VIRGIN (David Gregory and (?) John Wallis) and in CHRIST CHURCH CATHEDRAL (James Narborough and Lord Charles Somerset). His son, John Townesend, who died in 1746 and was mason to Christ Church, also

worked on the Radcliffe Camera, at St John's and Corpus Christi. He was succeeded in the family business by John Townesend the third, who died in 1784. He completed the work on the Radcliffe Camera, built the TOWN HALL to the designs of Isaac Ware, worked at The Queen's and Exeter Colleges and constructed the Gothic fan vault over the Convocation House beneath the Selden End of the BODLEIAN LIBRARY. He was also responsible for the monuments of Henry Bowles in New College chapel and of the Countess of Pomfret in St Mary the Virgin. His son, Stephen Townesend (1755–1800), carried on the business but worked for the most part outside Oxford. His foreman was Thomas Knowles, who in 1797 announced that, having conducted 'the business of Mr. S Townesend' for many years, he had opened a yard at the bottom of HOLYWELL STREET where he intended to carry on the business 'in its various branches' (*see* KNOWLES & SON *and also* PEISLEYS).

Tractarians *see* OXFORD MOVEMENT.

TRANSPORT
Carriers In 1448 the University decided that its licensed carriers were PRIVILEGED PERSONS. Members of the University were not allowed to use unlicensed carriers. The licensed carrier usually lived in his own district and conducted all business between there and Oxford, including the conveyance of students' belongings and books. The city appointed its own carriers from the 16th century onwards, which was a cause of dispute with the University. By 1731 the University could do little about it, as THOMAS HEARNE records, 'One Barnes of St. Aldates ... a freeman of the City, having set up a waggon last summer, to carry goods to and from London, without the Vice-Chancellor's licence . . . was put in the Vice-Chancellor's Court by Mr. Thos. Godfrey and the widow

455

Slatford, the two licenced waggoners. But he declined appearing, upon which he was removed by habeas corpus to London, where, no-one appearing against him, he was dismissed immediately, and . . . he returned to Oxford in a triumphant manner, with a laced hat, as if he designed to insult the University'. From the 1750s to the 1900s, Oxford's neighbouring towns and villages all had carriers and it is known that in 1846 there were almost 300 carriers' carts coming regularly to the city. Their horse-drawn carts took passengers and goods for sale into Oxford (eggs, butter, cheese, vegetables and country-craft ware, such as gloves from Woodstock). The carrier and his wife were entrusted by customers to do business on their behalf (selling, delivering, shopping, etc.) and on his return to the countryside the carrier delivered requirements such as food and clothes and also, in the 19th century, laundry (a cottage industry). They also met trains at stations and distributed goods to areas away from the RAILWAY. In Oxford the carriers left their carts at inns, including, in the 1880s, the CROWN, the BLUE ANCHOR and the WHITE HART, and in the 1900s the Crown, the New Inn, the ANCHOR, the CLARENDON and the Anchor Hotel. The rise of motor transport and the growth of country bus services after the First World War led to the eclipse of the carriers.

Coaches By 1667 a coach was making the journey to London three times a week. It left at 4 a.m., halted overnight at Beaconsfield and arrived at 4 p.m. on the next day. Two years later, the University's licensed 'flying-coach' was expected during the summertime to complete the trip in one day. Next year, the city licensed its own coach, provoking the VICE-CHANCELLOR to complain, 'These are to give notice that whereas Thomas Dye and John Fossett have, without licence from me . . . presumed to set up a flying-coach . . . to London. These are to require all scholars, privileged persons and members of the University not to travail in the said coach . . . nor to send letters or any goods whatsoever by the aforesaid flying-coach'. In 1671 the London fare was 12s and the summertime journey lasted thirteen hours. In 1751 Peregrine Pickle still took two days to reach Oxford but road improvements cut this time to one day in all seasons by 1754. In 1828 the journey took six hours although the 'Age' and 'Royal William' coaches, racing each other, did it in three hours, twenty minutes.

In the late 18th and early 19th centuries, Oxford was an important coaching centre with 100 coaches a day. Leading coaching inns included the ANGEL, GREYHOUND, MITRE and Vine (in HIGH STREET), the Star, Golden Cross, Roebuck and Bell (in CORNMARKET); the Three Cups in QUEEN STREET and the New Inn in ST ALDATE'S. ANGEL MEADOW and Greyhound Meadow provided hay for horses at their respective inns. Oxford's biggest coaching firm was Costar and Waddell, whose 1829 Angel timetable advertised six London coaches via Wycombe between 9 a.m. and midnight, and seven coaches via Henley between 7.45 a.m. and 2 a.m. These coaches were named Blenheim, Regulator, Retaliator, Champion and Telegraph (via Wycombe); Guide, Alert, Magnet, Sovereign, Triumph and Rocket (via Henley); two Royal Mail coaches left the Angel at 11.30 p.m., each following a different route to London. The timetable of a coach calling at the Roebuck Hotel, Cornmarket, was as follows: 'Mazeppa' left London at 6 a.m. and arrived

in Hereford at 10 p.m., having changed horses fifteen times. Breakfast was at High Wycombe (twenty minutes allowed). The horn was blown in West Wycombe as the signal for extra horses to pull Mazeppa up to Stokenchurch. Once over the Chilterns, a glass of Marlow beer was taken at the Lambert Arms. Oxford was reached at noon, after five team changes; for those travelling further, thirty minutes was allowed for lunch. Coaches left the Angel every morning for London, Cambridge, Northampton, Warwick, Birmingham, Cheltenham, Bristol, Southampton and, three days a week, Brighton. A coachguard of those days, William Bayzand, remembered the scene: 'The good old custom of the Oxford people . . . was, in the early morn, to see standing 10 coaches before the old Angel . . . the coachmen and porters busily loading, and waiting their time [for] Queen's College clock to strike 8, for the 9 coaches to make a start for their different destinations, East, West, North, and South. . . . I don't think you could witness in any other town in the kingdom the same number of coaches standing before an hotel, and 9 out of the 10 to start at the same time.' William Tuckwell recalled how along High Street or ST GILES' 'lumbered at midnight Pickford's vast wagons with their 6 musically-belled horses; sped stagecoaches all day long – Tantivy, Defiance, Rival, Regulator, Mazeppa, Dart, Magnet, Blenheim and some 30 more; heaped high with ponderous luggage and with cloaked passengers, thickly hung at Christmas time with turkeys, with pheasants in October; their guards picked buglers, sending before them as they passed Magdalen Bridge the now forgotten strains of "Brignall Banks", "The Troubadour", "I'd be a Butterfly", "The Maid of Llangollen", or "Begone Dull Care"; on the box their queer old purple-faced many-caped drivers – Cheesman, Steevens, Fowles, Charles Homes, Jack Adams, and Black Will.'

Two coach passengers probably had different thoughts about Oxford: Shelley left for London in March 1811 on the outside of a coach, having been sent down (see SHELLEY MEMORIAL); twenty years later WILLIAM GLADSTONE left Oxford on 'Champion' with a double First. After 1835 competition from the RAILWAY rapidly reduced the number of coaches. In 1840 Costar and Waddell sent a coach to meet every train at Steventon, the nearest station to Oxford. Horse-drawn omnibuses had started to run before Oxford station was opened in 1844. Two years later Hunt & Co.'s Directory noted that 'Omnibuses leave the principal Inns for the Railway Station to meet each up and down train'. The year 1846 also saw the withdrawal of the Oxford to Cambridge stagecoach after thirty years' service, and by 1854 there were only three coaches a week to London. The demolition of the main part of the Angel in 1866 symbolised the end of Oxford's coaching days, although a horse-drawn hackney carriage was licensed in Oxford as late as 1935.

River At Oxford, the THAMES splits into several streams which reunite south of IFFLEY; many of these once served the mills of monastic houses or the city. Navigation followed the Pot and Bulstake streams, to the west of the present main channel – which was OSENEY ABBEY mill stream until 1790 when Osney Lock was built by felons from the CASTLE gaol. In mediaeval times the city established a wharf at HYTHE BRIDGE and in the 16th century hay, wood, stone and

Henry Taunt's photograph of the coalyard on the Oxford Canal at Hayfield Wharf c.1890.

slate were unloaded here, city freemen paying $\frac{1}{2}d$ toll and 'foreigners' 1d. During James I's reign there were two Acts of Parliament to make the river navigable between Oxford and Burcot; one stated that this would be 'very convenient for the conveyance of Freestone, commonly called Oxford Stone or Headington Stone' to London (*see* STONE) and of 'coals, fuels and other necessaries [to Oxford] whereof there is now very great scarcity and want'. The Oxford–Burcot Commission was appointed to clear the river and to build locks and weirs; it had four representatives from the University and four from the city and was given power to tax both these bodies. This caused the city some trouble and in 1629 parish taxation was augmented by extra dues on Oxford's 300 alehouses. Furthermore, for some years afterwards, the MAYOR and bailiffs gave money to 'Bringing the Barges' instead of throwing their usual election dinners. The commissioners built the first pound-locks on the Thames at Culham, Sandford and Iffley; these helped towards the resumption of commercial traffic. The commissioners also built a wharf and wet-dock at FOLLY BRIDGE. River navigation remained dependent on the weather: in 1677 barges were aground for a month; in 1714 the Thames could be crossed on foot in places; in 1767 the barges were stuck at Oxford for ten weeks because of floods. One abiding problem for barges was the obstruction caused by the river's many privately owned mills, locks and weirs. Owners consistently delayed the passage of barges by controlling water-levels to suit their mills; they also charged tolls. In the 1750s tolls below Oxford were levied at thirty-two places, averaging 10s a time.

A typical 18th-century Thames barge measured 85 feet by 12 feet with a 4-foot draught, and weighed 60 tons. It was flat-bottomed, with square ends which sloped upwards like a punt; the tall central mast was hinged so that it could be lowered; there was only one sail (more were added later). When the wind was insufficient, the barge was towed by men or horses; the towline was fixed to the top of the mast. Punting poles were also used.

From the end of the 18th century onwards, CANAL competition reduced river trade and gradually the river was neglected and navigation became difficult. In Oxford, Folly Bridge was rebuilt to make the river passage easier (1824–7). The area was a commercial centre, including Mallam's Wharves, Clay Cross Coal Wharf, Plowman's Wharf, Wyatt's Wharf, L. and R. Wyatt's Wharf and Friar's Wharf (Oxford's largest wharf and wet-dock); one 1830s building survives as the Wharf House pub. As trade left the Thames for the RAILWAY, the state of the river deteriorated. The Victorians took their time rectifying the deficiencies, in spite of costly floods which had been exacerbated by land-drainage improvements. There were bad floods in 1821, 1825 and 1852–3, but the *impasse* between barge-masters and riparian owners blocked effective remedies. The floods of 1875–7 were followed by a lengthy enquiry and more inaction: there was not enough money for the required repairs because the rating area did not match the river drainage basin, even to the exclusion of Oxford. After further damage in 1882–3, widening and dredging were at last undertaken, restoring the riverbed's natural fall. At the same time, the New Cut was dug on the lower Cherwell to discourage it from flooding (*see* THAMES). In 1894 the Thames Conservancy was finally authorised to install pound-locks and weirs on the upper river. These meant that in the future, only the extremes of climate, such as occurred in 1918 and 1947, would cause serious flooding at Oxford.

Roads From around 1100 onwards, the King and Court often came through Oxford on their way to Woodstock, sometimes stopping at BEAUMONT PALACE outside the north wall of Oxford (*see* CITY WALL). In 1339 the royal party complained to the city that the condition of Oxford's roads presented a threat to Edward III's safety. At that time, and for long afterwards, road maintenance was the responsibility of each parish and residents naturally begrudged time and effort spent on easing the journey of strangers. In 1576 the Mileways Act bound inhabitants within 5 miles of Oxford to contribute labour on the roads within a mile of the city. In 1592 the city, expecting a royal visit, paid for road repairs in ST CLEMENT'S, even though it was reluctant to set a precedent. In 1604 the city again repaired the road through St Clement's but announced that it did so of 'mere goodwill'. From 1614 onwards, city freemen hung lanterns outside their doors at night to help light the way, and the city wanted thoroughfares 'cleane and sweete', so in 1615 it ordered each inhabitant to clean the street before his door every Saturday or pay a 12*d* fine. The Oxford mileways were poorly financed and repaired; by 1770 nobody even remembered statutory labour. Between 1719 and 1797, all main roads outside Oxford were taken over by turnpike trusts (*see below*). Between 1731 and 1835, five Acts of Parliament – known collectively as the Oxford Mileways Act – enabled the city to improve street conditions: the four routes crossing at CARFAX were widened; the last two city gates (East and North) were removed; MAGDALEN BRIDGE was rebuilt; St Clement's was widened; all streets were paved and lit, and effective provision was made for their cleaning; the market was transferred from the open streets to the COVERED MARKET. The first Act appointed commissioners, representing both University and city, authorising them to erect toll-gates at the city entrances and to impose a rate to pay for road cleaning and lighting. Oil lamps were erected and penalties were threatened against any University member who 'shall wilfully break, throw down, or otherwise damage, any of the Lamps . . . or any of the Posts, Irons, or other Furniture thereof, or extinguish any of the said Lamps'. In 1819 HIGH STREET was 'illuminated' with gas, and the 1835 Act provided a gas supply to light all the streets. Motor traffic was a later problem. The 30 m.p.h. speed limit was imposed in 1933 and the Carfax traffic-lights were installed in 1934. In the Chief Constable's Annual Report, 'Street Traffic' first appeared under a separate heading in 1925. Two years later, the far-sighted Chief Constable wanted to see 'the matter of By-pass Roads . . . receive the serious consideration of the City Council'. A road by-passing the city was opened from BOTLEY to HINKSEY HILL in the 1930s and other by-passes were built subsequently (*see* RING ROAD).

Trams and Buses Horse-tramways were authorised by the 1879 Oxford Tramways Order and the City of Oxford & District Tramways Company was incorporated for the purpose. Oxford was considered suitable for trams because of its broad and level streets and its potentially large number of passengers. In spite of protests from aesthetically minded University members, construction began of a 4-foot gauge track. The widening of MAGDALEN BRIDGE to accommodate the tramway caused an outcry because of the change in proportion. Once the work was completed, however, the 'Balaams of High Art . . . appeared somewhat inclined to regard the widening as not so objectionable after all'. On 1 December 1881 the tramway opened between the Magdalen Road cricket grounds and the PARK END STREET railway stations, via COWLEY ROAD, THE PLAIN, Magdalen Bridge, HIGH STREET, CARFAX, QUEEN STREET and NEW ROAD. A second line was

Horse-drawn trams operated from the Park End Street railway stations and the Magdalen Road cricket grounds from 1881.

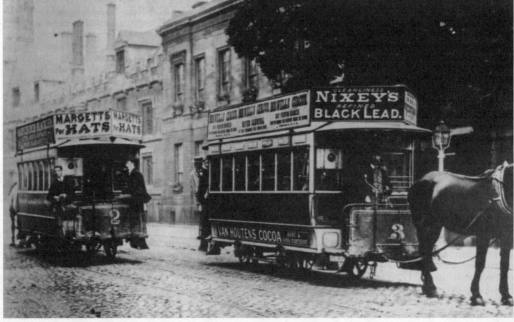

opened one month later from the bottom of ST ALDATE'S to Rackham's Lane (now ST MARGARET'S ROAD) via Carfax, CORNMARKET, ST GILES' and BANBURY ROAD. Each of the sixteen single-deck cars was pulled by one horse and carried up to twenty-five passengers on seats lengthwise along the sides. Soon, over 16,000 passengers were being carried every week and in March 1882 double-deckers were introduced. A third line was opened in July 1884 which branched off the second line at BEAUMONT STREET and went down WALTON STREET as far as Leckford Road. The sharp corners at both ends of Beaumont Street led to derailments, with the trams ending up against the TAYLOR INSTITUTION or the railings in front of Worcester College. In 1898 the second line was extended to run between SOUTH PARADE and Lake Street. With this addition, the tramway network reached its final length of 6¼ miles. The track was single-line with crossing loops, apart from double-track along High Street. The main depot was in Leopold Street and there were secondary depots at JERICHO HOUSE in Walton Street, the Cape of Good Hope (The Plain) and BREWER STREET stables (St Aldate's). The centre of the system was Carfax, where cars could be switched from one line to another. The fare from Carfax to the end of any line was 1*d*. Drivers were instructed to keep within a speed limit of 8 m.p.h., to slow down when going through a crowd of people or a herd of cattle and to stop dead when faced by a flock of sheep. There were no fixed 'stops' along the way; instead, conductors and drivers were instructed to look out for passengers and a notice on the tram asked passengers not to ring the bell unnecessarily in order to spare the horses. Not allowed inside the tram were anyone smoking, 'a sweep in his dirt', or a 'miller in his dust'. Inspectors were forbidden to converse with conductors except in the line of business. The Tramway Company also ran horse-buses along routes where no tramlines had been laid.

By 1900, electric tramcars were running in some cities; they were cheaper than horse-drawn trams and twice as fast. The following plans were made for the Oxford tramway in the 1900s: electrification; new lines along BOTLEY, IFFLEY and WOODSTOCK ROADS; present lines to be extended. The University described the proposal for overhead power lines in Oxford as unthinkable. The City Corporation wanted to wait until 1908 when the Tramway Company's lease ran out and the city could then take it over. Local rate-payers, however, wanted a private system of either electric trams or motor buses. In 1905 the Tramway Company agreed to a 1907 city takeover. In 1906 the city chose electric trams that would use the Dolter ground-orientated current collection (at a cost of £93,000). A public meeting was held at the TOWN HALL to debate the issue and the city's plans were heavily defeated. Realising that citizens were against a publicly owned tramway, the city decided to lease out the system and it received two tenders, one from the Tramway Company itself and one from the National Electric Construction Company. The latter's was accepted and the City of Oxford Electric Tramway Company was formed as its subsidiary. In 1907 the Oxford & District Tramways Act was passed to enable this company to build its electric network going out to COWLEY, IFFLEY and HEADINGTON and the ends of Woodstock and Banbury Roads. The Dolter system

would only be bought after it had been in use elsewhere for six months; when it did not prove a success, alternatives were proposed, involving the use of overhead wires in the suburbs. By 1913 the cost of the unbuilt electric tramway had risen to £230,000. The Oxford Electric Tramway Company, desperately short of funds, had been virtually inactive since 1907. Oxford inhabitants now wanted a fleet of motor buses at the lower cost of £25,000.

On 4 November 1913 a local ratepayer in the motor trade, William Morris (later LORD NUFFIELD), wrote to the town clerk requesting licences to run Daimler motor buses between the stations and Cowley Road. The city refused but the service started all the same on 5 November. In the absence of a licence, money could not legally be taken on Morris's buses; instead, coupons could be purchased from shops and presented for travel on the buses which soon proved popular. 'They run very smoothly,' a newspaper reported, 'almost noiselessly, are comfortably uphol-stered inside, brilliantly lighted by electricity at night – a marked contrast in every way to the old trams – and do the journey from Cowley Road terminus to the stations in about 10 minutes.' On 6 November the Electric Tramway Company informed the city that it would willingly provide a service of motor buses instead of trams. The city replied by threatening to sue it for non-completion of contract. After four days of service, Morris's buses had carried 17,000 people, leaving the trams deserted. The city eventually decided not to issue a writ for damages and on 30 December the Tramway Company started running its own unlicensed motor buses. Morris's Oxford Motor Omnibus Company now had services from BROAD STREET to Iffley, from Cornmarket to Hayfield Road and from Carfax to Wolvercote or New Hinksey. His buses called at stops which were marked by red-and-blue signs. Morris and the Tramway Company eventually altered their timetables to run a com-plementary service. On 7 January 1914 the city decided to grant both operators five licences each (later amended to twelve). On 28 January Morris proposed that the Tramway Company should take all twenty-six licences, since the competition was wasteful. The city approved and on 22 May promised the Tramway Company exclusive rights to ply for hire with motor buses for thirty-seven years. This was confirmed by the 1914 Oxford & District Tramways Act. Somewhat confusingly, therefore, the first official bus service in Oxford was run by the Oxford Electric Tramway Company until 1921, when it became the City of Oxford Motor Services Ltd. Some discarded tramcars served as holiday chalets at WOLVERCOTE until the 1930s.

From Oxford, bus services quickly spread into the surrounding country, though not without resistance. An action was successfully brought against the Tramway Company by Abingdon Rural District Council, who felt that the new motor bus service to BOAR'S HILL and Abingdon was 'extraordinary' traffic. Lord Justice Scrutton commented: 'Here one day is a country lane along which pass two or three trades-men's carts and an occasional motor car then, suddenly, there comes upon the road a fleet of omnibuses making 90 journeys a week. That is not a slow and normal increase – that is an eruption.' During the First World War conductors were replaced by conductresses or 'clippies'. The wartime

459

petrol shortage led to experiments with both paraffin and coal gas; the latter proved quite efficient and it was carried in a bag which occupied the whole of the top deck. In July 1928 roofed double-deckers arrived for the first time and some young people rode up and down in them all day. Traffic congestion at Carfax now prompted the search for another departure point for the country bus services. The city suggested Broad Street but it was considered too remote. In 1929 a site was cleared between Church Street and CASTLE STREET but this location was a failure and a move followed to GLOUCESTER GREEN in 1935. Here, the CENTRAL SCHOOL FOR GIRLS became the parcels and enquiries office and the old Settling Room belonging to the cattle market became a café. During the Second World War the bus fleet was dispersed every night to the Northern Bypass and CHENEY LANE to avoid any bombing of Cowley. Women drivers and conductresses were employed as staff left for the Forces. In 1943 some buses ran on gas, towing behind them anthracite-burning trailers. They kept poor time, however, and became unpopular as a result, so the scheme was abandoned in 1944. The number of bus passengers continued to grow until the early 1950s, when the private car began to establish itself. The subsequent boom in car ownership forced the bus company to run fewer services more economically. In 1966 double-deckers with drivers acting as ticket collectors became legal, and by 1978 all Oxford buses were one-person operated. The City Council's Balanced Transport Policy (1973) sought to discourage all non-essential traffic within the city centre by establishing bus lanes along the main routes, closing Queen Street and Cornmarket to all traffic except buses, and building Park and Ride sites around the peripheries of the city. The latest innovation has been the introduction of minibuses which provide a door-to-door service from residential areas to the city centre.

Turnpikes In 1719 the Stokenchurch Turnpike Trust became responsible for the road from Stokenchurch to New Woodstock, excluding the Oxford mileways. Before 1775 the London road from Oxford followed CHENEY LANE, Old Road and Shotover Hill; then, the Trust opened the new main road from HEADINGTON HILL to Wheatley. In 1736 the Henley and Dorchester road was also turnpiked, once more as far as the mileway. In 1756 the road to Abingdon was turnpiked. When FOLLY BRIDGE was rebuilt (1815–27) the toll-gate was on the south side of the bridge; when GRANDPONT railway station (see RAILWAY) opened in 1844 the toll-gate was moved to the north side to catch the train passengers. The toll-house is now a shop. In 1767, the Botley and Newland Turnpike Trust was made responsible for the Botley causeway. The Trust was composed of representatives from the University and city; it was empowered by Parliament 'to widen the said Causeway to the Breadth of Thirty Feet, and to raise, fence, and repair the same, so as to prevent Inconvenience or Danger in Time of Floods or otherwise; and also to rebuild the several Bridges which connect the different Parts of the said Causeway to each other . . . making the said Bridges at least Twenty Feet wide in the Clear for the passage of Cattle and Carriages.' PARK END STREET was laid out as part of these western improvements and NEW ROAD was cut through the CASTLE bailey. In 1770 New Road was, therefore, only the second new street to be built within the CITY WALL (BLUE BOAR STREET being the

first). In 1850 the BOTLEY ROAD toll-house was demolished to make way for the railway to Banbury; a smart new toll-house was built and is today part of the Old Gatehouse public house. In 1771 the ST CLEMENT'S mileway was turnpiked, and in 1818 a large toll-house was built on THE PLAIN, with toll-gates on either side to catch all travellers over MAGDALEN BRIDGE. All except one, that is: Richard Costar, Oxford's leading coach proprietor, who lived on the present site of MAGDALEN COLLEGE SCHOOL and whose house had entrance drives on both sides of the toll-gate. In 1797 the Adderbury, Kidlington and Oxford Turnpike Trust took over the BANBURY ROAD mileway; their 19th-century toll-house, 'Old Man's Gate', still stands as No. 566 Banbury Road. The start of the railway age meant that between 1865 and 1878 turnpikes were removed from all these roads, which then waited for the internal combustion engine to bring them back to life.

(See also BICYCLES, BRIDGES, CANAL, PARKING, POSTAL SERVICES and RAILWAY.)

(Jolly, S., & Taylor, N., *The Book of Oxford Buses and Trams*, Oxford, 1981; Bayzand, W., 'Coaching In and Out of Oxford', *Collecteanea*, Vol. IV, Oxford, 1905; 'Communications', No. 8, Local History Pack, Central Library, Oxford, 1973; Wastie, I., 'The Carrier's Cart', Local History Collections pamphlet, Oxford, 1982.)

Trees Since the early 19th century Oxford has been the home of an increasing variety of exotic and ornamental trees. Many, but by no means all, of these are to be found in the gardens of the older colleges, where the 17th-century introduction of fig and mulberry trees, the occasional curiosity such as the oriental plane in the Priory House garden at Christ Church, and the simultaneous planting of groves of elm, lime and walnut, gave way at the end of the 18th century to a fashion for specimen trees. One or two college gardens, notably those of Wadham and Worcester Colleges and the former bowling green at New College, all replanted between 1780 and 1820, are principally tree gardens, with fine displays of ruined purple beeches, catalpas, robinias, cedars of Lebanon, tulip-trees and London planes. Important collections of trees can also be found in the early 17th-century BOTANIC GARDEN and in the mid-19th-century University PARKS. The oldest tree in the Botanic Garden is one of an original pair of yews believed to date from about 1650, both of which grew there until the female of the pair blew down in 1976. A fine manna ash (*Fraxinus ornus*), a hornbeam (*Carpinus betulus*), a ginkgo (*Ginkgo biloba*) and a service-tree (*Sorbus domestica 'maliformis'*) all date from the end of the 18th century. The far more comprehensive collection in the University Parks includes a fine pagoda-tree (*Sophora japonica*), a great shellbark hickory (*Carya laciniosa*), a well-grown Turkish hazel (*Corylus colurna*), a striking cottonwood (*Populus deltoides*), a group of wellingtonias, several weeping beeches and Atlas cedars, and avenues of different varieties of thorn-tree and of western catalpas, alternating with tulip-trees.

Until the last century, the most characteristic of all Oxford trees was the elm. Rows of elms lined the approaches to the city by MAGDALEN BRIDGE and, from the north, along ST GILES', where the present London planes were introduced in the early 1860s. Many elms had been planted soon after the Restoration, reaching full maturity some 200 years later when they began to weaken and occasionally to blow down. These included the elms of the famous BROAD WALK in CHRIST CHURCH MEADOW (finally destroyed by Dutch elm disease in the 1970s), many of those in Magdalen College grove and in the gravel walk which screened the front of the college from the HIGH STREET, and those which lined the approach from the east side of the city northwards to the present University Parks.

Of the groves planted in the 17th century at Magdalen, Merton, University, Trinity, Balliol and St John's Colleges, all but the deer park at Magdalen, now much depleted of its elms, have disappeared. At Trinity the Fellows planted lime and walnut trees in the 1670s. University College had a grove of walnut trees on the site of the present Kybald Street, off MAGPIE LANE; but these, like most other walnuts in Oxford, had been cut down before the middle of the 18th century. A fine, mature walnut can be found in the courtyard of FREWIN HALL off NEW INN HALL STREET, while several colleges have recently planted new walnut trees in their gardens.

Lime trees were popular from the 17th century onwards for shady walks, like the surviving lime walk in the Fellows' Garden at Merton College, or for screening the edges of college gardens, like the Victorian limes at Pembroke, Keble and Corpus Christi. Sycamores, used at New College for a pleached hedge along one side of the bowling green in the 18th century, and at Merton for the fine, informal group still to be seen in the Fellows' Garden, were not otherwise much in demand as garden trees. The All Souls sycamore, which has overhung the High Street from an alleyway since the early 19th century, seems purely accidental.

Several horse chestnuts, now among the most noticeable trees in Oxford, seem to date from at least the end of the 18th century. These include the trees at Merton, at Exeter College (overhanging BRASENOSE LANE), at Jesus College (overhanging TURL STREET) and behind the LAMB AND FLAG in St Giles'. Only at New College, where they flank the CITY WALL, has there been any attempt at planting them in a formal arrangement. One or two London planes are almost as old – such as that in Magdalen College garden, planted by Henry Phillpotts in 1801, and the very dominant, early 19th-century plane at Worcester College. One or two tulip-trees, as at New College and University College, and catalpas, as at Worcester College, have reached striking heights in the last 150 years. Ordinary beeches are unusual, except at Worcester College and at St John's, which has two 19th-century weeping beeches and a cut-leaved beech. Purple or copper beeches, however, can be found in the gardens of many of the colleges, spreading northwards up the late Victorian WOODSTOCK and BANBURY ROADS, where their foliage alternates disturbingly with that of the light-green, ash-leaved maple and the duller, purple-leaved plum.

Evergreen oaks and yews occur sporadically between the centre of the city and the northern suburbs. Among the most striking are the yew walk at Trinity College, planted in the first half of the 18th century, and the evergreen oaks in the Trinity and Wadham gardens and the cloister at New College. The groups of Lombardy poplars, which in the early 19th century followed the line of BROAD STREET from Wadham College to Worcester College, have now entirely disappeared. Instead, the spiry shape of the ginkgo appears in a number of college gardens; while a more recent fashion for another fossil tree, *Metasequoia glyptostroboides* (the dawn redwood), can be seen at New College, Wadham and Merton Colleges, the Botanic Garden and elsewhere.

(*See also* BOTANIC GARDEN *and* GARDENS.)

(*Guide to the Oxford Botanic Gardens*, Oxford, 1971; *Guide to the Trees and Shrubs in the University Parks*, Oxford, 1978; Günther, R.C., *Oxford Gardens*, Oxford, 1912; Batey, M., *Oxford Gardens*, 1982.)

Trill Mill Stream   A branch of the THAMES which was a considerable watercourse in the Middle Ages. It ran along the eastern side of GRANDPONT, through ST ALDATE'S, across CHRIST CHURCH MEADOW towards the Cherwell (*see* THAMES). It was canalised in the 13th century and was crossed by two bridges, Preachers' or Littlegate Bridge between Littlegate and Black Friars, and Trill Mill Bow between St Aldate's and Grandpont. Both were demolished in the 1860s (*see* BRIDGES). The stream's mill was in operation at least as early as the 12th century, when it was granted by one Benet Kepeharm to ST FRIDESWIDE'S PRIORY, but it had disappeared by the time of the CIVIL WAR. The stream was a notorious danger to health in the middle of the 19th century, when much of the sewage and rubbish of ST EBBE'S were poured into it (*see* PUBLIC HEALTH). At that time it was known as 'Pactolus' in ironic allusion to the river in Asia Minor whose sands contained particles of gold, traditionally left there after Midas had bathed in it. It was recommended in 1854 that the stream should be made into a covered sewer connected to new sewers in ST CLEMENT'S and ABINGDON ROAD; but it was not finally culverted until 1863. It now emerges sluggishly from the culvert north of Christ Church Memorial Gardens before entering the Cherwell. In the 1920s the remains of a Victorian punt with two skeletons in it were found in the subterranean waterway. Intrepid punters still enter its dark cavern.

Trinity College   When Sir Thomas Pope resolved to found a college in Oxford, he decided, like some other benefactors of his period, not to build from the ground but to profit from the upheavals of the Reformation. Accordingly he bought in 1554 the surviving fabric of Durham College (*see* MONASTIC COLLEGES) from the then owners, Dr George Owen and William Martyn. It was a shrewd purchase and the quadrangle which he acquired proved adequate for his new foundation for most of its first hundred years.

Durham College had been begun in 1291 to furnish a University education for some of the monks of the great northern cathedral–monastery. It contained the essentials for collegiate life: a chapel for prayer and worship, a hall, a library and dwelling space for teachers and taught. Today the main survival is the east range, which included the library on the first floor and below it what became the earliest President's lodging, built in 1417–21. The land which Pope obtained was an L-shaped plot with a southern access on to BROAD STREET and a wide strip running eastwards down to what is now PARKS ROAD. Only in the 18th century were properties acquired which gave access to ST GILES'.

Sir Thomas Pope was of Oxfordshire stock. Trained as a lawyer, he had prospered in the service of

David Loggan's bird's-eye view of Trinity College in 1675, showing the by then dilapidated plain Perpendicular 15th-century chapel in the foreground.

the Crown and held the office of Treasurer – in effect second-in-command – of the Court of Augmentations, the great department created to handle the disposition of the vast monastic resources at the Dissolution of the Monasteries. He was one of the executors of Henry VIII. Although twice married, he was himself childless. On 8 March 1555 he obtained a charter of foundation from Philip and Mary and on the 28th issued his own charter establishing his college. The first plan was for a President, twelve Fellows, eight scholars and a school at Hook Norton; but in his own charter Pope raised the number of scholars to twelve and abandoned the idea of a school. Before his death in 1559 he was lavish in material benefactions of PLATE, vestments and books, including three volumes bound in doeskin which had been given to him by King Henry. He was buried at first in St Stephen Walbrook in London, but in about 1567 his widow moved his body to a tomb in the college chapel and later was buried there herself; he is believed to be the only founder of an Oxford or Cambridge college to lie under a monument within his own foundation. No provision was made for FOUNDER'S KIN. The territorial endowments were centred in Oxfordshire, particularly round Wroxton; Pope had acquired considerable estates in that county. On 30 May 1556 the original members were formally admitted to the premises. The statutes were of a conventional character, and like all Oxford colleges with Presidents (save Wolfson) the VISITOR was the Bishop of Winchester.

There can be little doubt that the sympathies of the founder were with the old religion; those of his widow

were undoubtedly so (*see* ROMAN CATHOLICS). In the last half of the 16th century several scholars fled abroad, including Thomas Forde (beatified in 1886); but Anglican churchmen also figured. The 1st and 2nd Lords Baltimore, founders of the tolerant colony of Maryland, were alumni (1594 and 1621 respectively). The college's Presidents were long lived: Arthur Yeldard (1559–99) and RALPH KETTELL (1599–1643) covered nearly a century. The latter was a striking character, living vividly in the pages of JOHN AUBREY, perhaps the most attractive of all Trinity chroniclers. Kettell made the first additions and alterations to the Durham fabric. An upper storey of cocklofts was added to the east range. Then, in 1618, excavation of cellars under the old Durham hall caused its collapse, and the main structure of the present hall was erected. Kettell also established a plate fund, but, alas, its proceeds went almost entirely to the MINT of Charles I, as did the bulk of the founder's plate. The undergraduates of his day were an able body. Numerous prelates (including GILBERT SHELDON of Canterbury), RALPH BATHURST, Aubrey and others speak for learning; in the larger world, the Earls of Craven and Cleveland (1623 and 1602 respectively), Sir Henry Blount, the traveller (1615) and Sir Thomas Glemham were on the royalist side. Two regicides, Henry Ireton (1628) and Edmund Ludlow (1634), represent a different standpoint: when Glemham surrendered Oxford to the former in 1646, it is permissible to wonder what words passed between them. By then Kettell was dead.

The original appearance of Durham had now been altered by a new hall, with rooms above it, by rooms on the east range (1602) and by an earlier third storey (1576–8) on the north range. In about 1620 Kettell acquired a long lease from Oriel of Baner Hall on Broad Street, and there built privately the handsome edifice which bears his name; it did not become a permanent part of the college till the 19th century.

In its contribution of college silver to the royal cause, Trinity ranked fifth (after Magdalen, All Souls, Exeter and Queen's). During the CIVIL WAR and the Commonwealth the college seems to have been almost empty. A few Fellows contrived to keep tradition alive – and among them Ralph Bathurst, who was to reign as President from 1664 to 1704 and radically to change the whole appearance of the foundation. Bathurst was very much a figure of his age: well connected (his mother was a Villiers), a Doctor of Medicine, a founding member of the group at Wadham from which grew the Royal Society, and a lively patron of the arts. At once he set about adding to the accommodation available. In 1665–8 his friend CHRISTOPHER WREN designed a freestanding building on the north side of the garden, topped by a pediment and a high mansard roof. It marked the first appearance in Oxford of the French style which Wren followed, and cost about £1500. Unhappily, since then his plan has been disfigured by alteration: it can however be clearly seen in DAVID LOGGAN's engraving of 1675, which serves Trinity particularly well. The college grew under Bathurst's care and soon this addition was not enough. In 1682 a matching building was erected on the west side of what now became an open court looking eastwards down the garden. It may be convenient to follow the fortunes of this Garden Quadrangle down to today. In 1728 the north side of Durham Quadrangle (and consequently the south face of the Garden Quad) was remodelled from the Gothic to match Wren's style, three storeys in height. More seriously, in 1802, the rooms in the upper storeys of the two Wren sides were considered cramped and the mansard roofs and pediments were sacrificed to comfort. Slight improvements to the proportions of the windows were made when these faces of the quadrangle were repaired in 1958–9 and 1963.

Early in Bathurst's reign it was decided to institute a common room for the Fellows; hitherto they had gathered in the rooms of individuals. The room now chosen and known today as the Old Bursary was a surviving portion of Durham College in the former west range; in 1681 it was most effectively clad in panelling at a cost of £54. The chimneypiece displays the founder's dragon crest. In 1687, and at his own cost, Bathurst erected a simple building containing six sets of rooms which occupied the site of the present President's lodging and lasted until these were built in 1885.

Bathurst laboured hard to interest men of importance in the college, and a number of his undergraduates rose to eminence. John Somers, 1st Baron Somers (1667), was Lord Keeper and then Lord Chancellor and a key figure in Whig politics; among others were the 1st Earl Stanhope (1688) and the 1st Earl Bathurst (1700); Spencer Compton (1690), Earl of Wilmington and a transient Prime Minister; and two Chief Justices of the Common Pleas, Thomas Reeve (1688) and John Willes (1663). DISCIPLINE was good; learning flourished under the President's guidance and he himself was in steady contact with the principal scientists of the day. A lower library was established for the use of undergraduates: lectures were given in Physics as well as on classical themes. 'The Education & Manner of Life in this Coll. was Manly and Gentle & free from abundance of the Pedantry and Impertinence in other Houses...' wrote John Harris, a scholar of 1684. It was a golden age in the story of Trinity.

The outstanding achievement of Bathurst's rule was the rebuilding of the chapel. The chapel of Durham was a work of 1406–8 in a plain Perpendicular style: it too can be seen clearly in Loggan's engraving of 1675. It had served Pope's college for over a hundred years, but it was becoming dilapidated and out of date. Bathurst began to raise funds in 1680 but eventually paid some £2000 from his own purse for the actual fabric: the sums collected went to providing the internal decoration. The first design was circulated in 1691 and the edifice was complete by 1694. Unluckily, the bursarial accounts for the crucial years are missing. It is generally believed that the main design came from HENRY ALDRICH, Dean of Christ Church, and the style is quite certainly close to that of ALL SAINTS CHURCH (now Lincoln Library) at the south end of TURL STREET. Wren, however, gave some help and advice from 1692. The whole concept was revolutionary: this was the first Oxford chapel not to be built in a derivative version of the Gothic style. The effect at the time must have been dazzling in its novelty as well as in its grace. The design involved the demolition of the one-time Durham entrance (and the treasury which stood above it) and the whole of the Durham chapel; fortunately it made no inroads on the former Durham library in the east range of the quadrangle. Basically, the new building consisted of a chapel of three bays and an antechapel of one; to the west stands a tower over an arched entrance, including a handsome set of rooms originally intended for the Dean and an archival chamber above. The tower is crowned with statues of Theology, Medicine, Geometry and Astronomy, which may have been the work of Caius Cibber but are today sadly battered by wind and rain. In the post-war period of refacing, it was decided not to replace them (see STATUES).

Within, the chapel is mainly panelled with *Juniperus bermudiana*, often referred to at the time as being cedar. Above the altar a discreetly cross-patterned reredos is surrounded by brilliant carving in lime wood. We have the testimony of that inveterate traveller, Celia Fiennes, that this was the work of Grinling Gibbons; the craftsmanship and beauty speak for themselves. The screen separating the antechapel is decorated with four figures of the Evangelists and is again covered with juniper veneer. Some of this must be the work of Arthur Frogley, who was master-carpenter in the crucial years; the chief mason was Bartholomew Peisley (see PEISLEYS), whose widow married Trinity's President Huddesford (1731–76). Heraldic emblems of the monarchy around the cornice would date the chapel to William III even if there were no other evidence. The painting on the ceiling, of the Ascension, is by the Huguenot Pierre Berchet (d.1720). The new chapel was consecrated on 12 April 1694 by the BISHOP OF OXFORD, acting for the Visitor. Two parcloses in the north-east and south-east corners contained the tomb of the founder, his first wife and his widow, and an enclosure where the wife of the President might worship in modesty, seeing but unseen. Pope's tomb shows him in full armour, which he can but rarely have worn in his influential, but administrative career. All the woodwork cost £1140.

The interior of this lovely building, wonderfully sympathetic to worship, has been little altered. In 1885 President Woods gave seven stained-glass windows by Powell, of moderate aesthetic value, showing saints with north-country or Durham connection. An unfortunate Munich glass window in the north-west light, in memory of the Tractarian Isaac Williams, has been removed and stored. An organ was introduced at the west end in 1896, but was replaced in 1965 by a more modern instrument, the gift of J.H. Britton (1923). The beams of the roof had to be extensively restored in 1932 and again in 1959 after a minor fire. Unhappily the local stone used for the exterior facing decayed badly and had to be replaced with Bath stone in 1959–63 – except for the east end which preserves its original dilapidation (*see* STONE).

The completion of the new chapel allowed the library of Durham College still to remain in use. This fine room, not generally shown to the public, contains good stained glass which probably came originally from the old chapel. Formerly in the western lights, the figures of saints have for some time been in the eastern windows. They were reset in 1765 and 1878 and again extensively re-leaded, repaired, and finally replaced in 1983. There are some interesting shields in the tracery. One is of John Wessington, who was Bursar here from 1398 to 1403 and later Prior of Durham itself, and belonged to the family which produced George Washington. Heraldists will note the arms of Thomas Grey and his Mowbray wife,

where contrary to general practice the bordure is carried right round the impalement. The books are a fine working collection for the 18th century, strongest in Theology and Classics, though with a good section on local history. All the manuscripts belonging to the college have been deposited in the BODLEIAN LIBRARY. Traces of painting survive on the beams and ceiling and (lately discovered) on the walls of the fine rooms below, which constituted the lodging of the President until 1885. The outer walls of the Durham building did not need refacing, as did the rest of the college in the post-war years.

After the lustrous régime of Bathurst, the 18th-century Presidents were less significant. The outstanding figure within the college was THOMAS WARTON, Camden Professor of Ancient History, Poet Laureate and friend of SAMUEL JOHNSON, who gave the library a fine Virgil. It was through Warton and at Trinity that Johnson met his friends Topham Beauclerk and Bennet Langton. He loved the library and found it a fine place to work, though 'if a man has a mind to prance, he must study at Christ Church and All Souls.' The outstanding name of this period is that of William Pitt (1727), Earl of Chatham and Prime Minister, who must compete with JOHN HENRY NEWMAN in the next century for first place among Trinity men. But there were also the 1st and 2nd Earls of Guilford (1721 and 1749 respectively), the latter better known as Lord North and head of the government which witnessed the loss of the American colonies. The pious Earl of Dartmouth (1749) was his lifelong friend and they gave the college two noble pieces of plate. Mention may be made of Sir John Sinclair (1775), the Scottish agriculturalist; Brownlow North (1760), Bishop of Winchester; and John Gilbert (1713), Archbishop of York. The poet Walter

Trinity College chapel, completed in 1694, was the first Oxford chapel not to be built in the derivative version of the Gothic style.

Savage Landor was sent down in 1794 for discharging a firearm across the Garden Quad. A distinguished line of poets not in the first rank has been maintained in more recent years by James Elroy Flecker (1902), Laurence Binyon (1888) and Robert Nichols (1913).

The 18th century witnessed no major pieces of building. The Almanack for 1732 portrays an elaborate plan for extended wings of the Garden Quad into the garden, which would have involved sad demolition of surviving Durham work, but it does not seem that this was seriously contemplated. The lime walk was first planted in 1713, but no original tree remains today. At the same time was erected the ironwork screen, supported by two fine stone piers at the east end of the garden. The tourist guide's legend that the gates are to be opened only for the true (i.e. Jacobite) King is utterly without foundation; they were, in fact, opened in the mid-19th century for the then Prince of Wales. In 1737 Lord North presented to the college a fine set of iron gates on the Broad Street frontage: only in 1889 were they given massive stone piers based on those in Parks Road. In 1772 the interior of the hall was redecorated and an elaborate ceiling introduced. There were two important territorial acquisitions: between 1780 and 1787 a strip of land between Balliol and St John's, formerly the DOLPHIN AND ANCHOR, was bought, and in 1786 the college acquired from Oriel and Magdalen the area lying north of Kettell Hall. This purchase substantially broadened the access strip to the college, and was of enormous value a hundred years later, while the Dolphin land effectually altered the ground plan of the college from an L to an irregular T.

Trinity played a leading part in throwing off the decadence of the 18th-century University arrangements. Some simple form of examination was instituted as early as 1789 and twenty years later a more rigid system was introduced. Two tutors who probably led the way were Henry Kett and Thomas Short, the latter of whom was a Fellow for sixty-three years. President Thomas Lee (1808–24) was VICE-CHANCELLOR when the allied sovereigns came to Oxford after Waterloo. In 1817 a young freshman wrote to his mother: 'If anyone wishes to study much, I believe that there can be no college that will encourage him more than Trinity. It is wishing to rise in the University and is rising fast. The scholarships were formerly open only to members of the college; last year, for the first time, they were thrown open to the whole University. In discipline it has become one of the strictest of the colleges. There are lamentations in every corner of the increasing rigour; it is laughable, but it is delightful, to hear the groans of the oppressed.' The writer was John Henry Newman. In 1843 fellowships were thrown open to members of other colleges, and Trinity rapidly gained a number of distinguished names, including the historians WILLIAM STUBBS (Fellow 1848–51) and Edward Augustus Freeman (Fellow 1845–7) and the classical scholar Robinson Ellis (Fellow 1858–93). But the student body also produced men of varied talents: the travellers Richard Ford (1813) and Sir Richard Burton (1840; rusticated 1842); James Lord Bryce (1857), historian and statesman; the gentle Tractarian Isaac Williams (1822); Lord Chancellor Selborne and the civil servant Lord Lingen (1837) form a remarkable group for a small college. When the first ROYAL COMMISSION issued its Ordinances in 1857,

little needed to be done at Trinity; the secretary to the Commission, Samuel Wayte, himself a Trinity man, became President (1866–78). JAMES INGRAM (President 1824–50) was a profuse but untidy scholar in Anglo-Saxon and bequeathed an important collection of books to the library; their accession unfortunately entailed raising in height the original Jacobean bookcases. By 1870 eight of the twelve fellowships had been thrown open to laymen, but they still had formally to be resigned on marriage.

Not surprisingly, the success of the college brought increasing pressure on the available accommodation. In 1864 a new staircase (now numbered XIV) filled in the gap in the north-west corner between the two Wren buildings of the Garden Quad; it incorporated four floors to their more spacious three. In 1882 only fifty-seven undergraduates were living in college, though others used the cottages adjacent to the lodge which were incorporated into the college in 1885. Kettell Hall was bought from Oriel in 1883, and after a period of use as a private house (by Bishop Stubbs among others) was brought into the college in 1898. In the meantime more substantial works had been undertaken. In 1883–5 a new range of buildings was erected on what had been the garden of Kettell Hall. The design, in a Jacobean style, was by SIR THOMAS JACKSON, who had not however at that date discovered the great virtues of Clipsham stone (see STONE). In 1885–7 Bathurst was demolished and a new President's lodging built on a slightly larger site, but preserving the traditional President's garden. What had been the President's yard and orchard to the south of Bathurst's building now became the front

De La Motte's drawing of the interior of Trinity College chapel. The limewood carvings surrounding the reredos are attributed to Grinling Gibbons.

quadrangle, and the whole access to Trinity assumed a more spacious air. The New Buildings included twenty-seven sets of rooms for undergraduates, one for the Dean, a lecture room and a Junior Common Room. Small purchases were also made behind the Broad Street houses (which include BLACKWELL'S bookshop) and later provided the site for the library.

Another feature of development was the rise of interest in science. A benefaction in 1873 by Thomas Millard, who, curiously, was not a member of the college, was devoted to exhibitions in Natural Science and to the construction of LABORATORIES. Balliol had already embarked on a basement for chemical research, but from 1877 Trinity shared in the work and later provided most of the site. This was in the north-west corner of the college, once occupied by the Dolphin Inn, which also housed a servant's cottage and a block of lavatories, replacing those of Durham College. The original site is now a carpenter's workshop and linked with the basement under Balliol hall – an addition which sorely spoiled the view of Trinity from its gardens – but gradual expansion took place and later extensions ran right down to the line of St Giles'. Further space was acquired by the demolition of the old lavatories and the erection of new ones on the other side of the passageway. Perhaps the greatest work done here was by SIR CYRIL HINSHEL-WOOD in the 1930s on the kinetic properties of gases: a recent tablet marks the spot and the achievement. The use made of limited resources and space underlines the value of the research done here, sometimes in situations almost of comedy. The opening, at the beginning of the Second World War, of the new University Physical Chemistry Laboratory marked the end of the Trinity–Balliol area, and research there ceased in 1941. Most of the site is today used as a car park. In 1947–8 the college built a handsome gatehouse over the entrance to Dolphin Yard, to the designs of Sir Hubert Worthington. The old servant's cottage was replaced by more modern accommodation in 1959. A squash court was later built beside it.

The long presidency of H.E.D. Blakiston (1907–38), able historian of the college and an idiosyncratic though charming character of whom many legends are still told, saw great and grave changes to the college, especially the onslaught of the First World War and the approach of the Second. The college continued to produce men of distinction: Randall Davidson (1867), Archbishop of Canterbury (and before that Visitor of the college as Bishop of Winchester); Rayner Goddard (1895–8), Lord Chief Justice; Charles Cannan (Fellow 1884–98), secretary to the OXFORD UNIVERSITY PRESS; R.W. Raper, an influential Fellow (1871–1915) and instigator of the Delegacy for Employment; Sir Arthur Quiller-Couch (1882); Cyril Alington (1891), headmaster of Eton and Dean of Durham; Sir Henry Stuart-Jones (Fellow 1890–1919), lexicographer; A.E.W. Mason (1884), novelist. Many of the Fellow-Chaplains rose to ecclesiastical fame – Charles Gore (1875–80), RONALD KNOX (1912–17), Kenneth Kirk (1922–33) and Austin Farrer (1935–60). In more recent years the college mourns Anthony Crosland (1937), Secretary of State for Foreign Affairs, and Sir Peter Kirk (1946), MP.

Like most Oxford colleges, Trinity suffered savage losses in the First World War: 155 names are on the memorial tablet in the library. This building was constructed by J. Osborne Smith, but the inspiration was that of President Blakiston himself, on land acquired from premises behind Broad Street. Nothing of note was added to the fabric between the wars but the second conflict brought losses almost as heavy as the first, with 132 names on the list – a contrast to the memorials in many a country church. During the Second World War the college housed under graduates, in diminished numbers, from Balliol and Keble as well as its own (in the First it had been used by the War Office for cadets). A bath-house was installed for the latter, which, with typical ingenuity President Blakiston succeeded in taking over free of cost.

In 1955 Trinity celebrated its 400th anniversary sharing the occasion with St John's, which had been established later in 1555. Two years afterwards the college received a large bequest from an old member Hugh Charles Cumberbatch (1904), including silver and furniture and also four fine leaden urns which now decorate the Garden Quadrangle. A building bearing his name was put up at the north end of the War Memorial Library; at the same time a link was built across the Kettell Hall garden and a huge under ground bookstore constructed for the benefit of Blackwell's, which, in honour of the then President also a former secretary of the Oxford University Press was given the title of the Norrington Room Cumberbatch was opened in June 1966; the architects were Robert Maguire and Keith Murray. It included a very successful public room named from the gifts of Colonel John Raymond Danson. It seems unlikely that the college can expand further on its present site without grave detriment to the garden. Steps have accordingly been taken to acquire property in NORTH OXFORD to house graduates and others.

Naturally the college has grown in numbers. In 1939 there were twelve Fellows and about 160 undergraduates. In recent years those reading for first degree have totalled about 245 and graduate students about sixty. The Senior Common Room contains twenty-six Fellows, including holders of professorial CHAIRS. The most striking change came with the advent of women in 1979; but it has not seemed greatly to have altered the life of the college With these figures, Trinity remains one of the smallest colleges; the ordinary undergraduate can still expect to pass his first two years within its walls, most of which were refaced with Bath stone in the years 1957–71, largely thanks to the generosity of the Oxford Historic Buildings Fund.

When President Ogston (1970–8) retired, he was painted in a conversation piece with two Nobel prizewinners (Sir Hans Krebs and Professor Porter CH) and two holders of the OM (Lord Clark and Sir Ronald Syme).

The corporate designation of the college is The President, Fellows and Scholars of the College of the Holy and Undivided Trinity in the University of Oxford of the Foundation of Sir Thomas Pope Knight. The President in 1990 was Sir John Burgh.

(Blakiston, H.E.D., *Trinity College*, 1898; *Victoria County History of Oxfordshire*, Vol. III, Oxford, 1954, pp. 238–51; Maclagan, Michael, *Trinity College: Short Guide and History*, revised edition, Oxford 1963.)

Trout *Godstow Road.* Originally a fisherman's house in the 16th century, it was an inn by 1625 and

A photograph of c.1885 of the Trout Inn, Godstow, which has been an inn since 1625.

was largely rebuilt in 1737 with separate stables which are still visible. The present two-storey building of grey stone and pitched roof of Stonesfield slate contains two flagstoned rooms, large oak beams, fireplaces and leaded windows. Famous for its wandering peacocks and its river terrace, it is mentioned in Matthew Arnold's poem 'The Scholar Gipsy'.

Turf Tavern *St Helen's Passage/Bath Place.* Begun as a malthouse, it became a cider house in 1775 and an inn, the Spotted Cow, in about 1790. At this time building land was scarce inside the CITY WALL, so many small tenements were erected just outside it. This small timbered inn became the Turf Tavern in 1847. It was closed suddenly in November 1986, following a dispute concerning the terms of the will of the late landlord, who had run it for more than thirty years on lease from Merton College, but reopened in 1987.

Turl Street An ancient street which connects BROAD STREET with HIGH STREET. It almost certainly gets its name from a revolving or twirling gate which was in a postern in the CITY WALL at the Broad Street or north end, until demolished in 1722. The street was very narrow at that point, but was set back and widened in 1785. It is joined by MARKET STREET in the centre. At the south end stands the former ALL SAINTS CHURCH, now the library of Lincoln College. This building appears to block off the end of the street, which in fact curves to the right and narrows before entering High Street. Almost the whole of the east side of the street is taken up by two colleges, Lincoln and Exeter. The former extends from High Street to BRASENOSE LANE, a narrow pedestrian lane which still has a gutter or kennel running down the centre in the mediaeval manner. On the north side of Brasenose Lane is Exeter College, with the new building

containing PARKER'S bookshop on the corner with Broad Street. On the opposite side of the street, the row of late 18th-century houses, stucco and timber-framed, between Broad Street and SHIP STREET, now contain shops. On the south side of Ship Street is Jesus College, with a large horse chestnut tree on the corner. The college extends to Market Street, and beyond that is a row of shops as far as the MITRE. Lincoln House, designed by G.T. Gardner and built in 1938–9 on the site of Lincoln College stables, is on the corner with Market Street. No. 14 is a timber-framed house of 17th-century origin. The building occupied by WALTERS & CO., the tailors, at Nos 10–12 was from 1607 to 1899 the MAIDEN'S HEAD INN. ROWELL & SON, the silversmiths, moved here from High Street in 1986.

In 1985 the southern part of the street from Market Street to the High was closed to traffic except for BICYCLES and vehicles requiring access.

Turn Again Lane The old name for this lane was revived in 1972 after it had been known as Charles Street for many years. A deed of 1737 shows 'Charles Street, known as Turn Again Lane'. Wood Street ran off the lane to the south, ending in a blank wall at the TRILL MILL STREAM, where a flight of steps led down to the water. This meant that people had to turn back again along Wood Street. HENRY TAUNT, the photographer, wrote in 1912 to H.E. SALTER, 'It was well-named Turn Again Lane when the old river gate was standing, as there was no outlet excepting the one entrance at Littlegate.' Two mid-17th-century and one 18th-century gabled stone houses (formerly Nos 8, 8a, 9 and 10) remain in an area dominated by the WESTGATE CENTRE and new buildings in LITTLEGATE STREET. They were threatened with demolition in the 1960s at a time when commercial development was being planned for the area by the City Council, but were saved by the perseverance of a few individuals and the OXFORD PRESERVATION TRUST's willingness to buy them. The Trust's offices are now in No. 10. The houses were restored in 1971. The lane now lies between Littlegate Street and OLD GREYFRIARS STREET.

Turner, William, of Oxford *(1789–1862).* After the death of his parents, when he was fourteen years old, William Turner went to live with his uncle, also William Turner, at the Manor House, Shipton-on-Cherwell, near Woodstock. As he showed an interest in drawing, he was sent in 1804 to join the household of John Varley in London. He had his first exhibition at the Royal Academy in 1807 and the following year, at the age of seventeen, was elected an Associate of the Royal Society of Painters in Water Colours. He is always referred to as William Turner of Oxford to distinguish him from his more famous contemporary, J.M.W. Turner. Although living in London, many of his subjects were of the countryside round Oxford. In 1812 he returned to Oxford and settled in ST JOHN STREET, where he lived until his death, though frequently staying with his uncle at Shipton-on-Cherwell.

He occasionally painted in oils, but preferred watercolours. He described himself in a census return as 'Artist and Teacher of Landscape Painting'. Many of his paintings depict broad landscapes, often with dramatic cloud effects and frequently with sheep. In

A self-portrait of William Turner of Oxford, who lived in St John Street from the 1820s until his death in 1862.

1838 he made a tour of Scotland and Scottish scenes figure largely in his later work. Some of his drawings of Oxford are in the ASHMOLEAN MUSEUM, and other works are in Exeter College, Worcester College, and in the City Council's collection in the TOWN HALL. A lover of nature, he was much influenced by John Varley. A reviewer of his early work, writing in 1808, said, 'By the mere dint of his superior art he has rolled such clouds over these landscapes as has given to a flat country an equal grandeur with mountain scenery.'

An exhibition of Turner's work was mounted at Woodstock in 1984 by the Oxfordshire County Museum Services and was later on show at the Bankside Gallery in London and at Bolton. This was the first major exhibition of the artist's work since the memorial exhibition held in the Ashmolean, then the University Galleries, in 1895.

Tutorials It is, above all, the tutorial system – a system integral to the college structure – which differentiates Oxford and Cambridge from most other Universities. The tutorial is the period, normally of an hour, which an undergraduate spends each week with his tutor or tutors, reading an essay, discussing his work and considering academic matters generally. Traditionally an undergraduate would have only one or two tutorials per week, and those would be *tête-à-tête*. However, an increasing degree of specialisation, together with an ever-widening range of options, has tended to mean that now an undergraduate will have more tutorials per week than would once have been the case; but equally they are less commonly *tête-à-tête*, as there may be two or three undergraduates at a tutorial, with the result that the distinction between a tutorial and a class can readily become blurred. However, there can be little doubt that the old-style tutorial remains what it always has been – namely an unrivalled method of ensuring that an undergraduate's strengths and weaknesses can be seen, and, where necessary, improved or corrected. It is arguable that an undergraduate's relationship with his or her tutor is often the closest that he or she will form during a University career; and the friendships thus made are not infrequently lifelong. Most experienced tutors would agree that it is essential in a tutorial not only to test the pupil's work but also to use it to enhance and broaden his interest in the subject.

There is an amusing account of a tutorial in Stephen Leacock's 'My Discovery of England', in which he sums up the system with the words: 'Men who have been systematically smoked at for four years turn into ripe scholars.'

Twining's Alderman Francis Twining founded the grocery firm of Twining Bros in the 19th century at the age of twenty-three. He had worked at GRIMBLY HUGHES shop in CORNMARKET after leaving school, but set up on his own in a grocer's shop in ST EBBE'S. The firm eventually had seven branches in Oxford, but was forced to close by the onset of the supermarket era in the 1960s. Francis Twining was also a land developer. In 1895 he bought some 25 acres at Hawkswell Farm, SUMMERTOWN, which, with 25 acres of Stone's Estate, was developed for housing and now comprises Portland Road, Lonsdale Road, King's Cross Road, Victoria Road, Hamilton Road and Lucerne Road, all to the east of BANBURY ROAD. Allotment land and tennis courts off King's Cross Road, part of the land which Twining bought, were developed in 1960 by Hawkswell Estates Ltd as Hawkswell Gardens. The houses were built by KNOWLES & SON, with front gardens owned by the estate company. Francis Twining lived at Summertown House, a large house north of Apsley Paddox. He was MAYOR of Oxford in 1905 and died in 1929. Apsley Road and a block of flats for University graduates and visiting academics were built in the grounds of the house.

Twyne, Brian (*c.1579–1644*). Entered Corpus Christi College in 1594 and, after election to a fellowship in 1605, was appointed lecturer in Greek in 1614. He resigned his lectureship in 1623 and thereafter devoted his time to antiquarian research. He had already published his *Antiquitatis Academiae Oxoniensis Apologia*, the earliest history of Oxford, in 1608; but the body of his published work is exceedingly small compared with the sixty volumes of his manuscripts of which ANTHONY WOOD was to make such free and barely acknowledged use. Twyne, with the help of Richard Zouche (1590–1661), Regius Professor of Civil Law, was largely responsible for editing the statutes known as the LAUDIAN CODE and was, in recognition of his labours, appointed the first curator of the University ARCHIVES. He died in lodgings in ST ALDATE'S and was buried in the chapel of Corpus Christi College, to whose library he bequeathed 'many choice books'.

(*See also* HISTORIANS.)

——U——

UCCA Oxford University, together with all other British universities, is a member of the Universities Central Council on Admissions (UCCA), which has its headquarters in Cheltenham. All applicants for admission to Oxford (other than those who are already graduates) have to make application through UCCA, naming Oxford as one of the five universities they list in an order of preference on the UCCA form. The date for the submission of that form, for application to Oxford or Cambridge, is 15th October of the year before that for which entry is sought, which is two months earlier than the general closing date for students who are not applying to Oxford or Cambridge.

From a copy of the UCCA form, Oxford colleges can obtain information about their applicants' school record, GCE qualifications, and other interests, plus an academic reference. As part of their agreement with UCCA, Oxford colleges have to complete their decisions on all applicants by the end of January each year. This information is relayed by UCCA to the candidates and to all other universities involved with each student's application.

(*See also* ADMISSIONS.)

Union Society The Oxford Union Society was established in December 1825 out of the Oxford United Debating Society which had been founded in 1823. It is, in the words of Harold Macmillan, later EARL OF STOCKTON, 'unique in that it has provided an unrivalled training ground for debates in the Parliamentary style which no other debating society in any democratic country can equal'. Past officers of the Union have included five Prime Ministers – GLADSTONE (Christ Church), Salisbury (Christ Church), Asquith (Balliol), Macmillan (Balliol) and Heath (Balliol) – Cabinet Ministers and leading politicians, judges, bishops, and men and women distinguished in many walks of life. (A list of Presidents since 1900 is given in Appendix 6.)

The Union's first debating rooms were in Wyatt's, the picture dealer's, at No. 115 HIGH STREET. In 1852

The Committee of the Union in 1895. Seated in the middle row are (from left to right): *John Bradbury, Brasenose (later 1st Baron, government official); F.E. Smith, Wadham (later 1st Earl of Birkenhead, statesman and lawyer); P.J. Macdonell, Brasenose, President of the Union (later High Court Judge); Hilaire Belloc, Balliol, and J.A. Simon, Wadham (later Viscount Simon, statesman and lawyer).*

a site in ST MICHAEL'S STREET was bought and the building of a permanent home for the society began. It was not, however, until 1857 that the debating hall (now the Old Library) was built. It was designed by Benjamin Woodward in a Gothic style and built of brick. It has a gallery all round and in the centre of the room are two fireplaces back to back, covered by a slab of marble. There is a system of flues under the floor to remove the smoke. WILLIAM MORRIS and EDWARD BURNE-JONES, were then undergraduates at Exeter College. During the Long Vacation of 1857 Morris brought his friend Dante Gabriel Rossetti to Oxford, where they met Benjamin Woodward, who asked them to see his new debating hall, the walls of which were then bare. Rossetti recorded that 'without taking into consideration the purpose it was intended for (indeed hardly knowing of the latter) I offered to paint figures of some kind on the blank spaces of one of the gallery window bays; and another friend who was with us, William Morris, offered to do the same for the second bay. Woodward was greatly delighted with the idea'. The Building Committee agreed and scenes from the *Morte d'Arthur* were decided upon. Rossetti started on a picture of 'Sir Lancelot's Vision of the Holy Grail'. Morris did 'Tristram and Iseult' and then started decorating the ceiling with a 'vast pattern-work of grotesque creatures'. John Hungerford Pollen, a Fellow of Merton who had decorated the roof of Merton College chapel, joined the group to paint 'King Arthur Receiving his Sword Excalibur', while Burne-Jones did the 'Death of Merlin'. Val Prinsep, a young man of nineteen, painted 'Sir Pelleas and the Lady Ettard'. Arthur Hughes did the 'Death of Arthur', and Rodham Spencer Stanhope from Christ Church painted 'Sir Gawain and the Three Damsels at the Fountain'.

The paintings were highly praised by JOHN RUSKIN, who described Rossetti's picture as 'the finest piece of colour in the world'. Coventry Patmore called the colours 'so brilliant as to make the walls look like the margin of an illuminated manuscript'. Unfortunately the pictures were painted in distemper on a coat of whitewash applied to damp walls which had not been properly prepared and the colours very soon began to fade. Morris repainted his roof pictures in 1875 in 'a new and lighter design', but, in spite of a restoration carried out by Professor Tristram in 1930, most of the other murals were so faded that they were hardly recognisable. Only the carving in stone of 'King Arthur and his Knights' designed by Rossetti and carved by Alexander Munro in the tympanum over the door of what was formerly the entrance could still be seen clearly. William Rivière, a teacher of painting, was later commissioned to paint pictures of 'Arthur's Education under Merlin', 'Arthur's First Victory', and the 'Wedding of Arthur and Guinevere' in the three empty bays. Coloured photographs of the paintings, with a description of each, are now mounted on a board in the Old Library. The murals were restored in 1986 and can now be illuminated by electric light.

In 1863 a library, by William Wilkinson, was added to the old debating hall, and in 1878 a new debating hall was built, designed by Alfred Waterhouse. This, like the old one, has a gallery for visitors to the debates and contains busts of Asquith, Gladstone, Salisbury, Simon, Birkenhead, and LORD CURZON. Further extensions to the Union buildings were added in 1910–11, comprising a new library, a dining room and steward's house. They were designed in Gothic style by W.E. Mills & Thorpe

and were built in brick. The buildings of the Union now surround the garden on three sides, the fourth side having a row of flowering trees on the St Michael's Street front. In the past, when the Union's finances have been at a low ebb – notably in 1972 – attempts have been made to develop this front on a commercial basis.

In 1859 the Oxford Union Society had the Victorian penny stamps which were sold to its members overprinted with its initials, O.U.S., between two wavy lines as a precaution against theft (*see* POSTAL SERVICES). The Union's premises now include, apart from the debating hall, the largest lending library in the University. The old dining room on the first floor is now the Macmillan Restaurant. Next to it is the billiard room, and also on the first floor are the Gladstone Room (used for discussions, conferences, parties and similar functions) and the Morris Room. There is a large bar on the ground floor.

The Oxford Union is well known for the wit of its speakers, and debates have been enlivened by, among many others, F.E. Smith (Lord Birkenhead), Norman St John Stevas, Jeremy Thorpe, Kenneth Tynan and Robin Day. 'Do I hear hissing?' said one speaker. 'There is always hissing when the waters of heaven fall upon the fires of hell.' Possibly the best known debate in the history of the Union was the famous 'King and Country' debate in February 1933. The motion was 'that this House will in no circumstances fight for its King and its Country'. The guest speaker supporting the motion was the pacifist C.E.M. Joad. The opposer was the twenty-five-year-old Quintin Hogg, then a Fellow of All Souls and a barrister; he was later MP for Oxford and subsequently, as Lord Hailsham, became

Mrs (later Dame) Millicent Garrett Fawcett, a leading member of the women's suffrage movement, speaking at the Union in November 1908, the first woman to do so.

470

Lord Chancellor. The motion was carried by 275 votes to 153. The debate caused heated controversy in the press. A box containing 275 white feathers was sent to the Union, and at the next debate the minutes of the previous one were torn out of the Minute Book. Randolph Churchill later moved a motion that the debate be formally expunged from the Minute Book. The debate on this motion was better attended than the original debate, but the motion was defeated by a large majority. There have been other pacifist motions before and since; fifty years later, in 1983, a similar motion was debated and heavily defeated. Among those supporting the motion were Helen John of the Greenham Common Peace Movement, Lord Soper, and Tariq Ali, who had been President of the Union in 1965. Those opposing it included Lord Beloff and Lord Home. The Prime Minister in 1959, Harold Macmillan (later EARL OF STOCKTON), spoke at the Farewell Debate (the final debate of each term) on 3 December in that year, and Queen Elizabeth attended a debate on 2 May 1968.

The first woman to address the Union was the suffragette Mrs Millicent Garrett Fawcett in 1908, but it was not until 1968 that a woman was elected President; she was Geraldine Jones (St Hugh's). One of the best-known women Presidents was Benazir Bhutto (1977, Lady Margaret Hall), who, following the death in 1979 of her father, the Prime Minister of Pakistan, became leader of the Pakistan People's Party and in 1988 Prime Minister of Pakistan. In Hilary Term 1986, for the first time in the Union's history, the offices of President, Librarian and Treasurer were all held by women.

In 1989 the Chancellor of the University and Mr Takiyi Shidachi, President of the Mitsubishi Trust and Banking Corporation, unveiled a plaque to mark a £1 million donation by the banking group for the renovation of the Union building.

(Morrah, Herbert Arthur, *The Oxford Union, 1823–1923*, London, 1923; Hollis, Christopher, *The Oxford Union*, London, 1965; Walter, David, *The Oxford Union, Playground of Power*, London, 1984.

The Story of the Painting of the Pictures on the Walls and the Decorations on the Ceiling of the Old Debating Hall (now the Library) in the Years 1857–8–9, by W. Holman Hunt, 1906, was reprinted at the University Press in a limited edition for the Union Society.)

University Founded at an unknown date towards the middle of the 12th century, the University, centred on the church of ST MARY THE VIRGIN, was well established by the beginning of the 13th when quarrels between scholars and townspeople erupted into RIOTS which almost destroyed it. Thereafter, supported by the papal legate and by the patronage of the Crown and the Bishop of Lincoln, in whose diocese Oxford then lay, the University prospered, gradually gaining a large measure of independence under a CHANCELLOR elected by the masters, whose interests were represented by the PROCTORS and whose collective decisions were made known in CONVOCATION. Most of the undergraduates at first lived in ACADEMIC HALLS, of which there were sixty-nine in 1444 and of which ST EDMUND HALL is the only survivor. Soon, however, colleges were established: University, Balliol, Merton, Exeter, Oriel, The Queen's College and New College all being founded before the 15th century. In addition to these there were also MONASTIC COLLEGES.

Education was then principally theological, but Logic, Philosophy and Mathematics were also taught;

and, since books were few and LIBRARIES limited, information was generally imparted by means of lectures – the quality of which, by the end of the 14th century, was acknowledged to be high. Duns Scotus and William of Ockham had both taught at Oxford in the 14th century; so had JOHN WYCLIF, the arguments of whose followers demonstrated the vigour and vitality of the mediaeval University's intellectual life (*see* LOLLARDS).

The University was as yet a small seat of learning by comparison with the universities of Paris, Bologna and Padua; but its reputation continued to grow and the DEGREES it conferred became increasingly valued and, in many cases, hard to obtain – a Doctor's degree might involve a course of study extending over eighteen years, while in 1456–7 fewer than thirty Master's degrees were awarded. By then the character of the University had begun to change: humanistic ideas had been introduced into the syllabus and there were growing numbers of gentlemen's and noblemen's sons, preparing for careers in law, diplomacy and politics, in addition to those undergraduates intent upon entering the Church. At the same time Oxford was renowned for the number of exponents of the new learning who lived and taught here, including WILLIAM GROCYN, JOHN COLET, THOMAS LINACRE, William Lily (*c.*1468–1522) of Magdalen, and William Latimer (*c.*1460–1545) of All Souls. Both Christ Church and Corpus Christi College were founded in the early 16th century specifically to promote the ideas of the Renaissance.

The religious upheavals of the 16th century caused further alarm amid conservative clerical circles in the University still clinging to the old scholastic learning; and in the 1530s, at the time of the Dissolution of the Monasteries, their fears were intensified by the appearance in Oxford of King Henry VIII's VISITORS (*see also* ROMAN CATHOLICS *and* VISITATIONS).

In the reign of Queen Elizabeth I the ferment in the University subsided. Most dons, placated by the Queen's flatteringly avowed interest in Oxford and their own concern to retain their places and privileges, accepted the Elizabethan Settlement. And as the 16th century progressed, so Oxford became more and more a university to which the wealthy felt impelled to send their sons, not so much to make them scholars or clergymen but to make them gentlemen; of the five colleges created in the eighty years after 1550 four were founded by rich laymen. Nevertheless, Oxford was still largely a clerical institution; most of its dons were clergymen; many of its undergraduates intended to be so; and its curriculum had changed but little in the past century, though there were both students and dons of eager intellectual curiosity and CHAIRS were being founded in such disciplines as Geometry and Astronomy, Natural Philosophy, Anatomy and Medicine. A chair of Arabic was founded by WILLIAM LAUD, whose influence on the 17th-century University was profound. The LAUDIAN CODE of 1636, however, was soon followed by the upheavals of the CIVIL WAR and by the Parliamentary Visitation of 1647. Yet the threat to Oxford posed by such men as the Digger, Gerrard Winstanley (*fl.*1648–52), who condemned all universities as standing ponds of 'stinking waters', was averted with the help of less extreme reformers like John Selden, Oxford's BURGESS in the Long Parliament (*see* BODLEIAN LIBRARY) and Oliver Cromwell, who became Chancellor in 1650. When Charles II was

Oxford University Amusements, *an aquatint by R.W. Buss, 1842.*

restored to the throne in 1660 the University adjusted itself to the new order with an ease which, in the words of Dr V.H.H. Green, 'suggests that the influence of the Puritan regime was superficial'.

There were, indeed, many voices, including that of ANTHONY WOOD, which were raised to deplore the laxity and dissoluteness of University life. And throughout the rest of the 17th century and for most of the 18th there were recurring scandals involving drunkenness, fornication, sodomy and what Wood called general 'sauciness'. These scandals were accompanied by a deterioration in the relations between the government and Oxford (*see* RIOTS *and* VISITATIONS) and in academic standards, in the quality of lectures and the size of their audiences, in the standard of disputations (still the usual method of instruction) and in the rigour of examinations. In a celebrated passage, Edward Gibbon described his days as a gentleman-commoner at Magdalen College as the most 'idle and unprofitable' of his whole life; while John Scott (1751–1838), later Lord Chancellor Eldon, maintained that his examination in Hebrew and History for his Bachelor's degree in 1770 consisted of just two questions:

Examiner: What is the Hebrew for the place of a skull?
Scott: Golgotha.

Examiner: Who founded University College?
Scott: King Alfred.

Examiner: Very well, sir, you are competent for your degree.

As the reputation of the University declined, so did the numbers of those attending it. By the middle of the 18th century there were fewer than half as many freshmen as had been admitted in the 1630s. Poorer parents could not afford Oxford's high fees and expenses; the richer preferred to send their sons on a Grand Tour of the Continent.

Yet although there were certainly many idle dons and numerous unsupervised undergraduates who did not trouble their tutors by seeking any instruction, it does seem that several of the better-known accounts of University life, such as Jeremy Bentham's of his life at The Queen's College, where he 'learnt nothing' and had 'no encouragement', were highly coloured. There were more than a few conscientious tutors, such as John Russell under whom Richard Edgeworth studied at Corpus Christi in the 1760s: 'I applied assiduously not only to my studies, under my excellent tutor Mr Russell, but also to the perusal of the best English writers, both in prose and verse. Scarcely a day passed without my having added to my stock of knowledge.' Against the names of Joseph Hunter, Fellow of Queen's, whom THOMAS HEARNE dismissed as 'a drunken old sot', and Robert Thistlewaite, Warden of Wadham, who – confessing that he 'did not give a Farthing for the finest Woman in the World, and that he loved a Man as he did his Soul' – went 'tickling about the Breeches' of both the college butler and the barber, may be set those of JOHN FELL and HENRY ALDRICH.

By the beginning of the 19th century demands for reform had nevertheless become difficult to resist (*see* ROYAL COMMISSIONS) and, after a series of complaints had been investigated and reported upon, reforms were gradually made. The first of the University Reform Acts was passed in 1854, and thereafter numerous alterations were made in the University's syllabus. Jurisprudence and History became separate SCHOOLS in 1872, the year in which the Honour School of Oriental Languages was established. The new School of English was instituted in 1893; and this was shortly followed by several other new Schools – among them those of Modern Greats (or Philosophy, Politics and Economics) and later Joint-Honour Schools. At the same time graduate research was greatly extended, while the number of research students increased so fast that by the beginning of the

1970s there were over 3000 post-graduate students compared with 8011 undergraduates.

While such scholars as BENJAMIN JOWETT and MARK PATTISON enhanced the reputation of Oxford as a centre of Classical Studies in the late Victorian period, it later became renowned for studies in wider fields – in History and Law, in Science and Philosophy. To single out but two of these fields, in our own day the Oxford philosophers A.J. Ayer (Wykeham Professor of Logic 1959–78), J.L. Austin (White's Professor of Moral Philosophy 1952–60), GILBERT RYLE and Sir Peter Strawson (Waynflete Professor of Metaphysical Philosophy since 1968) have aroused international controversy, while the names of some recent Oxford scientists provide an indication of the contribution made by the University to scientific research – Frederick Soddy (1877–1956), for seventeen years Professor of Chemistry; SIR CYRIL HINSHELWOOD, President of the Classical Association as well as of the Royal Society; LORD CHERWELL and his successor Francis Simon (1893–1956); LORD FLOREY; William Hume-Rothery (1899–1968), Wolfson Professor of Metallurgy; Sir Hans Krebs (1900–1981), Whitley Professor of Biochemistry; and Dorothy Hodgkin (b.1910), the chemist and Nobel prizewinner (see also CLARENDON LABORATORY).

Professor Hodgkin was at Somerville College, which had been founded in 1879 as a residential hall for women (the year after the establishment of the first such hall, Lady Margaret Hall). The Society of Oxford Home Students, which became St Anne's College in 1952, had also been founded in 1879. In 1884 Convocation decided by 464 votes to 321 that women should be allowed to take certain examinations, though it was not until 1920 that they were allowed to matriculate and to take all degrees except those in Theology, and it was not until 1956 that a limit imposed by the HEBDOMADAL COUNCIL upon the number of women who could be admitted to the University was finally lifted. In 1972 five men's colleges – Brasenose, Wadham, Jesus, St Catherine's and Hertford – changed their statutes so that they could admit women as graduates and undergraduates, an example since followed by all men's colleges.

After the First World War, which reduced the number of undergraduates from 1400 in 1914 to 369 in 1918, the finances of the University were in so serious a condition that a government grant had to be sought (see ROYAL COMMISSIONS). The reforms which this entailed, and those implemented after the report of the FRANKS COMMISSION, permanently changed the character of certain aspects of the University; while state grants, and a sharp increase in the number of students taking school examinations at advanced levels, made a marked difference to the kind of undergraduates that Oxford attracted. For long some colleges – Christ Church and Trinity among them – contrived to take most of their undergraduates from public schools; but the number of undergraduates at Oxford who have come up from independent schools is now a minority. By the 1980s the total number of undergraduates at the University had risen to nearly 10,000, almost half of them women.

Another notable change in University life has been the establishment of new graduate societies. Linacre College was founded in 1962, St Cross in 1965 and Wolfson College in 1966. Nuffield and St Antony's

Colleges had already been established in 1963. Green College was instituted in 1977.

(See also ACADEMIC HALLS, COLLEGES and MONASTIC COLLEGES.)

University and City Arms *288 Cowley Road*. The original inn stood from 1850–1938, when the present inn was built by HALL'S BREWERY to the design of their architect J.C. Leed. It was Oxford's largest inn from 1957 to 1977, when the HEAD OF THE RIVER was opened.

University Appointments Committee Founded in 1892 under the secretaryship of R.W. Raper of Trinity, it became a statutory department in 1907. Its objects are to assist members of the University by giving advice on careers, by seeking and receiving information of openings for employment, and by supplying this information to members. The services of the committee are now regularly sought and used by a very high percentage of undergraduate (and, increasingly, graduate) members of the University. Its staff and facilities (especially word processors and visual display units) have expanded to meet the University's growing size and needs; in 1985–6 its income and expenditure exceeded £400,000. The committee's staff and offices are now situated at No. 56 BANBURY ROAD. The secretary's staff normally includes a senior assistant secretary and nine assistant secretaries – all of whom are full-time officers of the University. There is almost certainly no University department which is better known to the University's junior members, or more highly valued by them; and its high reputation is fully borne out by its very high rate of success in helping graduates and undergraduates to find employment.

University Archives *see* ARCHIVES, UNIVERSITY.

University Chest Has three distinct meanings: an ancient mediaeval coffer, now in the ASHMOLEAN MUSEUM; the committee of University members dealing with University finance; and a part of the University secretariat in WELLINGTON SQUARE. The evolution from the first to the third spans seven centuries of the history of relations between the University and the colleges.

The earliest endowment of the University is recorded in 1214, an annual fine of £2 12s on the Oxford townsmen for an unlawful hanging of students. In 1240 ROBERT GROSSETESTE, an early CHANCELLOR, ordered the payments to be deposited in 'the Common Chest' which became the first of some dozen chests used as safe deposits from which loans were made to needy students in return for pledged valuables placed in them.

In 1427 the direct ancestor of the present University Chest makes its appearance, intended for the University's money and PLATE. It was provided with five locks, for five keyholders acting simultaneously. To distinguish it from other chests in use it was known as 'the Chest of the Five Keys'. Up to the mid-16th century accounts of University income and expenditure were maintained by the two PROCTORS but following alleged irregularities, the VICE-CHANCELLOR became responsible for the University's monies. In 1545 the Chest of the Five Keys was repaired, five new keyholders were appointed and all pledges were sold.

473

The Chest of the Five Keys, as the sole survivor, became *the* University Chest.

In 1668 another chest of five keys, but of lighter construction, replaced the original one; it became known as 'the Painted Chest'. Its appointed place of safe-keeping – and that of the Chest of the Five Keys – was the tower of Corpus Christi College. The Painted Chest was the sole repository of the University's cash and accounts until the University opened a bank account in 1756. A century later, the Painted Chest was deposited in the office of the secretary to the Curators of the Chest, where it remains. The Chest of the Five Keys has been on display in the Ashmolean since 1935.

The opening of a bank account by the University still left the handling of its finances the personal responsibility of the Vice-Chancellor, which successive Vice-Chancellors found increasingly onerous, with the squaring-up of accounts and the handing-over of the balance a disturbing process. Hence, in 1868, the handling of the University's finances and the management of its estates were placed in the hands of a committee – the Curators of the University Chest – with a full-time salaried secretary.

In the subsequent history of University reform two topics regularly cropped up: the anomalous position of the Curators and the disparity between the financial resources of the University and those of the colleges. The Curators of the Chest, though having considerable independence, never developed into a means of dealing with University finance as a whole. Following the ROYAL COMMISSION of 1872, which calculated the annual income of the University and of the colleges as £48,589 and £397,015 respectively, a system of taxing colleges for University purposes was set up, the product being paid into a specially established fund over which the Chest had no control.

The situation of a poor and weak University, with no central financial authority, dealing with richly endowed colleges persisted into the first half of the 20th century. Since 1945, however, a transformation has taken place. In 1919 the University first received a government grant – £30,000. This had grown to £57,000,000 in 1988–9, within the University's total annual income of £132,000,000, the colleges' annual income being £79,000,000, including £31,000,000 from endowments. Increasing contributions of public money have made it necessary for the University to evolve central machinery for financial control. One outcome is that, although 'the Chest' retains its ancient title, it is now part of the UNIVERSITY OFFICES under the REGISTRAR.

University Church see ST MARY THE VIRGIN.

University College The first collegiate foundation in Oxford, and therefore in Great Britain. The churchman–scholar William of Durham in 1249 bequeathed to the University 310 marks to be used to buy property, the rents from which were to maintain ten or twelve Masters of Arts studying Divinity. The University accordingly bought some properties. The first, in 1253, became known as Aula Universitatis (the hall of the University, or University Hall). In 1280 an 'inquisition' into what had become of William's benefaction was held by the University. (The document reporting the findings is in the college muniment room.) The 'inquisition' also drew up

statutes for the college. These antedate those of Balliol but not those of Merton. The three colleges amiably dispute the seniority, which may be determined thus: University College had the first benefactor and – indirectly – founder, and the first property; Balliol the first actual site; Merton the first statutes.

After 1280 more buildings were acquired, including (from 1332) some on the south side of HIGH STREET. Gradually the properties were amalgamated, and further purchases extended the site, which the college has occupied ever since and from time to time enlarged by purchase.

The history of 'Univ.' (as the college is commonly known) is long, but mostly uneventful – though it would not have seemed so to its early members, for it remained small in numbers and poor in endowment for the first two and a half centuries of its existence, and was several times on the verge of penury and perhaps extinction. Of course there were some dramas: the whole society was excommunicated in 1411 for supporting the LOLLARD 'heresies'; the Master and four Fellows were expelled during the CIVIL WAR; and there was a schism, with two rival Masters entrenched, in the early 18th century.

In about 1380, because of a dispute over property in which the college seemed likely to lose calamitously, the Fellows petitioned the Crown, asserting that Univ. had been founded by King Alfred and that his descendant Richard II was therefore its patron and should be its protector. The spurious claim was upheld and the college benefited. King Alfred is still prayed for on college feast days, although in discreetly ambiguous terms, for 'his encouragement of learning in this land'. Univ. has normally asserted its royal origins lightheartedly, but in the 18th century did so more seriously. After a disputed election to the mastership in 1722, when the Southern candidate narrowly defeated the Northern (*see* NATIONS) and two 'Masters' in residence disputed the mastership, an appeal was made again to the Crown, and in 1727 the court of King's Bench confirmed 'the fact' of royal foundation by King Alfred. (In 1872 the college unblushingly celebrated its millennium; it was presented with a parcel of burnt cakes at the celebratory dinner by the Regius Professor of History. It was more historically minded – or solemn – in 1972, allowing the occasion to pass uncelebrated.)

The strong northern connection, especially with Durham and Yorkshire, was strengthened in the 1440s by a valuable gift of land and property in Yorkshire for the support of three new Fellows from the northern dioceses by Henry Percy, Earl of Northumberland. This and other gifts enabled the college to build in the mid-15th century a new hall, kitchen and buttery, and to achieve the collegiate respectability of a gate-tower, but all were on a modest scale.

The 16th-century college did not lose ground, but did not much advance under a succession of briefly ruling Masters (five in the fifteen years between 1546 and 1561; two of these died after a year in office, one was a Catholic overtaken by the death of Mary I (*see* ROMAN CATHOLICS), and another was deprived for refusing to take the oath of the Queen's (Elizabeth's) Supremacy. Yet the college seems to have been spared deep divisions during the period of national religious oscillation from the time of Henry VIII; and the same was true even in the late 17th century under James II,

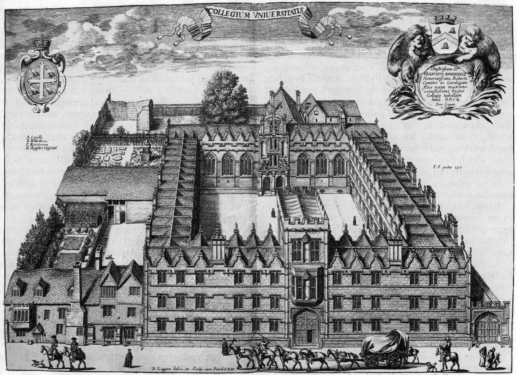

A bird's-eye view from David Loggan's Oxonia Illustrata *of 1675, depicting the recently rebuilt University College.*

when the Catholic Master, Obadiah Walker, set up a Mass-chapel in rooms in the quadrangle, a statue of James II on the tower, and a printing press for Catholic propaganda. And in the 20th century a rather markedly conservative college accommodated itself to becoming an inadvertent focus for social and political discussion and reform over several decades: William Beveridge (Master 1937–45) was a Prize Fellow (1902–9); Alec Paterson (1902) the future prison reformer, and Clement Attlee (1901), later Labour leader and Prime Minister, were undergraduates. Fellows included the early socialist A.J. Carlyle (1893 and Honorary Fellow 1963), G.D.H. Cole (1925–44 and Honorary Fellow 1944) and later J. Harold Wilson (1944 and Honorary Fellow 1963), the college's future second socialist Prime Minister.

A distinguished period for the still small college began with the mastership (1572–84) of William James, later Dean of Christ Church and Bishop of Durham, and his successor, the first layman Master, Anthony Gate (1584–97). By this time the Reformation had made possible the gradual secularisation – in some respects – of the college and the introduction of 'lay' subjects, notably Classics. The college now admitted undergraduates, and established properly organised teaching under praelectors in Greek, Philosophy and Logic as well as in Divinity. The northern connection continued, and was further strengthened by two Yorkshire benefactions, one of which provided for scholars from four Yorkshire schools. In 1618 the bequest of a southerner added scholarships from two schools in Kent. It is worth noting in passing, now that closed scholarships have been abolished in the University, that even what was

for so long a very small college was regularly able to give the chance of advancement to five or six poor boys a year for nearly 400 years.

In the early 17th century further benefactions made possible the building of a newly designed complete new college. The operation took more than thirty years, long delays being caused by the Civil War and by periodic shortages of money. Pulling down the small, old ranges and building anew was clearly a sign of confidence: it made the college larger and more considerable, and marked a turning-point in its fortunes, despite the troubles of the Civil War, and, not long afterwards, of the mercifully short period of James II's reign. Indeed the second half of the 18th century was another distinguished period for the college, largely due to the ability and personality of Robert Chambers (Fellow 1761–73). The fellowship included the Vinerian Professor of Law (Chambers), the Camden Professor of Ancient History (William Scott, later Lord Stowell, 1767–74); the botanist Sibthorpe (Radcliffe Fellow 1781); two future great orientalists and men of Law, Chambers himself and William Jones (1764–83); and the brothers Scott, a future Attorney-General and a future Lord Chancellor. A University College Club was founded at the end of the period; it had thirty-three members of whom eleven were or had been MPs, four ministers of the Crown, thirteen judges, two Lords Lieutenant, and one Commander-in-Chief in Scotland.

This period of intellectual and public prominence was inevitably followed by a decline – or rather a period of quite different quality – when Univ. was renowned for the number of hunting men 'in pink' it could turn out, and it ranked with or next to Christ

475

Church for aristocratic or landed-gentry members. The Cecil family for a time deserted Christ Church, between 1880 and 1890 sending the future Marquess of Salisbury, the future Viscount Cecil of Chelwood, a future Bishop of Exeter and Lord Hugh Cecil in turn to Univ. But this was after another swing, when again a devoted and enlightened Fellow, Arthur Penrhyn Stanley (1838–51), elevated the college's intellectual aims and, eventually, achievements, at the same time concerning himself, as the college historian William Carr expressed it, 'to facilitate social intercourse among those under his charge both rich and poor, hard-working and otherwise ... and the friendly social tone which for many years has been, and still is, characteristic of University as a college may be traced in great measure to the work and influence of this popular tutor.'

In the 20th century the college has increased in size, in its finances and greatly in distinction. It is now among the five or six leading colleges in academic and intellectual standing – higher probably than at any time in its long history.

No buildings earlier than 1634 survive at University College (with the exception of the earlier No. 90 High Street, which was taken into the college later). The ranges of the new front quadrangle, begun in 1634, slowly rose one by one behind the simple but apparently pretty ranges of the early small college, which were demolished in turn. The work was not finally completed until 1677. It is a conventional Oxford Gothic building and plan: a battlemented gate-tower with a porter's lodge; chapel and hall adjacent to each other across the quadrangle; separate staircases punctuating the ranges and giving access to the Fellows' and undergraduates' rooms; regular fenestration, and in the case of Univ., a parapet of rather heavy ogee gablets, the loop of the gablet held by a somewhat heavy 'brooch'. (The master-mason

came direct from completing work at St John's, where the President's Garden façade of the Canterbury Quadrangle has the same odd detail.) The south range, formed by the chapel and hall, originally had a rather rustic classical centrepiece, and the ogee gablets crowded the parapet and so made a virtually continuous sequence all round the quadrangle. It was mediaeval Gothic Univ.'s clumsy acknowledgement that the classical Renaissance had arrived in English architecture. Later, Gothicism revived, and in 1802 James Griffith, a Fellow with an itch – and some talent – for architecture, designed and saw constructed a Gothic façade for the south range, with crenellation, pinnacled buttresses (much crocketed) and a high gabled centrepiece with a tall oriel. As this had been built in poor limestone, 160 years later it needed reconstruction and, as the cost of faithful replacement would have been very high, the college decided on a simplification, lowering (and de-Gothicising) the crenellation and dispensing with pinnacles to the design of S. Dykes Bower (1957). The gate-tower has a stone statue of Queen Anne on the street front, and one of James II on the inner front, the latter being one of only two known statues of that monarch. The oak door is the original one, the fan-vaulting spectacularly anachronistic, yet functional.

The chapel interior, originally a good 17th-century Caroline interior save for the traceried Gothic windows, suffered Gothicising by SIR GEORGE GILBERT SCOTT in 1862. He installed an inappropriate large five-light east window, a high-pitched roof and a gallimaufry of Scott-Gothic at the east end (later mercifully concealed by the replacement of as much of the original panelling as survived and by curtaining): ball-flower, tessellation, arcading, stiff foliation, Purbeck marble shafts, all based on his favoured Decorated period. The glass in the north and south windows – seven windows in all – is wonderful painted

A steel engraving of Frederick Mackenzie's drawing of University College seen from the High Street c.1853.

476

glass by Abraham van Ling, dated 1641, full of colour, vigour and humanity and with many delightful landscape scenes (*see also* STAINED GLASS). The screen (1694) is of high quality, and the stalls, candle-holders and paving are all original. There is a pleasing monument to Sir William Jones, showing him with Indian scholars forming 'a digest of Hindu and Mohammedan Laws', by Flaxman, who also did three other memorials (to Chambers, Wetherell (Master 1764–1807) and Rolleson). A tablet to A.J. Melly (1919) was designed and cut by Eric Gill. The organ by J.W. Walker (1864) was enlarged and improved, and a new case for it designed by Sir Albert Richardson in 1955.

The hall is basically the original 17th-century hall (a truss next to the central roof-lantern bears the date 1656), although it was extended westwards by two bays in 1904. Much of the furnishing – oak tables and benches, but not the panelling – is original. The portraits include a fine Lawrence of William Windham, two good Hoppners of the Marquess of Hastings and Lord Stowell; a resplendent Sir Roger Newdigate by Kirkby; and good conventional Elizabethan/Jacobean portraits of Bishop Bancroft and Archbishop Abbot. There are some unusually good Victorian portraits by little-known and, one is inclined to think, unfairly ignored Victorian painters, notably Eddis – Dean Stanley and Master Plumptre – and Solomon – Lord Davey. The modern portraits include a splendid Greiffenhagen of Master Macan; an affectionate and perceptive portrait of Lord Beveridge in his eightieth year by Allan Gwynne-Jones; and a powerful, brooding study of Lord Goodman (Master) by Graham Sutherland, as well as portraits of the two Univ. Prime Ministers, Lords Attlee and Wilson. (In the common room hang a reputed Zuccharo – now thought to be by Segar – of Robert Dudley, Earl of Leicester, a reputed Lely of Sir Edward Hales, and a contemporary portrait of Lord Herbert of Cherbury.)

The 17th-century kitchen range lies behind the hall to the south. The first floor (the original library) is now the Alington Room – a panelled and wainscotted common room designed by Sir Albert Richardson (1956), gift of Master Goodhart in memory of a much-loved Dean, Giles Alington (1944–56).

To the west of the front quadrangle is New Buildings, a plain, seemly Gothic piece of 1842 by Charles Barry, the great architect already involved with his design for the Houses of Parliament. On the way to it you pass the figure in Carrara marble of the drowned Shelley – a moving and underrated conception by Onslow Ford – in a small domed mausoleum by Basil Champneys (1894) (*see* SHELLEY MEMORIAL).

To the east of the front quadrangle a central passage gives on to the Radcliffe Quadrangle, begun in 1716 and named after the donor, an old member and great benefactor of the college, DR JOHN RADCLIFFE. It was built by TOWNESEND and PEISLEY. Although nearly 100 years later than the design of the front quadrangle, it looks exactly coeval, for Radcliffe wanted it to be built 'answerable to the old'. In fact it is more attractive, being a three-sided building open to the south. A robust Dr Radcliffe in lead by Francis Bird stands on the inside face of the gate-tower, and a lead statue of Queen Mary II on the outside; so Univ. commemorates in statuary the last three Stuart

sovereigns. The fan-vaulting below the tower is almost certainly the last *functional* fan-vaulting in the country, and was constructed – a pleasing example of Gothic survival – only a few years before merely decorative Gothic Revival fan-vaulting began to appear.

The Master's lodgings in LOGIC LANE, east of the Radcliffe Quadrangle, is a charming 16th–17th-century Cotswold manor house by G.F. BODLEY (1879). It now faces a modern building, partly aiming to be quadrangular, by Mathew and Johnson-Marshall (1962), named after the munificent Master, Dr A.L. Goodhart (1951–6).

The library, west of the hall and cutting off the sun from a fair part of the Fellows' Garden, is Decorated Gothic, again by Sir George Gilbert Scott (1861). One would have called it unyieldingly ecclesiastical for its purpose but that the fenestration was altered when it became necessary to insert another floor into the wasteful spaces of its height. In the vestibule respectively glower and gloom the mammoth figures in Carrara marble of the two legal brothers and Fellows, Lords Stowell and Eldon (1767–74 and 1764–82 respectively), intended for Westminster Abbey but rejected.

The chief glory among the college's possessions is the original set of seven chapel windows in painted glass by Abraham van Ling of 1641, referred to above; of which the Adam and Eve, the Sacrifice of Isaac, and Jonah Disgorged by the Whale are the most enjoyed and admired. The most notable of several good oak-panelled rooms is the Summer Common Room; the elaborate chimneypiece with caryatids bears the date 1575, only one year after the publication in Antwerp of Plantin's edition of Alciati's *Emblematum Liber* (original Italian edition, 1532) from the wood-engravings in which most of the small carved scenes, some clumsy but all vigorous, have fairly recently been shown to be derived by the probably local carvers.

In the Civil War the college loyally rendered up its silver to the King (over 60 lb of it) and its earliest surviving piece is a noble 2-quart flagon, bought in 1651; there is some excellent communion plate of 1660. The college loving-cup dates from 1666. An early 18th-century punch-bowl by Paul de Lamerie is dated 1730. There is a large collection of silver beer-cups, given from the late 17th century onwards by individual undergraduates on going down; more recently graduands of the year have often combined to keep the generous custom going.

The college's nearly 200 manuscripts have long been on revocable loan to the BODLEIAN. They include a lively bestiary of about 1300, along with a striking collection of 15th-century English devotional and mystical works, including a *Piers Plowman* and three by Richard Rolle of Hampole. The finest is a copy of Bede's *Life of St Cuthbert* (the college's patron saint), probably executed at Durham in the 12th century. A collection of early printed books (including a few of the 15th century), chiefly Theology and scientific and medical works, is kept in the Master's Library in the lodgings.

In the Middle Ages the college, although small and poor, produced many English bishops and some archbishops, and for long its greatest contribution to the country must have been the supply of distinguished (and undistinguished) clerics, including – in

477

An aquatint after A.C. Pugin's drawing of University College's 17th-century hall in 1814 a few years after it had been remodelled.

the first category of course – Abbot (1597), Archbishop of Canterbury, who was a member of the Oxford 'company' responsible for part of the Authorised Version of the Bible (1611), and, 350 years later, Professor C.H. Dodd (1902), who was Director of the translation of the New English Bible. After the Reformation and with the great Elizabethan 'expansion' of England, the range of opportunity widened immensely, and Univ. men have always had a good share of achievement. In this century there have been many notable civil servants and ambassadors, scholars and teachers, industrialists and merchants, and men prominent in the media and arts. Among the college's distinguished members are Leonard Digges (*fl.*1540–70), the inventor of the theodolite; Twysden and Strode, the mathematicians (1623 and 1642 respectively); the early orientalists Dudley Loftus (MA 1640) and Thomas Maurice (1774), author of *Indian Antiquities*; Cartwright, the inventor of the power-loom (1757); the poets, Lord Herbert of Cherbury (1596; elder brother of the immeasurably greater George) and Percy Bysshe Shelley (1810). In this century a Lord Chief Justice, Hewart of Bury (1887); Lord Swinton, the pre-war Air Minister who played an important part in the development of radar and of the Hurricane and Spitfire fighter-planes (Honorary Fellow 1959); K.A. Busia, Prime Minister of Ghana 1969–72 (1939); R.J.L. Hawke, Prime Minister of Australia from 1983 (1953); the scholar, teacher and writer C.S. LEWIS; the poet, Stephen Spender (1917); the novelists V.S. Naipaul (1950), S.S. Naipaul (1964), Thomas Hinde (1947) and Dornford Yates (1904); Professor S.W. Hawking, the physicist and astronomer (1959); the legal philosopher H.L.A. Hart and the philosopher Sir Peter Strawson, both Fellows (1952–73 and 1948–68 respectively); General Sir Philip Christison (Honorary Fellow 1980), and General B.W. Rogers (USA), Supreme Allied Commander in Europe (Honorary Fellow 1980). This century, too, the college has had a number of most distinguished Masters: Sir Michael Sadler, the educationalist (1924–34); Lord Beveridge; Dr A.L. Goodhart, Fellow and Professor of Jurisprudence and the first American head of a college in either Oxford or Cambridge (1951–63); Lord Redcliffe-Maud, civil servant and ambassador (1963–76); Lord Goodman, lawyer (1976–86); and the second American Master in Kingman Brewster, lawyer, ex-President of Yale University and ex-Ambassador to the Court of St James (1986–88). He was succeeded in January 1989 by Professor John Albery, F.R.S.

The corporate designation of the college is The Master and Fellows of the College of the Great Hall of the University commonly called University College in the University of Oxford.

(Carr, W., *University College*, College Histories Series, London, 1902; 'University College', in *Victoria County History of Oxford*, Vol. III, Oxford, 1954;

478

University College Record, 1925– , an annual college publication, contains many articles on details of the history of the college, and on the buildings and possessions and on objects and persons of interest.)

University Museum *Parks Road.* At a meeting held in 1849 a resolution was passed that a building should be erected to bring together all 'the materials explanatory of the organic beings placed upon the globe'. At that time facilities for teaching science were severely limited and highly diffuse. The Honour School of Natural Science was started in 1850; but, despite the energetic advocacy of SIR HENRY ACLAND, who was appointed Aldrichian Professor of Clinical Medicine in 1851, it was not until 20 June 1855 that the foundation stone of the museum was laid – and then in the face of determined opposition from certain conservative factions in the University. When the building was completed in 1860 it was appropriately the scene of the meeting of the British Association at which the fundamentalist BISHOP OF OXFORD, SAMUEL WILBERFORCE, argued with Professor Thomas Huxley about Darwin's theory of evolution.

In his efforts to bring his scheme to fruition, Acland had had the support of JOHN RUSKIN, with whom he had been an undergraduate at Christ Church; and the influence of Ruskin, whose *Stones of Venice* was published in 1851–3, is clearly evident in the design of the Museum. The architect was the retiring Benjamin Woodward of the Dublin firm of Sir Thomas Deane, Son and Woodward, whose designs were shortlisted, with those of E.M. Barry, after a competition in which thirty others were submitted. Barry's designs were Italian, Woodward's Gothic, and, by a majority of eighty-one to thirty-eight, CONVOCATION decided upon the Gothic – a choice, as Howard Colvin has observed, 'of some importance in English architectural history. Gothic churches, country houses and collegiate buildings there were in plenty. But since the Houses of Parliament [begun in 1837] there had been

no major public building in the Gothic style, and certainly no museum. . . . This double victory – of Science over obscurantism, and of Gothic over classic – was not easily won.' Tennyson thought Woodward's design 'perfectly indecent'; a Fellow of Oriel, reflecting the views of those who considered it 'inappropriate to use Gothic for a secular purpose', described it as 'strange, bizarre and detestable'. Peculiarly bizarre to its critics was the Chemistry Laboratory which, attached to the south of the museum, was a copy of the Abbot's kitchen at Glastonbury.

Approached through an elaborately decorated portal, carved in marble, designed by Hungerford Pollen and executed by Thomas Woolner, the interior is a large square court, divided into three main aisles by iron pillars supporting a glass roof. The stone columns of the arcades are in themselves exhibits, each being hewn from a different British rock. The ornamentation incorporates natural forms. The wrought-ironwork embellishing the spandrels between the arches of the main aisles 'is formed into branches,' in the words of the Museum guide, 'with leaves, flowers and fruits of lime, chestnut, sycamore, walnut, palm and other trees and shrubs, and the leaves of many different plants are incorporated in the capitals. The carved stone capitals of the columns and piers of the arcades represent a series of plants, often with birds and animals too, and are remarkable in that the stonemasons, including the colourful, mercurial O'Shea brothers, conceived as well as executed the designs themselves, on the basis of actual specimens provided by the Botanic Garden'. The O'Sheas eventually left in high dudgeon, exasperated by interference from dons, but not before one of them had carved, between parrots and owls, various likenesses of members of Convocation, which he was ordered to obliterate – a task he did not fully perform. Before the work was complete, and after the fine craftsman in iron, Francis Skidmore, had been paid

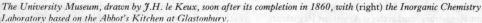

The University Museum, drawn by J.H. le Keux, soon after its completion in 1860, with (right) *the Inorganic Chemistry Laboratory based on the Abbot's Kitchen at Glastonbury.*

£3000, money ran out and the proposed wall-frescoes and further carving had to be abandoned.

Soon after the building was finished the Departments of Astronomy, Geometry, Experimental Physics, Mineralogy, Chemistry, Geology, Zoology, Anatomy, Physiology and Medicine all moved here. But as they grew in size new buildings had to be erected for them around the museum and in SOUTH PARKS ROAD, and in this way the SCIENCE AREA developed. Although the museum's principal function is to preserve the University's collections of zoological, entomological, mineralogical and geological specimens – known as the Scientific Collections – the staff is also involved in teaching and research and the four curators are selected from the teaching staff of the departments whose specimens are kept here. The nucleus of the collections which were transferred to the museum on its completion were the natural history items from the ASHMOLEAN, including many assembled by the Tradescants; the collections of the explorer William Burchell, and of WILLIAM BUCKLAND, the geologist, also from the Ashmolean; a large collection of osteological and physiological material from Christ Church, largely assembled by Acland; and the huge collection of insects and crustaceans presented to the University in 1849 by the Rev. F.W. Hope. These collections have since been considerably enlarged and now contain, for example, no fewer than 3 million specimens of insects and 300,000 specimens of fossils and rocks. For the large number of busts and statues of great scientists in the museum, which is open to the general public, *see* STATUES.

(Vernon, H.M., and Vernon K.D., *A History of the Oxford Museum*, 1909; Acland, H.W., and Ruskin, John, *The Oxford Museum*, enlarged edition, 1893.)

University Officers *see* OFFICERS OF THE UNIVERSITY.

University Offices The offices of the University are in WELLINGTON SQUARE. The REGISTRAR is assisted by a Deputy Registrar (Administration), five Senior Assistant Registrars, and sixteen Assistant Registrars. The staff additionally consists of the Secretary of the Chest and Chief Accountant, the Secretary of Faculties, the Establishment Officer, the Head of Data Processing and Management Services, three Deputy Chief Accountants, the Information Officer, the Investment Secretary, the Land Agent, two Principal Accountants, the Head Clerk, the Accommodation Officer, the Administration Officer, Graduate Studies Officer and the Superannuation Officer.

At the Malthouse, TIDMARSH LANE, are the offices of the Surveyor to the University, three Deputy Surveyors, the Senior Assistant Surveyor, the Electrical Engineer and eight members of the professional staff.

(*See also* OFFICERS OF THE UNIVERSITY *and* REGISTRAR.)

University Reform Acts *see* ROYAL COMMISSIONS.

University Sermon Preached every Sunday in full term at 10 or 10.30 a.m. in the University Church of ST MARY THE VIRGIN, but also occasionally in CHRIST CHURCH CATHEDRAL, New College Chapel, Magdalen College Chapel or Hertford College Chapel, the

The congregation stands in the University Church of St Mary the Virgin as the Vice-Chancellor arrives for a University Sermon in 1834.

preacher normally being a divine of distinction. The University is represented by the procession of VICE-CHANCELLOR, PROCTORS and Doctors, preserving some of the ancient ceremonial and symbolising the religious allegiance of the University in its public capacity. Although the sermon was in the past chiefly for senior members, undergraduates have for many years been encouraged to attend.

Some special benefactions have been given to ensure the preaching of sermons on particular subjects on certain Sundays during the year, as on Humility or Pride on Quinquagesima Sunday and the last Sunday before Advent; while the sermon on the second Sunday of Hilary Term, given in Hertford College, is known as the Macbride Sermon, and is preached upon 'the application of the prophecies in Holy Scripture respecting the Messiah to our Lord and Saviour Jesus Christ, with an especial view to confute the arguments of Jewish commentators and to promote the conversion to Christianity of the ancient people of God', a benefaction for this purpose having been given in 1848 by J.D. Macbride, Principal of MAGDALEN HALL.

It has to be observed that interest in the University Sermon, which dates back at least to the time of Queen Elizabeth I, is now much less than it was in the 1830s, when it might have been given by J.H. NEWMAN, then vicar of St Mary's, to listen to whose lengthy orations undergraduates would (it has been claimed) even give up their evening meal in college.

Urquhart, Francis Fortescue (*1868–1934*). Became a Fellow of Balliol in 1896, the first ROMAN

CATHOLIC to hold a Tutorial Fellowship in Oxford. By 1916 he was Senior Fellow, and became Dean (having reluctantly become Junior Dean soon after his election to a fellowship). From 1907 to 1919 he was also Junior Bursar. By profession a historian, his fame rests in his teaching and in his many friendships of every generation in Balliol and other colleges. Many of those friendships were fostered at his chalet (the Chalet des Mélèzes) near Chamonix, where parties were held for forty years between 1891 and 1931: the original chalet was burned down in 1906, but was rebuilt by 1909. The lists of those going to the chalet are still extant and include Roger Casement, H.H. Asquith, R.A. KNOX, Julian Huxley, Harold Macmillan (later EARL OF STOCKTON), Cyril Connolly, Quintin Hogg (later Lord Hailsham), R.H.S. Crossman and John Sparrow, among many other scarcely less famous names. Urquhart's devotion of his life to his undergraduate friends has left its mark in many autobiographies and memoirs. The belief that he is one of the models on which the Oxford don Sillery is based in Anthony Powell's sequence of novels, *A Dance to the Music of Time*, is emphatically refuted by the novelist himself. According to SIR JOHN BETJEMAN 'he liked people to be well-born and, if possible, Roman Catholic'. His nickname started as 'Sleeker' – 'the sleek one', with the Harrow termination 'er', and was later corrupted to 'Sligger'.

V

Vanbrugh House *St Michael's Street*. Vanbrugh house in ST MICHAEL'S STREET has been described as 'a minor work of the great eighteenth century architect Vanbrugh, the designer of Blenheim Palace'. It is now generally agreed that the 17th-century house was remodelled with a stone front, highly characteristic of Vanbrugh, by the master-mason, Bartholomew Peisley (*see* PEISLEYS), and that the ideas for the design were certainly acquired by him from his experience of working with Vanbrugh at Blenheim. Bartholomew Peisley the second (*c.*1654–1715) built the Grand Bridge over the lake at Blenheim to the design of Sir John Vanbrugh. Peisley and his family lived in Vanbrugh House. His son, also named Bartholomew, helped his father on the Grand Bridge and later went into partnership with William Townesend, another Oxford master-mason (*see* TOWNESENDS). They built many of the Oxford college buildings of this period, as well as Radley Hall, now part of Radley College, near Abingdon. Mary Peisley married Henry Joynes, who was clerk of works at Blenheim.

During building work in 1950 a Sun fire-mark was found in the yard. The number on the fire-mark enabled the policy to be traced as having been issued to Bartholomew Peisley in 1722 'for his new Dwelling house in St. Michael's Parish'. Peisley died at Vanbrugh House in 1727. His widow later married the President of Trinity College.

The building – now a Grade II listed building – is described by Pevsner as 'almost a parody of Blenheim' and 'understandably called Vanbrugh House. It is overloaded with motifs for its five bays; two broad giant pilasters, a piece of entablature above them projecting like a hood, and cubic aprons to some of the windows'. Laurence Whistler agreed that 'the appearance of this remarkable house, with its Doric centre, justified the name'. A drawing by J.C. BUCKLER in the BODLEIAN LIBRARY shows the house as it looked in 1822.

Inside there is a beautiful staircase with twisted balusters, two rooms with early 18th-century panelling, and an unusual 18th-century painted alcove of tulips, roses and other flowers in a bowl on a shell decoration. Below is a marble slab tiled behind with forty-four blue-and-white Delft tiles in twelve different patterns.

The building belongs to the City Council and has been occupied for over fifty years by Marshall & Galpin, one of Oxford's oldest firms of solicitors, established in 1782. The practice was carried on in the 19th century by members of the Walsh family from the adjoining house, No. 22. In the basement can be seen a section of the old CITY WALL.

Vanbrugh House, St Michael's Street, in 1822. It was probably remodelled by Vanbrugh's master-mason Bartholomew Peisley.

Varsity Match Although other sporting fixtures between the universities of Oxford and Cambridge are also known by this name, it is the annual rugby football or rugger match between the two universities which is widely acknowledged as the 'Varsity Match'. It is now played at Twickenham on the second Tuesday in December before a crowd of some 30,000–40,000 spectators; but the first match was played in the PARKS on 10 February 1872. Oxford won by a goal and a try to nil. The second match was played the following year at Parker's Piece in Cambridge, when Cambridge won. Since then the match has been played on a neutral ground in London, first at The Oval, then at Blackheath, and from 1887 to 1920 at the Queen's Club, West Kensington. In 1921 the venue was moved to Twickenham where it has remained ever since, except for the war years. Up to and including 1990 Cambridge have won forty-nine of the 109 matches (excluding the wartime series), Oxford have won forty-seven and thirteen have been drawn, including one in 1874 in which Oxford scored two tries but to win the match a goal had to be scored. It was not until the 1893–4 season that both sides employed a formation of four three-quarters. The record number of BLUES for rugger is held by Harry Fuller of Cambridge (1878–83) and Nick Herrod (1982–7) – six each. The highest number of points in a match is held by Oxford, who beat Cambridge 35–3 in 1909, the biggest winning margin. Cambridge won for five years running between 1972 and 1976, and again between 1980 and 1984.

(Marshall, Howard, *Oxford versus Cambridge: the Story of the University Rugby Match*, 1951.)

Vice-Chancellor Now the principal administrative officer of the University, holding office for four years. Originally he was merely the temporary commissary or deputy of the CHANCELLOR, exercising all the Chancellor's powers when he was absent. The term did not become official until 1549. From the early 16th century, however, he became the chief executive officer of the University. He was usually a Fellow of a college or a canon of Christ Church and was at first elected by CONVOCATION, as laid down in the Edwardian Code of 1549; from 1569, in the chancellorship of the Earl of Leicester, he was nominated by the Chancellor. He was henceforward always the head of a college, as the LAUDIAN CODE of 1636 laid down; by convention the nomination was made of heads of houses in order of seniority. The way in which this system developed reflected the government's wish to keep a tighter control over the affairs of the University. The system of nominating the Vice-Chancellor from heads of houses was left unchanged by the reforms made in the University's constitution by the University Reform Act of 1854, but in the post-Second World War period nomination was vested in a committee which proposed a name for appointment to CONGREGATION. The committee is under no obligation to restrict its choice to heads of houses, any member of Congregation being eligible for appointment provided that he (or she) can serve the full period of office before reaching the age of sixty-five; but in practice all recent Vice-Chancellors have been heads of houses.

(A full list of Vice-Chancellors will be found in Appendix 6.)

Victoria Arms *Mill Lane, Marston Ferry*. An isolated stone inn by the River Cherwell (*see* THAMES), originally built in the 17th century and reconstructed in 1840. There was once a ford here which had been in use since the 12th century and a line-ferry was in operation up till 1971. The inn was closed in 1958 when the tenant was bankrupted; and the building was left empty until 1961 when it was purchased by the OXFORD PRESERVATION TRUST. The new leaseholders, Wadsworth's Brewery of Devizes, spent rather more than £100,000 on renovation, retaining the old fireplaces and flagstone floors. The Vicky, as it is traditionally known, re-opened in the summer of 1986.

Victoria Fountain *The Plain*. Built in 1899 as a belated tribute to Queen Victoria for her Diamond Jubilee. The fountain occupies an island site at THE PLAIN, where ST CLEMENT's toll-house used to stand. Jets of water inside the fountain were used by the public and troughs were provided outside for horses. The Latin inscription on the fountain may be translated as 'The water drips, the hours go by. Be warned, drink, catch them ere they fly.' The fountain was designed by E.P. Warren and paid for by G.H. Morrell, the brewer (*see* MORRELL'S BREWERY). It was inaugurated by Princess Louise, daughter of Queen Victoria.

Vincent's Club *1a King Edward Street*. Formed in 1863 by W.B. Woodgate of Brasenose College and named after the printer whose premises in HIGH STREET were used for the inaugural meeting. 'The theory of this Club', Woodgate wrote, 'was that it should consist of the picked hundred of the University, selected for all-round qualities, social, physical and intellectual qualities being considered'. Woodgate had considered calling the club 'the Century' and the president 'the Centurion of Oxford'. Vincent's moved in 1931 to its present address where, by happy coincidence, it was reunited with Vincent the printer, who occupied the ground floor. The club has become more sporting in atmosphere than it was at its inception and most BLUES belong to it. The membership is limited to 250 male undergraduates by election (women guests are allowed in the club in the evenings). The club has a resident steward and provides not only refreshments, lunches and dinners but also rooms for social events. It is traditionally the meeting place of the Blues Committee. Originally, free beer, tea and coffee were provided and letters were stamped free of charge. The club tie has the University crowns emblazoned on a dark-blue background.

Among past and present members are two kings – Edward VIII and Olaf of Norway; two Japanese princes; two British prime ministers – Harold Macmillan, later the EARL OF STOCKTON, and Lord Home; a Viceroy of India; several bishops and numerous judges.

Past Presidents of the club include Sir Roger Bannister, the first athlete to run a mile in less than four minutes and now Master of Pembroke College; Jack Lovelock, the 1936 1500-metre Olympic champion; England cricket captains Colin Cowdrey and M.J.K. Smith; and the University's greatest all-rounder, C.B. FRY. Vincent's is normally open during term time only.

Members of Vincent's Club before a dinner, c.1900.

Visitations At the time of the Dissolution of the Monasteries, Richard Layton, a Cambridge-educated lawyer who became Dean of York, was empowered to visit the University with various assistants. Oxford's MONASTIC COLLEGES seemed threatened, although Henry VIII had declared, 'I tell you, sirs, that I judge no land in England better bestowed than that which is given to our Universites, for by their maintenance our Realm shall be governed when we be dead and rotten.' For the moment, however, Layton contented himself with tightening the discipline of students in monastic colleges, forbidding them to enter taverns, with condemning scholastic studies and with relegating the works of Duns Scotus to the town's latrines. He also established lectures in Greek, Latin and Civil Law. The monastic colleges did not long survive, however; and the houses of the Austin Friars, the Franciscans, the Dominicans and the Carmelites all disappeared too.

In the reign of Edward VI, Oxford's other colleges, where Masses were said for founders and benefactors, had cause to fear expropriation. But, while they were spared this, they had to admit to Visitations by government officials who were authorised to alter statutes, to abolish the study of Canon Law, to require practical work in Anatomy for degrees in Medicine, to remove heads and Fellows of colleges, to oversee finances, to provide new syllabuses, to strengthen discipline, to do everything necessary, in fact, to secure obedience to the new Protestant order (*see* ROMAN CATHOLICS). The VISITORS certainly succeeded in rooting out those images and symbols of popery which were not successfully concealed, in purging libraries of popish books and in removing such objectionable chapel furnishing as the reredos of All Souls. Yet, while Protestant ardour was encouraged, many outspoken adherents of the old religion contrived to remain in office – James Brooks, Master

of Balliol, for instance, whom the Roman Catholic Queen Mary was to make Bishop of Gloucester.

The Visitation of Oxford carried out soon after the accession of Elizabeth I, to reform the University in accordance with the Statutes of Supremacy and Uniformity, was conducted tactfully. The instructions issued in Mary's reign by Cardinal Reginald Pole, the CHANCELLOR, were quietly withdrawn; papist symbols which had reappeared in his time were removed or hidden; some exiled Protestant Fellows returned to their colleges; a few Roman Catholics were removed. But the Visitors were intent upon appeasement rather than coercion; and when the Queen herself came to Oxford in 1566 she told the dons, 'I know that I am not worthy of your praises. But if my speech be full of barbarisms, I will end it with a prayer: that you may prosper greatly in my lifetime and be happy for generations after I am dead.'

The Visitation of the University after the CIVIL WAR, which was intended to 'reform and regulate' it, aroused far more hostility. It began inauspiciously. The Parliamentary Visitors commanded the PROCTORS and the heads of houses to appear before them in the CONVOCATION house between nine and ten o'clock on the morning of 4 June 1647. The Visitors had not arrived by eleven, so the VICE-CHANCELLOR, Dr Samuel Fell, led his fellow heads out of the building and, on passing the Visitors on the way in, he 'very civilly moved his cap to them, saying "Good-morrow, gentlemen, 'tis past eleven of the clock," and so passed on, without taking any further notice of them'.

Fell was then dismissed both as Vice-Chancellor and as Dean of Christ Church. The Proctors were also deprived of their positions, as were several heads of houses and recalcitrant Fellows such as Samuel Jackson of Christ Church, who staunchly asserted, 'I can acknowledge the King only to be Visitor of Christ Church.' In all, between 300 and 400 members of the

University were expelled. About the same number submitted to the Visitors, however; and, although the men appointed to the vacant positions were dismissed by Samuel Fell's son, JOHN FELL, as 'illiterate rabble', there were scholars enough among them, so that the damage done to the University by this Visitation was not quite as severe as some diehard royalists protested. Although in 1652 a new Board of Visitors was appointed to regulate the curriculum and ensure the maintenance of DISCIPLINE and the Protestant religion, eight years later the Restoration Visitation reinstated ejected Fellows, together with the traditional government of the University and colleges.

There were threats of a further Visitation by representatives of the government after Jacobite RIOTS in 1715, when it was suggested that admissions to the University, as well as nominations to all its offices, should be controlled by the new Hanoverian administration. These threats were repeated after Dr William King, the Vice-Chancellor, had made a provocative speech in favour of the Jacobites on the occasion of the opening of the RADCLIFFE CAMERA in 1749. Placatory rather than coercive measures were decided upon, however; and in 1761 a new and lasting understanding between the government and the University was marked by the election as Chancellor of King George III's chief minister, Lord North.

(*See also* ROYAL COMMISSIONS, UNIVERSITY *and* VISITORS.)

Visiting Students Members of a college (or other society) who are not matriculated members of the University (*see* MATRICULATION). Normal college fees are payable, but University fees are charged at a special rate, normally half (or less) of what the student would have paid if he or she had formally matriculated. Visiting students may use libraries and attend lectures, but are not eligible for University examinations, PRIZES AND SCHOLARSHIPS. The studentship is held for up to three terms, and a typical visiting student would be, for example, an undergraduate of an American university spending one year at Oxford as part of the American course.

Visitors The final arbiters in the older colleges, who still possess substantial legal powers but rarely exercise them. All the early colleges, except University College, had bishops as their Visitors – for instance, at Merton the Archbishop of Canterbury (replacing in 1274 the Bishop of Rochester) and at Exeter the Bishop of Exeter. At University College the Visitor until the 18th century was the CHANCELLOR and scholars of the University (i.e. visitorial powers were exercised by the University). Balliol had a Visitorial Board until in 1364 the Bishop of London was made Visitor – a situation which remained until, by the 1506 statutes of Bishop Foxe, the college was given the right to elect its own Visitor, which it still does. The original Visitor of Oriel College was the Chancellor of Edward I, but with his fall from power on the accession of Edward II in 1307 the office passed to the Bishop of Lincoln until 1726, when the Crown became the Visitor. The Archbishop of York was the Visitor of The Queen's College (which has a patroness in the Queen or, more recently, the Queen Mother), reflecting its northern bias. The Visitor was both patron and protector of the college, as well as a judge in the interpretation of its statutes or in disputes between the Fellows. At Lincoln, the Visitor, the Bishop of Lincoln, had until 1948 the right of appointment to the chaplaincy fellowship. In the 20th century the Visitor's function has become principally ceremonial.

(*See also* VISITATIONS *and* ROYAL COMMISSIONS.)

W

Wadham College In October 1609 Nicholas Wadham, a seventy-seven-year-old gentleman, very rich and also childless, lay dying at his house at Merifield in Somerset. He proceeded to issue his last instructions for the foundation of a college at Oxford to be known as Wadham College. He had been contemplating the design for years and setting money aside for the purpose, but in a rather desultory way; he made only passing reference to it in the will he had drawn up three years before, and on his deathbed he was still thinking of a possible take-over bid for either GLOUCESTER HALL (later Worcester College) or Jesus College. The imprecision was to cause a deal of trouble for his executors, not least his widow.

The Wadham family had originally farmed in the parish of Knowestone in North Devon, where the remote Wadham Farm still stands. By the middle of the 14th century they had moved into the ranks of the landed gentry and established themselves at the manor of Edge, near Branscombe in the south of the county. A Sir John Wadham was a judge in the reign of Richard II. After that the family remained inconspicuous on a national level, marrying well, extending their estates into Somerset, sitting on the local bench, elected occasionally to Parliament. Nicholas Wadham, however, seems to have shunned even local office. He was never elected to Parliament, not even becoming a justice of the peace, and was never knighted in spite of a landed income of over £3000 a year, which was more than that of most peers of the realm. His retiring disposition seems to have puzzled his contemporaries. Some thought he had Catholic sympathies and even that he had originally intended to found a college for English exiles in Venice; but these stories seem without foundation.

If, as we may suspect, Nicholas Wadham was a somewhat ineffectual character, that was certainly not the case of his widow, the seventy-five-year-old Dorothy. Daughter of Sir William Petre, a self-made Tudor politician and a major benefactor, indeed 'second founder' of Exeter College, she was clearly a formidable lady. Faced with untangling her husband's muddled instructions, she flung herself with zest into fighting off the legal challenges of his relatives, and those of her fellow trustees, who had assumed that she would be a cypher. She was determined to run things her own way; and she moved fast, taking care first to cultivate good

The front of Wadham College, which faces on to Parks Road, as it appeared c.1820 before the removal of the wall and railings.

connections at the Court of James I, often quite expensively.

Incredibly, within five months, Dorothy acquired from Oxford City Council a suitable site; royal intervention helped beat the price down from £1000 to £600. Before the Dissolution of the Monasteries the great church of the Austin Friars had stood there, but that building had been entirely demolished and the site was now gardens and orchards, leased like modern 'allotments' to the citizens (*see* AUGUSTINIAN FRIARY). By the end of 1610 formal authorisation had been obtained from the Crown for the establishment of a collegiate body of Warden, Fellows and scholars. By the spring of 1613 the building was substantially complete, at a cost of some £12,000, and, less than five years after Nicholas Wadham's death, thirty-five members moved into the new foundation.

The architect (described as 'head workman' and doubling, in modern terms, as clerk of works) was William Arnold, described by Dorothy Wadham as 'an honest man, a perfect workman, and my near neighbour'. He was possibly related to Dorothy's factotum and man-of-business John Arnold. He had an extensive practice in the West Country, including the building of the great house at Montacute for Dorothy Wadham's neighbour, Speaker Edward Phelips. Dorothy Wadham directed operations at long-range from her home in the West Country; she did not visit Oxford and never saw her foundation. But she kept very tight control of the college's affairs, drawing up the statutes, sending detailed instructions and reserving to herself the nomination to every post from Warden to college cook until her death in 1618 at the age of eighty-four. She also provided from her own resources about £7000 of the total of £26,000 spent on building and endowing the college.

Wadham College was fashionable in its early days with the sons of the West Country gentry, among them, in 1619, Carew Ralegh, son of Sir Walter, who had been executed the previous year. Carew presented a copy of his father's *History of the World* to the college. In spite of royal favour at its foundation, the college was prepared to stand up to James I, especially when he tried to impose on it a Scotsman from St Andrews as a Fellow. Just senior to Carew Ralegh in the college was one Robert Blake (1615), son of a 'plebian' rather than a gentleman (in fact his father was a Bridgewater merchant), who in Cromwell's time was to become one of England's greatest admirals.

The CIVIL WAR hit Wadham hard; and it led to a purge of royalist sympathisers by the victorious Parliament: Warden John Pitt (1644–8), one of the foundation Fellows (and a protégé of the Wadhams), nine of the thirteen Fellows, nine of the fourteen scholars and eleven of the fourteen COMMONERS (college numbers had been drastically reduced by the war) were expelled. In 1648 the Parliamentary Commission which had been sent to purge the University appointed John Wilkins as Warden; he attracted to the college a distinguished set of Fellows, including Seth Ward (1647–59), mathematician and astronomer and royalist refugee from Cambridge. The young CHRISTOPHER WREN was also a member of the college (1650–3). Wilkins held informal meetings of friends to discuss scientific papers; and, after the Restoration, they were to fuse with a similar group to found the Royal Society. The college thereby had played an important part in the foundation of modern science.

Wilkins married Oliver Cromwell's sister Robina, widow of a canon of Christ Church, who must have been the first woman, officially at least, to live in college. Her nephew Richard Cromwell appointed Wilkins to the mastership of Trinity College, Cambridge, in 1659; and, though he lost that post when the monarchy was restored in 1660, he was on good enough terms with the new King (mainly through his scientific interests) eventually to become Bishop of Chester in spite of his parliamentarian past and embarrassing marital connections.

Two celebrated Restoration wits, poets and libertines passed briefly through Wadham: Sir Charles Sedley in 1656, and John Wilmot, later Earl of Rochester, in 1660–1. It was Rochester who wrote the immortal lines on Charles II:

> Restless he rolls about from whore to whore,
> A merry monarch, scandalous and poor.

But a more substantial legacy of the Wilkins era was the college's reputation for sober Whig politics in opposition to the largely Tory inclination of Oxford generally. Warden Ironside (1666–89) happened to be VICE-CHANCELLOR during the 1688–9 Revolution, and keenly supported the new regime. Lord Lovelace, an old member of the college (1655–61), commanded James II's troops in the Oxford region and made them over to William III; Lovelace's portrait, painted in 1689, and commemorating his role in helping 'to rid this nation from popery and slavery' looks down on the college hall from the gallery. Wadham showed its loyalty by acquiring a portrait of William III –

The hall of Wadham College, with its great hammerbeam roof, shown in this watercolour of c.1860, is one of the largest college halls in Oxford.

apparently the only college in Oxford to do so – and was also extremely unusual in possessing one of George I, until it was irreparably damaged in storage during the Second World War. Among its students was Arthur Onslow (1708), Speaker of the House of Commons for thirty-four years (1727–61).

During the 18th century Wadham built up something of a reputation in oriental studies, thanks initially to the initiative of Humphrey Hody, Regius Professor of Greek, who made a munificent bequest (1707) for the foundation of scholarships in Hebrew. But apart from this Wadham shared in the general stagnation or decline of 18th-century Oxford. Admissions dropped to an average of about twelve a year, as against twenty-five to thirty in the early 17th century. The majority of Fellows were absentees; sometimes there was only one in residence, deputising for his colleagues as Bursar, Dean, Divinity lecturer, librarian and tutor. Particularly unfortunate was the scandal of 1739 which resulted in the precipitate resignation of the Warden, Robert Thistlethwayte (1724–39), accused of homosexual assault on an undergraduate and on the college butler and barber. Thistlethwayte fled the country and died in exile at Boulogne.

The college's revival dates from the wardenship of John Wills (1783–1806), who was also a very considerable benefactor, bequeathing property worth over £27,000. Under his successor William Tournay (1806–31) the college rapidly won an excellent reputation in the newly created examinations for Honours, and in the competition for University PRIZES. As a 'sound reading college' Wadham had at this time a two- to three-year waiting list for admission.

The fiercely evangelical Benjamin Parsons Symons (Warden 1831–71) was, as Vice-Chancellor, the inveterate opponent of JOHN HENRY NEWMAN and the OXFORD MOVEMENT. Symons is unlikely to have had much sympathy, either, for a remarkable group of younger Fellows and students (Richard Congreve, Frederic Harrison, J.H. Bridges, and E.S. Beesly) busy promulgating in England the 'positivist' creed of the Frenchman Auguste Comte, a firmly secularist doctrine of scientific and social progress. Its adherents were to involve themselves in such causes as trade union reform and the foundation of county councils. SIR THOMAS JACKSON, the architect of so much of Victorian Oxford (although he built very little in his own college, which was fortunately spared his plan for an enlarged porters' lodge in front of the main doorway), was scholar and Fellow from 1854 to 1880. The country diarist and clergyman Francis Kilvert came up in 1859 (taking a fourth-class degree in History and Law); coming back in 1876, he dined at high table, 'an object of my undergraduate ambition realized at last'. There is a story, much repeated (even in print), that the entire college was sent down in 1879 after a rowdy undergraduate demonstration turned into a minor riot – but the sober bursarial records show that only a handful of men were rusticated for a few days at the end of term; only one was not allowed to return subsequently.

Wadham was particularly badly affected by plummeting rent-rolls on its estates due to the agricultural depression at the end of the 19th century. By pure chance, however, the early 1890s brought together at Wadham a remarkable group of under-graduates. F.E. Smith (1891–6) went on to become brilliant advocate, Tory politician, and, as Earl of Birkenhead, a reforming Lord Chancellor in the Lloyd George coalition (1919–22). His friend, John Simon (1892–7), who went into politics as a Liberal was to hold successively all the leading offices of State except that of Prime Minister in the National Governments of the 1930s, eventually becoming Lord Chancellor in Churchill's wartime government. C.B. FRY (1891–5) was the epitome of the all-round sportsman. He broke a string of athletics records, got three BLUES in the same year (athletics, cricket and football) and would have got a fourth (rugby) but for injury, and went on to notch up tremendous achievements as a batsman for Sussex and England. Sir Thomas Beecham was briefly at the college a little later (1897–8), but he quickly abandoned Oxford to study music in Germany. F.E. Smith was later to tell the college, 'I am no musician, but I am told by those who understand these matters well, that Beecham is the most brilliant conductor now living in the world. Anyone who does anything non-criminal better than anyone else in the world is evidently remarkable. I have never myself witnessed his efforts and I am sure that if I did they would cause me great inconvenience.'

In the early part of the 20th century Wadham was a respectable but modest college, catering largely to the solid sons of the less-affluent professional classes, its clientele drawn from minor public schools and well-established grammar schools, with a total undergraduate body of about 100–130. The college expanded dramatically in numbers and academic reputation under the twin impetus of the wardenship of SIR MAURICE BOWRA (1938–70) and the easier access to university education by the less well-off which followed the 1944 Education Act. Under Bowra's aegis, the college acquired a reputation for generally 'progressive' attitudes, an easy-going informality and lack of censoriousness ('humbug' was for Maurice Bowra the greatest sin), allied to a serious attitude to academic work – 'Whig principles and Cavalier taste' in the words of Michael Foot. The college's openness to innovation continued during the wardenship of Sir Stuart Hampshire (1970–84). It was, for instance, one of the first colleges to open its membership to women – a development which would have surprised Dorothy Wadham, whose statutes had, following tradition, decreed that no woman should be allowed past the gate except a laundress, and she to be of 'such age, condition and reputation' as to 'raise no sinister suspicion'.

In 1987 the college comprised a Warden (Sir Claus Moser, appointed 1984), some forty-three Fellows spread over the range of academic disciplines, about 100 graduate students and some 370 undergraduates. Among recent old members are Cecil Day-Lewis (1923), Poet Laureate from 1968 to 1972; Michael Foot (1931), Deputy Prime Minister from 1976 to 1979 and Leader of the Opposition 1980–83; and R.V. Jones (1929), son of an army sergeant, whose contribution to the war effort as scientific boffin (detailed in *Most Secret War*) is legendary. Frederick Lindemann, LORD CHERWELL (Fellow 1919–56 and Honorary Fellow 1956–7), Churchill's scientific adviser and head of the CLARENDON LABORATORY was Fellow for many years; so, more briefly, was A.J. Ayer (Fellow 1944–6 and Honorary Fellow from 1957), whose *Language, Truth and Logic* (1936) argued the

A lithograph from a pen-and-body-colour drawing by C.R.T. Cowern of Wadham College before the completion of the new buildings in 1954.

propositions (such as those of metaphysics or theology) not in principle susceptible to empirical validation are literally 'nonsense'.

The visitor enters the college through the fan-vaulted gateway into the main quadrangle built by William Arnold for Dorothy Wadham. The entrance tower, battlements and Tudor-Gothic arches are in the traditional mediaeval style. But this impression is offset by the strict classical symmetry of the whole; and by the Renaissance details of the east range, which faces the visitor across the lawn. Its elaborate frontispiece is composed of columns in the classical orders surrounding statues of King James I, of Nicholas Wadham (in armour and clutching a model of the college) and of Dorothy Wadham (*see* STATUES). The door to the left, with its open segmental pediment and urn, leads to the chapel; the identical one to the right is false, built purely for symmetry. The clock face dates from 1673; probably given and possibly designed by Wren, the original mechanism is now in the MUSEUM OF THE HISTORY OF SCIENCE. The insertion of sash windows in the studies and bedrooms and the replacement of the original gravelled court by the present lawn in 1809 has considerably changed the appearance of the quadrangle since 1613. So too the original Headington stone had grown very dark and had begun to crumble. The present honey-coloured appearance of the building is due to its refacing in Clipsham stone in 1957–66 (*see* STONE).

The central doorway leads to the hall, one of the largest in Oxford (due to Dorothy Wadham's original ambitious plan), with its great hammerbeam roof and the Jacobean screen carved by John Bolton. The fireplace was inserted in 1827, as was the present heraldic glass. Out again into the quadrangle, and into the chapel, the visitor confronts another timber screen

by John Bolton. The two screens, in hall and chapel, cost a total of £82. The chapel screen includes stalls for the Warden and Sub-Warden; behind them are some dark stalls for the 'college servants', used by them as late as the 1860s. The woodwork originally ran right round the chapel proper, and was painted; but in 1832 it was removed from the sanctuary and the present stone panelling and reredos (by Edward Blore) was inserted. Blore was also responsible for the plaster ceiling. The glass in the lower lights of the side-windows, of prophets and apostles, was inserted at the foundation; the upper lights are Flemish work from Louvain, rescued during the French Revolution. The great east window is the work of the Dutchman Bernard van Ling (recommended to the Warden as 'an excellent pencil man of sober and good carriage not given to drink'). It depicts the life of Christ, with, at the top, prophetic Old Testament scenes, including a splendid Jonah and whale. Van Ling was paid £113 for the window in 1623. In the antechapel are some monuments, including that of a languid young man, Sir John Portman, 3rd Baronet (who died as a nineteen-year-old undergraduate in 1624), and an ingenious pile of books (stacked, by modern standards, back to front) commemorating Thomas Harris, one of the foundation Fellows, who died in 1614 also aged nineteen; his father had been MAYOR of Oxford when the foundation stone was laid in 1610.

The chapel doorway gives on to the Fellows' Garden, one of the best in Oxford. F.E. Smith, indeed, described the 'haunting beauty' of the college buildings seen from the garden by moonlight as 'the most enchanting spectacle which Oxford can afford'. The gardens were planned in their present form by Mr Shipley, the Duke of Marlborough's gardener, in 1796; before that they had been laid out in neat

489

Harry Lamb's portrait of Sir Maurice Bowra, Warden of Wadham College from 1938 to 1970 and one of the most remarkable Oxford personalities of his day.

geometrical blocks in 17th-century style. The great copper beech in the north-east corner dates from 1796. Going round the chapel the visitor enters the cloister garden with the chapel on the right, and on the left a corresponding wing with, on the ground floor, the college kitchen and, above it, the original college library, now converted into a common room. In the cloister garden is a seated bronze statue of Sir Maurice Bowra, a work which attracts immediate attention and varied responses (*see* STATUES). Behind is the new library (*see below*).

From the main quadrangle, passages on the right give on to the much more informal back quadrangle. In one corner there is what appears to be a large Queen Anne-style house (Staircase IX), which was in fact built as student accommodation in 1693; it is not, as is often thought, by Christopher Wren. Next to it are some rather dark 18th-century buildings which had a varied history as brewhouse, and as typestore and Bible warehouse for the CLARENDON PRESS before being taken over by the college. The other old buildings are the backs of houses (and the KING'S ARMS public house) which front on to HOLYWELL and have been taken over by the college. There is a good deal of ingenious modern in-filling by Gillespie, Kidd and Coia (1971–2), which includes the small Holywell Court and a raised 'deck', with prominent light-well for BLACKWELL'S subterranean music shop (entrance in Holywell). The copper-roofed building in Cotswold stone is by H.G. Goddard, and dates from 1951–4. The flight of stairs next to it leads to a massive new building in glass and concrete with a large lead-clad roof, also by Gillespie, Kidd and Coia. The first stage, opened in 1978, includes the new college

library. The college also owns the HOLYWELL MUSIC ROOM, the entrance to which is in Holywell.

The corporate designation of the college is The Warden, Fellows and Scholars of Wadham College in the University of Oxford of the Foundation of Nicholas Wadham, Esquire, and Dorothy his wife.

(Jackson, T.G., *Wadham College*, 1893 (for architecture); Wells, Joseph, *Wadham College*, 1898 (for anecdote); Briggs, Nancy, 'The Foundation of Wadham College', *Oxoniensia*, xxi, 1956; Shapiro, Barbara, *John Wilkins*, Berkeley, Calif., 1969 (for Wadham and the scientific movement); Campbell, John, *F.E. Smith, First Earl of Birkenhead*, London, 1984 (turn of the century); Bowra, C.M., *Memories*, London, 1969 (for the inter-war period); Gardiner, R.B., *Registers of Wadham College, 1613–1871*, 2 vols, London, 1887–94 (list of members).)

Walters & Co. The men's outfitters and tailors known as 'Walters of the Turl' was founded in 1887 by F.C. Taylor, who opened a shop at the southern end of TURL STREET. He was joined by W.R. Walters, who came to Oxford from Plymouth. When Taylor died Walters took over the business. In 1910 the firm took over Bradbury and Hay, a firm of tailors in HIGH STREET. Walters died in 1947. The firm was bought in 1985 by SHEPHERD AND WOODWARD.

Walton Manor *see* WALTON MANOR ESTATE.

Walton Manor Estate Lies between Norham Manor and JERICHO, to the north of ST GILES'. It is part of the old manor of Walton. The name means the tun by the wall or well – a tun being an enclosed piece of ground or homestead, and the wall meaning the CITY WALL. The first written record is of Waltone in 1086. In 1279 the manor had about ten habitations, but by the 17th century these had disappeared and only a farmhouse remained. The early manor was very extensive and Walton Field was the name given to most of the present NORTH OXFORD. It was mainly farming land until the 19th century, when market gardening took over.

In 1086 Roger d'Ivri was owner of the manor. It was later granted to ST GEORGE'S IN THE CASTLE, which in 1149 passed to OSENEY ABBEY. ST FRIDESWIDE'S PRIORY owned property in the manor from at least 1122 until about 1358, at which date it exchanged its lands for some in GODSTOW. In 1541 it was owned by George Owen (*see* WOLVERCOTE) and it was his son, Richard, who sold it to St John's College in 1573. Walton Manor Farm was near where LUCY'S EAGLE IRON-WORKS now stand in WALTON WELL ROAD. The modern development of the Walton Manor Estate began in the 1860s when St John's commissioned S.L. Seckham to lay out the land for housing. Seckham had himself built Nos 121–3 WOODSTOCK ROAD (1856–7) in the same style as the houses in PARK TOWN. By 1862 the development had been taken over by William Wilkinson, who was joined by his nephew, H.W. Moore, in 1881. Their buildings are mainly Gothic, in red or yellow brick with stone facings.

Walton Street Runs north from BEAUMONT STREET by Worcester College to Kingston Road. Stockwell(e) Street, the early name for WORCESTER STREET, stretched northwards into the present Walton Street and a track led from its end to the road to Walton

Manor and Walton Well (*see* WALTON WELL ROAD). THOMAS HEARNE says that Thomas Rowney, MP, told him that he had read in some 200-year-old book that Stockwell Street once extended from GLOUCESTER HALL (now Worcester College) as far as Walton.

On the west side of the road, starting at Worcester College, are Nos 1, 1a and 2 – a row of cottages beneath the level of the road, probably built in the 18th century. They are listed Grade II, as are Nos 4–15 further north beyond Ruskin College. These are three-storeyed, early 19th-century houses with red and variegated brick fronts. Nos 10, 11, 13, 14 and 15 have contemporary Regency-style balconies. The OXFORD UNIVERSITY PRESS has a wide frontage finishing at the corner of GREAT CLARENDON STREET. No. 58 is the Phoenix Cinema – formerly the Scala, which had been on the site since 1913 (*see* CINEMAS). CAPE'S, the drapers and furnishers, once had a branch at Nos 71 and 72. In St Sepulchre's Cemetery, the entrance to which is between Nos 78 and 81, many Oxford worthies, including BENJAMIN JOWETT, are buried. It has a 19th-century Gothic-style lodge designed by E.G. Bruton. On the east side the Victoria public house (No. 90) of about 1840 has a variegated brick front and a mansard roof. No. 95 was once the home of the YMCA. ST PAUL'S CHURCH, formerly occupied by the ST PAUL'S ARTS CENTRE, was described by Pevsner as the 'finest Grecian Church in Oxford'. Next to the back entrance to the RADCLIFFE INFIRMARY is No. 119, formerly St Paul's School, built in the Gothic style in 1848 by T. Grimsley and restored by H.W. Moore in 1888. No. 172 (part of Worcester College) is 17th century, although much altered and, like No. 119, is a Grade II listed building.

Walton Well Road *Running from No. 88*

WALTON STREET to PORT MEADOW, the road is so called from an old well situated on the right-hand side as one walks towards the Meadow. There is some confusion (*see* ARISTOTLE LANE) over whether the well was the same as Aristotle's (or Brumman's or Brimmanes) Well. It is now more likely that Aristotle's Well was Wolward's Well and Brumman's the same as Walton Well. However, in the 19th century the well in this road was called Aristotle's and was so marked on Alden's map of the city (*see* MAPS). On the site now is a fountain put up in 1885 'by the liberality of Alderman Ward'. When the road was made up a stonemason joked that they had 'put a fireplace' over the well 'to keep it warm'. A tramway carted gravel from the vicinity of Chalfont Road as ballast for a railway (1849–52), but this was covered up in about 1898. The narrow road which led over the CANAL to the meadow in early days was the subject of frequent arguments between the city and the Abbess of GODSTOW ABBEY. The city, complaining that the Abbess narrowed, encroached upon and blocked the road, eventually built a house there in order to keep a watchful eye on it. Herbert Hurst, in *Oxford Topography* (1899), wrote of 'All this pother about a miserable road nine feet only in width in Elizabethan days'. Actually, the road was important because not only did it lead to the meadow but to BINSEY by traversing a ford. A bridge, replacing Walton Well ford, was built by Sheriff Hunt in 1841, paid for partly by the city, partly by subscription and partly by the Sheriff himself. This bridge, which was opened with 'a jubilee', was not popular with all the freemen, who

believed that the peace of the cattle on the meadow should not be disturbed. It was superseded by Walton Well Road railway bridge in 1881.

Warnborough College *Boar's Hill.* Founded in

1973 as an independent college giving overseas students the opportunity to study in Oxford. The college started in Warnborough Road, but in 1976 the present premises on BOAR'S HILL were acquired. The main house was successively known as Brumcombe, Glynde House and Sandridge. In 1939 it became the official residence of the BISHOP OF OXFORD and in 1954 was acquired by PLATER COLLEGE. In 1978 Warnborough purchased the adjoining property known as Yatscombe. Built in 1905, this was first occupied by the Shawcross family and then, in 1919, became the home of GILBERT MURRAY and the scene of many gatherings of distinguished scholars, writers and statesmen, including George Bernard Shaw, Bertrand Russell, Albert Einstein, H.G. Wells, Aldous Huxley, G.K. Chesterton, Madame Curie and Arnold Toynbee, who married Murray's daughter. In 1980 Warnborough College became part of the International University Foundation. It has an average of 100 students, sixty of whom are resident, and retains its original identity as a small, independent, co-educational, international university college run on American lines.

Warneford Hospital *Old Road, Headington.*

Opened in July 1826 as the Oxford Lunatic Asylum, it later became the Radcliffe Asylum (in recognition of a donation from the JOHN RADCLIFFE trustees) and in 1843, the Warneford Asylum. First proposals to found an asylum, as a sister-institution to the RADCLIFFE INFIRMARY (whose rules precluded the admission of lunatics), were submitted by the infirmary governors in 1812. The delays in acquiring a site enabled the Asylum Building Committee to procure advice on design and planning from well-known philanthropists, asylum superintendents and private mad-house keepers. The Oxford Asylum was purpose-built, to the plans of Richard Ingleman of Southwell (1777–1838), architect of the Lincoln and Nottingham asylums, who used stone from Headington Quarry (*see* STONE). The foundation stone was laid by the BISHOP OF OXFORD on 27 August 1821. It was planned as a small establishment, financed by voluntary subscription, for middle-class inmates capable of making some contribution to the cost of their treatment. It remained a private hospital until it became part of the National Health Service in 1948.

The asylum opened as a family establishment which tried to recreate the atmosphere of a gentleman's country house, with a chapel and chaplain and gracious landscaped grounds. It flourished under the superintendence of two dedicated resident directors – Dr Frederick Wintle (1828–53) and Mr Thomas Allen (1853–72), assisted by their wives as matrons. The early staff comprised three male keepers, two female attendants, six domestics and a gardener. Members of the honorary medical and surgical staff of the Radcliffe Infirmary acted as visiting consultants. Patients came principally from Oxfordshire and adjoining counties, but occasionally from Wales and Ireland. A Committee of Management supervised the affairs of the asylum closely, particularly during the thirty-year chairmanship of the Rev. Vaughan

Warneford Hospital, opened in 1826 as the Oxford Lunatic Asylum, was considerably enlarged in the later 19th century, the extensions of the 1880s being based on drawings by John Oldrich Scott.

Thomas (1775–1858), an intimate friend of the asylum's chief benefactor, the Rev. Samuel W. Warneford, rector of Bourton-on-the-Hill, Gloucestershire. During a lifetime of philanthropy, Samuel Warneford donated £70,000 to the asylum, visiting it regularly and advising on the use made of the money. It was due to the calibre and devotion of such men, assisted by the interest and influence of the University of Oxford, that the Warneford acquired a reputation for humane, enlightened care at a time when many institutions were shadowed by scandals and allegations of ill-treatment. There were many distinguished visitors, including European medical men and Dr John Conolly, superintendent of the Hanwell Asylum, Middlesex, the champion of non-coercive treatment of the insane. As with all successful institutions, demands increased as the late 19th century saw a greater chronicity among patients. The original buildings had been increased by the chapel (which had been begun in 1841 by Thomas Greenshields of Oxford, but was completed in 1852 by J.M. Derick) and by two small wings (J.C. BUCKLER, 1852) for patient accommodation. A very substantial extension was built in two stages (1877 and 1887), based on drawings by John O. Scott; this functions as the present entrance to the hospital. Its reception area contains a plaster bust of Vaughan Thomas (1845) and a white marble statue of Samuel Warneford (1849), both by Peter Hollins of Birmingham.

Twentieth-century developments have included the building of the first nurses' home (1914); the introduction, in combination with LITTLEMORE HOSPITAL, of out-patient clinics for patients of the Radcliffe Infirmary with mental and nervous disorders (1918); the purchase of premises in Hill Top Road (1931) for mild neurasthenic cases; and the acquisition of Highfield Park House as a convalescent villa (1936). With the creation of the W.A. Handley Chair of Psychiatry (1969), the new University Department of Psychiatry was set up in the Warneford grounds. The most recent addition (1971)

was the Highfield Unit (sixteen beds) for the treatment of adolescent psychiatric problems. By 1986 the Warneford had 120 beds and incorporated a busy day hospital and out-patient clinics.

Warton, Thomas (*1728–1790*). The son of Thomas Warton, Professor of Poetry at Oxford, he entered Trinity College in 1744. He became a Fellow of the college in 1751 and for the rest of his life remained a don. He was elected Professor of Poetry in 1757 and Poet Laureate in 1785. A prolific writer and editor of poetry, he edited *The Oxford Sausage* (*see* MAGAZINES) and in 1774–81 published his *History of English Poetry* in three volumes.

Water Supply Most people in Oxford until the late 19th century obtained water by means of innumerable pumps and shallow wells that tapped the plentiful supply lying just beneath the gravel terrace on which the city was built: twenty disused wells were discovered, for instance, on the site cleared in 1931 for the NEW BODLEIAN LIBRARY. Brewers and other industrial users took water straight from the river. Large institutional users, however, and particularly the religious houses built beyond the CITY WALLS on Oxford clay, faced problems in providing a supply of fresh water for drinking. In about 1220 OSENEY ABBEY brought in fresh spring water by aqueduct from NORTH HINKSEY, south-west of Oxford, as, by 1285, did BLACKFRIARS. GREYFRIARS, which, like Blackfriars, stood upon the clay of the ST EBBE'S district, was said to have a system of lead pipes miles long. St John's Hospital, later Magdalen College, obtained its water by aqueduct from Crowell, a spring at the north-east corner of the city ditch in HOLYWELL. In 1279 Merton College obtained permission to bring water from the Cherwell (*see* THAMES) by a system of ditches and gutters.

Between 1615 and 1617 a new supply of fresh water was provided through the generosity of Otho Nicholson, a wealthy London lawyer. Although not a member of the University, he was a benefactor of Christ Church, and the intention originally may have been to provide water for that college. A London plumber, Hugh Justyce, was employed to supervise the scheme, which gathered the water from several springs on Hinksey Hill into a lead cistern there holding 20,000 gallons. Water was then conveyed underground in lead pipes encased in elm to LITTLEGATE, crossing various branches of the THAMES and Osney mill stream. From Littlegate, the pipes passed along PEMBROKE STREET and ST ALDATE'S to CARFAX, where a stone conduit was built (*see* CARFAX CONDUIT). The total distance was 2564 yards. The conduit contained two cisterns – an upper for the University and an overflow cistern for the town. Pipes from the upper cistern took water to seven colleges and to a cistern by ALL SAINTS CHURCH, HIGH STREET, which supplied another three colleges and some private houses. Only a handful of citizens made arrangements to receive water from the lower cistern. It was intended that the University and the city should jointly control the conduit, but, after a period of financial difficulty, the University assumed liability for the works in 1635. There were constant problems with damaged pipes and with unauthorised tapping of the supply, and the conduit itself was regularly presented as an obstruction. In 1787, as part of the Paving Commission's street-widening programme, it was replaced by a new conduit on the north side of Carfax. The water system was purchased by the Corporation in 1869, by which time it had almost ceased to be capable of delivering water.

In 1694 the Corporation leased to a consortium headed by Fleetwood Dormer some waste ground and water at FOLLY BRIDGE to build a force-pump and water-wheel for conveying water to the city's principal streets. In August 1695 a letter writer was reporting excitedly that 'great waterworks are making here for the good of the city. Pipes are and must be laid all over Oxford'. In fact, wooden pipes were laid in CORNMARKET, QUEEN STREET, St Aldate's and CATTE STREET. In 1699 Dormer and his associates leased the first two arches of Folly Bridge so that floodgates could be built and the fall of water improved. The venture was unsuccessful because it could never attract enough consumers; and the waterworks were unsatisfactory technically. When the river was in flood there was insufficient fall; when the water was low it froze in winter, while in summer the quality was bad, for it was pumped, unfiltered, straight into the pipes. A new engine and a second water-wheel were built in 1767; and in 1776 the Corporation ordered all tenants of city property to take the water. In 1808 the Corporation decided to take over the works itself, chiefly because of the need to ensure an efficient supply in the event of fire. When Folly Bridge was rebuilt in 1825 the waterworks were re-sited on the newly cut river channel at the end of Isis Street. Wooden pipes were replaced in 1835 by 5320 yards of iron pipes; eighty fireplugs and thirty-two brass cocks were installed on street corners. In 1836 a modest profit was made, for the first time. There were further improvements in 1849 when a new wheel and pumps were fitted.

Meanwhile, the question of water supply was becoming inextricably caught up in the urgent debate on PUBLIC HEALTH in the city. In their response to questions put by the Health of Towns Association in 1848, Oxford's doctors stated that the city's sanitary state was 'so defective as to demand immediate

Carfax Conduit, seen on the left of this engraving, Carfax as it appeared in 1775, *was built in 1610, the upper part supplying water to a number of colleges, the lower part to the city.*

alteration', and they singled out the water supply as 'intermittent and deficient . . . the works are at the lowest level of the city and below nearly all the sewers'. Asked if the city was likely to undertake improvements to water supply, sewerage, drainage, street-cleansing, and fire protection, the reply was, 'Never . . . the "let-alone" system prevails and nothing but the interference of the government will change it.' The debate gathered pace following the outbreak of cholera in 1849. It might be thought to have been a blessing that so few households took the polluted water (only 340 of 4600), were it not for the fact that the wells still preferred by most were themselves contaminated. In 1851 Sir William Cubitt and Thomas Macdougall Smith were employed to conduct an inquiry. Among their recommendations was the building of a reservoir at WOLVERCOTE PAPER MILL, from where water would be pumped to Carfax and thence to a head reservoir on HEADINGTON HILL. That scheme was not adopted, and instead the Corporation bought in 1854 the 12-acre lake at SOUTH HINKSEY created by the Great Western Railway's extraction of gravel for ballast. A pumping station was built adjacent. There had been no time, however, for improvements to make themselves felt before cholera returned to the city in 1854.

The new scheme eventually transformed Oxford's water supply. In 1874 an analyst's report was published, praising the water as 'of excellent quality, well suited for domestic use'. By 1866 almost half the houses in the city were connected to the supply, and new pipes continued to be installed until, by 1884, there were 42 miles of them, and every house was connected to mains water. In 1875 an Act was obtained enabling the city to buy land at Headington for a high-level storage reservoir, fed from the lake at Hinksey. It was built in 1878. In 1884 the University set up an informal committee, headed by SIR HENRY ACLAND and Professor Joseph Prestwich, to inquire into the supply of water. Their concern stemmed from a felt need to supervise sanitary conditions in the rapidly increasing number of student lodging-houses. The inquiry was inconclusive but seemed happy to go along with the city's new scheme, embodied in an Act of 1885, to pipe water from the THAMES at King's Weir, above WOLVERCOTE, to the lake at Hinksey, where new filters would be installed. A reservoir was opened at Shotover in 1903 and, under the provisions of the Oxford Corporation (Water) Act of 1928, additional storage reservoirs were opened at Shotover, Headington, and Beacon Hill between 1929 and 1932. New waterworks were opened at Swinford in 1934, and the old works at Hinksey closed down. The city's rapid expansion and the consequent increased demand for water led to the construction of reservoirs at BOAR'S HILL in 1935 and 1948. The first stage of a raw-water storage reservoir at Farmoor, holding 960 million gallons of water pumped from the Thames, was opened in 1962 and the second stage, holding 1550 million gallons, in 1976.

The Act of 1875 covered the parliamentary borough and the parishes of St Aldate's, South Hinksey, COWLEY, Headington, IFFLEY, LITTLEMORE, and Wolvercote; MARSTON and North Hinksey were added in 1885. Following further extensions in 1932 and 1935, a total area of 113 square miles was supplied by the works. In 1967 the Oxford and District Water Board was created by grouping together several water

undertakings. The area served covered Oxfordshire and North Berkshire, and in 1974 the Board became the Vales division of the Thames Water Authority.

Webber's A department store which occupied premises at Nos 9–15 HIGH STREET. James Clark, a mercer, began business on the site in 1774. The building which he used at No. 13 High Street was designed by John Gwynn, who also designed MAGDALEN BRIDGE, and one of the others was formerly the King's Head Tavern. In 1905 Charles Webber bought the row of shops from Edward Beaumont junior, who had traded since the 1870s as the City Drapery Stores. The firm's advertisements claimed that it pioneered the introduction in a department store of telephones, cash railways and electric lifts. It had a long, ashlar front to High Street of thirteen bays, and the ground floor was divided by three pedestrian avenues to the COVERED MARKET. Like many of the early department stores, some of the staff lived in in its early days (*see* CAPE'S). The family firm was bought by Hide & Co. in 1952. It closed in October 1971 and the premises are now divided and leased to separate businesses.

Wellington Square Situated at the northern end of ST JOHN STREET and connected to LITTLE CLARENDON STREET by a footway. The square was formerly the site of the workhouse (House of Industry), which was built in 1772. A stone building of two storeys, it housed up to 200 paupers. In the 1790s a nursery and a ward for elderly and infirm people were added. The workhouse moved to COWLEY ROAD in 1860. In the vicinity was Rats and Mice Hill, referred to by ANTHONY WOOD and mentioned in the 1772 Survey, although its exact site is not known. It was probably a hillock of rubbish inhabited by rodents. The houses in the square, which were built between 1869 and 1876, were a speculative development. It was no doubt at this time that it was named after the Duke of Wellington, who had been CHANCELLOR of the University until 1852. An advertisement in the *Oxford Times* (*see* NEWSPAPERS) of April 1885 advertised for sale houses containing '10 bed and living rooms, excellent offices; the city water laid on to first floors and speaking tubes from the first to second floors'. Houses on the northern side of the street were pulled down in 1969–73 and the UNIVERSITY OFFICES were built on the site. Since 1960 the Department of Social and Administrative Studies has been at Barnett House. The Department of EXTERNAL STUDIES is at Rewley House in the south-eastern corner. The OXFORD EYE HOSPITAL, founded by R.W. Doyne, was in the square in two adjoining houses between 1886 and 1894, before moving to WALTON STREET. The Acland Nursing Home (now ACLAND HOSPITAL) also began its life here in 1879, at Nos 36, 37 and 38, before moving to Northgate in BANBURY ROAD.

Welsh Pony *16 Gloucester Street and 48 George Street*. One of the five GLOUCESTER GREEN market inns, it was built in 1830. It was named after the animals sold at the cattle market which it originally fronted.

Wesley, John (*1703–1791*). The founder of the Methodist Church, Wesley was born in Epworth, Lincolnshire, where his father was Rector. One of nineteen children, he was educated at home by his mother, Susanna, then at Charterhouse before obtaining an exhibition to Christ Church in 1720. He came 'to love the very sight of Oxford'. In the college's Great Hall hangs a copy of Romney's portrait. Elected a Fellow of Lincoln College in 1726, he was ordained priest in 1725 in CHRIST CHURCH CATHEDRAL, with which he was so familiar as an undergraduate. The rooms in Lincoln traditionally thought to have been Wesley's are situated on the right of the main quadrangle. They were restored in 1928 by the generosity of American Methodists and can be visited by arrangement with the Bursar. Dr V.H.H. Green has recently concluded, however, that Wesley actually occupied rooms on the TURL STREET side of Chapel Quadrangle.

Wesley joined a small undergraduate group led by his brother Charles, who had followed him to Christ Church. Variously known as 'Bible Moths', 'the Holy Club', and 'Methodists', they were dedicated to regular (hence 'Methodist') devotions and good works, visiting prisoners almost daily in the CASTLE and the BOCARDO, the debtors' prison. He preached in most of the city churches but is principally associated with ST MARY THE VIRGIN, where he preached the UNIVERSITY SERMON seven times and from where he was eventually excluded after a sermon on Scriptural Christianity in 1744. He left Oxford in 1735 to be chaplain to the English community in Savannah, Georgia. Three years later, at a meeting in Aldersgate Street, London, on 24 May 1738, 'about a quarter before nine', he felt his heart 'strangely warmed'. This evangelical conversion marked the beginning of his itinerant ministry, largely on horseback, throughout the British Isles. 'I look upon the world as my parish', he wrote, and all is meticulously recorded in his

John Wesley, the founder of Methodism, painted by Nathaniel Hone c.1766. An undergraduate at Christ Church in the 1720s, Wesley was ordained in Christ Church Cathedral and preached in most of the city's churches.

journal. Excluded from most parish churches, Wesley preached in the open air, drawing large and sometimes hostile crowds. He organised his followers into small groups or 'Societies', using the new-found gifts of local people in teaching, administration and preaching. In 1778 Wesley opened his chapel in City Road, London, and this became the centre of his work. His ordination in Bristol, in 1784, of Richard Whatcoat and Thomas Vazey for work in North America was the decisive act in separating Methodism from the Anglican Church, although Wesley maintained that he lived and died a member of the Church of England. On 14 July 1783, on one of his many visits to Oxford, he came to the new preaching house in NEW INN HALL STREET, described by him as 'a lightsome, cheerful place, and well filled with rich and poor, scholars as well as townsmen'. A plaque now marks Oxford's first Methodist Church at Nos 32 and 34. Nearby, the WESLEY METHODIST MEMORIAL CHURCH continues the tradition.

Wesley Memorial Methodist Church *New Inn Hall Street.* Designed by Charles Bell of London and built by Joshua Symm, a local man, it was opened in October 1878, its fine spire forming part of the Oxford skyline. The present church was built in front of an earlier one opened in 1818 and designed by William Jenkins. This was sold to St Peter's College in 1932 and demolished in 1968 to make way for student accommodation. NEW INN HALL STREET has long associations with JOHN WESLEY, his first preaching house in Oxford having been at Nos 32 and 34. Before him, however, his father, Samuel, was a member of NEW INN HALL.

Victorian Gothic in inspiration, the church has a full gallery and originally had a central pulpit behind the Communion table in true Nonconformist tradition. Polished granite pillars support the roof, and their capitals, carved by Henry Frith of Gloucester, show twelve species of English plants. The gallery window continues the theme of the countryside. The organ, by Nicholsons, dates from the opening of the church but was rebuilt by Henry Willis and Sons in 1950. A bastion of the ancient CITY WALL is to be seen to the right of the ancillary premises.

In 1978 the interior of the church was extensively modernised under the direction of Geoffrey Beard of the Oxford Architects Partnership. The flexibility of the sanctuary area, which includes the original pulpit, enables the church to be used not only for worship but also for concerts and plays. In the side-chapel can be seen a tapestry by Pat Russell of Abingdon, incorporating words from the Methodist Covenant Service.

Wesley Memorial Church is the centre for Methodist work among Oxford students through the John Wesley Society. The ancillary premises provide a home for several of Oxford's voluntary organisations.

Westgate Centre A shopping centre built in 1970–2 on the site of the old West Gate of the city. CASTLE STREET was re-aligned to enable the centre to be built. Archaeological excavations carried out by the Oxford Archaeological Unit before building began uncovered a stone coffin on the site of St Budoc's Church, which was destroyed in 1216; the remains of the GREYFRIARS' church were also discovered. Queen

Elizabeth II visited the site on 2 May 1968. The Centre incorporates the new CENTRAL LIBRARY and a covered shopping arcade leading from BONN SQUARE to the multi-storey Westgate Car Park (*see* PARKING). It was designed by the City Architect, Douglas Murray, and was built by Taylor Woodrow. In 1986 the Centre was sold by the City Council to Arrowcroft, the firm of developers which constructed the CLARENDON CENTRE. They refurbished the Centre, installing new lighting and doors across the entrance, and erected the Westgate pavilion in Bonn Square.

Westminster College *North Hinksey*. Founded in 1851 as the Wesleyan Training College, its first premises were in Horseferry Road, Westminster. It was intended to train teachers for a projected total of 700 Methodist elementary schools throughout the country. By 1939 all its students were automatically enrolled on a four-year course, which included a London University external degree. In 1955 the Horseferry Road site was sold to the General Post Office for £400,000 and in 1959 the college moved to Oxford with about 200 students, a few of them women. By 1962 there were 400 students, half of whom were women. The college was attached to the Oxford University Department of Educational Studies, through which the students took the Certificate of Education or, if already graduates, the Diploma of Education. From 1967 they studied for the degree of B.Ed (Oxon). Following the Bullock Committee's Report of 1973, the college's formal connection with the University ceased, and from 1976 students began to take the Council for National Academic Awards B.Ed degree instead. In 1985 the full-time teaching staff numbered forty-six, with nearly 600 students.

The college occupies some 88 acres of a site on HARCOURT HILL, owned in the 1930s by Lord Harcourt and intended to be sold for residential development. This was refused on environmental grounds in the 1950s; but planning permission was granted for a college. The buildings, in brick, designed by Lord Mottistone and Paul Paget, cover 25 acres, with gardens and playing fields of 63 acres, 16 of which are planted as an arboretum. Residential accommodation, indoor swimming pool, library, theatre, gymnasium and lecture rooms surround the central chapel, the east window of which, designed in 1912 by H.J. Salisbury, was moved from the college chapel in Westminster and is dedicated to D.J. Walker, DD (1835–1911), for thirty years secretary of the Wesleyan Educational Committee.

Whately, Richard (*1787–1863*). Fellow of Oriel College from 1811 to 1822 and Principal of ST ALBAN HALL from 1825 until his advancement in 1831 to the archbishopric of Dublin. He became Drummond Professor of Political Economy in 1829 and was one of the pioneers of Social Science. A man of 'blatant voice, great stride, rough dress', he loved teaching and had great powers of argument. He was uninterested in the Humanities and in the beauty of nature, though he was a great walker. His best known work is *Logic* (1826); another, *Historic Doubts relative to Napoleon Buonaparte*, sought to show that 'as a well-authenticated fact' Napoleon's existence was open to question.

According to the DICTIONARY OF NATIONAL BIOGRAPHY, 'In the Oxford of his day Whately's was a name to mention with bated breath'. Charles Greville, the diarist, however, found him 'a very ordinary man in appearance and conversation', though he admitted that he had heard that 'when he is with such men as [Nassau William] Senior [the economist], and those with whom he is very intimate, he shines'.

White Hart *21 Cornmarket Street*. In 1483 the site was occupied by a large house with shops and cellars. In 1657 this became the Globe, which remained its name until the late 17th century when it became the White Hart. It ceased trading in 1901 and became the Buol Restaurant (*see* RESTAURANTS).

White Hart Inn *Wytham*. A 17th-century stone-built inn, listed as being of special architectural or historic interest. It was bought by HALL'S BREWERY from the Wilkinson Trust and is the only house in the village of WYTHAM which does not belong to the University. The inn has an attractive walled garden and in the car park is a 16th-century dovecot – a square, timber-framed plastered building on a base of stone rubble with a pyramidal, tiled roof. This too is a listed building (Grade II).

White Horse *52 Broad Street*. A small, two-roomed 18th-century timber-framed tavern. Its frontage was completely rebuilt in 1951.

Wilberforce, Samuel (*1805–1873*). The third son of William Wilberforce, the philanthropist, he was educated privately before going up to Oriel College in 1823. At Oxford he excelled at public speaking and was one of the leading members of the UNION; after taking Holy Orders he became a celebrated preacher. Appointed one of the Prince Consort's chaplains in 1841, and Dean of Westminster in May 1845, he became BISHOP OF OXFORD in October, holding that appointment for almost twenty-five years, during which he became a national figure, speaking regularly in the House of Lords on secular as well as ecclesiastical matters, taking a prominent part in various controversies, and in the revival of CONVOCATION. He was highly energetic in his diocese, in which £2 million were spent during his episcopate, mostly on churches, endowments, schools, rectories and vicarages. He himself founded the theological college at Cuddesdon and a college for training schoolmasters at Culham. His reputation for evasiveness and his ingratiating manner earned him the nickname of 'Soapy Sam'. BENJAMIN JOWETT remarked of him, 'Samuel of Oxford is not unpleasing if you will resign yourself to being semi-humbugged by a semi-humbug.'

In 1860 Wilberforce confronted Thomas Huxley in a famous debate about the theory of evolution in the recently opened UNIVERSITY MUSEUM. 'The Bishop spoke for full half an hour with inimitable spirit, emptiness and unfairness,' recalled a woman who was present. 'In a light, scoffing tone, florid and fluent, he assured us that there was nothing in the idea of evolution; rock pigeons were what rock-pigeons had always been. Then turning to his antagonist with a smiling insolence, he begged to know, was it through his grandfather or his grandmother that he claimed his descent from a monkey. On this Mr Huxley slowly and deliberately rose ... a slight tall figure, stern and pale, very quiet and very grave. . . . He was not

The eloquent and ingratiating Samuel Wilberforce, Bishop of Oxford for almost twenty-five years from 1845.

ashamed to have a monkey for his ancestor; but he would be ashamed to be connected with a man who used great gifts to obscure the truth.'

Wilberforce lived at No. 39a ST GILES' where his arms are above the door (*see* HERALDRY). He left Oxford to become Bishop of Winchester in 1869.

Wilkins, John *(1614–1672)*. The son of an Oxford goldsmith whose 'head ran much upon the perpetuall motion', Wilkins was sent to a private school in the town run by one Edward Sylvester, 'the common drudge of the university'. He entered NEW INN HALL in 1627, then moved to MAGDALEN HALL, taking his MA degree in 1634. A supporter of the parliamentary side during the CIVIL WAR, he was appointed Warden of Wadham College by the Parliamentary Visitors (*see* VISITATIONS) of 1648. In 1656 he married Oliver

Cromwell's sister, the widow of a canon of Christ Church, and was given a dispensation which allowed him to remain Warden of Wadham despite the statute requiring holders of that office to be celibate. During his wardenship the college flourished, highly regarded by both Royalists and Parliamentarians, and Wilkins's rooms became the meeting place of those 'most inquisitive' members of the University, including RALPH BATHURST and CHRISTOPHER WREN, who met to discuss 'natural philosophy and other parts of human learning' and who later founded the Royal Society, of which Wilkins was to be the first secretary. At the Restoration, Wilkins's moderation in his support of the Parliamentarians ensured the success of his later career. He was obliged to resign his mastership of Trinity College, Cambridge, to which he had been appointed in 1660, but was appointed Prebendary of York that same year and in 1668 became Bishop of Chester.

Wolfson College Established by the University in 1964 as Iffley College. Its original purpose was to enhance the opportunities for graduate students and to increase the availability of college fellowships to holders of University teaching, research and other senior library and administrative posts. Thirty-six Fellows were assigned to Iffley College, which effectively came into existence in September 1965, though with no head and no constitutionally approved procedure for transforming the college into a living community. That has been the achievement of the first Fellows and their successors in the twenty years of its existence. Early meetings of the Fellows established the main themes of the college. It was to be large, serving the needs of many graduate students, but with a definite bias towards the natural sciences. This reflected the interests of a majority of the original Fellows, but the policy remains that students in every academic discipline are encouraged. The ratio of students in the natural sciences to the humanities continues to be two to one. In government the college maintains its egalitarian thrust: students are represented in all spheres of its procedures, with representatives on the governing body. This spirit is maintained by the inclusion of graduate students and member's families in the general college life.

These ambitions underlined the need for a large site with a generous endowment to extend that made by twelve of the older Oxford colleges at its foundation. The original site proposed by the University was Court Place at IFFLEY, but a lucky chance made available a much larger site known as Cherwell, between the end of Linton Road and the River Cherwell (*see* THAMES). It was on 26 June 1966 that the Fellows learned that the University had allocated the Cherwell site to the college; that the Wolfson Foundation was prepared to make a building grant of £1,500,000 and the Ford Foundation an endowment of $4,500,000; that Professor Sir Isaiah Berlin, Fellow of All Souls College and Chichele Professor of Social and Political Theory, had accepted the office of first President; and the college became Wolfson College. Initially with no corporate existence, trustees were appointed to receive grants and enter into building commitments on behalf of the college, with LORD FLOREY, Provost of The Queen's College, as first chairman. The Charter of Incorporation was granted by the Queen in Council on 18 February 1981 and

Wolfson reached its self-governing, truly independent modern self. The Queen herself had laid the foundation stone for the new buildings on 2 May 1968 and they were formally opened by the Rt Hon. Harold Macmillan (later LORD STOCKTON), CHANCELLOR of the University, on 12 November 1974. Designed by Powell and Moya, the distinction of the building was recognised by the Gold Medal awarded them by the Royal Institute of British Architects. They are now a vivid feature of every northward punt ride up the Cherwell.

During the years 1966–74 Wolfson College grew into a thriving community in various buildings in the BANBURY ROAD and there were over 100 graduate admissions a year by the time it moved to its permanent site. In 1987 the College had over 800 members, including students of thirty nationalities, a third of them women and many with families living in the college. As well as students there are Research and Junior Research Fellows, post-doctoral and other affiliated members of the college to complement the sixty governing-body Fellows. The annual Wolfson series of lectures is an important feature of Oxford academic life.

The college's second President, from 1975–85, was the Hon. Sir H.A.P. Fisher, also a former Fellow of All Souls; he was succeeded by Sir Raymond Hoffenberg, President of the Royal College of Physicians.

The corporate title of the college is The President and Fellows of Wolfson College in the University of Oxford.

(Jessup, F.W., *Wolfson College, Oxford: the Early Years*, Oxford, 1979.)

Wolsey, Thomas (?1475–1530).

The son of a prosperous butcher from Ipswich, Wolsey was sent to Oxford at an early age, took his BA before he was sixteen and was elected a Fellow of Magdalen when he was about twenty-two. He soon afterwards became Master of MAGDALEN COLLEGE SCHOOL, remaining there until 1500 when the Marquess of Dorset, father of three of his pupils, obtained for him a living in Somerset and embarked him upon his remarkable career, which ended in his becoming Archbishop of York, a Cardinal and Lord Chancellor. Having acquired enormous wealth, Wolsey founded Cardinal College, which developed into Christ Church.

(*See also* CHRIST CHURCH.)

Wolsey Hall

66 Banbury Road. Founded in Cirencester in 1894 by the pioneer teacher J. William Knipe (whose grandson Peter M. Newell was chairman of Wolsey Hall in 1986). The establishment moved in 1907 to Oxford, where it originally occupied a building known as Wolsey Hall on the site of the Christ Church Memorial Garden. It moved to its present address in 1930 and in 1961 a new wing of 5,000 square feet was added. As well as providing correspondence courses for GCE O- and A-level, Wolsey Hall offers courses for several external degrees of London University, the external MBA of the University of Warwick and a number of business and professional qualifications. It also organises seminars, summer schools, a residential college and law school. Until his death in December 1986, the Principal was the Hon. F.F. Fisher, a former master of Wellington College and Warden of ST EDWARD'S SCHOOL. He was succeeded by John Coffey.

Wolvercote

A village to the north-west of Oxford known by this name since 1185, although in 1220–30 it was called Wolgarcote and in 1285 Wolgaricote. It was sometimes spelt Wolvercot. Contrary to what some people (including THOMAS HEARNE) surmised, the village was not named after the number of wolves which inhabited its woods, but after Ulfgar (or Wulfgar), the Saxon, who had a cottage here. In Domesday it was known as Ulfgarcote.

The land was given to the manor of GODSTOW in 1171. For generations the Wolvercote Commoners have owned and controlled Wolvercote Common (adjoining PORT MEADOW), Goose Green and Wolvercote Green (to the north and south of Godstow Road respectively). From 1894 until 1929 the village was part of Woodstock District Council and had its own parish council. The parish included much of what is now CUTTESLOWE, and the ecclesiastical parish still extends to the Templar Road Estate, adjoining CUTTESLOWE PARK in the east. When taken into the city in 1929, the commoners formed their own committee and still act in some ways as a parish council. They have always been mindful of their rights over common land and have, throughout the centuries, been anxious to curb unauthorised use of both Port Meadow and Wolvercote Common. Nowadays any resident of the ecclesiastical parish of Wolvercote is entitled to attend and vote at commoners' meetings, held twice a year at the village hall. In earlier times there were many disputes over rights of pasture and common, most notably in 1552, when George Owen, owner of Wolvercote Manor and mill, and physician to Henry VIII, petitioned the King to prevent the MAYOR and BURGESSES of Oxford from enclosing the Wolvercote part of Port Meadow, as enclosure would have prevented the tenants and villagers from pasturing their animals there. (The town had already enclosed Cripley meadow to the south.)

At the time of the CIVIL WAR there were two mills at Wolvercote: one was used by the armourers of King Charles for grinding sword-blades. Sir John Walter had bought this mill from the descendants of Sir George Owen in 1616. Sir John was Chief Baron of the Exchequer and Justice of England and his family tomb, defaced during the siege of Oxford, is in ST PETER'S, the parish church. David Walter, his son, Lieutenant of the Ordnance, was also buried at Wolvercote when he died in 1679; his marble bust is on the north wall of the church. Such was David's loyalty to the King that he burned down his own house at Godstow (which included much beautiful antique glass) in order that it should not fall into the hands of the Parliamentarians. He was High Sheriff of Oxfordshire as well as Lord of the Manor of Wolvercote, and later was appointed one of Charles II's Grooms of the Bedchamber. He was a stout defender of the rights of Wolvercote, especially those concerning the division of the meadow among the freeholders.

As well as with the city of Oxford, Wolvercote was often at odds with the University too. In 1662, according to ANTHONY WOOD, scholars trying to steal geese at Wolvercote were set upon and one was put in the stocks still wearing his gown. He was later rescued by a band of forty University men, who then broke all the windows in Wolvercote before marching off with a goose on the end of a long pole.

Wolvercote now consists of the village itself, which extends from just east of the TROUT inn, Godstow, in the west, to Wolvercote Green on the edge of the Common. Upper Wolvercote includes the church, school (County First), post-office stores, the St Peter's Road (Council) Estate, and a large built-up area mainly on the west side of WOODSTOCK ROAD. Although much developed over the last two centuries (it was described in 1817 as a 'rather extensive village'), it still has some old houses and much of the village is a CONSERVATION AREA. WOLVERCOTE PAPER MILL has been there for three centuries, and until 1978 was owned by the University. Water-power was used until 1943. Later it was one of the first paper-mills in the country to be computerised. The Pre-Raphaelite painter Holman Hunt loved Wolvercote and said that he and Thomas Combe, who bought the paper mill in 1855, 'wended our way there not infrequently in the character of searchers after the picturesque'. Lewis Carroll (*see* CHARLES DODGSON) wrote *Alice's Adventures in Wonderland* after an outing on the river near Wolvercote with Alice Liddell and her sisters (*see* ALICE).

In the Middle Ages, Wolvercote was part of the parish of ST PETER-IN-THE-EAST and St Peter's Church, in First Turn, Upper Wolvercote, was a chapel-of-ease. Behind the church is a small church hall, which was erected in the 19th century and was once a schoolroom. It is a Grade II listed building. Church Farmhouse, to the west of the church, another listed building, is 16th century with a 19th-century addition. Its extensive orchard was sold in the late 1950s and Dove House Close was built upon it. Godstow Road, which winds from the Woodstock Road roundabout to the Trout inn, has several listed houses. At the eastern end on the north side is Manor Farm, a 17th-century farmhouse which has been much altered. Nos 67 and 139 Godstow Road are both 17th and 18th century, and No. 187 is 17th century, though restored. The village has three public houses, two of which are listed Grade II: these are the White Hart, at No. 126 Godstow Road, which is 17th–18th century but with a restored front, and the Red Lion, which is probably 18th century but has been much restored; the third is the Plough, situated at the corner of First Turn and Wolvercote Green with a view over canal and meadow.

The toll-bridge over the river by the bathing place on the way to Godstow was probably there in the Middle Ages, but it was rebuilt in 1892 when the road was widened. On its northern parapet is a granite memorial plaque to Lieutenant C.A. Bettington and Second Lieutenant E. Hotchkiss of the Royal Flying Corps, who were killed in a plane crash near here in 1912. The nearby bathing place, with its view across the meadows to the spires of Oxford, is one of the most beautiful in England. The new pound in which animals are temporarily placed after the Sheriff's Drive (*see* PORT MEADOW) is next to the bathing place on Wolvercote Common. Two roads in Wolvercote, Rosamund Road and Clifford Place, are named after Fair Rosamund and her family. The daughter of Walter de Clifford, a benefactor of GODSTOW ABBEY, she died in Woodstock in 1176 and was buried at Godstow. Blenheim Drive, Bladon Close and Blandford Avenue in Upper Wolvercote reflect the association with the Dukes of Marlborough; the present Duke still owns much of the land, although many of the leaseholds have now been purchased by residents. The Wolvercote Boys' Club is in St Peter's Road, and the Royal British Legion headquarters is off Ulfgar Road.

Wolvercote Paper Mill The paper mill at WOLVERCOTE has been associated with PRINTING at Oxford for some three centuries. Originally a water mill, it was part of the endowment of GODSTOW ABBEY. After the Dissolution of the Monasteries, the mill passed through several hands until it was bought by the 1st Duke of Marlborough. Paper made at the mill was used for the printing of books in Oxford from the 17th century. Towards the end of the 18th century the tenancy was acquired by John Swann, who carried out improvements to the mill to enlarge its capacity. His brother James took a new lease in 1823 and also bought Sandford Mill at Sandford-on-Thames. A watercolour drawing by J.C. BUCKLER, dated 1826, shows *The Paper Mill at Wolvercote, Oxfordshire,*

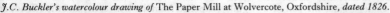

J.C. Buckler's watercolour drawing of The Paper Mill at Wolvercote, Oxfordshire, *dated 1826.*

belonging to James Swan, Esqre. In 1855 the mill was bought by Thomas Combe, Printer to the University. Holman Hunt, in his book on the Pre-Raphaelite Brotherhood, said that Combe bought the mill because he thought that the right of the University to print bibles might be withdrawn and believed that being able to make its own paper would be an advantage to the OXFORD UNIVERSITY PRESS. The existing mill was pulled down and a new one built, with a steam engine and other machinery for making paper. The first consignment of paper from the new mill was delivered in 1857 to the Bible Press (*see* OXFORD UNIVERSITY PRESS). No hand-made paper was produced at the new mill. In 1872 Combe sold the property to the University.

The machine house, which adjoins the mill on the north side, was built in the 1890s and extended in 1953. The old chapel built by Thomas Combe was converted into a modern office and laboratory block in the same year. Combe's mill, which had been driven by water-power until 1943, was then demolished and a new one, designed by Booth, Ledeboer & Pinckheard and built by KINGERLEE LTD, was opened in 1957. The building housed a Millspaugh 120-inch deckle paper machine capable of producing various grades and weights of paper. In 1965 the first on-line paper-machine control computer in the United Kingdom was opened. The method of paper-making was changed in 1966 from acid to neutral or slightly alkaline to produce long-life papers. High-quality coated papers are now produced at the mill by Star Paper Ltd, who took a long lease of the building from the University in 1978. The paper-making machine was rebuilt in 1987 so that it can produce paper coated on both sides. Ninety per cent of the mill's production is now specially coated paper supplied to the packaging industry and used to label goods sold in cans and cartons. The computer-control system was replaced by a more modern one at the same time.

(Carter, Harry, *Wolvercote Mill: A Study in Paper-Making at Oxford*, Oxford, 1957.)

Wood, Anthony (*1632–1695*). Anthony à Wood, as he preferred to style himself in later life, was born in a house opposite Merton College gate, the son of a man who owned property in Oxford, let lodgings and kept a tennis court. For a time he attended NEW COLLEGE SCHOOL, entering Merton in 1647 and graduating BA after five undistinguished years. He had hoped for a fellowship but this was not forthcoming, largely because of his bitter, suspicious and quarrelsome nature; so he pursued the antiquarian and historical studies, to which he was to devote his life, in the garret of the family home in MERTON STREET, making frequent visits to the University ARCHIVES to consult the collections on Oxford formed by BRIAN TWYNE and to Oxford's bookshops to buy books and pamphlets, many of which, together with his correspondence, autobiography and diaries he left to the ASHMOLEAN, whence they passed to the BODLEIAN LIBRARY. With the encouragement of RALPH BATHURST and the financial help of JOHN FELL, in 1674 Wood published his *Historia et Antiquitates Universitatis Oxoniensis* in two big volumes, many copies of which Fell distributed together with DAVID LOGGAN's *Oxonia Illustrata* (1675). By then the cantankerous and opinionated author · had quarrelled with almost everyone with whom he was associated – with both

Anthony Wood, the cantankerous antiquarian and author of The History and Antiquities of the University of Oxford, in 1695 at the age of sixty-four.

Fell and Bathurst, with his family and the Fellows of Merton, and with JOHN AUBREY, who provided him with much of his biographical material and whom he later described as 'a shiftless person, roving and maggotty-headed and sometimes little better than crazed'.

Aubrey also helped Wood with his other great work, *Athenae Oxonienses* (1691–2), a huge biographical dictionary of Oxford writers and ecclesiastics for which Andrew Allam (1655–85), another antiquarian, and Vice-Principal of ST EDMUND HALL, also supplied material. In the second volume of this work it was suggested that Edward Hyde, 1ST EARL OF CLARENDON, had accepted bribes. The Earl's son consequently took proceedings against Wood, who was prosecuted in the VICE-CHANCELLOR's court (*see* COURTS). He was found guilty, expelled from the University and the offending parts of the *Athenae* were publicly burned. Wood died two years later. He was buried in Merton College chapel, where a commemorative monument was erected by Thomas Rowney, Member of Parliament for the city. THOMAS HEARNE wrote of Wood: '[He] was always looked upon in Oxford as a most egregious, illiterate, dull Blockhead, a conceited, impudent Coxcombe'.

(*See also* HISTORIANS.)

Woodstock Road Once the Turnpike Road to Woodstock (*see* TRANSPORT). Two of the old mile-stones still survive. The west side begins at the north-west corner of LITTLE CLARENDON STREET and continues to WOLVERCOTE. In the early days of its residential development, the southern part was known as St Giles' Road West. When first built the road had a trench on its west side, continuing northwards to SUMMERTOWN. Scrapings from the road, which in those days consisted of horse manure and excavations for house cellars, were thrown into the ditch, and this is the reason why so many healthy trees grew at the roadside.

Between Nos 17 and 19 Woodstock Road is Radcliffe Row, formerly Cock's Row. The last remaining house, Radcliffe House (No. 17a Woodstock Road), is halfway down on the south side. The row used to run through to WALTON STREET but is now blocked off beyond Radcliffe House. The Row (like 'Yard', a traditional name for slums) had many small houses in it at one time, with the result that when ST ALOYSIUS CHURCH was built in 1873–5 (by James Hansom), it stood on a restricted site. Radcliffe Row was demolished between 1893 and 1904. St Aloysius Presbytery (No. 25) was built in 1877–8 by William Wilkinson, and beyond it is Somerville College, which stands on the site of the Waggon and Horses Public House, and which now owns Nos 11–21 Woodstock Road. To the north is the RADCLIFFE INFIRMARY, which once stood in open countryside remote from the town. There is a copy of Bernini's Triton fountain in the infirmary quad and on the north side of the quad is the chapel of St Luke by Arthur Blomfield. Between the infirmary and a terrace of three-storey red brick houses (listed Grade II) is Green College. Belsyre Court, a large linked block of flats with five shops and one office below, lies between OBSERVATORY STREET and ST BERNARD'S ROAD. It was built in 1936 by Ernest Barrow. The St Giles Brewery stood on the site between 1830 and the First World War.

On the north corner of St Bernard's Road is the HORSE AND JOCKEY public house. Nos 71–9 form a group of two-storey stucco houses, listed Grade II, which were built in about 1830. Nos 91 and 93–7 are all Grade II listed houses. On the south corner of Leckford Road is No. 111, which is possibly by Wilkinson and which is now a private old people's home. Nos 113–19 now form Butler Close, a large development of flats jointly called after Edwin Butler, for whom William Wilkinson built (in 1860) No. 113 (Butler paid £1180 for it), and Miss C.V. (Violet) Butler, Fellow of St Anne's College and prominent in Oxford voluntary social work. Wilkinson describes the original No. 113 in his *English Country Houses*, in which it is illustrated (Plate 15). The house was pulled down in the mid-1960s to make way for the flats. No. 115 was formerly St Faith's School; which was started in 1900 by the sisters of the Holy and Undivided Trinity; it was closed in 1965. A pair of Italianate houses by S.L. Seckham, built in 1856–7, are Nos 121–3. The houses from No. 71 to about No. 125 were part of WALTON MANOR ESTATE. No. 125 is now Stevens Close, Jesus College student accommodation. On the north corner of ST MARGARET'S ROAD is St Aloysius First School, occupying new low buildings built in the grounds of Notre Dame Convent and Hostel at Nos 145–7 (St Julie Hall), connected by a red brick chapel.

In a stretch of Woodstock Road between Nos 209 and 271 there are no fewer than three sports grounds. St John's College cricket ground and tennis courts are reached by a driveway between Nos 209 and 211. Further north is Keble College cricket ground, followed by ST EDWARD'S SCHOOL's sports ground, which is joined to the school by a pedestrian tunnel under the road. No. 271 is Corfe House, also owned by the school. The old city boundary ran near this point. Between First Turn and Godstow Road is the last remnant of a raised pathway (*see* FIVE MILE DRIVE). First Turn is so named because it was the first stop of the omnibuses for WOLVERCOTE, the second being Godstow Road. To the west of the roundabout on the

A typical Woodstock Road house, No. 113, built by William Wilkinson in 1860.

corner of Godstow Road is the Queen's Moathouse Hotel, which, in the 1960s, was called the Oxford Motel (of Watney Lyon Ltd).

The east side of Woodstock Road begins to the north of ST GILES' CHURCH. No. 10 is the St Giles' Parish Room, which was built in 1887–91 by H.W. Moore; during the Second World War it was a municipal restaurant. Next door is a building which was once a big-game museum and later the first home of the PLAYHOUSE. To the north is St Giles Terrace, Nos 14–36, which are of the late 18th century, cement-faced and rendered to give the impression of stone blocks. They are listed Grade II, as is the ROYAL OAK inn (Nos 42–4). No. 46 (dated 1904) is part of the ACLAND HOSPITAL and then come St Anne's and St Antony's Colleges. Nos 64–70 are all owned by St Antony's, as are most of the houses (except the new vicarage) in Church Walk. The old vicarage (No. 68) is by H.G.W. Drinkwater (1886–7) and No. 1 Church Walk is by F.J. Codd (1870s). The church of ST PHILIP AND ST JAMES, by G.E. STREET, was built in 1862. On the northern corner of Canterbury Road is No. 72, a Grade II listed house built in about 1840 for Thomas Mallam. An auctioneer, who had been a tobacconist, he was MAYOR in 1839 and 1846 (see MALLAMS). The house was called 'The Shrubbery', but people nicknamed it Quidville. Nos 78–82 are owned by St Hugh's College. RYE ST ANTONY SCHOOL, now in HEADINGTON, was once at No. 84; it then became part of Notre Dame Preparatory School, before being demolished for Hartley Court flats (built 1971–2), a large development on the north corner of ST MARGARET'S ROAD. The Squirrel School, a nursery and pre-preparatory school, is at No. 90 (once at No. 92); and on the north corner of Rawlinson Road is Ogston House, Trinity College graduate accommodation. This is a fine example of a restored and renovated late Victorian house which was once threatened with demolition. The annexe of University College (Nos 102 and 104) is on the corner of Staverton Road. Lord (then Sir William) Beveridge lived for a time at No. 104.

Further north, on the southern corner of Beechcroft Road, is the Woodstock Road Baptist Church (Evangelical) housed in a modern, fawn-coloured brick building. From No. 238 to No. 250 is St Edward's School, and beyond SOUTH PARADE are two public houses – the Red Lion with its green-tiled roof, and the Woodstock Arms. Between them lies the entrance to Alexandra Courts, a municipal playground and tennis courts. Beside it are the offices and clothing depot of the Royal Women's Voluntary Service. Beyond the newsagent at No. 274 was Wyatt's Yard, still there in the late 1960s. By the Summertown Garage, near the site of the former City Corporation depot, is Reborn Cottage, a renovated stone house. Ridgemont Close, to the north, is a new private development which takes its name from the brick used. Between that and Osberton Road is a row of early Victorian cottages (Nos 286–96), and down Osberton Road on the south side are two new developments, Woodstock Court (1985) and Charles Ponsonby House (1984–5) (named after a major supporter of the Wyndham Housing Association, whose development this is), while opposite on the north side are Newcombe Court flats (1977–8), named after Mrs Elizabeth Newcombe, who lived in No. 300 Woodstock Road which was demolished for the flats.

Beyond Richards Lane, an unadopted lane leading to MIDDLE WAY, is Henley House, until recently Cranes Court School, founded by Miss Dorothy Crane in 1935. The old boundary of the city ran just beyond SQUITCHEY LANE and this is still the southern boundary of the (ecclesiastical) parish. FIELD HOUSE DRIVE, the next road north, takes its name from Field House of St Edward's School – a large house in the drive, which now consists mainly of post-war houses. To the north is the Roman Catholic Church of ST GREGORY AND ST AUGUSTINE. No. 322 is the presbytery.

Worcester College   Established by royal charter in 1714 on the site of and incorporating the buildings of the Benedictine Gloucester College (see MONASTIC COLLEGES), which was founded in 1283 and re-founded in 1560 as GLOUCESTER HALL after the Dissolution of the Monasteries in 1540. The surviving 'cottages' on the south side of the present main quadrangle were mediaeval monastic quarters (camerae), and still bear over their doors the carved shields of arms of several of the monasteries associated with Gloucester College. The mediaeval chapel, partly on the site of the present chapel, was completely in ruins by 1675, but there are remnants in several parts of the college, even on the north side of the present quadrangle, where a new terrace was built between 1753 and 1759. The present buttery was the camera of Malmesbury Abbey. Changes in earth levels and 'improvements' over the centuries have not destroyed a sense of architectural continuity, although it is the lack of symmetry in the main quadrangle between the mediaeval cottages on the south and the 18th-century terrace on the north – along with the gardens and lake – which has given the college its present distinctive visual identity. GLOUCESTER GREEN, opposite the college, retains the old place-names.

A sense of what Gloucester Hall looked like around 1675 can be obtained from a contemporary engraving by DAVID LOGGAN, the earliest visual record, which suggests that between the Dissolution of the Monasteries and then there had been additions to the fabric as well as demolitions. A new chapel, for example, at the north end of the present nine-arch loggia, was erected after 1720. The building used as the Principal's lodgings had formerly belonged to St Albans Abbey. Gloucester Hall never controlled the whole of the monastic property: meadows to the north and west were not recovered until the 18th century. The mediaeval library was never recovered: only one manuscript survives – a 15th-century collection of tracts against Lollardy (see LOLLARDS).

In its life of more than 150 years, from 1560 to 1714, Gloucester Hall had many uses: there were also many breaks in academic continuity. The first Elizabethan owner of the site and buildings, William Doddington, had sold them in 1560, the year when he acquired them, to Sir Thomas White, the founder of St John's College, but the sale was disputed by the BISHOP OF OXFORD, who had held the site and buildings from 1542 to 1560; an agreement was not reached until 1605. A Fellow of St John's, William Stock, became the first Principal of the Hall. He was succeeded in 1576 by another St John's Fellow, Henry Russell (1576–80). Lodgings were provided for both graduates and undergraduates – the numbers of both varied substantially from year to year – but there was much that was makeshift: there is, documentary

Beaumont Street under construction in the late 1820s, with the remains of Beaumont Palace to the right and the front of Worcester College in the background.

evidence, for example, that in 1567 St John's was using the old monastic library as a 'garner or place for the College to lay their corn'.

In 1577 the hall under Russell housed numbers of ROMAN CATHOLIC recusants, although Russell's successor as Principal in 1597, Christopher Bagshaw (1579–80), not a Fellow of St John's, was a firm Protestant, and the Puritan Philip Stubbes, author of *The Anatomie of Abuses*, lived for a time in the hall. John Hawley, who was Principal from 1593 to 1626 and deputy to SIR THOMAS BODLEY, founder of the BODLEIAN LIBRARY, resisted efforts by Nicholas Wadham to establish his new college on the site, but the numbers of residents declined under his principalship and there were only three or four matriculations a year.

St John's continued to own the land and buildings of Gloucester Hall after Hawley's death, but it lost its academic connections under the distinguished principalship of Degory Wheare (1626–47), a Fellow of Exeter College and first Camden Professor who, despite ill-health, raised donations for the hall; Sir Kenelm Digby, a member of the hall from 1618 to 1620, gave £2. Wheare also restored old buildings and increased the number of residents, among them the gentleman-commoner Richard Lovelace (1634–6), who was to become one of the best known Restoration poets. The CIVIL WAR destroyed Wheare's work, however, in what he himself described in his notebook as 'so uncivil a manner', and after he died in 1647 the premises seem to have been used for a time for the quartering of soldiers.

In the year in which Loggan's engraving is said to have been made (1675), 'the paths' of the college, according to ANTHONY WOOD, were 'overgrown with grass' and 'the way into the hall and chappell made up with boards'. There were no scholars, and three families had moved into former undergraduate rooms. Twelve years later, twelve armed men broke into the lodgings of the second post-Restoration Principal, Byrom Eaton (1662–92), tied up members of his household and escaped with his PLATE. (Nonetheless,

some plate has survived.) Moreover, there were contemporaries who recognised that the site and buildings of the hall had considerable potential for educational and other purposes. Thus, JOHN AUBREY, fifty of whose books were presented to the library, wrote to Wood in 1675 that if he could become Principal, it would be 'a fine way of ending my dayes in peace and ingeniose Innocency. I would undertake to make it an ingeniose Nest, and would decoy thither, severall honest and ingeniose persons of either University.'

Eaton's successor, Benjamin Woodroffe, Student, Canon, Sub-dean and for a few days Dean of Christ Church, appointed Principal of Gloucester Hall in 1692, was as distinguished a scholar as any of his predecessors, and was made a Fellow of the Royal Society. A controversial and eccentric figure, he had made many enemies inside and outside Oxford. He had been appointed Dean of Christ Church by James II, and one of his critics called him 'a man of a magotty brain'. At first Woodroffe attracted a number of undergraduates to Gloucester Hall – there were eleven matriculations in 1697 – but in 1701 there were none. He decided, therefore, to develop a scheme for educating Greek students in Oxford along lines discussed earlier (1677) by the Archbishop of Canterbury and the Archbishop of Samos. Woodroffe was a Greek scholar himself, backed by the Bishop of London, the Levant Company and small gifts from the Crown, a series of Greek students – the maximum number was ten – were welcomed to Gloucester Hall, in the face of satire and of Turkish and other opposition. Hopes were high, and a new building was erected for them opposite the hall, incorporating some of the remains of BEAUMONT PALACE. Again, however, numbers fell, and there were bitter quarrels, with serious financial implications. Indeed, in 1706, Woodroffe, heavily in debt, was imprisoned in the Fleet. His new building came to be thought of as a folly and was eventually demolished in 1806. Woodroffe himself died in 1711, to be succeeded by another Fellow of St John's, three times its Vice-President,

Richard Blechinden, who three years later became the first Provost of Worcester College.

Already, however, Woodroffe had been involved in discussions which were to point the way to the future Worcester College. In 1696 he had heard that Sir Thomas Cookes, a Worcestershire baronet, was contemplating the foundation of a new college in Oxford and was prepared to donate £10,000 for the purpose. At once he wrote to him expressing interest, subsequently writing a pamphlet, *Model for a College*. Prematurely assuming Cookes' agreement, he bought land and secured royal approval in 1698 for college statutes. Cookes was anxious that his family should appoint the first Provost, rather than the CHANCELLOR of the University, who had hitherto appointed the Principal of Gloucester Hall; and for a time it seemed likely that Cookes's money would pass to Balliol. It was not until Woodroffe had died that Principal Blechinden, who did not raise Oxford hackles as his predecessor had done but who had not been Gloucester Hall's first choice as Principal, was able to secure the Cookes funds and the lease of the site from St John's. Cookes's portrait now hangs in Worcester College hall – a hall smaller in size than the Benedictine *refectorium* – and the college still bears his coat of arms.

New statutes were drafted in a new charter in 1714 and passed the great seal two days before Queen Anne's death. On 29 July 1714, Gloucester Hall ceased to exist and Worcester College was brought into existence with the old Principal, in his late forties, as first Provost. Of its six Fellows, only one had been a Fellow of Gloucester Hall. Blechinden was a capable administrator, and although there were critics of his scholarship, he left nearly 200 books for his successor, William Gower (a foundation Fellow, who succeeded him in 1736), to incorporate in the college library, in which he himself had taken great interest.

Blechinden's friendship with GEORGE CLARKE, politician, virtuoso, Member of Parliament for Oxford University from 1717 until his death, and a restive Fellow of All Souls, was of immense importance to Worcester College. The papers of Clarke's father, Sir William, who had held offices of state under the Commonwealth and Charles II, made their way to Worcester, along with a remarkable collection of Civil War documents, tracts and pamphlets, and, along with George Clarke's own collection (which included unique Inigo Jones and other architectural drawings) constitute the college's greatest treasure. Clarke provided money and estates, too, for fellowships, scholarships and buildings, and well deserves to be remembered in the words inscribed on a silver-gilt loving-cup which he presented to the college: *tantum nos Fundator*, 'almost our Founder'.

Work on the first new Worcester College buildings had been begun with money from a legacy and according to a plan made by Clarke in 1720, providing for a loggia, a chapel and hall behind it, and a new and handsome library – an essential part of the scheme – above it. In his will Clarke left further funds for residential accommodation on the terrace. The college was beginning to acquire some of its present appearance – including the sunken quadrangle – but it is fortunate that Clarke's plan as a whole was not followed: although his collaborator NICHOLAS HAWKSMOOR had interesting ideas for the frontage, the plan

would have involved the destruction of the cottages and the building of a parallel second wing for the terrace.

Further benefactions, notably a sizeable gift in 1739 from Sarah Eaton, daughter of Byrom Eaton, the former Principal of Gloucester Hall, brought with them more fellowships and scholarships. Further land was acquired from St John's in the 1740s, but it was not until parliamentary approval had been given more than a generation later that the terrace was completed during the 1770s, that the old Provost's lodgings were demolished, and a handsome new lodgings at the west end of the block was built, as Clarke had intended, in the form of a Palladian country house. The architect was HENRY KEENE, who died in 1776, the year that the buildings were completed. He was succeeded by James Wyatt, who was responsible for much of the internal structure of other college buildings.

Gower, who had done much to develop Worcester – his portrait was painted by Gainsborough – was a sick man and himself died in the same year as Keene. He never lived, therefore, in the lodgings of which he had dreamed, and his successor, William Sheffield, formerly Vice-Provost, and Fellow since 1758, moved in instead when he was appointed by the Chancellor, Lord North. Sheffield and Gower had long been on bad terms, having quarrelled about the election procedures for Cookes and Eaton Fellowships; Sheffield, on appeal to the VISITOR, had won.

Sheffield was an able and lively man, who corresponded with Gilbert White, the naturalist, on equal terms and who from 1772 until his death in 1795 served as Keeper of the ASHMOLEAN MUSEUM. Yet he left remarkably few college records behind him. As one of his 20th-century successors, J.C. MASTERMAN (1947–61) has noted, one of the few records that do survive is an order of October 1785 'that any Member of the College who keeps a Dog in his Room should be sconced half a Crown: as shall every one, who walk upon the grass plot in the Quadrangle.' The latter part of this order, at least, has remained in force as the undisturbed 'grass plot', carefully nurtured, has become one of the main features of the college.

Undergraduate numbers were low during the 18th-century: under Sheffield's provostship, for example, MATRICULATIONS ranged from two in 1779–80 to nine in 1789–90, and twelve in his last year. There is occasional documented evidence of disorderly behaviour, and some records relating to admissions. Thus, Blechinden turned down two candidates for scholarships recommended by Sir Thomas Cookes's heir, telling him firmly that 'notwithstanding our foundation is young and our society very small, yet we esteem ourselves as firm in our establishment . . . as any of the oldest and largest Colleges in Oxford.' There were losses in the 18th century, however, as well as gains – particularly in 1788, when, following an agreement with the Oxford Canal Company (*see* CANAL), the college was cut off from the river to which its grounds had previously extended. The agreement was invoked successfully in a legal dispute with the company about drainage in 1911.

There was another big change to the geographical orientation of Worcester when BEAUMONT STREET was built in the 1820s: this provided an important link not only with ST GILES' but also with other colleges. The opportunity was not taken at the same time to

At Worcester College, established in 1714, 18th-century buildings face the mediaeval monastic quarters of the Benedictine monastic college from which Worcester developed.

'improve' the front of the college, although drawings survive of Greek and Italianate plans by Daniel Robertson, Charles Barry and Edward Blore. There were important improvements to the GARDENS, however, beginning in 1827 under the active bursarship of Richard Gresswell. (Gresswell is better remembered than Provost Whittington Landon (1795–1839), although the latter was Worcester's first VICE-CHANCELLOR, in 1802, and in 1814, in the absence of the then Vice-Chancellor, was host for the spectacular visit of the Allied Sovereigns to Oxford. Gresswell was responsible, less dramatically, for the draining of PORT MEADOW.) The college's gardens have been described as 'the only fashioned true landscape garden in Oxford', and Gresswell was not the last of a line of Worcester Bursars – and Provosts – who took a keen interest in them. The lake, often the subject of Victorian and later watercolours, was a major feature, described in 1821 as 'a large sheet of water, well stocked with fish'. The trees, however, were equally noteworthy in the general scheme, as were the new *cottage ornée* redecorations of the west end of the cottages, and the small hanging garden attached to one of the Fellows' rooms, contrasting with, yet complementary to, the Provost's lodgings. It was fitting, too, that an arch from the monastic buildings was sited on the lakeside path. At the end of the 19th century the creation of the playing fields, which involved the reduction of the Provost's demesne, used in part for grazing cattle, was highly controversial: so, too, was the design of the pavilion, conceived in 1903. F.J. Lys, who became Bursar in 1908 and Provost in 1919, was a powerful supporter: he was responsible, too, for herbaceous borders and for the planting of flowers round the quadrangle. His predecessor as Provost, C.H.O. Daniel (1903–19), closely associated with the Arts and Crafts movement and founder of one of the best-known private presses, the Daniel Press, concentrated on parts of the Provost's garden near to the lodgings which, influenced by Alfred Parsons,

acquired what has been called 'Cotswold nook quality' design.

Daniel's predecessors, Dr Robert Lynch Cotton (1839–81) and William Inge (1881–1903), were contrasting personalities. Cotton, an old member of the college, was, like Gresswell, a generous and active man, who was Vice-Chancellor in the politically difficult years for Oxford from 1852 to 1856. He was still Provost when, following university reform, the statutes of the college were revised in 1877, the number of fellowships (all but one of which were now open to laymen) reduced from nineteen to nine, and marriage for Fellows permitted (*see* ROYAL COMMISSIONS). Inge, by contrast, was a surprise appointment, made by the Chancellor rather than by the Fellows as would have been the case had the new statutes already come into operation. A former Fellow of Worcester, a University cricketer, and a parish priest for over twenty years, he was known as a scholar, but from the start he was on bad terms with some of his new colleagues and played a minor part in college affairs. It was during his provostship, too, that the financial position of the college, imperfectly managed, deteriorated sharply under the impact of the so-called 'agricultural depression', with the result that the Fellows never received the full stipends allowed for in the new statutes.

There had been little premonition of this under Cotton, who is best remembered for the lavish Victorian transformation of the college chapel by William Burges in 1863–4 – a transformation which was at least as controversial in the 19th century as the return to the original decoration of the hall (also transformed by Burges at a more modest cost in 1877) in 1966 under the provostship of Lord Franks (1962–76). The chapel, partially cleaned, repaired and re-lit under the provostship of Lord Franks's successor Lord Briggs (1976 to date), remains one of the most fascinating examples of Burges's luxuriant architecture and decoration. The animals and birds at the ends of the pews, the elaborate floor mosaics, the rich ceiling patterns, the once highly controversial statues of the Evangelists in Wyatt's corner niches, and the text round the wall culminating in the word 'God' above the Provost's stall, reveal different but integrated facets of Burges's creative imagination. On one side of the altar a Benedictine monk is shown offering a model of Gloucester College and on the other Cookes is depicted offering a model of Worcester College. Three new windows were added on the north side, as well as a new altar window, the design by Henry Holiday.

Undergraduate numbers were small in the 19th century, when the best-remembered student was Thomas de Quincey (1803), little though he gained from his Worcester experience. The brothers of two eminent Victorians – contrasting and antagonistic – Francis Newman (1822) and Henry Kingsley (1850), were distinguished in their later lives, the former having religious views which were as different from those of his more famous brother as were those of Henry from Charles Kingsley's. As an undergraduate, Henry Kingsley was remembered, however, for different reasons: he is said to have performed the feat of running a mile, riding a mile, and rowing a mile within the space of fifteen minutes.

Some of the Fellows left their mark. Among those of the 18th century Dr T.R. Nash (1740–57) had bequeathed to the college a superb painting by Jacob van Ruisdael, and other paintings; William Palmer (1831) was described by Francis Newman as the 'only really learned man' among the early Tractarians (*see* OXFORD MOVEMENT); H.A. Pottinger, who had matriculated in 1842 but did not become a Fellow until 1883, was a dedicated collector of books and pamphlets, which were also bequeathed to the college; and J.E. Thorold Rogers, who took his degree in the same year, 1846, was a distinguished radical economic historian who never became a Fellow. Later in the century, W.H. (later Sir Henry) Hadow, examiner in three schools and editor of the *Oxford History of Music*, was both a versatile and powerful figure before he left Oxford for other universities in 1909. The undergraduate, C.H. Wilkinson, a very different personality but equally compelling, went down a year later, becoming a Fellow of the college in 1919, and served for many years as its often formidable but usually greatly respected Dean. He died in 1960.

After the Second World War, during which from 1940 Wilkinson served as Defence Commander of Oxford City, Worcester increased greatly in size – the number of undergraduates more than doubled – and in range. Several members of domestic staff offered the college more than fifty years service, but it was not until 1956 that it appointed its first Tutorial Fellow in a science subject, and it was only during the 1960s that its postgraduate numbers grew rapidly until they reached a quarter of its total student strength. The number of Fellows rose from ten in 1945 to thirty-nine in 1985. There was also a strengthening of the professorial element among them, with many distinguished academics, including the orthopaedic surgeon Professor Joseph Trueta (1949–77), and the historian Richard Cobb (1973).

Provost Masterman (Provost 1946–61), who left a deep mark on Worcester, was an old college man and a friend for fifty years of Wilkinson; Lord Franks, with a unique experience of statecraft and administration,

came in from outside and interested himself in college affairs as much as in those of the University; and Lord Briggs (like Masterman, a historian), who had been a Fellow from 1945 to 1955, had served for sixteen years, for ten of them as Vice-Chancellor, at the first of Britain's new universities of the 1960s – Sussex.

There were many changes in the appearance of the college during these years. Already under Provost Lys a new Nuffield Building had been completed in 1939 – largely due to his initiative – with W.G. Newton as a safe and uncontroversial architect. Among other new developments, garden buildings designed by Hugh Casson (1961); the Wolfson Building, financed by the Wolfson Foundation (1971); and the Sainsbury Building, financed by two Sainsbury old members of the college and designed by Richard MacCormac (1984), were necessary additions to a transformed college. The last of these won a Civic Trust Award. At the same time, the undergraduate library was completely overhauled within the shell of the 18th-century building, after a generous benefaction from Rupert Murdoch, a 1950s' undergraduate.

The building programme under Briggs's provost-ship has probably been the largest in the college's history. Worcester's finances have been precarious, however, and a major appeal was launched in 1980 and successfully carried through under the direction of the Provost and the Vice-Provost, David Mitchell. Meanwhile, the college has moved into new academic areas such as Information Technology, and by 1986 there were eighteen Tutorial Fellows, including two Fellows in Physics, two in Engineering and two in Chemistry. There were large-scale celebrations in 1983 for the seventh centenary of the opening of Gloucester College.

The corporate designation of the college is The Provost, Fellows and Scholars of Worcester College in the University of Oxford. Mr R.G. Smethurst was elected to succeed Lord Briggs as Provost in autumn 1991.

(Daniel, C.H.O., and Barker, W.R., *Worcester College*, London, 1900; Galbraith, V.H., *Some Documents on Gloucester College*, 1924; Pantin, W.A., 'Gloucester College', in *Oxoniensia*, 1946; Sutherland, L.S., 'The Foundation of Worcester College', in *Oxoniensia*, 1979; Lys, F.J., *Worcester College, 1882–1943, and Some Account of a Stewardship*, Oxford, 1944; Colvin, H.M., *A Catalogue of Architectural Drawings of the Eighteenth and Nineteenth Centuries in the Library of Worcester College, Oxford*, Oxford, 1964; Masterman, J.C., *Bits and Pieces*, London, 1961; *C.H. Wilkinson, 1888–1960, A Memoir*, Oxford, 1965.)

Worcester Street Formerly Stockwelle Street, which ran along the line of the present WALTON STREET and LITTLE CLARENDON STREET, and seems to have been built up by 1279. The well at the corner of the street and the road to HYTHE BRIDGE was once known as Cornwell or Cornwall. It was called Plato's Well in Tudor times to distinguish it from Aristotle's Well, half a mile further north (*see* ARISTOTLE LANE), which, according to Hurst, sprang from the same gravel bed. Stockwelle Street was probably so named because Stoke (or Stock) is nearly always associated with streams. The Carmelites, or Whitefriars, first settled in the street in 1256 but moved to BEAUMONT PALACE in 1317. On the east side of the road, which had become Worcester Street by about 1850, is GLOUCESTER GREEN.

Workhouse, City *see* COWLEY ROAD HOSPITAL.

Wren, Sir Christopher (*1632–1723*). Entered Wadham College, probably in 1650. From his undergraduate days his polymathic skills as experimentalist, designer, illustrator and model-maker were exercised in many fields. In 1653 he was elected to a fellowship at All Souls; in 1657 (at the age of twenty-five) he became Professor of Astronomy at Gresham College in London; and in 1661 was appointed Savilian Professor of Astronomy in Oxford (*see* CHAIRS). He retained his All Souls fellowship until 1661, and his first contribution to Oxford architecture is the notably accurate sun-dial which he designed for the college chapel (1659). His second, major, contribution was the SHELDONIAN THEATRE, built between 1664 and 1669, which ingeniously solved the problem of the large, medially unsupported, ceiling. He was responsible for a new building at Trinity College (1665–8), and other Oxford works were chancel-screens at All Souls (1664), St John's College (*c*.1670) and Merton (1671–4), and Tom Tower at Christ Church (1681–2). After the Great Fire of London in 1666 and his appointment as Surveyor-General in 1669, St Paul's, the London churches and the 'King's Works' became his main concerns. His last Oxford commission was the rescue of Duke Humfrey's Library in the BODLEIAN (1701–3), though his expert opinion on other Oxford projects was often sought thereafter (as, indeed, it had been earlier).

Wychwood School *74 Banbury Road*. An independent school for girls aged eleven–eighteen, it began in 1897 when Miss A.S. Batty, Vice-Principal of Miss Clarke's 'Eton for Girls' in Warrington Crescent, London, joined her former pupil, Miss M.L. Lee, lecturer in English to women students at Oxford, Reading and London Universities, at No. 41 BANBURY ROAD. They took a few girls daily in standard subjects. From 1898 to 1906 some fifteen girls were taught at No. 77 Banbury Road, the group being known familiarly as 'the Dons' School' or 'Miss Batty's'. In 1906 the school moved to No. 12 Park Crescent (now No. 31 PARK TOWN) and in 1912 to No. 3 Bradmore Road, where it became known as 'the Bradder' and a few boarders were taken. A brief description of those days appears in Joanna Cannan's *The Misty Valley*. Annual picnics to Wychwood Forest, near Miss Lee's home at Leafield Vicarage, gave the school its name. In 1917 Miss G. Coster joined as a partner and in 1918 inaugurated the 'constitution' to replace a prefectorial system with one of co-operative government, in which the individuality, independence and initiative of each girl are emphasised within a framework of democratic discussion and embodied in a school council consisting of staff and girls. In that year, to accommodate increasing numbers, the school moved to No. 74 Banbury Road. In 1928 it acquired No. 2 BARDWELL ROAD; shortly afterwards, No. 72 Banbury Road; and in 1938, No. 4 Bardwell Road. In 1944 the school became a limited company and in 1952 was registered as an Educational Trust. By 1947, the year of its jubilee, there were some 3000 names on the register. A science laboratory was built in 1960, connecting Nos 72 and 74 Banbury Road. In 1986 the numbers were some seventy-five boarders and eighty day girls.

Wyclif, John (*c.1330–1384*). Educated at Oxford and appointed Master of Balliol College, a position he resigned in 1361 to become vicar of Fillingham, Lincolnshire, the best living in the gift of the college. In 1368 he was again studying at the University, and became a Doctor of Divinity in 1372. In about 1374 he became active in politics, urging disendowment of the Church and a return to evangelical poverty. He recommended King Edward III and Parliament to withhold treasure of the kingdom from Rome, whereupon, in 1377, Pope Gregory XI issued no less than five bulls against him and demanded his arrest. Oxford, however, refused to condemn him. Nevertheless, in 1381 a council of Oxford theologians, convened by the CHANCELLOR, William Barton, did arraign him for his denial of the doctrine of transubstantiation. His dogma was condemned in the school of the Austin Friars and was forbidden to be taught in the University under pain of imprisonment, academical suspension and the greater excommunication.

In about 1380 Wyclif set about reforming popular ignorance of religion. From 1363 to 1381 he was at The Queen's College working on his two translations of the Bible into the vernacular so that the scriptures could be available to everyone who could read. He also 'gathered around him many disciples ... in Oxford', his 'poor priests' who went about the country preaching his controversial doctrines. The LOLLARDS, as they were called, were held to be partly responsible for the outbreak, in 1381, of the Peasants' Revolt in which Simon Sudbury, Archbishop of Canterbury, was murdered. He was succeeded by William Courtenay who, intolerant of Wyclif's heretical ideas, took action against him. His writings, condemned by the 1382 synod of Blackfriars, were banned at Oxford after much controversy, at least half the University being in sympathy with the beliefs of the 'flower of Oxford'. Wyclif died on the last day of 1384 at Lutterworth, where he had been Rector for the last ten years of his life.

Wycliffe Hall *Banbury Road*. Founded in 1877 as a theological college within the evangelical movement and named after JOHN WYCLIF. It was intended as a counterweight to the clericalism of Anglo-Catholicism and had a missionary commitment to prepare men for ordination to the ministry of the Church of England. At first there were only four students at Old Lodge, No. 52 BANBURY ROAD, but by 1893 there were fifty-three. No. 54 Banbury Road was acquired in the 1890s, and a chapel built between the two houses in 1896 to the designs of William Wallace. To celebrate the hall's jubilee in 1927, stained glass depicting Christ and the four Evangelists was added to the east window. The former dining hall, built in 1912–13, is now a lecture room; in the First World War it was used variously as temporary accommodation for St Hugh's College, for Serbian refugees, for the Army, and for the Royal Air Force, who fitted up its interior as a dummy aeroplane. In 1933 Nos 2 and 4 NORHAM GARDENS were acquired, thus forming a triangular group of buildings, lawns and trees at the junction of Banbury Road and Norham Gardens. In 1979 the Talbot-Rice Dining Hall, built to the designs of Peter Bosanquet and John Perryman, was completed as an addition to the main buildings to celebrate the hall's centenary. At present courses are provided for some eighty men and ten women students from a number of domestic and overseas denominations who require graduate and non-graduate training for a variety of theological qualifications. Courses in lay-teaching and preaching, and refresher courses for clergy, are also available. Between 1877 and 1927 some 600 ordinands were trained, and since 1927 a further 1000.

Among distinguished Principals of the hall have been F.J. Chavasse (1889–1900), later Bishop of Liverpool, and founder of St Peter's Hall (now College); J.P. Thornton-Duesbury (1943–55), later Master of St Peter's Hall; F.J. Taylor (1955–62), later Bishop of Sheffield; G.F. Graham Brown (1925–32), later Bishop of Jerusalem; and J.R.S Taylor (1932–42), later Bishop of Sodor and Man. Both Archbishop Coggan of Canterbury and Archbishop Blanch of York were former students (1934 and 1946–9 respectively). Although not incorporated by the University, from its earliest days the hall has been closely associated with undergraduate religious life, and in 1879 was the birthplace of the Oxford Inter-Collegiate Christian Union (OICCU).

Wykeham, William of (*1324–1404*). A 'mighty pluralist', the founder of Winchester College and of New College, William of Wykeham acquired numerous prebends and livings before becoming Archdeacon of Lincoln, Canon of Lichfield, Bishop of

William of Wykeham, Bishop of Winchester and Chancellor of England, who founded New College in 1379.

willus·wykhm·eps winton· Fundator·Collegn·bnte Marie Winton in Oxon·

Winchester in 1367, and Chancellor of England the following year. He had already started buying land for his Oxford college and by 1376 seventy poor scholars were living at his expense on the site. The foundation stone was laid on 5 March 1380.

Wytham A small stone-built village with many thatched cottages to the north-west of Oxford, just beyond the RING ROAD. The name is derived from the Old English words *wiht*, meaning 'bend', and *ham*, a village, estate or manor. Wytham lies near a sharp bend in the THAMES. The manor belonged to Abingdon Abbey and was held by the family of de Wytham from the 12th century until 1479; it was then in the possession of the Harcourt family until the 16th century. At the Dissolution of the Monasteries it was bought by Lord Williams of Thame and, through his daughter, passed to the Earls of Abingdon. The 7th Earl sold it to Raymond ffennell in 1920. The Manor House itself – known as Wytham Abbey though never an abbey in more than name – was built during the ownership of the estate by the Harcourts, but was substantially altered in the 19th century. Some fittings from Rycote Place near Thame were incorporated in the house by the 5th Earl of Abingdon.

The whole village is now owned by the University of Oxford, who acquired the estate of over 3000 acres by an agreement with Raymond ffennell in 1943. Under this agreement, the agricultural land, amounting to 1579 acres, was to be purchased by the University; the abbey and 300 acres attached to it were given to the University, though Mr and Mrs ffennell were to continue in occupation during their lifetimes; and the 960 acres of Wytham Woods were also given to the University. Wytham Hill, above the village, is over 500 feet above sea-level and is covered with woodland. The main part of Wytham Woods is known as 'the Woods of Hazel' after Raymond ffennell's daughter, Hazel, his only child, who died at an early age. She was described in *The Times* as 'a girl of rare promise, with a strange and beautiful genius for the understanding of birds and animals, which before her early death she had begun to express through the gift of sculpture'. Mr ffennell was 'an enthusiastic promoter of education', inviting classes from the elementary schools of Oxford to spend a day at Wytham and to carry on their schoolwork in the open air. Wytham Woods are now owned and managed by the University for scientific research. They are not open to the public but can be visited by permit-holders. Neither is the abbey open to the public, being let in separate apartments. Oxford University Field Station is a mile to the north of the village.

(*See also* ALL SAINTS CHURCH, WYTHAM, *and* WHITE HART INN, WYTHAM.)

(*Wytham. A record issued by The Oxford Preservation Trust on the acquisition of Wytham Abbey and Estate by the University of Oxford 1943*, Oxford, 1943; Grayson, A.J., and Jones, E.W., *Notes on the History of Wytham Estate with special reference to the Woodland*, Oxford, 1955.)

YWCA The Alexandra Club, hostel premises for the Young Women's Christian Association (YWCA) in WOODSTOCK ROAD, was built in 1964 in red brick, designed by Elsworth Sykes Partnership. The headquarters of the YWCA moved from London in November 1985 to Clarendon House, CORNMARKET.

Zacharias and Co. A firm of waterproofers which carried on business in CORNMARKET STREET until 1983. It was founded by Abraham Zacharias, a Jewish Lithuanian immigrant, who was in business in the 1850s as a silversmith and jeweller. In the 1870s he established his son Joel in business at No. 27 Cornmarket as a china and glass dealer, also selling souvenir china. In the late 1880s the business expanded into No. 26. In about 1896 the firm stopped selling china and specialised in the sale of riding gear and waterproof clothing of all sorts. They were also tailors and outfitters. They had stands at agricultural and county shows throughout the country and in 1898 sent a display stand to the Chicago World Fair. When Joel Zacharias died in 1905 the business was taken over by Henry Osborn King of WOLVERCOTE, who was succeeded in 1942 by his son Cecil. The business, whose slogan was 'Zacs for Macs', closed in 1983. The premises were restored in 1986 by Jesus College, the owners, to the designs of John Fryman of the Architects Design Partnership at a cost of £500,000. In 1987 they were occupied by Laura Ashley.

Zuleika Dobson SIR MAX BEERBOHM'S only novel, a satire published in 1911. Within two months of publication, for his own pleasure, he illustrated the text with colour-wash caricatures, but these were not published until some time after his death. Zuleika, the eponymous heroine, is so ravishing that on her arrival in Oxford 'as the landau rolled by, sweat started from the brows of the Emperors' (*see* EMPERORS' HEADS). She stays with her grandfather, the Warden of Judas College, in EIGHTS WEEK. All the undergraduates in Oxford fall madly in love with her, including the Duke of Dorset who 'had already taken (besides a brilliant First in Mods) the Stanhope, the Newdigate, the Lothian, and the Gaisford Prize for Greek Verse . . . and was reading, a little, for Literae Humaniores. There is no doubt that but for his untimely death he

Max Beerbohm whose satire of Oxford life, Zuleika Dobson, *was published in 1911.*

would have taken a particularly brilliant First in that school also'. On the final day of the BUMPING RACES there is a mass suicide in Zuleika's honour when all the young men with 'great single cries of "Zuleika!"' hurl themselves into the Isis (*see* THAMES). That evening Zuleika asks her maid to consult Bradshaw. 'See if it is possible to go direct from here to Cambridge,' she says.

In 1952 Beerbohm gave permission for Sir Osbert Lancaster to paint twelve scenes from the novel for the RANDOLPH HOTEL. He suggested which scenes might be chosen and added that he hoped the poor Emperors' Heads would not be 'ignored altogether'. They were not. The pictures still hang in the hotel.

APPENDIX 1

Bishops of Oxford

542 Robert King, Suffragan of Lincoln, first Bishop of Oxford, the seat of the bishopric being at Osney until 1545
558 Thomas Goldwell, Bishop of St Asaph, nominated, but died before institution

See vacant nine years)

567 Hugh Coren or Curwen, Archbishop of Dublin

See vacant twenty-one years)

589 John Underhill, Rector of Lincoln College

See vacant eleven years)

604 John Bridges, Dean of Salisbury
619 John Howson, Student of Christ Church
628 Richard Corbet, Dean of Christ Church
632 John Bancroft, Master of University College
641 Robert Skinner, Bishop of Bristol (deprived during the Commonwealth, but restored 1660)
663 William Paul, Dean of Lichfield
665 Walter Blandford, Warden of Wadham College
671 Nathaniel, Lord Crewe, Rector of Lincoln and Dean of Chichester
674 Henry Compton, Canon of Christ Church
676 John Fell, Dean of Christ Church
686 Samuel Parker, Archdeacon of Canterbury
688 Timothy Hall (denied installation by the chapter of Christ Church)
690 John Hough, President of Magdalen College
699 William Talbot, Dean of Worcester

1715 John Potter, Regius Professor of Divinity
1737 Thomas Secker, Bishop of Bristol
1758 John Hume, Bishop of Bristol
1766 Robert Louth, Bishop of St David's
1777 John Butler, Prebendary of Winchester
1788 Edward Smallwell, Bishop of St David's
1799 John Randolph, Regius Professor of Divinity
1807 Charles Moss
1812 William Jackson, Regius Professor of Greek
1816 Hon. Edward Legge, Dean of Windsor
1827 Charles Lloyd, Regius Professor of Divinity
1829 Richard Bagot, Dean of Canterbury
1845 Samuel Wilberforce, Dean of Westminster
1870 John Fielder Mackarness, Prebendary of Exeter
1889 William Stubbs, Bishop of Chester
1901 Francis Paget, Dean of Christ Church
1911 Charles Gore, Bishop of Birmingham (resigned See of Oxford 1919)
1919 Hubert Murray Burge, Bishop of Southwark
1925 Thomas Banks Strong, Bishop of Ripon (resigned See of Oxford 1937)
1937 Kenneth Escott Kirk, Regius Professor of Moral and Pastoral Theology
1955 Harry James Carpenter, Warden of Keble (resigned See of Oxford 1970)
1971 Kenneth John Woollcombe, Principal of Edinburgh Theological College (resigned See of Oxford 1978)
1978 Patrick Campbell Rodger, Bishop of Manchester
1987 Richard Douglas Harries, Dean of King's College, London

APPENDIX 2

Mayors and Lord Mayors of Oxford

MAYORS

122/3	Turchillus, Provost of Oxon	1207	Henrieus, Praetor	1241–2	Laurence Wyth
134	Johannes, son of Radulph	1208	Thomas, son of Walter	1243–4	Peter Torald
		1209	Nic. de Stockwell	1245	Adam Fetiplace
136/9	W. de Cheneto	1214	Philip	1246	Nic. de Stockwell
178	Laurence Kepeharm, Praetor	1216	Torald	1247	Thomas, son of Walter
	T. de Tadmarton, Praetor	1224	T., son of Edwyn	1248	Nic. de Stockwell
		1227–9	T., son of Edwyn	1249	Wyda, son of Robert
		1232–6	J. Pady	1250	Thomas, son of Walter
180	Peter, son of Torald	1237–9	Peter Torald	1251–2	Nic. de Heureth
182	Willus, Praetor	1240	Galf de Stockwell	1253–60	Adam Fetiplace
			Peter Torald	1261–3	Nic. de Kyngston

1264–5	Nic. de Stockwell	
1266–7	Adam de Fetiplace	
1268	Nic. de Kyngston	
1269	J. de Coleshull	
1270–2	Nic. de Kyngston	
1273	H. Owayn	
1275	Nic. de Kyngston	
1276	Philip de O.	
1277	Nic. de Kyngston	
1279	Andrew de Wormenhale	
1280	H. Oxen, *alias* Owain	
1281–4	Nic. de Kyngston	
1285	J. Culvert	
1286	Philip de O., *alias* de Ew.	
1287	J. de Dokelinton	
1288	H. Owayn, or Hewen, or Oyn	
1289	Nic. le Orseur	
1290–1	H. Owayn	
1292–3	J. Culvert	
1294	T. de Sowy	
1295–6	Philip de Ew.	
1297	Andrew de Pyrie	
1298	Robert de Wormenhale	
1299	Dnus. Phil. de Ho., *alias* de Ew.	
1300	Jo. de Eu	
1301–3	T. de Sowy	
1304	John de Ew.	
1305–9	Sir J. de Dokelinton	
1310	Philip de Wormenhale	
1311–14	W. de Burcestre	
1315–16	Sir J. de Dokelinton	
1317	W. de Burcestre	
1318	H. de Lynne	
1319–20	J. Hampton	
1321	Sir J. de Dokelinton	
1322	J. de Hampton	
1323	Robert de Watlington	
1324	Sir J. de Dokelinton	
1325	W. de Burcestre	
1326	Sir J. de Dokelinton	
1327	Sir Andrew de Wormenhale	
1328	R. Cary	
1329–34	W. de Burcestre	
1335	R. Cary	
1336	Simon de Gloucestre	
1337	H. Stodleigh	
1338	Stephen de Adynton	
1339	W. de Burcestre	
1340–1	R. Cary	
1342	J. Hampton	
1343	R. Cary	
1344	H. de Stodle	
1345	R. Cary	
1346–7	R. de Selewade	
1348–51	J. de Bereford	
1352	J. de St Frideswide	
1353	J. de Stodle	
1354	J. de Bereford	
1355–6	J. de St Frideswide	
1357–61	J. de Stodle	
1362–4	R. de Wodehay	
1365	J. de Stodle	
1366	R. de Wodehay	
1367	J. de Hertwell	
1368	J. de Stodle	
1369	W. de Northerne	
1370–1	W. Codeshall	
1372	J. Hertwell	
1373–5	W. Codeshall	
1376	Sir W. Northerne	
1377–8	J. Gybbes	
1379	W. Codeshall	
1380–1	W. Dagvile	
1382	R. Merser	
1383–4	J. Gybbes	
1385	W. Dagvile	
1386	R. Gerston	
1387–8	R. Merser	
1389	W. Dagvile	
1390–1	R. Merser	
1392	T. Somerset	
1393	R. Merser	
1394	W. Dagvile	
1395–6	R. Garston	
1397–8	Walter Bowne	
1399	Sir R. de Garston	
1400	J. Merston	
1401	Edmund Kenyan	
1402	J. Sprunt	
1403	J. Merston	
1404	Edmund Kenyan	
1405–8	J. Sprunt	
1409–10	Walter Daundsey	
1411	Sir R. Garston	
1412	Edmund Kenyan	
1413–15	Sir J. Gybbes or Gibbes	
1416–18	Walter Daundsey	
1419	T. Coventre	
1420–2	Sir W. Brampton	
1423	Walter Daundsey	
1424	W. Offord	
1425	Sir W. Brampton	
1426	W. Offord	
1427–9	T. Coventre	
1430–1	Sir W. Brampton	
1432–3	W. Herkefield	
1434–5	T. Dagvile	
1436	Sir W. Brampton	
1437–8	J. North	
1439	Sir W. Brampton	
1440–3	T. Bayley	
1444–5	Rob. Walford	
1446	J. North	
1447–8	J. Spraget	
1449–50	J. Fitzalan	
1451–2	R. Spraget	
1453–8	R. Attwode, *alias* à Wode	
1459–60	J. Clerk	
1461–2	Sir R. Spraget	
1463	J. Clerk	
1464	Sir R. Spraget	
1465–7	W. Dagvile	
1468	J. Clerk	
1469	J. Dobbes	
1470	J. Dagvile	
1471	Sir R. Spraget	
1472	W. Dagvile	
1473	Sir R. Spraget	
1474	W. Dagvile	
1475	J. Clerk	
1476–7	J. Seman	
1478–9	J. Clerk	
1480–1	Ed. Wodeward	
1482	J. Seman	
1483	Sir Ed. Wodeward	
1484–5	Sir J. Edgecombe	
1486	J. Seman	
1487	Sir Ed. Wodeward	
1488	Ed. Wade	
1489–90	R. Howes, *alias* Hewys	
1491	Sir J. Edgecombe	
1492–3	Richard Kent	
1494	Sir Ed. Wodeward	
1495	R. Hewis, or Howes	
1496	Richard Kent	
1497	Sir J. Edgecombe	
1498	J. Rogers	
1499	J. Hedde	
1500	J. Rogers	
1501–2	Richard Kent	
1503	William Bulcombe	
1504–6	J. Hedde	
1507	William Bulcombe	
1508	Richard Kent	
1509	William Bulcombe	
1510	John Hedde	
1511	Richard Kent	
1512	John Broke	
1513	John Broke	
1514	John Haynes	
1515	John Haynes	
1516	William Bulcombe	
1517	John Hedde	
1518	Richard Millett	
	William Bulcombe	
1519	John Traves	
1520	John Traves	
1521	Thomas Shelton	
1522	Thomas Shelton	
1523	Thomas Shelton	
1524	John Awsten	
1525	Michael Heth	
1526	Michael Heth	
1527	William Flemyng	
1528	William Flemyng	
1529	Michael Hethe	
1530	William Friar	
1531	William Frere	
1532	John Pye	
1533	John Pye	
1534	William Frere	
1535	William Freurs	
1536	William Freurs	
1537	William Banister	
1538	William Banister	
1539	John Barry	
1540	John Barry	
1541	William Freurs	
1542	William Freurs	
1543	Edmund Irysshe	
1544	Edmund Irysshe	
1545	Richard Gonter	
1546	Richard Gonter	
1547	John Pye	
1548	Richard Atkinson	
1549	Richard Atkinson	
1550	Edmund Irysshe	

1551	Ralphe Flaxney	1617	Walter Payne	1685	Edward Coombes
1552	Ralphe Flaxney	1618	William Potter	1686	Thomas Hunsdon
1553	Richard Atkynson	1619	Oliver Smyth	1687	John Payne
1554	Edmund Irysshe	1620	Anthony Fyndall	1688	Richard Carter
1555	John Wayte	1621	John Davenant		Robert Harrison
1556	William Tylcock	1622	William Boswell	1689	Richard Hawkins
1557	Thomas Willyams	1623	William Potter	1690	Richard Carter
1558	Richard Whittington	1624	Oliver Smyth	1691	Henry White
1559	Richard Atkynson	1625	Henry Boswell	1692	John Croney
1560	William Tylcock	1626	John Dewe	1693	Tobie Browne
1561	John Wayte	1627	John Sare	1694	Richard Wood
1562	Ralphe Flaxney	1628	William Goode	1695	John Tayler
1563	Roger Taylor	1629	Henry Southam	1696	Timothy Browne
1564	William Mathew	1630	Thomas Cooper	1697	Thomas Hunsdon
	Richard Williams	1631	Oliver Smyth	1698	John Knibb
1565	Thomas Williams	1632	William Charles	1699	Sir Robert Harrison
1566	Richard Whittington	1633	Francis Harris	1700	Daniel Webb
1567	Richard Atkynson	1634	John Sare	1701	William Claxon
1568	William Tylcock	1635	Martin Wright	1702	James Pinnell
1569	Roger Taylor	1636	John Nixon	1703	Thomas Sellar
1570	Nicholas Todde	1637	Henry Southam	1704	Michael Cripps
1571	Richard Williams	1638	Thomas Smith	1705	Tobias Payne
1572	William Levens	1639	John Smith	1706	Daniel Webb
1573	Roger Hewett	1640	Hum. Whistler	1707	Timothy Bourne
1574	Roger Taylor	1641	Leonard Bowman	1708	John Tayler
1575	William Tylcock	1642	Thomas Dennis	1709	Thomas Sellar
1576	Thomas Williams	1643	Thomas Smith	1710	John Knibb
1577	Ralphe Flaxney	1644	William Chillingworth	1711	Henry Wise
1578	Richard Williams	1645	Henry Silvester	1712	Daniel Webb
1579	William Levinz	1646	John Nixon	1713	Richard Broadwater
1580	John Harteley	1647	Humphrey Boddicot	1714	Daniel Webb
1581	William Noble	1648	Thomas Wickes	1715	Tobias Payne
1582	Edmund Bennett	1649	George Potter	1716	Richard Wise
1583	William Furnesse	1650	Walter Cave	1717	Oliver Greenway
1584	John Barkesdale	1651	Matthew Langley	1718	Henry Wise
1585	Thomas Smythe	1652	Richard Millar	1719	John Nicholes
1586	William Levinz	1653	Thomas Williams	1720	John Townesend
1587	Thomas Rowe	1654	John Nixon	1721	Oliver Greenway
1588	James Almonte	1655	Martin Wright	1722	John Boyce
1589	William Furnesse	1656	William Wright	1723	John Halifax
1590	Thomas Smythe	1657	Thomas Dennis	1724	William Applebee
1591	Richard Browne	1658	Hum. Whistler	1725	Robert Vicaris
1592	Henry Dodwell	1659	John Lambe	1726	Robert Brocks
1593	Thomas Rowe	1660	Sampson White	1727	Sir John Boyce
1594	William Levinz	1661	Leonard Bowman	1728	Jeremy Franklin
1595	Thomas Smythe	1662	Roger Griffin	1729	Sir Oliver Greenway
1596	Richard Browne	1663	John Harris	1730	Henry Wise
1597	William Furnesse	1664	John White	1731	John Nicholes
1598	John Williams	1665	Sir Sampson White	1732	William Applebee
1599	Isaac Bartholomew	1666	William Bailey	1733	John Knibb
1600	Thomas Smythe	1667	William Wright	1734	John Wilkins
	William Levinz	1668	John Lambe	1735	Robert Vicaris
1601	Richard Goode	1669	John Townsend	1736	Jeremy Franklin
1602	Richard Browne	1670	Francis Greneway	1737	Thomas Lawrence
1603	Thomas Harris	1671	Francis Heyword	1738	William Ives
1604	Thomas Cossam	1672	William Cornish	1739	Sir John Boyce
1605	Richard Bryan	1673	Anthony Hall	1740	Daniel Shilfox
1606	Richard Goode	1674	William Walker	1741	John Treacher
1607	Walter Payne	1675	Tobias Browne	1742	John Austin
1608	Richard Hannes	1676	Thomas Fifield	1743	William Turner
1609	Thomas Harris	1677	William Morrell	1744	John Wilkins
1610	William Potter	1678	Thomas Fustace	1745	Thomas Lawrence
1611	Matthew Harrison	1679	Robert Pawling	1746	Thomas Wise
1612	Ralphe Flaxney	1680	John Bowell	1747	John Knibb
1613	Henry Toldervey	1681	William Bayley	1748	Richard Tawney
1614	William Wright	1682	John Townsend	1749	William Ives
1615	John Bird	1683	William Walker	1750	Thomas Munday
1616	Richard Smyth	1684	William Walker	1751	Anthony Weston

1752	John Nicholes	1816	William Folker		John Galpin (Nov.)
1753	Daniel Shilfox	1817	Thomas Robinson	1880	James Stanley Lowe
1754	John Treacher	1818	Thomas Fox Bricknell	1881	James Jenkin
1755	William Wickham	1819	James Adams	1882	Alfred Wheeler
1756	Philip Ward	1820	Herbert Parsons	1883	James Hughes
1757	John Phillips	1821	Sir E. Hitchings	1884	James Hughes
1758	Thomas Treadwell	1822	John Wise Thorp	1885	Robert Buckell
1759	Isaac Lawrence	1823	Richard Cox	1886	James Hughes
1760	Sir Thomas Munday	1824	William Slatter	1887	Charles Underhill
1761	John Austin	1825	William Slatter	1888	Walter Gray
1762	Anthony Weston		Thomas Emsworth	1889	James Hughes
1763	William Ives (died)	1826	Richard Ferd. Cox	1890	Robert Buckell
	John Treacher	1827	John Hickman	1891	Frederick William
1764	Richard Tawney	1828	Thomas Fox Bricknell		Ansell
1765	Philip Ward	1829	Sir Joseph Lock	1892	Thomas Lucas
1766	John Phillips	1830	Thomas Wyatt	1893	Walter Gray
1767	William Applebee	1831	Richard Sheen	1894	George W. Cooper
1768	Isaac Lawrence	1832	James Banting	1895	John Seary
1769	William Wickham	1833	William Thorp	1896	Robert Buckell
1770	Sir Thomas Munday	1834	Richard Wootten	1897	Walter Gray
1771	John Austin	1836	William H. Butler	1898	Thomas Henry
1772	Edward Tawney		(Jan.)		Kingerlee
1773	Ralph Kirby		Charles James Sadler	1899	Frederick Parker
1774	Samuel Culley		(Nov.)		Morrell
1775	William Thorp	1837	Charles Tawney	1900	George Claridge Druce
1776	Edward Lock	1838	Richard Sheen	1901	Sir Walter Gray
1777	Richard Holloway	1839	Thomas Mallam	1902	John Henry Salter
1778	Richard Tawney	1840	Charles Tawney	1903	Edmund Augustine
1779	John Phillips	1841	Jonathan S. Browning		Bevers
1780	Vincent Shortland	1842	James Wyatt	1904	Thomas William
1781	George Tonge	1843	Richard Dry		Taphouse
1782	William Fletcher	1844	William Thorp		Robert Buckell
1783	John Watson	1845	John Thorp	1905	Francis Twining
1784	Isaac Lawrence	1846	Thomas Mallam	1906	Edmund John Brooks
	(March)	1847	Richard C. Godfrey	1907	Frederick William
	Edward Tawney (July)	1848	William Thorp		Ansell
	John Treacher (Sept)	1849	Charles James Sadler	1908	Edmund Augustine
1785	Nicholas Hulse	1850	George H. Warburton		Bevers
1786	Richard Weston	1851	William Ward	1909	James Edward Salter
1787	Francis Guiden	1852	John Crews Dudley	1910	Sydney Francis
1788	John Parsons	1853	Richard James Spiers		Underhill
1789	William Thorp	1854	Charles James Sadler	1911	Thomas Henry
1790	Sir Richard Tawney	1855	James Pike		Kingerlee
1791	Edward Lock	1856	John Towle	1912	Samuel Hutchins
1792	Christopher Yeats	1857	Isaac Grubb	1913	William Edward
1793	James Pears	1858	Nathaniel Castle		Sherwood
1794	Vincent Shortland	1859	Thomas Randall	1914	William Edward
1795	George Tonge	1860	Charles James Sadler		Sherwood
1796	William Fletcher	1861	William Ward	1915	Cyril Mosson Vincent
1797	Edward Tawney	1862	William Thompson	1916	Sir Robert Buckell
1798	Thomas Hardy	1863	John Richard Carr	1917	James Hastings
1799	Richard Cox	1864	James Hughes	1918	Sir Robert Buckell
1800	Edward Hitchings	1865	John Caldecott Cavell	1919	Col. Stanier Waller
1801	Richard Weston	1866	Edwin Thomas Spiers	1920	Edmund Butterworth
1802	William Folker	1867	John Richard Carr		Lewis
1803	Thomas Fox Bricknell	1868	Joseph Castle	1921	Frederick Ferris
1804	James Adams	1869	James Hughes		Vincent
1805	John Wise Thorp	1870	Daniel Hanley	1922	Tom Basson
1806	Edward Lock	1871	John Richard Carr	1923	William Henry Perkins
1807	Christopher Yeats	1872	Robert Pike	1924	Amos John George
1808	John Parsons	1873	John Galpin	1925	Rev. John Carter
1809	William Fletcher	1874	Joseph Round	1926	William Henry Perkins
1810	Herbert Parsons	1875	Jason Saunders	1927	William Matthew Gray
1811	Edward Hitchings	1876	William Eagleston	1928	William Matthew Gray
1812	Richard Cox	1877	John Caldecott Cavell	1929	George Tinline Button
1813	Joseph Lock	1878	James Grainge	1930	William Stobie
1814	William Tubb	1879	John Caldecott Cavell	1931	Fred William Albert
1815	Richard Wootten		(April)		Bennett

1932	Charles Henry Brown	1941	Arthur Edward Skipper	1954	William Richard
1933	Lily Sophia Tawney	1942	Maud Amy Margaret		Gowers
1934	George Castle Pipkin		White	1955	Marcus Anthony Lower
1935	Mary Georgiana	1943	Harry Charles Ingle	1956	Wilfred John Allaway
	Townsend	1944	Reginald Philip Capel	1957	Robert Frank Knight
1936	Leonard Henry Alden	1945	David Oliver	1958	Harry Gordon Lionel
	(died)	1946	Edgar Alfred Smewin		Gordon-Roberts
	Mary Georgiana	1947	James William Heading		Mary Georgiana
	Townsend (July)	1948	James William Heading		Townsend
1937	Harold Sydney Rogers	1949	Norman Whatley	1959	Frederick Mason
1938	Henry Tregelles Gillett	1950	Florence Mary		Brewer
1939	Clement James Victor		Andrews	1960	Arthur Henry Kinchin
	Bellamy	1951	William Osborn King	1961	Lionel Ernest Harrison
1940	Clement James Victor	1952	William Charles Walker		
	Bellamy	1953	Alan Brock Brown		

LORD MAYORS

1962	Evan Owen Roberts	1973	Frederick George	1982	Anthony William
1963	Alec Percival Parker		Ingram		Williamson
1964	John Leonard Norman	1974	Mrs Olive Frances	1983	Mrs Janet Gillespie
	Baker		Gibbs		Todd
1965	Mrs Florence Kathleen	1975	William George Robert	1984	Frank Arnold Garside
	Lower		Fagg	1985	Roger Alan Dudman
1966	William Foster	1976	Miss Ann Hazel Spokes	1986	John George William
	Macneece Foster	1977	Mrs Dora Minnie Carr		Parker
1967	Francis Vincent	1978	William Eaton Simpson	1987	Mrs Elizabeth Florence
	Pickstock	1979	John Arundel Hamilton		Mary Standingford
1968	Peter Spencer Spokes	1980	Gordon Woodward	1988	Mrs Queenie Whorley
1969	Percy Dudley Bromley	1981	Henry Briskol	1989	Mrs Patricia Anne
1970	Michael Maclagan		Nicholson Myers		Tempest Yardley
1971	Thomas James		Nimmo	1990	Mrs Queenie Hamilton
	Meadows		Mrs Olive Frances	1991	Alan David Pope
1972	Arthur Bernard		Gibbs		
	Conners				

APPENDIX 3

Members of Parliament for Oxford

1295	Thomas de Sowy	1307 Jan.	Andrew de Pirie
	Andrew de Pirie		Christopher, son of Simon
1298	Christopher de Oxon	Oct.	Andrew de Pirie
	John de Weston		William Deveneys
1300	Andrew de Pirie	1309	Andrew de Pirie
	John le Orfevre		John le Orfevre
1301	Andrew de Pirie	1311	Andrew de Pirie
	John Aurifaber		John de Fallele
1302	Andrew de Pirie	Nov.	*The same*
	John le Orfevre	1313 March	Andrew de Pirie
1305	Andrew de Pirie		John le Orfevre
	Christopher, son of Simon	Sept.	Andrew de Pirie
1306	Andrew de Pirie		John Aurifaber
	Christopher, son of Simon		

1314		John Aurifaber	1348 Jan.	John de Falle
		John de Fallele		John de Aleston
1315		John, son of William le Spicer	March	John de Bereford
		John de Fallele		John de Bybury
1318		John Mymekan	1351	John de Bereford
		John de Cudelynton		John de Falle
1319		John, son of William Bost	1353	John de Bereford
		William de Spaldyng		John de Stodle
1320		Richard Cary	1355	John de St Frideswide
		John de Fallele		Henry de Malmesbury
1321		John Aurifaber	1358	John de Stodle
		John de Fallele		John de St Frideswide
1322	May	John de Fallele	1360	Peter le Paynter
		John, son of William Bost		John de Wyndesore
	Nov.	John Aurifaber	1361	John de Stodle
		John de Fallele		John de Bereford
1324		John de Fallele	1362	John de Wyndesore
		John, son of William Bost		Galfridus de Brehull
1325		Andrew de Wormenhale	1363	Richard Wydehay
		John, son of William Bost		John Wyndesore
1327		*The same*	1365	Richard Wydehay
1328		Andrew de Wyrcestre		John Hertewelle
		John, son of William de Oxon	1366	John de ——
	April	John Culverd		William Northern
		John, son of William Bost	1368	John Dadynton
	July	John Mymekan		John de Benham
		John, son of William Bost	1369	William de Codeshale
1330	March	John Culverd		John Gybbes
		Stephen de Adynton	1371 Feb.	William de Codeshale
	Nov.	Andrew de Wormenhale		John de Stodle
		Henry de Stodlegh	June	William de Codeshale
1331		Andrew de Wormenhale	1372	William Northern
		John Culverd		John de Wyndesore
1332	March	Andrew de Wormenhale	1373	William de Codeshale
		Henry de Stodlegh		William Dagvile
	Sept.	John Culverd	1376	William de Codeshale
		John Mymekan		John Gybbes
	Dec.	*The same*	1377 Jan.	Richard de Garston
1334		John Mymekan		William Dagvile
		John de Falle	Oct.	William de Codeshale
1335		Richard Cary		John Gybbes
		John de Pershore	1378	William Dagvile
1336	March	Henry de Stodlegh		Alan le Spicer
		John Mymekan	1379	Thomas Somerset
	Sept.	Andrew de Wormenhale		Edmund Kenyan
		John, son of William Bost	1380 Jan.	Richard Mercer
1337	Jan.	Andrew de Wormenhale		John Hickes
		John Bost	Nov.	Richard de Adyngton
	Sept.	Stephen de Adynton		Edmund Kenyan
		Andrew de Wormenhale	1381	Edmund Kenyan
1338	Feb.	John de Pershore		Walter Bon
		John Mymekan	1382 May	*The same*
	July	John Mymekan	Oct.	William Dagvile
		Nicholas de Peplesbury		William Northern
1339	Jan.	Richard Cary	1383 Feb.	William Northern
		Andrew de Wormenhale		William Dagvile
	Oct.	Henry de Stodlegh	Oct.	William Dagvile
		John, son of William Bost		John Hickes
1340	Jan.	Simon de Gloucestr	1384 April	*The same*
		John, son of William Bost	Nov.	*The same*
	March	John, son of William Bost	1385	Peter Welynton
		John de Bybury		Edmund Kenyan
1341		John, son of William de Oxon	1386	Edmund Kenyan
		Nicholas de Peplesbury		Thomas Houkyn
1344		John de Bereford	1388 Feb.	John Hickes
		Nicholas de Peplesbury		Thomas Somerset
1346		John de Bybury	Sept.	John Shawe
		John de Falle		Thomas Baret

1390	Jan.	Richard Garston
		Alan Lekenesfeld
	Nov.	Edmund Kenyan
		Adam de la Ryver
1391		Edmund Kenyan
		John Utteworth
1393		Richard Garston
		John Merston
1394		Edmund Kenyan
		John Forster
1395		John Lodelowe
		Adam de la Ryver
1397	Jan.	Adam de la Ryver
		Walter Benham
	Sept.	Adam de la Ryver
		John Otteworth
1399		John Spicer
		John Burbrigge
1401		Thomas Forsthull
		Adam de la Ryver
1402		John Spicer
		Walter Benham
1403		John Spicer
		Thomas Coventre
1404		John Merston
		Michael Salesbury
1406		Thomas Couele
		John Otteworth
1407		Thomas Coventre
		Hugo Benet
1410		The same
1413		The same
1414	April	John Shawe
		Walter Colet
	Oct.	John Merston
		Thomas Coventre
1416		William Brampton
1417		Thomas Coventre
		Hugo Benet
1419		Thomas Coventre
		William Brompton
1420		Thomas Coventre
		William Offord, or Ufforde
1421	April	William Brampton
		Thomas Coventre
	Nov.	William Offord
		John Quarame
1422		Thomas Coventre
		William Offord
1423		Thomas Coventre
		Thomas Wilde
1425		William Brampton
		Thomas Wilde
1426		William Offord
		Thomas Goldesmyth
1427		Thomas Coventre
		Thomas Swanne
1429		Thomas Coventre
		Richard Wythigg
1431		Thomas Coventre
		Richard Wythigg
1432		William Herberfeld
		Thomas Wylde
1433		Thomas Dagvile
		John Estbury
1435		Thomas Dagvile
		Thomas Coventre

1436		John Buntyng
		Thomas Bailly
1442		Thomas Bailly
		John Michell
1447		Thomas Dagvile
		Robert Walford
1449	Jan.	Thomas Wythyg
		William Dagvile
	Oct.	William Newman
		Oliver Urry
1450		William Newman
		John Fitzalan
1453		Robert atte Wood
		William Newman
1459		John Kenyngton
		Reginald Skyres
1460		Richard Spraget
		Robert atte Wood
1467		William Bedston
		William Dagvile
1472		John Goylyn
		Stephen Havell
1478		John Seman
		Henry Gay
1491		Edward Woodward
		Robert Caxton
1529		John Latton
		William Flemyng
1541		William Lenthall
1547		Ralphe Flaxney
		Edward Freurs
1553	Feb.	Christopher Edmonds
		Edward Glynton
	Aug.	John Wayte
		Thomas Williams
1554	March	Thomas Mallynson
		Edward Glynton
	Oct.	John Wayte
		William Tylcock
1555		John Wayte
		William Pantre
1558		John Barton
		Richard Williams
1559		Thomas Wood
		Roger Taylor
1562		William Page
		Thomas Wood
1571		Edward Knollys
		William Frier
1572		Edward Knollys
		William Owen
1575	Dec.	Francis Knollys
1584		Francis Knollys
		William Noble
1586		Francis Knollys
		George Calfielde
1588		Sir Francis Knollys jun.
		George Calfielde
1593		Hon. Sir Edmund Carye
		George Calfeilde
1597		Anthony Bacon
		George Calfielde
1601		Francis Leighe
		George Calfielde
1604		Sir Francis Leighe
		Thomas Wentworth
1614		Sir John Ashley
		Thomas Wentworth

517

1621		Sir John Brooke	1768		George Nares (Tory)
		Thomas Wentworth			Hon. W. Harcourt (Tory)
1624		Thomas Wentworth	1771		Lord Robert Spencer (Tory)
		John Whistler	1774		Lord Robert Spencer (Tory)
1625		*The same*			Hon. Peregrine Bertie (Whig)
1626		*The same*	1780		Hon. Peregrine Bertie (Whig)
1628		*The same*	1782		Lord Robert Spencer (Whig)
1640	March	Charles Lord Howard	1784		Lord Robert Spencer (Whig)
		Thomas Cooper			Hon. Peregrine Bertie (Whig)
	Oct.	Charles Lord Howard	1790	June	Hon. Peregrine Bertie (Whig)
		John Whistler			Francis Burton (Tory)
	Nov.	John Smith of Oxford		Dec.	Arthur Annesley (Tory)
1646		John Nixon	1796		Henry Peters (Tory)
		John Doyley			Francis Burton (Tory)
1654		Richard Croke	1802		J. A. Wright (Tory)
1656		Richard Croke			Francis Burton (Tory)
1659		Unton Croke	1806		Francis Burton (Tory)
		Richard Croke			J. A. Wright (Tory)
1660		Viscount Falkland	1807		Francis Burton (Tory)
		James Haxley			J. I. Lockhart (Tory)
1661		Richard Croke	1812		J. A. Wright (Tory)
		Brome Whorwood			J. I. Lockhart (Tory)
1679	Feb.	William Wright	1818		J. A. Wright (Tory)
		Brome Whorwood			Gen. F. St John (Tory)
	Aug.	William Wright	1820		Charles Wetherell (Tory)
		Brome Whorwood			J. I. Lockhart (Tory)
1681		William Wright	1824		Charles Wetherell (Tory)
		Brome Whorwood	1826		J. H. Langston (Whig)
1685		Hon. Henry Bertie			J. I. Lockhart (Tory)
		Sir George Pudsey	1830		J. H. Langston (Whig)
1689		Hon. Henry Bertie (Tory)			W. H. Hughes (Whig)
		Sir Edward Norreys (Tory)	1831		J. H. Langston (Whig)
1690		*The same*			W. H. Hughes (Whig)
1695		Sir Edward Norreys (Tory)	1832		J. H. Langston (Whig)
		Thomas Rowney (Tory)			Thomas Stonor (Whig)
1698		*The same*	1833		W. H. Hughes (Whig)
1701	Jan.	Thomas Rowney (Tory)	1835		W. H. Hughes (Tory)
		Francis Norreys (Tory)			Donald Maclean (Tory)
	Nov.	*The same*	1837		Donald Maclean (Tory)
1702		*The same*			William Erle (Whig)
1705		*The same*	1841		J. H. Langston (Whig)
1706		Sir John Walter (Tory)			Donald Maclean (Tory)
1708		Thomas Rowney (Tory)	1847		J. H. Langston (Liberal)
		Sir John Walter (Tory)			W. Page Wood (Liberal)
1710		*The same*	1851		W. Page Wood (Liberal)
1711		Sir John Walter (Tory)	1852		J. H. Langston (Liberal)
1713		Thomas Rowney (Tory)			Sir W. Page Wood (Liberal)
		Sir John Walter (Tory)	1853		Rt Hon. Edward Cardwell (Liberal)
1715		*The same*	1857	March	J. H. Langston (Liberal)
1722	March	Sir John Walter (Tory)			Charles Neate (Liberal)
		Thomas Rowney (Tory)		July	Rt Hon. Edward Cardwell (Liberal)
	Oct.	Francis Knollys (Tory)	1859	April	J. H. Langston (Liberal)
1727		Thomas Rowney (Tory)			Rt Hon. Edward Cardwell (Liberal)
		Francis Knollys (Tory)		June	Rt Hon. Edward Cardwell (Liberal)
1734		Thomas Rowney (Tory)	1861		Rt Hon. Edward Cardwell (Liberal)
		Matthew Skinner (Whig)	1863		Charles Neate (Liberal)
1739		James Herbert (Tory)	1864		Rt Hon. Edward Cardwell (Liberal)
1740		Philip Herbert (Tory)	1865		Rt Hon. Edward Cardwell (Liberal)
1741		Thomas Rowney (Tory)			Charles Neate (Liberal)
		Philip Herbert (Tory)	1868	Nov.	Rt Hon. Edward Cardwell (Liberal)
1747		*The same*			W. V. Harcourt (Liberal)
1749		Viscount Wenman		Dec.	Rt Hon. Edward Cardwell (Liberal)
1754		Thomas Rowney (Tory)	1873		W. V. Harcourt (Liberal)
		Hon. Robert Lee (Tory)	1874	Feb.	Sir W. V. Harcourt (Liberal)
1759		Sir Thomas Stapleton (Tory)			Rt Hon. Edward Cardwell (Liberal)
1761		Hon. Robert Lee (Tory)		March	A. W. Hall (Conservative)
		Sir Thomas Stapleton (Tory)			

1880	April	Sir W. V. Harcourt (Liberal)
		J. W. Chitty (Liberal)
	May	A. W. Hall (Conservative)
1885		A. W. Hall (Conservative)
1886		A. W. Hall (Conservative)
1892	April	Viscount Valentia (Conservative)
	July	Sir G. T. Chesney (Conservative)
1895		Viscount Valentia (Conservative)
1898		Viscount Valentia (Conservative)
1918		J. A. R. Marriott (Conservative)
1922		Frank Gray (Liberal)
1924		R. C. Bourne (Conservative)
1938		Quintin Hogg (Conservative)
1950		H. F. L. Turner (Conservative)

1959	Hon. C. M. Woodhouse (Conservative)
1966	D. E. T. Luard (Labour)
1970	C. M. Woodhouse (Conservative)
1974	D. E. T. Luard (Labour)
1979	J. H. C. Patten (Conservative)

Following boundary changes:

1983	J. H. C. Patten (Conservative), Oxford West and Abingdon
	S. J. Norris (Conservative), Oxford East
1987	J. H. C. Patten (Conservative), Oxford West and Abingdon
	A. D. Smith (Labour), Oxford East

(Williams, W. R., *The Parliamentary History of the County of Oxford*, 1899.)

APPENDIX 4

Burgesses for the University

1604	Sir Daniel Dunne, DCL, sometime Fellow of All Souls and Principal of New Inn Hall
	Sir Thomas Crompton, DCL, Merton
1609	Sir William Byrde, DCL, sometime Fellow of All Souls
1614	Sir John Bennett, DCL, sometime Student of Christ Church
	Sir Daniel Dunne
1620	Sir John Bennett
	Sir Clement Edmonds, MA, sometime Fellow of All Souls
1621	Sir John Danvers
1624	Sir George Calvert, MA, Trinity
	Sir Isaac Wake, MA, sometime Fellow of Merton
1625	Sir Thomas Edmonds
	Sir John Danvers
1626 Jan.	*The same*
March	Sir Francis Stewart, MA, Christ Church
1628	Sir Henry Marten, DCL, New College
	Sir John Danvers
1640 March	Sir Francis Windebank, BA, St John's
	Sir John Danvers
Oct.	Sir Thomas Roe, Magdalen
	John Selden, Hart Hall
1653	Jonathan Goddard, DM, Warden of Merton, alone
1654	John Owen, DD, Dean of Christ Church, alone
1656	Hon. Nathaniel Fiennes, alone
1659	Matthew Hale, Magdalen Hall, Serjeant at Law

	John Mills, DCL, sometime Canon of Christ Church
1660	Thomas Clayton, DM, sometime Fellow of Pembroke and Regius Professor of Medicine
	John Mills
1661	Hon. Lawrence Hyde, MA
	Sir Heneage Finch, Bart, Christ Church
1674	Thomas Thynne, Christ Church
1679 Feb.	Hon. Heneage Finch
	John Edisbury, DCL, Brasenose
Aug.	Sir Leoline Jenkins, DCL, sometime Principal of Jesus College
	Charles Perrott, DCL, Fellow of St John's
1684	*The same*
1685 March	*The same*
Nov.	George Clarke, MA, Fellow of All Souls
1688	Sir Thomas Clarges, Wadham
	Hon. Heneage Finch, now DCL
1689–90	*The same*
1695	Sir William Trumbull, DCL, sometime Fellow of All Souls
	Hon. Heneage Finch
1698	Sir Christopher Musgrave, Bart, Queen's
	Sir William Glynne, Bart, St Edmund Hall
1701 Jan.	Sir Christopher Musgrave
	Hon. Heneage Finch
March	William Bromley, BA, Christ Church
Nov.	Hon. Heneage Finch
	William Bromley

519

1702	*The same*
1703	Sir William Whitlock
1705	Sir William Whitlock
	William Bromley, now DCL
1708	*The same*
1710	*The same*
1713	*The same*
1715	*The same*
1717	George Clarke, now DCL
1722	William Bromley
	George Clarke
1727	*The same*
1732	Henry Hyde, Viscount Cornbury, DCL, Christ Church
1734	Viscount Cornbury
	George Clarke
1737 Feb.	William Bromley, DCL, Oriel
March	Edward Butler, DCL, President of Magdalen
1741	Viscount Cornbury
	Edward Butler
1745	Peregrine Palmer, MA, sometime Fellow of All Souls
1747	Viscount Cornbury
	Peregrine Palmer
1750	Sir Roger Newdigate, Bart, DCL, University College
1754	Sir Roger Newdigate
	Peregrine Palmer, now DCL
1761	*The same*
1762	Sir Walter Wagstaffe Bagot, Bart, DCL, Magdalen
1768 Feb.	Sir William Dolben, Bart, DCL, sometime Student of Christ Church
March	Sir Roger Newdigate
	Francis Page, DCL, New College
1774	*The same*
1780	Sir William Dolben
	Francis Page
1784	*The same*
1790	*The same*
1796	*The same*
1801	Sir William Scott, DCL, sometime Fellow of University College
1802	Sir William Dolben
	Sir William Scott
1806	Rt Hon. Sir William Scott
	Rt Hon. Charles Abbot, DCL, sometime Student of Christ Church
1807	*The same*
1812	*The same*
1817	Rt Hon. Robert Peel, MA, Christ Church
1818	Rt Hon. Sir William Scott
	Rt Hon. Robert Peel, now DCL
1820	*The same*
1821	Richard Heber, MA, Brasenose
1822	Rt Hon. Robert Peel, re-elected after accepting office
1826 Feb.	Thomas Grimston Bucknall-Estcourt, MA, Corpus Christi
June	Rt Hon. Robert Peel
	Thomas G. Bucknall-Estcourt, now DCL
1828	Rt Hon. Robert Peel
1829	Sir Robert Harry Inglis, Bart, DCL, Christ Church
1830	Thomas Grimston Bucknall-Estcourt
	Sir Robert Harry Inglis
1831	*The same*

1832	*The same*
1835	*The same*
1837	*The same*
1841	*The same*
1847	Sir Robert Harry Inglis
	Rt Hon. William Ewart Gladstone, MA, sometime Student of Christ Church
1852	*The same*
1853	Rt Hon. William Ewart Gladstone, now DCL
1854	Sir William Heathcote, Bart, DCL, sometime Fellow of All Souls
1857	*The same*
1859 Feb.	Rt Hon. William Ewart Gladstone
April	*The same*
1865	Sir William Heathcote, Bart
	Gathorne Hardy, MA, Oriel
1866	Rt Hon. Gathorne Hardy, DCL
1868	Rt Hon. Gathorne Hardy
	Rt Hon. John Robert Mowbray, MA, late Student of Christ Church, DCL
1874 Jan.	*The same*
March	Rt Hon. Gathorne Hardy
1878	John Gilbert Talbot, MA, Christ Church, DCL
1880	Rt Hon. John Robert Mowbray
	John Gilbert Talbot
1885	*The same*
1886	*The same*
1892	*The same*
1895	*The same*
1899	Sir William Reynell Anson, Bart, DCL, Warden of All Souls
1900	Rt Hon. John Gilbert Talbot
	Sir William Reynell Anson, Bart
1910	Sir William Reynell Anson
	Lord Hugh Cecil
1914	Lord Hugh Cecil
	Rowland Edmund Prothero, afterwards Baron Ernle
1918	Rt Hon. Lord Hugh Cecil
1919	Rt Hon. Rowland Edmund Prothero
	Professor Charles William Chadwick Oman, MA, Hon. DCL, Fellow of All Souls
	Professor George Gilbert Aimé Murray, Fellow of New College
1922	Rt Hon. Lord Hugh Cecil
	Sir Charles William Chadwick Oman
1923	*The same*
1924	*The same*
1929	Rt Hon. Lord Hugh Richard Heathcote Gascoyne Cecil, MA, Hon. DCL, Fellow of Hertford, afterwards Rt Hon. Lord Quickswood, Hon. Fellow of Hertford
	Sir Charles William Chadwick Oman
1931	*The same*
1935	Alan Patrick Herbert, MA, New College, afterwards Sir A. P. Herbert
	Rt Hon. Lord Hugh Cecil
1937	Sir (James) Arthur Salter, MA, Hon. DCL, Fellow of All Souls, PC, Hon. Fellow of Brasenose, afterwards Lord Salter
	Sir E. F. Buzzard, Bart
1945	Rt Hon. Sir (James) Arthur Salter
	Alan Patrick Herbert

Chancellors of the University

c.1224	Robert Grosseteste	1338	Robert Paynink?
1231	Ralph [Cole?]		John Leech
	Richard Batchden?	1339	William de Skelton, sometimes Fellow of
1233	Ralph Cole		Merton
1238	Simon de Bovill	1341	Walter de Scauren
1239	John de Rygater		William de Bergeveney
1240	Richard de la Wyke	1345	John de Northwode
	Ralph de Heyham	1349	William de Hawkesworth, Provost of Oriel
1241	*The same*		[John Wylyot, sometime Fellow of Merton,
1244	Simon de Bovill		intruded himself into the office, contrary
1246	Gilbert de Biham		to the statutes of the University]
1252	Ralph de Sempringham	1350–1	William de Palmorna, sometime Rector of
1255	William de Lodelawe		Exeter
1256	Richard de S. Agatha	1354	Humphrey de Cherlton
1262	Thomas de Cantilupe	1357	Lewis Charlton?
1264	?Henry de Cicestre		John de Hotham, Provost of Queen's
1267	Nicholas de Ewelme	1358	John Renham, or Reigham
1269	Thomas Bek	1359	John de Hotham
1273	William de Bosco	1360	Richard Fitz Ralph?
1276	Eustace de Normanville		Nicholas de Aston, sometime of Queen's
1280	Henry de Stanton	1363	John de Renham, resigned
	John de Pontissara		John de Echingham, or Hethingham
1282	William de Montfort	1366	Adam de Toneworth
1283	Roger de Rowell, or Rodewell	1367	Adam de Toneworth
1284	William Pikerell		William Courtney
1285	Hervey de Saham	1369	Adam de Toneworth
1288	Robert de Winchelsey	1371	William de Heytisbury, sometime Fellow of
1289	William de Kingescote		Merton
1290	John de Ludlow	1372	William de Remmyngton
	John of Monmouth	1373	William de Wylton, sometime Fellow of
1291	Simon de Gaunt		Balliol, afterwards of University College
1292	Henry Swayne?		and Queen's
1293	Roger de Martival	1376	John Turke, sometime Fellow of Merton
1294	Peter de Medburn	1377	Adam de Toneworth
	Roger de Weseham	1379	Robert Aylesham, Merton
1297	Richard de Clyve, sometime of Merton		William Berton, sometime of Merton
1300	James de Cobeham	1381	Robert Rygge, or Rugge, Exeter, afterwards
1302	Walter de Wetheringsete		Fellow of Merton
1304	Simon de Faversham	1382	William Berton
1306	Walter Burdun		Robert Rygge
1308	William de Bosco		Nicholas Hereford, sometime Fellow of
1309	Henry de Maunsfeld, sometime Fellow of		Queen's
	Merton		William Rygge?
1311	Walter Giffard	1383	Robert Rygge
	Henry de Maunsfeld	1388	Thomas Brightwell, sometime Fellow of
1313	Henry de Harcia		Merton
1316	Richard de Nottingham?	1390	Thomas Cranley, Merton, Warden of New
1317	John Lutterell		College
1322	Henry Gower, sometime Fellow of Merton	1391	Robert Rygge
1324	William de Alburwyke, Merton, Principal	1392	Ralph Redruth, sometime of Oriel,
	of Broadgates Hall		afterwards of Exeter
1326	Thomas Hotham	1393	Thomas Prestbury
1328	Ralph of Shrewsbury	1394	Robert Arlyngton, sometime of Queen's
1329	Roger de Streton	1395	Thomas Hyndeman, sometime Fellow of
1330	Nigel de Wavere, sometime Fellow of		Exeter
	Merton	1397	Philip Repyngdon
1332	Ralph Radyn		Henry Beaufort
1334	Hugh de Willoughby	1399	Thomas Hyndeman
1335	Robert de Stratford, Merton	1400	Philip Repyngdon
1336	*The same*	1403	Robert Alum, or Halam

1407	Richard Courtney	1588	Sir Christopher Hatton, sometime of St Mary Hall
	Richard Ullerston, sometime of Queen's		
1408	William Clynt, Fellow of Merton	1591	Thomas Sackville, Lord Buckhurst, afterwards Earl of Dorset, sometime (it is believed) of Hart Hall
1409	Thomas Prestbury		
1410	William Sulburge		
1411	John Banard	1608	Richard Bancroft
	Richard Courtney	1610	Thomas Egerton, Lord Ellesmere
1412	William Sulburge	1616	William Herbert, Earl of Pembroke
	Richard Courtney	1630	William Laud, sometime President of St John's
1413	William Sulburge		
	William Barrow	1641	Philip Herbert, Earl of Pembroke
1414	Richard Snetisham, sometime Fellow of Oriel	1643	William Seymour, Marquis of Hertford, sometime of Magdalen
1415	William Barrow	1648	Philip Herbert, Earl of Pembroke, restored; died Jan. 1649; office vacant until Jan. 1650
1416	Thomas Clare		
	William Barrow		
1417	Thomas Clare	1650	Oliver Cromwell
	Walter Treugof, sometime of Exeter	1657	Richard Cromwell
1419	Robert Colman	1660	William Seymour, Marquis of Hertford and Duke of Somerset, restored
	Walter Treugof		
1420	Thomas Rodborne, sometime of Merton		Sir Edward Hyde, Earl of Clarendon, sometime of Magdalen Hall
	Walter Treugof		
1421	John Castell, Master of University College	1667	Gilbert Sheldon, DD, sometime Warden of All Souls, but never sworn or installed
1426	Thomas Chase, sometime Master of Balliol		
1431	Gilbert Kymer, Principal of Hart Hall	1669	James Butler, 1st Duke of Ormonde, DCL
1433	Thomas Bouchier	1688	James Butler, 2nd Duke of Ormonde, DCL, Christ Church
1437	John Carpenter, Provost of Oriel		
1438	?Richard Praty, sometime Fellow of Oriel	1715	Charles Butler, Earl of Arran, DCL
1439	John Norton, sometime Fellow of New College	1759	John Fane, Earl of Westmorland, DCL
		1762	George Henry Lee, Earl of Lichfield, DCL, St John's College
1440	Richard Roderham, Balliol		
	William Grey, Balliol	1772	Frederick North, Lord North, MA, Trinity College, DCL, afterwards Earl of Guilford
1442	Thomas Gascoigne, Oriel		
	Henry Sever, Merton		
1443	Thomas Gascoigne	1792	William Henry Cavendish Bentinck, Duke of Portland, DCL
1445	Robert Thwaits, Balliol		
1446	Gilbert Kymer	1809	William Wyndham Grenville, Lord Grenville, BA, sometime student of Christ Church, DCL
1453	George Nevill, Balliol		
1457	Thomas Chaundeler, Warden of New College		
		1834	Arthur Wellesley, Duke of Wellington, DCL
1461	George Nevill		
1472	Thomas Chaundeler, Warden of New College	1852	Edward Geoffrey Smith Stanley, Earl of Derby, Christ Church, DCL
		1869	Robert Arthur Talbot Gascoyne-Cecil, Marquis of Salisbury, DCL, sometime Fellow of All Souls
1479	Lionel Woodvill		
1483	William Dudley		
	John Russell, sometime Fellow of New College	1903	George Joachim, Viscount Goschen, DCL, Oriel
1494	John Morton, sometime of Balliol	1907	George Nathaniel, Baron (afterwards Marquess) Curzon of Kedleston, DCL, sometime Fellow of All Souls, Hon. Fellow of Balliol
1500	William Smyth		
1502	Richard Mayew, President of Magdalen and Archdeacon of Oxford		
1506	William Warham, sometime Fellow of New College	1925	Alfred, Viscount Milner, MA, Hon. DCL, Hon. Fellow of Balliol and of New College
1532	John Longland, sometime Fellow of Magdalen and Principal of Magdalen Hall		
			George, Viscount Cave, DCL, Hon. Fellow of St John's
1547	Richard Coxe, Dean of Christ Church		
1552	Sir John Mason, sometime Fellow of All Souls	1928	Edward, Viscount Grey of Fallodon, DCL, Hon. Fellow of Balliol
1556	Reginald Pole, sometime of Magdalen College	1933	Edward Frederick Lindley Wood, Rt Hon. the Viscount Halifax, afterwards Rt Hon. the Earl of Halifax
1558	Henry Fitz-Alan, Earl of Arundel		
1559	Sir John Mason, sometime Fellow of All Souls	1960	Maurice Harold Macmillan, DCL, Hon. Fellow of Balliol, afterwards Rt Hon. the Earl of Stockton
1564	Robert Dudley, Earl of Leicester		
1585	Sir Thomas Bromley, Deputy Chancellor during the Earl of Leicester's absence in Holland	1987	Rt Hon. Lord Jenkins of Hillhead, Hon. Fellow of Balliol

Vice-Chancellors of the University

1230	Elyas de Daneis		William Westkarre
1270	Robert Steeton?	1444	William Dowson, sometime Fellow of
1288	John Heigham		Merton, afterwards Fellow of University
1304	John de Oseworhd		College
1311	Walter Gifford		Richard Hall
1325	Richard Kamshale, Merton, sometime of		William Westkarre
	Balliol	1445	William Dowson
1333	Richard, son of Radulph, or Fitzrauf		John Selot, New College
1336	John de Ayllesbury, sometime of Merton	1446	William Westkarre, DD
1337	John de Reigham		John Moreton, LLD, Balliol
1347?	Hugh de Willoughby		William Dowson, DD
1348	William de Hawkesworth, Provost of Oriel	1447	John Burneby, DD, Durham College
1367	John de Codeford		(Trinity)
1368	*The same*		William Dowson, DD
1377	Robert Aylesham, Merton	1448	John Burneby, DD
1382	Fr Peter Stokes	1449	John Willey, University College
1386	Henry Nafford, or Yafford		John Burneby, DD
1389?	John Lyndon, Fellow of Merton		William Dowson, DD
1391	John Ashwardby	1450	Richard Ringstede, DD, Gloucester College
1394	Richard Ullerston, sometime of Queen's		John Beke, DD, Lincoln
1396	Nicolas Faux		Roger Bulkeley, DD, Principal of Hart Hall
1397	William Farendon, or Faringdon, sometime		John Van
	of Merton?	1451	John Beke, DD
1399	John Snappe and others		John Van
1401	William Farendon	1452	John Beke, DD
1404	Griffin Kirkadam		Thomas Tweyn, or Yweyn, *alias* Chalke,
1405	William Farendon		Fellow of New College
1406	John Whytehede, University College		Thomas Saunders
1407	John Orum, University College	1453	Luke Lacock
1422	John Daventry, University College		Robert Thwayts, DD, Master of Balliol
1426	Richard Roderham, Balliol		Thomas Saunders
1430	Thomas Eglesfield, Queen's	1454	Thomas Tweyn
1431	Richard Roderham		Thomas Saunders
1433	John Burbach or Hurbach, Fellow of	1455	Thomas Twynge, *alias* Bonifaunt, DD,
	Merton		Queen's
1434	Thomas Gascoigne, Oriel	1456	Thomas Saunders
	Christopher Knolles	1457	Thomas Chippenham, LLD
	John Burbach	1458	Walter Wynhale, DD
1435	*The same*		Thomas Twynge
	Thomas Bonyngworth	1459	John Danvers
1436	John Burbach		Thomas Jaune, or Jane, New College
	Thomas Greneley, Oriel	1460	Thomas Tweyn
1437	John Gorsuch, Lincoln	1461	William Ive, DD, Magdalen
	Thomas Greneley		Roger Bulkeley, DD, Magdalen
1438	John Gorsuch	1462	William Ive, DD, Magdalen
	William Hawtrine, Fellow of New College	1463	John Watts, DD
1439	John Gorsuch		Thomas Chaundler, DD, Warden of New
	John Burbach		College
	Thomas Southam?		David Husband, LLD
	Thomas Gascoigne?		John Mulcaster, DD, University College,
1440	John Gorsuch		sometime of Queen's
1441	*The same*	1464	Laurence Cokkys, New College
	Robert Thwaytes, Balliol		Thomas Chaundeler, DD
	William Babington		Roger Bulkeley, DD
1442	William Grey		John Caldbeck, DD, Queen's
	William Babington		Thomas Person
	John Gorsuch	1465	Thomas Smith, DD, Magdalen
	William Westkarre		Robert Ixworth, Gloucester College
1443	William Dowson, sometime Principal of		John Caldbeck, DD, Queen's
	Little University Hall		Thomas Chaundler, DD

1466	*The same*	1508	William Fauntleroy, DD
	John Caldbeck, DD, Queen's		John Thornden, DD
	Thomas Stevyn, DD, Exeter	1509	William Fauntleroy, DD
	Laurence Cokkys	1510	John Thornden, DD
	Thomas Hill, DD, New College		John Mychell, DD, Exeter
1467	Thomas Chaundler, DD	1511	William Fauntleroy, DD
	Thomas Stevyn, DD, Exeter		Thomas Drax, DD, Rector of Lincoln
	Thomas Walton, LLD		John Roper, DD
1468	Thomas Stevyn, DD		John Cockys, LLD, sometime Fellow of All
	Thomas Jaune, LLD		Souls
1469	Robert Tulley, DD		Edmund Wylsford, DD, Provost of Oriel
	Thomas Jaune, LLD	1512	Edmund Wylsford, DD
1470	Thomas Stevyn, DD		William Fauntleroy, DD
1480	John Lane, DD		John Kynton, DD
	William Sutton, DD, Principal of	1513	William Fauntleroy, DD
	Brasenose Hall		John Kynton, DD
1481	Richard Fitzjames, DD, Merton		John Thornden, DD
	William Sutton, DD, Principal of	1514	John Thornden, DD
	Brasenose Hall		Lawrence Stubbs, DD, Magdalen,
1482	Robert Wrangwais, Queen's		afterwards President
	William Sutton, DD, Principal of		Edmund Wylsford, DD
	Brasenose Hall		Hugh Whytehead, DD
1484	Richard Mayew, DD, President of	1515	Edmund Wylsford, DD
	Magdalen	1516	Lawrence Stubbs, DD, Magdalen
	Thomas Pawnton, DD, sometime of	1517	Richard Duck, or Doke, Exeter
	Lincoln	1518	*The same*
1485	Richard Mayew, DD, President of	1519	Ralph Barnack, DD, sometime of New
	Magdalen		College
1486	John Taylor, DD, Provost of Oriel		Richard Duck, or Doke
1487	Richard Estmond	1520	William Broke, or Brook, Warden of All
1488	John Coldale, DD		Souls
1489	*The same*		Richard Benger, Fellow of New College
1490	*The same*	1521	Richard Benger
1491	Richard Fitzjames, DD, Warden of Merton	1522	*The same*
	John Coldale, DD, sometime Fellow of	1523	Thomas Musgrave, MD, sometime Fellow
	Queen's		of Merton
1492	*The same*	1527	Martin Lyndsey, DD, Fellow of Lincoln
1493–6	Robert Smith, DD, Lincoln		John Cottisford, DD, Rector of Lincoln
1497	William Atwater, DD, Magdalen		College
1498	Thomas Harpur, DD, Merton, afterwards	1528	*The same*
	Warden	1531	Henry White, LLD
1499	David Hays, DD	1532	John Cottisford, DD
	William Atwater, DD, Magdalen		William Tresham, DD, sometime Fellow of
	Thomas Chaundeler, DD, Warden of		Merton
	Canterbury College	1547	Walter Wright, LLD
1500	William Atwater, DD, Magdalen	1550	William Tresham, DD, Merton
1501	Thomas Banke, DD, Rector of Lincoln	1551	Owen Oglethorpe, DD, President of
	Hugh Saunders, *alias* Shakspeere, DD,		Magdalen
	Principal of St Alban Hall, Fellow of	1552	James Brokes, *alias* Brooks, DD, sometime
	Merton		Fellow of Corpus Christi, Master of
1502	William Atwater, DD, Magdalen		Balliol
	Thomas Banke, DD, Rector of Lincoln		Richard Martiall, DD, Christ Church
	Hugh Saunders	1553	*The same*, now Dean of Christ Church
1503	John Thornden, or Thornton, DD	1554	John Warner, MD, Warden of All Souls
	John Kynton, DD	1555	Richard Smyth, DD, sometime Fellow of
	Simon Grene, *alias* Fotherby, DD,		Merton, Canon of Christ Church
	Lincoln	1556	William Tresham, DD
1504	John Kynton, DD		Thomas Raynolds, DD, Warden of Merton
	Robert Tehy, or Thay, DD, Magdalen	1557	Thomas Raynolds, DD
1505	Simon Grene, DD, Lincoln		Thomas Whyte, LLD, Warden of New
	John Roper, DD, sometime of Magdalen		College
	John Adams, DD, Merton	1558	William Tresham, DD
1506	John Thornden, DD	1559	John Warner, MD, Warden of All Souls
	William Fauntleroy, DD, sometime of New	1560	Francis Babington, DD, Master of Balliol
	College	1561	*The same*
1507	John Thornden, or Thornton, DD	1562	Thomas Whyte, LLD, Warden of New
	John Avery, DD, Lincoln		College
	John Kynton, DD		*The same*

1564	John Kennall, LLD, Canon of Christ Church
1567	Thomas Cowper, DD, Dean of Christ Church, sometime of Magdalen
1570	*The same*
1571	Lawrence Humphrey, DD, President of Magdalen
1576	Herbert Westphaling, DD, Canon of Christ Church
1577	William Cole, DD, President of Corpus Christi
1578	Martyn Colepeper, DM, Warden of New College
1579	Toby Mathew, DD, sometime President of St John's, now Dean of Christ Church
1580	Arthur Yeldard, DD, President of Trinity
1581	William James, DD, Master of University College, afterwards Dean of Christ Church
1582	Robert Hovenden, DD, Warden of All Souls
1583	Thomas Thornton, BD, Canon of Christ Church
1584	John Underhill, DD, Rector of Lincoln
1585	Edmund Lilly, DD, Master of Balliol
1586	Daniel Bernard, DD, Canon of Christ Church
1587	Francis Wyllis, MA, President of St John's
1588	Martin Heton, DD, Canon of Christ Church
1589	Nicholas Bond, DD, President of Magdalen
1590	William James, DD, now Dean of Christ Church
1592	Nicholas Bond, DD, President of Magdalen
1593	Edmund Lilly, DD, Master of Balliol
1596	Thomas Ravys, DD, Dean of Christ Church
1598	Thomas Singleton, DD, Principal of Brasenose
1599	Thomas Thornton, DD, Canon of Christ Church
1600	George Abbot, DD, Master of University College
1601	George Ryves, DD, Warden of New College
1602	John Howson, DD, Canon of Christ Church
1603	George Abbot, DD, Master of University College
1604	John Williams, DD, Principal of Jesus College
1605	George Abbot, DD, Master of University College
1606	Henry Airay, DD, Provost of Queen's
1607	John King, DD, Dean of Christ Church
1611	Thomas Singleton, DD, Principal of Brasenose
1614	William Goodwyn, DD, Dean of Christ Church
1616	Arthur Lake, DD, Warden of New College
1617	William Goodwyn, DD, Dean of Christ Church
1619	John Prideaux, DD, Rector of Exeter
1621	William Piers, DD, Canon of Christ Church
1624	John Prideaux, DD, Rector of Exeter
1626	William Juxon, DD, President of St John's
1628	Accepted Frewen, DD, President of Magdalen

1630	William Smyth, DD, Warden of Wadham
1632	Brian Duppa, DD, Dean of Christ Church
1634	Robert Pincke, DD, Warden of New College
1636	Richard Baylie, DD, President of St John's
1638	Accepted Frewen, DD, President of Magdalen
1640	Christopher Potter, DD, Provost of Queen's
1641	John Prideaux, DD, Rector of Exeter
1642	Dr Prideaux
1643 Feb.	John Tolson, DD, Provost of Oriel
Nov.	Robert Pincke, DD, Warden of New College
1645	Samuel Fell, DD, Dean of Christ Church
1648	Edward Reynolds, MA, Dean of Christ Church, afterwards Warden of Merton
1650	Daniel Greenwood, DD, Principal of Brasenose
1652	John Owen, MA, Dean of Christ Church
1657	John Conant, DD, Rector of Exeter
1660	Paul Hood, DD, Rector of Lincoln
1661	Richard Baylie, DD, President of St John's
1662	Walter Blandford, DD, Warden of Wadham
1664	Robert Say, DD, Provost of Oriel
1666	John Fell, DD, Dean of Christ Church
1669	Peter Mews, DCL, President of St John's
1673	Ralph Bathurst, DM, President of Trinity
1676	Henry Clerk, DM, President of Magdalen
1677	John Nicholas, DD, Warden of New College
1679	Timothy Halton, DD, Provost of Queen's
1682	John Lloyd, DD, Principal of Jesus
1685	Timothy Halton, DD, Provost of Queen's
1686	John Venn, DD, Master of Balliol
1687	Gilbert Ironside, DD, Warden of Wadham
1689	Jonathan Edwards, DD, Principal of Jesus
1692	Henry Aldrich, DD, Dean of Christ Church
1695	Fitzherbert Adams, DD, Rector of Lincoln
1697	John Meare, DD, Principal of Brasenose
1698	William Paynter, DD, Rector of Exeter
1700	Roger Mander, DD, Master of Balliol
1702	William Delaune, DD, President of St John's
1706	William Lancaster, DD, Provost of Queen's
1710	Thomas Brathwaite, DCL, Warden of New College
1712	Bernard Gardiner, DCL, Warden of All Souls
1715	John Baron, DD, Master of Balliol
1718	Robert Shippen, DD, Principal of Brasenose
1723	John Mather, DD, President of Corpus Christi
1728	Edward Butler, DCL, President of Magdalen
1732	William Holmes, DD, President of St John's
1735	Stephen Niblett, DD, Warden of All Souls
1738	Theophilus Leigh, DD, Master of Balliol
1741	Walter Hodges, DD, Provost of Oriel
1744	Euseby Isham, DD, Rector of Lincoln
1747	John Purnell, DD, Warden of New College
1750	John Browne, DD, Master of University College
1753	George Huddesford, DD, President of Trinity

1756	Thomas Randolph, DD, President of Corpus Christi
1759	Joseph Browne, DD, Provost of Queen's
1765	David Durell, DD, Principal of Hertford
1768	Nathan Wetherell, DD, Master of University College
1772	Thomas Fothergill, DD, Provost of Queen's
1776	George Horne, DD, President of Magdalen
1780	Samuel Dennis, DD, President of St John's
1784	Joseph Chapman, DD, President of Trinity
1788	John Cooke, DD, President of Corpus Christi
1792	John Wills, DD, Warden of Wadham
1796	Scrope Berdmore, DD, Warden of Merton
1797	Edmund Isham, DD, Warden of All Souls
1798	Michael Marlow, DD, President of St John's
1802	Whittington Landon, DD, Provost of Worcester
1806	Henry Richards, DD, Rector of Exeter
1807	John Parsons, DD, Master of Balliol
1810	John Cole, DD, Rector of Exeter
1814	Thomas Lee, DD, President of Trinity
1818	Frodsham Hodson, DD, Principal of Brasenose
1820	George William Hall, DD, Master of Pembroke
1824	Richard Jenkyns, DD, Master of Balliol
1828	John Collier Jones, DD, Rector of Exeter
1832	George Rowley, DD, Master of University College
1836	Ashhurst Turner Gilbert, DD, Principal of Brasenose
1840	Philip Wynter, DD, President of St John's
1844	Benjamin Parsons Symons, DD, Warden of Wadham
1848	Frederick Charles Plumptre, DD, Master of University College
1852	Richard Lynch Cotton, DD, Provost of Worcester
1856	David Williams, DCL, Warden of New College
1858	Francis Jeune, DCL, Master of Pembroke
1862	John Prideaux Lightfoot, DD, Rector of Exeter
1866	Francis Knyvett Leighton, DD, Warden of All Souls
1870	Henry George Liddell, DD, Dean of Christ Church
1874	James Edwards Sewell, DD, Warden of New College
1878	Evan Evans, MA, Master of Pembroke, DD
1882	Benjamin Jowett, MA, Master of Balliol
1886	James Bellamy, DD, President of St John's
1890	Henry Boyd, DD, Principal of Hertford
1894	John Richard Magrath, DD, Provost of Queen's
1898	Sir William Reynell Anson, DCL, Warden of All Souls
1899	Thomas Fowler, DD, President of Corpus Christi
1901	David Binning Monro, MA, Provost of Oriel, Hon. DCL
1904	William Walter Merry, DD, Rector of Lincoln
1906	Thomas Herbert Warren, MA, President of Magdalen, Hon. DCL
1910	Charles Buller Heberden, MA, Hon. DCL, Principal of Brasenose
1913	Thomas Banks Strong, DD, Dean of Christ Church, Hon. DMus
1917	Herbert Edward Douglas Blakiston, DD, President of Trinity
1920	Lewis Richard Farnell, MA, DLitt, Rector of Exeter
1923	Joseph Wells, MA, Warden of Wadham, Hon. DCL
1926	Francis William Pember, DCL, Warden of All Souls
1929	Frederick Homes Dudden, DD, Master of Pembroke
1932	Francis John Lys, MA, Provost of Worcester, Hon. DCL
1935	Alexander Dunlop Lindsay, MA, Master of Balliol
1938	George Stuart Gordon, MA, President of Magdalen, Hon. DCL
1941	Sir William David Ross, MA, DLitt, Provost of Oriel
1944	Sir Richard Winn Livingstone, MA, President of Corpus Christi
1947	William Teulon Swan Stallybrass, DCL, Principal of Brasenose
1948	Very Rev. John Lowe, MA, Dean of Christ Church
1951	Sir Cecil Maurice Bowra, MA, DLitt, Warden of Wadham
1954	Alic Halford Smith, MA, Warden of New College
1957	John Cecil Masterman, MA, Provost of Worcester
1958	Thomas Sherrer Ross Boase, MA, President of Magdalen, Hon. DCL
1960	Arthur Lionel Pugh Norrington, MA, President of Trinity
1962	Walter Fraser Oakeshott, MA, Rector of Lincoln, later Sir Walter
1964	Kenneth Clinton Wheare, MA, DLitt, Rector of Exeter, later Sir Kenneth
1966	Kenneth Charlton Turpin, MA, BLitt, Provost of Oriel
1969	Sir Alan Louis Charles Bullock, MA, DLitt, Master of St Catherine's
1973	Sir Hrothgar John Habakkuk, MA, Principal of Jesus College
1977	Sir Rex Edward Richards, MA, DPhil, DSc, Warden of Merton
1981	Geoffrey James Warnock, MA, Principal of Hertford, later Sir Geoffrey
1985	Sir Francis Patrick Neill, QC, BCL, MA, Warden of All Souls
1989	Professor Sir Richard Southwood, FRS, Linacre Professor of Zoology and Fellow of Merton.

Presidents of the Union since 1900

Year	Name	Died	College	Career
1900	R. C. K. Ensor	1958	Balliol	academic at Corpus Christi and Nuffield Colleges
	Raymond Asquith	1916	Balliol	killed in action in First World War
	Rt Hon. Harold Baker	1960	New College	Liberal MP for Accrington 1910–18
1901	Algernon Cecil	1953	New College	author, *British Foreign Secretaries*, etc.
	T. Cuthbertson		Corpus Christi	
	Sir George Tomlinson	1963	University College	Colonial Service
1902	Lord Lindsay of Birker	1952	University College	Master of Balliol College
	Sir Eric Macfadyen	1966	Wadham	Liberal MP for Devizes 1923–4; pioneer of rubber industry
	Lord du Parcq	1949	Exeter	Judge of the Appeal Court
1903	Herbert Asquith	1947	Balliol	author, *The Volunteer*, etc.
	F. W. Curran		Lincoln	
	Sir John Brooke	1937	Corpus Christi	public servant; Ministry of Transport and Electricity Commission
1904	Most Rev. William Temple	1944	Balliol	Archbishop of Canterbury
	W. A. Moore	1962	St John's	editor, *The Calcutta Statesman*
	E. S. Jose		Hertford	
1905	J. St G. C. Heath		Corpus Christi	
	Lord Craigmyle (A. Shaw)	1944	Trinity	Liberal MP for Kilmarnock 1915–23; Director, the Bank of England
	M. H. Woods	1929	Trinity	journalist, *The Times*
1906	H. M. Paul		New College	
	Hon. H. Lygon		Magdalen	London County Councillor
	Sir Gervais Rentoul	1946	Christ Church	Conservative MP for Lowestoft 1922–34; Chairman 1922 Committee
1907	Rt Rev. N. S. Talbot	1943	Christ Church	Bishop of Pretoria
	William Gladstone	1915	New College	MP for Kilmarnock Boroughs 1911–15: killed in First World War
	W. S. Armour		Jesus College	editor, *Northern Whig*, Belfast
1908	C. T. le Quesne, QC	1954	Exeter	barrister; Recorder of Plymouth
	Sir Hugh Hallett	1967	Christ Church	High Court Judge
	Rev. M. H. Richmond		New College	Hon. Canon of Norwich
1909	Rt Rev. Monsignor Ronald Knox	1957	Balliol	translator of the Bible
	Rt Rev. Edgar Swain	1949	St John's	Bishop of Burnley
	R. G. D. Laffan	1972	Balliol	Bursar of Queen's College, Cambridge
1910	Hon. R. S. A. Palmer	1916	University College	killed in First World War
	L. J. Stein	1973	Balliol	President of the Anglo-Jewish Association
	A. W. Cockburn, QC	1969	New College	Chairman of the County of London Sessions
1911	Rev. Nathaniel Micklem	1976	New College	Principal of Mansfield College; President of the Liberal Party
	R. Bevir	1916	Hertford	killed in First World War
	Philip Guedalla	1944	Balliol	historian and biographer
1912	Frank Griffith	1962	Balliol	County Court Judge and Liberal MP for Middlesbrough W. 1928–40
	Robert Barrington-Ward	1948	Balliol	editor, *The Times*
	G. S. Woodhouse	1916	Lincoln	killed in First World War
1913	Lord Monckton of Brenchley	1965	Balliol	Minister of Labour and Defence
	W. J. Bland	1918	Lincoln	killed in First World War
	Godfrey Talbot	1916	Christ Church	killed in First World War

Year	Name	Died	College	Career
1914	Sir Ernest Roberts	1969	Trinity	Conservative MP for Flintshire 1924–9; Chief Justice in Rangoon
	A. H. M. Wedderburn, KC	1968	Balliol	barrister; LCC Member
	A. F. H. Wiggin	1935	Oriel	Diplomatic Service
1919	Lord Hore-Belisha	1957	St John's	Liberal Nationalist, then Independent MP; Minister of Transport; Secretary for War
	Thomas Earp	1958	Exeter	literary and artistic critic
1920	Constantine Gallop, QC	1967	Balliol	Master of the Bench, Middle Temple
	Sir John Russell	1978	New College	barrister; Chairman of the London Conservative Union 1953–5
	Beverley Nichols	1983	Balliol	journalist, author and composer
1921	Alec Beechman, QC	1965	Balliol	Liberal Nationalist MP and Chief Whip
	Captain Cecil Ramage		Pembroke	barrister; Liberal MP 1923–4
	Kenneth Lindsay		Worcester	Independent MP; Parliamentary Secretary, Board of Education
1922	J. Victor Evans	1957	St John's	barrister; Independent Nationalist MP
	Ralph Carson	1977	Oriel	lawyer on Wall Street
	Edward Marjoribanks	1932	Christ Church	MP; biographer and poet
1923	J. Douglas Woodruff	1978	New College	journalist; editor, *The Tablet*
	Gordon Bagnall		St John's	journalist
	Christopher Hollis	1977	Balliol	author and journalist; Conservative MP for Devizes
1924	Prof. Christopher Scaife		St John's	academic; Professor of English in Cairo and Beirut
	Lord Gardiner		Magdalen	Lord Chancellor, 1964–70
	The Earl of Dundee (Scrymgeour Wedderburn)	1983	Balliol	Conservative MP; Foreign Office Minister; Deputy Leader, House of Lords
1925	Robert Bernays	1945	Worcester	Liberal MP; Health and Transport Minister
	Sir Vincent Lloyd-Jones	1986	Jesus College	High Court Judge
	Lord Molson		New College	Conservative MP; Minister of Works 1957–9
1926	Sir Gyles Isham	1976	Magdalen	actor and farmer
	Prof. Lindley Fraser	1963	Balliol	Professor of Political Economy, Aberdeen University; Head of BBC German and Austrian Services
	Lord Boyd of Merton (Alan Lennox-Boyd)	1983	Christ Church	Colonial Secretary 1954–9
1927	Sir Roger Fulford	1983	Worcester	writer and historian; President of the Liberal Party
	John Playfair Price		New College	Foreign Office – series of diplomatic and consular posts
	Malcolm Brereton	1942	Balliol	lawyer; BBC; killed in Second World War
1928	Sir Dingle Foot, QC	1978	Balliol	Liberal and Labour MP; Solicitor-General 1964–7
	Aubrey Herbert	1981	University College	broadcaster and Liberal politician
	S. Stopford Brooke	1976	Balliol	stockbroker and Liberal candidate
1929	Prof. Roger Wilson		Queens	Professor of Education, University of Bristol
	Lord Hailsham (Quintin Hogg)		Christ Church	Lord Chancellor 1970–4, 1979–87
	Lord Stewart of Fulham		St John's	Labour Cabinet Minister 1964–70
1930	Edgar Lustgarten	1978	St John's	barrister, journalist and broadcaster
	J. P. W. Mallalieu	1980	Trinity	Labour MP for Huddersfield 1945–79 and junior minister
	Lord Boyd-Carpenter (J. A. Boyd-Carpenter)		Balliol	Chief Secretary to the Treasury 1962–4; Chairman of the Civil Aviation Authority
1931	Lord Foot (John Foot)		Balliol	solicitor and Liberal peer; Chairman of the UK Immigrants Advisory Service

528

Year	Name	Died	College	Career
1931	Sir Geoffrey Wilson		Oriel	civil servant; Chairman of the Race Relations Board; Chairman of Oxfam
	Toby O'Brien	1979	Exeter	Director of Information for the Conservative Party
1932	Sir Arthur Irvine	1978	Oriel	Liberal and Labour MP; Solicitor-General 1967–70
	Brian Davidson		New College	businessman; Director of Bristol Siddeley
	Lt-Col. J. C. Smuts	1979	University College	Army
1933	Frank Hardie		Christ Church	author and academic
	Lord Greenwood of Rossendale (Anthony Greenwood)	1982	Balliol	Labour MP 1946–70; Cabinet Minister 1964–70
	Michael Foot		Wadham	Leader of the Labour Party 1980–3
1934	Dosoo Karaka	1974	Lincoln	journalist; editor, *The Current* of Bombay
	Sir Keith Steel-Maitland	1965	Balliol	businessman; chairman of an estates company
	W. G. Murray	1938	Balliol	journalist and broadcaster
1935	David Lewis	1981	Lincoln	Leader of the Canadian New Democratic Party
	Rev. James Hickerton		St Catherine's	Baptist minister
	Brian Farrell		Balliol	Reader in Mental Philosophy, Oxford University
1936	Ian Harvey		Christ Church	Conservative MP for Harrow E. 1950–8; President of the Conservative Group for Homosexual Equality
	Bill Shebbeare	1944	Christ Church	killed in the Second World War
	James Brown		Balliol	Judge; Recorder of Belfast 1978–82
1937	Lord Mayhew (Christopher Mayhew)		Christ Church	Navy Minister 1964–6; Labour and Liberal MP; Liberal peer
	Patrick Anderson	1979	Worcester	writer
	Alan Fyfe	1944	Balliol	killed in Second World War
1938	Sir Raymond Walton		Balliol	Judge
	Philip Toynbee	1982	Christ Church	author and critic
	Alan Wood	1957	Balliol	writer
1939	Edward Heath		Balliol	Prime Minister 1970–4
	Sir Hugh Fraser	1984	Balliol	Conservative MP since 1945; Air Secretary 1962–4
	Sandy Giles*		Balliol	Colonial Service
	Sir Nicholas Henderson		Hertford	diplomat; Ambassador to Bonn, Paris and Washington
1940	Madron Seligman, MEP		Balliol	businessman; Member of the European Parliament
	Sir Robert Edmonds		Brasenose	diplomat; High Commissioner for Cyprus
	Sir James Comyn		New College	Judge
1941	Indar Bahadoorsingh		St Catherine's	
	Rev. Kenneth Riddle		St Catherine's	Anglican priest
	Michael Kinchin-Smith		Christ Church	BBC; Secretary, Crown Appointments Commission
1942	Gershon Hirsch (now Avner)		Brasenose	Israeli diplomat
	F. P. R. Hinchcliffe		New College	Judge
	Cameron Tudor		Keble	High Commissioner for Barbados in London
1943	Rev. Herbert Clarke		Jesus College	Anglican priest
	Courtney Blackmore		Keble	Lloyds
	Sir Godfrey le Quesne		Exeter	Judge in Jersey
1944	Hon. Kenneth Lamb		Trinity	broadcasting; Director of Public Affairs of the BBC
	Prof. Fernando Henriques	1976	Brasenose	Director, Centre for Multi-Racial Studies, Exeter University
	Tony Pickford		Oriel	

*Elected but did not hold office because of war service

Year	Name	Died	College	Career
1945	Alan Gibson*		Queen's	broadcaster; BBC radio commentator
	Rudi Weisweiller		New College	international financial consultant
	Anthony Walton, QC		Hertford	barrister
	Dr John Long		Queen's	chemist; Director of ICI
1946	Lord Wigoder, QC (Basil Thomas Wigoder)		Oriel	Liberal Chief Whip, House of Lords
	Anthony Crosland	1977	Trinity	Labour Cabinet Minister 1965–70, 1974–7
	Group Captain Ronald Brown		Brasenose	surgeon, RAF Medical Branch
1947	Roger Gray, QC		Queen's	Recorder of the Crown Court
	Tony Benn		New College	Labour Minister 1964–70, Cabinet Minister 1974–9
	Peter Kroyer		Christ Church	
1948	Clive Wigram	1956	Oriel	barrister
	Lord Boyle	1981	Christ Church	Cabinet Minister; Vice-Chancellor of Leeds University
	Seymour Hills	1964	St Catherine's	printer; industrial consultant
1949	Sir Peter Kirk	1977	Trinity	Conservative Minister and Leader of European Parliament Delegation
	Rodney Donald		Christ Church	financier
	Sir Richard Faber		Christ Church	diplomat; Ambassador to Algeria 1977–81
1950	Uwe Kitzinger		New College	Director of Oxford Centre for Management Studies
	Sir Robin Day		St Edmund Hall	broadcaster
	Godfrey Smith		Worcester	author; *Sunday Times* columnist
1951	Jeremy Thorpe		Trinity	Leader of the Liberal Party 1967–76
	Sir William Rees-Mogg		Balliol	editor, *The Times*; Chairman of the Arts Council
	Ivan Yates	1975	Pembroke	journalist, the *Observer*
1952	Sir Peter Blaker		New College	MP for Blackpool S. since 1964; Foreign Office and Defence Minister
	Howard Shuman		New College	administrative assistant to American senators
	Sir Patrick Mayhew		Balliol	MP for Royal Tunbridge Wells since 1974; Solicitor-General
1953	Bryan Magee		Keble	writer, Labour and SDP MP for Leyton 1974–83
	John Peters		Balliol	Civil Servant; Assistant Undersecretary, MoD
	Sir Andrew Cuninghame	1959	Worcester	Foreign Office
1954	Tyrell Burgess		Keble	Director of Institutional Studies, NE London Polytechnic
	Raghavan Iyer		Magdalen	academic in California
	Michael Heseltine		Pembroke	Cabinet Minister 1979–86; MP for Henley
1955	Jeremy Isaacs		Merton	Chief Executive, Channel 4 Television
	Anthony Howard		Christ Church	deputy editor, the *Observer*
	Desmond Watkins		Keble	industrialist with Shell
1956	Alec Grant		Merton	barrister; former Labour member of the GLC
	Roy Dickson		Exeter	Jamaican Civil Service
	Edmund Ions		Merton	academic; Reader in Politics, York University
1957	Jeremy Lever, QC		University College	lawyer; Fellow of All Souls College
	Hon. Peter Brooke		Balliol	MP for City of London since 1977; Education Minister; Chairman of the Conservative Party 1987
	Brian Walden		Queen's	MP for Birmingham All Saints 1964–77; television presenter; journalist

*Elected but did not hold office because of war service

Year	Name	Died	College	Career
1958	Lalithe Athulathmudali		Jesus College	Minister of Trade and Shipping in Sri Lanka
	Stuart Griffiths		Magdalen	script editor, Plays, BBC TV
	Ron Owen		Christ Church	personnel officer in industry
1959	Lashman Kadirgamer		Balliol	lawyer in Sri Lanka
	Anthony Newton		Trinity	MP for Braintree since 1974; Health Minister
	Joe Trattner		St Catherine's	American lawyer
1960	Ian Lyon		Oriel	journalist; editor, *International Tax Free Trader*
	Peter Jay		Christ Church	television presenter; journalist; Ambassador to USA 1977–9
	Robert Rowland		Keble	BBC, Open University
1961	Phillip Whitehead		Exeter	Labour MP for Derby N. 1970–83; television producer
	Paul Foot		University College	journalist on the *Daily Mirror*
	Howard Preece		Merton	journalist
1962	Hugh Stephenson		New College	editor, *New Statesman*
	John McDonnell		Balliol	barrister
	Michael Beloff, QC		Magdalen	academic and barrister
1963	G. R. Karnad		Magdalen	actor
	Jeffrey Jowell		Hertford	barrister
	Anthony Hart		New College	Civil Servant
1964	Garth Pratt		Christ Church	Liberal political activist
	Lord James Douglas-Hamilton		Balliol	Conservative MP for Edinburgh W. since 1974
	Eric Abrahams		St Peter's	Minister of Tourism in Jamaica
1965	Prof. Neil MacCormick		Balliol	Regius Professor of Public Law, Edinburgh University
	Tariq Ali		Exeter	journalist and Marxist politician
	Douglas Hogg		Christ Church	Conservative MP for Grantham since 1979; Whip
1966	Joshua Bamfield		Pembroke	
	Jeremy Beloff		St Catherine's	businessman, Procter and Gamble
	Montek Singh		Magdalen	World Bank
1967	Ronald Cohen		Exeter	investment banker
	Stephen Marks		New College	journalist, *International Socialism*
	Robert Jackson		St Edmund Hall	MP for Wantage since 1983; MEP since 1979
1968	Geraldine Greineder (née Jones)		St Hugh's	housewife
	Hon. William Waldegrave		Corpus Christi	Conservative MP for Bristol W. since 1979; Environment Minister
	Ian Glick		Balliol	barrister
1969	David Walter		Trinity	political correspondent, ITN
	Colin Youlden		Merton	academic
	Gyles Brandreth		New College	writer and broadcaster
1970	Guy Harkin		Hertford	polytechnic lecturer and Labour councillor
	Stephen Milligan		Magdalen	foreign editor, the *Sunday Times*
	Eric Parsloe		Ruskin and Corpus Christi	businessman
1971	Michael House		Exeter	barrister
	Susan Kramer (née Richards)		St Hilda's	housewife in USA
	Christopher Tookey		Exeter	television producer, TV-AM
1972	Julian Priestley*		Balliol	EEC administrator and Labour candidate
	Pradeep Mitra		Balliol	academic
	Patric Dickinson		Exeter	Rouge Dragon Pursuivant, College of Arms
	Philip McDonagh		Balliol	Irish Foreign Office
1973	Michael Austerberry		Trinity	Civil Service
	Colin Maltby		Christ Church	businessman
	David Warren		Exeter	Foreign Office

*Resigned

Year	Name	Died	College	Career
1974	Simon Walker		Balliol	journalist, USA
	Michael Soole		University College	barrister
	Robert McDonagh		Balliol	Irish Foreign Office
1975	Robert Scoble		Nuffield	Australian Foreign Office
	Victor van Amerongen		Magdalen	BBC producer
	David Soskin		Magdalen	business consultant
1976	Andrew Bell		University College	Shell-UK
	Hon. Colin Moynihan		University College	Conservative Minister for Sport, 1987–
	Hon. Richard Norton		New College	merchant banker
1977	Benazir Bhutto		LMH	Former Prime Minister of Pakistan
	Victoria Schofield		LMH	BBC Radio producer
	Damian Green		Balliol	news editor, Times Business News
1978	Nicholas O'Shaughnessy		Keble	academic; lecturer at the University of Wales
	John Harrison		Merton	schoolmaster at Rugby School
	Daniel Moylan		Queen's	banking
1979	Alan Duncan		St John's	oil trader
	Philip May		Lincoln	stockbroker
	Michael Crick		New College	journalist, ITN
1980	Warwick Lightfoot		Exeter	bond trader
	Nicholas Prettejohn		Balliol	management consultant
	Rupert Soames		Worcester	industry, Marconi
1981	Andrew Sutcliffe		Worcester	barrister
	Alexandra Jones		New College	graduate student in USA
	William Hague		Magdalen	Shell-UK; aide to Sir Geoffrey Howe during 1983 election
1982	Kevin Brennan		Pembroke	journalist on a community newspaper
	Paul Thompson		Corpus Christi	stockbroker
	Christopher Wortley		New College	Jardine Matheson
1983	Hilali Nordeen		Balliol	
	Andrew Sullivan		Magdalen	journalist
	Neale Stevenson		Christ Church	
1984	Malcolm Bull		Balliol	
	Melvyn Stride		St Edmund Hall	
	Laurence Grafstein		Balliol	
1985	Roland Rudd		Regent's Park	
	Neil Sherlock		Christ Church	
	Anthony Goodman		New College	
1986	Mrs Jaya Wilson		St Antony's	
	Boris Johnson		Balliol	
	Angus McCullough		Pembroke	
1987	Simon Stevens		Balliol	
	Jessica Pulay		Christ Church	
	Anthony Frieze		Balliol	
1988	Michael Grove		LMH	
	Duncan Gray		University	
	Andrew McCulloch		Jesus	
1989	The Hon. Adam Bruce		Balliol	
	Stefan Green		Queen's	
	Diana Gerald		Balliol	
1990	Ed Lazarus		St Anne's	
	Jeremy Quin		Hertford	
	Melanie Johnson		St Anne's	
1991	Oliver Campbell		St Hugh's	
	Damian Hinds		Trinity	
	Nicholas Edgar		University	

(Walter, David, *The Oxford Union: Playground of Power*, 1984.)

Glossary

This glossary is limited to those words and phrases which do not have separate entries elsewhere in the *Encyclopædia*.

The Act	*see* ENCAENIA.
Austins	a kind of disputation, so called because it was originally conducted at the convent of the Austin Friars (*see* AUGUSTINIAN FRIARY).
BNC	Brasenose College.
The Broad	BROAD STREET
Censor	senior tutor and administrative Dean of Christ Church.
Choragus	a senior member of the Faculty of Music, originally appointed in 1626 to superintend the practice of music. *See* MUSIC.
Come up	take up residence at the University.
The Corn	CORNMARKET STREET.
Cuppers	*see* OXFORD UNIVERSITY RUGBY FOOTBALL CLUB.
Don	University teacher (Latin: *dominus*).
Freshman	a man in his first year at the University.
Gated	*see* DISCIPLINE.
Giler	ST GILES' STREET.
Go down	leave the University.
Greats	*see* LITERAE HUMANIORES.
Hanasters	*see* PRIVILEGED PERSONS.
The High	HIGH STREET.
The House	Christ Church.
Littlego	MODERATIONS.
LMH	Lady Margaret Hall.
Manciple	officer who buys provisions for a college.

Mods	MODERATIONS.
Oxbridge	Oxford and Cambridge Universities collectively.
Plough	fail an examination.
Preliminaries	'Prelims' – the first of the two examinations for a Bachelor's degree in some subjects.
Proxime accessit	(person gaining) next place in merit to prizewinner in examination, etc.
Rusticated	temporarily expelled from the University (Latin: *rusticari*, live in the country).
Scarlet Days	occasions in the University year marked by the wearing of special ACADEMIC DRESS.
Screwing up	fastening the outer doors of college rooms from the outside as a practical joke (*see also* SPORTING ONE'S OAK).
Sent down	permanently expelled.
Smalls	*see* RESPONSIONS.
Steward	Domestic Bursar at Christ Church.
Student	*see* CHRIST CHURCH.
Teddy Hall	St Edmund Hall
Treasurer	Estates Bursar at Christ Church.
Tufts	titled undergraduates, from the gold tassel formerly worn on the cap – hence tuft-hunter. (*See also* ACADEMIC DRESS.)
The Turl	Turl Street.
Univ	University College.
Varsity	once a colloquial abbreviation of 'university', now used in connection with sport.

Notes on Sources

In an encyclopædia such as this the debt owed to previous writers is prodigious; but since more books have probably been published about Oxford than about any other English city except London, a comprehensive bibliography is obviously impracticable. The Local History Library in the Westgate Library has a very extensive collection of books on Oxford, both on the city and on the University, running to several hundred volumes, as well as maps, pamphlets, newspaper cuttings and records on microfilm.

In the encyclopædia the college entries, some other of the longer articles, and shorter entries based to a large extent upon one or more particular sources, have their own brief bibliographies. Fuller bibliographies will be found in *A Bibliography of Printed Works relating to the University of Oxford*, eds E. H. Cordeaux and D. H. Merry (3 vols, 1968); in Falconer Madan's *Oxford Books: A Bibliography of Printed Works relating to the University and City of Oxford or Printed or Published There* (1895–1931); and in the same editor's *Rough List of Manuscript Materials relating to the History of Oxford contained in the Printed Catalogues of the Bodleian and College Libraries* (1887).

The entry on HISTORIANS mentions the principal sources for the history of the University and the city. Indispensable as sources for this book have been volumes 3 (University) and 4 (City) of *The Victoria History of the County of Oxford*; and the section on Oxford by Nikolaus Pevsner in the volume on *Oxfordshire* by Jennifer Sherwood and Nikolaus Pevsner (1974) in *The Buildings of England* series. Other important sources are the *Royal Commission on Historical Monuments: An Inventory of the Historical Monuments in the City of Oxford* (1939); the annual volumes of *Oxoniensia*; Malcolm Graham's series of *On Foot in Oxford*; the Rev. James Ingram's *Memorials of Oxford* (3 vols, 1837); *Anthony Wood's History and Antiquities of the University of Oxford* (4 vols, ed. J. Gutch, 1792–6); Wood's *Survey of the Antiquities of the City of Oxford* (3 vols, ed. Andrew Clark, 1889–99); and *Remarks and Collections of Thomas Hearne* (11 vols, eds C. E. Doble, D. W. Rannie and H. E. Salter, 1885–1921). Sir Charles Edward Mallet's *A History of the University of Oxford* (3 vols, 1924–7) is gradually being superseded by the eight-volume history published by the Oxford University Press, of which three volumes had appeared by the end of 1987 (*see* HISTORIANS). A good single-volume history is V. H. H. Green's *A History of Oxford University* (1974). Complementary to this is Ruth Fasnacht's *A History of the City of Oxford* (1954).

Other books of which use has been made and which do not appear in the brief bibliographies appended to individual entries include:

ABRAHAMS, H. M., AND BRUCE-KERR, J., *Oxford versus Cambridge: A Record of Inter-University Contests from 1827 to 1930* (1931), and *Supplement* for 1931
Ackermann's Oxford, with notes by H. M. Colvin (1954)

ALEXANDER, SALLY, *St Giles's Fair, 1830–1914: Popular Culture and the Industrial Revolution in 19th-century Oxford* (1970)
Alumni Oxonienses: The Members of the University of Oxford, 1500–1886 (ed. Joseph Foster, 8 vols, 1887–92)
Annual Reports of the Oxfordshire Architectural Society
Archaeologia Oxoniensis, 1892–1895 (1895)
Aspects of Modern Oxford by a Mere Don [A. D. Godley] (1894)
AVELING, H., AND PANTIN, W. A. (eds), *The Letter Book of Robert Joseph ... 1530–32* (1967)
BALSDON, DACRE, *Oxford Life* (2nd edition, 1962) *Now and Then* (1970)
BARDOUX, JACQUES, *Memories of Oxford* (1899)
BATTISCOMBE, GEORGINA, *John Keble* (1963)
BEADLE, MURIEL, *These Ruins are Inhabited* (1961)
BETJEMAN, JOHN, *An Oxford University Chest* (1938) (with David Vaisey) *Victorian and Edwardian Oxford from Old Photographs* (1971)
BOAS, F. S., *University Drama in the Tudor Age* (1914) (ed.) *The Diary of Thomas Crosfield* (1935)
BOASE, CHARLES W., *Oxford* (1887)
The Book of Oxford (printed for the 104th Annual Meeting of the BMA, 1936)
BOWRA, C. M., *Memoirs* (1966)
BRIANT, KEITH, *Oxford Limited* (1937)
BRITTAIN, VERA, *The Women at Oxford* (1960)
BUTLER, C. V., *Social Conditions in Oxford* (1912)
BUXTON, L. H. DUDLEY, AND GIBSON, STRICKLAND, *Oxford University Ceremonies* (1935)
CHEETHAM, HAL, *Portrait of Oxford* (1971)
CLARK, ANDREW (ed.), *The Life and Times of Anthony Wood, Antiquary of Oxford ... Described by Himself and Collected from His Diaries and Other Papers* (5 vols, 1891–1900)
CLARK, G. N., *Open Fields and Enclosures at Marston near Oxford* (1924)
COLVIN, H. M., *Unbuilt Oxford* (1983) *A Biographical Dictionary of British Architects, 1600–1840* (1978)
COX, G. V., *Recollections of Oxford* (1868)
CREE, ANTHONY (ed.), *1871: An Oxford Diary* (1974)
CURTIS, M. H., *Oxford and Cambridge in Transition 1558–1642* (1959)
DALE, LAWRENCE, *Towards a Plan for Oxford City* (1941)
DATALLER, ROGER, *A Pitman Looks at Oxford* (1933)
DAVIDSON, MAURICE, *Memoirs of a Golden Age* (1958)
DENT, C. M., *Protestant Reformers in Elizabethan Oxford* (1983)
DICKENS, CHARLES (ed.), *A Dictionary of the University of Oxford, 1886–1887* (1886)
ELMHIRST, W., *A Freshman's Diary, 1911–12* (1969)
EMDEN, A. B., *An Oxford Hall in Mediaeval Times* (1927) *A Biographical Register of the University of Oxford to AD1500* (3 vols, 1957–59) *A Biographical Register of the University of Oxford, 1501–1540* (1974)
ENGEL, A. J., *From Clergyman to Don: The Rise of the Academic Profession in 19th-century Oxford* (1983)

FABER, G., *Benjamin Jowett* (1957)

FARNELL, L. R., *An Oxonian Looks Back* (1934)

FEILING, KEITH, *In Christ Church Hall* (1960)

FIRTH, SIR CHARLES, *Modern Languages at Oxford 1724–1929* (1929)

FISHER, H. A. L., *An Unfinished Autobiography* (1940)

FLETCHER, C. J. H., *History of the Church and Parish of St Martin* (1896)

FOOT, M. D. R. (ed.), *Gladstone's Diary* (Vol. 1, 1968)

Formularies which bear on the History of Oxford c.1204–1420 (eds. H. E. Salter, W. A. Pantin and H. G. Richardson, 2 vols, 1942)

GAUNT, WILLIAM, *Oxford* (1965)

GIBSON, A. J., *The Radcliffe Infirmary* (1926)

GODLEY, A. D., *Oxford in the Eighteenth Century* (1908)

GREEN, J. R., *The Early History of Oxford* (1871–2)
Oxford During the Eighteenth Century (1908) (with G. Robertson) *Studies in Oxford History* (1901)

GREEN, V. H. H., *Religion at Oxford and Cambridge: A History c.1160–1960* (1964)

GREENRIDGE, T., *Degenerate Oxford* (1930)

GRETTON, R. H., *Ancient Remains of Oxford Castle* (1936)

GRUNDY, G. B., *Fifty-five Years at Oxford* (1945)

GUNTHER, R. T., *Early Science in Oxford* (14 vols, 1920–45)

HARGREAVES-MAWDSLEY, W. N., *Oxford in the Age of John Locke* (1973)
(ed.) *Woodforde at Oxford 1759–1776* (1969)

HASSALL, T. G., *Oxford: The City Beneath Your Feet* (1972)

HAYTER, SIR WILLIAM, *Spooner* (1977)

HEADLAM, CECIL, *The Story of Oxford* (1907)

HIGHAM, T. F., *Dr Blakiston Recalled* (1967)

HISCOCK, W. G., *A Christ Church Miscellany* (1946)
Henry Aldrich (1960)

Historical Register of the University of Oxford, 1220–1900 (1900)

HOBHOUSE, CHRISTOPHER, *Oxford: As it was and As it is Today* (1948)

HOLLAND, HENRY SCOTT, *A Bundle of Memories* (1915)

HOLLIS, CHRISTOPHER, *Oxford in the Twenties: Recollections of Five Friends* (1976)

INGRAM, JAMES, *Memorials of Oxford* (3 vols, 1837)
Memorials of the Churches and Parishes of Oxford (1848)

JEUNE, M. D., *Pages from the Diary of an Oxford Lady, 1845–1862* (ed. M. J. Gifford, 1932)

KEARNEY, HUGH, *Scholars and Gentlemen: Universities and Society in Pre-Industrial England, 1500–1700* (1970)

KIBRE, PEARL, *Scholarly Privileges in the Middle Ages* (1961)
The Nations in the Medieval Universities (1948)

LAWSON, F. H., *The Oxford Law School, 1850–1965* (1968)

LEGGE, H. EDITH, *The Divinity School, Oxford* (1923)

LIDDON, H. P., AND JOHNSTON, J. O., *E. B. Pusey* (4 vols, 1893–7)

LITTLE, A. G., *The Grey Friars at Oxford* (1892)
AND PELSTER, F., *Oxford Theology and Theologians* (1934)

LOCK, WALTER, *Oxford Memories* (1932)

LONGMATE, NORMAN, *Oxford Triumphant* (1954)

MABBOTT, JOHN, *Oxford Memories* (1987)

MACKINNON, ALAN, *Oxford Amateurs: A Short History of Theatricals at the University* (1910)

MADAN, FALCONER, *Oxford Outside the Guide-Books* (1925)

MARKHAM, FELIX, *Oxford* (1967)

MARRIOTT, SIR JOHN A. R., *Oxford: Its Place in National History* (1933)

MARTIN, A. F., AND STEEL, R. W. (eds), *The Oxford Region: A Scientific and Historical Survey* (1954)

MASTERMAN, J. C., *To Teach the Senators Wisdom* (1962)

MIDDLETON, R. D., *Newman at Oxford* (1950)
Dr Routh (1938)

MORRIS, JAMES (JAN), *Oxford* (revised edition, 1978)
(ed.) *The Oxford Book of Oxford* (1978)

MAYCOCK, A. L., *An Oxford Note-Book* (1931)

New Pocket Companion to Oxford (1802)

OMAN, CAROLA, *An Oxford Childhood* (1976)

OMAN, SIR CHARLES, *Memories of Victorian Oxford* (1941)

Oxford Studies Presented to D. Callus (1964)

Oxford University and City Guide (1823)

Oxford University Calendar (various editions)

Oxford University Commission Report (1852)

Oxford University Handbook (various editions)

PANTIN, W. A., *Oxford Life in Oxford Archives* (1972)

PARKER, J., *Early History of Oxford, 727–1100* (1885)

PATTISON, MARK, *Suggestions on Academical Organization* (1868)
Memoirs (1885; intro. by J. Manton, 1969)

Place Names of Oxfordshire (general editor A. H. Smith, 1953)

PLUMMER, C., *Elizabethan Oxford* (1886)

POTTER, DENNIS, *The Glittering Coffin* (1960)

PREST, JOHN, *Balliol Studies* (1982)

PRIOR, MARY, *Fishermen, Bargemen and Boatmen in Oxford* (1982)

PYCROFT, JAMES, *The Collegian's Guide or Recollections of College Days* (1858)
Oxford Memories: A Retrospect after Fifty Years (2 vols, 1886)

QUARRELL, W. H. AND W. J. C., *Oxford in 1710: From the Travels of Zacharias Conrad von Uffenbach* (1928)

QUILLER COUCH, LILIAN M. (ed.), *Reminiscences of Oxford* (1892)

RASHDALL, HASTINGS, *The Universities of Europe in the Middle Ages* (eds F. M. Powicke and A. B. Emden, Vol. III, 1936)

REED, DAVID, AND OPHER, PHILIP, *New Architecture in Oxford* (1977)

Report of a Committee of the Hebdomadal Board (1853)

Report of Commission of Enquiry (2 vols, 1966)

Report on the Committee on Relations with Junior Members (1969)

REX, M. B., *University Representation, 1604–1690* (1964)

REYNOLDS, J. S., *The Evangelicals at Oxford, 1755–1871* (1953 and 1975)

RICE-OXLEY, L., *Oxford Renowned* (1925)

ROBSON, J. A., *Wycliff and the Oxford Schools: The Relation of the 'Summa de Ente' to the Scholastic Debates at Oxford in the later 14th century* (1966)

ROGERS, ANNIE, *Degrees by Degrees* (1938)

ROGERS, J. E. THOROLD, *Oxford City Documents, 1268–1665* (1890)

Round About "The Mitre" at Oxford (R. A. H. Spiers; 2nd edition, 1929)

ROWSE, A. L., *Oxford in the History of the Nation* (1975)
A Cornishman at Oxford (1965)

SALTER, H. E., *Mediaeval Oxford* (1936)
 Mediaeval Archives of the University of Oxford (2 vols, 1920–1)
 Oxford City Properties (1926)
 The Historic Names of the Streets and Lanes of øOxford (1921)
SCOTT, DRUSILLA, *A. D. Lindsay* (1971)
SECCOMBE, THOMAS (with H. Spencer Scott), *In Praise of Oxford: An Anthology in Prose and Verse* (2 vols, 1912)
SELINCOURT, HUGH DE, *Oxford from Within* (1910)
 Shopping in Oxford: A Brief History (Oxford Preservation Trust, Occasional Papers, No. 4)
SIMCOCK, A., *The Ashmolean Museum and Oxford Science* (1984)
SINCLAIR, H. M., AND ROBB-SMITH, A. H. T., *A Short History of Anatomical Teaching at Oxford* (1950)
SPARROW, JOHN, *Mark Pattison and the Idea of a University* (1967)
SQUIRES, THOMAS W., *In West Oxford* (1928)
Statutes, Decrees and Regulations of the University of Oxford (1983)
STEDMAN, A. M. N., *Oxford: Its Life and Schools* (1887)
 Oxford: Its Social and Intellectual Life (1878)
STONE, LAWRENCE (ed.), *University in Society: vol. 1, Oxford and Cambridge from the 14th to the early 19th century* (1974)
Survey of Oxford in 1772 (1912)

THOMAS, EDWARD, *Oxford* (1903)
THWAITE, ANN (ed.), *My Oxford* (1977)
TREVOR-ROPER, H. R., *Archbishop Laud* (2nd edition, 1962)
TUCKWELL, REV. W., *Reminiscences of Oxford* (1907)
TURNER, W. H., *Records of the City of Oxford, 1509–83* (1880)
TYERMAN, L., *The Oxford Methodists* (1873)
VARLEY, F. J., *The Siege of Oxford 1642–46* (1932)
WADE, W. M., *Walks in Oxford* (1821)
WARD, W. R., *Victorian Oxford* (1965)
 Georgian Oxford (1958)
WARNER, P. F., AND ASHLEY-COOPER, F. S., *Oxford versus Cambridge at the Wicket* (1926)
WELLS, J., *The Oxford Degree Ceremony* (1906)
 (ed.) *Oxford and Oxford Life* (1892)
WOODWARD, E. L., *Short Journey* (1942)
WOOLLEY, A. R., *Oxford: University and City* (1951)
WORDSWORTH, CHRISTOPHER, *Social Life at the English Universities in the Eighteenth Century* (1874)

Among the best modern guide-books to Oxford are A. R. Woolley's *Clarendon Guide to Oxford*, *Alden's Oxford Guide* and Peter Heyworth's *The Oxford Guide to Oxford*. *The Oxford Handbook*, published by the Oxford University Students' Union, provides a guide to all aspects of Oxford life for the student and for other young people living in the city.

Picture Acknowledgements

The publishers wish to thank the following for their permission to reproduce the illustrations in this book: Ashmolean Museum, Oxford: 16, 22, 23, 25, 54, 57, 81, 130, 169, 195, 255, 258, 292, 309, 352, 468, 509. The Master and Fellows of Balliol College, Oxford: 27 (photo/Courtauld Institute of Art), 29, 162, 226 (photo/Thomas-Photos, Oxford). Bodleian Library, Oxford: 1 (Ms.Top.Oxon.d.493.f.55), 11 (Ms.Don.a.2.(46)), 51, 72 (Ms.Don.a.3.(101)), 93, 103 (Ms.Top.Don.d.495.f.118r), 196, 203, 256 (Arch.Kc.f.175), 261 (Ms.Top.Oxon.d.505 (32), 279 (Ms.Don.a.2.(19)), 281 (Ms.Top.Oxon.d.496.f.8v), 289 (Ms.Don.a.2.(10)), 308 (Ms.Adds.124.c.38), 319 (GA.Oxon.a.57.f.6), 325 (GA.Oxon.a.65.p.94), 331 (Ms.Top.Oxon.d.502.f.4), 358, 368 (Ms.Don.d.14.f.23r), 378 (GA.Oxon.a.69.p.23), 395 (GA.Oxon.a.91a), 419 (Ms.Don.a.3.no.93), 430 (GA.Oxon.a.86f.53), 482 (Ms.Don.a.3.(94)), 503 (GA.Oxon.a.95). British Motor Industry Heritage Trust: 228, 263. The Governing Body, Christ Church, Oxford: 84. David Collett:152. Mary Evans Picture Library: 300. Fotomas, London: 12, 49, 86, 149, 200, 296, 354 below, 403, 428, 462, 475, 478. Edward Hibbert: 66, 335. A.F. Kersting: 135. Keystone Collection/Photo Source: 192. Lady Margaret Hall, Oxford: 214. The Trustees of the Lloyd-Baker Settled Estates: 34. Mrs Barbara Lynam: 125 below. The President and Fellows of Magdalen College, Oxford: 231, 233 (photos by Thomas-Photos, Oxford). The Mansell Collection: 2, 10, 35, 48, 53, 65, 92, 118, 123, 145, 160, 161, 230, 252, 343 below, 355, 411, 412, 437, 441, 464, 472. National Portrait Gallery, London: 66, 124, 216, 262, 277, 495, 497. Oxford Preservation Trust and Edith Gollnast: 52. Oxford Union Society Library: 469 (photo/B.J. Harris, Oxford). Oxford University Press: 266, 285, 376, 406, 489, 499 (photo/Thomas-Photos, Oxford). Words of the clerihew 'Napoleon' by E. Clerihew Bentley, as published in *The First Clerihews*, 1982. Reproduced by courtesy of Oxford University Press: 23 below. Oxfordshire County Libraries. The Local Studies Collection, Central Library, Oxford. Photos by John Peacock, Oxford: 4, 6, 7, 14, 36, 38, 58, 62, 64, 68, 69, 71, 74, 82, 83, 89, 96, 97, 102, 110, 111, 117, 122, 126, 127, 129, 131, 139, 143, 144, 154, 167, 181, 183, 184, 189, 191, 201, 207, 210, 224, 232, 237, 244, 247, 250, 259, 274, 278, 288, 294, 295, 307, 316, 317, 321, 328, 342, 343 above, 354 above, 365, 383, 389, 396, 397, 405, 409, 416, 420, 426, 434, 435, 448, 449, 451, 457, 458, 465, 467, 476, 479, 480, 484, 492, 493. Juliet Pannett: 218. Pitt Rivers Museum, Oxford: 324. Private Collections: 26, 115, 163, 290, 298, 318, 444, 508. Provost and Fellows of The Queen's College, Oxford: 348. The Royal Aeronautical Society, London: 370. The Principal and Fellows of St Anne's College, Oxford: 374. St Edward's School Archives, Oxford: 41, 392. The Principal and Fellows of St Hugh's College, Oxford: 400 (photo/Thomas-Photos, Oxford). The Principal and Fellows of Somerville College, Oxford: 432 (photo/Thomas-Photos, Oxford). Thomas-Photos, Oxford: 9, 55, 151, 164, 193, 205, 206, 209, 215, 249, 257, 264, 399. University of Oxford: 181. University Museum, Oxford: 63. The Warden and Fellows of Wadham College, Oxford: 486, 487, 490 (photos/Thomas-Photos, Oxford). *The Adventures of Mr Verdant Green* (1853–7) by 'Cuthbert Bede, B.A.' (Rev. Edward Bradley): 141, 341, 360, 429, 437. B. Coles, *Map of Port Meadow* (c. 1720): 323. *Illustrated London News*, 28 November, 1908: 745. *Memorials of Oxford* (1832–7) by James Ingram: 23, 50, 79, 106, 124, 133, 188 above right, 188 below left, 219, 272, 351, 388, 422, 455, 505. *Oxonia Illustrata, etc.* (1675) by David Loggan: 105, 128, 132, 198, 222, 270. *Punch*, 2 December 1936: 287. *Rowlandson's Oxford* (1911) by A. Hamilton Gibbs: 120, 234, 346. *Vanity Fair*, 13 June 1901: 18. *English Country Houses* (1875, 2nd edition) by William Wilkinson: 31, 282, 501. *History and Antiquities, etc.* (1792) by Anthony à Wood: 500.

Maps on pages x–xiii are based upon Ordnance Survey material with the permission of the Controller of Her Majesty's Stationery Office, Crown copyright reserved. The map of Oxford c.1375 on page x incorporates information from a map by K.J. Wass. The maps have been redrawn by Hilary Evans.

The publishers have endeavoured to acknowledge all known persons and collections holding copyright or reproduction rights for the illustrations in this book.

——INDEX OF PEOPLE——

542

543

Numbers in bold type refer to main entries. Numbers in italic refer to illustrations.

552

561